American Government

POWER AND PURPOSE
2010 ELECTION UPDATE

11TH EDITION
2010 ELECTION UPDATE

American Government

POWER AND PURPOSE

Theodore J. Lowi
CORNELL UNIVERSITY

Benjamin Ginsberg
THE JOHNS HOPKINS UNIVERSITY

Kenneth A. Shepsle
HARVARD UNIVERSITY

Stephen Ansolabehere
HARVARD UNIVERSITY

W. W. NORTON & COMPANY
NEW YORK • LONDON

W. W. Norton & Company has been independent since its founding in 1923, when William Warder Norton and Mary D. Herter Norton first published lectures delivered at the People's Institute, the adult education division of New York City's Cooper Union. The firm soon expanded its program beyond the Institute, publishing books by celebrated academics from America and abroad. By mid-century, the two major pillars of Norton's publishing program—trade books and college texts—were firmly established. In the 1950s, the Norton family transferred control of the company to its employees, and today—with a staff of four hundred and a comparable number of trade, college, and professional titles published each year—W. W. Norton & Company stands as the largest and oldest publishing house owned wholly by its employees.

Editor: Ann Shin
Assistant editor: Jake Schindel
Project editor: Kate Feighery
Design director: Rubina Yeh
Production manager: Christine D'Antonio
E-media editor: Dan Jost
Manuscript editor: Barbara Curialle
Graphic artist: John McAusland
Composition: TexTech, Inc.
Manufacturing: Worldcolor

ISBN 978-0-393-11820-9 (hardcover)

W. W. Norton & Company Inc.,
500 Fifth Avenue, New York, N.Y. 10110
www.wwnorton.com

W. W. Norton & Company Ltd.,
Castle House, 75/76 Wells Street, London W1T 3QT
2 3 4 5 6 7 8 9 0

FOR OUR FAMILIES

Angele, Anna, and Jason Lowi
Sandy, Cindy, and Alex Ginsberg
Rise, Nilsa, and Seth Shepsle
Laurie Gould and Rebecca and
Julia Ansolabehere

Contents

4   Civil Liberties and Civil Rights   98

PART 2   INSTITUTIONS   165

5   Congress: The First Branch   166

Analyzing the 2010 Midterm Elections (following page 584)

PART 4 GOVERNANCE 585

14 Economic Policy 586

APPENDIX   A1

Preface

This book was written for faculty and students who are looking for a little more than just "nuts and bolts," and who are drawn to an analytical perspective. No fact about American government is intrinsically difficult to grasp, and in an open society such as ours, facts abound. The philosophy of a free and open media in the United States makes information about the government that would be suppressed elsewhere readily available. The advent of the Internet and other new communication technologies has further expanded the opportunity to learn about our government. The ubiquity of information in our society is a great virtue. Common knowledge about the government gives our society a vocabulary that is widely shared among its citizens and enables us to communicate effectively with each other about politics. But it is also important to reach beyond that common vocabulary and develop a more sophisticated understanding of politics and government. The sheer quantity of facts in our society overwhelms us at times. In a 24/7 news cycle it can be hard to pick out what stories are important and to stay focused on them. The single most important task of the teacher of political science is to confront popular ideas and to choose from among them the small number of really significant concepts that help us make better sense of the world. This book aims to help instructors and students accomplish this task.

The analytical framework of this book is oriented around five principles that we use to help make sense of politics:

1. All political behavior has a purpose.
2. Institutions structure politics.
3. All politics is collective action.
4. Political outcomes are the products of individual preferences and institutional procedures.
5. History matters.

This Eleventh Edition represents a major revision of the text. We have not changed the approach of the book. Rather, in this new edition, we have both sharpened the analytical approach developed in earlier editions and made it more teachable. Those who have used this book in the past are familiar with the narrative it presents about American government and politics—the storyline of how the United States government has evolved, how it operates, and the characters involved in the unfolding development of our polity. This book also presents an analytical approach based on the five principles outlined above. We are guided by the belief that students of government need an analytical framework for understanding political phenomena—a framework rooted in some of the most important insights the discipline of political science has to offer and that encourages students to draw out the general lessons about collective action and collective decision-making.

The 2008 elections and the Obama presidency represent a dramatic change in our politics. The Obama and McCain campaigns of 2008 inspired new participation by voters; they brought many new voters to politics and many older-but-discouraged voters back in. Voter turnout hit its highest point since the 1964 election. Shifts in public opinion about the government since 2004 have altered the political terrain in the United States, and the new communications technologies have eroded traditional media, especially print media. The 2006 and 2008 elections altered control of Congress, from a Republican majority to a Democratic majority sufficiently large enough to prevent a partisan filibuster in the Senate. In this revision, particular attention has been given to these changes.

The major changes in this Eleventh Edition are intended to amplify the benefits of the Five Principles of Politics framework and provide a more contemporary and unified perspective on the key topics in American government. The most significant changes include:

- *Part 3 on "Democratic Politics" has been thoroughly revised to provide a more current and integrated treatment of mass political behavior.* Chapter 9 (Public Opinion) presents an up-to-date account of what motivates people's political preferences, and sets up a more unified discussion of political behavior in the chapters that follow. The chapter also includes new sections on how today's media—including new media—influence public opinion, and on the debate over how polarized America really is. Chapter 10 (Elections) has been completely rewritten to highlight how the design of our electoral institutions and laws has important consequences for how people's preferences are (or aren't) reflected in government. The new section on how voters decide takes full account of recent research, providing a more nuanced perspective on voter knowledge in particular. Likewise, the other chapters in Part 3, on parties, interest groups, and the media, have been deeply revised.

- *Throughout the text, the analytical framework from Chapter 1 has been more deeply integrated into the body of each chapter.* Each chapter's analysis focuses on the principles from Chapter 1 that are most relevant to the topic at hand. New chapter introductions preview how the Five Principles framework will help us understand the chapter's topic, setting up the analysis that runs through the body of the chapter. New chapter conclusions return to points raised in the introduction and reinforce the chapter's analysis. This deeper integration of the key principles within the body of the chapter was widely requested by instructors as a way to maximize the usefulness of the Five Principles of Politics framework.

- *New "Core of the Analysis" sections at the start of each chapter highlight and reinforce the key analytic insights from the chapter.* We want the pedagogy to reinforce the chapter's analysis, signaling to students that they are not just responsible for the key terms and "nuts and bolts" but also for the chapter's analysis of the topic. These bulleted points highlight the analytical insights that students will want to watch for and master as they read the chapter, drawing on the Five Principles framework.

- *A new primer on "Analyzing the Evidence" has been added to Chapter 1,* to offer the student guidance in how to understand a graph, table, or chart, and how to use data to draw conclusions. As in the Tenth Edition, an "Analyzing the Evidence" unit in each subsequent chapter—including many that are new to the Eleventh Edition—takes a closer look at how political scientists analyze empirical data to understand political phenomena discussed in the book in greater depth.

For the Eleventh Edition we have profited greatly from the guidance of many teachers who have used earlier editions, and from the suggestions of numerous thoughtful reviewers. We thank them by name in the Acknowledgments. We recognize that there is no one-best-way to craft in an introductory text, and we are grateful for the advice we have received.

Theodore J. Lowi
Benjamin Ginsberg
Kenneth A. Shepsle
Stephen Ansolabehere

Acknowledgments

Our students at Cornell, Johns Hopkins, and Harvard have already been identified as an essential factor in the writing of this book. They have been our most immediate intellectual community, a hospitable one indeed. Another part of our community, perhaps a large suburb, is the discipline of political science itself. Our debt to the scholarship of our colleagues is scientifically measurable, probably to several decimal points, in the footnotes of each chapter. Despite many complaints that the field is too scientific or not scientific enough, political science is alive and well in the United States. Political science has never been at a loss for relevant literature, and without that literature, our job would have been impossible.

We are pleased to acknowledge our debt to the many colleagues who had a direct and active role in criticism and preparation of the manuscript. The First Edition was read and reviewed by Gary Bryner, Brigham Young University; James F. Herndon, Virginia Polytechnic Institute and State University; James W. Riddlesperger, Jr., Texas Christian University; John Schwarz, University of Arizona; Toni-Michelle Travis, George Mason University; and Lois Vietri, University of Maryland. We also want to reiterate our thanks to the four colleagues who allowed us the privilege of testing a trial edition of our book by using it as the major text in their introductory American Government courses: Gary Bryner, Brigham Young University; Allan J. Cigler, University of Kansas; Burnet V. Davis, Albion College; and Erwin A. Jaffe, California State University—Stanislaus.

For subsequent editions, we relied heavily on the thoughtful manuscript reviews we received from David Canon, University of Wisconsin; Russell Hanson, Indiana University; William Keech, Carnegie Mellon University; Donald Kettl, University of Wisconsin; Anne Khademian, University of Wisconsin; William McLauchlan, Purdue University; J. Roger Baker, Wittenburg University; James

Lennertz, Lafayette College; Allan McBride, Grambling State University; Joseph Peek, Jr., Georgia State University; Grant Neeley, Texas Tech University; Mark Graber, University of Maryland; John Gilmour, College of William and Mary; Victoria Farrar-Myers, University of Texas at Arlington; Timothy Boylan, Winthrop University; Robert Huckfeldt, University of California—Davis; Mark Joslyn, University of Kansas; Beth Leech, Rutgers University; Charles Noble, California State University, Long Beach.

For the Eighth Edition, we benefited from the comments of Scott Ainsworth, University of Georgia; Thomas Brunell, Northern Arizona University; Daniel Carpenter, Harvard University; Brad Gomez, University of South Carolina; Paul Gronke, Reed College; Marc Hetherington, Bowdoin College; Gregory Huber, Yale University; Robert Lowry, Iowa State University; and Anthony Nownes, University of Tennessee; Scott Adler, University of Colorado—Boulder; John Coleman, University of Wisconsin—Madison; Richard Conley, University of Florida; Keith Dougherty, University of Georgia; John Ferejohn, Stanford University; Douglas Harris, Loyola College; Brian Humes, University of Nebraska—Lincoln; Jeffrey Jenkins, Northwestern University; Paul Johnson, University of Kansas; Andrew Polsky, Hunter College—CUNY; Mark Richards, Grand Valley State University; Charles Shipan, University of Iowa; Craig Volden, Ohio State University; and Garry Young, George Washington University.

For the Ninth Edition, we were guided by the comments of John Baughman; Lawrence Baum, Ohio State University; Chris Cooper, Western Carolina State University; Charles Finochiaro, State University of New York—Buffalo; Lisa Garcia-Bellorda, University of California—Irvine; Sandy Gordon, New York University; Steven Greene, North Carolina State University; Richard Herrera, Arizona State University; Ben Highton, University of California—Davis; Trey Hood, University of Georgia; Andy Karch, University of Texas—Austin; Glen Krutz, University of Oklahoma; Paul Labedz, Valencia Community College; Brad Lockerbie, University of Georgia; Wendy Martinek, State University of New York—Binghamton; Nicholas Miller, University of Maryland Baltimore County; Russell Renka, Southeast Missouri State University; Debbie Schildkraut, Tufts University; Charles Shipan, University of Iowa; Chris Shortell, California State University, Northridge; John Sides, University of Texas—Austin; Sean Theriault, University of Texas—Austin; and Lynn Vavreck, University of California, Los Angeles.

For the Tenth Edition, we were grateful for the detailed comments of Christian Grose, Vanderbilt University; Kevin Esterling, University of California—Riverside; Martin Johnson, University of California—Riverside; Scott Meinke, Bucknell University; Jason MacDonald, Kent State University; Alan Wiseman, Ohio State University; Michelle Swers, Georgetown University; William Hixon, Lawrence University; Gregory Koger, University of Miami; and Renan Levine, University of Toronto.

For their advice on the Eleventh Edition, we thank Scott Ainsworth, University of Georgia; Bethany Albertson, University of Washington; Brian Arbour, John Jay College; James Battista, University at Buffalo, State University of New York; Lawrence Becker, California State University, Northridge; Damon Cann, Utah State University; Jamie Carson, University of Georgia; Suzanne Chod, Pennsylvania

State University; Michael Crespin, University of Georgia; Ryan Emenaker, College of the Redwoods; Kevin Esterling, University of California—Riverside; Brad Gomez, Florida State University; Sanford Gordon, New York University; Christian Grose, Vanderbilt University; James Hanley, Adrian College; Ryan Hurl, University of Toronto; Josh Kaplan, University of Notre Dame; Wendy Martinek, Binghamton University; Will Miller, Southeast Missouri State University; Evan Parker-Stephen, Texas A&M University; Melody Rose, Portland State University; Eric Schickler, University of California—Berkeley; John Sides, George Washington University; Lynn Vavreck, University of California—Los Angeles.

An important contribution to the Tenth and Eleventh Editions was made by the authors of the "Analyzing the Evidence" units. Jamie Carson of the University of Georgia authored the "Analyzing the Evidence" spreads for Chapters 2, 3, 5, 6, 7, 8, and 10. Andrea Campbell of MIT contributed the "Analyzing the Evidence" unit for Chapter 9, and Kevin Esterling wrote the unit for Chapter 12. We thank the three of them for their excellent contributions to the book.

This Election Update Edition includes two substantial new sections, one on the first two years of the Obama presidency and one on the 2010 elections. For their extensive help developing these new sections, we wish to thank Joseph Williams and Eitan Hersh.

Perhaps above all, we wish to thank those who kept the production and all the loose ends of this Eleventh Edition coherent and in focus. Ann Shin has been a talented editor, offering numerous suggestions for this edition. Kate Feighery has been a superb project editor, following in the great tradition of her predecessors. Christine D'Antonio has been an excellent production manager, and Mollie Eisenberg has been a helpful assistant editor. Dan Jost brought a vision to the Web site and spent countless hours making it a reality.

We are more than happy, however, to absolve all these contributors from any flaws, errors, and misjudgments that this book contains. We wish it could be free of all production errors, grammatical errors, misspellings, misquotes, missed citations, etc. From that standpoint, a book ought to try to be perfect. But substantively we have not tried to write a flawless book; we have not tried to write a book to please everyone. We have again tried to write an effective book, a book that cannot be taken lightly. Our goal was not to make every reader a political scientist. Our goal was to restore politics as a subject of vigorous and enjoyable discourse, releasing it from the bondage of the thirty-second sound bite and the thirty-page technical briefing. Every person can be knowledgeable because everything about politics is accessible. One does not have to be a television anchorperson to profit from political events. One does not have to be a philosopher to argue about the requisites of democracy, a lawyer to dispute constitutional interpretations, an economist to debate public policy. We will be very proud if our book contributes in a small way to the restoration of the ancient art of political controversy.

Theodore J. Lowi
Benjamin Ginsberg
Kenneth A. Shepsle
Stephen Ansolabehere

PART ONE

Foundations

1

Five Principles of Politics

American government and politics are extraordinarily complex. The United States has many levels of government: federal, state, county, city, and town—to say nothing of a host of special and regional authorities. Each of these governments operates under its own rules and statutory authority and is related to the others in complex ways. In many nations, regional and local governments are appendages of the national government. This is not true in the United States. America's state and local governments possess a considerable measure of independence and authority. Each level of government, moreover, consists of an array of departments, agencies, offices, and bureaus, each with its own policy, jurisdiction, and responsibilities, and undertaking a variety of sometimes overlapping tasks. Sometimes this complexity gets in the way of effective governance, as in the case of governmental response to emergencies. America's federal, state, and local public safety agencies seldom share information and frequently use incompatible communications equipment, so they are often not even able to speak to each other. For example, on September 11, 2001, New York City's police and fire departments could not effectively coordinate their responses to the terrorist attack on the World Trade Center because their communications systems were not linked.

The complexity of America's government is no accident. Complexity was one element of the Founders' grand constitutional design. The framers of the Constitution hoped that an elaborate division of power among institutions and between the states and the federal government would allow a variety of competing groups, forces, interests, and ideas to have access to arenas of decision making and a voice in public affairs—while preventing any single group or coalition from monopolizing power. One set of interests might be active and powerful in some states, other forces would be influential in the national legislature, and still other groups might prevail in the executive branch. The overall pattern would disperse power and opportunity, allowing many groups to achieve at least some of their political goals. In this way, America's political tradition associates complexity with liberty and political opportunity.

But although America's institutional complexity creates many avenues and possibilities for political action, its complexity also places a considerable burden on citizens who might wish to achieve something through political participation, for they may not easily discern where particular policies are actually made, who the influential decision makers are, and what forms of political participation are most likely to be effective. This is one of the paradoxes of political life: In a dictatorship, lines of political authority may be simple, but opportunities to influence the use of power are few; in America, political opportunities are plentiful, but how they should be used is far from obvious. Indeed, precisely because America's institutional and political arrangements are so complex, many Americans are mystified by government. As we shall see in Chapter 9, many Americans have difficulty making sense of even the basic features of the Constitution.

CORE OF THE ANALYSIS

- Five principles of politics can help us think analytically about American government and make sense of the apparent chaos and complexity of the political world. These five principles are:
- All political behavior has a purpose (rationality principle).
- Institutions structure politics (institution principle).
- All politics is collective action (collective-action principle).
- Political outcomes are the products of individual preferences and institutional procedures (policy principle).
- How we got here matters (history principle).

If America's government seems complex, its politics can be utterly bewildering. Like the nation's governmental structure, its political processes have numerous components. For most Americans, the focal point of politics is the electoral process. As we shall see in Chapter 10, tens of millions of Americans participate in a host of national, state, and local elections, during which they listen to thousands of candidates debate a perplexing array of issues. Candidates inundate the media with promises, charges, and countercharges while an army of pundits and journalists, whom we also discuss in Chapter 9, adds its own clamor to the din.

Politics, however, does not end on Election Day. Indeed, given the growing tendency of losers to challenge election results in the courts, even elections do not end on Election Day. The most famous of these, of course, was the resolution of the 2000 presidential election by the Supreme Court in *Bush v. Gore*. Long after the voters have spoken, political struggles continue in Congress, the executive branch, and the courts and embroil political parties, interest groups, and the mass media. In some instances, the participants in political struggles and their goals seem fairly obvious. For example, it is no secret that businesses and upper-income wage earners strongly support programs of tax reduction, farmers support maintenance of agricultural subsidies, and labor unions oppose "outsourcing" of production. Each of these forces has created or joined organized groups to advance its cause. We examine some of these groups in Chapter 12.

In other instances, though, the participants in political struggles and their goals are not so clear. Sometimes corporate groups hide behind environmental causes to surreptitiously promote their economic interests. Strong environmental requirements make it difficult for prospective competitors to enter their markets. Other times groups claiming to want to help the poor and downtrodden seek only to help themselves. And to make matters worse, many of the government's policies are made behind closed doors, away from the light of publicity. Ordinary citizens can hardly be blamed for failing to understand bureaucratic rule making and other obscure techniques of government.

MAKING SENSE OF GOVERNMENT AND POLITICS

Can we find order in the apparent chaos of politics? The answer is that we can, and doing so is the purpose of this text. Finding order in the apparent chaos of politics is precisely what political scientists do. The discipline of political science, and especially the study of American politics, is devoted to identifying patterns and regularities in all the noise and maneuvering of everyday political life. This is motivated by two fundamental questions: What do we observe? And why?

The first question makes clear that political science is an *empirical* enterprise. By this we mean that it is ultimately interested in identifying facts and patterns that are true in the world around us. What do voters decide when they enter the polling booth? What strategies and tactics do candidates employ to capture votes? What decisions do legislators make about how to vote on bills? What groups organize and put pressure on the institutions of government? How do the media report politics? What tools are available to the president so he can get what he wants in dealing with Congress? How have courts intervened in regulating political life? How do they come to the decisions they have made? These and many other questions have been explored by political science in an effort to observe and ascertain what is true about the political world, and will be taken up in great detail in later chapters.

The second question—why?—is the fundamental concern of science. We not only would like to know that something is true about the world. We also want to know why it is true. Knowing why something is true requires us to create a theory of how the world works. And a theory is constructed from basic principles. The remainder of this chapter will present a set of such basic principles. They will help us navigate the apparent chaos of politics and make sense of what we observe. In this way we not only describe politics, we analyze it.

One of the most important purposes of this book is to help readers learn to analyze what they observe in American politics.[1] Analysis requires abstracting. For example, in political science, we are not much interested in an analysis that *only* explains why the Republicans gained congressional seats in the 2010 elections. Explanations that provide an account of a unique circumstance are the sorts of things in which pundits, journalists, and other commentators engage as soon as the polls close. You find them on television news programs as well as on the op-ed pages of newspapers. Rather, as political scientists, we would seek a more general theory of voting choice that we can apply to particular instances—such as the 2010 elections.

In this chapter, we will first discuss what we mean by *government* and *politics*. Then we introduce our five principles of politics. These principles are intentionally somewhat abstract, because we want them to apply to a wide range of circumstances. However, we shall provide concrete illustrations along the way, and in later chapters we apply the principles presented here more extensively to help us understand the specific features of politics and government in the United States. We conclude this chapter with a brief guide to analyzing evidence, something you will find useful as we examine empirical information throughout the rest of the book.

---

[1] For an entire book devoted to the issue of analysis, the reader should consult Kenneth A. Shepsle and Mark S. Bonchek, *Analyzing Politics: Rationality, Behavior, and Institutions* (New York: Norton, 1997).

What Is Government?

Government is the term generally used to describe the formal political arrangements by which a land and its people are ruled. Government is composed of institutions and processes that rulers establish to strengthen and perpetuate their power or control over a land and its inhabitants. A government may be as simple as a tribal council that meets occasionally to advise the chief or as complex as our own vast establishment, with its elaborate procedures, laws, governmental bodies, and bureaucracies. This more complex government is sometimes called the state, an abstract concept referring to the source of all public authority.

government The institutions and procedures through which a land and its people are ruled.

Forms of Government

Governments vary in their institutional structure, in their size, and in their modes of operation. Two questions are of special importance in determining how governments differ from each other: Who governs? How much government control is permitted?

In some nations political authority is vested in a single individual—a king or dictator, for example. This state of affairs is called an **autocracy.** When a small group of landowners, military officers, or wealthy merchants controls most of the governing decisions, the government is said to be an **oligarchy.** If more people participate and the populace is deemed to have some influence over decision making, the government is tending toward **democracy.**

autocracy A form of government in which a single individual rules.

oligarchy A form of government in which a small group of landowners, military officers, or wealthy merchants controls most of the governing decisions.

Governments also vary considerably in terms of how they govern. In the United States and some other nations, governments are severely limited in terms of *what* they are permitted to control (they are restricted by substantive limits) as well as *how* they go about exercising that control (they are restricted by procedural limits). Governments that are so limited are called **constitutional** (or liberal) governments. In other nations, although the law imposes few real limits, a government is nevertheless kept in check by other political and social institutions that it is unable to control but must come to terms with, such as autonomous territories, an organized church, organized business groups, or organized labor unions. Such governments are generally called **authoritarian.** In a third, very small, group of nations, including the Soviet Union under Joseph Stalin, Nazi Germany, and perhaps pre–World War II Japan and Italy, governments not only are free of legal limits but also seek to eliminate those organized social groupings that might challenge or limit their authority. These governments typically attempt to dominate or control every sphere of political, economic, and social life and, as a result, are called **totalitarian.** North Korea is a current example, and Cambodia under the Khmer Rouge is another from the late twentieth century.

democracy A system of rule that permits citizens to play a significant part in the governmental process, usually through the selection of key public officials.

constitutional government A system of rule in which formal and effective limits are placed on the powers of the government.

Politics

In its broadest sense, the term **politics** refers to conflicts over the character, membership, and policies of any organization to which people belong. As Harold Lasswell, a famous political scientist, once put it, politics is the struggle over "who gets what, when, how."[2] Although politics is a phenomenon that can be found in any organization, in this book *politics* will refer only to conflicts and struggles over the leadership, structure, and policies of governments. The goal of politics, as we define it, is to have a share or a say in the composition of the government's leadership, how the government is organized, or what its policies are going to be.

Politics takes many forms. As they attempt to influence the policies and leadership of the government, individuals may run for office, vote, join political parties and movements, contribute money to candidates, lobby public officials, participate in demonstrations, write letters, talk to their friends and neighbors, go to court, and engage in numerous other activities. Some forms of politics are aimed at gaining power, some at influencing those in power, and others at bringing new people to power and throwing the old leaders out. Those in power use myriad means and strategies to try to achieve their goals. But even though it takes many forms, politics possesses an underlying logic that can be understood in terms of five simple principles:

1. All political behavior has a purpose.
2. Institutions structure politics.
3. All politics is collective action.
4. Political outcomes are the products of individual preferences, institutional procedures, and collective action.
5. History matters.

Some of these principles may seem obvious or abstract. They will prove useful, however, because they possess a distinct kernel of truth on the one hand, yet on the other hand are sufficiently general to help us understand politics in a wide variety of settings. Armed with these principles, we can perceive the order underlying the apparent chaos of political events whenever and wherever they take place.

FIVE PRINCIPLES OF POLITICS

The Rationality Principle: All Political Behavior Has a Purpose

One compelling reason that governments do what they do is that they respond to what people want. All people have goals and work to achieve those goals through their political behavior. For many citizens, political behavior is as simple as reading a headline or an editorial in the newspaper while drinking their morning coffee or discussing the latest local political controversy with a neighbor over the back fence. Though political, these actions are normal routines of everyday life. Beyond these very basic acts, citizens' political behavior broadens to include still relatively modest activities, such as watching a political debate on television, arguing about politics with a coworker, signing a petition, or attending a city-council meeting. These are understood to be explicitly political activities that require some forethought. Political

authoritarian government A system of rule in which the government recognizes no formal limits but may nevertheless be restrained by the power of other social institutions.

totalitarian government A system of rule in which the government recognizes no formal limits on its power and seeks to absorb or eliminate other social institutions that might challenge it.

politics The conflicts and struggles over the leadership, structure, and policies of government.

---

[2] Harold D. Lasswell, *Politics: Who Gets What, When, How* (1936; repr., New York: Meridian, 1958).

behavior requiring even more premeditation and effort includes going to the polls and casting a vote in the November election (having first registered in a timely manner), contacting one's legislative representatives about a political issue, contributing time or money to a political campaign, or even running for local office.

Some of these acts require time, effort, financial resources, and resolve, whereas others place small, even insignificant demands on a person. Nevertheless, all of them are done for specific reasons. They are not random; they are not entirely automatic or mechanical, even the smallest of them; they are purposeful. Sometimes they are engaged in for the sake of entertainment (reading the front page in the morning) or just to be sociable (chatting about politics with a neighbor, coworker, or family member). At other times, they take on considerable personal importance explicitly because of their political content—because an individual cares about, and wants to influence, an issue, a candidate, a party, or a cause. We will treat all of this political activity as purposeful, as having a goal. Indeed, our attempts to identify the goals of various political activities will help us understand them better.

We've just noted that many of the political activities of ordinary citizens are hard to distinguish from conventional everyday behavior—reading newspapers, watching television news, discussing politics, and so on. For the professional politician, on the other hand—the legislator, executive, judge, party leader, bureau chief, or agency head—nearly every act is political. The legislator's decision to introduce a particular piece of legislation, give a speech in the legislative chamber, move an amendment to a pending bill, vote for or against that bill, or accept a contribution from a particular group requires his or her careful attention. There are pitfalls and dangers, and the slightest miscalculation can have huge consequences. Introduce a bill that appears to be too pro-labor in the eyes of your constituents, for example, and before you know it you're charged with being in bed with the unions during the next election campaign. Give a speech against job quotas for minorities, and you risk your standing with the minority communities in your state or district. Accept campaign contributions from industries known to pollute, and environmentalists think you are no friend of the earth. Nearly every move a legislator makes is fraught with risks. And because of these risks, legislators think about their moves before they make them—sometimes carefully, sometimes not; sometimes correctly, sometimes not. But whatever actions they take or decide against taking, they make their choices with forethought, with deliberation, with calculation. Their actions are not knee-jerk but are, in a word, **instrumental**. Individuals think through the benefits and the costs of a decision, speculate about future effects, and weigh the risks of their decision. Making decisions is all about weighing probabilities of various events and determining the personal value of various outcomes.

instrumental
Done with purpose, sometimes with forethought, and even with calculation.

To find examples of instrumental behavior, consider elected officials. Most politicians want to keep their positions or move up the political ladder to even more important positions. They like their jobs for a variety of reasons—salary, privileges, prestige, stepping-stones, and opportunities for accomplishment, to name just a few. So we can understand why politicians do what they do by thinking of their behavior as instrumental, with a goal of keeping their jobs. This is quite straightforward in regard to elected politicians. They often see no further than the next election and think mainly about how to prevail in that contest. To understand their routines and behaviors, it is essential to figure out who can help them win. "Retail" politics involves dealing directly with constituents, as when a politician helps an individual navigate a federal agency, find a misplaced Social Security check, or apply to a service academy. "Wholesale" politics involves appealing to collections of constituents, as when a legislator introduces a bill that would benefit a group that is active in her state or district (say, veterans), secures money for a bridge or public building in his hometown, or intervenes in an official proceeding on behalf of an interest group that will, in turn, contribute to the next campaign. Politicians may do any and all of these things because it is "right" or for ideological reasons. But we institute elections and provide incentives for politicians to do such things as a means of winning those elections, just in case their generosity of spirit and personal ideology are insufficient. Elections and electoral politics are thus premised on instrumental behavior by politicians.

Political scientists have found it useful to explain the behavior of elected politicians by making the "electoral connection" the principal motivation.[3] Elected politicians, in this view, base their behavior on the goal of maximizing votes at the next election, or maximizing their probability of winning. Of course, politicians seek other things as well—public policy objectives, power in their institution (for legislators, this includes acquiring committee chairs and party leadership posts), and ambition for higher office (members of the House may want to become senators, and senators may want the presidency).[4] Primary emphasis on the electoral motivation is premised on the fact that reelection is a necessary condition for pursuing any of the other objectives.[5]

But what about political actors who are not elected? What do they want? Consider a few examples:

- Agency heads and bureau chiefs, motivated by policy preferences and power, seek to maximize their budgets.

- Legislative committee chairs (who are elected to Congress but appointed to committees) are "turf minded," intent on maximizing their committee's policy jurisdiction and thus its power.

- Voters cast ballots to influence the policies of government, with an eye to their own personal welfare as well as their conception of "what's best for the country."

- Justices, serving lifetime terms, maximize the prospects for their view of constitutional interpretation to prevail.[6]

---

[3]The classic statement of this premise is David R. Mayhew, *Congress: The Electoral Connection* (New Haven, Conn.: Yale University Press, 1974). Although now more than three decades old, this book remains a source of insight and wisdom.

[4]The classic statement of this additional premise is Richard F. Fenno, *Congressmen in Committees* (Boston: Little, Brown, 1973), another book that remains relevant decades after its publication.

[5]As Vince Lombardi, the famous coach of the Green Bay Packers football team, once said, "Winning isn't everything; it's the only thing."

[6]For most political actors, self-interest motivates their behavior. The motivations or purposes of judges and justices have proved more difficult to ascertain in light of the fact that they typically enjoy lifetime appointments (and thus are not looking ahead to the next election or occasion for "contract renewal"). For an interesting discussion of judicial motivations by an eminent law professor and incumbent judge, see Richard Posner, "What Do Judges Maximize? (The Same Thing Everybody Else Does)," *Supreme Court Economic Review* 3 (1993): 1–41.

In each of these instances, we can postulate motivations for political actors that seem to fit the political context in which they are found. These motivations often have a strong element of self-interest, but they may be broadened out to incorporate "enlightened self-interest," including the welfare of others (such as their families), the entire society, or even all of humanity.

The Institution Principle: Institutions Structure Politics

Because people, especially elected leaders and other government officials, confront certain recurring problems, they develop routines and standard ways of addressing those problems. Routinized, structured relations are what we call institutions. **Institutions** are the rules and procedures that provide incentives for political behavior, thereby shaping politics. Institutions may discourage conflict, encourage coordination, enable bargaining, and thus facilitate decision making, cooperation, and collective action.

Institutions are part script and part scorecard. As scripts, they choreograph political activity. As scorecards, they list the players, their positions, what they want, what they know, what they can do, and when they can do it. Although the Constitution sets the broad framework, much adaptation and innovation takes place as the institutions themselves are bent to the various purposes of strategic political actors who want to win for their side and defeat the other side. Our focus here will be on the authority that institutions provide politicians for the pursuit of public policies. The discussion is divided into four broad subjects: jurisdiction, decisiveness, agenda and veto power, and delegation.

Jurisdiction. A critical feature of an institution is the domain over which institutional members have the authority to make decisions; other members impose limits and sanctions if they feel jurisdictional authority has been exceeded. Political institutions are full of specialized jurisdictions over which individuals or subsets of members have authority. One feature of the U.S. Congress, for example, is the existence of "standing committees," whose jurisdictions are carefully defined by law. Most members of Congress become specialists in all aspects of the jurisdiction of their committees—and they often seek committee assignments based on the subjects in which they want to specialize. Committee members are granted specific authority within their jurisdiction to set the agenda of the larger parent chamber. For example, proposed legislation related to the military must pass through the Armed Services Committee before it can be voted on by the entire House or Senate. Thus the politics of the legislative institution in the United States is affected by the way its jurisdiction-specific committees are structured. Similarly, a bureau or agency is established by law, and its jurisdiction—its scope of authority—is firmly fixed. Thus, the Food and Drug Administration possesses well-defined authority to regulate the marketing of pharmaceuticals but is not permitted to regulate products falling outside its jurisdiction. (An ongoing conflict revolves around whether tobacco falls within its jurisdiction. Presently it does not.)

Decisiveness. Another crucial feature of an institution is its rules for making decisions. It might sound like a straightforward task to lay out the rules for decision

institutions The rules and procedures that provide incentives for political behavior, thereby shaping politics.

making, but in practice such rules often require a raft of conditions and qualifications. Every organization has rules of some sort, and the more an organization values participation by the broadest range of its members, the more it needs those rules: The requirement of participation must be balanced with the need to bring discussion and activity to a close at some point so that a decision can be made. This is why one of the motions that can be made on the floor of a legislature is to "move" the previous question, a motion to close the debate and move immediately to a vote.[7] In some legislatures, though, inaction seems to take precedence over action. In the U.S. House of Representatives, for example, a motion to adjourn (and thus not vote on a measure) takes precedence over a motion to move the previous question. In the U.S. Senate, to take another example, a supermajority (sixty votes) is required to close debate and move to a vote. Decisiveness rules thus specify when votes may be taken and the sequence in which votes may occur, and—most important of all—how many individuals supporting a motion are sufficient for it to pass.

Agenda Power and Veto Power. If decisiveness characterizes what it takes to win, then **agenda power** describes who determines what will be taken up for consideration in the first place. Those who exercise some form of agenda power are said to engage in gatekeeping. They determine which alternatives may pass through the gate onto the institution's agenda and which alternatives will have the gate slammed in their face. Gatekeeping, in other words, consists of the power to make proposals and the power to block proposals from being made. The ability to keep something off an institution's agenda should not be confused with **veto power**. Veto power is the ability to defeat something even if it does become part of the agenda. In the legislative process, for example, the president has no general gatekeeping authority—he or she has no agenda power and thus cannot force the legislature to take up a proposal—but does have (limited) veto power provided by the Constitution. Congress, on the other hand, controls its own agenda—its members can place matters on the legislative agenda. It cannot be prevented from passing a measure, but a presidential veto can prevent a measure from becoming the law of the land. Thus, when it comes to legislation, agenda power is vested in the legislature. Veto power is possessed both by the legislature and the president (the assent of each is required for a bill to become a law). We'll examine these processes in more detail in Chapters 5 and 6.

Delegation. Representative democracy is the quintessential instance of **delegation**. Citizens, through voting, delegate the authority to make decisions on their behalf to representatives—chiefly legislators and executives—rather than exercising political authority directly. We can think of our political representatives as our *agents*, just as we may think of professionals and craftspeople whose services we retain—doctors, lawyers, accountants, plumbers, mechanics, and so

agenda power The control over what a group will consider for discussion.

veto power The ability to defeat something even if it has made it on to the agenda of an institution.

delegation The transmission of authority to some other official or body for the latter's use (though often with the right of review and revision).

---

[7] For a general discussion of motions to close debate and get on with the decision, see Henry M. Robert, *Robert's Rules of Order* (1876), items III. 21 and VI. 38. *Robert's* has achieved the status of an icon and now exists in an enormous variety of forms and shapes.

on—as agents whom we hire to act on our behalf. Why would those with authority, whom we will call *principals*, delegate some of their authority to agents? This has to do with the virtues of decentralization and of division and specialization of labor. The answer is that both principals and agents benefit from it. Principals benefit because they are able to off-load to experts and specialists tasks that they themselves are less capable of performing. Ordinary citizens, for example, are not so well versed in the tasks of governance as are professional politicians. Thus by delegating, citizens do not have to be specialists and can focus their energies on other things. This is the rationale for representative democracy. Agents benefit as well, since delegation means there is a demand for their services, which enables them to exercise authority and receive compensation for their efforts.

This same rationale applies to the division and specialization of labor we often observe in specific political institutions. Legislators generally benefit from a decentralized arrangement in which they focus on those aspects of public policy for which they are best equipped—issues of special interest to their constituents or with which their occupational and other experiences have given them familiarity and perspective. In exchange, they are freed from having to be policy generalists and can avoid areas of little interest or relevance to them. The legislative committee system accomplishes this task by partitioning policy into different jurisdictions and allowing legislators to gravitate to those committees that most suit their purposes.

The benefits of delegation, in which a principal delegates authority to an agent, may seem almost too good to be true. But there is a dark side to this **principal-agent relationship.** As the eighteenth-century economist Adam Smith noted in his classic work, *The Wealth of Nations* (1776), economic agents are not motivated by the welfare of their customers to grow vegetables, make shoes, or weave cloth; rather, they do those things out of their own self-interest. Thus a principal must take care when delegating to agents that those agents are properly motivated to serve the principal's interests, either by sharing his or her interests or by deriving something of value (reputation, compensation, and so on) for acting to advance those interests. The principal will need to have some instruments by which to monitor and validate what his or her agent is doing and then reward or punish the agent accordingly. Nevertheless, a principal will not bother to eliminate entirely the agent's prospective deviations from the principal's interests. The reason is **transaction costs.** The effort necessary to negotiate and then police every aspect of a principal-agent relationship becomes, at some point, more costly than it is worth. In sum, the upside of delegation consists of the assignment of activities to precisely those agents who possess a comparative advantage in performing them. (A corollary is that those who are poorly prepared to conduct these activities are relieved of performing them.) The downside is the prospective misalignment of the goals of agents with the goals of principals and thus the possibility of agents marching to the beat of their own drummers. Delegation is a double-edged sword.

Characterizing institutions in terms of jurisdiction, decisiveness, agenda and veto power, and delegation covers an immense amount of ground. Our purpose here has been to introduce the many ways collectivities arrange their business and routinize it, thereby enabling cooperation and facilitating political bargaining and decision making. A second purpose has been to highlight the potential diversity in

principal-agent relationship The relationship between a principal and his or her agent. This relationship may be affected by the fact that each is motivated by self-interest, yet their interests may not be well aligned.

transaction costs The cost of clarifying each aspect of a principal-agent relationship and monitoring it to make sure arrangements are complied with.

institutional arrangements—there are so many ways to do things collectively. This diversity underscores the amazing sophistication and intelligence of the framers of the U.S. Constitution in the institutional choices they made more than two centuries ago, as we will discuss in the following chapter. Finally, we want to make clear that institutions not only make rules for governing but also present strategic opportunities for various political interests. As George Washington Plunkitt, the savvy and candid political boss of Tammany Hall, said of the institutional situations in which he found himself, "I seen my opportunities, and I took 'em."[8]

The Collective-Action Principle: All Politics Is Collective Action

The third factor that helps explain why governments do what they do is that political action is collective, involving the building, combining, mixing, and amalgamating of people's individual goals. People join together to achieve those goals. But as we shall see, collective action can be difficult to orchestrate because the individuals involved in the decision-making process often have different goals and preferences. The result is mixed motives for cooperation. Conflict is inevitable; the question is how it can be resolved. The most typical and widespread means of resolving collective dilemmas is bargaining among individuals. But when the number of parties involved is too large to engage in face-to-face bargaining, incentives must be provided to get everyone to act collectively.

Informal Bargaining. Political bargaining may be highly formal or entirely informal. Relations among neighbors, for example, are usually based on informal give-and-take. To present a personal example, one of this book's authors has a neighbor with whom he shares a hedge on their property line. First one takes responsibility for trimming the hedge and then the other, alternating from year to year. This arrangement (or bargain) is merely an understanding, not a legally binding agreement, and it was reached amicably and without much fuss or fanfare after a brief conversation. No organizational effort—such as hiring lawyers, drafting an agreement, and having it signed, witnessed, notarized, filed at the county courthouse, and so on—was required to reach this bargain.

Bargaining in politics can be similarly informal and unstructured. Whether called horse trading, back-scratching, logrolling, or wheeling and dealing, it has much the same flavor as the casual, over-the-fence negotiation between neighbors that was just described. Deals will be struck depending on the preferences and beliefs of the participants. If preferences are too incompatible or beliefs too inconsistent with one another, then a deal simply may not be possible. On the other hand, if preferences and beliefs are not too far out of line, then there will be a range of possible bargaining outcomes, some of which slightly advantage one party, others of which advantage other parties. In short, there will be room for a compromise.

---

[8] In the nineteenth century and well into the twentieth, Tammany Hall was the club that ran New York City's Democratic Party like a machine.

In fact, much of politics *is* informal, unstructured bargaining. First, many disputes subjected to bargaining are of sufficiently low impact that establishing elaborate formal machinery for dealing with them is just not worth the effort. Rules of thumb often develop as a benchmark—such as "split the difference" or "take turns" (the outcome of the hedge-trimming example just given). Second, repetition can contribute to successful cooperation. If a small group engages in bargaining today over one matter and tomorrow over another—as neighbors bargain over draining a swampy meadow one day, fixing a fence another, and trimming a hedge on still another occasion—then patterns develop. If one party constantly tries to extract maximal advantage, then the other parties will cease doing business with him. If, on the other hand, each party "gives a little to get a little," then a pattern of cooperation develops over time. It is the repetition of similar, mixed-motive occasions that allows this pattern to emerge without formal trappings. Many political circumstances are either amenable to informal rules of thumb like those mentioned or are repeated with sufficient frequency as to allow cooperative patterns to emerge.[9]

Formal Bargaining.   Formal bargaining entails interactions that are governed by rules. The rules describe such things as who gets to make the first offer, how long the other parties have to consider it, whether other parties must take it or leave it or can make counteroffers, the method by which they convey their assent or rejection, what happens when all (or some decisive subset) of the others accept or reject it, what happens next if the proposal is rejected, and so on. It may be hard to imagine two neighbors deciding how to trim their common hedge under procedures as explicit and formal as these. It makes more sense, however, to imagine a bargaining session over wages and working conditions between labor and management at a large manufacturing plant proceeding in just this manner. The distinction suggests that some parties are more appropriately suited to formal proceedings, whereas others get on well enough without them. The same may be said about situations. A husband and wife are likely to divide household chores by informal bargaining, but this same couple would employ a formal procedure if they were dividing household assets in a divorce settlement.

Formal bargaining is often associated with events that take place in official institutions—legislatures, courts, party conventions, administrative and regulatory agencies. These are settings in which mixed-motive situations arise over and over again. Year in and year out, legislatures pass statutes, approve executive budgets, and oversee the administrative branch of government. Courts administer justice, determine guilt or innocence, impose sentences, resolve differences between disputants, and render interpretive opinions about the meaning of the law. Party conventions nominate candidates and approve the platforms on which they base their campaigns. Administrative and regulatory agencies implement policy and make rulings about its applicability. All of these are instances of mixed-motive circumstances in which gains from cooperation are possible but bargaining failures are also

---

[9] A wonderful description of how ranchers in Shasta County, California, organized their social lives and collective interactions in just this fashion is found in Robert C. Ellickson, *Order without Law: How Neighbors Settle Disputes* (Cambridge, Mass.: Harvard University Press, 1991).

a definite possibility. Consequently, the formal bargaining that takes place through institutions is governed by rules that regularize proceedings both to maximize the prospects of reaching agreement and to guarantee that procedural wheels don't have to be reinvented each time a similar bargaining problem arises. This is our first application of the institution principle: institutions facilitate collective action.

Collective Dilemmas and Bargaining Failures.   Even when gains are possible from collective action—when people share some common objective, for example—it still may not be feasible to arrive at a satisfactory conclusion. Let us take the simple example of two farmers interested in mending a piece of fence that separates their properties. For simplicity, suppose that Farmer Jones and Farmer Smith each value the mended fence at some positive level, V. Suppose further that the total cost (in terms of time or effort) to do this chore is c, a big enough cost to make the job not worth the effort if a farmer had to do it all by himself. For example, if each farmer values the mended fence at $700, but the cost to repair it on his own is $1,000, the net benefit to one farmer repairing it alone ($700 minus $1,000) is less than zero—and thus not an attractive option. If they shared the cost equally, their net benefit would each be $V-c/2$, in our example, $700 minus $500—a positive net benefit of $200 to both. If one of the farmers, however, could off-load the entire project on his neighbor, then he would not have to bear any of the cost and would enjoy the mended fence valued by him at V ($700). The situation is displayed in the accompanying Figure 1.1. Each row gives the options available to Jones and each column the options available to Smith. The lower left entry in each cell of the figure is the payoff to Jones if he selects the row option and Smith selects the column option; the upper right entry in each cell is Smith's payoff. Thus if both choose to mend the fence (the upper left cell), then they each enjoy a (positive) net benefit of $V-c/2$. If, on the other hand, Jones takes on the job, but Smith does not—this is the upper right cell of the figure—then Jones pays the full price and receives $V-c$ (which is negative) and Smith gets the full value, V. The other two cells are filled in according to this logic.

FIGURE 1.1 A COLLECTIVE DILEMMA

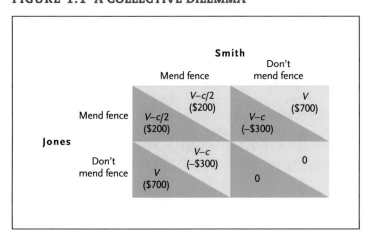

Consider now how Jones might think about this problem. On the one hand, if Smith chooses to mend the fence (left column in the figure), then Jones gets $V–c/2$ if he does too, but he does even better, V, if he lets Smith do the whole job. On the other hand, if Smith chooses not to mend the fence (right column in the figure), then Jones gets $V–c$ if he goes ahead and does the job himself (this is negative) but gets zero if he too does not take up the task. Putting these together, Jones realizes that *no matter what Smith does, Jones is better off not mending the fence.* Following the same logic, Smith will arrive at the same conclusion. So, each chooses "don't mend fence," and each gets a payoff of zero, even though both would have been better off if both had chosen to "mend the fence."

This is a famous dilemma.[10] It is a dilemma because the two individuals actually share a common goal—mending the fence—but each person's individual rationality causes both of them to do worse than they needed to. Had they only "suspended" their rationality and contributed to the common objective, then each would have been better served than when both are behaving in a fully rational manner. Even if the two farmers sat down and tried to overcome this dilemma, the dilemma still persists, as each has a rational temptation to defect from a bargain in which both agree to mend the fence. Moreover, each is nervous that the other will defect, given the incentives of the situation, and so feels compelled to defect himself.

The broad point of this example is that bargaining, even with common values and objectives, is no guarantee that a positive outcome will occur. We will encounter dilemmas and bargaining failures like the one facing the two farmers frequently in politics. We will also discover that people have invented some methods that partially mitigate bargaining failures.

Collective Action, Free Riders, Public Goods, and the Commons. The idea of political bargaining suggests an intimate kind of politics, involving face-to-face relations, negotiation, compromise, give-and-take, and so on. Such bargaining results from the combination of mixed motives and small numbers. When the numbers of individuals or other actors become large, bargaining may no longer be practical. If 100 people own property bordering a swampy meadow, how does this community solve the swamp's mosquito problem? How does the community secure the benefits that arise from cooperation? In short, what happens if a simple face-to-face interaction, possibly amenable to bargaining, now requires coordination among a large number of people?

In the swamp meadow example, everyone shares some common value—eliminating the mosquito habitat—but they may disagree on other matters. Some may want to use pesticides in the meadow, while others are concerned about the environmental impact. And there are bound to be disagreements over how to pay for the project. A collective-action problem arises, as in this example, when there is something to be gained if the group can cooperate and assure group members that some do not get away with bearing less than their fair share of the effort. Face-to-face bargaining, however, is made impractical by sheer numbers. (And as we saw with the example of the two farmers in the previous section, even face-to-face bargaining is no guarantee of

---

[10] In another context, it is known as the prisoner's dilemma. We will encounter it again in Chapter 12 when we discuss interest groups.

success.) The issue, then, is how to accomplish some common objective among a large number of interested parties.

Groups of individuals intent on **collective action** will ordinarily establish some decision-making procedures—relatively formal arrangements by which to resolve differences, coordinate the group to pursue a course of action, and sanction slackers, if necessary. Most groups will also require a leadership structure, which is necessary even if all the members of the group are in agreement about how to proceed. This structure is necessary to deal with a phenomenon known as **free riding**. Imagine that each owner of land bordering a swamp wants the area cleared of mosquitoes. If one or a few owners were to clear the swamp alone, their actions would benefit all the other owners as well, without any efforts on the part of these others. They would be free riders, enjoying the benefit of others' efforts without contributing themselves. (The same issue faced farmers Smith and Jones in the fence-mending problem described earlier.) It is this prospect of free riding that risks undermining collective action. A leadership structure will have to be in place to threaten and, if necessary, inflict punishments to discourage individuals from reneging on the individual contributions required to enable the group to pursue its common goals.

Another way to think about this is to describe a commonly shared goal—in the present example a mosquito-free meadow—as a public good. A **public good** is a benefit that others cannot be denied from enjoying, once it has been provided. Once the meadow is mosquito free, it will constitute a benefit to *all* the members of the group, even those who have not contributed to its provision. More generally, a public good is one that can be "consumed" by individuals without using it up, and for which there are no means at hand to exclude individuals easily. A classic example is a lighthouse. Once it is erected, it aids all ships, and there is no simple way to charge a ship for its use. Another classic example is national defense. It protects tax payers and tax avoiders alike. A third example is clean air. Once enough people restrict their polluting, the air is cleansed and may be enjoyed even by those who have not restricted their polluting. (Imagine owners of hybrid vehicles whose reduced pollution makes for cleaner air enjoyed even by those whose automobiles produce lots of noxious exhaust.) Because public goods have these properties, it is easy for some members of a group to free-ride on the efforts shouldered by others. And as a result, it may be difficult to get anyone to provide it in the first place. Collective action is required, and this in turn often requires leaders (or governments) with the capacity to induce all to contribute to its provision.

Various solutions to the collective-action problem have been proposed. The most famous is Mancur Olson's **by-product theory**.[11] Briefly, Olson's idea is this: The nub of free riding derives from the fact that most individuals in a large group don't make much difference to the final result, and they know it. This is why they may comfortably abstain from participation: They know that in following their

---

collective action
The pooling of resources and the coordination of effort and activity by a group of people (often a large one) to achieve common goals.

free riding
Enjoying the benefits of some good or action while letting others bear the costs.

public good A good that (1) may be enjoyed by anyone if it is provided and (2) may not be denied to anyone once it has been provided.

by-product theory The idea that groups provide members with private benefits to attract membership. The possibility of group collective action emerges as a consequence.

---

[11] Mancur Olson, *The Logic of Collective Action: Public Goods and the Theory of Groups* (1965; repr., Cambridge, Mass.: Harvard University Press, 1971). On the general subject of collective action, the interested reader should also consult Kenneth A. Shepsle and Mark S. Bonchek, *Analyzing Politics: Rationality, Behavior, and Institutions* (New York: Norton, 1997), chap. 9, where Olson's work, among that of others, is taken up.

inclination to avoid the costs of participation, they do not damage their prospects (or anyone else's) for receiving benefits. The problem is that although no one person's free riding does much harm, if enough people free ride, then the collective action will be compromised. What if, however, something of value were at stake that would be lost if the person abstained from participation? What if participants were given something special that nonparticipants were denied? That is, what if some benefits were contingent on contributing to the group effort? Many organizations use this tactic, giving dues-paying or effort-contributing members special insurance or education benefits, reduced-fare travel, free or subsidized subscriptions to magazines and newsletters, bowling and golf tournaments, soccer leagues, access to members-only social events, and so on. Olson argued that if members were prepared to "pay their dues" to join an organization partially (or even mainly) for these special benefits, of which they would otherwise be deprived—what Olson called **selective benefits**—then the collective cooperation would end up being provided as well, as a by-product, with whatever surplus the dues structure generated. A member's inclination to free ride would be diminished, not because of feelings of obligation to his or her fellow members, not because of a moral imperative to participate, and not even because of a desire for the collective benefit supplied by the group, but rather because of naked self-interest—the desire for selective benefits. Clearly this is an extreme version of the argument; the main point is that the selective benefits available only to participants and contributors—and denied to nonparticipants and noncontributors—are the key to successful collective action. A group that appeals to its members *only* on the basis of its common collective purposes is a group that will have trouble achieving those purposes.[12]

One of the most notorious collective-action problems involves too much of a good thing. Known as the *tragedy of the commons*, this type of problem reveals how unbridled self-interest can have damaging collective consequences. A political party's reputation, for example, can be seen as something that benefits all politicians affiliated with the party. This collective reputation is not irreparably harmed if one legislator in the party pushes her advantage by getting approval for a minor amendment helpful to a special interest in her district. But if lots of party members do it, the party comes to be known as the champion of special interests, and its reputation is tarnished. A pool of resources is not much depleted if someone takes a little of it. But it does become depleted if lots of people take from it—a forest is lost a pine tree at a time; an oil reserve declines a barrel at a time; the atmosphere is polluted a particle at a time. The party's reputation, the forest, the oil reserve, and the atmosphere are all *commons*.[13] The problem to which they are vulnerable is

selective benefits Benefits that do not go to everyone but, rather, are distributed selectively— only to those who contribute to the group enterprise.

---

[12] Getting such an organizational effort up and running, however, is no small feat. Olson's argument appreciates what is necessary to keep a group going but underestimates what it takes to organize collective action in the first place. Put differently, a prior collective-action problem needs to be solved—and that is an organizational problem. The solution is leadership, and the individuals imaginative enough to see this need are referred to as political entrepreneurs. That is, there must be a selective benefit available to those who bear organizational burdens, thereby facilitating the collective action; the selective benefits of leadership include perquisites of office, financial reward, and honor and status.

[13] The original meaning is of a pasture on which cows graze. A most insightful discussion of "commons problems," of which these are examples, is Elinor Ostrom, *Governing the Commons: The Evolution of Institutions for Collective Action* (New York: Cambridge University Press, 1990).

overgrazing. Thus, a common resource that is irreparably depleted by individual actions is known as "the tragedy of the commons."[14]

To summarize, individuals try to accomplish things not only as individuals but also as members of larger collectivities (families, friendship groups, clubs and associations, and political parties) and even larger categories (economic classes, ethnic groups, and nationalities). The rationality principle covers individual initiative. The collective action principle describes the paradoxes encountered, the obstacles that must be overcome, and the incentives necessary for individuals to work with others to coordinate their energies, accomplish collective purposes, and secure the dividends of cooperation. Much of politics is about doing this or failing to do this. The institution principle discussed previously takes this argument to its logical conclusion, focusing on collective activities that are regularized because they are both important and frequently occurring. Institutions do the public's business while relieving communities of having to reinvent collective action each time it is required. Thus we have a rationale for government.

The Policy Principle: Political Outcomes Are the Products of Individual Preferences and Institutional Procedures

At the end of the day, we are interested in the results of politics—the collective decisions that emerge from the political process. A Nebraska farmer, for example cares about how public laws and rulings affect his welfare and that of his family, friends, and neighbors. He cares about how export policies affect the prices his crops and livestock products earn in international markets and how monetary policy influences inflation and, as a result, the cost of purchasing fuel, feed, seed, and fertilizer; about the funding of public and private research and development efforts in agriculture and their effect on the quality and reliability of the scientific information he obtains; and about the affordability of the state university, where he hopes to educate his children. He also cares, eventually, about inheritance laws and their effect on his ability to pass his farm on to his kids without Uncle Sam taking a huge chunk of it in estate taxes. As students of American politics, we need to consider the link between individual goals, institutional arrangements, collective action, and policy outcomes. How do all of these leave their marks on policy? What biases, predilections, and tendencies manifest themselves in public decisions?

The linchpin is the motivations of political actors. As we saw in our discussion of the rationality principle, their ambitions—ideological, personal, electoral, and institutional—provide politicians with the incentives to craft policies in particular ways. In fact, most policies make sense only as reflections of individual politicians' interests, goals, and beliefs. Examples include

Personal interests: Congressman X is an enthusiastic supporter of subsidizing home heating oil (but opposes regulation to keep its price down) because some of his friends own heating-oil distributorships.[15]

---

[14] The classic statement is Garrett Hardin, "The Tragedy of the Commons," *Science* 162 (1968): 1243–48.

[15] These friends would benefit from people's having the financial means to buy home heating oil but would not want the price they charge for the oil restricted.

Electoral ambitions:	Senator Y, a well-known political moderate, has lately been introducing very conservative amendments to bills dealing with the economy to appeal to more conservative financial donors, who might then contribute to her budding presidential campaign.
Institutional ambitions:	Representative Z has promised his vote and given a rousing speech on the House floor supporting a particular amendment because he knows it is near and dear to his party leader. He hopes his support will earn him her endorsement next year for an assignment to the prestigious Appropriations Committee.

These examples illustrate how policies are politically crafted according to both institutional procedures and individual aspirations. The procedures, as we saw in a previous discussion, are a series of chutes and ladders that shape, channel, filter, and prune the alternatives from which ultimate policy choices are made. The politicians who populate these institutions, as we have just noted, are driven both by private objectives and by public purposes, pursuing their own private interests while working on behalf of their conception of the public interest.

Because the institutional features of the American political system are complex and policy change requires success at every step, change is often impossibly difficult, meaning the status quo usually prevails. A long list of players must be satisfied with the change, or it won't happen. Most of these politicians will need some form of "compensation" to provide their endorsement and support.

Majorities are usually built by legislators drafting bills so as to spread the benefits to enough members of the legislature to get the requisite number of votes for that particular bill. Derisively, this is called pork-barrel legislation. It can be better understood by remembering that the overwhelming proportion of pork-barrel projects that are distributed to build policy majorities are justified to voters as valuable additions to the public good of the various districts. What may be pork to the critic is actual bridges, roads, and post offices.

Elaborate institutional arrangements, complicated policy processes, and intricate political motivations make for a highly combustible mixture. The policies that emerge are inevitably lacking in the neatness that citizens desire. But policies in the United States today are sloppy and slapdash for a clear reason: The tendency to spread the benefits broadly results when political ambition comes up against a decentralized political system.

The History Principle: How We Got Here Matters

There is one more aspect of our analysis that is important: We must ask how we have gotten where we are. By what series of steps? When by choice and when by accident? Every question and problem we confront has a history. History will not tell the same story for every institution. Nevertheless, without history, we have neither a sense of causation nor a full sense of how institutions are related to one another. In explaining the answer to why governments do what they do, we must turn to history to see what choices were available to political actors at a given time, what consequences resulted from those choices and what consequences might have flowed from the paths not chosen.

Imagine a tree growing from the bottom of the page. Its trunk grows upward from some root ball at the bottom, dividing into branches that continue to grow upward, further dividing into smaller branches. Imagine a path through this tree, from its very roots at the bottom of the page to the end of one of the highest branches at the top of the page. There are many such paths, from the one point at the bottom to many possible points at the top. If instead of a tree this were a time diagram, then the root ball at the bottom would represent some specific beginning point and all of the top-branch endings would represent some terminal time. Each path is now a possible history, the delineation of movement from some specific beginning to some concluding time. Alternative histories, like paths through trees, entail irreversibilities. Once one starts down a historical path (or up a tree), one cannot always retrace one's steps.[16] Once things happen, they cannot always unhappen. Some futures are foreclosed by the choices people have already made or, if not literally foreclosed, then made extremely unlikely.

It is in this sense that we explain a current situation at least in part by describing the historical path by which we arrived at it. Some scholars use the term **path dependency** to suggest that some possibilities are more or less likely because of events that occurred, and choices that were made, earlier in history. Both the status quo and the path from it significantly delimit future possibilities.

path dependency
The idea that certain possibilities are made more or less likely because of the historical path taken.

Three factors that help to explain why history commonly matters in political life are rules and procedures, loyalties and alliances, and historically conditioned points of view. As for the first of these factors, rules and procedures, choices made during one point in time continue to have important consequences for years, decades, or even centuries. For example, America's single-member-district plurality voting rules, established in the eighteenth century, continue to shape the nation's party system today.[17] Those voting rules, as we shall see in Chapter 11, help explain why the United States has a two-party system rather than the multiparty systems found in many other Western democracies. Thus a set of choices made 200 years ago affects party politics today.

A second way in which history often matters in politics is through the persistence of loyalties and alliances. Many of the political alliances that are important in American politics today are products of events that took place decades ago. For example, Jewish voters are among the Democratic Party's most loyal supporters, consistently giving 80 or 90 percent of their votes to Democratic presidential candidates. Yet on the basis of economic interest, Jews, one of the wealthier social groups in America, might be expected to vote for the Republicans. In recent years, moreover, the GOP has been a stronger supporter of Israel than the Democrats. Why, then, do Jews overwhelmingly support the Democrats? Part of the answer has to do with history. In the late nineteenth and early twentieth centuries, Jews

---

[16] Clearly with tree climbing this is not literally true, or once we started climbing a tree, we would never get down! So the tree analogy is not perfect here.

[17] Single-member districts are arrangements in which one legislator is selected from each district. (Some electoral systems select multiple members from each district.) A plurality voting rule declares that the one legislator selected in a district is the one with the most votes (not necessarily a majority).

suffered considerable discrimination in the United States. In the 1930s, though, under the leadership of Franklin Roosevelt, the Democratic Party was one vehicle through which Jews in America began their climb to the success they enjoy today. This historical experience continues to shape Jewish political identity. Similar historical experiences help to explain the political loyalties of African Americans, Cuban Americans, and others.

A third factor explaining why history matters is the fact that past events and experiences shape current viewpoints and perspectives. For example, many Americans now in their fifties and sixties view events in Iraq through the lens of the Vietnam War. Those influenced by the memory of Vietnam often see U.S. military involvement in a Third World country as likely to lead to a quagmire of costs and casualties. Interestingly, in the 1960s, many older Americans viewed events in Vietnam through the lens of the 1930s, when the Western democracies were slow to resist Adolf Hitler's Germany. Thus to those influenced by events of the 1930s and World War II, failure to respond strongly to aggression was seen as a form of appeasement that would only encourage hostile powers to use force against American interests. Both groups saw the world through perspectives that they had learned from their own histories.

CONCLUSION

This introductory chapter has asked much of the reader. We have set the stage for an analytical treatment of the phenomena that constitute American politics. This analytical approach requires attention to *argument* and *evidence*. To construct an argument about some facet of American politics—why were young voters attracted to Barack Obama in 2008 or Ronald Reagan in 1980? why do incumbent legislators in the House and Senate have so much success in securing reelection? why does the president dominate media attention?—we can draw on a set of five principles. The linchpin is the rationality principle, emphasizing individual goal seeking as a key explanation for behavioral patterns. But politics is a collective undertaking, and it is often structured by political arrangements, so we also focus on collective action and the institutions in which such action takes place (collective action principle, institution principle). The combination of goal-seeking individuals engaging in collective activity in institutional contexts provides leverage for understanding why governments govern as they do—making laws, passing budgets, implementing policies, rendering judicial judgments (policy principle). But we could not make entire sense of these activities without an appreciation of the broader historical path (history principle). These five principles, then, are tools of analysis. They are also tools of discovery, permitting the interested observer to uncover new ideas about why politics works as it does.

Arguments may be tight or loose, compelling or questionable, persuasive or dubious. To know if an argument truly contributes to our understanding of the real world around us, we need to sift through evidence. In the study of American politics, much of this evidence takes the form of quantitative data, and much of it is easily accessible on significant Web sites. How to make sense of such evidence is what political scientists do in their workaday world. In the "Analyzing the Evidence" section beginning on the following page, we provide a brief glimpse of how to go about this task. We hope it proves helpful in allowing you to think analytically about political information as we move through the remaining chapters of the book.

Drawing on the lesson of the history principle, we begin in the remaining chapters of Part One by setting the historical stage. With analytical principles and strategies for analyzing evidence in hand, we are in a position to understand what influenced and inspired the founding generation more than two centuries ago to create a national government and a federal political system, while preserving individual rights and liberties.

FOR FURTHER READING

Bianco, William T. *American Politics: Strategy and Choice.* New York: Norton, 2001.

Dahl, Robert A. *Who Governs? Democracy and Power in an American City.* New Haven, Conn.: Yale University Press, 1961.

Downs, Anthony. *An Economic Theory of Democracy.* New York: Harper & Row, 1957.

Ellickson, Robert C. *Order without Law: How Neighbors Settle Disputes.* Cambridge, Mass.: Harvard University Press, 1991.

Hardin, Garrett, "The Tragedy of the Commons," *Science* 162 (1968): 1243–48. ◯ reader selection

Hindmoor, Andrew. *Rational Choice.* New York: Palgrave-Macmillan, 2006.

Kiewiet, D. Roderick, and Matthew McCubbins. *The Logic of Delegation.* Chicago: University of Chicago Press, 1991. ◯ reader selection

Mayhew, David R. *Congress: The Electoral Connection.* New Haven, Conn.: Yale University Press, 1974.

Mueller, Dennis. *Public Choice III.* New York: Cambridge, 2003.

Olson, Mancur, Jr. *The Logic of Collective Action: Public Goods and the Theory of Groups.* 1965. Reprinted with new preface and appendix. Cambridge, Mass.: Harvard University Press, 1971. ◯ reader selection

Putnam, Robert D. *Making Democracy Work: Civic Traditions in Modern Italy.* Princeton, N.J.: Princeton University Press, 1993.

Riker, William H. *Liberalism against Populism: A Confrontation between the Theory of Democracy and the Theory of Social Choice.* San Francisco: Freeman, 1982.

Shepsle, Kenneth A. "Rational Choice Institutionalism," in R.A.W. Rhodes, Sarah A. Binder, and Bert A. Rockman, eds. *The Oxford Handbook of Political Institutions.* New York: Oxford University Press, 2006, pp. 23–39.

————, and Mark S. Bonchek. *Analyzing Politics: Rationality, Behavior, and Institutions.* New York: Norton, 1997.

Ⓢ Additional study and review materials are available online at wwnorton.com/studyspace/

How Do Political Scientists Know What They Know?

The five principles introduced in this chapter provide a foundation for understanding and explaining the facts of political life. There are two things, however, that we need to appreciate before proceeding—things that political scientists regularly do in their analysis of politics. The first we have already mentioned earlier in this chapter. In order to make effective use of our principles, we need to know how to make analytical arguments; the assumptions we make about the structure of politics and the behavior of political actors decisively affect how we interpret the data of everyday political life. Our five principles of politics attempt to capture these assumptions; they constitute the raw input for reasoning about politics. Second, we need to understand how political scientists uncover facts about politics and what tools they use to analyze and interpret these facts. What data are relevant to an argument about politics? Where can we find such data? How do we learn things from these data? How do we test arguments about the data? In short, we need both an analytical frame of reference (as provided by the five principles) and a set of empirical tools that allow us to explore questions with this frame of reference and tease out conclusions from relevant data. This is what constitutes the *systematic* study of politics.

In each of the empirical chapters to follow, you will find an "Analyzing the Evidence" box, highlighting arguments and evidence on some of the subjects of that chapter. In this first "Analyzing the Evidence" section, however, we provide a more methodological discussion. Here we introduce some simple ways in which political scientists examine arguments about politics—ways in which political scientists know what they know. This is no more than a basic primer on how political scientists work with political data, but we believe you will find it helpful in assessing arguments and evidence in succeeding chapters.

Consider just a few arguments about American politics:

1. Most Americans have strong psychological attachments to parties, and they vote in line with their party attachments.

2. Members of Congress seek reelection, and they will vote for laws that majorities in their constituencies would also support.

3. The chief executive of a government—the president, governor, or mayor—is the most powerful person in that government, and on important policy questions will win more often than any other politician.

How should we think critically about such claims? What is the reasoning that sustains a claim, and what is the evidence to support it? What are alternative explanations? Throughout this book we will present some of the most important facts about American political behavior and government and discuss how they help us understand the motivations of individuals and the nature of politics.

Consider one of the most basic questions about voting. In elections, Americans face two main alternatives in the form of the two major political parties—the Democratic Party and the Republican

Party. Each party promises to pursue distinctive economic policies. Since at least the 1930s, the Democratic Party has favored economic policies that redistribute income to poorer segments of society; Republicans, on the other hand, favor lower taxes and little or no redistribution. Such policies, if enacted into law, have real consequences for people's livelihoods. If those are the choices, it makes perfect sense to vote according to your economic self interest: Choose the party that maximizes your income.

This is quite a compelling argument. Indeed, many economists take it as axiomatic that people vote to maximize their personal income or economic self-interest. On reflection, however, we see that other factors also affect election outcomes and voting, including personal qualities of candidates, important noneconomic issues, and even the force of habit. These other factors suggest alternative explanations, including the possibility that people try to choose the ablest individuals to serve in office, that people vote according to beliefs or ideologies or issues that bear little relation to their income, and that people vote in line with psychological attachments to parties that they developed in childhood.

The criterion for a good argument is how well it helps us understand reality. Is it consistent with past experience? Does it do a good job of predicting events, such as current legislative outcomes or a future election? How well does it fit current circumstances or repeated observations over time? Familiarity with some basic concepts and tools will help us grapple with these issues.

What are Data?

The first step in any systematic study is to define terms. Often, research begins with a puzzling or sensational event. For example, elections are exciting events, and we want to understand many facets of them. Perhaps the central question about elections for political scientists is, Why do people vote the way they do? There is, in this example, a behavior that we generally want to explain, *vote choice*. We represent this general construct mathematically as a variable. A variable defines all possible outcomes that might have occurred and assigns them a unique label or value. Vote choice, for instance, may take four possible values or outcomes: Vote for the Democratic candidate, vote for the Republican candidate, vote for another party or candidate, or don't vote.[1]

The second step is to measure the behavior of interest. This stage requires the collection of data. Observation of a small set of events can be quite enlightening. We might, for instance, conduct in-depth interviews with a dozen or so people about how they decided to vote. However, we usually require more evidence to support a given claim; a small number of people might not be sufficiently representative.

Censuses and random sample surveys are staples of social science data collection. With a *census* we observe all individuals in the population at a given moment. Every ten years, the United States conducts a comprehensive enumeration of all people living in the country. The U.S. Constitution requires a decennial

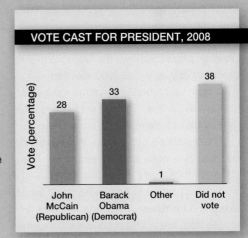

VOTE CAST FOR PRESIDENT, 2008

Source: Federal Election Commission, www.fec.gov (accessed 7/6/09).

[1]We could complicate our analysis by expanding the number of potential descriptions of vote choice. For example, vote for Democratic presidential candidate and Democratic congressional candidate, Democratic presidential candidate and Republican congressional candidate, and so on. The set of categories or values that our variable can take on is an important decision the researcher must make.

census for the purposes of apportionment of seats in the U. S. House. Today, the census provides a unique and comprehensive view of the American population, including information on families, education levels, income, race and ethnicity, commuting, housing, and employment.[2] An election is a census of sorts, because it is a comprehensive count of all votes cast in a given election. Likewise, the set of all roll-call votes cast by members of Congress in a given session is also a census.

A *survey*, on the other hand, consists of a study of a relatively small subset of individuals. We call this subset a sample. One of the most important social science research projects of the second half of the twentieth century is the American National Election Study, or ANES for short. The ANES is a national survey that has been conducted during every presidential election and most midterm congressional elections since 1948 to gauge how people voted and to understand why. Today, many important surveys examine American society and politics, including the General Social Survey, the Current Population Survey, and the American Community Survey (all by the Census Bureau), and exit polls conducted by national news organizations.[3] Most of the information used by public policy makers, businesses, and academic researchers— including estimates of unemployment and inflation, television and radio ratings, and most demographic characteristics of the population (used to distribute federal funds)—are measured using surveys.

Summarizing Data. Communicating the information in a census or survey requires tools for summarizing data. The summary of data proceeds in two steps. First, we compute the frequency with which each value of a variable occurs. Frequency may be either the number of times that a specific behavior or value of a variable occurs or the percent of the observations in which it occurs. Second, we construct a graph or statistic that summarizes the frequencies of all values of the variable.

The *distribution* of a variable expresses the frequencies of the values of a variable. That distribution may be represented graphically with a bar chart (also called a histogram) or a pie chart. It may also be represented by a statistical table. On its horizontal axis, a *bar chart* displays all possible values of a variable; the heights of the bars equal the frequency or percent of cases observed for each value. In the 2008 U.S. presidential election, 38% of the people did not vote, 28% of the people voted for Republican John McCain, 33% of the people voted for Democrat Barack Obama, and 1% of the people voted for third-party candidates. The frequencies sum to 100 percent. It is common to restrict the analysis to voters only, in which case McCain won 45.7% of the votes cast and Obama won 52.9% of the votes cast, with the remaining votes scattered across other candidates. The bar chart on page 25 shows the histogram of the presidential vote in the 2008 election.

A *statistical table* displays the values of the variable along the left-hand side of the table and the frequencies to the right.

The distribution of income in the United States offers a somewhat different example. The U.S. Census offers many different definitions of income, so we must settle on one: household income before taxes and transfers. This variable takes a range of values from the smallest household income to the

VOTE CAST FOR PRESIDENT, 2008	
John McCain	28%
Barack Obama	33%
Other candidates	1%
Did not vote	38%

Source: Federal Election Commission, www.fec.gov (accessed 7/6/09).

[2]www.census.gov
[3]All of these resources are publicly available. We encourage you to consult them on the Web or at the library.

largest household income, and then reports frequencies by categories. Category 1 is "less than $10,000"; category 2 is "$10,000 to $14,999"; category 3 is "$15,000 to $24,999"; and so forth up to the top category, which is "over $200,000." All possible income levels are covered in this classification, and the categories can be ordered from lowest to highest. The histogram below presents the distribution of incomes in the U. S. population in 2007.

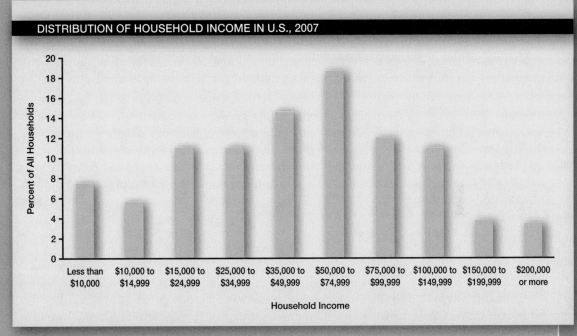

DISTRIBUTION OF HOUSEHOLD INCOME IN U.S., 2007

Source: U.S. Census Bureau, www.census.gov (accessed 7/6/09).

Variables such as income can be characterized with statistics, such as the median or mean. In this example, the *median* is the value of household income such that half of all households have income below that value and half have income above it. Fifty percent of all cases have income above the median value, and fifty percent have income below it; thus, the median is also called the fiftieth percentile. The median household income in the United States in 2007 was $50,233. We can see this in the histogram by beginning with the lowest value and adding up the percentages associated with each successive value until the cumulated percentage equals 50 percent. The *mean*, or average, equals the sum of each household's income (or personal income of all people in the United States) divided by the number of households. Personal income totaled approximately $11.6 trillion in 2007, and there are 117 million households. So, in the United States in 2007, the average household income was $99,800.

Why do the mean and median differ? When we calculate the median, every household is equal. We merely count the percent above and below a certain income level. The mean value weights households according to their incomes; consequently, a household with $200,000 income contributes 10 times as much to the calculation of the mean as a household with $20,000. If there were only small differences in income among households, the mean would be very close to the median. The difference between the median and the mean thus provides a measure of inequality.

The median is particularly important in thinking about voting. In an election involving two parties or candidates, it takes at least 50 percent of the votes to win. In a legislature, any bill must receive at least half of the votes of those present in order to pass. Suppose a piece of legislation directly affects people's incomes by taxing those with income above a certain level, say $75,000, and transferring that income to people who make less than that amount. Suppose also that people only care about their personal income when thinking about this bill. We may use the distribution of incomes to calculate directly what percent of people will support the bill and what percent of people will oppose it. If we use the data on the preceding page, we find that approximately one-quarter of households have income higher than $75,000, and three-quarters have income less than $75,000. If people voted only on the basis of their income—their economic self-interest—then 23 percent would oppose the tax bill and 77 percent would support it. In such a setting we can see that democracy would inevitably tax the rich.

Testing Arguments Using Data. The argument that democracy will tend to redistribute income depends on an important assumption—that people vote their economic self-interest. Is that assumption correct? Political science involves entertaining propositions, such as the claim that people vote their economic self-interest, and then testing those ideas using quantitative and other sorts of data.

Testing a claim or argument requires making comparisons: Compare the predictions from a given argument or proposition with data relevant to that idea. Usually, such conjectures take the form of a hypothesis that there is a strong relationship between two variables, such as income and the vote. To test for such a relationship, we examine how the distribution of one variable (called the dependent variable, in this case the vote) depends on the values of another variable (the independent variable). The difference in the outcome across values for the independent variable is called an *effect*.

In the case of income and vote choice, we want to know how much voting decisions depend on individuals' income levels. Compare two types of people—those who live in high-income households (income above $120,000) and those who live in low-income households (income below $15,000). Do these two types of people differ in the frequency with which they support policies that lead to greater income redistribution, and parties and candidates that favor such policies? As stated earlier, in the United States today, the Republican Party generally favors lower income taxes and less income redistribution, and the Democratic Party favors higher income taxes and more income redistribution. We therefore want to know if those in high-income households vote Republican at a much higher rate than those in low-income households. The difference in voting behavior between these two groups is the *effect* of income on the vote.

Tables offer a convenient way to display the relationship between two variables. As we saw earlier, a table presents all possible combinations of the values of two variables in a rectangular array. The top of the array corresponds to one of the variables and is divided into

VOTE BY LEVEL OF INCOME IN 2008 NATIONAL EXIT POLLS			
Income (% of people)	Obama	McCain	Other
Under $15,000 (6%)	73%	25%	2%
$15,000–30,000 (12%)	60%	37%	3%
$30,000–50,000 (19%)	55%	43%	2%
$50,000–75,000 (21%)	48%	49%	3%
$75,000–100,000 (15%)	51%	48%	1%
$100,000–150,000 (14%)	48%	51%	1%
$150,000–200,000 (6%)	48%	50%	2%
$200,000 or More (6%)	52%	46%	2%

Source: www.cnn.com/ELECTION/2008/results/polls/USP00p1 (accessed 5/21/09).

columns, one for each of the values of the variable. The left side of the array corresponds to the other variable and is divided into rows, one for each value of this variable. Each cell, then, corresponds to a unique pair of values of the two variables (the intersection of a given row and a given column). In our example the variables are income and vote choice. The first cell corresponds to survey respondents who voted for Obama and who are from families with income below $15,000. The cells in the table on page 28 correspond to the percent of people in each income group who chose Obama, McCain, or someone else.

To see whether the income gap in voting is indeed large, we can use the data in this table to examine the actual voting behavior of different sorts of individuals. The national exit polls in 2008 reveal that 73 percent of voters with income less than $15,000 chose Barack Obama (and approximately 25 percent John McCain). In contrast, 52 percent of those with income over $200,000 chose Barack Obama (and only about 46 percent John McCain). The difference in the support for Obama across these two income groups is 21 percentage points (73–52). This large difference reveals that income is associated with vote choice, but it is not absolutely determinative. In particular, no income group voted overwhelmingly Republican in this election.

Consider an alternative argument, offered by the political scientists Angus Campbell, Philip Converse, Warren Miller, and Donald Stokes in *The American Voter*. People have a psychological attachment to party from which they rarely deviate. This argument suggests that those who identify personally with one of the parties vote almost entirely along party lines. The following table shows that is true; the effect of party identity is much larger than the effect of income. Knowing someone's party identity provides a strong indicator of how he or she will likely vote.

VOTE BY PARTY IDENTIFICATION IN 2008 NATIONAL EXIT POLLS			
	Obama	McCain	Other
Democrat (39%)	89%	10%	1%
Republican (32%)	9%	90%	1%
Independent (29%)	52%	44%	4%

Source: www.cnn.com/ELECTION/2008/results/polls/USP00p1 (accessed 5/21/09).

As we explore many alternative arguments about vote choice, we can make many different comparisons—Democrats versus Republicans, men versus women, college graduates versus high school graduates, and so forth. In each case, we begin by making a table of the frequencies and compute the percentages within each group that voted Democratic or Republican. Our goal is to find which, if any of these potential explanations, best accounts for the variation in voting. Throughout this book, we will consider other outcomes beside voter behavior, such as members' of Congress support for different types of legislation and the percent of times that the executive succeeds in passing legislation—in each case, what we know about these phenomena in American politic is informed by an analytical approach to evidence.

2 Constructing a Government: The Founding and the Constitution

To really understand the character of the American Founding and the meaning of the American Constitution, it is essential to look beyond myths and rhetoric. Our first principle of politics is that all political behavior has a purpose. The men and women who became revolutionaries were guided by a number of purposes. Most of the nation's Founders, though highly educated, were not political theorists. They were, rather, hardheaded and pragmatic in their commitments and activities. Although their interests were not identical, they did agree that a relationship of political and economic dependence on a colonial power, one that did not treat them as full-fledged citizens of the empire, was intolerable. In the end, the decision to break away from Britain and, over the succeeding decade, fashion institutions of self-governance was the consequence.

Many of those most active in the initial days of the Revolution felt backed into a corner, their decisions forced. For years, the imperial center in London, preoccupied by a war with France that had spread across several continents, had left the colonists to their own devices. These were years in which the colonists enjoyed an immense amount of local control and home rule. These institutional arrangements suited merchants, farmers, and planters in the separate colonies. Local control under the mild direction of colonial governors left colonists to tend to their own business for the most part. But suddenly, as the war with France drew to a close in the 1760s, the British presence became more onerous and more intrusive. This historical experience incited collective action. In reaction to English attempts to extract tax revenues to pay for the troops that were being sent to defend the colonial frontier, protests erupted throughout the colonies against the infamous Stamp Act of 1765. This act required that all printed and legal documents, including newspapers, pamphlets, advertisements, notes and bonds, leases, deeds, and licenses, be printed on official paper stamped and sold by English officials. To show their displeasure with the act, the colonists held mass meetings, participated in parades, lit bonfires, and conducted other demonstrations throughout the spring and summer of 1765. In Boston, for example, a stamp agent was hanged and burned in effigy. Later the home of the lieutenant governor was sacked, leading to his resignation and those of his colonial commission and stamp agents. By November 1765, business was proceeding and newspapers were being published without the stamp; in March 1766, Parliament repealed the detested law. Through their protest, the nonimportation agreements that the colonists subsequently adopted, and the Stamp Act Congress that met in October 1765, the colonists took the first steps down a path that ultimately would lead to war and the establishment of a new nation.

This is where we begin our story in the present chapter. We first assess the political backdrop of the American Revolution. From the history principle we know that nearly a century of relatively light-handed colonial administration by London had produced a set of expectations among the colonists that later British actions unmistakably violated. Then we examine the Constitution that ultimately emerged—after a rather

CORE OF THE ANALYSIS

- The framers of the Constitution, although guided by underlying values, also had conflicting goals and interests.
- These conflicting interests were accommodated through the rules and procedures—the institutions—set forth in the Constitution.
- The Constitution not only provides a framework for government but also often guides the policy process—even to this day.

bumpy experience in self-government just after the Revolution—as the basis for America's government. This document is the quintessential institutional setup that structures political relationships, facilitates collective action, and encourages peaceful conflict resolution. We conclude with a reflection on the Founding period by emphasizing a lesson to be learned from the Founding that continues to be important throughout American history. The lesson is that politics, as James Madison said in *The Federalist*, generally involves struggles among conflicting interests. In 1776, the main conflict was between pro-Revolutionary and anti-Revolutionary forces. In 1787, the major struggle was between the Federalists and the Antifederalists. Today the struggle is between the Democratic and Republican parties, each representing competing economic, social, and sectional interests. Often political ideas are the weapons developed by competing interests to further their own causes. The New England merchants who cried "no taxation without representation" cared more about lower taxes than expanded representation. Yet today representation is one of the foundations of American democracy.

The policy principle tells us that institutional procedures help shape political outcomes. And in the United States, no set of institutional procedures is more important than the Constitution, which was drafted during our Founding period. What are the basic rules embodied in the Constitution? What significance have constitutional precepts had for American life? These are the important questions addressed in this chapter.

THE FIRST FOUNDING: INTERESTS AND CONFLICTS

Competing ideals often reflect competing interests, and so it was in Revolutionary America. The American Revolution and the Constitution were outgrowths and expressions of a struggle among economic and political forces within the colonies. Five sectors of society had interests that were important in colonial politics: (1) the New England merchants; (2) the southern planters; (3) the "royalists"— holders of royal lands, offices, and patents (licenses to engage in a profession or business activity); (4) shopkeepers, artisans, and laborers; and (5) small farmers. Throughout the eighteenth century, these groups were in conflict over issues of taxation, trade, and commerce. For the most part, however, the southern planters, the New England merchants, and the royal officeholders and patent holders— groups that together made up the colonial elite—were able to maintain a political alliance that held in check the more radical forces representing shopkeepers, laborers, and small farmers. After 1750, however, by seriously threatening the interests of New England merchants and southern planters, British tax and trade policies split the colonial elite. This split permitted radical forces to expand their political influence, and set into motion a chain of events that culminated in the American Revolution.[1]

British Taxes and Colonial Interests

Beginning in the 1750s, the debts and other financial problems faced by the British government forced it to search for new revenue sources. This search rather quickly led to the Crown's North American colonies, which on the whole paid remarkably little in taxes to the mother country. The British government reasoned that a sizable fraction of its debt was, in fact, attributable to the expenses it had incurred in defense of the colonies during the recent French and Indian Wars, as well as to the continuing protection from Indian attacks that British forces were giving the colonists and to the protection that the British navy was providing for colonial shipping. Thus during the 1760s, Britain sought to impose new, though relatively modest, taxes on the colonists.

Like most governments of the period, the British regime had at its disposal only limited ways to collect revenues. The income tax, which in the twentieth century became the single most important source of government revenue, had not yet been developed. For the most part in the mid-eighteenth century, governments relied on tariffs, duties, and other taxes on commerce, and it was to such taxes, including the Stamp Act, that the British turned during the 1760s. British interests (revenue) and institutions (Parliament and colonial administration) combined to produce a plausible solution to an existing problem, as suggested by the policy principle.[2]

The Stamp Act and other taxes on commerce, such as the Sugar Act of 1764, which taxed sugar, molasses, and other commodities, most heavily affected the two groups in colonial society whose commercial interests and activities were most extensive: the New England merchants and southern planters. Under the famous slogan "no taxation without representation," the merchants and planters together

---

[1] The social makeup of colonial America and some of the social conflicts that divided colonial society are discussed in Jackson Turner Main, *The Social Structure of Revolutionary America* (Princeton, N.J.: Princeton University Press, 1965).

[2] Parliament also enacted the Quebec Act as part of the British settlement with the Native Americans. This withdrew the right of colonists to settle lands west of the Allegheny Mountains, preserving them for native populations. Among others, the families of George Washington and Benjamin Franklin had speculated on these lands and thus faced serious financial loss. See Norman Schofield, *Architects of Political Change: Constitutional Quandaries and Social Choice Theory* (New York: Cambridge University Press, 2006), chap. 3. A compact version is found in Norman Schofield, "Evolution of the Constitution," *British Journal of Political Science* 32 (2002): 1–23.

purposefully organized opposition to the new taxes. In the course of the struggle against British tax measures, the planters and merchants broke with their royalist allies and turned to their former adversaries—the shopkeepers, small farmers, laborers, and artisans—for help. With the assistance of these groups, the merchants and planters organized demonstrations and a boycott of British goods that ultimately forced the Crown to rescind most of its new taxes. It was in the context of this unrest that a confrontation between colonists and British soldiers in front of the Boston customs house on the night of March 5, 1770, resulted in what came to be known as the Boston Massacre. Nervous British soldiers opened fire on the mob surrounding them, killing five colonists and wounding eight others. News of this event quickly spread throughout the colonies and was used by radicals to fan anti-British sentiment.

From the perspective of the merchants and planters, however, the British government's decision to eliminate most of the hated taxes meant a victorious end to their struggle with the mother country. They were eager to end the unrest they had helped arouse, and they supported the British government's efforts to restore order. Indeed, most respectable Bostonians supported the actions of the British soldiers involved in the Boston Massacre. In their subsequent trial, the soldiers were defended by John Adams, a pillar of Boston society and a future president of the United States. Adams asserted that the soldiers' actions were entirely justified, provoked by a "motley rabble of saucy boys, negroes and mulattoes, Irish teagues and outlandish Jack tars." All but two of the soldiers were acquitted.[3]

Despite the efforts of the British government and the better-to-do strata of colonial society, it proved difficult to bring an end to the political strife. The more radical forces representing shopkeepers, artisans, laborers, and small farmers, who had been mobilized and energized by the struggle over taxes, continued to agitate for political and social change within the colonies. Dramatic events helped them to overcome early collective action problems. These radicals, led by individuals such as Samuel Adams, a cousin of John Adams, asserted that British power supported an unjust political and social structure within the colonies, and they began to advocate an end to British rule.[4] That the British revenue-raising policies backfired so dramatically was a result of their greatly underestimating colonial resistance. Although they seemed rational and sensible before the fact, the policies appeared mistaken after the fact and were rescinded. The rationality principle only requires people to do the best they can at the time they act. There are bound to be uncertainties that can only imperfectly be taken into account, and thus necessitate subsequent adaptation. So the British attempts to raise revenue and then to adapt this strategy in the face of the resulting unrest were rational, but it proved difficult to undo the damage caused by their initial misreading of the situation.

---

[3] Quoted in George B. Tindall and David E. Shi, *America: A Narrative History*, 6th ed. (New York: Norton, 2004), p. 199.

[4] For a discussion of events leading up to the Revolution, see Charles M. Andrews, *The Colonial Background of the American Revolution: Four Essays in American Colonial History* (New Haven, Conn.: Yale University Press, 1924).

Organizing resistance to the British authorities required widespread support. Collective action, as noted, may emerge spontaneously in certain circumstances, but the colonists' campaign against the British imperial power in late-eighteenth-century America was a series of encounters, maneuvers, and ultimately, confrontations that required planning, coalition building, bargaining, compromising, and coordinating—all elements of the give-and-take of politics. Conflicts among the colonists had to be resolved by bargaining, persuasion, and even force. Cooperation needed cultivation and encouragement. Leadership was clearly a necessary ingredient.

Political Strife and the Radicalizing of the Colonists

The political strife within the colonies was the background for the events of 1773–74. In 1773, the British government granted the politically powerful East India Company a monopoly on the export of tea from Britain, eliminating a lucrative form of trade for colonial merchants. To add to the injury, the East India Company sought to sell the tea directly in the colonies instead of working through the colonial merchants. Tea was an extremely important commodity in the 1770s, and these British actions posed a mortal threat to the New England merchants. The merchants once again called on their radical adversaries for support. The most dramatic result was the Boston Tea Party of 1773, led by Samuel Adams.

This event was of decisive importance in American history. The merchants had hoped to force the British government to rescind the Tea Act, but they did not support any demands beyond this one. They certainly did not seek independence from Britain. Samuel Adams and the other radicals, however, hoped to provoke the British government to take actions that would alienate its colonial supporters and pave the way for a rebellion. This was precisely the purpose of the Boston Tea Party, and it succeeded. By dumping the East India Company's tea into Boston Harbor, Adams and his followers goaded the British into enacting a number of harsh reprisals. Within five months of the incident in Boston, the British Parliament had passed a series of acts that closed the port of Boston to commerce, changed the provincial government of Massachusetts, provided for the removal of accused persons to Britain for trial, and most important, restricted movement to the West from the southern colonies—further alienating the southern planters who depended on access to new western lands. These acts of retaliation confirmed the worst criticisms of England and helped radicalize Americans and move them toward collective resistance to British rule.[5]

The choice of this course of action by British politicians looks puzzling in retrospect, but at the time it appeared reasonable to those who prevailed in Parliament that a show of force was required. The toleration of lawlessness and the making of concessions, they felt, would only egg on the more radical elements in the colonies to take further liberties and demand further concessions. The British, in effect, drew a line in the sand. Their repressive reactions became a clear point around

---

[5] For an intriguing take on the role of dense population networks in cities that promoted collective action against the British, see Edward L. Glaeser, "Revolution of Urban Rebels," *Boston Globe*, July 4, 2008, Section A.

which dissatisfied colonists could rally. Radicals such as Samuel Adams had been agitating for more violent measures to deal with Britain. But ultimately they needed Britain's political repression to create widespread support for independence.[6]

Thus the Boston Tea Party set into motion a cycle of provocations and retaliations that in 1774 resulted in the convening of the First Continental Congress, an assembly consisting of delegates from all parts of the colonies, which called for a total boycott of British goods and, under the prodding of the radicals, began to consider the possibility of independence from British rule. The eventual result was the Declaration of Independence.

The Declaration of Independence

In 1776, the Second Continental Congress appointed a committee consisting of Thomas Jefferson of Virginia, Benjamin Franklin of Pennsylvania, Roger Sherman of Connecticut, John Adams of Massachusetts, and Robert Livingston of New York to draft a statement of American independence from British rule. The Declaration of Independence, written by Jefferson and adopted by the Second Continental Congress, was an extraordinary document in both philosophical and political terms. Philosophically, the Declaration was remarkable for its assertion that certain rights, called "unalienable rights"—including life, liberty, and the pursuit of happiness—could not be abridged by governments. In the world of 1776, a world in which some kings still claimed to rule by divine right, this was a dramatic statement. Politically, the Declaration was remarkable because, despite the differences of interest that divided the colonists along economic, regional, and philosophical lines, it identified and focused on problems, grievances, aspirations, and principles that might unify the various colonial groups. The Declaration was an attempt to identify and articulate a history and a set of principles that might help to forge national unity.[7]

The Articles of Confederation

Having declared their independence, the colonies needed to establish a governmental structure—a set of institutions through which to govern. In November of 1777, the Continental Congress adopted the **Articles of Confederation and Perpetual Union**—the United States' first written constitution. Although it was not ratified by all the states until 1781, it was the country's operative constitution for almost twelve years, until March 1789.

The Articles of Confederation formed a constitution concerned primarily with limiting the powers of the central government. The central government, first of all, was based entirely in Congress. Because it was not intended to be a powerful government, it was given no executive branch. Execution of its laws was to be left

Articles of Confederation and Perpetual Union America's first written constitution. Adopted by the Continental Congress in 1777, the Articles of Confederation and Perpetual Union were the formal basis for America's national government until 1789, when they were superseded by the Constitution.

---

[6] For an extensive discussion of how misunderstandings and incorrect beliefs caused the situation to spin out of control, see Jack N. Rakove, Andrew R. Rutten, and Barry R. Weingast, "Ideas, Interest, and Credible Commitments in the American Revolution" 2008, http://ssrn.com/abstract=1153515 (accessed 2/3/09).

[7] A "biography" of the Declaration is found in Pauline Maier, *American Scripture: Making the Declaration of Independence* (New York: Knopf, 1997).

to the individual states. Second, Congress had little power. Its members were not much more than delegates or messengers from the state legislatures. They were chosen by the state legislatures, their salaries were paid out of the state treasuries, and they were subject to immediate recall by state authorities. In addition, each state, regardless of its size, had only a single vote.

Congress was given the power to declare war and make peace, to make treaties and alliances, to coin or borrow money, and to regulate trade with Native Americans. It could also appoint the senior officers of the U.S. Army. But it could not levy taxes or regulate commerce among the states. Moreover, the army officers it appointed had no army to serve in because the nation's armed forces were composed of the state militias. An especially dysfunctional aspect of the Articles of Confederation was that the central government could not prevent one state from discriminating against other states in the quest for foreign commerce.

In brief, the relationship between Congress and the states under the Articles of Confederation was much like the contemporary relationship between the United Nations and its member states, a relationship in which virtually all governmental powers are retained by the states. It was properly called a confederation because, as provided under Article II, "each state retains its sovereignty, freedom, and independence, and every power, jurisdiction, and right, which is not by this Confederation expressly delegated to the United States, in Congress assembled." Not only was there no executive, but there was also no judicial authority and no other means of enforcing Congress's will. If there were to be any enforcement at all, it would be done for Congress by the states.[8] All told, the Articles of Confederation were an inadequate institutional basis for collective action. The states collectively could act only if each state individually were prepared to participate in and enforce that action.

THE SECOND FOUNDING: FROM COMPROMISE TO CONSTITUTION

Institutional arrangements, devised to accomplish various collective purposes by creating routines and processes, aren't always well suited to these tasks. The Declaration of Independence and the Articles of Confederation were not sufficient to hold the nation together as an independent and effective nation-state. Almost from the moment of armistice with the British in 1783, moves were afoot to reform and strengthen the Articles of Confederation.

International Standing and Balance of Power

There was a special concern for the country's international position. Competition among the states for foreign commerce allowed the European powers to play the states against one another, creating confusion on both sides of the Atlantic. At one

---

[8] See Merrill Jensen, *The Articles of Confederation* (Madison: University of Wisconsin Press, 1963).

point during the winter of 1786–87, John Adams, a leader in the struggle for independence, was sent to negotiate a new treaty with the British, one that would cover disputes left over from the war. The British government responded that because the United States under the Articles of Confederation was unable to enforce existing treaties, it would negotiate with each of the thirteen states separately.

At the same time, well-to-do Americans—in particular the New England merchants and southern planters—were troubled by the influence that "radical" forces exercised in the Continental Congress and in the governments of several of the states. The colonists' victory in the Revolutionary War not only had meant the end of British rule but also had significantly changed the balance of political power within the new states. As a result of the Revolution, one key segment of the colonial elite—the royal land, office, and patent holders—was stripped of its economic and political privileges. In fact, many of these individuals, along with tens of thousands of other colonists who considered themselves loyal British subjects, had left for Canada after the British surrender. And although the pre-Revolutionary elite was weakened, the pre-Revolutionary radicals were now better organized than ever before and were the controlling forces in such states as Pennsylvania and Rhode Island, where they pursued economic and political policies that struck terror in the hearts of the pre-Revolutionary political establishment. In Rhode Island, for example, between 1783 and 1785 a legislature dominated by representatives of small farmers, artisans, and shopkeepers had instituted economic policies, including drastic currency inflation, that frightened businessmen and property owners throughout the country. Of course, the central government under the Articles of Confederation was powerless to intervene.

The Annapolis Convention

The continuation of international weakness and domestic economic turmoil led many Americans to consider whether their newly adopted form of government might not already require revision. Experiments in governance don't always work out. After nearly a decade under the Articles, in the fall of 1786, many state leaders accepted an invitation from the Virginia legislature to attend a conference of representatives of all the states. Delegates from five states actually attended. This conference, held in Annapolis, Maryland, was the first step toward the second Founding. One positive thing that came out of the Annapolis Convention was a carefully worded resolution calling on Congress to send commissioners to Philadelphia at a later time "to devise such further provisions as shall appear to them necessary to render the Constitution of the Federal Government adequate to the exigencies of the Union."[9] This resolution was drafted by Alexander Hamilton, a thirty-four-year-old New York lawyer who had played a significant role in the Revolution as George Washington's secretary and would play a still more significant role in framing the Constitution and forming the new government in the 1790s. But the resolution did not necessarily imply any desire to do more than improve and reform the Articles of Confederation.

---

[9] Quoted in Samuel Eliot Morison, Henry Steele Commager, and William E. Leuchtenburg, *The Growth of the American Republic*, 6th ed. (New York: Oxford University Press, 1969), I, p. 244.

Shays's Rebellion

It is possible that the Constitutional Convention of 1787 in Philadelphia would never have taken place at all except for a single event that occurred soon after the Annapolis Convention: Shays's Rebellion. Like the Boston Tea Party, this was a focal event. It concentrated attention, coordinated beliefs, produced widespread fear and apprehension, and thus convinced waverers that something was broken and needed fixing. In short, it prompted collective action by providing politicians who had long been convinced that the Articles were flawed and insufficient with just the ammunition they needed to convince a much broader public of these facts.[10]

Daniel Shays, a former army captain, led a mob of farmers in a rebellion against the government of Massachusetts. The purpose of the rebellion was to prevent foreclosures on their debt-ridden land by keeping the county courts of western Massachusetts from sitting until after the next election. The state militia dispersed the mob, but for several days Shays and his followers terrified the state government by attempting to capture the federal arsenal at Springfield, provoking an appeal to Congress to help restore order. Within a few days, the state government regained control and captured fourteen of the rebels (all were eventually pardoned). In 1787, a newly elected Massachusetts legislature granted some of the farmers' demands. Although the incident ended peacefully, its effects lingered and spread.

Congress under the Confederation had been unable to act decisively in a time of crisis. This inadequacy provided critics of the Articles of Confederation with precisely the evidence they needed to push Hamilton's Annapolis resolution through the Congress. Thus the states were asked to send representatives to Philadelphia to discuss constitutional revision. Delegates were eventually sent by every state except Rhode Island.

The drama of Shays's Rebellion underscores the robustness and resistance to change of an institutional status quo—the Articles of Confederation regime. As the history principle suggests, the status quo prevails until and unless it is replaced. And to accomplish the latter, a spark or focal event is often necessary to coalesce the forces of change and enable them to overcome the biases in favor of doing nothing and keeping the status quo in place. In effect, Shays's Rebellion strengthened the resolve of supporters of change, convinced waverers, and generally coordinated the beliefs of many that something comprehensive needed to be done about the existing regime. Thus, the event facilitated collective action.

The Constitutional Convention

Twenty-nine of a total of seventy-three delegates selected by the state governments convened in Philadelphia in May 1787, with political strife, international embarrassment, national weakness, and local rebellion fixed in their minds. Recognizing that these issues were symptoms of fundamental flaws in the Articles of Confederation, the delegates soon abandoned the plan to revise the Articles and committed themselves to a second Founding—a second and ultimately successful attempt to create a legitimate and effective national system. This effort occupied the convention for the next five months.

---

[10] For an easy-to-read argument that supports this view, see Keith L. Dougherty, *Collective Action under the Articles of Confederation* (New York: Cambridge University Press, 2001).

A Marriage of Interest and Ideals.　For years, scholars have disagreed about the motives of the Founders in Philadelphia. Among the most controversial views of the framers' motives is the "economic" interpretation put forward by the historian Charles Beard and his disciples.[11] According to Beard's account, America's Founders were a collection of securities speculators and property owners whose only aim was personal enrichment. From this perspective, the Constitution's lofty principles were little more than sophisticated masks behind which the most venal interests sought to enrich themselves. Although Beard's arguments are extreme in their exclusive emphasis on economics, there is some foundation for them. Northern economic interests feared debtor revolts, while southern planters feared slave revolts. Capital investment and its protection were weak under the Articles not only because of potential rebellions, but also because of inflated currencies, limited credit markets, and outstanding public debt. Also, manufacturers needed protection from foreign competition, and exporters (primarily of southern cotton) needed the security of safe passage for their cargoes on the high seas.

Contrary to Beard's approach is the view that the framers of the Constitution were concerned with philosophical and ethical ideas. Indeed, the framers sought to devise a system of government consistent with the dominant philosophical and moral values of the day.[12]

Lurking in the background was a generalized suspicion of distant central government. As the historian Joseph Ellis observed, this was the "core argument used to discredit the authority of Parliament and the British monarch . . . 'Whig principles,' an obsessive suspicion of any centralized political power that operated in faraway places . . . "[13] But in fact, these interests and ideals belong together: The Founders' interests were reinforced by their principles. The convention that drafted the U.S. Constitution was chiefly organized by the New England merchants and southern planters. Although the delegates representing these groups did not all hope to profit personally from an increase in the value of their securities, as Beard would have it, they did hope to benefit in the broadest political and economic sense by breaking the power of their radical foes and establishing a system of government more compatible with their long-term economic and political interests. Thus the framers—inline with the rationality principle—sought to create a new government capable of promoting commerce and protecting property from radical state legislatures. They also sought to liberate the national government from the power of individual states and their sometimes venal and corrupt local politicians. At the same time, they hoped to fashion a government less susceptible than the existing state and national regimes to populist forces hostile to the interests of the commercial and propertied classes. These highly educated but practically experienced politicians were instrumentally motivated by both interests and ideals. The Constitutional Convention was a grand exercise in rationality and collective action.

---

[11] Charles A. Beard, *An Economic Interpretation of the Constitution of the United States* (New York: Macmillan, 1913).

[12] For an analytical treatment see Schofield, *Architects of Political Change*, chap. 4.

[13] Joseph J. Ellis, *Founding Brothers: the Revolutionary Generation* (New York: Knopf, 2000), p. 7.

The Great Compromise.   The proponents of a new government fired their opening shot on May 29, 1787, when Edmund Randolph of Virginia offered a resolution that proposed corrections and enlargements in the Articles of Confederation. The proposal, which showed the strong influence of James Madison, was not a simple motion. It provided for virtually every aspect of a new government. Randolph later admitted it was intended to be an alternative draft constitution, and it did in fact serve as the framework for what ultimately became the Constitution.[14]

This proposal, known as the Virginia Plan, provided for a system of representation in the national legislature based on the population of each state, the proportion of each state's revenue contribution, or both. (Randolph also proposed a second branch of the legislature, but it was to be elected by the members of the first branch.) Because the states varied enormously in size and wealth, the Virginia Plan was thought to be heavily biased in favor of the large states.

While the convention was debating the Virginia Plan, additional delegates arriving in Philadelphia were beginning to mount opposition to it. Their resolution, introduced by William Paterson of New Jersey and known as the New Jersey Plan, did not oppose the Virginia Plan point for point. Instead, it concentrated on specific weaknesses in the Articles of Confederation, in the spirit of revision rather than radical replacement of that document. Supporters of the New Jersey Plan did not seriously question the convention's commitment to replacing the Articles. But their opposition to the Virginia Plan's scheme of representation was sufficient to send its proposals back to committee to be worked into a common document. In particular, delegates from the less populous states, which included Delaware, New Jersey, Connecticut, and New York, asserted that the more populous states, such as Virginia, Pennsylvania, North Carolina, Massachusetts, and Georgia, would dominate the new government if representation were to be determined by population. The smaller states argued that each state should be equally represented in the new regime regardless of its population.

The issue of representation was one that threatened to wreck the entire constitutional enterprise. Delegates conferred, factions maneuvered, and tempers flared. James Wilson of Pennsylvania told the small-state delegates that if they wanted to disrupt the Union they should go ahead. The separation could, he said, "never happen on better grounds." Small-state delegates were equally blunt. Gunning Bedford of Delaware declared that the small states might look elsewhere for friends if they were forced. "The large states," he said, "dare not dissolve the confederation. If they do the small ones will find some foreign ally of more honor and good faith, who will take them by the hand and do them justice." These sentiments were widely shared. The Union, as Oliver Ellsworth of Connecticut put it, was "on the verge of dissolution, scarcely held together by the strength of a hair." Convention delegates,

---

[14]There is no verbatim record of the debates, but Madison was present during virtually all of the deliberations and kept full notes on them. Madison's notes, along with the somewhat less complete records kept by several other participants in the convention, are available in a four-volume set. See Max Farrand, ed., *The Records of the Federal Convention of 1787*, rev. ed., 4 vols. (New Haven, Conn.: Yale University Press, 1966).

acting as agents for the interests of their respective states, bargained, cajoled, and made attempts at persuasion in the rational pursuit of a result they would prefer.

The outcome of this debate was the Connecticut Compromise, also known as the **Great Compromise**. Under the terms of this compromise, in the first chamber of Congress—the House of Representatives—the representatives would be apportioned according to the number of inhabitants in each state. This, of course, was what delegates from the large states had sought. But in the second chamber—the Senate—each state would have an equal vote regardless of its size; this was to deal with the concerns of the small states. This compromise was not immediately satisfactory to all the delegates. Indeed, two of the most vocal members of the small-state faction, John Lansing and Robert Yates of New York, were so incensed by the concession that their colleagues had made to the large-state forces that they stormed out of the convention.

In the end, however, both sets of forces preferred compromise to the breakup of the Union, and the plan was accepted. The "Analyzing the Evidence" unit for this chapter explores, in more detail, the states' conflicting interests and how these shaped the eventual compromise.

The Question of Slavery: The Three-fifths Compromise.   Many of the conflicts that emerged during the Constitutional Convention were reflections of the fundamental differences between the slave and nonslave states, differences that pitted the southern planters and New England merchants against each other. This was the first premonition of a conflict that would almost destroy the Republic in later years.

Over 90 percent of all slaves resided in five states—Georgia, Maryland, North Carolina, South Carolina, and Virginia—where they accounted for 30 percent of the total population. In some places, slaves outnumbered nonslaves by as much as 10 to 1. If the Constitution were to embody any principle of national supremacy, some basic decisions would have to be made about the place of slavery in the general scheme.

Northerners and southerners eventually reached agreement through the **Three-fifths Compromise.** The seats in the House of Representatives would be apportioned according to a "population" in which five slaves would count as three people. The slaves would not be allowed to vote, of course, but the number of representatives would be apportioned accordingly. This arrangement was supported by the slave states, which included some of the biggest and some of the smallest states at that time. It was also accepted by many delegates from nonslave states who strongly supported the principle of property representation, whether that property were expressed in slaves or in land, money, or stocks. The concern exhibited by most delegates was over how much slaves would count toward a state's representation rather than whether the institution of slavery would continue.

The issue of slavery was the most difficult one faced by the framers, and it nearly destroyed the Union. Although some delegates believed slavery to be morally wrong, an evil and oppressive institution that made a mockery of the ideals and values espoused in the Constitution, morality was not the issue that caused the framers to support or oppose the Three-fifths Compromise. Whatever they thought of the institution of slavery, most delegates from the northern states opposed

Great Compromise An agreement reached at the Constitutional Convention of 1787 that gave each state an equal number of senators regardless of its population but linked representation in the House of Representatives to population.

Three-fifths Compromise An agreement reached at the Constitutional Convention of 1787 stipulating that for purposes of the apportionment of congressional seats, every slave would be counted as three fifths of a person.

counting slaves in the distribution of congressional seats. Wilson of Pennsylvania, for example, argued that if slaves were citizens, they should be treated and counted like other citizens. If, on the other hand, they were property, then why should not other forms of property be counted toward the apportionment of Congress? But southern delegates made it clear that if the northerners refused to give in, they would never agree to the new government. Even southerners such as Edmund Randolph of Virginia, who conceded that slavery was immoral, insisted on including slaves in the allocation of congressional seats. This conflict between the southern and northern delegates was so divisive that many came to question the possibility of creating and maintaining a union of the two. Pierce Butler of South Carolina declared that the North and the South were as different as Russia and Turkey. Eventually the North and the South compromised on the issue of slavery and representation. Indeed, northerners even agreed to permit a continuation of the odious slave trade to keep the South in the Union. But in due course, Butler proved to be correct, and a bloody war was fought when the disparate interests of the North and the South could no longer be reconciled.

THE CONSTITUTION

The political significance of the Great Compromise and the Three-fifths Compromise was to reinforce the unity of the mercantile and planter forces that sought to create a new government. The Great Compromise reassured those who feared that the importance of their own local or regional influence would be reduced by the new governmental framework. The Three-fifths Compromise temporarily defused the rivalry between the merchants and the planters. Their unity secured, members of the alliance supporting the establishment of a new government moved to fashion a constitutional framework consistent with their economic and political interests.

The framers of the Constitution understood that well-designed institutions make it easier to achieve collective goals. They understood also that the institutions they built could affect political outcomes for decades, if not centuries, to come. Accordingly, the framers took great care to construct institutions that over time would help the nation accomplish what they viewed as important political purposes.

In particular, the framers sought first a new government that would be strong enough to promote commerce and protect property from radical state legislatures such as Rhode Island's. This goal became the basis for national control over commerce and finance, as well as for both the establishment of national judicial supremacy and the effort to construct a strong presidency. Second, the framers sought to prevent what they saw as the threat posed by the "excessive democracy" of the state and national governments under the Articles of Confederation. Here again the framers' historical experience mattered. This goal led to such constitutional principles as **bicameralism** (division of the Congress into two chambers), checks and balances, staggered terms of office, and indirect election (selection of the president by an electoral college rather than directly by the voters). Third, the framers, lacking the power to force the states or the public at large to accept the new form of government, sought to identify principles that would help secure support. This goal

bicameralism
The division of a legislative assembly into two chambers, or houses.

Voting at the Constitutional Convention

Under the Articles of Confederation, there was a unicameral Congress in which each state delegation received a single vote, regardless of state population. So Virginia, with roughly 700,000 people, had the same share of votes as Rhode Island, with a population closer to 70,000.** Among the issues considered by the framers at the Constitutional Convention, one of the most contentious involved how representation in the Congress would work under the new Constitution.

On May 29, 1787, Edmund Randolph proposed the Virginia Plan, which later came to be associated with James Madison. This plan initially called for the creation of three semi-independent branches of government with a bicameral legislature and introduced the idea of checks and balances. On June 11, a series of votes were taken on the Virginia Plan, which consistently received the support of the larger, more populous states—because under this plan at least one of the chambers of Congress would be elected with representation proportional to population, giving the more populous states more of a voice in the national government.

Given that the smaller, less populous states were poised to lose representation if votes in Congress were based on population, delegates from those states decided to propose their own plan for the national government. On June 15, William Patterson proposed the New Jersey Plan, which called for the creation of a unicameral legislature with one vote per state. When a vote was scheduled on June 19 that pitted the Virginia Plan against the New Jersey Plan, the states voted exactly the same way as they did on the vote for proportional representation in the Virginia Plan (see below). Moreover, many of the delegates from the smaller states threatened to leave the convention if the Virginia Plan was ratified. In an attempt to prevent the smaller states from departing, Roger Sherman proposed the Connecticut Compromise, which was voted on on June 23. This plan called for a bicameral legislature, with representation based on population in the lower house and equal representation of states in the upper house. The Connecticut Compromise ultimately passed by a 5–4 vote.

State*	Total population**	Slave population**	Vote on Virginia Plan	Vote on Connecticut Compromise
Virginia	747,550	292,627	Y	N
Pennsylvania	433,611	3,707	Y	N
Massachusetts	378,556	0	Y	–
New York	340,241	21,193	N	–
Maryland	319,728	103,036	–	Y
North Carolina	395,005	100,783	Y	Y
South Carolina	249,073	107,094	Y	N
Connecticut	237,655	2,648	Y	Y
New Jersey	184,139	11,423	N	Y
Georgia	82,548	29,264	Y	N
New Hampshire	141,899	157	–	–
Delaware	59,096	8,887	N	Y
Rhode Island	69,112	958	–	–

*Maryland's delegates were split equally and thus did not vote. Delegates from New Hampshire never attended at the same time as those from New York, hence their lack of participation. Rhode Island did not send any delegates to the convention.

**Population data are based on the 1790 census and therefore are only approximate with respect to populations in 1787.

If we consider the number of representatives in Congress that each state would receive under the various plans (see below), it becomes clear why individual states voted the way they did. Under the Articles and the proposed New Jersey Plan, even the smallest states had 1 out of 13 votes in the Congress. We can express their share of the total votes as .077.

State*	Under Articles: Each state has one out of 13 total votes	Population-based system like Virginia Plan: Each state has one vote per 30,000 constituents, out of 65 total votes*
Virginia	.077	10/65 = .154
Pennsylvania	.077	8/65 = .123
Massachusetts	.077	8/65 = .123
New York	.077	6/65 = .092
Maryland	.077	6/65 = .092
North Carolina	.077	5/65 = .077
South Carolina	.077	5/65 = .077
Connecticut	.077	5/65 = .077
New Jersey	.077	4/65 = .062
Georgia	.077	3/65 = .046
New Hampshire	.077	3/65 = .046
Delaware	.077	1/65 = .015
Rhode Island	.077	1/65 = .015

*Note that the framers calculated the number of representatives per state using population estimates. The first census was not taken until 1790.

Under a population-based system such as the Virginia Plan, the smaller states would lose voting power in Congress. For example, in a population-based system with one representative per 30,000 people, Delaware would only have 1 out of 65 votes, or a .015 share of total votes. This is significantly less voting power than the 1 out of 13 (.077) share that these states enjoyed under the Articles and other arrangements that would give each state equal representation in Congress.

By providing for equal representation of the states in one house of Congress and population-weighted representation in the other, the Connecticut Compromise mitigated the loss of voting power that the small states would suffer. As the right-hand column in the table on the previous page indicates, a majority of the states accepted this compromise, which eventually became part of the Constitution. As this case demonstrates, the conflicting interests of the framers are reflected in the rules and procedures of the institutions they established.

Sources: Keith L. Dougherty and Jac C. Heckelman, "A Pivotal Voter from a Pivotal State: Roger Sherman at the Constitutional Convention," *American Political Science Review* 100 (May 2006): 297–302; Clinton L. Rossiter, *1787: The Grand Convention* (New York: Macmillan, 1996.)

became the basis for the constitutional provision for direct popular election of representatives and, subsequently, the basis for the addition of the Bill of Rights to the Constitution. Finally, the framers wanted to be certain that the government they created did not use its power to pose even more of a threat to its citizens' liberties and property rights than did the radical state legislatures they feared and despised. To prevent the new government from abusing its power, the framers incorporated into the Constitution such principles as the separation of powers and federalism.

The framers provided us with a grand lesson in instrumental behavior. They came to Philadelphia united by a common distaste for government under the Articles and animated by the agitation following Shays's Rebellion. They didn't always agree on what it was they disliked about the Articles. They certainly didn't agree on how to proceed—hence the necessity for the historic compromises we have just described. But they did believe that the acts of fostering commerce and protecting property could be served better by a set of institutional arrangements other than that provided by the Articles. They agreed that the institutional arrangements of government mattered for their lives and for those of their fellow citizens. They believed that both too much democracy and too much governmental power were threats to the common good, and they felt compelled to find instruments and principles that weighed against them. Let us assess the major provisions of the Constitution's seven articles to see how each relates to these objectives.

The Legislative Branch

The first seven sections of Article I of the Constitution provide for a Congress consisting of two chambers—a House of Representatives and a Senate. Members of the House of Representatives are given two-year terms of office and are to be elected directly by the people. Members of the Senate are to be appointed by the state legislatures (this provision was changed in 1913 by the Seventeenth Amendment, which instituted direct election of senators) for six-year terms. These terms, moreover, are staggered so that the appointments of one third of the senators expire every two years. The Constitution assigns somewhat different tasks to the House and the Senate. Though the approval of each body is required for the enactment of a law, the Senate alone is given the power to ratify treaties and approve presidential appointments. The House, on the other hand, is given the sole power to originate revenue bills.

The character of the legislative branch is directly related to the framers' major goals. The House of Representatives was designed to be directly responsible to the people, to encourage popular consent for the new Constitution and to help enhance the power of the new government. At the same time, to guard against "excessive democracy," the power of the House of Representatives is checked by the Senate, whose members are to be appointed rather than elected directly by the people and are to serve long (six-year) terms. The purpose of this provision, according to Alexander Hamilton, was to avoid "an unqualified complaisance to every sudden breeze of passion, or to every transient impulse which the people may receive."[15] Staggered terms of service in the Senate, moreover, were intended to make that

---

[15] Alexander Hamilton, James Madison, and John Jay, *The Federalist*, E.M. Earle, ed. (New York: Modern Library, 1937), no. 71.

body even more resistant to popular pressure. Because only one-third of the senators would be selected at any given time, the composition of the institution would be protected from changes in popular preferences transmitted by the state legislatures. This would prevent what James Madison called "mutability in the public councils arising from a rapid succession of new members."[16] Thus the structure of the legislative branch was designed to contribute to governmental power, promote popular consent for the new government, and at the same time place limits on the popular political currents that many of the framers saw as a radical threat to the economic and social order.

The issues of power and consent are important throughout the Constitution. Section 8 of Article I lists the specific powers of Congress, which include the authority to collect taxes, borrow money, regulate commerce, declare war, and maintain an army and navy. By granting it these powers, the framers indicated clearly that they intended the new government to be far more influential than its predecessor. At the same time, by defining the new government's most important powers as belonging to Congress, the framers sought to promote popular acceptance of this critical change by reassuring citizens that their views would be fully represented whenever the government exercised its new powers.

As a further guarantee to the people that the new government would pose no threat to them, the Constitution implies that any powers not listed are not granted at all. This is the doctrine of **expressed power**. The Constitution grants only those powers specifically expressed in its text. But the framers intended to create an active and powerful government, and so they included the **necessary and proper clause**, sometimes known as the elastic clause, which signifies that the enumerated powers are meant to be a source of strength to the national government, not a limitation on it—that the government may employ means "necessary and proper" to implement the expressed powers. No new powers can be seized on by the national government without a constitutional amendment. In the absence of such an amendment, any power not enumerated is conceived to be "reserved" to the states (or the people).

The Executive Branch

The Constitution provides for the establishment of the presidency in Article II. As Alexander Hamilton commented, the presidential article was aimed toward creating "energy in the Executive." It did so in an effort to overcome the natural stalemate that was built into both the bicameral legislature and the separation of powers among the legislative, executive, and judicial branches. The Constitution afforded the president a measure of independence from the people and from the other branches of government, particularly the Congress.

In line with the framers' goal of increased power in the national government, the president is granted the unconditional power to accept ambassadors from other countries; this provision amounts to the power to "recognize" other countries. The president is also given the power to negotiate treaties, although their acceptance requires the approval of the Senate. The president is given the unconditional right to grant reprieves and pardons, except in cases of impeachment. And the president is provided

expressed power
The notion that the Constitution grants to the federal government only those powers specifically named in its text.

necessary and proper clause
Article 1, Section 8, of the Constitution, which enumerates the powers of Congress and provides Congress with the authority to make all laws "necessary and proper" to carry them out; also referred to as the elastic clause.

---

[16] *The Federalist*, no. 62.

with the power to appoint major departmental personnel, convene Congress in a special session, and veto congressional enactments. (The veto power is formidable, but it is not absolute because Congress can override it by a two-thirds vote.)[17]

The framers hoped to create a presidency that would make the federal government, rather than the states, the agency capable of timely and decisive action to deal with public issues and problems. This goal is the meaning of the "energy" that Hamilton hoped to impart to the executive branch.[18] At the same time, however, the framers sought to help the president withstand (excessively) democratic pressures by making the office subject to indirect rather than direct election (through selection by a separate electoral college). The extent to which the framers' hopes were realized is the topic of Chapter 6.

The Judicial Branch

In establishing the judicial branch in Article III, the Constitution reflects the framers' preoccupations with enhancing the power of the national government and checking radical democratic impulses while guarding against potential interference with liberty and property from the new national government itself.

Under the provisions of Article III, the framers created a court that was to be literally a supreme court of the United States and not merely the highest court of the national government. The most important expression of this intention was granting the Supreme Court the power to resolve any conflicts that might emerge between federal and state laws. In particular, the Supreme Court was given the right to determine whether a power was exclusive to the federal government, concurrent with the states, or exclusive to the states. The significance of this was noted by Justice Oliver Wendell Holmes, Jr., who observed, "I do not think the United States would come to an end if we lost our power to declare an act of Congress void. I do think the union would be imperilled if we could not make that declaration as to the laws of the several states."[19]

In addition, the Supreme Court was assigned jurisdiction over controversies between citizens of different states. The long-term significance of this provision was that as the country developed a national economy, it came to rely increasingly on the federal judiciary, rather than the state courts, for the resolution of disputes.

Judges were given lifetime appointments to protect them from popular politics and interference by the other branches. This did not mean, however, that the judiciary would remain totally impartial to political considerations or to the other branches, for the president is to appoint the judges and the Senate is to approve the appointments. Congress also has the power to create inferior (lower) courts,

---

[17] A modern description of executive-legislature relations is, "The president proposes; the Congress disposes." The president may propose to the legislature when the subject is a treaty or a major departmental appointment or a federal judge or justice, which must be approved by the Senate; then the president is a legislative "agenda setter." When, however, it is a proposed law or budget, it is a "suggestion" that the legislature may choose to ignore altogether. Such proposals are then said to be "dead on arrival" because Congress marches to the beat of its own drummer.

[18] *The Federalist*, no. 70.

[19] Oliver Wendell Holmes, Jr., *Collected Legal Papers* (New York: Harcourt, Brace, 1920), pp. 295–96.

change the jurisdiction of the federal courts, add or subtract federal judges, and even change the size of the Supreme Court.

No direct mention is made of **judicial review**—the power of the courts to render the final decision when a conflict of interpretation of the Constitution or of laws arises between the courts and Congress, the courts and the executive branch, or the courts and the states. Scholars generally feel that judicial review is implicit in the very existence of a written constitution and in the power given directly to the federal courts over "all Cases . . . arising under this Constitution, the Laws of the United States, and Treaties made, or which shall be made, under their Authority" (Article III, Section 2). The Supreme Court eventually assumed the power of judicial review. Its assumption of this power, as we shall see in Chapter 8, was based not on the Constitution itself but on the politics of later decades and the membership of the Court.

National Unity and Power

Various provisions in the Constitution address the framers' concern with national unity and power, including Article IV's provisions for comity (reciprocity) among states and among the citizens of all states.

Each state is prohibited from discriminating against the citizens of other states in favor of its own citizens, with the Supreme Court charged with deciding in each case whether a state has discriminated against goods or people from another state. The Constitution restricts the power of the states in favor of ensuring that the national government holds enough power to give the country a free-flowing national economy.

The framers' concern with national supremacy was also expressed in Article VI, in the **supremacy clause**, which provides that national laws and treaties "shall be the supreme Law of the Land." This means that all laws made under the "Authority of the United States" are superior to all laws adopted by any state or any other subdivision, and the states are expected to respect all treaties made under that authority. This provision was a direct effort to keep the states from dealing separately with foreign nations or businesses. The supremacy clause also binds the officials of all state and local, as well as federal, governments to take an oath of office to support the national Constitution. This means that every action taken by the U.S. Congress must be applied within each state as though the action were in fact state law.

Amending the Constitution

The Constitution establishes procedures for its own revision in Article V. Its provisions are so difficult that Americans have availed themselves of the amending process only seventeen times since 1791, when the first ten amendments were adopted. Many other amendments have been proposed in Congress, but fewer than forty of them have come even close to fulfilling the Constitution's requirement of a two-thirds vote in Congress, and only a fraction have gotten anywhere near adoption by three-fourths of the states. The Constitution can also be amended by a constitutional convention. Occasionally proponents of particular measures, such as a balanced-budget amendment, have called for a constitutional convention to

judicial review
The power of the courts to declare actions of the legislative and executive branches invalid or unconstitutional. The Supreme Court asserted this power in *Marbury v. Madison* (1803).

supremacy clause
A clause of Article VI of the Constitution, that states that all laws passed by the national government and all treaties are the supreme laws of the land and superior to all laws adopted by any state or any subdivision.

consider their proposals. Whatever the purpose for which it was called, however, such a convention would presumably have the authority to revise America's entire system of government.

It should be noted that any body of rules, including a national constitution, must balance the need to respond flexibly to changes on the one hand with the caution not to be too flexible on the other. An inflexible body of rules is one that cannot accommodate major change. It risks being rebelled against, a circumstance in which the slate is wiped clean and new rules are designed—or ignored altogether. Too much flexibility, however, is disastrous. It invites those who lose in normal everyday politics to replay battles at the constitutional level. If institutional change is too easy to accomplish, the stability of the political system becomes threatened. This means, as stated in the institution principle, that the institutional arrangements characterized in a constitution should structure politics by providing a framework, not rigidly specify political outcomes explicitly.

Ratifying the Constitution

The rules for ratification of the Constitution of 1787 are set forth in Article VII of the Constitution. This provision actually violated the amendment provisions of the Articles of Confederation. For one thing, it adopts a nine-state rule in place of the unanimity required by the Articles. For another, it provides for ratification to occur in special state conventions called for that purpose rather than in the state legislatures. All the states except Rhode Island eventually did set up state conventions to ratify the Constitution.

Constitutional Limits on the National Government's Power

As we have indicated, although the framers sought to create a powerful national government, they also wanted to guard against possible misuse of that power. To that end, the framers incorporated two key principles into the Constitution: the **separation of powers** and **federalism** (see Chapter 3). A third set of limitations, in the form of the **Bill of Rights**, was added to the Constitution to help secure its ratification when opponents of the document charged that it paid insufficient attention to citizens' rights.

The Separation of Powers. No principle of politics was more widely shared at the time of the 1787 Founding than the principle that power must be used to balance power. The French political theorist Baron de la Brède et de Montesquieu (1689–1755) believed that this balance was an indispensable defense against tyranny. His writings, especially his major work, *The Spirit of the Laws*, "were taken as political gospel" at the Philadelphia Convention. Although the principle of the separation of powers was not explicitly stated in the Constitution, the entire structure of the national government was built precisely on Article I, the legislature; Article II, the executive; and Article III, the judiciary (see Figure 2.1).

However, separation of powers is nothing but mere words on parchment without a method to maintain the separation. The method became known by the popular label "**checks and balances.**" Each branch is given not only its own powers but

separation of powers The division of governmental power among several institutions that must cooperate in decision making.

federalism The system of government in which a constitution divides power between a central government and regional governments.

Bill of Rights The first ten amendments to the U.S. Constitution, adopted in 1791. The Bill of Rights ensures certain rights and liberties to the people.

checks and balances The mechanisms through which each branch of government is able to participate in and influence the activities of the other branches.

FIGURE 2.1 THE SEPARATION OF POWERS

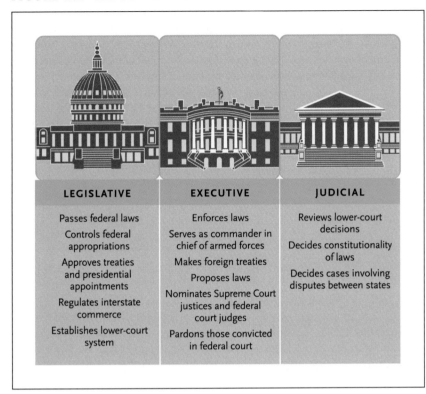

LEGISLATIVE	EXECUTIVE	JUDICIAL
Passes federal laws	Enforces laws	Reviews lower-court decisions
Controls federal appropriations	Serves as commander in chief of armed forces	Decides constitutionality of laws
Approves treaties and presidential appointments	Makes foreign treaties	Decides cases involving disputes between states
Regulates interstate commerce	Proposes laws	
Establishes lower-court system	Nominates Supreme Court justices and federal court judges	
	Pardons those convicted in federal court	

also some power over the other two branches. Among the most familiar checks and balances are the president's veto as a power over Congress and Congress's power over the president through its control of appointments to high executive posts and to the judiciary. Congress also has power over the president with its control of appropriations and (by the Senate) the right of approval of treaties. The judiciary was assumed to have the power of judicial review over the other two branches.

Another important feature of the separation of powers is the principle of giving each of the branches a distinctly different constituency. Theorists such as Montesquieu called this a "mixed regime," with the president chosen indirectly by electors, the House by popular vote, the Senate (originally) by state legislature, and the judiciary by presidential appointment. By these means, the occupants of each branch would tend to develop very different outlooks on how to govern, different definitions of the public interest, and different alliances with private interests.

Federalism.　Compared with the confederation principle of the Articles of Confederation, federalism was a step toward greater centralization of power. The delegates agreed that they needed to place more power at the national level, without completely undermining the power of the state governments. Thus they devised a system of two sovereigns—the states and the nation—with the hope that competition between the two would be an effective limitation on the power of both.

The Bill of Rights.   Late in the Philadelphia convention, a motion was made to include a bill of rights in the Constitution. After a brief debate, in which hardly a word was said in its favor and only one speech was made against it, the motion to include it was almost unanimously turned down. Most delegates sincerely believed that because the federal government was already limited to its expressed powers, any further protection of citizens was not needed. The delegates argued that the states should adopt bills of rights because their greater powers needed greater limitations. But almost immediately after the Constitution was ratified, there was a movement to adopt a national bill of rights. This is why the Bill of Rights, adopted in 1791, makes up the first ten amendments to the Constitution and is not incorporated into the body of it. We shall have a good deal more to say about the Bill of Rights in Chapter 4.

THE FIGHT FOR RATIFICATION: FEDERALISTS VERSUS ANTIFEDERALISTS

The first hurdle faced by the new Constitution was ratification by state conventions of delegates elected by the people of each state. This struggle for ratification was carried out in thirteen separate campaigns. Each involved different men, moved at a different pace, and was influenced by local as well as national considerations. Two sides faced off throughout the states, however, calling themselves Federalists and Antifederalists (Table 2.1).[20] The Federalists (who ought to have called themselves Nationalists but took their name to appear to follow in the Revolutionary tradition) supported the Constitution and preferred a strong national government. The Antifederalists opposed the Constitution and preferred a decentralized federal government; they took their name by default, in reaction to their better-organized opponents. The Federalists were united in their support of the Constitution, whereas the Antifederalists were divided in what they believed the alternative to the Constitution should be.

During the struggle over ratification of the proposed Constitution, Americans argued about great political issues and ideals. How much power should the national government be given? What safeguards were most likely to prevent the abuse of power? What institutional arrangements could best ensure adequate representation for all Americans? Was tyranny to be feared more from the many or from the few?

In political life, of course, ideals—and values—are seldom completely divorced from some set of interests. In 1787, Americans were divided along economic, regional, and political lines. These divisions inevitably influenced their attitudes toward the profound political questions of the day. Many well-to-do merchants and planters, as we saw earlier, favored the creation of a stronger central government that

---

[20]An excellent analysis of the ratification campaigns—based on a quantitative assessment of the campaigners' own words as found in campaign documents, pamphlets, tracts, public letters, and the eighteenth-century equivalent of op-ed pieces (such as the individual essays that make up the *Federalist Papers*)—is William H. Riker, *The Strategy of Rhetoric: Campaigning for the American Constitution* (New Haven, Conn.: Yale University Press, 1996).

TABLE 2.1 FEDERALISTS VERSUS ANTIFEDERALISTS

	Federalists	Antifederalists
Who were they?	Were property owners, creditors, merchants	Were small farmers, frontiersmen, debtors, shopkeepers
What did they believe?	Believed that elites are best fit to govern and that "excessive democracy" is dangerous	Believed that government should be close to the people and that the concentration of power in the hands of the elites is dangerous
What system of government did they favor?	Favored strong national government; believed in "filtration" so that only elites would obtain governmental power	Favored retention of power by state governments and protection of individual rights
Who were their leaders?	Were led by Alexander Hamilton, James Madison, George Washington	Were led by Patrick Henry, George Mason, Elbridge Gerry, George Clinton

would have the capacity to protect property, promote commerce, and keep some of the more radical state legislatures in check. At the same time, many powerful state leaders, such as Governor George Clinton of New York, feared that strengthening the national government would reduce their own influence and status. Each of these interests, of course, justified its position with an appeal to basic values.

Ideas are often important weapons in political warfare, and seeing how and by whom they are wielded can illuminate their otherwise obscure implications. Even if an idea is invented and initially brandished to serve an interest, however, once it has been articulated, it can take on a life of its own and prove to have implications that transcend the narrow interests it was created to serve. For example, some opponents of the Constitution who criticized the absence of a bill of rights in the initial document did so simply with the hope of blocking the document's ratification. Yet the bill of rights that was added to the Constitution has proved for over two centuries to be a bulwark of civil liberty in the United States.

As this example shows, truly great political ideas transcend the interests that initially set them forth. The first step in understanding a political value is understanding why and by whom it is espoused. The second step is understanding the full implications of the idea itself—implications that may go far beyond the interests that launched it. Whatever the underlying clash of interests that may have guided them, the Federalists and the Antifederalists presented important alternative visions of America.

During the ratification struggle, thousands of essays, speeches, pamphlets, and letters were presented in support of and in opposition to the proposed Constitution. The best-known pieces supporting ratification of the Constitution were the eighty-five essays written under the name Publius by Alexander Hamilton, James Madison, and John Jay between the fall of 1787 and the spring of 1788. These *Federalist Papers,* as they are collectively known today, defended the principles of the Constitution and sought to dispel fears of a national authority. The Antifederalists published essays of their own, arguing that the new Constitution betrayed the Revolution and was a step toward monarchy. Among the best of the Antifederalist works were the essays, usually attributed to the New York Supreme Court justice Robert Yates, that were written under the name Brutus and published in the *New York Journal* at the same time the *Federalist Papers* appeared. The Antifederalist view was also ably presented in pamphlets and letters written by a former delegate to the Continental Congress and future U.S. senator, Richard Henry Lee of Virginia, using the pen name the Federal Farmer. These essays highlight the major differences of opinion between Federalists and Antifederalists. Federalists appealed to basic principles of government in support of their nationalist vision. Antifederalists cited equally fundamental precepts to support their vision of a looser confederacy of small republics.

The two sides engaged in what was almost certainly the very first nationwide political campaign in the history of the world. Though each side was itself only loosely organized, they did address their collective-action problem—a rudimentary form of coordination and cooperation was manifest. This was especially evident in the division of labor among Hamilton, Madison, and Jay as they alternately wrote under the Publius pseudonym on different aspects of the newly drafted Constitution in an effort to effect its ratification in the state of New York.

Representation

One major area of contention between the two sides was the question of representation. The Antifederalists asserted that representatives must be "a true picture of the people, . . . [possessing] the knowledge of their circumstances and their wants."[21] This could be achieved, argued the Antifederalists, only in small, relatively homogeneous republics such as the existing states. In their view, the size and extent of the entire nation precluded the construction of a truly representative form of government.

The absence of true representation, moreover, would mean that the people would lack confidence in and attachment to the national government and would refuse to obey its laws voluntarily. As a result, according to the Antifederalists, the national government described by the Constitution would be compelled to resort to force to secure popular compliance. The Federal Farmer averred that laws of the remote federal government could be "in many cases disregarded, unless a multitude of officers and military force be continually kept in view, and employed to enforce the execution of the laws, and to make the government feared and respected."[22]

---

[21] Melancton Smith, quoted in Herbert J. Storing, *What the Anti-Federalists Were For: The Political Thought of the Opponents of the Constitution* (Chicago: University of Chicago Press, 1981), p. 17.

[22] "Letters from the Federal Farmer," no. 2, in *The Complete Anti-Federalist,* Herbert J. Storing, ed., 7 vols. (Chicago: University of Chicago Press, 1981).

Federalists, for their part, did not long for pure democracy and saw no reason that representatives should be precisely like those they represented. In their view, government must be representative *of* the people but must also have a measure of autonomy *from* the people. Their ideal government was to be constructed such that it would be capable of serving the long-term public interest even if doing so conflicted with the public's current preference. In more contemporary terms, Federalists sought representatives who were *trustees* whereas Antifederalists sought *delegates*.

Federalists also dismissed the Antifederalist claim that the distance between representatives and constituents in the proposed national government would lead to popular disaffection and compel the government to use force to secure obedience. Federalists replied that the system of representation they proposed was more likely to produce effective government. In Hamilton's words, there would be "a probability that the general government will be better administered than the particular governments."[23] Competent government, in turn, should inspire popular trust and confidence more effectively than simple social proximity between rulers and ruled.

The Threats Posed by the Majority

A second important issue dividing Federalists and Antifederalists was the threat of **tyranny**—unjust rule by the group in power. Both opponents and defenders of the Constitution frequently affirmed their fear of tyrannical rule. Each side, however, had a different view of the most likely source of tyranny and, hence, of the way in which the threat was to be forestalled.

From the Antifederalist perspective, the great danger was the tendency of all governments—including republican governments—to become gradually more and more "aristocratic" in character, with the small number of individuals in positions of authority using their stations to gain more and more power over the general citizenry. In essence, the few would use their power to tyrannize the many. For this reason, Antifederalists were sharply critical of those features of the Constitution that divorced governmental institutions from direct responsibility to the people—institutions such as the Senate, the executive, and the federal judiciary. The latter, appointed for life, presented a particular threat: "I wonder if the world ever saw . . . a court of justice invested with such immense powers, and yet placed in a situation so little responsible," protested Brutus.[24]

The Federalists, too, recognized the threat of tyranny. They were not naive about the motives and purposes of individuals and took them to be no less opportunistic and self-interested than the Antifederalists did. But the Federalists believed that the danger particularly associated with republican governments was not aristocracy but, instead, majority tyranny. The Federalists were concerned that a popular majority, "united and actuated by some common impulse of passion, or of interest, adverse to the rights of other citizens," would endeavor to "trample on the

tyranny Oppressive government that employs the cruel and unjust use of power and authority.

---

[23] *The Federalist*, no. 27.

[24] "Essays of Brutus," no. 15, in *The Complete Anti-Federalist*.

rules of justice."[25] From the Federalist perspective, it was precisely those features of the Constitution attacked as potential sources of tyranny by the Antifederalists that offered the best hope of averting the threat of oppression. The size and extent of the nation, for instance, were for the Federalists a bulwark against tyranny. In Madison's famous formulation, reflecting the logic of the collective action principle,

> The smaller the society, the fewer probably will be the distinct parties and interests . . . the more frequently will a majority be found of the same party; and the smaller the number of individuals composing a majority, and the smaller the compass within which they are placed, the more easily will they concert and execute their plans of oppression. Extend the sphere, and you take in a greater variety of parties and interests; you make it less probable that a majority of the whole will have a common motive to invade the rights of other citizens; or if such a common motive exists, it will be more difficult for all who feel it to discover their own strength, and to act in unison with each other.[26]

The Federalists understood that in a democracy, temporary majorities could abuse their power. The Federalists' misgivings about majority rule were reflected in the constitutional structure. The indirect election of senators, the indirect election of the president, the judicial branch's insulation from the people, the separation of powers, the president's veto power, the bicameral design of Congress, and the federal system were all means to curb majority tyranny. These features of the Constitution suggest, following the institution principle, the framers' awareness of the problems of majority rule and the need for institutional safeguards. Except for the indirect election of senators (which was changed in 1913), these aspects of the constitutional structure remain in place today.[27]

To some extent, the Federalists were influenced by an understanding of history that differed from that of the Antifederalists. Federalists believed that colonial history, to say nothing of the history of the Greeks, showed that republican governments were often endangered by mob rule. The Antifederalists, by contrast, thought that history revealed the dangers of aristocratic conspiracies against popular liberties. History matters, but it is always subject to interpretation.

Governmental Power

A third major difference between Federalists and Antifederalists was the issue of governmental power. Both the opponents and the proponents of the Constitution agreed on the principle of limited government. They differed, however, on the fundamentally important question of how to place limits on governmental action. Antifederalists favored limiting and enumerating the powers granted to the national

---

[25] *The Federalist*, no. 10.

[26] *The Federalist*, no. 10.

[27] A classic development of this theme is found in James M. Buchanan and Gordon Tullock, *The Calculus of Consent: Logical Foundations of Constitutional Democracy* (Ann Arbor: University of Michigan Press, 1962). For a review of the voting paradox and a case study of how it applies today, see Kenneth A. Shepsle and Mark S. Bonchek, *Analyzing Politics: Rationality, Behavior, and Institutions* (New York: Norton, 1997), pp. 49–81.

government in relation to both the states and the people at large. To them, the powers given the national government ought to be "confined to certain defined national objects."[28] Otherwise, the national government would "swallow up all the power of the state governments."[29] Antifederalists bitterly attacked the supremacy clause and the necessary and proper clause of the Constitution as unlimited and dangerous grants of power to the national government.[30]

Antifederalists also demanded that a bill of rights be added to the Constitution to place limits on the government's exercise of power over the citizenry. "There are certain things," wrote Brutus, "which rulers should be absolutely prohibited from doing, because if they should do them, they would work an injury, not a benefit to the people."[31] Similarly, the Federal Farmer maintained that "there are certain unalienable and fundamental rights, which in forming the social compact . . . ought to be explicitly ascertained and fixed."[32]

Federalists favored the construction of a government with broad powers. They wanted a government that had the capacity to defend the nation against foreign foes, guard against domestic strife and insurrection, promote commerce, and expand the nation's economy. Antifederalists shared some of these goals but still feared governmental power. Hamilton pointed out, however, that these goals could not be achieved without allowing the government to exercise the necessary power. Federalists acknowledged, of course, that every power could be abused but argued that the way to prevent misuse of power was not by depriving the government of the powers needed to achieve national goals. Instead, they argued that the threat of abuse of power would be mitigated by the Constitution's internal checks and controls. As Madison put it,

> The power surrendered by the people is first divided between two distinct governments, and then the portion allotted to each subdivided among distinct and separate departments. Hence a double security arises to the rights of the people. The different governments will control each other, at the same time that each will be controlled by itself.[33]

The Federalists' concern with avoiding unwarranted limits on governmental power led them to oppose a bill of rights, which they saw as nothing more than a set of unnecessary restrictions on the government.

The Federalists acknowledged that abuse of power remained a possibility but felt that the risk had to be taken because of the goals to be achieved. "The very idea of power included a possibility of doing harm," said the Federalist John Rutledge during South Carolina's ratification debates. "If the gentleman would show the power that could do no harm," Rutledge continued, "he would at once discover it to be a power that could do no good."[34]

---

[28] "Essays of Brutus," no. 7.

[29] "Essays of Brutus," no. 6.

[30] Storing, *What the Anti-Federalists Were For*, p. 28.

[31] "Essays of Brutus," no. 9.

[32] "Letters from the Federal Farmer," no. 2.

[33] *The Federalist*, no. 51.

[34] Quoted in Storing, *What the Anti-Federalists Were For*, p. 30.

CHANGING THE INSTITUTIONAL FRAMEWORK: CONSTITUTIONAL AMENDMENT

The Constitution has endured for more than two centuries as the framework of government. But it has not endured without change. Without change, the Constitution might have become merely a sacred relic, stored under glass.

Amendments: Many Are Called, Few Are Chosen

The need for change was recognized by the framers of the Constitution, and the provisions for amendment were incorporated into Article V. Since 1791, when the first 10 amendments, the Bill of Rights, were added, only 17 amendments have been adopted. And two of them—Prohibition and its repeal—cancel each other out, so that for all practical purposes only 15 amendments have been added to the Constitution since 1791. Despite vast changes in American society and its economy, only 12 amendments have been adopted since the Civil War amendments in 1868.
　　Four methods of amendment are provided for in Article V:

1. Passage in House and Senate by two-thirds vote; then ratification by majority vote of the legislatures of three-fourths (now thirty-eight) of the states.

2. Passage in House and Senate by two-thirds vote; then ratification by conventions called for that purpose in three-fourths of the states.

3. Passage in a national convention called by Congress in response to petitions by two-thirds (now thirty-four) of the states; ratification by majority vote of the legislatures of three-fourths of the states.

4. Passage in a national convention, as in method 3; then ratification by conventions called for that purpose in three-fourths of the states.

(Figure 2.2 illustrates each of these methods.) Because no amendment has ever been proposed by national convention, however, routes 3 and 4 have never been employed. And route 2 has been employed only once (for the Twenty-first Amendment, which repealed the Eighteenth, or Prohibition, Amendment). Thus route 1 has been used for all the others.

The Twenty-seven Amendments

The Constitution and its amendments are reproduced at the end of this book. Most of the Constitution's twenty-seven amendments share a common characteristic: All but two are concerned with the structure or composition of government. This is consistent with the dictionary, which defines *constitution* as the "makeup or composition of a thing"—anything. And it is consistent with the concept of a constitution as higher law because the whole point and purpose of a higher law is to establish a framework within which government and the process of making ordinary law can take place. Even those who would have preferred more changes in the Constitution would have had to agree that there is great wisdom in this principle. A constitution ought to enable legislation and public policies to take place, but it should not determine what that legislation or those public policies ought to be.

FIGURE 2.2 ROUTES OF AMENDMENT

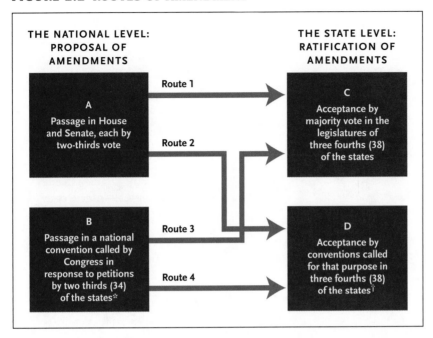

THE NATIONAL LEVEL: PROPOSAL OF AMENDMENTS		THE STATE LEVEL: RATIFICATION OF AMENDMENTS
A Passage in House and Senate, each by two-thirds vote	Route 1 / Route 2	**C** Acceptance by majority vote in the legislatures of three fourths (38) of the states
B Passage in a national convention called by Congress in response to petitions by two thirds (34) of the states*	Route 3 / Route 4	**D** Acceptance by conventions called for that purpose in three fourths (38) of the states†

*This method of proposal has never been employed. Thus amendment routes 3 and 4 have never been attempted.

†In each amendment proposal, Congress has the power to choose the method of ratification, the time limit for consideration by the states, and other conditions of ratification.

The purpose of the ten amendments in the Bill of Rights was basically structural: to give each of the three branches clearer and more restricted boundaries. The First Amendment clarifies the jurisdiction of Congress. Although the powers of Congress under Article I, Section 8, do not justify laws regulating religion, speech, and the like, the First Amendment makes this limitation explicit: "Congress shall make no law . . . " The Second, Third, and Fourth Amendments similarly spell out limits on the executive branch. Such limits were seen as a necessity given the abuses of executive power Americans had endured under British rule.

The Fifth, Sixth, Seventh, and Eighth Amendments contain some of the most important safeguards for individual citizens against the arbitrary exercise of governmental power. And these amendments sought to accomplish their goal by defining the judicial branch more concretely and clearly than had been done in Article III of the Constitution. Table 2.2 analyzes the ten amendments included in the Bill of Rights.

Five of the seventeen amendments adopted since 1791 are directly concerned with expansion of the electorate (Table 2.3). These occasional efforts to expand the electorate were made necessary by the fact that the Founders were unable to establish a national electorate with uniform voting qualifications. Stalemated on that issue, the delegates decided to evade it by providing in the final draft of Article I, Section 2, that eligibility to vote in a national election would be the same as "the Qualifications requisite for Electors of the most numerous Branch of the State

TABLE 2.2 THE BILL OF RIGHTS: ANALYSIS OF ITS PROVISIONS

Amendment	Purpose
I	Limits on Congress: Congress is not to make any law establishing a religion or abridging the freedom of speech, press, or assembly or the right to petition the government.
II, III, IV	Limits on the executive: The executive branch is not to infringe on the right of people to keep arms (II), is not to arbitrarily take houses for use by a militia (III), and is not to engage in the search or seizure of evidence without a court warrant swearing to a belief in the probable existence of a crime (IV).
V, VI, VII, VIII	Limits on the courts: The courts are not to hold trials for serious offenses without provision for a grand jury (V), a petit (trial) jury (VII), a speedy trial (VI), presentation of charges, and confrontation of hostile witnesses (VI). Individuals may not be compelled to testify against themselves (V) and are immune from trial more than once for the same offense (V). Neither bail nor punishment can be excessive (VIII), and no property can be taken without just compensation (V).
IX, X	Limits on the national government: All rights not enumerated are reserved to the states or the people.

Legislature." Article I, Section 4, added that Congress could alter state regulations as to the "Times, Places and Manner of holding Elections for Senators and Representatives." Nevertheless, this meant that any important expansion of the American electorate would almost certainly require a constitutional amendment.

Six more amendments are also electoral in nature, although not concerned directly with voting rights and the expansion of the electorate (Table 2.4). These six amendments are concerned with the elective offices themselves (the Twentieth, Twenty-second, and Twenty-fifth) or with the relationship between elective offices and the electorate (the Twelfth, Fourteenth, and Seventeenth).

Another five amendments have sought to expand or limit the powers of the national and state governments (Table 2.5).[35] The Eleventh Amendment protects the states from suits by private individuals and takes away from the federal courts any

---

[35]The Fourteenth Amendment is included in this table as well as in Table 2.3 because it not only seeks to define citizenship but also *seems* to intend that this definition of citizenship include, along with the right to vote, all the rights of the Bill of Rights, regardless of the state in which the citizen resides. A great deal more will be said about this in Chapter 4.

TABLE 2.3 AMENDING THE CONSTITUTION TO EXPAND THE ELECTORATE

Amendment	Purpose	Year Proposed	Year Adopted
XIV	Provided, in Section 1, a national definition of citizenship*	1866	1868
XV	Extended voting rights to all races	1869	1870
XIX	Extended voting rights to women	1919	1920
XXII	Extended voting rights to residents of the District of Columbia	1960	1961
XXIV	Extended voting rights to all classes by abolition of poll taxes	1962	1964
XXVI	Extended voting rights to citizens aged 18 and over	1971	1971

*In defining citizenship, the Fourteenth Amendment actually provided the constitutional basis for expanding the electorate to include all races, women, and residents of the District of Columbia. Only the "eighteen-year-olds' amendment" should have been necessary because it changed the definition of citizenship. The fact that additional amendments were required after the Fourteenth suggests that voting is not considered an inherent right of U.S. citizenship. Instead, it is viewed as a privilege.

TABLE 2.4 AMENDING THE CONSTITUTION TO CHANGE THE RELATIONSHIP BETWEEN THE ELECTED OFFICES AND THE ELECTORATE

Amendment	Purpose	Year Proposed	Year Adopted
XII	Provided a separate ballot for the vice president in the electoral college	1803	1804
XIV	Eliminated, in Section 2, the counting of slaves in the apportionment of House seats	1866	1868
XVII	Provided for the direct election of senators	1912	1913
XX	Eliminated "lame duck" sessions of Congress	1932	1933
XXII	Limited the presidential term	1947	1951
XXV	Provided for presidential succession in case of disability	1965	1967

TABLE 2.5 AMENDING THE CONSTITUTION TO EXPAND OR LIMIT THE POWER OF GOVERNMENT

Amendment	Purpose	Year Proposed	Year Adopted
XI	Limited the jurisdiction of federal courts over suits involving the states	1794	1798
XIII	Eliminated slavery and the rights of states to allow property in the form of persons	1865*	1865
XIV	In Section 2, applied due process of the Bill of Rights to the states	1866	1868
XVI	Established the national power to tax income	1909	1913
XXVII	Limited Congress's power to raise its own salary	1789	1992

*The Thirteenth Amendment was proposed on January 31, 1865, and adopted less than a year later, on December 6, 1865.

power to hear suits by private individuals of one state (or a foreign country) against another state. Three other amendments in Table 2.5 are obviously designed to reduce state power (the Thirteenth), reduce state power and expand national power (the Fourteenth), and expand national power (the Sixteenth). The Twenty-seventh puts a limit on Congress's ability to raise its own salary.

The two missing amendments underscore the meaning of the rest: the Eighteenth, or Prohibition, Amendment and the Twenty-first, its repeal. They represent the only instance in which the country tried to *legislate* by constitutional amendment. In other words, the Eighteenth is the only amendment that was designed to deal directly with some substantive social problem. And it was the only amendment ever to have been repealed. Two other amendments—the Thirteenth, which abolished slavery, and the Sixteenth, which established the power to levy an income tax—can be said to have had the effect of legislation. But the purpose of the Thirteenth Amendment was to restrict the power of the states by forever forbidding them to treat any human being as property. As for the Sixteenth Amendment, it is certainly true that income-tax legislation followed immediately; nevertheless, the amendment concerns itself strictly with establishing the power of Congress to enact such legislation. The legislation came later; and if down the line a majority in Congress had wanted to abolish the income tax, they could also have done so by legislation rather than through the arduous path of a constitutional amendment repealing the income tax.

For those whose hopes for change center on the Constitution, it must be emphasized that the amendment route to social change is, and always will be, extremely limited. This is "path dependency," as captured in the history principle, with a vengeance. The status quo—the original Constitution—and the arduousness of its amendment process provide durability on the one hand and constrain the prospects for change on the other. Through a constitution it is possible to establish a working structure of government, and through a constitution it is possible to establish basic rights of citizens by placing limitations and obligations on the powers of that government. Once these things have been accomplished, the real problem is how to extend rights to those people who do not already enjoy them.

REFLECTIONS ON THE FOUNDING: IDEALS OR INTERESTS?

At the start of this chapter, we stressed the need to look beyond the myths and rhetoric of the Founding era to analyze the goals of the Founders, their struggle to resolve their conflicts and reach their collective goals, and the institutions that resulted from their endeavor. The story of the Founding—the initial decision of Britain's New World colonies to chart a separate course (the Declaration of Independence), a successful revolution and the creation of a confederation of states with a weak central government (the Articles of Confederation), and the re-creation of an entirely elaborated new body of institutional arrangements (the Constitution), what Seymour Martin Lipset called the "first new nation"[36]—is a chronicle of purposeful collective action leading to the creation of a unique political scaffolding for governance.

The revolutionary generation, the politicians of the Articles years, and those who met in Philadelphia to create a new nation were rational actors with specific goals and purposes in mind. As we've seen, some scholars, such as Charles Beard, put a premium on economic self-interest. Northern merchants and manufacturers wanted property protection and security, unfettered opportunities to trade in domestic and international markets, and the financial security of sound currency, low taxes, and limited public debt. Southern planters also wanted property protection (with some of that property human in form), low tariffs to enable them to obtain manufactured goods cheaply, and access to international markets for their products and for slaves. Small farmers, tradesmen, and artisans wanted easy credit, relief from onerous taxes, and permissive policies toward debt. Other scholars have emphasized the idea of liberty and the "rights of Englishmen" that were compromised by clumsy interventions on the part of the mother country. Independence, loose federation, and finally a new nation with a central government capable of effective action were the goals, at different times, toward which the economic and political purposes of many of these groups pointed.

To orchestrate a revolution, organize a confederation, or draft a constitution requires a large variety of collective actions. Behaviors of many must be coordinated, participation must be induced, efforts must be focused on common objectives, and free riding must be discouraged. To accomplish all this, bargaining, cooperation, and

---

[36] Seymour Martin Lipset, *The First New Nation* (New York: Norton, 1979).

compromise must prevail, and during the Founding period, political leaders facilitated this process. Jefferson and Adams brought the colonies to the point of separating from the motherland; Washington was pivotal in the revolutionary phase; a variety of politicians came together to bargain over the directions to be taken by the Confederation, often without success; Madison, Hamilton, Washington, and ultimately Franklin presided over the drafting of the Constitution. In sum, collective action, coordinated by motivated leadership, paved the historical path from colony to new nation.

We've also seen that new institutions were needed to organize the new government successfully. Colonial institutions were satisfactory for 150 years, especially in a context in which the mother country was preoccupied with events elsewhere. Independence and self-governance became institutional objectives when the burdens of colonialism began to weigh heavily on the economic circumstances and political freedoms of the colonists. Over a fifteen year period (roughly 1775–90), the Founders experimented with and ultimately crafted a political order that, in most of its aspects, has survived more than two centuries. The final product of the Constitutional Convention has to be considered an extraordinary victory for the groups that had most forcefully called for the creation of a new system of government to replace the Articles of Confederation. Antifederalist criticisms forced the Constitution's proponents to accept the addition of a bill of rights designed to limit the powers of the national government. In general, however, it was the Federalist vision of America that triumphed. The Constitution adopted in 1789 created the framework for a powerful national government that has defended the nation's interests, promoted its commerce, and maintained national unity in the years since.

Though the Constitution was the product of a particular set of political forces, the form of government it established has a significance that goes far beyond the interests of its authors. As we have observed, political ideals often take on lives of their own. The great political values incorporated into the Constitution continue, more than two centuries later, to shape our political lives in ways that the framers may not have anticipated. For example, when they empowered Congress to regulate commerce among the states in Article I, Section 8, of the Constitution, they could hardly have anticipated that this provision would become the basis for many of the federal government's regulatory activities in areas as diverse as the environment and civil rights.

Two great constitutional notions, federalism and civil liberties, will be discussed in Chapters 3 and 4. As we close our discussion of the Founding and move on to an examination of federalism, it is worth reflecting on the Antifederalists. Although they were defeated in 1789, the Antifederalists present us with an important picture of a road not taken, an America that might have been. Would we have been worse off as a people if we had been governed by a confederacy of small republics linked by a national administration with severely limited powers? Were the Antifederalists correct in predicting that a government given great power in the hope that it might do good would, through "insensible progress," inevitably come to serve the interests of the few at the expense of the many? More than two centuries of government under the federal Constitution are not necessarily enough to definitively answer these questions. Only time will tell.

FOR FURTHER READING

Amar, Akhil Reed. *America's Constitution: A Biography*. New York: Random House, 2005.

Bailyn, Bernard. *The Ideological Origins of the American Revolution*. Cambridge, Mass.: Harvard University Press, 1967.

Beard, Charles A. *An Economic Interpretation of the Constitution of the United States*. New York: Macmillan, 1913.

Breyer, Stephen. *Active Liberty: Interpreting Our Democratic Constitution*. New York: Knopf, 2005.

Chernow, Ron. *Alexander Hamilton*. New York: Penguin, 2004.

Ellis, Joseph. *Founding Brothers: The Revolutionary Generation*. New York: Knopf, 2000.

———. *His Excellency, George Washington*. New York: Knopf, 2004.

Farrand, Max, ed. *The Records of the Federal Convention of 1787*. Rev. ed. 4 vols. New Haven, Conn.: Yale University Press, 1966.

Glaeser, Edward C. "Revolution of Urban Rebels." *Boston Globe,* July 4, 2008, Section A.

Hamilton, Alexander, James Madison, and John Jay. *The Federalist Papers*. Isaac Kramnick, ed. New York: Viking Press, 1987. ○ reader selection

Keller, Morton. *America's Three Regimes: A New Political History*. New York: Oxford University Press, 2007.

Maier, Pauline. *American Scripture: Making the Declaration of Independence*. New York: Knopf, 1997.

Riker, William H. *The Strategy of Rhetoric: Campaigning for the American Constitution*. New Haven, Conn.: Yale University Press, 1996.

Storing, Herbert J., ed. *The Complete Anti-Federalist*. 7 vols. Chicago: University of Chicago Press, 1981. ○ reader selection

Ⓢ Additional study and review materials are available online at wwnorton.com/studyspace/

3

Federalism and the Separation of Powers

The great achievement of American politics was the fashioning of an effective constitutional structure of political institutions. Although it is an imperfect and continuously evolving work in progress, this structure of law and political practice has served its people well for more than two centuries by managing conflict, providing inducements for bargaining and cooperation, and facilitating collective action. It has had at least one major failure: the cruel practice of slavery, which ended only after a destructive civil war. But the basic configuration of institutions first formulated in Philadelphia in 1787 survived that tragedy and has otherwise stood the test of time.

Two of America's most important institutional features are federalism and the separation of powers. Federalism seeks to limit government by dividing it into two levels, national and state, each with sufficient independence to compete with the other, thereby restraining the power of both.[1] The separation of powers seeks to limit the power of the national government by dividing government against itself—by giving the legislative, executive, and judicial branches separate functions, thus forcing them to share power.

In Chapter 1 we observed that institutions organize political life. Institutions, however, take many forms and can choreograph collective action in a variety of ways. One important difference among political institutions is the manner in which

---

[1] The notion that federalism requires separate spheres or jurisdictions in which lower and higher levels of government are uniquely decisive is developed fully in William H. Riker, *Federalism: Origin, Operation, Significance* (Boston: Little, Brown, 1964). This American version of federalism is applied to the emerging federal arrangements in the People's Republic of China during the 1990s in a paper by Barry R. Weingast, "The Economic Role of Political Institutions: Market-Preserving Federalism and Economic Development," *Journal of Law, Economics, and Organization* 11 (1995): 1–32.

they distribute decision, agenda, and veto powers. The institutions established by authoritarian regimes are usually designed to concentrate power in the hands of a small group of leaders who determine what will be considered, make the final decisions, and seek to block the actions of others. In democratic states, in contrast, political institutions are usually designed to allow a variety of groups to participate in decision making and provide at least a measure of agenda and veto power to a number of actors.

In the United States, the framers of the Constitution created institutions that would widely disperse involvement in decision making, along with agenda and veto power. Federalism assigns agenda-setting power, decision-making power, and veto powers to the federal government and to each of the fifty states. The separation of powers gives several federal institutions a degree of control over the agenda, the power to affect decisions, and the ability to block the actions of the others. The framers feared that concentrating power in a small number of hands would threaten citizens' liberties, and they were surely correct. Yet, although the constitutional dispersion of power among federal institutions and between the federal government

CORE OF THE ANALYSIS

- Two of the most important institutional features of America's government are federalism and the separation of powers.

- Federalism assigns agenda-setting, decision-making, and veto powers to the federal government and the fifty states. The apportionment of these powers between the federal government and the states has shifted over time.

- The separation of powers delineates the authority of the executive, Congress, and the courts, giving each a degree of control over the agenda, the power to affect decisions, and the ability to block the actions of the others.

and the states may well protect our liberties, it often seems to make it impossible to get anything done collectively. This lack of decisiveness sometimes appears to negate the most important reason for building institutions in the first place.

Since the adoption of the Constitution, ambitious politicians have developed a variety of strategies for overcoming the many impediments to policy change that inevitably arise in our federal system of separated powers. Most commonly, those seeking to promote a new program may try to find ways of dispersing the program's benefits so that other politicians controlling institutional veto powers will be persuaded that it is in their interest to go along. Thus, federalism and the separation of powers have given rise to the federal pork barrel, to the defense subcontracting system, and to grants-in-aid and other forms of policy that reflect the dispersion of decision, agenda, and veto powers. For example, if the executive branch hopes to win congressional support for a new weapons system, it generally sees to it that portions of the new system are subcontracted to firms in as many congressional districts as possible. In this way, dispersion of benefits helps to overcome the separation of powers between the executive and legislative branches. Similarly, as we shall see below, federal officials often secure state cooperation with national programs by offering the states funding, called grants-in-aid, in exchange for their compliance. These programs help to overcome the limitations of federalism. Thus, consistent with our discussion of the five principles of politics in Chapter 1, America's public policies are shaped by the institutional arrangements through which individual efforts must flow.

However, institutions are not carved in stone. Once created, they are subject to revision and modification as competing forces seek new decision rules that will give them an advantage, and as the leaders of institutions seek to strengthen their own power and expand their own jurisdictions at the expense of other institutions. In recent decades, the presidency has increased in power relative to Congress, and the federal government has grown in jurisdiction relative to the states. Nevertheless, these two core institutional features, federalism and the separation of powers, remain at the heart of the American system of government. Let us examine these features and assess their consequences for American government.

WHO DOES WHAT? FEDERALISM AND INSTITUTIONAL JURISDICTIONS

Federalism can be defined as the division of powers and functions between the national government and the state governments. Federalism limits national and state power by creating two levels of government—the national government and the state governments, each with a large measure of **sovereignty** and thus the ability to restrain the power of the other. As we saw in Chapter 2, the states existed as individual colonies before independence, and for nearly thirteen years they were virtually autonomous units under the Articles of Confederation. In effect, the states had retained too much power relative to the national government, a problem that led directly to the Annapolis Convention in 1786 and to the Constitutional Convention in 1787. Under the Articles, disorder within states was beyond the reach of the national government (see Shays's Rebellion, discussed in Chapter 2), and conflicts of interest between states were not manageable. For example, states were making their own trade agreements with foreign countries and companies, which might then play off one state against another for special advantages. Some states adopted trade tariffs and further barriers to foreign commerce that were contrary to the interests of other states.[2] Tax and other barriers were also being erected between the states.[3] But even after the ratification of the Constitution, the states continued to be more important than the national government. For nearly a century and a half, virtually all of the fundamental policies governing the lives of Americans were made by the state legislatures, not by Congress.

Why Keep the States: The Importance of History.   Many of the Constitution's framers, particularly Alexander Hamilton, had hoped to create something close to a unitary national government and to circumscribe severely the power of the individual states. The fact that the framers established a federal system in which the states retained significant powers is an illustration of the importance of history. Each of the states had a well-established set of governmental institutions staffed by legislators, judges, and executive officials who had no desire to see their power and autonomy submerged in a new national government. New York's governor George Clinton, for example, opposed the idea of a stronger national government mainly because he enjoyed his position as the chief executive of what amounted to an important independent nation. At the same time, citizens identified with their own states. The people of North America were not Americans. Instead, they had already had several generations to become Virginians, New Yorkers, Pennsylvanians, and so on. Well-established popular identification with the thirteen states was another reason that even the most nationalistic of the framers was forced to accept the idea that the states would continue as important entities. In a

federalism The system of government in which a constitution divides power between a central government and regional government.

sovereignty Supreme and independent political authority.

---

[2] For a good treatment of these conflicts of interest between states, see Forrest McDonald, *E Pluribus Unum: The Formation of the American Republic, 1776–1790* (Boston: Houghton Mifflin, 1965), chap. 7, esp. pp. 319–38.

[3] See David M. O'Brien, *Constitutional Law and Politics*, 3rd ed. (New York: Norton, 1997), I: pp. 602–3.

sense, the framers were faced by the same historically given realities faced today by advocates of a stronger European Union (EU). The nations of Europe have historically distinct identities, well-entrenched governments, and loyal citizens. Given the force of history, uniting these nations is no easy matter. Like America's Founders, the architects of the EU, bowing to history, have generally sought to erect the new regime on federal foundations.

Federalism in the Constitution: Who Decides What

American federalism recognized two sovereigns in the original Constitution and reinforced the principle in the Bill of Rights by granting a few **expressed powers** to the national government and reserving the rest to the states. Thus, the Constitution defined the jurisdiction of each level of government.

The Powers of the National Government.   As we saw in Chapter 2, the expressed powers granted to the national government are found in Article I, Section 8, of the Constitution. These seventeen powers include the powers to collect taxes, coin money, declare war, and regulate commerce (which, as we shall see, became a very important power for the national government). Article I, Section 8, also contains an important source of power for the national government: the **implied powers** that enable Congress "to make all Laws which shall be necessary and proper for carrying into Execution the foregoing Powers." Not until several decades after the Founding did the Supreme Court allow Congress to exercise the power granted in this **necessary and proper clause,** but as we shall see later in this chapter, this doctrine allowed the national government to expand considerably the scope of its authority, although the process was a slow one. In addition to these expressed and implied powers, the Constitution affirms the power of the national government in the supremacy clause (Article VI), which makes all national laws and treaties "the supreme Law of the Land."

The Powers of State Government.   One way in which the framers sought to preserve a strong role for the states was through the Tenth Amendment to the Constitution. The Tenth Amendment presents a decision rule, or general principle governing decisions, stating that the powers the Constitution does not delegate to the national government or deny to the states are "reserved to the States respectively, or to the people." The Antifederalists, who feared that a strong central government would encroach on individual liberty, repeatedly pressed for such an amendment as a way of limiting national power. Federalists agreed to the amendment because they did not think it would do much harm, given the powers the Constitution already granted to the national government. The Tenth Amendment is also called the **reserved powers** amendment because it aims to reserve powers to the states.

The most fundamental power retained by the states is that of coercion—the power to develop and enforce criminal codes, administer health and safety rules, and regulate the family via marriage and divorce laws. The states have the power to regulate individuals' livelihoods: If you're a doctor or a lawyer or a plumber or a barber, you must be licensed by the state. Even more fundamental, the states had the

expressed powers
The notion that the Constitution grants to the federal government only those powers specifically named in its text.

implied powers
Powers derived from the necessary and proper clause (Article I, Section 8) of the Constitution. Such powers are not specifically expressed but are implied through the expansive interpretation of delegated powers.

necessary and proper clause
Article I, Section 8, of the Constitution, which enumerates the powers of Congress and provides Congress with the authority to make all laws "necessary and proper" to carry them out; also referred to as the elastic clause.

reserved powers
Powers, derived from the Tenth Amendment to the Constitution, that are not specifically delegated to the national government or denied to the states.

power to define private property: Private property exists because state laws against trespass define who is and who is not entitled to use a piece of property. If you own a car, your ownership isn't worth much unless the state is willing to enforce your right to possession by making it a crime for anyone else to drive your car without your permission. These are fundamental matters, and the powers of the states regarding such domestic issues are much greater than the powers of the national government, even today. For example, in its 2008 decision in the case of *District of Columbia v. Heller*, the Supreme Court ruled that a District of Columbia handgun control ordinance that made it virtually impossible for a district resident to legally possess a handgun was unconstitutional.[4] The Court based its ruling on the Second Amendment, which guarantees the right to bear arms. The Court's majority, however, indicated that the Second Amendment applies only to the federal government and that the District's ordinance was invalidated only because the District of Columbia is legally an agency of the federal government.[5] Two years later, in the case of *McDonald v. Chicago*, the Court struck down a Chicago gun ordinance, this time declaring that the Second Amendment applied to the states as well as the federal government.[6]

A state's authority to regulate these fundamental matters is commonly referred to as the **police power** of the state and encompasses the state's power to regulate the health, safety, welfare, and morals of its citizens. Policing is what states do—they coerce you in the name of the community in order to maintain public order. And this was exactly the type of power the Founders intended the states to exercise.

In some areas, the states share **concurrent powers** with the national government: They retain and share some power to regulate commerce and affect the currency—for example, by chartering banks, granting or denying corporate charters, granting or denying licenses to engage in a business or practice a trade, and regulating the quality of products or the conditions of labor. This issue of concurrent versus exclusive power has come up from time to time in our history, but wherever there has been a direct conflict of laws between the federal and the state levels, the issue has most often been resolved in favor of national supremacy.

States' Obligations to Each Other.   The Constitution also creates obligations among the states. These obligations, spelled out in Article IV, were intended to promote national unity. By requiring the states to recognize actions and decisions taken in other states as legal and proper, the framers aimed to make the states less like independent countries and more like parts of a single nation.

Article IV, Section 1, calls for "Full Faith and Credit" among states, meaning that each state is normally expected to honor the "public Acts, Records, and Proceedings" that take place in any other state. So, for example, if two people are married in Texas—marriage being regulated by state law—Missouri must recognize that marriage even though the couple was not married under Missouri state law.

This **full faith and credit clause** has recently become entangled in the controversy over gay marriage. In several states, individuals of the same gender may

> **police power** The power reserved to the government to regulate the health, safety, and morals of its citizens.

> **concurrent powers** The authority possessed by *both* state and national governments, such as the power to levy taxes.

> **full faith and credit clause** The provision in Article IV, Section 1, of the Constitution requiring that each state normally honors the public acts and judicial decisions that take place in another state.

---

[4] *District of Columbia v. Heller*, 07-290 (2008).

[5] Jess Bravin and Susan Davis, "In a First, High Court Affirms Gun Rights," *Wall Street Journal*, June 22, 2008, p. A1.

[6] *McDonald v. Chicago*, 08-1521 (2010).

marry. A number of other states, though, have passed "defense of marriage acts" that define marriage only as a union between a man and a woman. Eager to show its disapproval of gay marriage, Congress passed the federal Defense of Marriage Act in 1996, declaring that states will *not* have to recognize a same-sex marriage legally contracted in another state. The Supreme Court may eventually be asked to clarify this issue.

Article IV, Section 2, known as the comity clause, also seeks to promote national unity. It provides that citizens enjoying the **privileges and immunities** of one state should be entitled to similar treatment in other states. What this clause has come to mean is that a state cannot discriminate against someone from another state or give special privileges to its own residents. For example, in the 1970s, when Alaska passed a law that gave residents preference over nonresidents in obtaining work on the state's oil and gas pipelines, the Supreme Court ruled the law illegal because it discriminated against citizens of other states.[7] This clause also regulates criminal justice among the states by requiring states to return fugitives to the states from which they have fled. Thus in 1952, when an inmate escaped from an Alabama prison and sought to avoid being returned to Alabama on the grounds that he was being subjected to "cruel and unusual punishment" there, the Supreme Court ruled that he must be returned, according to Article IV, Section 2.[8] This example highlights the difference between the obligations among states and those among different countries. Recently France refused to return an American fugitive because he might be subject to the death penalty, which does not exist in France.[9] The Constitution clearly forbids states from doing something similar.

Limitations on the States. Although most of the truly coercive powers of government are reserved to the states, the Constitution does impose some significant limitations. One example was given in the discussion of the privileges and immunities clause: that one state cannot discriminate against a person residing in another state. But the most prominent application of this clause is extradition; any person in any state "who shall flee from Justice . . . [to] another State, shall on Demand . . . be delivered up . . . to the State having Jurisdiction" (Article IV, Section 2). In the last section, we gave the example of the case of an Alabama inmate.

Another potential on states is in a clause in Article I, Section 10, that provides that "no State shall, without the Consent of Congress, . . . enter into any Agreement or Compact with another State." Compacts are a way for two or more states to reach a legally binding agreement about how to solve a problem that crosses state lines. In the early years of the Republic, states turned to compacts primarily to settle border disputes. Today with the support of the federal government they are used for a wide range of issues but are especially important in regulating the distribution of river water, addressing environmental concerns, and operating transportation systems

privileges and immunities The provision in Article IV, Section 2, of the Constitution stating that a state cannot discriminate against someone from another state or give its own residents special privileges.

---

[7] *Hicklin v. Orbeck,* 437 U.S. 518 (1978).

[8] *Sweeney v. Woodall,* 344 U.S. 86 (1953).

[9] Marlise Simons, "France Won't Extradite American Convicted of Murder," *New York Times,* December 5, 1997, p. A9.

that cross state lines.[10] A well-known contemporary example is the Port of New York Authority, a compact formed between New York and New Jersey in 1921. Without it, such public works as the bridge connecting Brooklyn and Staten Island, the bridges connecting New Jersey and Staten Island, the Lincoln Tunnel, the George Washington Bridge, the expansion and integration of the New York port area, and the expansion and integration of the three major airports and countless approaches and transfer facilities could not have been financed or completed.[11] In 1972, the name of the agency was appropriately changed to the Port Authority of New York and New Jersey.

Local Government and the Constitution. Local government, including counties, cities, and towns occupies a peculiar but very important place in the American system. In fact, the status of American local government is probably unique in world experience. First, it must be pointed out that local government has no status in the American Constitution. *State* legislatures created local governments, and *state* constitutions and laws permit local governments to take on some of the responsibilities of the state governments. Most states amended their own constitutions to give their larger cities **home rule**—a guarantee of noninterference in various areas of local affairs. But local governments enjoy no such recognition in the Constitution. Local governments have always been mere conveniences of the states.[12]

Local governments became administratively important in the early years of the Republic because the states possessed little administrative capability. They relied on local governments—cities and counties—to implement the laws of the state. Local government was an alternative to a statewide bureaucracy.

The Slow Growth of the National Government's Power

Before the 1930s, America's federal system could have been characterized as one of **dual federalism**, a two-layered system—national and state—in which the states and their local principalities did most of the governing. That is, the jurisdiction of the states was greater than that of the federal government. The structure of dual federalism is demonstrated in Table 3.1. The items in each column (disregarding the local-level functions discussed in the previous section) are the important types of public policies that governed America for the first century and a half under the

home rule The power delegated by the state to a local unit of government to manage its own affairs.

dual federalism The system of government that prevailed in the United States from 1789 to 1937, in which fundamental governmental powers were shared between the federal and state governments, with the states exercising the most important powers.

---

[10] Patricia S. Florestano, "Past and Present Utilization of Interstate Compacts in the United States" *Publius* (Fall 1994): 13–26.

[11] A good discussion of the status of the New York Port Authority in politics is found in Wallace Sayre and Herbert Kaufman, *Governing New York City—Politics in the Metropolis* (New York: Russell Sage Foundation, 1960), chap. 9.

[12] A good discussion of the constitutional position of local governments is in York Y. Willbern, *The Withering Away of the City* (Bloomington: Indiana University Press, 1971). For more on the structure and theory of federalism, see Thomas R. Dye, *American Federalism: Competition among Governments* (Lexington, Mass.: Lexington Books, 1990), chap. 1; and Martha Derthick, "Up-to-Date in Kansas City: Reflections on American Federalism," *PS: Political Science and Politics* 25 (December 1992): 671–75.

TABLE 3.1 THE FEDERAL SYSTEM: SPECIALIZATION OF GOVERNMENTAL FUNCTIONS IN THE TRADITIONAL SYSTEM, 1789–1937

National Government Jurisdiction (Domestic)	State Government Jurisdiction	Local Government Jurisdiction
Internal improvements	Property laws (including slavery)	Adaptation of state laws to local conditions (variances)
Subsidies	Estate and inheritance laws	Public works
Tariffs	Commerce laws	Contracts for public works
Public lands disposal	Banking and credit laws	Licensing of public accommodations
Patents	Corporate laws	Assessable improvements
Currency	Insurance laws	Basic public services
	Family laws	
	Morality laws	
	Public health laws	
	Education laws	
	General penal laws	
	Eminent domain laws	
	Construction codes	
	Land-use laws	
	Water and mineral laws	
	Criminal procedure laws	
	Electoral and political party laws	
	Local government laws	
	Civil service laws	
	Occupations and professions laws	

Constitution. We refer to it here as the traditional system precisely because almost nothing about our pattern of government changed during two thirds of our history. That is, of course, with the exception of the four years of the Civil War, after which we returned to the traditional system.

But there was more to dual federalism than merely the existence of two tiers. The two tiers were functionally quite different from one another. There have been debates every generation over how to divide responsibilities between the two tiers. As we have seen in this chapter, the Constitution delegated a list of specific powers to the national government and reserved all the rest to the states. That left a lot of room for interpretation, however, because of the final, "elastic" clause of Article I, Section 8. The three formal words *necessary and proper* amounted to an invitation to struggle over the distribution of powers between national and state governments. We shall confront this struggle throughout the book. However, the most remarkable thing about the history of American federalism is that federalism remained dual for nearly two thirds of that history, with the national government remaining steadfastly within a "strict construction" of Article I, Section 8. The results are clear in Table 3.1.

The best example of the potential elasticity inherent in Article I, Section 8, is in the **commerce clause**, which delegates to Congress the power "to regulate Commerce with foreign Nations, and *among the several States* and with the Indian Tribes" [emphasis added]. It is obvious that this clause can be interpreted broadly or narrowly, and in fact the Supreme Court embraced the broad interpretation throughout most of the nineteenth century. Yet Congress chose not to take the Court's invitation to be expansive. The first and most important case favoring national power was *McCulloch v. Maryland.*[13] The issue was whether Congress had the power to charter a bank, in particular the Bank of the United States (created by Congress in 1791 over Thomas Jefferson's constitutional opposition), because no express power to create banks was found anywhere in Article I, Section 8. Chief Justice John Marshall, speaking for the Supreme Court, answered that such a power could be "implied" from the other specific powers in Article I, Section 8, plus the final clause enabling Congress "to make all Laws which shall be necessary and proper for carrying into Execution the foregoing Powers." Thus the Court created the potential for significant increases in national governmental power by creating a decision rule that favored the national government over the states. Essentially, Marshall's ruling said that if a goal was allowed in the Constitution and Congress's chosen means to achieve the goal was not prohibited by the Constitution, Congress could act. This ruling gave the national government wide latitude.

A second question of national power arose in *McCulloch v. Maryland:* the question of whether Maryland's attempt to tax the bank was constitutional. Once again Marshall and the Supreme Court took the side of the national government, arguing that a legislature representing all the people (Congress) could not be taxed out of business by a state legislature (Maryland) representing only a small portion of the American people. This opinion was accompanied by Marshall's immortal dictum that "the power to tax is the power to destroy." It was also in this case that the

commerce clause Article I, Section 8, of the Constitution, which delegates to Congress the power "to regulate Commerce with foreign Nations, and among the several States, and with the Indian Tribes." This clause was interpreted by the Supreme Court to favor national power over the economy.

---

[13] *McCulloch v. Maryland,* 4 Wheaton 316 (1819).

Supreme Court recognized and reinforced the supremacy clause: Whenever a state law conflicts with a federal law, the state law should be deemed invalid because "the Laws of the United States . . . shall be the supreme Law of the Land." (This concept was introduced in Chapter 2 and will come up again in Chapter 8.)

This nationalistic interpretation of the Constitution was reinforced by another major case, that of *Gibbons v. Ogden* in 1824. The important but relatively narrow issue was whether the state of New York could grant a monopoly to Robert Fulton's steamboat company to operate an exclusive service between New York and New Jersey. Aaron Ogden had secured his license from Fulton's company, whereas Thomas Gibbons, a former partner of Ogden's, had secured a competing license from the U.S. government. Chief Justice Marshall argued that Gibbons could not be kept from competing because the state of New York did not have the power to grant this particular monopoly affecting other states' interests. To reach his decision, it was necessary for Marshall to define what Article I, Section 8, meant by "Commerce . . . among the several States." Marshall insisted that the definition was "comprehensive" but added that the comprehensiveness was limited "to that commerce which concerns more states than one." This opinion gave rise to what later came to be called interstate commerce.[14]

Although *Gibbons* was an important case, the precise meaning of interstate commerce would remain uncertain for several decades of constitutional discourse. However, one thing was certain: "Interstate commerce" was a source of power for the national government as long as Congress sought to improve commerce through subsidies, services, and land grants (Table 3.1, col. 1). Later in the nineteenth century, when the national government sought to use its power to *regulate* the economy rather than merely promote economic development, the concept of interstate commerce began to operate as a restraint rather than as a source of national power. Any effort by the federal government to regulate commerce in such areas as fraud, the production of impure goods, the use of child labor, or the existence of dangerous working conditions or long hours was declared unconstitutional by the Supreme Court as a violation of the concept of interstate commerce. Regulation in these areas would mean the federal government was entering the factory and the workplace, areas inherently local because the goods produced there had not yet passed into commerce and crossed state lines. Any effort to enter these local workplaces was an exercise of police power, a power reserved to the states. No one questioned the power of the national government to regulate certain kinds of businesses, such as railroads, gas pipelines, and waterway transportation, because they intrinsically involved interstate commerce.[15] But well into the twentieth century, most other efforts by Congress to regulate commerce were blocked by the Supreme Court's interpretation of federalism, with the concept of interstate commerce as the primary barrier.

---

[14] *Gibbons v. Ogden*, 9 Wheaton 1 (1824).

[15] In *Wabash, St. Louis, and Pacific Railway Company v. Illinois*, 118 U.S. 557 (1886), the Supreme Court struck down a state law prohibiting rate discrimination by a railroad; in response, Congress passed the Interstate Commerce Act of 1887, creating the Interstate Commerce Commission (ICC), the first federal regulatory agency.

After 1937, the Supreme Court threw out the old distinction between interstate and intrastate commerce, creating a new decision rule and converting the commerce clause from a barrier to a source of power. The Court began to refuse even to review appeals challenging acts of Congress that protected the rights of employees to organize and engage in collective bargaining, regulated the amount of farmland in cultivation, extended low-interest credit to small businesses and farmers, and restricted the activities of corporations dealing in the stock market, as well as many other laws that contributed to the construction of the "regulatory state" and the "welfare state."

Cooperative Federalism and Grants-in-Aid: Institutions Shape Policies

If the traditional system of two sovereigns performing highly different functions can be called dual federalism, the system since the 1930s can be called **cooperative federalism,** which generally refers to supportive relations, sometimes partnerships, between the national government and the state and local governments. It comes in the form of federal subsidization of special state and local activities; these subsidies are called **grants-in-aid.** But make no mistake about it: Although many of these state and local programs would not exist without the federal grant-in-aid, the grant-in-aid is also an important form of federal influence. (Another form of federal influence, the mandate, is covered in the next section.)

A grant-in-aid is really a kind of bribe, or a "carrot," whereby Congress appropriates money for state and local governments with the condition that the money be spent for a particular purpose as defined by Congress. Congress uses grants-in-aid because it does not have the political or constitutional power to command local governments to do its bidding. Federalism gives the states the power to veto many national government efforts. For example, some states are opting out of the federal No Child Left Behind education law and effectively vetoing it in their own jurisdictions. When you can't command, a monetary inducement becomes a viable alternative. The grant-in-aid is one more example of the fact that institutions shape policies. America's constitutional system gives the states de facto vetoes over many potential national government programs. As a result, the central government has learned to craft policies likely to elicit the states' cooperation.

Beginning in the late 1930s, this approach was applied to cities. Congress set national goals, such as public housing and assistance to the unemployed, and provided grants-in-aid to meet them. World War II temporarily stopped the distribution of these grants. But after the war, Congress resumed the provision of grants for urban development and school lunches. The value of such **categorical grants-in-aid** increased from $2.3 billion in 1950 to over $450 billion in 2008 (Figure 3.1). Sometimes Congress requires the state or local government to match the national contribution dollar for dollar, but for some programs, such as the interstate highway system, the congressional grant-in-aid provides a significant percentage of the cost. The nationwide speed limit of fifty-five miles per hour was not imposed on individual drivers by an act of Congress. Instead, Congress bribed the state legislatures by threatening to withdraw the federal highway grants-in-aid if the states did not set that speed limit. In the early 1990s, Congress began to ease up on the states,

cooperative federalism A type of federalism existing since the New Deal era, in which grants-in-aid have been used strategically to encourage states and localities (without commanding them) to pursue nationally defined goals. Also known as intergovernmental cooperation.

grants-in-aid A general term for funds given by Congress to state and local governments.

categorical grants-in-aid Funds given by Congress to states and localities and that are earmarked by law for specific categories, such as education or crime prevention.

FIGURE 3.1 THE HISTORICAL TREND OF FEDERAL GRANTS-IN-AID

ANALYZING THE EVIDENCE

Federal grants-in-aid began to expand dramatically during the 1960s. What political trends might explain this expansion?

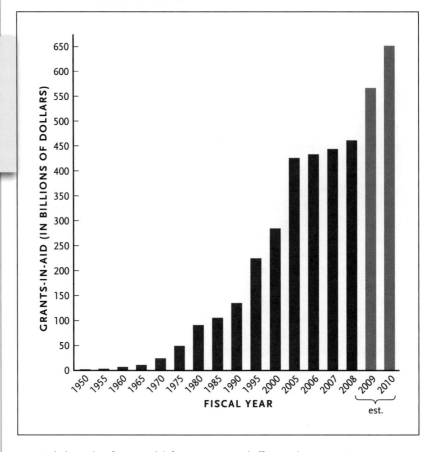

NOTE: Excludes outlays for national defense, international affairs, and net interest.

SOURCE: Office of Management and Budget, *Budget of the U.S. Government, Fiscal Year 2010*, www.whitehouse.gov/omb/budget/fy2010/pdf/hist.pdf.

permitting them, under certain conditions, to go back to the sixty-five-mile-per-hour (or higher) limit without losing their highway grants.

For the most part, the categorical grants created before the 1960s simply helped the states perform their traditional functions, such as educating and policing.[16] In the 1960s, however, the national role expanded, and the number of categorical grants increased dramatically. For example, during the Eighty-ninth

---

[16] Kenneth T. Palmer, "The Evolution of Grant Policies," in *The Changing Politics of Federal Grants*, Lawrence D. Brown, James W. Fossett, and Kenneth T. Palmer, eds. (Washington, D.C.: Brookings Institution, 1984), p. 15.

Congress (1965–66) alone, the number of categorical grant-in-aid programs grew from 221 to 379.[17] The grants authorized during the 1960s announced national purposes much more strongly than did earlier grants. Central to that national purpose was the need to provide opportunities to the poor.

Many of the categorical grants enacted during the 1960s were **project grants**, which require state and local governments to submit proposals to federal agencies. In contrast to the older **formula grants**, which used a formula (composed of such elements as need and state and local capacities) to distribute funds, the new project grants made funding available on a competitive basis. Federal agencies would give grants to the proposals they judged to be the best. In this way, the national government acquired substantial control over which state and local governments got money, how much they got, and how they spent it.

One of the most important scholars of the history of federalism, Morton Grodzins, characterized the shift to post–New Deal cooperative federalism as a move from "layer cake federalism" to "marble cake federalism,"[18] in which the line distinguishing intergovernmental cooperation and sharing has blurred, making it difficult to say where the national government ends and the state and local governments begin. Figure 3.2 demonstrates the basis of the marble cake idea. At the high point of grant-in-aid policies, in the late 1970s, federal aid contributed 25 to 30 percent of the operating budgets of all the state and local governments in the country (Figure 3.3).

> **project grants**
> Grant programs in which state and local governments submit proposals to federal agencies and for which funding is provided on a competitive basis.
>
> **formula grants**
> Grants-in-aid in which a formula is used to determine the amount of federal funds a state or local government will receive.

Regulated Federalism and National Standards

Developments from the 1960s to the present have moved well beyond cooperative federalism to what might be called regulated federalism.[19] Regulated federalism is an important new decision rule, enhancing the national government's power. In some areas, the national government actually regulates the states by threatening to withhold grant money unless state and local governments conform to national standards. The most notable instances of this kind of regulated federalism are in the areas of civil rights, poverty programs, and environmental protection. This focus reflects a general shift in federal regulation away from the oversight and control of strictly economic activities toward "social regulation"—intervention on behalf of individual rights and liberties, environmental protection, workplace safety, and so on. In these instances, the national government provides grant-in-aid

---

[17] Palmer, "Grant Policies," p. 6.

[18] Morton Grodzins, "The Federal System," in *Goals for Americans*, ed. President's Commission on National Goals (Englewood Cliffs, N.J.: Prentice-Hall, 1960), p. 265. In a marble cake, the white cake is distinguishable from the chocolate cake, but the two are streaked rather than arranged in distinct layers.

[19] The concept and the best discussion of this modern phenomenon are found in Donald F. Kettl, *The Regulation of American Federalism* (1983; repr., Baltimore: Johns Hopkins University Press, 1987), esp. pp. 33–41.

FIGURE 3.2 FOUR VIEWS OF FEDERALISM

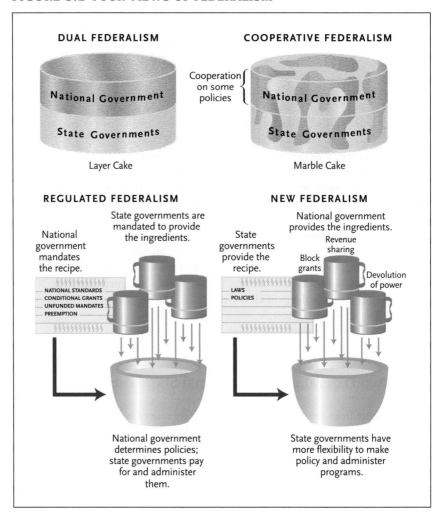

financing but sets conditions the states must meet to keep the grants (see again Figure 3.2). The national government refers to these policies as "setting national standards." Important examples include the Asbestos Hazard Emergency Act of 1986, which requires school districts to inspect for asbestos hazards and remove them from school buildings when necessary, and the Americans with Disabilities Act of 1990, which requires all state and local governments to promote access for the handicapped to all government buildings. The net effect of these national standards is that state and local policies are more uniform from coast to coast. National regulations and standards provide coordination across states and localities and solve collective-action problems. However, there are a number of other programs in which the national government engages in regulated federalism by imposing

FIGURE 3.3 THE RISE, DECLINE, AND RECOVERY OF FEDERAL AID

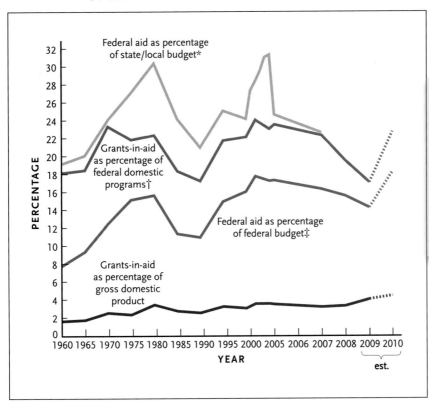

*Federal aid as a percentage of state and local expenditures after transfers.

†Federal aid as a percentage of federal expenditures from the federal government's own funds.

‡Excludes outlays for national defense, international affairs, and net interest.

SOURCE: Office of Management and Budget, *Budget of the U.S. Government, Fiscal Year 2010,* www.whitehouse.gov/omb/budget/fy2010/pdf/hist.pdf.

national standards on the states without providing any funding at all. These have come to be called **unfunded mandates.**[20]

These burdens became a major part of the rallying cry that produced the famous Republican Congress elected in 1994 and its Contract with America. One of the first measures adopted by the Republican 104th Congress in 1995 was an act to

unfunded mandates National standards or programs imposed on state and local governments by the federal government without accompanying funding or reimbursement.

---

[20] John J. DiIulio and Donald F. Kettl report that in 1980 there were thirty-six laws that could be categorized as unfunded mandates. And despite the concerted opposition of the administrations of Ronald Reagan and George H.W. Bush, another twenty-seven laws qualifying as unfunded mandates were adopted between 1982 and 1991. See John DiIulio, Jr., and Donald F. Kettl, *Fine Print: The Contract with America, Devolution, and the Administrative Realities of American Federalism* (Washington, D.C.: Brookings Institution, 1995), p. 41.

limit unfunded mandates: the Unfunded Mandates Reform Act (UMRA). UMRA was considered a triumph of lobbying efforts by state and local governments, and it was "hailed as both symbol and substance of a renewed congressional commitment to federalism."[21] Under this law, any mandate with an uncompensated state and local cost estimated at greater than $50 million a year, as determined by the Congressional Budget Office, can be stopped by a point of order raised on the House or Senate floor. This so-called stop, look, and listen requirement forced Congress to take positive action to own up to a mandate and its potential costs. During 1996, the first full year in which UMRA was in effect, only eleven bills included mandates that exceeded the $50 million threshold. Examples included a minimum wage increase, parity for mental health and health insurance, mandated use of Social Security numbers on driver's licenses, and extension of the federal Occupation Safety and Health Administration's standards to state and local employees. Most of these bills were modified in the House to reduce their costs. However, as one expert put it, "the primary impact of UMRA came not from the affirmative blockage of [mandate] legislation, but rather from its effect as a deterrent to mandates in the drafting and early consideration of legislation."[22]

As indicated by the first year of its operation, the effect of UMRA has not been revolutionary. UMRA does not prevent members of Congress from passing unfunded mandates; it only makes them think twice before they do. Moreover, the act exempts several areas from coverage. And states must still enforce antidiscrimination laws and meet other requirements in order to receive federal assistance. On the other hand, UMRA is a serious effort to move the national-state relationship a bit further toward the state side.

President George W. Bush made opposition to this shift in focus a key feature of his electoral campaign of 2000 and his legislative agenda of 2001. Yet the most heralded item in his domestic policy agenda, the No Child Left Behind (NCLB) Act, a concept going back to his successful program as governor of Texas, *is a very expensive unfunded mandate!* Signed into law in January 2002, NCLB set a national standard for steady improvement in students' performance on standardized tests and punishes schools whose students fail to improve. It also set rules for educating disabled students and presents detailed requirements that, as lobbyists for the states put it, "fail to recognize the tapestry of educational challenges faced by teachers in the nation's 15,000 school districts."[23] President Bush's promise that NCLB would provide the money for compliance brought him support from his leading Democratic voice of opposition in the Senate, Senator Edward Kennedy, but so far the cost of NCLB has been borne mainly by the states.

Opposition lobbying of Congress and the president by state government representatives became so intense that in 2004 the National Conference of State Legislatures (NCSL) began publishing *Mandate Monitor*, which itemizes the "gap" in

---

[21] Paul Posner, "Unfunded Mandate Reform: How Is It Working?" *Rockefeller Institute Bulletin* (1998): 35.

[22] Posner, "Unfunded Mandate Reform," 36.

[23] Sam Dillon, "Report from States Faults Bush's Education Initiative," *New York Times*, February 24, 2005, p. A18.

funding it claims is directly attributable to Congress's failure to appropriate the support necessary to comply with unfunded mandates. The first results of this analysis produced a list of fifteen major federal programs, the largest being education (NCLB and Americans with Disabilities), state drug costs, and the Department of Homeland Security. These programs have contributed to a total "cost shift" from the federal government to the states. According to the NCSL, the cost shift in federal funding to the states for fiscal years 2004 and 2005 collectively was $51 billion and $30 billion for 2006 alone. However, the NCSL insists that these are estimates and that "additional research . . . strongly suggests the cost shift to the states is double these amounts."[24] Although the measurement of these gaps can be criticized, the scale of unfunded and underfunded mandates is undeniable. Note also that the responsibility for this enormous shortfall is not attributable only to the party in power.

New Federalism and the National-State Tug-of-War

Federalism in the United States can best be understood today as a tug-of-war between those seeking more uniform national standards and those seeking more room for variability from state to state. This is a struggle over federalism's script and scorecard—over who does what and how the various activities are structured and sequenced. Presidents Richard Nixon and Ronald Reagan called their efforts to reverse the trend toward national standards and reestablish traditional policy making and implementation the new federalism. They helped craft national policies whose purpose was to return more discretion to the states. Examples of these policies include Nixon's revenue sharing and Reagan's **block grants**, which consolidated a number of categorical grants into one larger category, leaving the state (or local) government more discretion to decide how to use the money. Presidents Nixon and Reagan, as well as former president George H.W. Bush, were sincere in wanting to return somewhat to a traditional notion of freedom of action for the states. They called it new federalism, but their concepts and their goals were really much closer to the older traditional federalism that predated the 1930s.

block grants Federal funds given to state governments to pay for goods, services, or programs, with relatively few restrictions on how the funds may be spent.

In effect, President Bill Clinton adopted the new federalism of Nixon and Reagan even while expanding federal grant activity: He signed the UMRA of 1995 and the Personal Responsibility and Work Opportunity Reconciliation Act of 1996, which goes further than any other act of Congress in the past sixty years to relieve the states of national mandates, funded or unfunded. This new law replaced the sixty-one-year-old program of Aid to Families with Dependent Children (AFDC) and its education, work, and training program with block grants to states for Temporary Assistance for Needy Families (TANF). Although some national standards remain, the place of the states in the national welfare system has been virtually revolutionized through **devolution**, the strategy of delegating to the states more and more authority over a range of policies that had until then been under national government authority, plus providing the states with a substantial portion of the cost of these programs. Since the mid-1990s, devolution has been quite consequential for the national-state tug-of-war.

devolution The policy of removing a program from one level of government by deregulating it or passing it down to a lower level, such as from the national government to the state and local governments.

---

[24] *Mandate Monitor*, 2, no. 1 (March 2005).

By changing welfare from a combined federal-state program into a block grant to the states, Congress gave the states more responsibility for programs that serve the poor. One argument in favor of devolution is that states can act as "laboratories of democracy" by experimenting with many approaches and thus find one that best meets the needs of their citizens.[25] As states have altered their welfare programs in the wake of the new law, they have indeed designed diverse approaches. For example, Minnesota has adopted an incentive-based approach that offers extra assistance to families that take low-wage jobs. Other states, such as California, have more sticks than carrots in their new welfare programs.[26]

Former president George W. Bush, though sometimes compared with Ronald Reagan, was not an unwavering supporter of smaller national government, new federalism, and states' rights. On a number of very important matters dear to his heart, Bush was closer to the spirit of the New Deal and "regulated federalism" in terms of both direct expansion of the national government and increasing imposition of national standards on the states. The former went by the name compassionate conservatism, and it was not altogether popular among Bush's own partisan supporters. The latter takes the form of unfunded mandates, which not only rankled his supporters but also went against strict rules established by his administration. Some of the expansions of national government under George W. Bush are clearly attributable to 9/11 and the gigantic reaction to world terrorism, the creation of the Department of Homeland Security, the war in Iraq, and the cost of Hurricane Katrina, all complicated by failed implementation. But President Bush had other plans for the national government that he brought with him from his experience as a governor. His No Child Left Behind Act increased by 51 percent the budget of the Department of Education, a department that conservatives had vowed since the Reagan administration to abolish. Agriculture subsidies were increased by 40 percent. The 2005 Public Transportation Act included a commitment of $286 billion, of which $24 billion was for pork-barrel projects for favorite congressional districts. The prescription drug benefit that he added to Medicare was another enormous national government commitment; its estimated cost is $534 billion, the largest expansion of the welfare state since Lyndon Johnson.[27] In 2009, President Barack Obama proposed a record-shattering $3 trillion national budget that included hundreds of millions of dollars in grants to the states for public works and infrastructural improvements as part of his plan to stimulate the nation's faltering economy. Obama, however, told the state governors that he would be watching to see that they spent the money wisely and in a manner consistent with the federal government's purposes. Once again, the national government seemed to view the states as administrative arms more than independent laboratories.

---

[25] The phrase *laboratories of democracy* was coined by Supreme Court Justice Louis Brandeis in his dissenting opinion in *New State Ice Company v. Liebman*, 285 U.S. 262 (1932).

[26] For assessments of welfare grants to states, see both Frances Fox Piven, "Welfare and Work," and Dorothy Roberts, "Welfare's Ban on Poor Motherhood," in *Whose Welfare?*, Gwendolyn Mink, ed. (Ithaca, N.Y.: Cornell University Press, 1999), pp. 83–99 and 152–67.

[27] The figures and judgments in this paragraph are provided by George F. Will, one of America's most distinguished conservative columnists and philosophers, in "The Last Word," *Newsweek*, October 27, 2005, p. 78.

The Supreme Court as Referee. The courts establish the decision rules that determine the relationship between federal and state power. For much of the nineteenth century, federal power remained limited. The Tenth Amendment was used to bolster arguments about **states' rights**, which in their extreme version claimed that the states did not have to submit to national laws when they believed the national government had exceeded its authority. Arguments in favor of states' rights were voiced less often after the Civil War. But the Supreme Court continued to use the Tenth Amendment to strike down laws that it thought exceeded national power, including the Civil Rights Act passed in 1875.

In the early twentieth century, however, the Tenth Amendment appeared to lose its force. Reformers began to press for national regulations to limit the power of large corporations and to preserve the health and welfare of citizens. The Supreme Court approved of some of these laws, but it struck down others, including a law combating child labor. The Court stated that the law violated the Tenth Amendment because only states should have the power to regulate conditions of employment. By the late 1930s, however, the Supreme Court had approved such an expansion of federal power that the Tenth Amendment appeared irrelevant. In fact, in 1941, Justice Harlan Fiske Stone declared that the Tenth Amendment was simply a "truism," that it had no real meaning.[28]

Recent years have seen a revival of interest in the Tenth Amendment and important Supreme Court decisions limiting federal power. Much of the renewed interest stems from conservatives who believe that a strong federal government encroaches on individual liberties. They believe freedom is better protected by returning more power to the states through the process of devolution. In 1996, the Republican presidential candidate, Bob Dole, carried a copy of the Tenth Amendment in his pocket as he campaigned, pulling it out to read at rallies.[29] Around the same time, the Eleventh Amendment concept of **state sovereign immunity** was revived by the Court. This legal doctrine holds that states are immune from lawsuits by private individuals or groups claiming that the state violated a statute enacted by Congress.

The Supreme Court's ruling in *United States v. Lopez* in 1995 fueled further interest in the Tenth Amendment. In that case, the Court, stating that Congress had exceeded its authority under the commerce clause, struck down a federal law that barred handguns near schools.[30] It was the first time since the New Deal that the Court had limited congressional powers in this way. The Court further limited the power of the federal government over the states in a 1996 ruling based on the Eleventh Amendment. That ruling prevented Seminole Indians from suing the state of Florida in federal court. A 1988 law had given Indian tribes the right to sue a state in federal court if the state did not negotiate in good faith issues related to gambling casinos on tribal land. The Supreme Court's ruling appeared to signal a much broader limitation on national power by raising new questions about whether individuals can sue a state if it fails to uphold federal law.[31]

states' rights The principle that states should oppose increases in the authority of the national government. This view was most popular before the Civil War.

state sovereign immunity A legal doctrine holding that states cannot be sued for violating an act of Congress

---

[28] *United States v. Darby,* 312 U.S. 100 (1941).

[29] W. John Moore, "Pleading the 10th," *National Journal,* July 29, 1995, p. 1940.

[30] *United States v. Lopez,* 514 U.S. 549 (1995).

[31] *Seminole Tribe v. Florida,* 517 U.S. 44 (1996).

Another significant decision involving the relationship between the federal government and state governments was the 1997 case of *Printz v. United States*, in which the Court struck down a key provision of the Brady bill, enacted by Congress in 1993 to regulate gun sales. Under the terms of the act, state and local law enforcement officers were required to conduct background checks on prospective gun purchasers. The Court held that the federal government cannot require states to administer or enforce federal regulatory programs.[32] Because the states bear administrative responsibility for a variety of other federal programs, this decision could have far-reaching consequences. Finally, in another major ruling from the 1996–97 term, in *City of Boerne v. Flores*, the Court ruled that Congress had gone too far in restricting the power of the states to enact regulations they deemed necessary for the protection of public health, safety, or welfare (see Chapter 4).[33] These rulings signal a move toward a much more restricted federal government.

In 1999, the Court's ruling on another Eleventh Amendment case further strengthened the doctrine of state sovereign immunity by finding that "the federal system established by our Constitution preserves the sovereign status of the States. . . . The generation that designed and adopted our federal system considered immunity from private suits central to sovereign dignity."[34] In 2000, in *United States v. Morrison*, the Supreme Court invalidated an important provision of the 1994 Violence against Women Act, which permitted women to bring private damage suits if their victimization was "gender-motivated." Although the 1994 act did not add any new national laws imposing liability or obligations on the states, the Supreme Court still held the act to be "an unconstitutional exercise" of Congress's power.[35] And although *Morrison* is a quite narrow decision on federalism, when it is coupled with *United States v. Lopez*, there is a definite trend toward questioning the need for federal intervention in American sociey. This trend continued with the 2006 *Gonzales v. Oregon* case.

The *Gonzales* case involved Oregon's physician-assisted suicide law, which permitted doctors to prescribe lethal doses of medication for terminally ill patients who requested help ending their lives. In 2001, then U.S. attorney general John Ashcroft issued an order declaring that any physician involved in such a procedure would be prosecuted for violating the federal Controlled Substances Act. The state of Oregon joined several physicians and patients in a suit against Ashcroft's order. Eventually, the U.S. Supreme Court ruled that the federal government could not overrule state laws determining how drugs should be used so long as the drugs were not prohibited by federal law.[36]

These developments put federalism and the Court directly in the line of fire. But there is nothing new in this. The Court under John Marshall was, in essence, a nationalizing court. Marshall's successor, Chief Justice Roger Taney, gave us the most extreme denationalizing period, virtually inventing the concept of states'

[32] *Printz v. United States*, 521 U.S. 898 (1997).

[33] *City of Boerne v. Flores*, 521 U.S. 507 (1997).

[34] *Alden v. Maine*, 527 U.S. 706 (1999).

[35] *United States v. Morrison*, 529 U.S. 598 (2000).

[36] *Gonzales v. Oregon*, 546 U.S. 243 (2006).

rights, as slavery and its extension were endangering the Union. The Court in place when Franklin Roosevelt was first elected was extremely antinational; it declared virtually all the novel New Deal programs unconstitutional. And most notoriously, that same Court, after Roosevelt's landslide 1936 reelection, followed public opinion into the longest and most profound pro-nationalizing era. (It should be explained once again that the national government was permitted to expand, but not at the expense of the states.) The only remarkable thing about the current era has been the moderation and patience of the Burger and Rehnquist Courts in turning the tendency back toward the states.

This tug-of-war between state and national levels of government will almost certainly continue. The Roberts Court will surely take us further back toward the state level, but how far back will depend on new judicial appointments as presidents and parties change and vacancies on the Court arise. The respective jurisdictions of the state and federal governments are always matters of contention and, hence, changes in the decision rules established by the courts always have important implications for the relative power of the nation and the states.

THE SEPARATION OF POWERS

As we noted at the beginning of this chapter, the separation of powers gives several different federal institutions the ability to influence the nation's agenda, to affect decisions, and to prevent the other institutions from taking action—dividing agenda, decision and veto power. This arrangement may be cumbersome, but the Constitution's framers saw it as an essential means of protecting liberty.

In his discussion of the separation of powers, James Madison quoted the originator of the idea, the French political thinker Baron de Montesquieu: "There can be no liberty where the legislative and executive powers are united in the same person . . . [or] if the power of judging be not separated from the legislative and executive powers."[37] Using this same reasoning, many of Madison's contemporaries argued that there was not *enough* separation among the three branches, and Madison had to backtrack to insist that complete separation was not required:

> Unless these departments [branches] be so far connected and blended as to give
> to each a constitutional control over the others, the degree of separation which
> the maxim requires, as essential to a free government, can never in practice be
> duly maintained.[38]

This is the secret of how Americans have made the separation of powers effective: They have made it self-enforcing by giving each branch of government the means to participate in, and partially or temporarily obstruct, the workings of the other branches.

---

[37] Alexander Hamilton, James Madison, and John Jay, *The Federalist Papers*, Clinton L. Rossiter, ed. (New York: New American Library, 1961), no. 47, p. 302.

[38] *The Federalist Papers*, no. 48, p. 308.

Checks and Balances: A System of Mutual Vetoes

The means by which each branch of government interacts with the others is known informally as **checks and balances.** This arrangement gives each branch agenda and veto power, under a decision that requires all the branches to agree on national policies. The best-known examples are the presidential power to veto legislation passed by Congress; the power of Congress to override the veto by a two-thirds majority vote, the power of Congress to impeach the president, and the power of the Senate to approve presidential appointments; the power of the president to appoint the members of the Supreme Court and the other federal judges with Senate approval; and the power of the Supreme Court to engage in judicial review (discussed below). These and other examples are shown in Figure 3.4. The framers sought to guarantee that the three branches would in fact use the checks and balances as weapons against each other by giving each branch a different political constituency: direct, popular election of the members of the House and indirect election of senators (until the Seventeenth Amendment, adopted in 1913); indirect election of the president (still in effect, at least formally); and appointment of federal judges for life. All things considered, the best characterization of the separation-of-powers principle in action is, as we said in Chapter 2, "separated institutions sharing power."[39]

Legislative Supremacy

Although each branch was to be given adequate means to compete with the other branches, it is also clear that within the system of separated powers the framers provided for **legislative supremacy** by making Congress the preeminent branch. Legislative supremacy made the provision of checks and balances in the other two branches all the more important.

The most important indication of the intention of legislative supremacy was made by the framers when they decided to place the provisions for national powers in Article I, the legislative article, and to treat the powers of the national government as powers of Congress. In a system based on the "rule of law," the power to make the laws is the supreme power. Section 8 provides in part that "*Congress* shall have Power To lay and collect Taxes . . . ; To borrow Money . . . ; To regulate Commerce" [emphasis added]. The Founders also provided for legislative supremacy in their decision to give Congress the sole power over appropriations and to give the House of Representatives the power to initiate all revenue bills. Madison recognized legislative supremacy as part and parcel of the separation of powers:

> It is not possible to give to each department an equal power of self-defense. In republican government, the legislative authority necessarily predominates. The remedy for this inconveniency is to divide the legislature into different branches; and to render them, by different modes of election and different principles of action, as little connected with each other as the nature of their common functions and their common dependence on the society will admit.[40]

---

[39] Richard E. Neustadt, *Presidential Power and the Modern Presidents: The Politics of Leadership from Roosevelt to Reagan* (1960; rev. ed., New York: Free Press, 1990), p. 33.

[40] *The Federalist Papers,* no. 51, p. 322.

FIGURE 3.4 CHECKS AND BALANCES

LEGISLATIVE

Executive over Legislative
- President can veto acts of Congress.
- President can call a special session of Congress.
- President carries out, and thereby interprets, laws passed by Congress.
- Vice president casts tie-breaking vote in the Senate.

Legislative over Executive
- Congress can override presidential veto.
- Congress can impeach and remove president.
- Senate can reject president's appointments and refuse to ratify treaties.
- Congress can conduct investigations into president's actions.
- Congress can refuse to pass laws or provide funding that president requests.

Legislative over Judicial
- Congress can change size of federal court system and number of Supreme Court justices.
- Congress can propose constitutional amendments.
- Congress can reject Supreme Court nominees.
- Congress can impeach and remove federal judges.
- Congress can amend court jurisdictions.
- Congress controls appropriations.

Judicial over Legislative
- Court can declare laws unconstitutional.
- Chief Justice presides over Senate during hearing to impeach the president.

Executive over Judicial
- President nominates Supreme Court justices.
- President nominates federal judges.
- President can pardon those convicted in federal court.
- President can refuse to enforce the court's decisions.

JUDICIAL

EXECUTIVE

Judicial over Executive
- Court can declare executive actions unconstitutional.
- Court has the power to issue warrants.
- Chief Justice presides over impeachment of president.

In other words, Congress was so likely to dominate the other branches that it would have to be divided against itself, into House and Senate. One almost could say that the Constitution provided for four branches, not three.

Although "presidential government" gradually supplanted legislative supremacy after 1937, the relative power position of the executive and legislative branches since that time has varied. The degree of conflict between the president and Congress has changed with the rise and fall of political parties, and it has been

especially tense during periods of **divided government**, when one party controls
the White House and another controls the Congress, as has been the case almost
continuously since 1969.

Checks and Balances: The Rationality Principle at Work

The framers' idea that the president and Congress would check and balance one
another rests, in part, on an application of the rationality principle. The framers
assumed that each branch would seek to maintain or even expand its power and
would resist what the framers called "encroachments" on its prerogatives by the
other branch. This idea certainly seems consistent with the behavior of presidents
and congressional leaders. At least since the Nixon administration, presidents and
members of Congress have battled almost constantly over institutional prerogatives.
For example, what culminated in the Watergate struggle between Congress and
President Nixon began when Nixon sought to implement a reorganization of the executive branch that would have increased presidential control and reduced congressional oversight powers.[41] After Nixon's resignation, Congress enacted several pieces
of legislation, including the War Powers Act, to delimit presidential power. When
he took office, President Ronald Reagan worked to undo Congress's efforts and to
bolster the power of the White House. Reagan had a good deal of success, though
Congress ultimately put a stop to his efforts through investigations into presidential wrongdoing in the so-called Iran-Contra affair. During the Clinton era, Congress impeached the president but failed to convict him. During President George
W. Bush's second term in office, Congress and the president battled constantly over
the president's frequent refusals to disclose information to Congress on the basis of
executive privilege and his assertions that only the White House was competent to
manage the nation's security. "I am the decider," the president famously averred.
During his first months in office, President Obama had little reason to clash with
Congress. Both houses were controlled by Democrats, and the Democratic leadership was eager to cooperate with the new president. If history is any guide, however,
this "honeymoon" between Obama and Congress will not last forever.

Though each institution has registered success and failures in this struggle, over
time, the president has possessed a distinct advantage. The president is a unitary
actor, whereas Congress, as a collective decision maker, suffers from collective-
action problems (see Chapter 12). That is, each member of Congress may have
individual interests that are inconsistent with the collective interests of Congress
as a whole. For example, when Congress initially registered its support for President Bush's plan to use force in the Middle East, members were uneasy about the
fact that the president was asserting that he actually did not need congressional
approval—that he was the only decider. The president was using the war to underline claims of institutional power, but few members of Congress thought it would be
politically safe to express that viewpoint when the public was clamoring for action.
These considerations help to explain why, over time, the powers of the presidency

---

[41] Benjamin Ginsberg and Martin Shefter, *Politics by Other Means*, 3rd ed. (New York: Norton, 2002),
chap. 1.

have grown and those of the Congress diminished.[42] The "Analyzing the Evidence" section on the following page explains some of the ways presidents attempt to bypass the system of checks and balances. We will return to this topic in Chapter 6.

The Role of the Supreme Court: Establishing Decision Rules

The role of the judicial branch in the separation of powers has depended on the power of judicial review (see Chapter 8), a power not provided for in the Constitution but asserted by Chief Justice Marshall in 1803:

> If a law be in opposition to the Constitution; if both the law and the Constitution apply to a particular case, so that the Court must either decide that case conformable to the law, disregarding the Constitution, or conformable to the Constitution, disregarding the law; the Court must determine which of these conflicting rules governs the case: This is of the very essence of judicial duty.[43]

Marshall's decision was an extremely important assertion of judicial power and has been the basis of the judiciary's influence in American life ever since. In effect, Marshall declared that whenever there was doubt or disagreement about which rule should apply in a particular case, the Court would decide. In this way, Marshall made the Court the arbiter of all future debates between Congress and the president and between the federal and state governments.

In terms of numbers of cases, judicial review of the constitutionality of acts of the president or Congress is relatively rare. For example, there were no Supreme Court reviews of congressional acts in the fifty plus years between *Marbury v. Madison* (1803) and *Dred Scott v. Sandford* (1857). In the century or so between the Civil War and 1970, eighty-four acts of Congress were held unconstitutional (in whole or in part), but there were long periods of complete Supreme Court deference to Congress, punctuated by flurries of judicial review during times of social upheaval. The most significant of these was 1935–36, when twelve acts of Congress were invalidated, blocking virtually the entire New Deal program.[44] Then, after 1935, when the Court made its great reversals, no significant acts were voided until 1983, when the Court declared unconstitutional the legislative veto, a practice in which Congress authorized the president to take action but reserved the right to rescind presidential actions with which it disagreed.[45] Another decision, in 1986, struck down the Gramm-Rudman Act of 1985, which mandated a balanced budget. That act, the Court held, delegated too much power to the comptroller general, a congressional

---

[42] Matthew Crenson and Benjamin Ginsberg, *Presidential Power: Unchecked and Unbalanced* (New York: Norton, 2007).

[43] *Marbury v. Madison*, 1 Cranch 137 (1803).

[44] The Supreme Court struck down eight out of ten New Deal statutes. For example, in *Panama Refining Company v. Ryan*, 293 U.S. 388 (1935), the Court ruled that a section of the National Industrial Recovery Act of 1933 was an invalid delegation of legislative power to the executive branch. And in *Schechter Poultry Corporation v. United States*, 295 U.S. 495 (1935), the Court found the National Industrial Recovery Act itself to be invalid for the same reason.

[45] *Immigration and Naturalization Service v. Chadha*, 462 U.S. 919 (1983).

Bypassing Checks and Balances?

Although the system of checks and balances envisioned by the Founders seems to apportion checks equally among the branches, this has not stopped political actors from attempting to consolidate power. A recent example of one branch claiming greater power at the expense of the others is the increased use of presidential *signing statements*. Presidents use signing statements to offer their opinions on legislation and how it should be interpreted and implemented. However, recent presidents have made more frequent and calculated use of signing statements to nullify legislation they disagree with. An April 2006 article in the *Boston Globe* reported that President Bush used the practice to claim the authority to bypass over 750 statutes passed by Congress.[1]

Criticism of this use of signing statements to reinterpret and nullify legislation has been sharp. A *New York Times* editorial blasted the Bush administration for "disrupt[ing] the founders' careful allocation of power among the president, Congress and the courts."[2] Senator Patrick Leahy (D-Vt.) accused the administration of utilizing "an extra-constitutional, extra-judicial step to enhance the power of the president."[3] Senator Arlen Specter (R-Pa.) introduced legislation to curb the practice, and Senator Robert Byrd (D-Va.) and Congressman John Conyers (D-Mich.) commissioned a study to gauge the impact of the practice. As the figure below demonstrates, the threats and rhetoric from critics seem to have effectively reduced the total number of signing statements issued in the last two years of the Bush presidency. Further, soon after taking office in 2009, President Obama announced plans to use the practice much more modestly than the previous administration.[4]

SIGNING STATEMENTS PER YEAR

Statements / Year (vertical axis: 0, 20, 40, 60, 80, 100; horizontal axis: 1948, 1958, 1969, 1978, 1988, 1998, 2008)

Use of signing statements to bypass Congress was high in the first few years of the Bush presidency.

In 2007 and 2008, Bush's use of signing statements dropped off considerably, suggesting that efforts by members of Congress and others to check the presidency had been effective.

Source: Data from the American Presidency Project, www.presidency.ucsb.edu/index.php (accessed 5/28/09).

[1] Charles Savage, "Bush Challenges Hundreds of Laws." *Boston Globe*, April 30, 2006.
[2] "On Signing Statements," *New York Times*, March 16, 2009.
[3] Carl Hulse, "Lawmakers to Investigate Bush on Laws and Intent," *New York Times*, June 20, 2007.
[4] "Charles Salvage, "Obama Looks to Limit Impact of Tactic Bush Used to Sidestep New Laws," *New York Times*, March 9, 2009.

Presidents have also attempted to circumvent constitutional checks on their power by using the Constitution's *recess appointment clause*. The recess appointment clause in Article II, Section 2 allows presidents to "fill up all Vacancies that may happen during the Recess of the Senate, by granting Commissions which shall expire at the End of their next Session." The George W. Bush administration seized this language and regularly used recess appointments to bypass the Senate, which normally has the power to confirm (or not confirm) appointees to the executive and judicial branches. As the figure below demonstrates, early in his term, Bush used recess appointments at a higher rate than previous administrations.[5]

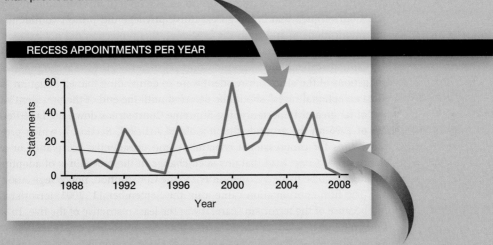

Not only did President Bush make a large number of recess appointments, but he made many controversial ones as well. Bush's recess appointments of Charles W. Pickering and William Pryor to federal appellate courts and John Bolton to the United Nations outraged Senate Democrats who had been blocking those nominations. However, it was not until his 2007 recess appointment of Sam Fox to be the United States' ambassador to Belgium that the Democrats took action. Fox's nomination was likely to be defeated by the Democratic-controlled Senate Foreign Relations Committee when the president withdrew it and gave him a recess appointment to the position. The move prompted Senate Majority Leader Harry Reid (D-Nev.) to declare his intention of keeping the Senate in permanent session. This maneuver, though highly unorthodox, was aimed at blocking the president from making further recess appointments. As the data demonstrates, it was effective in restoring the Senate's ability to check executive nominations. Following threats by Democrats in Congress, President Bush made a mere four recess appointments in 2007, and none in 2008. In this respect, then, it appears that the system of checks and balances envisioned by the framers had been restored.

[5]Ryan C. Black, Anthony J. Madonna, Ryan J. Owens, and Michael S. Lynch, "Adding Recess Appointments to the President's 'Tool Chest' of Unilateral Powers," *Political Research Quarterly* 60, no. 4 (December 2007): 645–54.

official, to direct the president to reduce the budget.[46] The Supreme Court became much more activist (that is, less deferential to Congress) after the elevation of Justice William H. Rehnquist to the position of chief justice (in 1986).[47] All of the cases in Table 3.2 altered some aspect of federalism by declaring unconstitutional all or an important portion of an act of Congress, and the end of this episode of judicial activism against Congress is not over. Between 1995 and 2002, at least twenty-six acts or parts of acts of Congress were struck down on constitutional grounds.[48]

Since the New Deal period, the Court has been far more deferential toward the president, with only five significant confrontations. One was the so-called steel seizure case of 1952, in which the Court refused to permit President Harry Truman to use "emergency powers" to force workers back into the steel mills during the Korean War.[49] A second case was *United States v. Nixon*, in which the Court declared unconstitutional President Nixon's refusal to respond to a subpoena to make available the infamous White House tapes as evidence in a criminal prosecution. The Court argued that although executive privilege did protect confidentiality of communications to and from the president, this protection did not extend to data in presidential files or tapes linked to criminal prosecutions.[50] During the heat of the Clinton scandal, the Supreme Court rejected the claim that the pressures and obligations of the office of president were so demanding that all litigation "but the most exceptional cases" should be deferred until the end of the president's term.[51] But of far greater importance, the Supreme Court struck down the Line Item Veto Act of 1996 on the grounds that it violated Article I, Section 7, which prescribes procedures for congressional enactment, and presidential acceptance or veto, of statutes. The Court held that any such change in the procedures of adopting laws would have to be made by amendment to the Constitution, not by legislation.[52]

The fifth confrontation came after the September 11, 2001, terrorist attacks. But because of the terrorism scare, it was the least restrictive of the five. In *Rasul v. Bush,* the Court held that the estimated 650 "enemy combatants" detained without formal charges at the U.S. Naval Station at Guantánamo Bay, Cuba, had the right to seek release through a **writ of *habeas corpus*.**[53] However, in Section 7 of the 2006 Military Commissions Act, Congress declared that enemy combatants held at Guantánamo Bay could not avail themselves of the right of *habeas corpus*. Then, in 2008, the Supreme Court responded by striking down Section 7 and affirming that the Guantánamo detainees had the right to challenge their detentions in federal court.[54] The Court noted that *habeas corpus* was among the most fundamental

writ of *habeas corpus* A court order demanding that an individual in custody be brought into court and shown the cause for detention. *Habeas corpus* is guaranteed by the Constitution and can be suspended only in cases of rebellion or invasion.

---

[46] *Bowsher v. Synar*, 478 U.S. 714 (1986).

[47] Cass R. Sunstein, "Taking Over the Courts," *New York Times*, November 9, 2002, p. A19.

[48] Sunstein, "Taking Over the Courts."

[49] *Youngstown Sheet and Tube Company v. Sawyer*, 343 U.S. 579 (1952).

[50] *United States v. Nixon*, 418 U.S. 683 (1974).

[51] *Clinton v. Jones*, 520 U.S. 681 (1997).

[52] *Clinton v. City of New York*, 524 U.S. 417 (1998).

[53] *Rasul v. Bush*, 542 U.S. 466 (2004).

[54] *Boumediene v. Bush*, 06-1195 (2008).

TABLE 3.2 A NEW FEDERAL SYSTEM? THE CASE RECORD, 1995–2006

Case	Date	Court Holding
United States v. Lopez, 514 U.S. 549	1995	Voids federal law barring handguns near schools: It is beyond Congress's power to regulate commerce.
Seminole Tribe v. Florida, 517 U.S. 44	1996	Voids federal law giving tribes the right to sue a state in federal court: "Sovereign immunity" requires a state's permission to be sued.
Printz v. United States, 521 U.S. 898	1997	Voids key provision of Brady law requiring states to make background checks on gun purchases: As "unfunded mandate," it violated state sovereignty under the Tenth Amendment.
City of Boerne v. Flores, 521 U.S. 507	1997	Restricts Congress's power under the Fourteenth Amendment to regulate city zoning and health and welfare policies to "remedy" rights: Congress may not expand those rights.
Alden v. Maine, 527 U.S. 706	1999	Declares states "immune" from suits by their *own* employees for overtime pay under the Fair Labor Standards Act of 1938. (See also the *Seminole* case.)
United States v. Morrison, 529 U.S. 598	2000	Extends *Seminole* case by invalidating Violence against Women Act: States may not be sued by individuals for failing to enforce federal laws.
Gonzales v. Oregon, 546 U.S.	2006	Upholds state assisted-suicide law over attorney general's objection.

constitutional rights and was included in the Constitution even before the Bill of Rights was added.

Like federalism, the separation of powers is an ongoing struggle. Deference to the president is not necessarily a permanent condition. However, more and more activities of the executive branch are being put beyond the reach of the courts.

FEDERALISM AND THE SEPARATION OF POWERS: COLLECTIVE ACTION OR STALEMATE?

Institutions are designed to solve collective action problems, but the solutions can take many different forms. The framers of the American Constitution believed that agenda, decision, and veto power should be dispersed among many different institutions. And because history matters and the thirteen existing states already possessed considerable autonomy when the Constitution was drafted, the framers had little choice but to relinquish a considerable measure of agenda, decision, and veto power to them, as well. The result was our federal system of separated powers.

Critics of the American constitutional framework have often pointed to this dispersion of governmental power as a source of weakness and incoherence in America's policy-making processes. Because of federalism, America's national government is often unable to accomplish what might be a matter of course in most nations. For example, in the case of *United States v. Lopez*, cited above, the Supreme Court invalidated a federal statute prohibiting the possession of firearms near schools, saying that it was an unconstitutional encroachment on the sovereignty of the states. In a country with a unitary system of government, this statute would not face this type of hurdle.

Because of the separation of powers, Congress often finds itself stymied by the president—or the president by Congress—in efforts to bring about changes in policy. The president possesses a veto over congressional action. Congress can, by legislation, seek to limit the powers of the executive. In 2006, for example, Congress sought, via legislation, to circumvent President Bush's refusal to permit federal dollars to be spent on stem-cell research. The president greeted this congressional initiative with a veto. In 2008, Congress attempted to express its displeasure with the president's conduct of the war on terrorism by enacting legislation outlawing a number of harsh methods authorized by the president for the interrogation of terrorist suspects. The president responded with a veto. Sometimes it seems that the dispersion of power among different institutions of government merely ensures that there will be no collective action.

The framers, though, did not want to make collective action too easy. They thought it was important to provide checks and balances that would protect the nation from the tyrannical actions of a small number of leaders, as well as from precipitous and thoughtless actions on the part of larger groups—the framers called this latter possibility "majority tyranny." The framers believed that well-constructed institutions should diminish the likelihood of inappropriate and unwise collective action, even at the cost of occasional stalemate. In recent years, the U.S. government has been criticized more for what it *has* done, especially with regard to the war in

Iraq, than what it *has not* done. Many Americans believe that Congress should have done more to thwart presidential war policies and hope the judiciary will do more to delimit presidential war powers in the future. The framers likely would have understood this desire to check the executive branch. Stalemate is not always the worst collective outcome.

FOR FURTHER READING

Bednar, Jenna. *The Robust Federation.* New York: Cambridge University Press, 2008. ○ reader selection

Campbell, Tom. *Separation of Powers in Practice.* Palo Alto, Calif.: Stanford University Press, 2004.

Crenson, Matthew, and Benjamin Ginsberg. *Presidential Power: Unchecked and Unbalanced.* New York: Norton, 2007.

Ferejohn, John A., and Barry R. Weingast, eds. *The New Federalism: Can the States Be Trusted?* Stanford, Calif.: Hoover Institution Press, 1997.

Fisher, Louis. *Constitutional Conflicts Between Congress and the President,* 7th ed. Lawrence: University of Kansas Press, 2007.

Hamilton, Alexander, James Madison, and John Jay. *The Federalist Papers.* Issac Kramnick, ○ reader selection
ed. New York: Viking Press, 2007.

Karmis, Dimitrios, and Wayne Norman. *Theories of Federalism: A Reader.* New York: Palgrave, Macmillan, 2005.

Nagel, Robert. *The Implosion of American Federalism.* New York: Oxford University Press, 2001.

Noonan, John T. *Narrowing the Nation's Power: The Supreme Court Sides with the States.* Berkeley: University of California Press, 2002.

Posner, Richard. *Not a Suicide Pact: The Constitution in a Time of National Emergency.* New York: Oxford University Press, 2006.

Riker, William H. *Federalism: Origin, Operation, Significance.* Boston: Little, Brown, 1964. ○ reader selection

Smith, Rogers M. *Civic Ideals: Conflicting Visions of Citizenship in U.S. History.* New Haven, Conn.: Yale University Press, 1997.

Van Horn, Carol E. *The State of the States,* 4th ed. Washington, D.C.: CQ Press, 2004.

Winston, Pamela. *Welfare Policymaking in the States: The Devil in Devolution.* Washington, D.C.: Georgetown University Press, 2002.

Additional study and review materials are available online at wwnorton.com/studyspace/

4 Civil Liberties and Civil Rights

Institutions are designed to solve collective-action problems. To "solve," however, does not necessarily mean to promote or facilitate collective action. Solving a problem may entail blocking or redirecting some forms of collective action. For example, nearly every nation has created police and judicial institutions designed to discourage or prevent mob violence. These institutions solve a collective-action problem by regulating or discouraging a form of collective action deemed to be undesirable and dangerous. As we saw in Chapter 3, the Constitution's framers viewed federalism and the separation of powers as institutional solutions that often would make collective action more difficult by dispersing decision, agenda, and veto powers. The benefit, from the framers' perspective, was to lessen the chance of rash and unwise collective action.

Another important set of constitutional instruments designed to solve collective-action problems are civil liberties and civil rights. Here, too, "solve" does not mean simply to facilitate collective action. Instead, the constitutional principles of civil liberties and civil rights presented by the Bill of Rights regulate collective action. Civil liberties are limitations or restrictions on collective action. In effect, the concept of civil liberties defines certain spheres of activity, such as speech or worship, in which the government's authority to interfere with individual conduct is limited. Civil rights, on the other hand, are rules governing collective decision-making processes and outcomes. Under the Constitution, for example, no American may be excluded from participation or representation in collective decision-making processes or treated adversely by decision makers on account of such factors as race, gender or ethnic background. Thus, generally speaking, civil liberties limit collective action by restricting the government's *jurisdiction*. Civil rights, on the other hand, regulate collective action through their impact on the government's rules for makind decisions, or *decisiveness*. That is, citizens' constitutional rights affect the manner in which decision makers are chosen, the process of decision making, and the range of permissible collective choices. In essence, civil rights are curbs on the power of majorities, and civil liberties are limits on the power of the government itself.

Constitutional guarantees of civil rights and civil liberties often seem clear in the abstract, but they inevitably produce thousands of complex questions and controversies every year when they are applied to concrete cases. Every government agency, for example, is constitutionally required to respect Americans' civil liberties. The government, though, is also obligated to protect the public's health and safety. This duty is sometimes called the "police power" and is exercised by the federal government and the governments of the states. Suppose that Congress enacts a law allowing national security agencies to sift through millions of phone calls searching for evidence of terrorist plots. Is such a law an unjustified intrusion on civil liberties or a necessary and legitimate effort to prevent bloodshed? In 2008, the Supreme Court declined to hear a case brought by a civil liberties group that wanted to halt a large-scale federal wiretapping program aimed at identifying

CORE OF THE ANALYSIS

- Civil liberties are rules that limit the government's authority to interfere in certain spheres of activity. They restrict the government's jurisdiction in areas such as free speech and religion.

- Civil rights are rules that govern collective decision-making processes and outcomes. They curb the power of majorities to exclude or harm individuals on the basis of factors such as race, gender, or ethnic background.

- Today's conception of civil liberties and civil rights has been shaped by the historical development of these ideas and their interpretation by key political actors, especially the Supreme Court.

possible terrorist communications.[1] This action let stand a lower-court ruling that had allowed the program to continue.

As in the wiretap case, jurisdiction over civil liberties and civil rights issues is primarily exercised by the courts, which have developed myriad decision rules and procedures designed to resolve controversies in these realms. The United States Supreme Court, in particular, asserts a good deal of agenda and veto power when it comes to the interpretation of constitutional principles, and we will examine many Supreme Court decisions in this chapter. But consistent with the concept of checks and balances, other actors, particularly the U.S. Congress, also claim agenda and veto power in these realms. The Supreme Court's jurisdiction over constitutional issues is derived from Article III of the Constitution, from statutes, and from decisions of the Court itself. Congress's jurisdiction stems from Article II of the Constitution, which gives Congress the power to make the laws, and from its role in the process of amending the Constitution, as defined in Article V. As we will see in this chapter and Chapter 8, Congress and the Court sometimes clash over the interpretation of constitutional principles in the areas of civil liberties and civil rights. Usually, the Court prevails in these battles by asserting the power of judicial review (which we will discuss in Chapter 8) and declaring acts of Congress to be unconstitutional. In some instances, though, Congress is able to use its powers to write new laws or to initiate constitutional amendments to thwart the Court. In addition, the so-called exceptions clause of Article III, Section II of the Constitution gives Congress the power to limit the jurisdiction of the federal courts.

As we observed in our discussion of federalism and the separation of powers, institutional principles are not carved in stone. Over the past century, a number of civil liberties have been strengthened, placing greater limits on collective action. In the realm of civil rights, African Americans and others who were once excluded from participation in many collective processes have won the right to be included.

---

[1] *ACLU v. NSA*, 07-468 (2008).

In both areas, change came as a result of political struggles and was punctuated by battles within and between Congress and the courts. With these considerations in mind, let us examine the character and evolution of civil liberties and civil rights in America.

ORIGINS OF THE BILL OF RIGHTS

When the first Congress under the new Constitution met in late April of 1789 (having been delayed since March 4 by the lack of a quorum because of bad winter roads), the most important item of business was consideration of a proposal to add a bill of rights to the Constitution. Such a proposal by the Virginia delegate George Mason had been turned down with little debate in the waning days of the Constitutional Convention in September 1787 because of arguments by Alexander Hamilton and other Federalists that a bill of rights was irrelevant in a constitution providing the national government with only delegated powers. How could the national government abuse powers not given to it in the first place? Hamilton was also concerned that a bill of rights would weaken the new government by limiting its jurisdiction even before it had an opportunity to organize itself. But when the Constitution was submitted to the states for ratification, Antifederalists, most of whom had *not* been delegates in Philadelphia, picked up on the argument of Thomas Jefferson (who also had not been a delegate) that the omission of a bill of rights was a major imperfection of the new Constitution. Whatever the merits of Hamilton's or Jefferson's positions, to gain ratification, the Federalists in Massachusetts, South Carolina, New Hampshire, Virginia, and New York made an "unwritten but unequivocal pledge" to add a bill of rights and a promise to confirm (in what became the Tenth Amendment) the understanding that all powers not delegated to the national government or explicitly prohibited to the states were reserved to the states.[2]

James Madison, who had been a delegate to the Philadelphia convention and later became a member of Congress, may still have believed privately that a bill of rights was not needed. But in 1789, recognizing the urgency of obtaining the Antifederalists' support for the Constitution and the new government, he fought for the bill of rights, arguing that the ideals it embodied would acquire "the character of fundamental maxims of free Government, and as they become incorporated with the national sentiment, counteract the impulses of interest and passion."[3]

"After much discussion and manipulation . . . at the delicate prompting of Washington and under the masterful prodding of Madison," the House adopted

---

[2]Clinton L. Rossiter, *1787: The Grand Convention* (New York: Norton, 1987), p. 302.

[3]Quoted in Milton Konvitz, "The Bill of Rights: Amendments I–X," in *An American Primer,* 2 vols., Daniel J. Boorstin, ed. (Chicago: University of Chicago Press, 1966), I, p. 159.

seventeen amendments; the Senate adopted twelve of these. Ten of the amendments were ratified by the necessary three-fourths of the states, making them part of the Constitution on December 15, 1791—from the start, these ten were called the Bill of Rights.[4]

The Bill of Rights—its history and the controversy of interpretation surrounding it—can be usefully subdivided into two categories: civil liberties and civil rights. This chapter is divided accordingly. **Civil liberties** are defined as protections of citizens from improper governmental action. When adopted in 1791, the Bill of Rights was seen as guaranteeing a private sphere of personal liberty free of governmental restrictions. As Jefferson had put it, a bill of rights "is what people are entitled to against every government on earth." In this sense, we could call the Bill of Rights a bill of liberties because the amendments focus on what government must *not* do. For example (with emphasis added),

civil liberties The protections of citizens from improper governmental action.

1. "Congress shall make *no* law . . . " (I)

2. "The right . . . to . . . bear Arms, shall *not* be infringed." (II)

3. "*No* Soldier shall . . . be quartered . . . " (III)

4. "*No* Warrants shall issue, but upon probable cause . . . " (IV)

5. "*No* person shall be held to answer . . . unless on a presentment or indictment of a Grand Jury . . . " (V)

6. "Excessive bail shall not be required . . . *nor* cruel and unusual punishments inflicted." (VIII)

Thus the Bill of Rights is a series of "thou shalt nots"—restraints addressed to government, limiting its jurisdiction. Some of these restraints are *substantive*, putting limits on *what* the government shall and shall not have the power to do, such as establishing a state religion, quartering troops in private homes without consent, or seizing private property without just compensation. Other restraints are procedural, dealing with how the government is supposed to act. For example, even though the government has the substantive power to declare certain acts to be crimes and to arrest and imprison persons who violate its criminal laws, it may not do so except by fairly meticulous observance of procedures designed to protect the accused. The best-known procedural rule is that a person is presumed innocent until proven guilty. This rule does not question the government's power to punish someone for committing a crime; it questions only the way the government determines who committed the crime. Substantive and procedural restraints together identify the realm of civil liberties. Proponents of the Bill of Rights wished to make it clear that their enumeration of rights and liberties should not be deemed exhaustive. Americans might be entitled to other constitutional protections not formally included in the Bill of Rights. This concern was addressed by the Ninth Amendment, which declares that the enumeration in the Constitution of some rights "shall not be construed" to mean that the people do not retain others rights as well.

---

[4]Rossiter, *1787*, p. 303, where he also reports that "in 1941 the States of Connecticut, Massachusetts, and Georgia celebrated the sesquicentennial of the Bill of Rights by giving their hitherto withheld and unneeded assent."

Civil rights are obligations imposed on the government to guarantee equal citizenship and protect citizens from discrimination when collective decisions are made and implemented. Civil rights did not become part of the Constitution until 1868, with the adoption of the Fourteenth Amendment, which addresses the issue of who is a citizen and provides for each citizen "the equal protection of the laws." In legal terms, civil liberties issues arise under the "due process of law" clause, and civil rights issues arise under the "equal protection of the laws" clause of the Constitution.

We turn first to civil liberties and the long effort to make personal liberty a reality for every citizen in America. The struggle for freedom against arbitrary and discriminatory actions by governments continues to this day. And inevitably it is tied to the continuing struggle for civil rights, to persuade those same governments to take positive action. We deal with that in the second section of this chapter.

CIVIL LIBERTIES: NATIONALIZING THE BILL OF RIGHTS

The First Amendment provides that "Congress shall make no law respecting an establishment of religion . . . or abridging the freedom of speech, or of the press; or the right of . . . [assembly and petition]." But this is the only amendment in the Bill of Rights that addresses itself exclusively to the national government. For example, the Second Amendment provides that "the right of the people to keep and bear Arms, shall not be infringed." The Fifth Amendment says, among other things, that *no person* "shall . . . be twice put in jeopardy of life or limb" for the same crime, that *no person* "shall be compelled in any criminal case to be a witness against himself," that *no person* shall "be deprived of life, liberty, or property, without due process of law," and that private property cannot be taken "without just compensation."[5] Because the First Amendment is the only part of the Bill of Rights that is explicit in its intention to put limits on the national government, a fundamental question inevitably arises: Do the remaining amendments of the Bill of Rights put limits on state governments, or do they put them only on the national government?

Dual Citizenship

The question of whether the Bill of Rights also limits state governments was settled in 1833 in a way that seems odd to Americans today. The 1833 case was *Barron v.*

---

[5] It would be useful at this point to review all the provisions of the Bill of Rights to confirm this distinction between the wording of the First Amendment and the wording of the rest (see the Appendix). The emphasis in the examples is not in the original. For a spirited and enlightening essay on the extent to which the entire Bill of Rights is about equality, see Martha Minow, "Equality and the Bill of Rights," in *The Constitution of Rights: Human Dignity and American Values,* Michael J. Meyer and William A. Parent, eds. (Ithaca, N.Y.: Cornell University Press, 1992), pp. 118–28.

Baltimore, and the facts were simple. In paving its streets, the city of Baltimore had disposed of so much sand and gravel in the water near John Barron's wharf that the value of the wharf for commercial purposes was virtually destroyed. Barron brought the city into court on the grounds that it had, under the Fifth Amendment, unconstitutionally deprived him of his property. Barron had to take his case all the way to the Supreme Court, despite the fact that the argument made by his attorney seemed airtight. This is Chief Justice John Marshall's characterization of Barron's argument:

> The plaintiff [Barron] . . . contends that it comes within that clause in the Fifth Amendment of the Constitution which inhibits the taking of private property for public use without just compensation. He insists that this amendment, being in favor of the liberty of the citizen, ought to be so construed as to restrain the legislative power of a state, as well as that of the United States.[6]

Then Marshall, in one of the most significant Supreme Court decisions ever handed down, disagreed:

> The Constitution was ordained and established by the people of the United States for themselves, for their own government, and not for the government of individual States. Each State established a constitution for itself, and in that constitution provided such limitations and restrictions on the powers of its particular government as its judgment dictated. . . . If these propositions be correct, *the fifth amendment must be understood as restraining the power of the General Government, not as applicable to the States.*[7]

In other words, if an agency of the *national* government had deprived Barron of his property, there would have been little doubt about Barron's winning his case. But if the constitution of the state of Maryland contained no such provision protecting citizens of Maryland from such action, then Barron had no legal leg to stand on against Baltimore, an agency of the state of Maryland.

Barron v. Baltimore confirmed "dual citizenship"—that is, that each American was a citizen of the national government and separately a citizen of one of the states. This meant that the Bill of Rights did not apply to decisions or procedures of state (or local) governments. Even slavery could continue because the Bill of Rights could not protect anyone from state laws treating people as property. In fact, the Bill of Rights did not become a vital instrument for the extension of civil liberties for anyone until after a bloody civil war and the revolutionary Fourteenth Amendment intervened. And even so, as we shall see, nearly another century would pass before the Bill of Rights would truly come into its own. This is a case where America's history has truly mattered. America's states predated the creation of the federal government. The states joined the Union voluntarily, retaining many of their sovereign powers. In many other nations, subnational governments were created by and for the administrative convenience of the central government. In the United States, the nationalization of governmental powers has proceeded slowly and in fits and starts.

---

[6] *Barron v. Mayor and City of Baltimore*, 32 U.S. 243 (1833).

[7] *Barron v. Baltimore* [emphasis added].

The Fourteenth Amendment

From a constitutional standpoint, the defeat of the South in the Civil War settled one question and raised another. It probably settled forever the question of whether secession was an option for any state. After 1865, there was to be more "united" than "states" to the United States. But this left unanswered just how much the states were obliged to obey the Constitution and, in particular, the Bill of Rights. Just reading the words of the Fourteenth Amendment, anyone might think it was almost perfectly designed to impose the Bill of Rights on the states and thereby reverse *Barron v. Baltimore*. The very first words of the Fourteenth Amendment point in that direction:

> All persons born or naturalized in the United States, and subject to the juris-diction thereof, are citizens of the United States and of the State wherein they reside.

This provides for a single national citizenship, and at a minimum that means civil liberties should not vary drastically from state to state. That would seem to be the spirit of the Fourteenth Amendment: to nationalize the Bill of Rights by national-izing the definition of citizenship.

This interpretation of the Fourteenth Amendment is reinforced by the next clause of the Amendment:

> No State shall make or enforce any law which shall abridge the privileges or immunities of citizens of the United States; nor shall any State deprive any per-son of life, liberty, or property, without due process of law.

All of this sounds like an effort to extend the Bill of Rights in its entirety to citizens wherever they might reside. But this was not to be the Supreme Court's inter-pretation for nearly a century. Within five years of ratification of the Fourteenth Amendment, the Court was making decisions as though the amendment had never been adopted. The shadow of *Barron* grew longer and longer. In an important 1873 decision known as *the Slaughter-House Cases*, the Supreme Court determined that the federal government was under no obligation to protect the "privileges and immunities" of citizens of a particular state against arbitrary actions by that state's government. The case had its origins in 1867, when a corrupt Louisiana legislature conferred upon a single corporation a monopoly on the slaughterhouse business in the city of New Orleans. The other slaughterhouses, facing bankruptcy, brought suits claiming, like John Barron, that this was a seizure of their property in viola-tion of Fifth Amendment rights. But unlike Barron, they believed that they were protected now because, they argued, the Fourteenth Amendment incorporated the Fifth Amendment, applying it to the states. The suits were all rejected. The Supreme Court argued, first, that the primary purpose of the Fourteenth Amendment was to protect "Negroes as a class." Second, and more to the point here, the Court argued, without trying to prove it, that the framers of the Fourteenth Amendment could not have intended to incorporate the entire Bill of Rights.[8] Yet when the Civil Rights Act of 1875 attempted to protect blacks from discriminatory treatment by proprietors of

---

[8] *The Slaughter-House Cases*, 83 U.S. 36 (1873).

hotels, theaters, and other public accommodations, the Supreme Court disregarded its own primary argument in the previous case and held the act unconstitutional, declaring that the Fourteenth Amendment applied only to discriminatory actions by state officials, "operating under cover of law," and not to discrimination against blacks by private individuals, even though these private individuals were companies offering services to the public.[9] Such narrow interpretations raised the inevitable question of whether the Fourteenth Amendment had incorporated any of the Bill of Rights. The Fourteenth Amendment remained shadowy until the mid-twentieth century. The shadow was *Barron v. Baltimore* and the Court's unwillingness to "nationalize" civil liberties—that is, to interpret the civil liberties expressed in the Bill of Rights as imposing limitations not only on the federal government but also on the states.

It was not until the very end of the nineteenth century that the Supreme Court began to nationalize the Bill of Rights by incorporating its civil liberties provisions into the Fourteenth Amendment. Table 4.1 outlines the major steps in this process. The only change in civil liberties during the first sixty years after the adoption of the Fourteenth Amendment came in 1897, when the Supreme Court held that the due process clause of the Fourteenth Amendment did in fact prohibit states from taking property for a public use without just compensation.[10] This effectively over-ruled *Barron* because it meant that the citizen of Maryland, or any state, was hence-forth protected from a "public taking" of property even if the state constitution did not provide such protection. The power of public agencies to seize private property is called eminent domain. According to the Fifth Amendment, private owners must be paid "just compensation" by the government if it decides that it needs their property. In a broader sense, however, *Barron* still cast a shadow because the Supreme Court had "incorporated" into the Fourteenth Amendment only the property protection provision of the Fifth Amendment and no other clause, let alone the other amendments of the Bill of Rights. In other words, although due process applied to the taking of life and liberty as well as property, only property was incorporated into the Fourteenth Amendment as a limitation on state power.

No further expansion of civil liberties through incorporation occurred until 1925, when the Supreme Court held that freedom of speech is "among the fundamental personal rights and 'liberties' protected by the due process clause of the Fourteenth Amendment from impairment by the states."[11] In 1931, the Court added freedom of the press to that short list of civil rights protected by the Bill of Rights from state action; in 1934, it added freedom of religion; and in 1939, it added freedom of assembly.[12] But that was as far as the Court was willing to go. This one-by-one application of the provisions of the Bill of Rights is known as *selective incorporation* as distinguished from the notion of "total incorporation" advocated by some scholars. Total incorporation is the idea that all of the provisions of

---

[9] *The Civil Rights Cases*, 109 U.S. 3 (1883).

[10] *Chicago, Burlington, and Quincy Railroad Company v. Chicago*, 166 U.S. 226 (1897).

[11] *Gitlow v. New York*, 268 U.S. 652 (1925).

[12] *Near v. Minnesota ex rel. Olson*, 283 U.S. 697 (1931); *Hague v. Committee for Industrial Organization*, 307 U.S. 496 (1939).

TABLE 4.1 INCORPORATION OF THE BILL OF RIGHTS INTO THE FOURTEENTH AMENDMENT

Selected Provisions and Amendments	Date "Incorporated"	Key Cases
Eminent domain (V)	1897	Chicago, Burlington, and Quincy Railroad v. Chicago
Freedom of speech (I)	1925	Gitlow v. New York
Freedom of the press (I)	1931	Near v. Minnesota ex rel. Olson
Free exercise of religion (I)	1934	Hamilton v. Regents of the University of California
Freedom of assembly (I)	1939	Hague v. Committee for Industrial Organization
Freedom from unnecessary search and seizure (IV)	1949	Wolf v. Colorado
Freedom from warrantless search and seizure ("exclusionary rule") (IV)	1961	Mapp v. Ohio
Freedom from cruel and unusual punishment (VIII)	1962	Robinson v. California
Right to counsel in any criminal trial (VI)	1963	Gideon v. Wainwright
Right against self-incrimination and forced confessions (V)	1964	Mallory v. Hogan Escobedo v. Illinois
Right to privacy (III, IV, and V)	1965	Griswold v. Connecticut
Right to remain silent (V)	1966	Miranda v. Arizona
Right against double jeopardy (V)	1969	Benton v. Maryland

the Bill of Rights were applied to the states by the Fourteenth Amendment. As late as 1937, the Supreme Court was still loath to nationalize civil liberties beyond the First Amendment. In fact, the Court in that year took one of its most extreme turns backward toward *Barron v. Baltimore.*

The state of Connecticut had indicted a man named Frank Palko for first-degree murder, but a lower court found him guilty of only second-degree murder and sentenced him to life in prison. Unhappy with the verdict, the state of Connecticut appealed the conviction to its highest court, won the appeal, got a new trial, and succeeded in getting Palko convicted of first-degree murder. Palko appealed to the Supreme Court on what seemed an open-and-shut case of double jeopardy—being tried twice for the same crime. Yet though a majority of the Court agreed that this could indeed be considered a case of double jeopardy, the justices decided that double jeopardy was *not* one of the provisions of the Bill of Rights incorporated into the Fourteenth Amendment as a restriction on the powers of the states. Justice Benjamin Cardozo, considered one of the ablest Supreme Court justices of the twentieth century, rejected the argument made by Palko's lawyer that "whatever is forbidden by the Fifth Amendment is forbidden by the Fourteenth also." Cardozo responded tersely, "There is no such general rule." As far as Cardozo and the majority were concerned, the only rights from the Bill of Rights that ought to be incorporated into the Fourteenth Amendment as applying to the states as well as to the national government were those that were "implicit in the concept of ordered liberty." He asked the questions, Does double jeopardy subject Palko to a "hardship so acute and shocking that our polity will not endure it? Does it violate those 'fundamental principles of liberty and justice which lie at the base of all our civil and political institutions?' . . . The answer must surely be 'no.'"[13] Palko was eventually executed for the crime—because he lived in the state of Connecticut rather than in a state whose constitution included a guarantee against double jeopardy.

Cases like *Palko* extended the shadow of *Barron* into its second century, despite adoption of the Fourteenth Amendment. The Constitution, as interpreted by the Supreme Court, left standing the framework in which the states had the power to determine their own law on a number of fundamental issues. It left states with the power to pass laws segregating the races—and thirteen states chose to exercise that power. The constitutional framework also left states with the power to engage in searches and seizures without a warrant, indict accused persons without benefit of a grand jury, deprive persons of trial by jury, force persons to testify against themselves, deprive accused persons of their right to confront adverse witnesses, and as we have seen, prosecute accused persons more than once for the same crime.[14] All of these were implicitly identified in the *Palko* case as "not incorporated" into the Fourteenth Amendment as limitations on the powers of the states. Few states chose the option to use those kinds of powers, but some states did, and the authority to do so was there for any state whose legislative majority so chose.

The Constitutional Revolution in Civil Liberties

For more than thirty years after the *Palko* case, the nineteenth-century framework was sustained, but signs of change came after 1954, in *Brown v. Board of Education,* when the Supreme Court overturned the infamous *Plessy v. Ferguson.*[15] *Plessy* was a civil rights case involving the "equal protection" clause of the Fourteenth Amendment but was not an issue of applying the Bill of Rights to the states. (We will discuss *Plessy's* significance for civil rights later in this chapter.) Nevertheless, *Brown* indicated clearly that the Supreme Court was going to be expansive about civil liberties

---

[13] *Palko v. Connecticut,* 302 U.S. 319 (1937).

[14] *Palko* was explicitly reversed in *Benton v. Maryland,* 395 U.S. 784 (1969), in which the Court said that double jeopardy was in fact incorporated into the Fourteenth Amendment as a restriction on the states.

[15] *Brown v. Board of Education,* 347 U.S. 483; *Plessy v. Ferguson,* 163 U.S. 537 (1896).

because in that case the Court effectively promised that it was actively going to subject the states and all actions affecting civil rights and civil liberties to *strict scrutiny*. In retrospect, one could say that this constitutional revolution was given a jump start by the *Brown* decision,[16] even though the results were not apparent until after 1961, when the number of incorporated civil liberties increased (Table 4.1).

Nationalizing the Bill of Rights.   As with the federalism revolution, the constitutional revolution in civil liberties was a movement toward nationalization. But the two revolutions required opposite motions on the part of the Supreme Court. In the area of commerce (the first revolution), the Court had to decide to assume a passive role by not interfering as Congress expanded the meaning of the commerce clause of Article I, Section 8. This expansion has been so extensive that the national government can now constitutionally reach a single farmer growing twenty acres of wheat or a small restaurant selling barbecue to local "whites only" without the farmer's or the restaurant's being anywhere near interstate commerce routes. In the second revolution, involving the Bill of Rights and the Fourteenth Amendment rather than the commerce clause, the Court had to assume an active role, which required close review not of Congress but of the laws of state legislatures and the decisions of state courts to apply a single national Fourteenth Amendment standard to the rights and liberties of all citizens.

Table 4.1 shows that until 1961, only the First Amendment had been fully and clearly incorporated into the Fourteenth Amendment.[17] After 1961, several other important provisions of the Bill of Rights were incorporated. Of the cases that expanded the Fourteenth Amendment's reach, among the most famous (partly because it became the subject of a best-selling book and a popular movie) is *Gideon v. Wainwright,* which established the right to counsel in a criminal trial.[18] In *Mapp v. Ohio,* the Court held that evidence obtained in violation of the Fourth Amendment ban on unreasonable searches and seizures would be excluded from trial.[19] This "exclusionary rule" was particularly irksome to police and prosecutors because it meant that patently guilty defendants sometimes got to go free because the evidence that clearly damned them could not be used. In *Miranda,* the Court's ruling required that arrested persons be informed of the rights to remain silent and have counsel present during interrogation.[20] This is the basis of the **Miranda rule** of reading persons their rights, which is familiar to most Americans from movies and

Miranda rule The convention derived from the Supreme Court's 1966 ruling in the case of *Miranda v. Arizona* whereby persons under arrest must be informed of their legal rights, including their right to counsel, before undergoing police interrogation.

---

[16] The first constitutional revolution began with *National Labor Relations Board v. Jones and Laughlin Steel Corporation,* 301 U.S. 1 (1937).

[17] The one exception was the right to a public trial (the Sixth Amendment), but the 1948 case did not mention the right to a public trial as such; it was cited in a 1968 case as establishing the right to a public trial as part of the Fourteenth Amendment. The 1948 case was *In re Oliver,* 333 U.S. 257, where the issue was put more generally as "due process," and public trial itself was not mentioned. Later opinions, such as *Duncan v. Louisiana,* 391 U.S. 145 (1968), cited the *Oliver* case as the precedent for incorporating public trials as part of the Fourteenth Amendment.

[18] Anthony Lewis, *Gideon's Trumpet* (New York: Random House, 1964); *Gideon v. Wainwright,* 372 U.S. 335 (1963).

[19] *Mapp v. Ohio,* 367 U.S. 643 (1961).

[20] *Miranda v. Arizona,* 384 U.S. 436 (1966).

TV police shows. By 1969, in *Benton v. Maryland,* the Supreme Court had come full circle regarding the rights of the criminally accused, explicitly reversing the *Palko* ruling and thereby incorporating double jeopardy.

During the 1960s and early 1970s, the Court expanded another important area of civil liberties: rights to privacy. When the Court began to take a more activist role in the mid-1950s and the 1960s, the idea of a right to privacy was revived. In 1958, the Supreme Court recognized "privacy in one's association" in its decision to prevent the state of Alabama from using the membership list of the National Association for the Advancement of Colored People (NAACP) in its investigations.[21] As we shall see later in this chapter, legal questions about the right to privacy have come to the fore in more recent cases concerning birth control, abortion, homosexuality, and assisted suicide.

THE BILL OF RIGHTS TODAY

Since liberty requires restraining the power of government, the general status of civil liberties can never be considered fixed and permanent.[22] Every provision in the Bill of Rights is subject to interpretation, and in any dispute involving a clause of the Bill of Rights, interpretations will always be shaped by the interpreter's interest in the outcome. As we have seen, the Court continuously reminds everyone that if it has the power to expand the Bill of Rights, it also has the power to contract it.[23]

The best way to examine the Bill of Rights today is the simplest way: to take the provisions one at a time. Some of these provisions are settled areas of law, and some are not. Any one of them can be reinterpreted by the Court at any time.

The First Amendment and Freedom of Religion

> Congress shall make no law respecting an establishment of religion, or prohibiting the free exercise thereof; or abridging the freedom of speech, or of the press; or the right of the people peaceably to assemble, and to petition the Government for a redress of grievances.

The Bill of Rights begins by guaranteeing freedom, and the First Amendment provides for that freedom in two distinct clauses: "Congress shall make no law [1] respecting an establishment of religion, or [2] prohibiting the free exercise thereof." The first clause is called the establishment clause, and the second is called the free exercise clause. Let us examine the meaning of each clause.

---

[21] *NAACP v. Alabama,* 357 U.S. 449 (1958).

[22] This section is taken from Benjamin Ginsberg, Theodore J. Lowi, and Margaret Weir, *We the People: An Introduction to American Politics,* 6th ed. (New York: Norton, 2006).

[23] For a lively and readable treatment of the possibilities of restricting provisions of the Bill of Rights without actually reversing prior decisions, see David G. Savage, *Turning Right: The Making of the Rehnquist Supreme Court* (New York: Wiley, 1992).

Separation between Church and State.   The **establishment clause** and the idea of "no law" regarding the establishment of religion could be interpreted in several possible ways. One interpretation, which probably reflects the views of many of the First Amendment's authors, is that the government is prohibited from establishing an official church. Official state churches, such as the Church of England, were common in the eighteenth century and were viewed by many Americans as inconsistent with a republican form of government. Indeed, many American colonists had fled Europe to escape persecution for having rejected state-sponsored churches. A second possible interpretation is the "nonpreferentialist" or "accommodationist" view, which holds that the government may not take sides among competing religions but is not prohibited from providing assistance to religious institutions or ideas so long as it shows no favoritism. The United States accommodates religious beliefs in a variety of ways, from the reference to God on U.S. currency to the prayer that begins every session of Congress. These forms of establishment have never been struck down by the courts.

The third view regarding religious establishment, which for many years dominated Supreme Court decision making in this realm, is the idea of a "wall of separation" between church and state that cannot be breached by the government. The concept of a wall of separation was Jefferson's own formulation, and it has figured in many Supreme Court cases arising under the establishment clause. For two centuries, Jefferson's words have had a powerful impact on our understanding of the proper relationship between church and state in America.

Despite the absolute sound of the phrase *wall of separation,* there is ample room to disagree on how high the wall is or of what materials it is composed. For example, the Court has been consistently strict in cases of school prayer, striking down such practices as Bible reading,[24] nondenominational prayer,[25] a moment of silence for meditation, and pregame prayer at public sporting events.[26] In each of these cases, the Court reasoned that school-sponsored observations, even of an apparently nondenominational character, are highly suggestive of school sponsorship and therefore violate the prohibition against establishment of religion. On the other hand, the Court has been quite permissive (and some would say inconsistent) about the public display of religious symbols, such as city-sponsored Nativity scenes in commercial or municipal areas.[27] And although the Court has consistently disapproved of government-financed support for religious schools, even when the purpose has been purely educational and secular, it has permitted certain direct aid to students of such schools in the form of busing, for example. In 1971, after thirty years of cases involving religious schools, the Court attempted to specify some criteria to guide its decisions and those of lower courts, indicating, for example, in a decision invalidating state payments for the teaching of secular subjects in parochial schools, circumstances under which the Court might allow certain financial assistance. The case was *Lemon v. Kurtzman;* in its decision, the Supreme Court

establishment clause The First Amendment clause that says, "Congress shall make no law respecting an establishment of religion." This law means that a wall of separation exists between church and state.

---

[24] *Abington School District v. Schempp,* 374 U.S. 203 (1963).

[25] *Engel v. Vitale,* 370 U.S. 421 (1962).

[26] *Wallace v. Jaffree,* 472 U.S. 38 (1985).

[27] *Lynch v. Donnelly,* 465 U.S. 668 (1984).

Lemon test Rule
articulated in
Lemon v. Kurtzman
according to which
governmental ac-
tion in respect to
religion is permis-
sible if it is secular
in purpose, does
not lead to "exces-
sive entanglement"
with religion, and
neither promotes
nor inhibits the
practice of religion.

established three criteria to guide future cases, in what came to be called the **Lemon test.** The Court held that government aid to religious schools would be accepted as constitutional if (1) it had a secular purpose, (2) its effect was neither to advance nor to inhibit religion, and (3) it did not entangle government and religious institutions in one another's affairs.[28]

Although these restrictions make the *Lemon* test a hard test to pass, imaginative authorities have found ways to do so, and the Supreme Court has demonstrated a willingness to let them, perhaps moving toward a more accommodationist view of the establishment clause. In 1995, for example, the Court narrowly ruled that a student religious group at the University of Virginia could not be denied student activities funds merely because it was a religious group espousing a particular viewpoint about a deity. The Court called the denial "viewpoint discrimination" and declared that it violated the free speech rights of the group.[29] This led two years later to a new, more conservative approach to the separation of church and state. In 1997, the Court accepted the practice of sending public-school teachers into parochial schools to provide remedial education to disadvantaged children.[30]

The establishment clause has also been put under pressure by the school-voucher and charter-school movements. Vouchers financed by public revenues are supporting tuition to religious schools, where common prayer and religious instruction are known parts of the curriculum. In addition, many financially needy church schools are actively recruiting students with tax-supported vouchers, considering the vouchers an essential source of revenue if they are to keep their schools operating. In both these respects, vouchers and charter schools are creating the impression that public support is aiding the establishment of religion.[31] Yet the Supreme Court has refused to rule on the constitutionality of these programs.

In 2004, the question of whether the phrase "under God" in the Pledge of Allegiance violates the establishment clause was brought before the Court. Written in 1892, the Pledge had been used in schools without any religious references. But in 1954, in the midst of the Cold War, Congress voted to change the Pledge, in response to the "godless Communism" of the Soviet Union. The conversion was made by adding two key words, so that the revised version read, "I pledge allegiance to the flag of the United States of America and to the Republic for which it stands, one nation *under God,* indivisible, with liberty and justice for all" [emphasis added].

Ever since the change was made, there has been a constant murmuring of discontent from those who object to an officially sanctioned profession of belief in a deity as a violation of the religious freedom clause of the First Amendment. When saying the pledge, those who object to the phrase have often simply stayed silent

---

[28] *Lemon v. Kurtzman,* 403 U.S. 602 (1971). The *Lemon* test is still good law, but as recently as the 1994 Court term, four justices urged that it be abandoned. Here is a settled area of law that may become unsettled.

[29] *Rosenberger v. University of Virginia,* 515 U.S. 819 (1995).

[30] *Agostini v. Felton,* 521 U.S. 203 (1997). The case being overruled was *Aguilar v. Felton,* 473 U.S. 402 (1985).

[31] For good coverage of voucher and charter-school experiments, see Peter Schrag, "The Voucher Seduction," *American Prospect,* November 23, 1999, pp. 46–52.

during the recitation of the two key words. In 2003, Michael Newdow, the father of a kindergarten student in a California elementary school, forced the issue to the surface when he brought suit against the local school district. Newdow, an atheist, argued that the reference to God turned the daily recitation of the pledge into a religious exercise. A federal court ruled that although students were not required to recite the pledge at all, having to stand and listen to others say "under God" still violated the First Amendment's establishment clause. The case was appealed to the Supreme Court, and on June 14, 2004—fifty years to the day after the adoption of "under God" in the Pledge—the Court ruled that Newdow lacked a sufficient personal stake in the case to bring the complaint.[32] This inconclusive decision by the Court left "under God" in the Pledge while keeping the issue alive for possible resolution in a future case.

Free Exercise of Religion.   The **free exercise clause** protects the right to believe and practice whatever religion one chooses; it also protects the right to be a non-believer. Generally speaking, problems arise under the free exercise clause not because the government specifically decides to interfere with religion. Rather, they arise, because generally applicable secular laws happen to intrude on the beliefs of one or another group. The precedent-setting case involving free exercise was *West Virginia State Board of Education v. Barnette* (1943), which involved the children of a family of Jehovah's Witnesses who refused to salute and pledge allegiance to the American flag on the grounds that their religious faith did not permit it. Three years earlier, the Court had upheld such a requirement and had permitted schools to expel students for refusing to salute the flag. But the entry of the United States into a war to defend democracy coupled with the ugly treatment to which the Jehovah's Witnesses' children had been subjected induced the Court to reverse itself and endorse the free exercise of religion even when it may be offensive to the beliefs of the majority.[33]

Although the Supreme Court has been fairly consistent and strict in protecting the free exercise of religious belief, it has taken pains to distinguish between religious beliefs and *actions* based on those beliefs. In one case, for example, two Native Americans had been fired from their jobs for smoking peyote, an illegal drug. They claimed they had been fired from their jobs illegally because smoking peyote was a religious sacrament protected by the free exercise clause. The Court disagreed with their claim in an important 1990 decision,[34] but Congress supported the claim and went on to engage in an unusual controversy with the Court, involving the separation of powers as well as the proper application of the separation of church and state. Congress literally reversed the Court's 1990 decision with the enactment of the Religious Freedom Restoration Act (RFRA) of 1993, which forbids any federal agency or state government to restrict a person's free exercise of religion unless the federal agency or state government demonstrates that its

free exercise clause   The First Amendment clause that protects a citizen's right to believe and practice whatever religion he or she chooses.

---

[32] *Elk Grove Unified School District v. Newdow,* 542 U.S. 1 (2004).

[33] *West Virginia State Board of Education v. Barnette,* 319 U.S. 624 (1943). The case it reversed was *Minersville School District v. Gobitis,* 310 U.S. 586 (1940).

[34] *Employment Division v. Smith,* 494 U.S. 872 (1990).

action "furthers a compelling government interest" and "is the least restrictive means of furthering that compelling governmental interest." One of the first applications of the RFRA was to a case brought by St. Peter's Catholic Church against the city of Boerne, Texas, which had denied permission to the church to enlarge its building because the building had been declared a historic landmark. The case went to federal court on the argument that the city had violated the church's religious freedom as guaranteed by Congress in the RFRA. The Supreme Court declared the RFRA unconstitutional, but on grounds rarely utilized, if not unique to this case: Congress had violated the separation-of-powers principle, infringing on the powers of the judiciary by going so far beyond its lawmaking powers that it ended up actually expanding the scope of religious rights rather than just enforcing them. The Court thereby implied that questions requiring a balancing of religious claims against public policy claims were reserved strictly to the judiciary.[35]

The *City of Boerne* case did settle some matters of constitutional controversy over the religious exercise and the establishment clauses of the First Amendment, but it left a lot more unsettled. What about polygamy, a practice that has been allowed by some factions in the Mormon faith? Or the refusal of some Amish parents to send their children to school beyond eighth grade because of their belief that exposing their children to "modern values" undermines their religious commitment? In this last example, the Court decided in favor of the Amish and endorsed a very strong interpretation of the protection of free exercise.[36]

The First Amendment and Freedom of Speech and the Press

> Congress shall make no law . . . abridging the freedom of speech, or of the press.

Because democracy depends on an open political process and politics is basically talk, freedom of speech and freedom of the press are considered critical. For this reason, they were given a prominence in the Bill of Rights equal to that of freedom of religion. In 1938, freedom of speech (which in all important respects includes freedom of the press) was given extraordinary constitutional status when the Supreme Court established that any legislation that attempts to restrict these fundamental freedoms "is to be subjected to a more exacting judicial scrutiny . . . than are most other types of legislation."[37]

The Court was saying that the democratic political process must be protected at almost any cost. This higher standard of judicial review came to be called *preferred position*. Preferred position implies that speech—at least some kinds of speech—will be protected almost absolutely. But as it turns out, only some types of speech are

---

[35] *City of Boerne v. Flores*, 521 U.S. 507 (1997).

[36] *Wisconsin v. Yoder*, 406 U.S. 205 (1972).

[37] *United States v. Carolene Products Company*, 304 U.S. 144 (1938), 384. This footnote is one of the Court's most important doctrines. See Alfred H. Kelly, Winfred A. Harbison, and Herman Belz, *The American Constitution: Its Origins and Development*, 7th ed., 2 vols. (New York: Norton, 1991), II, pp. 519–23.

fully protected against restrictions. As we shall see, many forms of speech are less than absolutely protected—even though they are entitled to a preferred position.

Political Speech.   Political speech was the activity of greatest concern to the framers of the Constitution, even though they found it the most difficult provision to observe. Within seven years of the ratification of the Bill of Rights, Congress adopted the infamous Alien and Sedition Acts, which, among other things, made it a crime to say or publish anything that might tend to defame or bring into disrepute the government of the United States. Quite clearly, the acts' intentions were to criminalize the very conduct given absolute protection by the First Amendment. Fifteen violators, including several newspaper editors, were indicted, and a few were convicted before the relevant portions of the acts were allowed to expire.

The first modern free speech case arose immediately after World War I. It involved persons who had been convicted under the federal Espionage Acts of 1917 for opposing American involvement in the war. The Supreme Court upheld the act and refused to protect the speech rights of the defendants on the grounds that their activities—appeals to draftees to resist the draft—constituted a **"clear and present danger"** to security.[38] This is the first and most famous test of when government intervention or censorship can be permitted, though it is no longer used by courts.

It was only after the 1920s that real progress toward a genuinely effective First Amendment was made. Since then, political speech has been consistently protected by the courts even when it has been deemed "insulting" or "outrageous." Here is the way the Supreme Court put it in one of its most important statements on the subject:

> The constitutional guarantees of free speech and free press do not permit a State to forbid or proscribe advocacy of the use of force or of law violation *except where such advocacy is directed to inciting or producing imminent lawless action and is likely to incite or produce such action.*[39] [Emphasis added]

This statement was made in the case of a Ku Klux Klan leader, Charles Brandenburg, who had been arrested and convicted of advocating "revengent" action against the president, Congress, and the Supreme Court, among others, if they continued "to suppress the white, Caucasian race." Although Brandenburg was not carrying a weapon, some members of his audience were. Nevertheless, the Supreme Court reversed the state courts and freed Brandenburg while declaring Ohio's Criminal Syndicalism Act unconstitutional because it punished persons who "advocate, or teach the duty, necessity, or propriety [of violence] as a means of accomplishing industrial or political reform" or who publish materials or "voluntarily assemble . . . to teach or advocate the doctrines of criminal syndicalism." The Supreme Court argued that the statute did not distinguish "mere advocacy" from "incitement to imminent lawless action." It would be difficult to go much further in protecting freedom of speech. Typically, the federal courts will strike down restrictions on

clear and present danger The criterion used to determine whether speech is protected or unprotected, based on its capacity to present a "clear and present danger" to society.

---

[38] *Schenck v. United States*, 249 U.S. 47 (1919).

[39] *Brandenburg v. Ohio*, 395 U.S. 444 (1969).

speech if they are deemed to be "overbroad," "vague," or lacking "neutrality" in terms of the content of the speech, for example, if a statute prohibited the views of the political left but not the political right, or vice versa.

Another area of recent expansion of political speech—the participation of wealthy persons and corporations in political campaigns—was opened up in 1976 with the Supreme Court's decision in *Buckley v. Valeo*.[40] Campaign finance reform laws of the early 1970s, arising out of the Watergate scandal, sought to put severe limits on campaign spending, and a number of important provisions were declared unconstitutional on the basis of a new principle that spending money by or on behalf of candidates is a form of speech protected by the First Amendment. The issue came up again in 2003, after passage of a new and still more severe campaign finance law, the Bipartisan Campaign Reform Act (BCRA) (2002). In *McConnell v. Federal Election Commission*, the majority seriously reduced the area of speech protected by the *Buckley v. Valeo* decision by holding that Congress was well within its power to put limits on the amounts individuals could spend, plus severe limits on the amounts of "soft money" that could be spent by corporations and their PACs and limits on issue advertising prior to election day. The Court argued that "the selling of access . . . has given rise to the appearance of undue influence [that justifies] regulations impinging on First Amendment rights . . . in order to curb corruption or the appearance of corruption."[41] In 2007, however, in the case of *Federal Election Commission v. Wisconsin Right to Life*, the Supreme Court struck down a key portion of BCRA, finding that the act's limitations on political advertising violated the First Amendment's guarantee of free speech.[42] In 2008, in the case of *Davis v. Federal Election Commission*, the Supreme Court struck down another element of BCRA, the so-called millionaire's amendment, which had increased contribution limits for opponents of self-funded, wealthy candidates.[43] And, in *Citizens United v. Federal Election Commission*, the Court ruled that corporate funding of independent election ads could not be limited under the First Amendment.[44]

Symbolic Speech, Speech Plus, and the Rights of Assembly and Petition.   The First Amendment treats the freedoms of assembly and petition as equal to the freedoms of religion and political speech. Freedom of assembly and freedom of petition are closely associated with speech but go beyond it to speech associated with action. Since at least 1931, the Supreme Court has sought to protect actions that are designed to send a political message. (Usually the purpose of a symbolic act is not only to send a direct message but also to draw a crowd—to do something spectacular in order to draw spectators to the action and thus strengthen the message.) Thus the Court held unconstitutional a California statute making it a felony to display a red flag "as a sign, symbol or emblem of opposition to organized government."[45]

---

[40] *Buckley v. Valeo*, 424 U.S. 1 (1976).

[41] *McConnell v. Federal Election Commission*, 540 U.S. 93 (2003).

[42] *Federal Election Commission v. Wisconsin Right to Life*, 09-969 (2007).

[43] *Davis v. Federal Election Commission*, 07-320 (2008).

[44] *Citizens United v. FEC*, 08-205 (2010).

[45] *Stromberg v. California*, 283 U.S. 359 (1931).

Although today there are limits on how far one can go with actions that symbolically convey a message, the protection of such action is very broad. Thus although the Court upheld a federal statute making it a crime to burn draft cards to protest the Vietnam War on the grounds that the government had a compelling interest in preserving draft cards as part of the conduct of the war itself, it considered the wearing of black armbands to school a protected form of assembly. In these sorts of cases, a court will often use the standard it articulated in the draft card case, *United States v. O'Brien*, and now known as the "*O'Brien* test."[46] Under the terms of the *O'Brien* test, a statute restricting expressive or symbolic speech must be justified by a compelling government interest and be narrowly tailored toward achieving that interest.

Another example is the burning of the American flag as a symbol of protest. In 1984, at a political rally held during the Republican National Convention in Dallas, a political protester burned an American flag in violation of a Texas statute that prohibited desecration of a venerated object. In a 5–4 decision, the Supreme Court declared the Texas law unconstitutional on the grounds that flag burning is expressive conduct protected by the First Amendment.[47] Congress reacted immediately with a proposal for a constitutional amendment reversing the Court's decision, and when the amendment failed to receive the necessary two-thirds majority in the Senate, Congress passed the Flag Protection Act of 1989. Protesters promptly violated this act, and their prosecution moved quickly into the federal district court, which declared the new law unconstitutional. The Supreme Court, in another 5–4 decision, affirmed the lower court's decision.[48] A renewed effort began in Congress to propose a constitutional amendment that would reverse the Supreme Court and place this form of expressive conduct outside the realm of protected speech or assembly. Since 1995, the House of Representatives has six times passed a resolution for a constitutional amendment to ban flag burning, but each time the Senate has failed to go along.[49] In 2003, the Supreme Court struck down a Virginia cross-burning statute, ruling that states could make cross burning a crime as long as the statute required prosecutors to prove that the act of setting fire to the cross was intended to intimidate. Justice Sandra Day O'Connor wrote for the majority that the First Amendment permits the government to forbid cross burning as a "particularly virulent form of intimidation" but not when the act was "a form of symbolic expression."[50] This decision will almost inevitably become a more generalized First Amendment protection of any conduct, including flag burning, that can be shown to be a form of symbolic expression.

Closer to the original intent of the assembly and petition clause is the category of **speech plus**—following speech with physical activity such as picketing, distributing leaflets, and other forms of peaceful demonstration or assembly. Such assemblies are consistently protected by courts under the First Amendment; state and local laws regulating such activities are closely scrutinized and frequently overturned. But the same assembly on private property is quite another matter and can

speech plus
Speech accompanied by activities such as sit-ins, picketing, and demonstrations. Protection of this form of speech under the First Amendment is conditional, and restrictions imposed by state or local authorities are acceptable if properly balanced by considerations of public order.

---

[46] *United States v. O'Brien*, 391 U.S. 367 (1968).

[47] *Texas v. Johnson*, 491 U.S. 397 (1989).

[48] *United States v. Eichman*, 496 U.S. 310 (1990).

[49] Carl Hulse, "Flag Amendment Narrowly Fails in Senate Vote," *New York Times*, June 28, 2006.

[50] *Virginia v. Black*, 538 U.S. 343 (2003).

in many circumstances be regulated. For example, the directors of a shopping center can lawfully prohibit an assembly protesting a war or supporting a ban on abortion. Assemblies in public areas can also be restricted under some circumstances, especially when the assembly or demonstration jeopardizes the health, safety, or rights of others. This condition was the basis of the Supreme Court's decision to uphold a lower-court order restricting the access that abortion protesters had to the entrances of abortion clinics.[51]

Freedom of the Press.   For all practical purposes, freedom of speech implies and includes freedom of the press. With the exception of the broadcast media, which are subject to federal regulation, the press is protected under the doctrine prohibiting **prior restraint**. Beginning with the landmark 1931 case of *Near v. Minnesota*,[52] the Supreme Court has held that except under the most extraordinary circumstances, the First Amendment prohibits government agencies from seeking to prevent newspapers or magazines from publishing whatever they wish. Indeed, in the case of *New York Times v. United States*, the so-called Pentagon Papers case, the Supreme Court ruled that the government could not even block publication of secret Defense Department documents furnished to the *New York Times* by an opponent of the Vietnam War who had obtained the documents illegally.[53] In a 1990 case, however, the Supreme Court upheld a lower-court order restraining the Cable News Network (CNN) from broadcasting tapes of conversations between the former Panamanian dictator Manuel Noriega and his lawyer, supposedly recorded by the American government. By a vote of 7–2, the Court held that CNN could be restrained from broadcasting the tapes until the trial court in the Noriega case had listened to the tapes and decided whether their broadcast would violate Noriega's right to a fair trial.[54]

Libel and Slander.   Some speech is not protected at all. If a written statement is made in "reckless disregard of the truth" and is considered damaging to the victim because it is "malicious, scandalous, and defamatory," it can be punished as **libel**. If an oral statement of such nature is made, it can be punished as **slander.**

Today most libel suits involve freedom of the press, and the realm of free press is enormous. Historically, newspapers were subject to the law of libel, which provided that newspapers that printed false and malicious stories could be compelled to pay damages to those they defamed. In recent years, however, American courts have greatly narrowed the meaning of libel and made it extremely difficult, particularly for politicians or other public figures, to win a libel case against a newspaper. In the important case of *New York Times v. Sullivan*, the Court held that to be deemed libelous a story about a public official not only had to be untrue but also

---

prior restraint
An effort by a government agency to block the publication of material it deems libelous or harmful in some other way; censorship. In the United States, the courts forbid prior restraint except under the most extraordinary circumstances.

libel   A written statement made in "reckless disregard of the truth" and considered damaging to a victim because it is "malicious, scandalous, and defamatory."

slander   An oral statement made in "reckless disregard of the truth" and considered damaging to a victim because it is "malicious, scandalous, and defamatory."

---

[51] For a good general discussion of "speech plus," see Louis Fisher, *American Constitutional Law* (New York: McGraw-Hill, 1990), pp. 544–46. The case upholding the buffer zone against the abortion protesters is *Madsen v. Women's Health Center*, 512 U.S. 753 (1994).

[52] *Near v. Minnesota ex rel. Olson*, 283 U.S. 697 (1931).

[53] *New York Times v. United States*, 403 U.S. 713 (1971).

[54] *Cable News Network v. Noriega*, 111 S.Ct. 451 (1990).

had to result from "actual malice" or "reckless disregard" for the truth.[55] In other words, the newspaper had to *deliberately* print false and malicious material. In practice, it is nearly impossible to prove that a paper deliberately printed maliciously false information, and it is especially difficult for a politician or other public figure to win a libel case. Essentially, the print media have been able to publish anything they want about a public figure.

In at least one recent case, however, the Court has opened up the possibility of public officials' filing libel suits against the press. In 1985, the Court held that the press was immune from libel only when the printed material was "a matter of public concern." In other words, in future cases a newspaper would have to show that the public official was engaged in activities that were indeed *public*. This new principle has made the press more vulnerable to libel suits, but it still leaves an enormous realm of freedom for the press. For example, the Reverend Jerry Falwell, a cofounder of the Moral Majority, lost his libel suit against *Hustler* magazine even though the magazine had published a cartoon depicting Falwell having drunken intercourse with his mother in an outhouse. A unanimous Supreme Court rejected a jury verdict in favor of damages for "emotional distress" on the grounds that parodies, no matter how outrageous, are protected because "outrageousness" is too subjective a test and thus would interfere with the free flow of ideas protected by the First Amendment.[56]

Obscenity and Pornography.

If libel and slander cases can be difficult because of the problem of determining the truth of statements and whether those statements are malicious and damaging, cases involving pornography and obscenity can be even stickier. It is easy to say that pornography and obscenity fall outside the realm of protected speech, but it is impossible to draw a clear line defining where protection ends and unprotected speech begins. Not until 1957 did the Supreme Court confront this problem, and it did so with a definition of obscenity that may have caused more confusion than it cleared up. Justice William Brennan, in writing the Court's opinion, defined obscenity as speech or writing that appeals to the "prurient interest"—that is, books, magazines, films, and other material whose purpose is to excite lust as this appears "to the average person, applying contemporary community standards." Even so, Brennan added, the work should be judged obscene only when it is "utterly without redeeming social importance."[57] Brennan's definition, instead of clarifying the Court's view, caused more confusion. In 1964, Justice Potter Stewart confessed that although he found pornography impossible to define, "I know it when I see it."[58]

All attempts by the courts to define pornography and obscenity have proved impractical because each instance required courts to screen thousands of pages of print material or feet of film alleged to be pornographic. The vague and impractical standards that had been developed meant ultimately that almost nothing could be

---

[55] *New York Times v. Sullivan*, 376 U.S. 254 (1964).

[56] *Hustler Magazine v. Falwell*, 485 U.S. 46 (1988).

[57] *Roth v. United States*, 354 U.S. 476 (1957).

[58] Concurring opinion in *Jacobellis v. Ohio*, 378 U.S. 184 (1964).

banned on the grounds that it was pornographic and obscene. An effort was made to strengthen the restrictions in 1973, when the Supreme Court expressed its willingness to define pornography as a work that as a whole is deemed prurient by the "average person" according to "community standards," depicts sexual conduct "in a patently offensive way," and lacks "serious literary, artistic, political, or scientific value." This definition meant that pornography would be determined by local rather than national standards. Thus a local bookseller might be prosecuted for selling a volume that was a best-seller nationally but was deemed pornographic locally.[59] This new definition of standards did not help much either, and not long after 1973 the Court again began to review all such community antipornography laws, reversing most of them. Consequently, today there is a widespread fear that Americans are free to publish any and all variety of intellectual expression, whether there is any "redeeming social value" or not. Yet this area of free speech is far from settled.

In recent years, the battle against obscene speech has focused on pornography on the Internet. Opponents of this form of expression argue that it should be banned because of the easy access children have to the Internet. The first major effort to regulate the content of the Internet occurred on February 1, 1996, when the 104th Congress passed major telecommunications legislation. Attached to the Telecommunications Act was an amendment, called the Communications Decency Act (CDA), that was designed to regulate the online transmission of obscene material. The constitutionality of the CDA was immediately challenged in court by a coalition of interests led by the American Civil Liberties Union (ACLU). In the 1997 Supreme Court case of *Reno v. ACLU*, the Court struck down the CDA, ruling that it suppressed speech that "adults have a constitutional right to receive" and that governments may not limit the adult population to messages that are fit for children. Supreme Court Justice John Paul Stevens described the Internet as the "town crier" of the modern age and said that it was entitled to the greatest degree of First Amendment protection possible.[60] Congress again tried to limit children's access to Internet pornography with the 2001 Children's Internet Protection Act, which required public libraries to install antipornography filters on all library computers with Internet access. Though the act made cooperation a condition for receiving federal subsidies, it did permit librarians to unblock a site at the request of an adult patron. The law was challenged, and in 2003 the Court upheld it, asserting that its provisions did not violate library patrons' First Amendment rights.[61] In 2003, Congress enacted the Prosecutorial Remedies and Other Tools to end the Exploitation of Children Today (PROTECT) Act, which outlawed efforts to sell child pornography via the Internet. The Supreme Court upheld this act in the 2008 case of *United States v. Williams*, in which the majority said that criminalizing efforts to pander child pornography did not violate free-speech guarantees.[62]

In 2000, the Supreme Court also extended the highest degree of First Amendment protection to cable (not broadcast) television. In *United States v. Playboy*

---

[59] *Miller v. California*, 413 U.S. 15 (1973).

[60] *Reno v. ACLU*, 521 U.S. 844 (1997).

[61] *United States v. American Library Association*, 539 U.S. 194 (2003).

[62] *United States v. Williams*, 06-694 (2008).

Entertainment Group, the Court struck down a portion of the Telecommunications Act of 1996 that required cable TV companies to limit the broadcast of sexually explicit programming to late-night hours. In its decision, the Court noted that the law already provided parents with the means to restrict access to sexually explicit cable channels through various blocking devices. Moreover, such programming could come into the home only if parents decided to purchase such channels in the first place.[63]

Fighting Words. Speech can also lose its protected position when it moves toward the sphere of action. "Expressive speech," for example, is protected until it moves from the symbolic realm to the realm of actual conduct—to direct incitement of damaging conduct with the use of so-called **fighting words.** In 1942, the Supreme Court upheld the arrest and conviction of a man who had violated a state law forbidding the use of offensive language in public. He had called the arresting officer a "goddamned racketeer" and "a damn Fascist." When his case reached the Supreme Court, the arrest was upheld on the grounds that the First Amendment provides no protection for such offensive language because such words "are no essential part of any exposition of ideas."[64] This case was reaffirmed in a much more famous and more important case decided at the height of the Cold War, when the Supreme Court held that

fighting words
Speech that directly incites damaging conduct.

> there is no substantial public interest in permitting certain kinds of utterances: the lewd and obscene, the profane, the libelous, and the insulting or "fighting" words—those which by their very utterance inflict injury or tend to incite an immediate breach of the peace.[65]

Since that time, however, the Supreme Court has reversed almost every conviction based on arguments that the speaker had used "fighting words." But again, it does not mean this is an absolutely settled area. In recent years, the increased activism of minority and women's groups has prompted a movement against words that might be construed as offensive to members of a particular group. This movement has come to be called, derisively, political correctness, or PC. In response to this movement, many organizations have attempted to impose codes of etiquette that acknowledge these enhanced sensitivities. These efforts to formalize the restraints on the use of certain words in public are causing great concern over their possible infringement on freedom of speech. But how should we determine what words are "fighting words" and therefore fall outside the protections of the freedom of speech?

One category of conditionally protected speech is the free speech of high school students in public schools. In 1986, the Supreme Court backed away from a broad protection of student free speech rights by upholding the punishment of a high

---

[63] *United States v. Playboy Entertainment Group, Inc.,* 529 U.S. 803 (2000).

[64] *Chaplinsky v. State of New Hampshire,* 315 U.S. 568 (1942).

[65] *Dennis v. United States,* 341 U.S. 494 (1951), which upheld the infamous Smith Act of 1940, which provided criminal penalties for those who "willfully and knowingly conspire to teach and advocate the forceful and violent overthrow and destruction of the government."

school student for making a sexually suggestive speech. The Court opinion held that such speech interfered with the school's goal of teaching students the limits of socially acceptable behavior.[66] Two years later the Supreme Court took another conservative step by restricting students' speech and press rights even further, defining them as part of the educational process and not to be treated with the same standard as adult speech in a regular public forum.[67] An even more recent case involving high school students is the 2007 case of *Morse v. Frederick*.[68] This case dealt with the policies of Juneau-Douglas High School in Juneau, Alaska. In 2002, the Olympic torch relay passed Juneau on its way to Salt Lake City for the opening of the Winter Olympics. As the torch passed Juneau-Douglas High, a senior, Joseph Frederick, unfurled a banner that read, "Bong Hits 4 Jesus." The school's principal promptly suspended Frederick, who then brought suit for reinstatement, alleging that his free-speech rights had been violated. Like most of America's public schools, Juneau High prohibits assemblies or expressions on school grounds that advocate illegal drug use. Schools say that some federal aid is contingent on this policy. Civil libertarians, of course, see such policies as restricting students' right to free speech—a right that has been recognized by the Supreme Court since a 1969 case in which it said an Iowa public school could not prohibit students from wearing antiwar armbands. Unfortunately for Frederick, today's Supreme Court has a much more conservative cast than its 1969 counterpart. Speaking for the Court's majority, Chief Justice Roberts said that the First Amendment did not require schools to permit students to advocate illegal drug use.

In addition, scores of universities have attempted to develop speech codes to suppress utterances deemed to be racial or ethnic slurs. What these universities find, however, is that the codes often produce more problems than they solve. Speech codes at public universities have been struck down by federal judges as unconstitutional infringements of speech. Such concerns are not limited to universities, although universities have probably moved furthest toward efforts to formalize "politically correct" speech guidelines. Similar developments have taken place in large corporations, both public and private, in which many successful complaints and lawsuits have been brought, alleging that the words of employers or their supervisors create a "hostile or abusive working environment." The Supreme Court has held that "sexual harassment" that creates a "hostile working environment" includes "unwelcome sexual advances, requests for sexual favors, and other *verbal* or physical conduct of a sexual nature"[69] [emphasis added]. A fundamental free speech issue is involved in these regulations of hostile speech.

Hate Speech. Many jurisdictions have drafted ordinances banning forms of expression designed to assert hatred toward one or another group, be they African Americans, Jews, Muslims, or others. Such ordinances seldom pass constitutional muster. The leading Supreme Court case in this realm is the 1992 decision in

---

[66] *Bethel School District No. 403 v. Fraser*, 478 U.S. 675 (1986).

[67] *Hazelwood School District v. Kuhlmeier*, 484 U.S. 260 (1988).

[68] *Morse v. Frederick*, 06-278 (2007).

[69] *Meritor Savings Bank v. Vinson*, 477 U.S. 57 (1986).

R.A.V. v. City of St. Paul.[70] Here, a white teenager was arrested for burning a cross on the lawn of a black family in violation of a municipal ordinance that banned cross burning. The Court ruled that such an ordinance must be *content neutral,* that is, not prohibiting actions directed at some groups but not others. The statute in question prohibited only cross burning—typically an expression of hatred of African Americans. Since a statute banning all forms of hateful expression would be deemed overly broad, the *R.A.V.* standard suggests that virtually all hate speech is constitutionally protected.

Commercial Speech. Commercial speech, such as newspaper or television advertising, does not have full First Amendment protection because it cannot be considered political speech. Initially considered to be entirely outside the protection of the First Amendment, commercial speech has made gains during the twentieth century. Some commercial speech is still unprotected and therefore regulated. For example, the regulation of false and misleading advertising by the Federal Trade Commission is an old and well-established power of the federal government. The Supreme Court long ago approved the constitutionality of laws prohibiting the electronic media from carrying cigarette advertising.[71] The Court has upheld a state-university ban on Tupperware parties in college dormitories.[72] It has upheld city ordinances prohibiting the posting of all signs on public property (as long as the ban is total, so that there is no hint of censorship).[73] And the Supreme Court, in a heated 5–4 decision written by Chief Justice William Rehnquist, upheld Puerto Rico's statute restricting gambling advertising aimed at residents of Puerto Rico.[74]

However, the gains far outweigh the losses in the effort to expand the protection commercial speech enjoys under the First Amendment. As the scholar Louis Fisher explains, "In part, this reflects the growing appreciation that commercial speech is part of the free flow of information necessary for informed choice and democratic participation."[75] For example, the Court in 1975 struck down a state statute making it a misdemeanor to sell or circulate newspapers encouraging abortions; the Court ruled that the statute infringed on constitutionally protected speech and the right of the reader to make informed choices.[76] On a similar basis, the Court reversed its own earlier decisions upholding laws that prohibited dentists and other professionals from advertising their services. For the Court, medical-service advertising was a matter of health that could be advanced by the free flow of information.[77] In a 1983 case, the Supreme Court struck down a congressional statute that prohibited the unsolicited mailing of advertisements for contraceptives. In

---

[70] *R.A.V. v. City of St. Paul,* 506 U.S. 377 (1992).

[71] *Capital Broadcasting Company v. Acting Attorney General,* 405 U.S. 1000 (1972).

[72] *Board of Trustees, State University of New York v. Fox,* 492 U.S. 469 (1989).

[73] *City Council v. Taxpayers for Vincent,* 466 U.S. 789 (1984).

[74] *Posadas de Puerto Rico Associates v. Tourism Company of Puerto Rico,* 478 U.S. 328 (1986).

[75] Fisher, *American Constitutional Law,* p. 546.

[76] *Bigelow v. Virginia,* 421 U.S. 809 (1975).

[77] *Virginia State Board of Pharmacy v. Virginia Citizens Consumer Council,* 425 U.S. 748 (1976). Later cases restored the rights of lawyers to advertise their services.

1996, the Court struck down Rhode Island laws and regulations banning the advertisement of liquor prices as a violation of the First Amendment.[78] And in a 2001 case, the Court ruled that a Massachusetts ban on all cigarette advertising violated the First Amendment right of the tobacco industry to advertise its products to adult consumers.[79] These instances of commercial speech are significant in themselves, but they are all the more significant because they indicate the breadth and depth of the freedom existing today to direct appeals broadly to a large public, not only to sell goods and services but also to mobilize people for political purposes.

The Second Amendment and the Right to Bear Arms

> A well regulated Militia, being necessary to the security of a free State, the right of the people to keep and bear Arms, shall not be infringed.

The point and purpose of the Second Amendment is the provision for militias; they were to be the backing of the government for the maintenance of local public order. *Militia* was understood at the time of the Founding to be a military or police resource for state governments, and militias were specifically distinguished from armies and troops, which came within the sole constitutional jurisdiction of Congress. Some individuals, though, have always argued that the Second Amendment also establishes an individual right to bear arms. In its 2008 decision in the case of *District of Columbia v. Heller*, the Supreme Court ruled that the federal government could not prohibit individuals from owning guns for self-defense in their homes.[80] The case involved a District of Columbia ordinance that made it virtually impossible for residents to possess firearms legally. The District of Columbia is an entity of the federal government, and the Court did not indicate that its ruling applied to state firearms laws. However, in the 2010 case of *McDonald v. Chicago*, the Court struck down a Chicago firearms ordinance and applied the Second Amendment to the states as well.[81]

Rights of the Criminally Accused

Except for the First Amendment, most of the battle to apply the Bill of Rights to the states was fought over the various protections granted to individuals who are accused of a crime, who are suspects in the commission of a crime, or who are brought before the court as a witness to a crime. The Bill of Rights entitles every American to **due process** of law. The concept of due process of law means that the government must respect all the legal rights to which every individual is entitled. The Fourth, Fifth, Sixth, and Eighth Amendments, taken together, are the essence of the due process of law, even though this fundamental concept does not appear until the very last words of the Fifth Amendment. In the next sections, we shall

due process
Proceeding according to law and with adequate protection for individual rights.

---

[78] *44 Liquormart, Inc., and Peoples Super Liquor Stores, Inc., Petitioners v. Rhode Island and Rhode Island Liquor Stores Association*, 517 U.S. 484 (1996).

[79] *Lorillard Tobacco v. Reilly*, 533 U.S. 525 (2001).

[80] *District of Columbia v. Heller*, 07-290 (2008).

[81] *McDonald v. Chicago*, 08-1521 (2010).

look at specific cases that illuminate the dynamics of this important constitutional issue. The procedural safeguards that we shall discuss may seem remote to most law-abiding citizens, but they help define the limits of governmental action against the personal liberty of every citizen. Many Americans believe that "legal technicalities" are responsible for setting many criminals free. In many cases, that is absolutely true. In fact, setting defendants free is the very purpose of the requirements that constitute due process. One of America's traditional and most strongly held juridical values is that "it is far worse to convict an innocent man than to let a guilty man go free."[82] In civil suits, verdicts rest on "the preponderance of the evidence"; in criminal cases, guilt has to be proved "beyond a reasonable doubt"—a far higher standard. The provisions for due process in the Bill of Rights were added in order to improve the probability that the standard of reasonable doubt will be respected.

The Fourth Amendment and Searches and Seizures

The right of the people to be secure in their persons, houses, papers, and effects, against unreasonable searches and seizures, shall not be violated, and no Warrants shall issue, but upon probable cause, supported by Oath or affirmation, and particularly describing the place to be searched, and the persons or things to be seized.

The purpose of the Fourth Amendment is to guarantee the security of citizens against unreasonable (that is, improper) searches and seizures. In 1990, the Supreme Court summarized its understanding of the Fourth Amendment brilliantly and succinctly: "A search compromises the individual interest in privacy; a seizure deprives the individual of dominion over his or her person or property."[83] But how are we to define what is reasonable and what is unreasonable?

The 1961 case of *Mapp v. Ohio* illustrates the beauty and the agony of one of the most important of the procedures that have grown out of the Fourth Amendment— the **exclusionary rule**, which prohibits evidence obtained during an illegal search from being introduced in a trial. Dollree (Dolly) Mapp was "a Cleveland woman of questionable reputation" (by some accounts), the ex-wife of one prominent boxer, and the fiancée of an even more famous one. Acting on a tip that Dolly Mapp was harboring a suspect in a bombing incident, several policemen forcibly entered her house, claiming they had a warrant to look for the suspect. The police did not find the suspect but did find some materials connected to the local numbers racket (an illegal gambling operation) and a quantity of "obscene materials," which were in violation of an Ohio law banning possession of such materials. Although the warrant was never produced, the evidence that had been seized was admitted by a court, and Mapp was charged and convicted of illegal possession of obscene materials.

By the time Mapp's appeal reached the Supreme Court, the issue of obscene materials had faded into obscurity, and the question before the Court was whether any evidence produced under the circumstances of the search of her home was

> **exclusionary rule** The ability of courts to exclude evidence obtained in violation of the Fourth Amendment.

---

[82] *In re Winship*, 397 U.S. 358 (1970). An outstanding treatment of due process in issues involving the Fourth through Seventh Amendments is found in Fisher, *American Constitutional Law*, chap. 13.

[83] *Horton v. California*, 496 U.S. 128 (1990).

admissible. The Court's opinion affirmed the exclusionary rule: Under the Fourth Amendment (applied to the states through the Fourteenth Amendment), "all evidence obtained by searches and seizures in violation of the Constitution . . . is inadmissible." This means that even people who are clearly guilty of the crime of which they are accused must not be convicted if the only evidence for their conviction was obtained illegally. This idea was expressed by Supreme Court Justice Benjamin Cardozo nearly a century ago when he wrote that "the criminal is to go free because the constable has blundered."

The exclusionary rule is the most severe restraint ever imposed by the Constitution and the courts on the behavior of the police. The exclusionary rule is a dramatic restriction because it rules out precisely the evidence that produces a conviction; it frees those people who are *known* to have committed the crime of which they have been accused. Because it works so dramatically in favor of persons known to have committed a crime, the Court has since softened the application of the rule. In recent years, the federal courts have relied on a discretionary use of the exclusionary rule, whereby they make a judgment as to the "nature and quality of the intrusion." It is thus difficult to know ahead of time whether a defendant will or will not be protected from an illegal search under the Fourth Amendment.[84]

Another recent issue involving the Fourth Amendment is the controversy over mandatory drug testing. Such testing is most widely used on public employees, and in an important case the Supreme Court upheld the U.S. Customs Service's drug-testing program for its employees.[85] That same year the Court approved drug and alcohol tests for railroad workers if the workers were involved in a serious accident.[86] After Court approvals of those two cases in 1989, more than forty federal agencies initiated mandatory employee drug tests. The practice of drug testing was reinforced by a presidential executive order widely touted as the "campaign for a drug-free federal workplace." These growing practices gave rise to public appeals against the general practice of "suspicionless testing" of employees. Regardless of any need to limit the spread of drug abuse, doing so by testing public employees seemed patently unconstitutional, in violation of the Fourth Amendment. A 1995 case, in which the Court upheld a public school district's policy requiring that all students participating in interscholastic sports submit to random drug tests, surely contributed to the efforts of federal, state, and local agencies to initiate random and suspicionless drug and alcohol testing.[87] The most recent cases suggest, however, that the Court is beginning to consider limits on the "war" against drugs. In a decisive 8–1 decision, the Court applied the Fourth Amendment as a shield against "state action that diminishes personal privacy" when the officials in question are not performing high-risk or safety-sensitive tasks.[88] Using random and suspicionless drug testing as a symbol to fight drug use was, in the Court's opinion, carrying the exceptions to the Fourth Amendment too far.

---

[84] For a good discussion of the issue, see Fisher, *American Constitutional Law*, pp. 884–89.

[85] *National Treasury Employees Union v. Von Raab*, 489 U.S. 656 (1989).

[86] *Skinner v. Railroad Labor Executives Association*, 489 U.S. 602 (1989).

[87] *Vernonia School District v. Acton*, 515 U.S. 646 (1995).

[88] *Chandler et al. v. Miller, Governor of Georgia et al.*, 520 U.S. 305 (1997).

More recently, the Court found it unconstitutional for police to use trained dogs in roadblocks set up to look for drugs in cars. Unlike drunk-driving roadblocks, where public safety is directly involved, narcotics roadblocks "cannot escape the Fourth Amendment's requirement that searches be based on suspicion of individual wrongdoing."[89] The Court also ruled that the police may not use thermal-imaging devices to detect suspicious patterns of heat emerging from private homes without obtaining the usual search warrant.[90] In 2009 the court ruled against an Arizona school district that conducted a strip search of a 13-year-old student suspected of hiding drugs in her underwear.[91]

The Fifth Amendment

> No person shall be held to answer for a capital, or otherwise infamous crime, unless on a presentment or indictment of a Grand Jury, except in cases arising in the land or naval forces, or in the Militia, when in actual service in time of War or public danger; nor shall any person be subject for the same offense to be twice put in jeopardy of life or limb; nor shall be compelled in any criminal case to be a witness against himself, nor be deprived of life, liberty, or property, without due process of law; nor shall private property be taken for public use, without just compensation.

Grand Juries.   The first clause of the Fifth Amendment, the right to have a **grand jury** determine whether a trial is warranted, is considered "the oldest institution known to the Constitution."[92] Grand juries play an important role in federal criminal cases. However, the provision for a grand jury is the one important civil liberties provision of the Bill of Rights that was not incorporated by the Fourteenth Amendment to apply to state criminal prosecutions. Thus some states operate without grand juries. In such states, the prosecuting attorney simply files a "bill of information" affirming that there is sufficient evidence available to justify a trial. If the accused person is to be held in custody, the prosecutor must take the available information before a judge to determine whether the evidence shows probable cause.

grand jury A jury that determines whether sufficient evidence is available to justify a trial. Grand juries do not rule on the accused's guilt or innocence.

Double Jeopardy.   "Nor shall any person be subject for the same offense to be twice put in jeopardy of life or limb" is the constitutional protection from **double jeopardy**, or being tried more than once for the same crime. The protection from double jeopardy was at the heart of the *Palko* case in 1937, which, as we saw earlier in this chapter, also helped establish the principle of selective incorporation of the Bill of Rights. It took more than thirty years for the Court to nationalize the constitutional protection against double jeopardy.

double jeopardy The Fifth Amendment right providing that a person cannot be tried twice for the same crime.

---

[89] *Indianapolis v. Edmund*, 531 U.S. 32 (2000).

[90] *Kyllo v. United States*, 533 U.S. 27 (2001).

[91] *Safford Unified School District No.1 v. Redding*, 08-479 (2009).

[92] E.S. Corwin and Jack Peltason, *Understanding the Constitution*, p. 286.

Self-Incrimination. Perhaps the most significant liberty found in the Fifth Amendment, and the one most familiar to many Americans who watch television crime shows, is the guarantee that no citizen "shall be compelled in any criminal case to be a witness against himself." The most famous case concerning self-incrimination is one of such importance that Chief Justice Earl Warren assessed its results as going "to the very root of our concepts of American criminal jurisprudence." Twenty-three-year-old Ernesto Miranda was sentenced to between twenty and thirty years in prison for the kidnapping and rape of an eighteen-year-old woman. The woman had identified him in a police lineup, and, after two hours of questioning Miranda confessed, subsequently signing a statement that his confession had been made voluntarily, without threats or promises of immunity. These confessions were admitted into evidence, served as the basis for Miranda's conviction, and also served as the basis of the appeal of his conviction all the way to the Supreme Court. In one of the most intensely and widely criticized decisions ever handed down by the Supreme Court, Ernesto Miranda's case produced the rules the police must follow before questioning an arrested criminal suspect. The reading of a person's "Miranda rights" has become a standard scene in every police station and on virtually every dramatization of police action on television and in the movies. *Miranda* advanced the civil liberties of accused persons not only by expanding the scope of the Fifth Amendment clause covering coerced confessions and self-incrimination but also by confirming the right to counsel. The Supreme Court under Warren Burger and William Rehnquist considerably softened the Miranda restrictions, making the job of the police a little easier, but the Miranda rule still stands as a protection against egregious police abuses of arrested persons. The Supreme Court reaffirmed Miranda in *Dickerson v. United States.*[93]

Eminent Domain. Another fundamental clause of the Fifth Amendment is the "takings clause," which extends to each citizen a protection against the taking of private property "without just compensation." Although this part of the amendment is not specifically concerned with protecting persons accused of crimes, it is nevertheless a fundamentally important instance where the government and the citizen are adversaries. As discussed earlier in this chapter, the power of any government to take private property for a public use is called **eminent domain.** This power is essential to the very concept of sovereignty. The Fifth Amendment neither invented eminent domain nor took it away; its purpose was to put limits on that inherent power through procedures that require a demonstration of a public purpose and the provision of fair payment for the seizure of someone's property. This provision is now universally observed in all American principalities, but it has not always been meticulously observed.

The first modern case confronting the issue of public use involved a mom-and-pop grocery store in a rundown neighborhood on the southwest side of the District of Columbia. In carrying out a vast urban-redevelopment program in the 1950s, the city government of Washington, D.C., took the property as one of a large number of privately owned lots to be cleared for new housing and business construction.

eminent domain
The right of the government to take private property for public use, with reasonable compensation awarded for the property.

---

[93] *Dickerson v. United States,* 530 U.S. 428 (2000).

The owner of the grocery store and his successors, after his death, took the government to court on the grounds that taking property from one private owner and eventually turning that property back, in altered form, to another private owner was an unconstitutional use of eminent domain. The store owners lost their case. The Supreme Court's argument was a curious but very important one: The "public interest" can mean virtually anything a legislature says it means. In other words, since the overall slum clearance and redevelopment project was in the public interest, according to the legislature, the eventual transfers of property that were going to take place were justified.[94] In 1984 and again in 2005 the Supreme Court reaffirmed that decision.[95]

The Sixth Amendment and the Right to Counsel

> In all criminal prosecutions, the accused shall enjoy the right to a speedy and public trial, by an impartial jury of the State and district wherein the crime shall have been committed, which district shall have been previously ascertained by law, and to be informed of the nature and cause of the accusation; to be confronted with the witnesses against him; to have compulsory process for obtaining witnesses in his favor, and to have the Assistance of Counsel for his defense.

Like the exclusionary rule of the Fourth Amendment and the self-incrimination clause of the Fifth Amendment, the "right to counsel" provision of the Sixth Amendment is notable for freeing defendants who seem to the public to be patently guilty as charged. Other provisions of the Sixth Amendment, such as the right to a speedy trial and the right to confront witnesses before an impartial jury, are less controversial in nature.

Gideon v. Wainwright is the perfect case study because it involved a disreputable person who seemed patently guilty of the crime for which he was convicted. In and out of jails for most of his fifty-one years, Clarence Earl Gideon received a five-year sentence for breaking into and entering a poolroom in Panama City, Florida. While serving time in jail, Gideon became a fairly well qualified "jailhouse lawyer," made his own appeal on a handwritten petition, and eventually won the landmark ruling on the right to counsel in all felony cases.[96] *Gideon* was decided in 1963, and the following year, in *Escobedo v. Illinois*, the Supreme Court ruled that suspects had a right to counsel during police interrogations, not just when their cases reached trial.[97]

The right to counsel has been expanded during the past few decades. For example, although at first the right to counsel was met by judges' assigning lawyers

---

[94] *Berman v. Parker,* 348 U.S. 26 (1954). For a thorough analysis of the case, see Benjamin Ginsberg, "*Berman v. Parker:* Congress, the Court, and the Public Purpose," *Polity* 4 (1971): 48–75.

[95] *Hawaii Housing Authority v. Midkiff,* 469 U.S. 2321 (1984) and *Kelo v. City of New London,* 545 U.S. (2005).

[96] For a full account of the story of the trial and release of Clarence Earl Gideon, see Lewis, *Gideon's Trumpet.* See also David M. O'Brien, *Storm Center,* 2nd ed. (New York: Norton, 1990).

[97] *Escobedo v. Illinois,* 378 U.S. 478 (1964).

from the community as a formal public obligation, most states and cities have now created an office of public defender whose state-employed professional defense lawyers typically provide poor defendants with much better legal representation. And although these defendants cannot choose their private defense attorneys, they do have the right to appeal a conviction on the grounds that the counsel provided by the state was deficient. For example, in 2003 the Supreme Court overturned the death sentence of a Maryland death-row inmate, holding that the defense lawyer had failed to fully inform the jury of the defendant's history of "horrendous childhood abuse."[98] Moreover, the right to counsel extends beyond serious crimes to any trial, with or without a jury, that holds the possibility of imprisonment.[99]

The Eighth Amendment and Cruel and Unusual Punishment

The Eighth Amendment prohibits "excessive bail," "excessive fines," and "cruel and unusual punishment." Virtually all the debate over Eighth Amendment issues focuses on the last clause of the amendment: the protection from "cruel and unusual punishment." One of the greatest challenges in interpreting this provision consistently is that what is considered "cruel and unusual" varies from culture to culture and from generation to generation. And unfortunately, it also varies by class and race.

By far the biggest issue in the inconsistency of class and race as constituting cruel and unusual punishment arises over the death penalty. In 1972, the Supreme Court overturned several state death-penalty laws not because they were cruel and unusual but because they were being applied in a capricious manner.[100] Very soon after that decision, a majority of states revised their capital-punishment provisions to provide clear standards.[101] Since 1976, the Court has consistently upheld state laws providing for capital punishment, although it also continues to review numerous death-penalty appeals each year.

Between 1976 and 2000, states executed 683 people. Most of those executions occurred in southern states, with Texas leading the way at 239. As of 2002, thirty-eight states had adopted some form of capital punishment, a move approved of by about three-quarters of all Americans.

Although virtually all criminal conduct is regulated by the states, Congress has also jumped on the bandwagon, imposing capital punishment for more than fifty federal crimes. Despite the seeming popularity of the death penalty, the debate has become, if anything, more intense. In 1997, for example, the American Bar Association passed a resolution calling for a halt to the death penalty until concerns about its fairness—that is, whether its application violates the principle of equality—and concerns about ensuring due process are addressed. In 2000, the governor of Illinois imposed a moratorium on the death penalty and created a commission to

---

[98] *Wiggins v. Smith,* 539 U.S. 510 (2003).

[99] For further discussion of these issues, see Corwin and Peltason, *Understanding the Constitution,* pp. 319–23.

[100] *Furman v. Georgia,* 408 U.S. 238 (1972).

[101] *Gregg v. Georgia,* 428 U.S. 153 (1976).

review the capital-punishment system. After a two-year study by the commission, Illinois adopted a number of reforms, including a ban on executions of the mentally retarded. In June 2002, the Supreme Court banned all executions of mentally retarded defendants, a decision that could move 200 or more people off death row. In 2008, the Court issued a number of death penalty opinions, declaring that death was too harsh a penalty for a child rapist[102] and invalidating a death sentence for black defendant where the prosecutor had improperly excluded African Americans from the jury.[103] In a decision which received worldwide attention, the Court ruled that the International Court of Justice had no authority to order a Texas court to reopen a death penalty case involving a foreign national.[104]

Many death-penalty supporters praise its deterrent effects on other would-be criminals. Although studies of capital crimes usually fail to demonstrate any direct deterrent effect, the punishment's failure to act as a deterrent may be due to the lengthy delays—typically years and even decades—between convictions and executions. A system that eliminates undue delays would surely enhance deterrence. And deterring even one murder or other heinous crime, proponents argue, is more than ample justification for such laws. Beyond that argument, the death penalty is seen as a proper expression of retribution, echoed in the biblical phrase "an eye for an eye." People who commit vicious crimes deserve to forfeit their lives in exchange for the suffering they have inflicted. If the world applauded the execution of Nazis after World War II, for example, how could it deny the right of society to execute a serial killer?

Constitutional objections to the death penalty often invoke the Eighth Amendment's protection against punishments that are "cruel and unusual." Yet the death penalty can hardly be considered a violation of this protection, say supporters, since it was commonly used in the eighteenth century and was supported by most early American leaders. And although the poor, men, and blacks and Latinos are more likely than others to find themselves sitting on death row, this fact reflects the painful reality that these categories of individuals are more likely to commit crimes.

Death-penalty opponents are quick to point out that the death penalty has not been proved to deter crime, either in the United States or abroad. In fact, America is the only Western nation that still executes criminals. The fact that American states execute criminals debases rather than elevates society by extolling vengeance. If the government is to serve as an example of proper behavior, say foes, it has no business sanctioning killing when incarceration will similarly protect society. As for the Constitution, most of the Founders surely supported the death penalty. But, foes note, they also countenanced slavery and lived at a time when society was both less informed about, and more indifferent to, the human condition. Modern Americans' greater civility should be reflected in how the society defines individual rights.

Furthermore, according to death-penalty foes, execution is expensive—more expensive than life imprisonment—precisely because the government must make

---

[102] *Kennedy v. Louisiana,* 07-343 (2008).

[103] *Snyder v. Louisiana,* 06-10119 (2008).

[104] *Medellin v. Texas,* 06-984 (2008).

every effort to ensure that it is not executing an innocent person. Curtailing legal appeals would make the possibility of a mistake too great. And although most Americans do support the death penalty, people also support life without the possibility of parole as an alternative. Race also intrudes in death-penalty cases: People of color (who are more likely to face economic deprivation) are disproportionately more likely to be sentenced to death, whereas whites charged with identical crimes are less likely to be given the ultimate punishment. Finally, according to opponents, a life sentence may be a worse punishment than the death penalty.

The Right to Privacy

Some of the people all of the time and all of the people some of the time would just like to be left alone, to have their own private domain into which no one—friends, family, government, church, or employer—has the right to enter without permission.

Many Jehovah's Witnesses felt that way in the 1930s. They risked serious punishment in 1940 by telling their children not to salute the flag or say the Pledge of Allegiance in school because of their understanding of the first commandment's prohibition of the worship of "graven images." As noted in our discussion of the free exercise of religion, they lost their appeal, the children were expelled, and the parents were punished. However, the Supreme Court concluded that the 1940 decision had been "wrongly decided." These two cases arose under the freedom of religion provisions of the First Amendment, but they were also the first cases to confront the possibility of another right that is not mentioned anywhere in the Constitution or the Bill of Rights: the right to be left alone. When the Court began to take a more activist role in the mid-1950s and 1960s, the idea of a **right to privacy** was revived. In 1958, the Supreme Court recognized "privacy in one's association" in its decision to prevent the state of Alabama from using the membership list of the NAACP in the state's investigations. The Constitution does not specifically mention a right to privacy, but recall that the Ninth Amendment declares that the rights enumerated by the Constitution are not an exhaustive list.

right to privacy The right to be let alone, which has been interpreted by the Supreme Court to entail free access to birth control and abortions.

Birth Control. The sphere of privacy was drawn in earnest in 1965, when the Court ruled that a Connecticut statute forbidding the use of contraceptives violated the right of marital privacy. Estelle Griswold, the executive director of the Planned Parenthood League of Connecticut, was arrested by the state of Connecticut for providing information, instruction, and medical advice about contraception to married couples. She and her associates were found guilty as accessories to the crime and fined $100 each. The Supreme Court reversed the lower court's decisions and declared the Connecticut law unconstitutional because it violated "a right of privacy older than the Bill of Rights—older than our political parties, older than our school system." Justice William O. Douglas, author of the majority decision in the *Griswold* case, argued that this right of privacy is also grounded in the Constitution because it fits into a "zone of privacy" created by a combination of the Third, Fourth, and Fifth Amendments. A concurring opinion, written by Justice Arthur Goldberg, attempted to strengthen Douglas's argument by adding that "the concept of liberty . . . embraces the right of marital privacy though that right is not mentioned explicitly in the Constitution [and] is supported by numerous decisions of this Court . . . and *by the language and history of the Ninth Amendment*" [emphasis added].[105]

Abortion.   The right to privacy was confirmed and extended in 1973 in the most important of all privacy decisions and one of the most important Supreme Court decisions in American history: *Roe v. Wade*. This decision established a woman's right to seek an abortion and prohibited states from making abortion a criminal act.[106] The Burger Court's decision in *Roe* took a revolutionary step toward establishing the right to privacy. It is important to emphasize that the preference for privacy rights and for their extension to include the rights of women to control their own bodies was not something invented by the Supreme Court in a vacuum. Most states did not regulate abortions in any fashion until the 1840s, at which time only six of the twenty-six states had any regulations governing abortion at all. In addition, many states had begun to ease their abortion restrictions well before the 1973 *Roe* decision, although in recent years a number of states have reinstated some restrictions on the procedure.

By extending the umbrella of privacy, this sweeping ruling dramatically changed abortion practices in America. In addition, it galvanized and nationalized the abortion debate. Groups opposed to abortion, such as the National Right to Life Committee, organized to fight the new liberal standard, while abortion rights groups sought to maintain that protection. In recent years, the legal standard shifted against abortion rights supporters in three key Supreme Court cases.

In *Webster v. Reproductive Health Services,* the Court narrowly upheld (by a 5–4 majority) the constitutionality of restrictions on the use of public medical facilities for abortion.[107] And in the 1992 case of *Planned Parenthood v. Casey,* another 5–4 majority of the Court upheld *Roe* but narrowed its scope, refusing to invalidate a Pennsylvania law that significantly limits freedom of choice. The Court's decision defined the right to an abortion as a "limited or qualified" right subject to regulation by the states as long as the regulation does not constitute an "undue burden."[108] More recently, the Court had another opportunity to rule on what constitutes an undue burden. In the 2000 case of *Stenberg v. Carhart,* the Court, by a vote of 5–4, struck down Nebraska's ban on partial-birth abortions because the law had the "effect of placing a substantial obstacle in the path of a woman seeking an abortion."[109]

Homosexuality.   In the last two decades, the right to be left alone began to include the privacy rights of homosexuals. One morning in Atlanta in the mid-1980s,

---

[105] *Griswold v. Connecticut*, 381 U.S. 479 (1965) and *Griswold v. Connecticut*, concurring opinion. In 1972, in *Eisenstadt v. Baird*, 405 U.S. 438 (1972), the Court extended the privacy right to unmarried women.

[106] *Roe v. Wade*, 410 U.S. 113 (1973).

[107] *Webster v. Reproductive Health Services*, 492 U.S. 490 (1989), which upheld a Missouri law that restricted the use of public medical facilities for abortion. The decision opened the way for other states to limit the availability of abortion.

[108] *Planned Parenthood v. Casey*, 505 U.S. 833 (1992).

[109] *Stenberg v. Carhart*, 530 U.S. 914 (2000).

Michael Hardwick was arrested by a police officer who discovered him in bed with another man. The officer had come to serve a warrant for Hardwick's arrest for failure to appear in court to answer charges of drinking in public. One of Hardwick's unknowing housemates invited the officer to look in Hardwick's room, where he found Hardwick and another man engaging in "consensual sexual behavior." Hardwick was then arrested under Georgia's laws against heterosexual and homosexual sodomy. Hardwick filed a lawsuit against the state, challenging the constitutionality of the Georgia law, and won his case in the federal court of appeals. The state of Georgia, in an unusual move, appealed the court's decision to the Supreme Court. The majority of the Court reversed the lower-court decision, holding against Hardwick on the grounds that "the federal Constitution confers [no] fundamental right upon homosexuals to engage in sodomy" and that there was therefore no basis to invalidate "the laws of the many states that still make such conduct illegal and have done so for a very long time." The Court majority concluded its opinion with a warning that it ought not and would not use its power to "discover new fundamental rights embedded in the Due Process Clause." In other words, the Court under Chief Justice Rehnquist was expressing its determination to restrict quite severely the expansion of the Ninth Amendment and the development of new substantive rights. The four dissenters argued that the case was not about a fundamental right to engage in homosexual sodomy but was in fact about "the most comprehensive of rights and the right most valued by civilized men, [namely,] the right to be let alone."[110]

Seventeen years later, and to most everyone's surprise, the Court overturned *Bowers v. Hardwick* with a dramatic pronouncement that gays are "entitled to respect for their private lives" as a matter of constitutional due process. With *Lawrence v. Texas,* state legislatures no longer had the authority to make private sexual behavior a crime.[111] Drawing from the tradition of negative liberty, the Court maintained, "In our tradition the State is not omnipresent in the home. And there are other spheres of our lives and existence outside the home, where the State should not be a dominant presence." Explicitly encompassing lesbians and gay men within the umbrella of privacy, the Court concluded that the "petitioners are entitled to respect for their private lives. The State cannot demean their existence or control their destiny by making their private sexual conduct a crime." This decision added substance to the Ninth Amendment "right of privacy."

The Right to Die. Another area ripe for further litigation and public discourse is the so-called right to die. A number of highly publicized physician-assisted suicides in the 1990s focused attention on whether people have a right to choose their own death and receive assistance in carrying it out. Can this become part of the privacy right, or is it a new substantive right? A tentative answer came in 1997, when the Court ruled that a Washington State law establishing a ban on "causing" or "aiding"

---

[110] *Bowers v. Hardwick,* 478 U.S. 186 (1986). The dissenters were quoting an earlier case, *Olmstead v. United States,* 277 U.S. 438 (1928), to emphasize the nature of their disagreement with the majority in the *Bowers* case.

[111] *Lawrence and Garner v. Texas,* 539 U.S. 558 (2003).

a suicide did not violate the Fourteenth Amendment or any clauses of the Bill of Rights incorporated into the Fourteenth Amendment. Thus if a state can constitutionally adopt such a prohibition, there is no constitutional right to suicide or assisted suicide. However, the Court left open the narrower question of "whether a mentally competent person who is experiencing great suffering has a constitutionally cognizable interest in controlling the circumstances of his or her imminent death." "Americans are engaged in an earnest and profound debate about the morality, legality, and practicality of physician-assisted suicide. Our holding permits this debate to continue, as it should in a democratic society."[112] Never before has the Supreme Court more openly invited further litigation on a point.

The War on Terrorism. In response to the September 11, 2001, terrorist attacks on the United States, Congress enacted new legislation—the USA PATRIOT Act—designed to make it easier for federal law enforcement agencies to investigate and prosecute suspected terrorists. In addition, the president issued a series of orders allowing the National Security Agency to eavesdrop on domestic communications and the military to detain and try terrorism suspects. Civil libertarians have argued that the government's new surveillance and eavesdropping authority poses a threat to free speech and privacy. Critics have also declared that the open-ended military detention of terrorism suspects, along with the special military tribunals and procedures established by the president to try such suspects, violates many of the fundamental constitutional protections provided to those accused of criminal actions.

Some of these questions have been raised in the federal courts. In June 2004, the Supreme Court ruled in three cases involving the president's antiterrorism initiatives and claims of executive power and in two of those cases appeared to place some limit on presidential authority. Indeed, the justices were clearly influenced by revelations that U.S. troops abused prisoners in Iraq, and they sought in those cases to make a statement against the absolute denial of procedural rights to individuals in the custody of U.S. military authorities.[113]

In its June 2004 rulings, the Supreme Court did assert that presidential actions were subject to judicial scrutiny and placed some constraints on the president's unfettered power. At the same time, the Court affirmed the president's single most important claim: the unilateral power to declare individuals, including U.S. citizens, "enemy combatants" who can be detained by federal authorities under adverse legal circumstances. Future presidents are likely to cite the Court's decisions as precedents for, rather than limits on, the exercise of executive power.

The same is likely to be true of the Court's June 2006 decision in the case of *Hamdan v. Rumsfeld*.[114] Salim Ahmed Hamdan, a Taliban fighter captured in Afghanistan in 2001 and held at Guantánamo since 2002, was slated for trial by a special military tribunal. Such tribunals, operating outside both the civilian and the

---

[112] *Washington v. Glucksberg,* 521 U.S. 702 (1997).

[113] *Hamdi v. Rumsfeld,* 542 U.S. 507 (2004); *Rasul v. Bush,* 542 U.S. 466 (2004); *Rumsfeld v. Padilla,* 542 U.S. 426 (2004).

[114] *Hamdan v. Rumsfeld,* 548 U.S. (2006).

military court systems, were created by the Bush administration to deal with suspected terrorists in the wake of the September 11 attacks and the U.S. invasion of Afghanistan. Hamdan challenged the propriety of the tribunals. In its decision, the Supreme Court held that tribunals must either be authorized by statute or follow rules and procedures consistent with the Uniform Code of Military Justice (UCMJ) and the Geneva Conventions. The Court found that President Bush's tribunals were not authorized by statute and were operating under procedures that provided defendants with fewer rights and safeguards than they would receive under the UCMJ. Hence, the tribunals were declared invalid.

Though invalidating these particular tribunals, however, the Supreme Court accepted the principle that the president could order persons he deemed unlawful combatants to be tried by military tribunals so long as the tribunals were lawfully constituted. Accordingly, the president asked Congress to authorize the creation of special tribunals that would operate under the same rules and procedures as those declared unconstitutional by the Supreme Court, a request to which Congress acceded in the 2006 Military Commissions Act (MCI). One provision of that act, however, was subsequently overturned by the Supreme Court. Congress had declared in the MCI that terrorist suspects held at Guantánamo could not seek their release in federal court by filing writs of *habeas corpus*. This provision, contained in Section 7 of the MCI, was a response to the Supreme Court's 2004 decision in *Rasul v. Bush* (see Chapter 3). In its 2008 decision in *Boumediene v. Bush*, however, the Court overturned Section 7, declaring that *habeas corpus* was a fundamental right.[115] This fight over *habeas corpus* is another example of the struggle that often breaks out between Congress and the judiciary over who will exercise ultimate power in the realm of civil liberties and civil rights.

Civil Liberties and the History Principle.   In their rulings, the courts are heavily influenced by history. Every court decision recites the history of prior court decisions relating to the principles at hand. This use of history is called *precedent*. When courts issue their decisions, they constantly refer to the opinions of prior courts to justify their interpretations, logic, and ultimate findings. Seldom will a court depart from established precedent. Even the Supreme Court is always careful to justify its decisions by pointing to numerous precedents and will seldom overturn established legal principles. Because the job of a court is to apply rather than to make the law, history in the form of precedent is an important factor limiting judicial discretion. But history does not merely limit judicial discretion. When the courts apply precedent, they also limit the discretion of other governmental institutions. Take the *Boumediene* case. The Bush administration, at that time supported by a Republican Congress, had secured the enactment of legislation stripping the Guantánamo detainees of their right of *habeas corpus*. When it struck down Section 7 of the MCI, the Court pointed to our nation's history for justification. Indeed, the Court cited the history of *habeas corpus* going back to the Magna Carta to support the contention that Congress could not so easily deny the application of *habeas* to any particular group. Writing for the Court, Justice Kennedy declared:

---

[115] *Boumediene v. Bush*, 06-1195 (2008).

Magna Carta decreed that no man would be imprisoned contrary to the law of the land. Art. 39, in Sources of Our Liberties 17 (R. Perry & J. Cooper eds. 1959) ("No free man shall be taken or imprisoned or dispossessed, or outlawed, or banished, or in any way destroyed, nor will we go upon him, nor send upon him, except by the legal judgment of his peers or by the law of the land"). Important as the principle was, the Barons at Runnymede prescribed no specific legal process to enforce it. Holdsworth tells us, however, that gradually the writ of habeas corpus became the means by which the promise of Magna Carta was fulfilled. 9 W. Holdsworth, A History of English Law 112 (1926) (hereinafter Holdsworth).

In this as in other opinions, the Court insisted that the nation be bound by its historical traditions and principles. One reason that history matters is that when they cite precedent, the courts impose our history on us.

CIVIL RIGHTS

With the adoption of the Fourteenth Amendment in 1868, civil rights became part of the Constitution, guaranteed to each citizen through "equal protection of the laws." These words launched a century of political movements and legal efforts to press for racial equality. African Americans' quest for civil rights in turn inspired many other groups—including members of other racial and ethnic groups, women, people with disabilities, and gay men and lesbians—to seek new laws and constitutional guarantees of their civil rights.

Congress passed the Fourteenth Amendment and the states ratified it in the aftermath of the Civil War. Together with the Thirteenth Amendment, which abolished slavery, and the Fifteenth Amendment, which guaranteed voting rights to black men, it seemed to provide a guarantee of civil rights for the newly freed enslaved blacks. But the general language of the Fourteenth Amendment meant that its support for civil rights could be far reaching. The very simplicity of the **equal protection clause** of the Fourteenth Amendment left it open to interpretation:

> No State shall make or enforce any law which shall . . . deny to any person within its jurisdiction the equal protection of the laws.

equal protection clause The provision of the Fourteenth Amendment guaranteeing citizens "the equal protection of the laws." This clause has been the basis for the civil rights of African Americans, women, and other groups.

Plessy v. Ferguson: "Separate but Equal"

The Supreme Court was no more ready to enforce the civil rights aspects of the Fourteenth Amendment than it was to enforce the civil liberties provisions. The Court declared the Civil Rights Act of 1875 unconstitutional on the grounds that it sought to protect blacks from discrimination by *private* businesses, whereas the Fourteenth Amendment, according to the Court's interpretation, was intended to protect individuals from discrimination only in the case of actions by *public* officials of state and local governments.

In 1896, the Court went still further, in the infamous case of *Plessy v. Ferguson.* It upheld a Louisiana statute that *required* segregation of the races on trolleys and other public carriers (and, by implication, in all public facilities, including schools). Homer Plessy, a man defined as "one-eighth black," had violated a Louisiana law that provided for "equal but separate accommodations" on trains and a $25 fine for any white passenger who sat in a car reserved for blacks or any black passenger who sat in a car reserved for whites. The Supreme Court held that the Fourteenth Amendment's "equal protection of the laws" was not violated by racial distinction as long as the law applied to both races equally. People generally pretended they were treated equally as long as some accommodation existed. The Court said that although

> the object of the [Fourteenth] Amendment was undoubtedly to enforce the absolute equality of the two races before the law, . . . it could not have intended to abolish distinctions based on color, or to enforce social, as distinguished from political, equality, or a commingling of the two races upon terms unsatisfactory to either.[116]

What the Court was saying in effect was that the use of race as a criterion of exclusion in public matters was not unreasonable. This was the origin of the **"separate but equal" rule**, which was not reversed until 1954.

"separate but equal" rule The doctrine that public accommodations could be segregated by race but still be equal.

Racial Discrimination after World War II

The Supreme Court had begun to change its position on racial discrimination before World War II by defining more strictly the criterion of equal facilities in the "separate but equal" rule. In 1938, the Court rejected Missouri's policy of paying qualified blacks' tuition to out-of-state law schools rather than admitting them to the University of Missouri Law School.[117]

After the war, modest progress resumed. In 1950, the Court rejected Texas's claim that its new "law school for Negroes" afforded education equal to that of the all-white University of Texas Law School; without confronting the "separate but equal" principle itself, the Court's decision anticipated *Brown v. Board of Education* by opening the question of whether any segregated facility could be truly equal.[118] The same was true in 1944, when the Supreme Court struck down the southern practice of "white primaries," which legally excluded blacks from participation in the process of nominating candidates. Here the Court simply recognized that primaries could no longer be regarded as the private affairs of the parties but were an integral aspect of the electoral process. This decision made parties "an agency of the State," and any practice of discrimination against blacks was therefore "state action within the meaning of the Fifteenth Amendment."[119] The most important pre-1954 decision was probably *Shelley v. Kraemer*,[120] in which the Court ruled against the widespread practice of "restrictive covenants," whereby the seller of a home added

---

[116] *Plessy v. Ferguson*, 163 U.S. 537 (1896).

[117] *Missouri ex rel. Gaines v. Canada*, 305 U.S. 337 (1938).

[118] *Sweatt v. Painter*, 339 U.S. 629 (1950).

[119] *Smith v. Allwright*, 321 U.S. 649 (1944).

[120] *Shelley v. Kraemer*, 334 U.S. 1 (1948).

a clause to the sales contract requiring the buyers to agree not to sell their home to any nonwhite, non-Christian, and so on. The Court ruled that although private persons could sign such restrictive covenants, they could not be judicially enforced because the Fourteenth Amendment prohibits any organ of the state, including the courts, from denying equal protection of its laws.

However, none of these pre-1954 cases confronted head on the principle of "separate but equal" as such and its legal and constitutional support for racial discrimination. Each victory by the Legal Defense Fund of the NAACP was celebrated for itself and was seen, it was hoped, as a trend, but each was still a small victory, not a leading case. The massive effort by the southern states to resist direct desegregation and to prevent further legal actions against it by making a show of equalizing the quality of white and black schools convinced the NAACP that the Supreme Court was unready for a full confrontation with the constitutional principle sustaining segregation. But the continued unwillingness of Congress after 1948 to consider fair employment legislation seemed to convince the NAACP that the courts were its only hope. Thus by 1951, the NAACP had decided to attack the principle of segregation itself as unconstitutional and, in 1952, instituted cases in South Carolina, Virginia, Kansas, Delaware, and the District of Columbia. The strategy was to file suits simultaneously in different federal districts so that inconsistent results between any two states would more quickly lead to Supreme Court acceptance of at least one appeal.[121] Of these suits, the Kansas case became the chosen one. It seemed to be ahead of the pack in its district court, and it had the special advantage of being located in a state outside the Deep South.[122]

Oliver Brown, the father of three girls, lived "across the tracks" in a low-income, racially mixed Topeka neighborhood. Every school-day morning, Linda Brown took a school bus to the Monroe School for black children, about a mile away. In September 1950, Oliver Brown took Linda to the all-white Sumner School, which was closer to home, to enter her in the third grade, in defiance of state law and local segregation rules. When they were refused, Brown took his case to the NAACP, and soon thereafter *Brown v. Board of Education* was born. In mid-1953, the Court announced that the several cases on their way up would be reargued within the context of a set of questions having to do with the intent of the Fourteenth Amendment. Almost exactly a year later, the Court responded to those questions in one of the most important decisions in its history.

In deciding the case, the Court, to the surprise of many, basically rejected as inconclusive all the learned arguments about the intent and the history of the

---

[121] The best reviews of strategies, tactics, and goals is found in John Hope Franklin, *From Slavery to Freedom: A History of Negro Americans*, 4th ed. (New York: Knopf, 1974), chap. 22; and Richard Kluger, *Simple Justice: The History of* Brown v. Board of Education *and Black America's Struggle for Equality* (New York: Vintage, 1977), chaps. 21 and 22.

[122] The District of Columbia case came up too, but because the District of Columbia is not a state, the case did not directly involve the Fourteenth Amendment and its "equal protection" clause. It confronted the Court on the same grounds, however: that segregation is inherently unequal. Its victory in effect was "incorporation in reverse," with equal protection moving from the Fourteenth Amendment to become part of the Bill of Rights. See *Bolling v. Sharpe,* 347 U.S. 497 (1954).

Fourteenth Amendment and committed itself to considering only the consequences of segregation:

> Does segregation of children in public schools solely on the basis of race, even though the physical facilities and other "tangible" factors may be equal, deprive the children of the minority group of equal educational opportunities? We believe that it does. . . . We conclude that, in the field of public education, the doctrine of "separate but equal" has no place. Separate educational facilities are inherently unequal.[123]

The *Brown* decision altered the constitutional framework in two fundamental respects. First, after *Brown*, the states would no longer have the power to use race as a criterion of discrimination in law. Second, the national government would from then on have the constitutional basis for extending its power (hitherto in doubt, as we saw earlier) to intervene with strict regulatory policies against the discriminatory actions of state or local governments, school boards, employers, and many others in the private sector.

Civil Rights after *Brown v. Board of Education*

Although *Brown v. Board of Education* withdrew all constitutional authority to use race as a criterion of exclusion, this historic decision was merely a small opening move. First, most states refused to cooperate until sued, and many ingenious schemes were employed to delay obedience (such as paying the tuition of white students to attend newly created "private" academies). Second, even as southern school boards began to cooperate by eliminating their legally enforced (**de jure**) segregation, extensive actual (**de facto**) school segregation remained in the North and the South as a consequence of racially segregated housing, which could not be affected by the 1954 *Brown* principles. Third, discrimination in employment, public accommodations, juries, voting, and other areas of social and economic activity was not directly touched by *Brown*.

A decade of frustration following *Brown* made it fairly obvious that adjudication alone would not succeed. The goal of equal protection required positive, or affirmative, action by Congress and administrative agencies. And given massive southern resistance and generally negative national public opinion toward racial integration, progress would not be made through courts, Congress, or agencies without intense, well-organized support. The number of peaceful civil rights demonstrations for voting rights and public accommodations increased greatly during the first fourteen years following *Brown*.[124]

Organized civil rights demonstrations began to mount slowly but surely after *Brown v. Board of Education*. By the 1960s, the many organizations that made up the civil rights movement had accumulated experience and built networks capable of launching massive direct-action campaigns against southern segregationists. The Southern Christian Leadership Conference, the Student Nonviolent Coordinating

de jure segregation Racial segregation that is a direct result of law or official policy.

de facto segregation Racial segregation that is not a direct result of law or government policy but is, instead, a reflection of residential patterns, income distributions, or other social factors.

---

[123] *Brown v. Board of Education*, 347 U.S. 483 (1954).

[124] Jonathan D. Casper, *The Politics of Civil Liberties* (New York: Harper & Row, 1972), p. 90.

Committee, and many other organizations had built a movement that stretched across the South. That movement used the media to attract nationwide attention and support. In the massive March on Washington in 1963, the Reverend Martin Luther King, Jr. staked out the movement's moral claims in his "I Have a Dream" speech. Also in the 1960s, images of protesters being beaten, attacked by police dogs, and set on with fire hoses did much to win broad sympathy for the cause of black civil rights and discredit state and local governments in the South. In this way, the movement created intense pressure for a reluctant federal government to take more assertive steps to defend black civil rights.

Why Fight for Civil Rights? Collective Action and Selective Benefits.

One of the tenets of our five principles of politics from Chapter 1 is that individuals have little incentive to participate in mass-action politics. After all, what possible difference could one person make by taking part in a civil rights protest? Participation is costly in terms of time, and in the case of civil rights marchers even one's health or life was endangered. The risks outweighed the potential benefits, yet hundreds of thousands of people *did* participate. Why?

Even though little scholarly attention has been paid by those who apply this perspective to the civil rights movements,[125] a general answer is available. Most rational analysis takes behavior to be *instrumental*—motivated by and directed toward some purpose or objective. But behavior may also be *experiential*. People do things, on this account, because they like doing them—they feel good inside, they feel free of guilt, they take pleasure in the activity for its own sake. We maintain that this second view of behavior is entirely compatible with rational accounts. Instrumental behavior may be thought of as *investment activity*, whereas experiential behavior may be thought of as *consumption activity*. With the latter, it is the behavior itself that generates utility, rather than the consequences produced by the behavior. To take a specific illustration of collective action, many people certainly attended the 1963 March on Washington because they cared about civil rights. But it is unlikely that many deluded themselves into thinking their individual participation made a large difference to the fate of the civil rights legislation they supported through the march. Rather, they attended because they wanted to be part of a social movement, hear Martin Luther King, Jr. speak, and identify with the hundreds of thousands of others who felt the same way. Also—and this should not be minimized—many participated because they anticipated that the march would be fun, an adventure of sorts.

So experiential behavior is consumption-oriented activity predicated on the belief that the activity in question is fulfilling, apart from its consequences. Individuals are bound to be animated both by the consumption value of a particular behavior and by its instrumental value, the rational (investment) explanation that we have used throughout this book. To insist on only one of these complementary forms of rationality while excluding the other is to provide but a partial explanation.

---

[125] One notable exception is Dennis Chong, *Collective Action and the Civil Rights Movement* (Chicago: University of Chicago Press, 1991).

1950's

JUDICIAL AND LEGAL ACTION

Brown v. Board of Education (1954)

Brown v. Board of Education II (1955) implementation of Brown v. Board of Education (1954)

Federal courts order school intergration and order Autherine Lucy admitted to University of Alabama (1956)

Civil Rights Act creates Civil Rights Commission; President Dwight D. Eisenhower sends paratroopers to Little Rock, Arkansas, to enforce integration of Central Hight School (1957)

POLITICAL ACTION

Montgomery, Alabama, bus boycott (1955)

Southern Christian Leadership Conference (SCLC) formed with Martin Luther King, Jr. as president. (1957)

School Desegregation, Phase One.   Although the District of Columbia and some of the school districts in the border states began to respond almost immediately to court-ordered desegregation, the states of the Deep South responded with a carefully planned delaying tactic known as *massive resistance.* Southern politicians stood shoulder to shoulder to declare that the Supreme Court's decisions and orders were without effect. The legislatures in these states enacted statutes ordering school districts to maintain segregated schools and state superintendents to terminate state funding wherever there was racial mixing in the classroom. Some southern states violated their own long traditions of local school autonomy by centralizing public-school authority under the governor or the state board of education and giving states the power to close schools and provide alternative private schooling wherever local school boards might be tending to obey the Supreme Court.

Most of these plans of massive resistance were tested in the federal courts and struck down as unconstitutional.[126] But southern resistance was not confined to legislation. In 1957, for example, Governor Orval Faubus mobilized the Arkansas National Guard to intercede against enforcement of a federal court order to integrate Little Rock's Central High School, and President Dwight D. Eisenhower was forced to deploy U.S. troops and place the city under martial law. The Supreme

---

[126] The two most important cases were *Cooper v. Aaron,* 358 U.S. 1 (1958), which required Little Rock, Arkansas, to desegregate, and *Griffin v. Prince Edward County School Board,* 377 U.S. 218 (1964), which forced all the schools of that Virginia county to reopen after they had been closed for five years to avoid desegregation.

1960's

JUDICIAL AND LEGAL ACTION

First substantive Civil Rights Act, primarily guaranteeing voting rights (1960)

Interstate Commerce Commission orders desegregation on all buses, on all trains, and in terminals; President John F. Kennedy favors executive action over civil rights legislation (1961)

President Kennedy shifts gears, supporting strong civil rights law; President Lyndon B. Johnson asserts strong support for civil rights (1963)

Congress passes historic Civil Rights Act covering voting, employment, public accomodations, education (1964)

War on Poverty in full swing (1966)

Voting rights Act (1965)

POLITICAL ACTION

Student Nonviolent Co-ordinating Committee (SNCC) formed to organize protests, sit-ins, freedom rides (1960)

Nonviolent demonstrations in Birmingham, Alabama, lead to King's arrest and "Letter from Birmingham Jail"; march on Washington (1963)

King announces drive to register 3 million blacks in the South (1965)

Movement dissipates with remains focusing on litigation, community action programs, anti-war protest, and more militant "Black Power" actions (1966)

Court considered the Little Rock confrontation so historically important that the opinion it rendered in that case not only was agreed to unanimously but also and unprecedentedly was signed personally by every one of the justices. The end of massive resistance, however, became the beginning of still another southern strategy, "pupil placement" laws, which authorized school districts to place each pupil in a school according to a variety of academic, personal, and psychological considerations, never mentioning race at all. These laws put the burden of transferring to an all-white school on the nonwhite children and their parents, making it almost impossible for a single court order to cover a whole district, let alone a whole state. The effect was to delay desegregation a while longer.[127]

As the southern states invented new devices to avoid desegregation, the federal courts followed with cases and decisions quashing them. Ten years after *Brown*, fewer than 1 percent of black school-age children in the Deep South were attending schools with whites. It had become unmistakably clear well before that time that the federal courts could not do the job alone. The first modern effort to legislate in the field of civil rights was made in 1957, but the law contained only a federal guarantee of voting rights, without any powers of enforcement, although it did create

---

[127] *Shuttlesworth v. Birmingham Board of Education,* 358 U.S. 101 (1958), upheld a pupil placement plan purporting to assign pupils on various bases, with no mention of race. This case interpreted *Brown* to mean that school districts must stop explicit racial discrimination but were under no obligation to take positive steps to desegregate. For a while, black parents were doomed to case-by-case approaches.

the Civil Rights Commission to study abuses. Much more important legislation for civil rights followed, especially the Civil Rights Act of 1964. It is important to observe here the mutual dependence of the courts and the legislatures—not only do the legislatures need constitutional authority to act, but the courts also need legislative and political assistance, through the power of the purse, the power to organize administrative agencies to implement court orders, and the ability to focus political support. Consequently, even as Congress finally moved into the field of school desegregation (and other areas of equal protection), the courts continued to exercise their powers, not only by issuing court orders against recalcitrant school districts but also by extending and reinterpreting aspects of the equal protection clause to support legislative and administrative actions.

School Desegregation: Busing and Beyond. The most important judicial extension of civil rights in education after 1954 was probably the *Swann* decision of 1971, which held that state-imposed desegregation could be brought about by busing children across school districts even where relatively long distances were involved. But the decision went beyond that, adding that under certain limited circumstances even racial quotas could be used as the "starting point in shaping a remedy to correct past constitutional violations" and that the pairing or grouping of schools and the reorganizing of school attendance zones would also be acceptable (Figure 4.1).[128]

Three years later, however, the *Swann* case was severely restricted when the Supreme Court determined that only cities found guilty of deliberate and de jure racial segregation (segregation in law) would have to desegregate their schools. This decision was handed down in the 1974 case of *Milliken v. Bradley,* involving the city of Detroit and its suburbs.[129] The *Milliken* ruling had the effect of exempting most northern states and cities from busing because school segregation in northern cities is generally de facto (segregation in fact), resulting from segregated housing and thousands of acts of private discrimination against blacks and other minorities.

Additional progress in the desegregation of schools is likely to be extremely slow unless the Supreme Court decides to permit federal action against de facto segregation and the various kinds of private schools and academies that have sprung up for the purpose of avoiding integration. The prospects for further school integration diminished with a series of Supreme Court decisions handed down in the 1990s. In 1995, for example, in *Missouri v. Jenkins,* the Court signaled to the lower courts that they should "disengage from desegregation efforts."[130] This is a direct and explicit threat to the main basis of the holding in the original 1954 *Brown v. Board of Education* decision.

The Rise of the Politics of Rights

Despite the agonizingly slow progress of school desegregation, there was some progress in other areas of civil rights during the 1960s and 1970s. Voting rights were

---

[128] *Swann v. Charlotte-Mecklenburg Board of Education,* 402 U.S. 1 (1971).

[129] *Milliken v. Bradley,* 418 U.S. 717 (1974).

[130] *Missouri v. Jenkins,* 515 U.S. 70 (1995). The quotation is from David M. O'Brien, *Supreme Court Watch 1996* (New York: Norton, 1996), p. 220.

FIGURE 4.1 THE PERCENTAGE OF SOUTHERN BLACK SCHOOLCHILDREN ATTENDING SCHOOL WITH WHITES, 1955–73

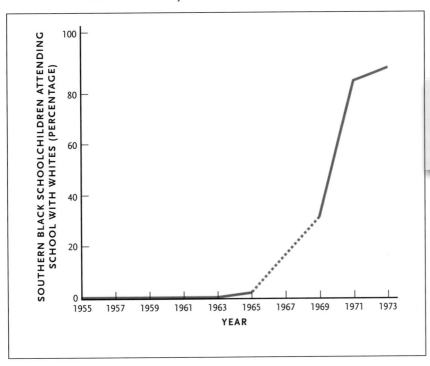

NOTE: Dashed line indicates missing data.

SOURCE: Gerald N. Rosenberg, *The Hollow Hope: Can Courts Bring About Social Change?* (Chicago: University of Chicago Press, 1991), pp. 50–51.

ANALYZING THE EVIDENCE

What happened in 1964 that accounts for the upward trend beginning in 1965?

established and fairly quickly began to revolutionize southern politics, and service on juries was no longer denied to minorities. But progress in securing the right to participate in politics and government dramatized the relative lack of progress in the economic domain, and it was in this area that battles over civil rights were increasingly fought. (See the "Analyzing the Evidence" unit on the following page.)

Outlawing Discrimination in Employment.   The federal courts and the Justice Department entered this area through Title VII of the Civil Rights Act of 1964, which outlaws job discrimination by all private and public employers, including government agencies (such as fire and police departments), that employ more than fifteen workers. We have already seen that the Supreme Court gave "interstate commerce" such a broad definition that Congress had the constitutional authority to ban discrimination by virtually any local employers.[131] Title VII makes it unlawful to discriminate in employment on the basis of color, religion, sex, or national origin, as well as race.

---

[131] See especially *Katzenbach v. McClung,* 379 U.S. 294 (1964).

Racial Equality

As we discuss in this chapter, civil rights is a major political issue in the United States. Especially since the 1960s, most forms of racial discrimination have been prohibited by law, and a large number of government programs have been designed to promote greater political, social, and economic equality between black and white Americans. Despite these efforts, progress in the direction of racial equality has been uneven. As we can see in the following figures and tables, some data suggest that the United States has made great strides toward the color-blind society envisioned by the early leaders of the civil rights movement. Other data, though, indicate that we have a long way to go. The fact that America's president is black does not mean that complete racial equality has been achieved in the U.S.

In assessing racial equality in the United States, we could also consider numerous other statistics and other racial and ethnic groups. Depending upon which evidence is selected, one might argue that racial equality in the United States has increased substantially in recent years or that it has not.

HIGH-SCHOOL GRADUATION RATES

White Americans

African Americans

Percentage

Year

One encouraging statistic is the change in black versus white levels of educational attainment over the past 45 years. In 1960, black Americans were less than half as likely to finish high school or graduate from college as whites. Today, the percentage of blacks graduating from high school is nearly identical to the percentage of whites who earn diplomas.

Source: U.S. Census Bureau, www.census.gov (accessed 6/22/09).

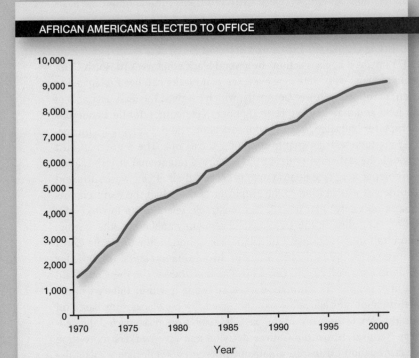

AFRICAN AMERICANS ELECTED TO OFFICE

Year

Progress has also been made in the political arena. As recently as 1970, only 1,469 African Americans held elected office in the United States—out of approximately half a million federal, state, and local offices. By 2001, the last year for which the government collected data, there were more than 9,000 black elected officials, an increase of more than 600 percent.

Source: Joint Center for Political and Economical Studies, "Black Elected Officials," jointcenter.org/BD/detail/BEO.htm (accessed 6/22/09).

In the economic realm the gap between blacks and whites has decreased more slowly. In 2007, the *mean* income of black men was only 66 percent of the mean income for white men. This represented only slight progress for black men since 1980. Although black women's mean income was close to that of white women in 2007, it was even closer in 1980—so black women have lost ground relative to white women during this period. The table below shows *median* incomes, which also reflect the gap between blacks and whites, especially among men.

MEDIAN INCOME (2005 Dollars)

	Men				Women			
	1980	1990	2000	2007	1980	1990	2000	2007
White	31,931	32,557	35,877	35,141	11,852	15,866	19,360	21,069
Black	19,188	19,789	25,698	25,822	10,973	12,807	19,121	19,752

Source: U.S. Census Bureau, www.census.gov (accessed 6/22/09).

A possible problem with Title VII is that the complaining party has to show that deliberate discrimination was the cause of the failure to get a job or a training opportunity. Rarely does an employer explicitly admit discrimination on the basis of race, sex, or any other illegal reason. Recognizing the rarity of such an admission, the courts have allowed aggrieved parties (the plaintiffs) to make their case if they can show that an employer's hiring practices had the *effect* of exclusion. A leading case in 1971 involved a "class action" by several black employees in North Carolina attempting to show with statistical evidence that blacks had been relegated to one department of the Duke Power Company, which involved the least desirable of manual-labor jobs, and that they had been kept out of contention for the better jobs because the employer had added high-school education and passing grades on specially prepared aptitude tests as qualifications for those jobs. The Supreme Court held that although the statistical evidence did not prove intentional discrimination and the requirements were race neutral in appearance, their effects were sufficient to shift the burden of justification to the employer to show that the requirements were a "business necessity" that bore "a demonstrable relationship to successful performance."[132] The ruling in this case was subsequently applied to other hiring, promotion, and training programs.[133] In recent years, though, the Supreme Court has placed a number of limits on employment discrimination suits. In 2007, for example, in the case of *Ledbetter v. Goodyear Tire and Rubber Co.* the Court said that a complaint of gender discrimination must be brought within 180 days of the time the discrimination was alleged to have occurred.[134] This blocks suits based on events that might have taken place in the past. In 2009, Congress enacted the Ledbetter Fair Pay Act to overturn the Court's decision and give workers more time to file pay discrimination claims. In a pair of important 2008 decisions, also, the Court helped individuals who sought to bring employment discrimination complaints by declaring that employers were barred from retaliating against them.[135] Fear of retaliation is a powerful force discouraging employees from seeking to assert their legal rights.

Gender Discrimination. Title VII provided a valuable tool for the growing women's movement in the 1960s and 1970s.[136] In fact, in many ways the law fostered the growth of the women's movement. The first major campaign of the National Organization for Women (NOW) involved picketing the Equal Employment Opportunity Commission (EEOC) for its refusal to ban sex-segregated employment advertisements. NOW also sued the *New York Times* for continuing to publish such ads after the passage of Title VII. Another organization, the Women's Equity Action League (WEAL), pursued legal action on a wide range of sex discrimination issues, filing lawsuits against law schools and medical schools for their discriminatory admission policies, for example.

---

[132] *Griggs v. Duke Power Company*, 401 U.S. 424 (1971). See also Allan P. Sindler, *Bakke, DeFunis, and Minority Admissions: The Quest for Equal Opportunity* (New York: Longman, 1978), pp. 180–89.

[133] For a good treatment of these issues, see Charles O. Gregory and Harold A. Katz, *Labor and the Law*, 3rd ed. (New York: Norton, 1979), chap. 17.

[134] *Ledbetter v. Goodyear Tire and Rubber Co.*, 05-1074 (2007).

[135] *CBOC West v. Humphries*, 06-1431 (2008), *Gomez-Perez v. Potter*, 03-1321 (2008).

[136] This and the next five sections are from Ginsberg et al., *We the People*.

Building on these victories and the growth of the women's movement, feminist activists sought an equal rights amendment (ERA) to the Constitution. The proposed amendment was short: Its substantive passage stated that "equality of rights under the law shall not be denied or abridged by the United States or by any State on account of sex." The amendment's supporters believed that such a sweeping guarantee of equal rights was a necessary tool for ending all discrimination against women and for making gender roles more equal. Opponents charged that it would be socially disruptive and would introduce changes—such as coed restrooms—that most Americans did not want. The amendment easily passed Congress in 1972 and won quick approval in many state legislatures but fell three states short of the thirty-eight needed to ratify the amendment by the 1982 deadline for its ratification.[137]

Despite the failure of the ERA, gender discrimination expanded dramatically as an area of civil rights law. In the 1970s, the conservative Burger Court helped to establish gender discrimination as a major and highly visible civil rights issue. Although the Burger Court refused to treat gender discrimination as the equivalent of racial discrimination,[138] it did make it easier for plaintiffs to file and win suits on the basis of gender discrimination by applying an "intermediate" level of review to these cases.[139] This **intermediate scrutiny** is midway between traditional rules of evidence, which put the burden of proof on the plaintiff, and the doctrine of strict scrutiny, which requires the defendant to show not only that a particular classification is reasonable but also that there is a need or compelling interest for it. Intermediate scrutiny shifts the burden of proof partially onto the defendant, rather than leaving it entirely on the plaintiff.

One major step was taken in 1992, when the Court decided in *Franklin v. Gwinnett County Public Schools* that violations of Title IX of the 1972 Education Act could be remedied with monetary damages.[140] Title IX forbids gender discrimination in education, but it initially sparked little litigation because of its weak enforcement provisions. The Court's 1992 ruling opened the door for more legal action in the area of education. The greatest impact has been in the areas of sexual harassment—the subject of the *Franklin* case—and in equal treatment of women's athletic programs. The potential for monetary damages has made universities and public schools take the problem of sexual harassment more seriously. Colleges and universities have also started to pay more attention to women's athletic programs. In the two years after the *Franklin* case, complaints to the Education Department's Office for Civil Rights about unequal treatment of women's athletic programs nearly tripled. In several high-profile legal cases, some prominent universities have been ordered to create more women's sports programs; many other colleges and universities have begun to add more women's programs in order to avoid potential litigation.[141] In 1997, the Supreme Court refused to hear a petition by Brown

intermediate scrutiny The test used by the Supreme Court in gender discrimination cases. Intermediate scrutiny places the burden of proof partially on the government and partially on the challengers to show that the law in question is constitutional.

---

[137] See Jane J. Mansbridge, *Why We Lost the ERA* (Chicago: University of Chicago Press, 1986); and Gilbert Steiner, *Constitutional Inequality* (Washington, D.C.: Brookings Institution, 1985).

[138] See *Frontiero v. Richardson*, 411 U.S. 677 (1973).

[139] See *Craig v. Boren*, 423 U.S. 1047 (1976).

[140] *Franklin v. Gwinnett County Public Schools*, 503 U.S. 60 (1992).

[141] Jennifer Halperin, "Women Step Up to Bat," *Illinois Issues* 21 (September 1995): 11–14.

University challenging a lower-court ruling that the university establish strict sex equity in its athletic programs. The Court's decision meant that in colleges and universities across the country, varsity athletic positions for men and women must reflect their overall enrollment numbers.[142]

In 1996, the Supreme Court made another important decision about gender and education by putting an end to all-male schools supported by public funds. It ruled that the Virginia Military Institute's policy of not admitting women was unconstitutional.[143] Along with the Citadel, an all-male military college in South Carolina, Virginia Military Institute (VMI) had never admitted women. It argued that the unique educational experience it offered, including intense physical training and the harsh treatment of freshmen, would be destroyed if women were admitted. The Court, however, ruled that the male-only policy denied "substantial equality" to women. Two days after the Court's ruling, the Citadel announced that it would accept women. VMI considered becoming a private institution in order to remain all male, but in September 1996 the school board finally voted to admit women. The legal decisions may have removed formal barriers to entry, but the experience of the female cadets at these schools has not been easy. The first female cadet at the Citadel, Shannon Faulkner, won admission in 1995 under a federal court order but quit after four days. Although four women were admitted to the Citadel after the Supreme Court decision, two of them quit several months later. They charged harassment by male students, including attempts to set the female cadets on fire.[144]

Courts began to find sexual harassment a form of sex discrimination during the late 1970s. Although sexual harassment law applies to education, most of the law of sexual harassment has been developed by courts through interpretation of Title VII of the Civil Rights Act of 1964. In 1986, the Supreme Court recognized two forms of sexual harassment—the quid pro quo type, which involves sexual extortion, and the hostile-environment type, which involves sexual intimidation.[145] Employers and many employees have worried that hostile-environment sexual harassment is too ambiguous. When can an employee bring charges? When is the employer liable? In 1986, the Court said that sexual harassment may be legally actionable even if the employee did not suffer tangible economic or job-related losses in relation to it. And in 1993, the Court said that sexual harassment may be legally actionable even if the employee did not suffer tangible psychological costs as a result of it.[146] In two 1998 cases, the Court further strengthened the law when it said that whether or not sexual harassment results in economic harm to the employee, an employer is liable for the harassment if it was committed by someone with authority over the employee—by a supervisor, for example. But the Court also said

---

[142] Joan Biskupic and David Nakamura, "Court Won't Review Sports Equity Ruling," *Washington Post,* April 22, 1997, p. A1.

[143] *United States v. Virginia,* 518 U.S. 515 (1996).

[144] Judith Havemann, "Two Women Quit Citadel over Alleged Harassment," *Washington Post,* January 13, 1997, p. A1.

[145] *Meritor Savings Bank v. Vinson* (1986).

[146] *Harris v. Forklift Systems,* 510 U.S. 17 (1993).

that an employer may defend itself by showing that it had a sexual harassment prevention and grievance policy in effect.[147]

The development of gender discrimination as an important part of the civil rights struggle has coincided with the rise of women's politics as a discrete movement in American politics. As with the struggle for racial equality, the relationship between changes in government policies and political action suggests that changes in government policies to a great degree produce political action. Today the existence of a powerful women's movement derives in large measure from the enactment of Title VII of the Civil Rights Act of 1964 and from the Burger Court's vital steps in applying that law to the protection of women. The recognition of women's civil rights has become an issue that in many ways transcends the usual distinctions of American political debate. In the heavily partisan debate over the federal crime bill enacted in 1994, for instance, the section of the bill that enjoyed the widest support was the Violence against Women Act, whose most important feature was that it defined gender-biased violent crimes as a matter of civil rights and created a civil rights remedy for women who have been the victims of such crimes. But since the act was ruled unconstitutional by the Supreme Court in 2000, the struggle for women's rights will likely remain part of the political debate.

Latinos and Asian Americans.   The labels "Latino" or "Hispanic" and "Asian American" encompass a wide range of groups with diverse national origins, distinctive cultural identities, and particular experiences. For example, the early political experiences of Mexican Americans were shaped by race and region. In 1898, Mexican Americans were given formal political rights, including the right to vote. In many places, however, and especially in Texas, Mexican Americans were segregated and prevented from voting by such means as the white primary and the poll tax.[148] Region made a difference too. In contrast to the northeastern and midwestern cities in which most European immigrants settled, the Southwest did not have a tradition of ethnic mobilization associated with machine politics. Particularly after the political reforms enacted in the first decade of the twentieth century, city politics in the Southwest was dominated by a small group of white elites. In the countryside, when Mexican Americans participated in politics, it was often as part of a political organization dominated by a large white landowner, or *patron*.

The earliest independent Mexican American political organizations, the League of United Latin American Citizens (LULAC) and the American GI Forum, worked to stem discrimination against Mexican Americans in the years after World War II. By the late 1950s, the first Mexican American had been elected to Congress, and four others followed in the 1960s. In the late 1960s, a new kind of Mexican American political movement was born. Inspired by the black civil rights movement, Mexican American students launched boycotts of high-school classes in Los

---

[147] *Burlington Industries v. Ellerth*, 524 U.S. 742 (1998); *Faragher v. City of Boca Raton*, 524 U.S. 775 (1998).

[148] New Mexico had a different history because not many Anglos settled there initially. (*Anglo* is the term for a non-Hispanic white of European background.) Mexican Americans had considerable power in territorial legislatures between 1865 and 1912. See Lawrence H. Fuchs, *The American Kaleidoscope* (Hanover, N.H.: University Press of New England, 1990), pp. 239–40.

Angeles, Denver, and San Antonio. Students in colleges and universities across California joined in as well. Among their demands were bilingual education, an end to discrimination, and greater cultural recognition. In Crystal City, Texas, which had been dominated by Anglo politicians despite a population that was over-whelmingly Mexican American, the newly formed La Raza Unida Party took over the city government.[149]

Since that time, Mexican American political strategy has developed along two tracks. One is a traditional ethnic-group path of voter registration and voting along ethnic lines. The second is a legal strategy using the various civil rights laws designed to ensure fair access to the political system. The Mexican American Legal Defense and Education Fund (MALDEF) has played a key role in designing and pursuing the latter strategy.

The early Asian experience in the United States was shaped by a series of naturalization laws dating back to 1790, the first of which declared that only white aliens were eligible for citizenship. Chinese immigrants had begun arriving in California in the 1850s, drawn by the boom of the gold rush. They were immediately met with hostility. The virulent antagonism toward Chinese immigrants in California led Congress in 1870 to declare Chinese immigrants ineligible for citizenship. In 1882, the first Chinese Exclusion Act suspended the entry of Chinese laborers.

At the time of the Exclusion Act, the Chinese community was composed predominantly of single male laborers, with few women and children. The few Chinese children in San Francisco were initially denied entry to the public schools; only after parents of American-born Chinese children pressed legal action were the children allowed to attend public school. Even then, however, they were made to attend a separate Chinese school. American-born Chinese children could not be denied citizenship, however; this right was confirmed by the Supreme Court in 1898, when it ruled in *United States v. Wong Kim Ark* that anyone born in the United States was entitled to full citizenship.[150] Still, new Chinese immigrants were barred from the United States until 1943; China by then had become a key wartime ally, and Congress repealed the Chinese Exclusion Act and permitted Chinese residents to become citizens.

Immigration climbed rapidly after the 1965 Immigration and Nationality Services Act, which lifted discriminatory quotas. In spite of this and other developments, limited English proficiency barred many Asian Americans and Latinos from full participation in American life. Two developments in the 1970s, however, established rights for language minorities. In 1974, the Supreme Court ruled in *Lau v. Nichols,* a suit filed on behalf of Chinese students in San Francisco, that school districts have to provide education for students whose English is limited.[151] It did not mandate bilingual education, but it established a duty to provide instruction that students could understand. The 1970 amendments to the Voting Rights Act of 1965 permanently outlawed literacy tests in all fifty states and mandated

---

[149] On the La Raza Unida Party, see Carlos Muñoz, Jr. and Mario Barrera, "La Raza Unida Party and the Chicano Student Movement in California," in *Latinos and the Political System,* F. Chris Garcia, ed., (Notre Dame, Ind.: University of Notre Dame Press, 1988), pp. 213–35.

[150] *United States v. Wong Kim Ark,* 169 U.S. 649 (1898).

[151] *Lau v. Nichols,* 414 U.S. 563 (1974).

bilingual ballots or oral assistance for those who speak Spanish, Chinese, Japanese, Korean, Native American languages, or Eskimo languages.

Asian Americans and Latinos have also been concerned about the impact of immigration laws on their civil rights. Many Asian American and Latino organizations opposed the Immigration Reform and Control Act of 1986 because it imposes sanctions on employers who hire undocumented workers. Such sanctions, they feared, would lead employers to discriminate against Latinos and Asian Americans. These suspicions were confirmed in a 1990 report by the General Accounting Office that found employer sanctions had created a "widespread pattern of discrimination" against Latinos and others who appear foreign.[152] Organizations such as MALDEF and the Asian Law Caucus monitor and challenge such discrimination. These groups have turned their attention to the rights of legal and illegal immigrants as anti-immigrant sentiment has grown in recent years.

The Supreme Court has ruled that illegal immigrants are eligible for education and medical care but can be denied other social benefits; legal immigrants are to be treated much the same as citizens. But growing immigration—including an estimated 300,000 illegal immigrants per year—and mounting economic insecurity have undermined these practices. Groups of voters across the country now strongly support drawing a sharper line between immigrants and citizens. Not surprisingly, the movement to deny benefits to noncitizens began in California, which experienced sharp economic distress in the early 1990s and has the highest levels of immigration of any state. In 1994, Californians voted in favor of Proposition 187, which denied illegal immigrants all services except emergency medical care. Supporters of the measure hoped to discourage illegal immigration and pressure illegal immigrants already in the country to leave. Opponents contended that denying basic services to illegal immigrants risked creating a subclass of residents in the United States whose lack of education and poor health would threaten all Americans. In 1994 and 1997, a federal court declared most of Proposition 187 unconstitutional, affirming previous rulings that illegal immigrants should be granted public education.

The question of the rights of legal immigrants points to an even tougher problem. Congress has the power to deny public benefits to this group, but doing so would go against long-standing traditions in American political culture. Legal immigrants have traditionally enjoyed most of the rights and obligations of citizens (such as paying taxes). As the constitutional scholar Alexander Bickel points out, the Constitution begins with "We the People of the United States"; likewise the Bill of Rights refers to the rights of *people,* not the rights of citizens. But even as Congress continues to debate immigration policy, several states, led by Arizona, have enacted their own laws aimed at identifying and deporting illegal immigrants within their borders. Immigration continues to be a divisive issue in American politics.

Native Americans.   The political status of Native Americans was left unclear in the Constitution. But by the early 1800s, the courts had defined each of the Indian tribes as a nation. As members of Indian nations, Native Americans were declared

---

[152] Dick Kirschten, "Not Black and White," *National Journal,* March 2, 1991, p. 497.

noncitizens of the United States. The political status of Native Americans changed in 1924, when congressional legislation granted citizenship to all those who were born in the United States. A variety of changes in federal policy toward Native Americans during the 1930s paved the way for a later resurgence of their political power. Most important was the federal decision to encourage Native Americans on reservations to establish local self-government.[153]

The Native American political movement gathered force in the 1960s as Indians began to use protest, litigation, and assertion of tribal rights to improve their situation. In 1968, Dennis Banks cofounded the American Indian Movement (AIM), the most prominent Native American protest organization. AIM won national attention in 1969 when 200 of its members, representing twenty tribes, took over the famous prison island of Alcatraz in San Francisco Bay, claiming it for Native Americans. In 1973, AIM members took over the town of Wounded Knee, South Dakota, the site of the massacre of over 200 Sioux men, women, and children by the U.S. Army in December 1890. The federal government responded to the rise in Indian activism with the Indian Self-determination and Education Assistance Act (1975), which began to give Indians more control over their own land.[154]

As a language minority, Native Americans were also affected by the 1975 amendments to the Voting Rights Act and the *Lau* decision, which established the right of Native Americans to be taught in their own languages. This ruling marked quite a change from the boarding schools once run by the Bureau of Indian Affairs, at which members of Indian tribes were forbidden to speak their own languages. Native Americans have also sought to expand their rights on the basis of their sovereign status. Since the 1920s and 1930s, Native American tribes have sued the federal government for illegally seizing land, seeking monetary reparations and land as damages. Both types of damages have been awarded in such suits, but only in small amounts. Native American tribes have been more successful in winning federal recognition of their sovereignty. Sovereign status has, in turn, allowed them to exercise greater self-determination. Most significant economically was a 1987 Supreme Court decision that freed Native American tribes from most state regulations prohibiting gambling.[155] The establishment of casino gambling on Native American lands has brought a substantial flow of new income into desperately poor reservations.

Americans with Disabilities.   The concept of rights for people with disabilities began to emerge in the 1970s as the civil rights model spread to other groups. The seed was planted in a little-noticed provision of the 1973 Rehabilitation Act that outlawed discrimination against individuals on the basis of disabilities. As in many

---

[153] Not all Indian tribes agreed with this, including the Navajos. See Ronald Takaki, *A Different Mirror: A History of Multicultural America* (Boston: Little, Brown, 1993), pp. 238–48.

[154] On the resurgence of Indian political activity, see Stephen Cornell, *The Return of the Native: American Indian Political Resurgence* (New York: Oxford University Press, 1990); and Dee Brown, *Bury My Heart at Wounded Knee* (New York: Holt, 1971).

[155] *California v. Cabazon Band of Mission Indians*, 480 U.S. 202 (1987).

other cases, the law itself helped give rise to the movement demanding rights.[156] Modeling itself on the NAACP's Legal Defense Fund, the disability movement founded a Disability Rights Education and Defense Fund to press its legal claims. The movement achieved its greatest success with the passage of the Americans with Disabilities Act (ADA) of 1990, which guarantees the disabled equal employment rights and access to public businesses. Claims of discrimination in violation of this act are considered by the EEOC. The impact of the law has been far reaching as businesses and public facilities have installed ramps, elevators, and other devices to meet its requirements.[157]

In 1998, the Supreme Court interpreted the ADA to apply to people with HIV. Until then, ADA was interpreted as applying to people with AIDS but not people with HIV. The case arose when a dentist was asked to fill a cavity for a woman with HIV; he would do it only if the procedure was done in a hospital setting. The woman sued, and her complaint was that HIV had already disabled her because it was discouraging her from having children. (The act prohibits discrimination in employment, housing, and health care.) Although there have been widespread concerns that the ADA was being expanded too broadly and the costs were becoming too burdensome, corporate America did not seem to be disturbed by the Court's ruling. Stephen Bokat, general counsel of the U.S. Chamber of Commerce, said businesses in general had already been accommodating people with HIV as well as those with AIDS and the case presented no serious problem.[158]

The Aged.   The 1967 federal Age Discrimination in Employment Act (ADEA) makes age discrimination illegal when practiced by employers with at least twenty employees. Many states have added to the federal provisions with their own age-discrimination laws, and some of the state laws are stronger than the federal provisions. The major lobbyist for seniors, AARP (formerly the American Association of Retired Persons), with its claim to more than 30 million members, has been active in keeping these laws on the books and making sure they are vigorously implemented.

Gays and Lesbians.   In less than thirty years, the gay movement has become one of the largest civil rights movements in contemporary America. Beginning with street protests in the 1960s, it has grown into a well-financed and sophisticated lobby. The Human Rights Campaign is the primary national PAC focused on gay rights; it provides campaign financing and volunteers to work for candidates

---

[156] See the discussion in Robert A. Katzmann, *Institutional Disability: The Saga of Transportation Policy for the Disabled* (Washington, D.C.: Brookings Institution, 1986).

[157] For example, after pressure from the Justice Department, one of the nation's largest rental-car companies agreed to make special hand controls available to any customer requesting them. See "Avis Agrees to Equip Cars for Disabled," *Los Angeles Times*, September 2, 1994, p. D1.

[158] The case and the interview with Stephen Bokat were reported in Margaret Warner, "Expanding Coverage: Defining Disability," *Online NewsHour*, June 30, 1998, www.pbs.org/newshour/bb/law/jan-june98/hiv_6-30.html (accessed 2/16/09).

endorsed by the group. The movement has also formed legal rights organizations, including the Lambda Legal Defense and Education Fund.

Gay rights drew national attention in 1993, when President Bill Clinton confronted the question of whether gays should be allowed to serve in the military. As a candidate, Clinton had said he favored lifting the ban on homosexuals in the military. The issue set off a huge controversy in the first months of his presidency. After nearly a year of deliberation, the administration enunciated a compromise: its "don't ask, don't tell" policy, which allows gays and lesbians to serve in the military as long as they do not openly proclaim their sexual orientation or engage in homosexual activity. The administration maintained that the ruling would protect gay men and lesbians from witch-hunting investigations, but many gay advocates expressed disappointment, charging the president with reneging on his campaign promise.

But until 1996, there was no Supreme Court ruling or national legislation explicitly protecting gays and lesbians from discrimination. The first gay rights case that the Court decided, *Bowers v. Hardwick* (1986), ruled against a right to privacy that would protect consensual homosexual activity. After the *Bowers* decision, the gay rights movement sought suitable legal cases to test the constitutionality of discrimination against gays and lesbians, much as the civil rights movement had done in the late 1940s and 1950s. As one advocate put it, "lesbians and gay men are looking for their *Brown v. Board of Education*."[159] Among the cases tested were those stemming from local ordinances restricting gay rights (including the right to marry), job discrimination, and family-law issues such as adoption and parental rights. In 1996, in *Romer v. Evans,* the Supreme Court explicitly extended fundamental civil rights protections to gays and lesbians by declaring unconstitutional a 1992 amendment to the Colorado state constitution that prohibited local governments from passing ordinances to protect gay rights.[160] The decision's forceful language highlighted the connection between gay rights and civil rights as it declared discrimination against gay people unconstitutional.

In *Lawrence v. Texas* (2003), the Court overturned *Bowers* and struck down a Texas statute criminalizing certain intimate sexual conduct between consenting partners of the same sex.[161] A victory for lesbians and gay men every bit as significant as *Roe v. Wade* was for women, *Lawrence v. Texas* extends at least one aspect of civil liberties to sexual minorities: the right to privacy. However, this decision by itself does not undo the various exclusions that deprive lesbians and gay men of full civil rights, including the right to marry, which became a hot-button issue.

Early in 2004, the Supreme Judicial Court of Massachusetts ruled that under that state's constitution same-sex couples were entitled to marry. The state senate then requested the court to rule on whether a civil-union statute (avoiding the word *marriage*) would, as it did in Vermont, satisfy the court's ruling, in response

---

[159] Quoted in Joan Biskupic, "Gay Rights Activists Seek a Supreme Court Test Case," *Washington Post,* December 19, 1993, p. A1.

[160] *Romer v. Evans,* 517 U.S. 620 (1996).

[161] *Lawrence and Garner v. Texas,* 539 U.S. 558 (2003).

to which the court ruled negatively, asserting that civil unions are too much like the "separate but equal" doctrine that maintained legalized racial segregation from 1896 to 1954. In San Francisco, meanwhile, hundreds of gay men and lesbians responded to the opportunity provided by the mayor, who had directed the city clerk to issue marriage licenses to same-sex couples in defiance of California law. At the same time, signs indicated that Massachusetts might move toward a state constitutional amendment that would ban gay unions by whatever name. Voters in Missouri and Louisiana approved a ban on same-sex marriages, joining Alaska, Hawaii, Nebraska, and Nevada in implementing such a ban. Voters in eleven other states approved similar bans in the November 2004 elections. In 2008, California voters changed the state constitution to prohibit same-sex marriage.

Affirmative Action

The politics of rights not only spread to increasing numbers of groups in society but also expanded its goal. The relatively narrow goal of equalizing opportunity by eliminating discriminatory barriers had been developing toward the far broader goal of **affirmative action**—compensatory action to overcome the consequences of past discrimination and encourage greater diversity. An affirmative action policy tends to involve two novel approaches: (1) positive or benign discrimination in which race or some other status is taken into account, but for compensatory action rather than mistreatment, and (2) compensatory action to favor members of the disadvantaged group who themselves may never have been the victims of discrimination. Quotas may be—but are not necessarily—involved in affirmative action policies.

In 1965, President Lyndon Johnson attempted to inaugurate affirmative action by executive orders directing agency heads and personnel officers to pursue vigorously a policy of minority employment in the federal civil service and in companies doing business with the national government. But affirmative action did not become a prominent goal until the 1970s.

affirmative action A policy or program designed to redress historic injustices committed against specific groups by making special efforts to provide members of these groups with access to educational and employment opportunities.

The Supreme Court and the Burden of Proof. As this movement spread, it began to divide civil rights activists and their supporters. The whole issue of qualification versus minority preference was addressed in the case of Allan Bakke. Bakke, a white man with no minority affiliation, brought suit against the University of California Medical School at Davis on the grounds that in denying him admission the school had discriminated against him on the basis of his race (that year the school had reserved 16 of 100 available slots for minority applicants). He argued that his grades and test scores had ranked him well above many students who had been accepted at the school and that the only possible explanation for his rejection was that the others were black or Hispanic and he was white. In 1978, Bakke won his case before the Supreme Court and was admitted to the medical school, but he did not succeed in getting affirmative action declared unconstitutional. The Court rejected the procedures at the University of California because its medical school had used both a quota and a separate admissions system for minorities. The Court agreed with Bakke's argument that racial categorizations are suspect categories that place a severe burden of proof on those using them to show a "compelling public purpose." The Court went on to say that achieving "a diverse student body" was such a public purpose, but the method of a rigid quota of student slots assigned on the basis of race was incompatible with the equal protection clause. Thus the Court permitted universities (and other schools, training programs, and hiring authorities) to continue to take minority status into consideration but limited severely the use of quotas to situations in which previous discrimination had been shown and the quotas were used more as a guideline for social diversity than as a mathematically defined ratio.[162]

For nearly a decade after *Bakke*, the Supreme Court was tentative and permissive about efforts by corporations and governments to experiment with affirmative action programs in employment.[163] But in 1989, the Court returned to the *Bakke* position, ruling that any "rigid numerical quota" is suspect. In *Wards Cove v. Atonio*, the Court further weakened affirmative action by easing the way for employers to prefer white men, holding that the burden of proof of unlawful discrimination should be shifted from the defendant (the employer) to the plaintiff (the person claiming to be the victim of discrimination).[164] This decision virtually overruled the Court's prior holding.[165] That same year, the Court ruled that any affirmative action program already approved by federal courts could be challenged by white men who alleged that the program discriminated against them.[166]

In 1995, the Supreme Court's ruling in *Adarand Constructors v. Pena* further weakened affirmative action. This decision stated that race-based policies, such as preferences given by the government to minority contractors, must survive strict scrutiny, placing the burden on the government to show that such affirmative action programs serve a compelling government interest and are narrowly tailored to address identifiable past discrimination.[167] President Clinton responded to the *Adarand* decision by ordering a review of all government affirmative action policies and practices. Although many observers suspected that the president would use the review as an opportunity to back away from affirmative action, the conclusions of the task force largely defended existing policies. Reflecting the influence of the Supreme Court's decision in *Adarand*, President Clinton acknowledged that some government policies would need to change. But on the whole, the review found that most affirmative action policies were fair and did not "unduly burden nonbeneficiaries."[168]

Although Clinton sought to "mend, not end" affirmative action, developments in the courts and the states continued to restrict it in important ways. One of the most significant was the *Hopwood* case, in which white students challenged admissions practices at the University of Texas Law School, charging that the school's

---

[162] *Regents of the University of California v. Bakke*, 438 U.S. 265 (1978).

[163] *United Steelworkers of America v. Weber*, 443 U.S. 193 (1979), and *Fullilove v. Klutznick*, 448 U.S. 448 (1980).

[164] *Wards Cove Packing Company v. Atonio*, 490 U.S. 642 (1989).

[165] *Griggs v. Duke Power Company* (1971).

[166] *Martin v. Wilks*, 490 U.S. 755 (1989).

[167] *Adarand Constructors v. Pena*, 515 U.S. 200 (1995).

[168] Ann Devroy, "Clinton Study Backs Affirmative Action," *Washington Post*, July 19, 1995, p. A1.

affirmative action program discriminated against whites. In 1996, a federal court ruling on the case (the U.S. Court of Appeals for the Fifth Circuit) stated that race could never be considered in granting admissions and scholarships at state colleges and universities.[169] This decision effectively rolled back the use of affirmative action permitted by the 1978 *Bakke* case. In *Bakke,* as noted earlier, the Supreme Court had outlawed quotas but said that race could be used as one factor among many in admissions decisions. Many universities and colleges have since justified affirmative action as a way of promoting racial diversity among their student bodies. What was new in the *Hopwood* decision was the ruling that race could *never* be used as a factor in admissions decisions, even to promote diversity.

In 1996, the Supreme Court refused to hear a challenge to the *Hopwood* case. This meant that its ruling remains in effect in the states covered by the Fifth Circuit—Texas, Louisiana, and Mississippi—but does not apply to the rest of the country. The impact of the *Hopwood* ruling is greatest in Texas because Louisiana and Mississippi are under conflicting court orders to desegregate their universities. In Texas in the year after the *Hopwood* case, minority applications to state universities declined. Concerned about the ability of Texas public universities to serve the state's minority students, the Texas legislature quickly passed a new law granting students who graduate in the top 10 percent of their class automatic admission to the state's public universities. State officials hoped that this measure would ensure a racially diverse student body.[170]

The weakening of affirmative action in the courts was underscored in a case the Supreme Court agreed to hear in 1998. A white schoolteacher in New Jersey who had lost her job had sued her school district, charging that her layoff was racially motivated: A black colleague hired on the same day was not laid off. Under former president George H.W. Bush, the Justice Department had filed a brief on her behalf in 1989, but in 1994 the Clinton administration formally reversed course in a new brief supporting the school district's right to make distinctions based on race as long as they did not involve the use of quotas. Three years later, the administration, worried that the case was weak and could result in a broad decision against affirmative action, reversed course again and filed a brief with the Court urging a narrow ruling in favor of the dismissed worker. Because the school board had justified its actions on the grounds of preserving diversity, the administration feared that a broad ruling by the Supreme Court could totally prohibit the use of race in employment decisions, even as one factor among many designed to achieve diversity. But before the Court could issue a ruling, a coalition of civil rights groups brokered and arranged to pay for a settlement. This unusual move reflected the widespread fear of a sweeping negative decision. Cases involving dismissals, as the New Jersey case did, are generally viewed as much more difficult to defend than cases that concern hiring. In addition, the particular facts of the New Jersey

---

[169] *Hopwood v. State of Texas,* 78 F. 3d 932 (Fifth Cir., 1996).

[170] See Lydia Lum, "Applications by Minorities Down Sharply," *Houston Chronicle,* April 8, 1997, p. A1; R.G. Ratcliffe, "Senate Approves Bill Designed to Boost Minority Enrollments," *Houston Chronicle,* May 8, 1997, p. A1.

case—two equally qualified teachers hired on the same day—were seen as unusual and unfavorable to affirmative action.[171]

This betwixt-and-between status of affirmative action was where things stood in 2003, when the Supreme Court took two cases against the University of Michigan that were virtually certain to clarify, if not put closure on, affirmative action. The first suit, *Gratz v. Bollinger,* alleged that by using a point-based ranking system that automatically awarded 20 points (out of 150) to African American, Latino, and Native American applicants, the university's undergraduate admissions policy discriminated unconstitutionally against white students with otherwise equal or superior academic qualifications. The Supreme Court agreed, 6–3, arguing that something tantamount to a quota was involved because undergraduate admissions lacked the necessary "individualized consideration," employing instead a "mechanical one," based too much on the favorable minority points.[172] The Court's ruling in *Gratz v. Bollinger* was not surprising, given *Bakke's* holding against quotas and recent decisions calling for strict scrutiny of all racial classifications, even those that are intended to remedy past discrimination or promote future equality.

The second case, *Grutter v. Bollinger,* broke new ground. Barbara Grutter sued the University of Michigan Law School on the grounds that it had discriminated in a race-conscious way against white applicants with grades and law boards equal or superior to those of minority applicants. A precarious vote of 5–4 aligned the majority of the Supreme Court with Justice Lewis Powell's opinion in *Bakke* for the first time. In *Bakke,* Powell had argued that diversity in education is a compelling state interest and that constitutionally race could be considered a positive factor in admissions decisions. In *Grutter,* the Court reiterated Powell's holding and, applying strict scrutiny to the law school's policy, found that its admissions process was narrowly tailored to the school's compelling state interest in diversity because it gave a "highly individualized, holistic review of each applicant's file," in which race counted but was not used in a "mechanical way."[173]

Throughout the 1990s, federal courts, including the Supreme Court, had subjected public affirmative action programs to strict scrutiny to invalidate them. *Adarand Constructors v. Pena* (1995) definitively established the Supreme Court's view that constitutionally permissible use of race must serve a compelling state interest. Between *Korematsu v. United States* (1944)[174] and *Grutter,* no consideration of race had survived strict scrutiny. Such affirmative action plans that had survived constitutional review did so before 1995, under a lower standard of review, one reserved for policies intended to remedy racial injustice. For affirmative action to survive under the post-1995 judicial paradigm, the Court needed to find that sometimes racial categories can be deployed to serve a compelling state interest. That the Court found exactly this in *Grutter* puts affirmative action on stronger

---

[171] Linda Greenhouse, "Settlement Ends High Court Case on Preferences," *New York Times,* November, 22 1997, p. A1; Barry Bearak, "Rights Groups Ducked a Fight, Opponents Say," *New York Times,* November, 22 1997, p. A1.

[172] *Gratz v. Bollinger,* 539 U.S. 244 (2003).

[173] *Grutter v. Bollinger,* 539 U.S. 306 (2003).

[174] *Korematsu v. United States,* 323 U.S. 214 (1944).

ground—at least if its specific procedures pass the Supreme Court's muster and until the Court's majority changes. A recent affirmative action case that attracted wide attention was *Ricci v. DeStefano,* in which the Court ruled that New Haven, Connecticut officials had discriminated against white firefighters when they threw out a promotions exam because no nonwhite candidate received a high enough score for promotion.[175] The Court said that employers must show "a strong basis in evidence" under Title VII of the Civil Rights Act and may not rely simply on a test's outcome to show racial discrimination.

Referendums on Affirmative Action. The courts have not been the only center of action: Challenges to affirmative action have also emerged in state and local politics, in the form of ballot initiatives or referendums that ask voters to decide the issue. One of the most significant state actions was the passage of the California Civil Rights Initiative, also known as Proposition 209, in 1996. Proposition 209 outlawed affirmative action programs in the state and local governments of California, thus prohibiting state and local governments from using race or gender preferences in their decisions about hiring, contracting, and university admissions. The political battle over Proposition 209 was heated, and supporters and defenders took to the streets and airwaves to make their case. When the referendum was held, the measure passed with 54 percent of the vote, including 27 percent of the black vote, 30 percent of the Latino vote, and 45 percent of the Asian American vote.[176] In 1997, the Supreme Court refused to hear a challenge to the new law.

Many observers predicted that the success of California's ban on affirmative action would provoke similar movements in states and localities across the country. But the political factors that contributed to the success of Proposition 209 in California may not exist in many other states. Winning a controversial state referendum takes leadership and lots of money. The popular California Republican governor Pete Wilson led with a strong anti-affirmative action stand (favoring Proposition 209), and his campaign had a lot of money for advertising. But similar conditions did not exist elsewhere. Few prominent Republican leaders in other states were willing to come forward to lead the anti-affirmative action campaign. Moreover, the outcome of any referendum, especially a complicated and controversial one, depends greatly on how the issue is drafted and placed on the ballot. California's Proposition 209 was framed as a civil rights initiative: "The state shall not discriminate against, or grant preferential treatment to, any individual or group on the basis of race, sex, color, ethnicity, or national origin." Different wording can produce quite different outcomes, as a 1997 vote on affirmative action in Houston revealed. There the ballot initiative asked voters whether they wanted to ban affirmative action in city contracting and hiring, not whether they wanted to end preferential treatment. In that city, 55 percent of voters decided in favor of affirmative action.[177]

---

[175] *Ricci v. DeStefano,* 07-1428 (2009).

[176] Michael A. Fletcher, "Opponents of Affirmative Action Heartened by Court Decision," *Washington Post,* April 13, 1997, p. A21.

[177] See Sam Howe Verhovek, "Houston Vote Underlined Complexity of Rights Issue," *New York Times,* November 6, 1997, p. A1.

Civil Liberties and Civil Rights: Limiting and Regulating Collective Action

Over the past century, America has strengthened its citizens' liberties and expanded their rights. Both civil liberties and civil rights are solutions to collective-action problems. Strengthening the former means imposing more restrictions on some forms of collective action. Expanding the later means allowing more individuals to take part in collective decision making and imposing restrictions on the sorts of decisions that can be reached.

Institutions help to solve collective action problems, but no particular solution is carved in stone. Contending political forces continually seek to change the institutional rules to serve their particular purposes. In the United States today, for example, some groups argue that the government's jurisdiction needs to be expanded to counter the threat of terrorism. Others assert that the nation's security can be protected without compromising liberty. The outcomes of this and other struggles over liberties and rights are never certain. Institutions matter, but exactly how they will matter in the years to come is always subject to change.

FOR FURTHER READING

Ackerman, Bruce. *Before the Next Attack: Preserving Civil Liberties in an Age of Terrorism.* New Haven, Conn.: Yale University Press, 2006.

Baer, Judith, and Leslie Goldstein. *The Constitutional and Legal Rights of Women.* Los Angeles: Roxbury, 2006.

Dawson, Michael. *Behind the Mule: Race and Class in African-American Politics.* Princeton, N.J.: Princeton University Press, 1995.

Dworkin, Ronald. *Justice in Robes.* Cambridge, Mass.: Belknap Press, 2006.

Garrow, David J. *Bearing the Cross: Martin Luther King, Jr., and the Southern Christian Leadership Conference: A Personal Portrait.* New York: Morrow, 1986.

Gerstmann, Evan. *Same-Sex Marriage and the Constitution.* New York: Cambridge University Press, 2004.

Glendon, Mary Ann. *Rights Talk: The Impoverishment of Political Discourse.* New York: Free Press, 1991.

Greenberg, Jack. *Crusaders in the Courts: How a Dedicated Band of Lawyers Fought for the Civil Rights Revolution.* New York: Basic Books, 1994.

Jackson, Thomas. *From Civil Rights to Human Rights.* Philadelphia: University of Pennsylvania Press, 2006.

Klarman, Michael. *From Jim Crow to Civil Rights: The Supreme Court and the Struggle for Racial Equality.* New York: Oxford University Press, 2004.

Levy, Leonard W. *Freedom of Speech and Press in Early America: Legacy of Suppression.* New York: Harper & Row, 1963.

reader selection

Lewis, Anthony. *Gideon's Trumpet.* New York: Random House, 1964.

Meltsner, Michael. *The Making of a Civil Rights Lawyer.* Charlottesville: University of Virginia Press, 2006.

Posner, Richard. *Not a Suicide Pact: The Constitution in a Time of National Emergency.* New York: Oxford University Press, 2006.

Rosenberg, Gerald N. *The Hollow Hope: Can Courts Bring About Social Change?* 2nd ed. Chicago: University of Chicago Press, 2008.

Tushnet, Mark, and Michael Olivas. *Colored Men and Hombres Aqui:* Hernandez v. Texas *and the Emergence of Mexican American Lawyering.* Houston: Arte Publico Press, 2006.

Yoshino, Kenji. *Covering: The Hidden Assault on Our Civil Rights.* New York: Random House, 2007.

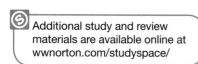

Additional study and review materials are available online at wwnorton.com/studyspace/

PART TWO

Institutions

5

Congress: The First Branch

The U.S. Congress is the "first branch" of government under Article I of our Constitution and is also among the world's most important representative bodies. Many of the world's representative bodies only represent—that is, their governmental functions consist mainly of affirming and legitimating the national leadership's decisions. The only national representative body that actually possesses powers of governance is the U.S. Congress. For example, the U.S. Congress never accedes to the president's budget proposals without making major changes, but both the British House of Commons and the Japanese Diet always accept the budget exactly as proposed by the government.

This unique status of the American Congress provides an illustration of the institution principle. In the separation-of-powers regime institutionalized by the U.S. Constitution, the American executive cannot govern alone. The legislature, in particular, actively participates. In Richard Neustadt's memorable phrase, the executive and the legislature in the United States are "separated institutions sharing power."[1] In parliamentary regimes, such as Britain or Japan, in contrast, the executive controls its majority in parliament. These different institutional arrangements give different powers to different players. In the American case, the institutional arrangements were intended to give Congress a great deal of power relative to the president.

Congress controls a formidable battery of powers that it uses to shape policies and, when necessary, defend its prerogatives against the executive branch. Congress has vast authority over the two most important powers given to any government: the power of force (control over the nation's military forces) and the power over money. Specifically, according to Article I, Section 8, Congress can "lay and collect Taxes,"

---

[1] Richard E. Neustadt, *Presidential Power: The Politics of Leadership* (New York: Wiley, 1960), p. 42.

deal with indebtedness and bankruptcy, impose duties, borrow and coin money, and generally control the nation's purse strings. It also may "provide for the common Defence and general Welfare," regulate interstate commerce, undertake public works, acquire and control federal lands, promote science and "useful Arts" (pertaining mostly to patents and copyrights), and regulate the militia.

In the realm of foreign policy, Congress has the power to declare war, deal with piracy, regulate foreign commerce, and raise and regulate the armed forces and military installations. These powers over war and the military are supreme—even the president, as commander in chief of the military, must obey the laws and orders of Congress *if* Congress chooses to assert its constitutional authority. (In the past century, Congress has usually surrendered this authority to the president.) Further, the Senate has the power to approve treaties (by a two-thirds vote) and the appointment of ambassadors. Capping these powers, Congress is charged to make laws "which shall be necessary and proper for carrying into Execution the foregoing Powers, and all other Powers vested by this Constitution in the Government of the United States, or in any Department or Officer thereof."

CORE OF THE ANALYSIS

- Members of Congress, like all politicians, are ambitious and thus eager to serve the interests of their constituents in order to improve their chances of reelection.
- Congress is the most important representative institution of American government. In many ways, Congress works because its system of representation harnesses individual legislators' ambitions and puts them to use.
- The internal organization of Congress solves the collective-action problems that arise due to the many and varied goals of individual legislators.
- Rules matter in the legislative process, and the process through which a bill becomes a law affects which proposed bills succeed and in what form.

If it seems to you that many of these powers, especially those having to do with war and spending, actually belong to the president, that is because modern presidents do exercise great authority in these areas. The modern presidency is a more powerful institution than it was two centuries ago, and much of that power has come from Congress, either because Congress has delegated the power to the president by law or because Congress has simply allowed, or even urged, presidents to be more active in these areas.[2] As we noted in Chapter 1, institutions evolve over time, as the various players seek to adapt them to their purposes. This helps explain why today the executive branch seems like a more important branch of government than Congress. Still, the constitutional powers of Congress remain intact in the document. As we shall see, congressional power cannot be separated from congressional representation. Indeed, there is a reciprocal relationship between the two. Without its array of powers, Congress could do little to represent effectively the views and interests of its constituents. At the same time, the power of Congress is ultimately a function of its capacity to represent important groups and forces in American society effectively. As we will see, all five principles of politics from Chapter 1 are important to our understanding of the institutional structure of the contemporary Congress.

We begin our discussion with a brief consideration of representation. Then we examine the institutional structure of the contemporary Congress and the manner in which congressional powers are organized and employed. Throughout, we point out the connections between these two aspects—the ways in which representation affects congressional operations (especially through "the electoral connection") and the ways in which congressional institutions enhance or diminish representation (especially Congress's division-of-labor and specialization-of-labor committee system).

---

[2] On the issue of congressional delegation to the executive, two valuable sources are D. Roderick Kiewiet and Mathew D. McCubbins, *The Logic of Delegation: Congressional Parties and the Appropriations Process* (Chicago: University of Chicago Press, 1991); and David Epstein and Sharyn O'Halloran, *Delegating Powers: A Transaction Cost Politics Approach to Policy Making under Separate Powers* (New York: Cambridge University Press, 1999).

REPRESENTATION

Congress is the most important representative institution in American government. Each member's primary responsibility is to the district, to his or her **constituency**, not to the congressional leadership, a party, or even Congress itself. Yet the task of representation is not a simple one. Views about what constitutes fair and effective representation differ, and constituents can make very different kinds of demands on their representatives. Members of Congress must consider these diverse views and demands as they represent their districts (Figure 5.1).

Legislators generally vary in the weight they give to personal priorities and the things their campaign contributors and past supporters desire. Some see themselves as perfect agents of others: They have been elected to do the bidding of those who sent them to the legislature, and they act as **delegates**. Others see themselves as having been selected by their fellow citizens to do what they think is "right," and they act as **trustees**. Most legislators are a mix of these two types. And all, one way

FIGURE 5.1 HOW MEMBERS OF CONGRESS REPRESENT THEIR DISTRICTS

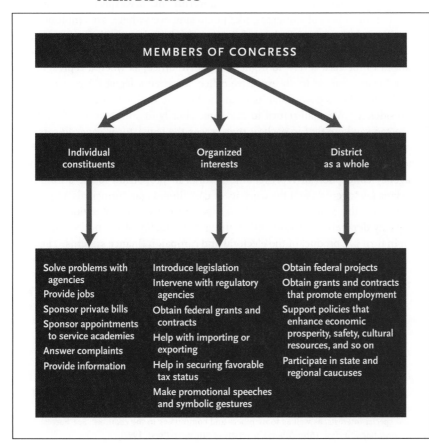

or another, need to survive the next election in order to pursue whatever role they formulate for themselves. Rational agents necessarily must focus on survival.

As we discussed in Chapter 1, one person might be trusted to speak for another if the two are formally bound together so that the representative is in some way accountable to those he or she purports to represent. If representatives can somehow be punished or held to account for failing to speak properly for their constituents, then we know they have an incentive to provide good representation even if their own backgrounds, views, and interests differ from those of the people they represent. This idea is called **agency representation**—the sort of representation that takes place when constituents have the power to hire and fire their representatives (who act as their agents). Frequent competitive elections are an important means by which constituents hold their representatives to account and keep them responsive to their own views and preferences. The idea of a representative as agent is similar to the relationship between lawyer and client. True, the relationship between the member of Congress and as many as 630,000 "clients" in the district or that between the senator and millions of clients in the state is very different from that of the lawyer and client. But the criteria of performance are comparable.

We would expect at the very least that each representative will constantly be seeking to discover the interests of the constituency and will be speaking for those interests in Congress and other centers of government.[3] We expect this because we believe that members of Congress, like politicians everywhere, are ambitious. For many, this ambition is satisfied simply by maintaining a hold on their present office and advancing up the rungs of power in that body. Some, however, may be looking ahead to the next level—to higher legislative office, as when a representative seeks a Senate seat, or to an executive office, as when a legislator returns home to run for the state's governorship, or at the highest level, when a legislator seeks the presidency.[4] We shall return to this topic shortly in a discussion of elections. But we can say here that in each of these cases the legislator is eager to serve the interests of constituents, either to enhance his or her prospects of contract renewal at the next election or to improve the chances of moving to another level. In short, the agency conception of representation works in proportion to the ambition of politicians (as "agents") and the capacity of constituents (as "principals") to reward or punish on the basis of the legislator's performance and reputation.[5] This latter capacity depends on, among other things, the quality of political competition, which in turn is a product of the electoral and campaign finance systems. These institutional arrangements set the strategic context for electoral competition and thus

---

[3] The classic description of interactions between politicians and "the folks back home" is given by Richard F. Fenno, Jr., *Home Style: House Members in Their Districts* (Boston: Little, Brown, 1978). Essays elaborating on Fenno's classic are found in Morris P. Fiorina and David W. Rohde, eds., *Home Style and Washington Work* (Ann Arbor: University of Michigan Press, 1989).

[4] For more on political careers generally, see John R. Hibbing, "Legislative Careers: Why and How We Should Study Them," *Legislative Studies Quarterly* 24 (1999): 149–71. See also Cherie D. Maestas, Sarah Lutton, L. Sandy Maisel, and Walter J. Stone, "When to Risk It? Institutions, Ambitions, and the Decision to Run for the U.S. House," *American Political Science Review* 100, no. 2 (May 2006): 195–208.

[5] Constituents aren't a legislative agent's only principals. He or she may also be beholden to party leaders and special interests, as well as to members and committees in the chamber. See Forrest Maltzman, *Competing Principals* (Ann Arbor: University of Michigan Press, 1997).

agency representation The type of representation according to which representatives are held accountable to their constituents if they fail to represent them properly. That is, constituents have the power to hire and fire their representatives.

determine how effectively constituent-principals can keep their legislator-agent's nose to the grindstone.

House and Senate: Differences in Representation

The framers of the Constitution provided for a **bicameral legislature**—a legislative body consisting of two chambers. As we saw in Chapter 2, the framers intended each of these chambers, the House and the Senate, to represent a different constituency. Members of the House were to be "close to the people," elected by popular vote every two years. Members of the the Senate, on the other hand, were appointed by state legislatures for six-year terms, were to represent the elite members of society, and were to be attuned more to the interests of property than to those of the population. Today members of both the House and the Senate are elected directly by the people. The 435 members of the House are elected from districts apportioned according to population; the 100 members of the Senate are elected by state, with two senators from each. Senators continue to have longer terms in office and usually represent much larger and more diverse constituencies than do their counterparts in the House of Representatives (Table 5.1).

The House and the Senate play different roles in the legislative process. In essence, the Senate is the more deliberative of the two bodies: It is the forum in which any and all ideas can receive a thorough public airing. The House is the more centralized and the more organized of the two bodies: It is better equipped to play a routine role in the governmental process. In part, this difference stems from the different rules governing the two bodies. These rules give House leaders more control over the legislative process and provide for House members to specialize in certain legislative areas. The rules of the much smaller, more free-wheeling Senate give its leadership relatively little power and discourage specialization. This is the institution principle at work. The two legislative chambers are organized in very different ways, reflecting not only their differences in size but also their differences in

bicameral legislature
A legislative assembly composed of two chambers, or houses.

TABLE 5.1 DIFFERENCES BETWEEN THE HOUSE AND THE SENATE

	House	Senate
Minimum age of member	25 years	30 years
Length of U.S. citizenship	At least 7 years	At least 9 years
Length of term	2 years	6 years (staggered)
Number per state	Depends on population: 1 per 30,000 in 1789; 1 per 630,000 today	2 per state
Constituency	Tends to be local	Is both local and national

electoral rhythm, constituencies, and roles. House members specialize, their specialized activities take place mainly in committees, and deliberations by the full House take place mainly in response to committee proposals. The institution is organized to facilitate expeditious consideration of committee bills. The Senate does many of the same things. But senators are less specialized, partly because of their more heterogeneous constituencies, and therefore involve themselves in many more areas of policy. Senate proceedings permit wider participation and more open-ended deliberation.

Both formal and informal factors also contribute to the differences between the two chambers of Congress. Differences in the length of terms and the requirements for holding office specified by the Constitution generate differences in how the members of each body develop their constituencies and exercise their powers of office. The result is that members of the House more effectively and more frequently serve as the agents of well-organized local interests with specific legislative agendas—for instance, used-car dealers seeking relief from regulation, labor unions seeking more favorable legislation, or farmers looking for higher subsidies. The small size and relative homogeneity of their constituencies and the frequency with which they must seek reelection make House members more attuned than senators to the legislative needs of local interest groups. This is what the framers intended when they drafted the Constitution—namely, that the House of Representatives would be "the people's house" and that its members would reflect and represent public opinion in a timely manner.

Senators, on the other hand, serve larger and more heterogeneous constituencies. As a result, they are somewhat better able than members of the House to serve as the agents of groups and interests organized on a statewide or national basis. Moreover, with longer terms in office, senators have the luxury of considering "new ideas" or seeking to bring together new coalitions of interests, rather than simply serving existing ones. This, too, was the intent of the Constitution's drafters—that the Senate should provide a balance to the more responsive House, with its narrower and more homogenous constituencies. The Senate was said to be the saucer that cools the tea, bringing deliberation, debate, inclusiveness, calm, and caution to policy formulation.

In recent years, the House has exhibited considerably more intense partisanship and ideological division than the Senate. Because of their diverse constituencies, senators are more inclined to seek compromise positions that will offend as few voters and interest groups as possible. Members of the House, in contrast, with their party's domination in more homogeneous districts, are less inclined to seek compromises and more willing to stick to their partisan and ideological guns. For instance, the House divided almost exactly along partisan lines on the 1998 vote to impeach President Bill Clinton. In the Senate, by contrast, ten Republicans joined Democrats to acquit Clinton of obstruction of justice charges, and in a separate vote five Republicans joined Democrats to acquit Clinton of perjury.[6] During the presidency of George W. Bush, even the Senate grew more partisan

---

[6] Eric Pianin and Guy Gugliotta, "The Bipartisan Challenge: Senate's Search for Accord Marks Contrast to House," *Washington Post,* January 8, 1999, p. 1.

and polarized—especially on social issues and the war in Iraq.[7] More recently, in the early days of Barack Obama's presidency in the winter of 2009, the president's attempt to cope with economic crisis, legislation known as the "stimulus package," received no votes from Republicans in the House, and only three votes from moderate Republicans in the Senate.

The Electoral System

In light of their role as agents of various constituencies in their states and districts and the importance of elections as a mechanism by which principals (constituents) reward and punish their agents, representatives are very much influenced by electoral considerations. Three factors related to the American electoral system affect who gets elected and what he or she does once in office. The first set of issues concerns who decides to run for office and which candidates have an edge over others. The second issue is that of the incumbency advantage. Finally, the way congressional district lines are drawn can greatly affect the outcome of an election. Let us examine more closely the impact of these considerations on who serves in Congress.

Running for Office. Voters' choices are restricted from the start by who decides to run for office. In the past, decisions about who would run for a particular elected office were made by local party officials. A person who had a record of service to the party, or who was owed a favor, or whose "turn" had come up might be nominated by party leaders for an office.[8] Today few party organizations have the power to slate candidates in that way. Instead, the decision to run for Congress is a more personal choice. One of the most important factors determining who runs for office is a candidate's ambition.[9] A potential candidate may also assess whether he or she

---

[7] However, on the confirmation of Supreme Court nominations, even in an atmosphere of elevated partisanship moderates from both parties in the Senate have prevented partisan extremism from dominating. Chief Justice John Roberts was easily confirmed in 2005, and Justice Samuel Alito, though given a rougher ride during confirmation hearings, was approved with support from both parties in 2006. Nevertheless, Senate Democrats have blocked a number of lower court appointments proposed by the Republican administration. And the same is expected of Senate Republicans in response to Obama judicial nominations.

[8] In the nineteenth century, it was often an *obligation*, not an honor, to serve in Congress. The real political action was back home in the state capital or a big city, not in Washington. So the practice of "rotation" was devised, according to which a promising local politician would do a tour of duty in Washington before being slated for an important local office. This is not to say that electoral incentives—the so-called electoral connection, in which a legislator's behavior was motivated by the desire to retain the seat for himself or his party—was absent in nineteenth-century America. See, for example, Jamie L. Carson and Erik J. Engstrom, "Assessing the Electoral Connection Evidence from the Early United States," *American Journal of Political Science* 49 (2005): 746–57. See also William T. Bianco, David B. Spence, and John D. Wilkerson, "The Electoral Connection in the Early Congress: The Case of the Compensation Act of 1816," *American Journal of Political Science* 40 (1996): 145–71.

[9] See Linda L. Fowler and Robert D. McClure, *Political Ambition: Who Decides to Run for Congress* (New Haven, Conn.: Yale University Press, 1989); and Alan Ehrenhalt, *The United States of Ambition: Politicians, Power, and the Pursuit of Office* (New York: Times Books, 1991).

can attract enough money to mount a credible campaign. The ability to raise money depends on connections to other politicians, interest groups, and the national party organization. Wealthy individuals may finance their own races. In 2000, for example, the New Jersey Democrat and former investment banker Jon Corzine spent more than $60 million of his own money to win a U.S. Senate seat. (In 2005, he spent a similar amount of money to win the governorship of New Jersey.)

Features distinctive to each congressional district also affect the field of candidates. Among them are the range of other political opportunities that may lure potential candidates away. In addition, the way the congressional district overlaps state legislative boundaries may affect a candidate's decision to run. A state-level representative or senator who is considering a run for the U.S. Congress is more likely to assess his or her prospects favorably if the state district coincides with the congressional district (because the voters will already know him or her). For similar reasons, U.S. representatives from small states, whose congressional districts overlap a large portion of the state, are far more likely to run for statewide office than members of Congress from large states. For example, John Thune was elected as the lone representative from South Dakota in 1996. His constituency thus completely overlapped those of Senators Tim Johnson and Tom Daschle. In 2002, Thune challenged Johnson, losing by barely 500 votes. In 2004, he defeated Daschle, then the Democratic leader in the Senate. For any candidate, decisions about running must be made early because once money has been committed to declared candidates, it is harder for new candidates to break into a race. Thus the outcome of a November election is partially determined many months earlier, when decisions to run are finalized.[10]

Incumbency. **Incumbency** plays a very important role in the American electoral system and in the kind of representation citizens get in Washington. Once in office, members of Congress are typically eager to remain in office and make politics a career. Over the twentieth century, Congress developed into a professional legislature, a legislature whose members serve full time for multiple terms (Figure 5.2).[11] The career ambitions of members of Congress are helped by an array of tools that they can use to stack the deck in favor of their reelection. These tools have been created by incumbent legislators themselves to aid their own cause—the rationality principle at work once again. Through effective use of this arsenal of weapons, an incumbent establishes a reputation for competence, imagination, and responsiveness—the attributes most principals look for in an agent. One tool of incumbency is the franking privilege. Under a law enacted by the First Congress in 1789, members of Congress may send mail to their constituents free of charge to keep them informed of governmental business and public affairs. Under current law, members receive an average of about $100,000 in free postage for mailings to their constituents. There is a great variety of franked mail. Some target

---

[10] Thus the timing of Hurricane Katrina was especially propitious for the Democrats and unfortunate for the Republicans. Occurring in September 2005, the hurricane gave the Democrats a long lead time in which to recruit high-quality candidates to contest the November 2006 congressional elections while discouraging high-quality Republican candidates. On the thesis of "strategic candidacy," see Gary C. Jacobson, *The Politics of Congressional Elections*, 6th ed. (New York: Pearson Longman, 2004).

[11] Nelson W. Polsby, "The Institutionalization of the U.S. House of Representatives," *American Political Science Review* 62, no. 1 (March 1968): 144–68.

FIGURE 5.2 TURNOVER IN THE HOUSE REPRESENTATIVES

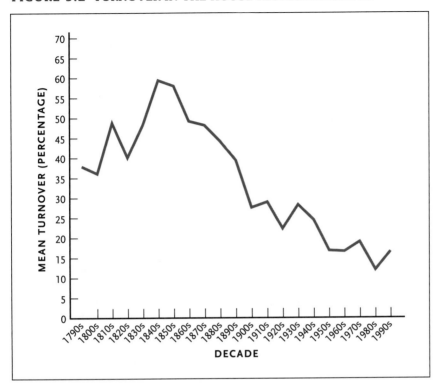

NOTE: Overall for this period, the mean turnover was 30.7 percent.

SOURCE: Based on John Swain, Stephen A. Borelli, Brian C. Reed, and Sean F. Evans, "A New Look at Turnover in the U.S. House of Representatives, 1789–1998," *American Politics Quarterly* 28 (2000): 435–57.

special groups on issues of direct interest to them—for example, news about minimum wage legislation sent to union households in the district. Most common of all are "your congressman at work" newsletters, which are sent to households in an entire district on a regular basis.

Members may not use these funds to send mail outside their districts, however, or to send mass mailings within ninety days of a primary or general election. Despite the restrictions, the franking privilege provides incumbents with a valuable resource for publicizing their activities and making themselves visible to voters.

A particularly important tool is the incumbent's reputation for constituency service: taking care of the problems and requests of individual voters. Through such services and their advertisement by word of mouth, the incumbent seeks to establish an attractive political reputation and a "personal" relationship with his or her constituents. Well over a quarter of the representatives' time and nearly two-thirds of the time of their staff members is devoted to constituency service (termed **casework**). This service is not merely a matter of writing and mailing letters. It includes talking to constituents, providing them with minor services, presenting special bills for them, and attempting to influence decisions by regulatory

casework An effort by members of Congress to gain the trust and support of constituents by providing personal service. One important type of casework consists of helping constituents obtain favorable treatment from the federal bureaucracy.

commissions on their behalf. Indeed, one might think of the member's legislative staff and office operation as a congressional enterprise, much like a firm, with the member himself or herself as the chief executive officer.[12]

One very direct way in which incumbent members of Congress serve as the agents of their constituencies is through **patronage.** Patronage refers to a variety of forms of direct services and benefits that members provide for their districts. One of the most important forms of patronage is **pork-barrel legislation.** Through pork-barrel legislation, representatives seek to capture federal projects and federal funds for their districts (or states in the case of senators) and thus "bring home the bacon."

A common form of pork barreling is the earmark, the practice through which members of Congress insert into otherwise pork-free bills language that provides special benefits for their own constituents.[13] For example, among the more outrageous earmarks in a 2005 transportation bill was a bridge in Alaska that cost more than $10 million and connected the mainland to an island on which no one lives (the so-called "bridge to nowhere"). This earmark proved so embarrassing to the Republicans once they began receiving adverse publicity that they rescinded the appropriation.

So why do legislators continue this practice? One answer is that each legislator can credibly and visibly claim personal responsibility, and thus take personal credit, for earmarked programs and special highway projects. This credit enhances the legislator's reputation back home as a Washington mover and shaker while enhancing his or her reelection prospects. If the same money came to the states or districts through an existing program, such as the Highway Trust Fund, the individual legislator would get little credit for it. (As with the bridge to nowhere, however, sometimes this practice can backfire.)

Pork-barrel activities by incumbent legislators bring a number of our principles from Chapter 1 into play. Incumbent legislators engage in the practice because it furthers their electoral objectives (the rationality principle). They succeed to the degree that they are able to join with fellow legislators in exchanging support for each other's projects (the collective-action principle). These efforts are facilitated by institutional procedures: amendments to appropriations bills, omnibus legislation, opportunities to insert special provisions into bills (the institution principle). And they decidedly influence the mix and location of spending by the federal government (the policy principle). From time to time, as with the "bridge to nowhere," the practice becomes so egregious that Congress establishes procedures to restrict the activity, thereby constraining the actions of members of Congress in the future (the history principle). Contemporary excesses have led many in Congress

[12] For more on the congressional office as an enterprise that processes the casework demands of constituents, see Robert H. Salisbury and Kenneth A. Shepsle, "Congressman as Enterprise," *Legislative Studies Quarterly* 6 (1981): 559–76.

[13] For a study of academic earmarking, see James D. Savage, *Funding Science in America: Congress, Universities, and the Politics of the Academic Pork Barrel* (New York: Cambridge University Press, 1999). For a general study of pork-barrel activity, see the excellent book by Diana Evans, *Greasing the Wheels: Using Pork Barrel Projects to Build Majority Coalitions in Congress* (New York: Cambridge University Press, 2004).

patronage The resources available to higher officials, usually opportunities to make partisan appointments to offices and confer grants, licenses, or special favors to supporters.

pork-barrel legislation The appropriations made by legislative bodies for local projects that often are not needed but are created so that local representatives can carry their home district in the next election.

FIGURE 5.3 THE POWER OF INCUMBENCY

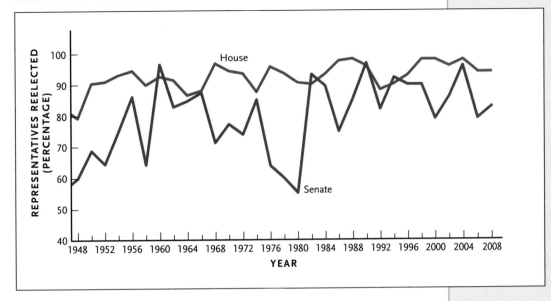

SOURCE: Center for Responsive Politics, www.opensecrets.org/bigpicture/reelect, and authors' update.

to begin considering ways to limit earmarks. The 110th Congress (2007–2008) instituted the practice of identifying the legislator who sponsored an earmark. This may decrease those projects introduced on behalf of narrow special interests. But the rationality principle tells us that it will not diminish those aimed at the geographic constituency, because reelection-oriented incumbents benefit from their ability to target their states and districts for federal spending.

The incumbency advantage is evident in the high rates of reelection among congressional incumbents: over 90 percent for House members and nearly 90 percent for members of the Senate in recent years (Figure 5.3).[14] In 2006, 93 percent of House incumbents won reelection: an amazing 100 percent of the Democratic incumbents and 87 percent of the Republicans. In the Senate in 2006, most incumbents also prevailed. In 2008, 95 percent of House incumbents running in the general election were successful, and 85 percent of incumbent senators were reelected. In the 2010 elections, dozens of incumbent Democrats lost their seats to Republican challengers, but still a majority of all incumbents (from both parties) who ran held onto their seats.

---

[14] Norman J. Ornstein, Thomas E. Mann, and Michael J. Malbin, *Vital Statistics on Congress, 1995–1996* (Washington, D.C.: Congressional Quarterly Press, 1996), pp. 60–61 (see also subsequent editions); Robert S. Erickson and Gerald C. Wright, "Voters, Candidates, and Issues in Congressional Elections," in *Congress Reconsidered*, 8th ed., Lawrence C. Dodd and Bruce I. Oppenheimer, eds. (Washington, D.C.: CQ Press, 2005), pp. 77–106; and John R. Alford and David W. Brady, "Personal and Partisan Advantage in U.S. Congressional Elections, 1846–1990," in *Congress Reconsidered*, pp. 141–57.

The incumbency advantage is also evident in what is called sophomore surge—the tendency for candidates to win a higher percentage of the vote when seeking their second term in office than they won in their initial election victory. Once in office, members of Congress find it much easier to raise campaign funds and are thus able to outspend their challengers (Figure 5.4).[15] Over the past quarter century, and despite many campaign finance regulations that were meant to level the playing field, the gap between incumbent and challenger spending has grown. Members of the majority party in the House and Senate are particularly attractive to donors who want access to those in power.[16]

Incumbency can help a candidate by scaring off potential challengers. In many races, potential candidates may decide not to run because they fear that the incumbent has simply brought too many benefits to the district, has too much money, or is too well liked or too well known.[17] Potentially strong challengers may also decide that a district's partisan leanings are too unfavorable.

The eighth district of Massachusetts provides a notable example. Represented by, among others, John F. Kennedy (1947–52) and Thomas "Tip" O'Neill (1953–86), who became president and Speaker of the House, respectively, this seat became vacant when the incumbent Joseph Patrick Kennedy (1987–98) left office. A wide-open Democratic primary, attracting more than a dozen candidates, selected the mayor of Somerville, Mike Capuano, who went on to win the general election easily in this urban, heavily Democratic district. Capuano has remained in this seat ever since, facing only token opposition in each election and rolling up huge majorities.

The advantage of incumbency thus tends to preserve the status quo in Congress by discouraging potentially strong challengers from running. When incumbents do face strong challengers, they are often defeated.[18] The reason is that strong challengers are willing to throw their hat into the ring only when they believe the incumbent is weak, out of touch, too preoccupied with national affairs, or plagued by scandal or declining capabilities. Indeed, incumbents afflicted in any of these ways may choose to retire voluntarily (strategic retirement) instead of facing the high probability of defeat. Another source of incumbent vulnerability is the unpopularity of their party label. In 2006, Senator Lincoln Chafee (R-R.I.) illustrated the latter. Despite a personal popularity rating of 62 percent in the polls, he was defeated as many Rhode Islanders signaled their displeasure with the Bush administration and the Republican Congress.

The role of incumbency also has implications for the social composition of Congress. For example, the incumbency advantage makes it harder for women to increase their numbers in Congress because most incumbents are men. Female candidates who run for open seats (for which there are no incumbents) are just as

---

[15] Stephen Ansolabehere and James Snyder, "Campaign War Chests and Congressional Elections," *Business and Politics* 2 (2000): 9–34.

[16] Gary W. Cox and Eric Magar, "How Much Is Majority Status in the U.S. Congress Worth?" *American Political Science Review* 93, no. 2 (June 1999): 299–309.

[17] Kenneth Bickers and Robert Stein, "The Electoral Dynamics of the Federal Pork Barrel," *American Journal of Political Science* 40 (1996): 1300–26.

[18] Jacobson, *The Politics of Congressional Elections.*

FIGURE 5.4 HOUSE AND SENATE CAMPAIGN EXPENDITURES

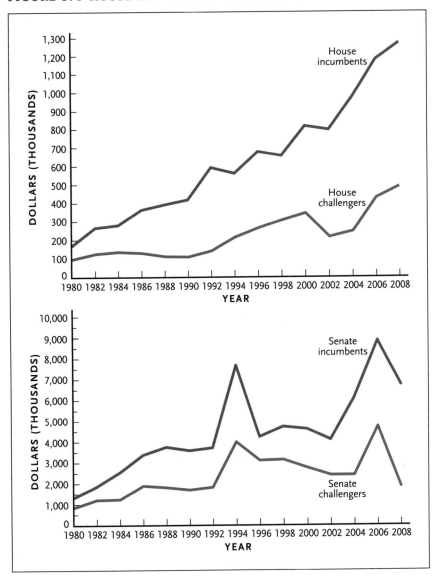

SOURCE: Norman J. Ornstein, Thomas E. Mann, and Michael J. Malbin, *Vital Statistics on Congress, 2001–2002* (Washington, D.C.: American Enterprise Institute, 2002), pp. 87, 93, and Campaign Finance Institute, www.cfinst.org.

likely to win as male candidates but they have to wait until a seat opens up.[19] Supporters of term limits argue that such limits are the best way to get new faces into Congress. They believe that the incumbency advantage and the tendency of many legislators to view politics as a career mean that very little turnover will occur in Congress unless limits are imposed on the number of terms a legislator can serve.

But the tendency toward the status quo is not absolute. In recent years, political observers have suggested that the incumbency advantage may be declining. In the 1992 and 1994 elections, for example, voters expressed considerable anger and dissatisfaction with incumbents, producing a 25 percent turnover in the House in 1992 and a 20 percent turnover in 1994. Yet the defeat of incumbents was not the main factor at work in either of these elections; 88.3 percent of House incumbents who sought reelection were reelected in 1992, and 90.2 percent won reelection in 1994. In 1992, it was an exceptionally high retirement rate (20 percent, as opposed to the norm of 10 percent) among members of Congress that created more open seats and brought new faces into Congress.[20] In 1994, a large number of open seats combined with an unprecedented mobilization of Republican voters to shift control of Congress to the Republican Party. In 2006, the reverse happened. The Democrats needed to gain fifteen seats to capture the House, and they won double that number; in the Senate, they captured the six Republican seats they needed to win control of that chamber.

Congressional Districts.   The final factor that affects who wins a seat in Congress is the way congressional districts are drawn. Every ten years, state legislatures must redraw congressional districts to reflect population changes. In 1929, Congress enacted a law fixing the total number of congressional seats at 435. As a result, when states with growing populations gain districts, they do so at the expense of states with slower population growth. In recent decades, this has meant that the nation's growth areas in the South and West have gained congressional seats at the expense of the Northeast and the Midwest (Figure 5.5). After the 2000 census, for example, Arizona, Texas, Florida, and Georgia each gained two seats, whereas New York and Pennsylvania each lost two seats. Redrawing congressional districts is a highly political process: Districts are shaped to create an advantage for the majority party in the state legislature, which controls the redistricting process. In this complex process, those charged with drawing districts use sophisticated computer technologies to come up with the most favorable district boundaries. Redistricting can create open seats and may pit incumbents of the same party against each other, ensuring that one of them will lose. Redistricting can also give an advantage to one party by clustering voters with some ideological or sociological characteristics in a single district or by separating those voters into two or more districts. **Gerrymandering** can have a major effect on the outcome of congressional elections. Before 1980, for example, California's House seats had been almost evenly divided between the two

gerrymandering
The apportionment of voters in districts in such a way as to give unfair advantage to one political party.

---

[19] See Barbara C. Burrell, *A Woman's Place Is in the House, Campaigning for Congress in the Feminist Era* (Ann Arbor: University of Michigan Press, 1994); and David Broder, "Key to Women's Political Parity: Running," *Washington Post*, September 8, 1994, p. A17.

[20] The reason for the high voluntary retirement rate that year is interesting. Congress had passed a reform making it impossible for members to pocket money left in their office accounts when they retired. The last year in which pocketing this money was permitted was 1992, and a number of members took that opportunity to retire, some enriching themselves by hundreds of thousands of dollars.

FIGURE 5.5 APPORTIONMENT OF HOUSE SEATS BY REGION, 1910 AND 2000

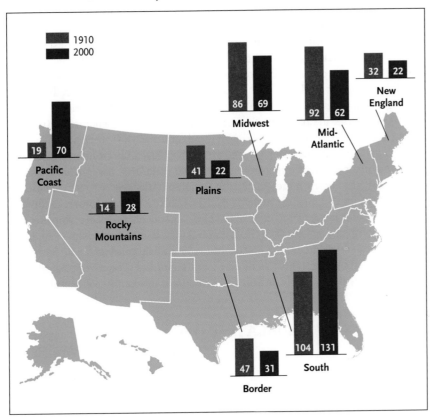

SOURCE: Norman J. Ornstein, Thomas E. Mann, and Michael J. Malbin, *Vital Statistics on Congress, 2001–2002* (Washington, D.C.: American Enterprise Institute, 2002), p. 59.

parties. After the 1980 census, a redistricting effort controlled by the Democrats, who held both houses of the state legislature as well as the governorship, resulted in Democrats' taking control of two-thirds of the state's seats in the U.S. House of Representatives.[21] Another more recent case benefited the Republicans. The 2002 congressional election was the first one under the redistricting required by the 2000 census. In 2003, the Texas legislature, controlled by the Republicans, set to work drawing up a *new* set of congressional districts. Ordinarily this exercise is performed once per decade, after the constitutionally required census. But, argued the Texas Republicans, nothing prohibits a state from doing it more frequently. Democrats in the Texas state legislature were furious and twice staged walkouts, even fleeing across the border to Oklahoma to avoid a posse of Texas Rangers sent to retrieve them. These walkouts delayed proceedings by making it difficult to assemble enough

---

[21] David Butler and Bruce Cain, *Congressional Redistricting: Comparative and Theoretical Perspectives* (New York: Macmillan, 1992).

legislators to meet the minimum requirements to do legislative business. Finally, however, the Republicans prevailed, redrawing the federal districts in a way that was very favorable to them. In the next election in 2004, the Republicans gained five seats in Texas, defeating four Democratic incumbents, in part as a result of their redistricting maneuver.[22] Examples such as these explain why the two parties invest substantial resources in state legislative and gubernatorial contests during the electoral cycle that precedes the year in which congressional district boundaries will be redrawn. The "Analyzing the Evidence" unit in Chapter 10 takes a closer look at redistricting, looking ahead to how district lines may be redrawn after the 2010 census.

As we shall see in Chapter 10, since the passage of the 1982 amendments to the 1965 Voting Rights Act, race has become a major—and controversial—consideration in drawing voting districts. These amendments, which encouraged the creation of districts in which members of racial minorities have decisive majorities, have greatly increased the number of minority representatives in Congress. After the 1991–92 redistricting, the number of predominantly minority districts doubled, from twenty-six to fifty-two. Among the most fervent supporters of the new minority districts were white Republicans, who used the opportunity to create more districts dominated by white Republican voters.[23] These developments raise thorny questions about representation. Some analysts argue that although the system may grant minorities greater sociological representation, it has made it more difficult for them to win substantive policy goals.[24]

PROBLEMS OF LEGISLATIVE ORGANIZATION

The U.S. Congress is not only a representative assembly. It is also a legislative body. For Americans, representation and legislation go hand in hand. Many parliamentary bodies, however, are representative yet lack the power to legislate. It is no small achievement that the U.S. Congress both represents *and* governs.

Governing is a challenge. It is extraordinarily difficult for a large, representative assembly to formulate, enact, and implement laws. Just the internal complexities of conducting business within Congress—the legislative process—are daunting. In addition, many individuals and institutions have the capacity to influence the legislative process. Because successful legislation requires the confluence of so many distinct factors, it is little wonder that most of the thousands of bills considered by Congress each year are defeated long before they reach the president.

The supporters of legislative proposals often feel that the formal rules of the congressional process are deliberately designed to prevent their own deserving

---

[22] In late 2004, the U.S. Supreme Court ordered a lower federal court to reconsider the "extra" Texas redistricting plan. This case worked its way back to the Supreme Court. In June 2006, the Court ruled that the Texas legislature was within its rights to redistrict more than once per decade; however, it also ruled that some of the particular decisions about district boundaries violated the rights of Latino voters

[23] David Lublin, *The Paradox of Representation: Racial Gerrymandering and Minority Interests in Congress* (Princeton, N.J.: Princeton University Press, 1997).

[24] Lani Guinier, *The Tyranny of the Majority: Fundamental Fairness in Representative Democracy* (New York: Free Press, 1995). See also David Epstein and Sharyn O'Halloran, "Measuring the Electoral and Policy Impact of Majority-Minority Voting Districts," *American Journal of Political Science* 42 (1999): 367–95.

proposals from ever seeing the light of day. But these rules allow Congress to play an important role in lawmaking. If it wants to be more than a rubber stamp for the executive branch, like so many other representative assemblies around the world, a national legislature such as the Congress must develop a division of labor, set an agenda, maintain order through rules and procedures, and place limits on discussion. If it wants to accomplish these things in a representative setting in which a veritable diversity of political preferences exists, then it must find the ways and means to allow cooperation despite the variety of interests and coalitions and to make compromises despite conflicts. We will first take up the general issues that face any legislature or decision-making group possessing diverse preferences: the problems of cooperation, coalitions, and compromises.

Cooperation in Congress

A popularly elected legislative assembly—the Boston City Council, the Kansas state legislature, the U.S. Congress, the French National Assembly, or the European Parliament—consists of politicians who harbor a variety of political objectives. Because they got where they are by winning an election and many hope to stay where they are or possibly advance their political careers, these politicians are intimately aware of whom they must please to do so:

- Because campaigns are expensive propositions, most politicians are eager to please those who can supply resources for the next campaign—campaign donors, PACs, important endorsers, party officials, volunteer activists.

- The most recent campaign—one that the politicians won—provides them with information about just why their victory was secured. It is sometimes quite difficult to sort out the myriad factors, but at the very least the politicians have a good sense of what categories of voters supported them and may be prepared to support them again if performance is adequate.

- Many politicians not only aim to please campaign contributors and voters but also have an agenda of their own. Whether for private gain or public good, politicians come to the legislature with policy goals of personal importance.

Congress consists of a heterogeneous group of legislators, and the specific public policies that they want to pursue are thus many and varied. They may be considered from two perspectives. First, owing to their different constituencies, legislators will give priority to different realms of public policy. A Cape Cod congressman will be interested in shipping, fishing, coastal preservation, harbor development, tourism, and shipbuilding. An inner-city Philadelphia congresswoman may not care much at all about those issues, focusing instead on welfare reform, civil rights policy, aid to inner-city school systems, and job-retraining programs. Montana's sole member of Congress is probably not interested in coastal preservation or inner-city schools but rather in ranching, agriculture, mining, and public land use. Evidently, Congress encompasses a mélange of legislative priorities.

Second, the opinions its members hold on any given issue are diverse. Although interest in environmental protection, for example, ranges from high among those who count many Sierra Club members among their constituents to low among those who have other fish to fry, once environmental protection is on the agenda there is a broad range of preferences for specific initiatives. Some want pollution discharges carefully monitored and regulated by a relatively powerful watchdog agency. Others believe that more decentralized and less intrusive means, such as marketable pollution permits, are the way to go. Still others think the entire issue is overblown, that any proposed cure is worse than the disease, and that the country would be best served by leaving well enough alone.

Diversity in both priorities and preferences among legislators is sufficiently abundant that the view of no group of legislators predominates. Legislative consensus must be built—this is what legislative politics is all about. Each legislator clamors to get his or her priority issue the attention he or she believes it deserves or to make sure his or her position on a given issue prevails. But neither effort is likely to succeed on its own merits. Support must be assembled, deals consummated, and promises and threats used. In short, legislators intent on achieving their objectives must cooperate, coalesce, and compromise. And these activities are facilitated by rules and procedures. This system leads to the division and specialization of legislative work, the regularization of procedures, and the creation of agenda power. All of these organizational features of Congress arise as part of a governance structure to allow for cooperation and coalition building—activities that yield compromise policies.

Underlying Problems and Challenges

Before we can understand why Congress selects particular ways to institutionalize its practices, we need a finer appreciation of other underlying problems with which legislators must grapple. Then we can consider how the U.S. Congress deals with these problems.

Matching Influence and Interest.   Legislatures are highly egalitarian institutions. Each legislator has one vote on any issue coming before the body. Whereas a consumer has a cash budget that she may allocate in any way she wishes to categories of consumer goods, a legislator is not given a vote budget in quite the same sense. Instead, his budget of votes is "dedicated"—one vote for each motion before the assembly. He cannot aggregate the votes in his possession and cast all or some large fraction of them for a motion on a subject near and dear to his heart (or the hearts of his constituents). This is a source of frustration because, as we have noted, the premise of instrumental behavior dictates that legislators would, if they could, concentrate whatever resources they commanded on those subjects of highest priority to them. The egalitarian arrangement thus forces legislators to make deals with one another— "I'll support you on this motion if you support me on a future motion."

Information.   Legislators do not vote for outcomes directly but, rather, for instruments (or policies) whose effects produce outcomes. Thus legislators, to vote intelligently, must know the connection between the instruments they vote for and the effects they desire. In short, they must have information and knowledge about how the world works.

Few legislators—indeed, few people in general—know how the world works in very many policy domains except in the most superficial of ways. Nearly everyone in the legislature would benefit from the production of valuable information, at the very least information that would allow all of them to eliminate policy instruments that make very little difference in solving social problems or even make matters worse. Producing such information, however, is not a trivial matter. Simply to digest the knowledge that is being produced outside the legislature by knowledge-industry specialists (academics, scientists, journalists, interest groups) is a taxing task. Clearly institutional arrangements that provide incentives to some legislators to produce, evaluate, and disseminate this knowledge for others will permit public resources to be used more effectively. Because legislatures are in competition with other branches of government—particularly the executive—legislators need to meet certain informational requirements just to keep up with the competition.

Compliance.   The legislature is not the only game in town. The promulgation of public policies is a joint undertaking in which judges, executives, bureaucrats, and others participate alongside legislators. If the legislature develops no means with which to monitor what happens after a bill becomes law, then it risks seeing public policies implemented in ways other than those it intended when the law was passed. Cooperation does not end with the successful passage of a law. If legislators wish to have an impact on the world around them, especially on those matters to which their constituents give priority, then it is necessary to attend to policy implementation, not just policy formulation. But it is just not practical for all 435 representatives and all 100 senators to march down to this or that agency on Pennsylvania Avenue to ensure appropriate implementation by the executive bureaucracy. Compliance will not just happen, and like the production and dissemination of reliable information at the policy-formulation stage, the need for oversight of the executive bureaucracy is but an extension of the cooperation that produced legislation in the first place. It, too, must be institutionalized.

What we have suggested in this abstract discussion about legislative institutions and practices is that Congress is a place in which different kinds of representatives congregate and try to accomplish things so that they may reap the support of their respective constituents back home. This very diversity is problematic—it requires cooperation, coalitions, and compromise. In addition, there is a mismatch of influence and interest (owing to one person, one vote), information about the effectiveness of alternative policies is in short supply, and the legislature must worry about how its product—public laws—gets treated by the other branches of government. These are the problems that legislatures, including the U.S. Congress, devise institutional arrangements to solve or at least mitigate. This is where the rationality principle and institution principle join forces.

THE ORGANIZATION OF CONGRESS

We shall now examine the organization of Congress and the legislative process, particularly the basic building blocks of congressional organization: political parties, the committee system, congressional staff, the caucuses, and the parliamentary rules of the House and Senate. Each of these factors plays a key role in the organization of Congress and in the process through which Congress formulates and enacts laws. We will also look at powers Congress has in addition to lawmaking and explore the future role of Congress in relation to the powers of the executive.

Party Leadership and Organization in the House and the Senate

One significant aspect of legislative life is not even part of the *official* organization: political parties. The legislative parties—primarily Democratic and Republican in modern times but numerous others over the course of American history—are organizations that foster cooperation, coalitions, and compromise. They are the vehicles of collective action, both for legislators sharing common policy objectives inside the legislature and for those very same legislators as candidates in periodic election contests back home.[25] In short, political parties in Congress are the fundamental building blocks from which policy coalitions are fashioned to pass legislation and monitor its implementation, thereby providing a track record on which members build electoral support.

Every two years at the beginning of a new Congress, the members of each party gather to elect their House leaders. This gathering is called the **party caucus** by the Democrats and the **party conference** by the Republicans. The elected leader of the majority party is later proposed to the whole House and is automatically elected to the position of **Speaker of the House**, with voting along straight party lines. The House majority caucus (or conference) also elects a **majority leader.** The minority party goes through the same process and selects the **minority leader.** Both parties also elect "whips," who line up party members on important votes and relay voting information to the party leaders.

In December 2006, in the wake of the November elections, the Democrats become the majority party in both chambers. In the House, they selected Nancy Pelosi of California as Speaker, Steny Hoyer of Maryland as majority leader, and James Clyburn of South Carolina as whip. The Republicans, who had in the previous Congress made John Boehner of Ohio their majority leader, kept him on as minority leader, as well as Roy Blunt of Missouri as minority whip. In 2008, Republicans chose Eric Cantor of Virgina to replace Blunt as whip, but otherwise the leadership from both parties remained the same.

At one time, party leaders strictly controlled committee assignments, using them to enforce party discipline. Today representatives often expect to receive the

---

party caucus, or party conference A normally closed meeting of a political or legislative group to select candidates or leaders, plan strategy, or make decisions regarding legislative matters.

Speaker of the House The chief presiding officer of the House of Representatives. The Speaker is elected at the beginning of every Congress on a straight party vote. He or she is the most important party and House leader.

majority leader The elected leader of the party holding a majority of the seats in the House of Representatives or the Senate. In the House, the majority leader is subordinate in the party hierarchy to the Speaker.

minority leader The elected leader of the party holding less than a majority of the seats in the House or Senate.

---

[25] For a historically grounded analysis of the development of political parties as well as a treatment of their general contemporary significance, see John H. Aldrich, *Why Parties? The Origin and Transformation of Political Parties in America* (Chicago: University of Chicago Press, 1995). For an analysis of the parties in the legislative process, see Gary W. Cox and Mathew D. McCubbins, *Legislative Leviathan: Party Government in the House,* 2nd ed. (Berkeley: University of California Press, 2006). See also their *Setting the Agenda: Responsible Party Government in the U.S. House of Representatives* (New York: Cambridge University Press, 2005). A provocative essay questioning the role of parties is Keith Krehbiel, "Where's the Party?" *British Journal of Political Science* 23 (1993): 235–66.

assignments they want and resent leadership efforts to control assignments. The leadership's best opportunities to use committee assignments as rewards and punishments come when more than one member seeks a seat on a committee.

Generally representatives seek assignments that will allow them to influence decisions of special importance to their districts. Representatives from farm districts, for example, may request seats on the Agriculture Committee.[26] This is one method by which the egalitarian allocation of power in the legislature is overcome. Even though each legislator has just one vote on each issue in the full chamber, he or she, by serving on the right committees, is able to acquire extra influence in areas important to his or her constituents. Seats on powerful committees such as Ways and Means, which is responsible for tax legislation, and Appropriations are especially popular.

We now turn to the Senate, where the president pro tempore, a position designated in the Constitution, exercises mainly ceremonial leadership. Usually the majority party designates the member with the greatest seniority to serve in this capacity. Real power is in the hands of the majority and minority leaders, each elected by party caucus. Together they control the Senate's calendar, or agenda, for legislation. In addition, the senators from each party elect a whip.

The 2002 elections gave the Republican Party a one-seat majority in the Senate. In the 2004 election, they gained an additional four seats, for a 55–45 majority. Republicans reelected Bill Frist of Tennessee as majority leader, while Democrats replaced the recently defeated Tom Daschle of South Dakota with Harry Reid of Nevada as the minority leader. After their six-seat gain in the 2006 election, the Democrats named Reid majority leader. The Republicans elected Mitch McConnell of Kentucky to the post of minority leader. Both were reelected to these positions after the 2008 and 2010 elections.

In recent years, party leaders have sought to augment their formal powers by reaching outside Congress for resources that might enhance their influence within the institution. One aspect of this strategy is the increased use of national communications media, including televised speeches and talk-show appearances, by party leaders. The former Republican House Speaker Newt Gingrich, for example, used television extensively to generate support for his programs among Republican loyalists.[27] As long as it lasted, Gingrich's support among the Republican rank and file gave him an added measure of influence over Republican members of Congress. The Democratic leaders Reid and Pelosi, and the Republican leaders McConnell and Boehner, have followed this pattern as regulars on the Sunday-morning talk shows.

---

[26] For an extensive discussion of the committee-assignment process in the U.S. House, see Kenneth A. Shepsle, *The Giant Jigsaw Puzzle: Democratic Committee Assignments in the Modern House* (Chicago: University of Chicago Press, 1978); and Scott A. Frisch and Sean Q. Kelly, *Committee Assignment Politics in the U.S. House of Representatives* (Norman: University of Oklahoma Press, 2006). See also E. Scott Adler, *Why Congressional Reforms Fail: Reelection and the House Committee System* (Chicago: University of Chicago Press, 2002).

[27] Douglas Harris, "The Public Speaker" (Ph.D. diss., Johns Hopkins University, 1998).

A second external strategy involves fund-raising. In recent years, congressional leaders have frequently established their own political action committees. Interest groups are usually eager to contribute to these "leadership PACs" in order to curry favor with powerful members of Congress. The leaders, in turn, use the funds to support the various campaigns of their party's candidates and thereby create a sense of obligation and loyalty among those they help.[28]

In addition to the tasks of organizing Congress, congressional party leaders set the legislative agenda. Not only do the party leaders have considerable sway over Congress's agenda in the large, but they also regulate the fine-grained deliberation over specific items on the agenda. This aspect of agenda setting is multifaceted. At the outset, for example, a bill is initially filed with the Clerk of the House as a legislative proposal. The Speaker of the House then determines which committee has jurisdiction over it. Indeed, since the mid-1970s, the Speaker has been given additional bill-assignment powers, known as multiple referral, permitting him or her to assign different parts of a bill to different committees or the same parts sequentially or simultaneously to several committees.[29] The steering and agenda setting by party leaders work, however, within an institutional framework consisting of structures and procedures. The "Analyzing the Evidence" unit on page 190 takes a closer look at parties and agenda control.

Having described some of the powers of party leaders, we might pause and ask an even more basic question: Why do members allow themselves to be governed by powerful party leaders? Leaders, after all, are elected by their rank-and-file members, and in their respective party caucuses the rank and file determine how powerful they will permit their leaders to be. Indeed, the power of party leaders has ebbed and flowed over time. From the end of World War II until as late as the 1970s, for example, when the Democrats were the majority party most of the time, party leaders were relatively weak. Speaker of the House Sam Rayburn (D-Tex.), to give one example, was beloved by his followers and was quite successful at persuading members to toe the party line during the 1940s and 1950s. But persuasion was just about the only tool at his disposal. Later party leaders possessed more potent tools. Jim Wright (D-Tex.), for example, who served as Speaker in the 1980s, was provided with considerable power over committee assignments and chaired most of the party committees that formulated policy objectives for the Democrats. Why did party leaders become more powerful?

The political scientists John Aldrich and David Rohde have sought to understand these ebbs and flows in the power of a party over its members, or what they

---

[28] Rank-and-file members, especially those from safe districts who face limited electoral challenges, have also created their own PACs, which enable them to contribute to their party and its candidates. See Eric S. Heberlig, "Congressional Parties, Fundraising, and Committee Ambition," *Political Research Quarterly* 56 (2003): 151–61.

[29] For a historical look, see David W. Rohde and Kenneth A. Shepsle, "Leaders and Followers in the House of Representatives: Reflections on Woodrow Wilson's *Congressional Government*," *Congress and the Presidency* 14 (1987): 111–33. A recent analysis of the House leadership is Eric Schickler and Kathryn Pearson, "The House Leadership in an Era of Partisan Warfare," in *Congress Reconsidered*, 8th ed., pp. 207–26. A companion piece on the Senate is C. Lawrence Evans and Daniel Lipinski, "Obstruction and Leadership in the U.S. Senate," in *Congress Reconsidered*, pp. 227–48.

call "conditional party government." They suggest that the institutional strength of party leaders is conditional; it depends on particular circumstances. The circumstance they emphasize is the degree to which party members share policy goals. If the rank and file are relatively homogeneous in this respect, they will endow their leaders with considerable power to prosecute the shared agenda. If, on the other hand, party members are heterogeneous in their goals, they will be less disposed to empower a leader (indeed, they will be suspicious of any exercise of power by a leader). Thus the Democratic Party of the 1940s and 1950s, with its northern liberal wing and its southern conservative wing, was heterogeneous in the extreme and provided its leaders with few power resources. The effects of the Voting Rights Act of 1965, one of which was that formerly Democratic constituencies in the South started electing Republicans, began to be felt in the 1970s, reducing the diversity in the Democratic ranks and thus rendering the party more homogeneous. Under this changed circumstance, Democratic Party legislators, who were more focused than before on moderate and liberal goals, were prepared to empower their leaders.[30] Let us now turn to the committee system—the backbone of Congress—and the role of the party leadership in guiding it.

The Committee System: The Core of Congress

If the system of leadership in each party and chamber constitutes the first set of organizational arrangements in the U.S. Congress, then the committee system provides it with a second set of organizational structures. But these are more a division-of-labor and specialization-of-labor system than the hierarchy-of-power system that determines leadership arrangements.

Congress began as a relatively unspecialized assembly, with each legislator participating equally in every step of the legislative process in all realms of policy. By the time of the War of 1812, if not earlier, Congress had begun employing a system of specialists—the committee system—because members with different interests and talents wished to play disproportionate roles in some areas of policy making while ceding influence in areas in which they were less interested.[31] If, Rip van Winkle–like, a congressman had fallen asleep in 1805 and woke up in 1825, he would have found

---

[30] A now-classic treatment of the ebbs and flows of parties and their leaders in the modern era is David W. Rohde, *Parties and Leaders in the Post-reform House* (Chicago: University of Chicago Press, 1991). For a more historical perspective, see David W. Rohde, John H. Aldrich, and Mark M. Berger, "The Historical Variability in Conditional Party Government, 1877–1986," in *Party, Process, and Political Change in Congress: New Perspectives on the History of Congress*, David W. Brady and Mathew D. McCubbins, eds. (Palo Alto, Calif.: Stanford University Press, 2002), pp. 17–35. For a development of the analytical argument, see David W. Rohde and John H. Aldrich, "The Logic of Conditional Party Government: Revisiting the Electoral Connection," in *Congress Reconsidered*, 7th ed., Lawrence C. Dodd and Bruce I. Oppenheimer, eds. (Washington, D.C.: CQ Press, 2001), pp. 265–92. A complementary theoretical perspective is offered by the political scientists Gary Cox and Mathew McCubbins in both *Legislative Leviathan* and *Setting the Agenda*. Finally, for a recent assessment of the party in light of the 2006 election results, see David W. Rohde, "Political Command and Control," *New York Times*, November 18, 2006, p. A24.

[31] The story of the evolution of the standing committee system in the House and the Senate in the early part of the nineteenth century is told in Gerald Gamm and Kenneth A. Shepsle, "Emergence of Legislative Institutions: Standing Committees in the House and Senate, 1810–1825," *Legislative Studies Quarterly* 14 (1989): 39–66.

Parties and Agenda Control in Congress

In assessing the influence of political parties on legislative politics, political scientists often ask how parties affect outcomes in Congress. One approach might be to look for evidence of arm twisting or promised favors by party leaders, both of which can be used to influence members' roll-call vote choices. Yet, increasingly, scholars have responded to this question by looking for evidence of agenda manipulation by the majority party. If the majority party can control *what* gets voted on—through its control of committees, including the Rules Committee, and the party leaders' scheduling power—then it can affect outcomes even when the party leaders cannot effectively twist arms or promise favors. Thus, a question that has taken center stage in congressional research is, Who controls the agenda in Congress?

REPUBLICAN AGENDA (Pre-Obama)	DEMOCRATIC AGENDA (Post-Obama)
Tax Cuts	Economic Recovery
War in Iraq and Afghanistan	Energy Independence
Education (No Child Left Behind)	Iraq Troop Withdrawal
National Security	Health Care Reform
Budget Management	College Access
Terrorism (Homeland Security)	Mortgage Reform
Social Security Reform	Banking Industry Reform
Faith Based and Community Initiatives	Equal Pay

Source: Republican National Committee, www.rnc.org; Office of the Speaker, U.S. House of Representatives, "A New Direction for America," www.speaker.gov/pdf/thebook.pdf (accessed 7/9/09).

Why is majority party status so important in Congress? Whichever party controls a greater number of seats in either the House or the Senate decides which issues will come to the floor for consideration. To illustrate this point, consider the recent instances when the Republicans controlled both chambers of Congress and the presidency (from 2003–2006) and when the Democrats achieved unified party control of these two branches of government (beginning in 2009). In addition to all the other perks that come with majority control, each party was able to push its specific agenda. As we see from the table above, there are clear differences between Republicans and Democrats in terms of the legislative policies they chose to pursue.

Congress	Majority Party	Total Final Passage Votes	Majority Party Rolls	Majority Party Roll Rate (%)	Minority Party Rolls	Minority Party Roll Rate (%)
99th	Democrats	89	1	1.1	35	39.3
100th	Democrats	116	2	1.7	40	34.5
101th	Democrats	108	1	0.93	39	36.1
102th	Democrats	142	0	0	39	27.5
103th	Democrats	160	1	0.63	56	35
104th	Republicans	136	1	0.74	63	46.3
105th	Republicans	133	3	2.3	51	38.4
106th	Republicans	136	4	2.9	51	37.5
107th	Republicans	93	1	1.1	31	33.3
108th	Republicans	119	1	0.84	46	38.7
109th	Republicans	146	2	1.37	64	43.8
110th	Democrats	161	4	2.48	102	63.4

Source: Gary W. Cox and Mathew D. McCubbins, *Setting the Agenda: Responsible Party Government in the U.S. House of Representatives*, New York: Cambridge University Press, 2005; calculated by author.

One specific way to think about agenda control in Congress is in terms of the winners and losers on particular pieces of legislation, because this may tell us how much influence the majority party actually has. The most prominent example of this approach has been to look at partisan roll rates. A party (or group of members) is "rolled" when a majority of its members winds up on the losing side of a vote that passes. In focusing specifically on final passage votes in the U.S. House, the political scientists Gary Cox and Mathew McCubbins have found that, at the aggregate level, the majority party is almost never rolled. In contrast, and as we see from the table above, the minority party is significantly more likely to be on the losing side of final-passage votes. This suggests that the majority party controls the agenda and prevents legislation that it opposes (and is likely to lose on) from coming to a vote.

himself in an entirely transformed legislative world. The legislative chambers in the beginning of that period consisted of bodies of generalists. By the end of the period, in policy area after policy area, the legislative agenda was dominated by groups of specialists serving on standing committees. If, on the other hand, our legislator had fallen asleep in 1825 and awoke a *century* later, the legislature would not seem so very different. In short, organizational decisions in the first quarter of the nineteenth century affected legislative activity over a long horizon. This is the history principle at work.

The congressional committee system consists of a set of standing committees, each with its own jurisdiction, membership, and authority to act. Each **standing committee** is given a permanent status by the official rules, with a fixed membership, officers, rules, a staff, offices, and above all, a jurisdiction that is recognized by all other committees and, usually, the leadership as well (Table 5.2). The jurisdiction of each standing committee is defined by the subject matter of legislation. Except for the Rules Committee in the House and the Rules and Administration Committee in the Senate, all the important committees receive proposals for legislation and process them into official bills. The House Rules Committee decides the order in which bills come up for a vote and determines the rules that govern the length of debate and opportunity for amendments. The jurisdictions of the standing committees usually parallel those of the major departments or agencies in the executive branch. There are important exceptions—Appropriations and Rules in both chambers, for example—but by and large the division of labor is self-consciously designed to parallel executive-branch organization.

Jurisdiction. The world of policy is partitioned into policy jurisdictions, which become the responsibility of committees. The members of the Armed Services Committee, for example, become specialists in all aspects of military affairs, the subject matter defining their committee's jurisdiction. Legislators tend to have disproportionate influence in their respective committee jurisdictions, not only because they have become the most knowledgeable members of the legislature in that area of policy but also because they are given the opportunity to exercise various forms of agenda power, a subject we develop further in the next section.

Dividing up institutional activities among jurisdictions, thereby encouraging participants to specialize, has its advantages. But it has its costs, too. If the Armed Services Committee of the House of Representatives had no restraints, its members would undoubtedly shower their districts with military facilities and contracts. In short, the delegation of authority and resources to specialist subunits exploits the advantages of the division and specialization of labor but risks jeopardizing the collective objectives of the group as a whole. The monitoring of committee activities thus goes hand in hand with delegation.

Sometimes new issues arise that fit neatly into no jurisdiction. Some, such as the issue of energy supplies that emerged during the 1970s, are so multifaceted that bits and pieces of them are spread across many committee jurisdictions. Other issues, such as the regulation of tobacco products, fall into the gray area claimed by several committees. In this case in the House, the Energy and Commerce Committee, with its traditional claim on health-related issues, fought with the Agriculture Committee, whose traditional domain includes crops such as tobacco, for jurisdiction over this issue. Turf battles between committees of Congress are

TABLE 5.2 STANDING COMMITTEES OF CONGRESS, 2009

House Committees

Agriculture	Natural Resources
Appropriations	Oversight and Government Reform
Armed Services	Rules
Budget	Science and Technology
Education and Labor	Small Business
Energy and Commerce	Standards of Official Conduct (Ethics)
Financial Services	Transportation and Infrastructure
Foreign Affairs Homeland Security	Veterans' Affairs
House Administration	Ways and Means
Judiciary	

Senate Committees

Agriculture, Nutrition, and Forestry	Foreign Relations
Appropriations	Health, Education, Labor, and Pensions
Armed Services	Homeland Security and Governmental Affairs
Banking, Housing, and Urban Affairs	
Budget	Judiciary
Commerce, Science, and Transportation	Rules and Administration
Energy and Natural Resources	Small Business and Entrepreneurship
Environment and Public Works	Veterans' Affairs
Finance	

notorious.[32] These battles involve committee chairs, the Office of the Parliamentarian, the political leadership of the chamber, and from time to time, select committees appointed to realign committee jurisdictions.

---

[32] An outstanding description and analysis of these battles is found in David C. King, "The Nature of Congressional Committee Jurisdictions," *American Political Science Review* 88, no. 1 (March 1994): 48–63. See also King's *Turf Wars: How Congressional Committees Claim Jurisdiction* (Chicago: University of Chicago Press, 1997).

Authority.   Committees may be thought of as agents of the parent body to which jurisdiction-specific authority is provisionally delegated. In this section, we describe committee authority in terms of gatekeeping and after-the-fact authority.

Normally any member of the legislature can submit a bill calling for changes in some policy area. Almost automatically this bill is assigned to the committee of jurisdiction, and very nearly always, there it languishes. In a typical session in the House of Representatives, about 8,000 bills are submitted, fewer than 1,000 of which are acted on by the appropriate committee of jurisdiction. In effect, then, although any member is entitled to make proposals, committees get to decide whether to open the gates and allow the bill to be voted on by the full chamber. Related to **gatekeeping authority** is a committee's **proposal power.** After a bill is referred to a committee, the committee may take no further action on it, amend the legislation in any way, or even write its own legislation before bringing the bill to the floor for a vote. Committees, then, are lords of their jurisdictional domains, setting the table, so to speak, for their parent chamber.[33]

A committee also has responsibilities for bargaining with the other chamber and for conducting oversight, or **after-the-fact authority.** Because the U.S. Congress is bicameral, once one chamber passes a bill, the bill must be considered by the other chamber. If the other chamber passes a bill different from the one passed in the first chamber and the first chamber refuses to accept the changes made, then the two chambers ordinarily meet in a **conference committee**, in which representatives from each chamber hammer out a compromise. In the great majority of cases, conferees are drawn from the committees that had original jurisdiction over the bill. For example, in a sample of Congresses in the 1980s, of the 1,388 House members who served as conferees for various bills during a three-year period, only 7 were not on the committee of original jurisdiction; similarly, in the Senate on only 7 of 1,180 occasions were conferees not drawn from the "right" committee.[34] The committee's effective authority to represent its chamber in conference-committee proceedings constitutes the first manifestation of after-the-fact power that complements its before-the-fact gatekeeping and proposal powers.

A second manifestation of after-the-fact committee authority consists of the committee's primacy in legislative **oversight** of policy implementation by the executive bureaucracy. Even after a bill becomes a law, it is not always (indeed, it is rarely) self-implementing. Executive agents—bureaucrats in the career civil service, commissioners in regulatory agencies, political appointees in the executive branch—march to their own drummers. Unless legislative actors hold their feet to the fire, they may not do precisely what the law requires (especially in light of the fact that

---

[33] This setup clearly gives committee members extraordinary power in their respective jurisdictions, allowing them to push policy into line with their own preferences—but only up to a point. If the abuse of their agenda power becomes excessive, the parent body has structural and procedural remedies available to counteract the committee's actions—such as stacking the committee with more compliant members, deposing a particularly obstreperous committee chair, or removing policies from a committee's jurisdiction. These are the clubs behind the door that only rarely have to be employed; their mere presence suffices to keep committees from the more outrageous forms of advantage taking.

[34] See Kenneth A. Shepsle and Barry R. Weingast, "The Institutional Foundations of Committee Power," *American Political Science Review* 81, no. 1 (March 1987), pp. 85–104.

---

gatekeeping authority The right and power to decide if a change in policy will be considered.

proposal power The capacity to bring a proposal before the full legislature.

after-the-fact authority The authority to follow up on the fate of a proposal once it has been approved by the full chamber.

conference committee A joint committee created to work out a compromise for House and Senate versions of a piece of legislation.

oversight The effort by Congress, through hearings, investigations, and other techniques, to exercise control over the activities of executive agencies.

statutes are often vague and ambiguous). Congressional committees are continuously watchful of the manner in which legislation is implemented and administered. They play this after-the-fact role by allocating staff and resources to track what the executive branch is doing and, from time to time, holding oversight hearings in which particular policies and programs are given intense scrutiny. This, in turn, gives congressional committees an additional source of leverage over policy in their jurisdictions. Oversight is discussed further in Chapter 7 on the bureaucracy.

Subcommittees. The standing committees of the U.S. House are divided into about 100 even more specialized subcommittees. These subcommittees serve their full committees in precisely the same manner as the full committees serve the parent chamber. Thus, in their narrow jurisdictions they have gatekeeping, proposal, interchamber-bargaining, and oversight powers. For a bill on wheat to be taken up by the full Agriculture Committee, for example, it first has to clear the Subcommittee on General Farm Commodities. All of the issues involving assignments, jurisdictions, and authority that we discussed earlier regarding full committees apply at the subcommittee level as well.

Hierarchy. At the committee level, the mantle of leadership falls on the committee chair. He or she, together with the party leaders, determines the committee's agenda and then coordinates the committee's staff, investigatory resources, and subcommittee structure.[35] This coordination includes scheduling hearings, "marking up" bills—that is, transforming legislative drafts into final versions—and scripting the process by which a bill goes from committee to floor proceedings to final passage. For many years, the Congress followed a rigid **seniority** rule for the selection of committee chairs. The benefits of this rule are twofold. First, the chair will be occupied by someone knowledgeable in the committee's jurisdiction, familiar with interest-group and executive-branch players, and politically experienced. Second, the larger institution will be spared divisive leadership contests that reduce the legislative process to efforts in vote grubbing. There are costs, however: Senior individuals may be unenergetic, out of touch, even senile.

> **seniority** The priority or status ranking given to an individual on the basis of length of continuous service on a congressional committee.

The U.S. House operated according to a strict seniority principle from about 1910 (and, informally, even earlier) until the mid-1970s, when most members felt that the burdens of this arrangement were beginning to outweigh its advantages. Committee chairs are now elected by the majority-party members of the full legislature, though there remains a presumption (which may be rebutted) that the most senior committee member will normally assume the chair.[36]

Decisiveness on Committees. When a committee goes about its business, its chair exercises agenda power, as noted. But he or she is not a dictator. Any proposal made to the committee by the chair must ultimately secure the support of a committee majority. In this setting, who is *decisive*? That is, whose vote is necessary and

---

[35] Because subcommittee chairs do essentially the same things in their narrower jurisdictions, we won't provide a separate discussion of them.

[36] Beginning with the Republican takeover of the House in 1995, committee chairs have been term limited. After three terms, a chair must step down.

FIGURE 5.6 THE MEDIAN VOTER IN CONGRESSIONAL COMMITTEES

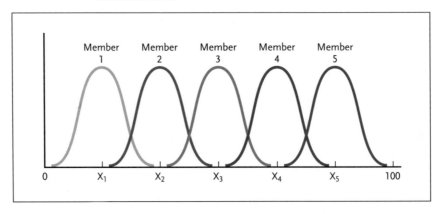

sufficient for a motion to pass? The answer is provided by the *median-voter theorem.* This theorem can be stated as follows: If the alternatives under consideration can be represented as points on a line, if individuals have a most-preferred point, and their preferences decrease steadily for points farther away, then the most-preferred point of the median (middle) voter can defeat any other point in a majority contest.

In Figure 5.6 we have a five-person committee that must choose a point on the line ranging from 0 to 100. Each member has a favorite point, represented by the peak of her curve, and her preferences decline steadily as points farther and farther away are considered. The median-voter theorem asserts that the favorite point of member 3 can beat any other point in a majority contest. A majority comprising members 3, 4, and 5 prefers 3's favorite to any point to its left; a majority comprising members 1, 2, and 3 prefers 3's favorite to any point to its right; therefore 3's favorite can prevail against *any* point. We will discuss the median-voter theorem again in Chapter 10 in the context of elections. To familiarize yourself further with how this concept applies to congressional committee decisions, see the "Analyzing the Evidence" unit on the following page.

Monitoring Committees.   If unchecked, committees might easily take advantage of their authority. Indeed, what prevents committees from exploiting their before-the-fact proposal power and their after-the-fact bargaining and oversight authority? As we saw in Chapter 1, in our discussion of the principal-agent problem, principals must be certain that agents are properly motivated to serve the principal's interests, either by actually sharing the principal's interests themselves or by deriving something of value (reputation, compensation, and so on) for acting to advance those interests. Alternatively, the principal will need to have some instruments by which to monitor and validate what his or her agent is doing, rewarding or punishing the agent accordingly.

Consider again the example of congressional committees. The House or Senate delegates responsibility to its Committee on Agriculture to recommend legislative policy in the field of agriculture. Not surprisingly, legislators from farm districts are most eager to get onto this committee, and for the most part their wishes are

The Median Voter in Congressional Committees

HOUSE RULES COMMITTEE COMPOSITION

109th U.S. Congress

Representative	State	Party	Rank
McGovern	MA	D	23
Slaughter	NY	D	25
Hastings, Alcee	FL	D	27
Matsui	CA	D	72
Capito	WV	R	227
Diaz-Balart	FL	R	255
COLE	**OK**	**R**	**310**
Dreier	CA	R	320
Hastings, Doc	WA	R	339
Putnam	FL	R	345
Bishop	UT	R	366
Gingrey	GA	R	390
Sessions	TX	R	404

House Median: 218
Democratic Median: 102
Republican Median: 320

110th U.S. Congress

Representative	State	Party	Rank
McGovern	MA	D	20
Slaughter	NY	D	22
Hastings, Alcee	FL	D	30
Welch	VT	D	48
Sutton	OH	D	57
Matsui	CA	D	74
CASTOR	**FL**	**D**	**88**
Arcuri	NY	D	144
Cardoza	CA	D	188
Diaz-Balart	FL	R	283
Dreier	CA	R	316
Hastings, Doc	WA	R	346
Sessions	TX	R	405

House Median: 218
Democratic Median: 118
Republican Median: 335

The Rules Committee is a (perhaps *the*) central gate keeper in the House of Representatives. In order for a bill proposed by a committee to find its way to the floor of the House for full-chamber consideration, it must secure a rule from the Rules Committee that governs when it will be taken up, the amendments to it that are in order, and other procedural matters. The Rules Committee is dominated by the majority party; it is composed of nine majority party members and four minority party members. The median member of the committee is "pivotal" in the sense that he or she can combine with colleagues to her left or her right to form a majority. If we rank-order all legislators, based on their voting behavior, from most liberal (legislator no. 1) to most conservative (legislator no. 435), we can assess where Rules Committee members stand. In the 109th Congress (2005–2006), dominated by the Republicans, Tom Cole of Oklahoma (in bold in the table above) was the median member of the Rules Committee. At no. 310 he was very conservative-indeed, much more conservative than the median member of the entire House chamber (no. 218). The Rules Committee in this Congress pulled legislation to the right, either refusing more liberal bills access to the floor or forcing them to be revised in a more conservative direction. In the 110th Congress (2007-2008), the Democrats were in the majority. The median Rules member, Kathy Castor of Florida, was among the most liberal (no. 88)—far to the left of the House median (no. 218) and even more liberal than the median of the majority party (no. 118). This Rules Committee favored moves to the left, sometimes even further than the majority party might prefer. A comparison of the two Congresses gives us a sense of how the matter of which party has a majority in the chamber can affect its politics and its policy decisions.

Source: These data were assembled by Joseph Williams, PhD candidate in government, Harvard University.

accommodated. The Committee on Agriculture, consequently, is composed mainly of farm legislators. And nonfarm legislators are relieved at not having to spend their time on issues of little material interest to them or their constituents. In effecting this delegation, however, the parent legislature is putting itself in the hands of its farm colleagues, benefiting from their expertise on farm-related matters, to be sure, but laying itself open to the danger of planting the fox squarely in the henhouse. The Committee on Agriculture becomes not only a collection of specialists but also a collection of advocates for farm interests. How can the parent body know for certain, therefore, that a recommendation from that committee is not more a reflection of its advocacy than a reflection of its expertise? This is the risk inherent in delegation in principal-agent relationships.

And it is for this reason that the parent legislature maintains a variety of tools and instruments to protect itself from being exploited by its agents. First, it does not allow committees to make final decisions on policy; it allows only recommendations, which the parent legislature retains the authority to accept, amend, or reject. A committee has agenda power, but it is not by itself decisive. Second, the parent body relies on the committee's concern for its own reputation. Making a recommendation on a piece of legislation is not a one-shot action; the committee knows it will return to the parent body time and time again with legislative recommendations, and it will not want to tarnish its reputation for expertise by too much advocacy. Third, the parent body relies on competing agents—interest groups, expert members not on the committee, legislative specialists in the other chamber of the legislature, executive-branch specialists, and even academics—to keep its own agents honest. Finally, in the House there is an institutional club behind the door—the discharge petition. A committee that is sitting on a bill, not permitting it to be taken up by the full chamber, can be discharged of responsibility for the bill if a petition to that effect is signed by a majority of the chamber.

Nevertheless, a principal will not bother to eliminate *entirely* these prospective deviations from his or her interests by agents who have interests of their own. A principal will suffer some **agency loss** from having delegated authority to a "hired hand"; therefore, nearly all principal-agent relationships will be imperfect in some respects from the principal's perspective. Agents will be in a position to extract some advantage from the privileged relationship they have with their principal—not too much, or it will undermine the relationship altogether, but enough to diminish the benefits of the relationship a bit from the principal's point of view. The Committee on Agriculture, for example, cannot get away with spending huge proportions of the federal budget on agricultural subsidies to farmers. But it can insert small items into agriculture bills from time to time—an experimental grain-to-fuel conversion project in an important legislator's state or district, for example, or special funds to the U.S. trade representative to give priority to agriculture-related trade issues. The parent body, as we suggested, will find it worth its while to keep an eye on the Agriculture Committee, but it won't be worth its while to take action on every instance of indulgence by the committee. The cost of doing that—the transaction cost of monitoring and overseeing committee performance—gets excessive if perfection is the objective.

Thus we see the institution principle providing some guidance on how a group of legislators organizes itself for business. The legislators take advantage of the division and specialization of labor, dividing themselves into specialized subgroups

agency loss The difference between what a principal would like an agent to do and the agent's performance.

(committees and subcommittees) and thus enjoying the benefits of expertise from these subunits. But they also guard against the subunits' going off half cocked in pursuit of their own narrower interests. The parent legislature in effect uses institutional arrangements to regulate and oversee its subunits' activities.

Committee Reform.   Over the years, Congress has reformed its organizational structure and operating procedures. Most changes have been made to improve efficiency, but some reforms have also represented a response to political considerations. In the 1970s, a series of reforms substantially altered the organization of power in Congress. Among the most important changes put into place at that time were an increase in the number of subcommittees, greater autonomy for subcommittee chairs, the opening of most committee deliberations to the public, and a system of multiple referral of bills that allowed several committees to consider one bill at the same time. One of the driving impulses behind these reforms was an effort to reduce the power of committee chairs.

As a consequence of those reforms, power became more fragmented, making it harder to reach agreement on legislation. In 1995, the Republican leadership of the 104th Congress sought to concentrate more authority in the party leadership. One of the ways the House achieved this was by abandoning the principle of seniority in the selection of a number of committee chairs, appointing them instead according to their loyalty to the party. This move tied committee chairs more closely to the leadership. In addition, the Republican leadership eliminated 25 of the House's 115 subcommittees and gave committee chairs more power over their subcommittees. The result was an unusually cohesive congressional majority, which pushed forward a common agenda. House Republicans also agreed to impose a three-term limit on committee and subcommittee heads. As a result, all the chairs were replaced in 2001, when the 107th Congress convened. In many instances, chairs were replaced by the most senior Republican committee member, but the net result was a redistribution of power in the House of Representatives. Since 2001 some of the earlier practices have slowly begun to reassert themselves. Speaker Nancy Pelosi and her new Democratic majority in 2007 observed seniority in the appointment of nearly all committee chairs. But it is not automatic, and committee chairs are on notice that significant deviations from a party policy consensus will not be tolerated. For example, in 2009 a newly enlarged Democratic majority replaced John Dingell (D-Mich), a fixture in the House for half a century, as chair of the Commerce and Energy Committee with Henry Waxman (D-Calif), a less senior member of the committee.

The Staff System: Staffers and Agencies

A congressional institution ranking just below committees and parties in importance is the staff system. Every member of Congress employs a large number of staff members, whose tasks include handling constituency requests and, to a large and growing extent, dealing with legislative details and the activities of administrative agencies. Increasingly, staffers bear the primary responsibility for formulating and drafting proposals, organizing hearings, dealing with administrative agencies, and negotiating with lobbyists. Indeed, legislators typically deal with each other through staff members rather than through direct, personal contact. Representatives and senators together employ nearly 11,000 staffers in their Washington and home offices. In addition to the personal staffs of individual senators and representatives, Congress also employs roughly 2,000 committee staffers. These individuals make up the permanent staff, who often stay regardless of turnover in Congress and are attached to every House and Senate committee. They are responsible for organizing and administering the committee's work, doing research, scheduling, organizing hearings, and drafting legislation.

Not only does Congress employ personal and committee staffs, but it has also established three **staff agencies** designed to provide the legislative branch with resources and expertise independent of the executive branch. These agencies enhance Congress's capacity to oversee administrative agencies and evaluate presidential programs and proposals. They are the Congressional Research Service, which performs research for legislators who wish to know the facts and competing arguments relevant to policy proposals or other legislative business; the Government Accountability Office, through which Congress can investigate the financial and administrative affairs of any government agency or program; and the Congressional Budget Office, which assesses the economic implications and likely costs of proposed federal programs, such as the Bush administration rescue packages for the failing financial system in 2008 and Barack Obama's stimulus package in 2009.

Informal Organization: The Caucuses

In addition to the official organization of Congress, an unofficial organizational structure also exists: the caucuses, formally known as legislative service organizations (LSOs). A **congressional caucus** is a group of senators or representatives who share certain opinions, interests, or social characteristics. There are ideological caucuses such as the liberal Democratic Study Group and the conservative Democratic Forum. There are also a large number of caucuses composed of legislators representing particular economic or policy interests, such as the Travel and Tourism Caucus, the Steel Caucus, the Mushroom Caucus, and the Concerned Senators for the Arts. Legislators who share common backgrounds or social characteristics have organized such caucuses as the Congressional Black Caucus, the Congressional Caucus for Women's Issues, and the Hispanic Caucus. All these caucuses seek to advance the interests of the groups they represent by promoting legislation, encouraging Congress to hold hearings, and pressing administrative agencies for favorable treatment.

RULES OF LAWMAKING: HOW A BILL BECOMES A LAW

The institutional structure of Congress is one key factor that helps shape the legislative process. A second and equally important set of factors is made up of the rules of congressional procedure. These rules govern all the procedures from introducing a

staff agencies
The agencies responsible for providing Congress with independent expertise, administration, and oversight capability.

congressional caucus An association of members of Congress based on party, interest, or social characteristics such as gender or race.

bill through submitting it to the president for signing. Not only do these regulations influence the fate of every bill, but they also help determine the distribution of power in Congress.[37]

Committee Deliberation

Even if a member of Congress, the White House, or a federal agency has spent months developing and drafting a piece of legislation, it does not become a bill until a senator or a representative officially submits it to the clerk of the House or Senate and it is referred to the appropriate committee for deliberation. No floor action on any bill can take place until the committee with jurisdiction over it has taken all the time it needs to deliberate.[38] During the course of its deliberations, the committee typically refers the bill to one of its subcommittees, which may hold hearings, listen to expert testimony, and amend the proposed legislation before referring it to the full committee for its consideration. The full committee may accept the recommendation of the subcommittee or hold its own hearings and prepare its own amendments. Even more frequently, the committee and subcommittee may do little or nothing with a bill and simply allow it to die in committee. In a typical congressional session, roughly 8,000 bills are introduced, and 85 to 90 percent of them die in committee—an indication of the power of the congressional committee system.

Once a bill's assigned committee or committees in the House of Representatives have acted affirmatively, the whole bill or various parts of it are transmitted to the Rules Committee, which determines the specific rules under which the legislation will be considered by the full House. Together with the Speaker, it influences when debate will be scheduled, for how long, what amendments will be in order, and the order in which they will be considered. The Speaker also rules on all procedural points of order and points of information raised during the debate. A bill's supporters generally prefer what is called a **closed rule**, which puts severe limits on floor debate and amendments. Opponents of a bill usually prefer an **open rule**, which permits potentially damaging floor debate and makes it easier to add amendments that may cripple the bill or weaken its chances of passing.

closed rule The provision by the House Rules Committee that prohibits the introduction of amendments during debate.

open rule The provision by the House Rules Committee that permits floor debate and the addition of amendments to a bill.

Debate

Party control of the agenda is reinforced by the rule giving the Speaker of the House and the majority leader of the Senate the power of recognition during debate on a bill. Usually the chair knows the purpose for which a member intends to speak well in advance of the occasion. Spontaneous efforts to gain recognition

---

[37] We should emphasize, although we don't mean to confuse the reader, that a legislature "suspends" its rules as often as it follows them. There are unorthodox ways to proceed in order to avoid procedural logjams, and the House and, especially, the Senate frequently resort to these unorthodox ways. See Barbara Sinclair, *Unorthodox Lawmaking: New Legislative Processes in the U.S. Congress*, 3rd ed. (Washington, D.C.: Congressional Quarterly Press, 2007).

[38] A bill can be pulled from a committee by a discharge petition, but this is an extreme measure and is resorted to only rarely. Other parliamentary tricks may also be attempted, but it is fair to say that most of the time at least it is the committee of jurisdiction that influences the course of a bill.

are often foiled. For example, the Speaker may ask, "For what purpose does the member rise?" before deciding whether to grant recognition. In general, the party leadership in the House has total control over debate. In the Senate, each member has substantial power to block the close of debate. A House majority can override opposition, whereas it takes an extraordinary majority (sixty votes) to close debate in the Senate; thus the Senate tends to be far more tolerant in debate, far more accommodating of various views, and far less partisan. In recent years, however, partisanship in both chambers has been on the rise.

In the House, virtually all of the time allotted by the Rules Committee for debate on a given bill is controlled by the bill's sponsor and its leading opponent. These two participants are, by rule and tradition, granted the power to allocate most of the debate time in small amounts to members who are seeking to speak for or against the measure.

In the Senate, other than the power of recognition, the leadership has much less control over floor debate. Indeed, the Senate is unique among the world's legislative bodies for its commitment to unlimited debate. Once given the floor, a senator may speak for as long as he or she wishes unless an extraordinary majority votes to end debate. On a number of memorable occasions, senators have used this right to prevent action on legislation they opposed. Through this tactic, called the **filibuster**, small minorities or even one individual in the Senate can force the majority to give in to his or her demands. During the 1950s and 1960s, for example, opponents of civil rights legislation often sought to block its passage by adopting the filibuster. Sixty votes are needed to end a filibuster. This procedure is called **cloture.**

Although it is the best known, the filibuster is not the only technique used to block Senate action. Under Senate rules, members have a virtually unlimited ability to propose amendments to a pending bill. Each amendment must be voted on before the bill can come to a final vote. The introduction of new amendments can be stopped only by unanimous consent. This, in effect, can permit a determined minority to filibuster by amendment, indefinitely delaying the passage of a bill.

Senators can also place "holds," or stalling devices, on bills to delay debate. Senators place holds on bills when they fear that openly opposing them will be unpopular. Because holds are kept secret, the senators placing the holds do not have to take public responsibility for their actions.

Once a bill is debated on the floor of the House and the Senate, the leaders schedule it for a vote on the floor of each chamber. By then, congressional leaders know what the vote will be; leaders do not bring legislation to the floor unless they are fairly certain it is going to pass. As a consequence, it is unusual for the leadership to lose a bill on the floor. On rare occasions, however, the last moments of the floor vote can be dramatic, as each party's leadership puts its whip organization into action to make sure wavering members vote with the party. In October 2008, a massive Treasury-sponsored plan to rescue failing financial institutions was defeated in the House, *despite* the support of the leadership of both parties. Because the vote came just before the 2008 elections, members were afraid to buck strong constituency opposition to the rescue plan. (A modified version passed a week later, though still with substantial and vocal opposition.)

filibuster A tactic used by members of the Senate to prevent action on legislation they oppose by continuously holding the floor and speaking until the majority backs down. Once given the floor, senators have unlimited time to speak, and it requires a cloture vote of three-fifths of the Senate to end a filibuster.

cloture A rule allowing a super-majority of the members of a legislative body to set a time limit on debate over a given bill.

Conference Committee: Reconciling House and Senate Versions of a Bill

Getting a bill out of committee and through one of the houses of Congress is no guarantee that it will be enacted. Frequently bills that began with similar provisions in both chambers emerge with little resemblance to one another. Alternatively, a bill may be passed by one chamber but undergo substantial revision in the other chamber. In such cases, a conference committee composed of the senior members of the committees or subcommittees that initiated the bills may be required to iron out differences between the two pieces of legislation. Sometimes members or leaders will let objectionable provisions pass on the floor with the idea that they will be eliminated in conference. Conference agreement requires majority support from each of the two delegations. Legislation that emerges successfully from a conference committee is more often a compromise than a clear victory of one set of forces over another.

When a bill comes out of conference, it faces one more hurdle. Before it can be sent to the president for signing, the House-Senate conference report must be approved on the floor of each chamber. It must be voted up or down; no amendments are in order. Usually such approval is given quickly. Occasionally, however, a bill's opponents use the report as one last opportunity to defeat a piece of legislation.

Presidential Action

Once adopted by the House and the Senate, a bill goes to the president, who may choose to sign the bill into law or **veto** it (Figure 5.7). The veto is the president's constitutional power to reject a piece of legislation. To veto a bill, the president returns it within ten days to the house of Congress in which it originated, along with objections to it. If Congress adjourns during the ten-day period and the president has taken no action, the bill is also considered to have been vetoed—by means of the **pocket veto.** The possibility of a presidential veto affects the willingness of members of Congress to push for different pieces of legislation at different times. If they think a proposal is likely to be vetoed, they might shelve it for a later time. Alternatively, the sponsors of a popular bill opposed by the president might push for passage to force the president to pay the political costs of vetoing it.[39] During the entire first term of President George W. Bush (2001–2005), not one bill was vetoed. In the next two years, the president vetoed a single bill, the Stem Cell Research Enhancement Act, on July 19, 2006. This unusual record of veto inactivity reflects the fact that the Republicans controlled both legislative chambers throughout the period and thus were able to work hand in glove with a Republican president. In the 110th Congress (2007–2008) the Republican president faced a Congress controlled by the Democrats. The president vetoed eight bills, and four of his vetoes were overridden.

A presidential veto may be overridden by a two-thirds vote in both the House and the Senate. A veto override says much about the support that a president can expect from Congress, and it can deliver a stinging blow to the executive branch.

veto The president's constitutional power to turn down acts of Congress within ten days of their passage while Congress is in session. A presidential veto may be overridden by a two-thirds vote of each house of Congress.

pocket veto A veto that is effected when Congress adjourns during the time a president has to approve a bill and the president takes no action on it.

---

[39] John B. Gilmour, *Strategic Disagreement: Stalemate in American Politics* (Pittsburgh: University of Pittsburgh Press, 1995).

FIGURE 5.7 HOW A BILL BECOMES A LAW

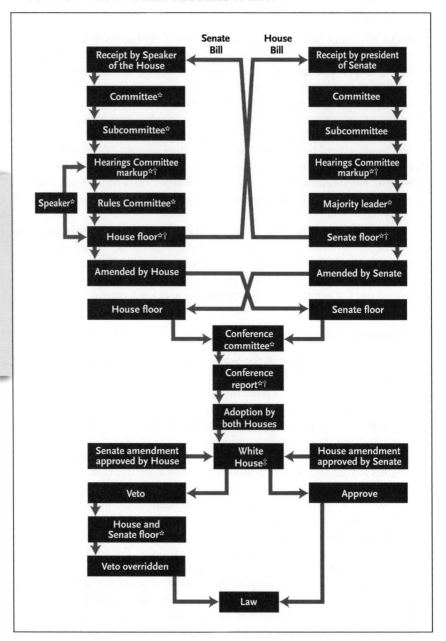

* Points at which the bill can be amended.
† Points at which the bill can die.
‡ If the president neither signs nor vetoes the bill within ten days, it automatically becomes law.

In 2007, a popular pork-barrel bill, the Water Resources Development Act, was vetoed by President Bush. His message to Congress, in part, stated:

> I am returning herewith without my approval H.R. 1495, the "Water Resources Development Act of 2007."
>
> This bill lacks fiscal discipline. I fully support funding for water resources projects that will yield high economic and environmental returns to the Nation and each year my budget has proposed reasonable and responsible funding. . . . However, this authorization bill makes promises to local communities that the Congress does not have a track record of keeping. The House of Representatives took a $15 billion bill into negotiations with a $14 billion bill from the Senate and instead of splitting the difference, emerged with a Washington compromise that costs over $23 billion. This is not fiscally responsible. . . . The bill's excessive authorization for over 900 projects and programs exacerbates the massive backlog of ongoing Corps construction projects, which will require an additional $38 billion in future appropriations to complete.[40]

Despite his opposition, both houses overwhelmingly overrode his veto. Presidents will often back down from their threat to veto a bill if they believe Congress will override the veto. These strategic interactions between the legislature and the executive branch are taken up in the next chapter.

Normal and Abnormal Procedures in Congress

We have noted that although there is a "normal" procedure in each chamber, it is often the case that the normal is abandoned and an abnormal, or unorthodox, procedure is devised. The treatment of appropriations bills in the period leading up to the November 2004 election provides an excellent example.

"Normally" the House passes thirteen separate appropriations bills after each one has passed through an appropriations process, beginning with a subcommittee hearing, followed by full Appropriations Committee deliberations, and concluding with passage by the full House. These thirteen measures are then transmitted to the Senate, which subjects each of them to its own "regular" appropriations process. Each of the bills (thirteen in all) now has a House version and a Senate version. Thirteen separate conference committees are set up to compromise on the differences between each pair. The thirteen compromised versions are then sent back to each chamber for final approval. And in principle, though rarely in practice, this entire process is completed before October 1, the day on which the new fiscal year begins.

But 2004 was an election year, and members up for reelection really did not want to remind the voters that the appropriations bills they were passing were going to produce the largest deficit in history. So an unorthodox procedure was invented. One of the thirteen appropriations bills passed the House and the Senate through the normal process and was sent to conference. During the conference, the other twelve bills were tacked on, making a single appropriations bill. This

---

[40] *Congressional Record*, at 2007 H12458.

omnibus bill was sent to each chamber for a single up-or-down vote. In voting for the omnibus measure, a member was "innoculated" against local objections from constituents. He or she could respond, "I know, I know. The omnibus bill is not ideal. But what was I to do? Defeating it would have shut the government down."

Before leaving this topic, it is worth noting that normal and abnormal procedures involve either the conventional or the creative application of existing rules. Each chamber, however, is granted by the Constitution the privilege of formulating its own rules of procedure. So from time to time, the House or the Senate will change its rules of procedure. At other times, a dominant coalition in a chamber will threaten to do this unless it is allowed its way under the existing rules. Here we see the confluence of the rationality principle and the institution principle as rational legislators seek to (re)arrange their chamber's institutional procedures in order to accomplish particular purposes or realize particular goals.

This phenomenon was dramatically illustrated in May 2005. Even though Republicans were in the majority in the Senate, President Bush's judicial nominations were threatened by a filibuster by Democratic senators. (The Senate must formally approve a president's nominations to the federal judiciary.) In the face of nominations whose approval looked vulnerable to a blocking action by the minority party, Bill Frist, the Senate majority leader, unveiled what came to be known as the *nuclear option*. It entailed a clever parliamentary maneuver in which debate could be brought to a close not by securing the sixty votes normally required (which the Republicans did not control) but by a simple majority. This would be executed by formally requesting the president of the Senate (Vice President Dick Cheney) to end debate without a cloture vote because the issue before the Senate was the constitutional one of "advising and consenting" on a presidential judicial nomination. It was expected that any such move on the part of the Republicans would be followed by the Democrats' appealing any ruling by the Senate president to end debate. But that ruling required only a majority vote to be sustained. In this manner, the Republicans could end-run the practice of unlimited debate that normally prevails in the Senate, on constitutional issues at least. The nuclear option was never implemented, however. The very threat of it induced a number of moderate senators to agree to support a motion to end debate (thereby producing the sixty needed votes) and bring a presidential nominee forward for a final vote. These senators were willing to accommodate a vote so long as the president and the Republican majority did not abuse this concession by bringing forward "extremist" nominees.[41]

The Distributive Tendency in Congress

To pass a policy, it is necessary to authorize the policy—that is, to provide statutory authority to a government agency to implement the legislation—and then provide appropriations to fund the implementation. The list of politicians whose consent is required in these processes is extraordinarily long. At a minimum, it includes majorities of the relevant committee and subcommittee of each chamber (almost

---

[41] For a model of the judicial confirmation process, see David W. Rohde and Kenneth A. Shepsle, "Advising and Consenting in the 60-Vote Senate: Strategic Appointments to the Supreme Court," *Journal of Politics* 69 (2007): 664–77.

certainly including their chairs), the Appropriations Committee and the appropriate subcommittee in each chamber (including their chairs), the House Rules Committee, chamber majorities (including leaders of the majority party), and the president. Some of the legislators may go along without requiring much for their states or districts on the assumption that their turn will come on another bill. But most of these politicians will need some form of "compensation" in order to provide their endorsement and support.

With so many hurdles to clear before a legislative initiative can become a law, the benefits must be spread broadly. It is as though a bill had to travel on a toll road past a number of tollbooths, each one housing a collector with his or her hand out for payment. On rare occasions, the required toll takes the form of a personal bribe—a contract to a firm run by a congressman's brother, a job for a senator's daughter, a boondoggle "military inspection" trip to a Pacific isle for a legislator and his or her companion. Occasionally there is a wink-and-a-nod understanding, usually given by the majority leader or committee chair, that support from a legislator today will result in reciprocal support for legislation of interest to him or her down the road. Most frequently features of the bill are drafted initially or revised so as to be more inclusive, spreading the benefits widely among beneficiaries. This is the **distributive tendency**.

The distributive tendency is part of the American system of representative democracy. Legislators, in advocating the interests of their constituents, are eager to advertise their ability to deliver for their state or district. They maneuver to put themselves in a position to claim credit for good things that happen there and duck blame for bad things. This is the way they earn trust back home, deter strong challengers in upcoming elections, and defeat those who do run against them. It means that legislators must take advantage of every opportunity that presents itself. In some instances, the results may seem bizarre. In April 2003, for example, Senator Thad Cochran (R-Miss.) was able to insert into the bill funding the war in Iraq language that provided $250 million for "disaster relief" for southern catfish farmers.[42] Most Americans would never have guessed that driving Saddam Hussein from power would have an effect on catfish farming in Mississippi.

This system, which is practiced in Washington and most state capitals, means that political pork gets spread around; it is not controlled by a small clique of politicians or concentrated in a small number of states or districts. But it also means that public authority and appropriations do not go where they are most needed. The most impoverished cities do not get so much money as is appropriate because some of the available money must be diverted to buy political support. The neediest individuals often do not get tax relief, health care, or occupational subsidies for reasons unrelated to philosophy or policy grounds. It is the distributive tendency at work. And it is one of the unintended consequences of the separation of powers and multiple veto points.[43] As the policy principle suggests, rationality combines with institutional practices to leave their marks on the shape of policy.

distributive tendency The tendency of Congress to spread the benefits of a policy over a wide range of members' districts.

---

[42] Dan Morgan, "War Funding Bill's Extra Riders," *Washington Post*, April 8, 2003, p. A4.

[43] See George Tsebelis, *Veto Players: How Political Institutions Work* (Princeton, N.J.: Princeton University Press, 2002).

HOW CONGRESS DECIDES

What determines the kinds of legislation that Congress ultimately produces? The process of creating a legislative agenda, drawing up a list of possible measures, and deciding among them is very complex. In this process, a variety of influences from inside and outside government play important roles. External influences include a legislator's constituency and various interest groups. Influences from inside government include party leadership, congressional colleagues, and the president. Let us examine each of these influences individually and then consider how they interact to produce congressional policy decisions.

Constituency

Because members of Congress want to be reelected, we would expect the views of their constituents to have a key influence on the decisions legislators make. Yet constituency influence is not so straightforward as we might think. In fact, most constituents do not even know what policies their representatives support. The number of citizens who *do* pay attention to such matters—the attentive public—is usually very small. Nonetheless, members of Congress spend a lot of time worrying about what their constituents think because these representatives realize that their choices may be scrutinized in a future election and used as ammunition by an opposing candidate. Because of this possibility, members of Congress will try to anticipate their constituents' policy views.[44] Legislators are more likely to act in accordance with those views if they think voters will take them into account during elections. In this way, constituents may affect congressional policy choices even when there is little direct evidence of their awareness of those choices.[45]

Interest Groups

Interest groups are another important external influence on the policies that Congress produces. When members of Congress are making voting decisions, interest groups that have some connection to constituents in the districts of particular members are most likely to be influential. For this reason, interest groups with the ability to mobilize followers in many congressional districts may be especially influential in Congress. The small-business lobby, for example, played an important role in defeating President Clinton's proposal for comprehensive health-care

---

[44] See John W. Kingdon, *Congressmen's Voting Decisions* (New York: Harper & Row, 1973), chap. 3, and R. Douglas Arnold, *The Logic of Congressional Action* (New Haven, Conn.: Yale University Press, 1990). See also Joshua Clinton, "Representation in Congress: Constituents and Roll Calls in the 106th House," *Journal of Politics* 68 (2006): 397–409.

[45] Interest groups from the state or district (which we discuss below) can be useful to legislators in this respect when they provide information concerning the significance of particular issues for various constituency groups. In effect, they provide legislators with heads-up signals and wake-up calls. See Kenneth W. Kollman, *Outside Lobbying: Public Opinion and Interest Group Strategies* (Princeton, N.J.: Princeton University Press, 1998).

reform in 1993–94. The mobilization of networks of small businesses across the country meant that virtually every member of Congress had to take their views into account.

In the 2010 electoral cycle, interest groups and PACs gave many millions of dollars in campaign contributions to incumbent legislators and challengers. What does this money buy? A popular conception is that campaign contributions buy legislative votes. In this view, legislators vote for whichever proposal favors the bulk of their contributors. Although the vote-buying hypothesis makes for good campaign rhetoric, it has little factual support. Empirical studies by political scientists show little evidence that contributions from large PACs influence legislative voting patterns.[46]

If contributions don't buy votes, what do they buy? Our claim is that campaign contributions influence legislative behavior in ways that are difficult for the public to observe and political scientists to measure. The institutional structure of Congress provides opportunities for interest groups to influence legislation outside the public eye, which legislators and contributors prefer.

Committee proposal power enables legislators, if they are on the relevant committee, to introduce legislation that favors contributing groups. Gatekeeping power enables committee members to block legislation that harms contributing groups. The fact that certain provisions are *excluded* from a bill is as much an indicator of PAC influence as the fact that certain provisions are *included*. The difference is that it is hard to measure what you don't see. Committee oversight powers enable members to intervene in bureaucratic decision making on behalf of contributing groups.

The point here is that voting on the floor, the alleged object of campaign contributions according to the vote-buying hypothesis, is a highly visible, highly public act, one that could get a legislator in trouble with his or her broader electoral constituency. The committee system, on the other hand, provides loads of opportunities for legislators to deliver "services" to PAC contributors and other donors that are more subtle and better hidden from public view. Thus we suggest that the most appropriate places to look for traces of campaign-contribution influence on the legislative process are in the manner in which committees deliberate, mark up proposals, and block legislation from the floor; outside public view, these are the primary arenas for interest-group influence.[47]

Party Discipline

In both the House and the Senate, party leaders have a good deal of influence over the behavior of their party members. This influence, sometimes called party discipline,

---

[46] See Janet M. Grenke, "PACs and the Congressional Supermarket: The Currency Is Complex," *American Journal of Political Science* 33, no. 1 (February 1989): 1–24. More generally, see Jacobson, *The Politics of Congressional Elections*. For a view that interest groups spend too little, not too much, money, see Stephen Ansolabehere, John de Figueiredo, and James Snyder, "Why Is There So Little Money in U.S. Politics?" *Journal of Economic Perspectives* 17 (2003): 105–30.

[47] A complementary effect of campaign contributions is not to buy votes that would otherwise be unavailable to a contributor. It is, rather, to increase the likelihood that legislators *already sympathetic* will be reelected. Interest groups thus primarily support their friends with contributions rather than attempting to convert opponents to their cause.

FIGURE 5.8 PARTY UNITY SCORES BY CHAMBER

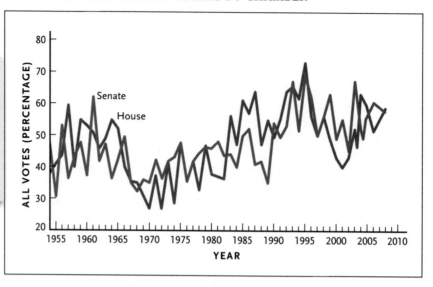

SOURCE: Party Polarization: 1879–2008, updated January 2, 2009,
http://voteview.com/Polarized_America.htm#politicalpolarization (accessed 6/18/09).

ANALYZING THE EVIDENCE

Party voting has ticked up since the 1970s but began to tail off after reaching a peak in the mid-1990s. What contributes to party voting?

party vote A roll-call vote in the House or Senate in which at least 50 percent of the members of one party take a particular position and are opposed by at least 50 percent of the members of the other party. Party votes are less common today than they were in the nineteenth century.

roll-call votes Votes in which each legislator's yes or no vote is recorded.

was once so powerful that it dominated the lawmaking process. Let us define as a **party vote** a vote on which 50 percent or more of the members of one party take one position while at least 50 percent of the members of the other party take the opposing position. At the beginning of the twentieth century, most **roll-call votes** in the House of Representatives were party votes. The frequency of party votes declined through most of the twentieth century as legislative parties grew more ideologically diverse. Democrats included liberals from the big cities and conservatives from the South. Republicans included conservatives from the Midwest and West and moderates from the Northeast. The tail end of this decline in party voting can be observed in Figure 5.8 between 1955 and 1970. Beginning in the 1970s, however, legislative parties grew more homogeneous and more polarized. Conservative southern districts began electing Republicans, and liberal northeastern districts began sending Democrats to Congress. The data shown in the figure reflect this, with party votes ticking upward from the 1970s onward. Some of this change is the result of the intense partisan struggles that began during the administrations of Ronald Reagan and George H. W. Bush. Straight party-line voting was also seen briefly in the 103rd Congress (1993–94) after Bill Clinton's election in 1992. The situation soon gave way, however, to the many long-term factors working against party discipline in Congress, as seen in the decline in party voting over the rest of the 1990s.[48] Since the election of George W. Bush, accompanied by Republican congressional control, party voting

---

[48] There were fluctuations during George W. Bush's presidency—declines in party voting following September 11 and then surges and declines in subsequent years (see Figure 5.8).

again ticked upward. And in the first two years of the Obama administration, party voting in both chambers was strong—Republican votes supporting Obama initiatives are quite rare.

To some extent, party divisions are based on ideology and background. Republican members of Congress are more likely than Democrats to be drawn from rural or suburban areas. Democrats are likely to be more liberal on economic and social questions than their Republican colleagues. This ideological gap has been especially pronounced since 1980 (Figure 5.9). Ideological differences certainly help explain roll-call divisions between the two parties.[49] Ideology and background, however, are only part of the explanation of party unity. The other part has to do with party organization and leadership. Although party organization has weakened since the beginning of the twentieth century, today's party leaders still have some resources at their disposal: (1) committee assignments, (2) access to the floor, (3) the whip system, (4) logrolling, and (5) the presidency. These resources are regularly used and are often effective in securing the support of party members.[50]

Committee Assignments.   Leaders can create debts among members by helping them get favorable committee assignments. These assignments are made early in the congressional careers of most members and ordinarily cannot be taken from them if they later balk at party discipline. Nevertheless, if the leadership goes out of its way to get the right assignment for a member, the effort is likely to create a bond of obligation that can be called on without any other payments or favors.

In 2005, the Republicans removed several members from the House Ethics Committee because of their participation, in the previous Congress, in investigating the House Republican leader, Tom DeLay. Inasmuch as the Ethics Committee

---

[49] Keith T. Poole and Howard Rosenthal, *Congress: A Political-Economic History of Roll Call Voting* (New York: Oxford University Press, 1997).

[50] Legislative leaders may behave in ways that enhance their reputation for being willing to punish party members who stray from the party line. The problem of developing such a credible reputation is analyzed in Randall Calvert, "Reputation and Legislative Leadership," *Public Choice* 55 (1987): 81–120, and is summarized in Kenneth A. Shepsle and Mark S. Boncheck, *Analyzing Politics: Rationality, Behavior, Institutions* (New York: Norton, 1997), pp. 397–403. The classic example of such punishment occurred after the 1964 election, in which two prominent House Democrats, John Bell Williams of Mississippi and Albert Watson of South Carolina, were disciplined for having supported the Republican presidential nominee, Barry Goldwater. The party leaders pushed for, and the Democratic caucus supported, a punishment in which each was demoted to the bottom of the seniority roster on the committees of which they were members. In Williams's case, the punishment was serious because he was the second-highest-ranking Democrat on the House Energy and Commerce Committee. Each resigned from the House in the wake of this punishment and ran for elective office (both successfully) as Republicans. The message was clear: Party members cross some partisan lines at their peril! The famous mid-twentieth-century House Speaker Sam Rayburn is known to have believed that deviation from the party position would be tolerated for "reasons of conscience or constituency." Of one wayward Democrat, he is alleged to have said that the departure from the party line "better be a matter of conscience, because it damn sight isn't because of his constituency." In short, there would be hell to pay! More recently, Senator Joseph Lieberman (I-Conn.), an independent who caucuses with the Democrats, and in past years had been elected as one, endorsed and campaigned for the 2008 Republican standard bearer, John McCain. Many Democrats sought severe sanctions against him, but he managed to escape with only a mild rebuke (because Democrats were so desperate for his vote on the Obama legislature program and nominations).

FIGURE 5.9 THE WIDENING IDEOLOGICAL GAP BETWEEN THE PARTIES

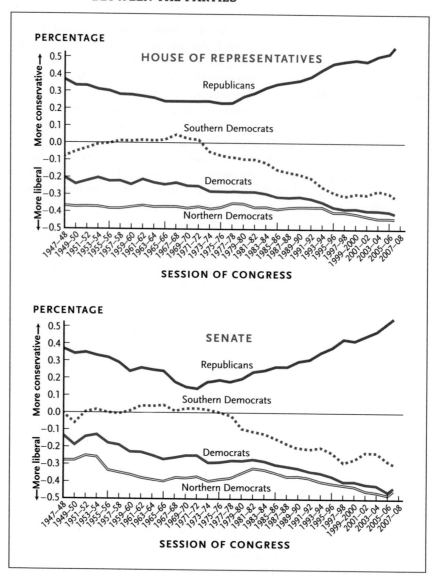

SOURCE: Party Polarization: 1879–2008, updated January 2, 2009, http://voteview.com/Polarized_America.htm#politicalpolarization (accessed 3/30/09).

is seen as a bipartisan watchdog, these actions were regarded as muscle-flexing responses by the Republican leadership. Bipartisan or not, the leadership seemed to be saying, as noted above, that some lines should not be crossed.

Access to the Floor.   The most important everyday resource available to the parties is control over access to the floor. With thousands of bills awaiting passage and most members clamoring for access to influence a bill or publicize themselves, floor time is precious. In the Senate, the leadership allows ranking committee members to influence the allocation of floor time—who will speak for how long. In the House, the Speaker, as head of the majority party (in consultation with the minority leader), allocates large blocks of floor time. Thus floor time is allocated in both houses of Congress by the majority and minority leaders. More important, the Speaker of the House and the majority leader in the Senate possess the power of recognition. Although this power may not appear to be substantial, it is a formidable authority and can be used to stymie a piece of legislation completely or to frustrate a member's attempts to speak on a particular issue. Because the power is significant, members of Congress usually attempt to stay on good terms with the Speaker and the majority leader to ensure that they will continue to be recognized.[51]

The Whip System. Some influence accrues to party leaders through the **whip system**, which is primarily a communications network. Between twelve and twenty assistant and regional whips are selected by geographic zones to operate at the direction of the majority or minority leader and the whip. They take polls of all the members to learn their intentions on specific bills. This information enables the leaders to know if they have enough support to allow a vote and whether the vote is so close that they need to put pressure on a few swing votes. Leaders also use the whip system to convey their wishes and plans to the members, but only in very close votes do they exert pressure on a member. In those instances, the Speaker or a lieutenant will go to a few party members who have indicated they will switch if their votes are essential. The whip system helps the leaders limit the practice of pressuring members to a few times per session. It helps maintain party unity in both houses of Congress, but it is particularly critical in the House of Representatives because of the large number of legislators whose positions and votes must always be accounted for.

Logrolling. An agreement between two or more members of Congress who have nothing in common except the need for mutual support is called **logrolling**. The agreement states, in effect, "You support me on bill X, and I'll support you on a bill of your choice." Because party leaders are the center of the communications networks in the two chambers, they can help members create large logrolling coalitions. Hundreds of logrolling deals are made each year, and although there are no official records, it would be a poor party leader whose whips did not know who owed what to whom.[52] In some instances, logrolling produces strange alliances.

whip system A communications network in each house of Congress. Whips poll the membership to learn their intentions on specific legislative issues and assist the majority and minority leaders in various tasks.

logrolling A legislative practice wherein reciprocal agreements are made between legislators, usually in voting for or against a bill. In contrast to bargaining, logrolling unites parties that have nothing in common but their desire to exchange support.

---

[51] A recent analysis of how floor time is allocated is found in Cox and McCubbins, *Setting the Agenda*.

[52] For an analysis of the formal problems that logrolling (or vote trading) both solves and creates, see Shepsle and Bonchek, *Analyzing Politics*, pp. 317–19. They argue that logrolling cannot be the entire solution to the problem of assembling majority coalitions out of the diverse preferences found in any political party. The reason is that although party leaders can try to keep track of who owes what to whom, the bookkeeping is imperfect and highly complex at best. Nevertheless, if anyone is positioned to orchestrate a system of logrolling, it is the party leaders. And of all those who have tried to facilitate such "cooperation," Robert Byrd (D-W.Va.), who served as both majority whip and majority leader in the Senate, has been the acknowledged master. For an insightful analysis of the ways party leaders build majority coalitions through the strategic use of pork-barrel projects, see Evans, *Greasing the Wheels*.

A seemingly unlikely alliance emerged in Congress in June 1994, when 119 mainly conservative senators and representatives from oil-producing states met with President Clinton to suggest that they might be willing to support the president's health-care proposals in exchange for his support for a number of tax breaks for the oil industry. Senator J. Bennett Johnston of Louisiana, a leader of the oil-state representatives, contended that the issues of health care and oil production were closely related because both "affected the long-term economic security of the nation." Ironically, the oil-producing groups that promoted this alliance are generally among the most conservative forces in the nation. When asked what he thought of the president's health-care proposal, George Alcorn, a leading industry lobbyist involved in the logrolling effort, dismissed Clinton's plan as "socialized medicine." Another alliance of strange bedfellows was the 1994 "corn for porn" logroll in which liberal urbanites supported farm programs in exchange for rural support for National Endowment for the Arts funding (at a time when many conservatives thought that the art produced by some NEA grantees bordered on the pornographic). Good logrolling, it would seem, is not hampered by minor ideological concerns.[53] In this case, the rationality principle (exemplified by a willingness to support a policy to which one is opposed in exchange for reciprocal support for a policy one cares passionately about) and the institution principle (in which the separation of powers allows the president and legislators to cut deals) work in unusual ways to produce policy outcomes.

The Presidency.   Of all the influences that maintain the clarity of party lines in Congress, the influence of the presidency is probably the most important. Indeed, it is a touchstone of party discipline in Congress. Since the late 1940s, under President Harry Truman, presidents each year have identified a number of bills to be considered part of their administration's program. By the mid-1950s, both parties in Congress began to look to the president for these proposals, which became the most significant part of Congress's agenda. The president's support is a criterion for party loyalty, and party leaders are able to use it to rally some members.

Weighing Diverse Influences

Clearly many factors affect congressional decisions. But at various points in the decision-making process, some are likely to be more influential than others. For example, interest groups may be more effective at the committee stage, when their expertise is especially valued and their visibility is less obvious. Because committees play a key role in deciding what legislation reaches the floor of the House or the Senate, interest groups can often put a halt to bills they dislike, or they can ensure that the options that do reach the floor are those that the group's members support.

Once legislation reaches the floor and members of Congress are deciding among alternatives, constituent opinion will become more important. Legislators are also influenced very much by other legislators: Many of their assessments about the substance and politics of legislation come from fellow members of Congress.

---

[53] Allen R. Meyerson, "Oil-Patch Congressmen Seek Deal with Clinton," *New York Times,* June 14, 1994, p. D2.

The influence of the external and internal forces described in the preceding section also varies according to the kind of issue being considered. On policies of great importance to powerful interest groups—farm subsidies, for example—those groups are likely to have considerable influence. On other issues, members of Congress may be less attentive to narrow interest groups and more willing to consider what they see as the general interest.

Finally, the mix of influences varies according to the historical moment. The Republicans' 1994 electoral victory allowed their party to control both houses of Congress for the first time in forty years. That fact, combined with an unusually assertive Republican leadership, meant that party leaders became especially important in decision making. The willingness of moderate Republicans to support measures they had once opposed indicated the unusual importance of party leadership in this period. As the House Democratic minority leader, Richard Gephardt, put it, "When you've been in the desert forty years, your instinct is to help Moses."[54] In a reversal of fortune, the Democrats bounced back in 2006, with party leaders both working with the president *and* investigating the executive branch with equal levels of energy and commitment. The Bush administration's financial "rescue package" of 2008 was itself rescued by *Democratic* leadership activism and *Democratic* votes.

BEYOND LEGISLATION: ADDITIONAL CONGRESSIONAL POWERS

In addition to the power to make the law, Congress has at its disposal an array of other instruments through which it can influence the process of government.

Advice and Consent: Special Senate Powers

The Constitution has given the Senate a special power, one that is not based on lawmaking: The president has the power to make treaties and appoint top executive officers, ambassadors, and federal judges—but only "with the Advice and Consent of the Senate" (Article II, Section 2). For treaties, two-thirds of those senators present must concur; for appointments, a majority is required.

The power to approve or reject presidential requests also involves the power to set conditions. The Senate only occasionally exercises its power to reject treaties and appointments. Only nine Supreme Court nominees have been rejected by the Senate during the past century, while many times that number have been approved.[55]

More common than the Senate rejection of presidential appointees is a senatorial "hold" on an appointment. By Senate tradition, any member may place an indefinite hold on the confirmation of a mid- or lower-level presidential appointment. The hold may be a signal of a senator's willingness to filibuster a nomination, but it is typically used by senators trying to wring concessions from the White House on matters

---

[54] Quoted in David Broder, "At 6 Months, House GOP Juggernaut Still Cohesive," *Washington Post*, July 17, 1995, p. A1.

[55] Of President George W. Bush's three nominees, however, although two were confirmed, one nominee withdrew because of a concern that she could not succeed.

having nothing to do with the appointment in question. After Bush came to power in January 2001, the Democrats in the Senate actively scrutinized judicial nominations. Senate Democrats prevented final confirmation votes on a dozen especially conservative nominees, a matter about which President Bush frequently complained during the 2004 reelection campaign. Of course, Republicans had done exactly the same thing to many judicial nominations in the preceding Clinton administration.

Judicial nomination politics loomed large during Bush's second term. In May of 2005, Senate majority leader Frist, responding to the obstructionist tactics by the minority Democrats, threatened the nuclear option, as we reported earlier. Had the option been exercised, it is believed it would have constituted a procedural watershed in the Senate, making this chamber much more like the more majoritarian House. In yielding to the nuclear-option threat, the Democrats permitted a number of previously controversial federal court nominees to be confirmed.

Into this highly charged environment, in the summer of 2005, came a number of bolts from the blue. Bush, who had not had a single opportunity to name a Supreme Court justice in his first term, was confronted with a flurry of opportunities during a few short months in his second term. During the summer, Justice Sandra Day O'Connor (the first woman to serve on the Court) announced her retirement. Bush nominated John Roberts, a sitting federal judge, as her replacement. But before he could be confirmed, Chief Justice William Rehnquist died. O'Connor agreed to remain on the Court until her replacement was confirmed, so President Bush withdrew Roberts's nomination and then renominated him to replace Rehnquist as chief justice. Roberts was confirmed in time for the opening of the Court's term in October. Bush now turned to O'Connor's replacement. His initial nominee, presidential confidante and White House Counsel Harriet Miers, was forced to withdraw amid charges of cronyism and lack of experience. In addition, conservative Republicans thought Miers was not sufficiently conservative. Bush then nominated Samuel Alito, a federal appeals court judge with a substantial track record and solidly conservative credentials.

During his first term in office, President Obama had the opportunity to name two new justices when David Souter and John Paul Stevens announced their retirements. To replace Souter, Obama chose federal appeals court judge Sonia Sotomayor, the first Hispanic to serve on the Supreme Court. To take Stevens's place, Obama named Solicitor General Elena Kagan. Republicans grumbled that both nominees were too liberal, but made only token objections since Sotomayor and Kagan would be replacing liberal justices and so would not change the balance of power on the Court.

Senatorial advice and consent is also required on treaties. Most presidents make every effort to take potential Senate opposition into account in treaty negotiations and will frequently resort to **executive agreements** with foreign powers instead of treaties. The Supreme Court has held that such agreements are equivalent to treaties, but they do not need Senate approval.[56] In the past, presidents sometimes concluded secret agreements without informing Congress of the agreements' contents or even their existence. For example, American involvement in the Vietnam

executive agreement An agreement between the president and another country that has the force of a treaty but does not require the Senate's "advice and consent."

---

[56] *United States v. Pink*, 315 U.S. 203 (1942). For a good discussion of the problem, see James W. Davis, *The American Presidency: A New Perspective* (New York: Harper & Row, 1987), chap. 8. A recent analysis is found in William G. Howell, *Power without Persuasion: The Politics of Direct Presidential Action* (Princeton, N.J.: Princeton University Press, 2003).

War grew in part out of a series of secret arrangements made between American presidents and the South Vietnamese during the 1950s and 1960s. Congress did not even learn of the existence of these agreements until 1969. In 1972, Congress passed the Case Act, which requires that the president inform Congress of any executive agreement within sixty days of its having been reached. This provides Congress with the opportunity to cancel agreements that it opposes. In addition, Congress can limit the president's ability to conduct foreign policy through executive agreement by refusing to appropriate the funds needed to implement an agreement. In this way, for example, Congress can modify or even cancel executive agreements to provide economic or military assistance to foreign governments.

Impeachment

The Constitution, in Article II, Section 4, also grants Congress the power of **impeachment** over the president, vice president, and other executive officials. Impeachment means charging a government official (president or otherwise) with "Treason, Bribery, or other high Crimes and Misdemeanors" and bringing him or her before Congress to determine guilt. Impeachment is thus like a criminal indictment, in which the House of Representatives acts like a grand jury, voting (by simple majority) on whether the accused ought to be impeached. If a majority of the House votes to impeach, the impeachment trial is held in the Senate, which acts like a trial jury by voting whether to convict and forcibly remove the person from office (this vote requires a two-thirds majority).

Controversy over Congress's impeachment power has arisen over the grounds for impeachment, especially the meaning of "high Crimes and Misdemeanors." A strict reading of the Constitution suggests that the only impeachable offense is an actual crime. But a more commonly agreed on definition is that "an impeachable offense is whatever the majority of the House of Representatives considers it to be at a given moment in history."[57] In other words, impeachment, especially impeachment of a president, is a political decision.

The United States came closest to impeaching and convicting a president in 1867. Andrew Johnson, a southern Democrat who had battled a congressional Republican majority over Reconstruction, was impeached by the House but saved from conviction by one vote in the Senate. At the height of the Watergate scandal in 1974, the House started impeachment proceedings against President Richard Nixon, but Nixon resigned before the House could proceed. The possibility of impeachment arose again in 1998, when President Clinton was accused of lying under oath and obstructing justice in the investigation into his sexual affair with the White House intern Monica Lewinsky. In October 1998, the House voted to impeach the president. At the conclusion of the Senate trial in 1999, Democrats, joined by a handful of Republicans, acquitted the president of both charges.

The impeachment power is a considerable one; its very existence in the hands of Congress is a highly effective safeguard against the executive tyranny so greatly feared by the framers of the Constitution.

impeachment
The charging of a government official (president or otherwise) with "Treason, Bribery, or other high Crimes and Misdemeanors" and bringing him or her before Congress to determine guilt.

---

[57] Carroll J. Doherty, "Impeachment: How It Would Work," *Congressional Quarterly Weekly Report*, January 31, 1998, p. 222.

POWER AND REPRESENTATION

Because they feared both executive and legislative tyranny, the framers of the Constitution pitted Congress and the president against each other. And as the history principle suggests, this has provided us with a legacy of interbranch competition. During the first century of American government, Congress was the dominant institution. American foreign and domestic policy was formulated and implemented by Congress, and generally the most powerful figures in American government were the Speaker of the House and the leaders of the Senate—not the president. During the nineteenth century, Congress—not the president—dominated press coverage on "the affairs of government."[58] The War of 1812 was planned and fought by Congress. The great sectional compromises before the Civil War were formulated in Congress without much intervention from the executive branch. Even during the Civil War, a period of extraordinary presidential leadership, a joint congressional committee on the conduct of the war played a role in formulating war plans and campaign tactics—and even had a hand in the promotion of officers. After the Civil War, when President Andrew Johnson sought to interfere with congressional plans for Reconstruction, he was summarily impeached, saved from conviction by only one vote. Subsequent presidents understood the moral and did not attempt to thwart Congress.

This congressional preeminence began to diminish at the beginning of the twentieth century, so that by the 1960s the executive had become, at least temporarily, the dominant branch of American government. The major domestic policy initiatives of the twentieth century—Franklin Roosevelt's New Deal, Harry Truman's Fair Deal, John F. Kennedy's New Frontier, and Lyndon Johnson's Great Society—all included some congressional involvement but were essentially developed, introduced, and implemented by the executive. In the area of foreign policy, although Congress continued to be influential during the twentieth century, the focus of decision-making power clearly moved into the executive branch. The War of 1812 may have been a congressional war, but in the twentieth century American entry into World War I, World War II, Korea, Vietnam, Iraq, Afghanistan, and a host of lesser conflicts was essentially a presidential—not a congressional—decision. In the last forty years, there has been a good deal of resurgence of congressional power vis-à-vis the executive. This has occurred mainly because Congress has sought to represent many important political forces, such as the civil rights, women's, environmental, consumer, and peace movements, which in turn became constituencies for congressional power. During the mid-1990s, Congress became more receptive to a variety of new conservative political forces, including groups on the social and religious right as well as more traditional economic conservatives. After Republicans won control of both houses in the 1994 elections, Congress took the lead in developing programs and policies supported by these groups. These efforts won Congress the support of conservative forces in its battles for power against a Democratic White House.

To herald the new accessibility of Congress, Republican leaders instituted a number of reforms designed to eliminate many of the practices that they had long

---

[58] Samuel Kernell and Gary C. Jacobson, "Congress and the Presidency as News in the Nineteenth Century," *Journal of Politics* 49 (1987): 1016–35.

criticized as examples of Democratic arrogance. Republican leaders reduced the number of committees and subcommittees, eliminated funding of the various unofficial caucuses, imposed term limits on committee chairs, eliminated the practice of proxy voting, reduced committee staffs by one-third, ended Congress's exemption from the labor, health, and civil rights laws that it imposed on the rest of the nation, and prohibited members from receiving most gifts. With these reforms, Republicans hoped to make Congress both more effective and more representative. Term limits and bans on gifts were seen as increasing the responsiveness of Congress to new political forces and to the American people in general. Simplification of the committee structure was seen as making Congress more efficient and thus potentially more effective and more powerful. To some extent, unfortunately, the various reforms worked at cross-purposes. Simplification of the committee structure and elimination of funding for the caucuses increased the power of the leadership, thereby muting the effectiveness of more representative elements. In another instance, when term limits for committee and subcommittee chairs were finally imposed in 2001, the result was confusion because experienced leaders were forced to step down, spreading power around in a more representative manner but diminishing committee effectiveness. This is the dilemma of congressional reform. Efficiency and representation are often competing principles in our system of government, and we must be wary of gaining one at the expense of the other. In the next chapter, we turn to the second branch of American government, the presidency, to view this dilemma from a somewhat different angle.

CONCLUSION

Our discussion in this chapter has been both descriptive and analytical. The Constitution sets the stage by describing Congress's role in politics. The U.S. Congress is a two-chamber legislature with the authority to develop and pass legislation (with the concurrence of the president) on the one hand, and the power to oversee policy implementation by the president and executive bureaucracy on the other hand. It is present at the creation, so to speak, and has a continuing responsibility after a law is crafted. Each chamber keeps an eye on the other chamber and ultimately must come to terms with that other chamber on joint legislative products that are sent on to the president for his or her signature. But each chamber has a life of its own as well. Each is organized by its majority party, itself possessing an organizational structure of leaders and followers. For efficiency reasons, and to accommodate the career and policy ambitions of its members, committee systems in the House and Senate allow for the division and specialization of labor; each of these committees is a "little legislature"[59] with committee leaders and a subcommittee structure. In addition to pursuing substantive policy objectives through legislation by authorizing new programs and reauthorizing existing ones, the two chambers have a special

---

[59] The classic statement is George Goodwin, *The Little Legislatures* (Amherst, Mass.: University of Massachusetts Press, 1970).

role to play in the financial realm—raising revenue from taxes and appropriating monies to fund authorized programs. In addition, the Constitution gives the Senate further responsibilities, including the approval of treaties and the confirmation of federal judges, Supreme Court justices, and high administrative officers.

In analytical terms, the U.S. Congress is an institutional arrangement. First, in light of the rationality principle, it arranges itself in accordance with the policy and career ambitions of its members. These goals encompass reelection, the achievement of personal policy objectives, and the attainment of influence and position inside the legislative chamber. Politicians are ambitious for themselves, their party, and their constituencies. To accomplish at least some of the personal objectives of 435 individuals in one chamber and 100 in the other, politicians must engage in bargaining, coordination, and cooperation. These activities are orchestrated by institutional rules, structures, and procedures, the effects of which are found in the policies ultimately produced. It should be noted that, given the size of majorities required in each chamber to produce results, policy benefits must be distributed widely in what we called the *distributive tendency*. The resulting product isn't always pretty; there are occasional "bridges to nowhere" and other undesirable pork-barrel projects. But this is what it takes to accomplish things in a diverse, multiperson, elected body. Over the course of more than two centuries, each chamber has created ways of doing business, reformed them, and sometimes engineered entirely new ways of conducting its affairs. The history of what has gone before channels this institutional engineering.

The two chambers of the American legislature do not operate in a vacuum. In front of them are the president, the executive bureaucracy, and the courts, which jointly participate in lawmaking and its implementation. Behind them is public opinion, which ultimately renders judgment on their efforts by rewarding or punishing individuals through elections. In the next three chapters we take up the presidency, the executive branch, and the court system. In Part III we explore public opinion and elections.

FOR FURTHER READING

Adler, E. Scott. *Why Congressional Reforms Fail: Reelection and the House Committee System.* Chicago: University of Chicago Press, 2002.

Aldrich, John H., and David W. Rohde. "The Republican Revolution and the House Appropriations Committee," *Journal of Politics* 62 (2000): 1–33.

Arnold, R. Douglas. *The Logic of Congressional Action.* New Haven, Conn.: Yale University Press, 1990.

Binder, Sarah. *Stalemate: Causes and Consequences of Legislative Gridlock.* Washington, D.C.: Brookings Institution, 2003.

——— and Paul Quirk, eds. *Institutions of Democracy: The Legislative Branch.* New York: Oxford University Press, 2004.

reader selection

Brady, David W., and Mathew D. McCubbins, eds. *Party, Process, and Political Change in Congress: New Perspectives on the History of Congress.* Palo Alto, Calif.: Stanford University Press, 2002 (vol. 1); 2007 (vol. 2).

Brady, David W., and Craig Volden. *Revolving Gridlock: Politics and Policy from Carter to Bush,* 2nd ed. Boulder, Colo.: Westview Press, 2005.

Cox, Gary C., and Jonathon Katz, *Elbridge Gerry's Salamander: The Electoral Consequences of the Reapportionment Revolution.* Cambridge: Cambridge University Press, 2002.

———, and Mathew D. McCubbins. *Setting the Agenda: Responsible Party Government in the U.S. House of Representatives.* New York: Cambridge University Press, 2005.

———. *Legislative Leviathan: Party Government in the House.* 2nd ed. Berkeley: University of California Press, 2006.

Fenno, Richard F., Jr. *Home Style: House Members in Their Districts.* Boston: Little, Brown, 1978.

———. *The United States: A Bicameral Perspective.* Washington, D.C.: American Enterprise Institute, 1982.

Fiorina, Morris P. *Congress: Keystone of the Washington Establishment.* 2nd ed. New Haven, Conn.: Yale University Press, 1989.

Frisch, Scott A., and Sean Q. Kelly. *Committee Assignment Politics in the U.S. House of Representatives.* Norman: University of Oklahoma Press, 2006.

Gamm, Gerald, and Kenneth A. Shepsle. "Emergence of Legislative Institutions: Standing Committees in the House and the Senate, 1810–1825," *Legislative Studies Quarterly* 14 (1989): 39–66.

Jacobson, Gary C. *The Politics of Congressional Elections.* 6th ed. New York: Longman, 2004.

Krehbiel, Keith. *Pivotal Politics: A Theory of U.S. Lawmaking.* Chicago: University of Chicago Press, 1998.

Mayhew, David R. *Congress: The Electoral Connection.* New Haven, Conn.: Yale University Press, 1974.

Polsby, Nelson W. *How Congress Evolves.* New York: Oxford University Press, 2004.

Rohde, David W. *Parties and Leaders in the Post-reform House.* Chicago: University of Chicago Press, 1991.

Smith, Steven S., and Christopher J. Deering. *Committees in Congress.* 3rd ed. Washington, D.C.: Congressional Quarterly Press, 1997.

Stewart, Charles H. *Analyzing Congress.* New York: Norton, 2001.

Strom, Gerald. *The Logic of Lawmaking.* Baltimore: Johns Hopkins University Press, 1990.

Wawro, Gregory, and Eric Schickler. *Filibuster: Obstruction and Lawmaking in the United States Senate.* Princeton, N.J.: Princeton University Press, 2006.

reader selection

reader selection

reader selection

Ⓢ Additional study and review materials are available online at wwnorton.com/studyspace/

6 The Presidency as an Institution

America's last eight presidents have left office under political clouds and, in five cases, sooner than they wanted. Lyndon Johnson did not run for reelection in 1968 when the Vietnam War turned large segments of his own party against him. Richard Nixon was forced to resign in 1974, before completing his second term, as the Watergate scandal unfolded. Nixon's appointed successor, Gerald Ford, was defeated for election to a full term in 1976. Jimmy Carter, who ousted Ford, was, himself, denied reelection by Ronald Reagan. Reagan won reelection to a second term but left office with a reputation damaged by the Iran-Contra scandal. Reagan's successor, George H. W. Bush, was defeated for reelection by Bill Clinton. Clinton served two full terms, but only after surviving an impeachment and numerous scandals. And, of course, Clinton's successor, George W. Bush, will be remembered as the least popular president in the history of opinion polling. Given this backdrop, it might be difficult to understand why our current president, Barack Obama, ever aspired to the office.

Yet even as our presidents have limped out of the White House, the presidency as an institution has grown in power and prominence. Indeed, over the past century, the presidency has become America's most powerful institution in the realms of foreign and military policy and in most arenas of domestic policy as well. One reason that presidential power has grown despite the difficulties presidents have faced has to do with the character of the presidency as an institution. The presidency is America's only political institution characterized by unitary rather than collective decision-making processes. Members of Congress and the judiciary must deliberate, compromise, and vote before reaching decisions. The president may wish to seek advice from many sources but, in the end, exercises the powers of the office on his or her own authority. As former president George W. Bush once said, "I am the decider."

Unitary "deciders" are usually better able to accrue power than collective decision makers. To begin with, the unitary decider usually sees a direct relationship between the power of the institution and the ability to achieve whatever political goals he or she might have. Presidents Reagan and Clinton, for example, worked diligently and successfully to expand the president's power of regulatory review (discussed later in the chapter), so that they could use the bureaucratic rule-making process to achieve their policy goals without the need for congressional approval. For members of collective decision-making bodies such as Congress, on the other hand, the situation is not so simple. Members of Congress are often confronted with collective-action problems and motivated to put their immediate political interests ahead of the long-term power of the institution. For example, in October 2008, Congress responded to enormous political pressure for quick action to deal with the nation's financial crisis by giving the executive branch unprecedented new economic powers. Few members considered how their vote would affect the long-term balance of power between the legislative and executive branches. Typically, as one observer put it in an

CORE OF THE ANALYSIS

- The Constitution endows the president with only a small number of expressed powers, so the presidency is an office whose powers are primarily delegated to it by Congress or claimed by presidents without specific statutory authority.

- Over time, the presidency has accumulated more and more power relative to the other institutions of government, partly because the president doesn't face the same collective-action problems as Congress.

- Presidents can broaden their powers through successful execution of the law.

- Presidential power can also be enhanced through strategic interactions with other political actors, and through a president's ability to build popular support.

- Historic events requiring bold action and leadership by the president, such as the Great Depression, can also contribute to the president's power.

earlier context, few members are prepared to "speak up for the institutional interests of Congress."[1]

At the same time, as the foregoing example suggests, collective decision makers often feel pressure to cede power to unitary deciders when expeditious action seems of paramount importance. During times of crisis, when a quick response seems obligatory and the public is impatient with constitutional limitations on collective action, Congress and the judiciary typically accede to political appeals and presidential demands for new executive powers to deal expeditiously with the emergency. This pattern is almost always manifest in times of war and national emergency. Most recently, in the wake of the 2001 terrorist attacks against the United States, Congress quickly enacted legislation granting sweeping powers to the president to provide for the nation's defense. Similarly, during the Great Depression, Congress gave the White House unprecedented power and discretion to work to salvage the nation's economy. The same pattern recurred during the economic crisis that began in 2008.

Hence, the character of the presidency as an institution—the fact that the presidency is a unitary decider—helps to explain why the presidency has gained in power over time at the expense of other institutions, particularly Congress. Of course, the fact that the president is a unitary decider, coupled with the growth of presidential power, also helps to explain why presidents usually become quite unpopular. Unlike members of Congress and other participants in collective decision making, presidents cannot escape responsibility for their decisions and are invariably blamed when things go wrong. The problem with being the decider in more and more policy spheres is that presidents have opportunities to make more mistakes and generate

---

[1] Robert G. Kaiser, "Congress-s-s-s: That Great Hissing Sound You Hear Is Congress Giving Up Its Clout," *Washington Post*, March 14, 2004, p. B1.

more opposition. Thus, ironically, the growing power of the presidency as an institution is one reason that so many of our recent presidents have seen their own popularity fade after a few years in office.

Our focus in this chapter is on the development of the institutional character of the presidency, the power of the presidency, and the relationship between the two. The chapter concerns itself with three major topics. First, we review the constitutional origins and powers of the presidency. In particular, we examine the constitutional basis for the president's foreign and domestic roles. Second, we review the history of the American presidency to see how the office has evolved from its original status under the Constitution. We look in particular at the ways in which Congress has augmented the president's constitutional powers by deliberately delegating to the presidency many of its own responsibilities. Third, we assess the means by which presidents can enhance their own ability to govern.

THE CONSTITUTIONAL BASIS OF THE PRESIDENCY

The presidency as an institution was established by Article II of the Constitution. Article II begins by asserting, "The executive Power shall be vested in a President of the United States of America." It goes on to describe the qualifications for the office (one must be a natural-born citizen, at least thirty-five years of age, and a resident of the United States for at least fourteen years), the manner in which the president is to be chosen, and the basic powers of the presidency. By vesting the executive power in a single president, the framers were emphatically rejecting proposals for various forms of collective leadership. Some delegates to the Constitutional Convention had argued in favor of a multiheaded executive or an "executive council" to avoid undue concentration of power in the hands of one individual. Most of the framers, however, hoped the president would be capable of taking quick and aggressive action. The framers thought a unitary executive would be more energetic than some form of collective leadership. They believed that a powerful executive would help protect the nation's interests vis-à-vis other nations and promote the federal government's interests relative to the states. In other words, the framers opted for a decider rather than a deliberative body.

Immediately following the first sentence of Article II, Section 1, of the Constitution, the manner in which the president is to be chosen is defined. This is an odd sequence, and it says something about the struggle the delegates were having over how to provide great power of action to the executive and at the same time balance that power with limitations. The struggle was between those delegates who wanted the president to be selected by, and thus responsible to, Congress and those delegates who preferred that the president be elected directly by the people. Direct popular election would create a more independent and more powerful presidency. With the adoption of a scheme of indirect election through an electoral college, in which the electors would be selected by the state legislatures (and close elections would be resolved in the House of Representatives), the framers hoped to achieve a "republican" solution: a strong president responsible to state and national legislators rather than directly responsible to the electorate. This indirect method of electing the president dampened the power of most presidents in the nineteenth century.

The presidency was strengthened somewhat in the 1830s with the introduction of the national convention system of nominating presidential candidates. Until then, candidates had been nominated by their party's congressional delegates. That was the **caucus system** of nominating candidates, and it was derisively called King Caucus because any candidate for president had to be beholden to the party's leaders in Congress to get the party's nomination and the support of the party's congressional delegation in the presidential election. The convention system quickly became the most popular method of nominating candidates for all elective offices and remained so until well into the twentieth century, when it succumbed to the criticism that it was a nondemocratic method dominated by a few leaders in a "smoke-filled room." But in the nineteenth century, it was seen as a victory for democracy over the congressional elite. And the national convention gave the presidency a base of power independent of Congress.

This additional independence did not immediately transform the presidency into the office we recognize today, but the national convention did begin to open the presidency to larger social forces and newly organized interests in society. In other words, it gave the presidency a mass popular base that would eventually support and demand increased presidential power. Improvements in the telephone, the telegraph, and other forms of communication allowed individuals to share their complaints and allowed national leaders—especially presidential candidates and presidents—to reach out directly to people and ally themselves with, and sometimes even create, popular groups and forces. Eventually, though more slowly, the presidential selection process began to be further democratized with the adoption of primary elections, through which millions of ordinary citizens were given an opportunity to take part in the nominating process by popular selection of convention delegates.

But despite political and social conditions favoring the enhancement of the presidency, the development of presidential government as we know it today did not mature until the middle of the twentieth century. For a long period, even as the national government began to grow, Congress was careful to keep tight reins on the president's power. The real turning point in the history of American national government came during the administration of Franklin Roosevelt, when the institutional powers of the presidency were greatly expanded.

THE CONSTITUTIONAL POWERS OF THE PRESIDENCY

Whereas Article II, Section 1, explains how the president is to be chosen, Sections 2 and 3 outline the powers and duties of the president. These two sections identify two sources of presidential power. One source is the specific language of the Constitution. For example, the president is specifically authorized to make treaties, grant pardons, and nominate judges and other public officials. These clearly defined powers are called the **expressed powers** of the office and cannot be revoked by the

---

caucus system
A normally closed meeting of a political or legislative group to select candidates, plan strategy, or make decisions regarding legislative matters.

expressed powers
Specific powers granted to the president under Article II, Sections 2 and 3, of the Constitution.

Congress or any other agency without an amendment to the Constitution. Other expressed powers include the power to receive ambassadors and to command the military forces of the United States.

The second source of presidential power lies in the declaration in Article II that the president "shall take Care that the Laws be faithfully executed." Because the laws are enacted by Congress, this language implies that Congress is to delegate to the president the power to implement or execute its will. Powers given to the president by Congress are called **delegated powers.** In principle, Congress delegates to the president only the power to identify or develop the means through which to carry out its decisions. So, for example, if Congress determines that air quality should be improved, it might delegate to a bureaucratic agency in the executive branch the power to identify the best means of bringing about such an improvement, as well as the power to implement the cleanup process. In practice, of course, decisions about how to clean the air are likely to have an enormous effect on businesses, organizations, and individuals throughout the nation. As it delegates power to the executive, Congress substantially enhances the importance of the presidency and the executive branch. In most cases, Congress delegates power to bureaucratic agencies in the executive branch rather than to the president. As we shall see, however, contemporary presidents have found ways to capture a good deal of this delegated power for themselves.

Presidents have claimed a third source of institutional power beyond expressed and delegated powers. These are powers that are not specified in the Constitution or the law but are said to stem from "the rights, duties and obligations of the presidency."[2] They are referred to as the **inherent powers** of the presidency and are most often asserted by presidents in times of war or national emergency. For example, after the fall of Fort Sumter and the outbreak of the Civil War, President Lincoln issued a series of executive orders although he had no clear legal basis for doing so. Without even calling Congress into session, Lincoln combined the state militias into a ninety-day national volunteer force, called for 40,000 new volunteers, enlarged the regular army and navy, diverted $2 million in unspent appropriations to military needs, instituted censorship of the U.S. mails, ordered a blockade of southern ports, suspended the writ of *habeas corpus* in the border states, and ordered military police to arrest individuals whom he deemed to be guilty of engaging in or even contemplating treasonous actions.[3] Lincoln asserted that these extraordinary measures were justified by the president's inherent power to protect the nation.[4] Subsequent presidents, including Franklin Roosevelt and George W. Bush, have had similar views.

delegated powers
Constitutional powers that are assigned to one government agency but exercised by another agency with the express permission of the first.

inherent powers
Powers claimed by a president that are not expressed in the Constitution but are inferred from it.

---

[2] In the case of *In re Neagle*, 135 U.S. 1 (1890), David Neagle, a deputy U.S. marshal, had been authorized by the president to protect a Supreme Court justice whose life had been threatened by an angry litigant. When the litigant attempted to carry out his threat, Neagle shot and killed him. Neagle was then arrested by local authorities and tried for murder. His defense was that his act was "done in pursuance of a law of the United States." Although the law was not an act of Congress, the Supreme Court declared that it was an executive order of the president and that the protection of a federal judge was a reasonable extension of the president's power to "take Care that the Laws be faithfully executed."

[3] James G. Randall, *Constitutional Problems under Lincoln* (New York: Appleton, 1926), chap. 1.

[4] E. S. Corwin, *The President: Office and Powers,* 4th ed. (New York: New York University Press, 1957), p. 229.

Expressed Powers

The president's expressed powers, as defined by Article II, Sections 2 and 3, fall into several categories:

1. *Military.* Article II, Section 2, provides for the power as "Commander in Chief of the Army and Navy of the United States, and of the Militia of the several States, when called into the actual Service of the United States."

2. *Judicial.* Article II, Section 2, provides the "Power to grant Reprieves and Pardons for Offences against the United States, except in Cases of Impeachment."

3. *Diplomatic.* Article II, Section 2, provides the "Power, by and with the Advice and Consent of the Senate, to make Treaties." Article II, Section 3, provides the power to "receive Ambassadors and other public Ministers."

4. *Executive.* Article II, Section 3, authorizes the president to see to it that all the laws are faithfully executed. Section 2 gives the chief executive power to appoint, remove, and supervise all executive officers and appoint all federal judges.

5. *Legislative.* Article I, Section 7, and Article II, Section 3, give the president the power to participate authoritatively in the legislative process.

Military Power. The president's military powers are among the most important of the powers exercised by the chief executive. The position of **commander in chief** makes the president the highest military authority in the United States, with control of the entire defense establishment. The president is also head of the nation's intelligence network, which includes not only the Central Intelligence Agency (CIA) but also the National Security Council (NSC), the National Security Agency (NSA), the Federal Bureau of Investigation (FBI), and a host of less well known but very powerful international and domestic security agencies.

War and Inherent Presidential Power. The Constitution, of course, gives Congress the power to declare war. Presidents, however, have gone a long way toward capturing this power for themselves. Congress has not declared war since December 1941, and yet since then American military forces have engaged in numerous campaigns throughout the world under orders of the president. When North Korean forces invaded South Korea in June 1950, Congress was prepared to declare war, but President Harry S. Truman decided not to ask for congressional action. Instead, Truman asserted the principle that the president, and not Congress, could decide when and where to deploy America's military might. Truman dispatched U.S. forces to Korea without a congressional declaration, and in the face of the emergency Congress felt it had to acquiesce. It passed a resolution approving the president's actions, and this sequence of events became the pattern for future congressional-executive relations in the military realm. The wars in Vietnam, Bosnia, Afghanistan, and Iraq, as well as a host of lesser conflicts, were all fought without declarations of war.

In 1973, Congress responded to presidential unilateralism by passing the **War Powers Resolution**—over President Richard Nixon's veto. This resolution reasserted the principle of Congress's power to declare war, required the president to inform Congress of any planned military campaign, and stipulated that forces

---

commander in chief The power of the president as commander of the national military and the state national guard units (when called into service).

War Powers Resolution A resolution of Congress declaring that the president can send troops into action abroad only by authorization of Congress or if U.S. troops are already under attack or seriously threatened.

must be withdrawn within sixty days in the absence of a specific congressional authorization for their continued deployment. Presidents have generally ignored the War Powers Resolution, however, claiming inherent executive power to defend the nation. Thus, for example, in 1989 President George H. W. Bush ordered an invasion of Panama without consulting Congress. In 1990, the same President Bush received congressional authorization to attack Iraq but had already made it clear that he was prepared to go to war with or without congressional assent. In 1995, President Bill Clinton ordered a massive bombing campaign against Serbian forces in the former nation of Yugoslavia without congressional authorization. And of course President George W. Bush responded to the 2001 attacks by Islamic terrorists by organizing a major military campaign to overthrow the Taliban regime in Afghanistan, which had sheltered the terrorists. In 2002, Bush ordered a major U.S. campaign against Iraq, which he accused of posing a threat to the United States. American forces overthrew the government of the Iraqi dictator Saddam Hussein and occupied the country. In both of these most recent instances, Congress passed resolutions approving the president's actions, but President Bush was careful to assert that he did not need congressional authorization. The War Powers Resolution was barely mentioned on Capitol Hill and was ignored by the White House.

Most American presidents have been attentive to the importance of history. George Washington, for example, always carried himself in a regal manner to establish, from the start, the dignity of the office. Beginning with Ronald Reagan, presidents were very conscious of the fact that the more times they ignored the War Powers Act and got away with so doing, the weaker the act became. Reagan, Clinton, and both Bushes deliberately refrained from using the law's procedures to undermine and, ultimately, negate the War Powers Act. Congress, for its part, seldom had the stomach to confront presidential claims that the nation's security demanded quick action and could not wait for the cumbersome war-powers process to run its course. Precisely because presidents know that history matters, they seize every opportunity to write a history favorable to their own goals and to the power of the presidency as an institution.

However, the fact that presidents since 1974 have ignored the War Powers Resolution, with virtually no objection from Congress, does not mean that tensions stemming from the separation of powers between the president and Congress have ceased. The relationship between the branches is encased in layers of institutional fabric, and as our institution principle suggests, tensions emerge within this complex institutional arrangement. The powers of the purse and of investigation give Congress levers with which to constrain even the most freewheeling executive.

Military Sources of Domestic Power.   The president's military powers extend into the domestic sphere. Article IV, Section 4, provides that "the United States shall . . . [protect] every State . . . against Invasion . . . and . . . domestic Violence." Congress has made this an explicit presidential power through statutes directing the president as commander in chief to discharge these obligations.[5] The Constitution restrains the president's use of domestic force by providing that a state legislature

---

[5] These statutes are contained mainly in Title 10 of the United States Code, Sections 331, 332, and 333.

(or governor when the legislature is not in session) must request federal troops before the president can send them into the state to provide public order. Yet this proviso is not absolute. First, presidents are not obligated to deploy national troops merely because a state legislature or governor makes such a request. And more important, the president may deploy troops in a state or city without a specific request from a state legislature or governor if the president considers it necessary to maintain an essential national service during an emergency, enforce a federal judicial order, or protect federally guaranteed civil rights.

One historic example of the unilateral use of presidential emergency power to protect the states against domestic disorder, even when the states do not request it, was the decision by President Dwight Eisenhower in 1957 to send troops into Little Rock, Arkansas, against the wishes of the state of Arkansas in order to enforce court orders to integrate Little Rock's Central High School. As we saw in Chapter 4, the governor, Orval Faubus, had posted the Arkansas National Guard at the entrance of the school to prevent the court-ordered admission of nine black students. After an effort to negotiate with the governor failed, President Eisenhower reluctantly sent 1,000 paratroopers to Little Rock; they stood watch while the black students took their places in the all-white classrooms. This case makes quite clear that the president does not have to wait for a request by a state legislature or a governor before acting as a domestic commander in chief.[6] More recently, President George W. Bush sent various military units to the Gulf Coast in response to Hurricanes Katrina and Rita in 2005. In most instances of domestic disorder—whether a result of human or natural events—presidents tend to exercise unilateral power by declaring a "state of emergency," thereby making available federal grants, insurance, and direct assistance.

Military emergencies have typically also led to expansion of the domestic powers of the executive branch. This was true during World Wars I and II and has been the case during the "war on terrorism" as well. Within a month of the September 11 attacks, the White House had drafted, and Congress had enacted, the USA PATRIOT Act, expanding the power of government agencies to engage in domestic surveillance, including electronic surveillance, and restricting judicial review of such efforts. The following year Congress created the Department of Homeland Security, combining offices of twenty-two federal agencies into one huge new cabinet department that would be responsible for protecting the nation from attack.

Judicial Power. The presidential power to grant reprieves, pardons, and amnesties involves the power of life and death over all individuals who may be a threat to the security of the United States. Presidents may use this power on behalf of a particular individual, as did Gerald Ford when he pardoned Richard Nixon in 1974 "for all offenses against the United States which he . . . has committed or may have committed." Or they may use it on a large scale, as Andrew Johnson did in 1868 when

---

[6]The best study covering all aspects of the domestic use of the military is that of Adam Yarmolinsky, *The Military Establishment* (New York: Harper & Row, 1971). Probably the most famous instance of a president's unilateral use of the power to protect a state "against domestic violence" was President Grover Cleveland's response to the Pullman strike of 1894. The famous Supreme Court case that ensued was *In re Debs*, 158 U.S. 564 (1895).

he gave full amnesty to all Southerners who had participated in the "Late Rebellion" and as Jimmy Carter did in 1977 when he declared an amnesty for all Vietnam War draft evaders. President Clinton issued a number of controversial pardons during his last weeks in office. This power of life and death over others helped elevate the president to the level of earlier conquerors and kings, by establishing him as the person before whom supplicants might come to make their pleas for mercy.

Diplomatic Power. The president is America's "head of state," its chief representative in dealings with other nations. As head of state, the president has the power to make treaties for the United States (with the advice and consent of the Senate). When President George Washington received Edmond Genet ("Citizen Genet") as the formal emissary of the revolutionary government of France in 1793 and had his cabinet officers and Congress back his decision, he established a greatly expanded interpretation of the power to "receive Ambassadors and other public Ministers," extending it to the power to "recognize" other countries. That power gives the president the almost unconditional authority to review the claims of any new ruling group to determine whether it indeed controls the territory and population of its country and therefore can, in the president's opinion, legitimately commit it to treaties and other agreements.

In recent years, presidents have expanded the practice of using executive agreements instead of treaties to establish relations with other countries.[7] An **executive agreement** is like a treaty because it is a contract between two countries, but an executive agreement does not require a two-thirds vote of approval by the Senate. (A treaty does require approval by the Senate.) Ordinarily executive agreements are used to carry out commitments already made in treaties or to arrange for matters well below the level of policy. But when presidents have found it expedient to use an executive agreement in place of a treaty, Congress has typically acquiesced.

executive agreement An agreement between the president and another country that has the force of a treaty but does not require the Senate's "advice and consent."

Executive Power. The most important basis of the president's power as chief executive is found in Article II, Section 3, which stipulates that the president must see that all the laws are faithfully executed, and Section 2, which provides that the president will appoint, remove, and supervise all executive officers and appoint all federal judges (with Senate approval). The power to appoint the principal executive officers and to require each of them to report to the president on subjects relating to the duties of their departments makes the president the true chief executive officer (CEO) of the nation. In this manner, the Constitution focuses executive power and legal responsibility on the president. The famous sign on President Truman's desk, "The buck stops here," was not merely an assertion of Truman's personal sense of responsibility but was in fact evidence of his recognition of the legal and constitutional responsibility of the president. The president is subject to some limitations because the appointment of all such officers, including ambassadors, ministers,

---

[7] In *United States v. Pink*, 315 U.S. 203 (1942), the Supreme Court confirmed that an executive agreement is the legal equivalent of a treaty despite the absence of Senate approval. This case approved the executive agreement that was used to establish diplomatic relations with the Soviet Union in 1933. An executive agreement, not a treaty, was used in 1940 to exchange "fifty over-age destroyers" for ninety-nine-year leases on some important military bases.

and federal judges, is subject to majority approval by the Senate. The Congress, through its committees and the budgetary process has oversight responsibilities for executive agencies. The George W. Bush administration, supported by conservative scholars, argued that congressional power vis-à-vis the bureaucracy was actually quite limited. Article II of the Constitution, they asserted, vests all executive power in the president, who, by implication, is in full control of the executive branch. This idea is called the theory of the unitary executive. The theory is often disputed in principle, but all presidents act as though they believe it.

Another component of the president's power as chief executive is **executive privilege.** Executive privilege is the claim that confidential communications be-tween a president and close advisers should not be revealed without the consent of the president. Presidents have made this claim ever since George Washington refused a request from the House of Representatives to deliver documents con-cerning negotiations of an important treaty. Washington refused (successfully) on the grounds that, first, the House was not constitutionally part of the treaty-making process and, second, that diplomatic negotiations required secrecy.

Executive privilege became a popular part of the checks-and-balances coun-terpoint between president and Congress, and presidents have usually had the upper hand when invoking it. Although many presidents have claimed executive privilege, the concept was not tested in the courts until the 1971 Watergate affair, during which President Nixon refused congressional demands that he turn over secret White House tapes that congressional investigators thought would establish Nixon's complicity in illegal activities. In *United States v. Nixon*, the Supreme Court ordered Nixon to turn over the tapes.[8] The president complied with the order and was forced to resign from office. *United States v. Nixon* is often seen as a blow to presidential power, but in actuality the Court's ruling recognized for the first time the validity of a claim of executive privilege, although holding that it did not apply in this instance. Subsequent presidents have cited *United States v. Nixon* in support of their claims of executive privilege. For example, the administration of George W. Bush invoked executive privilege when it refused to give Congress documents relating to the president's decision to make use of warrantless wiretaps and the so-called CIA leak case, in which the identity of a CIA operative revealed after her hus-band criticized the administration. The Bush administration also invoked executive privilege when it refused to obey congressional subpoenas demanding materials pertaining to the firing of a number of assistant U.S. attorneys. The exercise of presidential power through the executive-privilege doctrine has been all the more frequent in the past twenty years, when we have been living nearly 90 percent of the time under conditions of "divided government;" that is, the party that is not in control of the White House is in control of one or both chambers of Congress.[9]

The President's Legislative Power. The president plays a role not only in the administration of government but also in the legislative process. Two constitutional provisions are the primary sources of the president's power in the legislative arena.

---

[8] *United States v. Nixon*, 418 U.S. 683 (1974).

[9] A recent extension of executive power by President George W. Bush is the "signing statement" which is discussed later in this chapter.

The first of these is the provision in Article II, Section 3, providing that the president "shall from time to time give to the Congress Information of the State of the Union, and recommend to their Consideration such Measures as he shall judge necessary and expedient." The second of the president's legislative powers is of course the veto power assigned by Article I, Section 7.[10]

Delivering a "State of the Union" address might not appear to be of any great import. It is a mere obligation on the part of the president to make recommendations for Congress's consideration. But as political and social conditions favored an increasingly prominent role for presidents, each president, especially since Franklin D. Roosevelt, has relied on this provision to become the primary initiator of proposals for legislative action in Congress and the principal source for public awareness of national issues, as well as the most important single individual participant in legislative decisions. Few today doubt that the president, together with the executive branch as a whole, is the primary source of many important congressional actions.[11]

The **veto** is the president's constitutional power to turn down acts of Congress (Figure 6.1). It alone makes the president the most important single legislative leader.[12] No bill vetoed by the president can become law unless both the House and Senate override the veto by a two-thirds vote. In the case of a **pocket veto**, Congress does not have the option of overriding the veto but must reintroduce the bill in the next session. A pocket veto can occur when the president is presented with a bill during the last ten days of a legislative session. Usually if a president does not sign a bill within ten days, it automatically becomes law. But this is true only while Congress is in session. If a president chooses not to sign a bill presented within the

veto The president's constitutional power to turn down acts of Congress within ten days of their passage while Congress is in session. A presidential veto may be overridden by a two-thirds vote of each house of Congress.

pocket veto A veto that is effected when Congress adjourns during the time a president has to approve a bill and the president takes no action on it.

---

[10] There is a third source of presidential power implied in the provision for faithful execution of the laws. This is the president's power to impound funds—that is, to refuse to spend money Congress has appropriated for certain purposes. One author referred to this as a "retroactive veto power" (Robert E. Goosetree, "The Power of the President to Impound Appropriated Funds," *American University Law Review*, January 1962). This impoundment power was used freely and to considerable effect by many modern presidents, and Congress occasionally delegated such power to the president by statute. But in reaction to the Watergate scandal, Congress adopted the Budget and Impoundment Control Act of 1974, which was designed to circumscribe the president's ability to impound funds by requiring the president to spend all appropriated funds unless both houses of Congress consent to an impoundment within forty-five days of a presidential request. Since 1974, therefore, the use of impoundment has declined significantly. Presidents have had to bite their tongues and accept unwanted appropriations or revert to the older and more dependable but politically limited method of vetoing an entire bill.

[11] For a different perspective, see William F. Grover, *The President as Prisoner: A Structural Critique of the Carter and Reagan Years* (Albany: State University of New York Press, 1989).

[12] Although the veto power is the most important legislative resource in the hands of the president, it can often end in frustration, especially when the presidency and Congress are held by opposing parties. George H. W. Bush vetoed forty-six congressional enactments during his four years, and only one was overridden. Ronald Reagan vetoed thirty-nine bills in his eight years, and nine were overridden. Compare these numbers with thirty-one vetoes during Jimmy Carter's four years, with two overridden. In 1993–94, Bill Clinton did not veto a single bill, a record unmatched since the days of President Millard Fillmore (1850–53); both, of course, were working with Congresses controlled by their own political party. President George W. Bush had not vetoed a single bill in more than five years, thus topping Clinton's record, until he vetoed a bill on stem-cell research. For more on the veto, see Chapter 5 and Robert J. Spitzer, *The Presidential Veto: Touchstone of the American Presidency* (Albany: State University of New York Press, 1988).

FIGURE 6.1 THE VETO PROCESS

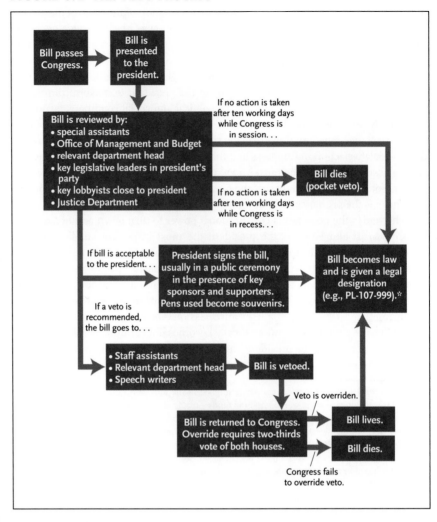

*PL stands for "public law"; 107 is the Congress (e.g., the 107th Congress was in session in 2001–2); 999 is the number of the law.

last ten days that Congress is in session, then the ten-day limit expires while Congress is out of session, and instead of becoming law, the bill is considered vetoed. In 1996, a new power was added to the president's lineup—the **line-item veto**—giving the president power to strike specific spending items from appropriations bills passed by Congress unless they are reenacted by a two-thirds vote of both the House and the Senate. In 1997, President Clinton used this power eleven times to strike eighty-two items from the federal budget. But in 1998 the Supreme Court ruled that the Constitution does not authorize the line-item veto.[13] Only a constitutional amendment would restore this power to the president.

line-item veto
The power of the executive to veto specific provisions (lines) of a bill passed by the legislature.

---

[13] *Clinton v. City of New York*, 524 U.S. 417 (1998).

The Games Presidents Play: The Veto.   Use of the veto varies according to the political situation that each president confronts. During Bill Clinton's first two years in office, when Democrats controlled both houses of Congress, the president vetoed no bills. After the congressional elections of 1994, however, Clinton confronted a Republican-controlled Congress with a definite agenda, and he began to use his veto power vigorously. Likewise, George W. Bush vetoed no bill during his first term, a period in which his party controlled both houses of Congress. He vetoed only one bill during the first two years of his second term, another period during which Congress was controlled by his party.[14] In 2008, Bush vetoed a bill prohibiting the CIA from using harsh methods to interrogate terrorist suspects. In general, presidents have used the veto to equalize or perhaps upset the balance of power with Congress. While the simple power to reject or accept legislation in its entirety might seem like a crude tool for making sure that legislation adheres to a president's preferences, the politics surrounding the veto is complicated, and it is rare that vetoes are used simply as bullets to kill legislation. Instead, vetoes are usually part of an intricate bargaining process between the president and Congress, involving threats of vetoes, the repassage of legislation, and second vetoes.[15]

The fact that presidents rarely veto legislation does not mean that vetoes and veto bargaining have an insignificant influence over the policy process. The fact that presidents vetoed only several hundred of the 17,000 public bills that Congress sent to them between 1945 and 1992 belies the centrality of the veto to presidential power. Many of these bills were insignificant and not worth the veto effort. Thus it is important to separate "significant" legislation, for which vetoes frequently occur, from insignificant legislation.[16] Vetoes can also be effective—even though they are rarely employed—because individuals will condition their actions on the basis of how they think others will respond.[17] With respect to vetoes, this means that members of Congress will alter the content of a bill to make it more to a president's liking in order to preempt a veto. Thus the veto power can be influential even when the veto pen rests in its inkwell.[18]

Rhetoric and reputation take on particular importance when vetoes become part of a bargaining process. Bargaining between Congress and the president is strategic and an example of the rationality principle in action. The president tries to influence legislators' beliefs about what they must do to keep the president from using the veto power. The key to veto bargaining is uncertainty. Members of Congress are often unsure about the president's policy preferences and therefore don't

---

[14] A caveat: President George W. Bush, as observed in an earlier footnote, relied on signing statements as something of a substitute for the veto. Were the Supreme Court to declare the maneuver unconstitutional, the president would be forced to face squarely the decision to use the power of the veto.

[15] Charles M. Cameron, *Veto Bargaining: Presidents and the Politics of Negative Power* (New York: Cambridge University Press, 2000). See also David W. Rohde and Dennis Simon, "Presidential Vetoes and Congressional Response: A Study of Institutional Conflict," *American Journal of Political Science* 29 (1985): 397–427.

[16] David R. Mayhew, *Divided We Govern: Party Control, Lawmaking, and Investigations, 1946–1990* (New Haven, Conn.: Yale University Press, 1991).

[17] Jack H. Nagel, *The Descriptive Analysis of Power* (New Haven, Conn.: Yale University Press, 1975).

[18] See Rohde and Simon, "Presidential Vetoes and Congressional Response."

know which bills the president is willing to sign. When the policy preferences of the president and Congress diverge, as they typically do in a divided government, the president tries to convince Congress that his preferences are more extreme than they really are in order to get Congress to enact legislation that is closer to what he really wants. If members of Congress knew the president's preferences ahead of time, they would pass a bill that was close to what *they* wanted, subject to minimally satisfying the president. Through strategic use of the veto and veto threats, a president tries to shape Congress's beliefs about his policy preferences in order to gain greater concessions from Congress. Reputation is central to presidential effectiveness in this process.[19] By influencing congressional beliefs, the president is building a policy reputation that will affect future congressional behavior.

During the first year of his presidency, Barack Obama threatened to veto a defense spending bill that contained $369 billion in funding for the production of the F-22 fighter as well as a congressional resolution that would have blocked the release of about $350 billion in economic stimulus funds. After meeting with the president, members of Congress agreed to release the stimulus funds. On the issue of the F-22, however, Congress has, as of this writing, ignored the president's threat. The White House says that the F-22 "Raptor," an advanced air-superiority fighter, is not needed by the United States military. Members of Congress with ties to the Air Force or whose states and districts stand to benefit from the F-22 program, assert that the aircraft is needed. Despite the president's veto threat, a bill containing funding for the F-22 passed the House and seemed likely to pass the Senate as well. Even when the president's party controls both houses of Congress, there is no guarantee that every element of the president's program will pass congressional muster. However, when Congress and the White House are held by the same party, both sides prefer to avoid bruising veto battles and try to reach a compromise instead. The "Analyzing the Evidence" unit on page 238 takes a closer look at veto politics.

What about the relationship between mass public support for the president and the use of the veto? At least for the modern presidency, a crucial resource for the president in negotiating with Congress has been public approval as measured by opinion polls.[20] In some situations, members of Congress pass a bill not because they want to change policy but because they want to force the president to veto a popular bill that he disagrees with in order to hurt his approval ratings.[21] The key is that the public, uncertain of the president's policy preferences, uses information implied by vetoes to reassess what it knows about his preferences. As a result, vetoes may come at a price to the president. A president must, according to the rationality principle, weigh the advantages of using the veto or threatening to do so—to gain concessions

---

[19]Richard E. Neustadt, *Presidential Power and the Modern Presidents: The Politics of Leadership from Roosevelt to Reagan* (1960; rev. ed., New York: Free Press, 1990).

[20]Theodore J. Lowi, *The Personal President: Power Invested, Promise Unfulfilled* (Ithaca, N.Y.: Cornell University Press, 1985).

[21]Timothy Groseclose and Nolan McCarty, "The Politics of Blame: Bargaining before an Audience," *American Journal of Political Science* 45 (2001): 100–119.

from Congress—against the hit he may take in his popularity. The president may be reluctant to use the veto or the threat of a veto to gain concessions from Congress if it will hurt him in the polls. But in some cases, the president will take a hit in his approval ratings by vetoing a bill if it is drastically inconsistent with his policies.

Legislative Initiative. Although the power not explicitly stated, the Constitution provides the president with the power of **legislative initiative.** To initiate means to originate, and in government that can mean power. The framers of the Constitution clearly saw legislative initiative as one of the keys to executive power. Initiative obviously implies the ability to formulate proposals for important policies, and the president, as an individual with a great deal of staff assistance, is able to initiate decisive action more frequently than Congress, with its large assemblies that have to deliberate and debate before taking action. With some important exceptions, Congress banks on the president to set the agenda of public policy. And quite clearly there is power in initiative: There is power in being able to set the terms of discourse in the making of public policy.

For example, during the weeks immediately following September 11, 2001, George W. Bush took many presidential initiatives to Congress, and each was given almost unanimous support: from commitments to pursue Al Qaeda, remove the Taliban, and reconstitute the Afghanistan regime all the way to almost unlimited approval for mobilization of both military power and power over the regulation of American civil liberties. After winning reelection in 2004, Bush sought to push forward his domestic legislative agenda, which included making changes in the nation's Social Security system and reforming the tax structure. Bush also called on Congress to act quickly to limit lawsuit awards in medical malpractice cases and to push for tougher educational standards for high schools. Bush said, "I earned capital in this campaign, political capital, and now I intend to spend it. . . . There is a feeling that the people have spoken and embraced your point of view, and that's what I intend to tell the Congress."[22] Bush's second term, however, was difficult. Growing problems (and casualties) in Iraq, administrative scandals, and a financial crisis plagued the president. As presidential popularity ebbed in the polls, so, too, did Bush's agenda power.

In 2009, soon after taking office, President Obama presented Congress with a record-breaking $3 trillion budget proposal that included a host of new programs in such areas as health and human services, transportation, housing, and education. Obama told Congress that he would soon be requesting several hundred billion more for the financial bailout designed to rescue America's banks and revive the nation's credit markets. Not only was Congress responsive to the president's initiatives but lawmakers also expected the president to take the lead in responding to America's financial emergency and other problems.

The president's initiative does not end with policy making involving Congress and the making of laws in the ordinary sense of the term. The president has still

legislative initiative The president's inherent power to bring a legislative agenda before Congress.

---

[22]Quoted in Richard W. Stevenson, "Focus on Social Security and the Tax Code," *New York Times,* November 5, 2004, p. A1.

Veto Politics

Although vetoes are relatively rare in the legislative process, scholars are drawn to study them because vetoes carry clear policy implications. Indeed, a president's use of the veto is an ideal example of negative agenda control—it creates an opportunity to block legislative action, but does not give the executive the power to alter proposed legislation after the fact. Nonetheless, chief executives regularly use the threat of a veto in their attempts to shape legislative outcomes.[1] In many cases, a credible veto threat may be sufficient to force compliance on the part of reluctant legislators who would like to avoid a prolonged legislative battle over a controversial bill or resolution, especially near the end of a legislative session. Instead of "losing" to the president, one or both chambers of the legislature may be willing to make concessions if the price of passage necessitates it.

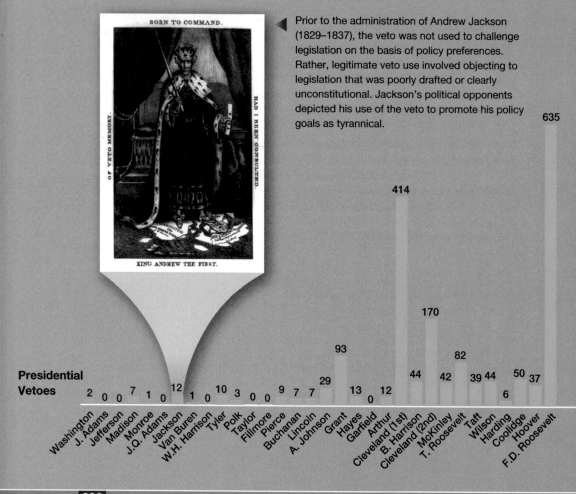

BORN TO COMMAND.

OF VETO MEMORY.

HAD I BEEN CONSULTED.

KING ANDREW THE FIRST.

Prior to the administration of Andrew Jackson (1829–1837), the veto was not used to challenge legislation on the basis of policy preferences. Rather, legitimate veto use involved objecting to legislation that was poorly drafted or clearly unconstitutional. Jackson's political opponents depicted his use of the veto to promote his policy goals as tyrannical.

Presidential Vetoes

President	Vetoes
Washington	2
J. Adams	0
Jefferson	0
Madison	7
Monroe	1
J.Q. Adams	0
Jackson	12
Van Buren	1
W.H. Harrison	0
Tyler	10
Polk	3
Taylor	0
Fillmore	0
Pierce	9
Buchanan	7
Lincoln	7
A. Johnson	29
Grant	93
Hayes	13
Garfield	0
Arthur	12
Cleveland (1st)	414
B. Harrison	44
Cleveland (2nd)	170
McKinley	42
T. Roosevelt	82
Taft	39
Wilson	44
Harding	6
Coolidge	50
Hoover	37
F.D. Roosevelt	635

Veto power is by no means absolute. Consistent with the Madisonian notion of checks and balances, the legislature has the opportunity to override a veto if legislators can muster the necessary votes. In the U.S. Congress, two-thirds of both chambers must successfully vote to override a presidential veto. Although many override attempts fail as a result of this supermajority requirement, the risk of a successful override attempt provides an important check on executive power.[2]

PRESIDENTIAL VETOES AND CONGRESSIONAL OVERRIDES, 1945–2007

	Years in Office	Vetoes	Divided Government	Override Attempts		Successes	
Truman	1945–1953	250	1947–1949	22	8.8%	12	54.5%
Eisenhower	1953–1961	181	1955–1961	11	6.1%	2	18.2%
Kennedy	1961–1963	21		0	0.0%	0	0.0%
Johnson	1963–1969	30		0	0.0%	0	0.0%
Nixon	1969–1974	43	1969–1974	21	48.8%	7	33.3%
Ford	1974–1977	66	1974–1977	28	42.4%	12	42.9%
Carter	1977–1981	31		4	12.9%	2	50.0%
Reagan	1981–1989	78	1981–1989	15	19.2%	9	60.0%
G. H. W. Bush	1989–1993	44	1989–1993	21	47.7%	1	4.8%
Clinton	1993–2001	37	1995–2001	11	29.7%	2	18.2%
G. W. Bush	2001–2009	12	2007–2009	6	50.0%	4	66.6%

Sources: "Congressional Bills Vetoed: 1789–2001." Contributed by John P. McIver. *Historical Statistics of the United States,* Millennial Edition On Line, edited by Susan B. Carter, Scott S. Gartner, Michael R. Haines, Alan L. Olmstead, Richard Sutch, and Gavin Wright. © Cambridge University Press, 2006; calculated by author.

Veto override attempts and successes are more likely to occur under divided government than unified government, which is most likely a function of divergent preferences across the institutions. Note that few or no overrides were attempted during presidencies that enjoyed unified government, with the president's party controlling at least one chamber of Congress.

250
181
66
78
21 30 43 31 44 37
12

Truman
Eisenhower
Kennedy
Johnson
Nixon
Ford
Carter
Reagan
G.H.W. Bush
Clinton
G.W. Bush

Since Jackson left office in 1837, presidents have routinely vetoed legislation for political reasons. During the twentieth century, for instance, the incidence of presidential vetoes was almost always greater under divided government, in which the executive is controlled by one political party and at least one chamber of Congress by the other.

[1]Charles M. Cameron, *Veto Bargaining: Presidents and the Politics of Negative Power.* (New York: Cambridge University Press, 2000).
[2]David W. Rohde and Dennis M. Simon, "Presidential Vetoes and Congressional Response: A Study of Institutional Conflict," *American Journal of Political Science* 29 (1985): 397–427.

another legislative role (in all but name) within the executive branch. This is designated as the power to issue **executive orders.** The executive order is foremost a normal tool of management, a power virtually any CEO possesses to make company policy—rules setting procedures, etiquette, chains of command, functional responsibilities, and so on. But evolving from this normal management practice is a recognized presidential power to promulgate rules that have the effect and formal status of legislation. Most of the executive orders of the president provide for the reorganization of structures and procedures or otherwise direct the affairs of the executive branch—either to be applied across the board to all agencies or to be applied in some important respect to a single agency or department.

The power to issue executive orders illustrates that although reputation and persuasion are typically required in presidential policy making, the practice of issuing executive orders, within limits, allows a president to govern without the necessity to persuade.[23] One of the most important examples is Executive Order No. 8248 of 1939, which established the divisions of the Executive Office of the President. Of equal importance is President Nixon's executive order establishing the Environmental Protection Agency (EPA) in 1971, which included establishment of the Environmental Impact Statement. President Reagan's Executive Order No. 12291 of 1981 provided a regulatory reform process that has been responsible for more deregulation in the past twenty-five years than was accomplished by any acts of congressional legislation. In May 2007, President Bush issued a controversial order giving the president sole responsibility for determining when and how constitutional government could be reestablished in the event of a catastrophic attack on the United States.

On his second full day in office—January 22, 2009—President Obama issued four executive orders reversing several of former president Bush's policies in the "war on terror." Among other things, Obama ordered the closing of the Guantánamo Bay detention camp where terror suspects were being held, ended the policy of "extraordinary renditions" under which suspects had been sent to countries known to torture prisoners, abolished the secret prisons the United States had maintained around the world, and ordered that the Geneva Convention be applied to terror suspects. Though Congress had objected to Bush's orders, lawmakers' ability to countermand an executive order is limited. It took a new president to undo what a prior president had done.

Delegated Powers

Many of the powers exercised by the president and the executive branch are not set forth in the Constitution but are the products of congressional statutes and resolutions. Over the past three quarters of a century, Congress has voluntarily delegated a great deal of its own legislative authority to the executive branch. To some extent, this delegation of power has been an almost inescapable consequence of the expansion of governmental activity in the United States since the New Deal.

---

[23]This point is developed in both Kenneth R. Mayer, *With the Stroke of a Pen: Executive Orders and Presidential Power* (Princeton, N.J.: Princeton University Press, 2001), and William G. Howell, *Power without Persuasion: The Politics of Direct Presidential Action* (Princeton, N.J.: Princeton University Press, 2003).

Given the vast range of the federal government's responsibilities, Congress cannot execute and administer all the programs it creates and the laws it enacts. Inevitably Congress must turn to the hundreds of departments and agencies in the executive branch or, when necessary, create new agencies to implement its goals. Thus, for example, in 2002, when Congress sought to protect America from terrorist attacks, it established the Department of Homeland Security and gave it broad powers in the realms of law enforcement, public health, and immigration. Similarly, in 1970, when Congress enacted legislation designed to improve the nation's air and water quality, it assigned the task of implementing its goals to the new Environmental Protection Agency created by Nixon's executive order. Congress gave the EPA substantial power to set and enforce air- and water-quality standards.

As they implement congressional legislation, federal agencies collectively develop thousands of rules and regulations and issue thousands of orders and findings every year. Agencies interpret Congress's intent, promulgate rules aimed at implementing that intent, and issue orders to individuals, firms, and organizations throughout the nation designed to impel them to conform to the law. When it establishes an agency, Congress sometimes grants it only limited discretionary authority, providing very specific guidelines and standards that must be followed by the administrators charged with the program's implementation. Take the Internal Revenue Service (IRS), for example. Most Americans view the IRS as a powerful agency whose dictates can have an immediate and sometimes unpleasant effect on their lives. Yet congressional tax legislation is specific and detailed and leaves little to the discretion of IRS administrators.[24] The agency certainly develops numerous rules and procedures to enhance tax collection. It is Congress, however, that establishes the structure of the tax liabilities, tax exemptions, and tax deductions that determine each taxpayer's burdens and responsibilities.

In most instances, however, congressional legislation is not very detailed. Often Congress defines a broad goal or objective and delegates enormous discretionary power to administrators to determine how that goal is to be achieved. For example, the 1970 act creating the Occupational Safety and Health Administration (OSHA) states that Congress's purpose is "to assure so far as is possible every working man and woman in the nation safe and healthful working conditions." The act, however, neither defines such conditions nor suggests how they might be achieved.[25] The result is that agency administrators have enormous discretionary power to draft rules and regulations that have the effect of law. Indeed, the courts treat these administrative rules like congressional statutes. For all intents and purposes, when Congress creates an agency such as OSHA or the EPA, giving it a broad mandate to achieve some desirable outcome, it transfers its own legislative power to the executive branch.

In the nineteenth and early twentieth centuries, Congress typically wrote laws that provided fairly clear principles and standards to guide executive implementation. For example, the 1922 Tariff Act empowered the president to increase or decrease duties on certain manufactured goods in order to reduce the difference in

---

[24] Kenneth F. Warren, *Administrative Law*, 3rd ed. (Upper Saddle River, N.J.: Prentice-Hall, 1996), p. 250.

[25] Theodore J. Lowi, *The End of Liberalism: The Second Republic of the United States*, 2nd ed. (New York: Norton, 1979), pp. 117–18.

cost between products produced domestically and those manufactured abroad. The act authorized the president to make the final determination, but his discretionary authority was quite constrained. The statute listed the criteria the president was to consider, fixed the permissible range of tariff changes, and outlined the procedures to be used to calculate the cost differences between foreign and domestic goods. When an importer challenged a particular executive decision as an abuse of delegated power, the Supreme Court had no difficulty finding that the president was merely acting in accordance with Congress's directives.[26]

At least since the New Deal, however, Congress has tended to give executive agencies broad mandates and draft legislation that offers few clear standards or guidelines for implementation by the executive. For example, the 1933 National Industrial Recovery Act gave the president the authority to set rules to bring about fair competition in key sectors of the economy without ever defining what the term meant or how it was to be achieved. Similarly, the 1938 Agricultural Adjustment Act, which led to a system of commodity price supports and agricultural production restrictions, authorized the secretary of agriculture to make agricultural marketing "orderly" without offering any guidance regarding the commodities to be affected, how markets were to be organized, or how prices should be determined. All these decisions were left to the discretion of the secretary and his or her agents.[27] This pattern of broad delegation became typical in the ensuing decades. The 1972 Consumer Product Safety Act, for example, authorizes the Consumer Product Safety Commission to reduce unreasonable risk of injury from household products but offers no suggestions to guide the commission's determination of what constitutes reasonable and unreasonable risks or how these are to be reduced.[28]

This shift from the nineteenth-century pattern of issuing relatively well defined congressional guidelines to administrators to the more contemporary pattern of broadly delegating congressional power to the executive branch is, to be sure, partially a consequence of the great scope and complexity of the tasks that America's contemporary government has undertaken. During much of the nineteenth century, the federal government had relatively few domestic responsibilities, and Congress could pay close attention to details. Today the operation of an enormous executive establishment and thousands of programs under varied and changing circumstances requires that administrators be allowed some considerable measure of discretion to carry out their jobs. Nevertheless, the result is to shift power from Congress to the executive branch.

THE RISE OF PRESIDENTIAL GOVERNMENT

Most of the real influence of the modern presidency derives from the powers granted by the Constitution and the laws made by Congress. Presidential power is institutional. Thus any person properly elected and sworn in as president will

---

[26] *J. W. Hampton & Company. v. United States*, 276 U.S. 394 (1928).

[27] David Schoenbrod, *Power without Responsibility: How Congress Abuses the People through Delegation* (New Haven, Conn.: Yale University Press, 1993), pp. 49–50.

[28] Lowi, *The End of Liberalism*, p. 117.

possess almost all the power held by the strongest presidents in American history. Even when they are lame ducks, presidents still possess all the power of the office. For example, in 2008, lame-duck president Bush secured the enactment of a major piece of legislation aimed at ameliorating the nation's economic crisis.

What variables account for a president's success in exercising these powers? Why are some presidents considered great successes and others colossal failures? These questions relate broadly to the very concept of presidential power. Is it a reflection of the attributes of the person, or is it more characteristic of the political situations that a president encounters? The personal view of presidential power dominated political scientists' thinking for several decades,[29] but recently scholars have argued that presidential power should be analyzed in terms of the strategic interactions that a president has with other political actors.[30] With the occasional exception, however, it took more than a century, perhaps as much as a century and a half, before presidents came to be seen as consequential players in these strategic encounters. A bit of historical review will be helpful in understanding how the presidency has risen to its current level of influence.

The Legislative Epoch, 1800–1933

In 1885, a then-obscure political science professor named Woodrow Wilson titled his general textbook *Congressional Government* because American government was just that, congressional government. There is ample evidence that Wilson's description of the national government was consistent not only with nineteenth-century reality but also with the intentions of the framers. Within the system of three separate and competing powers, the clear intent of the Constitution was legislative supremacy. In the early nineteenth century, some observers saw the president as little more than America's chief clerk. Indeed, most historians agree that after Thomas Jefferson and until the beginning of the twentieth century, Presidents Andrew Jackson and Abraham Lincoln were the only exceptions to a succession of weak presidents. Both Jackson and Lincoln are considered great presidents because they used their great power wisely. But it is important in the history of the presidency that neither of them left his powers as an institutional legacy to his successors. That is to say, once Jackson and Lincoln left office, the presidency reverted to the subordinate role that it played during the nineteenth century.

One of the reasons that so few great men became president in the nineteenth century is that there was only occasional room for greatness.[31] As Chapter 3 indicated,

---

[29] Neustadt, *Presidential Power and the Modern Presidents*.

[30] Charles M. Cameron, "Bargaining and Presidential Power," in *Presidential Power: Forging the Presidency for the Twenty-first Century*, Robert Y. Shapiro, Martha Joynt Kumar, and Lawrence R. Jacobs, eds. (New York: Columbia University Press, 2000). See also Samuel Kernell, *Going Public: New Strategies of Presidential Leadership*, 3rd ed. (Washington, D.C.: Congressional Quarterly Press, 1998).

[31] For related appraisals, see Jeffrey Tulis, *The Rhetorical Presidency* (Princeton, N.J.: Princeton University Press, 1987); Stephen Skowronek, *The Politics Presidents Make: Leadership from John Adams to Bill Clinton* (Cambridge, Mass.: Harvard University Press, 1997); and Robert J. Spitzer, *President and Congress: Executive Hegemony at the Crossroads of American Government* (Philadelphia: Temple University Press, 1993).

the national government of that period was not a particularly powerful entity. The presidency of the nineteenth century was also weak because during this period the presidency was not closely linked to major national political and social forces. Indeed, there were few important *national* political or social forces to which presidents could have linked themselves even if they had wanted to. Federalism had taken very good care of this by fragmenting political interests and diverting the energies of interest groups toward the state and local levels of government, where most key decisions were being made.

As discussed earlier in the chapter, the presidency was strengthened in the 1830s when the national convention system of nominating presidential candidates was introduced. However, this additional independence did not change the presidency into the office we see today because the parties disappeared, returning to their states and Congress once the national election was over. In addition, as the national government grew, Congress kept a tight rein on the president's power. For example, when Congress began to make its first efforts to exert power over the economy (beginning in 1887 with the adoption of the Interstate Commerce Act and in 1890 with the adoption of the Sherman Antitrust Act), it sought to keep this power away from the president and the executive branch by placing the new regulatory policies in "independent regulatory commissions" responsible to Congress rather than to the president (see also Chapter 7).

The New Deal and the Presidency

As discussed earlier, the key moment in the history of American national government came during Franklin Roosevelt's administration. The Hundred Days at the outset of the Roosevelt administration in 1933 had no parallel in U.S. history. But it was only the beginning. The policies proposed by President Roosevelt and adopted by Congress during the first 1,000 days of his administration so changed the size and character of the national government that they constitute a moment in American history equivalent to the Founding or the Civil War. The president's constitutional obligation to see "that the laws be faithfully executed" became, during FDR's presidency, virtually a responsibility to shape the laws before executing them.

Many of the New Deal programs were extensions of the traditional national government approach, which was described in Chapter 3 (see especially Table 3.1). But the New Deal went well beyond the traditional approach, adopting types of policies never before tried on a large scale by the national government; it began intervening in economic life in ways that had hitherto been reserved to the states. In other words, the national government discovered that it, too, had "police power" and could directly regulate individuals as well as provide roads and other services.

The new programs were such dramatic departures from the traditional policies of the national government that their constitutionality was in doubt. The Supreme Court in fact declared several of them unconstitutional, mainly on the grounds that in regulating the conduct of individuals or their employers, the national government was reaching beyond "*inter*state" and involving itself in "*intra*state"—essentially local—matters. Most of the New Deal remained in constitutional limbo until 1937, five years after Roosevelt was first elected and one year after his landslide 1936 reelection.

The turning point came with *National Labor Relations Board v. Jones and Laughlin Steel Corporation*, a case challenging the federal government's authority over the regulation of labor relations. The Supreme Court affirmed a federal role in the regulation of the national economy.[32] After the end of the New Deal, the Supreme Court has never again seriously questioned the legitimacy of interventions of the national government in the economy or society.[33]

The most important constitutional effect of Congress's actions and the Supreme Court's approval of those actions during the New Deal was the enhancement of presidential power. Most major acts of Congress in this period involved significant exercises of control over the economy. But few programs specified the actual controls to be used. Instead, Congress authorized the president or, in some cases, a new agency to determine what the controls would be. Some of the new agencies were independent commissions responsible to Congress. But most of the new agencies and new programs of the New Deal were placed in the executive branch directly under presidential authority. The institutional power of the presidency had been greatly increased.

Technically this form of congressional act, as we noted earlier, is the delegation of power. In theory, the delegation of power works as follows: (1) Congress recognizes a problem, (2) Congress acknowledges that it has neither the time nor the expertise to deal with the problem, and (3) Congress therefore sets the basic policies and then delegates to an agency the power to fill in the details. But in practice, Congress was delegating to the executive branch not merely the power to fill in the details but also real policy-making powers—that is, real legislative powers.

No modern government can avoid the delegation of significant legislative powers to the executive branch. But the fact remains that this delegation produced a fundamental shift in the American constitutional framework. During the 1930s, the growth of the national government through acts delegating legislative power tilted the national structure away from a Congress-centered government toward a president-centered government.[34] Make no mistake, Congress continues to be

---

[32] *National Labor Relations Board v. Jones and Laughlin Steel Corporation*, 301 U.S. 1 (1937).

[33] Some will argue that there are exceptions to this statement. One was *National League of Cities v. Usery*, 426 U.S. 833 (1976), which declared unconstitutional Congress's effort to supply national minimum wage standards to state and local government employees. But the Court reversed itself on this nine years later, in *Garcia v. San Antonio Metropolitan Transit Authority*, 469 U.S. 528 (1985). Another was *Bowsher v. Synar*, 478 U.S. 714 (1986), which declared unconstitutional the part of the Gramm-Rudman law authorizing the comptroller general to make across-the-board budget cuts when total appropriations exceeded legally established ceilings. In 1999, executive authority was compromised somewhat by the Court's decision to question the Federal Communications Commission's authority to supervise telephone deregulation under the Telecommunications Act of 1996. But cases such as these are few and far between, and they touch on only part of a law, not the constitutionality of an entire program.

[34] The Supreme Court did in fact *dis*approve broad delegations of legislative power by declaring the National Industrial Recovery Act of 1933 unconstitutional on the grounds that Congress did not accompany the broad delegations with sufficient standards or guidelines for presidential discretion (*Panama Refining Co. v. Ryan*, 293 U.S. 388 [1935], and *Schechter Poultry Corporation v. United States*, 295 U.S. 495 [1935]). The Supreme Court has never reversed those two decisions, but neither has it really followed them. Thus broad delegations of legislative power from Congress to the executive branch can be presumed to be constitutional. See Sotirios A. Barber, *The Constitution and the Delegation of Congressional Power* (Chicago: University of Chicago Press, 1975).

the constitutional source of policy. Legislative supremacy remains a constitutional fact of life, even at the beginning of the twenty-first century, because delegations are contingent. And not all delegations are the same. A Democratic Congress, for example, is unwilling to empower a Republican president, and vice versa; unified governments are more likely than divided governments to engage in broad delegation.[35] In short, Congress can rescind these delegations of power, restrict them with subsequent amendments, and oversee the exercise of delegated power through congressional hearings, oversight agencies, budget controls, and other administrative tools. However, it is fair to say that presidential government has become an administrative fact of life as government by delegation has expanded greatly over the past century. The world of Woodrow Wilson's *Congressional Government* is forever changed. But Congress has many clubs behind its door with which to influence the manner in which the executive branch exercises its newly won power.

PRESIDENTIAL GOVERNMENT

The locus of policy decision making shifted to the executive branch because, as we just noted, Congress made delegations of authority to the president. Congress delegated authority to the executive for instrumental reasons, much as a principal delegates to an agent. An expanded agenda of political demands, necessitated first by economic crisis—the Great Depression—but also by an accumulation of the effects of nearly a century's worth of industrialization, urbanization, and greater integration into the world economy, confronted the national government, forcing Congress's hand. The legislature itself was limited in its ability to expand its own capacity to undertake these growing responsibilities, so delegation proved a natural administrative strategy. These acts of delegation gave a far greater role to the president, empowering this "agent" to initiate in his own right.

In the case of Franklin Roosevelt, it is especially appropriate to refer to his New Deal as launching an era of presidential government. Congress certainly retained many tools with which to threaten, cajole, encourage, and persuade its executive agent to do its bidding. But presidents in general, and Roosevelt in particular, are not *only* agents of the Congress and not *only* dependent on Congress for resources and authority. They are also agents of national constituencies for whom they are eager to demonstrate their capacity for leadership in executing constituency policy agendas.[36]

Likewise, congressional delegations of power are not the only resources available to a president. Presidents have at their disposal a variety of other formal and

[35] David Epstein and Sharyn O'Halloran, *Delegating Powers: A Transaction Cost Politics Approach to Policy Making under Separate Powers* (New York: Cambridge University Press, 1999).

[36] As the political scientist Terry Moe writes, "This is the rational basis for the institutional presidency. Throughout . . . [the twentieth] century, presidents have struggled to provide themselves with a structural capacity for leadership by building institutions of their own." See Terry M. Moe, "Presidents, Institutions, and Theory," in *Researching the Presidency: Vital Questions, New Approaches*, George C. Edwards III, John H. Kessel, and Bert A. Rockman, eds. (Pittsburgh: University of Pittsburgh Press, 1993), p. 367.

informal resources that have important implications for their ability to govern. Indeed, without these other resources, presidents would lack the ability—the tools of management and public mobilization—to make much use of the power and responsibility given to them by Congress. Let us first consider the president's formal or official resources and then turn to the more informal resources that affect a president's capacity to govern, in particular the president's base of popular support.

What Are the Formal Resources of Presidential Power?

The Cabinet. In the American system of government, the **Cabinet** is the traditional but informal designation for the heads of all the major departments of the federal government (Figure 6.2). The Cabinet has no constitutional status. In contrast to the United Kingdom and many other parliamentary countries, where the cabinet is the government, the American Cabinet is not a collective body. It meets but makes no decisions as a group. Each appointment must be approved by the Senate, but cabinet members are not responsible to the Senate or to Congress at large. Cabinet appointments help build party and popular support, but the Cabinet is not a party organ. The Cabinet is made up of directors but is not a true board of directors.

Aware of this fact, the president tends to develop a burning impatience with and a mild distrust of cabinet members, to make the Cabinet a rubber stamp for actions already decided on, and to demand results, or the appearance of results, more immediately and more frequently than most department heads can provide. Because cabinet appointees generally have not shared political careers with the president or with each other and because they may meet each other for the first time after their selection, the formation of an effective governing group out of this motley collection of appointments is unlikely. Although President Clinton's insistence on a Cabinet diverse enough to resemble American society could be considered an act of political wisdom, it virtually guaranteed that few of his appointees had ever spent much time working together or even knew the policy positions or beliefs of the other appointees.[37]

Some presidents have relied more heavily on an "inner cabinet," the **National Security Council (NSC).** The NSC, established by law in 1947, is composed of the president, the vice president, the secretary of state, the secretary of defense, and other officials invited by the president. It has its own staff of foreign policy specialists run by the assistant to the president for national security affairs. For these highest appointments, presidents usually turn to people from outside Washington, often longtime associates. President Obama (at least in his early months in office) relied heavily on his chief of staff, Rahm Emanuel, who resigned in 2010 and was replaced by Pete Rouse; his former chief campaign strategist and now senior adviser, David Axelrod; the deputy chief of staff, Jim Messina; and the press secretary, Robert Gibbs. Collectively, this tight-knit group of Obama loyalists is known in Washington as "the boys."

Cabinet The secretaries, or chief administrators, of the major departments of the federal government. Cabinet secretaries are appointed by the president with the consent of the Senate.

National Security Council (NSC) A presidential foreign policy advisory council composed of the president, the vice president, the secretary of state, the secretary of defense, and other officials invited by the president.

---

[37] Adam Clymer, "The Transition; Push for Diversity May Cause Reversal on Interior Secretary," *New York Times,* December 23, 1992, p. 1.

FIGURE 6.2 THE INSTITUTIONAL PRESIDENCY, 2009

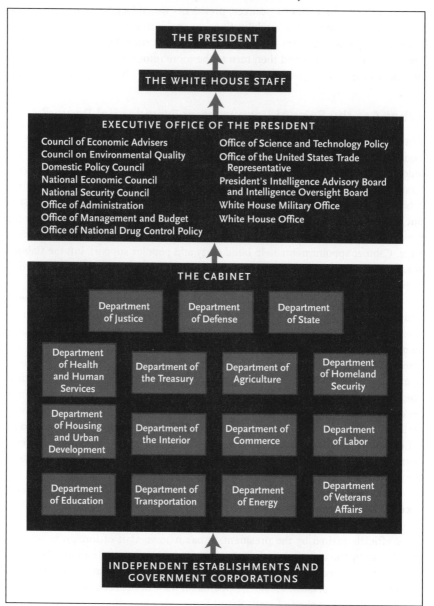

Presidents have obviously been uneven and unpredictable in their reliance on the NSC and other subcabinet bodies because executive management is inherently a personal matter. Despite all the personal variations, however, one generalization can be made: Presidents have increasingly preferred the White House staff to the Cabinet as their means of managing the gigantic executive branch.

The White House Staff.   The **White House staff** is composed mainly of analysts and advisers.[38] Although many of the top White House staff members are given the title "special assistant" for a particular task or sector, the types of judgments they are expected to make and the kinds of advice they are supposed to give are a good deal broader and more generally political than those coming from the Executive Office of the President or the cabinet departments. The members of the White House staff also tend to be more closely associated with the president than other presidentially appointed officials.

From an informal group of fewer than a dozen people (popularly called the **kitchen cabinet**) and no more than four dozen at the height of FDR's prewar administration, the White House staff has grown substantially with each successive president.[39] Richard Nixon employed 550 people in 1972. President Carter, who found so many of the requirements of presidential power distasteful and publicly vowed to keep his staff small and decentralized, built an even larger and more centralized staff. President Clinton reduced the White House staff by 20 percent, but a large White House staff is still essential.

The White House staff is a crucial information source and management tool for the president. But it may also insulate the president from other sources of information. Managing this trade-off between in-house expertise and access to independent outside opinion is a major challenge for the president. Sometimes it is botched, as when President George W. Bush depended too heavily on his staff for information about weapons of mass destruction (WMD) in Iraq, leading him to erroneous conclusions.[40]

The Executive Office of the President.   The development of the White House staff can be appreciated only in its relation to the still-larger **Executive Office of the President (EOP)**. Created in 1939, the EOP is a major part of what is often called the institutional presidency—the permanent agencies that perform defined management tasks for the president. The most important and the largest EOP agency is the Office of Management and Budget (OMB). Its roles in preparing the national budget, designing the president's program, reporting on agency activities, and overseeing regulatory proposals make OMB personnel part of virtually every conceivable presidential responsibility. The status and power of the OMB have grown in importance with each successive president. The process of budgeting at one time was a bottom-up procedure, with expenditure and program requests passing from the lowest bureaus through the departments to "clearance" in OMB and hence to Congress, where each agency could be called in to reveal what its original request had been before it was revised by the OMB. Now the budgeting process is top-down:

White House staff The analysts and advisers to the president, often given the title "special assistant."

kitchen cabinet An informal group of advisers to whom the president turns for counsel and guidance. Members of the official cabinet may or may not also be members of the Kitchen Cabinet.

Executive Office of the President (EOP) The permanent agencies that perform defined management tasks for the president. Created in 1939, the EOP includes the Office of Management and Budget, the Council of Economic Advisers, the National Security Council, and other agencies.

---

[38] A substantial portion of this section is taken from Lowi, *The Personal President,* pp. 141–50.

[39] All the figures since 1967, and probably since 1957, are understated because additional White House staff members have been on "detailed" service, borrowed from the military and various cabinet departments (some secretly assigned) and are not counted here because they were not on the White House payroll.

[40] See George Krause, "The Secular Decline in Presidential Domestic Policymaking: An Organizational Perspective," *Presidential Studies Quarterly* 34 (2004): 779–92. On the general issue, see James P. Pfiffner, ed., *The Managerial Presidency,* 2nd ed. (College Station: Texas A&M University Press, 1999).

OMB sets the terms of discourse for agencies as well as for Congress. The director of OMB is now one of the most powerful officials in Washington.

The staff of the Council of Economic Advisers (CEA) constantly analyzes the economy and economic trends and attempts to give the president the ability to anticipate events rather than waiting and reacting to events. The Council on Environmental Quality was designed to do for environmental issues what the CEA does for economic issues. The members of the National Security Council meet regularly with the president to give advice on the large national-security picture. The staff of the NSC assimilates and analyzes data from all intelligence-gathering agencies (the CIA, and so on). Other EOP agencies perform more specialized tasks.

Somewhere between 1,500 and 2,000 highly specialized staffers work for EOP agencies.[41] The importance of each agency in the EOP varies according to the personal orientation of the president. For example, the NSC staff was of immense importance under President Nixon, especially because it served essentially as the personal staff of the presidential assistant Henry Kissinger before his elevation to the office of secretary of state. But it was of less importance to President George H. W. Bush, who looked outside the EOP altogether for military policy matters, turning much more to the Joint Chiefs of Staff and its chair at the time, General Colin Powell.

The Vice Presidency. The vice presidency is a constitutional anomaly, even though the office was created by the Constitution along with the presidency. The vice president exists for two purposes only: to succeed the president in case of death, resignation, or incapacitation and to preside over the Senate, casting a tie-breaking vote when necessary.[42]

The main value of the vice presidency as a political resource for the president is electoral. Traditionally a presidential candidate's most important rule for the choice of a running mate is that he or she bring the support of at least one state (preferably a large one) not otherwise likely to support the ticket. Another rule holds that the vice-presidential nominee should provide some regional balance and, wherever possible, some balance among various ideological or ethnic subsections of the party. It is very doubtful that John Kennedy would have won in 1960 without his vice-presidential candidate, Lyndon Johnson, and the contribution Johnson made to winning in Texas. George W. Bush's choice of Dick Cheney in 2000 was completely devoid of direct electoral value, since Cheney comes from one of our least populous states (Wyoming, which casts only three electoral votes). But given Cheney's stalwart right-wing record both in Congress and as President George H. W. Bush's secretary of defense, coupled with his even more prominently right-wing wife, Lynne Cheney, his inclusion on the Republican ticket was clearly an effort to consolidate the support of the restive right wing of the Republican Party. In 2008, the Republican candidate, John McCain, chose Alaska's governor, Sarah Palin, as his running mate. Palin had no national visibility or experience but was well liked

---

[41]The actual number is difficult to estimate because, as with the White House staff, some EOP personnel, especially those in national-security work, are detailed to the office from outside agencies.

[42]Article I, Section 3, provides that "the Vice President . . . shall be President of the Senate, but shall have no Vote, unless they be equally divided." This is the only vote the vice president is allowed.

on the Republican right for her conservative views. Many conservative Republicans thought McCain was too liberal and had been threatening to sit out the election. Palin ignited their enthusiasm. At the same time, the Democratic candidate, Barack Obama, chose Senator Joseph Biden of Delaware as his vice-presidential running mate. Obama had often been criticized for lacking background in the realm of foreign policy. Biden, chair of the Senate Foreign Relations Committee, brought considerable foreign policy-experience to the ticket.

As the institutional presidency has grown in size and complexity, most presidents of the past twenty-five years have sought to use their vice presidents as management resources after the election. George H. W. Bush, as President Reagan's vice president, was kept within the loop of decision making because Reagan delegated so much power. Bush received a copy of virtually every document prepared for Reagan, especially during the first term, when Bush's close friend James Baker was chief of staff. Former president Bush did not take such pains to keep Vice President Dan Quayle in the loop, but President Clinton relied greatly on his vice president, Al Gore, and Gore emerged as one of the most trusted and effective figures in the Clinton White House. Gore's most important task was to oversee the National Performance Review (NPR), an ambitious program to "reinvent" the way the federal government conducts its affairs. The presidency of George W. Bush resulted in unprecedented power and responsibility for his vice president, Dick Cheney. Known as a hands-on vice president, Cheney played an active role in cabinet meetings and policy formation and directed the National Energy Policy Development Group. Cheney also played a key role in organizing the war on terror and launching the Iraq war. Cheney was widely viewed as one of the most—if not the most—influential vice presidents in American history. It remains to be seen just how much influence Vice President Joe Biden will wield in the Obama administration. It seems unlikely that Obama will need Biden's counsel quite as much as Bush felt compelled to rely on Cheney.

The President and Policy. The president's powers and institutional resources, taken together, give the chief executive a substantial voice in the nation's policy-making processes. Strictly speaking, presidents cannot introduce legislation. Only members of Congress can formally propose new programs and policies. However, presidents often do send proposals to Congress. Congress, in turn, takes up these proposals by referring them to the relevant committee of jurisdiction. Sometimes these proposals are said to be dead on arrival, an indication that presidential preferences are at loggerheads with those in the House or Senate. This is especially common during periods of divided government. In such circumstances, presidents and legislators engage in bargaining, although in the end the status quo may prevail. Presidents are typically in a weak position in these circumstances, especially if they have grand plans to change the status quo.[43] During periods of unified government, the president has fellow partisans in charge of each chamber; in these cases, the president may indeed seize the initiative, seeking to coordinate policy initiatives from the White House. The political scientist Charles Cameron suggests that the distinction between unified and

---

[43] D. Roderick Kiewiet and Mathew D. McCubbins, *The Logic of Delegation: Congressional Parties and the Appropriations Process* (Chicago: University of Chicago Press, 1991).

divided government is quite consequential for presidential "style": It makes the chief executive either bargainer in chief or coordinator in chief.[44]

Congress has come to expect the president to propose the government's budget, and the nation has come to expect presidential initiatives to deal with major problems. Some of these initiatives have come in the form of huge packages of programs—Franklin Roosevelt's New Deal and Lyndon Johnson's Great Society. Sometimes presidents craft a single program they hope will have a significant effect on both the nation and their political fortunes. For example, George W. Bush made the war on terrorism the centerpiece of his administration. To fight this war, Bush brought about the creation of a new cabinet department, the Department of Homeland Security, and the enactment of such pieces of legislation as the USA PATRIOT Act to give the executive branch more power to deal with the terrorist threat. Going beyond terrorism, Bush also presided over the enactment of a huge expansion of the Medicare program to provide prescription drug benefits to senior citizens. All this from a president who was said to lack a popular **mandate** in the wake of the controversial 2000 election. Bush may have lacked a mandate, but the expressed and delegated powers of the office gave him the resources with which to prevail. Ironically his 2004 reelection victory was more substantial than his victory in 2000, but it failed to provide him much leverage on new policy initiatives. His efforts to reshape and reinvigorate the Social Security system and reform the estate tax came to naught; the war in Iraq, the fight against terrorism, and the response to catastrophic hurricanes squeezed other domestic initiatives off the active to-do list.

At one time, historians and journalists liked to debate the question of strong versus weak presidents. Today every president is strong. This strength is not so much a function of personal charisma or political savvy as it is a reflection of the increasing power of the institution of the presidency.

The Contemporary Bases of Presidential Power

In the nineteenth century, when Congress was America's dominant institution of government, its members sometimes treated the president with disdain. Today, however, no one would assert that the presidency is an unimportant institution. Presidents seek to dominate the policy-making process and claim the inherent power to lead the nation in time of war. The expansion of presidential power over the course of the past century has come about not by accident but as the result of an ongoing effort by successive presidents to enlarge the powers of the office. Some of these efforts have succeeded, and others have failed. As the framers of the Constitution predicted, presidential ambition has been a powerful and unrelenting force in American politics.

Generally presidents can expand their power by three means: party, popular mobilization, and administration. In the first instance, presidents may construct or strengthen national partisan institutions with which to exert influence in the legislative process and through which to implement their programs. Alternatively or in addition to the first tactic, presidents may use popular appeals to create a mass base of support that will allow them to subordinate their political foes. This

mandate A claim by a victorious candidate that the electorate has given him or her special authority to carry out promises made during the campaign.

---

[44]Cameron, "Bargaining and Presidential Power."

tactic has sometimes been called the strategy of going public, or the "rhetorical" presidency.[45] In the third instance, presidents may seek to bolster their control of established executive agencies or create new administrative institutions and procedures that will reduce their dependence on Congress and give them a more independent governing and policy-making capability. Presidents' use of executive orders to achieve their policy goals in lieu of seeking to persuade Congress to enact legislation is, perhaps, the most obvious example.

Party as a Source of Power.   All presidents have relied on the members and leaders of their own party to implement their legislative agendas. President George W. Bush, for example, worked closely with congressional GOP leaders on such matters as energy policy and Medicare reform. But the president does not control his own party; party members have considerable autonomy. On immigration policy, for example, the Bush proposals in 2006 were supported in most respects by the Republican-controlled Senate. The Republican-controlled House, however, passed much more punitive policies. The two chambers, despite being controlled by the president's party, were unable to agree on a compromise and ended up settling on elements of the House bill that the president least desired. Nevertheless, he signed the measure in October 2006, noting it was only the first step in comprehensive immigration reform. The issue reemerged in 2007.

President Obama initially declared that he would seek bipartisan support for his programs. Congressional Republicans, however, calculated that they had little to gain from supporting Obama and much to lose if his administration was successful. Hence, the GOP opposed the president's domestic and foreign policy initiatives. With overwhelming Democratic majorities in both houses of Congress, President Obama found that he had no difficulty turning to the Democratic leadership for support. Indeed, Republican opposition helped Democratic leaders unite their fractious followers behind the president's budget proposals in 2009.

In America's system of separated powers, the president's party may be in the minority in Congress and unable to do much for the chief executive's programs (Figure 6.3). Consequently, although their party is valuable to chief executives, it has not been a fully reliable presidential tool. The more unified the president's party is in supporting his legislative requests, the more unified the opposition party is likely to be. Unless the majority of the president's party is very large, he must also appeal to the opposition to make up for the inevitable defectors within the ranks of his own party. Thus the president often poses as being above partisanship to win "bipartisan" support in Congress. But to the extent that he pursues a bipartisan strategy, he cannot throw himself fully into building the party loyalty and the party discipline that would maximize the value of his own party's support in Congress. This is a dilemma for every president, particularly those faced with an opposition-controlled Congress.

The role of the filibuster in the Senate should not be underestimated in this context (see Chapter 5). Even a president with a large majority in the House and a good working majority in the Senate may not have the 60 votes needed to shut down debate in the Senate. This is especially apparent in the case of presidential

---

[45] Kernell, *Going Public;* see also Tulis, *The Rhetorical Presidency.*

FIGURE 6.3 THE PRESIDENTIAL BATTING AVERAGE: PRESIDENTIAL SUCCESS ON CONGRESSIONAL VOTES

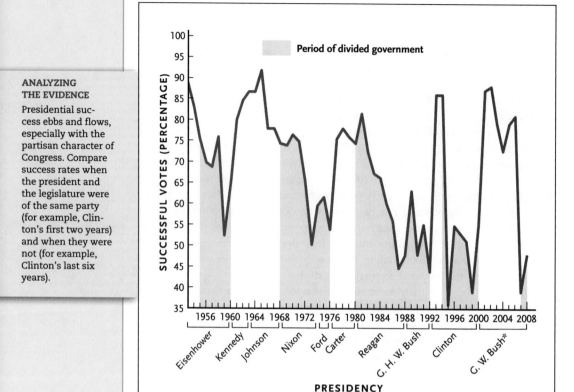

*In 2001, the government was divided for only part of the year.

NOTE: Percentages are based on votes on which presidents took a position.

SOURCE: *Congressional Quarterly Weekly Report*, January 3, 2004, p.18, and authors' update.

appointments, where individual senators can place a hold on a nomination, putting everyone on notice that the president's pursuit of a particular candidate will trigger a filibuster.[46] Filibuster power was especially prominent in 2005 as President Bush sought senate confirmation of federal judges and two Supreme Court justices. The Democrats, who were in the minority, were in a position to filibuster nominations they regarded as "extremist," forcing the president (and his majority partisans in the Senate) to negotiate. The Democrats lifted the filibuster threat in exchange for some moderation on the part of the president, and they allowed up-or-down votes on some nominees. Because they cannot always rely on their party in Congress,

---

[46] A powerful argument that invokes this logic is that of Keith Krehbiel in *Pivotal Politics: A Theory of U.S. Lawmaking* (Chicago: University of Chicago Press, 1998).

contemporary presidents are more likely to use two other methods—popular mobilization and executive administration—to achieve their political goals.

Going Public. Popular mobilization as a technique of presidential power has its historical roots in the presidencies of Theodore Roosevelt and Woodrow Wilson and subsequently became a weapon in the political arsenals of most presidents after the mid-twentieth century. During the nineteenth century, it was considered rather inappropriate for presidents to engage in personal campaigning on their own behalf or in support of programs and policies. When Andrew Johnson broke this unwritten rule and made a series of speeches vehemently seeking public support for his Reconstruction program, even some of his most ardent supporters were shocked at what was seen as a lack of decorum and dignity. The president's opponents cited his "inflammatory" speeches in one of the articles of impeachment drafted by Congress pursuant to the first effort in American history to oust an incumbent president.[47]

The president who used public appeals perhaps most effectively was Franklin Roosevelt. The political scientist Sidney Milkis observes that FDR was "firmly persuaded of the need to form a direct link between the executive office and the public."[48] FDR developed a number of tactics aimed at forging such a link. Like his predecessors, he often embarked on speaking trips around the nation to promote his programs. On one such tour, he told a crowd, "I regain strength just by meeting the American people."[49] In addition, FDR made limited but important use of the new electronic medium, radio, to reach millions of Americans. In his famous "fireside chats," the president, or at least his voice, came into every living room in the country to discuss programs and policies and generally to assure Americans that Franklin Delano Roosevelt was aware of their difficulties and working diligently toward solutions. Another executive, Mayor Fiorello La Guardia of New York City, also "went public," using radio to read comic strips to Depression-era city children during a long newspaper strike. A brilliant political ploy, it deeply impressed voting-age citizens while entertaining the young ones.

Roosevelt was also an innovator in the realm of what now might be called press relations. When he entered the White House, FDR faced a mainly hostile press typically controlled by conservative members of the business establishment. As the president wrote, "All the fat-cat newspapers—85 percent of the whole—have been utterly opposed to everything the Administration is seeking."[50] Roosevelt hoped to be able to use the press to mold public opinion, but to do so he needed to circumvent the editors and publishers who were generally unsympathetic to his goals. To this end, the president worked to cultivate the reporters who covered the White House. Roosevelt made himself available for twice-weekly press conferences,

---

[47] Tulis, *The Rhetorical Presidency*, p. 91.

[48] Sidney M. Milkis, *The President and the Parties: The Transformation of the American Party System since the New Deal* (New York: Oxford University Press, 1993), p. 97.

[49] Quoted in James MacGregor Burns, *Roosevelt: The Lion and the Fox* (New York: Harcourt, Brace, 1956), p. 317.

[50] Burns, *Roosevelt*, p. 317.

FIGURE 6.4 PUBLIC APPEARANCES BY PRESIDENTS

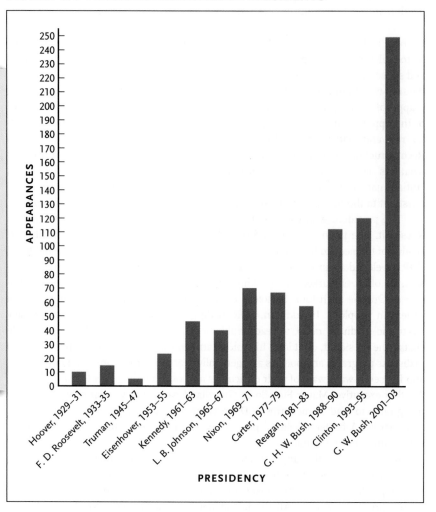

NOTE: Only the first two years of each term are included, because the last two years include many purely political appearances for the president's reelection campaign.

SOURCE: Samuel Kernell, *Going Public: New Strategies of Presidential Leadership*, 3rd ed. (Washington, D.C.: Congressional Quarterly Press, 1998), p.118, and authors' update.

during which he offered candid answers to reporters' questions and made certain to make important policy announcements that would provide the reporters with significant stories to file with their papers.[51] Roosevelt was the first president to designate a press secretary (Stephen Early), who was charged with organizing the press conferences and making certain that reporters observed the informal rules

---

[51] Kernell, *Going Public*, p. 79.

distinguishing presidential comments that were off the record from those that could be attributed directly to the president.

Every president since FDR has sought to craft a public relations strategy that emphasized his strengths and maximized his popular appeal. One Clinton innovation was to make the White House Communications Office an important institution within the EOP. In a practice continued by George W. Bush, the Communications Office became responsible not only for responding to reporters' queries but also for developing and implementing a coordinated communications strategy: promoting the president's policy goals, developing responses to unflattering news stories, and making certain that a favorable image of the president would, insofar as possible, dominate the news. Consistent with President Obama's successful use of social networking in his 2008 election campaign, the Obama administration's communications office has emphasized social networking techniques, including "twittering," to reach newsmakers and the American people directly. For example, in May 2009, the White House posted a 140 word "tweet" on the swine flu. Of course, unlike ordinary tweets, presidential tweets must, under the terms of the Presidential Records Act, be recorded and stored for posterity.

In addition to using the media, recent presidents, have reached out directly to the American public to gain its approval (see Figure 6.4). During his first full month in office, for example, President Obama addressed Congress and the American people on the nation's financial crisis. Obama said nothing new but sought to reassure the public and to mobilize its support for his policies. During his first year in office, Obama made additional major speeches in the United States and abroad designed to generate both domestic and international support for his programs. In his speeches, the president frequently sought to explain how his approaches would differ from those of the Bush administration. In a nationally-televised May 2009 speech on national security, for example, Obama declared that the security policies employed by the Bush administration, including harsh interrogations, indefinite detention of suspects, and other violations of America's customary rule of law were both inconsistent with American values and ineffective. He promised to craft an approach that would protect both liberty and the nation's security. In a June 2009 speech delivered in Cairo, Egypt, Obama sought to reassure the Arab world that the United States was not its enemy. Obama began his speech with the traditional Muslim greeting, "Assalamu Alaykum," and made reference in his text to the "holy Koran." The speech was well received, though many listeners wondered if the president's words would be followed by changes in policy.

The Limits of Going Public.   Some presidents have been able to make effective use of popular appeals to overcome congressional opposition. Popular support, though, has not been a firm foundation for presidential power. To begin with, it is notoriously fickle. President George W. Bush maintained an approval rating of over 70 percent for more than a year after the September 11 terrorist attacks. By 2003, however, his approval rating had fallen nearly twenty points as American casualties in Iraq mounted; by the end of 2005, it had fallen almost another twenty points, to the high 30s, where it remained through much of 2006. Such declines in popular approval during a president's term in office are nearly inevitable and follow

FIGURE 6.5 PRESIDENTIAL PERFORMANCE RATINGS

ANALYZING THE EVIDENCE

In the presidential performance-rating poll, respondents are asked, "Do you approve of the way the president is handling his job?" The graphs show the percentage of positive responses. What factors help explain changes in presidential approval ratings? Does popular approval really affect presidential power? How can popular feelings about the president affect the president's conduct and influence?

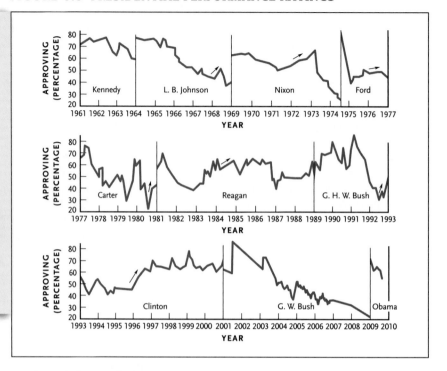

NOTE: Arrows indicate preelection upswings.
SOURCE: Courtesy of the Gallup Organization and Louis Harris and Associates.

a predictable pattern (Figure 6.5).[52] Presidents generate popular support by promising to undertake important programs that will contribute directly to the well-being of large numbers of Americans. Almost inevitably, presidential performance falls short of those promises and popular expectations, leading to a sharp decline in public support and an ensuing collapse of presidential influence.[53]

Presidents certainly have not abandoned the tool of going public, but they no longer use it frequently as they once did—there has been, for example, a decline in presidential appearances on prime-time television over the past five administrations.[54] Instead, presidents have employed institutionalized public and media relations efforts more to create a generally favorable public image than to promote specific policies. Thus in 2002, President George W. Bush made several speeches to boost the proposed creation of the Homeland Security Department. At the same time, however, the White House Communications Office was engaged in a nonstop, seven-day-a-week effort to promote news and feature stories aimed at bolstering the president's more general public image. Stories emphasized the president's

---

[52] Lowi, *The Personal President*.

[53] Lowi, *The Personal President*, p. 11.

[54] Kernell, *Going Public*, p. 114.

empathy for retirees hurt by the downturn of stock prices, the president's anger over corporate abuses, the president's concern for the environment, the president's determination to prevent terrorism, the president's support for Israel, and so forth. These are all examples of image polishing rather than going public on behalf of specific programs. Confronted with the limitations of a strategy of popular mobilization, presidents have shifted from an offensive strategy to a more defensive mode in this domain. The limitations of going public as a route to presidential power have also led contemporary presidents to make use of a third technique: expanding their administrative capabilities.

The Administrative State

Contemporary presidents have increased the administrative capabilities of their office in three ways. First, they have enhanced the reach and power of the EOP. Second, they have sought to increase White House control over the federal bureaucracy. Third, they have expanded the role of executive orders and other instruments of direct presidential governance. Taken together, these components of what might be called the White House administrative strategy have given presidents a capacity to achieve their programmatic and policy goals even when they are unable to secure congressional approval. Indeed, some recent presidents have been able to accomplish quite a bit without much congressional, partisan, or even public support.

The Executive Office of the President.   The Executive Office of the President has grown from 6 administrative assistants in 1939 to today's 39 assistants to the president, deputy assistants, and special assistants who work in the White House office, along with some 1,800 individuals staffing the nine divisions of the Executive Office.[55] The creation and growth of the White House staff give the president an enormously enhanced capacity to gather information, plan programs and strategies, communicate with constituencies, and exercise supervision of the executive branch. The staff multiplies the president's eyes, ears, and arms, serving as a critical instrument of presidential power.[56] In light of the degree to which Congress delegates to the executive branch, as described earlier in this chapter, the president has greatly enhanced his capacity as an agent of policy formulation and implementation.

In particular, the OMB serves as a potential instrument of presidential control over federal spending and hence as a mechanism through which the White House has greatly expanded its power. The OMB has the capacity to analyze and approve not only budgetary requests but all legislative proposals emanating from all federal agencies before they are submitted to Congress. This procedure, now a matter of routine, greatly enhanced the president's control over the entire executive branch. All executive orders also go through the OMB.[57] Thus through one White House agency the president has the means to exert major influence over the flow of money as well as the shape and content of national legislation.

---

[55] Harold W. Stanley and Richard G. Niemi, *Vital Statistics on American Politics, 2005–2006* (Washington, D.C.: Congressional Quarterly Press, 2005), pp. 250–51.

[56] Milkis, *The President and the Parties,* p. 128.

[57] Milkis, *The President and the Parties,* p. 160.

Regulatory Review. A second tactic that presidents have used to increase their power and reach is the process of regulatory review, through which they have sought to control rule making by the agencies of the executive branch (see also Chapter 14). Whenever Congress enacts a statute, its actual implementation requires the promulgation of hundreds of rules by the agency charged with administering the law and giving effect to the will of Congress. Some congressional statutes are quite detailed and leave agencies with relatively little discretion. Typically, however, Congress enacts a relatively broad statement of legislative intent and delegates to the appropriate administrative agency the power to fill in many important details.[58] In other words, Congress typically says to an administrative agency, "Here is the problem. Deal with it."[59]

The discretion Congress delegates to administrative agencies has provided recent presidents with an important avenue for expanding their power. For example, President Clinton believed the president had full authority to order agencies of the executive branch to adopt such rules as the president thought appropriate. During the course of his presidency, Clinton issued 107 directives to administrators ordering them to propose specific rules and regulations. In some instances, the language of the rule to be proposed was drafted by the White House staff; in other cases, the president asserted a priority but left it to the agency to draft the precise language of the proposal. Presidential rule-making directives covered a wide variety of topics. For example, Clinton ordered the Food and Drug Administration (FDA) to develop rules designed to restrict the marketing of tobacco products to children. White House and FDA staffers then spent several months preparing nearly 1,000 pages of new regulations affecting tobacco manufacturers and vendors.[60] Republicans denounced Clinton's actions as a usurpation of power.[61] After he took office, however, President George W. Bush made no move to surrender the powers Clinton had claimed. Bush has continued the Clinton-era practice of issuing presidential directives to agencies to spur them to issue new rules and regulations. When he assumed office, President Obama appointed the Harvard law professor Cass Sunstein to head his regulatory review effort. Sunstein, an expert on the regulatory process, was expected to make regulatory review an even more important arrow in the president's quiver.

Governing by Decree: Executive Orders. A third mechanism through which contemporary presidents have sought to enhance their power to govern unilaterally is the use of executive orders and other forms of presidential decrees, including executive agreements, national-security findings and directives, proclamations, reorganization plans, the signing of statements, and a host of others.[62] Executive

---

[58] The classic critique of this process is Lowi, *The End of Liberalism.*

[59] Kenneth Culp Davis, *Administrative Law Treatise* (St. Paul, Minn.: West, 1958), p. 9.

[60] Elena Kagan, "Presidential Administration," *Harvard Law Review* 114 (2001): 2265.

[61] For example, Douglas W. Kmiec, "Expanding Power," in *The Rule of Law in the Wake of Clinton*, Roger Pilon, ed. (Washington, D.C.: Cato Institute Press, 2000), pp. 47–68.

[62] A complete inventory is provided in Harold C. Relyea, *Presidential Directives: Background and Review*, Congressional Research Service Report for Congress, 98–611 GOV, 9 November 2001.

FIGURE 6.6 SIGNIFICANT EXECUTIVE ORDERS, 1900–1995

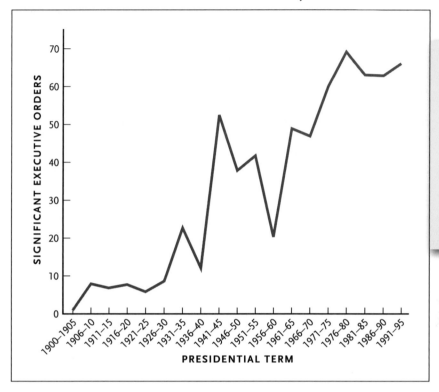

SOURCE: William G. Howell, "The President's Powers of Unilateral Action: The Strategic Advantages of Acting Alone" (Ph.D. diss., Stanford University, 1999).

ANALYZING THE EVIDENCE

During the twentieth century, presidents made increasingly frequent use of executive orders to accomplish their policy goals. What factors explain this development? How have Congress and the courts responded to increased presidential assertiveness?

orders have a long history in the United States and, as we saw earlier, have been the vehicles for a number of important government policies. These include the purchase of Louisiana, the annexation of Texas, the emancipation of the slaves, the internment of the Japanese, the desegregation of the military, the initiation of affirmative action, and the creation of important federal agencies, among them the Environmental Protection Agency (EPA), the Food and Drug Administration (FDA), and the Peace Corps.[63]

Although wars and national emergencies produce the highest volume of executive orders, such presidential actions also occur frequently in peacetime (Figure 6.6). In the realm of foreign policy, unilateral presidential actions in the form of executive agreements have virtually replaced treaties as the nation's chief foreign-policy instruments.[64] Presidential decrees, however, are often issued for purely domestic purposes.

---

[63]Terry M. Moe and William G. Howell, "The Presidential Power of Unilateral Action," *Journal of Law, Economics, and Organization* 15 (1999): 133–34.

[64]Moe and Howell, "Unilateral Action," p. 164.

Presidents may not use executive orders to issue whatever commands they please. The use of such decrees is bound by law. If a president issues an executive order, proclamation, directive, or the like, in principle he does so pursuant to the powers granted to him by the Constitution or delegated to him by Congress, usually through a statute. When presidents issue such orders, they generally state the constitutional or statutory basis for their actions. For example, when President Truman ordered the desegregation of the armed services, he did so pursuant to his constitutional powers as commander in chief. In a similar vein, when President Johnson issued Executive Order No. 11246, he asserted that the order was designed to implement the 1964 Civil Rights Act, which prohibited employment discrimination. Where an executive order has no statutory or constitutional basis, the courts have held it to be void. The most important case illustrating this point is *Youngstown Sheet and Tube Company v. Sawyer*, the so-called steel seizure case of 1952.[65] Here the Supreme Court ruled that President Truman's seizure of the nation's steel mills during the Korean War had no statutory or constitutional basis and was thus invalid.

A number of court decisions, though, have established broad boundaries that leave considerable room for presidential action. By illustration, the courts have held that Congress might approve a presidential action after the fact or, in effect, ratify a presidential action through "acquiescence"—for example, by not objecting for long periods of time or by continuing to provide funding for programs established by executive orders. In addition, the courts have indicated that some areas, most notably the realm of military policy, are presidential in character, and they have allowed presidents wide latitude to make policy by executive decree. Thus within the very broad limits established by the courts, presidential orders can be and have been important policy tools.

President Clinton issued numerous orders designed to promote a coherent set of policy goals: protecting the environment, strengthening federal regulatory power, shifting the focus of America's foreign policy from unilateral to multilateral, expanding affirmative action programs, and helping organized labor in its struggles with employers.[66] As in his use of regulatory review, President Clinton was able to craft through executive orders a policy agenda that he could not accomplish through legislation. Faced with a hostile Congress, Clinton turned to unilateral instruments of executive power, including regulatory review, executive orders, and the like. Clinton certainly did not issue more executive orders than previous presidents. His innovation was to take an instrument that had been used sporadically and show that an activist president could develop and implement a significant policy agenda without legislation—a lesson that surely was not lost on his successor.

Indeed, just as he continued the practice of using regulatory review as a policy instrument, President George W. Bush did not hesitate to use executive orders, issuing more than forty during his first year in office and continuing to employ this device (along with signing statements, described earlier) with great regularity during his presidency. During his first months in office, Bush issued orders placing

---

[65] *Youngstown Sheet and Tube Company v. Sawyer*, 343 U.S. 579 (1952).

[66] Todd Gaziano, "The New 'Massive Resistance,'" *Policy Review* (May/June 1998): 283.

limits on the use of embryonic stem cells in federally funded research projects and prohibiting the use of federal funds to support international family-planning groups that provide abortion-counseling services. Subsequently Bush made very aggressive use of executive orders in response to the threat of terrorism, which the president declared to be his administration's most important policy agenda. In November 2001, for example, Bush issued a directive authorizing the creation of military tribunals to try noncitizens accused of involvement in acts of terrorism against the United States. The presidential directive also prohibits defendants from appealing their treatment to any federal or state court. In 2005 and 2006, it came to light that Bush had ordered the National Security Administration to conduct a massive program of domestic surveillance of telephone traffic involving suspected terrorists.

In addition, the president issued orders freezing the assets of groups and individuals associated with terrorism, providing expedited citizenship for foreign nationals serving in the U.S. military, and empowering the CIA to use all means possible to oust President Saddam Hussein of Iraq, whom Bush accused of plotting terrorist acts. In *Hamdan v. Rumsfeld*, the Supreme Court in June 2006 determined that the military tribunals established by Bush's executive order to try detainees at the U.S. naval base at Guantánamo Bay, Cuba, violated both the Uniform Code of Military Justice and the Geneva Conventions.[67]

Although terrorism was certainly at the top of President Bush's agenda, he also issued a number of executive orders having to do with domestic policy. For example, the president was able to overcome congressional resistance to his efforts to increase domestic energy exploration and the rapid exploitation of domestic energy resources. Like Clinton, President Bush discovered that an executive order can often substitute for legislation. In May 2001, Bush signed an executive order that closely followed a recommendation from the American Petroleum Institute (API), an oil industry trade association, to free energy companies from a number of federal regulations. As we saw above, President Obama signed four executive orders on his second full day in office. These rescinded a number of Bush's orders regarding the treatment of suspected terrorists. Over the next two years, Obama issued orders changing government contracting policies, strengthening protections for endangered species, and changing children's health care programs.

Signing Statements. The signing statement has become another instrument of presidential power. To negate congressional actions to which they objected, recent presidents have made frequent and calculated use of presidential signing statements when signing bills into law.[68] A **signing statement** is an announcement made by the president at the time of signing a congressional enactment into law, sometimes presenting the president's interpretation of the law as well as usually innocuous remarks predicting the many benefits the new law would bring to the nation. Occasionally, presidents have used signing statements to point to sections of the law they deemed improper or even unconstitutional, and to instruct executive

signing statement Announcement made by the president when a bill is signed into law.

---

[67] *Hamdan v. Rumsfeld,* 548 U.S. (2006).

[68] Mark Killenback, "A Matter of Mere Approval: The Role of the President in the Creation of Legislative History," 48 *University of Arkansas Law Review* 239 (1995).

branch agencies how they were to execute the law.[69] President Harry Truman, for example, accompanied his approval of the 1946 Hobbs Anti-Racketeering Act with a message offering his interpretation of ambiguous sections of the statute and indicating how the federal government would implement the new law.[70]

Presidents have made signing statements throughout American history, though many were not recorded and so did not become part of the official legislative record. Ronald Reagan's attorney general, Edwin Meese, is generally credited with transforming the signing statement into a routine tool of presidential direct action.[71] Meese believed that carefully crafted signing statements would provide a basis for action by executive agencies and, perhaps even more important, would become part of the history and context of a piece of legislation if and when judicial interpretation became necessary. Indeed, to make certain that signing statements became part of the legislative history, Meese reached an agreement with the West Publishing Company to include them in its authoritative texts.[72]

With the way paved, Reagan proceeded to use detailed and artfully designed signing statements—prepared by the Department of Justice—to attempt to reinterpret congressional enactments. For example, when signing the Safe Drinking Water Amendments of 1986, President Reagan issued a statement that interpreted sections of the Act to allow discretionary enforcement when the Congress seemed to call for mandatory enforcement.[73] Reagan hoped the courts would accept his version of the statute when examining subsequent enforcement decisions. In other cases, Reagan used his signing statements to attempt to nullify portions of statutes. For example, in one signing statement, Reagan declared that portions of the 1988 Veterans Benefit Bill would intrude upon the integrity of the executive branch and said he would not enforce them.[74] In the same year, Reagan signed a bill prohibiting construction on two pristine Idaho waterways but declared that one portion of the bill was unconstitutional and would not be enforced.[75] This strategy, to be sure, was not always successful. When he signed the Competition in Contracting Act in 1984, President Reagan declared that portions of the law were unconstitutional and directed executive branch officials not to comply with them. Subsequently, U.S. District Court Judge Harold Ackerman upheld the act and decried the notion that the president had the power to declare acts of Congress unconstitutional.[76] The same conclusion was later reached by the Ninth Circuit Court of Appeals, which

---

[69] Philip J. Cooper, *By Order of the President: The Use and Abuse of Presidential Direct Action* (Lawrence: University Press of Kansas, 2002), p. 201.

[70] Edward S. Corwin, *The President: Office and Powers*, 4th ed. (New York: New York University Press, 1957), p. 283.

[71] Cooper, *By Order of the President*, p. 201.

[72] Cooper, *By Order of the President*, p. 203.

[73] Cooper, *By Order of the President*, p. 216.

[74] Ronald Reagan, Statement on Signing a Veterans' Benefit Bill, November 18, 1988, in *Public Papers of the President, 1988–1989* (Washington, D.C.: U.S. Government Printing Office, 1990), 2:1558.

[75] Ronald Reagan, Statement on Signing the Bill Prohibiting the Licensing or Construction of Facilities on the Salmon and Snake Rivers in Idaho, November 17, 1988, *Public Papers*, 2:1525.

[76] *AMERON, Inc. v. U.S. Army Corps of Engineers*, 610 F.Supp. 750 (D.N.J. 1985).

declared that the president did not have the authority to "excise or sever provisions of a bill with which he disagrees."[77]

Despite these adverse rulings, however, the same tactic of reinterpreting and nullifying congressional enactments was continued by Reagan's successor, George H. W. Bush. When he signed the 1991 Civil Rights Act, Bush asserted his concern that one of its provisions might be unfairly applied to businesses. By so doing, the president established his own reading to shape the act's legislative history, provided guidance to administrators regarding the law's implementation, and attempted to influence future court interpretations.[78] On another occasion, Bush signed a bill that he had unsuccessfully opposed and that required the Department of Energy to employ affirmative action in contracting for the construction of the Superconducting Super Collider. However, when he signed the bill, Bush declared that there was no valid constitutional basis for an affirmative action program involving this project and directed the energy secretary to ignore the requirement.[79] Bush had effectively nullified a law whose passage he had been unable to prevent.

For the most part, Presidents Reagan and Bush used signing statements to limit the scope of affirmative action programs, to block expansion of business regulation, to reduce the impact of environmental programs and to thwart new labor laws. Bill Clinton followed the examples set by Reagan and Bush and made extensive use of signing statements both to reinterpret and nullify congressional enactments. But, of course, Clinton's agenda was far different from that of his two immediate predecessors. Faced with Republican-controlled congresses for six of his eight years in office, Clinton used his signing statements to attempt to block constriction of affirmative action programs, to limit efforts to weaken environmental standards, and to protect the rights of individuals with disabilities. For example, in 1996 Congress enacted a defense appropriations bill that included a provision requiring that any member of the military who was HIV positive be discharged from the service. President Clinton signed the appropriations bill but asserted that this provision was unconstitutional.[80] He ordered the Justice Department not to defend the HIV ban in court if it was challenged. In effect, he was announcing that the provision would not be enforced.

Presidential use of signing statements to challenge legislative provisions and to declare that provisions not favored by the president would not be enforced increased sharply during the George W. Bush years. President Reagan used signing statements to attack 71 legislative provisions, and President Clinton made 105 significant signing statements. Bush challenged more than 800 legislative provisions with his signing statements, including a number of important domestic and security matters, such as a congressional effort, led by Senator John McCain, to ban the use of torture by American interrogators. During the 2008 presidential campaign, Democrats denounced Bush's use of signing statements. In March 2009, however, President Obama made use of the same tactic employed by his predecessors. After he signed a $410 budget bill into law, Obama declared five provisions of the Act to be unconstitutional and non-binding, including a provision to prevent punishment of whistleblowers.

---

[77] *Lear, Siegler v. Lehman*, 842 F.2nd 1102 (1988).

[78] Cooper, *By Order of the President*, p. 207.

[79] Cooper, *By Order of the President*, p. 206.

[80] Cooper, *By Order of the President*, p. 217.

Ed Meese's contrivance has become a full-blown instrument of presidential power. Adding to the importance of this power in recent years, as presidents had hoped, courts have given weight to presidential signing statements when interpreting the meaning of statutes.[81]

The Advantages of the Administrative Strategy. Through the course of American history, party leadership and popular appeals have played important roles in presidential efforts to overcome political opposition. Both parties and appeals to the people continue to be instruments of presidential power. Reagan's tax cuts and Clinton's budget victories were achieved with strong partisan support. George W. Bush, lacking the oratorical skills of a Reagan or a Roosevelt, nevertheless made good use of sophisticated communications strategies to promote his agenda. Yet, as we saw, in the modern era, parties have waned in institutional strength, and the effects of popular appeals have often proved evanescent. The limitations of the alternatives have increasingly impelled presidents to try to expand the administrative capabilities of the office and their own capacity for unilateral action as means of achieving their policy goals. And in recent decades, the expansion of the Executive Office, the development of regulatory review, and the use of executive orders, the signing of statements, and the like have given presidents a substantial capacity to achieve significant policy results despite congressional opposition to their legislative agendas.

To be sure, the administrative strategy does not always succeed. In some instances over the years, as just noted, the federal courts have struck down unilateral actions by the president. And occasionally Congress acts to reverse presidential orders. For example, in 1999, Congress enacted legislation prohibiting the Department of Education from carrying out a presidential directive to administer national tests of reading and mathematics.[82] And before that, in 1996, in response to President Clinton's aggressive regulatory review program, the Republican-controlled Congress moved to strengthen its capacity to block the president's use of administrative directives by enacting the Congressional Review Act (CRA). This piece of legislation requires federal agencies to send all proposed regulations to Congress for review sixty days before they take effect. It also creates a fast-track procedure to allow the House and the Senate to enact a joint resolution of disapproval that would not only void the regulation but also prohibit the agency from subsequently issuing any substantially similar rule. The first test of the act came after Clinton left office. In the early weeks of the Bush administration, Congress passed a joint resolution repealing an ergonomics standard that had been supported by the Clinton administration and adopted by OSHA. President Bush, who opposed the standard, signed the resolution, and the ergonomics standard was voided. While this outcome may be seen as an effective effort by Congress to thwart a presidential directive, it seems clear that Congress was successful only because Clinton was out of office. Had his term not expired, Clinton would almost certainly have vetoed the resolution. Indeed, one reason Clinton was willing to sign the CRA into law in the first place was

---

[81] Kristy Carroll, "Whose Statute Is It Anyway? Why and How Courts Should Use Presidential Signing Statements When Interpreting Federal Statutes," 16 *Catholic University Law Review* 475 (1997).

[82] Kagan, "Presidential Administration," 2351.

that the president retained the power to veto any action undertaken by Congress under the statute's authority.

In principle, perhaps, Congress could respond more vigorously than it has to unilateral policy making by the president. Certainly a Congress willing to impeach a president should have the mettle to overturn his administrative directives. But the president has significant advantages in such struggles with Congress. In battles over presidential directives and orders, Congress is on the defensive, reacting to presidential initiatives. The framers of the Constitution saw "energy," or the ability to take the initiative, as a key feature of executive power.[83] When the president takes action by issuing an order or an administrative directive, Congress must initiate the cumbersome and time-consuming lawmaking process, overcome internal divisions, and enact legislation that the president may ultimately veto. Moreover, as the political scientist Terry Moe has argued, in such battles Congress faces a significant collective-action problem insofar as members are likely to be more sensitive to the substance of a president's action and its effects on their constituents than to the more general implications of presidential power for the long-term vitality of their institution.[84]

PRESIDENTIAL POWER: MYTHS AND REALITIES

We began this chapter by observing that presidents had a distinct institutional advantage vis-à-vis other governmental actors. Presidents were unitary "deciders," whereas other political actors were members of institutions whose decision-making processes were collective, requiring deliberation, debate, compromise, and voting. This institutional difference has contributed to the steady growth of presidential power, which has occasioned an ongoing debate between the advocates of a strong presidency and those who favor America's traditional separation of powers system, with its built-in limitations and constraints on collective action, discussed in Chapter 1.

Emergency Power

Advocates of presidential power have typically advanced three arguments for deferring to the White House. The first, which echoes themes articulated by Alexander Hamilton and others among the nation's Founders, is that executive power is needed to deal with emergencies and to ensure the nation's security.[85] Although no one

---

[83] Alexander Hamilton, James Madison, and John Jay, *The Federalist Papers*, Clinton L. Rossiter, ed. (New York: Signet, 1961), no. 70, pp. 423–30.

[84] Terry M. Moe, "The Presidency and the Bureaucracy: The Presidential Advantage," in *The Presidency and the Political System*, 7th ed., Michael Nelson, ed. (Washington, D.C.: Congressional Quarterly Press, 2003), pp. 425–57.

[85] A contemporary statement of this position is Harvey C. Mansfield, Jr., *Taming the Prince: The Ambivalence of Modern Executive Power* (New York: Free Press, 1989), chap.1.

could argue with this position in the abstract, particularly in an age of global terrorism, the problem is that presidents can sometimes be too anxious to act forcefully in response to what they perceive as security threats. The framers of the Constitution gave Congress, and not the president, the power to make war precisely because they feared that presidents might be altogether too willing to commit the nation to armed conflicts. "The strongest passions and most dangerous weakness of the human breast," wrote James Madison, "ambition, avarice, vanity, the honorable or venial love of fame, are all in a conspiracy [within the executive branch] against the desire and duty of peace. Hence it has grown into an axiom that the executive is the department of power most distinguished by its propensity to war."[86]

But if the president is too anxious to go to war, is Congress too reluctant to respond to emergencies? The short answer is no. It would be difficult to identify an instance of the past half century in which the nation's security was compromised because Congress refused to act, though in a number of cases, including perhaps the recent Iraq war, the president was, as Madison feared, too quick to take vigorous action. When the nation has faced actual emergencies, Congress has seldom refused to grant appropriate powers to the president. Indeed, the legislative branch has generally been too pliable, granting presidents powers to deal with emergencies of their own making, as in the case of the Gulf of Tonkin Resolution, which President Lyndon Johnson used as the legislative basis for his Vietnam war policies.

Contemporary executive power, moreover, is not held in reserve for national emergencies but is, instead, employed by presidents on a routine basis, often to implement mundane elements of their agenda that lack sufficient support in Congress to be enacted into law. Thus, President Clinton used the power of regulatory review to launch an environmental program that had been blocked in the Congress. Similarly, President Bush used an executive order to place limits on stem-cell research, a decision that pleased religious conservatives but could never have mustered majorities in the House and Senate. Right or wrong, these decisions hardly involved national emergencies. Neither stem-cell researchers nor the foes of environmentalism posed imminent threats to the nation's security. In both instances, the president was simply asserting his policy preferences and using his executive powers to override or ignore those of his opponents.

The Public Interest

A second argument often made in favor of expanded presidential power is that the president champions the national interest as opposed to the particularistic interests defended by members of Congress, party politicians, bureaucrats, and most other political actors. This notion of the president's being above party seems reminiscent of the premodern yearning for a wise and beneficent king who would brush aside the selfish claims of manipulative courtiers and rule in the best interests of all his subjects. Perhaps such kings existed from time to time, but the behavior of the kingly stratum as a whole does not inspire much confidence in the notion that powerful executives are a good antidote to factional selfishness and rent-seeking special interests.

---

[86] Richard Loss, ed., *The Letters of Pacificus and Helvidius* (Delmar, N.Y.: Scholars Facsimiles and Reprints, 1976), pp. 91–92.

Presidents, to be sure, are unitary actors. As such they may find it more difficult than members of Congress to escape responsibility for their conduct or, through inaction, to become free riders on the efforts of others. To this extent, the presidentialist argument might have some merit. Empirically, however, presidents do not appear much less likely than senators and representatives to set aside personal concerns in favor of some abstract public good. Presidents often enough seem to promote programs designed mainly to reward important political backers and contributors even when such programs clearly do not serve the larger public interest. What public interest was served by President Clinton's decision to pardon the fugitive financier Marc Rich? Why did President Bush block stem-cell research even though such work is important to maintaining America's technological edge? In both instances, personal or political calculations appear to have outweighed presidential concern for the public interest.

Presidential Power and Democracy

Beyond assertions of the need for a strong presidency and the allegedly superior commitment of the president to the national interest, a third argument is frequently made in support of enhanced presidential power. This is the contention that the presidency is a more democratic institution than the Congress.[87] This argument has a certain surface plausibility. The president is, of course, the nation's only elected official who can claim to represent all the people. As a decision-making institution, however, the presidency is perhaps America's least democratic entity.

Presidential decision making generally takes place in private and is often shrouded in secrecy. Recent presidents have vehemently asserted that the secrecy of the processes leading up to their decisions is shielded by executive privilege. This was the Bush administration's claim when it refused to disclose information regarding the composition or deliberations of the task forces with whom Vice President Cheney met in 2001 to plan the administration's energy policies. The Supreme Court supported the administration's position on the grounds that the "energetic performance" of the executive branch's duties required protection from intrusive requests for information.[88] Successive presidents have also disciplined staffers who revealed information to Congress and worked to block legislation that would protect whistle-blowers. Not only are the deliberations leading up to presidential decisions often removed from the public domain, but even the decisions themselves are sometimes not revealed to the public or even to the Congress. Many so-called national security directives issued by presidents in recent years have been used to initiate secret missions by intelligence and defense agencies.[89] For many years, too, presidents have signed secret executive agreements with other governments obligating the United States to various forms of action without congressional knowledge, much less approval.

---

[87] Grant McConnell, *The Modern Presidency* (New York: St. Martin's, 1976). See also Steven Calabresi, "Some Normative Arguments for the Unitary Executive," 48 *Arkansas Law Review* 23 (1995), p. 58.

[88] *U.S. v. U.S. District Court of the District of Columbia* 124 S.Ct. 1391 (2004).

[89] Christopher Simpson, *National Security Directives of the Reagan and Bush Administrations* (Boulder, Colo.: Westview Press, 1995).

As long as fewer voters participate in congressional races than in presidential elections, the Congress is inherently a more democratic decision-making institution than the presidency. To exert influence, competing factions in Congress must maintain active and ongoing relationships with important groups and forces in civil society. For members of Congress, constituency mobilization and political power are closely connected. Journalists may cluck their tongues at the "senator from Boeing" or the "congressman from the UAW." But ties to these and a host of other key constituency forces help members of Congress exercise influence on Capitol Hill and strengthen the Congress as a collective body vis-à-vis the executive branch. Today, indeed, Congress must sometimes mobilize constituency pressure just to compel the president to implement its decisions. One of Congress's weaknesses as an institution is that it must depend on the executive to carry out and enforce most of its dictates. As we saw when we discussed presidential signing statements, presidents are increasingly wont to claim that they are not required to implement decisions with which they disagree.

Presidents, of course, can also mobilize supporters and interests. Indeed, some presidents, such as Andrew Jackson and Franklin D. Roosevelt, worked to expand the scope of political participation in order to overwhelm their political opponents at the polls and in the national legislature. When it comes to the routines of governance, however, presidents usually prefer processes that limit political debate and social mobilization. In an open political struggle, involving contestation among many interests and forces, presidents may win or they may lose. But where decisions are made discreetly if not covertly, in the corridors and offices of the White House with minimal external intervention, then surely the president will prevail. And unlike Congress, the president does not have to rely on an agency outside his sphere of control to implement his decisions. Presidents control bureaucrats and soldiers and contractors and mercenaries. They view the involvement of other political actors as more likely to hinder their plans than to help them govern. For these reasons, where possible, presidents seek to develop institutions and procedures that restrict the number and range of participants in decision making and limit rather than expand the scope of political debate.

The realm of national security policy is an important example. Rather than encourage open debate and discussion of security issues, presidents have conceived it to be in their interest to limit the possibilities for political disputation, interest-group conflict, and popular mobilization around national security matters. For example, presidents sought to bring conflicts and divisions among the services under control, in part, to delimit the opportunity for congressional intervention into military affairs. In a similar vein, after America's protracted struggle in Vietnam generated a political uproar and massive popular mobilization against the war, the White House pushed to end conscription and to create a fully professional military. Successive presidents and military planners reasoned that a force composed of professional soldiers recruited mainly from military families and sequestered from civilian society could be sent into combat without engendering the popular clamor that created opportunities for rival politicians and members of Congress to attack presidential policies during the Vietnam era. For the same reason, the White House also developed a host of schemes to prevent the news media from presenting unfavorable accounts of military campaigns. These efforts have been at least partially successful and help to explain why popular opposition to President Bush's Iraq policy was muted for several years despite a steady stream of casualties, an uncertain war purpose, and substantial evidence of mismanagement and duplicity on the part of the White House.

In sum, presidents seek to exercise power by preventing the sort of open debate and discussion that might allow other actors an opportunity to intervene in the security realm. Indeed, Presidents Reagan, George H. W. Bush, Clinton, and George W. Bush led the nation into significant armed conflicts without substantial prior debate. These observations would seem entirely inconsistent with the idea that the presidency is somehow a more democratic institution than the Congress. Hence, democracy has not necessarily been well served as our chief decider has accrued more power. Institutions matter a great deal.

FOR FURTHER READING

Cameron, Charles M. *Veto Bargaining: Presidents and the Politics of Negative Power.* New York: Cambridge University Press, 2000. ○ reader selection

Canes-Wrone, Brandice. *Who Leads Whom? Presidents, Policy, and the Public.* Chicago: University of Chicago Press, 2006. ○ reader selection

Crenson, Matthew, and Benjamin Ginsberg. *Presidential Power: Unchecked and Unbalanced.* New York: Norton, 2007.

Deering, Christopher, and Forrest Maltzman. "The Politics of Executive Orders: Legislative Constraints on Presidential Power," *Political Research Quarterly* 52 (1999): 767–83.

Howell, William G. *Power Without Persuasion: The Politics of Direct Presidential Action.* Princeton, N.J.: Princeton University Press, 2003. ○ reader selection

Krutz, Glen, and Jeffrey Peake. *Presidential-Congressional Governance and the Rise of Executive Agreements.* Ann Arbor: University of Michigan Press, 2009.

Lowi, Theodore J. *The Personal President: Power Invested, Promise Unfulfilled.* Ithaca, N.Y.: Cornell University Press, 1985.

Milkis, Sidney M. *The President and the Parties: The Transformation of the American Party System since the New Deal.* New York: Oxford University Press, 1993.

Nelson, Michael, ed. *The Presidency and the Political System.* 8th ed. Washington, D.C.: Congressional Quarterly Press, 2005.

Neustadt, Richard E. *Presidential Power and the Modern Presidents: The Politics of Leadership from Roosevelt to Reagan.* 1960. Rev. ed., New York: Free Press, 1990. ○ reader selection

Pfiffner, James P. *The Modern Presidency.* 4th ed. Belmont, Calif.: Wadsworth, 2005.

Skowronek, Stephen. *The Politics Presidents Make: Leadership from John Adams to Bill Clinton.* Cambridge, Mass.: Harvard University Press, 1997.

Yoo, John. *The Powers of War and Peace.* Chicago: University of Chicago Press, 2005.

Ⓢ Additional study and review materials are available online at wwnorton.com/studyspace/

7

The Executive Branch: Bureaucracy in a Democracy

The bureaucracy is the administrative heart and soul of government. It is where the rubber meets the road—where policies formulated, incubated, refined, and ultimately passed into law by elected officials (legislators, executives) are interpreted, implemented, and ultimately delivered to a nation's citizens. Government touches the life of the ordinary citizen most directly in his or her interactions with bureaucratic agents—at the Department of Motor Vehicles when obtaining a driver's license; in filing one's income-tax return with the Internal Revenue Service; at the recruiting center when enlisting in one of the armed services; at the Board of Elections when registering to vote. We examine the federal bureaucracy in this chapter both as an organizational setting within which policies are interpreted and implemented and as a venue in which politicians (bureaucrats or bureaucratic agents) pursue their own (and sometimes the public's) interests.

As an organizational setting, a bureaucracy is something created by elected politicians. These politicians seek to coordinate governmental effort in order to accomplish public purposes (and private objectives) as well as to solve collective action problems. Sometimes bureaucracies are created in the face of a pressing need, indeed at times of crisis. Consider the case of the Department of Homeland Security (DHS).

On March 1, 2003, twenty-two federal agencies with responsibilities for combating international terrorism in the United States were combined in the Department of Homeland Security (see Table 7.1). By all accounts, this event marked the most dramatic reform of the federal bureaucracy since the establishment of the Department of Defense in 1947. The story begins with the catastrophic events of September 11, 2001. Both Republicans and Democrats realized that the public was going to demand some ongoing response to the terrorist threat (beyond the immediate military response in Afghanistan).[1] A congressional investigation quickly revealed that serious security lapses and a lack of coordination among the various agencies with responsibility for domestic and foreign intelligence had occurred during the administrations of both President Bill Clinton and President George W. Bush. Both political parties might be blamed if the government did not respond aggressively enough to the terrorist threat. Furthermore, the major alternative solution—the creation of a homeland-security "czar"—was tried and proved inadequate. In the end, there seemed to be no alternative available to the president and members of Congress. The path to a cabinet-level agency was clear.

Whatever the initial stimulation or inspiration for the creation of a new bureaucracy, it

---

[1] John W. Kingdon calls events that limit and focus our political options "windows of political opportunity." See his *Agendas, Alternatives, and Public Policies* (Boston: Little, Brown, 1984).

- Bureaucratic institutions are created by Congress to achieve policy goals.

- By implementing the laws and policies passed by elected officials, bureaucrats can be seen as agents of Congress and the presidency. As is the case in any principal-agent relationship, the agent (the bureaucracy) is delegated authority and has a certain amount of leeway for independent action.

- Despite the efforts of elected officials (the principals) to check departments and agencies (the agents), bureaucrats have their own goals and thus exercise their own influence on policy.

- Although controling the growth of bureaucracy has been a concern in American politics, most Americans benefit in some way from government programs and thus are reluctant to cut back on specific programs.

should be clear that such an entity does not drop fully formed from the heavens. It is actively shaped by politicians who come at the problem from a variety of perspectives and must hammer out an agreement (often involving bargaining and compromise) about the size, shape, and authority of the new entity. DHS was an amalgam of twenty-two major units previously housed in seven cabinet departments and several other independent entities. They were stitched together through intense negotiations between President Bush's White House and legislators on Capitol Hill. Bureaucracies, thus, are administrative in purpose, but are born through a political process. Their features are designed by politicians who appreciate, as in our institution principle, that the institutional powers with which they endow a bureaucracy have consequences for the kinds of rulings and decisions subsequently made.

Bureaucracies are also venues in which bureaucratic actors pursue public and private purposes. Bureaucrats are politicians who make decisions, form coalitions, engage in bargaining; in short, they bring private preferences and values to the table as they engage in various administrative processes. We should no more think of them as automatons or cogs in some giant wheel than we do legislative, executive, or judicial politicians. The private hopes and aspirations they bring to this setting interact with the institutional features with which their bureaucracy has been endowed to produce policies, outcomes, and decisions. And these, as the policy principle tells us, will reflect both the private interests of bureaucratic politicians and the institutional ways in which they conduct their business.

In our focus on the federal bureaucracy—the administrative structure that on a day-by-day basis is the American government—we first define and describe bureaucracy as a social and political phenomenon. Second, we look in detail at American bureaucracy in action by examining the government's major administrative agencies, their role in the governmental process, and their political behavior.

TABLE 7.1 THE SHAPE OF A DOMESTIC SECURITY DEPARTMENT

Department of Homeland Security	Agencies and Departments Now Part of the Main Divisions of the DHS	Previously Responsible Agency or Department
Border and Transportation Security Directorate	U.S. Customs Service	Treasury
	Immigration and Naturalization Service*	Justice
	Federal Protective Service†	
	Transportation Security Administration	Transportation
	Federal Law Enforcement Training Center	Treasury
	Animal and Plant Health Inspection Service*	Agriculture
	Office for Domestic Preparedness	Justice
Emergency Preparedness and Response Directorate	Federal Emergency Management Agency‡	Health and Human Services
	Strategic National Stockpile and the National Disaster Medical System	
	Nuclear Incident Response Team	Energy
	Domestic Emergency Support Teams	Justice
	National Domestic Preparedness Office	FBI
Science and Technology Directorate	CBRN (Chemical, Biological, Radiological and Nuclear) Countermeasures Programs	Energy
	Environmental Measurements Laboratory	Energy
	National BW (Biological Warfare) Defense Analysis Center	Defense
	Plum Island Animal Disease Center	Agriculture
Information Analysis and Infrastructure Protection Directorate§	Federal Computer Incident Response Center	General Services Administration
	National Communications System	Defense
	National Infrastructure Protection Center	FBI
	Energy Security and Assurance Program	Energy
Secret Service		Treasury
Coast Guard		Transportation

*Only partially under the aegis of DHS; some functions remain elsewhere.

†New.

‡Previously independent.

§Established to analyze information provided by the CIA, the FBI, the Defense Intelligence Agency, the National Security Agency, and other agencies.

SOURCE: Department of Homeland Security, "History: Who Became Part of the Department?," www.dhs.gov/xabout/history/editorial_0133.sht.

WHY BUREAUCRACY?

Bureaucracies touch nearly every aspect of daily life. Government bureaucracies implement the decisions made by the political process. Bureaucracies are full of routine because routine ensures that services are delivered regularly and that each agency fulfills its mandate. For this reason, students often conclude that bureaucracy is mechanical, routinized, and just plain boring. But that is a mistake. Bureaucracy is not just about collecting garbage, training police, or mailing Social Security checks. It is all these things for sure, but it is much more besides. Mainly, it is a reflection of political deals consummated by elected politicians, turf wars among government agents and private-sector suppliers and contractors, policy-delivery successes and failures in the eyes of the public, and to complete the circle, reactions to these by the very same elected officials who cut the deals in the first place. It is politics through and through.

Public bureaucracies are powerful because legislatures and chief executives—and, indeed, the people—delegate to them vast power to make sure a particular job is done, enabling the rest of us to be freer to pursue our private ends. The public sentiments that emerged after September 11 revealed this underlying appreciation of public bureaucracies. When faced with the challenge of making air travel safe again, the public strongly supported giving the federal government responsibility for airport security even though this meant increasing the size of the federal bureaucracy in order to make the security screeners federal workers. The former House majority whip Tom DeLay sought to forestall this growth in the federal government, declaring that "the last thing we can afford to do is erect a new bureaucracy that is unaccountable and unable to protect the American public."[2] But the antibureaucratic language that had been so effective before September 11 no longer resonated with a fearful public. Instead, there was a widespread belief that a public bureaucracy would provide more effective protection than the cost-conscious private companies that had been charged with airport security in the past.

We can shed some systematic light on public attitudes toward government bureaucracy by examining one of the standard questions posed in election years by the American National Election Studies (ANES). As part of its survey of the American public, the ANES asks a range of questions, among which is "Do you think that people in the government waste a lot of money we pay in taxes, waste some of it, or don't waste very much of it?" Although not perfect for eliciting from the public a nuanced assessment of bureaucratic performance, the question allows respondents to register a blunt evaluation. Results from the past several decades are given in Figure 7.1.

Public unhappiness with bureaucratic inefficiency grew during the 1960s and 1970s and became one of Ronald Reagan's campaign themes in the 1980 election. In recent decades, this unhappiness declined from nearly 80 percent of the survey respondents believing government "wastes a lot" in 1980 to just over 60 percent in

---

[2] Janet Hook, "U.S. Strikes Back: Political Landscape; GOP Bypasses the Bipartisan Truce," *Los Angeles Times,* October 14, 2001, p. A8.

FIGURE 7.1 THE PUBLIC THINKS THERE IS A LOT OF WASTE IN GOVERNMENT

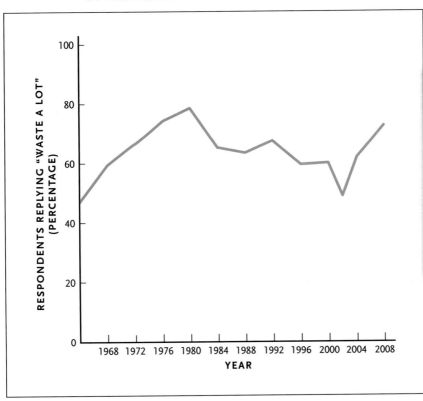

SOURCE: American National Election Studies, Cumulative Data File, 1948–2008, www.electionstudies.org/index.htm.

2004. This opinion has held steady near the low 60 percent range for twenty years, though there was a significant downward tick in 2002, just after September 11. But whatever honeymoon there might have been after the terrorist attacks, it appears that the public remains cynical about bureaucratic performance. The poor response of the Federal Emergency Management Agency (FEMA)—part of DHS—to the hurricane crises in the fall of 2005 and, especially, to charges of cronyism in personnel appointments surely contributed to further cynicism.

Bureaucratic Organization Enhances Efficiency

Despite this tendency to criticize bureaucracy, most Americans recognize that maintaining order in a large society is impossible without some sort of large governmental apparatus, staffed by professionals with some expertise in public administration. When we approve of what a government agency is doing, we give the phenomenon a positive name, administration; when we disapprove, we call the phenomenon bureaucracy. **Bureaucracy** refers to the actual offices, tasks, and principles of organization that are employed in the most formal and sustained administration. The core of bureaucracy is the division of labor. The key to bureaucratic effectiveness is the coordination of experts performing complex tasks. If each job is specialized to gain efficiencies, then each worker must depend on the output of other workers, and that dependence requires careful allocation of jobs and resources. Inevitably bureaucracies become hierarchical, often approximating a pyramid in form. At the base of the organization are workers with the fewest skills and specializations; one supervisor can deal with a relatively large number of these workers. At the next level of the organization, where there are more highly specialized workers, the supervision and coordination of work involves fewer workers per supervisor. Toward the top of the organization, a very small number of high-level executives engages in the "management" of the organization, meaning the organization and reorganization of all the tasks and functions, plus the allocation of the appropriate supplies and the distribution of the output of the organization to the market (if it is a private-sector organization) or to the public.

Bureaucracies Allow Governments to Operate

Bureaucracy, when used pejoratively, conjures up images of endless paperwork, red tape, and lazy, uncaring employees. But bureaucracy in fact represents a rather spectacular human achievement. By dividing up tasks, matching tasks to a labor force that develops appropriately specialized skills, routinizing procedure, and providing the incentive structure and oversight arrangements to get large numbers of people to operate in a coordinated, purposeful fashion, bureaucracies accomplish tasks and missions in a manner that would otherwise be unimaginable. The provision of an array of "government goods" as broad as the defense of people, property, and national borders or as narrow as a subsidy to a wheat farmer, a beef rancher, or a manufacturer of specialty steel requires organization, routines, standards, and at the end of the day, the authority that allows for someone to cut a check and put it in the mail. Bureaucracies are created to do these things. Although there are mistakes and miscalculations, a bureaucracy reflects instrumental thinking about how to accomplish particular tasks; it is the rationality principle at work. No large organization would be larger than the sum of its parts, and many would be smaller, without bureaucratizing its activities.

Bureaucracy also consolidates a range of complementary programs and insulates them from the predatory ambitions of out-of-sympathy political forces. Nothing in this world is permanent, but bureaucracies come close. By creating clienteles—in the legislature, the world of interest groups, and public opinion—a bureaucracy establishes a coalition of supporters, some of whom will fight to the end to keep it in place. It is a well-known rule of thumb that everyone in the political world cares deeply and intensely about a subset of policies and the agencies that produce them and opposes other policies and agencies, but not with nearly the same passion. Opponents, to succeed, must clear many hurdles, while proponents, to maintain the status quo, must marshal their forces only at a few veto points. In the final analysis, opponents typically meet obstacle after obstacle and eventually give up their uphill battles and concentrate on protecting and expanding what they care most deeply about. In a complex political system like that of the United States, it is much easier to do the latter. Politicians appreciate this fact of life. Consequently, both opponents and proponents of a particular set of governmental activities wage the fiercest battles at the time programs are enacted and a bureaucracy is created. Once created, these organizations assume a status of relative permanence.

This raises an interesting dilemma that we only flag here, because we will develop it more systematically in the next section. In principle, bureaucratic agents are "servants" of elected politicians. They are charged with implementing statutes and policies produced by their "masters," the elected politicians in the White House and on Capitol Hill. But the relative permanence enjoyed by bureaucracy is a form of insulation—servants have discretion and masters are limited in their ability to control them. Elected officials who might want to steer a bureaucracy in a different direction often find the obstacles substantial. Only those with intense concern for the jurisdiction of a bureaucracy are likely to persist in their efforts to guide it; others have more important fish to fry in different bureaucratic jurisdictions. Thus bureaucratic agents are most affected by legislators with extraordinary interest in the bureaucratic mission. Even among these, rational legislators in support of the bureaucratic mission are likely to dominate, because those in opposition succumb to the obstacles and move their attention elsewhere.

So in response to the question of how bureaucracy makes government possible, there is an efficiency part to the answer and a credibility part. The creation of a bureau is a way to deliver government goods efficiently, and it is a device by which to tie one's hands, thereby providing a credible commitment to the long-term existence of a policy.

Bureaucrats Fulfill Important Roles

"Government by offices and desks" conveys to most people a picture of hundreds of office workers shuffling millions of pieces of paper. There is a lot of truth in that image, but we have to look more closely at what papers are being shuffled and why. Seventy years ago, an astute observer defined bureaucracy as "continuous routine business."[3] Almost any organization succeeds by reducing its work to routines, with each routine being given to a different specialist. But specialization separates people from one another; one worker's output becomes another worker's input. The timing of the relationships is essential, requiring the workers to stay in communication with each other. In fact, bureaucracy was the first information network. Voluminous routine came as bureaucracies grew and specialized. It's no small irony that as bureaucracies have grown, the term *bureaucrat* has come to connote sluggishness and inefficiency.

Bureaucrats Implement Laws.   Bureaucrats, whether in public or in private organizations, communicate with each other to coordinate all the specializations within their organization. This coordination is necessary to carry out the primary task of bureaucracy, which is **implementation**—that is, implementing the objectives of the organization as laid down by its board of directors (if a private company) or by

implementation
The efforts of departments and agencies to translate laws into specific bureaucratic routines.

---

[3] Arnold Brecht and Comstock Glaser, *The Art and Technique of Administration in German Ministries* (Cambridge, Mass.: Harvard University Press, 1940), p. 6.

law (if a public agency). In government, the "bosses" are ultimately the legislature and the elected chief executive. As we saw in Chapter 1, in a principal-agent relationship it is the principal who stipulates what he wants done, relying on the agent's concern for her reputation, appropriate incentives, and other control mechanisms to secure compliance with his wishes. Thus we can argue that legislative principals establish bureaucratic agents—in departments, bureaus, agencies, institutes, and commissions of the federal government—to implement the policies promulgated by Congress and the president.

Bureaucrats Make and Enforce Rules. When the bosses—Congress, in particular, when it is making the law—are clear in their instructions to bureaucrats, implementation is a fairly straightforward process. Bureaucrats translate the law into specific routines for each employee of an agency. But what happens to routine administrative implementation when there are several bosses who disagree as to what the instructions ought to be? The agent of multiple principals who disagree among themselves often finds himself or herself in a bind. The agent must chart a delicate course, seeking to do the best he or she can and trying not to offend any of the bosses too much. This requires yet another job for the bureaucrats: interpretation. Interpretation is a form of implementation in that the bureaucrats have to carry out what they believe to be the intentions of their superiors. But when bureaucrats have to interpret a law before implementing it, they are in effect engaging in lawmaking.[4] Congress often deliberately delegates to an administrative agency the responsibility of lawmaking. Members of Congress often conclude that some area of industry needs regulating or some area of the environment needs protection, but they are unwilling or unable to specify just how that should be done. In such situations, Congress delegates to the appropriate agency a broad authority within which the bureaucrats have to make law, through the procedures of **rule making** and **administrative adjudication**.

Rule making is exactly the same as legislation; in fact, it is often referred to as quasi-legislation. The rules issued by government agencies provide more detailed and specific indications of what a policy will actually mean. For example, the Forest Service is charged with making policies that govern the use of national forests. Just before President Clinton left office, the agency issued rules that banned new road building and development in the forests. This was a goal long sought by environmentalists and conservationists. In 2005, the Forest Service relaxed the rules, allowing states to make proposals for building new roads within the national forests. Just as the timber industry opposed the Clinton rule banning road building, environmentalists have challenged the new ruling and have sued the Forest Service in federal court for violating clean-water and endangered-species legislation.

New rules proposed by an agency take effect only after a period of public comment. Reaction from the people or businesses that are subject to the rules may

rule making
A quasi-legislative administrative process that produces regulations by government agencies.

administrative adjudication The application rules and precedents to specific cases to settle disputes with regulated parties.

---

[4] When bureaucrats engage in interpretation, the result is what political scientists call bureaucratic drift. Bureaucratic drift occurs because, as we've suggested, the "bosses" (in Congress) and the agents (within the bureaucracy) don't always share the same purposes. Bureaucrats also have their own agendas to fulfill. A vast body of political science literature focuses on the relationship between Congress and the bureaucracy. For a review, see Kenneth A. Shepsle and Mark S. Bonchek, *Analyzing Politics: Rationality, Behavior, and Institutions* (New York: Norton, 1997), pp. 355–68.

cause an agency to modify the rules they first issue. The rule-making process is thus a highly political one. Once rules are approved, they are published in the *Federal Register* and have the force of law.[5]

Bureaucrats Settle Disputes. Administrative adjudication is very similar to what the judiciary ordinarily does: apply rules and precedents to specific cases to settle disputes. In administrative adjudication, the agency charges the person or business suspected of violating the law. The ruling in an adjudication dispute applies only to the specific case being considered. Many regulatory agencies use administrative adjudication to make decisions about specific products or practices. For example, product recalls are often the result of adjudication. To take another example, the National Labor Relations Board (NLRB) has used case-by-case administrative adjudication in a great many instances. One large class of cases involves union certification. Groups of workers seek the right to vote on the formation of a union or the right to affiliate with an existing union as their bargaining agent and are opposed by their employers, who assert that relevant provisions of labor law do not apply. The NLRB takes testimony case by case, considers evidence, and makes determinations for one side or the other, acting essentially like a court.

In sum, bureaucrats in government do essentially the same things that bureaucrats in large private organizations do, and neither type deserves the disrespect embodied in the term *bureaucrat*. But because of the authoritative, coercive nature of government, far more constraints are imposed on public bureaucrats than on private bureaucrats, even when their jobs are the same. Public bureaucrats are required to maintain a far more thorough paper trail. They are also subject to a great deal more access by the public—newspaper reporters, for example, have access to public bureaucrats. And public access has been vastly facilitated in the past half century; the adoption of the Freedom of Information Act (FOIA) in 1966 gave ordinary citizens the right of access to agency files and agency data so that they might determine whether those files (and data) contain derogatory information about them and learn what the agency is doing in general.

Finally, citizens are given opportunities to participate in the decision-making processes of public agencies. This kind of access is limited by time, money, and expertise, but it does exist, and it occupies a great deal of the time of mid-level and senior public bureaucrats. Such public exposure and access serve a purpose, but they also cut down significantly on the efficiency of public bureaucrats. Thus much of the lower levels of efficiency in public agencies can be attributed to the political, judicial, legal, and publicity restraints put on public bureaucrats.

Politics

We have provided two main answers to the question "Why bureaucracy?": (1) Bureaucracies enhance efficiency, and (2) they are the instruments of policy

---

[5] The *Federal Register* is the daily journal of the U.S. government. It is published every day by the Government Printing Office and contains publications and notices of government agencies.

implementation. We would be remiss if we didn't include a third important answer: Legislatures find it valuable to delegate.

In principle, the legislature could make all bureaucratic decisions itself, writing very detailed legislation each year, dotting every *i* and crossing every *t*. In some jurisdictions—tax policy, for example—this is in fact done. Tax policy is promulgated in significant detail by the House Ways and Means Committee, the Senate Finance Committee, and the Joint Committee on Taxation. The Internal Revenue Service, the administrative agency charged with implementation, engages in relatively less discretionary activity than many other regulatory and administrative agencies. But it is the exception.

The norm is for statutory authority to be delegated to the bureaucracy, sometimes with specificity but often in relatively vague terms. The bureaucracy is expected to fill in the gaps. This, however, is not a blank check to exercise unconstrained discretion. The bureaucracy is expected to be guided by legislative intent, and it will be held to account by the legislature's oversight of bureaucratic performance. The latter is monitored by the staffs of relevant legislative committees, which also serve as repositories for complaints from affected parties.[6] Poor performance or the exercise of discretion inconsistent with the preferences of important legislators invites sanctions ranging from the browbeating of senior bureaucrats to the trimming of budgets and the clipping of authority.

The delegation relationship will be revisited later in this chapter. For now, simply note that over and above the more conventional reasons for bureaucracy, politicians find it convenient to delegate many of the nuts-and-bolts decisions to bureaucratic agents. We will take up the reasons shortly.

HOW IS THE EXECUTIVE BRANCH ORGANIZED?

Cabinet departments, agencies, and bureaus are the operating parts of the bureaucratic whole. These parts can be separated into four general types: (1) cabinet departments, (2) independent agencies, (3) government corporations, and (4) independent regulatory commissions.

Although Figure 7.2 is an organizational chart of the Department of Agriculture, any other department could have been used as an illustration. At the top is the head of the department, called the secretary of the department. Below the department head and his or her deputy are several top administrators, such as the general counsel and the chief financial officer, whose responsibilities cut across the various departmental functions and provide the secretary with the ability to manage the entire organization. Of equal status are the undersecretaries and assistant secretaries, each of whom has management responsibilities for a group of operating agencies, which are arranged vertically below each of the undersecretaries.

---

[6] See Mathew D. McCubbins and Thomas Schwartz, "Congressional Oversight Overlooked: Police Patrols versus Fire Alarms," *American Journal of Political Science* 28 (1984): 165–79.

FIGURE 7.2 ORGANIZATIONAL CHART OF THE DEPARTMENT OF AGRICULTURE

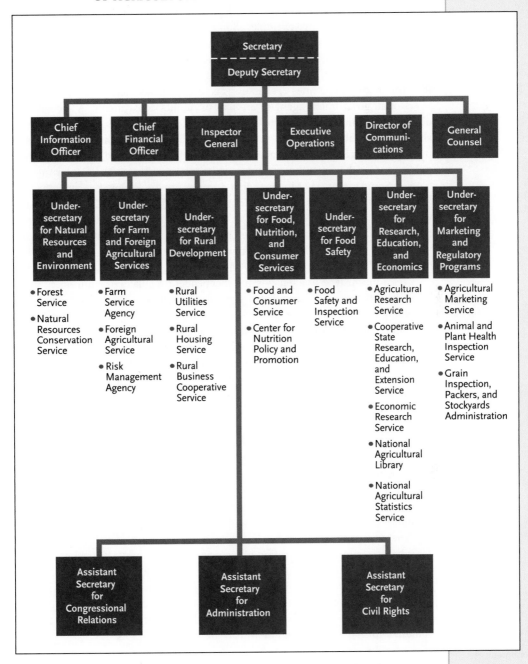

SOURCE: U.S. Department of Agriculture, www.usda.gov/img/content/org_chart_enlarged.jpg.

The next tier, generally called the bureau level, is the highest level of responsibility for specialized programs. The names of these "bureau-level agencies" are often very well known to the public: The Forest Service and the Food Safety and Inspection Service are two examples. Sometimes they are officially called bureaus, as in the FBI, which is a bureau in the Department of Justice. Nevertheless, *bureau* is also the generic term for this level of administrative agency. Within the bureaus, there are divisions, offices, services, and units—sometimes designating agencies of the same status, sometimes designating agencies of lesser status.

Not all government agencies are part of cabinet departments. A second type of agency, the independent agency, is set up by Congress outside the departmental structure altogether, even though the president appoints and directs the heads of these types of agencies. Independent agencies usually have broad powers to provide public services that are either too expensive or too important to be left to private initiatives. Some examples of independent agencies are the National Aeronautics and Space Administration (NASA), the Central Intelligence Agency (CIA), and the Environmental Protection Agency (EPA). Government corporations are a third type of government agency but are more like private businesses performing and charging for a market service, such as delivering the mail (the United States Postal Service) or transporting railroad passengers (Amtrak).

Yet a fourth type of agency is the independent regulatory commission, given broad discretion to make rules. The first regulatory agencies established by Congress, beginning with the Interstate Commerce Commission in 1887, were set up as independent regulatory commissions because Congress recognized that regulatory agencies are mini-legislatures, whose rules and rulings are the same as legislation and legislative interpretation but require the kind of expertise and full-time attention that is beyond the capacity of Congress. Until the 1960s, most of the regulatory agencies that were set up by Congress, such as the Federal Trade Commission (1914) and the Federal Communications Commission (1934), were independent regulatory commissions. But beginning in the late 1960s and early 1970s, all new regulatory programs, with a few exceptions (such as the Federal Election Commission), were placed within existing departments and made directly responsible to the president. Since the 1970s, no new major regulatory programs have been established, independent or otherwise. (During the financial crisis of 2008–09, Congress and the president formulated new regulatory arrangements involving the Federal Reserve System, the Federal Deposit Insurance Corporation, the Treasury, and related agencies.)

There are too many agencies in the executive branch to identify, much less to describe, so a simple classification of agencies will be helpful. Instead of dividing the bureaucracy into four general types, as we did above, an alternative classification organizes each agency by its mission, as defined by its jurisdiction: clientele agencies, agencies for maintenance of the Union, regulatory agencies, and redistributive agencies. We shall examine each of these types of agencies, focusing on both their formal structure and their place in the political process.

Clientele Agencies Serve Particular Interests

The entire Department of Agriculture is an example of a **clientele agency.** So are the Departments of the Interior, Labor, and Commerce. Although all administrative

clientele agency A department or bureau of government whose mission is to promote, serve, or represent a particular interest.

agencies have clienteles, certain agencies are singled out and called clientele agencies because they are directed by law to foster and promote the interests of their clientele. For example, the Department of Commerce and Labor was founded in 1903 as a single department "to foster, promote, and develop the foreign and domestic commerce, the mining, the manufacturing, the shipping, and fishing industries, and the transportation facilities of the United States."[7] It remained a single department until 1913, when the law created the separate departments of Commerce and Labor, with each statute providing for the same obligation: to support and foster each agency's respective clientele.[8] The Department of Agriculture serves the many farming interests that, taken together, are one of the largest economic sectors of the United States.

Most clientele agencies locate a relatively large proportion of their total personnel in field offices dealing directly with their clientele. The Extension Service of the Department of Agriculture is among the most familiar, with its numerous local "extension agents" who consult with farmers on farm productivity. These same agencies also seek to foster the interests of their clientele by providing "functional representation"—that is, they try to learn what their clients' interests and needs are and then operate almost as a lobby in Washington on their behalf. In addition to the Departments of Agriculture, the Interior, Labor, and Commerce, other clientele agencies include five of the newest cabinet departments: Housing and Urban Development (HUD), created in 1965; Transportation (DOT), created in 1966; Energy (DOE), created in 1977; Education (ED), created in 1979; and Health and Human Services (HHS), created in 1979.[9]

Agencies for the Maintenance of the Union Keep the Government Going

Agencies for the maintenance of the Union could be called public-order agencies were it not for the fact that the Constitution entrusts to the state governments so many of the vital functions of public order, such as the police. But some agencies vital to maintaining national bonds do exist in the national government, and they can be grouped for convenience into three categories: (1) agencies for managing the sources of government revenue, (2) agencies for controlling conduct defined as a threat to internal national security, and (3) agencies for defending American security from external threats. The departments of greatest power in these three areas are Treasury, Justice, Defense, State, and Homeland Security.

Revenue Agencies. The Internal Revenue Service (IRS) is the most important revenue agency. The IRS is also one of the federal government's largest bureaucracies. Over 100,000 employees are spread throughout four regions, sixty-three

---

[7] *U.S. Statutes at Large* 32 (1903): 825; 15 U.S. Code 1501.

[8] For a detailed account of the creation of the Department of Commerce and Labor and its division into separate departments, see Theodore J. Lowi, *The End of Liberalism: The Second Republic of the United States,* 2nd ed. (New York: Norton, 1979), pp. 78–84.

[9] Until 1979, the Department of Education and the Department of Health and Human Services were joined in a single department, Health, Education, and Welfare (HEW), which was established by Congress in 1953.

districts, ten service centers, and hundreds of local offices. In 2006, more than 130 million individual tax returns were filed. In that same year, the IRS collected nearly $2.2 trillion in taxes from individuals and corporations.

Agencies for Internal Security. As long as the country is not in a state of insurrection, most of the task of maintaining the Union takes the form of legal work, and the main responsibility for that lies with the Department of Justice. It is indeed a luxury, and rare in the world, when national unity can be maintained by routines of civil law rather than imposed by military force. The largest and most important agency in the Justice Department is the Criminal Division, which is responsible for enforcing all the federal criminal laws except a few specifically assigned to other divisions. Criminal litigation is actually conducted by the U.S. attorneys. A presidentially appointed U.S. attorney is assigned to each federal judicial district, and he or she supervises the work of assistant U.S. attorneys. The work or jurisdictions of the Antitrust and Civil Rights Divisions are described by their official names. Although it looms so very large in American folklore, the FBI is simply another bureau of the Department of Justice. The FBI handles no litigation but instead serves as the information-gathering agency for all the other divisions.

In 2002, Congress created the Department of Homeland Security to coordinate the nation's defense against the threat of terrorism. The new department is responsible for a number of tasks, including protecting commercial airlines from would-be hijackers.

Agencies for External National Security. Two departments occupy center stage here, State and Defense. A few key agencies outside State and Defense also have external national-security functions. They are treated in this chapter only as bureaucratic phenomena and as examples of the political problems relevant to administration.

Although diplomacy is generally considered the primary task of the State Department, diplomatic missions make up only one of its organizational dimensions. The State Department is also composed of geographic, or regional, bureaus concerned with all problems within the defined regions of the world; "functional" bureaus, which handle such things as economic and business affairs, intelligence, and research; and international organizations and bureaus of internal affairs, which handle such areas as security, finance and management, and legal issues.

Despite the importance of the State Department in foreign affairs, fewer than 20 percent of all U.S. government employees working abroad are directly under its authority. By far the largest number of career government professionals working abroad are under the authority of the Defense Department.

The creation of the Department of Defense by legislation enacted between 1947 and 1949 was an effort to unify the two historic military departments, the War Department and the Navy Department, and integrate into them a new department, the Air Force Department. Real unification did not occur, however. Instead, the Defense Department added more pluralism to national security.

America's primary political problem with its military has not been the historic one of how to keep the military out of the politics of governing, a problem that has plagued so many countries in Europe and Latin America. The American military problem is instead the more mundane politics of the pork barrel. President Clinton's long list of proposed military-base closings, a major part of his budget-cutting drive for 1993, caused a firestorm of opposition even in his own party, with some of the opposition coming from members of Congress who otherwise prominently favored significant reductions in the Pentagon budget. Emphasis on jobs rather than strategy and policy means pork-barrel use of the military for political purposes. This is a classic way for a bureaucracy to defend itself politically in a democracy. It is the distributive tendency, in which the bureaucracy ensures political support among elected officials by making sure to distribute things—military bases, contracts, facilities, and jobs—to the states and districts that elected the legislators. As is commonly known, it is hard to bite the hand that feeds you! Thus the best way to understand the military in American politics is to study it within the bureaucratic framework that is used to explain the domestic agencies.

Regulatory Agencies Guide Individual Conduct

As we saw in Chapter 3, our national government did not even begin to get involved in the regulation of economic and social affairs until the late nineteenth century. Until then, regulation was strictly a state and local affair. The federal **regulatory agencies** are, as a result, relatively new, most dating from the 1930s. But they have come to be extensive and important. In this section, we look at these regulatory agencies as an administrative phenomenon, with its attendant politics.

regulatory agency A department, bureau, or independent agency whose primary mission is to eliminate or restrict certain behaviors defined as negative in themselves or negative in their consequences.

The United States has no "department of regulation," but it has many regulatory agencies. Some of these are bureaus within departments, such as the Food and Drug Administration (FDA) in the Department of Health and Human Services, and the Occupational Safety and Health Administration (OSHA) in the Department of Labor. Other regulatory agencies are independent regulatory commissions—for example, the Federal Trade Commission (FTC). But whether departmental or independent, an agency or commission is regulatory if Congress delegates to it relatively broad powers over a sector of the economy or a type of commercial activity and authorizes it to make rules governing the conduct of people and businesses within that jurisdiction. Rules made by regulatory agencies have the force and effect of legislation; indeed, the rules they make are referred to as **administrative legislation.** And when these agencies make decisions or orders settling disputes between parties or between the government and a party, they are acting like courts.

administrative legislation Rules made by regulatory agencies and commissions.

Because regulatory agencies exercise a tremendous amount of influence over the economy and because their rules are a form of legislation, Congress was at first loath to turn them over to the executive branch as ordinary agencies under the control of the president. Consequently, most of the important regulatory programs were delegated to independent commissions with direct responsibility to Congress rather than to the White House. This is the basis of the 1930s reference to them as the "headless fourth branch."[10] With the rise of presidential government, most

---

[10] *Final Report of the President's Committee on Administrative Management* (Washington, D.C.: Government Printing Office, 1937). The term *headless fourth branch* was invented by a member of the committee staff, the Cornell University government professor Robert Cushman.

recent presidents have supported more regulatory programs but have successfully opposed the expansion of regulatory independence. The 1960s and 1970s witnessed the adoption of an unprecedented number of new regulatory programs but only four new independent commissions.

Agencies of Redistribution Implement Fiscal or Monetary and Welfare Policies

Welfare agencies and fiscal or monetary agencies are responsible for the transfer of hundreds of billions of dollars annually between the public and the private spheres, and through such transfers these agencies influence how people and corporations spend and invest trillions of dollars annually. We call them agencies of redistribution because they influence the amount of money in the economy and because they directly influence who has money, who has credit, and whether people will want to invest or save their money rather than spend it.

Fiscal and Monetary Agencies. Governmental activity affecting or relating to money may be partitioned into **fiscal** and **monetary policy.** Fiscal policy includes taxing and spending activities. Monetary policies focus on banks, credit, and currency.

Administration of fiscal policy is primarily performed in the Treasury Department. It is no contradiction to include the Treasury both here and with the agencies for maintenance of the Union. This duplication indicates (1) that the Treasury is a complex department, performing more than one function of government; and (2) that traditional controls have had to be adapted to modern economic conditions and new technologies.

Today, in addition to administering and policing income tax and other tax collections, the Treasury is responsible for managing the enormous federal debt. The Treasury Department also prints the currency that we use, but currency is only a tiny proportion of the entire money economy. Most of the trillions of dollars used in the transactions that make up the private and public sectors of the American economy exist on printed accounts and computers, not in currency.

Another important fiscal agency (although for technical reasons it is called an agency of monetary policy) is the **Federal Reserve System**, headed by the Federal Reserve Board. The Federal Reserve System (the Fed) has authority over the credit rates and lending activities of the nation's most important banks. Established by Congress in 1913, the Fed is responsible for adjusting the supply of money to both the needs of banks in the different regions and the commerce and industry in each. The Fed helps shift money from where there is too much to where there is too little. It also ensures that banks do not overextend themselves by adopting lending policies that are too liberal. The basis for this responsibility is the fear that if there is a sudden economic scare, a run on a few banks might be contagious and cause another terrible crash like the one in 1929. The Federal Reserve Board sits at the top of a pyramid of twelve district Federal Reserve Banks, which are "bankers' banks," serving the monetary needs of the hundreds of member banks in the national bank system. The subprime mortgage crisis of 2008 and 2009, which resulted after banks and other lenders provided home mortgages that proved unusually risky and led to home foreclosures, reflected gaps and loopholes in the regulation of the banking sector.

fiscal policy
Policies that use spending and taxing to accomplish policy purposes.

monetary policy
Policies that control the supply of money, the price of money (interest rate), and the availability of credit.

Federal Reserve System (the Fed)
Consisting of twelve Federal Reserve districts, the Fed facilitates exchanges of cash, checks, and credit; it regulates member banks; and it deploys monetary policies to fight inflation and deflation.

Welfare Agencies.   No single government agency is responsible for all the programs making up the "welfare state." The largest agency in the field is the Social Security Administration (SSA), which manages the social insurance aspects of Social Security and Supplemental Security Income (SSI). As the baby-boom generation ages, a growing bloc of voters (and their children) have become concerned about the solvency of this system. It is a live political issue that has figured prominently in presidential election campaigns for the past quarter century. Many argue that without some adjustments in benefit schedules, taxes, or retirement age, the present population will begin drawing down the enormous amount of funds in the Social Security Trust Fund in two decades and exhaust it in forty years.

Agencies in the Department of Health and Human Services administer Temporary Assistance to Needy Families (TANF) and Medicaid, and the Department of Agriculture is responsible for the Food Stamp Program. With the exception of Social Security, these are *means-tested* programs, requiring applicants to demonstrate that their total annual cash earnings fall below an officially defined poverty line. These public-assistance programs create a large administrative burden. In August 1996, virtually all of the means-tested public-assistance programs were legally abolished as national programs and "devolved" to the states (see also Chapter 3).

THE PROBLEM OF BUREAUCRATIC CONTROL

Two centuries, millions of employees, and trillions of dollars after the Founding, we must return to James Madison's observation that "you must first enable the government to control the governed; and in the next place oblige it to control itself."[11] Today the problem is the same, but the form has changed. The problem today is bureaucracy and our inability to keep it accountable to elected political authorities.

Bureaucrats Have Their Own Motivational Considerations

The economist William Niskanen proposed that we regard a bureau or department of government as analogous to a division of a private firm and conceive of the bureaucrat just as we would the manager who runs that division.[12] In particular, Niskanen stipulated that the behavior of a bureau chief or department head be thought of as following the rationality principle. In this view the bureaucrat is a rational maximizer of his or her budget (just as the private-sector counterpart is a maximizer of his or her division's profits).

There are quite a number of motivational bases on which bureaucratic budget maximizing might be justified. A cynical (though some would say realistic) basis for budget maximizing is that the bureaucrat's own compensation is often tied to the size of his or her budget. Not only might bureaus with large budgets have higher-salaried executives with more elaborate fringe benefits but there also may

---

[11] Alexander Hamilton, James Madison, and John Jay, *The Federalist Papers,* Clinton L. Rossiter, ed. (New York: New American Library, 1961), no. 51.

[12] William A. Niskanen, Jr., *Bureaucracy and Representative Government* (Chicago: Aldine, 1971).

be enhanced opportunities for career advancement, travel, a poshly appointed office, possibly even a chauffeur-driven limousine.

A second, related motivation for large budgets is nonmaterial personal gratification. An individual understandably enjoys the prestige and respect that comes from running a major enterprise. You can't take these things to the bank or put them on your family's dinner table, but your sense of esteem and your stature are surely buoyed by the conspicuous fact that your bureau or division has a large budget. That you are also boss of a large number of subordinates, made possible by a large bureau budget, is another aspect of this sort of ego gratification.

But personal salary, "on-the-job consumption," and power tripping are not the only forces driving a bureaucrat toward gaining as large a budget as possible. Some bureaucrats, perhaps most, actually *care* about their mission.[13] They initially choose to go into public safety, or the military, or health care, or social work, or education—as police officers, soldiers, hospital managers, social workers, and teachers, respectively—because they believe in the importance of helping people in their community. As they rise through the ranks of a public bureaucracy and assume management responsibilities, they take this mission orientation with them. Thus as chief of detectives in a big-city police department, as head of procurement in the air force, as director of nursing services in a public hospital, as supervisor of the social work division in a county welfare department, or as assistant superintendent of a town school system, individuals try to secure as large a budget as they can to succeed in achieving the mission to which they have devoted their professional lives.

Whether for cynical, self-serving motives or for the noblest of public purposes, it is entirely plausible that individual bureaucrats seek to persuade others (typically legislators or taxpayers) to provide them with as many resources as possible. Indeed, it is sometimes difficult to distinguish the saint from the sinner because each sincerely argues that he or she needs more to do more. This is one nice feature of the rationality principle in general, and Niskanen's assumption of budget maximizing in particular: It doesn't really matter *why* a bureaucrat is interested in a big budget; what matters is simply that he or she prefers more resources to fewer.

This does not mean that the legislature, which controls the bureau's budget, has to fork over whatever the bureau requests. Critics of Niskanen's budget-maximizing theory call into question precisely this assumption about the passivity of the legislature. The legislature, the only customer of the bureau's product, in essence tells the bureau how much it is willing to pay for various levels of the bureau's product; the bureau then figures out how much it can extract from the legislature and, according to Niskanen, goes for the maximum. The critics suggest that this is akin to a customer walking onto a used-car lot and telling the salesman the most he or she is willing to spend for each vehicle.[14]

In a representative democracy, it may be difficult for the legislature to keep silent about its valuation of the bureau's product. The bureau, at any rate, can do some research to judge the preferences of various legislators. For example, the bureau can

---

[13] John Brehm and Scott Gates, *Working, Shirking, and Sabotage: Bureaucratic Response to a Democratic Public* (Ann Arbor: University of Michigan Press, 1997).

[14] This and other related points are drawn from Gary J. Miller and Terry M. Moe, "Bureaucrats, Legislators, and the Size of Government," *American Political Science Review 77*, no. 2 (June 1983): 297–323.

draw inferences about the importance of its product for a legislator from the characteristics of the legislator's constituency. But legislators can do research, too. Indeed, we suggested in Chapter 5 that the collection, evaluation, and dissemination of information—in this case information about bureaucratic supply—are precisely the things in which specialized legislative committees engage. Committees hold hearings, request documentation on production, assign investigatory staff to various research tasks, and query bureau personnel on the veracity of their data and their use of the lowest-cost technologies (making it more difficult for the bureau to disguise on-the-job consumption). After the fact, the committees engage in oversight, making sure that what the legislature was told at the time when authorization and appropriations were voted actually holds in practice. In short, the legislature can be much more proactive than the Niskanen budget-maximizing theory gives it credit for. And in the real world, the legislature is more proactive, as we shall see later in this chapter. This doesn't mean budget maximizing is an implausible hypothesis about bureau motivations; it simply means that bureaus don't always get (all of) what they want.

Before leaving motivational considerations, we should remark that budget maximizing is not the only objective that bureaucrats pursue. It needs to be emphasized and reemphasized that career civil servants and high-level political appointees are *politicians.* They spend their professional lives pursuing political goals, bargaining, forming alliances and coalitions, solving cooperation and collective-action problems, making policy decisions, operating within and interfacing with political institutions—in short, doing what other politicians do. They do not have elections to win, but even elections affect their conditions of employment by determining the composition of the legislature and the partisan and ideological complexion of the chief executive. Bureaucrats are politicians beholden to other politicians for authority and resources. They are servants of many masters.

As politicians subject to the oversight and authority of others, bureaucrats must make contingency plans. They must be strategic and forward thinking. Whichever party wins control of the House or the Senate, whichever candidate wins the presidency, whoever becomes chair of the legislative committee with authorization or appropriation responsibility over their agency, life will go on and bureau chiefs will have to adjust to the prevailing political winds. To protect and expand authority and resources, bureaucratic politicians seek, in the form of autonomy and discretion, insurance against political change. They don't always succeed in acquiring this freedom, but they do try to insulate themselves from changes in the broader political world.[15] So bureaucratic motivations include budget-maximizing behavior, to be sure, but bureaucrats also seek the autonomy to weather changes in the political atmosphere and the discretion and flexibility to achieve their goals.

Control of the Bureaucracy Is a Principal-Agent Problem

Two broad categories of control mechanisms enable a principal to guard against opportunistic or incompetent agent behavior. They can be illustrated by a homeowner

---

[15] For an expanded view of bureaucratic autonomy and insulation with historical application to the U.S. Department of Agriculture and the Post Office Department, see Daniel P. Carpenter, *The Forging of Bureaucratic Autonomy: Reputations, Networks, and Policy Innovation in Executive Agencies, 1862–1928* (Princeton, N.J.: Princeton University Press, 2001).

(the principal) who seeks out a contractor (the agent) to remodel a kitchen. The first category is employed before the fact and depends on the reputation an agent possesses. One guards against selecting an incompetent or corrupt agent by relying on various methods for authenticating the promises made by the agent. These include advice from people you trust (your neighbors who just had their kitchen remodeled), certification by various official boards (an association of kitchen contractors), letters of recommendation and other testimonials, credentials (specialized training programs), and interviews. Before-the-fact protection relies on the assumption that an agent's reputation is a valuable asset that he or she does not want to depreciate.

The second class of control mechanisms operates after the fact. Payment may be made contingent on completion of various tasks by specific dates, so that it may be withheld for nonperformance. Alternatively, financial incentives (for example, bonuses) for early or on-time completion may be part of the arrangement. The agent may be required to post a bond that would be forfeited for lack of performance. An inspection process, after the work is completed, may lead to financial penalties, bonuses, or possibly even legal action. Of course, the principal can always seek legal relief for breach of contract, either in the form of an injunction stipulating that the agent comply or in the form of an order demanding that the agent pay damages.

How does the principal-agent problem apply to the president's and Congress's control of the bureaucracy?

Suppose the legislation that created the EPA required that after ten years new legislation be passed renewing its existence and mandate. The issue facing the House, the Senate, and the president in their consideration of renewal involves how much authority to give this agency and how much money to permit it to spend. Suppose the House is conservative on environmental issues and prefers limited authority and a limited budget. The Senate wants the agency to have wide-ranging authority but is prepared to give it only slightly more resources than the House is (because of its concern with the budget deficit). The president is happy to split the difference between House and Senate on the matter of authority but feels beholden to environmental types and is thus prepared to shower the EPA with resources. Bureaucrats in the EPA want more authority than even the Senate is prepared to grant and more resources than even the president is willing to grant. Eventually relevant majorities in the House and the Senate (including the support of relevant committees) and the president agree on a policy reflecting a compromise among their various points of view.

The bureaucrats are not particularly pleased with this compromise because it gives them considerably less authority and funding than they had hoped for. If they flout the wishes of their principals and implement a policy exactly to their liking, they risk the unified wrath of the House, the Senate, and the president. Undoubtedly the politicians would react with new legislation (and they would also presumably find other political appointees and career bureaucrats at the EPA to replace the current bureaucratic leadership). If, however, the EPA implements some policy located between its own preferences and the preferences of its principals, it might be able to get away with it.

Thus we have a principal-agent relationship in which a political principal—a collective principal consisting of the president and coalitions in the House and Senate—formulates policy and creates an implementation agent to execute its details. The agent, however, has policy preferences of its own and, unless subjected to further controls, will inevitably implement a policy that drifts toward its ideal.

A variety of controls might conceivably restrict this **bureaucratic drift.** Indeed, legislative scholars often point to congressional hearings in which bureaucrats may be publicly humiliated; annual appropriations decisions that may be used to punish out-of-control bureaus; and watchdog agents, such as the Government Accountability Office, that may be used to monitor and scrutinize the bureau's performance. But these all come after the fact and may be only partially credible threats to the agency.[16]

Before-the-Fact Controls.　The most powerful before-the-fact political weapon is the appointment process. The adroit control of the political stance of a given bureau by the president and Congress, through their joint powers of nomination and confirmation (especially if they can arrange for appointees who closely share the political consensus on policy) is a self-enforcing mechanism for ensuring reliable agent performance.

A second powerful before-the-fact weapon, following from the institution principle, is procedural controls. The general rules and regulations that direct the manner in which federal agencies conduct their affairs are contained in the Administrative Procedure Act. This act is almost always the boilerplate of legislation creating and renewing federal agencies. It is not uncommon, however, for an agency's procedures to be tailored to suit particular circumstances.

Coalitional Drift as a Collective-Action Problem.　Not only do politicians want the legislative deals that they strike to be faithfully implemented by the bureaucracy, but they also want those deals to endure. This is especially problematic in American political life, with its shifting alignments and absence of permanent political cleavages. Today's coalition transforms itself overnight. Opponents today are partners tomorrow, and vice versa. A victory today, even one implemented in a favorable manner by the bureaucracy, may unravel tomorrow. What is to be done?

To some extent, legislators are disinclined to undo legislation. If a coalition votes for handsome subsidies to grain farmers, say, it is very hard to reverse this policy without the gatekeeping and agenda-setting assistance of members on the House and Senate Agriculture Committees, yet their members undoubtedly participated in the initial deal and are unlikely to turn against it. But even these structural units are unstable; old politicians depart and new ones are enlisted.

In short, legislatively formulated and bureaucratically implemented output is subject to **coalitional drift.**[17] To prevent shifting coalitional patterns among

bureaucratic drift The oft-observed phenomenon of bureaucratic implementation that produces policy more to the liking of the bureaucracy than faithful to the original intention of the legislation that created it, but without triggering a political reaction from elected officials.

coalitional drift The prospect that enacted policy will change because the composition of the enacting coalition is temporary and provisional.

---

[16] For the classic statement that, despite before-the-fact and after-the-fact tools available to the political principals, the bureau-agent will "drift" in policy implementation toward its own preferences, see Mathew D. McCubbins, Roger G. Noll, and Barry R. Weingast, "Structure and Process; Politics and Policy: Administrative Arrangements and the Political Control of Agencies," *Virginia Law Review* 75 (1989): 431–82.

[17] This idea, offered as a supplement to the analysis of bureaucratic drift, is found in Murray J. Horn and Kenneth A. Shepsle, "Administrative Process and Organizational Form as Legislative Responses to Agency Costs," *Virginia Law Review* 75 (1989): 499–509. It is further elaborated in Kenneth A. Shepsle, "Bureaucratic Drift, Coalitional Drift, and Time Consistency," *Journal of Law, Economics, and Organization* 8 (1992): 111–18.

politicians from endangering carefully fashioned policies, one thing the legislature might do is insulate the bureaucracy and its implementation activities from legislative interventions. If an enacting coalition makes it difficult for its *own* members to intervene in implementation, then it also makes it difficult for enemies of the policy to disrupt the flow of bureaucratic output. This political insulation can be provided by giving bureaucratic agencies long lives, their political heads long terms of office and wide-ranging administrative authority, and other political appointees overlapping terms of office and secure sources of revenue. This insulation comes at a price, however. The civil servants and political appointees of bureaus insulated from political overseers are thereby empowered to pursue independent courses of action. Protection from coalitional drift comes at the price of an increased potential for bureaucratic drift. It is one of the great trade-offs in the field of intergovernmental relations.

The President, as Chief Executive, Can Direct Agencies

In 1937, President Franklin Roosevelt's Committee on Administrative Management gave official sanction to an idea that had been growing increasingly urgent: "The president needs help." The national government had grown rapidly during the preceding twenty-five years, but the structures and procedures necessary to manage the burgeoning executive branch had not yet been established. The response to the call for help for the president initially took the form of three management policies: (1) All communications and decisions that related to executive policy decisions must pass through the White House; (2) to cope with such a flow, the White House must have an adequate staff of specialists in research, analysis, legislative and legal writing, and public affairs; and (3) the White House must have additional staff to follow through on presidential decisions—to ensure that those decisions are made, communicated to Congress, and carried out by the appropriate agency.

Establishing a management capacity for the presidency began in earnest with FDR, but it did not stop there. The story of the modern presidency can be told largely as a series of responses to the plea for managerial help. Indeed, each expansion of the national government into new policies and programs in the twentieth century was accompanied by a parallel expansion of the president's management authority. This pattern began even before FDR's presidency, with the policy innovations of President Woodrow Wilson between 1913 and 1920. Congress responded to Wilson's policies with the 1921 Budget and Accounting Act, which conferred on the White House agenda-setting power over budgeting. The president, in his annual budget message, transmits comprehensive budgetary recommendations to Congress. Because Congress retains ultimate legislative authority, a president's proposals are sometimes said to be dead on arrival on Capitol Hill. Nevertheless, the power to frame deliberations is potent and constitutes an important management tool. Each successive president has continued this pattern of setting the congressional agenda, creating what we now know as the managerial presidency.

Along with the development of the managerial presidency came expectations of administrative competence. Presidents are now *expected* to be CEOs, and are roundly criticized for ineptitude. For example, President Clinton was often disparaged for the way he managed his administration. (Clinton's easygoing approach led critics to liken his management style to college bull sessions.) George W. Bush was the first president with a graduate degree in business. His management strategy followed a standard business-school dictum: Select skilled subordinates and delegate responsibility to them. Bush followed this model closely in his appointment of highly experienced officials to cabinet positions. This was no guarantee of policy success as doubts emerged about the conduct of the Iraq war, especially about the leadership of the highly experienced Secretary of Defense, Donald Rumsfeld. The incompetence of less experienced leadership became evident in the administration's mishandling of relief to New Orleans and the Gulf Coast after Hurricane Katrina.

Congress Can Promote Responsible Bureaucracy through Oversight and Incentives

Congress is constitutionally essential to responsible bureaucracy because the key to governmental responsibility is legislation. When a law is passed and its intent is clear, then the president knows what to "faithfully execute," and the responsible agency understands what is expected of it. In our modern age, legislatures rarely make laws directly for citizens; most laws are really instructions to bureaucrats and their agencies. But when Congress enacts vague legislation, agencies must rely on their own interpretations. The president and the federal courts step in to tell them what the legislation intended. And so do intensely interested organized groups. But when everybody—from the president to the courts to interest groups—gets involved in the interpretation of legislative intent, to whom is the agency responsible?

The answer lies in the process of **oversight**. The more legislative power Congress has delegated to the executive bureaucracy, the more it has sought to get back into the game through committee and subcommittee oversight of the agencies. The standing committee system in Congress is well suited for oversight, inasmuch as most of the congressional committees and subcommittees are organized with jurisdictions roughly parallel to one or more executive departments or agencies. Appropriations committees as well as authorization committees have oversight powers, as do their respective subcommittees. In addition to these, there is a committee on government operations in both the House and the Senate, each with oversight powers not limited by departmental jurisdiction.

The best indication of Congress's oversight efforts is the holding of public hearings, before which bureaucrats and other witnesses are summoned to discuss and defend agency budgets and decisions. The data drawn from systematic studies of congressional committee and subcommittee hearings and meetings show dramatically that Congress has tried through oversight to keep pace with the expansion of the executive branch. Between 1950 and 1980, the annual number of committee and subcommittee meetings in the House of Representatives rose steadily. Yet beginning in 1980 in the House and 1978 in the Senate, the number of committee and subcommittee hearings and meetings slowly began to decline. New questions about the ability of Congress to exercise oversight arose when the Republicans took

oversight The effort by Congress, through hearings, investigations, and other techniques, to exercise control over the activities of executive agencies.

over Congress in 1995. Reductions in committee staffing and an emphasis on using investigative oversight to uncover scandal meant that much less time was spent on programmatic oversight. On matters of major national importance, however, multiple committees may initiate oversight hearings simultaneously. No less than a dozen congressional committees (along with the Justice Department and the Securities and Exchange Commission) launched investigations into the collapse of the giant energy company Enron. Likewise, the failure of the Bush administration's response to the Gulf Coast hurricanes of 2005 drew the attention of a number of congressional panels.

Although congressional oversight is potent because of Congress's power to make—and therefore change—the law, often the most effective and the most influential control over bureaucratic accountability is the power of the purse—the ability of the House and Senate committees and subcommittees on appropriations to look at agency performance through the microscope of the annual appropriations process. This process makes bureaucrats attentive to Congress, especially members of the relevant authorizing committee and appropriations subcommittee, because they know that Congress has a chance each year to reduce their authority or funding.[18] This may be another explanation for why there may be some downsizing but almost no terminations of federal agencies.

Oversight can also be carried out by individual members of Congress. Such inquiries addressed to bureaucrats are considered standard congressional "casework" and can turn up significant questions of public responsibility even when the motive is only to meet the demand of an individual constituent. Oversight also very often takes place through communications between congressional staff and agency staff. Congressional staff has grown tremendously since the Legislative Reorganization Act of 1946, and the legislative staff, especially the staff of the committees, is just as professionalized and specialized as the staff of an executive agency. In addition, Congress has created for itself three quite large agencies whose obligations are to engage in constant research on problems taking place in the executive branch: the Government Accountability Office, the Congressional Research Service, and the Congressional Budget Office. Each is designed to give Congress information independent of the information it can get through hearings and other communications directly with the executive branch.[19]

---

[18] See Aaron Wildavsky, *The New Politics of the Budgetary Process,* 2nd ed. (New York: HarperCollins, 1992), pp. 15–16.

[19] Until 1983, there was still another official tool of legislative oversight, the legislative veto. Each executive agency was obliged to submit to Congress proposed decisions or rules. These were to lie before both houses for thirty to sixty days; then, if Congress took no explicit action by a one-house or two-house resolution to veto a proposed measure, it became law. The legislative veto was declared unconstitutional by the Supreme Court in 1983 on the grounds that it violated the separation of powers because the resolutions Congress passed to exercise its veto were not subject to a presidential veto, as required by the Constitution. See *Immigration and Naturalization Service v. Chadha,* 462 U.S. 919 (1983). On the congressional staff more generally, see Robert H. Salisbury and Kenneth A. Shepsle, "Congressman as Enterprise," *Legislative Studies Quarterly* 6 (1981): 559–76. On the role and activities of the Government Accountability Office, see Anne Joseph O'Connell, "Auditing Politics or Political Auditing?" UC Berkeley Public Law Research Paper no. 964656 (2007), http://ssrn.com/abstract=964656 (accessed 2/27/09).

Congressional Oversight: Abdication or Strategic Delegation? Congress often grants the executive-branch bureaucracies discretion in determining certain features of a policy during the implementation phase. Although the complexities of governing a modern industrialized democracy make the granting of discretion necessary, some argue that Congress not only gives unelected bureaucrats too much discretion but also delegates too much policy-making authority to them. Congress, they say, has transferred so much power that it has created a "runaway bureaucracy" in which unelected officials accountable neither to the electorate nor to Congress make important policy decisions.[20] By enacting vague statutes that give bureaucrats broad discretion, so the argument goes, members of Congress effectively abdicate their constitutionally designated roles and effectively remove themselves from the policy-making process. Ultimately this extreme delegation has left the legislative branch weak and ineffectual and has dire consequences for the health of our democracy.

Others claim that even though Congress may possess the tools to engage in effective oversight, it fails to use them simply because we do not see Congress actively engaging in much oversight activity.[21] However, Mathew McCubbins and Thomas Schwartz argue that these critics have focused on the wrong type of oversight and have missed a type of oversight that benefits members of Congress in their bids for reelection.[22] McCubbins and Schwartz distinguish between two types of oversight: police patrol and fire alarm. Under the police-patrol variety, Congress systematically initiates investigation into the activity of agencies. Under the fire-alarm variety, members of Congress do not initiate investigations but wait for adversely affected citizens or interest groups to bring bureaucratic perversions of legislative intent to the attention of the relevant congressional committee. To make sure that individuals and groups bring these violations to members' attention—to set off the fire alarm, so to speak—Congress passes laws that help individuals and groups make claims against the bureaucracy, granting them legal standing before administrative agencies and federal courts.

McCubbins and Schwartz argue that fire-alarm oversight is more efficient than the police-patrol variety, given costs and the electoral incentives of members of Congress. Why should members spend their scarce resources (mainly time) to initiate investigations without having any evidence that they will reap electoral rewards? Police-patrol oversight can waste taxpayers' dollars too, because many investigations will not turn up any evidence of violations of legislative intent. It is much more cost effective for members to conserve their resources and then claim credit for fixing the problem (and saving the day) after the fire alarms have been sounded (also see "Analyzing the Evidence," page 300).

On the other hand, bureaucratic drift might be contained if Congress spent more of its time clarifying its legislative intent and less of its time on oversight

---

[20] Lowi, *The End of Liberalism*; and Lawrence C. Dodd and Richard L. Schott, *Congress and the Administrative State* (New York: Wiley, 1979).

[21] Morris S. Ogul, *Congress Oversees the Bureaucracy: Studies in Legislative Supervision* (Pittsburgh: University of Pittsburgh Press, 1976); and Peter Woll, *American Bureaucracy*, 2nd ed. (New York: Norton, 1977).

[22] McCubbins and Schwartz, "Congressional Oversight Overlooked."

activity. If its original intent in the law were clearer, Congress could then afford to defer to presidential management to maintain bureaucratic responsibility. Bureaucrats are more responsive to clear legislative guidance than to anything else. But when Congress and the president are at odds (or coalitions within Congress are at odds), bureaucrats have an opportunity to evade responsibility by playing one side off against the other.

Policy Implications.   Because the bureaucracy finds itself squarely in the middle of the separation of powers between the legislature and the executive, it manages to elude systematic and comprehensive review and oversight. The institution principle suggests as much. Rational political actors in both branches will pay some attention to the bureaucracy, but as we have just seen, their own goals and objectives may not be well served by obsessive attention. The result is a bureaucracy that retains some discretion—partly because political actors' own specialization and expertise warrant it, but also because political arrangements permit their oversight to fall between the institutional cracks. Bureaus, in turn, perform their missions in ways that aim to maintain this kind of independence. They produce rulings, interpretations, and particular implementations of policy in order to deter after-the-fact oversight, allowing sleeping dogs (potential overseers) to lie.

Rational political adaptations to these institutional arrangements have policy consequences. In particular, bureaucrats will be extraordinarily attentive to the policy needs of those legislators who are in a position to help or harm them. Thus, states and districts represented on the House and Senate authorizing committees, as well as on the relevant appropriations subcommittees, can expect to have government largesse steered their way. Legislative lore points to instances in which, for example, a major weapons system is sustained politically by an implicit agreement between Defense Department agents and private sector contractors to ensure that subcontracts are distributed, geographically, to politically significant locations.

Repeat this pattern of deals among agency officials, powerful legislators, and private-sector special interests over many projects in many policy areas and we have a "distributive tendency" in which successful play of the political game by legislators and bureaucrats requires the wide distribution of spending. More efficient targeting of spending takes a backseat to the practical politics of making sure the "right" states and districts are taken care of. One classic example of the distributive tendency is found in the attempt by President Lyndon Johnson in the mid-1960s to focus federal assistance on those central cities in direst need of economic stimulus. His Model Cities program identified ten cities in desperate straits. But ten was too small a number in a political system with fifty states and 435 legislative districts. By the time Johnson's proposal had worked its way through the legislative process, the relevant bureaucratic entities had been given discretion to spread funds to many distressed cities—numbering in the hundreds when all was said and done—rather than concentrating assistance on the most desperate ones. The policy principle suggests that institutional arrangements (bicameralism and the separation of powers in this instance) combined with rational political behavior (reelection motivations of legislators and programmatic survival instincts of bureaucrats) produce policy distortions (the wide distribution of programmatic funds to sustain programs and to avoid the risk of critical oversight).

HOW CAN BUREAUCRACY BE REDUCED?

Americans like to complain about bureaucracy. Americans don't like big government because big government means big bureaucracy, and bureaucracy means the federal service—about 2.7 million civilian and 1.4 million military employees.[23] Promises to cut the bureaucracy are popular campaign appeals; "cutting out the fat," with big reductions in the number of federal employees, is held out as a sure-fire way of cutting the deficit.

Despite fears of bureaucratic growth's getting out of hand, however, the federal service has hardly grown at all during the past thirty years; it reached its peak postwar level in 1968 with 2.9 million civilian employees plus an additional 3.6 million military personnel (a figure swollen by the war in Vietnam). The number of civilian federal executive-branch employees has since remained close to that figure. The growth of the federal service is even less imposing when placed in the context of the total workforce and compared to the size of state and local public employment, which was 19.4 million full- and part-time employees in 2009.[24] Figure 7.3 indicates that since 1950 the ratio of federal service employment to the total workforce has been fairly steady, declining only slightly in the past twenty-five years. Another useful comparison is to be found in Figure 7.4: Although the dollar increase in federal spending shown by the bars looks impressive, the red line indicates that even here the national government has simply kept pace with the growth of the economy. During the Clinton years, federal outlays as a percent of the size of the economy (GDP) actually declined. During the Bush years, it steadily grew (from 18.5 percent to over 20 percent).

In sum, the national government is indeed very large, but the federal service has not been growing any faster than the economy or the society. The same is roughly true of the growth pattern of state and local public personnel. Our bureaucracy keeps pace with our society, despite our seeming dislike for it, because we cannot operate the control towers, the prisons, the Social Security system, and other essential elements of the state without it. And we certainly could not conduct wars in Iraq and Afghanistan without a gigantic military bureaucracy.

Nevertheless, some Americans continue to argue that bureaucracy is too big and that it should be reduced. In the 1990s, Americans seemed particularly enthusiastic about reducing (or to use the popular contemporary word, *downsizing*) the federal bureaucracy. During the deep economic recession beginning in December 2007, popular sentiment toward an enlarged role for government has softened.

Termination

The only *certain* way to reduce the size of the bureaucracy is to eliminate programs. But most agencies have a supportive constituency that will fight to reinstate any cuts that are made. Termination is the only way to ensure an agency's reduction, and it is a rare occurrence.

---

[23] U.S. Bureau of the Census, *Statistical Abstract of the United States, 2009* (Washington, D.C.: Government Printing Office, 2009), Tables 443 and 478.

[24] U.S. Bureau of the Census. www.census.gov/govs/

Keeping a Growing Bureaucracy in Check

The federal government is the United States's largest employer, with over 1.8 million civilian employees. This graph shows how the overall size of the federal bureaucracy has changed from 1940 to the present. During World War II, the number of civilian employees vastly increased, although the growth was largely concentrated in the Department of Defense. Since the war ended, the number of other civilian employees has steadily increased.

We can also use this graph to evaluate the views of the two political parties on the size of government. Generally speaking, Democrats are in favor of more government intervention and programs, while Republicans support a more limited role for the federal government. If this translates into policy, we should observe an increased number of federal employees during Democratic administrations. However, based on the figure, there does not seem to be a distinct pattern for either party. The total number of non-military federal employees ("other civilian employees") has risen steadily since the 1940s, regardless of which party was in power.

GROWTH OF EXECUTIVE BRANCH CIVILIAN EMPLOYEES, 1940–2007

As the size of the government increases, it may become more difficult to make sure the bureaucrats are doing their jobs. Although we often think of the Congress as a lawmaking body, it also carries out another important task—checking the executive branch through the oversight process. If Congress thinks the bureaucracy is no longer serving the public's interest as defined by the legislative branch, it can use its oversight powers to pull the agency back where it belongs. The political scientists Mathew McCubbins and Thomas Schwartz (1984) define two types of oversight: Police-Patrols and Fire-Alarms.

Under the police-patrol method, Congress systematically initiates investigations into the activity of agencies. The goal is to catch and punish enough violators so that the rest of the bureaucracy will be discouraged from straying too far from legislative intent. However, Congress cannot monitor all agencies at once. Police-patrol oversight is especially difficult because of the vast number of employees spread out over many government departments and agencies. The table below lists the number of employees in each of the fifteen executive Cabinet departments and the six largest independent agencies.

EXECUTIVE BRANCH EMPLOYEES

Executive Departments		Independent Agencies	
Defense	623,000	Social Security Administration	62,000
Veterans Affairs	239,000	National Aeronautics and Space Administration	18,000
Homeland Security	149,000		
Justice	105,000	Environmental Protection Agency	18,000
Agriculture	92,000		
Treasury	109,000	Tennessee Valley Authority	12,000
Interior	66,000	General Services Administration	12,000
Health and Human Services	60,000	Federal Deposit Insurance Corporation	5,000
Transportation	53,000		
Commerce	39,000		
Labor	16,000		
Energy	15,000		
State	14,000		
Housing and Urban Development	10,000		
Education	4,000		

Source: Bureau of Labor Statistics, U.S. Department of Labor, *Career Guide to Industries*, Federal Government, Excluding the Postal Service, www.bls.gov/oco/cg/cgs041.htm (accessed 4/28/09).

The fire-alarm method relies on the public. Members of Congress do not initiate investigations but wait for adversely affected citizens or interest groups to bring bureaucratic perversions of legislative intent to the attention of the relevant congressional committee. McCubbins and Schwartz argue that this method is more effective because, "Instead of sniffing for fires, Congress places fire-alarm boxes on street corners, builds neighborhood fire houses and sometimes dispatches its own hook-and-ladder in response to an alarm."[1] Since concerned citizens are out looking for bureaucratic fires, members of Congress will have more time to engage in other activities, such as securing reelection.

[1]Mathew McCubbins and Thomas Schwartz. 1984. "Congressional Oversight Overlooked: Police Patrols and Fire Alarms." *American Journal of Political Science* 28(1): 165–179.

FIGURE 7.3 EMPLOYEES IN THE FEDERAL SERVICE: TOTAL NUMBER AS A PERCENTAGE OF THE WORKFORCE

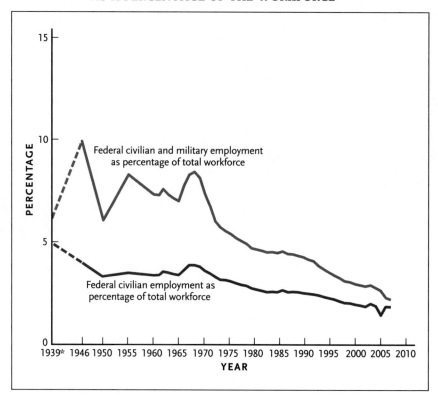

Federal civilian and military employment as percentage of total workforce

Federal civilian employment as percentage of total workforce

*Lines between 1939 and 1946 are broken because they connect the last prewar year with the first postwar year, disregarding the temporary ballooning of federal employees, especially in the military, during the war years.

NOTE: Workforce includes unemployed persons.

SOURCE: Tax Foundation, *Facts and Figures on Government Finance* (Baltimore: Johns Hopkins University Press, 1990), pp. 22, 44; Office of Management and Budget, *Budget of the U.S. Government, Fiscal Year 2009*, Table 17.5; and U.S. Bureau of Labor Statistics, "Employment Status of the Civilian Population by Sex and Age," *Labor Force Statistics from the Current Population Survey*, stats.bls.gov/webapps/legacy/cpsatab1.htm, table A1.

The Republican-led 104th Congress (1995–96) was committed to the termination of programs. Newt Gingrich, the Speaker of the House, took Congress by storm with his promises of a virtual revolution in government. But when the dust had settled at the end of the first session of the first Gingrich-led Congress, no significant progress had been made toward downsizing through the termination of agencies and programs.[25] The only two agencies eliminated were the Office of Technology Assessment, which provided research for Congress, and the Advisory Council on Intergovernmental

---

[25] A thorough review of the first session of the 104th Congress can be found in "Republican's Hopes for 1996 Lie in Unfinished Business," *Congressional Quarterly Weekly Report*, January 6, 1996, pp. 6–18.

FIGURE 7.4 ANNUAL FEDERAL OUTLAYS

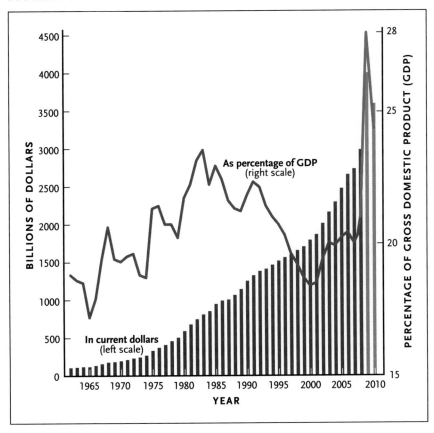

*Data for 2008–2009 are estimated.

SOURCE: Office of Management and Budget, *Budget of the U.S. Government, Fiscal Year 2010*, Tables 1.1 and 1.2.

Relations, which studied the relationship between the federal government and the states. Significantly, neither of these agencies had a strong constituency to defend it.[26]

The overall lack of success in terminating bureaucracy is a reflection of Americans' love-hate relationship with the national government. As antagonistic as Americans may be toward bureaucracy in general, they grow attached to the services rendered and protections offered by particular bureaucratic agencies—that is, they fiercely defend their favorite agencies while perceiving no inconsistency between that defense and their antagonistic attitude toward the bureaucracy in

---

[26] The Interstate Commerce Commission, created in 1887, was also terminated in 1995, by which time many of its functions had been dispersed to other agencies. In that year, its remaining functions were transferred to the newly created Surface Transportation Board.

general. A good case in point was the agonizing problem of closing military bases in the wake of the end of the Cold War, when the United States no longer needed so many bases. Because every base is in some congressional member's district, it proved impossible for Congress to decide to close any of them. Consequently, between 1988 and 1990, Congress established the Defense Base Closure and Realignment Commission to decide on base closings. Even though the matter is now out of Congress's hands altogether, the process has been slow and agonizing.

Elected leaders have come to rely on a more incremental approach to downsizing the bureaucracy. They have done much by budgetary means, reducing the budgets of all agencies across the board by small percentages and cutting some poorly supported agencies by larger amounts. Yet these changes are still incremental, leaving the existence of agencies unaddressed.

An additional approach has been taken to thwart the highly unpopular regulatory agencies, which are so small (relatively) that cutting their budgets contributes virtually nothing to reducing the deficit. This approach is called **deregulation**, simply defined as a reduction in the number of rules promulgated by regulatory agencies. But deregulation by rule reduction is still incremental and has certainly not satisfied the hunger of the American public in general and Washington representatives in particular for a genuine reduction in the size of the bureaucracy.

deregulation The policy of reducing or eliminating regulatory restraints on the conduct of individuals or private institutions.

Devolution

An alternative to genuine reduction in the size of the bureaucracy is **devolution**—downsizing the federal bureaucracy by delegating the implementation of programs to state and local governments. Indirect evidence for this is seen in Figure 7.5, which shows the increase in state and local government employment against a backdrop of flat or declining federal employment. This evidence suggests a growing share of governmental actions taking place on the state and local levels.

Devolution often alters the pattern of who benefits most from government programs. In the early 1990s, a major devolution in transportation policy sought to open up decisions about transportation to a new set of interests. Since the 1920s, transportation policy had been dominated by road-building interests in the federal and state governments. Many advocates for cities and many environmentalists believed that the emphasis on road building hurt cities and harmed the environment. The 1992 reform, initiated by environmentalists, put more power into the hands of metropolitan planning organizations and lifted many federal restrictions on how the money should be spent. Reformers hoped that these changes would open up the decision-making process so that those advocating alternatives to road building, such as mass transit, bike paths, and walkways, would have more influence over how federal transportation dollars were spent. Although the pace of change has been slow, devolution has indeed brought new voices to decisions about transportation spending, and alternatives to highways have received increasing attention.

Often the central aim of devolution is to provide more efficient and more flexible government services. Yet by its very nature, devolution entails variation across the states. In some states, government services may improve as a consequence of

devolution The policy of removing a program from one level of government by deregulating it or passing it down to a lower level, for example, from the national government to the state and local governments.

FIGURE 7.5 GOVERNMENT EMPLOYMENT

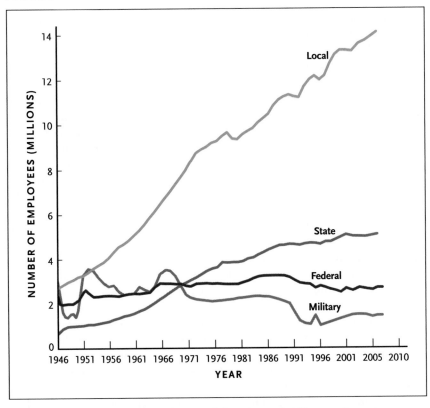

NOTE: Federal government employment figures include civilians only. Military employment figures include only active-duty personnel.

SOURCE: U.S. Bureau of the Census, *Statistical Abstract of the United States 2009* (Washington, D.C.: Government Printing Office, 2009), Tables 443 and 478.

devolution. In other states, services may deteriorate as the states use devolution as an opportunity to cut spending and reduce services. This has been the pattern in the implementation of the welfare reform passed in 1996, the most significant devolution of federal social programs in many decades. Some states, such as Wisconsin, have used the flexibility of the reform to design innovative programs that respond to clients' needs; other states, such as Idaho, have virtually dismantled their welfare programs. Because the legislation placed a five-year lifetime limit on receiving welfare, the states will take on an even greater role in the future as existing clients lose their eligibility for federal benefits. Welfare reform has been praised by many for reducing welfare rolls and responding to the public desire that welfare be a temporary program. At the same time, it has placed more low-income women and their children at risk of being left with no form of assistance at all.

This variation is the dilemma that devolution poses. Up to a point, variation can be considered one of the virtues of federalism. But in a democracy dangers are inherent in large variations in the provision of services and benefits.

Privatization

Privatization, another downsizing option, seems like a synonym for termination, but that is true only at the extreme. Most of what is called privatization is not termination at all but the provision of government goods and services by private contractors under direct government supervision. Except for top-secret strategic materials, virtually all of the production of military hardware, from boats to bullets, is done on a privatized basis by private contractors. Billions of dollars of research services are bought under contract by governments; these private contractors are universities as well as ordinary industrial corporations and private think tanks. **Privatization** simply means that a public purpose is provided under contract by a private company.[27] But such programs are still very much government programs; they are paid for by government and supervised by government. Privatization downsizes the government only in that the workers providing the service are no longer counted as part of the government bureaucracy.

privatization The act of moving all or part of a program from the public sector to the private sector.

The central aim of privatization is to reduce the cost of government. When private contractors can perform a task as well as a government but for less money, taxpayers win. Government workers are generally unionized and, therefore, receive good pay and generous benefits. Private-sector workers are less likely to be unionized, and private firms often provide lower pay and fewer benefits. For this reason, public-sector unions have been one of the strongest voices arguing against privatization. Other critics of privatization observe that private firms may not be more efficient or less costly than government. This is especially likely when there is little competition among private firms and public bureaucracies are not granted a fair chance to bid in the contracting competition. When private firms have a monopoly on service provision, they may be more expensive than government.

There are important questions about how private contractors can be held accountable. As one analyst of Pentagon spending put it, "The Pentagon is supposed to be representing the taxpayer and the public interest—its national security. So it's really important to have transparency, to be able to see these competitions and hold people accountable."[28] As security has become the nation's paramount concern, new worries about privatization have surfaced. Some Pentagon officials fear that too many tasks vital to national security may have already been contracted out and that national security might best be served by limiting privatization.

The new demands of domestic security have altered the thrust of bureaucratic reform. The emphasis on reducing the size of government that was so prominent during the previous two decades is gone. Instead, there is an acceptance of the idea that the federal government will grow as needed to ensure the safety of American citizens. The administration's security effort, focusing the entire federal bureaucracy on a single central mission, will require unprecedented levels of coordination

---

[27] A more general term is *outsourcing*. Privatization is outsourcing to the private sector. Devolution is outsourcing to a lower level of government. A third example is the opposite of devolution, as when a small community contracts with a county for, say, police services.

[28] Ellen Nakashima, "Defense Balks at Contract Goals: Essential Services Should Not Be Privatized, Pentagon Tells OMB," *Washington Post*, January 30, 2002, p. A21.

among federal agencies. Despite the strong agreement on the goal of fighting terrorism, the effort to streamline the bureaucracy by focusing on a single purpose is likely to face considerable obstacles along the way. Reform of public bureaucracies is always complex because strong constituencies may attempt to block changes that they believe will harm them. Initiatives that aim to improve coordination among agencies can easily provoke political disputes if the proposed changes threaten to alter the access of groups to the bureaucracy. And groups that oppose bureaucratic changes can appeal to Congress to intervene on their behalf.

CONCLUSION

Bureaucracy is one of humanity's most significant inventions. It is an institutional arrangement that employs both division and specialization of labor, harnesses expertise, and coordinates collective action for social, political, and economic purposes. It enables governments to exist and perform. In this chapter, we have focused on what public bureaucracies do, how they are organized at the national level in the United States, and how they are controlled (or not) by elected politicians.

At a theoretical level, public bureaucracy is the concrete expression of rational, purposeful, political action. Elected politicians have goals—as broad as defending the realm, maintaining public health and safety, or promoting economic growth; as narrow as securing a post office for Possum Hollow, Pennsylvania, or an exit off the interstate highway for Springfield, Massachusetts. Bureaucracy is the instrument by which political objectives, established by elected legislators and executives, are transformed from ideas, concepts, and intentions into the actual "bricks and mortar" of implemented policies.

At a practical level, this transformation depends upon the motivations of bureaucratic agents and the institutional machinery created when a bureaucratic entity is formed or reformed. Elected politicians engage in institutional design in creating agencies. They have their greatest impact at this point. Once an agency is up and running, elected officials only imperfectly control their bureaucratic agents. Institutional arrangements, and simple human nature, provide a certain amount of insulation to agencies, enabling bureaucrats to march to their own drummers, at least some of the time. Of course, bureaucrats are not entirely free agents. But control is a constant and recurring problem for elected officials.

The policy principle suggests that the combination of bureaucratic arrangements and individual motivations produce evident patterns in policy. Because of its insulation, an agency's policies, once underway, are difficult to reverse. Insulation thwarts only but the most intensely expressed interventions in the affairs of an agency. This has the benefit of commitment—interested parties are reassured about the continued provision of a bureaucratic product or service. The farmer can rely on his subsidy check; the senior citizen can count on her monthly Social Security stipend; truckers and other motorists can be secure in the expectation that the interstate highways will be there for them.

But it has distributive costs. Bureaucrats will be most attentive to the most intense interested parties. As a consequence, policies will come to be skewed in particular ways. The efficiency gains that come from the expertise and coordinating services of bureaucracy are thus dissipated by these political pressures. For example, highway funds will find their way disproportionately to the states and districts of legislators who sit on the public works authorizing and appropriating committees. For the last quarter century, until 2009, Alaska was a major beneficiary of infrastructure expenditures precisely because one of its senators (Ted Stevens) and its lone representative (Don Young) were powerhouses in their respective legislative chambers.

In describing the federal bureaucracy in this chapter, we hope we have made clear the ways in which rationality, institutional ways of doing things, and the resulting policy outputs are a consequence of the way in which agencies straddle the divide produced by the separation of powers. Attuned partly to the executive and partly to the legislature, bureaucratic agents tread a careful line between their several masters, protected in part by the natural insulation associated with bureaucracy but vulnerable to intense political pressure. Politics is at the very heart of these organizations and the policies they produce.

FOR FURTHER READING

Aberbach, Joel, and Bert A. Rockman. *In the Web of Politics: Three Decades of the U.S. Federal Executive.* Washington, D.C.: Brookings Institution, 2000.

Besley, Timothy. *Principled Agents? Motivations and Incentives in Politics.* Oxford: Oxford University Press, 2006.

Brehm, John, and Scott Gates. *Working, Shirking, and Sabotage: Bureaucratic Response to a Democratic Public.* Ann Arbor: University of Michigan Press, 1997.

Downs, Anthony. *Inside Bureaucracy.* Boston: Little, Brown, 1966.

Esman, Milton J. *Government Works: Why Americans Need the Feds.* Ithaca, N.Y.: Cornell University Press, 2000.

Fiorina, Morris P. "Legislative Choice of Regulatory Forms: Legal Process or Administrative Process." *Public Choice* 39 (1982): 33–66.

Goodsell, Charles. *The Case for Bureaucracy.* 4th ed. Washington, D.C.: Congressional Quarterly Press, 2003.

Heclo, Hugh. *On Thinking Institutionally.* Boulder, Colo.: Paradigm, 2007.

Huber, John, and Charles Shipan. *Deliberate Discretion? The Institutional Foundations of Bureaucratic Autonomy.* New York: Cambridge University Press, 2002.

Kerwin, Cornelius M. *Rulemaking.* 3rd ed. Washington, D.C.: Congressional Quarterly Press, 2003.

Kettl, Donald F., and James Fesler. *The Politics of the Administrative Process.* 3rd ed. Washington, D.C.: Brookings Institution, 2005.

Light, Paul C. *The True Size of Government*. Washington, D.C.: Brookings Institution, 1999.

McCubbins, Mathew, Roger Noll, and Barry Weingast. "Structure and Process; Politics and Policy: Administrative Arrangements and the Political Control of Agencies." *Virginia Law Review* 75 (1989): 431–82.

McCubbins, Mathew, and Thomas Schwartz. "Congressional Oversight Overlooked: Police reader selection
Patrols versus Fire Alarms." *American Journal of Political Science* 28 (1984): 165–79.

Meier, Kenneth J., and John Bohte. *Politics and the Bureaucracy*. 5th ed. Belmont, Calif.: Wadsworth, 2006.

Seidman, Harold. *Politics, Position, and Power: The Dynamics of Federal Organization*. 5th ed. New York: Oxford University Press, 1998.

Wilson, James Q. *Bureaucracy: What Government Agencies Do and Why They Do It*. New reader selection
York: Basic Books, 1989.

 Additional study and review materials are available online at wwnorton.com/studyspace/

8

The Federal Courts:
Structure and Strategies

Courts serve an essential and ancient function. When disputes arise, those involved need an impartial arbiter to help settle the matter. When laws must be enforced, justice requires an impartial judge to determine guilt and innocence and, if the accused is found guilty, the appropriate punishment. And when questions arise about the meaning of those laws, we rely on the wisdom of judges to divine what Congress meant and how that meaning applies in a given circumstance. It is not possible, or even wise, to pass a law to cover every contingency. Thus, nearly every nation today has established a system of courts to satisfy the need for an arbiter and interpreter.

A significant feature of the American judiciary is that it is independent, with powers to check Congress and the president. At the time of the Founding, this independence from the other branches of government was unique. The Constitution of the United States, as it was written and as it has evolved over time, sets up the system of courts as a separate entity from the legislature, the executive, and the states, and insulated from electoral politics. As we will see in this chapter, four important features of the institutions of the American Judiciary ensure a powerful, independent judiciary. First, the Constitution establishes the federal courts as a separate branch of government from Congress and the president. Second, authority among the courts is hierarchical, with federal courts able to overturn state courts and the United States Supreme Court the ultimate authority. Third, the U.S. Supreme Court and other federal courts of appeals can strike down actions of Congress, the president, or the states if the judges deem those acts to be violations of the constitution. This is the power of judicial review. And fourth, federal judges are appointed for life. Federal judges are not subject to the pressures of running for reelection and need not be highly responsive to changes in public opinion.[1]

---

[1] Judges in many state and local courts are elected.

An independent judiciary has been one of the most distinctive and successful institutions of the American government. It has settled constitutional crises, when Congress and the president are at odds. It has guaranteed that no person is above the law, even members of Congress and the president.[2] It has helped ensure that all people, even noncitizens, enjoy the equal protection of the laws. It has made it possible for small businesses, large corporations, and workers to engage in economic activities and agreements, knowing that their rights will be protected. It has even ensured that the democratic branches of government operate in a democratic manner and that every citizen's vote counts equally in the selection of the legislature. The cumulative effect of an independent judiciary has been a stable, successful democracy and economy.[3]

---

[2] The case of *United States v. Nixon* dealt head on with the question of whether President Nixon was beyond prosecution for alleged obstruction of justice in the case of the break-in at the Democratic Party headquarters in the Watergate hotel. See *United States v. Nixon*, 418 U.S. 683 (1974).

[3] Douglass C. North, *Institutions, Institutional Change, and Economic Performance* (New York: Cambridge University Press, 1990).

CORE OF THE ANALYSIS

- Just like presidents and legislators, judges have preferences about what government should do, and they use their powers to shape public policy.

- Judicial decisions are highly constrained by the past, in the form of common law and precedents, but every decision also contributes to the evolution of the law.

- The courts maintain their independence from the legislature and executive because federal judges are appointed for life and not elected. Independence allows the courts to act as a check on the democratically chosen branches of government, to protect individual rights.

- Courts can block or overturn political decisions of the legislature or executive if those decisions violate the constitution or conflict with other laws, a power called *judicial review.*

- However, the courts are also constrained by the checks and balances built into the institutional setting within which they operate.

The sources and nature of judicial power in American government are, however, quite subtle. The Constitution of the United States defines judicial power as primarily a negative power—the power to stop the actions of others or to decide between conflicting state laws. It says little about the normal operation of courts, except to empower the Congress to set up a federal judiciary. Courts lack Congress's power of the purse or the president's ability to move troops or to order other branches of the executive to act. Courts are also passive and must wait for people to file lawsuits in order to make any decisions or issue any decree. They lack the staff that the other branches have to conduct independent research or to launch their own investigations.

The real power of the courts emanates from their ability to interpret the meaning of the laws in a way that society accepts. Courts are powerful to the extent that the parties involved accept the decrees that judges issue. In nearly all cases, judges' edicts are ultimately accepted. However, if people ignored the decrees of judges in local courts or if Congress routinely passed legislation contradicting the U.S. Supreme Court, the judicial function in our society would vanish. Herein lies the ability of the judiciary not just to interpret but to make law. The decree of any one judge in any single case may not seem very important, but each decision or settlement in a court is an act of lawmaking, a function as important as the passage of a statute by the legislature. The accumulation of many such decisions, accepted by common practice, is eventually cited by others as the norm. It becomes part of the common law of the land.

Even though judges can influence the future, they are also greatly constrained by the past. Common law consists of all past agreements that we accept when we reach any decision. A contract for a real estate sale, for example, consists of many pages of language pertaining to the possible contingencies that might arise, what would happen in each case, and who would bear responsibility. Each clause has been developed through past legal decisions accumulated over centuries, indeed millennia, dating back in some instances to ancient Rome. The Supreme Court is similarly constrained by decisions that it has made in the past. When a majority of justices have issued an opinion interpreting the law a particular way, that opinion has the standing of precedent and constrains future courts. History matters more fundamentally for the judiciary than for the other branches of government, and its influence is instrumental to their success. If the judges themselves were to ignore precedent wholesale, they would undercut the power of the courts and their own authority.

The accumulation of centuries of legal agreements and precedents would seem to leave little leeway for innovation and change. Indeed, for much of U.S. history, the Supreme Court has appeared to act cautiously, so as to not overstep its bounds and the constraints of the past. But society changes, and the law and the courts must adapt. At times, the courts have made sweeping changes in the interpretation of American laws. With industrialization in the late nineteenth century came new ideas about the enforcement of contracts that dominated the thinking of the courts. The New Deal eventually won the support of the Supreme Court and with that a new acceptance of the role of government in the economy and society. The Great Society witnessed the expansion of individual rights, ranging from voting rights to the rights of the accused to rights of employment and education. And with the new technologies of the late twentieth and early twenty-first centuries came new thinking about the nature of property rights and constraints on the government. All of these eras in American legal thought have responded to great changes in our society and the need for the courts to interpret anew the meaning of the law.

The place of the judiciary in the American system of government points to a basic lesson about the U.S. courts and courts in general: they are fundamentally political. Just like presidents and legislators, judges have preferences about what the government should do, and they use their powers to interpret, apply, and review laws to shape public policy. Judges are also constrained by the institutional setting within which they operate. They are mindful that others in the political process may try to alter or undo a court's rulings.

The constraints of the U.S. political system and the weight of history and precedent can give the impression that courts are not powerful, or at least that they have little opportunity to shape public policy. But there are moments in American history when the judiciary's authority and political power are clearly evident. The most striking recent examples come from the years 1954 through 1967. During this era, the U.S. Supreme Court, under the leadership of Chief Justice Earl Warren, asserted new individual rights across a wide range of areas from education and employment to voting to sexual relations. These rulings shaped the way American society addressed a wide range of pressing social issues, such as race relations, family structures, and representation in the political arena. The tremendous changes in the Court's agenda and reach under Earl Warren demonstrate both the political importance and potential power of the judiciary in American politics.

In this chapter, we examine the judicial process first, including the types of cases that the federal courts consider and the types of laws with which they deal. Second, we assess the organization and structure of the federal court system and explain how judges are appointed to the courts. Third, we analyze courts as political institutions and consider their roles in the political system. Fourth, we consider judicial review and how it makes the Supreme Court a lawmaking body. Fifth, we examine the flow of cases through the courts and various influences on the Supreme Court's decisions. Finally, we analyze the process of judicial decision making and the power of the federal courts in the American political process, looking in particular at the growth of judicial power in the United States.

THE JUDICIAL PROCESS

Originally a court was the place where a sovereign ruled—where a king and his entourage governed. Judging—settling disputes between citizens—was part of governing. Over time, however, the function of settling disputes was slowly separated from the king and the king's court and made into a separate institution of government. Courts have taken over from kings the power to settle controversies by hearing the facts on both sides and deciding which side possesses the greater merit. But because judges are not kings, they must have a basis for their authority. That basis in the United States is the Constitution and the law. Courts decide cases by applying the relevant law or principle to the facts.

Court cases in the United States proceed under two broad categories of law: criminal and civil. One form of civil law, public law, is so important that we consider it as a separate category (Table 8.1).

criminal law The branch of law that deals with disputes or actions involving criminal penalties (as opposed to civil law).

Cases of **criminal law** are those in which the government charges an individual with violating a statute that has been enacted to protect the public health, safety, morals, or welfare. In criminal cases, the government is always the plaintiff (the party that brings charges) and alleges that a criminal violation has been committed by a named defendant. Most criminal cases arise in state and municipal courts and involve matters ranging from traffic offenses to robbery and murder. Although the great bulk of criminal law is still a state matter, a large and growing body of federal criminal law deals with such matters as tax evasion, mail fraud, and the sale of narcotics. Defendants found guilty of criminal violations may be fined or sent to prison.

civil law A system of jurisprudence, including private law and governmental action, for settling disputes that do not involve criminal penalties.

Cases of **civil law** involve disputes between individuals or between individuals and the government where no criminal violation is charged. Unlike criminal cases, the losers in civil cases cannot be fined or sent to prison, although they may be required to pay monetary damages for their actions. In a civil case, the one who brings a complaint is the plaintiff and the one against whom the complaint is brought is the defendant. The two most common types of civil cases involve contracts and torts. In a typical contract case, an individual or corporation charges that it has suffered because of another's violation of a specific agreement between the two. For example, the Smith Manufacturing Corporation may charge that Jones Distributors failed to honor an agreement to deliver raw materials at a specified time, causing Smith to lose business. Smith asks the court to order Jones to compensate it for the damage allegedly suffered. In a typical tort case, one individual charges that he or she has been injured by another's negligence or malfeasance. Medical malpractice suits are one example of tort cases.

TABLE 8.1 TYPES OF LAWS AND DISPUTES

Type of Law	Type of Case or Dispute	Form of Citation
Criminal law	Cases arising out of actions that violate laws protecting the health, safety, and morals of the community. The government is always the plaintiff.	*U.S. (or state) v. Jones* *Jones v. U.S. (or state)* if Jones lost and is appealing
Civil law	Law involving disputes between citizens or between a government and a citizen where no crime is alleged. Two general types are contract law and tort law. Contract cases are disputes that arise over voluntary actions. Tort cases are disputes that arise out of obligations inherent in social life. Negligence and slander are examples of torts.	*Smith v. Jones* *New York v. Jones* *U.S. v. Jones* *Jones v. New York*
Public law	All cases in which the powers of government or the rights of citizens are involved. The government is the defendant. Constitutional law involves judicial review of the basis of a government's action in relation to specific clauses of the Constitution as interpreted in Supreme Court cases. Administrative law involves disputes over the statutory authority, jurisdiction, or procedures of administrative agencies.	*Jones v. U.S. (or state)* *In re Jones* *Smith v. Jones* if a license or statute is at issue in their private dispute

precedents Prior cases whose principles are used by judges as the bases for their decisions in present cases.

stare decisis Literally, "let the decision stand." The doctrine whereby a previous decision by a court applies as a precedent in similar cases until that decision is overruled.

public law Cases involving the action of public agencies or officials.

In deciding cases, courts apply statutes (laws) and legal **precedents** (prior decisions). State and federal statutes often govern the conditions under which contracts are and are not legally binding. Jones Distributors might argue that it was not obliged to fulfill its contract with the Smith Corporation because actions by Smith—the failure to make promised payments—constituted fraud under state law. Attorneys for a physician being sued for malpractice, on the other hand, may search for prior instances in which courts ruled that actions similar to those of their client did not constitute negligence. Such precedents are applied under the doctrine of *stare decisis*, a Latin phrase meaning "let the decision stand."

A case becomes a matter of a third category, **public law**, when a plaintiff or defendant in a civil or criminal case seeks to show that his or her case involves the powers of government or the rights of citizens as defined under the Constitution or by statute. One major form of public law is constitutional law, under which a court will examine the government's actions to see if they conform to the Constitution as it has been interpreted by the judiciary. Thus what began as an ordinary criminal case may enter the realm of public law if a defendant claims that his or her constitutional rights were violated by the police. Another important arena of public law is administrative law, which involves disputes over the jurisdiction, procedures, or authority of administrative agencies. Under this type of law, civil litigation between an individual and the government may become a matter of public law if the individual asserts that the government is violating a statute or abusing its power under the Constitution. For example, landowners have asserted that federal and state restrictions on land use constitute violations of the Fifth Amendment's restrictions on the government's ability to confiscate private property. Recently the Supreme Court has been very sympathetic to such claims, which effectively transform an ordinary civil dispute into a major issue of public law.

Most of the Supreme Court cases we will examine in this chapter involve judgments concerning the constitutional or statutory basis of the actions of government agencies. As we shall see, it is in this arena of public law that Court decisions can have significant consequences for American politics and society.

THE ORGANIZATION OF THE COURT SYSTEM

Types of Courts

In the United States, systems of courts have been established both by the federal government and by the governments of the individual states. Both systems have several levels, as shown in Figure 8.1. Nearly 99 percent of all court cases in the United States are heard in state courts. The overwhelming majority of criminal cases, for example, involve violations of state laws prohibiting such actions as murder, robbery, fraud, theft, and assault. If such a case is brought to trial, it will be heard in a state **trial court** in front of a judge and sometimes a jury, who will determine whether the defendant violated state law. If the defendant is convicted, he or she may appeal the conviction to a higher court, such as a state **court of appeals**, and from there to a state's **supreme court**. Similarly, in civil cases, most litigation is brought in the courts established by the state in which the activity in question took place. For example, a patient bringing suit against a physician for malpractice would file the suit in the appropriate court in the state where the alleged malpractice occurred. The judge hearing the case would apply state law and state precedent to the matter at hand. (It should be noted that in both criminal and civil matters, most cases are settled before trial through negotiated agreements between the parties. In criminal cases, these agreements are called plea bargains. Such bargains may affect the severity of the charge and/or the severity of the sentence.)

In addition, the U.S. military operates its own court system under the Uniform Code of Military Justice, which governs the behavior of men and women in the armed services. On rare occasions, the government has constituted special military

trial court
The first court to hear a criminal or civil case.

court of appeals (or appellate court) A court that hears the appeals of trial-court decisions.

supreme court
The highest court in a particular state or in the United States. This court primarily serves an appellate function.

FIGURE 8.1 THE U.S. COURT SYSTEM

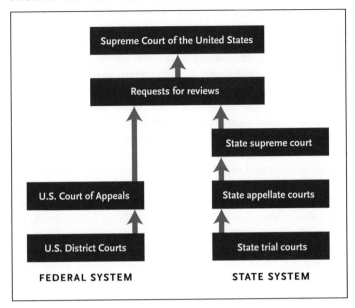

tribunals to hear cases deemed inappropriate for the civil courts. Such tribunals tried Nazi saboteurs apprehended in the United States during World War II. More recently, President George W. Bush ordered the creation of military tribunals to try individuals suspected of acts of terrorism against the United States.

Federal Jurisdiction

Cases are heard in the federal courts if they involve federal laws, treaties with other nations, or the U.S. Constitution; these areas are the official jurisdiction of the federal courts. In addition, any case in which the U.S. government is a party is heard in the federal courts. If, for example, an individual is charged with violating a federal criminal statute, such as evading the payment of income taxes, charges would be brought before a federal judge by a federal prosecutor. Civil cases involving the citizens of more than one state and in which more than $70,000 is at stake may be heard in either the federal or the state courts, usually depending on the preference of the plaintiff.

But even if a matter belongs in federal court, how do we know which federal court should exercise jurisdiction over the case? The answer to this seemingly simple question is somewhat complex. The jurisdiction of each federal court is derived from the U.S. Constitution and federal statutes. Article III of the Constitution gives the Supreme Court appellate jurisdiction in all federal cases and original jurisdiction in cases involving foreign ambassadors and issues in which a state is a party. Article III assigns original jurisdiction in all other federal cases to the lower courts that Congress was authorized to establish. Over the years, as Congress enacted statutes creating the federal judicial system, it specified the jurisdiction of each type of court it established. For the most part, Congress has assigned jurisdictions on the basis of geography. The nation is currently, by statute, divided into ninety-four judicial districts, including one court for each of three U.S. territories: Guam, the U.S. Virgin Islands, and the Northern Marianas. Each of the ninety-four U.S. district courts exercises jurisdiction over federal cases arising within its territorial domain. The judicial districts are, in turn, organized into eleven regional circuits and the District of Columbia circuit (Figure 8.2). Each circuit court exercises appellate jurisdiction over cases heard by the district courts within its region.

Geography is not the only basis for federal court jurisdiction. Congress has also established several specialized courts that have nationwide original jurisdiction in certain types of cases. These include the U.S. Court of International Trade, created to deal with trade and customs issues, and the U.S. Court of Federal Claims, which handles damage suits against the United States. Congress has, in addition, established a court with nationwide appellate jurisdiction. This is the U.S. Court of Appeals for the Federal Circuit, which hears appeals involving patent law and those arising from the decisions of the trade and claims courts. Other federal courts assigned specialized jurisdictions by Congress include the U.S. Court of Appeals for Veterans Claims, which exercises exclusive jurisdiction over cases involving veterans' claims, and the U.S. Court of Appeals for the Armed Forces, which deals with questions of law arising from trials by court-martial.

FIGURE 8.2 GEOGRAPHIC BOUNDARIES OF U.S. COURTS OF APPEALS AND U.S. DISTRICT COURTS

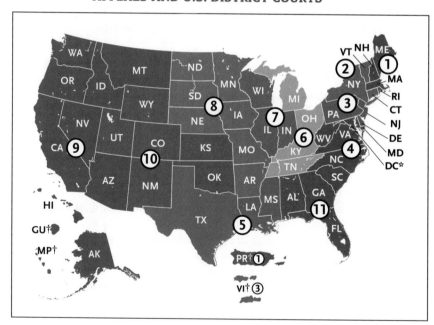

* The District of Columbia has its own circuit, called the D.C. Circuit.

† U.S. Postal Service abbreviations for Guam (GU), Northern Mariana Islands (MP), Puerto Rico (PR), and the U.S. Virgin Islands (VI).

SOURCE: Administrative Office of the U.S. Courts, www.uscourts.gov/images/CircuitMap.pdf.

With the exception of the claims court and the Court of Appeals for the Federal Circuit, these specialized courts were created not in accordance with Article III of the Constitution but by Congress on the basis of the powers the legislature exercises under Article I. Article III was designed to protect judges from political pressure by granting them life tenure and prohibiting reduction of their salaries while they serve. The judges of Article I courts, by contrast, are appointed by the president for fixed terms of fifteen years and are not protected by the Constitution from salary reduction. As a result, these so-called legislative courts are generally viewed as less independent than the courts established under Article III of the Constitution. The three territorial courts were also established under Article I, and their judges are appointed for ten-year terms.

The appellate jurisdiction of the federal courts also extends to cases originating in the state courts. In both civil and criminal cases, a decision of the highest state court can be appealed to the U.S. Supreme Court by raising a federal issue. Appellants might assert, for example, that they were denied the right to counsel or otherwise deprived of the **due process** guaranteed by the federal Constitution, or they might assert that important issues of federal law were at stake in the case. The U.S. Supreme Court is not obligated to accept such appeals and will accept them only if it believes that the matter has considerable national significance. (We shall return to this topic later in this chapter.) In addition, in criminal cases defendants who have been convicted in a state court may request a **writ of *habeas corpus*** from a federal district court. Sometimes known as the Great Writ, *habeas corpus* is a court order to the authorities to release a prisoner deemed to be held in violation of his or her legal rights. In 1867, its distrust of southern courts led Congress to authorize federal district judges to issue such writs to prisoners they believed had been deprived of their constitutional rights in state court. Generally speaking, state defendants seeking a federal writ of *habeas corpus* must show that they have exhausted all available state remedies and raise issues not previously raised in their state appeals. Federal courts of appeals and, ultimately, the U.S. Supreme Court have appellate jurisdiction over federal district court *habeas* decisions.

Over the past three decades, the caseload of the federal courts has nearly quadrupled, to nearly 350,000 cases a year. This has come about because Congress has greatly expanded the number of federal crimes, particularly in the realm of drug possession and sale. Behavior that was once exclusively a state criminal matter has, to some extent, come within the reach of federal law. In 1999, Chief Justice William Rehnquist criticized Congress for federalizing too many offenses and intruding unnecessarily into areas that should be handled by the states.[4] About 80 percent of federal cases end in the district courts, and the remainder are appealed to the circuit courts. In the past five years, moreover, between 8,500 and 9,500 circuit court decisions per year were appealed to the Supreme Court. Most of the cases filed with the Supreme Court are dismissed without a ruling on their merits. The Court has broad latitude to decide what cases it will hear and generally

due process
The guarantee that no citizen may be subjected to arbitrary action by national or state government.

writ of *habeas corpus* A court order demanding that an individual in custody be brought into court and shown the cause for detention. *Habeas corpus* is guranteed by the Constitution and can be suspended only in cases of rebellion or invasion.

---

[4] Roberto Suro, "Rehnquist: Too Many Offenses Are Becoming Federal Crimes," *Washington Post*, January 1, 1999, p. A2.

listens only to those it deems to raise the most important issues. Thus in the last five years, between 84 and 91 cases per year were given full-dress Supreme Court review (the nine justices actually sitting *en banc*—in full court—and hearing lawyers argue the case).[5]

Even seemingly unimportant events can raise fundamental questions of law, such as when the First Amendment protects speech. The case of *Morse v. Frederick*, although not the most serious matter facing the nation, exemplifies the appellate process at work in the United States. On January 24, 2002, the Olympic torch relay passed through Juneau, Alaska, on its way to Salt Lake City and the winter games. The parade, to be carried on local television, passed immediately in front of Juneau-Douglas High School. The high school's principal Deborah Morse, decided to allow staff and students to cheer on the relay as it paraded down the street in front of the high school. As the torch relay passed by the school, Joseph Frederick, a senior, and several of his friends unfurled a fourteen-foot banner that read BONG HiTS 4 JESUS. Principal Morse promptly confiscated the banner and later suspended Frederick for ten days for promoting illegal drug use at a school-sponsored event. Frederick appealed his suspension to the Juneau School Committee. The expression BongHits4Jesus, he argued, did not advocate drug use. It was a meaningless phrase that merely attracted the attention of the television cameras. The school committee was not sympathetic.

Frederick felt that his right to free speech under the First Amendment was violated. He went to court. The federal district court ruled that the school committee had qualified immunity from the First Amendment. Frederick pushed his appeal onward and won. The Ninth Circuit Court of Appeals ruled that "a school cannot censor or punish students' speech merely because the students advocate a position contrary to government policy." The school committee did not let the matter end there. It appealed the circuit court's ruling to the United States Supreme Court, which in the U.S. system has the last say. The Court agreed to hear the case because it raised interesting legal questions about the reach of the First Amendment. Citing a 1969 "school speech" decision involving antiwar protests, a majority of the justices ruled in favor of Principal Morse and the school committee. "Schools may reasonably take steps to safeguard those entrusted to their care from speech that can reasonably be regarded as encouraging illegal drug use," Chief Justice Roberts wrote for the majority.[6]

Although the federal courts hear only a small fraction of all the civil and criminal cases decided each year in the United States, their decisions are extremely important. (See Table 8.2.) It is in the federal courts that the Constitution and federal laws that govern all Americans are interpreted and their meaning and significance established. Moreover, it is in the federal courts that the powers and limitations of the increasingly powerful national government are tested. Finally, through their power to review the decisions of the state courts, it is ultimately the federal courts that dominate the American judicial system.

---

[5] Administrative Office of the U.S. Courts, 2006, www.uscourts.gov/adminoff.html.

[6] *Mouse v. Frederick*, 551 U.S. 393 (2007).

TABLE 8.2 LANDMARK COURT CASES

Not all cases and decisions are equally important. "Landmark" cases are decisions that revolutionize an area of law and announce new legal standards or have far-reaching political consequences. Here are some of the more significant decisions made by the U.S. Supreme Court.

Marbury v. Madison (1804). The Court declared part of the Judiciary Act unconstitutional, establishing judicial review.

McCulloch v. Maryland (1819). The Supreme Court justified the "implied powers" of the government under the Constitution, enabling Congress and the president to assert their authority beyond those activities explicitly mentioned in the Constitution.

Gibbons v. Ogden (1824). This decision establishes the supremacy of the federal government over the states in the regulation of commerce so as to create uniform business law.

Dred Scott v. Sandford (1857). The Court declared that people of African origin brought to the United States as part of the slave trade were not given the rights of citizenship under the Constitution and could, therefore, claim none of the rights and privileges that the Constitution provides.

Plessy v. Ferguson (1896). The Court interpreted the post–Civil War amendments to the Constitution in such a way as to allow segregation, so long as facilities were "separate but equal."

Lochner v. New York (1905). The Court established a general right to enter freely into contracts as part of business, including the right to purchase and sell labor. The decision made it more difficult for unions to form.

Schenck v. United States (1919). The Court declared that the right to free speech does not extend to words that are "used in such circumstances and are of such a nature as to create a clear and present danger."

Korematsu v. United States (1944). The Court allowed the United States government to intern Japanese-Americans in concentration camps during World War II as a safeguard against insurrection or spying.

Brown v. Board of Education (1954). The Court ruled that separate educational facilities could not be equal, overturning *Plessy*, and ordering an end to segregation "with all deliberate speed."

Baker v. Carr (1962). The justices established that the Court had the authority to hear cases involving legislative districting, even though that is a "political matter," ultimately guaranteeing equal representation in the state legislatures and the U.S. House of Representatives.

Mapp v. Ohio (1961). The Court ruled that all evidence obtained by searches and seizures in violation of the federal Constitution is inadmissible in a court of law.

Griswold v. Connecticut (1965). The Court struck down a Connecticut law prohibiting counseling on the use of contraceptives, and declared that the Bill of Rights implied a right to privacy.

Roe v. Wade (1973). The Court held that a mother may abort her baby for any reason up to the point that the fetus becomes "viable," and that any law passed by a state or Congress inconsistent with this holding violated the right to privacy and the right to enter freely into contracts.

Kelo v. City of New London (2005). The Court upheld the power of local government to seize property for economic development.

Boumediene v. Bush (2008). The Court declared that foreign terrorism suspects have the constitutional right to challenge their detention (using the writ of *habeas corpus*) at the Guantánamo Bay naval base in U.S. courts, even though the detainees are not citizens.

Federal Trial Courts

The federal district courts are trial courts of general jurisdiction, and their cases are, in form, indistinguishable from cases in the state trial courts.

There are eighty-nine district courts in the fifty states, one each in the District of Columbia and Puerto Rico, and one in each of the three U.S. territories. There are 663 district judgeships. District judges are assigned to district courts according to the workload; the busiest of these courts may have as many as 28 judges. Only one judge is assigned to each case, except where statutes provide for three-judge courts to deal with special issues. The routines and procedures of the federal district courts are essentially the same as those of the lower state courts except that federal procedural requirements tend to be stricter. States, for example, do not have to provide a grand jury, a twelve-member trial jury, or an unanimous jury verdict. Federal courts must provide all these things. As we saw above, in addition to the district courts, cases are handled by several specialized courts, including the U.S. Tax Court, the Court of Federal Claims, and the Court of International Trade.

Federal Appellate Courts

Roughly 20 percent of all lower-court cases, along with appeals of some federal agency decisions, are subsequently reviewed by a federal appeals court. As noted, the country is divided into twelve judicial circuits, each with a U.S. Court of Appeals. Every state and the District of Columbia are assigned to the circuit in the continental United States that is closest to it. A thirteenth appellate court, the U.S. Court of Appeals for the Federal Circuit, is defined by subject matter (patent law and decisions of trade and claims courts) rather than geographic jurisdiction.

Except for cases selected for review by the Supreme Court, decisions made by the appeals courts are final. Because of this finality, certain safeguards have been built into the system. The most important is the provision of more than one judge for every appeals case. Each court of appeals has from three to twenty-eight permanent judgeships, depending on the workload of the circuit. Although normally three judges hear appealed cases, in some instances a larger number of judges sit together *en banc.*

Another safeguard is provided by the assignment of a Supreme Court justice as the circuit justice for each of the twelve circuits. The circuit justice deals with requests for special action by the Supreme Court. The most frequent and best-known action of circuit justices is that of reviewing requests for stays of execution when the full Court is unable to do so—mainly during the summer, when the Court is in recess.

The Supreme Court

The Supreme Court is America's highest court. Article III of the Constitution vests "the judicial Power of the United States" in the Supreme Court, and this court is supreme in fact as well as form. The Supreme Court is made up of a chief justice and eight associate justices. The **chief justice** presides over the Court's public sessions and conferences. In the Court's actual deliberations and decisions, however, the chief justice has no more authority than his colleagues. Each justice casts one

chief justice
The justice on the Supreme Court who presides over the Court's public sessions.

vote. The chief justice, though, is always the first to speak and the last to vote when the justices deliberate. In addition, if the chief justice has voted with the majority, he decides which of the justices will write the formal opinion for the Court. To some extent, the influence of the chief justice is a function of his leadership ability. Some chief justices, such as Earl Warren, have been able to lead the court in a new direction. In other instances, a forceful associate justice, such as Felix Frankfurter, is the dominant figure on the Court.

The Constitution does not specify the number of justices that should sit on the Supreme Court; Congress has the authority to change the Court's size. In the early nineteenth century, there were six Supreme Court justices; later there were seven. Congress set the number of justices at nine in 1869, and the Court has remained that size ever since. In 1937, President Franklin D. Roosevelt, infuriated by several Supreme Court decisions that struck down New Deal programs, asked Congress to enlarge the Court so that he could add sympathetic justices to the bench. Although Congress balked at Roosevelt's "Court-packing" plan, the Court gave in to FDR's pressure and began to take a more favorable view of his policy initiatives. The president, in turn, dropped his efforts to enlarge the Court. The Court's surrender to FDR came to be known as "the switch in time that saved nine."[7]

How Judges Are Appointed

Federal judges are appointed by the president and are generally selected from the more prominent or politically active members of the legal profession. Many federal judges previously served as state court judges or state or local prosecutors. Before the president formally nominates a candidate for a district judgeship, however, the senators from the nominee's state must indicate that they support him or her. This is an informal but seldom violated practice called **senatorial courtesy**. If one or both senators from a prospective nominee's home state belong to the president's political party, the president will almost invariably consult them and secure their blessing for the nomination. Because the president's party in the Senate will rarely support a nominee opposed by a home-state senator from their ranks, this arrangement gives these senators virtual veto power over appointments to the federal bench in their own states. Senators often see such a nomination as a way to reward important allies and contributors in their states. If the state has no senator from the president's party, the governor or members of the state's House delegation may make suggestions. In general, presidents endeavor to appoint judges who possess legal experience and good character and whose partisan and ideological views are similar to theirs. During the presidencies of Richard Nixon, Ronald Reagan, George H. W. Bush, and George W. Bush, most federal judicial appointees were conservative Republicans. Bill Clinton's appointees to the federal bench, on the other hand, tended to be liberal Democrats. Following the example of Jimmy Carter, Clinton also made a major effort to appoint women and African Americans to the federal courts. Nearly half his nominees were drawn from these groups.

senatorial courtesy The practice whereby the president, before formally nominating a person for a federal judgeship, finds out whether the senators from the candidate's state support the nomination.

---

[7] For an alternative view, see David R. Mayhew, "Supermajority Rule in the Senate," *PS: Political Science and Politics* 36 (2003): 31–36.

Once the president has formally nominated an individual, the nominee must be considered by the Senate Judiciary Committee and confirmed by a majority vote in the full Senate. In recent years, the Senate Judiciary Committee has sought to signal the president when it has qualms about a judicial nomination. After the Republicans won control of the Senate in 1994, for example, the Judiciary Committee chair, Orrin Hatch of Utah, let President Clinton know that he considered two of the president's nominees to be too liberal. The president withdrew the nominations.

Federal appeals court nominations follow much the same pattern. Because appeals court judges preside over jurisdictions that include several states, however, senators do not have so strong a role in proposing potential candidates. Instead, potential candidates are generally suggested to the president by the Justice Department or by members of the administration. The senators from the nominee's state are still consulted before the president formally acts.

During President George W. Bush's first two years in office, Democrats controlled the Senate and used their majority on the Judiciary Committee to block eight of the president's first eleven federal court nominations. After the GOP won a narrow Senate majority in the 2002 national elections, Democrats used a filibuster to block action on several other federal appeals court nominees. Both Democrats and Republicans saw struggles over lower-court slots as practice and preparation for all-out partisan warfare over the next Supreme Court vacancy. President Bush occasionally followed a successful strategy when nominees were victimized by partisan fighting. Instead of withdrawing a nominee blocked by Democrats in the Senate, he waited until the Senate was in recess and then appointed the nominee provisionally, the appointment lasting until the end of the Congress. The appointment then terminated unless the president resubmitted the nomination.

If political factors play an important role in the selection of district and appellate court judges, they are decisive when it comes to Supreme Court appointments. Because the high court has so much influence over American law and politics, virtually all presidents have made an effort to select justices who share their own political philosophy. Presidents Ronald Reagan and George H. W. Bush, for example, appointed five justices whom they believed to have conservative perspectives: Sandra Day O'Connor, Antonin Scalia, Anthony Kennedy, David Souter, and Clarence Thomas. Reagan also elevated William Rehnquist to the position of chief justice. Reagan and George H. W. Bush sought appointees who believed in reducing government intervention in the economy and supported the moral positions taken by the Republican Party in recent years, particularly opposition to abortion. However, not all the Reagan and Bush appointees fulfilled their sponsors' expectations. David Souter, for example, appointed by President George H. W. Bush, was attacked by conservatives as a turncoat for his decisions on school prayer and abortion rights. Nevertheless, through their appointments, Reagan and George H. W. Bush were able to create a far more conservative Supreme Court. For his part, President Clinton endeavored to appoint liberal justices. He named Ruth Bader Ginsburg and Stephen Breyer to the Court, hoping to counteract the influence of the Reagan and Bush appointees.

In 2005, President George W. Bush was given an opportunity to put his own stamp on the Supreme Court after Justice O'Connor announced her decision to

TABLE 8.3 SUPREME COURT JUSTICES, 2009

Name	Year of Birth	Prior Experience	President Who Made the Appointment	Year of Appointment
John G. Roberts, Jr., *Chief Justice*	1955	Federal judge	G. W. Bush	2005
Antonin Scalia	1936	Federal judge	Reagan	1986
Anthony M. Kennedy	1936	Federal judge	Reagan	1988
Clarence Thomas	1948	Federal judge	G. H. W. Bush	1991
Ruth Bader Ginsburg	1933	Federal judge	Clinton	1993
Stephen G. Breyer	1938	Federal judge	Clinton	1994
Samuel A. Alito, Jr.	1950	Federal judge	G. W. Bush	2006
Sonia Sotomayor	1954	Federal judge	Obama	2009
Elena Kagan	1960	Solicitor General	Obama	2010

retire and Chief Justice Rehnquist died (Table 8.3). Bush quickly nominated the federal appeals court judge John Roberts, initially to replace O'Connor and then as Chief Justice after Rehnquist's death. Roberts, a moderate conservative with a brilliant legal record, provoked some Democratic opposition but was confirmed without much difficulty. Bush's next nominee, though, sparked an intense battle within the president's party. To the surprise of most observers, the president named a long-time associate, White House counsel Harriet Miers, to replace O'Connor. Many Republicans viewed Miers as merely a Bush crony who lacked judicial qualifications and was insufficiently supportive of conservative causes. Opposition to Miers within the GOP was so intense that Democrats remained gleefully silent as the president was forced to allow her to withdraw her name from consideration. In the wake of the Miers debacle, President Bush turned to a more conventional nominee, the federal appeals court judge Samuel Alito, who pleased conservative Republicans. Democrats and liberal political forces attempted to block the nomination but ultimately failed, and Alito was confirmed in February 2006. Barack Obama's nominations of Sonia Sotomayor and Elena Kagan to the Court were easily approved, despite Republican criticisms, thanks to a strong Democratic majority in the Senate.

Typically in recent years, after the president has named a nominee, interest groups opposed to the nomination have mobilized opposition in the media, the public, and the Senate. When former president Bush proposed the conservative judge Clarence Thomas in 1991, for example, liberal groups launched a campaign to discredit the nominee. After extensive research into his background, opponents of the nomination were able to produce evidence suggesting that Thomas had sexually harassed a former subordinate, Anita Hill, a charge Thomas steadfastly denied. After contentious Senate Judiciary Committee hearings, highlighted by testimony by Thomas and Hill, Thomas narrowly won confirmation.

Likewise, conservative interest groups carefully scrutinized Bill Clinton's more liberal nominees, hoping to find information about them that would sabotage their appointments. During his two opportunities to name Supreme Court justices, Clinton was compelled to drop several potential appointees because of information unearthed by political opponents.

The matter of judicial appointments became an important issue in the 2000 and 2004 elections. Democrats charged that if he were elected president, George W. Bush would appoint conservative judges who might, among other things, reverse the *Roe v. Wade* decision[8] and curb abortion rights. Bush would say only that he would seek judges who would uphold the Constitution without reading their own political biases into the document.

These struggles over judicial appointments indicate the growing intensity of partisanship in the United States today. They also indicate how much importance competing political forces attach to Supreme Court appointments. Because the contending forces see the outcome as critical, they are willing to engage in a fierce struggle when Supreme Court appointments are at stake.

HOW COURTS WORK AS POLITICAL INSTITUTIONS

Judges are central players in important political institutions, and this role makes them politicians. To understand what animates judicial behavior, we need to place the judge or justice in context by considering the role of the courts in the political system more generally. In doing so, we emphasize the role of the courts as dispute resolvers, coordinators, and interpreters of rules.

Dispute Resolution

So much productive activity occurs in a modern society because its members do not have to devote substantial resources to protecting themselves and their property or monitoring compliance with agreements.[9] For any potential violation of person or property or defection from an agreement, all parties know in advance that an aggrieved party may take an alleged violator to court. The court, in turn, is a venue in which the facts of a case are established, punishment is meted out to violators, and compensation awarded to victims. An employee, for example, may sue his or her employer

---

[8] *Roe v. Wade*, 410 U.S. 113 (1973).

[9] If extraordinary resources had to be devoted to those activities, their rising cost would cause the frequency of productive activities to decline. Indeed, because the costs of negotiating, monitoring, and enforcing agreements (what political economists call transaction costs) can be very high, they are a serious impediment to social interaction and productive activities of all sorts. Economizing on them—by providing the services of courts and judges, for example—is one of the modern state's great contributions to social welfare.

for allegedly violating the terms of a privately negotiated employment contract. Or a consumer may sue a producer for violating the terms of a product warranty. The court, then, is an institution that engages in fact-finding and judgment. It provides the service of dispute resolution. In criminal cases, the "aggrieved party" is not only the victim of the crime but also the entire society whose laws have been violated.

Coordination

Dispute resolution occurs after the fact—that is, after a dispute has occurred. We may also think of courts and judges as before-the-fact coordination mechanisms inasmuch as the anticipation of legal consequences allows private parties to form rational expectations and thereby coordinate their actions in advance of possible disputes. A prospective embezzler, estimating the odds of getting caught, prosecuted, and subsequently punished, may think twice about cheating his partner. Conversely, the legal system can work as an incentive: Two acquaintances, for example, may confidently entertain the possibility of going into business together, knowing that the sword of justice hangs over their collaboration.

In this sense, the court system is as important for what it doesn't do as for what it does. The system of courts and law coordinates private behavior by providing incentives and disincentives for specific actions. To the extent that these work, there are fewer disputes to resolve and thus less after-the-fact dispute resolution for courts and judges to engage in.

Rule Interpretation

Dispute resolution and coordination affect private behavior and the daily lives of ordinary citizens tremendously. Judges, however, are not entirely free agents. In matching the facts of a specific case to judicial principles and statutory guidelines, judges must engage in interpretive activity: They must determine what particular statutes or judicial principles mean, which of them fit the facts of a particular case, and then, having determined this, ascertain the disposition of the case at hand. Does the statute of 1927 regulating the electronic transmission of radio waves apply to television, cellular phones, ship-to-shore radios, fax machines, and e-mail? Does the law governing the transportation of dangerous substances, passed in 1937, apply to nuclear fuels, infected animals, and artificially created biological hazards? Often the enacting legislative body has not been entirely clear about the scope of the legislation it passed.

Interpreting the rules is probably the single most important activity in which higher courts engage. This is because the court system is hierarchical in the sense that judgments by higher courts constrain the discretion of judges in lower courts. If the Supreme Court rules that nuclear fuels are covered by the 1937 law on transporting dangerous substances, then lower courts must render subsequent judgments in a manner consistent with this ruling.

As we shall see in the following section, courts and judges engage not only in statutory interpretation but in constitutional interpretation as well. Here they interpret the provisions of the U.S. Constitution, determining their scope and content. In determining, for example, whether the act of Congress regulating the transportation of dangerous substances from one state to another is constitutional, the justices of the Supreme Court might invoke the commerce clause of the Constitution (allowing the federal government to regulate interstate commerce) to justify the constitutionality of the act. On the other hand, a Supreme Court majority might also rule that a shipment of spent fuel rods from a nuclear reactor in Kansas City to a nuclear-waste facility outside St. Louis is *not* covered by this law because the shipment took place entirely within the boundaries of a single state and thus did not constitute interstate commerce.

In short, judges and justices are continually engaged in elaborating, embellishing, even rewriting the rules by which private and public life are organized. However, judicial interpretation—elaboration, embellishment, and "redrafting"—of statutes is naturally subject to review. Statutory interpretation, even if it is conducted by the highest court in the land, is exposed to legislative review. If Congress is unhappy with a specific statutory interpretation, then it may amend the legislation so as to overcome the Court's objection or even reverse its ruling. In January 2005, for example, the Supreme Court struck down the mandatory-sentencing rules enacted by Congress in 1984.[10] The rules severely limited judicial discretion in the realm of sentencing and had long been resented by the bench. Members of Congress vowed to reinstate the guidelines through new legislation. Senator Jeff Sessions (R-Ala.) said, "The challenge will be to . . . re-create the guidelines in a way that will meet the court's test."[11] Of course, if the court makes a *constitutional* ruling, Congress cannot then abrogate that ruling through new legislation. Congress would need to commence the process of constitutional amendment to overturn a constitutional interpretation with which it disagreed.

THE POWER OF JUDICIAL REVIEW

judicial review
The power of the courts to declare actions of the legislative and executive branches invalid or unconstitutional. The Supreme Court asserted this power in *Marbury v. Madison* (1803).

The phrase **judicial review** refers to the power of the judiciary to examine and, if necessary, invalidate actions undertaken by the legislative and executive branches. The phrase is sometimes also used to describe the scrutiny that appellate courts give to the actions of trial courts, but strictly speaking, that is an improper usage. A higher court's examination of a lower court's decisions might be called appellate review, but it is not judicial review (Figure 8.3).

Judicial Review of Acts of Congress

Because the Constitution does not give the Supreme Court the power of judicial review of congressional enactments, the Court's exercise of it may be seen as something of a usurpation. Among the proposals debated at the Constitutional Convention was one to create a council composed of the president and the judiciary

---

[10] *United States v. Booker*, 543 U.S. 220 (2005).

[11] Quoted in Carl Hulse and Adam Liptak, "New Fight over Controlling Punishments Is Widely Seen," *New York Times*, January 13, 2005, p. A27.

FIGURE 8.3 JUDICIAL REVIEW

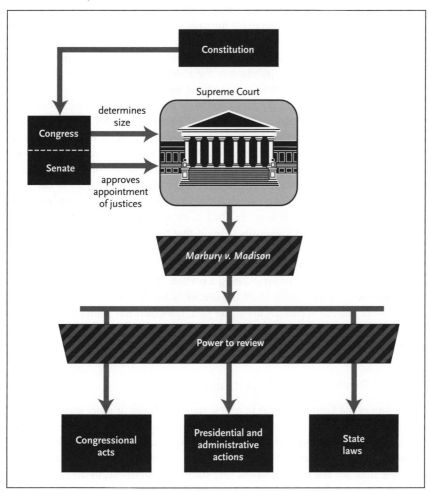

that would share the veto power over legislation. Another proposal was to route all legislation through both the Court and the president; overruling a veto by either one would have required a two-thirds vote of the House and the Senate. Those and other proposals were rejected by the delegates, and no further effort was made to give the Supreme Court review power over the other branches. This does not prove that the framers of the Constitution opposed judicial review, but it does indicate that "if they intended to provide for it in the Constitution, they did so in a most obscure fashion."[12]

Disputes over the intentions of the framers were settled in 1803 in the case of *Marbury v. Madison*.[13] In that case, William Marbury sued Secretary of State James

---

[12] C. Herman Pritchett, *The American Constitution* (New York: McGraw-Hill, 1959), p. 138.

[13] *Marbury v. Madison*, 1 Cranch 137 (1803).

Madison for Madison's failure to complete Marbury's appointment to a lower judgeship that had been initiated by the outgoing administration of President John Adams. Quite apart from the details of the case, Chief Justice John Marshall, speaking on behalf of the court, used the case to declare a portion of a law unconstitutional. In effect, he stated that although the substance of Marbury's request was not unreasonable, the Court's jurisdiction in the matter was based on a section of the Judiciary Act of 1789, which the Court declared unconstitutional.

Although Congress and the president have often been at odds with the Court, its legal power to review acts of Congress has not been seriously questioned since 1803. One reason is that judicial power has been accepted as natural, if not intended. Another reason is that during the early years of the Republic, the Supreme Court was careful to use its power sparingly, striking down only two pieces of legislation during the first seventy-five years of its history. One of these decisions was the 1857 *Dred Scott* ruling, which invalidated the Missouri Compromise and helped precipitate the Civil War. In *Dred Scott v. Sandford*, Chief Justice Roger Taney wrote in the Court's majority opinion that the fact that a slave, Dred Scott, had been transported to a free state (Illinois) and a free territory (Wisconsin) before returning to the slave state of Missouri did not alter the fact that he was property.[14] This ruling had the effect of invalidating a portion of the Missouri Compromise of 1820, thus permitting slavery in all the country's territories. In recent years, with the power of judicial review securely accepted, the Court has been more willing to use it. Between 1986 and 2007, the Supreme Court struck down more than thirty-six acts of Congress.

Judicial Review of State Actions

The power of the Supreme Court to review state legislation or other state action and to determine its constitutionality is neither granted by the Constitution nor inherent in the federal system. But the logic of the **supremacy clause** of Article VI of the Constitution—which declares the Constitution and laws made under its authority to be the supreme law of the land—is very strong. Furthermore, in the Judiciary Act of 1789, Congress conferred on the Supreme Court the power to reverse state constitutions and laws whenever they are clearly in conflict with the U.S. Constitution, federal laws, or treaties.[15] This power gives the Supreme Court jurisdiction over all of the millions of cases handled by American courts each year.

The civil rights area abounds with examples of state laws that were overturned because the statutes violated the guarantees of due process and equal protection contained in the Fourteenth Amendment to the Constitution. For example, in the 1954 case of *Brown v. Board of Education*, the Court overturned statutes in Kansas, South Carolina, Virginia, and Delaware that either required or permitted segregated public schools, on the basis that such statutes denied black schoolchildren equal protection of the law.[16] In 1967 in *Loving v. Virginia*, the Court invalidated a

supremacy clause A clause of Article VI of the Constitution that states that all laws passed by the national government and all treaties are the supreme laws of the land and superior to all laws adopted by any state or any subdivision.

---

[14] *Dred Scott v. Sandford*, 60 U.S. 393 (1857).

[15] This review power was affirmed by the Supreme Court in *Martin v. Hunter's Lessee*, 14 U.S. 304 (1816).

[16] *Brown v. Board of Education*, 347 U.S. 483 (1954).

Virginia statute prohibiting interracial marriages.[17] State statutes in other areas are equally subject to challenge. In *Griswold v. Connecticut*, the Court invalidated a Connecticut statute prohibiting the general distribution of contraceptives to married couples, on the basis that the statute violated the couples' right to marital privacy.[18]

Judicial Review of Federal Agency Actions

Although Congress makes the law, as we saw in Chapters 5 and 7, Congress can hardly administer the thousands of programs it has enacted and must delegate power to the president and to a huge bureaucracy to achieve its purpose. For example, if Congress wishes to improve air quality, it cannot possibly anticipate all the conditions and circumstances that may arise over the years with respect to its general goal. Inevitably Congress must delegate to the executive substantial discretionary power to make judgments about the best ways to bring about improved air quality in the face of changing circumstances. Thus, over time, almost any congressional program will result in thousands and thousands of pages of administrative regulations developed by executive agencies nominally seeking to implement the will of Congress.

The issue of delegation of power has led to a number of court decisions over the past two centuries, generally involving the question of the scope of the delegation. Courts have also been called on to decide whether the rules and regulations adopted by federal agencies are consistent with Congress's express or implied intent.

As presidential power expanded during the New Deal era, one measure of increased congressional subordination to the executive was the enactment of laws that contained few if any principles limiting executive discretion. Congress enacted legislation, often at the president's behest, that gave the executive virtually unfettered authority to address a particular concern. For example, the Emergency Price Control Act of 1942 authorized the executive to set "fair and equitable" prices without offering any indication of what those terms might mean. Although the Court initially challenged these delegations of power to the president during the New Deal, a confrontation with President Franklin Roosevelt caused the Court to retreat from its position. Perhaps as a result, no congressional delegation of power to the president has been struck down as impermissibly broad since then. In the last two decades in particular, the Supreme Court has found that as long as federal agencies developed rules and regulations "based upon a permissible construction" or "reasonable interpretation" of Congress's statute, the judiciary would accept the views of the executive branch.[19] Generally the courts give considerable deference to administrative agencies as long as those agencies have engaged in a formal rule-making process and can show that they have carried out the conditions prescribed by the various statutes governing agency rule making. These statutes include the 1946 Administrative Procedure Act, which requires agencies to notify parties

---

[17] *Loving v. Virginia*, 388 U.S. 1 (1967).

[18] *Griswold v. Connecticut*, 381 U.S. 479 (1965).

[19] *Cookman Realty Group, Inc. v. West Virginia Division of Environmental Protection*, no. 30116 (W.Va. S. Ct. App. 2002).

affected by proposed rules and to allow them ample time to comment on such rules before they go into effect.

Judicial Review and Presidential Power

The federal courts are also called on to review the actions of the president. As we saw in Chapter 6, presidents have increasingly made use of unilateral executive powers rather than relying on congressional legislation to achieve their objectives. On many occasions, presidential orders and actions have been challenged in the federal courts by members of Congress and by individuals and groups opposing the president's policies. In recent years, assertions of presidential power in such realms as foreign policy, war and emergency powers, legislative power, and administrative authority have, more often than not, been upheld by the federal bench. Indeed, the federal judiciary has sometimes taken extraordinary presidential claims that were made for limited and temporary purposes and rationalized them—that is, the Court has converted them into routine and permanent instruments of presidential government. Take, for example, Richard Nixon's sweeping claims of executive privilege. In *United States v. Nixon*, the Court, to be sure, rejected the president's refusal to turn over tape recordings to congressional investigators. For the first time, though, the justices recognized the validity of the principle of executive privilege and discussed the situations in which such claims might be appropriate.[20] This judicial recognition of executive privilege encouraged Presidents Bill Clinton and George W. Bush to base broad claims on that principle during their terms in office.[21] Executive privilege has even been invoked to protect the deliberations of the vice president from congressional scrutiny, in the case of Dick Cheney's consultations with representatives of the energy industry.

This pattern of judicial deference to presidential authority is also manifest in the Supreme Court's recent decisions regarding President Bush's war on terrorism. In June 2004, the Supreme Court ruled on three cases involving the president's antiterrorism initiatives and claims of executive power and in two of them appeared to place some limits on presidential authority. Indeed, the justices had clearly been influenced by revelations that U.S. troops had abused prisoners in Iraq, and the justices sought in these cases to make a statement against the absolute denial of procedural rights to individuals in the custody of U.S. military authorities. But although the Court's decisions were widely hailed as reining in the executive branch, they fell far short of stopping presidential power in its tracks.

The most important of these cases was *Hamdi v. Rumsfeld*.[22] Yaser Esam Hamdi, apparently a Taliban soldier, was captured by American forces in Afghanistan in late 2001 and brought to the United States. Hamdi was classified as an enemy combatant and denied civil rights, including the right to counsel, despite the fact that he was born in Louisiana and held U.S. citizenship. A federal district

---

[20] *United States v. Nixon*, 418 U.S. 683 (1974).

[21] On Clinton, see Jonathan Turley, "Paradise Lost: The Clinton Administration and the Erosion of Executive Privilege," *Maryland Law Review* 60 (2001): 295. On Bush, see Jeffrey P. Carlin, "*Walker v. Cheney*: Politics, Posturing, and Executive Privilege," *Southern California Law Review* 76 (November 2002): 235.

[22] *Hamdi v. Rumsfeld*, 542 U.S. 507 (2004).

court ordered that he be given unmonitored access to counsel. This ruling was reversed by the U.S. Court of Appeals for the Fourth Circuit, however. In its opinion, the court held that in the national-security realm, the president wields "plenary and exclusive power." In essence, said the court, the president had virtually unfettered discretion in dealing with emergencies, and it was inappropriate for the judiciary to saddle presidential decisions with what the court called the "panoply of encumbrances associated with civil litigation."

In June 2004, the Supreme Court ruled that Hamdi was entitled to a lawyer and "a fair opportunity to rebut the government's factual assertions." However, the Supreme Court affirmed that the president possessed the authority to declare a U.S. citizen an enemy combatant and order that such an individual be held in federal detention. Several of the justices intimated that once designated an enemy combatant, a U.S. citizen might be tried before a military tribunal, with the normal presumption of innocence suspended. In 2006, in *Hamdan v. Rumsfeld*, the Court ruled that the military commissions established to try enemy combatants and other detainees violated both the Uniform Code of Military Justice and the Geneva Conventions.[23]

Thus the Supreme Court did assert that presidential actions were subject to judicial scrutiny and placed some constraints on the president's power. But at the same time, the Court affirmed the president's single most important claim: the unilateral power to declare individuals, including U.S. citizens, "enemy combatants" who could be detained by federal authorities under adverse legal circumstances.

Judicial Review and Lawmaking

Much of the work of the courts involves the application of statutes to a particular case at hand. Over the centuries, however, judges have developed a body of rules and principles of interpretation that are not grounded in specific statutes. This body of judge-made law is called common law.

The appellate courts are in another realm. Their rulings can be considered laws, but they are laws governing only the behavior of the judiciary. They influence citizens' conduct only because, in the words of Justice Oliver Wendell Holmes, Jr. (who served on the Supreme Court from 1902 to 1932), lawyers make "prophecies of what the courts will do in fact."[24]

The written opinion of an appellate court is about halfway between common law and statutory law. It is judge made and draws heavily on the precedents of previous cases. In that it tries to articulate the rule of law controlling the case in question and future cases like it, it is like a statute. But a statute addresses itself to the future conduct of citizens, whereas a written opinion addresses itself mainly to the willingness or ability of courts in the future to take cases and render favorable opinions.

An example may help clarify the distinction. In *Gideon v. Wainwright*, the Supreme Court ordered a new trial for Clarence Earl Gideon, an indigent defendant, because he had been denied the right to legal counsel. This ruling said to all trial

---

[23] *Hamdan v. Rumsfeld*, 548 U.S. (2006).

[24] Oliver Wendell Holmes, Jr., "The Path of the Law," *Harvard Law Review* 10 (1897): 457.

judges and prosecutors that henceforth they would be wasting their time if they cut corners in the trials of indigent defendants.[25] The Court was thereby predicting what it would and would not do in future cases of this sort. It also invited thousands of prisoners to appeal their convictions.

Many areas of civil law have been constructed in the same way—by judicial messages to other judges, some of which are codified eventually in legislative enactments. It has become "the law," for example, that employers are liable for injuries in the workplace without regard to negligence. But the law in this instance is simply a series of messages to lawyers that they should advise their corporate clients not to appeal injury decisions.

In the realm of criminal law, almost all the dramatic changes in the treatment of criminals and persons accused of crimes have been made by the appellate courts, especially the Supreme Court. The Supreme Court brought about a veritable revolution in the criminal process with three cases over less than five years. The first, *Gideon v. Wainwright,* in 1963, was just discussed. The second, *Escobedo v. Illinois,* in 1964, gave suspects the right to remain silent and the right to have counsel present during questioning.[26] But the decision left confusion that allowed differing decisions to be made by lower courts. In the third case, *Miranda v. Arizona,* in 1966, the Supreme Court cleared up the confusion by setting forth what is known as the *Miranda* rule: Arrested people have the right to remain silent, the right to be informed that anything they say can be held against them, and the right to counsel before and during police interrogation.[27]

One of the most significant changes brought about by the Supreme Court was the revolution in legislative representation unleashed by the 1962 case of *Baker v. Carr.*[28] In this landmark case, the Supreme Court held that it could no longer avoid reviewing complaints about the apportionment of seats in state legislatures. Following that decision, the federal courts went on to force reapportionment of all state, county, and local legislatures in the country.

As these various cases illustrate, the appellate courts are intimately involved in creating and interpreting laws. Many experts on court history and constitutional law criticize the federal appellate courts for being too willing to introduce radical change, even when the experts agree with the general direction of the changes. Often they are troubled by the willingness of the courts (especially the Supreme Court) to jump into such cases prematurely—before the constitutional issues have been fully clarified by decisions of district and appeals courts in many related cases in various parts of the country.[29] But from the perspective of the appellate judiciary, and especially the Supreme Court, the situation is one of choosing between the lesser of two evils: They must take the cases as they come and then weigh the risks of opening new options against the risks of embracing the status quo.

---

[25] *Gideon v. Wainwright,* 372 U.S. 335 (1963).

[26] *Escobedo v. Illinois,* 378 U.S. 478 (1964).

[27] *Miranda v. Arizona,* 384 U.S. 436 (1966).

[28] *Baker v. Carr,* 369 U.S. 186 (1962).

[29] See Philip B. Kurland, *Politics, the Constitution, and the Warren Court* (Chicago: University of Chicago Press, 1970).

THE SUPREME COURT IN ACTION

How Cases Reach the Supreme Court

Given the millions of disputes that arise every year, the job of the Supreme Court would be impossible if it were not able to control the flow of cases and its own caseload. The Supreme Court has original jurisdiction in a limited variety of cases defined by the Constitution. Original jurisdiction includes (1) cases between the United States and one of the fifty states, (2) cases between two or more states, (3) cases involving foreign ambassadors or other ministers, and (4) cases brought by one state against citizens of another state or against a foreign country. The most important of these cases are disputes between states over land, water, or old debts. Generally the Supreme Court deals with these cases by appointing a "special master," usually a retired judge, to hear the case and present a report. The Supreme Court then allows the states involved in the dispute to present arguments for or against the master's opinion.[30]

Rules of Access.   Over the years, the courts have developed specific rules that govern which cases within their jurisdiction they will and will not hear. Thus the Court is an institution very much in control of its own agenda, which, according to the institution principle, gives it a great deal of independence to follow the preferences of its members. To have access to the courts, cases must meet certain criteria that are initially applied by the trial court but may be reconsidered by appellate courts. These rules of access can be broken down into three major categories: case or controversy, standing, and mootness.

Both Article III of the Constitution and Supreme Court decisions define judicial power as extending only to "cases and controversies." This means that the case before a court must be an actual controversy, not a hypothetical one, with two truly adversarial parties. The courts have interpreted this language to mean that they do not have the power to render advisory opinions to legislatures or agencies about the constitutionality of proposed laws or regulations. Furthermore, even after a law is enacted, the courts will generally refuse to consider its constitutionality until it is actually applied.

Parties to a case must also have **standing**—that is, they must show that they have a substantial stake in the outcome of the case. The traditional requirement for standing has been that one must show injury to oneself; that injury can be personal, economic, or even aesthetic, for example. In order for a group or class of people to have standing (as in class-action suits), each member must show specific injury. This means that a general interest in the environment, for instance, does not provide a group with a sufficient basis for standing.

The third criterion in determining whether the Supreme Court will hear a case is **mootness**. In theory, this requirement disqualifies cases that are brought too

standing The right of an individual or an organization to initiate a court case.

mootness A criterion used by courts to avoid hearing cases that no longer require resolution.

---

[30] Walter F. Murphy, "The Supreme Court of the United States," in *Encyclopedia of the American Judicial System: Studies of the Principal Institutions and Processes of Law,* Robert J. Janosik, ed. (New York: Scribner, 1987).

late—after the relevant facts have changed or the problem has been resolved by other means. The criterion of mootness, however, is subject to the discretion of the courts, which have begun to relax the rules pertaining to this criterion, particularly in cases in which a situation that has been resolved is likely to come up again. In the abortion case of *Roe v. Wade*, for example, the Supreme Court rejected the lower court's argument that because the pregnancy had already come to term, the case was moot. The Court agreed to hear the case because no pregnancy was likely to outlast the lengthy appeals process.

Putting aside the formal criteria, the Supreme Court is most likely to accept cases that involve conflicting decisions by the federal circuit courts, cases that present important questions of civil rights or civil liberties, and cases in which the federal government is the appellant.[31] Ultimately, however, the question of which cases are accepted can come down to the preferences and priorities of the justices. If a number of justices believe that the Court should intervene in a particular area of policy or politics, they are likely to look for a case or cases that will be vehicles for judicial intervention. For many years, for example, the Court was not interested in considering challenges to affirmative action or other programs designed to provide particular benefits to minorities. In recent years, however, several of the Court's more conservative justices have been eager to push back the limits of affirmative action and racial preference and have therefore accepted a number of cases that would allow them to do so. In 1995, the Court's decisions in *Adarand Constructors v. Pena, Missouri v. Jenkins*, and *Miller v. Johnson* placed new restrictions on federal affirmative action programs, school desegregation efforts, and attempts to increase minority representation in Congress through the creation of "minority districts" (see Chapter 10).[32] Similarly, the Court has taken on some social issues that it and other branches of the federal government have long avoided, such as gun control. Laws regulating gun ownership and licensing have been left to the states. Inconsistencies across states' gun laws have fueled debate at the national level between those activists who want strict, national regulation of gun ownership and those who want minimal regulations. The heart of the debate is the Second Amendment to the U.S. Constitution and the meaning of the "right to bear arms." The U.S. Supreme Court last heard a case dealing with the Second Amendment in 1939, the case of *United States v. Miller* (307 U.S. 134 [1939]). In 2003, six residents of the District of Columbia sued in federal district court to challenge a D.C. law banning residents from owing handguns. The federal district court dismissed the lawsuit, and the plaintiffs appealed to the U.S. Court of Appeals, which reversed the district court on a 2-to-1 vote, declaring the District of Columbia's gun law unconstitutional. The U.S. Supreme Court ruled that the District could require Heller and the other plaintiffs to register their handguns and obtain licenses to carry handguns, but that the plaintiffs clearly had a right to have handguns.

Most cases reach the Supreme Court through a **writ of *certiorari*** (Figure 8.4). *Certiorari* is an order to a lower court to deliver the records of a particular case to

writ of certiorari A formal request by an appellant to have the Supreme Court review a decision of a lower court. *Certiorari* is from a Latin word meaning "to make more certain."

---

[31] Gregory A. Caldeira and John R. Wright, "Organized Interests and Agenda Setting in the U.S. Supreme Court," *American Political Science Review* 82, no. 4 (December 1988): 1109–27.

[32] *Adarand Constructors v. Pena*, 115 U.S. 200 (1995); *Missouri v. Jenkins*, 515 U.S. 70 (1995); *Miller v. Johnson*, 515 U.S. 900 (1995).

FIGURE 8.4 REACHING THE SUPREME COURT THROUGH *CERTIORARI*

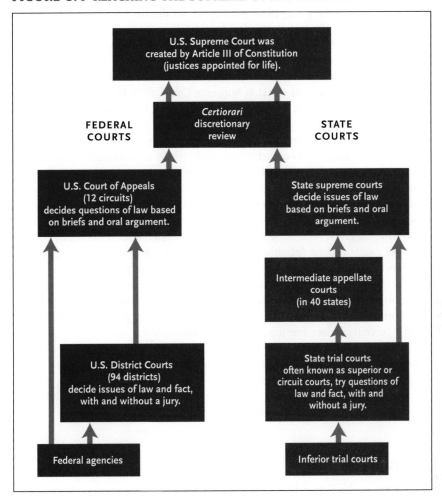

be reviewed for legal errors. The term is sometimes shortened to *cert,* and cases deemed to merit *certiorari* are referred to as *certworthy.* An individual who loses in a lower federal court or a state court and wants the Supreme Court to review the decision has ninety days to file a petition for a writ of *certiorari* with the clerk of the U.S. Supreme Court. There are two types of petitions: paid petitions and petitions *in forma pauperis* ("in the form of a pauper"). The former requires the payment of filing fees, submission of a certain number of copies, and compliance with a variety of other rules. For *in forma pauperis* petitions, which are usually filed by prison inmates, the Court waives the fees and most other requirements.

Since 1972, most of the justices have participated in a *"certiorari* pool" in which their law clerks work together to evaluate the petitions. Each petition is reviewed by one clerk, who writes a memo summarizing the facts and issues and making a recommendation for all the justices participating in the pool. Clerks for the other justices add their comments to the memo. After the justices have reviewed the memos, any one of them may place any case on the discuss list, which is circulated by the chief justice. If a case is not placed on the discuss list, it is automatically denied *certiorari*. Cases placed on the discuss list are considered and voted on during the justices' closed-door conference.

For *certiorari* to be granted, four justices must be convinced that the case satisfies Rule 10 of the Rules of the U.S. Supreme Court. Rule 10 states that *certiorari* is not a matter of right but is to be granted only when there are special and compelling reasons. These include conflicting decisions by two or more circuit courts, conflicts between circuit courts and state courts of last resort, conflicting decisions by two or more state courts of last resort, decisions by circuit courts on matters of federal law that should be settled by the Supreme Court, and a circuit court decision on an important question that conflicts with a Supreme Court decision. It should be clear from this list that the Court will usually take action under only the most compelling circumstances—when there are conflicts among the lower courts about what the law should be, when an important legal question has been raised in the lower courts and not definitively answered, or when a lower court deviates from the principles and precedents established by the high court. The support of four justices is needed for *certiorari*, and few cases are able to satisfy this requirement. In recent sessions, although thousands of petitions have been filed (Figure 8.5), the Court has granted *certiorari* to hardly more than eighty petitioners each year—about 1 percent of those seeking a Supreme Court review.

A handful of cases reach the Supreme Court through avenues other than *certiorari*. One of these is the writ of certification. This writ can be used when a U.S. Court of Appeals asks the Supreme Court for instructions on a point of law that has never been decided. A second alternative avenue is the writ of appeal, which is used to appeal the decision of a three-judge district court.

Controlling the Flow of Cases

In addition to the judges themselves, two other actors play an important role in shaping the flow of cases through the federal courts: the solicitor general and the federal law clerks.

The Solicitor General. If any single person has greater influence than the individual justices over the work of the Supreme Court, it is the solicitor general of the United States. The solicitor general is third in status in the Justice Department (below the attorney general and the deputy attorney general), but he or she is the top government lawyer in virtually all cases before the appellate courts in which the government is a party. Although others can regulate the flow of cases, the solicitor general has the greatest control, with no review of his or her actions by any higher authority in the executive branch. More than half the Supreme Court's total workload consists of cases under the direct charge of the solicitor general.

The solicitor general exercises especially strong influence by screening cases long before they approach the Supreme Court; indeed, the justices rely on the solicitor general to "screen out undeserving litigation and furnish them with an agenda

FIGURE 8.5 CASES FILED IN THE U.S. SUPREME COURT

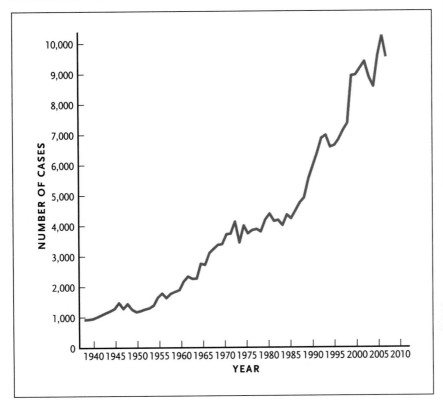

NOTE: Graph indicates the number of cases filed in the term beginning in the year indicated.

SOURCE: Years 1938–69 and 2000–2008: successive volumes of U.S. Bureau of the Census, *Statistical Abstract of the United States* (Washington, D.C.: Government Printing Office); 1970–83: Office of the Clerk of the Supreme Court; 1984–99: *The United States Law Week* (Washington, D.C.: Bureau of National Affairs), vol. 56, 3102; vol. 59, 3064; vol. 61, 3098; vol. 63, 3134; vol. 65, 3100; vol. 67, 3167; vol. 69, 3134.

to hear government cases that deserve serious consideration."[33] Typically, more re-quests for appeals are rejected than are accepted by the solicitor general. Agency heads may lobby the president or otherwise try to circumvent the solicitor general, and a few of the independent agencies have a statutory right to make direct appeals, but without the solicitor general's support these are seldom reviewed by the Court.

By writing an **amicus curiae** ("friend of the court") brief, the solicitor general, can enter a case even when the federal government is not a direct litigant. A "friend of the court" is not a direct party to a case but has a vital interest in its outcome. Thus when the government has such an interest, the solicitor general can file as

amicus curiae "Friend of the court," an individual or group who is not party to a lawsuit but seeks to assist the court in reaching a decision by presenting an additional brief.

---

[33] Robert Scigliano, *The Supreme Court and the Presidency* (New York: Free Press, 1971), p. 162. For an interesting critique of the solicitor general's role during the Reagan administration, see Lincoln Caplan, "Annals of the Law," *New Yorker*, August 17, 1987, pp. 30–62.

amicus curiae, or the Court can invite such a brief because it wants an opinion in writing. Other interested parties may file briefs as well.

In addition to exercising substantial control over the flow of cases, the solicitor general can shape the arguments used before the Court. Indeed, the Court tends to give special attention to the way the solicitor general characterizes the issues. The solicitor general is the person appearing most frequently before the Court and, theoretically at least, the most disinterested. The credibility of the solicitor general is not hurt when several times each year he or she comes to the Court to withdraw a case with the admission that the government has made an error.[34]

Law Clerks. Every federal judge employs law clerks to research legal issues and assist with the preparation of opinions. Each Supreme Court justice is assigned four clerks. The clerks are almost always honors graduates of the nation's most prestigious law schools. A clerkship with a Supreme Court justice is a great honor and generally indicates that the fortunate individual is likely to reach the very top of the legal profession. One of the most important roles performed by the clerks is screening the thousands of petitions for writs of *certiorari* that come before the Court.[35] It is also likely that some justices rely heavily on their clerks for advice in writing opinions and deciding whether an individual case ought to be heard by the Court. It is often rumored that certain opinions were actually written by a clerk rather than a justice.[36] Although such rumors are difficult to substantiate, it is clear that at the end of long judicial careers, justices such as William O. Douglas and Thurgood Marshall had become so infirm that they were compelled to rely on the judgments of their law clerks.

The Supreme Court's Procedures

The Preparation. The Supreme Court's decision to accept a case is the beginning of what can be a lengthy and complex process (Figure 8.6). First, the attorneys on both sides must prepare **briefs**—written documents in which the attorneys explain why the Court should rule in favor of their client. The document filed by the individual bringing the case is called the petitioner's brief. It summarizes the facts of the case and presents the legal basis on which the Supreme Court is being asked to overturn the lower court's decision. The document filed by the side that prevailed in the lower court is called the respondent's brief. It explains why the Supreme Court should affirm the lower court's verdict. The petitioners then file a brief answering and attempting to refute the points made in the respondent's brief. This document is called the petitioner's reply brief. Briefs are filled with references

brief A written document in which an attorney explains—using case precedents—why the Court should rule in favor of his or her client.

---

[34] On the strategic and informational role played by the solicitor general, see Kevin McGuire, "Explaining Executive Success in the U.S. Supreme Court," *Political Research Quarterly* 51 (1998): 505–26. Also see Michael Bailey, Brian Kamoie, and Forrest Maltzman, "Signals from the Tenth Justice: The Political Role of the Solicitor General in Supreme Court Decision Making," *American Journal of Political Science* 49 (2005): 72–85.

[35] H. W. Perry, Jr., *Deciding to Decide: Agenda Setting in the United States Supreme Court* (Cambridge, Mass.: Harvard University Press, 1991).

[36] Edward Lazarus, *Closed Chambers: The First Eyewitness Account of the Struggles inside the Supreme Court* (New York: Times Books, 1998).

FIGURE 8.6 THE SUPREME COURT'S DECISION-MAKING PROCESS

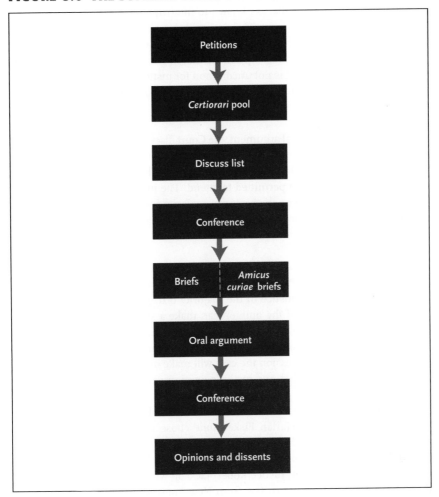

Petitions

Certiorari pool

Discuss list

Conference

Briefs | *Amicus curiae* briefs

Oral argument

Conference

Opinions and dissents

to precedents specifically chosen to show that other courts have frequently ruled in the same way that the Supreme Court is being asked to rule.

As the attorneys prepare their briefs, they often ask sympathetic interest groups for their help by means of *amicus curiae* briefs. In a case involving separation of church and state, for example, liberal groups such as the American Civil Liberties Union (ACLU) and People for the American Way are likely to be asked to file *amicus* briefs in support of strict separation, whereas conservative religious groups, the Family Research Council or Focus on the Family, for example, are likely to file *amicus* briefs advocating increased public support for religious ideas. Often dozens of briefs will be filed on each side of a major case.

Oral Argument. The next stage of a case is **oral argument**, in which attorneys for both sides appear before the Court to present their positions and answer the justices' questions. Each attorney has only a half hour to present his or her case,

oral argument
The stage in Supreme Court proceedings in which attorneys for both sides appear before the Court to present their positions and answer questions posed by the justices.

and this time includes interruptions for questions. Certain members of the Court, such as Justice Antonin Scalia, are known to interrupt attorneys dozens of times. Others, such as Justice Clarence Thomas, seldom ask questions. Oral argument can be very important to the outcome of a case. It allows justices to understand better the heart of a case and raise questions that might not have been addressed in the opposing sides' briefs. It is not uncommon for justices to go beyond the strictly legal issues and ask opposing counsel to discuss the implications of the case for the Court and the nation at large.[37]

The Conference.   After oral argument, the Court discusses the case in its Wednesday or Friday conference. The chief justice presides over the conference and speaks first; the other justices follow in order of seniority. The Court's conferences are secret, and no outsiders are permitted to attend. The justices discuss the case and eventually reach a decision on the basis of a majority vote. As the case is discussed, justices may try to influence or change each other's opinions. At times, this may result in compromise decisions.

Opinion Writing.   After a decision has been reached, one of the members of the majority is assigned to write the **opinion**. This assignment is made by the chief justice or the most senior justice in the majority if the chief justice is on the losing side. The assignment of the opinion can make a significant difference to the interpretation of a decision, as its wording and emphasis can have important implications for future litigation. Thus in assigning an opinion, the justices must give serious thought to the impression the case will make on lawyers and the public, as well as to the probability that one justice's opinion will be more widely accepted than another's.[38]

opinion The written explanation of the Supreme Court's decision in a particular case.

One of the more dramatic instances of this tactical consideration occurred in 1944, when Chief Justice Harlan Fiske Stone chose Justice Felix Frankfurter to write the opinion in the "white primary" case *Smith v. Allwright*, which overturned the southern practice of prohibiting black participation in primaries. The day after Stone made the assignment, Justice Robert Jackson wrote a letter to Stone arguing that Frankfurter, a foreign-born Jew from New England, would not win over the South with his opinion, regardless of his brilliance. Stone accepted the advice and substituted Justice Stanley F. Reed, an American-born Protestant from Kentucky and a southern Democrat in good standing.[39]

Once the majority opinion is drafted, it is circulated to the other justices. Some members of the majority may agree with both the outcome and the rationale but wish to emphasize or highlight a particular point and so draft a concurring opinion, called a regular concurrence. In other instances, one or more justices may agree

---

[37] On the consequences of oral argument for decision making, see Timothy R. Johnson, Paul J. Wahlbeck, and James F. Spriggs II, "The Influence of Oral Arguments on the U.S. Supreme Court," *American Political Science Review* 100, no. 1 (February 2006): 99–113.

[38] For this and other strategic aspects of the Court's process, see Forrest Maltzman, James F. Spriggs II, and Paul J. Wahlbeck, *Crafting Law on the Supreme Court: The Collegial Game* (New York: Cambridge University Press, 2001).

[39] *Smith v. Allwright*, 321 U.S. 649 (1944).

with the majority but disagree with the rationale presented in the majority opinion. Then the justices may draft a special concurrence, explaining their disagreements with the majority. The pattern of opinions that emerge on a case ultimately depends on bargaining among the justices, as suggested by the collective-action principle.

Dissent. Justices who disagree with the majority decision of the Court may choose to publicize the character of their disagreement in the form of a **dissenting opinion**. The dissenting opinion is generally assigned by the senior justice among the dissenters. Dissents can be used to express irritation with an outcome or to signal to defeated political forces in the nation that their position is supported by at least some members of the Court. Ironically, the most dependable way an individual justice can exercise a direct and clear influence on the Court is to write a dissent. Because there is no need to please a majority, dissenting opinions can be more eloquent and less guarded than majority opinions. The current Supreme Court often produces 5–4 decisions, with dissenters writing long and detailed opinions that, they hope, will help them convince a swing justice to join their side on the next round of cases dealing with a similar topic. Thus, for example, Justice David Souter wrote a thirty-four-page dissent in a 2002 case upholding the use of government-funded school vouchers to pay for parochial-school tuition. Souter called the decision "a dramatic departure from basic Establishment Clause principle" and went on to say that he hoped it would be reconsidered by a future court.[40]

> **dissenting opinion**
> A decision written by a justice who voted with the minority opinion in a particular case, in which the justice fully explains the reasoning behind his or her opinion.

Dissent plays a special role in the work and impact of the Court because it amounts to an appeal to lawyers all over the country to keep bringing cases of the sort at issue. Therefore, an effective dissent influences the flow of cases through the Court as well as the arguments that lawyers will make in later cases.

JUDICIAL DECISION MAKING

The judiciary is conservative in its procedures, but its effect on society can be radical. That effect depends on a variety of influences, two of which stand out above the rest. The first is the individual members of the Supreme Court, their attitudes and goals, and their relationships with each other. The second is the other branches of government, particularly Congress.

The Supreme Court Justices

The Supreme Court explains its decisions in terms of law and precedent. But although law and precedent do have an effect on the Court's deliberations and eventual decisions, it is the Supreme Court that decides what laws mean and what importance precedents will have. Throughout its history, the Court has shaped and reshaped the law. If any individual judges in the country influence the federal judiciary, the Supreme Court justices are the ones who do.

---

[40] Warren Richey, "Dissenting Opinions as a Window on Future Rulings," *Christian Science Monitor*, July 1, 2002, p. 1.

From the 1950s to the 1980s, the Supreme Court took an activist role in such areas as civil rights, civil liberties, abortion, voting rights, and police procedures. For example, the Supreme Court was more responsible than any other governmental institution for breaking down America's system of racial segregation. The Supreme Court virtually prohibited states from interfering with the right of a woman to seek an abortion and sharply curtailed state restrictions on voting rights. And it was the Supreme Court that placed restrictions on the behavior of local police and prosecutors in criminal cases.

But since the early 1980s, resignations, deaths, and new appointments have led to many shifts in the mix of philosophies and ideologies represented on the Court. In a series of decisions between 1989 and 2001, the conservative justices appointed by Ronald Reagan and George H. W. Bush were able to swing the Court to a more conservative position on civil rights, affirmative action, abortion rights, property rights, criminal procedure, voting rights, desegregation, and the power of the national government.

The importance of ideology was very clear during the Court's 2000–2001 term. In important decisions, the Court's most conservative justices—Scalia, Thomas, and Rehnquist, usually joined by Kennedy—generally voted as a bloc.[41] Indeed, Scalia and Thomas voted together in 99 percent of all cases. At the same time, the Court's most liberal justices—Breyer, Ginsburg, Souter, and Stevens—also generally formed a bloc, with Ginsburg and Breyer and Ginsburg and Souter voting together 94 percent of the time.[42] Justice O'Connor, a moderate conservative, was the swing vote in many important cases.[43] This ideological division led to a number of important 5–4 decisions. In the Florida election law case, *Bush v. Gore*, Justice O'Connor joined with the conservative bloc to give Bush a 5–4 victory. Indeed, more than 33 percent of all the cases heard by the Court in its 2000–2001 term were decided by a 5–4 vote. In the Court's 2003–2004 term, eight of the fourteen most important cases were also decided by a 5–4 margin.

However, precisely because the Court was so evenly split during this period, the conservative bloc did not always prevail. On some issues Justice O'Connor or Justice Kennedy sided with the liberal camp, producing a 5–4 and, sometimes, a 6–3 victory for the liberals. In the 2003 case of *Missouri v. Seibert*, for example, Justice Kennedy joined a 5–4 majority to strengthen Miranda rights.[44] Similarly, in *McConnell v. Federal Election Commission*, Justice O'Connor joined the liberal bloc to uphold the validity of the Bipartisan Campaign Reform Act.[45] On abortion, women's rights, and affirmative action, Justice O'Connor often joined the liberal bloc. With the departure of O'Connor and her replacment by Alito in 2006, many anticipated a series of new 5–4 decisions favoring the conservatives under new chief

---

[41] Linda Greenhouse, "In Year of Florida Vote, Supreme Court Also Did Much Other Work," *New York Times*, July 2, 2001, p. A12.

[42] Charles Lane, "Laying Down the Law," *Washington Post*, July 1, 2001, p. A6.

[43] For an insightful discussion about identifying the swing justice on the Court, see Andrew D. Martin, Kevin M. Quinn, and Lee Epstein, "The Median Justice on the U.S. Supreme Court," *North Carolina Law Review* 83 (2005): 1275–1322.

[44] *Missouri v. Seibert*, 542 U.S. 600 (2004).

[45] *McConnell v. Federal Election Commission*, 540 U.S. 93 (2003).

justice John Roberts.[46] In 2007, for example, the Court upheld the Partial Birth Abortion Ban Act—a law favored by conservatives—by a 5–4 majority. The "Analyzing the Evidence" section on the following page looks at the trend toward more closely decided cases in recent years. However, the Court's policy influence comes not from the "horse race" results often trumpeted by the media, but from the written opinions providing the constitutional or statutory rationale for policy in the future. These opinions establish the guidelines that govern how federal courts must decide similar cases in the future. The departure of Justice O'Connor shifted the center of the Court (the part that proves pivotal in formulating opinions) to Justice Kennedy, who by many measures does not significantly differ from O'Connor in his jurisprudence. The Court's policies may have drifted rightward since O'Connor's departure, but only from O'Connor's position to Kennedy's, not nearly so dramatic a difference as that between O'Connor and Alito.[47]

Activism and Restraint. One element of judicial philosophy is the issue of activism versus restraint. Over the years, some justices have believed that courts should interpret the Constitution according to the stated intentions of its framers and defer to the views of Congress when interpreting federal statutes. Justice Felix Frankfurter, for example, advocated judicial deference to legislative bodies and avoidance of the "political thicket," in which the Court would entangle itself by deciding questions that were essentially political rather than legal in character. Advocates of **judicial restraint** are sometimes called strict constructionists because they look strictly to the words of the Constitution in interpreting its meaning.

The alternative to restraint is **judicial activism**. Activist judges such as Chief Justice Earl Warren believe that the Court should go beyond the words of the Constitution or a statute to consider the broader societal implications of its decisions. Activist judges sometimes strike out in new directions, promulgating new interpretations or inventing new legal and constitutional concepts when they believe them to be socially desirable. For example, Justice Harry Blackmun's opinion in *Roe v. Wade* was based on a constitutional right to privacy that is not found in the words of the Constitution but was, rather, based on the Court's prior decision in *Griswold v. Connecticut*. Blackmun and the other members of the majority in the *Roe* case argued that the right to privacy is implied by other constitutional provisions. In this instance of judicial activism, the Court knew the result it wanted to achieve and was not afraid to make the law conform to the desired outcome.

Political Ideology. The second component of judicial philosophy is political ideology. The liberal or conservative attitudes of justices play an important role in their decisions.[48] The philosophy of activism versus restraint is sometimes a smoke screen

judicial restraint
The judicial philosophy whose adherents refuse to go beyond the text of the Constitution in interpreting its meaning.

judicial activism
The judicial philosophy that posits that the Court should see beyond the text of the Constitution or a statute to consider broader societal implications for its decisions.

---

[46] Adam Liptak, "Entrances and Exits: The New 5-to-4 Supreme Court," *New York Times*, April 22, 2007.

[47] For a development of this argument, see David W. Rohde and Kenneth A. Shepsle, "Advising and Consenting in the 60-Vote Senate: Strategic Appointments to the Supreme Court," *Journal of Politics* 69, no. 3 (August 2007): 664–77.

[48] C. Herman Pritchett, *The Roosevelt Court: A Study in Judicial Politics and Values* (New York: Macmillan, 1948); Jeffrey A. Segal and Harold J. Spaeth, *The Supreme Court and the Attitudinal Model* (New York: Cambridge University Press, 1993); and by the same authors, *The Supreme Court and Attitudinal Model Revisited* (New York: Cambridge University Press, 2002).

Consensus on the U.S. Supreme Court

For much of the nineteenth century and through the early part of the twentieth century, the Supreme Court publicly operated under what many considered to be a "norm of consensus." Justices believed that unanimity in decision making would serve to strengthen the authority of the Court and its rulings, even if disagreements persisted in private.[1] Over time, however, this behavioral norm appears to have declined among the justices serving on the Court.

▶

The proportion of unanimous decisions handed down by the Court declined sharply between 1930 and 1950, dropping from 90 percent of the cases heard to less than 20 percent. While a number of changes occurred within the judiciary during this period, no definitive explanation exists to account for this trend. Since the 1950s, there has been a modest increase in the proportion of unanimous decisions, but not to anywhere near the level that was common prior to the 1930s.

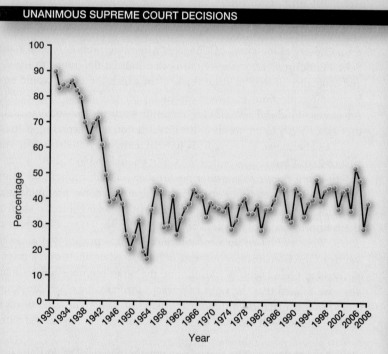

UNANIMOUS SUPREME COURT DECISIONS

Source: Lee Epstein, Jeffrey A. Segal, Harold J. Spaeth, and Thomas G. Walker, *The Supreme Court Compendium: Data, Decisions, and Developments,* 3rd edition. (Washington, DC: CQ Press, 2003). Updated by author.

[1] On these points, see Lee Epstein, Jeffrey A. Segal, and Harold J. Spaeth, "The Norm of Consensus on the U.S. Supreme Court," *American Journal of Political Science* 45 (April 2001): 362–77.

As Alexander Hamilton observed in *Federalist 78*, the federal judiciary was designed to be the weakest of the three branches of government. Given that the Supreme Court is reliant upon the other branches of government to enforce its decisions, it is much easier to defend a unanimous Court decision than one that reveals a sharp divide among the justices.

Federalist 78

The judiciary...has no influence over either the sword or the purse; no direction either of the strength or of the wealth of the society; and can take no active resolution whatever. It may truly be said to have neither FORCE nor WILL, but merely judgment; and must ultimately depend upon the aid of the executive arm even for the efficacy of its judgments.[2]

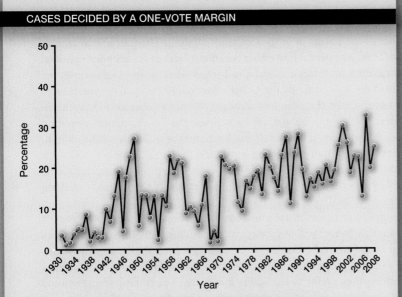

CASES DECIDED BY A ONE-VOTE MARGIN

Percentage vs. Year

Source: Lee Epstein, Jeffrey A. Segal, Harold J. Spaeth, and Thomas G. Walker, *The Supreme Court Compendium: Data, Decisions, and Developments,* 3rd edition. (Washington, DC: CQ Press, 2003). Updated by author.

What are the implications of the precipitous decline in unanimous decisions after 1930? Unanimously decided cases are less likely to be interpreted differently by lower court judges who consider these decisions to be established precedents, whereas decisions supported by a bare majority of justices may not be followed as strictly. Indeed, the proportion of Supreme Court cases decided by a one-vote margin has been steadily increasing since 1930.

[2]Alexander Hamilton, *Federalist No. 78*, in *The Federalist Papers*, Clinton Rossiter, ed. (New York, Penguin: 1961).

for political ideology. In the past, liberal judges have been activists, willing to use the law to achieve social and political change, whereas conservatives have been associated with judicial restraint. Conservative politicians often castigate "liberal activist" judges and call for the appointment of conservative jurists who will refrain from reinterpreting the law. It is interesting, however, that in recent years some conservative justices who have long called for restraint have become activists in seeking to undo some of the work of liberal jurists over the past three decades. To be sure, some liberal jurists are activists and some conservatives have been advocates of restraint, but the relationship is by no means one to one. Indeed, the Rehnquist Court, dominated by conservatives, was among the most activist Courts in American history, striking out in new directions in areas such as federalism and election law.

In our discussion of congressional politics in Chapter 5, we described legislators as policy oriented. In conceiving of judges as legislators in robes, we are effectively claiming that judges, like other politicians, have policy preferences that they seek to implement.

Other Institutions of Government

Congress. At both the national and the state level in the United States, courts and judges are players in the policy game because of the separation of powers. Essentially this means that the legislative branch formulates policy (defined constitutionally and institutionally by a legislative process), the executive branch implements policy (according to well-defined administrative procedures and subject to initial approval by the president or the legislative override of his veto), and the courts, when asked, rule on the faithfulness of the legislated and executed policy, either to the substance of the statute or to the Constitution itself. The courts, that is, may strike down an administrative action either because it exceeds the authority granted in the relevant statute (statutory rationale) or because the statute itself exceeds the authority granted the legislature by the Constitution (constitutional rationale).

If the Court declares the administrative agent's act as outside the permissible bounds prescribed by the legislation, we suppose the Court's majority opinion can declare whatever policy it wishes. If the legislature is unhappy with this judicial action, then it may either recraft the legislation (if the rationale for striking it down was statutory)[49] or initiate a constitutional amendment that would enable the stricken policy to pass constitutional muster (if the rationale for originally striking it down was constitutional).

In reaching their decisions, Supreme Court justices must anticipate Congress's response. As a result, judges will not always vote according to their true preferences because doing so may provoke Congress to enact legislation that moves the policy further from what the judges prefer. By voting for a lesser preference, the justices can get something they prefer to the status quo without provoking congressional action to overturn their decision. The most famous example of this phenomenon is the "switch in time that saved nine," when two justices voted in favor of New Deal legislation, the constitutionality of which they doubted, to diminish congressional

---

[49] William N. Eskridge, Jr., "Overriding Supreme Court Statutory Interpretation Decisions," *Yale Law Journal* 101 (1991): 331–55.

support for President Roosevelt's plan to "pack" the Court by increasing the number of justices. In short, the interactions between the Court and Congress are part of a complex strategic game.[50]

The President. The president's most direct influence on the Court is the power to nominate justices. Presidents typically nominate judges who they believe are close to their policy preferences and close enough to the preferences of a majority of senators, who must confirm the nomination.

Yet the efforts by presidents to reshape the federal judiciary are not always successful. Often in American history, judges have surprised and disappointed the presidents who named them to the bench. Justice Souter, for example, has been far less conservative than President George H. W. Bush and the Republicans who supported Souter's appointment in 1990 thought he would be. Likewise, Justices O'Connor and Kennedy disappointed conservatives by opposing limitations on abortion.

Nevertheless, with a combined total of twelve years in office, Reagan and Bush were able to exercise a good deal of influence on the composition of the federal district and appellate courts. By the end of Bush's term, he and Reagan together had appointed nearly half of all the federal judges. Thus, whatever impact Reagan and Bush ultimately had on the Supreme Court, their federal appointments have certainly had a continuing influence on the temperament and behavior of the district and circuit courts.

President Clinton promised to appoint more liberal jurists to the district and appellate courts and to increase the number of women and minorities serving on the federal bench. During his first two years in office, Clinton held to this promise (Figure 8.7). More than 50 percent of his 128 judicial nominees were women or members of minority groups.[51] A large number of judicial vacancies remained unfilled, however, when the Republicans took control of Congress at the end of 1994. Soon after the election, Senator Orrin Hatch of Utah, the new chair of the Senate Judiciary Committee, indicated his intention to oppose any nominee he deemed too liberal. Hatch's attitude prompted the Clinton White House to withdraw some nominations and to search for district and appellate nominees who would be more acceptable to the Republicans.[52]

During President George W. Bush's first term in office, Senate Democrats fought a pitched battle with the White House to block judicial nominees they deemed too conservative. Ten of Bush's nominees to the circuit courts were blocked by Democratic filibusters, though Bush infuriated Democrats by giving two of them, Charles Pickering, Sr. and William Pryor, temporary recess appointments. Democrats had hoped to block Bush's nominees until the 2004 elections and then see a Democratic president chosen. After Bush's reelection, however, the battle resumed, and Republicans threatened to change the Senate rules to prevent a continuation of

---

[50] A full strategic analysis of the maneuvering among legislative, executive, and judicial branches in the separation-of-powers arrangement choreographed by the U.S. Constitution may be found in William N. Eskridge, Jr. and John Ferejohn, "The Article I, Section 7, Game," *Georgetown Law Review* 80 (1992): 523–65. The entire issue of this journal is devoted to the theme of strategic behavior in American institutional politics.

[51] *Chicago Daily Law Bulletin*, October 5, 1994.

[52] R. W. Apple, Jr., "A Divided Government Remains, and with It the Prospect of Further Combat," *New York Times*, November 7, 1996, p. B6.

FIGURE 8.7 DIVERSITY OF FEDERAL DISTRICT COURT APPOINTEES

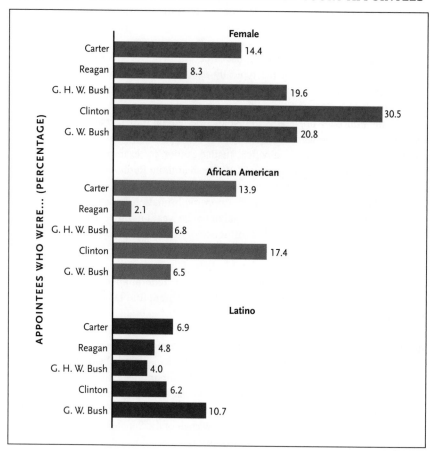

SOURCE: Harold W. Stanley and Richard G. Niemi, *Vital Statistics on American Politics, 2001–2002* (Washington, D.C.: Congressional Quarterly Press, 2001), pp. 277–79, plus updates by the authors.

the Democrats' filibuster. As noted earlier, this threat, known as the nuclear option, was ultimately shelved by the Republicans. The 2006 and 2008 elections changed the political landscape around judicial appointments further. Democrats gained control of the Senate in 2006, which meant that the Senate Judiciary Committee became majority Democratic. As a result, any Bush appointments to the federal bench had to satisfy the Democrats. The 2008 election saw the addition of eight more Democrats to close debate and end filibusters of Barack Obama's judicial appointments.

The Implementation of Supreme Court Decisions

The president and the rest of the executive branch, along with Congress, the states, the lower courts, and a variety of private organizations and individuals also play key roles in the implementation of Supreme Court decisions. Once the high court has made a decision, a variety of other government agencies must put it into effect. The lower courts must understand and apply to new cases the principles asserted by the Supreme Court. The executive branch must enforce the Court's decision. State legislators and governors must implement the decision in their own jurisdictions. And often individuals and organizations must take action in the courts and in the political arena to demand that the Supreme Court's verdicts be fully implemented. At each of these stages, opposition on the part of the revelant actors may delay full national implementation of a Supreme Court decision, sometimes for years.

For example, if lower-court judges strongly disagree with a Supreme Court decision, they may use a variety of tactics to avoid fully implementing it. Lower-court judges may, for example, avoid applying the case by disposing of similar cases on technical or procedural grounds. Similarly, they may apply the case as narrowly as possible or declare that some portion of the Court's opinion was merely "dicta"— useful as guidance but not binding.

As for executive agencies, most Supreme Court decisions must be implemented by federal, state, and local agencies. If these agencies are unsympathetic to the Court's decision, they may obstruct, delay, or even refuse to accept them. In the nineteenth century, President Andrew Jackson famously refused to obey a Supreme Court decision, declaring, "John Marshall has made his decision. Now let him enforce it." Although few executives or executive agencies have been as overtly defiant as Jackson, many have quietly ignored or sought to circumvent the Court. For example, many local school boards have searched for years for ways to circumvent the high court's various rulings prohibiting religious observance in the public schools.

Strategic Behavior in the Supreme Court

In describing the role and effect of the Supreme Court, we have occasionally referred to the strategic opportunities the Court provides. It is useful to gather some of them in one place to stitch together a more consistent strategic interpretation. Let's divide this strategic behavior into three stages. Stage 1 begins with a period of "normal" politics— in (local or national) legislatures, (local or national) executive and regulatory agencies, political processes like elections, and the stuff of everyday life involving interactions among public and private entities (citizens, corporations, nonprofits, voluntary associations, governments). Conflict arises, and interested parties must decide what to do: live with the results, pursue normal political channels using legislatures and agencies to resolve the conflict, or move the conflict into the courts. Stage 2 involves a court responding to its environment, with judges both reacting to demands from the outside and fashioning their own behavioral strategies within the legal process. Stage 3 involves what happens once a court renders a decision and how the actors in stages 1 and 2 anticipate the decision and adjust their behavior to its expectations. Although our discussion could be developed for all courts, we will focus on the U.S. Supreme Court. Indeed, we will narrow things even further by devoting the bulk of our remarks to the internal strategic environment of the Supreme Court at stage 2, when it both reacts to developments that have preceded its being drawn into a conflict (stage 1) and anticipates what will happen if it responds in a particular manner (stage 3).

Stage 1. Assume that a conflict has arisen and appeals have been made through normal channels. Administrative and regulatory agencies, for example, often have well-defined procedures for appealing a ruling within the agency, with the opportunity of a subsequent appeal to a court always being available. Dissatisfied with the outcome, one of the parties moves the dispute to the courts, and at some point in the process the option of appeal to the U.S. Supreme Court is available. The aggrieved party has a decision to make. It is a calculated, strategic decision in three respects.

First, an appeal will consume resources that might otherwise be redeployed and used for different purposes. A prospective appellant must weigh an appeal against this "opportunity cost." The Sierra Club, for example, might use resources to appeal a lower-court decision on environmental protection to the Supreme Court or, alternatively, devote some of those same resources to lobbying Congress on other issues.

Second, a high-court appeal sometimes competes with alternative political moves. An interest group such as the Sierra Club that lost its lower-court appeals might find it more sensible to lobby Congress for a change in the National Environmental Policy Act to ameliorate the condition addressed in the legal proceedings.

Third, all options are uncertain propositions whose resolution stretches out over time. Regarding uncertainty, a prospective appellant must recognize that the probability of successfully getting to the Court is slim, and even if it succeeds in obtaining *certiorari*, it may not win on the merits of its case. Regarding the time dimension, even if the appellant wins, the process may take years, making the delayed victory bittersweet.

Ultimately these strategic calculations revolve around what an appellant can expect in pursuing an appeal—that is, what might happen in stages 2 and 3. Let us turn to them.[53]

Stage 2. As we have already reported, thousands of cases are appealed to the Supreme Court. The decision to appeal from a lower federal or state court is consummated in a petition for a writ of *certiorari*. The nine justices of the Supreme Court (or, more accurately, their clerks) must sort through these petitions and, according to the **rule of four**, build their docket each session: A case is added to the docket if four justices vote to include it. The Court, in short, has the power to create its own agenda. Appellants for each session are competing with about 10,000 others to claim one of fewer than 100 slots.

rule of four The rule that *certiorari* will be granted only if four justices vote in favor of the petition.

In building their docket for the current session of the Court, how do justices think about the available options? They support some cases undoubtedly out of a strong belief that an area is ripe for constitutional clarification. They support others out of an interest in the development of legal principles in a particular area of the law—criminal rights, privacy, First Amendment, abortion, affirmative action, federal-state relations, and so on—or in the belief that contradictory decisions in lower courts need to be sorted out. They may oppose certain appeals because they believe a particular case will not provide a sufficiently clear-cut basis for clarifying a

---

[53] There are subtleties to the strategies of appellants. They may seek an appeal to the Supreme Court, for example, as a bluff to induce the winner in the lower court to accommodate in advance some of their preferences—in effect, to settle out of court. Why might the lower-court winners be induced to accommodate the losers? There are at least two reasons: first, to avoid the exorbitant costs of fighting an appeal to the Supreme Court and, second, to avoid the prospect that their victory in the lower court may be reversed.

legal issue. That is, even though a case might attract the interest of a justice on substantive grounds or might be perceived by a justice as containing procedural errors that could lead to a reversal, he or she might not support *certiorari* because of a strategic calculation that it is not a particularly good vehicle or that it would be prudent to wait until a better vehicle comes up through the appeals process in a subsequent session.[54]

Once a case is included on the docket and oral arguments have been delivered by the attorneys for the litigants and *amicus curiae* briefs filed by other interested parties, the case becomes the subject of two decisions.[55] The first takes place after it is discussed by the justices in one of the regularly scheduled conferences during the Court's term. When discussion has concluded and all attempts at persuasion have come to an end, there is a vote on the merits—a vote in favor of the appeal or against it. In principle, this vote affects only the parties to the case, either affirming or reversing the lower-court decision.

It is the second decision that has a wider bearing. Having decided one way or the other, the justices must determine whether there is agreement on the reasons for their decision. The most senior justice on the winning side—the chief justice if he is in this group—assigns a colleague to write the majority opinion or keeps it for himself to write. This is a highly strategic decision because the Court's impact over and above its effect on the contesting parties depends on the reasons it gives for the decision at hand. The reasons of a Court majority set legal precedent for similar cases in the future, thus influencing litigation in lower courts. If the majority cannot agree among themselves on why they decided as they did, there is no binding effect on other comparable cases. Drafting an opinion that can attract the signatures of at least five justices is therefore of pivotal significance. A justice on the winning side who stakes out an extreme position relative to the others is unlikely to be able to draft such an opinion, so moderate members of the Court usually do the heavy lifting of opinion drafting for especially controversial cases. Of course, in some cases a majority may agree on the merits of a case but are unable to come to a consensus on the reasons. In such cases, there will be no majority opinion, though each justice is free to write his or her own opinion (possibly cosigned by others), either supporting or dissenting from the decision on the merits, giving his or her particular reasons. These opinions have no binding effect on future lower-court cases but may still serve a strategic signaling role, conveying to the lower courts and the legal community where a justice stands on the issues involved in the case at hand.[56]

Stage 3. The Supreme Court is not an island unto itself. It is the top rung of one branch in a separation-of-powers system. Its decisions are not automatically implemented; it must depend on executive agencies for implementation and on

---

[54] An excellent discussion of this facet of Supreme Court decision making is found in Perry, *Deciding to Decide.*

[55] On the strategic decisions of *amicus* groups, see Thomas Hansford, "Information Provision, Organizational Constraints, and the Decision to Submit an Amicus Brief in a U.S. Supreme Court Case," *Political Research Quarterly* 57 (2004): 219–30.

[56] For an insightful discussion of the strategic elements influencing how the senior justice in the winning coalitions assigns opinion writing, see David W. Rohde, "Policy Goals, Strategic Choice, and Majority Opinion Assignments in the U.S. Supreme Court," *Midwest Journal of Political Science* 16 (1972): 652–82.

lower courts for enforcement of its dicta. In fact, it ultimately depends on the willingness of others, especially ordinary citizens, to conform to its rulings. In some instances, the Court may worry about resistance. Throughout the 1940s and 1950s, for example, there were concerns that issues relating to integration would meet with popular disapproval and defiance in the South. Indeed, in the famous *Brown* decision desegregating public schools in 1954, Chief Justice Earl Warren worried about precisely this. When he wrote the majority opinion for the Court, he strategically softened some of its language in order to attract the signatures of all nine justices. The 9–0 decision and opinion were a signal to a potentially defiant South that the Court was united and that it would take a very long time (the time needed to replace at least five justices) before there would be any prospect of reversal—that is, resistance would not pay off in the near or medium term.

In addition to compliance, enforcement, and resistance, the Court must also worry about reversal. On a decision taken by the Court on a statutory issue—for example, on whether an existing law covers a particular situation—majorities in both houses of Congress and the president may pass a new statute reversing the Court's interpretation. If, for example, the Court rules that the Radio Act of 1927 does not cover transmissions by cellular phones and Congress and the president think otherwise, then Congress may pass legislation, and the president may sign it into law, amending the Radio Act of 1927 to allow for its provisions to govern the regulation of cell phones. The Court may well say "what the law is" (to quote Justice Oliver Wendell Holmes), but Congress and the president are free to change the law.[57]

For decisions taken by the Court on constitutional (as opposed to statutory) grounds, no mere revision of existing law is sufficient to reverse the Court; an amendment to the Constitution is required. President George W. Bush, for example, gave his blessing to efforts to amend the Constitution to reverse the *Roe v. Wade* decision permitting a woman to choose an abortion in the first two trimesters of her pregnancy.

In the long run, the Supreme Court is the final legal authority on whether governmental and interpersonal practices satisfy statutory or Constitutional scrutiny. But as Yogi Berra put it, "It ain't over till it's over." The other branches of government must be taken into account as justices vote on cases and write legal opinions; the justices are not free agents. Hence strategic calculation can never be far from their thinking.

CONCLUSION: THE EXPANDING POWER OF THE JUDICIARY

Over the past fifty years, the place of the judiciary in American politics and society has changed dramatically. Demand for legal solutions has increased, and the reach of the judiciary has expanded. Some now call for reining in the power of the courts and discretion of judges in areas ranging from criminal law and sentencing to property rights to liability and torts. How our society deals with these issues will shape the nature of the judiciary—its independence and effectiveness—over the

---

[57] On the strategic interaction among Court, Congress, and the President, see Eskridge and Ferejohn, "The Article I, Section 7, Game."

generations to come. All indications now are that even the most conservative justices are reluctant to relinquish their new-found power, authority that, once asserted, has become accepted and thus established.

Let us summarize what we have learned so far: Judges enjoy great latitude because they are not subject to electoral pressures. Judges and justices, more than any other politicians in America, can pursue their own goals and preferences concerning what is right, their own ideologies. They are, however, constrained—by institutional rules governing access to the courts, by other courts, by Congress and the president, by their lack of enforcement powers, and, most important, by the past in the form of precedent and common law. For much of its history, the federal judiciary acted very cautiously. The Supreme Court rarely challenged Congress or the president. The justices instead tended to legitimate laws passed by Congress and the actions of the president. The scope of the Court's decisions were limited only to those individuals granted access to the courts.

Two judicial revolutions have expanded the power and reach of the federal judiciary in the decades since World War II. The first of these revolutions brought about the liberalization of a wide range of public policies in the United States. As we saw in Chapter 4, in policy areas—including school desegregation, legislative apportionment, and criminal procedure, as well as obscenity, abortion, and voting rights—the Supreme Court was at the forefront of a series of sweeping changes in the role of the U.S. government and, ultimately, the character of American society. The Court put many of these issues before the public long before Congress or the president were prepared to act. At the same time that the courts forged these policy innovations, they were bringing about a second, less visible revolution. During the 1960s and 1970s, the Supreme Court and other federal courts began a series of institutional changes in judicial procedures that had major consequences by fundamentally expanding the power of the courts in the United States. First, the federal courts liberalized the concept of standing to permit almost any group seeking to challenge the actions of an administrative agency to bring its case before the federal bench. In 1971, for example, the Supreme Court ruled that public interest groups could invoke the National Environmental Policy Act to challenge the actions of federal agencies by claiming that the agencies' activities might have adverse environmental consequences.[58] Congress helped make it even easier for groups dissatisfied with government policies to bring their cases to the courts by adopting Title 42, Section 1988, of the U.S. Code, which permits the practice of "fee shifting." Section 1988 allows citizens who successfully bring a suit against a public official for violating their constitutional rights to collect their attorneys' fees and costs from the government. Thus Section 1988 encourages individuals and groups to bring their problems to the courts rather than to Congress or the executive branch. These changes have given the courts a far greater role in the administrative process than ever before.

In a second institutional change, the federal courts broadened the scope of relief to permit themselves to act on behalf of broad categories or classes of persons in "class-action" cases, rather than just on behalf of individuals.[59] A **class-action suit**

---

[58] *Citizens to Preserve Overton Park v. Volpe*, 401 U.S. 402 (1971).

[59] See "Developments in the Law—Class Actions," *Harvard Law Review* 89 (1976): 1318.

class-action suit A lawsuit in which a large number of persons with common interests join together under a representative party to bring or defend a lawsuit, as when hundreds of workers join together to sue a company.

is a procedural device that permits a large number of persons with common interests to join together under a representative party to bring or defend a lawsuit. In 1999, for example, a consortium of several dozen law firms filed a class action suit against firearms manufacturers on behalf of victims of gun violence. Claims could ultimately amount to billions of dollars. Some of the same law firms had been involved earlier in the decade in a massive class action suit against cigarette manufacturers on behalf of victims of tobacco-related illnesses. This suit eventually led to a settlement in which the tobacco companies agreed to pay out several billion dollars. The beneficiaries of the settlement included the treasuries of all fifty states, which received compensation for costs allegedly borne by the states in treating illnesses caused by tobacco use. Of course, the attorneys who brought the case also received an enormous settlement, splitting more than $1 billion. Continuing litigation against tobacco firms remains to be resolved.

In the third major judicial change, the federal courts began to employ so-called structural remedies, in effect retaining jurisdiction of cases until a court's mandate had been implemented to its satisfaction.[60] The best-known of these instances was the effort by federal judge W. Arthur Garrity to operate the Boston school system from his bench to ensure its desegregation. Between 1974 and 1985, Judge Garrity issued fourteen decisions relating to different aspects of the Boston school desegregation plan that had been developed under his authority and put into effect under his supervision.[61]

Through these three judicial mechanisms, the federal courts paved the way for an unprecedented expansion of national judicial power. In essence, liberalization of the rules of standing and expansion of the scope of judicial relief drew the federal courts to link with important social interests and classes. The introduction of structural remedies enhanced the courts' ability to serve these constituencies. Thus during the 1960s and 1970s the power of the federal courts expanded in the same way the power of the executive expanded during the 1930s: through links with constituencies—such as groups advocating civil rights, consumers' rights, gay rights, women's rights, and environmental issues—that staunchly defended the Supreme Court in its battles with Congress, the executive, or other interest groups.

During the 1980s and 1990s, the Reagan and Bush administrations sought to end the relationship between the Court and liberal political forces. Conservative judges appointed by these Republican presidents modified the Court's position in areas such as abortion, affirmative action, and judicial procedure, though not so completely as some conservative writers and politicians had hoped. Within a one-week window in 2003, for example, the Supreme Court affirmed the validity of affirmative action, reaffirmed abortion rights, strengthened gay rights, offered new protection to individuals facing the death penalty, and issued a ruling in favor of a congressional apportionment plan that dispersed minority voters across several districts—a practice that appeared to favor the Democrats.[62] The Court hadn't

---

[60] See Donald L. Horowitz, *The Courts and Social Policy* (Washington, D.C.: Brookings Institution, 1977).

[61] *Morgan v. McDonough*, 540 F. 2nd 527 (1 Cir., 1976); *cert. denied* 429 U.S. 1042 (1977).

[62] David Van Drehle, "Court that Liberals Savage Proves to Be Less of a Target," *Washington Post*, June 29, 2003, p. A18.

changed, rather it had made these decisions based on the Justices' interpretations of precedent and law, not simply personal belief.

The current Court has not been conservative in another sense. It has not been eager to surrender the expanded powers carved out by earlier Courts, especially in areas that assert the power of the national government over the states. Indeed, the opponents to the U.S. Constitution (the Antifederalists in Chapter 2) feared the assertion of the national interest over the states through the independent judiciary. Over two centuries of U.S. history, the reach and authority of the federal judiciary has expanded greatly, and the judiciary has emerged as a powerful arm of our national politics. Whatever their policy beliefs or partisan orientations, judges and justices understand the new-found importance of the courts among the three branches of American government and act not just to interpret and apply the law but also to maintain the power of the courts.

FOR FURTHER READING

Abraham, Henry J. *The Judicial Process: An Introductory Analysis of the Courts of the United States, England, and France.* 7th ed. New York: Oxford University Press, 1998.

Baum, Lawrence. *The Puzzle of Judicial Behavior.* Ann Arbor: University of Michigan Press, 1997. ○ reader selection

Bickel, Alexander M. *The Least Dangerous Branch: The Supreme Court at the Bar of Politics.* Indianapolis, Ind.: Bobbs-Merrill, 1962. ○ reader selection

Epstein, Lee, and Jack Knight. *The Choices Justices Make.* Washington, D.C.: Congressional Quarterly Press, 1998.

Kahn, Ronald. *The Supreme Court and Constitutional Theory, 1953–1993.* Lawrence: University Press of Kansas, 1994.

O'Brien, David M. *Storm Center: The Supreme Court in American Politics.* 7th ed. New York: Norton, 2005.

Perry, H. W., Jr. *Deciding to Decide: Agenda Setting in the United States Supreme Court.* Cambridge, Mass.: Harvard University Press, 1991.

Segal, Jeffrey A., and Harold J. Spaeth. *The Supreme Court and the Attitudinal Model Revisited.* New York: Cambridge University Press, 2002.

Silverstein, Mark. *Judicious Choices: The New Politics of Supreme Court Confirmations.* New York: Norton, 1994.

Toobin, Jeffrey. *The Nine: Inside the Secret World of the Supreme Court.* New York: Knopf, 2008.

Whittington, Keith. *Political Foundations of Judicial Supremacy: The President, the Supreme Court, and Constitutional Leadership in U.S. History.* Princeton, N.J.: Princeton University Press, 2008.

 Additional study and review materials are available online at wwnorton.com/studyspace/

Analyzing the Obama Presidency: The First Two Years

In a historic election in November 2008, Barack Obama was chosen as the forty-fourth president of the United States. Inaugurated on January 20, 2009, he has served during a particularly rocky period of American history—two active wars, increased global economic competition, the most significant economic downturn since the Great Depression, and constituencies clamoring for action on the education, immigration, and environmental fronts: in short, a very full plate for any president. Though many problems were inherited from the Bush administration, President Obama was quickly forced to take ownership of these issues. Obama may have won the election partly because of his predecessor's poor performance, but now the performance under the microscope is his.

Although our focus in this secction is on the Obama administration, we will see that the story of Obama's presidency is inseparable from the stories of the other branches of government. We will also see how the concepts we have covered in this book so far can help us analyze and understand the politics of Obama's first two years. We can think of the Bush years as important background, but a new set of interests and objectives have been formulated under Obama. The attempt to pursue a very full agenda has constituted the stuff of politics these last two years and provides an illustration of how politicians act strategically in pursuit of their goals. The story of that effort is an institutional one, as the Obama administration decided on a strategy that put the U.S. Congress square in the middle and had the opportunity to appoint two new justices to the Supreme Court.

THE TEAM

The first task of any president-elect is, together with his transition team, to select a governing team—his cabinet and senior advisors. With his choice of Representative Rahm Emanuel (D-IL) to be White House chief of staff, President-elect Obama signaled to the political class that his administration was going to focus on securing an expansive legislative agenda. The rest of the administration was pieced together with this objective in mind, as well as other goals, including countering perceived weaknesses in the president's resumé, demonstrating seriousness of purpose, and repaying politicians who supported the president's election.

Throughout the primary and general election campaigns, Obama had to fend off criticisms of inexperience in foreign policy. The selection of Joe Biden of Delaware, a senator with extensive foreign policy experience, as Obama's running mate was one way his advisors attempted to address this. To shore up Obama's foreign policy credentials, the transition team surrounded the president with noted national security experts. Retaining Robert Gates, President Bush's secretary of defense, provided some continuity between administrations during a time in which the country was involved in two wars. The addition of General Jim Jones as the national security advisor lent even more weight to the national security team. Appointing his former rival Senator Hillary Clinton (D-NY) as the secretary of state harnessed the good will and energy of Senator Clinton and her husband, former president Bill Clinton. It also moved a potential critic into the administration.

Obama's nominee for treasury secretary, Timothy Geith- ▶
ner, was initially seen by some as too cozy with Wall
Street to push through needed financial reforms. How-
ever, Geithner was eventually confirmed and has been
instrumental in crafting and implementing Obama's
economic and financial initiatives.

On the domestic front, the transition team faced the daunting task of finding candidates for cabinet positions who could play to the president's political supporters and at the same time get confirmed by the Senate. In addition, several of them had to be credible with the financial industry. The principal financial appointee was Timothy Geithner to head the Treasury Department. Unfortunately, there were a few revelations of unpaid taxes, which were humbling for a man who would be chief of the department that oversees the Internal Revenue Service. However, the greater problem for Geithner's confirmation was the role he had played as head of the Federal Reserve Bank of New York in the period leading up to the financial crisis of late 2008. He had credibility on Wall Street, but this wasn't the best character reference in the stormy weeks following the passage of the Troubled Assets Relief Program (TARP), as many Americans held Wall Street responsible for the problems in the economy. Nonetheless, Geithner was confirmed. Another important member of the economic team was Lawrence Summers, the former vice president of the World Bank, Clinton treasury secretary and, more recently, president of Harvard University. Summers became the principal economic advisor to the president.

President Obama's focus on health care reform led to great speculation about whom he would choose to head the Department of Health and Human Services. His first choice, former South Dakota senator Tom Daschle, provided another strong signal that the president intended to get health care reform through Congress. Daschle had served as majority leader in the Senate and knew the inner workings of Congress. However, a significant tax delinquency derailed this nomination. Instead, the president settled on Kathleen Sebelius, the governor of Kansas.

In an attempt to repay an early declaration of support, President Obama named New Mexico governor Bill Richardson to be secretary of commerce. This bid failed when it was revealed that the governor was under investigation for improper conduct in his home state. The Commerce hot potato then landed in the lap of Senator Judd Gregg (R-NH), but Gregg later publicly repudiated the nomination in a spat with the president. The vacancy was finally filled by the former two-term governor of Washington, Gary Locke.

As all this suggests, former office holders were a major presence in the cabinet. Ray LaHood at the Department of Transportation had been a member of the House. The secretary of agriculture position went to a farm-state politician, Tom Vilsack, the former governor of Iowa. Janet Napolitano, the governor of Arizona, became the secretary of homeland security. Ron Kirk, the former mayor of Dallas, became the

U.S. trade representative. President Obama nominated Congresswoman Hilda Solis (D-CA) to head the Department of Labor. He named Senator Ken Salazar (D-CO) to become the secretary of the interior. The Obama cabinet also included academics like Secretary of Energy Steven Chu, Ambassador to the UN Susan Rice, and Chair of the Council on Economic Advisors Christina Romer. Eric Holder's appointment as attorney general added another former Clinton appointee to a top Obama administration post. David Axelrod, Obama's campaign manager, moved into a position as an advisor to the president, while Robert Gibbs took on the role of press secretary.

The diversity of backgrounds, genders, and races was an important sign of Obama's commitment to the different political constituencies within the Democratic Party. In addition to their political qualifications, that Salazar and Solis were Hispanic was important to the new administration. Eric Holder's appointment as attorney general was historic in that he was the first African American to hold that office. Kirk and Rice are also African American. Clinton, Napolitano, Romer, Rice, Sebelius, and Solis are women. Chu and Locke are Asian American. It is important to remember that every action a president takes is interpreted as a signal of support for different electoral constituencies. With his team in place, the president went to work on some of his legislative goals.

EARLY LEGISLATIVE ACHIEVEMENTS

Together with the Democratic 111th Congress, President Obama achieved a number of legislative results in his first two years. This section discusses some of Obama's significant legislative victories: the Lilly Ledbetter Fair Pay Act, the Children's Health Insurance Program Reauthorization Act of 2009, the American Recovery and Reinvestment Act of 2009, and financial reform legislation. The next section looks at the case of health care reform legislation in some detail and analyzes the politics surrounding its passage. Table 1 shows how Congress voted on each of these bills. In working to get these bills passed, Obama's team was strategic in how they pursued their goals and mindful of the institutional rules and practices that would affect the outcomes.

The Lilly Ledbetter Fair Pay Act

Obama championed the cause of Lilly Ledbetter, a former employee of the Goodyear Tire & Rubber Company, and other women who shared her plight. When Ledbetter retired from Goodyear in 1998, she was earning significantly less than her male peers. She sued the company, claiming that she was a victim of discrimination based on gender, and arguing that supervisors had prevented her from receiving the same pay raises as her male peers. The central claim of her case was that her current state of reduced retirement income was the result of previous acts of discrimination. Ledbetter won her case at the district court level, where she was awarded both back pay and damages. Goodyear then appealed the case based on the fact that her complaint was filed in 1998, which meant that the alleged discrimination took place well outside the 180-day time limit imposed by the Civil Rights Act of 1964. The appellate court agreed with Goodyear and overturned the lower court's decision. Ledbetter pursued an appeal to the Supreme Court, where she argued that pay discrimination was not a discrete event like being fired or other more overt job actions and that therefore the Court should use a different rule for establishing when the 180-day clock starts. The Court rejected her claim. Justice Samuel Alito, writing the majority opinion, cited several precedents where petitioners' claims had been rejected as a result of untimely filings. The Lilly Ledbetter Fair Pay Act, which Obama actively supported and signed into law in 2009, legislatively overturned the Supreme Court's decision. It amended U.S. law so that the 180-day time period starts each time the employee receives a paycheck that is affected by a discriminatory decision instead of when the discriminatory pay decision was made.

The Children's Health Insurance Program Reauthorization Act of 2009

Although the bill enjoyed considerable bipartisan support, President George W. Bush vetoed the Children's Health Insurance Plan Reauthorization Act of 2007 (CHIP). His principal objection to the bill was his belief that it was a step toward socialized medicine and that it provided incentives to middle- and upper-income parents to move their children off private insurance plans and onto the public plan. There was tremendous political fallout over this decision. Calling it a "heartless veto," Senate Majority Leader Harry Reid (D-NV) accused President Bush of denying health care to millions of children. Reauthorizing and expanding CHIP became a Democratic campaign promise that President Obama fulfilled early in his administration.

The American Recovery and Reinvestment Act of 2009

The economic downturn of 2008 gave a major boost to the campaign of Barack Obama. In fact, throughout most of the end stages of the presidential campaign, Senator Obama drew distinctions between his plan to get the economy growing, what his opponent, Senator John McCain (R-AZ), would do, and what the Republican Party, under President George W. Bush,

Although most Americans agreed that the gov- ▶
ernment needed to address the economic crisis,
Obama's specific plans for the economy were
controversial. Some Democrats complained that
the government was "bailing out" Wall Street
rather than ordinary Americans, while some Re-
publicans objected to the deep deficit that would
result from increased government spending.

had done. Obama proposed enacting a large stimulus package of federal spending mixed with some targeted tax cuts. The purpose of this spending was to spur economic demand. This constituted a 180-degree departure from the more conservative Republican emphasis on supply-side economics, which calls for stimulating the economy by giving incentives to producers, through tax breaks and subsidies, to employ their capital. Supply-side prescriptions for helping the economy favor reducing taxes and eliminating governmental regulation. The demand-side proponents argued that producers were not going to produce more when consumers were not inclined to buy what was being produced. The stimulus would put money into the hands of consumers, which would then enable producers to get back to employing their capital and ultimately would lead the economy out of the recession. As a result of this sharp ideological divide, support for the American Recovery and Reinvestment Act of 2009, Public Law 111-5, ran almost completely along partisan lines (see Table 1). No Republican members of the House and only three Republican senators supported passage.

Financial Reform Legislation

If the economic downturn gave the Obama campaign a general boost, the near complete meltdown of the global financial system created a major challenge for the new president. Political pressure for a response was intense. The Obama administration, along with its allies in Congress, delivered by enacting laws to protect consumers, restructure the financial system, and prevent a recurrence of the factors that led to the collapse in the first place. The Democrats enacted the Fraud Enforcement and Recovery Act of 2009, the Helping Families Save Their Homes Act of 2009, the Credit Card Accountability Responsibility and Disclosure Act of 2009, and the Dodd-Frank Wall Street Reform and Consumer Protection Act. As Table 1 shows, the Republicans were more supportive of these acts than of Obama's other major initiatives.

HEALTH CARE REFORM

No discussion of President Obama's legislative track record would be complete without treating the passage of the Patient Protection and Affordable Care Act and the Health Care and Education Reconciliation Act of 2010. Together, the two laws comprised Obama's landmark health care reform legislation. The last attempt at comprehensive health care reform in the United States, a failure, had severely weakened President Clinton. In fact, some argued that President Obama's plan to enact health care reform was based on a study of how opponents of health care reform had defeated the Clinton attempt.

Where President Clinton had used an executive branch approach to fashioning a plan, President Obama chose a plan driven by the legislative branch. He outlined the basic goals but left the details to the legislative leaders who would be responsible for getting the plan through Congress. Where Clinton's plan faced intense industry opposition, Obama sought buy-in from the industries to be regulated by his plan. Another crucial difference between the approaches of Clinton and Obama

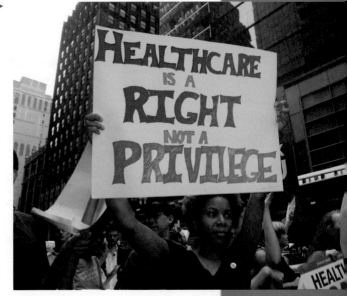

The issue of health care reform was highly divi- ▶
sive. Even Democrats who supported reform in
general disagreed over the details. Obama and
his allies in Congress struggled to devise a plan
that would win the necessary votes.

arose from the facts that Obama enjoyed
a bigger partisan seat advantage in each
chamber of Congress and that the Democrats were more ideologically unified than
they had been in 1993–94.

Even with this more inclusive strategy,
however, securing passage of Obama's
health care reform legislation was far from
simple. While the Democrats in the 111th
Congress were more ideologically unified
than their predecessors in Clinton's 103rd,
there was still a considerable diversity of
preferences. Some on the liberal end of

the spectrum wanted a single-payer system that was flatly opposed by all Republicans
and most centrist Democrats. At the same time, the minor modifications to the current system that more conservative members favored were insufficient for liberals.
Social issues that had not previously divided Democrats in the health care debate
started to gain traction when Democrats representing socially conservative districts
demanded provisions limiting funding for abortions and stem cell research.

Not to be completely left out of the debate, opponents of health care reform
used the opportunity of Democratic intra-party squabbling to project their own
views on the issue. Former Alaska governor Sarah Palin, the 2008 Republican vice-
presidential candidate, a vocal critic of the president, and a potential presidential
challenger in 2012, weighed in with her concerns about bureaucratic determination of end-of-life care, which she termed "death panels." The politics of the matter were further confused when opponents of health care reform argued that the
president's plan would endanger current Medicare benefits, leaving some Medicare recipients to object to "socialized medicine" even though they were already on
government-provided health insurance.

By late fall 2009, it had become clear that health care reform remained highly
divisive. In the January 2010 special election in Massachusetts to fill the U.S. Senate seat of Ted Kennedy, the eventual winner, Republican Scott Brown, campaigned
as being *the* vote to stop Obamacare. Ironically, Senator Brown's election may well
have made passage of health care reform possible, because it put to rest some of
the squabbles within the Democratic party over policy alternatives. The loss of the
Kennedy seat to the Republicans meant that some of the features preferred by
more liberal Democrats in the House were no longer viable. To understand why
requires an appreciation of the institutional context in which the parties and politicians contest policy.

When President Obama announced that he intended to make health care reform part of his legislative agenda for the 111th Congress, he had to rebut critics

TABLE 1 FINAL PASSAGE VOTE TALLIES: HOUSE OF REPRESENTATIVES

| | HOUSE OF REPRESENTATIVES | | | | | |
| | Total | | Democrats | | Republicans | |
Legislation	Yeas	Nays	Yeas	Nays	Yeas	Nays
The Lilly Ledbetter Fair Pay Act	250	177	247	5	3	172
The Children's Health Insurance Program Reauthorization Act of 2009	290	135	250	2	40	133
The American Recovery and Reinvestment Act of 2009	246	183	246	7	0	163
The Fraud Enforcement and Recovery Act of 2009	338	52	224	0	114	52
The Helping Families Save Their Homes Act of 2009	367	54	244	3	123	51
The Credit Card Accountability Responsibility and Disclosure Act of 2009	279	147	105	145	174	2
The Dodd-Frank Wall Street Reform and Consumer Protection Act	237	192	234	19	3	173
The Patient Protection and Affordable Care Act	219	212	219	34	0	178
The Health Care and Education Reconciliation Act of 2010	220	207	220	32	0	175

SOURCE: The Library of Congress, http://thomas.loc.gov/ (accessed 10/21/10).

who argued that his young administration already had too many issues to address. Obama faced the immediate tasks of waging the wars in Iraq and Afghanistan simultaneously and rescuing an economy on the brink of collapse. Both his supporters and his opponents suggested that attempting to pass health care reform was an unnecessary burden. However, reviewing the political situation from Obama's viewpoint allows one to see why a newly elected president would go for big-ticket legislative items early in his first term.

It may help to use an example from the military. When developing combat orders, military planners first assess the terrain, then try to determine the ways in which the enemy can use the terrain, and finally take stock of their assets and allies in order to try to use them to counter what the enemy might do to prevent the unit from achieving its objectives. This is summed up by three short commands: "see the terrain, see the enemy, see yourself." Upon becoming president of the United States of America, Barack Obama, along with his advisors, must have conducted a similar strategic review of the situation.

TABLE 1 (CONT.) FINAL PASSAGE VOTE TALLIES: SENATE

| | SENATE | | | | | |
| | Total | | Democrats | | Republicans | |
Legislation	Yeas	Nays	Yeas	Nays	Yeas	Nays
The Lilly Ledbetter Fair Pay Act	61	36	56	0	5	36
The Children's Health Insurance Program Reauthorization Act of 2009	66	32	57	0	9	32
The American Recovery and Reinvestment Act of 2009	60	38	57	0	3	38
The Fraud Enforcement and Recovery Act of 2009	92	4	56	0	36	4
The Helping Families Save Their Homes Act of 2009	91	5	56	0	35	5
The Credit Card Accountability Responsibility and Disclosure Act of 2009	90	5	55	1	35	4
The Dodd-Frank Wall Street Reform and Consumer Protection Act	60	39	57	1	3	38
The Patient Protection and Affordable Care Act	60	39	60	0	0	39
The Health Care and Education Reconciliation Act of 2010	56	43	56	3	0	40

"See the Terrain"

Instead of a physical terrain, political strategists see their battlefield as the institutions in which political actions take place. Instead of in mountains, forests, valleys, and rivers, political fights take place on the floor of the House and Senate, in the committee chambers, at the party caucuses/conferences, in political action committees, at regulatory commission hearings, in administrative law courts, in the judicial courts, and indeed in the "court" of public opinion. For achieving the president's agenda, the terrain is the Congress.

Barack Obama took office with huge majorities in both houses of Congress. Only Lyndon Johnson in 1965 enjoyed larger majorities. Possession of these majorities, however, is tempered by the fact that, with few exceptions, the party of the president loses seats in the president's first midterm election; accomplishments must come early.

The president also had to adapt to the unexpected. During Obama's inaugural luncheon on Capitol Hill, Senator Ted Kennedy (D-MA), one of Obama's key supporters, had to be taken away by ambulance. In a situation where every single vote counts, the age and relative health of the members of Congress start to factor into legislative strategies. The lesson here is that new presidents should go for the big-ticket items early in their terms because they may not get a second chance.

Strategists must also consider the rules of both bodies and their implications for the president's agenda. A central concern for the administration and in the media was the possibility of obstruction in the Senate. As we discussed in Chapter 5, 60 votes are needed to overcome a filibuster. So, the administration would need to assemble a coalition of 60 senators whose votes could close down debate. The necessity of "getting to 60" in the Senate means that an essential senator can hold hostage the policy preferences of majorities in both legislative chambers. President Obama's team was very close to "getting to 60" and knew the identity of the one or two senators who could take them over the top. These senators, in turn, knew their value to the president and were in a position to extract maximum reward for their votes.

Political terrain is different from geographic terrain. While mountains and valleys are relatively stable, political terrain is dynamic. The essential senators alluded to in the previous paragraph changed as the composition and/or political affiliation of the U.S. Senate changed for various reasons, one member at a time. The initial seating of 99 senators—the outcome of the Minnesota Senate race had not been determined—left the filibuster pivot among a trio of moderate Republicans: Arlen Specter (PA), Susan Collins (ME), and Olympia Snowe (ME). However, Specter's switching of his party affiliation from Republican to Democrat as a result of an intra-party challenge in Pennsylvania coupled with the declaration that Al Franken (D) had won the hotly contested Minnesota Senate seat changed the identity of the pivotal senator to Ben Nelson (D-NE).

"See the Enemy"

Military planners say that the enemy gets a vote. In the case of the president, the enemy is any political actor who wants to prevent the president from securing parts of his legislative agenda. There are different categories of those who oppose the president's goals. The Republicans in Congress executed a simple policy of confronting the president; they opted for no compromise, voting against almost everything he wanted to accomplish. As Table 1 shows, not a single Republican voted for either of the two health care bills passed in 2010. It is easy to suggest that this is just a case of sour grapes and of being ornery for the sake of being ornery. However, a more sophisticated reading of this tactic is that by forcing the administration to rely on strict party votes to pass legislation, it actually pulls the Democratic administration policy toward its most conservative members, instead of making it appealing to moderate Republicans. A secondary benefit of such opposition is that it frees the Republican Party from blame if something goes wrong. One of the few benefits of being in the minority is that the minority's political task is to point out how the majority party has screwed things up. The minority party is free of the responsibilities of governing.

In addition to members of the minority party in Congress, Republicans with national election ambitions made themselves known by going public in opposition. Sarah Palin was a constant critic of the Obama administration. Other high-profile critics—former speaker of the House Newt Gingrich, former governor of Massachusetts Mitt Romney, and former governor of Arkansas Mike Huckabee—were all rumored to be considering presidential bids in 2012.

"See Yourself"

Having a good understanding of the political situation in which he finds himself, the president is better able to evaluate methods for implementing his legislative agenda. What tools does the president have to get things done? Within the bounds of legislative and legal restrictions, he has nominal control over the immense federal bureaucracy and the resources it controls. The president has sticks and carrots to encourage legislators to work with him instead of against him. For example, suppose a vote in favor of health care reform will be secured if a senator is able to obtain more federal assistance for her state. Several years after Hurricane Katrina, mobile teams of federal health clinics descended upon Louisiana. One of Louisiana's senators, Mary Landrieu (D), initially uncertain, came to support Obamacare. In short, the president can, and President Obama did, use discretionary authority over federal activity and, as leader of his party, exert legislative guidance over the exact language and structure of legislation to assemble a winning coalition.

What Obama won did not please all his supporters; indeed, it undoubtedly fell short of his own aspirations. But a win is a win, and in this case a bare win was about as good as he could do. The point of this section has been to drive home the idea that the president must know the rules of the institutional game, the capabilities of his opponents, and the tools he controls in order to implement his legislative agenda. We devoted special attention to health care since passing health care reform was one of Obama's major domestic achievements.

LEGISLATIVE DISAPPOINTMENTS AND CHALLENGES

Obama took on enormous political risks when he staked his presidency on legislative accomplishments. The first risk was that he would fail to accomplish what he had set out to do. For example, President Jimmy Carter's inability to realize his big plans contributed greatly to his defeat in the 1980 election and to the impression that his presidency was "a failure," and Obama risks suffering the same consequences.

The second risk is that the messy and often ugly process of legislation will frustrate the president's efforts to meet these goals. There is a reason that the German statesman Otto von Bismarck said, "Laws are like sausages. It's better not to see them being made." Compromise is at the heart of politics in a democracy. When the president gives special favors to those whose vote might help his legislation pass or when the majority leader tries to pass amendments that favor a particular senator or representative, the seamy side of politics is rearing its head. During the attempt to pass health care reform, critics of bartering political favors for crucial votes had a field day. For example, Nebraska was given a Medicare exemption that no other state received solely to secure the vote for Obamacare of the pivotal Nebraska senator, something the media publicized and Obama opponents took great pains to point out. For a president who campaigned on "changing politics as we know it," it looked an awful lot like old-school politics. The Republicans were free to point out the inconsistencies between Democratic pledges for open, honest government and the closed-door negotiations, proposals, and counterproposals that were taking place. Even worse, elements of the coalitions that supported President Obama in the campaign had to watch as their objectives were sacrificed or ignored in the quest to get *something* done. Compromise is all well and good unless your pet policy is the one that's about to be compromised away, and public legislative bargaining alienated some supporters. In short, the messiness of the political process negatively affected the Democrats and left the Republicans largely unscathed.

Even when the president takes great pains to understand his political situation, he sometimes fails to meet his objectives. Most notably, Obama has not passed significant environmental legislation nor has he secured comprehensive immigration reform.

Environmental Legislation

Although the Democratic platform called for "implement[ing] a market-based cap and trade system to reduce carbon emissions by the amount scientists say is necessary to avoid catastrophic change and [setting] interim targets along the way to ensure that we meet our goal," Democrats were unable to muster the votes to pass the legislation in the Senate. Furthermore, the filibuster did not come into play as Democrats in the House were unable to obtain even a simple majority to pass the proposed legislation.

Immigration Reform

When Arizona governor Jan Brewer signed Arizona Senate Bill 1070, a controversial law that permitted Arizona police to stop and require identification from individuals who might be illegal aliens, comprehensive immigration reform jumped back to the forefront of U.S. political conversation. It is a topic that previous presidents have faced and not handled well. President George W. Bush attempted (and failed) to pass comprehensive immigration reform during his second term. A great deal of the opposition came from members of the president's own party.

Most federal immigration laws have aimed at limiting or reducing the immigration of national and racial minorities. In the wake of the terrorist attacks of September 11, 2001, the immigration debate became enmeshed in the dramatic confusion of national security policy, economic policy, and human rights. The Democrats recognized the intricacies of dealing with immigration reform, stating in their 2008 platform that "our current immigration system has been broken for far too long. We need comprehensive immigration reform, not just piecemeal efforts. We are committed to pursuing tough, practical, and humane immigration reform in the first year of the next administration."

With so many different dimensions, immigration reform is a topic with many losing positions and few winning ones. Even Senator John McCain (R-AZ), Obama's opponent in the 2008 presidential election and a strong supporter of President Bush's plans for comprehensive immigration reform, faced a tough primary challenge from the *right* in his 2010 bid for reelection to the Senate and altered his position on immigration to shore up his conservative credentials. It is no wonder that politicians avoid the topic of immigration reform even when they declare it to be a top priority.

This all leads us to ask how these apparently hopeless items end up on the president's legislative agenda. Some of these policy positions are personal preferences that stem from life experiences. Others result from trying to persuade large groups of voters to support one's candidacy for office. Obama, for example, sought the support of young voters and of highly educated ones, both of which groups would support increases in federal assistance for higher education. He also sought the support of Hispanic Americans; hence his emphasis on immigration reform.

OBAMA'S USE OF EXECUTIVE ORDERS

In many cases, the president opts to use nonlegislative tools to achieve his policy objectives. Clearly, the fastest, most direct, and easiest way to implement change is to issue an executive order. As we saw in Chapter 6, executive orders are instructions the president gives to the government, implementing his policy objectives using authority granted to the president by Congress through previous laws. Sometimes a president issues an executive order when attempts to arrive at a legislative solution fail.

The earliest actions of the Obama presidency were executive orders rescinding some of the more controversial policies of his predecessor. With the stroke of a pen, President Obama changed government policy on detention operations at the naval base at Guantanamo Bay; clarified his administration's stance on the use of torture and/or controversial interrogation techniques; reversed the previous administration's ban on certain types of stem cell research; and reversed the so-called "Mexico City gag rule," which restricted federal funding for groups who performed or advocated abortion in other countries as a component of family-planning services.

The executive order reversing the gag rule is a good example of why executive orders are in some ways less desirable than new laws. As easy as it was for President Obama to rescind the old order, it will be equally as easy for a future president to reinstate it. In fact, the gag rule was first imposed by President Reagan in 1984. Shortly after his inauguration, President Clinton issued an executive order rescinding Reagan's policy. Shortly after his inauguration, President George W. Bush issued an executive order rescinding President Clinton's executive order.

Finally, the president as a unitary actor and as the commander-in-chief of the military is free to issue commands that are either inherently beyond the scope of legislation or create a very high cost for Congress to do anything to reverse. While many Republicans supported President Obama's expansion of the war in Afghanistan, many Democrats in Congress were upset. Ultimately, both Republicans and Democrats have little control over the president's options in this realm. While

TABLE 2 NOMINATIONS TO FEDERAL COURTS

President	Congress	Nominations	Confirmed	Withdrawn	Rejected	Expired	Pending
George W. Bush	110th	104	68	6	0	30	N/A
Barack H. Obama	111th	97	41	1	7	N/A	48

SOURCE: The Library of Congress, http://thomas.loc.gov/ (accessed 10/21/10)

Congress does hold the purse strings, the political reality is that Congress will back down in the face of the president in his role as commander-in-chief. Congress will not allow itself to be accused of failing to support the members of the American military while they are engaged in foreign conflict.

CHANGES ON THE SUPREME COURT

Presidents have many opportunities to fill posts in the federal judiciary, the most common of which are naming district and appeals court judges. Table 2 compares President Obama's federal court nominations in his first two years in office to President Bush's from his last half-term. More than half of Obama's nominees have yet to be decided on. Rarer for presidents are opportunities to name justices to the Supreme Court. President Obama has been fortunate in his first two years; he has been able to fill *two* Supreme Court vacancies. Obama's selections partly reflected his commitment to diversity. He named, and the Senate confirmed, two women: Sonia Sotomayor, a Catholic Hispanic, and Elena Kagan, a Jew. The court now consists of six Catholics and three Jews (the first time in living memory that no Protestant serves), a Hispanic for the first time, and three women (a historical high). Given the age and health of the sitting justices, Obama may have additional opportunities before his present term concludes.

Sonia Sotomayor, Obama's first nominee, had served for eight years as a federal district judge (nominated by President George H. W. Bush) and for an additional ten years as a court of appeals judge (nominated by President Bill Clinton). Shortly after Justice David Souter announced his retirement in spring 2009, Obama nominated Sotomayor to the Supreme Court, and she was confirmed by the Senate in August 2009 by a 68–31 vote. Perhaps her most famous ruling as a federal judge was one in which she prevented major league baseball owners from hiring replacements for striking baseball players, thus bringing the 1994 baseball strike to an end. Her "paper trail" as a federal judge was quite extensive, with a mainly liberal cast (though she was not always predictable, especially on business-related issues). This provided her opponents with many opportunities to try to derail the nomination. But, after following the tried-and-true practice of nominees to provide little indication of their inclinations on current hot-button legal issues during confirmation hearings, Sotomayor was confirmed relatively easily.

Prior to her nomination to the Supreme Court, Elena Kagan had a varied legal career. From 1995 to 1999 she served as President Clinton's White House counsel. He nominated her to a federal judgeship in 1999, but the Republican-controlled Senate did not schedule a hearing and her nomination lapsed when Clinton left office at the end of the year. After returning to academia—she had been a professor of law at the University of Chicago—she was named professor, and then dean, at the Harvard Law School. In early 2009 President Obama appointed her solicitor general. A year later, Justice John Paul Stevens, the oldest member of the Supreme Court, announced he would retire that summer. Kagan was nominated by the president in May 2010 and confirmed later that summer, after another uneventful confirmation hearing, by a 63–37 vote.

EVALUATING THE OBAMA PRESIDENCY

As we have already noted, it is too early to evaluate Obama's record and the impact of his first two years as president. However, we can make a few observations about how Obama's early record might eventually be assessed.

President Obama will be evaluated not only for his legislative hits and misses but also for the implementation of policy during his administration. There his record of accomplishments is less clear. One way to assess the president is to look

FIGURE 1 PRESIDENT OBAMA'S APPROVAL RATING AND MONTHLY EMPLOYMENT, JANUARY 2008–SEPTEMBER 2010 (SEASONALLY ADJUSTED)

at the stated goals of his presidency before he took office and evaluate his success so far. As part of the party's platform, "Renewing America's Promise," the president vowed to renew the American dream, renew American leadership, renew the American community, and renew American democracy.

If the economic stimulus package and health care reform bring about the objectives of the laws, the president will have succeeded in renewing economic and social well-being. Renewing American leadership in the world is much more questionable. The situation in Afghanistan is deeply problematic; Pakistan remains a questionable ally; and the dismissal of the director of National Intelligence bodes poorly for intelligence reform. Iran seems on the brink of developing nuclear weapons, and North Korea will likely retain its nuclear capacity. American combat brigades have withdrawn from Iraq on schedule, but a resurgence of coordinated terrorist attacks is making permanent peace in the country questionable. Recent cyber-attacks on Google in China and U.S. government networks indicate that much work remains to be done on strengthening cyber-security. The successes in this broader category of American leadership largely stem from policies that focus on "revitalizing and supporting our military, keeping faith with veterans." The country is still a long way off from establishing energy security; and its efforts to provide international leadership to combat climate change are currently dead in Congress.

Renewing the American community is also a mixed bag for the president. The failure to enact significant immigration reform is a gaping hole. The catastrophic oil spill in the Gulf of Mexico underscores the federal government's Katrina-like inability to handle large-scale environmental crises. Of course, the president has also not scored many points for the government's continuing efforts to rebuild New Orleans and other areas affected by Hurricane Katrina.

Ultimately, President Obama's term in office will be judged by whether he is reelected in 2012. Research has shown that the economy is the single most important indicator of how well presidents will do in their bids for reelection. According to the Bureau of Economic Analysis, the economy had begun to expand by the end of Obama's first two years, but the rate of growth is slow. The rule of thumb is that voters punish incumbents when the economy underperforms. Figure 1 illustrates the relationship between presidential approval rating and economic performance with regards to employment. If the economy rebounds, all will be forgiven and President Obama will likely cruise to reelection. If the economy stagnates or deteriorates further, then the president's chances of remaining in office decline.

PART THREE

Democratic Politics

9

Public Opinion

Public support is the coin of the realm in Washington politics. Popular presidents succeed; unpopular presidents struggle. A president who has the backing of a large majority of the public gains leverage in dealing with Congress and the bureaucracy, but a president who lacks public support often meets resistance from members of Congress, even those in his own party. In 1981, Republican president Ronald Reagan had just won a landslide election when he proposed massive cuts in income and capital taxes. Reluctant to oppose such a popular president, the Democratic-controlled Congress readily passed the cuts, allowing Reagan to reduce radically the number of federal regulations. President George W. Bush later described Reagan's popularity as political capital, an asset that must be spent wisely on a few well-chosen issues.[1]

Members of Congress are perhaps even more attuned than the president to the ups and downs of public opinion. Representatives in the U.S. House must run for reelection every two years, a very short election cycle. They cannot afford to make many unpopular decisions for fear of being punished by their constituents in the next election. A saying among members of Congress goes, "It's okay to be on the losing side of a vote, but you don't want to be on the wrong side." That is, they worry about going against their constituents' preferences. Members of Congress and party leaders pay close attention to various indicators of public sentiment, including polls, visits back to their districts or home states, and letters, phone calls, and e-mails from constituents.

---

[1] Chris Suellentrop, "America's New Political Capital," *Slate*, November 30, 2004, www.slate.com/id/2110256/ (accessed 3/18/09). Also see Richard Neustadt, *Presidential Power and the Modern Presidents*, 4th ed. (New York: Free Press, 1990), and Brandice Canes-Wrone, *Who Leads Whom? Presidents, Policy, and the Public* (Chicago: University of Chicago Press, 2006).

Even the courts are not immune to the influence of public opinion. Courts lack the power to enforce their decisions; they depend on the compliance of those affected and the cooperation of Congress, the president, and political leaders in the states. That cooperation is not always forthcoming. As we saw in Chapter 4, *Brown v. Board of Education*, perhaps the most important court decision of the twentieth century, met with immediate opposition in the southern states. In 1963, Governor George Wallace of Alabama stood on the statehouse steps and declared his firm opposition to the Court's edict that the states desegregate "with all deliberate speed." Desegregation occurred slowly, often in the face of violent protests. Only after public opinion turned in support of equal rights for all races did Congress and the president act, accelerating the pace of desegregation.[2]

Aside from particular government decisions, public opinion is also the standard by which we judge democracy in America. Ideally, representative democracy approximates what the nation as a whole would choose to do were all

---

[2] Gerald Rosenberg, *The Hollow Hope* (Chicago: University of Chicago Press, 1991).

CORE OF THE ANALYSIS

- There are a wide range of interests at stake in any question that the government must decide, as well as differing preferences, beliefs, and opinions about what ought to be done.

- Public opinion is the aggregation of individuals' views. It expresses the range of attitudes and beliefs and on which side of any question a majority of people fall.

- Politicians follow public opinion as part of the representative process. They take signals from polls and other indicators of public sentiment to gauge whether a particular decision might affect their prospects at the next election.

- Politicians, interest groups, the media, and others try to shape public opinion by influencing what issues are debated, what alternatives are offered, and what information is presented.

300 million Americans to consider a given matter. Congress and the president are supposed to act as the public's agents, enacting laws that a clear majority of the public wants and rejecting laws that fail to achieve widespread support. Also ideally, representative democracy in the United States enacts laws that benefit society and that respond to changes in public sentiment, with the constraint that the laws not violate the freedoms and rights guaranteed in the Bill of Rights. If the norms of society shift strongly in one direction for a period of time, so too should the laws of the land. The nature and origins of public opinion are among the central concerns of modern political science precisely because democratic government is supposed to reflect the will of the people.

The rationality principle and, specifically, the idea that members of the public have goals and preferences can help us understand the role of public opinion in American politics. What does it mean when large majorities support or oppose the president? How can we measure what the majority of people want the government to do on important issues such as taxation, military intervention, or social issues? Do individuals know enough to make decisions about the direction of the government or public policies? The rationality behind democratic government is a key element in democracy. The translation of people's preferences into electoral decisions and public policies also depends on institutions, problems of collective action, and history. These factors will be emphasized in later chapters on elections, interest groups, political parties, and the media. Public opinion operates through these various institutions to determine who serves in government, what problems government must address, and the principles and values that shape public policy.

There are two levels on which to understand public opinion—aggregate and individual. The term *public opinion* itself refers to an aggregate, the public, and commonly the public is treated as if it were a thinking, rational organism. It is not. Rather, public opinion reflects the accumulation of millions of individuals' expressions of their opinions, attitudes, and choices. There are many different procedures for aggregating individual opinion, including public-opinion polls, voting, and other forms of political participation. Aggregate opinion may not always appear rational, but there is power in numbers. The basic idea behind democracy holds that the sum of many millions of votes produces a better outcome than the decision of a small number of people. This idea is brilliantly expressed in the Jury Theorem. The Marquis de Condorcet, a French political philosopher, argued that the majority of a jury would more likely reach the right decision in a trial than would a single individual who heard the same evidence. Every individual would like to make the right decision, but there is some chance that an individual will make a mistake. Adding up the private judgments of many separate individuals, however, reduces the probability of a mistake. A majority of a jury of twelve people, then, is less likely to reach the wrong decision than a single individual. And according to this idea, 130 million voters are even more likely to produce the right verdict.[3] This idea has been rediscovered at the beginning of the twenty-first century, as new information technology has expanded the opportunities and the possibility for millions of people to express their opinions on virtually any matter. Firms such as Amazon.com collect such information and aggregate the millions of decisions made by consumers to figure out who is likely to buy particular products. There is wisdom in masses, a lesson borne out in markets and democracy.[4]

Public opinion can also be understood at the level of individuals. Votes cast during elections, answers to surveys, letters, and e-mails to members of Congress, and other ways that people communicate their opinions reflect how individuals think and behave politically. Aggregate public opinion, after all, is the collection of these many expressions. The meaning of individual political opinions depends on three factors: the individual's underlying *preferences* (what he or she wants), his or her *beliefs* about the current circumstances and the consequences of different courses of action, and the *choices* presented. A person will make a given political choice among the options presented, say, in an election or on a survey, because he or she wants a certain outcome (such as higher income or better education for one's own children) and because he or she believes that a given political option is the best approach among the alternatives offered. The choices offered in any situation are usually few in number—Democrat or Republican, McCain or Obama, a proposed bill versus the status quo, vote yes or vote no, get involved or stay at home. The significance of the individual's actions depends on why he or she chooses one of the alternatives.

Preferences and beliefs are quite complex. Preferences reflect what people want, such as material goods and money, and also people's values, such as justice and morality. For example, income is often taken as the basis for political

[3] Marquis de Condorcet, "Essai sur l'application de l'analyse à la probabilité des décisions rendues à la pluralité des voix," http://gallica.bnf.fr/ark:/12148/bpt6k417181 (accessed 3/24/09). Condorcet also argued that democracy has a weakness in that it need not always produce a definite majority-rule winner and may be manipulated by a clever agenda setter. This idea was rediscovered in the middle of the twentieth century by the Nobel prize–winning economist Kenneth Arrow in *Social Choice and Individual Values* (New York: Wiley, 1963).

[4] See Cass Sunstein, *Infotopia: How Many Minds Produce Knowledge* (Oxford: Oxford University Press, 2006).

preferences—people want lower taxes and more spending on programs that benefit them directly. But it is also the case that moral values, shaped by religion and family and social conscience, influence the way Americans behave. Some observers argue that because of the collective nature of political choices, values matter even more in politics than narrow self-interest, and that politicians can win by emphasizing values, rather than narrow self-interest.[5] The intensity of preferences also matters in politics. Those who have strong opinions and attitudes are more likely to express their views and take political action than those who do not.

Beliefs reflect what people know and how they understand the world and the consequences of their actions. An individual who has developed considerable expertise about a topic usually has clearer beliefs about that subject. He or she will have more certainty about the choices involved and the consequences of different actions. However, strong beliefs about politics are not necessarily based only on fact. Often in politics, one encounters people who have strong convictions about a specific issue that are based on the intensity of their general political views. When the facts don't fit their theories, they may ignore fact and stick with their theory. Thus, Democrats and Republicans may observe the same event, such as a political debate, and come to completely opposite conclusions about who won. And public figures may, in the face of strong scientific evidence, reject the science if it does not favor their own political position. As in other aspects of life, people often find it easier to stick to their political beliefs than to change their minds. In this chapter we examine the basis for individuals' preferences and the origins of their beliefs, as well as aggregate public opinion.

In conceiving how democracy works, democratic theory and civics lessons often present a highly idealized notion of democratic citizens. It is assumed that people follow all the important issues of the day closely, are well informed about the decisions of their representatives, understand the consequences of their actions, and participate in public debate, elections, and even in public decision making. There is ample evidence that individuals fall far short of this ideal. Some people do not like the choices they are presented with in American politics and opt out altogether. Studies have suggested that the typical American may not know enough or have strong enough beliefs to make reasoned decisions about many political issues, especially where foreign policy is involved. Some research has even cast doubt on whether individuals know what they want and whether they have consistent preferences when it comes to politics. And some political leaders have exploited these inconsistencies and weaknesses to accomplish objectives not in line with the true preferences of the majority.[6]

The prospect that political leaders can readily manipulate the public presents a lingering and difficult problem. Do Americans in fact know enough to sustain democracy? Or are they easily led and misled? Are Americans sufficiently active and involved? Or do we need greater political participation in the United States?

---

[5] Benjamin Wattenberg, *Values Matter Most* (New York: Simon & Schuster, 1995).

[6] William Riker, *The Art of Political Manipulation* (New Haven, Conn.: Yale University Press, 1986).

Throughout this chapter and those that follow, we encourage you to keep these questions in mind. The United States continually grapples with these difficult problems. They motivate radical critiques of the failings of American politics and efforts at political reform, ranging from campaign finance to media regulation to election administration. A tacit assumption about the public lies behind most of the legal decisions and electoral laws governing the United States (as we will see in Chapters 10 through 13). That is the view that America is a wide-open democracy. Our system of government does not presume that people must have a minimum level of competence or literacy to participate, or even that they must participate at all. Rather, public opinion is the expression of what people prefer and believe, of their wants and experiences. Although a better informed and more engaged public is ideal, not all citizens are highly educated and engaged. Democracy works, as Condorcet observed, because aggregating opinions collects the knowledge widely held in society.

WHAT IS PUBLIC OPINION?

Public opinion is the aggregation of many citizens' views and interests. It encompasses assessments of those in office, attitudes toward political organizations and social groups, and preferences about how government ought to address important problems. The term sometimes gives the impression that the public has a single opinion on a given matter; however, that is rarely the case.

Americans do hold common views on questions vital to governance and society. There is consensus on the legitimacy of the Constitution of the United States and trust in the rule of law, the principle that no one is above the law. There is consensus that we are a democratic society and that the outcomes of elections, whether a person likes the winners or not, determine who governs. These commonly held opinions and values are essential to maintaining a well-functioning democracy in the United States. They ensure peaceful transitions of government after each election and respect for laws produced by a legitimately chosen government.

There is also wide agreement on fundamental political values, such as equality of opportunity, liberty, and democracy.[7] Nearly all Americans agree that all people have equal rights, regardless of race, gender, or social standing. Americans hold a common commitment to freedom. People who live in the United State are free to live where they want, travel where they want, work where they want, say what they want, and practice whatever religion they wish, including no religion at all. And Americans have an undying belief in democracy, that whenever possible public officials should be chosen by majority vote.[8] It makes sense to think of the American public as having a single opinion on these elemental questions.

public opinion
Citizens' attitudes about political issues, leaders, institutions, and events.

---

[7] See Louis Hartz, *The Liberal Tradition in America: An Interpretation of American Political Thought since the Revolution* (New York: Harcourt, Brace, 1955).

[8] For a discussion of political beliefs of Americans, see Everett Carl Ladd, *The American Ideology* (Storrs, Conn: Roper Center, 1994).

On most matters that come before the government, however, the public does not hold a single view. Usually, opinions are divided between those who support the government or a proposed action and those who do not. Politicians are still attuned to public opinion when it is divided, but what matters most are the balance and direction of opinion. What do the majority of constituents want? Which way is opinion trending? Is it possible to find a popular middle ground?

People express their views to those in power in a variety of ways. Constituents contact their members of Congress directly through letters, phone calls, e-mails, and even personal visits to the representatives' offices. Most questions before Congress elicit little reaction from the public, but some questions start a maelstrom of objections. During the fall of 2008, Congress considered a $700 billion bailout of financial institutions. The volume of e-mail related to this bill was so great that at one point the House of Representatives had to limit incoming e-mail to keep its computers from crashing.[9]

People also express their opinions more publicly, through blogs, letters to newspapers and op-ed pieces, and conversations with others. They express their support for candidates with lawn signs and bumper stickers; by working on campaigns; by giving money to candidates, groups, and party organizations; and, most simply, by voting.

Such expressions of opinions and preferences are not always easy to interpret. If a constituent votes against a member of Congress, did the voter do so because of a controversial decision that the legislator made in Congress or because the voter decided to vote against all politicians from the legislator's party?

Political scientists and political consultants try to provide more refined and structured descriptions of public opinion using surveys. On any important issue, the government may pursue different policies. Public opinion on a given issue can be thought of as the distribution of opinion across the different options. Likewise, public opinion may represent the division of support for a leader or party. We try to gauge where majority support lies and how intensely or firmly citizens across the spectrum hold their views. More and more, politicians rely on opinion polls to anticipate the effects of their decisions, to identify opportunities, and to develop ways to blunt the objections to controversial decisions. Answering a survey, then, can also be a form of political action, because it may influence political decisions.

Consider, for example, one of the most widely followed indicators of public support for the government—the approval rating of the president. Since the 1930s, the Gallup organization has asked in public-opinion polls whether the respondent to the survey approves or disapproves of the job the president is doing, or has no opinion. Over the eighty years that this measure has been taken, on average, approximately 55 percent approve the job that the president is doing and 45 percent disapprove. But those figures vary considerably from president to president and over time within a presidency. George W. Bush received the historically high

---

[9] Jordy Yeager, "House Limits Constituent E-mail to Prevent Crash," *The Hill*, September 30, 2008, http://thehill.com/leading-the-news/house-limits-constituent-e-mails-to-prevent-crash-2008-09-30.html (accessed 3/24/09).

approval rate of 90 percent of the public in the wake of the terrorist attacks on the World Trade Center in 2001. His approval rating remained above 50 percent through the 2004 election, but reached a historic low late in his second term as the stock market lost almost half of its value, a financial crisis caused a collapse of the investment banking industry, and the nation settled into a deep recession. At that point the Gallup poll documented that only 28 percent of the public approved of the way George Bush handled his job as president, whereas 68 percent disapproved; the remainder neither approved nor disapproved.

Political scientists characterize public opinion on issues in a similar way. We identify the possible views on an issue or possible outcomes of a debate and measure the percent of people who support a given view or outcome.

For instance, the debate over the legality of abortion quickly sorted into two polar positions in the 1970s—"pro-life" and "pro-choice." Survey research has since measured the percentage of the public that identifies as "pro-life" and as "pro-choice." As this issue has evolved over time, however, it has become clear that those are not the only possible policies that the government could pursue, and survey researchers have developed more refined questions to ascertain the conditions under which people would and would not allow abortion. Would a respondent allow abortion for teenagers if parents did not consent? What about cases of rape or incest? What if the pregnancy endangered the life of the mother? Such refinements have allowed for a more nuanced expression of public preference on this issue, and they have led Congress to make public policies that are more attuned to the public's preferences. Congress stopped Medicaid funding for abortions in the 1980s and passed a ban on late-term or "partial birth" abortions, both of which were opposed by large majorities. But Congress has not approved highly restrictive laws, even though they have been introduced frequently.[10] Public opinion, then, should not be thought of as a single-minded view or consensus on a given matter, but as a range of options. Social scientists call this a *variable*, and social scientists and political strategists try to gauge the frequency of support for each option or side in a public debate and try determine where the majority's favor lies.

Opinions themselves take a variety of forms, depending on what is at issue. It is helpful to keep in mind a few common examples in thinking about this subject.

Evaluations of Those in Government and Other Institutions. Survey researchers use a variety of questions to gauge support for or opposition to the government. They ask about approval of the job that the president is doing, approval of the job that Congress is doing, approval of individual members of Congress, and approval of the job the Supreme Court is doing. At elections, those who vote express their support for and opposition to members of government directly through their votes. In other disciplines, similar questions are asked about social and economic institutions and leaders.

---

[10]Throughout the 1980s and 1990s, Representative Henry Hyde of Illinois regularly introduced an amendment to appropriations and other bills to ban abortion in the United States. The Hyde Amendment, as it came to be called, was never passed.

Assessments of Public Policies.   Do you support or oppose a given policy? Do you think a problem is important or not? What do you think is the most important problem that the government should address? How people answer such questions depends on the choices that are presented and immediate circumstances. Views on specific issues may follow the same patterns as general political orientations, if they directly affect partisan groups or derive from ongoing political debates between parties or ideological groups. For instance, a bill that would alter wages for public employees affects unions directly, and thus touches a core constituency of the Democratic Party. So, we might find that Democrats are more likely to view this issue in a certain way.

Assessments of Current Circumstances.   Is the economy performing well or poorly? Is crime high or low? Is the country headed in the right direction? Such questions might seem to have objective answers, but often there are differences of opinion about the state of the economy and other aspects of our society, depending on each individual's own experiences and what he or she has read or heard through the media.

Political Orientations.   The two most important indicators of individuals' general political orientations are party identification and ideology. Do you consider yourself a Democrat, a Republican, of another party, or of no party in particular? Do you consider yourself liberal, moderate, or conservative? These concepts capture general political orientations that are usually quite stable. Researchers have shown that party identifications predict voting preferences very well and correlate strongly with evaluations of those in office. Party identification often acts as a filter for information, a tinted lens that colors the way people view the world and interpret any piece of information. Immediately after an election, members and supporters of the winning party express much greater optimism about the economy, about global affairs, and even about their own personal finances. Often a Democrat and a Republican will offer markedly different views on a presidential debate, with the Democrat concluding that the Democratic candidate clearly won and the Republican concluding that the Republican candidate was victorious.

Political scientists characterize the variation in public opinion by measuring the percentage of people who choose each particular option or variable. A bar chart in which the height of each bar is the percentage of people choosing each outcome of a variable represents the distribution of public opinion. Typically, we care about which option receives the most support or the support of a majority. In elections, for example, counties and states tally the votes received by each candidate. The candidate with the largest number of votes (not necessarily a majority) wins. Nationwide in 2008, Barack Obama received 53 percent of all votes cast (a total of 69,457,389 votes), John McCain received 46 percent of all votes (59,935,933 votes), and all other candidates combined received 1 percent of votes cast (1,703,136 votes). Obama won the largest share of the vote for a Democratic presidential candidate since Lyndon Johnson in 1964. Social scientists, journalists, and even politicians view the size of the winner's vote margin as an indication of the breadth and intensity of the support for the policies and ideology of the winner.

Opinion data, such as the information gathered in surveys, provide an even more subtle and varied measure of public attitudes and political orientations. Consider ideology (which we will discuss in more detail later in this chapter). According to a survey by the Pew Research Center in November 2008, shortly after Obama's victory, 38 percent of Americans described themselves as conservative, 36 percent as moderate, and 21 percent as liberal. Another 5 percent do not think of themselves in these terms.[11] For an indicator such as ideology, then, no single camp has a clear majority, but we can say that self-described conservatives outnumber self-described liberals.[12]

One particularly important debate about public opinion today concerns ideological polarization. Pundits and other observers have often argued that the public is deeply divided into very conservative and very liberal groups, with relatively few people in the middle. Observers assume that this view of "two Americas" holds true for questions about ideology and across a wide range of issues, such as taxation, health care, education, and foreign affairs. The political scientists Morris Fiorina, Jeremy Pope, and Samuel Abrams tackled this alleged polarization in their 2004 book *Culture War? The Myth of a Polarized America*. Fiorina and his coauthors made simple bar charts to describe the distribution of public opinion in the United States. Rather than a deep divide, they found that on most issues Americans are centrists, either completely moderate or leaning somewhat to the right or left. This finding has important implications about the ability to reach consensus in public debate. It also raises an even more elusive puzzle. Although most Americans are centrist, most representatives in Congress vote either on the very liberal end of the spectrum or on the very conservative end. The public, then, is not polarized, but Congress is. It is worth pausing to consider why this is the case. Political scientists have suggested that it is the nature of the debate in Washington and the choices put before Congress, or that it is due to the organization of parties in Congress or to the election process—who votes and who doesn't, primary elections, and campaign contributors. The debate over this question has yet to come to a definitive resolution; as yet a convincing answer has not been found.[13]

Just as we do not think of public opinion as consensus, nor do we think of the public as monolithic. From the start, American society was conceived to be a large, heterogeneous nation. The guarantees of freedom of religion, the press, and association in the Bill of Rights were meant to protect this diversity of opinion

---

[11] Juliana Horowitz, "Winds of Political Change Haven't Shifted Public's Ideology Balance," November 25, 2008, http://pewresearch.org/pubs/1042/winds-of-political-change-havent-shifted-publics-ideology-balance (accessed 3/24/09).

[12] As an exercise, we recommend that you (1) write down several concepts of interest (such as ideology, partisanship, policy preferences on taxes or abortion); (2) find surveys that have measured public opinion on those topics (for example, at the Roper Center or the Pew Research Center on People and the Press); and (3) make a bar chart showing the percent of people who chose each category for a given question.

[13] For five different views, see Fiorina et al., *Culture War?*; McCarty et al., *Polarization in America*; Gary Jacobson, *A Divider, Not a Uniter*; Alan Abramowitz, "Constraint, Ideology, and Polarization in the American Electorate," paper presented at the annual meeting of the American Political Science Association, August 30, 2007; and Stephen Ansolabehere et al., "Purple America," *Journal of Economic Perspectives* 29 (Winter 2006): 97–118.

and belief. Indeed, one of the problems the Founders faced was how to maintain a stable democracy in a large society. James Madison famously wrote that "expanding the sphere" of the United States would make it less likely for any single group to achieve a stable majority capable of riding roughshod over other groups. A large heterogeneous nation, then, would cure the "mischief of faction."

Madison's vision of diverse opinions and beliefs has indeed come to pass. American society is a hodgepodge of different ethnic and racial groups; Americans differ greatly in educational attainment, income, and religion. The United States Census, conducted every ten years, measures variations in housing, family, employment, and other demographic characteristics. The Census Bureau also conducts monthly surveys on everything from communication to employment to voting. These data provide a rich picture of the diversity and complexity of American society. Fifteen percent of Americans claim Hispanic ethnicity, 13 percent are black or African American, 5 percent are Asian, 1 percent are Native American, and 74 percent identify themselves as White. One person of every eight living in the United States today was not even born here. Although the large majority of Americans identify with some form of Christianity and most of those are Protestant, the single largest sect is Roman Catholicism. Slightly more than 25 percent of adults in the United States have a college degree; 15 percent did not complete high school. America is one of the richest nations on earth, but approximately one in ten Americans still lives in poverty. The most populous region of the country is the South, with approximately 35 percent of the people. American society can be divided in many other ways. The picture that emerges from the census data is indeed one of a heterogeneous society.[14] In describing and understanding the attitudes, opinions, needs, and wants of the American public, we must be mindful of the fact that the public itself is fractured into many subgroups and interests.[15]

ORIGINS OF PUBLIC OPINION

Public opinion is, ultimately, the reflection of millions of individuals' preferences and beliefs. To understand the meaning and origins of the public's opinions, we must have some sense of the basis for individual choice. An individual's opinions are the products of his or her personality, social characteristics, and interests. They mirror who a person is, what she wants, and the manner in which she is embedded in a family and community, and the broader economy and society. But opinions are also shaped by institutional, political, and governmental forces that make it more likely that an individual will hold some beliefs and less likely that he will hold others.

---

[14] *The Statistical Abstract of the United States.*

[15] As an exercise, we recommend that the student consult the *Statistical Abstract of the United States* and construct bar charts (distributions) for the following demographic variables: (1) household incomes; (2) residency (urban, suburban, and rural); (3) region; (4) race; and (5) religion. Note the largest category for each variable. For income, calculate the level of income such that half of the people have income below that level and half have income above it (the median).

Self-Interest

Individuals' preferences about politics and public policy are rooted partly in self-interest. Laws and other governmental actions directly affect people's interests—their disposable income, the quality of public services and goods, and personal safety, to give just a few examples. It is not surprising, then, that when people express their political opinions, they react to the effects that government actions have had on them personally.

Economic interests are perhaps the most salient preferences when it comes to people's opinions. Taxes cut into disposable income, whereas public expenditures provide goods worth thousands of dollars to the typical American households. Government regulations limit how people use their property and may raise the cost of operating a business, but they may also preserve the value of neighbors' property, protect consumers from potential harm, and even create the property rights necessary to maintain a well-functioning market economy. Government is the single largest employer in the United States. Twenty-one million people, 14 percent of the U.S. civilian labor force, work for federal, state, or local governments; another million people are in the armed services. Government spending comprises a substantial share of the national economy (though less than in most other nations). In the United States federal government expenditures account for 20 percent of gross domestic product (GDP).[16] Virtually every American has an interest in the government's role in the nation's economy and strong preferences about tax rates and expenditure priorities. Public opinion about taxes and spending reflect these preferences. Given the enormous influence of the federal government in the economy, assessments of the president and the party in power often correspond to how well the nation's economy performs.

Individuals' attitudes toward government reflect other forms of self-interest as well. Laws affect families, the status of civic and religious organizations, and neighborhoods. Zoning laws and urban redevelopment programs shape the nature of neighborhoods, including the mix of commercial and residential housing and the density of low-income housing in an area. Tax laws treat nonprofits, such as universities, religious organizations, and social clubs, differently from for-profit companies, making it easier for nonprofit organizations to exist. Family law affects how easy it is for families to stay together, what happens when they break down, and what rights and responsibilities parents have. Individuals have a personal stake in decisions bearing on their own communities and families. Proposed changes in such laws bring immediate reaction from those affected.

Political Socialization

Individuals' attitudes about political issues and personalities tend to be shaped by their underlying political beliefs and values. For example, an individual who has basically negative feelings about government intervention in America's economy and society would probably be predisposed to oppose the development of new

---

[16]The gross domestic product consists of the value of all goods and services produced in the United States. It is one measure of the nation's income.

political
socialization The
induction of indi-
viduals into the
political culture; the
process of learning
the underlying be-
liefs and values on
which the political
system is based.

agents of
socialization The
social institutions,
including families
and schools, that
help shape individ-
uals' basic political
beliefs and values.

health-care and social programs. Similarly, someone who distrusts the military would likely be suspicious of any call for the use of American troops. The processes through which such underlying political beliefs and values are formed are called **political socialization**.

The process of political socialization is important. Probably no nation and certainly no democracy could survive if its citizens did not share some fundamental beliefs. If Americans had few common values or perspectives, it would be very difficult for them to reach agreement on particular issues. In contemporary America, some elements of the socialization process tend to produce differences in outlook, whereas others promote similarities. Four of the most important **agents of socialization** that foster differences in political perspectives are the family, membership in social groups, education, and prevailing political conditions. Although these factors cannot fully explain the development of any one individual's political outlook, let us consider the ways in which they tend to influence most people.

The Family. Most people acquire their initial orientation to politics from their families. Although relatively few parents spend much time teaching their children about politics, political conversations occur in many households, and children tend to absorb the political views of their parents and other caregivers, perhaps without realizing it. Studies have suggested, for example, that party preferences are initially acquired at home. Children raised in households in which the primary caregivers are Democrats tend to become Democrats themselves, whereas children raised in homes where their caregivers are Republicans tend to favor the GOP.[17] Similarly, children reared in politically liberal households are more likely than not to develop a liberal outlook, whereas children raised in politically conservative settings are likely to see the world through conservative lenses. Obviously, not all children absorb their parents' political views. For instance, two of the four children of Ronald Reagan, a conservative Republican president, rejected their parents' conservative values. The late president's son Ron supported the Democrat John Kerry in the 2004 presidential race and Barack Obama in the 2008 presidential race. Moreover, even those children whose views are initially shaped by parental values may change their minds as they mature and experience political life for themselves. Nevertheless, the family is an important initial source of political orientation for everyone.

Social Groups. Another important source of divergent political orientations and values is the social groups to which individuals belong. Social groups include those to which individuals belong involuntarily—gender and racial groups, for example—as well as those to which people belong voluntarily—such as political parties, labor unions, religious organizations, and educational and occupational groups. Some social groups have both voluntary and involuntary attributes. For example, individuals are born with a particular social-class background, but as a result of their own efforts they may move up—or down—the class structure.

---

[17] See Angus Campbell, Philip E. Converse, Warren E. Miller, and Donald E. Stokes, *The American Voter* (New York: Wiley, 1960), p. 147. We shall discuss psychological attachments to political parties, called party identification, in Chapter 11.

FIGURE 9.1 DISAGREEMENT AMONG BLACKS AND WHITES

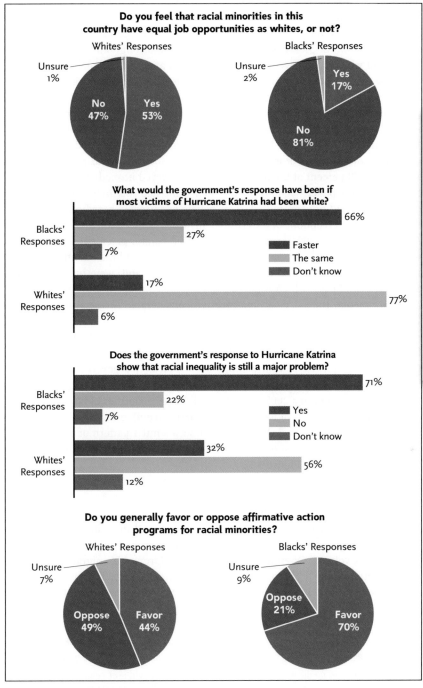

Do you feel that racial minorities in this country have equal job opportunities as whites, or not?

Whites' Responses
- Unsure 1%
- No 47%
- Yes 53%

Blacks' Responses
- Unsure 2%
- Yes 17%
- No 81%

What would the government's response have been if most victims of Hurricane Katrina had been white?

Blacks' Responses
- Faster 66%
- The same 27%
- Don't know 7%

Whites' Responses
- Faster 17%
- The same 77%
- Don't know 6%

Does the government's response to Hurricane Katrina show that racial inequality is still a major problem?

Blacks' Responses
- Yes 71%
- No 22%
- Don't know 7%

Whites' Responses
- Yes 32%
- No 56%
- Don't know 12%

Do you generally favor or oppose affirmative action programs for racial minorities?

Whites' Responses
- Unsure 7%
- Oppose 49%
- Favor 44%

Blacks' Responses
- Unsure 9%
- Oppose 21%
- Favor 70%

SOURCE: Gallup polls, June 8–25, 2006 and June 12–15, 2003, http://pollingreport.com; Pew Research Center for the People and the Press, "The Black and White of Public Opinion," October 31, 2005, http://people-press.org/commentary/?analysisid=121 (accessed 3/24/09).

ANALYZING THE EVIDENCE

Although America's system of legally mandated racial segregation ended nearly half a century ago, its effects continue to linger. In contemporary America, blacks and whites have different perspectives on race relations. Do you think that black-white differences have increased or decreased in the past few decades? Are these differences of opinion important?

Membership in social groups can affect political values in a variety of ways. Membership in a particular group can give individuals important experiences and perspectives that shape their views of political and social life. The experiences of blacks and whites, for example, can differ significantly. Blacks are a minority and have been victims of persecution and discrimination throughout American history. Blacks and whites also have different educational and occupational opportunities, often live in separate communities, and may attend separate schools. Such differences tend to produce distinctive political outlooks. For example, in 1995 blacks and whites had very different reactions to the murder trial of the former football star O. J. Simpson, who was accused of killing his ex-wife and one of her friends. Approximately 70 percent of the white Americans surveyed believed that Simpson was guilty, on the basis of evidence presented by the police and prosecutors. But an identical 70 percent of the black Americans surveyed immediately after the trial believed that the police had fabricated evidence and had sought to convict Simpson of a crime he had not committed, their beliefs presumably based on their experiences with and perceptions of the criminal justice system.[18] Similarly, the Reverend Al Sharpton's 2003–2004 campaign for the Democratic presidential nomination was not taken seriously by most white voters and received little attention from the mainstream news media. Black voters, on the other hand, were quite attuned to Sharpton's candidacy, which received considerable coverage in the African American news media. Indeed, Sharpton received considerable financial backing from black media executives.[19]

According to other recent surveys, blacks and whites in the United States differ on a number of issues. For example, in surveys conducted by the Pew Research Center, clear majorities of whites supported the ideas that government should do more to guarantee food and shelter (62 percent in a 2003 survey) and generally help the needy (55 percent in a 2005 survey). Much larger majorities of blacks expressed support for the guarantee of food and shelter (80 percent) and the provision of help for the needy (72 percent).[20] Other issues show a similar pattern of disagreement, reflecting the differences in experience, background, and interests between blacks and whites in America (Figure 9.1).

Of course, disagreements between blacks and whites are not the only important racial or ethnic differences to be found in contemporary America. Latinos are another major American subgroup with distinctive opinions on some public issues. A 2008 survey by the Pew Hispanic Center found that education is the top concern of Hispanic voters, whereas the economy ranked highest among white non-Hispanic voters.[21] Often immigrants or the children of immigrants, Hispanics view education as the ticket to a better life in America and attach great value to educational opportunity. Latinos also have a distinctive view of immigration. A 2004

---

[18] Richard Morin, "Poll Reflects Division over Simpson Case," *Washington Post*, October 8, 1995, p. A31.

[19] Paul Farhi, "Black Media Barons Back Sharpton Bid," *Washington Post*, November 9, 2003, p. A4.

[20] Pew Research Center for the People and the Press, "The Black and White of Public Opinion," October 31, 2005, http://people-press.org/commentary/?analysisid=121 (accessed 3/24/09).

[21] Mark Lopez and Susan Minushkin, "2008 National Survey of Latinos: Hispanic Voter Attitudes," Pew Hispanic Center, July 24, 2008, http://pewhispanic.org/files/reports/90.pdf (accessed 3/24/09).

TABLE 9.1 CHANGING PARTISAN DIVISION IN THE LATINO COMMUNITY

Background	2004		2008	
	Dem. %	Rep. %	Dem. %	Rep. %
Cuban	17	52	53	20
Mexican	47	18	50	18
Puerto Rican	50	17	61	11

SOURCE: Mark Hugo Lopez and Susan Minushkin, "2008 National Survey of Latinos: Hispanic Voter Attitudes," Pew Hispanic Center Report, July 24, 2008, http://pewhispanic.org/files/reports/90.pdf (accessed 4/30/09).

ANALYZING THE EVIDENCE
Members of America's Latino community share a linguistic heritage, but they are not politically homogeneous. What factors might account for these differences? Why might so many Cuban Americans have changed their party allegiance between 2004 and 2008?

Pew Hispanic Center survey found that more than 60 percent of Latinos believe that immigration is good for America. Among non-Latinos, though, more than 60 percent believe that immigration poses a major threat to the country. The Latino community itself is divided into subgroups based on national origin. Latinos of Mexican, Puerto Rican, Cuban, and Central American descent have traditionally had differing partisan attachments, with Cubans identifying much more strongly with the Republican Party. By 2008 that appeared to have changed; surveys during the presidential campaign found that Cuban Americans are now nearly as Democratic as other Hispanic groups (Table 9.1).

Religion has become another important source of variation in opinion. In recent years, contending political forces have placed a number of religious and moral issues on the national political agenda. The Republican Party, in particular, has emphasized its support for traditional "family values" and its opposition to abortion, same-sex marriage, and other practices opposed by conservative religious leaders. It is not surprising that public opinion on these issues differs along religious lines, with evangelical Protestants being most supportive of traditional values and respondents identifying themselves as "secular" manifesting the least support for them. For example, Table 9.2 shows how different religious groups view same-sex marriage.

Men and women have important differences of opinion as well. Reflecting differences in social roles, political experience, and occupational patterns, women tend to be less militaristic than men on issues of war and peace, more likely than men to favor measures to protect the environment, and more supportive than men of government social and health-care programs (Table 9.3). Perhaps because of these differences on issues, women are more likely than men to vote for Democratic candidates, whereas men have become increasingly supportive of the GOP.[22] This

---

[22] For data, see Center for American Women and Politics, Eagleton Institute of Politics, Rutgers, State University of New Jersey, www.cawp.rutgers.edu/fast_facts/voters/turnout.php (accessed 4/30/09).

TABLE 9.2 SHOULD SAME-SEX MARRIAGE BE LEGALIZED?

Religious Group	In Favor (%)	Opposed (%)
White evangelical Protestant	14	81
White nonevangelical Protestant	43	47
White non-Hispanic Catholic	41	49
Black Protestant	15	79
Secular	60	30

SOURCE: Pew Research Center for the People and the Press, "A Stable Majority: Most Americans Still Oppose Same-Sex Marriage," April 1, 2008, http://pewforum.org/docs/?DocID=290 (accessed 3/24/09).

gender gap A distinctive pattern of voting behavior reflecting the differences in views between women and men.

tendency for men's and women's opinions to differ is called the **gender gap**. Perhaps surprisingly, the gender gap has virtually vanished on the abortion issue. An August 2006 Pew Research Center poll indicated that men and women are nearly identical—52 percent versus 51 percent—on the issue of allowing abortion in general or on a limited basis, and 46 percent of both men and women believe abortion should always or almost always be illegal.[23]

As we shall see in Chapter 11, political party membership can be another factor affecting political orientation. Partisans tend to rely on party leaders and spokespersons for cues on the appropriate position to take on major political issues. In recent years, congressional redistricting and partisan realignment in the South have reduced the number of conservative Democrats and all but eliminated liberal Republicans from Congress and positions of prominence in the party. As a result, the leadership of the Republican Party has become increasingly conservative and that of the Democratic Party has become more and more liberal. These changes in the positions of party leaders have been reflected in the views of party adherents and sympathizers in the general public. According to recent studies, differences between Democratic and Republican partisans on a variety of political and policy questions are greater today than they were during any other period for which data are available. On issues of national security, for example, Republicans have become very "hawkish," whereas Democrats have become quite "dovish." This polarization was most evident throughout the war in Iraq. Nine months into the war, a large majority of Democrats opposed the war and supported withdrawal. A large majority of Republicans supported the war and continued efforts to stabilize the situation. In April 2008, a Gallup survey asked, "If you had to choose, which do you think is better for the U.S., to keep a significant number of troops in Iraq until the situation there gets better, even if that takes many years, or to set a timetable for

---

[23] Pew Research Center for the People and the Press, "Pragmatic Americans Liberal and Conservative on Social Issues: Most Want Middle Ground on Abortion," August 3, 2006, http://people-press.org/report/283/pragmatic-americans-liberal-and-conservative-on-social-issues (accessed 3/24/09).

TABLE 9.3 DISAGREEMENTS AMONG MEN AND WOMEN ON ISSUES OF WAR AND PEACE

Government Action	Approve of Action (%)	
	Men	Women
Going to war against Iraq (2003)	66	50
Brokering a cease-fire in Yugoslavia instead of using NATO air strikes (1999)	44	51
Ending the ban on homosexuals in the military (1993)	34	51
Engaging in a military operation against a Somali warlord (1993)	72	60
Going to war against Iraq (1991)	72	53

SOURCE: Gallup polls, 1991, 1993, and 1999; *Washington Post*, 2003.

removing troops from Iraq and to stick to that timetable regardless of what is going on in Iraq?" Eighty-one percent of Democrats chose a timetable for withdrawal, compared with 32 percent of Republicans. Sixty-five percent of Republicans favored continued engagement, compared with 15 percent of Democrats.[24]

Membership in a social group can affect individuals' political orientations in another way: through the efforts of groups themselves to influence their members. Labor unions, for example, often seek to "educate" their members through meetings, rallies, and literature. These activities are designed to shape union members' understanding of politics and make them more amenable to supporting the political positions favored by union leaders. Similarly, organizations can sharpen the effect of membership in an involuntary group. Women's groups, black groups, religious groups, and the like usually endeavor to structure their members' political views through intensive educational programs. The importance of such group efforts can be seen in the impact of group membership on political opinion. Women who belong to women's organizations, for example, are more likely than women without such group affiliation to differ from men in their political views.[25] Other analysts have found that African Americans who belong to black organizations are more likely than blacks who lack such affiliations to differ from whites in their political orientation.[26]

---

[24] Jeffrey M. Jones, "Iraq War Attitudes Politically Polarized," Gallup News, April 8, 2008, www.gallup.com/poll/106309/Iraq-War-Attitudes-Politically-Polarized.aspx (accessed 3/24/09).

[25] Pamela Johnston Conover, "The Role of Social Groups in Political Thinking," *British Journal of Political Science* 18 (1988): 51–78.

[26] See Michael C. Dawson, *Behind the Mule: Race and Class in African-American Politics* (Princeton, N.J.: Princeton University Press, 1994).

In many cases, no particular efforts are required by groups to affect their members' beliefs and opinions. Often individuals will consciously or unconsciously adapt their views to those of the groups with which they identify. For example, an African American who is dubious about affirmative action is likely to come under considerable peer pressure and internal pressure to modify his or her views. In this and other cases, dissenters are likely to gradually shift their own views to conform to those of the group. The political psychologist Elisabeth Noelle-Neumann has called this process the "spiral of silence."[27]

Another way in which membership in social groups can affect political beliefs is through what might be called objective political interests. On many economic issues, for example, the interests of the rich and the poor differ significantly. Inevitably, these differences of interest will produce differences of political outlook. James Madison and other framers of the Constitution thought that the inherent gulf between the rich and the poor would always be the most important source of conflict in political life. Certainly today struggles over tax policy, welfare policy, health-care policy, and so forth are fueled by differences of interest between wealthier and poorer Americans. In a similar vein, objective differences of interest between senior citizens and younger Americans can lead to very different views on such diverse issues as health-care policy, Social Security, and criminal justice.

It is worth noting again that, like the other agents of socialization, group membership can never fully explain a given individual's political views. Group membership is conducive to particular outlooks, but it is not determinative. It is also worth pointing out, in line with the rationality principle, that objective interests, though not always determinative, exert a strong influence on opinions and behavior—hence the small number of black Republicans and socialist businesspeople.

Differences in Education.   A third important source of differences in political perspectives is a person's education. In some respects, of course, schooling is a great equalizer. Governments use public education to try to teach all children a common set of civic values. It is mainly in school that Americans acquire their basic belief in liberty, equality, and democracy. In history classes, students are taught that the Founders fought for the principle of liberty. Through participation in class elections and student government, students are taught the virtues of democracy. In the course of studying such topics as the Constitution, the Civil War, and the civil rights movement, students are taught the importance of equality. These lessons are repeated at every grade level in a variety of contexts. No wonder they are such an important element in Americans' beliefs.

At the same time, however, differences in educational attainment are strongly associated with differences in political outlook. In particular, those who attend college are often exposed to philosophies and modes of thought that will forever

---

[27] Elisabeth Noelle-Neumann, *The Spiral of Silence: Public Opinion, Our Social Skin* (Chicago: University of Chicago Press, 1984).

TABLE 9.4 EDUCATION AND PUBLIC OPINION

Issues	Level of Education			
	Grade School	High School	Some College	College Graduate
Women and men should have equal roles.	73	82	90	90
Abortion should never be permitted.	27	17	12	9
The government should adopt national health insurance.	66	58	50	49
Helping to bring democracy to other nations is a very important.	36	27	21	12
Government should see to fair treatment in jobs for African Americans.	80	58	54	60
Government should provide fewer services to reduce government spending.	10	18	21	25

NOTE: The figures show the percentage of respondents in each category agreeing with the statement.

SOURCE: American National Election Studies 2008 data, Center for Political Studies, University of Michigan, www.electionstudies.org.

ANALYZING THE EVIDENCE

What factors might explain the relationship between education and opinion? Some commentators believe that many college courses have a liberal political orientation. Do you agree? How have your college courses affected your opinions on social and political issues?

distinguish them from their friends and neighbors who do not pursue college diplomas. Table 9.4 outlines some general differences of opinion that are found between college graduates and other Americans. One of the major differences is in levels of political participation. College graduates vote, write letters to the editor, join campaigns, take part in protests, and generally make their voices heard.

Political Conditions. A fourth set of factors shaping political orientation and values has to do with the conditions under which individuals and groups are recruited into and involved in political life—that is, the circumstances in which an individual comes of age politically. Although political beliefs are influenced by family background and group membership, the precise content and character of these views is, to a large extent, determined by political circumstances. For example, many Americans who came of political age during the Great Depression and World War II developed an intense loyalty to President Franklin Roosevelt and became permanently attached to his Democratic Party. In a similar vein, the Vietnam War and the social upheavals of the 1960s produced lasting divisions among Americans of the baby-boom generation. Indeed, arguments over Vietnam persisted into the 2004 presidential election, some thirty years after American troops left Southeast Asia. Perhaps the September 11 terrorist attacks and ongoing threats to America's security will have a lasting impact on the political orientation of contemporary Americans.

In a similar vein, the views held by members of a particular group can shift drastically over time as political circumstances change. For example, white southerners were staunch members of the Democratic Party from the Civil War through the 1960s. As members of this political group, they became key supporters of liberal New Deal and post-New Deal social programs that greatly expanded the size and power of the national government. Since the 1960s, however, southern whites have shifted in large numbers to the Republican Party. Now they provide a major base of support for efforts to scale back social programs and sharply reduce the size and power of the national government. The South's move from the Democratic to the Republican camp took place because of white southern opposition to the Democratic Party's racial policies and because of determined Republican efforts to win white southern support. It was not a change in the character of white southerners but a change in the political circumstances in which they found themselves that induced this major shift in political allegiances and outlook in the South.

The moral of this story is that a group's views cannot be inferred simply from the character of the group. College students are not inherently radical or inherently conservative. Jews are not inherently liberal. Southerners are not inherently conservative. Men are not inherently militaristic. Any group's political outlooks and orientations are shaped by the political circumstances in which the group finds itself, and those outlooks can change as circumstances change. Quite probably, the generation of American students now coming of political age will have a very different view of the use of American military power than their parents, members of a generation who reached political consciousness during the 1960s, when opposition to the Vietnam War and military conscription were important political phenomena.

Political Ideology

As we have seen, people's beliefs about government can vary widely. But for some individuals the set of underlying orientations, ideas, and beliefs through which they understand and interpret politics fits together in a political ideology.

In America today, people often describe themselves as liberals or conservatives. Liberalism and conservatism are political ideologies that include beliefs about the role of government, ideas about public policies, and notions about which groups in society should properly exercise power. In earlier times, these terms were defined somewhat differently. As recently as the nineteenth century, a liberal was an individual who favored freedom from state control, whereas a conservative was someone who supported the use of governmental power and favored continuation of the influence of church and aristocracy in national life.

Today, in the United States, the term **liberal** has come to imply support for political and social reform; extensive government intervention in the economy; the

liberal A liberal today generally supports political and social reform; extensive government intervention in the economy; the expansion of federal social services; more vigorous efforts on behalf of the poor, minorities, and women; and greater concern for consumers and the environment.

expansion of federal social services; more vigorous efforts on behalf of the poor, minorities, and women; and greater concern for consumers and the environment. In social and cultural areas, liberals generally support abortion rights and oppose state involvement with religious institutions and religious expression. In international affairs, liberal positions usually include support for arms control, opposition to the development and testing of nuclear weapons, support for aid to poor nations, opposition to the use of American troops to influence the domestic affairs of developing nations, and support for international organizations such as the United Nations. Of course, liberalism is not monolithic. For example, among individuals who view themselves as liberal, many support American military intervention when it is tied to a humanitarian purpose, as in the case of America's military action in Kosovo in 1998–99. Most liberals initially supported President George W. Bush's war on terrorism even when some of the president's actions seemed to curtail civil liberties.

By contrast, the term **conservative** today is used to describe those who generally support the social and economic status quo and are suspicious of efforts to introduce new political formulas and economic arrangements. Conservatives believe strongly that a large and powerful government poses a threat to citizens' freedom. Thus in the domestic arena conservatives generally oppose the expansion of governmental activity, asserting that solutions to social and economic problems can be developed in the private sector. Conservatives in particular oppose efforts to impose government regulation on business, pointing out that such regulation is frequently economically inefficient and costly and can ultimately lower the entire nation's standard of living. As for social and cultural positions, many conservatives oppose abortion and support school prayer. In international affairs, conservatism has come to mean support for the maintenance of American military power. Like liberalism, conservatism is far from a monolithic ideology. Some conservatives support many government social programs. George W. Bush, a Republican, called himself a compassionate conservative to indicate that he favored programs that assist the poor and the needy. Other conservatives oppose efforts to outlaw abortion, arguing that government intrusion in this area is as misguided as government intervention in the economy. The real political world is far too complex to be seen in terms of a simple struggle between liberals and conservatives.

There are many other ideologies beside liberal and conservative. Some people seek to expand liberty above all other principles and wish to minimize government intervention in the economy and society. Such a position is sometimes called libertarian. Other ideologies seek a particular outcome, such as environmental protection. Such a stance may lead to emphasis on certain issues, such as economic growth, and deemphasis of other issues, such as abortion. Communism and fascism are ideologies that involve government control of all aspects of the economy and society. These ideologies dominated politics in many European countries from the 1920s through the 1940s. Political discourse in the United States, however, has revolved around the division between liberals and conservatives for most of the last century.

Liberal and conservative differences manifest themselves in a variety of contexts. For example, the liberal approach to increasing airline safety in October 2001

conservative Today this term refers to those who generally support the social and economic status quo and are suspicious of efforts to introduce new political formulas and economic arrangements. Many conservatives also believe that a large and powerful government poses a threat to citizens' freedoms.

was to create a workforce of federal employees who would screen and inspect passengers' luggage. The conservative approach was to call for better training of current employees and better supervision of private-sector screeners. To some extent, contemporary liberalism and conservatism can be seen as blends of the fundamental American political values of liberty and equality. For liberals, equality is often the most important of the core values. Liberals are willing to tolerate government intervention in such areas as college admissions and business decisions to help remedy high levels of race, class, or gender inequality. For conservatives, on the other hand, liberty is the core value. Conservatives oppose most efforts by the government, however well intentioned, to intrude into private life or the marketplace. This simple formula for distinguishing liberalism and conservatism is of course not always accurate because political ideologies seldom lend themselves to neat or logical characterizations. Conservatives, for example, are sometimes more tolerant of, and liberals more resistant to, government intervention in social policy realms involving the family, marriage, homosexuality, and abortion.

Often political observers search for logical connections among the various positions identified with liberalism or conservatism, and they are disappointed or puzzled when they are unable to find a set of coherent philosophical principles that define and unite the several elements of either set of beliefs. On the liberal side, for example, what is the logical connection between opposition to U.S. government intervention in the affairs of foreign nations and calls for greater intervention in America's economy and society? On the conservative side, what is the logical relationship between opposition to government regulation of business and support for a ban on abortion?

Frequently, the relationships among the various elements of liberalism or the several aspects of conservatism are *political* rather than *logical*. One underlying basis of liberal views is that all or most of them are criticisms of or attacks on the foreign and domestic policies and cultural values of the business and commercial strata that have been prominent in the United States for more than a century. In some measure, the tenets of contemporary conservatism are this elite's defense of its positions against its enemies, who include organized labor, minority groups, and some intellectuals and professionals. Thus liberals attack business and commercial elites by advocating more government regulation, including consumer protection and environmental regulation; opposition to weapons programs; and support for expensive social programs. Conservatives counterattack by asserting that government regulation of the economy is ruinous and that military weapons are needed in a changing world.

Of course, it is important to note that many people who call themselves liberals or conservatives accept only part of the liberal or conservative ideology. Although it appears that Americans have adopted a more conservative outlook on some issues, their views in other areas have remained largely unchanged or have even become more liberal in recent years. Thus many individuals who are liberal on social issues are conservative on economic issues. There is certainly nothing illogical about these mixed positions. They simply indicate the relatively open and fluid character of American political debate.

PUBLIC OPINION AND POLITICAL KNOWLEDGE

As they read newspapers, listen to the radio, watch television, and chat with their friends and associates, citizens are constantly confronted by new political events, issues, and personalities. Often they will be asked what they think about a particular issue or whether they plan to support a particular candidate. Indeed, in our democracy we expect every citizen to have views about the major problems of the day as well as opinions about who should be entrusted with the nation's leadership.

Some Americans know quite a bit about politics, and many have general views and hold opinions on several issues. Few Americans, though, devote sufficient time, energy, or attention to politics to really understand or evaluate the myriad issues with which they are bombarded on a regular basis. In fact, many studies have shown that the average American knows very little about politics. In one major study, for example, only 25 percent of respondents could name their two senators, only 29 percent could name their U.S. representative, and fewer than half knew that the Constitution's first ten amendments are called the Bill of Rights.[28] Evidence that half of America's citizens—particularly those who have not attended college—are so unaware of the nation's history and politics is troubling.

Yet ignorance is probably a predictable and inevitable fact of political life. Some analysts have argued that political attentiveness is costly; it means spending time at the very least, and often money as well, to collect, organize, and digest political information.[29] Balanced against this cost to an individual is the very low probability that he or she will, on the basis of this costly information, take an action that would not otherwise have been taken *and* that such a departure in behavior would make a beneficial difference to him or her *and* that such a difference, if it existed, would exceed the cost of acquiring the information in the first place. Because individuals anticipate that informed actions that they take will rarely make much difference and that the costs of informing oneself are often not trivial, it may be rational to remain ignorant. In other words, the rationality principle suggests that many people should more profitably devote their personal resources—particularly their time—to more narrowly personal matters. This idea is in turn suggested by the collective-action principle, in which the bearing of burdens—such as the cost of becoming informed—is not likely to have much impact in a mass political setting. A more moderate version of "rational" ignorance recognizes that some kinds of information are inexpensive to acquire, such as sound bites from the evening news, or can be pleasant, such as reading the front page of the newspaper while drinking a cup of coffee. In such cases, an individual may become partially informed, but usually not in detail.

Precisely because becoming truly knowledgeable about politics requires a substantial investment of time and energy, many Americans seek to acquire political

---

[28] Michael X. Delli Carpini and Scott Keeter, *What Americans Know about Politics and Why It Matters* (New Haven, Conn.: Yale University Press, 1996), pp. 307–28.

[29] Anthony Downs, *An Economic Theory of Democracy* (New York: Harper & Row, 1957).

information and to make political decisions on the cheap, using shortcuts that seem to relieve them of having to engage in information gathering and evaluation. One "inexpensive" way to become informed is to take cues from trusted others—the local minister, the television commentator or newspaper editorialist, an interest-group leader, friends, and relatives.[30] Sometimes the cue giver is distrusted, in which case the cue leads the receiver in the opposite direction. For example, if a liberal is told that a Republican president is backing a major overhaul of the Social Security system, he or she will probably not read thousands of pages of economic projections before exhibiting suspicion of the president's efforts. Along the same lines, a common shortcut for political evaluation and decision making is to assess new issues and events through the lenses of one's general beliefs and orientation. Thus if a conservative learns of a plan to expand federal social programs, he or she might express opposition to the endeavor without carefully pondering the specifics of the proposal.

Neither of these shortcuts is entirely reliable, however. Taking cues from others may lead individuals to accept positions that they would not support if they had more information. And general ideological orientations are usually poor guides to decision making in concrete instances. For one thing, especially when applied to discrete issues, most individuals' beliefs turn out to be filled with contradictions. For example, what position should a liberal take on immigration? Should a liberal favor keeping America's borders open to poor people from all over the world, or should he or she be concerned that America's open borders create a pool of surplus labor that permits giant corporations to drive down the wages of poor American workers? Many other issues defy easy ideological characterization. What should liberals think about the intelligence reforms enacted by Congress in 2004? How should conservatives view America's military actions in Iraq? Each of these policies combines a mix of issues and is too complex to lend itself to simple ideological interpretation.

Although understandable and perhaps inevitable, widespread inattentiveness to politics weakens American democracy in two ways. First, those who lack political information or resort to inadequate shortcuts to acquire and assess information cannot effectively defend their political interests and can easily become victims or losers in political struggles. Second, the presence of large numbers of politically inattentive or ignorant individuals means that the political process can be more easily manipulated by the various institutions and forces that seek to shape public opinion.

As to the first of these problems, in our democracy millions of ordinary citizens take part in political life, at least to the extent of voting in national elections. Those with little knowledge of the election's issues or candidates or procedures can find themselves acting against their own preferences and interests. One example is U.S. tax policy. Over the past several decades, the United States has substantially

---

[30] For a discussion of the role of information in democratic politics, see Arthur Lupia and Mathew D. McCubbins, *The Democratic Dilemma: Can Citizens Learn What They Need to Know?* (New York: Cambridge University Press, 1998).

reduced the rate of taxation for its wealthiest citizens.[31] Tax cuts signed into law by President Bush in 2001 and mostly maintained throughout the decade provided a tax break mainly for the top 1 percent of the nation's wage earners, and further tax cuts proposed by the president offered additional benefits to this privileged stratum. It is surprising, however, that polling data show that millions of middle-class and lower-middle-class Americans who did not stand to benefit from the president's tax cuts seemed to favor them nonetheless. The explanation for this odd state of affairs appears to be a lack of political knowledge. Millions of individuals who were unlikely to derive much advantage from President Bush's tax policy thought they would. The political scientist Larry Bartels has called this phenomenon "misplaced self-interest."[32] Upper-bracket taxpayers, who are usually served by an army of financial advisers, are unlikely to suffer from this problem. Knowledge may not always translate into political power, but lack of knowledge is almost certain to translate into political weakness. And according to the policy principle, the lack of knowledge and concomitant political weakness mean policy disappointment.

Campaigns and other forums for public discourse can change public attitudes on issues by altering the nature of the choices or informing the public about the effects of policies. For example, during the 2008 presidential election campaign, Barack Obama seized on the tax issue at a time when the economy was worsening and people's economic prospects looked bleak. Then-candidate Obama promised to raise taxes on the incomes of those making more than $300,000 per year, a pledge that proved highly popular. In this way, Obama shifted the discourse away from taxes on inheritance and other assets that people hold and to the incomes of the top 1 percent of earners. The Democratic campaign used advertisements, debates, and other public events to remind voters that his proposal would increase taxes for only a small percentage of the population. The "Analyzing the Evidence" section on the following page looks at how public opinion on taxes has shifted over time.

SHAPING OPINION: POLITICAL LEADERS, PRIVATE GROUPS, AND THE MEDIA

The fact that many Americans are inattentive to politics and lack even basic political information renders public opinion and the political process more easily susceptible to manipulation. Although direct efforts to influence opinion don't always succeed, three forces play especially important roles in shaping opinion. These are the government, private groups, and the news media.

---

[31] One of the most detailed analyses of the distribution of the tax burden in advanced industrial democracies in the past half century is Thomas Piketty and Emmanuel Saez, "How Progressive Is the U.S. Federal Tax System? Historical and International Perspectives," working paper 12404, National Bureau of Economic Research, 2006, www.nber.org/papers/w12404 (accessed 3/25/09).

[32] Larry M. Bartels, "Homer Gets a Tax Cut: Inequality and Public Policy in the American Mind," *Perspectives on Politics* 3 (2005): 15–31.

Public Opinion and Taxes

Nobody likes to pay taxes. The United States was founded in part due to disputes over taxes. Talk of taxes dominates political campaigns. Americans simply hate taxes, right?

That wasn't always the case. Both the importance of taxes to politics and American dislike of taxes were lower during the 1950s and 1960s than during the period from the 1970s to the present. What changed after the 1960s? Why did taxes become more important to the public? What encouraged politicians to campaign on tax issues?

One measure of the centrality of taxes in political campaigns is the number of times the topic is mentioned in presidential nomination acceptance speeches. These data show that the word *taxes* barely passed the lips of the major-party nominees until after the 1960s. The numbers on the vertical axis represent the number of sentences mentioning taxes in nomination acceptance speeches.

Source: Author content analysis of acceptance speeches as compiled by the Woolley and Peters American Presidency Project.

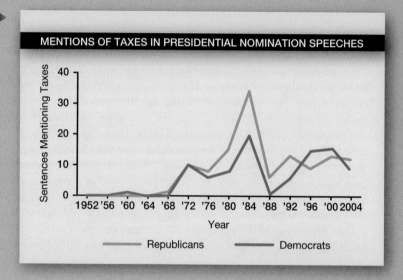

MENTIONS OF TAXES IN PRESIDENTIAL NOMINATION SPEECHES

In earlier decades, taxes weren't very important to members of the public, either. The National Election Study has asked respondents what they like and dislike about each of the political parties at least every four years since 1952. With the exception of 1952, when the presidential election featured talk of lowering taxes after World War II, the percentages of all "likes" and "dislikes" that concerned taxes were much lower during the 1950s and 1960s than in later decades. Here the vertical axis shows the percentages of all "likes" and "dislikes" (for Republicans and Democrats combined) that concern taxes.

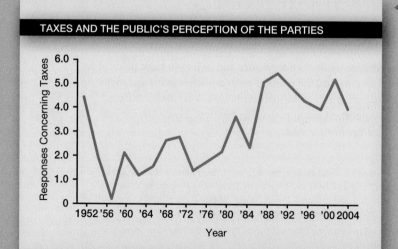

TAXES AND THE PUBLIC'S PERCEPTION OF THE PARTIES

Source: National Election Studies Cumulative File.

Political scientists don't have a definitive answer, but there are a number of plausible explanations. One factor could be the increasing effective costs of taxes. During the 1950s and 1960s, per capita taxes increased rapidly, but real wages grew even faster. With Americans' disposable income growing, the impact of taxes was muted. But during the 1970s, oil shocks and worldwide economic slowdown reduced wage growth. High inflation both ate into Americans' purchasing power and pushed them into higher and higher tax brackets (a phenomenon called *bracket creep*). As taxes took a bigger bite, their salience to the public grew.

Another explanation, popularized by the journalists Thomas and Mary Edsall in their 1992 book *Chain Reaction*, is that taxes became linked in the public mind with race-related policies. They hypothesized that with the Great Society policies of the 1960s, white Americans in particular came to resent the use of their tax dollars for welfare and other means-tested policies they believed they would never benefit from themselves.

The salience of taxes may also have been fueled by institutional changes within Congress. During the 1950s and 1960s, tax policy was dominated by the House Ways and Means Committee and its powerful chairman for much of this period, Wilbur Mills. The committee and its chair held both tight jurisdiction over taxes and tremendous power within the chamber, which allowed the containment of politics around taxes to a small tax policy community. Reforms in the late 1960s and early 1970s reduced the power of Ways and Means, which had to establish subcommittees for the first time, open its hearings to the public, and give up its control over committee assignments, previously an important source of leverage over House members. These changes opened up the insulated tax policy–making community, paving the way for tax politics as public spectacle.

Finally, tax revolts in some states demonstrated to politicians the expediency of taxes as a political issue. In 1978, California voters, frustrated that the state legislature had done nothing to cut taxes in a period of large budget surpluses and growing state and local tax burdens, took matters into their own hands by passing Proposition 13. The ballot initiative capped property tax rates and also instituted a two-thirds majority requirement in both houses of the state legislature for any subsequent increases in state taxes. Prop 13 convinced politicians, including the presidential candidate Ronald Reagan, that "tax cuts were good politics," according to the sociologist Isaac Martin.[1] Other entrepreneurial politicians, particularly in the Republican party, strove to keep taxes on the public agenda and to cement the GOP's image as the party of tax cuts.

It is likely that all of these factors contributed to the heightening of taxes as a political issue. And given the current budget deficit, growing national debt, and mismatch between projected revenues and likely spending on Social Security, Medicare, and Medicaid over the long term, taxes will undoubtedly be high on the political agenda for some time to come.

[1]Isaac William Martin, *The Permanent Tax Revolt* (Palo Alto, Calif.:Stanford University Press, 2008), p. 15.

Source: Adapted from *How Americans Think about Taxes* by Andrea Louise Campbell (Princeton, N.J.: Princeton University Press, 2009).

Government and the Shaping of Public Opinion

All governments attempt, to a greater or lesser extent, to influence, manipulate, or manage their citizens' beliefs. But the extent to which public opinion is affected by government public relations efforts is probably limited. The government—despite its size and power—is only one source of information in the United States. Very often government claims are disputed by the media and interest groups, and at times by opposing forces within the government itself. Often, too, government efforts to manipulate public opinion backfire when the public is made aware of the government's tactics. Thus in 1971 the government's efforts to build popular support for the Vietnam War were hurt when CBS News aired its documentary *The Selling of the Pentagon*, which purported to reveal the extent and character of government efforts to sway popular sentiment. In this documentary, CBS demonstrated the techniques, including planted news stories and faked film footage, that the government had used to misrepresent its activities in Vietnam. These revelations, of course, undermined popular trust in government claims.

A hallmark of the administration of President Bill Clinton was the steady use of election-campaign-type techniques to bolster popular enthusiasm for White House initiatives. The president established a political "war room" similar to the one that operated in his campaign headquarters. In the presidential version, representatives from all cabinet departments met daily to discuss and coordinate the president's public relations efforts. Many of the same consultants and pollsters who directed the successful Clinton campaign were also employed in the selling of the president's programs.[33]

After he assumed office in 2001, George W. Bush asserted that political leaders should base their programs on their own conception of the public interest, not on the polls. This did not mean that Bush ignored public opinion, however. He relied on the pollster Jan van Lohuizen to conduct a low-key operation, sufficiently removed from the limelight to allow the president to renounce polling while continuing to make use of survey data.[34] At the same time, the Bush White House developed an extensive public relations program, led initially by the former presidential aide Karen Hughes, to bolster popular support for the president's policies. Hughes, working with the conservative TV personality Mary Matalin, coordinated White House efforts to maintain popular support for the administration's war against terrorism. These efforts included presidential speeches, media appearances by administration officials, numerous press conferences, and thousands of press releases presenting the administration's views.[35] The White House also made a substantial effort to sway opinion in foreign countries, even sending officials to present the administration's views on television networks serving the Arab world.

Another example of a Bush administration effort to shape public opinion was a series of commercials it produced at taxpayer expense in 2004 to promote the new

---

[33] Gerald F. Seib and Michael K. Frisby, "Selling Sacrifice," *Wall Street Journal*, February 5, 1993, p. 1.

[34] Joshua Green, "The Other War Room," *Washington Monthly*, April 2002.

[35] Peter Marks, "Adept in Politics and Advertising, Four Women Shape a Campaign," *New York Times*, November 11, 2001, p. B6.

Medicare prescription drug program. The commercials, prominently featuring the president, were designed to look like news stories and were aired in English and Spanish by hundreds of local television stations. Called a video news release, this type of commercial is designed to give viewers the impression that they are watching a real news story. The presumption is that viewers are more likely to believe what they think is news coverage than material they know to be advertising. Democrats, of course, accused the administration of conducting a partisan propaganda campaign with public funds, but Republicans pointed out that the Clinton administration had engaged in similar practices.

In January 2005, it was revealed that the administration had paid the conservative African American radio pundit Armstrong Williams to comment favorably on its educational policies. Williams received $240,000 in taxpayer dollars for touting the administration's programs but never indicated that he was being paid for his support. Presumably, listeners were never aware that they were hearing what amounted to government propaganda disguised as editorial commentary. Rational politicians push the envelope in manipulating the information environment to show themselves off in the most favorable light. Sometimes they get caught.

Private Groups and the Shaping of Public Opinion

We have already seen how the government tries to shape public opinion. But the ideas that become prominent in political life are also developed and spread by important economic and political groups searching for issues that will advance their causes. Rational political entrepreneurs pursue strategies that—an application of the collective-action principle—give the groups they lead a decided advantage in the political arena in comparison with latent, unorganized groups. In some instances, in the hope of bringing others over to their side, private groups espouse values they truly believe in. Take, for example, the campaign against so-called partial birth abortion, which resulted in the Partial Birth Abortion Ban Act of 2003. Proponents of the act believed that prohibiting particular sorts of abortions would be a first step toward eliminating all abortions, something they view as a moral imperative.[36] In other cases, however, groups will promote principles designed mainly to further hidden agendas of political and economic interests. One famous example is the campaign against cheap imported handguns—the so-called Saturday-night specials—that was covertly financed by the domestic manufacturers of more expensive firearms. The campaign's organizers claimed that cheap handguns pose a grave risk to the public and should be outlawed. The real goal, though, was not safeguarding the public but protecting the economic well-being of the domestic gun industry. A more recent example is the campaign against the alleged "sweatshop" practices of some American companies manufacturing their products in third world countries. This campaign is mainly financed by U.S. labor unions seeking to protect their members' jobs by discouraging American firms from manufacturing their products abroad.[37]

---

[36] Cynthia Gorney, "Gambling with Abortion," *Harper's Magazine*, November 2004, pp. 33–46.

[37] David P. Baron and Daniel Diermeier, "Strategic Activism and Nonmarket Strategy," *Journal of Economics and Management Strategy* (2006).

Typically, ideas are marketed most effectively by groups with access to financial resources, public or private institutional support, and sufficient skill or education to select, develop, and draft ideas that will attract interest and support. Thus the development and promotion of conservative themes and ideas in recent years have been greatly facilitated by the millions of dollars that conservative corporations and business organizations such as the U.S. Chamber of Commerce and the Public Affairs Council spend each year on public information and what is now called in corporate circles "issues management." In addition, conservative business leaders have contributed millions of dollars to such conservative institutions as the Heritage Foundation, the Hoover Institution, and the American Enterprise Institute.[38] Many of the ideas that helped those on the right influence political debate were first developed and articulated by scholars associated with institutions such as these.

Although they do not usually have access to financial assets that match those available to their conservative opponents, liberal intellectuals and professionals have ample organizational skills, access to the media, and practice in creating, communicating, and using ideas. During the past three decades, the chief vehicle through which liberal intellectuals and professionals have advanced their ideas has been the "public interest group," an institution that relies heavily on voluntary contributions of time, effort, and interest on the part of its members. Through groups such as Common Cause, the National Organization for Women, the Sierra Club, Friends of the Earth, and Physicians for Social Responsibility, intellectuals and professionals have been able to use their organizational skills and educational resources to develop and promote ideas.[39] Often research conducted at universities and liberal "think tanks" such as the Brookings Institution provides the ideas on which liberal politicians rely. For example, the welfare reform plan introduced by the Clinton administration in 1994 originated with the work of the Harvard professor David Ellwood. Ellwood's academic research led him to the conclusion that the nation's welfare system would be improved if services to the poor were expanded in scope but limited in duration. His idea was adopted by the 1992 Clinton presidential campaign, which was searching for a position on welfare that would appeal to both liberal and conservative Democrats. The Ellwood plan seemed perfect: It promised liberals an immediate expansion of welfare benefits, yet it held out to conservatives the idea that welfare recipients would receive benefits for only a limited time. The Clinton welfare reform plan even borrowed phrases from Ellwood's book *Poor Support*.[40]

The journalist and author Joe Queenan has correctly observed that although political ideas can erupt spontaneously, they almost never do. Instead, he says,

---

[38] See David Vogel, "The Power of Business in America: A Reappraisal," *British Journal of Political Science* 13 (1983): 19–44.

[39] See David Vogel, "The Public Interest Movement and the American Reform Tradition," *Political Science Quarterly* 96 (Winter 1980): 607–27.

[40] Jason DeParle, "The Clinton Welfare Bill Begins Trek in Congress," *New York Times*, July 15, 1994, p. 1.

issues are usually manufactured by tenured professors and obscure employees of think tanks. . . . It is inconceivable that the American people, all by themselves, could independently arrive at the conclusion that the depletion of the ozone layer poses a dire threat to our national well-being, or that an immediate, across-the-board cut in the capital-gains tax is the only thing that stands between us and the economic abyss. The American people do not have that kind of sophistication. *They have to have help* [emphasis added].[41]

The Media and Public Opinion

The communications media are among the most powerful forces operating in the marketplace of ideas. Most Americans say that their primary source of information about public affairs is news media—newspapers, broadcast and cable news, radio, and Internet news providers. The alternative sources of political information are direct contact with politics, information provided by groups, and information conveyed by other individuals, such as family members or coworkers. Certainly few people actually go to Washington to find out what's going on in American politics, and the broad access people have to media outlets dwarfs the number of households that receive direct mail from organizations and elected officials. Personal conversation is also an important source for information, but people tend to avoid controversial topics. For example, at work or school, sports and weather are much safer topics for casual conversation than politics.

The mass media, as the term suggests, can be thought of as mediators. They are the conduits through which information flows. Through newspapers, radio and television, magazines, and the Internet we can learn about what's going on in our world and in our government. Providing this opportunity to learn about the world and politics is the most important way the media contribute to public opinion.

People rely on the media, rather than other sources of information, to find out what's going on in politics and public affairs because it is easy to do so. Media outlets are ubiquitous. More households in the United States have television than have indoor plumbing. Radio penetration is nearly as universal. Nearly every community has a newspaper, with 1,500 daily newspapers published throughout the United States. The number of news programs and the availability of news has also expanded tremendously in recent decades. In the 1960s there were only three television news outlets—CBS, NBC, and ABC. They aired evening and nightly news programs and allowed a half-hour slot for news from local affiliates. The rise of cable television in the 1980s brought a twenty-four-hour news station, CNN; expanded news programming through the Public Broadcasting System (PBS); and a network devoted exclusively to broadcasting proceedings of Congress and government agencies, C-SPAN. Important competitors to the big three networks emerged, including FOX, UPN, WB, and the Spanish-language networks Univision and Telemundo. Today there is no shortage of televised news programming available at all hours.[42]

---

[41] Joe Queenan, "Birth of a Notion," *Washington Post*, September 20, 1992, p. C1.

[42] See Stephen Ansolabehere, Roy Behr, and Shanto Iyengar, *The Media Game* (New York: Macmillan, 1993).

Technological innovations continue to push change in political communication in the United States. Today, more than 75 percent of Americans have Internet access.[43] To put that in historical perspective, Internet penetration in the United States today is comparable to television penetration in the late 1950s. This technology, then, has yet to reach its full power and potential. Nevertheless, the rise of the Internet has already opened the flow of communication further. Conventional media have moved much of their content online, provided for free. Internet users can gain access not only to U.S. media but also to media from around the world. The Internet has also changed the traditional media, leading to the development of interactive graphics and reader forums. We have also witnessed the rise of new forms of communications, most notably Web logs ("blogs" for short), which provide a platform for anyone to have their say. Several Web sites, such as Google News and realclearpolitics.com, are clearinghouses for traditional media, newswire stories, and blogs. This new, highly competitive media environment has put increased financial pressures on the traditional media, and it has radically changed the flow and nature of communication in the United States and the availability of information to the public. In Chapter 13, we discuss the media as a democratic institution at greater length. Our concern here is the media's role in how people learn about politics and public affairs.

Learning through mass media occurs both actively and passively. Active learning occurs when people search for a particular type of program or a particular type of information. If you turn on the nightly news to find out what has happened in national and international affairs, you are engaged in actively learning. If you search the Web for information about your member of Congress, you are engaged in active learning. Passive learning may be just as important. Many entertainment programs discuss current affairs and issues, such as social issues or an election. When that occurs, learning takes a passive form. You watch the program for entertainment but gain information about politics. One study of information gain among voters found that people learned as much from Oprah as from the evening news.[44] Political advertising is perhaps the most common form of passive information. During the last month of national political campaigns, it is not uncommon to see three or four political advertisements during one commercial break in a prime-time (7:00 to 11:00 P.M.) television program.

Mass media are our primary source for information about current affairs. They influence how Americans understand politics not just through the volume of information available but also through what is presented and how. Editors, reporters, and others involved in preparing the content of the news must ultimately decide what topics to cover, what facts to include, and whom to interview. Journalists usually try to present issues fairly, but it is difficult, perhaps impossible, to be perfectly objective. C-SPAN takes an unusual approach. It sets up a camera at an event and simply records what occurs; it adds no commentary and does not edit the material. Just the facts. However, even that approach necessar-

---

[43] These figures are tracked regularly by the Nielsen Corporation, www.nielsen-online.com/pr/pr_040318.pdf (accessed 3/25/09).

[44] See Matthew Baum, *Soft News Goes to War* (Princeton, N.J.: Princeton University Press, 2006).

ily involves some slant, depending on what events C-SPAN decides to cover. By choosing to cover some events and not others, it sends a message about what, in its view, is important.

What the media cover and how news is presented and interpreted can affect public opinion. Psychologists have identified two potential pathways through which media coverage shapes what people think. First, the news sets the public's agenda. It cues people to think about some issues rather than others; it makes some considerations more salient than others. Suppose, for example that the local news covers crime to the exclusion of all else. When someone who watches the local news regularly thinks about the mayoral election, crime is more likely to be his or her primary consideration, compared with someone who does not watch the local news. Psychologists call this **priming**.

Second, news coverage of an issue frames the way the issue is defined. News coverage of crime, to continue the example, may include a report on every murder that happens in a large city. Such coverage would likely make it seem that murder occurs very often and is much more common than it actually is. This in turn might heighten viewers' sense of insecurity or threat, leading to an exaggerated sense of risk of violent crime and increased support for tough police practices.[45] **Framing** refers to the media's power to influence how events and issues are interpreted.

Priming and framing are often viewed as twin evils. One can distract us from other important problems, and the other can make us think about an issue or a politician in a biased way. The cumulative effects of priming and framing on public opinion depend ultimately on the variety of issues covered and the diversity of perspectives represented. That, after all, is the idea behind the guarantee of a free press in the First Amendment to the Constitution. Free and open communication media allow the greatest likelihood that people will learn about important issues, that they will gain the information they need to distinguish good ideas from bad ones, and that they will learn which political leaders and parties can best represent their interests.

In this regard, the most significant framing effects take the form of the balance in the information available to people. Those in politics—elected officials, candidates, leaders of organized groups—work hard to influence what the news covers. A competitive political environment usually translates into a robust flow of information. However, some political environments are not very competitive, where only one view gets expressed and only one view is reflected in the media. Congressional elections are a case in point. Incumbent politicians today are able to raise much more money than their challengers (an advantage of about $3 to $1). As a result, House elections often have a gross imbalance in the amount of advertising and news coverage between the two campaigns, that of the incumbent member of Congress and that of the challenger. This will likely affect public opinion, because voters hear the incumbent's views and message more often than the challenger's.

priming A process of preparing the public to take a particular view of an event or a political actor.

framing The power of the media to influence how events and issues are interpreted.

---

[45] The seminal work on priming and framing in public policy and politics is Shanto Iyengar and Donald Kinder, *News That Matters* (Chicago: University of Chicago Press, 1987).

A further example of an imbalance in news coverage arises with the president and Congress. Presidential press conferences and events receive much more coverage than the press events of the leaders of the House or Senate. This gives the president the upper hand in setting the public agenda through the media, because members of the public are more likely to hear the president's arguments for a particular policy. That opportunity and power, of course, must be used wisely. A president who pursues an ill-advised policy can easily squander the advantage that is gained from disproportionate attention from the media. If a policy fails, the president's media advantage can be short lived. President Clinton, for example, used his 1993 State of the Union address to introduce an initiative to pass national health insurance. That initiative got bogged down in Congress, was challenged by the insurance industry in a nationwide advertising campaign, and failed, contributing to the Democrats' loss of Congress in 1994. In 2002, President George W. Bush convinced the nation that Iraq was developing weapons of mass destruction and the United States need to topple the regime of Saddam Hussein immediately. The invasion occurred and Hussein's regime quickly fell, but large caches of chemical and nuclear weapons were never found, and the United States remained in Iraq for the better part of a decade. The backlash against these policies cost the Republicans support among the public, control of Congress in the 2006 election, and ultimately the presidency in 2008. The power of the president is the power to persuade, but control of information for political aims is a power to be used with caution.

Today, it is easy to learn about public affairs and to hear different opinions— even when we don't want to. The rise of cable television and the Internet has weakened the old media outlets, such as ABC, CBS, and NBC, and the newspaper industry. But, it is widely conjectured, the new media have facilitated learning and muted some of the biases that may emerge through priming and framing. No one voice or perspective dominates our multifaceted media environment and competitive political system. And biases in the media often reflect not the lack of outlets or restrictive editorial control but, rather, failures of political competition.

MEASURING PUBLIC OPINION

As recently as fifty years ago, American political leaders gauged public opinion by people's applause and the size of crowds at meetings. This direct exposure to the people's views did not necessarily produce accurate knowledge of public opinion. It did, however, give political leaders confidence in their public support—and therefore confidence in their ability to govern by consent.

Abraham Lincoln and Stephen Douglas debated each other seven times in the summer and autumn of 1858, two years before they became presidential nominees. Their debates took place before audiences in parched cornfields and courthouse squares. A century later most presidential debates, although seen by millions, take place before a few reporters and technicians in television studios that might as well be on the moon. The public's response cannot be experienced firsthand. This distance between leaders and followers is one of the agonizing problems of modern democracy. The media provide information to millions of people, but they are not yet so efficient at providing leaders with information. Is government by consent possible when the scale of communication is so large and impersonal? To compensate for the decline in their ability to experience public opinion for themselves, leaders have turned to science, in particular the science of opinion polling.

It is no secret that politicians and public officials make extensive use of **public-opinion polls** to help them decide whether to run for office, what policies to support, how to vote on important legislation, and what types of appeals to make in their campaigns. President Lyndon Johnson was famous for carrying the latest Gallup and Roper poll results in his pocket, and it is widely believed that he began to withdraw from politics because the polls reported losses in public support. All recent presidents and other major political figures have worked closely with polls and pollsters.

Constructing Public Opinion from Surveys

The population in which pollsters are interested is usually quite large. To conduct their polls, they first choose a **sample** of the total population. The selection of this sample is important. Above all, it must be representative: The views of those in the sample must accurately and proportionately reflect the views of the whole. To a large extent, the validity of the poll's results depends on the sampling procedure used.

Sampling Techniques and Selection Bias. The most common techniques for choosing such a sample are probability sampling and random digit dialing. In the case of **probability sampling**, the pollster begins with a list of the population to be surveyed. This list is called the sampling frame. After each member of the population has been assigned a number, a table of random numbers or a computerized random selection process is used to pick those members of the population to be surveyed.

It is important to emphasize, first, that a sample selected in this manner produces a subset of the population that is representative of the population—it is a microcosm, so to speak. It is also important to point out that whatever is learned about this representative sample can also be attributed to the larger population with a high level of assurance. (We will discuss potential errors in generalizing to the full population shortly.) This technique is appropriate when the entire population can be identified. For example, all students registered at Texas colleges and universities can be identified from college records, and a sample of them can easily be drawn. When the pollster is interested in a national sample of Americans, however, this technique is not feasible, because no complete list of Americans exists.[46] National samples are usually drawn using a technique called **random digit dialing**—in which a computerized random-number generator produces a list of as many ten-digit numbers as the pollster deems necessary. Given that more than 95 percent of American households have telephones, this technique usually results in

public-opinion poll The scientific instrument for measuring public opinion.

sample A small group selected by researchers to represent the most important characteristics of an entire population.

probability sampling A method used by pollsters to select a representative sample in which every individual in the population has an equal probability of being selected as a respondent.

random digit dialing A poll in which respondents are selected at random from a list of ten-digit telephone numbers, with every effort made to avoid bias in the construction of the sample.

---

[46] Herbert Asher, *Polling and the Public* (Washington, D.C.: Congressional Quarterly Press, 2001), p. 64.

a random national sample. With the growth in cell-phone use, however, and the enactment of "do-not-call" legislation to discourage telemarketers, random digit dialing has become less reliable. (We will elaborate on this shortly.)

The importance of sampling was brought home early in the history of political polling. A 1936 *Literary Digest* poll predicted that the Republican presidential candidate, Alf Landon, would defeat the Democrat, Franklin D. Roosevelt, in that year's election. The election of course ended in a Roosevelt landslide. The main problem with the survey was what is called **selection bias** in drawing the sample. The pollsters had relied on telephone directories and automobile registration rosters to produce a sampling frame. During the Great Depression, however, only wealthy Americans owned telephones and automobiles. Thus the millions of working-class Americans who constituted Roosevelt's principal base of support were excluded from the sample. A more recent instance of polling error caused by selection bias occurred during the 1998 Minnesota gubernatorial election. A poll conducted by the *Minneapolis Star Tribune* just six weeks before the election showed the former professional wrestler Jesse Ventura running a distant third to the Democratic candidate, Hubert Humphrey III, who seemed to have the support of 49 percent of the electorate, and the Republican, Norm Coleman, whose support stood at 29 percent. Only 10 percent of those polled said they were planning to vote for Ventura. On election day, Ventura outpolled both Humphrey and Coleman. Analysis of exit-poll data showed why the preelection polls had been so wrong. In an effort to be accurate, preelection pollsters' predictions often take account of the likelihood that respondents will actually vote. They do this by polling only people who have voted in the past or correcting for past frequency of voting. The *Star Tribune* poll was conducted only among individuals who had voted in the previous election. Ventura, however, brought to the polls not only individuals who had not voted in the last election but also many people who had never voted before in their lives. Approximately 12 percent of Minnesota's voters in 1998 said they came to the polls only because Ventura was on the ballot. This surge in turnout was facilitated by the fact that Minnesota permits same-day voter registration. Thus the pollsters were wrong because Ventura changed the composition of the electorate.[47]

In recent years, the issue of selection bias has been further complicated by the fact that growing numbers of individuals refuse to answer pollsters' questions or use answering machines and caller ID to screen unwanted calls. If pollsters could be certain that those who responded to their surveys simply reflected the views of those who refused to respond, there would be no problem. Some studies suggest, however, that the views of respondents and nonrespondents can differ, especially along social-class lines. Middle- and upper-middle-class individuals are more likely to be willing to respond to surveys than their working-class counterparts.[48] Thus far, "nonresponse bias" has not undermined a major national survey, but the possibility of a future *Literary Digest* fiasco should not be ignored.

selection bias
A polling error in which the sample is not representative of the population being studied, so that some opinions are over- or under-represented.

---

[47] Carl Cannon, "A Pox on Both Our Parties," in *The Enduring Debate: Classic and Contemporary Readings in American Politics*, 2nd ed., David T. Canon, Anne Khademian, and Kenneth R. Mayor, eds. (New York: Norton, 2000), p. 389.

[48] John Goyder, Keith Warriner, and Susan Miller, "Evaluating Socio-economic Status Bias in Survey Nonresponse," *Journal of Official Statistics* 18, no. 1 (2002): 1–11.

FIGURE 9.2 IT DEPENDS ON HOW YOU ASK

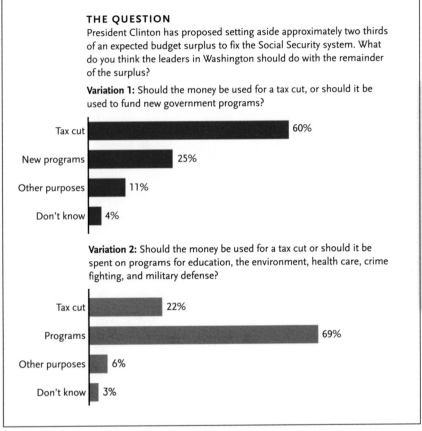

THE QUESTION
President Clinton has proposed setting aside approximately two thirds of an expected budget surplus to fix the Social Security system. What do you think the leaders in Washington should do with the remainder of the surplus?

Variation 1: Should the money be used for a tax cut, or should it be used to fund new government programs?

Tax cut	60%
New programs	25%
Other purposes	11%
Don't know	4%

Variation 2: Should the money be used for a tax cut or should it be spent on programs for education, the environment, health care, crime fighting, and military defense?

Tax cut	22%
Programs	69%
Other purposes	6%
Don't know	3%

SOURCE: Pew Research Center for the People and the Press, reported in the *New York Times*, January 30, 2000.

ANALYZING THE EVIDENCE
The public's desire for tax cuts can be hard to measure. Pollsters asking what should be done with the nation's budget surplus got different results, depending on the specifics of the question. What differences in the two versions of the question do you think account for the different answers?

Sample Size. The degree of reliability in polling is also a function of sample size. For polls of citizens of the United States, the typical size of a sample ranges from 450 to 1,500 respondents. This number reflects a trade-off between cost and degree of precision desired. A larger and hence more costly sample size is associated with greater precision in making generalizations to the full population than is a smaller sample size.

The chance that the sample used does not accurately represent the population from which it is drawn is called the **sampling error**, or *margin of error*. The sampling error measures the range of possibilities for a particular characteristic of a population based on the estimate of that characteristic in the sample drawn. The margin of error acknowledges that any given sample may not be perfectly representative of the full population. A typical survey of 1,500 respondents, for example, will have a sampling error of approximately 3 percent. When a preelection poll indicates that 51 percent of voters surveyed favor the Republican candidate and 49 percent support the Democratic candidate, the outcome is in fact too close to call because it is

sampling error
A polling error that arises on account of the small size of the sample.

TABLE 9.5 TWO POLLSTERS AND THEIR RECORDS

Year	Presidential Candidates	Harris	Gallup	Actual Outcome
2008	McCain	44	43	46
	Obama	50	51	53
2004	Bush, G. W.	49	49	51
	Kerry	48	49	48
	Nader	1	1	0
2000	Bush, G. W.	47	48	48
	Gore	47	46	49
	Nader	5	4	3
1996	Clinton	51	52	49
	Dole	39	41	41
	Perot	9	7	8
1992	Clinton	44	44	43
	Bush, G. H. W.	38	37	38
	Perot	17	14	19
1988	Bush, G. H. W.	51	53	54
	Dukakis	47	42	46
1984	Reagan	56	59	59
	Mondale	44	41	41
1980	Reagan	48	47	51
	Carter	43	44	41
	Anderson		8	
1976	Carter	48	48	51
	Ford	45	49	48
1972	Nixon	59	62	61
	McGovern	35	38	38
1968	Nixon	40	43	43
	Humphrey	43	42	43
	Wallace	13	15	14
1964	Johnson	62	64	61
	Goldwater	33	36	39
1960	Kennedy	49	51	50
	Nixon	41	49	49
1956	Eisenhower	NA*	60	58
	Stevenson		41	42
1952	Eisenhower	47	51	55
	Stevenson	42	49	44

ANALYZING THE EVIDENCE

Since their poor showing in 1948, the major pollsters have been close to the mark in every national presidential election. In 2000, though, neither Gallup nor Harris accurately predicted the outcome. From what you have learned about polling, what were some of the possible sources of error in these two national polls?

TABLE 9.5 (CONTINUED)

Year	Presidential Candidates	Harris	Gallup	Actual Outcome
1948	Truman	NA*	44.5	49.6
	Dewey		49.5	45.1

*Not asked

NOTE: Figures are percentages. All except those for 1948 are rounded.

SOURCE: Data from the Harris survey and the Gallup poll, Chicago Tribune–New York News Syndicate, various press releases, 1964–2008. Courtesy of Louis Harris & Associates and the Gallup Organization.

within the margin of error of the survey. A figure of 51 percent means that between 54 and 48 percent of voters in the population favor the Republicans, whereas a figure of 49 percent indicates that between 52 and 46 percent of all voters support the Democrats. Thus in this example, any outcome ranging from a 54–46 Republican victory to a 48–52 Republican loss is consistent with the survey evidence. The precision of the poll in this case does not permit a clear prediction of a winner.

Table 9.5 shows how accurate two of the major national polling organizations have been in predicting the outcome of presidential elections. In both the 2000 and the 2004 presidential elections, for example, in light of a 3 percent margin of error, both the Harris and the Gallup organizations predicted a "dead heat." Pollsters have been mostly correct in their predictions.[49]

Survey Design.   Even with reliable sample procedures, surveys may fail to reflect the true distribution of opinion within a target population. One frequent source of **measurement error** is the wording of survey questions. The precise words used in a question can have an enormous effect on the answers a survey elicits. The validity of survey results can also be adversely affected by poorly formatted questions, a faulty ordering of questions, inappropriate vocabulary, ambiguous questions, or questions with built-in biases. Often seemingly minor differences in the wording of a question can convey vastly different meanings to respondents and thus produce quite different response patterns (Figure 9.2). For example, for many years the University of Chicago's National Opinion Research Center has asked respondents whether they think the federal government is spending too much, too little, or about the right amount of money on "assistance for the poor." Answering the question posed this way, about two thirds of all respondents seem to believe that the government is spending too little. However, the same survey also asks whether

measurement error   The failure to identify the true distribution of opinion within a population because of errors such as ambiguous or poorly worded questions.

---

[49] For a recent paper on the difficulties with polls, especially in trying to assess the preferences of specific subgroups in the population, see David Leal, Matt Barreto, Jongho Lee, and Rodolfo O. de la Garza, "The Latino Vote in the 2004 Election," *PS: Political Science and Politics* 38 (January 2005): 41–49.

the government spends too much, too little, or about the right amount for "welfare." When the word *welfare* is substituted for *assistance for the poor*, about half of all respondents indicate that too much money is being spent.[50]

Push Polling.   In recent years, another form of bias has been introduced into surveys by the use of a technique called **push polling**. This technique involves asking a respondent a loaded question about a political candidate, with the question designed to elicit the response sought by the pollster and, simultaneously, to shape the respondent's perception of the candidate in question. For example, during the 1996 New Hampshire presidential primary, push pollsters employed by the campaign of one of Lamar Alexander's rivals called thousands of voters to ask, "If you knew that Lamar Alexander had raised taxes six times in Tennessee, would you be less inclined or more inclined to support him?"[51] More than 100 consulting firms across the nation now specialize in push polling, which is not a conventional use of legitimate survey methods and has been condemned by the American Association for Public Opinion Researchers.[52] Calling push polling the "political equivalent of a drive-by shooting," Representative Joe Barton (R-Tex.) launched a congressional investigation into the practice.[53] Push polls may be one reason why Americans are becoming increasingly skeptical of the practice of polling and increasingly unwilling to answers pollsters' questions.[54]

Illusion of Salience.   In the early days of a political campaign, when voters are asked which candidates they do or do not support, the answer they give often has little significance because the choice is not yet important to them. Their preferences may change many times before the election. This is part of the explanation for the phenomenon of the postconvention "bounce" in the popularity of presidential candidates, which is observed after Democratic and Republican national nominating conventions. Respondents' preferences reflected the amount of attention a candidate had received during the conventions rather than strongly held views.

The issues that are truly uppermost in the minds of voters at the time of an election, called **salient interests**, are often difficult to forecast very far in advance. These are interests that are of more than ordinary concern to respondents in a survey or to voters in the electorate. Politicians, social scientists, journalists, or pollsters who assume that something is important to the public when in fact it is not are creating an **illusion of salience**. This illusion can be created and fostered by polls despite careful controls in sampling, interviewing, and data analysis. In

push polling
A polling technique in which the questions are designed to shape the respondent's opinion.

salient interest
An attitude or view that is especially important to the individual holding it.

illusion of salience The impression conveyed by polls that something is important to the public when it actually is not.

---

[50] Michael R. Kagay and Janet Elder, "Numbers Are No Problem for Pollsters, Words Are," *New York Times*, August 9, 1992, p. E6.

[51] Donn Tibbetts, "Draft Bill Requires Notice of Push Polling," *Manchester Union Leader*, October 3, 1996, p. A6.

[52] See "AAPOR Statement on 'Push' Polls," www.aapor.org/aaporstatementonpushpolls?s=push%20 polling (accessed 3/25/09).

[53] Amy Keller, "Subcommittee Launches Investigation of Push Polls," *Roll Call*, October 3, 1996, p. 1.

[54] For a discussion of the growing difficulty of persuading people to respond to surveys, see John Brehm, *Phantom Respondents* (Ann Arbor: University of Michigan Press, 1993).

fact, the illusion is strengthened by the credibility that science gives survey results. The problem of salience has become especially acute as a result of the proliferation of media polls. The television networks and major national newspapers all make heavy use of opinion polls. Polls are also commissioned by local television stations and local and regional newspapers.

On the positive side, polls allow journalists to make independent assessments of political realities, assessments not influenced by the partisan claims of politicians. At the same time, however, media polls can allow journalists to make news when none exists. Polling diminishes journalists' dependence on news makers. A poll commissioned by a news agency can provide the basis for a good story even when candidates, politicians, and other news makers are not engaging in especially newsworthy activities. Thus on days when little or nothing is taking place in a political campaign, poll results, especially apparent changes in candidates' popularity margins, can provide exciting news. Several times during the 2008 presidential campaign, for example, small changes in the relative standing of the Democratic and Republican candidates produced banner headlines around the country. Stories about what the candidates actually did or said often took second place to reporting the "horse race."

Because rapid and dramatic shifts in candidates' margins tend to take place when voters' preferences are least fully formed, it is interesting that horse-race news is most likely to make the headlines when it is least significant. In other words, media interest in poll results is inversely related to the salience of voters' opinions and the significance of the polls' findings. However, by influencing perceptions, especially those of major contributors, media polls can influence political realities.

Bandwagon Effect. One of the most noted polling problems is the **bandwagon effect**, which occurs when polling results influence people to support the candidate marked as the probable victor. Some scholars argue that the bandwagon effect can be offset by an "underdog effect," in favor of the candidate who is trailing in the polls.[55] However, a candidate who demonstrates a lead in the polls usually finds it considerably easier to raise campaign funds than does a candidate whose poll standing is low. With these additional funds, poll leaders can often afford to pay for television time and other campaign activities that will cement their advantage.

bandwagon effect
A shift in electoral support to the candidate whom public opinion polls report as the front-runner.

HOW DOES PUBLIC OPINION INFLUENCE GOVERNMENT POLICY?

One of the fundamental notions on which the U.S. government was founded was that "the public" should not be trusted when it comes to governing. The framers designed institutions that, although democratic, somewhat insulated governmental

---

[55] See Michael Traugott, "The Impact of Media Polls on the Public," in *Media Polls in American Politics*, Thomas E. Mann and Gary Orren, eds. (Washington, D.C.: Brookings Institution, 1992), pp. 125–49.

decision making from popular pressure. For example, the indirect election of senators and presidents was supposed to prevent the government from being too dependent on the vagaries of public opinion.

Research from the 1950s and 1960s indicates that the framers' concerns were well founded. Individual-level survey analysis reveals that the respondents lacked fundamental political knowledge and had ill-formed opinions about government and public policy.[56] Their answers seemed nothing more than "doorstep opinions"—opinions given off the top of the head. When an individual was asked the same questions at different times, he or she often gave different answers. The dramatic and unpredictable changes seemed to imply that the public was indeed unreliable as a guide for political decisions.

However, the political scientists Benjamin Page and Robert Shapiro take issue with the notion that the public should not be trusted when it comes to policy making.[57] They contend that public opinion at the aggregate level is coherent and stable and that it moves in a predictable fashion in response to changing political, economic, and social circumstances.

How is this possible, given what previous studies have found? Page and Shapiro hypothesize that the individual-level responses are plagued by various types of errors that make people's opinions seem incoherent and unstable. When a large number of individual-level responses to survey questions are added up to produce an aggregate public opinion, the errors, or "noise," in the individual responses, if more or less random, will cancel each other out, revealing a collective opinion that is stable, coherent, and meaningful. From their results, Page and Shapiro concluded that the general public can indeed be trusted when it comes to governing.

In democratic nations, leaders should pay heed to public opinion, and most evidence suggests that they do. In many instances, public policy and public opinion do not coincide, but in general the government's actions are consistent with citizens' preferences. One study, for example, found that between 1935 and 1979, in about two-thirds of all cases significant changes in public opinion were followed within one year by changes in government policy consistent with the shift in the popular mood.[58] Other studies have come to similar conclusions about public opinion and government policy at the state level.[59] Do these results imply that elected leaders merely pander to public opinion? The answer is no.

A recent study on the role that public opinion played during the failed attempt to enact health-care reform in the early days of the Clinton presidency found that public opinion polls had very little influence on individual members of Congress,

[56] Campbell et al., *The American Voter;* Philip E. Converse, "The Nature of Belief Systems in Mass Publics," in *Ideology and Discontent,* David E. Apter, ed. (New York: Free Press, 1964).

[57] Benjamin I. Page and Robert Y. Shapiro, *The Rational Public: Fifty Years of Trends in Americans' Policy Preferences* (Chicago: University of Chicago Press, 1992).

[58] Benjamin I. Page and Robert Y. Shapiro, "Effects of Public Opinion on Policy," *American Political Science Review* 77, no. 1 (March 1983): 175–90.

[59] Robert S. Erikson, Gerald C. Wright, and John P. McIver, *Statehouse Democracy: Public Opinion and Policy in the American States* (New York: Cambridge University Press, 1993).

who used these polls first to justify positions they had already adopted and then to shape public thinking on the issue. In other words, opinion and policy were related because policy makers shaped opinion to support paths they already planned to take. This pattern is consistent with the opinion-manipulation efforts we examined earlier in this chapter. However, the study also found that congressional party leaders based their health-care legislation strategies on their concerns about the effects of public opinion on the electoral fortunes of individual members of Congress. Leaders' concerns about public opinion thus help explain why the congressional policy-making process follows public opinion even though individual members of Congress do not.[60] The salience of health care has remained high for more than a decade since the failure of Clinton's effort. President Bush's prescription drug plan for senior citizens came about in response to public concerns about rising prescription-drug costs. Even after Barack Obama and a Democratic Congress succeeded in passing health care legislation in 2010, many Americans remained concerned about the issue, and some Republicans promised to revisit the new legislation (or even repeal it) if they gained a majority in Congress.

There are always areas of disagreement between opinion and policy. For example, the majority of Americans favored stricter government control of handguns for years before Congress adopted the modest restrictions on firearms purchases embodied in the 1994 Brady gun-control bill and the amendment of the 1968 Omnibus Crime Control and Safe Streets Act. Similarly, most Americans, blacks as well as whites, oppose school busing to achieve racial balance, yet such busing continues to be used in many parts of the nation. Most Americans are also far less concerned with the rights of the accused than the federal courts seem to be. And most Americans oppose U.S. military intervention in other nations' affairs, yet such intervention continues to take place and often wins public approval after the fact.

Several factors can contribute to a lack of consistency between opinion and government policy. First, the nominal majority on a particular issue may not be as intensely committed to its preference as the adherents of the minority viewpoint. An intensely committed minority may often be more willing to commit its time, energy, efforts, and resources to the affirmation of its opinions than an apathetic majority, even if it is large. In the case of firearms, for example, although the proponents of gun control are in the majority by a wide margin, most do not regard the issue as being of critical importance to themselves and are not willing to commit much effort to advancing their cause. The opponents of gun control, by contrast, are intensely committed, well organized, and well financed and as a result are usually able to carry the day. In accordance with the institution principle, the collective-action principle, and the policy principle, intense commitment, organization, and financial resources are potent assets in the legislature, the executive bureaucracy, and the courts.

A second important reason why public policy and public opinion may not coincide has to do with the character and structure of the American system of government. The framers of the Constitution, as we saw in Chapter 2, sought to create a system of government that was based on popular consent but did not invariably

---

[60] Lawrence R. Jacobs, Eric D. Lawrence, Robert Y. Shapiro, and Steven S. Smith, "Congressional Leadership of Public Opinion," *Political Science Quarterly* 113 (Spring 1998): 21–41.

and automatically translate shifting popular sentiments into public policies. As a result, the American governmental process includes arrangements such as an appointed judiciary that can produce policy decisions that may run contrary to prevailing popular sentiment—at least for a time.

Perhaps the inconsistencies between opinion and policy could be resolved if we made broader use of a mechanism currently employed by a number of states: the ballot initiative. This procedure allows propositions to be placed on the ballot and voted into law by the electorate, bypassing most of the normal machinery of representative government. In recent years, several important propositions sponsored by business and conservative groups have been enacted.[61] For example, California's Proposition 209, approved by the state's voters in 1996, prohibited state and local government agencies in California from using race or gender preferences in hiring, contracting, or university admissions decisions. Responding to conservatives' success, liberal groups launched a number of ballot initiatives in 2000. In Washington State, for example, voters were asked to consider propositions sponsored by teachers unions that would have required annual cost-of-living raises for teachers and more than $1.8 billion in additional state spending over the next six years.[62]

Initiatives such as these seem to provide the public with an opportunity to express its will. During the 2006 and 2008 elections, propositions on social issues—gay marriage, stem-cell research, immigration—were on the ballot in many states, bypassing stalled efforts of the normal political process. In 2010, voters in numerous states decided questions related to taxes and the state's economy. The problem, however, is that government by initiative offers little opportunity for reflection and compromise. Voters are presented with a proposition, usually sponsored by a special interest group, and are asked to take it or leave it. Perhaps the true will of the people lies somewhere between the positions taken by the various interest groups. For example, California voters might have wanted affirmative action programs to be modified but not scrapped altogether, as Proposition 209 mandated. In a representative assembly, as opposed to a referendum campaign, a compromise position might have been achieved that would have been more satisfactory to all the residents of the state. This capacity for compromise is one reason the Founders strongly favored representative government rather than direct democracy.[63]

When all is said and done, however, the actions of the American government do not remain out of line with popular sentiment for long. A major reason for this is, of course, the electoral process, to which we shall next turn. Nonetheless, we should not forget that the close relationship between government and opinion in America may also be in part a result of the government's success in molding opinion.

---

[61] David Broder, *Democracy Derailed: Initiative Campaigns and the Power of Money* (New York: Harcourt, 2000).

[62] Robert Tomsho, "Liberals Take a Cue from Conservatives: This Election, the Left Tries to Make Policy with Ballot Initiatives," *Wall Street Journal*, November 6, 2000, p. A12.

[63] For the classic treatment of take-it-or-leave-it referendums and initiatives, see Thomas Romer and Howard Rosenthal, "Political Resource Allocation, Controlled Agendas, and the Status Quo," *Public Choice* 33 (1978): 27–44.

CONCLUSION

Representative democracy was a novel form of government when the United States created its Constitution. Behind this radical system lies one central idea—that the government reflects the will of the people. People have the opportunity to express their preferences through elections, public meetings and organizations, and free expression and debate. Public deliberations and public choices, it is conjectured, aggregate individuals' preferences and opinions to form the collective "will of the people" that would guide those in office. This chapter has explored the meaning of this idea today.

We no longer speak of the people of the United States as if they were an organic whole with a coherent will. Rather we characterize the "people" as the aggregation of individuals' preferences about the choices presented to them—in a phrase, public opinion. The individual is the foundation of public opinion. Politicians assume that individuals will pursue and express their own preferences and beliefs. They will act in ways to protect and expand their own property and wealth: they will express their own ideologies and ideals about what is right: they will pursue their own happiness and not sacrifice their own interests for those of the state or the community. When then vote, attend meetings, talk to others, or otherwise engage in democratic politics, people are free to say what they want, meet with whomever they want, and do what they want, so long as they don't harm others. The aggregation of all of those activities and actions expresses the public's opinion.

The succeeding chapters will consider how public opinion manifests itself through different institutions of democracy—elections, parties, organized interests, and communications media. As we discuss these institutions, it will be useful to keep in mind how we have described public opinion in this chapter. Specifically, every individual has his or her own preferences and own beliefs about the right policy or action to pursue. On any particular question or issue, individuals face a range of choices or options. Expressing their preferences, individuals choose the options that best reflect their preferences as to the outcomes and their beliefs about what is the best way to achieve those outcomes. On many issues, social scientists describe the range of people's preferences along a single dimension, such as ideology (from very liberal to very conservative) or partisanship (from strongly Democratic to strongly Republican). On general economic indicators, such as income, most people in the United States have what may be described as middle-class incomes; a significant percentage are poor, and a very small percentage are wealthy. Preferences about social spending and taxation often reflect these economic differences. On matters of ideology or public policy, social scientists guage the percentage of people adhering to each of the many possible views. Most people in the United States hold fairly centrist or moderate views on most questions. The tilt, depending on the issue and the choices offered, is slightly right of center or slightly left of center. Neither right nor left nor center, however, commands an outright majority of public support in the United States on any issue of importance. Anyone adhering to one of these views must reach out beyond his or her particular ideological slant in order to find a coalition large enough to capture the support of a majority.

Democracy in this free and open society is complicated further by the heterogeneity of American society. The nation's political institutions tolerate all manner of religious and political beliefs and all manner of social and economic relations, and the United States has long been a refuge for those from other countries seeking religious or political asylum or just a better way of life. As a result the United States is one of the most diverse societies in the world, with freedom to practice every major religion, with all manner of political and social organizations, and with great concentrations of wealth and poverty. This would seem to be a recipe not for consensus but for disagreement and conflict, even civil conflict.

The open society in the United States, however, has worked for over two centuries, and it works because there its members have a strong common commitment to democracy itself. Americans, in essence, agree to disagree. We agree that it is best to have a heterogeneous society and to tolerate many different opinions. We value liberty and restrain the government from imposing itself on how people think or express themselves politically. We further agree to allow the institutions of democracy to help us reach collective decisions about who should govern and how they should govern.

The next four chapters examine those institutions in detail. How do elections facilitate the choice of and control over the government? How do political parties simplify choices and compete in the political domain? How do people mobilize their interests to allow for the expression of interests in a more concerted way than just voting? And finally, how do the media help us overcome collective-action problems and allow us to learn from each other, communicate with each other, and find consensus?

FOR FURTHER READING

Althaus, Scott. *Collective Preferences and Democratic Politics.* New York: Cambridge University Press, 2003.

Ansolabehere, Stephen, Jonathan Rodden, and James M. Snyder, Jr. "Purple America." *Journal of Economic Perspectives* 20, no. 2 (Spring 2006): 97–118.

Bartels, Larry. *Unequal Democracy.* Princeton, N.J.: Princeton University Press, 2008.

Berinsky, Adam. *In Time of War: Understanding Public Opinion from World War II to Iraq.* Chicago: University of Chicago Press, 2009.

Erikson, Robert S., and Kent L. Tedin. *American Public Opinion: Its Origins, Content, and Impact.* 6th ed. New York: Longman, 2001.

reader selection ○ Fiorina, Morris, Samuel Abrams, and Jeremy Pope. *Culture War?* 2nd ed. New York: Pearson, Longman, 2005.

Frank, Thomas. *What's the Matter with Kansas?* New York: Macmillan, 2004.

Ginsberg, Benjamin. *The Captive Public: How Mass Opinion Promotes State Power.* New York: Basic Books, 1986.

Jacobson, Gary. *A Divider, Not a Uniter: George W. Bush, the American People, the 2006* ○   reader selection
    Election, and Beyond. White Plains, N.Y.: Longman, 2007.

Key, V. O. *Public Opinion and American Democracy.* New York: Knopf, 1961.

Lee, Taeku. *Mobilizing Public Opinion.* Chicago: University of Chicago Press, 2002.

Lupia, Arthur, and Matthew D. McCubbins. *The Democratic Dilemma: Can Citizens Learn* ○   reader selection
    What They Need to Know? New York: Cambridge University Press, 1998.

McCarty, Nolan, Keith Poole, and Howard Rosenthal. *Polarized America: The Dance of* ○   reader selection
    Ideology and Unequal Riches. Princeton, N.J.: Princeton University Press, 2007.

Page, Benjamin I., and Robert Y. Shapiro. *The Rational Public: Fifty Years of Trends in*
    Americans' Policy Preferences. Chicago: University of Chicago Press, 1992.

Stimson, James A. *Public Opinion in America: Moods, Cycles, and Swings.* 2nd ed. Boulder,
    Colo.: Westview Press, 1998.

Zaller, John R. *The Nature and Origins of Mass Opinion.* New York: Cambridge University
    Press, 1992.

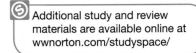

Ⓢ Additional study and review
materials are available online at
wwnorton.com/studyspace/

10 Elections

People convey their opinions to the government through many means, but the simplest and most profound expression of an individual's political preferences is the vote. Through the vote citizens can affirm a commitment to stay the course or to change their government when they think a new direction is needed. The vote, it is often said, is a blunt but effective instrument for controlling the government. In 2004, following a successful invasion of Iraq and with robust economic growth at hand, a majority of American voters reelected George W. Bush president and retained Republican majorities in the House and Senate. In 2006, with discontent over the war in Iraq growing, Americans elected Democratic majorities in the House and Senate. In 2008, facing an economic recession and ongoing involvement in Iraq, a majority of voters elected Barack Obama to the presidency and returned even larger Democratic majorities to the House and Senate. In each of these cases, voters expressed their political preferences through the institution of elections. Following the 2008 election, the administration of Barack Obama and the Democrats in Congress became the focus of the American electorate. As the new administration ascended to power, its members knew that they would be held accountable for their failings and rewarded for their successes in four short years. Indeed, only two years later, in the 2010 midterm elections, Republicans took control of the House of Representatives in what was widely seen as an electoral rebuke to the president.

Frequent, regular elections are the hallmark of democracy. Voters in the United States elect the president, governors, and other executive officers every four years, federal and state legislators every two years, and thousands of local mayors, councilors, and commissioners with similar frequency. All told there are over 88,000 governments at the federal, state, and local levels in the United States, nearly all of them run by elected bodies.[1] In a typical election, a voter may choose candidates for a dozen different offices, as well as deciding bond issues and other local questions put before the voters. In parliamentary systems, such as Britain, elections are held when the governing party in the legislature decides to hold elections, typically every four or five years. In parliamentary systems, voters in national elections usually only make one choice—which candidate should serve the district in parliament or which party should rule. In the United States, the regularity of elections makes the prospect of the next race a constant pressure on politicians. The wide use of elections, it is thought, keeps government policy close to the preferences and interests of its constituents. Electoral politics in the United States have functioned in this way for over two centuries. Elections have proved a

---

[1] There is one federal government. There are fifty state governments, over 3,000 county governments, about 36,000 municipal and town governments, about 13,500 school districts, and over 35,000 special districts (for example, water or utility), http://ftp2.census.gov/govs/cog/2002COGprelim_report.pdf (accessed 3/26/09) or http://www.census.gov/govs/www/cog2007.html. These data are compiled by the census of governments.

- The United States holds frequent elections as a means of keeping politicians close to the preferences of a majority of the people.

- The United States uses a system of plurality rule in which the candidate with the most votes wins the electoral district. Plurality rule creates a strong pressure toward two-party politics and makes it difficult for third parties to succeed.

- Plurality rule also shapes the incentives facing candidates and parties. It creates strong pressure on the parties or candidates to take more centrist policies so as to appeal to the median voter among the electorate as a whole.

- Most voters develop strong attachments to political parties, based on agreement on policy, social pressure, or upbringing. Those who identify with a party vote with that party nearly all of the time.

- Campaigns try to mobilize their candidate's supporters and persuade undecided voters. In the process, they provide information that helps solve some of the informational problems inherent in representative democracy.

remarkably successful method of bringing about continual renewal of government through peaceful means.

Why do elections work? How is it that elections generally create a government and policies that reflect and respond to the preferences of the public? In a representative democracy such as the United States, the electorate selects its leaders and representatives, rather than voting on each law and policy. Voters choose among the people and parties vying for office; they rarely consider the budget and other laws directly, except in the few legislative decisions put before voters in local and state politics, such as issuing school bonds or passing propositions. Elections, then, determine who will govern, not what they should do or what the laws should be. They are, to put the matter in terms we first considered in Chapter 1, occasions when multiple principals—the citizens—choose political agents to act on their behalf.

Two problems immediately arise for the principals (the citizens): First, are we selecting the best people for the job? Second, once elected, do the politicians do the job as we wish them to? Elections solve these problems by holding those in office accountable for their behavior and the results that their actions achieve. Politicians caught in scandals are usually voted out of office or decide to resign or retire rather than face the wrath of the voters. Voters usually take economic downturns as evidence of mismanagement of economic policy, and they vote against the incumbent president's party, as occurred in 2006 and 2008. They will also reward a party for economic good times and express their desire to continue with current economic policies, as occurred in 2004. They will reward Congress for the passage of legislation that addresses the concerns of the majority of people, as they did when the

Democratic minority brought along enough Republicans to pass an increase in the minimum wage in 2006. In this way the president and members of Congress are held accountable for the people around them and, sometimes, for events they only influence indirectly. Elections have proved a powerful mechanism for expressing the underlying desire of the majority either to continue down the present path, as in 2004, or to change the direction of public policy, as in 2006, 2008, and 2010.

The challenge of controlling the government through elections is compounded by problems of information. Voters cannot know everything about candidates for office or about politicians' actions once they are elected. In fact, the incentives to be highly knowledgeable are minimal. In a nation of 130 million voters or even a district of 650,000 voters, surely one's own ballot is unlikely to make a difference in the outcome and the cost of making a mistake is nil. Why, then, go to great lengths to find out the details of the candidates' backgrounds and personalities or to learn about the goings-on in Congress?

Incomplete information among the electorate magnifies the difficulties of choosing the best people and making sure they act in the electorate's interests. The first problem facing citizens, known as **adverse selection**, is a consequence of hidden information. When selecting one alternative over another, we often have incomplete information about just what we are choosing. Many aspects of our choices are hidden from view and may not become apparent until long after we have made our choice. The second problem facing voters is known as **moral hazard** and stems from hidden actions. Once selected, representatives cannot easily be monitored. Political leaders do many things that are public, such as making speeches and sending mail to constituents. But politicians necessarily engage in many acts that do not attract public attention, such as making deals with other politicians to build a winning coalition for a particular bill. The process of legislation typically goes unnoticed by most constituents, creating openings for politicians to act in ways contrary to the interests of the voters. How do we keep politicians from acting against our interests when the vast majority of people do not observe representatives' actions?

The answer to these problems of adverse selection and moral hazard are found partly in the fact that elections work through competition. Rival politicians or teams of politicians (parties) seek to hold elective office—we can consider that their primary motivation. Voters will choose those politicians who best fit their needs and wants, and the candidate or party fitting the preferences of the largest number of voters will win. Candidates and the parties actively seek victory: They present themselves to the public in ways that will make it most likely that they will win election. Candidates and parties will try to formulate positions on important policies that appeal to the greatest number of voters. Candidates also develop personal appeals. During campaigns, candidates advertise their own ability to do the job at hand, their honesty and strength of character, and their fidelity to the public; likewise, they draw attention to the failings of rival politicians. They try to meet as many people as possible, and they budget a large amount of time to attend public meetings and visit civic associations. Such activities do not end with the campaign season. While in office, politicians make decisions on public laws, organize their office staff, and budget their time and energy with their constituents and the next election in mind. They seek to publicize their own efforts on their constituents'

adverse selection The problem of incomplete information—of choosing alternatives without fully knowing the details of available options.

moral hazard Not knowing all aspects of the actions taken by an agent (nominally on behalf of the principal but potentially at the principal's expense).

behalf and to bring their rivals' shortcomings to their constituents' attention. Competition, then, creates strong incentives for those vying for office to reveal information to the electorate.

The details of how elections work differ from country to country, and in the United States they have changed greatly throughout our history. Electoral laws determine who can vote, what sorts of choices can be put before the voters, how campaigns are conducted, and how votes are cast and counted. Such rules may be thought of and ultimately assessed as mechanisms for dealing with the problems of moral hazard and adverse selection.

How well elections solve the problems of informing people and controlling those in office in the United States is a matter of great concern. Turnout in the United States tends to be much lower than in other countries, with somewhere between 50 and 60 percent of Americans voting in modern presidential elections. Low turnout and apparently underinformed voters are often taken as evidence of the need to reform election laws in the United States. Proponents of electoral reform point to the weakness of American political parties as compared with those in European democracies. They may also stress that the American system provides for less control over campaign finances and media usage, or the ways that the very rules for running elections affect the outcomes. Would American democracy be more engaging with limitations on how much is spent on campaigns and how public discourse is conducted during elections? Should we shift from a system that elects one member per legislative district to one in which seats in the legislature are divided up in proportion with the total support each party receives? Are there too few parties in American politics, and thus too few choices in elections? These questions have fueled debate over the conduct of U.S. elections for a century or more. In this chapter, we will look at how the institutional features of American elections shape the way citizens' goals and preferences are reflected in their government. Then, we will consider how voters decide among the candidates and questions put before them on the ballot.

INSTITUTIONS OF ELECTIONS

Elections don't just happen. They are not spontaneous affairs, but formal institutions for making collective decisions. As in Congress, the executive branch, and the courts, rules (institutions) determine the operations of elections—who is allowed to vote, how votes are cast and counted, and how we determine who wins office. Election rules consist of a mix of state and federal laws, legal decisions, and local administrative practices. Federal laws regulate the time of congressional and presidential elections, the qualifications for office, the allocation of seats, the structure of electoral districts, and the qualifications and rights of voters. State laws determine a wider range of factors, including how votes are cast and counted, the procedures for registering voters, candidate qualifications for all elected officials other than members of Congress and the president, the procedures for nominating candidates and getting on the ballot, the operations of the parties, and the conduct of all state and local elections. The responsibility for making all of this go smoothly on

Election Day falls, in turn, on the roughly 5,000 local election offices. Counties run the elections in most states; however, in the New England states and in Michigan and Wisconsin, that duty rests with the towns and cities. Workers in local election offices manage the registration lists, prepare the ballots and voting machinery, set up polling places, recruit and train poll workers, and tally and certify the votes. And at the polling places on Election Day the poll workers, roughly 1 million volunteers across the country, administer the election.

The laws and procedures governing election laws have important consequences for who votes and what choices are presented to the electorate. They can skew the electorate toward one interest or another; they can create barriers to some sorts of political organizations; and they can create a legislature that reflects the diversity in the population or one that has a clear majority.

Four features of U.S. election laws deserve particular emphasis.

- First, *who*. The United States provides for universal adult suffrage—all citizens over the age of eighteen have the right to vote.[2]

- Second, *how*. Americans vote in secret and choose among candidates for particular office using a form of the ballot called the "Australian ballot."

- Third, *where*. The United States selects almost all elected offices through single-member districts that have equal populations—one person, one vote.

- Fourth, *what* it takes to win. For most offices in the United States, the candidate who wins the most votes among all of those competing for a given seat wins the election.

Each of these rules has substantial effects on elections and representation. We will consider each and its consequences in turn. In short, we will see that in the United States these rules create a two-party system that broadly encompasses the entire adult population but that exaggerates the political power of the majority. Other features of American election law and procedure, including rules governing campaign expenditures and fund-raising, party nominations, and ballot access, further shape political competition in the United States. Also notable are rules that the United States does *not* have. Federal and state laws do not limit the amount of television and other forms of advertising, total campaign spending, the activities of groups and parties on behalf of candidates, or how the media cover the campaigns. Most other countries limit the use of television or forbid it altogether, restrict how candidates can campaign and how much they can spend, and tightly regulate the activities of organized interest groups. Compared with other countries, then, the United States has a relatively unregulated electoral system that allows candidates to run on their own separate from the parties and allows candidates to spend relatively freely on media and other aspects of their campaigns. We will turn to these campaign activities in the next section, especially as they bear on the important question of voter learning through campaigns. The features of election law considered here regulate the nature of the electorate and the choices that voters face.

---

[2] In addition, there is the restriction that those currently serving sentences for felonies cannot vote; some states prohibit ex-felons from voting.

Before we explore each of these rules in more detail, it is important to note that the rules governing elections are not static. The features of American electoral institutions have evolved over time through legislation, court decisions, administrative rulings of agencies, and public agitation for electoral reform. The nation has gradually converged to our present system of universal suffrage with secret voting and to the use of single-member districts with plurality rule. But this is only one era, and the future will likely bring further innovations in voting and elections. Society is always in flux, with continual changes in the population and its distribution across regions. With waves of immigration, new communication technologies, and other changes reshaping society, the institutions of democracy must change with the times. Perhaps the most dramatic changes under way involve the rise of "convenience voting"— voting by mail or early at a polling center or town hall. In 1972, approximately 5 percent of all votes nationwide were cast in absentia; in 2008, 30 percent of all votes were absentee or early ballots. The state of Oregon votes entirely by mail, as does every county in Washington State but King County. A few states, such as Virginia, accept absentee ballots by e-mail, which is particularly convenient for military personnel. The rise of these new modes of voting presents new questions about secrecy and about the form of the ballot; it provides new opportunities for reform and modes of voting (such as instant runoff voting). Such changes rarely come about through carefully planned federal legislation. Typically, new voting methods and rules emerge out of the experiences and experiments of local election officials and state laws. Let us now take a closer look at the key institutional features of American elections.

Who Votes: Electoral Composition

Over the course of American history the electorate has expanded greatly. At the beginning of the nineteenth century, America was unusually democratic compared with the rest of the world because the United States provided for universal suffrage for all adult white males, and in some cities even noncitizens. In contrast, during the nineteenth century, property qualifications restricted the electorate in European nations in a manner acceptable to the aristocracy and other ruling classes. In France before 1848, to cite just one example, limiting the suffrage to property owners restricted the electorate to just 240,000 out of 7 million men over age twenty-one.[3] No women were allowed to vote at this time. During the same era, other nations manipulated the electorate's composition by assigning unequal weights to different classes of voters. The 1831 Belgian constitution, for example, assigned individuals anywhere from one to three votes, depending on their property holdings, education, and social position. Even in the American context there were significant restrictions on the size of the electorate, especially on the basis of race and gender. In the southern states, blacks were not allowed to vote before the Civil War. The passage of the Fifteenth Amendment in 1870 gave blacks voting rights, but in the late nineteenth century, southern states passed "Jim Crow" laws establishing literacy tests, poll taxes, and all-white primaries. Local election officials administered these laws

---

[3] Stein Rokkan, *Citizens, Elections, Parties: Approaches to the Comparative Study of the Process of Development* (New York: David McKay, 1970), p. 149. Also see Daron Acemoglu and James A. Robinson, "Why Did the West Extend the Franchise?" *Quarterly Journal of Economics* 115 (2000): 1167–99.

FIGURE 10.1 VOTER TURNOUT AROUND THE WORLD

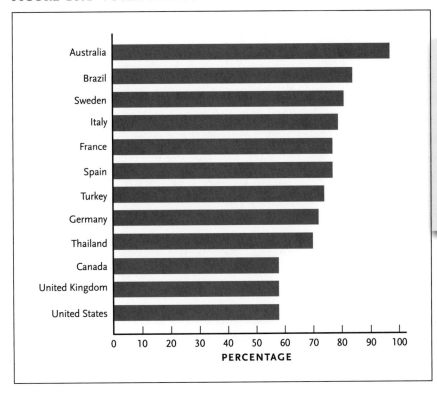

NOTE: Turnout as a percentage of voting-aged population in the most recent national presidential or parliamentary election between 2006 and 2008.

SOURCE: International Institute of Democracy and Electoral Assistance, www.idea.int/vt/ (accessed 4/30/09).

in ways that kept the large majority of blacks from voting. One by one, these institutions were struck down by the courts as violations of the Constitution, and finally forbidden by the Voting Rights Act of 1965 and the Twenty-third Amendment. Gender qualifications excluded an even larger segment of the population. In most states, women were not allowed to vote until 1920, following the passage of the Nineteenth Amendment. The most recent expansion of the franchise came in 1971, when Congress decided to lower the voting age from twenty-one to eighteen with the passage of the Twenty-sixth Amendment. If eighteen-year-olds could be drafted to serve their country in the military, it was argued, they deserved the full privileges of citizenship, including the right to vote.

Voting in the United States is treated as a right, not a requirement. Some countries, such as Australia and Germany, have compulsory voting: All eligible voters are required to vote or pay a modest fine. These societies treat electoral participation as a necessity. Americans view voting somewhat differently. Like most other activities in our society, voting is voluntary. If we do not feel strongly about government, we do not have to participate. If we want to send a message of disaffection or

FIGURE 10.2 VOTER TURNOUT IN U.S. PRESIDENTIAL ELECTIONS

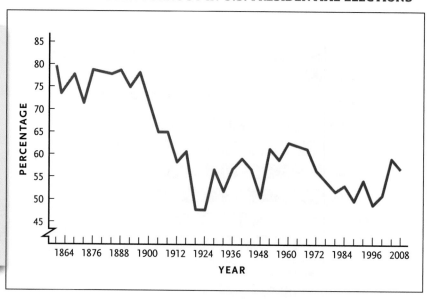

NOTE: Data reflect the population of eligible voters; the percentage of the voting-age population that voted would be smaller.

SOURCES: For 1860–1928, U.S. Bureau of the Census, *Historical Statistics of the United States, Colonial Times to 1970,* www.census.gov/prod/www/abs/statab.html (accessed 3/26/09); pt. 2, p. 1071; for 1932–92, U.S. Bureau of the Census, *Statistical Abstract of the United States,* 1993 (Washington, D.C.: Government Printing Office, 1993), p. 284; for 1996–2008, Federal Election Commission data.

dissatisfaction, one way to do so is to not vote. Of course, if no one voted, it would be a disaster for American democracy; it would signal the end of Americans' commitment to their form of government. When large numbers of people do participate in the collective decision making of the country at each election, it is evidence of a robust democracy. Governments at all levels in the United States also have so many elections that voters may not feel the need to participate in all elections all the time in order to weigh in on the activities of government. And there are many other ways that we can participate in electoral politics, such as blogging and speaking with others, joining organizations, and giving money. Compared with other nations, the United States is one of the best examples of participatory democracy in the world.[4]

That said, levels of voter participation in the latter half of the twentieth century were quite low in the United States as compared with those of the other Western democracies (Figure 10.1).[5] Indeed, voter participation in presidential elections in

---

[4] Sidney Verba, Kay Schlozman, and Henry Brady, *Voice and Equality: Civic Volunteerism in America* (Cambridge, Mass.: Harvard University Press, 1995).

[5] See Walter Dean Burnham, "The Changing Shape of the American Political Universe," *American Political Science Review* 59, no. 1 (March 1965): 7–28. It should be noted that other democracies, such as India and Switzerland, have even lower turnout rates, as do some of the new democracies in eastern Europe.

the United States barely averaged 50 percent (Figure 10.2). Turnout in the 2000 presidential election was 51 percent of voting-age Americans; in 2008, it was approximately 57 percent. During the nineteenth century, by contrast, voter turnout in the United States was extremely high, considerably higher than it is today.[6]

An important caveat about the quantitative measure of turnout is in order. When a turnout rate of 57 percent is reported, we may ask, fifty-seven percent of what? A turnout rate is a ratio comparing the number of people who voted to some baseline population. The first part of this ratio is relatively uncontroversial—it is the number of individuals who present themselves at polling stations or submit absentee ballots. Not all states report such figures in their certified tally of the vote. In fact, eleven states do not report total turnout, and researchers must substitute the total votes for all candidates for the presidency or another office on the top of the ballot. So, for example, if an individual voter in one of these states does not cast a vote for president but does turn out to vote on other questions on the ballot, this voter might not be counted in the total turnout. However, since nearly all voters who turn out do vote on the races at the top of the ticket, counting those totals is a reasonably accurate substitute for official turnout records. The appropriate baseline in the turnout ratio is more difficult to define. Conventionally, turnout is calculated as a percentage of the voting-age population. This understates turnout, because it includes some noncitizens (about 3 percent of the population) and those who are institutionalized or not allowed to vote in some states because they are ex-felons. Alternatively, it is possible to estimate from census reports the voting-*eligible* population, that is, the voting-age population minus noncitizens and institutionalized populations. Such calculations are somewhat controversial, but making these adjustments does increase participation rates noticeably. Following the usual conventions here, we will focus on the voting-*age* population, but there are some interesting differences in trends using various estimates of voting-eligible population.[7]

A further complication in gauging the overall rate of voter participation arises from the variation in turnout from election to election. Approximately 55 percent of the voting-age population turned out in 1992; 50 percent voted in 1996; 51 percent turned out in 2000; 55 percent in 2004, and 57 percent in 2008. The average of these numbers offers a succinct summary of the voting rate: approximately 53.6 percent of the public voted in the typical presidential election between 1990 and 2010. Averages permit ready comparison across nations and over long periods of time, and help guard against the distraction that might arise with an unusual election.

As Figure 10.2 indicates, voter turnout declined markedly in the United States between 1890 and 1910. These years coincide with the adoption of laws across much of the nation requiring eligible citizens to appear personally at a registrar's office to register to vote some time before the actual date of an election. Personal registration was one of several "progressive" reforms of political practices initiated

---

[6] See statistics of the U.S. Bureau of the Census and the Federal Election Commission. For voting statistics for 1960 to 2004, see "National Voter Turnout in Federal Elections: 1960–2004," at www.infoplease.com/ipa/A0781453.html (accessed 3/26/09).

[7] Michael McDonald and Samuel Popkin, "The Myth of the Vanishing Voter," *American Political Science Review* 95 (December 2001): 963–74.

at the beginning of the twentieth century. The ostensible purpose of registration was to discourage fraud and corruption. But to many progressive reformers, *corruption* was a code word, referring to the type of politics practiced in the large cities, where political parties had organized immigrant and ethnic populations. Reformers not only objected to the corruption that surely was a facet of party politics in this period but also opposed the growing political power of urban populations and their leaders.

Personal registration imposed a new burden on potential voters and altered the format of American elections. Under the registration systems adopted after 1890, it became the duty of individual voters to secure their own eligibility. This duty could prove to be a significant burden for potential voters, for a number of reasons. First, during a personal appearance before the registrar, individuals seeking to vote were (and are) required to furnish proof of identity, residence, and citizenship. Although the inconvenience of registration varied from state to state, usually voters could register only during business hours on weekdays. Many potential voters could not afford to lose a day's pay in order to register. Second, voters were usually required to register well before the next election, in some states up to several months earlier. Third, because most personal registration laws required a periodic purge of the election rolls, ostensibly to keep them up-to-date, voters often had to reregister to maintain their eligibility. Thus, although personal registration requirements helped diminish the widespread electoral corruption that accompanied a completely open voting process, they also made it much more difficult for citizens to participate in the electoral process. Rational citizens with busy lives might well be expected to forgo political participation as its complications and costs increase.

Registration requirements depress the participation of those with little education and low income in particular, because registration requires a greater degree of political involvement and interest than does the act of voting itself. To vote, a person need only be concerned with the particular election campaign at hand. Yet requiring individuals to register before a coming election forces them to make a decision to participate on the basis of an abstract interest in the electoral process rather than a simple concern with a specific campaign. Such an abstract interest in electoral politics is largely a product of education. Those with relatively little education may become interested in political events once the stimuli of a particular campaign become salient, but by that time it may be too late to register. As a result, personal registration requirements not only diminish the size of the electorate but also tend to create an electorate that is, in the aggregate, less representative of the voting-age population. The electorate is better educated, has a higher income and social status, and includes fewer African Americans and other minorities than the citizenry as a whole (Figure 10.3).

Over the years, voter registration restrictions have been modified somewhat to make registration easier. In 1993, for example, Congress approved and President Bill Clinton signed the "motor voter" bill to ease voter registration by allowing individuals to register when they applied for driver's licenses, as well as in public-assistance and military-recruitment offices.[8] In many jurisdictions, casting a vote

---

[8] Helen Dewar, "'Motor Voter' Agreement Is Reached," *Washington Post*, April 28, 1993, p. A6.

FIGURE 10.3 DIFFERENCES IN VOTER REGISTRATION RATES, 2004

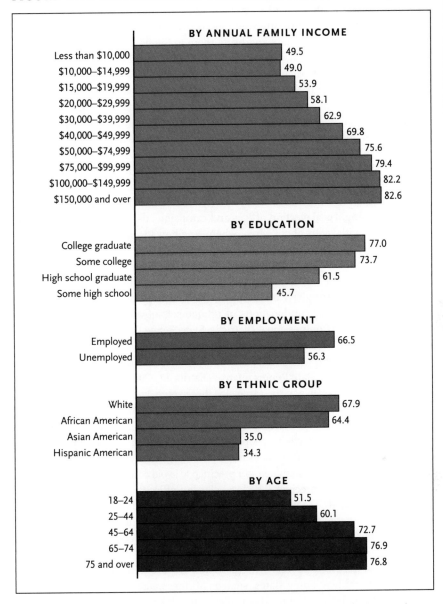

BY ANNUAL FAMILY INCOME

Income	Rate
Less than $10,000	49.5
$10,000–$14,999	49.0
$15,000–$19,999	53.9
$20,000–$29,999	58.1
$30,000–$39,999	62.9
$40,000–$49,999	69.8
$50,000–$74,999	75.6
$75,000–$99,999	79.4
$100,000–$149,999	82.2
$150,000 and over	82.6

BY EDUCATION

Education	Rate
College graduate	77.0
Some college	73.7
High school graduate	61.5
Some high school	45.7

BY EMPLOYMENT

Employment	Rate
Employed	66.5
Unemployed	56.3

BY ETHNIC GROUP

Ethnic Group	Rate
White	67.9
African American	64.4
Asian American	35.0
Hispanic American	34.3

BY AGE

Age	Rate
18–24	51.5
25–44	60.1
45–64	72.7
65–74	76.9
75 and over	76.8

SOURCE: U.S. Bureau of the Census, Population Division, Education and Social Stratification Branch, "Voting and Registration in the Election of November 2004," March 2006, www.census.gov/prod/2006pubs/p20-556.pdf (accessed 3/27/09).

automatically registers the voter for the next election. In Europe, there is typically no registration burden on the individual voter; voter registration is handled automatically by the government. This is one reason that voter turnout rates in Europe are higher than those in the United States.

Another factor explaining low rates of voter turnout in the United States is the relative weakness of the American party system. During the nineteenth century, American political party machines employed hundreds of thousands of workers to organize and mobilize voters and bring them to the polls. The result was an extremely high rate of turnout, typically more than 90 percent of eligible voters.[9] But political party machines began to decline in strength in the early twentieth century and by now have largely disappeared. Without party workers to encourage them to go to the polls and even take them there if necessary, many eligible voters will not participate. In the absence of strong parties, participation rates drop the most among poorer and less-educated citizens. Because of the absence of strong political parties, the American electorate is smaller and skewed more toward the middle class than toward the population of all those potentially eligible to vote.[10]

If registration systems create a hurdle to voting, they also facilitate the voting process. Registration systems contain a fairly reliable list of all people who are interested in voting. Local election offices and campaigns use the registration lists to communicate with voters about when, where, and how to vote. Campaigns also use these lists to prepare grassroots organizing efforts and direct-mail campaigns.

Registration lists serve another very important purpose: they enable local election offices to format ballots, set up precincts, and determine which voters should vote in which place. Any given area contains many overlapping election jurisdictions, creating many different combinations of unique sets of offices. For example, one voter might reside in Congressional District 1, State Senate District 7, State Representative District 3, City Council District 1, and so forth. Variations in district boundaries may mean that a few blocks away, another voter lives in Congressional District 2, State Senate District 4, State Representative District 12, City Council District 6, and so forth. Although they live in the same city, these voters live in very different sets of political districts and must vote on different ballots. The first voter is not supposed to vote in Congressional District 2, for instance. Registration lists have become vitally important in sorting out where people should vote. Using the definitions of the boundaries, local election offices determine how many distinct ballots they must prepare. Each distinct ballot is assigned to a precinct: to avoid confusion there is only one ballot constellation per precinct. The local election office then uses the registration list to assign individuals to precincts, and to communicate to the voter exactly where he or she is supposed to vote. Without this means of assigning voters to precincts and communicating to voters, there would be considerable confusion and practical difficulty running elections on Election Day.

Efforts to get rid of or reform registration requirements must confront this very practical problem. Some states, such as Minnesota and Wisconsin, allow registration at the polls on Election Day (called same-day registration or Election Day registration). These states have noticeably higher turnout, but also must recruit

---

[9] Erik W. Austin and Jerome M. Clubb, *Political Facts of the United States since 1789* (New York: Columbia University Press, 1986), pp. 378–79.

[10] In the 2008 election, both parties devoted considerable resources to targeting potential new voters, helping them register, and mobilizing them on Election Day. Elevated turnout in the election reflects this effort.

additional poll workers to handle the new registrants in the precincts. Other states, such as Colorado, are trying to get rid of traditional precincts and have experimented with vote centers. Electronic voting equipment now makes it possible to program many different ballots on a single machine. The voter need only key in his or her address to get the appropriate ballot and vote. Such machines enable people to vote anywhere and lessen the need for lists to assign voters to precincts. Innovations such as these may lead ultimately to an election system that does not require or rely heavily on registration before Election Day, but even these mechanisms still require the voter to register at some point. Wherever these innovations in voting may lead in the long term, the United States today relies heavily on registration to run elections, even though it creates a hurdle to voting.

With the exception of registration requirements, contemporary governments generally do not limit the composition of their electorate. Instead, they allow all adults to vote in an effort to make the government as responsive as possible to the needs and interests of the population as a whole.

How Americans Vote: The Ballot

The way Americans cast their votes reflects some of our most cherished precepts about voting rights. Most people today view voting as a private matter. They may tell others how they voted, but that is their prerogative. Polling places provide privacy for voters and keep an individual's vote secret. In some respects, the secret ballot seems incongruous with voting, because elections are a very public matter. Indeed, for the first century of the Republic, voting was conducted in the open. However, public voting led to vote buying and voter intimidation. American history is full of lore involving urban party workers paying poor voters for their support or intimidating members of the opposing party from voting. The secret ballot became widespread at the end of the nineteenth century in response to such corrupt practices.

The secret ballot has important implications for how people see themselves as voters. The secret ballot is a strong assertion of the individual. When a person votes, the law treats that person as an autonomous individual. The vote is meant to reflect the individual's own mind—what the individual knows about the choices and what his or her own preferences are about government—not the influences of others. In contrast, when voting is public, the choices individuals make reflect the group as well as their own thinking. American elections still have vestiges of public voting, in town meetings in New England states and at party nominating caucuses, such as in Iowa, Colorado, and Minnesota.

Attend a caucus or town hall meeting and you will appreciate the difference between these events and voting in the seclusion of a voting booth. Town meetings and caucuses often exhibit what social psychologists call groupthink, the tendency of the pack to follow particular individuals or to reflect a public conversation rather than each individual's private information. Public voting also demands more of the individual—more time and more attention to the decision-making process. Attending a caucus, for example, is an all-evening affair. As a result, public voting tends to draw in a much smaller and more committed electorate. These two methods can lead to radically different results. A good example comes from the

Democratic nominating process in Texas during the 2008 election. Primary elections determine how many delegates to the party's national convention are allotted to each candidate. The Texas Democratic Party allocates one-half of its delegates through a primary election involving secret ballots and the other half through caucuses. Primary voting runs throughout the day; the caucuses begin in the evening immediately after polls close. In 2008, Hillary Rodham Clinton won a decisive victory over Barack Obama in the primary voting in Texas, but Barack Obama won the caucuses by an equally large margin, offsetting the primary results entirely. Caucuses, however, are the exception. Almost all votes in the United States are cast by secret ballot.

With the secret ballot came another innovation, the **Australian ballot**. The Australian ballot lists the names of all candidates running for a given office and allows the voter to select any candidate for any office. This way of offering choices to voters was first introduced in Australia in 1851, and in the United States today it is universal. Before the 1880s Americans voted in entirely different ways. Some voted in public meetings; others voted on paper ballots printed by the political parties or by slates of candidates distributed to the voters. Voters chose which ballot they wished to submit—a Republican ballot, a Democratic ballot, a Populist ballot, a Greenback ballot, and so forth. The ballots were often printed on different-colored paper so that voters could distinguish among them—and so that the local party workers could observe who cast which ballots. With party ballots, voters could not choose candidates from different parties for different offices; they had to vote the party line.

In a ten-year period from 1885 to 1895, nearly every state adopted the Australian ballot, and with it the secret ballot. This new form of voting came about in an era of administrative reform in government throughout the United States. County governments took on the job of formatting and printing ballots, and the conduct of elections became an administrative task of government rather than a political activity of the parties. The move toward this new way of casting votes also reflected the efforts of the state governments to break the hold of local political organizations. All ballots are identical under the Australian form, making it difficult to observe who votes for which party. More importantly, voters could choose any candidate for any office, breaking the hold of parties over the vote. The introduction of the Australian ballot gave rise to the phenomenon of split-ticket voting, in which some voters select candidates from different parties for different offices.[11]

The secret and Australian ballot creates the opportunity for voters to choose candidates as well as parties and, as we shall discuss in more depth later, created a necessary condition for the rise of the personal vote and the incumbency advantage in American electoral politics. (See Chapter 5's discussion of the incumbency advantage in Congress.) The party ballot made it impossible to choose particular candidates without voting for an entire list of candidates nominated by a party or slate. Voters could not split their tickets, choosing, say, one party's nominee for president and another party's nominee for the House of Representatives. If a voter liked the

[11] Jerold G. Rusk, "The Effect of the Australian Ballot Reform on Split Ticket Voting, 1876–1908," *American Political Science Review* 64, no. 4 (December 1970): 1220–38.

Australian ballot
An electoral format that presents the names of all the candidates for any given office on the same ballot. Introduced at the end of the eighteenth century, the Australian ballot replaced the partisan ballot and facilitated split-ticket voting.

candidate for the House seat, but disliked the party's candidate for president, she would have to choose between sacrificing her choice for the House seat to bring about a new administration or voting for an unappealing presidential candidate in order to support her preferred candidate for the House. In the absence of a real possibility of split-ticket voting, the electorate could express a desire for change only as a vote against all candidates of the party in power. When the electorate voted to oust those in power at the national level, the election would sweep into power the opposing party or slate at the state and local levels as well. As a result, elections in the United States before 1896 were highly partisan affairs, often producing wholesale changes in control of government at all levels. The Australian ballot allows voters to cast a more sophisticated ballot that reflects both to the performance of individual officeholders and assessments of the political parties as a whole.

The possibility of split-ticket voting created greater fragmentation in the control of government in the United States. With the party ballot, an insurgent party could more readily be swept to power at all levels of government in a given election. A strong national tide toward one of the parties in the presidential election, resulting in a landslide victory, would change not just the presidency but also political control of every state and locality that gave a majority of its votes to that presidential candidate's party. The party ballot thus reinforced the effect of elections on party control of government and public policy. In contrast, because the Australian ballot permitted voters to choose for each office separately, it lessened the likelihood that the electorate would sweep an entirely new administration into power. Thus, ticket splitting led to increasingly divided control of government as well as the rise of personal voting.

Where: Electoral Districts

Elected officials in the United States represent places as well as people. Today, the president, representatives, senators, governors, and many other state officers, state legislators, and most local officers are elected by the people through geographic areas called electoral districts. Generally speaking, the United States employs **single-member districts** with equal populations. This means that the U.S. House of Representatives, the state legislatures, and almost all local governments have their own districts and elect one representative per district, and all of the districts for a given legislative body must have equal populations.

Elections for the U.S. Senate and the presidency are the odd cases. In the U.S. Senate, the states are the districts. Senate districts, then, have multiple members and unequal populations. In presidential elections, every state is allocated votes in the **electoral college** equal to the number of U.S. senators (two) plus the number of House members. The states are the districts, and each state chooses all of its electors, who commit to casting their votes for a certain candidate in the electoral college, in a statewide vote.[12] Within the political parties, the nomination process in most states allocates delegates to the parties' national conventions on the basis

single-member district An electorate that is allowed to elect only one representative from each district—the typical method of representation in the United States.

electoral college The presidential electors from each state who meet in their respective state capitals after the popular election to cast ballots for president and vice president.

---

[12] The exceptions are Maine and Nebraska, which choose the House electors in individual House districts and the Senate electors in a statewide vote.

of House districts, and thus population. However, some states choose their delegates on a statewide basis, with all districts selecting multiple delegates to the party conventions.

The system of single-member districts with equal populations was not part of the Founders' original design. Rather, it evolved over nearly two centuries, from 1790 to 1970. Article II of the Constitution designed the House to represent the people, with the number of seats elected by each state allocated on the basis of population following each decennial census, and the Senate to represent the states. The Constitution originally specified that the state legislatures would choose the U.S. senators, with each state choosing two senators to staggered six-year terms. That system was jettisoned in 1913 with the adoption of the Seventeenth Amendment, providing for direct election of senators.

The Constitution said nothing about the election of individual House members or electors to the electoral college. That task fell to the states, and in early times the states used many different electoral systems for choosing their House delegations. Most of the early state laws adopted single-member districts. The states divided their territory into as many districts as they had House seats, and each district elected one member. Some states created multimember districts, in which a district would elect more than one legislator. This was common in urban counties and cities, where the population exceeded the number required for two or more districts, but the legislature did not want to draw district boundaries. And some states elected all their House members in a single, statewide election (called an at-large election). An even greater hodgepodge of election procedures applied to the state legislatures and local councils.[13]

Congress tried to bring order to the election of House members with the 1842 Apportionment Act. Following the sixth decennial census (of 1840), Congress had to pass a new apportionment bill to assign House seats to the states. Through an amendment from Representative John Campbell of South Carolina, the act included an additional requirement on districts:

> [I]n every case where a State is entitled to more than one Representative, the number to which each State shall be entitled under this apportionment shall be elected by districts, composed of contiguous territory, equal in number to the number of Representatives to which said State may be entitled; no one district electing more than one Representative.[14]

Most states complied with this provision, even though it placed a new responsibility on the states of creating appropriate districts, especially around urban areas. Some states, however, insisted on using at-large and multimember districts up to the 1960s. Finally, in the 1967 Apportionment Act, Congress forbade the use of anything but single-member districts.

---

[13] For a history of districting politics, see Stephen Ansolabehere and James Snyder, Jr., *The End of Inequality: One Person, One Vote and the Transformation of American Politics* (New York: Norton, 2008).

[14] *Congressional Globe*, 27th Cong., 2d sess., 1842, 11, Part 1:471, 348.

A second important change in the nature of political districts in the United States occurred at that time as well. In a series of decisions beginning with *Baker v. Carr* in 1962, the United States Supreme Court ruled that all federal and state legislative districts have equal populations: one person, one vote. That simple aphorism today rings as the very definition of democracy, but before 1962 state legislative districts often had highly unequal populations, which meant that some votes in effect counted more than others. In the California state senate, Los Angeles County elected as many seats as Alpine County, even though Los Angeles had almost 500 times as many people. As a result, voters in Alpine County had greater representation (500 times greater) relative to the their population than did voters in Los Angeles County. Similar inequities reigned in every state legislature, producing a pattern of overrepresentation of rural areas and underrepresentation of most urban areas and, especially, suburban counties. In most states these inequalities arose from neglect. Most state constitutions require redistricting to keep district populations equal, but as urban populations grew, especially in the first half of the twentieth century, those in power realized that redistricting might jeopardize their own reelection. As a result, the legislatures chose to do nothing. With each successive decade, representation in the United States became more unequal, and there seemed to be no way to force the state legislatures to act. Finally, the U.S. Supreme Court ruled, in a series of important cases, that unequal representation violated the Fourteenth Amendment's guarantee of equal protection under the law. By 1971, nearly every legislative district in the United States elected one representative, and the populations of the districts for each legislative chamber were equal. Lawsuits brought by civil rights groups in the 1980s forced school districts and city councils to adopt single-member districts as well. Single-member districts with equal populations have become the rule in the United States, from city councils and school districts to the House of Representatives.

The United States Senate and the electoral college remain the two great exceptions to the requirements of single-member districts with equal populations. The apportionment of Senate seats to states makes that chamber inherently unequal. California's 35 million people have the same number of senators as Wyoming's 500,000 people. The allocation of electoral college votes creates a population inequity in presidential elections, with larger states selecting fewer electors per capita than smaller states. In the 1960s, the Supreme Court let stand the unequal district populations in the Senate and the electoral college, because the representation of states in the Senate is specified in the Constitution. The reason lies in the politics of the Constitutional Convention (see Chapter 2). That convention, as you may recall, consisted of delegations of states, each of which held equal numbers of votes under the Articles of Confederation. In order to create a House of Representatives to reflect the preferences of the population, the large states had to strike a deal with the smaller states, which stood to lose representation with the initial plan of a single chamber that reflected population. That deal, the Connecticut Compromise, created the U.S. Senate to balance representation of people with representation of places, and led to a clause in Article V of the Constitution that guarantees equal representation of the states in the Senate.

Even though they have unequal populations and select multiple representatives, the Senate and the electoral college share the salient feature of elections for the House and other elections in the use of districts to select representatives. All elections in the United States and all elected officials are tied to geographically based constituencies rather than to the national electorate as a whole. This is certainly true for the House and Senate. It applies also to presidential elections, in which candidates focus on winning key states in the electoral college rather than on winning a majority of the popular vote.

Electoral districts have a particularly important political consequence: the use of districts tends to magnify the power of the majority. In a system like that of the United States with two parties and single-member districts, the party that wins a majority of the vote nationwide tends to win a disproportionate share of the seats. In 2004, Republicans won 51.5 percent of the vote nationwide for the U.S. House, but 53.3 percent of the seats. As an empirical matter, in the United States, when the election is a tie, the parties win equal shares of the vote, and for every 1 percent of the vote above 50 percent a party gains an additional 2 percent of the seats. This is a pattern that has been observed in data on U.S. House elections over the last sixty years, and not a lawlike relationship. However, in the United States and other countries, such as the United Kingdom, that have single-member districts the share of seats for the party that wins a majority exceeds the share of votes. The electoral college tends to magnify the vote majority even more dramatically. Barack Obama won 53 percent of the vote nationwide, but he captured nearly 68 percent of the electoral college delegates. Electoral districts, then, create a very strong tendency toward majority rule.

This magnifying effect has been a particular problem for smaller parties and minority groups. Just as districts magnify the seats won by the majority party, they shrink the representation of small parties. If a party wins 5 percent of the vote nationwide, it is difficult for it to win any seats or electoral college delegates unless the support for that party is highly concentrated in a particular geographic area. The most successful third party in recent U.S. history was the Reform Party, started by Ross Perot in 1992. Perot won 19 percent of the presidential vote nationwide that year, a very strong third place throughout the country, but he won no electoral college delegates.

The majoritarian tendency of districts makes it very difficult for racial minorities to gain representation. Blacks and Hispanics constitute roughly a quarter of the population. Districts crafted without regard to race would spread the minority vote across many districts, making it unlikely that those groups would be a sufficiently large segment in any one district to elect proportionate numbers of blacks or Hispanics to the legislature. This problem, compounded by the historic discrimination against blacks and Hispanics, led Congress to amend the Voting Rights Act in 1982 to provide for the creation of legislative districts with sufficient numbers of black and Hispanic voters to elect House members representative of those groups. This law has been interpreted and implemented to mean that the state legislatures must create many districts, called majority-minority districts, containing majorities of black or Hispanic people. As we will discuss below, that provision has proved highly controversial in each subsequent round of districting, but the Voting Rights Act has been renewed repeatedly by Congress and has withstood legal challenges. It is a direct reaction against the strongly majoritarian pressures created by districts.

House districts and state legislative districts are not static. In order to comply with the dictum of equal population representation, they must be remade every decade. Responsibility for drawing new district boundaries rests, in most states, with the state legislatures and the governors, with the supervision of the courts and sometimes with the consultation of commissions (Figure 10.4). Every ten years, the U.S. Census updates the official population figures of the states, as well as population counts, to a fine level of geographical detail (census blocs). The politicians, their staffs, party consultants, and others with a stake in the outcome use the census data to craft a new district map; ultimately, the legislatures must pass and the governors must sign a law defining new U.S. House and state legislative districts. This job is forced on the legislatures by their constitutions and by the courts. As the history of unequal representation suggests, most legislatures would, if left to their own devices, leave the existing boundaries in place. Periodic redistricting, although it corrects one problem, invites another. Those in charge of redistricting may try to manipulate the new map to increase the likelihood of a particular outcome, such as the election of a majority of seats for one party or social interest. This problem arose with some of the earliest congressional district maps. A particularly egregious map of the 1812 Massachusetts House districts drawn with the imprimatur of Governor Elbridge Gerry prompted an editorial writer in the *Boston Gazette* to dub a very strangely shaped district the "Gerry-Mander." The term stuck, and **gerrymandering** refers broadly to any attempt at creating electoral districts for political advantage.

It is easy to draw an intentionally unfair electoral map, especially with the sophisticated software and data on local voting patterns and demographics that are available today. To facilitate districting, the Census Bureau divides the nation into very small geographic areas, called census blocks, that typically contain a few dozen people. U.S. House districts contain over 700,000 people. Political mapmakers combine various local areas, down to census blocks, to construct legislative districts. Those seeking political advantage try to make as many districts as possible that contain a majority of their own voters, maximizing the number of seats won for a given division of the vote. There are constraints on political cartography: the district populations must be equal, and all parts of the district must touch (be contiguous). Even with those constraints, the number of possible maps that could be drawn for any one state's legislative districts is extremely large.[15] The "Analyzing the Evidence" unit on page 430 shows how this works, using a hypothetical state to explain some basic strategies that politicians might implement to influence elections through the manipulation of district lines, as well as a real-world example of how redistricting affects election outcomes.

Political scientists examine the fairness of plans by assessing quantitatively the features of any given districting plan. Such measures are widely used by state

gerrymandering
The apportionment of voters in districts in such a way as to give unfair advantage to one political party.

---

[15] For definitions of these units, see Bureau of the Census, Geographic Area Reference Manual, www.census.gov/geo/www/garm.html (accessed 3/27/09).

FIGURE 10.4 CONGRESSIONAL REDISTRICTING

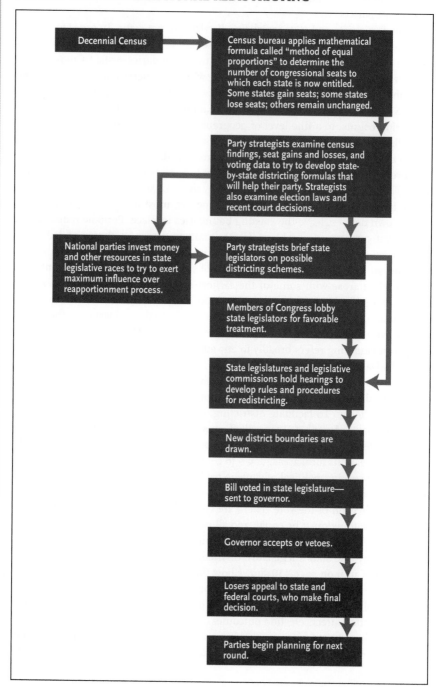

Decennial Census → Census bureau applies mathematical formula called "method of equal proportions" to determine the number of congressional seats to which each state is now entitled. Some states gain seats; some states lose seats; others remain unchanged.

Party strategists examine census findings, seat gains and losses, and voting data to try to develop state-by-state districting formulas that will help their party. Strategists also examine election laws and recent court decisions.

National parties invest money and other resources in state legislative races to try to exert maximum influence over reapportionment process.

Party strategists brief state legislators on possible districting schemes.

Members of Congress lobby state legislators for favorable treatment.

State legislatures and legislative commissions hold hearings to develop rules and procedures for redistricting.

New district boundaries are drawn.

Bill voted in state legislature—sent to governor.

Governor accepts or vetoes.

Losers appeal to state and federal courts, who make final decision.

Parties begin planning for next round.

legislatures, commissions, and courts in assessing districting plans. Of central importance is the notion of bias. In a hypothetical election where the vote is divided equally between the two major parties, what share of seats do we expect each party to win? An unbiased or fair districting plan would give both parties half of the seats in this hypothetical election. To gauge the magnitude of the bias, political scientists then simulate such hypothetical elections among a state's electorate under a given districting plan. A bias of, say, 5 points means that when the two parties split the vote evenly, one of the parties wins 55 percent of the seats and the other 45 percent. With each round of districting, experts weigh in with their assessments of the bias in the plans. Those who want fair elections will try to achieve no bias. Those who want to gain the upper hand try to inject bias into elections with a cleverly constructed map.

Empirical study of U.S. House and state legislative elections has documented several very important patterns in the bias of electoral districts. First, bias has declined greatly over the past half century. In 1960, the typical state legislative electoral map had approximately a 10- to 12-point bias in favor of one of the parties (depending on who drew the map). That means that around 1960, a dead-even election would actually produce a large majority for one of the parties in the legislature. Second, bias has declined substantially over time. In the 1990s and 2000s, the bias in the average state legislative district map was approximately 5 points, still substantial but much lower than in the past.[16] Since the 1960s, frequent redistricting and court oversight has forced state legislatures to create districting plans that treat both parties more fairly. Interestingly, this is one of the benefits of divided party control of the legislature and executive (see Chapter 6). When the legislature and executive are controlled by the same party, the legislature can create a map heavily biased toward that party, and the governor will likely sign it. However, when the legislature and executive are controlled by different parties, then the legislature might face a veto from the governor and must create districts that will be acceptable to the other party.[17]

Politicians can use gerrymandering to dilute the strength not only of a party but also of a group. Until recently, many state legislatures employed gerrymandering to dilute the strength of racial minorities. One of the more common strategies involved redrawing congressional district boundaries in such a way as to divide and disperse a black population that would have constituted a majority within the original district. This form of gerrymandering, sometimes called cracking, was used in Mississippi during the 1960s and 1970s to prevent the election of a black candidate to Congress. Historically, the black population of Mississippi was clustered in the western half of the state, along the Mississippi River Delta. From 1882 until 1966, the Delta constituted one congressional district. Although blacks were a clear majority within this district, discrimination against them in voter registration and at the polls guaranteed the continual election of white congressmen. With the passage

---

[16] See Ansolabehere and Snyder, *The End of Inequality*, chap. 11.

[17] See Gary King and Robert X. Browning, "Democratic Representation and Partisan Bias in Congressional Elections," *American Political Science Review* 81, no. 4 (December 1987): 1252–73.

Congressional Redistricting

The method by which electoral districts are drawn following each decennial census may directly impact who gets elected from those districts. Recent decades have witnessed more states utilizing independent commissions or panels to redraw congressional districts in an attempt to limit partisanship in the districting process, but the majority of states still rely on state legislatures to reapportion House seats. At the same time, technological innovations such as Geographic Information Systems (GIS) software allow mapmakers to be extremely precise in terms of how individual voters are allocated among districts. As a result, congressional redistricting remains a focal point for party strategy, with parties looking to increase their advantage after the 2010 census.

Partisan Districting

SCENARIO 1

Consider a hypothetical state where Republicans represent 60% of voters and Democrats represent the remaining 40% of voters. As a result of population changes during the preceding decade, this state now has five congressional districts. A state legislature controlled by a Republican majority could draw congressional districts so that Republican voters clearly dominate three of the five districts and Democratic voters dominate the remaining two. In this scenario, the Republicans could expect their candiates to win three of the five House districts.

SCENARIO 2

Another possibility might arise if the Republican state legislature decides to make the districts more competitive, but also attempts to gain control of all five House districts in the upcoming election.

SCENARIO 3

Now, suppose that the Democrats are in control of the state legislature. With the same distribution of voters in the state, they could draw the districts to favor Democratic candidates as much as possible (with Democratic voters dominating three of the districts).

IOWA DISTRICTS, 1990s

By contrast, a non-partisan, or independent commission may draw more competitive districts, with a more even distribution of Republican and Democratic voters. To take a real-world example, prior to the 2000 census, Iowa's districts were drawn by the state legislature. In the redistricting following the 1990 census, the Republican legislature established district boundaries.

Votes for Democratic candidates: 43%
House seats won by Democrats: 20%

After 2000, Iowa employed a commission to revise district boundaries in an effort to promote greater competitiveness.* Note that under the districting established by the Republican legislature in the 1990s, Democrats won only 20 percent of House races, although they won 43 percent of the vote. After the redistricting by the commission in the 2000s, the Democrats won a share of seats more closely in proportion to their share of total votes.

*Iowa uses both a commission and nonpartisan legislative staff.

IOWA DISTRICTS, 2000s

Votes for Democratic candidates: 48%
House seats won by Democrats: 40%

The Post–2010 Cycle: Who Draws District Lines?

State legislature
Commission

In the redistricting cycle following the 2010 census, the authority to redraw voting districts for congressional and state-level races remains in the hands of the state legislature in most states. In these states, the party with a majority in the legislature has the opportunity to draw districts that favor candidates from that party. However, a growing number of states are using commissions in the post–2010 cycle, which should lead to districts that are more competitive in these states.

of the Voting Rights Act in 1965, this district would almost surely be won by a black candidate or one favored by the black majority. To prevent that from happening, the Mississippi state legislature drew new House districts in 1965 in order to minimize the voting power of the black population. Rather than a majority of a single district that encompassed the Delta, the black population was split across three districts and constituted a majority in none. Mississippi's gerrymandering scheme was preserved in the state's redistricting plans in 1972 and 1982 and helped prevent the election of any black representative until 1986, when Mike Espy became the first African American since Reconstruction to represent Mississippi in Congress.

In recent years, the Republican Party has adopted an extremely aggressive redistricting strategy, in some instances not waiting for a new census before launching a redistricting effort that could serve its political interests. In Texas, for example, after the GOP took control of both houses of the state legislature in the 2002 elections, Republican lawmakers sought to enact a redistricting plan that promised to shift as many as five congressional seats to the Republican column. This Republican effort was masterminded by Tom DeLay, a Texan who was then majority leader in the U.S. House of Representatives. DeLay saw an opportunity to increase the Republican majority in the House and reduce Democratic prospects of regaining control of Congress. In an effort to block DeLay's plan, a group of fifty-one Democratic legislators refused to attend state legislative sessions, leaving the Texas legislature without a quorum and unable to conduct its business. The legislature's Republican leadership ordered the state police to apprehend the missing Democrats and return them to the state capitol. The Democrats responded by escaping to Oklahoma, beyond the jurisdiction of the Texas police. Eventually, the Democrats capitulated, and the GOP was able to enact its redistricting plan. In the 2004 election, the first under the new plan, the Republicans defeated four Democratic incumbents and won three of the five seats in which no incumbent was running. This Republican gain was equal to the total Republican gain in the House nationally. The redistricting plan was challenged in court by the League of United Latin American Citizens on the grounds that it violated the voting rights of Hispanic Americans. The case reached the Supreme Court in 2006, and parts of the redistricting plan were rejected.[18] A similar GOP redistricting effort in Colorado failed when it was ruled unconstitutional by the state's supreme court. The court declared that the Colorado constitution permitted the legislature to redistrict the state only once every ten years.

Examples such as the controversies in Texas have intensified criticism of the involvement of legislatures in drawing their own districts and raised profound concerns about the fairness of the political process in the states. Many states have created commissions to draw plans or appointed "special masters" to draw the maps. It has proved difficult to find a satisfactory reform. Perhaps the most unusual and creative attempt to engage the issue is that proposed by Ohio Secretary of State Jennifer Brunner. Working with the League of Women Voters of Ohio, Common Cause, and state representatives Joan Lawrence and Dan Stewart, the Ohio

---

[18] *League of Latin American Citizens v. Perry*, 548 U.S. (2006).

secretary of state developed a public contest in 2009 to develop the best districting plan—the Ohio Redistricting Competition. The purpose of the competition was not to produce a new districting law but to engage "a robust public conversation about the process can occur, leading to the development of the best possible redistricting recommendations for consideration by the Ohio General Assembly."[19] The Secretary of State developed comprehensive a Web site, including rules for judging the plans and constraints that all valid plans must meet, such as equal population. The Web site also gave access to the districting software used by the state and instruction in how to use the software. This was a way to inform the legislature and courts about what the public wanted in the districting plans and to produce a blueprint to guide those who would draw the official maps.

What It Takes to Win: Plurality Rule

The fourth prominent feature of U.S. electoral law is the criterion for winning. Americans often embrace majority rule as a defining characteristic of democracy. However, that is not quite right. The real standard is **plurality rule**. The candidate who receives the most votes in the relevant district or constituency wins the election, even if that candidate doesn't receive a majority of votes. Suppose, for example, three parties nominate candidates for a seat and divide the vote such that one wins 34 percent and the other two each receive 33 percent of the vote. Under plurality rule, the candidate with 34 percent wins the seat, even though she did not win a majority of votes (more than 50 percent). There are different types of plurality systems. The system currently used in the United States combines plurality rule with single-member districts and is called *first past the post*. The electoral college is a plurality system in which the candidate who receives the most votes wins all of the delegates: winner take all.[20] Some states set an even higher standard and require a candidate to receive at least 50 percent of all votes in order to win. This is **majority rule**. Louisiana and Georgia, for instance, require a candidate to receive an outright majority in an election in order to be declared the winner. If no candidate receives a majority in an election, a runoff election is held about one month later between the two candidates who received the most votes in the first round. Other systems also use plurality- and majority-rule criteria. For instance, some city councils still have multimember districts. The top vote getters win the seats. If there are, say, seven seats to fill, the seven candidates who win the most votes each win a seat.

Plurality rule is often criticized for yielding electoral results that do not reflect the public's preferences. The votes for the losing candidates seem wasted, because they do not translate directly into representation. Indeed, as the example of the three-candidate race above suggests, it is possible that a majority of voters wanted someone other than the winner. In the aggregate, plurality rule with single-member

plurality rule
A type of electoral system in which victory goes to the individual who gets the most votes in an election, but not necessarily a majority of the votes cast.

majority rule
A type of electoral system in which, to win a seat in a representative body, a candidate must receive a majority (50 percent plus 1) of all the votes cast in the relevant district.

---

[19] www.ohioredistricting.org (accessed 5/1/09).

[20] Over the centuries, many systems for voting and determining electoral outcomes have been devised. For an excellent analysis of voting systems and a complete classification see Gary Cox, *Making Votes Count* (New York: Cambridge University Press, 1997).

districts tends to inflate the share of seats won by the largest party and deflate the others' shares. A striking example of the effects comes from Great Britain. In 2005, the British Labour Party won 35 percent of the vote and 55 percent of the seats; the Conservatives finished second, with 31 percent of the vote and 31 percent of the seats; the Liberal Democrats garnered 22 percent of the popular vote, but won just 8 percent of the seats. The shares of all seats won by each party for a given division of the national vote depends on the districts. A particularly egregious gerrymander might bias the results heavily against one party and cause further deviations of election results from proportionality. Nevertheless, plurality rule offers certain advantages. It gives voters the ability to choose individuals to represent them personally, not just political parties, and it picks a definite winner without the need for runoff elections.

Among the democracies of the world, the main alternative to plurality rule is **proportional representation**, also called PR for short. Under proportional representation, competing parties win legislative seats in proportion to their share of the popular vote. For example, if three parties running for seats in the legislature seat divide the vote such that one wins 34 percent and the other two receive 33 percent of the vote, the first party received 34 percent of the seats and the other two receive 33 percent.

PR is used rarely in the United States. The most substantial elections in which it is employed are the Democratic presidential primary elections. During the 1988 primary season, Jesse Jackson routinely won 20 percent of the vote in the primaries, but ended up with only about 5 percent of the delegates. To make the Democratic National Convention and the party more representative of its disparate voting groups, Jackson negotiated with other party leaders to change the delegate allocation rules so that delegates within congressional districts would be assigned on a proportional basis. If a district elects five delegates, a candidate wins a delegate if the candidate receives at least 20 percent of the vote in the district, two delegates if the candidate wins at least 40 percent of the vote, and so forth. Prior to this rule change the Democratic Party awarded all delegates from a given congressional district to the candidate who won a plurality of the vote. Like any districted system with plurality rule, this created a strong majoritarian tendency.

Plurality rule in single-member districts has a very important consequence. It is the reason for two-party politics in the United States. Around the world, countries with plurality rule in single-member districts have far fewer political parties than other nations. Typically, elections under plurality rule boil down to just two major parties that routinely compete for power, with one of them winning a majority of legislative seats outright. Proportional representation systems, on the other hand, tend to have many more than two parties. Rarely does a single party win a majority of seats. Governments form as coalitions of many different parties. The political scientist Maurice Duverger described that pattern in a pathbreaking book, *Party Politics*, first published in 1951. Duverger formalized his law of politics quite simply: Plurality rule creates two-party politics; proportional representation encourages more than two parties.

The rationale behind **Duverger's law** has two components, the strategic behavior of politicians and the behavior of voters. Consider, first, how politicians would think about the prospects of forming a new party. Suppose that there already are

proportional representation (PR)
A multiple-member-district system that allows each political party representation in proportion to its percentage of the vote.

Duverger's law
Law of politics, formalized by Maurice Duverger, stating that plurality-rule electoral systems will tend to have two political parties.

two parties, a center-right party and a center-left party. A politician from the far right, for example, might be unhappy that the parties do not represent the ideals he espouses. He wants a far-right policy most, a center-right policy less, and least of all a center-left policy. One solution for the far-right politician is to leave the center-right party and form a far-right party. The problem with doing that is that it helps the center-left party. A far-right party in this circumstance splits the vote of those on the right without affecting the vote for the center-left party. Under plurality rule, the center-left party would almost certainly win, an outcome that the far-right politician likes even less. Thus, politicians on the extremes cannot gain by forming a new party. A politician with a centrist orientation also cannot win the election if the center-right and center-left parties are not too extreme. The center-right party would win all votes of voters on the right and on the center-right. The same is true for the center-left party. That would leave only a small segment of true centrists for a potential centrist party. Hence, if the current parties are not too extreme, there is no incentive for a third party to enter a two-party system when plurality rule is the criterion for winning.

Voters follow a similar logic. They do not want to waste their votes. If voters understand that the extremist party or candidate cannot win, they will vote for the more moderate alternative. Although second best for extremist voters, the moderate has a better chance of winning. This logic leads the extremist voters to choose the moderate party or candidate in order to have a better chance of selecting a candidate more to their liking. Extremist parties and candidates, then, have little incentive to enter a race, and when they do they usually attract few votes.

Such sophisticated voting occurs often in U.S. primary elections. John McCain was significantly more moderate than Mike Huckabee and Mitt Romney in the 2008 Republican presidential primaries, and he was more moderate than the typical Republican voter. Nevertheless, he won the nomination easily because many Republicans understood that McCain represented their best chance in the general election.

Proportional representation, in contrast, creates an incentive for more parties and candidates to enter, because they will win seats in proportion to their support among the national electorate. PR systems often have a multitude of parties, none of which represents a decisive majority. Elections in PR systems rarely decide which party will lead the government and often lead to coalition governments, because no one party wins enough seats to govern. In the Democratic Party, proportional representation has the further effect of stretching out the nominating season. If a candidate wins a plurality of 40 percent of the vote in a state's Democratic primary, he or she wins roughly 40 percent of the delegates. As a result, it takes many more victories in the Democratic primaries to accumulate sufficient delegates to lock the nomination. In 2008, the Democratic primaries came very close to being indecisive, which would have meant a convention at which neither Obama nor Clinton controlled a majority of delegates. Plurality rule and winner take all on the Republican side means that even when there are many candidates, as in 2008, the primary elections are decided rather quickly. John McCain won a smaller share of the vote in the primary elections through March 5, 2008 than either of the two main Democratic contestants, Hillary Clinton and Barack Obama, but by the beginning of March 2008, McCain had virtually sewn up the Republican nomination.

How votes are cast and counted, and what it takes to win a seat, then, have very substantial consequences for American politics. Plurality rule with single-member districts creates strong pressures toward two-party politics and majority rule in the legislature.

Direct Democracy: The Referendum and the Recall

referendum
A measure proposed or passed by a legislature that is referred to the vote of the electorate for approval or rejection.

In addition to voting for candidates, twenty-four states also provide for referendum voting. The **referendum** process allows citizens to vote directly on proposed laws or other governmental actions. In recent years, voters in several states have voted to set limits on tax rates, block state and local spending proposals, and prohibit social services for illegal immigrants. Although it involves voting, a referendum is not an election. The election is an institution of representative government. Through an election, voters choose officials to act for them. The referendum process, by contrast, is an institution of direct democracy; it allows voters to govern directly without intervention by government officials. The validity of referendum results, however, are subject to judicial action. If a court finds that a referendum outcome violates the state or national constitution, it can overturn the result. This happened in the case of a 1995 California referendum curtailing social services to illegal aliens.[21] It should be emphasized that the issues that emerge as referendum subjects are usually of the "hot-button" variety. It is not clear that these often emotional issues, which require deliberation and reflection, are best dealt with by direct democracy. In other words, referendum issues are often adversely selected.

initiative
A process by which citizens may petition to place a policy proposal on the ballot for public vote.

Twenty-four states also permit various forms of the initiative. Whereas the referendum process described above allows citizens to affirm or reject a policy produced by legislative action, the **initiative** provides citizens with a way forward in the face of legislative inaction. This is done by placing a policy proposal (legislation or a state constitutional amendment) on the ballot to be approved or rejected by the electorate. To have a place on the ballot, a petition must be accompanied by a minimum number of voters' signatures—a requirement that varies from state to state—that have been certified by the state's secretary of state.

The initiative is also vulnerable to adverse selection. Ballot propositions involve policies that the state legislature cannot (or does not want to) resolve. Like referendum issues, these are often highly emotional and, consequently, not always well suited to resolution in the electoral arena. One of the "virtues" of the initiative is that it may force action. That is, leaders in the legislature may induce recalcitrant legislators to move on controversial issues by using as a threat the possibility that a worse outcome will result from inaction.[22]

recall
The removal of a public official by popular vote.

Legal provisions for **recall** elections exist in eighteen states. The recall is an electoral device that was introduced by early-twentieth-century Populists to allow voters to remove governors and other state officials from office before the expiration of their term. Federal officials such as the president and members of Congress

---

[21] *League of United Latin American Citizens v. Wilson*, 908 F. Supp. 755 (C.D. Calif., 1995).

[22] This point is developed in Morton Bennedsen and Sven Feldmann, "Lobbying Legislatures," *Journal of Political Economy* 110 (2002): 919–46.

are not subject to recall. Generally speaking, a recall effort begins with a petition campaign. For example, in California—the site of a tumultuous recall battle in 2003—if 12 percent of those who voted in the last general election sign petitions demanding a special recall election, one must be scheduled by the state board of elections. Such petition campaigns are relatively common, but most fail to garner enough signatures to bring the matter to a statewide vote. In California in 2003, however, a conservative Republican member of Congress, Darrell Issa, led a successful effort to recall Governor Gray Davis, a Democrat. Voters were unhappy about the state's economy and dissatisfied with Davis's performance: They blamed him for the state's $38 billion budget deficit. Issa and his followers were able to secure enough signatures to force a vote, and in October 2003 Davis became the second governor in American history to be recalled by his state's electorate (the first was North Dakota governor Lynn Frazier, who was recalled in 1921). Under California law, voters in a special recall election are also asked to choose a replacement for the official whom they dismiss. In 2003 Californians elected the movie star Arnold Schwarzenegger to be their governor. Although critics charged that the Davis recall had been a "political circus," the campaign had the effect of greatly increasing voter interest and involvement in the political process. More than 400,000 new voters registered in California in 2003, many drawn into the political arena by the opportunity to participate in the recall campaign.

The referendum, initiative, and recall all entail shifts in agenda-setting power. The referendum gives an impassioned electoral majority the opportunity to reverse legislation that displeases it, thus affecting the initial strategic calculations of institutional agenda setters (who want to get as much of what they want *without* its being subsequently reversed). The initiative has a similar effect on institutional agenda setters, but here it inclines them toward action rather than inaction. Combining the two, an institutional agenda setter is caught on the two horns of an institutional dilemma: Do I act, risking a reversal via referendum, or do I maintain the status quo, risking an overturn via initiative? The recall complements both of these choices, keeping institutional agenda setters on their toes to avoid being ousted. As the institution principle implies, these arrangements do not just provide citizens with governance tools. They also affect the strategic calculations of institutional politicians—legislators and governors.

HOW VOTERS DECIDE

An election expresses the preferences of millions of individuals about whom they want as their representatives and leaders. Electoral rules and laws—the institutional side of elections—impose order on that process, but ultimately, elections are a reflection of the people, the aggregation of many millions of individuals' expressions of their preferences about politics.

The voter's decision can be understood as really two linked decisions: whether to vote and for whom. Social scientists have examined both facets of the electoral decision by studying election returns, survey data, and experiments conducted in laboratories as well as field experiments conducted during actual elections. Out of generations of research into these questions, a broad picture emerges of how voters decide. First, the decision to vote or not to vote correlates very strongly with the social characteristics of individuals, especially age and education, but it also depends on the electoral choices and context. An individual who does not know anything about the candidates or dislikes all of the choices is unlikely to vote. Second, which candidates or party voters choose depends primarily on three factors: partisan loyalties, issues, and candidate characteristics. Partisan loyalties have been found to be the strongest single predictor of the vote, though party attachments also reflect issues and experience with candidates. Party, issues, and candidates act together to shape vote choice.

Voters and Nonvoters

As we saw earlier in the chapter, turnout in modern American presidential elections ranges from 50 to 60 percent of the voting-age population. In other words, roughly half of those who may vote don't. This phenomenon has long puzzled social scientists and motivated reformers. A general explanation is elusive, but what social scientists do know about this phenomenon is that a few demographic characteristics routinely prove to be strong predictors of who votes. The most important of these characteristics are age, education, and residential mobility. Other factors, such as gender, income, and race also matter, but to a much smaller degree. In 2004, the Census Bureau found that 58.3 percent of those of voting age in the survey voted, compared with the actual figure of 55.5 percent. According to the study, 47 percent of those under age thirty voted, fully 11 points below the population average. Older cohorts exhibited higher turnout rates: 74 percent of those over age 65 voted in 2004. The difference between these groups was 27 percentage points, and the effect of age on voting surely translated into an electoral difference. Education shows similarly large differences. Those without a high school degree voted at half the rate of those with a college education. More than three in four people with a college education voted, and the rate was 84 percent among those with a professional degree. In contrast, slightly fewer than 40 percent of those without a high school diploma voted, and 56 percent of those with only a high school degree voted. Finally, consider residency and mobility. Only 53 percent of people who lived in their current residence less than a year report voting, compared with 76 percent of people who lived in their residence at least five years. Those who own their home or apartment vote at a 69 percent rate, but only 48 percent of those who rent vote.[23] Politicians listen to those who vote, and those who vote are disproportionately older, better educated, and more rooted in their communities.

One important concern is whether differences in voting reflect electoral institutions. Election laws have historically had a large effect on the size and character of the electorate, especially laws preventing racial discrimination at polling places (in 1965) and expanding the suffrage to women (in 1920). Those interested in encouraging

---

[23] The most reliable source of information about the demographics of voting is the Current Population Survey, conducted by the Bureau of the Census. For these and other statistics see Kelly Holder, "Voting and Registration in the Election of November 2004," March 2006, www.census.gov/prod/2006pubs/p20-556.pdf (accessed 3/27/09).

greater participation today have focused on voter registration requirements, which are thought to create an unnecessary hurdle and thus to depress turnout. The decision to vote itself consists of two steps—registration and turnout. In 2004, 88.5 percent of those who reported that they registered said they voted. Weakening registration requirements may increase participation. One approach to minimizing such requirements is Election Day registration. As of 2009, seven states allow people to register on election day at the polls or at a government office. The three states with the longest experience with same-day registration—Minnesota, Wisconsin, and Maine—do have higher turnout than most other states, and most studies suggest that in a typical state, adopting such a law would increase turnout by about 3 to 5 percent.[24]

Demographics and laws are only part of what accounts for voting and nonvoting. The choices presented to the voters are also quite important. The problem is not that many people have a hard time making up their minds, but that many people do not feel engaged by current elections, or dislike politics altogether. People who are disinterested, "too busy to vote," or do not like the candidates tend not to vote. The Census Bureau survey asks registered nonvoters why they did not vote. The top four reasons are "too busy," "sick or disabled," "not interested," and "did not like the choices."

Not voting may also stem partly from a sense that the election does not hinge on how any individual votes. There are, however, strong differences across demographic groups in their voting rates, and these might have political consequences. One hypothetical to consider is, What if everyone voted? In some specific domains, universal voting would certainly alter government policy. Increasing the voting rate of younger cohorts would probably affect government policy on Social Security, for instance. But would 100 percent turnout lead the country to elect a different person for president or put a different party in control of Congress? Interestingly, the answer seems to be no. Voters and nonvoters, for all of their demographic and political differences, hold fairly similar partisan views, ideological orientations, and preferences about the candidates.[25]

Partisan Loyalty

The single strongest predictor of how a person will vote is that individual's attachment to a political party. The American National Election Study (ANES), exit polls, and media polls have found that even in times of great political change in the United States, the overwhelming majority of Americans identifies with one of the two major political parties and votes almost entirely in accordance with that identity. Survey researchers ascertain **party identititification** with simple questions along the following lines: Generally speaking, do you consider yourself to be a Democrat, a Republican, an Independent, or what?[26] Survey researchers further classify people by asking of

party identification An individual's attachment to a particular political party, which might be based on issues or ideology, past experience, or upbringing.

---

[24] The classic study in this area is Raymond Wolfinger and Steven Rosenstone, *Who Votes?* (New Haven, Conn.: Yale University Press, 1978). See also Steven Rosenstone and John Mark Hansen, *Participation, Mobilization and American Democracy* (New York: Macmillan, 1993).

[25] See for instance Sidney Verba, Kay Schlozman, and Henry Brady, *Voice and Equality* (Cambridge, Mass.: Harvard University Press, 1995).

[26] This is the wording used by the Gallup Poll. Others ask "In politics today . . ." or offer "or another party" instead of "or what."

those who choose a party whether they identify strongly or weakly with that party, and by asking independents whether they lean toward one party or another.

Over the past three decades party identifications have broken evenly between the Democrats and Republicans. Figure 11.2, in the next chapter on political parties, shows the historical fluctuations in party identifications. From the 1930s to the 1970s, Democratic identifiers outnumbered Republican identifiers, sometimes by a sizable margin. In the 1980s, the parties reached parity in identifications, especially because younger Americans at that time identified very heavily with the Republican Party. The balance in party identifications remained fairly stable through 2000, even though from 1992 to 2004 those aged eighteen to twenty-five chose the Democrats by a sizable margin. Since 2002, however, Democrats have steadily gained in overall party identification and Republicans have lost ground. Because of generational changes and the backlash against the Iraq war, as of 2009 about 49 percent of Americans identified as Democrats or leaned toward the Democratic Party, while 42 percent of Americans identified as Republicans or leaned toward the Republican Party.[27] Interestingly, over a fifty-year period there has been little change in the percentage of people calling themselves independents and leaning toward neither party. Only 10 to 15 percent consider themselves pure independents.[28]

Party identifications capture the voters' predisposition toward their party's candidates. Although specific features of the choices and context matter as well, party identifications express how the voter would likely vote in a "neutral" election. Party identifications are extremely good predictors of voting behavior in less prominent elections, such as for state legislature or lower-level statewide offices, about which voters may know relatively little. Even in presidential elections, with their extensive advertising and very thorough news coverage, party predispositions predict individual voting behavior. Figure 10.5 displays the percentages of Democratic identifiers, Republican identifiers, and self-described independents who voted for McCain, Obama, or someone else in 2008. Approximately 90 percent of party identifiers voted for their own party's standard bearer. Independents (including independents who lean toward either party) broke 52 to 44 for Obama. The 2008 election was in this respect quite typical. Partisan loyalty is usually in the range of 90 percent, and the division among independent voters tips the balance.

Since the discovery of its importance in the 1950s, party identification has raised deeper questions about its origins and meaning. There are three distinct views about what party identification is. They are not necessarily exclusive of each other, but they point to very different understandings of the nature of party identification and its effect on elections.[29] Debate over the meaning of party identification cuts to the heart of the meaning of elections.

---

[27] www.gallop.com/poll/123362/independents–lean–gop–party–gap–smallest–since–05.aspx

[28] Marc Hetherington, "Resurgent Mass Partisanship: The Role of Elite Polarization," *American Political Science Review* 95, no. 3 (September 2001): 619–31. Pew Research Center for the People and the Press, "Obama Leads McCain 52% to 46% in Campaign's Final Days," November 2, 2008, http://pewresearch.org/pubs/1020/pew-final-pre-election-poll (accessed 3/31/09).

[29] For an excellent treatment of the meanings of party identification and analysis of the implications of different theories, see Donald Green, Bradley Palmquist, and Eric Schickler, *Partisan Hearts and Minds* (New Haven, Conn.: Yale University Press, 2003).

FIGURE 10.5 THE EFFECT OF PARTY IDENTIFICATION ON THE VOTE FOR PRESIDENT, 2008

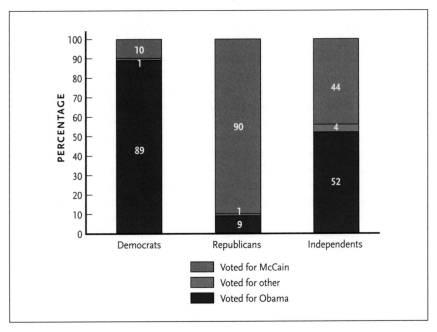

First, party identification is a psychological attachment that individuals hold, often throughout their adulthood, to one of the parties. Individuals learn as children and adolescents from parents, other adults, and even peers about politics, and as part of that socialization they develop attachments to a party, not unlike religion and community. Party identifications continue to form into early adulthood. The first few presidential elections that an individual experiences as an adult are thought to have particularly profound influence on that individual's understanding of the parties and politics. And as different cohorts come into politics, their experiences carry forward throughout their lives. Those who were eighteen to twenty-four years old in 1984, for example, identify overwhelmingly with the Republican party, because those elections marked the triumph of Ronald Reagan's presidency and political philosophy, the rise of a revitalized Republican Party, and the beginning of the end of the Cold War. Those eighteen to twenty-four years old in 2008, on the other hand, identify disproportionately with the Democratic Party, because the Obama campaign galvanized young voters around a new vision for the future. However it is developed, an individual's psychological affinity for a party makes that person want that party to win and want to support that party, even when he or she disagrees with the party on important policies or disapproves of the party's nominees for office.

Of course, the Democratic and Republican parties are quite different entities today than they were forty years ago or eighty years ago. On matters of race relations, for example, the Democratic Party has moved over the past century from supporting segregation to spearheading civil rights. The Republican Party, once a bastion of economic protectionism, now champions free trade. However strong generational transmission of party identifications may be, the dissonance between identities and issues must surely weaken the pull of party, which suggests a second theory of party. This second idea is that party identification reflects underlying ideologies of voters and policy positions of parties. Parties in government, as we discussed in Chapter 5, are meaningful organizations for producing public policies. The relatively high degree of party loyalty in Congress and other branches of government means that voters can reasonably anticipate how politicians will act in office. Citizens identify with parties that pursue public policies more to their liking. For example, a union worker will feel a stronger attachment to the Democratic Party because the Democrats have historically protected union interests. A high-income earner may feel a strong pull toward the Republican Party because that party pushes lower taxes overall, and the Democrats promote higher tax rates for higher-income households. In such cases, voters want to choose a party, not just a candidate, to be the agent for their interests. As mentioned in the introduction to this chapter, elections present an informational problem of adverse selection. The party labels act as brand names and help voters choose the candidates that will best match their preferences. Labels carry significant information to voters about the candidates. Voters need not know the details of an individual candidate's voting record or campaign promises in order to understand how that politician will likely behave on important matters. As such, party labels provide an informational short cut for voters. Party identification means, in part, that a voter feels that party represents his or her interests better than other parties; hence, an identifier is highly likely to vote for that party.[30]

Over the past two decades, the ideological alignments of voters and parties have shifted. Republicans have lost many of their moderate identifiers, especially in the Northeast, and conservative Southerners, who a generation ago would have called themselves Democrats, now overwhelmingly identify with the Republican Party. This shift reflects long-term changes in the ideological orientations of the parties at the elite level, and thus their brand names. The 1994 election was critically important in establishing a new label for the Republicans, because that election swept into office large numbers of Republican members of Congress in the South and eliminated much of the conservative wing of the Democratic Party. The parties, then, became more distinctive, presenting a much clearer choice to voters.[31]

Not all people fit neatly into one ideological camp or another. Some people do not think about politics in ideological or policy terms. Others are indifferent to the parties ideologically. A significant portion of Americans consider themselves to be centrists and feel that the Democrats are somewhat too liberal and the Republicans somewhat too conservative. They may turn one way or the other, but they do not have a strong affinity for either party. Other people feel pulled in

---

[30] For a detailed assessment of the political use of information-economizing devices such as party labels, see Arthur Lupia and Mathew D. McCubbins, *The Democratic Dilemma: Can Citizens Learn What They Need To Know?* (New York: Cambridge University Press, 1998).

[31] See Hetherington, "Resurgent Mass Partisanship."

different directions by different issues and concerns. A union member who strongly opposes abortion, for example, is drawn to the Democrats' labor policies and the Republicans' abortion policies. Campaigns target such cross-pressured voters, who are often pivotal in elections.[32]

A third explanation is that party identification reflects experiences with political leaders and representatives, especially the presidents from each of the parties. As the political scientist Morris Fiorina put it, party identifications are running tallies of experience. Americans hold their presidents, and to a lesser extent Congress, accountable for the economic performance of the country and success in foreign affairs. A bad economy or a disastrous military intervention will lead voters to disapprove of the president and to lower their assessment of the president's party's ability to govern. Parties are, by this account, teams seeking to run the government. They consist of policy experts, managers, and leaders who will conduct foreign policy, economic policy, and domestic policies (such as environmental protection and health care). When things go well, voters infer that the incumbent party has a good approach to running national affairs, but when things go badly, they learn that the party lacks the people needed to run the government competently or the approach needed to produce economic prosperity, international peace, and other outcomes desired by the public. With each successive presidency and their experience of it, individuals update their beliefs about which party is better able to govern.

Psychological attachments, ideological affinities, and past experiences add up to form an individual's current party identifications. But party is not the only factor in voting. Some partisans do defect, especially in elections when voters are dissatisfied with the incumbent party or are especially drawn to a particular candidate. Even in 2008, when 90 percent of partisans voted with their party's presidential candidate, significant defections occurred down the ticket. In the 2008 Virginia Senate election, for example, two ex-governors squared off against one another, the Democrat Mark Warner against the Republican Jim Gilmore. In a state where the Democratic presidential nominee, Barack Obama, won just 8 percent of the votes of Republican Party identifiers, Mark Warner received 25 percent of the vote of Republican identifiers. The issues at stake and the characteristics of the candidates overrode party attachments for large numbers of Republican identifiers and drew large numbers of independents and Republicans to Warner. We consider next how issues and candidates shape voting behavior.

Issues

Issues and policy preferences constitute a second factor influencing voters' decisions. Voting on issues and policies cuts to the core of our understanding of democratic accountability and electoral control over government. A simple, idealized account of **issue voting** goes as follows. Governments make policies and laws on a variety of issues that affect the public. Voters who disagree with those policies and laws on principle or who think those policies have failed will vote against those

issue voting An individual's propensity to select candidates or parties based on the extent to which the individual agrees with one candidate more than others on specific issues.

---

[32] For a more in-depth discussion of independent voters, policy indifference, and cross pressure, see Sunshine Hillygus and Todd Shields, *The Persuadable Voter: Wedge Issues in Presidential Campaigns* (Princeton, N.J.: Princeton University Press, 2008).

who made the decisions. Voters who support the policies or like the outcomes that government has produced will support the incumbent legislatures or party. It is important to note that policies are not taken as constants or fixed attributes of the candidates or parties. Rather, politicians choose what kinds of laws to enact and what kinds of administrative actions to take with the express aim of attracting electoral support. Voters, as we discussed in the previous chapter, have preferences about what policies the government pursues or what outcomes result, and they choose the candidates and parties that produce the best results or most preferred laws. Even party identifications, as we have noted, reflect the policy preferences of the voters and the policies pursued by the parties and candidates.

Voters' choice of issues usually involves a mix of their judgments about the past behavior of competing parties and candidates and their hopes and fears about candidates' future behavior. Political scientists call choices that focus on future behavior **prospective voting** and those based on past performance **retrospective voting**. To some extent, whether prospective or retrospective evaluation is more important in a particular election depends on the strategies of the competing candidates. Candidates always endeavor to define the issues of an election in terms that will serve their interests. Incumbents running during a period of prosperity will seek to take credit for the economy's happy state and define the election as revolving around their record of success. This strategy encourages voters to make retrospective judgments. By contrast, an insurgent running during a period of economic uncertainty will tell voters it is time for a change and ask them to make prospective judgments. Thus Bill Clinton focused on change in 1992 and on prosperity in 1996 and through well-crafted media campaigns was able to define voters' agenda of choices.

Not all issues, however, are alike. There are, as discussed in the previous chapter, different sorts of issues and dimensions to politics, such as economic concerns, moral questions, and foreign affairs. Voters may hold different views on each. Issues differ politically in another important respect, and that is according to differences in public preferences over the issue. Broadly speaking, issues may be distinguished as *spatial issues* and *valence issues*. We will consider each in turn.

Spatial Issues. Many issues are characterized by a range of different policies (usually represented by a line) and conflicting preferences over policies and outcomes. Minimum wages are an excellent example of what is called a **spatial issue.** Low-wage workers and unions favor minimum wages because they benefit from them. Low-wage workers will earn higher wages, and union members expect all wages to be pushed up with the minimum wage. Employers and investors tend not to like the minimum wage because it increases labor costs and reduces profit margins. Abortion rights provide another often-discussed example of a spatial issue. At one extreme are those who defend the legality of abortion under all circumstances; at the other extreme are those who want to ban the procedure under all circumstances. Between those two poles lie a range of policy alternatives, from putting some restrictions on access, such as parental consent or consultation with a medical professional, to regulations on the time during pregnancy and procedures used, to allowing the practice only when the life of the mother is threatened. Public-opinion research (as discussed in Chapter 9) has demonstrated that public preferences are distributed across such policy options, with many people favoring a moderate

---

prospective voting Voting based on the imagined future performance of a candidate.

retrospective voting Voting based on the past performance of a candidate.

spatial issue An issue for which a range of possible options or policies can be ordered, say, from liberal to conservative or from most expensive to least expensive.

approach of placing some restrictions on the practice. Minimum-wage laws and abortion laws exemplify the features of spatial issues—a range of policy options and a lack of consensus on the right policy.

Politicians compete for voters by pursuing particular policies that they think will attract the most voters. In 2004, President Bush emphasized his efforts to protect the nation from terrorists and his strong commitment to religious and moral values. On the other hand, the Democratic candidate, John Kerry, attacked Bush's decision to invade Iraq, questioned the president's leadership in the war on terrorism, and charged that the president's economic policies had failed to produce prosperity. When asked by exit pollsters which issue mattered most in deciding how they voted for president, 22 percent of all voters cited moral values as their chief concern. More than 80 percent of these voters supported President Bush. The economy was cited as the most important issue by 20 percent of those who voted, and 80 percent of those Americans voted for Senator Kerry. Terrorism ranked third in terms of the percentage of voters who indicated it was the most important issue for them. President Bush received more than 80 percent of the votes of those Americans concerned mainly with terrorism. The 2006 midterm elections were portrayed by Democrats as a referendum on President Bush's conduct of the war in Iraq. There was a considerable swing of votes to the Democrats, even in districts that had supported Bush over Kerry in 2004, with the result that the Democrats picked up twenty-five seats in the House and six in the Senate.[33] Similarly, the 2010 midterm elections, which were portrayed by Republicans as a referendum on President Obama's handling of the economy and health care, produced a considerable swing of votes to the GOP.

The ability of voters to make choices on the basis of issue or policy preferences is diminished, however, if competing candidates do not differ substantially or do not focus their campaigns on policy matters. Very often candidates deliberately take the safe course and emphasize topics that will not be offensive to any voters. Thus candidates often trumpet their opposition to corruption, crime, and inflation. Presumably, few voters favor these things. Although it may be perfectly reasonable for candidates to take the safe course and remain as inoffensive as possible, this strategy makes it extremely difficult for voters to make their issue or policy preferences the bases for their choices at the polls.

When voters engage in issue voting, competition between two candidates has the effect of pushing the candidates' issue positions toward the middle of the distribution of voters' preferences. This is known as the **median-voter theorem**, made famous by Duncan Black and Anthony Downs.[34] (Chapter 5 discussed the median-voter theorem in the context of congressional committees.) To see the logic of this claim in the context of elections, imagine a series of possible stances on a policy issue as points along a line, stretching from 0 to 100 (Figure 10.6). A voter is represented by an "ideal" policy and preferences, which decline as policy moves away from this ideal. Thus voters in group 1 prefer policy X_1 most, and their preference

median-voter theorem A proposition predicting that when policy options can be arrayed along a single dimension, majority rule will pick the policy most preferred by the voter whose ideal policy is to the left of half of the voters and to the right of exactly half of the voters. See Chapter 5 for further discussion.

---

[33] William F. Connelly, Jr., "Wall vs. Wave?" *The Forum* 4, no. 3 (2006), www.bepress.com/forum/vol4/iss3/art3 (accessed 3/31/09).

[34] See Duncan Black, *The Theory of Committees and Elections*, 2nd ed. (Boston: Kluwer, 1998), and Anthony Downs, *An Economic Theory of Democracy* (New York: Harper & Row, 1957). A general, accessible treatment of this subject is found in Shepsle and Bonchek, *Analyzing Politics*, chap. 5.

FIGURE 10.6 THE MEDIAN-VOTER THEOREM

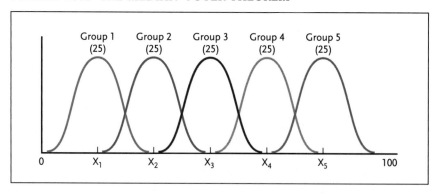

declines as the policy moves to the left or right of X_1. Voters whose ideal policy lies between, say, 0 and 25 are said to be liberal on this policy (groups 1 and 2), those whose ideal lies between 75 and 100 are conservative (groups 4 and 5), and those whose favorite policy is between 25 and 75 are moderate (group 3). An issue voter cares only about issue positions, not partisan loyalty or candidates' characteristics, and would, therefore, vote for the candidate whose announced policy is closest to his or her own most preferred policy.

Consider now an electorate of 125 voters evenly distributed among the five groups shown in Figure 10.6.[35] The middle group contains the median voter because half or more of this electorate has an ideal policy at or to the left of X_3 (groups 1, 2, and 3), and half or more has an ideal policy at or to the right of X_3 (groups 3, 4, and 5). Group 3 is in the driver's seat, as the following reasoning suggests. If a candidate announces X_3 as his policy—the most preferred alternative of the median voter—and if his opponent picks any point to the right, then the median voter and all those with ideal policies to the left of the median voter's (groups 1–3) will support the first candidate. They constitute a majority, by definition of the median, so this candidate will win. Suppose instead that the opponent chose as her policy some point to the left of the median ideal policy. Then the median voter and all those with ideal policies to the right of the median voter's (groups 3–5) will support the first candidate—and he wins, again. In short, the median-voter theorem says that the candidate whose policy position is closest to the ideal policy of the median voter will defeat the other candidate in a majority contest. We can conclude from this brief analysis that issue voting encourages candidate convergence (in which both candidates move to cozy up to the position of the median voter). Even when voters are not exclusively issue voters, two-candidate competition still encourages a tendency toward convergence, although it may not fully run its course.[36]

---

[35] For the sake of this illustration, we've put twenty-five voters in each group. One argument is the same with any distribution of voters among the groups.

[36] This convergence will also be a moderating force as candidates move toward what they believe will appeal to voters in the middle. But if the middle of the voter distribution of preferences tilts toward the right or the left, it may not be very moderate. If X_3, for example, were barely to the left of X_4, then the median voter would be fairly right wing rather than in the middle of the issue dimension.

Valence Issues. Some issues lack conflict: all people want the same outcome. All people want less crime, more prosperity and less poverty, less inflation, better health, peace, and security. They may have different beliefs about what to do to attain those objectives, but they don't really care about the means, they care about the outcome.

In the context of elections, economic conditions are the most important **valence issue**. If voters are satisfied with their economic prospects, they tend to support the party in power, while voters' unease about the economy tends to favor the opposition. Thus George H. W. Bush lost in 1992 during an economic downturn even though his victory in the Persian Gulf War had briefly given him a 90 percent favorable rating in the polls. And Bill Clinton won in 1996 during an economic boom even though voters had serious concerns about his moral fiber. Over the past quarter century, the Consumer Confidence Index, calculated by the Conference Board, a business research group, has been a fairly accurate predictor of presidential outcomes. The index is based on surveys asking voters how optimistic they are about the future of the economy. It would appear that a generally rosy view, indicated by a score greater than 100, augurs well for the party in power. An index score of less than 100, suggesting that voters are pessimistic about the economy's trend, suggests that incumbents should worry about their job prospects (Figure 10.7).

A common sort of empirical analysis uses economic growth (annual percentage changes in gross domestic product) to predict the vote. The idea is that large numbers of voters decide to vote against the incumbent party in bad times and with the incumbent party in good times. Every individual may have a different sense of the economy, but adding up the 100 million or so votes will aggregate every individual's experiences and reflect roughly what is going on in the economy and how the economy affects his or her voting. Although the fit between economic growth and vote for the incumbent party is hardly perfect, correlation is sufficient to allow statistically minded political scientists to make forecasts. Roughly speaking, every additional 1 percent growth in GDP corresponds to a 1 percentage point increase in the incumbent president's party's vote.[37]

Economic voting is one way that voters solve the moral hazard problems inherent in representative democracy. They cannot monitor every policy that the government initiates. They do, however, have a rudimentary way to hold the government accountable—staying the course when times are good and voting for change when the economy sours.

valence issue An issue or aspect of a choice for which all voters prefer a higher value, in contrast to a spatial issue. For example, voters prefer their politicians to be honest, and honesty is a valence issue.

Candidate Characteristics

Candidates' personal attributes always influence voters' decisions. The more important characteristics that affect voters' choices are race, ethnicity, religion, gender, geography, and social background. In general, voters prefer candidates who are closer to themselves in terms of these categories. Voters presume that such candidates

---

[37] Perhaps the most comprehensive study of the responsiveness of elections to fluctuations in the U.S. economy is Robert Erikson, Michael MacKuen, and James Stimson, *The Macro-Polity* (New York: Cambridge University Press, 2002).

FIGURE 10.7 CONSUMER CONFIDENCE AND PRESIDENTIAL ELECTIONS

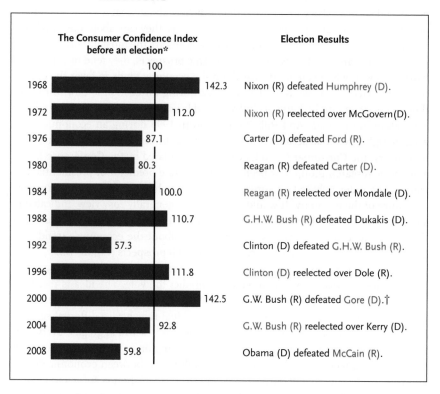

The Consumer Confidence Index before an election*

Election Results

1968	142.3	Nixon (R) defeated Humphrey (D).
1972	112.0	Nixon (R) reelected over McGovern (D).
1976	87.1	Carter (D) defeated Ford (R).
1980	80.3	Reagan (R) defeated Carter (D).
1984	100.0	Reagan (R) reelected over Mondale (D).
1988	110.7	G.H.W. Bush (R) defeated Dukakis (D).
1992	57.3	Clinton (D) defeated G.H.W. Bush (R).
1996	111.8	Clinton (D) reelected over Dole (R).
2000	142.5	G.W. Bush (R) defeated Gore (D).†
2004	92.8	G.W. Bush (R) reelected over Kerry (D).
2008	59.8	Obama (D) defeated McCain (R).

*Survey was bimonthly before 1977, so figures for 1968, 1972, and 1976 are for October; from 1980 on, they are for September.

†Gore won the popular vote, but Bush was elected by the Electoral College.

NOTE: The candidate representing the incumbent party appears in red.

SOURCE: *Bloomberg Markets.*

are likely to have views and perspectives close to their own. Moreover, they may be proud to see someone of their ethnic, religious, or geographic background in a position of leadership. This is why, for many years, politicians sought to "balance the ticket," making certain that their party's ticket included members of as many important groups as possible.

Just as a candidate's personal characteristics may attract some voters, so they may repel others. Many voters are prejudiced against candidates of certain ethnic, racial, or religious groups. And for many years, voters were reluctant to support the political candidacy of women, although this tendency appears to be changing.

Voters also pay attention to candidates' personality characteristics, such as their "decisiveness," "honesty," and "vigor." In recent years, integrity has become a key election issue. In the 2000 presidential race, Al Gore chose Joe Lieberman as his running mate in part because Lieberman had been sharply critical of Bill

Clinton's moral lapses. The senator's presence on the Democratic ticket thus helped defuse the GOP's efforts to link Gore to Clinton's questionable character. In the 2004 presidential race, President Bush and the Republicans accused Senator Kerry of being inconsistent, a "flip-flopper" who repeatedly changed his position when it was expedient to do so. Bush, on the other hand, emphasized his own constancy. "I say what I mean and I do what I say" was the president's frequent refrain. The president also pointed to his strong religious commitment as evidence of his exemplary character. For their part, Democrats emphasized Senator Kerry's intelligence, empathy for ordinary Americans, and record of wartime heroism, which, they said, stood in sharp contrast to Bush's own somewhat blemished military record. In the end, the GOP's characterization of Kerry as a "flip-flopper" and Bush as an individual with deep moral and religious commitments seemed to resonate with voters. Among those who said that it was important for the president to take a clear stand on issues, 80 percent voted for President Bush; among those for whom strong religious faith was important, 90 percent voted for Bush; and among those who cited honesty as the candidate quality that mattered most, more than 70 percent gave their votes to Bush. On the other hand, among Americans who thought a president should be empathic and care about people like them, 75 percent supported Kerry; and among those who thought intelligence was the most important personal characteristic of a president, 91 percent voted for Kerry and only 9 percent for Bush.[38]

One of the most distinctive features of American politics is the apparent advantage that incumbents have, as we saw in Chapter 5. Beginning around 1970, political scientists noted a peculiar change overtaking electoral politics, especially in congressional elections. Incumbents were winning reelection at higher rates than in previous generations and by wider margins. Closer examination of the election results revealed that this phenomenon appeared due to incumbency itself. As a simple natural experiment, Professor Robert Erikson compared the same politician running for election not as an incumbent and as an incumbent. In the first sort of election, the politician ran for a seat left vacant by an incumbent's retirement or against an incumbent and won. In the second sort of election, the politician had just won the previous election and had to defend the seat in the next election as a "sophomore." Erikson called the increase in the politician's vote share from the first election to the second the "sophomore surge." It is the increase in the vote attributable solely to the fact that the politician ran as an incumbent rather than as a nonincumbent. Erikson found an incumbency effect of approximately 5 percentage points around 1970. If the party division of the vote in a congressional district without an incumbent is, say, 50-50, then in a race where one candidate is the incumbent, that same district would vote for the incumbent with 55 percent to 45 percent.

---

[38] See Stephen Ansolabehere and James Snyder, "Valence Politics and Equilibrium in Spatial Election Models," *Public Choice* 103 (2000): 327–36; and Timothy Groseclose, "A Model of Candidate Location When One Candidate Has a Valence Advantage," *American Journal of Political Science* 45 (2001): 862–86.

Since Erikson documented it in 1970, the incumbency advantage has grown both in magnitude and in importance in U.S. elections. Incumbency advantages in House elections grew rapidly beginning in the mid-1950s, when they were worth only 1 to 2 percentage points, to 5 to 6 percentage points by the end of the 1960s. They have continued to inch upward, reaching as high as 15 points in the mid-1980s. Today, almost every elective office at the state and federal level exhibits an incumbency advantage. Those advantages have ranged from about 5 percent in state legislative elections to 10 percent for U.S. House, U.S. Senate, and governor. A 10 percent incumbency advantage is a massive electoral edge. It turns a 50-50 seat into a safe seat. It turns a competitive race into a blowout for the incumbent.[39]

Why the incumbency advantage has emerged and grown remains something of a puzzle. Redistricting is almost certainly not the explanation: Incumbency effects are as large in gubernatorial elections, where there are no districts, as in House elections. It is thought that about half of the incumbency advantage reflects the activities of the legislator in office; it is the result of voters rewarding incumbents for their performance. The other half of the incumbency advantage evidently reflects not the incumbents but their opponents.[40] The typical challenger in U.S. elections may not have the personal appeal of the typical incumbent; after all, the typical incumbent has already won office once. Moreover, challengers usually lack the experience and resources that the incumbent has for running a campaign. This is critical. The ability to communicate with the voters can give a politician the edge in close elections.

Although party, issues, and candidate characteristics are perhaps the three most important factors shaping voting decisions, there is much debate among political scientists as to the relative importance of each. Problems of measurement and the limitations of research methods have made it exceedingly difficult to parse the relative importance of these factors in voters' thinking. Recent scholarship suggests that they have roughly equal weight in explaining the division of the vote in national elections.[41] Part of the difficulty in understanding their importance is that the extent to which these factors matter depends on the information levels of the electorate. In the absence of much information, most voters rely almost exclusively on party cues. A highly informed electorate relies more heavily on issues and candidate characteristics.[42]

---

[39] See Stephen Ansolabehere and James M. Snyder, Jr., "The Incumbency Advantage in U.S. Elections: An Analysis of State and Federal Offices, 1942–2000," *Election Law Journal* 1 (2002), 315–38.

[40] The partitioning of the incumbency effect into officeholder advantages and challenger qualities begins with the important work of Gary Jacobson. See, for example, his excellent text *The Politics of Congressional Elections*, 7th ed. (White Plains, NY: Longman, 2008). Estimating exactly what fraction of the incumbency effect is due to officeholder benefits is tricky. See Stephen Ansolabehere, James M. Snyder, Jr., and Charles H. Stewart III, "Old Voters, New Voters, and the Personal Vote: Using Redistricting to Measure the Incumbency Advantage," *American Journal of Political Science* 44, no. 1 (January 2000), 17–34.

[41] See Stephen Ansolabehere, Jonathan Rodden, and James M. Snyder, Jr., "Issue Voting," *American Political Science Review* (May 2008).

[42] The classic study showing this is Philip Converse, "The Nature of Belief Systems in Mass Publics," in *Ideology and Discontent*, David Apter, ed. (New York: Free Press, 1964).

CAMPAIGNS: MONEY, MEDIA, AND GRASS ROOTS

American political campaigns are freewheeling events with few restrictions on what candidates may say or do. Candidates in hotly contested House and Senate races spend millions of dollars to advertise on television and radio, as well as direct mail and door-to-door canvassing. Those seeking office are in a race to become as well known and as well liked as possible and to get more of their supporters to vote. Federal laws limit how much an individual or organization may give to a candidate, but with the exception of the presidential campaigns, place no restrictions on how much a candidate or party committee may spend.

Adding to the freewheeling nature of campaigns is their organizational structure. Most political campaigns are temporary organizations. They form for the sole purpose of winning the coming elections and disband shortly afterward. To be sure, political parties in the United States have a set of permanent, professional campaign organizations that raise money, strategize, recruit candidates, and distribute resources. These are, on the Republican side, the Republican National Committee, the National Republican Senatorial Committee, and the National Republican Congressional Committee. On the Democratic side are the Democratic National Committee, the Democratic Senatorial Campaign Committee, and the Democratic Congressional Campaign Committee. They account for roughly a third of the money in politics and have considerable expertise. But most campaigns are formed by and around individual candidates, who often put up the initial cash to get the campaign rolling and rely heavily on family and friends as volunteers. Thousands of such organizations are at work during an election. The two presidential campaigns operate 50 different state-level operations, with other campaigns competing for 34 Senate seats, 435 House seats, dozens of gubernatorial and other statewide offices, and thousands of state legislative seats. There is relatively little coordination among these myriad campaigns, though they all simultaneously work toward the same end—persuading as many people as possible to vote for their candidate on Election Day.

All campaigns, big and small, face similar challenges—how to bring people in, how to raise money, how to coordinate activities, what messages to run, and how to communicate with the public. There is no one best way to run a campaign. There are many tried and true approaches, especially building up a campaign from many local connections, from the grass roots. Candidates have to meet as many people as possible and get their friends and their friends' friends to support them. In-person campaigning becomes increasingly difficult in larger constituencies. Candidates continually experiment with new ways of communicating with the public and new ways of organizing in order to more efficiently reach large segments of the electorate. In the 1920s, radio advertising eclipsed handbills and door-to-door canvassing, as broadcasting captured economies of scale. In the 1960s, television began to eclipse radio. In the 1980s and 1990s, cable television and innovations in marketing (especially phone polling and focus groups) allowed candidates to target very specific demographic groups through the media. The great innovation of the Obama campaign was to meld Internet networking tools with old-style organizing methods to develop a massive communications and fund-raising network, what came to be called a "netroots" campaign.

However they are organized, campaigns play an essential role in American democracy. They are the opportunity for the politicians to present themselves to the public to explain who they are, what they have accomplished, and what they will do in office. Television advertisements, get-out-the-vote activities, direct mail, and the like provide voters with factual information about the personal characteristics and ideologies of the candidates, about the meaning of the party labels, and about what issues distinguish the politicians.

Campaigns are also a time when the foibles and failures of those in office may be revealed. Challengers must make the case that a new direction is needed, and that case rests on showing that the incumbent is the wrong person to represent the constituency (a case of adverse selection) or has failed to do the job as constituents wanted (a case of moral hazard). Incumbents, for their part, try to appeal to voters on the basis of their ideological fit with their constituents and their performance in office. It has become an assumption of American elections and election law that candidates and parties will mount competitive campaigns to win office. They will spend millions, even billions of dollars, to persuade people to vote and how to vote. And because of those efforts voters will understand better what the choices they face in the elections. In short, campaigns inform voters, and they do so through competition.

In addition to being costly, American political campaigns are long, often spanning years. Campaigns for the presidency officially launch a year and a half to two years in advance of Election Day. Serious campaigns for the U.S. House of Representatives begin at least a year ahead of the general election date and often span the better part of two years. To use the term of the Federal Election Commission, an election is a two-year "cycle," not a single day or even the period between Labor Day and Election Day loosely referred to as "the general election."

The long campaigns in the United States are due in large part to the effort required to mount a campaign. There are roughly 300 million people in the United States, and the voting-age population exceeds 220 million people. Communicating with all of those people is an expensive and time-consuming enterprise. A simple calculation reveals the challenge. Suppose you ran for president of the United States. Sending one piece of mail to each household in the United States would cost approximately $100 million dollars. That is probably the minimum imaginable campaign effort. How long would it take to raise $100 million and mobilize such an effort to communicate with the American people? In the 2008 election cycle, Barack Obama spent $700 million dollars on his presidential bid; John McCain spent $326 million; the Democratic and Republican Party operations spent $1.8 billion. All told, candidates and organizations spent approximately $3 billion on the 2008 presidential election and perhaps another $1 billion on the 2008 congressional elections. The money came primarily from millions of individuals who gave small amounts through the personal networks that the campaigns built up over months, even years of effort. It takes extensive operations to reach out to so many people and to raise such vast sums. Simply putting such an organization in place takes months. Even a congressional campaign takes considerable time to cultivate. The typical U.S. House campaign raised and spent approximately $700,000 in 2006, with the lion's share of that money coming from hundreds of individual donors. Once a campaign has enough money to initiate operations, it begins to communicate with the voters, often starting small by attending meetings with various groups. A successful campaign builds on early successes, bringing in more supporters and volunteers, and culminating with intensive advertising campaigns in the final months or weeks before election day. Although the Democratic and Republican parties may help campaigns that have a good shot of succeeding, they typically come in late. Every campaign for Congress or president is built by the individual candidates and their close friends and associates from the ground up. The personal style of political campaigning that Americans have come to appreciate reflects an enormous investment of time and resources, an investment that takes the better part of a year to grow.

The campaign season is further extended by the election calendar. American elections proceed in two steps, the party primary elections and the general election. General elections for federal offices are set by the Constitution of the United States to take place on the first Tuesday after the first Monday in November. The first presidential caucuses and primaries come early in January and last through the beginning of June. State and congressional primaries do not follow the same calendar, but most occur in the spring and early summer, with a handful of some states waiting to hold their nominating elections until September of the election year. The immediate result of this year-long calendar of elections is to stretch the campaigns over the entire election year.

American electoral campaigns contrast starkly with those in other democracies, such as Germany, France, Japan, and even the United Kingdom. Parliamentary systems have short campaigns. Once the government calls for an election, the campaign proceeds for a few months, and an election is held. The years-long gestation of an American election is unheard of and even considered unseemly in most other democracies. Most democracies also limit candidates' campaign expenditures and fund-raising activities, constraining the ability of individual politicians to develop personal campaign organizations and appeals. Money and other resources in other democracies flow through party organizations, often with little government oversight. Most democracies also regulate how candidates and parties campaign. Very few countries permit television advertising, phone banks, or door-to-door canvassing. Posters and billboards are commonplace in other democracies, as are public campaign forums. These restrictions on campaign communications make the campaigns themselves less important, and make media coverage of the parties, the candidates, and the government more prominent. And however much leaders, candidates, and parties try to shape news coverage, they cannot control it.

The expense, duration, and chaos of American campaigns have prompted many efforts at reform, including attempts to limit campaign spending, shorten the campaign season, and restrict what candidates and organizations can say in advertisements. The most sweeping campaign reforms came in 1971, when Congress passed the Federal Elections Campaign Act (or FECA). It limited the amounts that a single individual could contributed to a candidate or party to $1,000 per election for individuals and $5,000 for organizations (these limits have since been increased, as Table 10.1 indicates). It further regulated how business firms, unions, and other organizations could give money, prohibiting donations directly from the organization's treasury and requiring the establishment of a separate, segregated fund—a **political action committee** (PAC for short). It established public funding for presidential campaigns and

political action committee (PAC) A private group that raises and distributes funds for use in election campaigns.

TABLE 10.1 FEDERAL CAMPAIGN FINANCE REGULATION

The Rules for Campaign Contributions

Who	may contribute ...	to ...	if ...
Individuals	up to $2,300	a candidate	they are contributing to a single candidate in a single election.
Individuals	up to $28,500	a national party committee.	
Individuals	up to $5,000	a PAC.	
PACs	up to $5,000	a candidate	they contribute to the campaigns of at least five candidates.
Individuals and PACs	unlimited funds	a 527 committee	the funds are used for issue advocacy and the 527 committee's efforts are not coordinated with any political campaign.
Individuals and PACs	up to $10,000	a state party committee	the money is used for voter registration and get-out-the-vote efforts.
Individuals and PACs	unlimited funds	an independent expenditure committee (super PAC)	the money is used for political ads advocating for or against candidates and the committee's efforts are not coordinated with any political campaign

The Rules for Campaign Advertising

Who	may not finance ...	if ...
Unions, corporations, and nonprofit organizations	broadcast issue ads mentioning federal candidates	they occur within sixty days of a general election or thirty days of a primary.

The Rules for Presidential Primaries and Elections

Candidates . . .	may receive . . .	if . . .
In primaries	federal matching funds, dollar for dollar, up to $5 million	they raise at least $5,000 in each of twenty states in contributions of $250 or less.
In general elections	full federal funding (but may spend no more than their federal funding)	they belong to a major party (minor-party candidates may receive partial funding).
In any election	money from independent groups (PACs and 527 committees)	the groups' efforts are not tied directly to the official campaign.

Important Definitions for Campaign Finance Regulation

- **Political action committee (PAC):** Private group that raises and distributes funds for use in election campaigns.
- **527 committee:** Tax-exempt organization that engages in political activities, often through unlimited "soft-money" contributions. The committee is not restricted by current law on campaign finance, thus exploiting a loophole in the Internal Revenue Service code.
- **501(c)4:** Not for profit group that may engage in unlimited political spending so long as amount spent does not exceed 50 percent of its budget. Unlike the 527s, 501(c)4s are not required to disclose contributor and recipient information.
- **Independent expenditure committee:** Organization that may engage in unlimited political spending to run advertising for and against candidates so long as their efforts are not coordinated with those of the candidates.
- **Federal matching funds:** Federal funds that match, dollar for dollar, all individual contributions of $250 or less received by a candidate. To qualify, the candidate must raise at least $5,000 in individual contributions of $250 or less in each of twenty states.
- **Federal Election Commission:** The commission that oversees campaign finance practices in the United States.

tied those funds to expenditure limits. And it set up the Federal Election Commission (FEC) to oversee public disclosure of information and to enforce the laws.[43] Congress has amended the act several times, most importantly in the Bipartisan Campaign Reform Act of 2002 (also called the McCain-Feingold Act, after Senators John McCain and Russell Feingold, its primary sponsors in the Senate). The McCain-Feingold Act prohibited unlimited party spending (called soft money) and banned certain sorts of political attack advertisements from interest groups in the last weeks of a campaign. See Table 10.1 for rules governing campaign finance in federal elections.

---

[43] The FEC's Web site is an excellent resource for those interested in U.S. campaign finance (www.fec.gov).

The FECA also established public funding for presidential campaigns. If a candidate agrees to abide by spending limits, that candidate's campaign is eligible for matching funds in primary elections and full public funding in the general election. The general election amount was set at $20 million in 1974 and allowed to increase with inflation. Until 2000, nearly all candidates bought into the system. George W. Bush chose to fund his 2000 primary election campaign outside this system and spent $500 million to win the Republican nomination. Barack Obama and Hillary Clinton ignored the public financing system in their 2008 primary contest, and Obama opted out of the public system in the general election as well, allowing him to spend several hundred million more dollars than the Republican nominee, John McCain.

FECA originally went much farther than the law that survives today. Congress originally passed mandatory caps on spending by House and Senate candidates and prohibited organizations from running their own independent campaigns on behalf of or in opposition to a candidate (and not coordinated with any candidate). James Buckley, a candidate for U.S. Senate in New York, challenged the law, arguing that the restrictions on spending and contributions limited his rights to free speech and that FEC had excessive administrative power. In the 1976 landmark case *Buckley v. Valeo*, the U.S. Supreme Court agreed in part.[44] The Court ruled that "money is speech," but the government also has a compelling interest in protecting elections from corrupt practices, such as bribery through large campaign donations. The justices declared the limits on spending unconstitutional because they violated free speech rights of candidates and groups. However, the need to protect the integrity of the electoral process led the justices to leave contribution limits in place. The presidential public-funding system was also validated because it is voluntary. Candidates can opt into the system, but they are not required to; hence, there is no violation of free speech. What survived *Buckley* is a system in which candidates, groups, and parties may spend as much as they like to win office, but donations must come in small amounts. In an expensive election, campaigns must accumulate their resources from large numbers of individuals and groups. This is a more democratic process of campaign finance, but it increases the effort and time needed to construct a campaign.

The Supreme Court's decision in *Buckley*, though highly controversial, rests on an essential truth of American democracy and elections. The First Amendment right to free speech amounts to a "profound national commitment to the principle that debate on public issues should be uninhibited, robust, and wide-open."[45] "In a republic where the people are sovereign," the Court continued, "the ability of the citizenry to make informed choices among candidates for office is essential, for the identities of those who are elected will inevitably shape the course that we follow as a nation. . . . It can hardly be doubted that the constitutional guarantee has its fullest and most urgent application precisely to the conduct of campaigns for political office."[46] Without competitive political campaigns, voters would lack the informa-

---

[44] *Buckley v. Valeo*, 424 U.S. 1 (1976).

[45] The majority opinion in *Buckley* quotes an earlier landmark case, *New York Times Co. v. Sullivan*, 376 U.S. 254 (1964).

[46] *Buckley v. Valeo*, 424 U.S. 1 (1976).

tion to make electoral decisions. Most of us might not even know when or how to vote; we would certainly lack basic information about the choices before us.

In this way, campaigns address the information problems discussed at the beginning of this chapter. In mass elections, individual voters have little incentive or opportunity to find information about the many candidates and ballot measures at issue. This situation creates an opportunity for candidates and parties. Through advertising, get-out-the-vote activities, and other campaign efforts, politicians try to shape the electorate and the outcome of the election. Candidates and parties bear much of the responsibility and costs for gathering and disseminating electoral information and for creating an informed electorate. Through their campaigns, parties and candidates present voters with the information they need to make a decision come Election Day—what the candidates and parties have done and what they promise to do, who they are, and which person is right for the job and the challenges the country faces.

Elections, of course, fail to serve this important function when competition is weak or lacking all together. At times in our history, there have been prolonged outages of electoral competition. Perhaps the most infamous example took the form of Democratic dominance in the South from the 1890s through 1960s—a political arrangement termed the Solid South. During this period, election laws were employed to exclude blacks and many poor whites from primary elections, and Republicans comprised a relatively small part of the electorate. As a result, Democrats won nearly every House seat, Senate seat, and gubernatorial race in the South from the end of Reconstruction through the passage of the Voting Rights Act in 1965. In some southern states, Democrats won every state legislative seat. Electoral competition, to the extent that it existed, resided only in the Democratic primary, and then only half of all seats saw competition. Shifting political alignments in the South during the 1960s and 1970s brought a rapid rise in Republican fortunes in the South and with that the benefits of electoral competition.

Today, some observers fear that the incumbency advantage stifles electoral competition. As we noted in the previous section, incumbents enjoy a sizable electoral advantage, a bonus of roughly 10 percentage points. Some of that advantage reflects the voters' reward of the incumbents' performance in office, but some of it may also reflect an imbalance in campaign politics. That imbalance is most obvious in campaign funds. The average House challenger in 2006 raised and spent $430,000; the typical incumbent raised and spent more than three times as much, approximately $1,310,000. To put matters another way, incumbents could spend roughly $2.50 per voting-age person in the district; the typical challenger could spend only $.80 per voting-age person. Incumbents' funding advantages allow them to communicate more extensively with constituents than their opponents.

THE 2008 ELECTION

The 2008 presidential election was in some ways predictable—voters wanted a change from a very unpopular Republican administration and, perhaps predictably, elected a Democrat—but in many ways the 2008 race was a groundbreaking

FIGURE 10.8 DISTRIBUTION OF ELECTORAL VOTES IN THE 2008 PRESIDENTIAL ELECTION

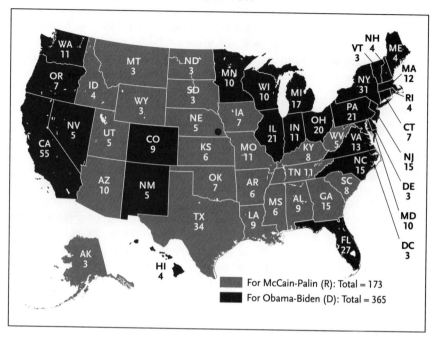

departure from politics as usual. In 2008, for the first time in the nation's history, Americans elected an African American to the White House as the Illinois senator Barack Obama led the Democratic Party to a solid electoral victory, securing 53 percent of the popular vote versus 46 percent for the Republican candidate, Senator John McCain. Obama won a 365-to-173 majority in the electoral college (see Figure 10.8), far more than the 270 electoral votes needed to claim the presidency. The 2008 presidential election was also notable because of the prominence of women candidates. Hillary Clinton's strong campaign for the Democratic nomination shattered the notion that a woman couldn't compete seriously for the nation's highest office, and John McCain's selection of Sarah Palin as his running mate seemed based at least partly on the advantages of having a woman on the ticket. The 2008 campaigns also brought about a significant shift in the electoral map, as states like Virginia and North Carolina that hadn't supported a Democratic candidate in decades went from "red" to "blue."

The Democrats increased their strength in both houses of Congress. The Democratic Party won seven Senate seats previously held by Republicans and lost none of the seats they previously held, giving them an effective majority of 59 to 41.[47] They fell two seats short of sixty, which would be sufficient to close debate if

---

[47] The Minnesota Senate seat was the subject of a contentious recount. The incumbent, Norm Coleman, beat the challenger, Al Franken, by just two hundred votes in the initial count and retabulation. The fate of the seat hung on a few thousand challenged and absentee ballots, and after the recount gave a narrow victory to Franken, legal challenges prevented Franken from taking his seat in the Senate until nearly eight months after Election Day.

the party voted in unison, but the Democrats in the Senate came out of the election with a very substantial majority. The Democrats fared almost as well in the House elections. They captured over two dozen seats previously held by Republicans, mostly open seats and seats defended by Republican freshmen, and the Republicans took five seats from the Democrats. On net, the Democrats added twenty-two seats total to win a 257-to-178 majority in the lower chamber. The defeat of three incumbent Republican senators—Ted Stevens of Alaska, John Sununu of New Hampshire, and Elizabeth Dole of North Carolina—underscored the magnitude of the shift toward the Democrats in 2008. Even the advantages of incumbency could not provide a sufficient levee against the rising tide of the Democratic Party.

The Path to 2008: Modern Electoral Politics and Race

At one level, the 2008 results are not so surprising. The outgoing Republican president George W. Bush had become one of the most unpopular chief executives in American history, the nation seemed mired in never-ending and inconclusive wars in Iraq and Afghanistan, and, to make matters even worse, the nation's fall 2008 financial crisis appeared to presage a deep economic recession. Was there any reason the GOP could even hope to survive the triple whammy of recession, war, and an extraordinarily unpopular Republican president? One reason Republicans might have hoped for survival in 2008 was the matter of race. The Democrat Barack Obama is the son of a black African father and white Kansan mother and was the first nonwhite major party presidential candidate in American history. Given America's tangled racial politics and sometimes violent racial antagonisms, many observers questioned whether white Americans were prepared to elect a black man to the highest office in the land. As late as September 2008, polls showed that more than one third of white Democratic and Independent voters harbored misgivings about the idea of a black president. That tens of millions of whites did vote for the Democratic candidate is a reflection both of Obama's unique attributes and of underlying changes in American race relations over the past several decades.

Race in Twentieth-Century Elections.   To understand the significance of the 2008 election, a bit of political history is in order. The roots of Obama's victory go back nearly half a century to the civil rights movement of the 1960s. In the New Deal era, the majority of northern blacks joined the Democratic Party, which they saw as the party of economic opportunity. Yet in the 1950s and early 1960s, when civil rights protests against the southern system of racial segregation and political exclusion initially broke out in the South, national Democratic leaders were reluctant to commit their support to the black cause. The white South had been a solid Democratic bastion since the end of Reconstruction and was a linchpin of Democratic power in the Congress and the White House. Indeed, during this era, many black Americans believed that the Republican Party, which had no ties to the South, was more likely to take up their cause than the Democrats. In 1960, nearly as many northern black voters cast ballots for Richard Nixon as for John F. Kennedy.

Though Kennedy is often remembered as having been a staunch supporter of civil rights, his administration was cautious and anxious not to offend white southerners. After Kennedy's assassination, Democratic liberals secured the support of

President Lyndon Johnson. Though a southerner, and knowing that his support for black civil rights would alienate the white South, Johnson felt a personal moral commitment to the civil rights cause and was also anxious to win the favor of the upper-middle-class intellectuals and professionals who had been devoted to Kennedy. Prodded by Johnson and against the backdrop of increasingly violent southern resistance to peaceful civil rights protests, Congress enacted the 1965 Voting Rights Act, under whose auspices federal voting officials presided over the registration of millions of African American voters in the former Confederacy.

Democratic support for black voting rights and affirmative action infuriated millions of white southerners and, at the same time, angered many blue-collar northern Democrats over what they saw as preferential treatment for blacks when they themselves were engaged in day-to-day economic struggles. With the Democratic Party divided by racial conflicts and struggles over the Vietnam War, and with Johnson choosing not to run for re-election, the 1968 election was won by the Republican Richard Nixon, who launched what he called his "southern strategy," to bring disaffected southern whites into the Republican camp. Nixon attacked racial preferences and declared that the civil rights movement had gone too far in its demands. In response to Nixon's appeals, millions of southern whites began to shift their political allegiance to the Republican Party.

Ronald Reagan built on but significantly modified Nixon's efforts. After taking office in 1980, Reagan eschewed the sorts of racial appeals that had been made by Nixon eight years earlier. Instead, Reagan used patriotic and religious symbols that would resonate not only among white southerners but also among blue-collar white northerners. Reagan and his advisers turned to "family values" issues, especially abortion, to appeal to Catholic and Protestant religious conservatives in the North and South.

As for the Democrats during this period, the nation's racial politics and racial polarization posed significant political dilemmas, especially at the presidential level. Championing the cause of civil rights had helped Democratic liberals greatly expand their power within the Democratic Party but had undermined the party's fortunes in national presidential elections. Racial divisions were one reason that the Democrats lost seven of ten presidential elections between 1968 and 2004, electing only two presidents in a forty-year period. Efforts by Democratic presidential candidates to rebuild their party's support among southern whites and blue-collar northerners were hampered by the harsh racial arithmetic of American politics. In the wake of the Voting Rights Act, the Democratic Party depended upon African Americans for more than 20 percent of its votes in national presidential elections. Yet at the same time, and for a somewhat larger percentage of Democratic and independent voters, the Democrats relied on whites who, for one or another reason, were unfriendly to blacks.

The 2000 and 2004 Elections.

In 2000 and 2004, George W. Bush generally followed the electoral game plan developed by Ronald Reagan. In 2000, Bush's own ineptitude and general voter satisfaction with the economics, if not the public morality, of the Clinton years, almost cost the Republicans the presidency. In fact, Bush lost the popular vote, but thanks to the vagaries of the electoral college system and the intervention of the Supreme Court, Bush became America's forty-third president.

As president, Bush reacted forcefully to the September 11, 2001, terrorist attacks against the United States and temporarily saw his standing in the polls rise to a stratospheric 90 percent level. Over the next two years, however, sluggish economic growth and the Bush administration's miscues in Iraq seemed to offer the Democrats an opportunity to reclaim the White House. Bush, however, made enormous efforts to register and mobilize the Republican base. Though Bush's dismal performance in the 2004 presidential debates briefly seemed to threaten his reelection, the Republican base rallied to his side and handed him a solid electoral victory.

Virtually unnoticed during the 2000 and 2004 elections, and during Bush's years in office, was a decline in the racial polarization of American politics. Some Americans, to be sure, continued to harbor animosities toward each other, but race seemed to be less salient in the political arena. To some extent, the credit for this development should go to Ronald Reagan. Reagan had made a deliberate decision to drop the racially charged Republican rhetoric of the Nixon years in favor of a focus on patriotism and religious values. This shift in rhetoric was not total and absolute, but it meant that the number of overtly racial appeals and even racial code words found in political debate gradually diminished and that issues of race were gradually deemphasized on the national political battlefield. It was significant that George W. Bush, a conservative president, appointed African Americans, such as the former secretaries of state Colin Powell and Condoleezza Rice and other non-white candidates to high government positions. Democrats accused Bush and the Republicans of racial tokenism, but these tokens were important.

In an atmosphere in which racially charged rhetoric was on the decline, other social processes could begin to have an effect. After the civil rights revolution of the 1960s and the erosion of America's many systems of segregation, both legal and customary, blacks and whites were more likely to live in the same neighborhoods, attend the same schools, work in the same factories and offices, serve in the military together, and frequent the same stores, restaurants, and entertainment venues. For many Americans, the end of segregation opened the way for a gradual lessening of racial antagonisms over the course of several decades. The nation's demographics also changed during this period. A huge influx of immigrants from Latin America as well as Asia and the Middle East meant that America was no longer a land of black and white. It now included many shades of brown as well, complicating the nation's racial divisions. In this new America, explicitly racist appeals from politicians would seem out of step and illegitimate.

The 2008 Campaigns

In this political landscape of shifting race relations and frustration with a Republican administration, Democrats saw that 2008 offered a major opportunity to reclaim the White House. Democratic strategists were determined not to repeat the errors of 2000 and 2004. In the 2006 congressional elections, the Democrats picked up momentum, winning majorities in both houses of Congress for the first time since 1994. By 2006, the electorate was already blaming the GOP for a sluggish economy and seemingly endless war. As voters became increasingly dissatisfied with the policies promoted by President Bush and supported by his Republican allies in Congress, it appeared that the stage was set for a Democratic victory in 2008.

The 2008 Primaries.   The 2008 Democratic and Republican primaries and caucuses to select the parties' candidates for the presidency began January 3 with the Iowa Democratic caucuses. The actual campaigns, of course, began early in 2007, when ambitious politicians assessed their chances and started the long process of raising the tens of millions of dollars required to launch a presidential candidacy. On the Republican side, the front-runner was John McCain. The Arizona senator had campaigned for the Republican nomination in 2000 only to be defeated by Bush in a primary contest remembered for the victor's smear tactics. McCain, the son and grandson of U.S. Navy admirals, was a Vietnam War hero. McCain had a distinguished career in the Senate and was the chief sponsor of several major pieces of legislation, including the McCain-Feingold campaign reform law. Despite his national prominence, McCain was generally not well liked in Republican circles. Traditional business-oriented Republicans might have preferred Mitt Romney, a successful businessman and former governor of Massachusetts, but the GOP's evangelical Protestant cadres did not like the idea of Romney, a Mormon, as their party's candidate. Social conservatives supported the former Arkansas governor and evangelical minister Mike Huckabee, an articulate politician whose sense of humor made him a successful guest on *Saturday Night Live.* Establishment Republicans, however, thought Huckabee was too closely associated with the party's religious element and would have no chance in a national campaign. Other Republicans—Ron Paul, Rudy Giuliani, and Fred Thompson—excited little interest. After losing the Iowa caucuses to Huckabee and struggling to raise money, McCain regained his political and financial footing and was able to drive his opponents from the race. McCain had effectively secured the Republican nomination by the beginning of March.

Clinton versus Obama.   On the Democratic side, the early front-runner for the presidential nomination was the New York senator and former first lady Hillary Rodham Clinton. Senator Clinton was famous, her husband was extraordinarily popular among Democrats, and her contacts and position as a New York senator meant that she would be able to count on tens of millions of dollars in campaign contributions. Most pundits predicted an easy Clinton victory. Other Democratic contenders included the former North Carolina senator and 2004 vice-presidential candidate John Edwards, the former New Mexico governor Bill Richardson, Congressman Dennis Kucinich, the former Alaska senator Mike Gravel, and senators Joe Biden, Chris Dodd, and Barack Obama. Biden, Dodd, and Richardson, along with Gravel and Kucinich, generated relatively little interest and quickly dropped out. Edwards was popular among his fellow trial lawyers, who contributed enough money to his campaign to keep him in through the end of January, though with little chance of success. The surprise of the Democratic primary contest was, of course, the Illinois senator Barack Obama.

Obama was a first-term senator, having arrived in Washington in 2005. He had won a measure of national celebrity by delivering a rousing keynote address at the 2004 Democratic national convention. Many Democrats' first opportunity to see Obama as a serious contender came in the Democratic debates. The Illinois senator was not necessarily more articulate, more knowledgeable, or more passionate about important issues than Clinton, Edwards, and the others, but observers were impressed that at debate after debate the virtually unknown senator stood toe-to-toe with his more seasoned and famous opponents and held his own. Obama's impressive performance electrified liberal Democrats, excited young voters, intrigued the media, and ignited the enthusiasm of black Democrats, even if most were initially dubious that Obama could succeed. This enthusiastic response to Obama's debate appearances swelled the ranks of Obama supporters, inspired donors to write checks, and gave Obama the means to compete against Clinton.

Throughout the primaries, Clinton and Obama battled furiously in state after state. Obama was particularly popular with younger voters and with liberals who resented what they saw as Clinton's early equivocation on the Iraq war. Black politicians—many of whom had considered Bill Clinton an important ally during his presidency—initially supported Hillary Clinton, assuming she would win. But as their constituents rallied to Obama and it became clear that Obama's candidacy actually had a chance, the Illinois senator was able to garner overwhelming black support. Some pundits said it was ironic that the first woman to mount a serious presidential bid and the first black person to mount such a bid were pitted against one another. For the news media, however, in this battle of the firsts. Obama's candidacy was the more important first.

By late spring, it became clear that Obama would be the Democratic presidential nominee. The result was close. Under Democratic rules, 2,118 delegates were needed to win the nomination. In the various primaries and caucuses, Obama had won 1,763 delegates to Clinton's 1,640. This effectively left the decision to the party's 796 "superdelegates," party officials and notables chosen to attend the convention. At the outset, most superdelegates had backed Clinton. As the race wore on, however, sentiment shifted toward Obama. Some saw Obama as the better candidate, while others worried that black Democrats—20 percent of the party's electoral strength—would stay home on Election Day if Obama was denied the nomination. With 438 superdelegates supporting Obama, he could count on 2,201 votes. Clinton briefly weighed taking her candidacy to the floor of the convention to be decided there, but ultimately, on June 3, withdrew and announced that she and her husband would staunchly support Obama in the general election.

The General Election. At the August 2008 Democratic national convention, speaker after speaker extolled Obama's virtues, and even Bill Clinton gave a speech in which he strongly supported Obama. Obama chose the Delaware senator Joseph Biden as his vice-presidential running mate. Biden, chair of the Senate Foreign Relations Committee, was selected at least partly in response to questions about Obama's scant foreign policy experience. In addition, Biden had working-class roots in Pennsylvania. Democrats hoped that Biden would appeal to the so-called Joe Sixpack voters, blue-collar workers whom the Democrats needed in such battleground states as Ohio and Pennsylvania.

The Republican convention, which opened a few days after the Democratic convention ended, began without much fanfare. Although John McCain had won the primary battle and was respected for his military service, he was not an especially beloved figure among rank-and-file Republicans. Nevertheless, McCain energized Republicans when he chose the little-known Alaska governor Sarah Palin as his vice-presidential running mate and "introduced" her to the GOP base at the convention. Palin, a religious conservative who opposed abortion, excited many Republicans who had been cool toward McCain. Unfortunately for the GOP, Palin's star faded rapidly as the inexperienced governor proved unequal to the demands of a national campaign. In television interviews, including one with Katie Couric on CBS, Palin seemed to know little about current political issues and problems and could do no more than repeat Republican talking points that she seemed to have committed to memory. Despite her reasonable performance in the nationally televised vice-presidential debate, Palin was declared "clearly out of her league," even by staunchly Republican commentators, who wondered aloud if Palin could seriously be entrusted with the presidency if anything happened to McCain.

Despite the brief surge of enthusiasm generated by the selection of Palin, the McCain ticket struggled throughout the campaign. From the beginning, the deck seemed stacked against the Republicans. Despite his assertions of independence, the fact remained that McCain was a Republican and, hence, was tied to the Bush administration. Obama and the Democrats, moreover, held an enormous fund-raising advantage over McCain and the Republicans. Knowing that he would have difficulty raising money from traditional GOP donors, McCain had decided to accept public funding for the general election. This would give his campaign some $84 million to spend on organizing, advertising, and voter registration. McCain hoped Republican Party fund-raising would add considerably to this figure. Obama, on the other hand, became the first major party candidate since the law was enacted to forgo general-election public funding. As a consequence, Obama was able to step up his Internet and conventional fund-raising, which eventually produced in the neighborhood of $700 million, an astonishing total that more than doubled the previous record, which had been set by the Republicans in 2004. His campaign's extraordinary fund-raising prowess gave Obama and the Democrats some $200 million more to spend than was available to McCain and the Republicans.

Lack of money was not McCain's only problem. In September 2008, the nation experienced a serious financial crisis that began with a decline in home sales and a wave of mortgage foreclosures and continued with billions of dollars of losses in mortgage-based securities. Since all these events took place while the Republicans controlled the White House, the Democrats were quick to blame the Bush administration's economic policies for the crisis.

The Debates.   Obama helped his cause enormously in the three televised presidential debates held in September and October. He responded with evident knowledge and intelligence to questions on domestic and foreign policy. So, for that matter, did McCain. But McCain, the Washington veteran, was expected to have answers to policy questions. Obama was the newcomer who had been chided for his inexperience. Like Kennedy, Reagan, and Clinton before him, Obama bore the burden of reassuring voters that he measured up to the job of being president. In the debates, Obama spoke clearly and incisively on education, economic policy, health policy, and the wars in Iraq and Afghanistan. Even more important was Obama's manner. By contrast with the often twitchy McCain, Obama was smooth, calm, and reassuring. Many commentators observed that Obama appeared "presidential" and that this helped more and more Americans feel comfortable with his candidacy. Following the debates, Obama's approval ratings rose steadily and the McCain campaign faltered.

Obama's Victory.   Throughout October, Obama consistently led by single-digit margins in the national polls. Given the faltering economy, an unpopular president, and the Democrats' enormous financial advantage, the GOP should have been heading for a train wreck of epic proportions, and yet, until Obama's lead increased in late October, McCain trailed by only three to five points in the polls: Some analysts of opinion data thought the problem was race. A white Democratic candidate, according to some mathematical models of public opinion, would have enjoyed a much stronger lead in the polls, perhaps an additional six or seven points. Some analysts worried whether Obama's lead was even as strong as it looked. These analysts pointed to the so-called Bradley effect, a phantom lead produced when white voters, reluctant to display overt signs of racism, lie to pollsters about their intentions. This is allegedly what happened in 1982, when the Los Angeles mayor Tom Bradley lost the California gubernatorial race after leading his white opponent in the polls.

In the end, racial antipathy did not determine the outcome of the 2008 presidential election. Though many forces were at work, Obama's victory was made possible by the softening of racial antagonisms in the United States over the past half century and the delegitimization of overtly racist rhetoric in the public forum. But the election of a black president does not mean the end of racism in America. Obama is an exceptional individual—a graduate of the Harvard Law School with a white mother, an African rather than an African American father, and raised by white grandparents. Some Democratic canvassers emphasized these facts to white voters, describing their candidate as a man from a multiracial background whose father was an African intellectual, not an American from the inner city.

Does Obama's victory represent the end of racism and the birth of a new America? Or is Obama an exception? Only time will help us to fully understand the significance of the 2008 election.

The 2008 election was remarkable in another respect. It was the highest turnout election in the United States since the 1960s. In 2008, 131 million Americans voted out of approximately 231 million voting-age people in the United States. That translates into a turnout rate of about 57 percent, the highest since 1968, and the continuation of a trend. The percentage of the voting-age population that voted was 49 percent in 1996, 51 percent in 2000, and 55 percent in 2004. The last two elections exhibit a tremendous increase in participation and perhaps, if the pattern continues, a resurgence of electoral participation in the United States.

CONCLUSION: ELECTIONS AND ACCOUNTABILITY

Elections should stir wonder in even the most jaded person. In an election, no one person matters much, and each person acts in apparent isolation, indeed secrecy. The individual voters' decisions reflect diverse experiences, opinions, and preferences about government and public policy. And the millions of votes cumulate into an expression of whom the majority wants to have as its representatives in state government, in Congress, in the presidency.

The design of the institutions of American elections facilitate majority rule. Single-member districts and plurality rule create strong pressures toward a two-party system and majoritarianism. Even in elections in which one party wins a plurality but not a majority, that party typically wins an outright majority of legislative seats. The election itself, then, determines the government. Other systems often produce multiparty outcomes, resulting in a period of negotiation and coalition formation among the parties in order to determine who will govern.

The significance of elections derives not so much from the laws as from the preferences of voters. Voting behavior depends in no small part on habit and the tendency to vote for a given party as a matter of ingrained personal identity. If that were all there is to voting behavior, then it is not clear that elections would provide a meaningful way of governing. Elections would be reduced to little more than a sporting event, in which people merely rooted for their own team. Voters' preferences are as strongly rooted in the issues at hand as in the choices themselves, the candidates. Voting decisions reflect individuals' assessments about whether it makes sense to keep public policies on the same track or to change direction, whether those in office have done a good job and deserve to be reelected, or whether they have failed and it is time for new representation. The aggregation of all voters' preferences responds collectively to fluctuations in the economy, to differences in the ideological and policy orientations of the parties, and to the personal abilities of the candidates.

FOR FURTHER READING

Ansolabehere, Stephen, and James M. Snyder, Jr. *The End of Inequality: One Person, One Vote and the Transformation of American Politics*. New York: Norton, 2008.

Brady, David W. *Critical Elections and Congressional Policy Making*. Palo Alto, Calif.: Stanford University Press, 1988.

Carmines, Edward G., and James A. Stimson. *Issue Evolution: Race and the Transformation of American Politics*. Princeton, N.J.: Princeton University Press, 1989.

Conway, M. Margaret. *Political Participation in the United States*. 3rd ed. Washington, D.C.: Congressional Quarterly Press, 2000.

Fowler, Linda L. *Candidates, Congress, and the American Democracy*. Ann Arbor: University of Michigan Press, 1994.

Gelman, Andrew, et al. *Red State, Blue State, Rich State, Poor State: Why Americans Vote the Way They Do*. Princeton, N.J.: Princeton University Press, 2008.

Ginsberg, Benjamin, and Martin Shefter. *Politics by Other Means: Politicians, Prosecutors, and the Press from Watergate to Whitewater*. 3rd ed. New York: Norton, 2002.

Green, Donald, and Alan Gerber. *Get Out the Vote: How to Increase Voter Turnout*. Washington, D.C.: Brookings Institution, 2004.

reader selection ○ Ifill, Gwen. *The Breakthrough: Politics and Race in the Age of Obama*. New York: Doubleday, 2009.

reader selection ○ Jacobson, Gary. *A Divider, Not a Uniter: George W. Bush and the American People, The 2006 Election and Beyond*. New York: Pearson, 2007.

——— *The Politics of Congressional Elections*. White Plains, N.Y.: Longman, 2008.

Morton, Rebecca B. *Analyzing Elections*. New York: Norton, 2006.

Reichley, A. James, ed. *Elections American Style*. Washington, D.C.: Brookings Institution, 1987.

Rosenstone, Steven, and John Mark Hansen. *Participation, Mobilization, and Democracy in America*. New York: Macmillan, 1993.

Tate, Katherine. *From Protest to Politics: The New Black Voters in American Elections*. Cambridge, Mass.: Harvard University Press, 1994.

Witt, Linda, Karen M. Paget, and Glenna Matthews. *Running as a Woman: Gender and Power in American Politics*. New York: Free Press, 1994.

 Additional study and review materials are available online at wwnorton.com/studyspace/

11

Political Parties

Political parties are defined as teams of politicians, activists, and voters whose goal is to win control of government. They do so by recruiting and nominating candidates to run for office; by accumulating the resources needed to run political campaigns, especially manpower and money; and by pursuing a policy agenda that can appeal to large numbers of voters and secure electoral majorities. As we saw in Chapter 5, once in office, parties organize the legislature and attempt to put their stamp on the laws passed by Congress and the president. Their potential political power is immense.

The prospect of "party rule" has long made Americans suspicious of these organizations. Indeed, the separation of powers into different branches was meant to blunt any attempts by a "faction" or party to gain control of government, as might more readily occur in a parliament.[1] Divided government, in which one party controls the presidency and the other has a majority in at least one chamber of the legislature, has been the norm in American national and state politics, especially over the past fifty years. In some elections, as in 1980, one party wins a landslide victory for the presidency but still fails to capture control of Congress. And, in some midterm elections, as in 1994, 2006, and 2010, the public decides to give control of Congress to the party opposing the president in order to rein in the executive. Our political system intentionally makes it difficult for any party or organized interest to gain complete control of American government, and when one does, unified government is often short lived. Separation of powers and divided government have not, however, put the parties out of business. Quite the contrary.

---

[1] James Madison famously made this argument in *Federalist 51* during the campaign to ratify the Constitution of the United States.

The Democratic and Republican parties remain essential to the day-to-day operation of the legislature and the conduct of elections. It is difficult to imagine how candidates would emerge and how individuals would vote without political parties to organize the electoral system. Our inability to conceive of democracy without parties is not a failure of our imaginations or an accident of American history. Rather, it reflects a law of democratic politics. Parties form to solve key problems of rationality and collective action in a democracy. They are not unlike businesses providing a service that consumers need. Parties offer clear choices to voters, lowering the costs of collecting information about the candidates and making it easier for voters to hold government accountable. Parties also ease the transition from elections to government. They bear the costs of bringing together representatives of disparate constituencies into coherent coalitions that can act collectively in government. Thus, parties link elections to governing. Throughout this chapter we will highlight some of the general functions of parties in any democracy, but we will be especially attentive to party politics in the United States.

CORE OF THE ANALYSIS

- Political parties are teams of politicians, activists, and interest groups organized to win control of government.

- The United States has a two-party system, in which two major parties, Democrats and Republicans, compete for most offices. This is a consequence of the form of government (presidential-congressional as opposed to parliamentary) and election laws, especially the use of single-member legislative districts.

- Parties offer distinctive views about how government ought to operate and what laws ought to be enacted and policies implemented, and they often serve distinct interests and communities.

- Parties help solve an important informational problem for voters. By offering distinctive "brands," the parties simplify the choices that voters must make and reduce the costs of gathering information about how to vote.

- The legislative and executive branches of the U.S. government are organized by the parties, with the party that won a majority of seats controlling most of the key positions and levers of power, especially congressional committees, the congressional agenda, and the appointment of agency heads.

The simplest observation about American parties is also perhaps the most important: the United States has just two major parties, the Democrats and the Republicans. The American two-party system is impressive in its durability and flexibility. Sustained third parties have not been able to compete with the Democrats and Republicans since the 1850s. The Democratic and Republican parties have, for the past 150 years, elected every president and nearly every member of Congress and governor and state legislator in the United States. Occasionally, a governor or legislator decides to run as a third-party candidate, but those independent candidacies usually fail unless the person eventually attaches him- or herself to one of the parties. When a faction breaks from one of the parties, as occurred with the Progressive Republicans in the 1920s and the Southern Democrats in 1948 and again in 1968, those factions eventually return to the fold or move into the other party. The parties have shifted their regional bases of support, with Democrats moving from a southern base to a northern one and the Republicans' base moving from the Northeast and Midwest increasingly to the South. And the two major parties have adapted to radical changes in the ideologies and social structure of American society.

The institutions of a two-party system, combined with majority rule, mean that the choice between the parties translates into the choice of government. Whichever party wins a majority of seats in House or Senate elections wins control of that chamber. Whichever party wins a majority of electoral votes wins the presidency. At election time, we choose between those who are in power and those who would like to be; those who are on the side of the president or the ruling coalition in the legislature, and those opposed to them. Choosing to change the government means voting against the party that currently holds the presidency and Congress.

In contrast, most parliamentary systems, especially those who allocate seats to parties based on the proportion of votes won nationwide, have more than two parties. In such systems, no party regularly wins a majority, and governments consist of coalitions of several parties. It is difficult to anticipate which coalitions might form, and it is hard to assign blame to any one party in a coalition government. There is a great simplicity in having a two-party system.

The Democratic and Republican parties have proved remarkably adept at accommodating diverse sets of interests and ideas while still presenting distinctive visions for governing. They each capture a range of ideological views while keeping successful third parties at bay. This situation arises in large measure because of the electoral and governmental institutions of the United States and the strategic skills of the party leaders. The opportunity for a third party to enter the races and win large numbers of congressional seats or the presidency is very limited.

The French political scientist Maurice Duverger laid out the reason for this state of affairs in his classic book *Political Parties*. As we discussed briefly in Chapter 10, any third-party movement that attempts to enter the American party system would likely fail, or worse, improve the electoral fortunes of the party it most opposes. The American electoral system is winner take all. Whoever gets the most votes wins the congressional seat. Whoever gets the most electoral votes wins the presidency. The Democratic and Republican parties have positioned themselves as center-left and center-right parties, neither extremely liberal nor extremely conservative. The ideological positions they have chosen maintain their policy distinctiveness and still divide the electorate about equally. If, for example, a far-left party (such as the Green Party) decided to make a strong play to win the presidency, it would split votes with the Democratic Party. This would not decrease votes of the Republican Party but would divide the votes of left-leaning voters between the Democrats and the Greens, effectively guaranteeing a Republican victory. A third party that entered in the middle, on the other hand, would be squeezed between the two parties and would have no hope of gaining sufficient support to win. Understanding this situation, most third parties decide to stay out. Getting on the ballot, recruiting candidates, building an organization—all create tremendous costs. The best that the party could do would be to come in a distant third. Even worse, it could cause the major party it likes less to win. Voters also appear to understand this situation. A voter who would normally want to vote for the third party sees that by doing so, he or she ends up boosting the electoral prospects of the major party that he or she favors less.

The same forces are less likely to influence elections in parliamentary systems, or systems that allocate seats in the legislature to parties in proportion to their share of the national vote. In parliaments, if no party wins a majority, the smaller parties can join with larger parties in a coalition. Systems that divvy up power based on the percentage of the vote won, rather than winner take all, occasionally have to form coalitions in order to form a government. That creates an incentive for small parties to fracture off larger parties or to form *de novo*.

Thus, U.S. government institutions and electoral rules create strong pressures to maintain just two parties, distinctive in their plans for governing but expansive in the interests and ideas that they encompass. This simplifies politics inside governing institutions, because one party will have a majority and control that institution (the presidency or one or both chambers of Congress). It also simplifies vote choice, because voters can readily sort into one of the two major party camps or use the party labels to figure out the most effective way to vote.

Parties, however, are not benevolent. They don't solve these problems simply to make democracy work. Those in the party recognize that these problems represent opportunities to secure elected office, to influence public policy, even to make a profit. For the politicians inside these organizations, the parties provide a clear path to office through the nominating system and to power through the party organization. For its activists, the party is a potential way to pull the policies of government in a direction more favorable to the party's views. For interest groups that sustain the parties, the parties offer the potential benefits of being closer to power and influencing what government does. At times, the influence of activists, party leaders, organized interests, and local bosses becomes too great. Regulations on campaign contributions and government contracting, sunshine laws and federal advisory rules, even civil-service reforms have all come about through efforts to prevent party bosses and interest groups from taking advantage of their power. Party organizations have been weakened by these reforms, but they have invariably found new resources to draw on. As a result, American history has witnessed eras of very strong party organization and periods of relative party weakness.

Today, American politics is characterized by relatively strong party organizations and disciplined legislative parties. They offer the American voter meaningful electoral choices and a simple strategy for changing the direction of government.

WHY DO POLITICAL PARTIES FORM?

political party
An organized group that attempts to influence government by electing its members to office.

Political parties, like interest groups, are organizations seeking influence over government. Ordinarily, they can be distinguished from interest groups on the basis of their orientation. A party seeks to control the entire government by electing its members to office, thereby controlling the government's personnel. Interest groups, through campaign contributions and other forms of electoral assistance, are also concerned with electing politicians—in particular, those who are inclined in their policy direction. But interest groups ordinarily do not sponsor candidates directly, and between elections they usually accept government and its personnel as givens and try to influence government policies through them. They are *benefit seekers*, whereas parties are composed mainly of *office seekers*.[2]

Political parties organize because of three problems with which politicians and other political activists must cope. The first is the problem of collective action. This is chiefly an outgrowth of elections in which a candidate for office must attract

---

[2] This distinction is from John H. Aldrich, *Why Parties? The Origin and Transformation of Party Politics in America* (Chicago: University of Chicago Press, 1995).

campaign funds, assemble a group of activists and workers, mobilize prospective voters, and persuade them to vote for him or her. Collective action is also a problem *inside* government, where kindred spirits in a legislature must arrange for, and then engage in, cooperation. The second problem for which parties are sometimes the solution is that of collective choice of policy.[3] The give-and-take within a legislature and between the legislature and the executive can make or break policy success and subsequent electoral success. The third problem follows from the fact that fellow politicians, like members of any organization, seek success simultaneously for the organization and for themselves. This problem of ambition can undermine the collective aspirations of fellow partisans unless astutely managed. We briefly examine each of these problems below.

To Facilitate Collective Action in the Electoral Process

Political parties as we know them today developed along with the expansion of suffrage and can be understood only in the context of elections. Parties and elections are so intertwined that American parties actually take their structure from the electoral process. The shape of party organization in the United States has followed a simple rule: For every district where an election is held, there should be some kind of party unit. These units provide the brand name, the resources—both human and financial—the "buzz," and the link to the larger national organization, which all help the party's candidates arouse interest in their candidacy, stimulate commitment, and ultimately overcome the free riding that diminishes turnout in general elections.

Party organization also enables and encourages electoral competition by groups. The Republican Party has long been the party of business interests (among other groups), especially small business and peak associations (organizations of organizations) such as the Chamber of Commerce and the National Association of Manufacturers. Since the 1930s, women have gravitated to the Democratic Party. Often, groups with significant numbers but lacking substantial economic and institutional resources find their voice in the party system. Women's organizations worked closely with the Progressive faction inside the Republican Party in the 1900s and 1910s in the struggle to gain the right to vote for women. By the 1970s, changing social issues and changed strategies by the parties led many newer womens' groups, such as the National Organization of Women, to align with the Democratic Party. Throughout American history, immigrant groups have aligned themselves with the parties. Irish immigrants attached themselves to the Democrats, whose urban political organizations helped those immigrants find jobs and negotiate the immigration system; Italian immigrants tended toward Republicans; most

---

[3] A slight variation on this theme is emphasized by Gary W. Cox and Mathew D. McCubbins in *Legislative Leviathan: Party Government in the House* (Berkeley: University of California Press, 1993). They suggest that parties in the legislature are electoral machines whose purpose is to preserve and enhance party reputation, thereby giving meaning to the party labels when elections are contested. By keeping order within their ranks, parties make certain that individual actions by members do not discredit the party label. This is an especially challenging task for party leaders when there is diversity within each party, as has often been the case in American political history.

Hispanic groups have gravitated to the Democrats because of its immigration policies; and Cubans aligned with the Republicans because that party took a harder line against the Castro regime. In the 1970s, disaffection with liberal policies concerning school prayer, funding of religious schools, abortion, and other social issues led fundamentalist church leaders to align with the Republican Party. Fundamentalist and born-again Christians became an essential and enduring part of the Republican electoral coalition that Ronald Reagan constructed leading up to the 1980 election.

The relationship between collective action by groups and party electoral strategy is clearly a two-way street. Groups that align with a party provide that party with essential electoral resources, including a reliable voting bloc, money, personnel, and even candidates. When the party they support wins, these interests gain influence over public policy. Of course there are risks as well. An organized interest may suffer if the party it supports loses the election.

To Resolve Collective Choice in the Policy-Making Process

Political parties are also essential elements in the process of making policy. Within the government, parties are coalitions of individuals with shared or overlapping interests who, as a rule, will support each other's programs and initiatives. Even though there may be areas of disagreement within each party, a common party label in and of itself gives party members a reason to cooperate. Because they are permanent coalitions, parties greatly facilitate the policy-making process. If alliances had to be formed from scratch for each legislative proposal, the business of government would slow to a crawl or halt altogether. Parties create a basis for coalition and thus sharply reduce the time, energy, and effort needed to advance a legislative proposal. For example, in January 1998, when President Bill Clinton considered a series of new policy initiatives, he met first with the House and Senate leaders of the Democratic Party. Although some congressional Democrats disagreed with the president's approach to a number of issues, all felt they had a stake in cooperating with Clinton in order to burnish the party's image in preparation for the next round of national elections. Without the support of a party, the president would be compelled to undertake the daunting and probably impossible task of forming a completely new coalition for every policy proposal—a virtually impossible task.

Sometimes party cohesion breaks down because of fundamental conflict between the public philosophy of the party and the need for action on a crucial issue. In September 2008, facing a collapse of the financial industry, President George W. Bush proposed a $700 billion intervention to unlock frozen credit markets. The government needed to act quickly. Democratic leaders in the House twisted enough arms to produce a sizable majority of Democratic votes in favor of the Republican president's plan. The competing presidential nominees, Barack Obama and John McCain, called for colleagues in their respective parties to back the bill. But Republican leadership in the House failed to produce enough Republican votes to pass the measure. Those voting against the bill argued that the plan would increase the size of government, that it rewarded irresponsible investors, and that it violated the free-market principles that lie at the heart of the Republican policy agenda. The failure of the president and his party to come to agreement on this plan in advance doomed the president's proposal. The following day the Dow Jones Industrial Index dropped 777 points, losing almost one-tenth of its value.[4]

To Deal with the Problem of Ambition

Parties are important vehicles that enable individual politicians to achieve their ambitions. The very "brand names" they provide are often a significant electoral asset. Moreover, once their candidates are elected, parties provide these politicians, who share principles, causes, and constituencies, with a basis for coordination, common cause, cooperation, and joint enterprise. But individual ambition, sometimes in the background but often in the foreground, constantly threatens to undermine any bases for cooperation. Political parties, by regulating career advancement, providing for the orderly resolution of ambitious competition, and attending to the postcareer care of elected and appointed party officials, do much to rescue coordination and cooperation and permit fellow partisans to pursue common causes where feasible. Simple devices such as primaries, for example, provide a context in which clashing electoral ambitions can be resolved. Representative partisan bodies, like the Democratic Committee on Committees in the House (with comparable bodies for the Republicans and for both parties in the Senate), resolve competing claims for power positions. In short, politics consists not of foot soldiers walking in lockstep but, rather, of ambitious and autonomous individuals seeking power. The unchecked and unregulated burnishing of individual careers is a formula for chaos and destructive competition in which the dividends of cooperation are rarely reaped. Political parties constitute organizations of relatively kindred spirits who try to capture some of those dividends by providing a structure in which ambition is not suppressed altogether but is not so destructive either.

WHAT FUNCTIONS DO PARTIES PERFORM?

Parties are mainly involved in nominations and elections—providing the candidates for office, getting out the vote, and facilitating mass electoral choice. That is, they help solve the problems of collective action and ambition to which we alluded earlier. They also influence the institutions of government—providing leadership as well as organization of the various congressional committees and activities on the floor in each chamber. That is, they help solve the problem of collective choice concerning institutional arrangements and policy formulation that we also noted earlier.

Recruiting Candidates

One of the most important but least noticed party activities is the recruitment of candidates for local, state, and national office. Each election year, candidates must

---

[4] Carl Hulse and David M. Herszenhorn, "Defiant House Rejects Huge Bailout; Next Step Is Uncertain," *New York Times*, September 29, 2008, www.nytimes.com/2008/09/30/business/30cong.html (accessed 4/3/09).

be found for thousands of state and local offices as well as for congressional seats. Where an incumbent is not running for reelection, party leaders attempt to identify strong candidates and interest them in entering the campaign. One reason for the great success of the Democrats in the 2006 midterm elections was the heightened role played by their campaign committees in the House and Senate and, especially, the active recruitment of new candidates by the chairs of the Democratic Congressional and Senatorial campaign committees.[5] The Democrats were able to recruit well-qualified candidates and to provide them with campaign resources. In 2010, the GOP worked to emulate the Democratic example.

An ideal candidate will have an unblemished record and the capacity to raise enough money to mount a serious campaign. Party leaders are usually not willing to provide financial backing to candidates who are unable to raise substantial funds on their own. For a House seat, this can mean several hundred thousand dollars; for a Senate seat, a serious candidate must be able to raise several million dollars. Often party leaders have difficulty finding attractive candidates and persuading them to run. In recent years, party leaders in several states have reported that many potential congressional candidates declined the opportunity to run for office, saying they were reluctant to leave their homes and families for the hectic life of a member of Congress. Candidate recruitment has become particularly difficult in an era when political campaigns often involve mudslinging and candidates must assume that their personal lives will be intensely scrutinized in the press.[6]

Nominating Candidates

Article I, Section 4, of the Constitution makes only a few provisions for elections. It delegates to the states the power to set the "Times, Places and Manner of holding Elections," even those for U.S. senators and representatives. It does, however, reserve to Congress the power to make such laws if it chooses to do so. The Constitution has been amended from time to time to expand the right to participate in elections. Congress has also occasionally passed laws regulating elections, congressional districting, and campaign practices. But the Constitution and the laws are almost completely silent on nominations, setting only citizenship and age requirements for candidates. The president must be at least thirty-five years of age, a natural-born citizen, and a resident of the United States for fourteen years. A senator must be at least thirty, a U.S. citizen for at least nine years, and a resident of the state he or she represents. A member of the House must be at least twenty-five, a U.S. citizen for seven years, and a resident of the state he or she represents.

Nomination is the process by which a party selects a single candidate to run for each elective office. Nomination is the parties' most serious and difficult business.

nomination The process by which political parties select their candidates for election to public office.

---

[5] See Adam Nagourney, "Eyeing '08: Democrats Nurse Freshmen at Risk," *New York Times*, December 22, 2006.

[6] For an excellent analysis of the parties' role in recruitment, see Paul S. Herrnson, *Congressional Elections: Campaigning at Home and in Washington* (Washington, D.C.: Congressional Quarterly Press, 1995).

FIGURE 11.1 TYPES OF NOMINATING PROCESSES

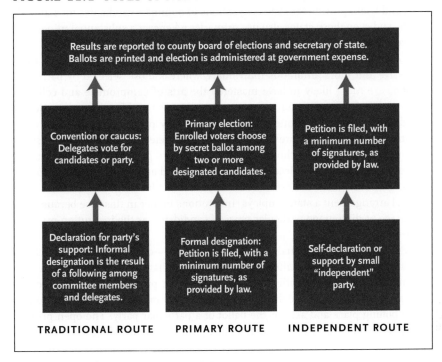

The nominating process can precede the election by many months (Figure 11.1), as it does when the many candidates for the presidency are eliminated from consideration through a grueling series of debates and state primaries until there is only one survivor in each party—that party's nominee.

Nomination by Convention. A nominating convention is a formal caucus bound by a number of rules that govern participation and nominating procedures. Conventions are meetings of delegates elected by party members from the relevant county (a county convention) or state (a state convention). Delegates to each party's national convention (which nominates the party's presidential candidate) are chosen by party members on a state-by-state basis; there is no single national delegate selection process.

Nomination by Primary Election. In primary elections, party members select the party's nominees directly rather than selecting convention delegates who then select the nominees. Primaries are far from perfect replacements for conventions because it is rare that more than 25 percent of the enrolled voters participate. Nevertheless, they have replaced conventions as the dominant method of nomination.[7]

---

[7] For a discussion of some of the effects of primary elections, see Peter F. Galderisi and Benjamin Ginsberg, "Primary Elections and the Evanescence of Third Party Activity in the United States," in *Do Elections Matter?* Benjamin Ginsberg and Alan Stone, eds. (Armonk, N.Y.: Sharpe, 1986), pp. 115–30.

At the present time, only a small number of states, including Connecticut, Delaware, and Utah, provide for state conventions to nominate candidates for statewide offices, and even those states also use primaries whenever a substantial minority of delegates has voted for one of the defeated aspirants.

Generally speaking, candidates chosen in primary elections tend to be more aggressive and more ambitious individuals, whereas those selected by party conventions are more likely to have mastered the arts of compromise and collegiality. The shift from party conventions to primary elections for the nomination of presidential candidates is one reason contemporary presidents tend to be more ambitious and, indeed, more driven than their nineteenth-century predecessors. Party conventions tend to choose candidates who can get along, whereas primary elections tend to favor politicians with the energy and enterprise to mount a public campaign.[8] Thus there is a "selection" effect that results from the particular institutional arrangement a state employs. Institutions matter in this case because they encourage or discourage particular types of candidates, as the institution principle suggests.

Primary elections fall mainly into two categories—closed and open. In a **closed primary**, participation is limited to individuals who have previously declared their affiliation by registering with the party. In an **open primary**, individuals declare their party affiliation on the day of the primary election. To do so, they simply go to the polling place and ask for the ballot of a particular party. The open primary allows each voter to consider candidates and issues before deciding whether to participate and in which party's contest to participate. Open primaries, therefore, are less conducive to strong political parties. But in either case, primaries are more open than conventions or caucuses to new issues and new types of candidates.

Getting Out the Vote

The election period begins immediately after the nominations. Historically, this has been a time of glory for the political parties, whose popular base of support is fully displayed. All the paraphernalia of party committees and all the committee members are activated in the form of local party workforces.

The first step in the electoral process involves voter registration. This aspect of the process takes place all year round. There was a time when party workers were responsible for virtually all of this kind of electoral activity, but they have been supplemented (and in many states virtually displaced) by civic groups such as the League of Women Voters, unions, and chambers of commerce.

Those who have registered have to decide on Election Day whether to go to the polling place, stand in line, and vote for the various candidates and referendums on the ballot. Political parties, candidates, and campaigning can make a big difference in persuading eligible voters to vote. Because it is costly for voters to participate in elections and because many of the benefits that winning parties bestow are public goods (that is, parties cannot exclude any individual from enjoying them), people

closed primary
A primary election in which voters can participate in the nomination of only those candidates of the party in which they have been enrolled for a period of time before primary day.

open primary
A primary election in which voters can choose on the day of the primary which party to enroll in to select candidates for the general election.

---

[8] Matthew Crenson and Benjamin Ginsberg, *Presidential Power: Unchecked and Unbalanced* (New York: Norton, 2007).

will often free ride by enjoying the benefits without incurring the costs of electing the party that provided the benefits. This is the free-rider problem (see Chapter 1), and parties are important because they help overcome it by mobilizing the voters to support the candidates.

In recent years, not-for-profit groups such as America Votes and MoveOn have registered and mobilized large numbers of people to vote and raised millions of dollars to devote to election organizing and advertising. These groups have legions of workers, often volunteers, and have proved especially effective at using new technologies to build networks of supporters and communicate through those networks. They are the "netroots" organizations of politics. To comply with federal election and tax law, these groups must maintain their independence from the political parties, although they have the same objectives as the parties and work very hard to elect politicians from just one party. Such organizations act as shadow appendages of the two parties, with some groups mobilizing Democratic supporters and others mobilizing Republicans. They proved vitally important in the political campaigns of 2004, 2006, and 2008. Since 2000 there has been a noticeable uptick in turnout in the United States, possibly attributable to the new partisan netroots organizations.

Facilitating Mass Electoral Choice

Parties make the electoral choice much easier. It is often argued that we should vote for the best person regardless of party affiliation. But on any general-election ballot, there are likely to be only two or three candidacies for which the characteristics and policy positions of the candidates are well-known to the voters. Without party labels, voters would be constantly confronted by a bewildering array of new faces and new choices and might have considerable difficulty making informed decisions. Without a doubt, their own party identifications and candidates' party affiliations help voters make reasonable choices.

Parties lower the information costs of participating by providing a recognizable "brand name." Without knowing a great deal about a candidate for office, voters can infer from party labels how the candidate will likely behave once elected. Individuals know about the parties through their past experience with those parties in state and federal office and from the actions of prominent political leaders from both parties. In the United States, the Democratic Party is associated with a commitment to more extensive government regulation of the economy and a larger public sector; the Republican Party favors a limited government role in the economy and reduced government spending paired with tax reductions. The Democrats favor aggressive protection of civil rights and a secular approach to religion in public life. The Republican Party wants to ban abortion and favors government participation in expanding the role of religious organizations in civil society. The parties' positions on the economy were cemented in the 1930s, and their division over civil society emerged during the 1960s and 1970s. The Democratic positions are loosely labeled liberal and those of the Republicans conservative.

Most Americans personally identify with one of the two parties. When asked in surveys whether they think of themselves as Democrats or as Republicans or neither, large majorities pick one of the two major parties. When voting, those who identify with a party are extremely likely to vote with that party (usually about

90 percent of the time). For these individuals, party simplifies the electoral decision. Except in rare circumstances, they vote with their team.

Even those who do not identify with one of the major parties derive value from the party labels. Nonpartisan voters are more conflicted about which party or candidate best represents their interests and ideals. But it would be the height of folly to try to learn about every politician running for every office. A voter would spend an enormous amount of time tracking down the information about dozens of different people. And if the entire electorate behaved this way, the advertising costs to politicians would be tremendous.

Party labels simplify the decision making of nonpartisan voters by reducing the choice to an evaluation of two competing policy positions or of the evaluation of the performance of those in office. The independent voter may ask, Which of the two parties will better represent my ideals and interests? The voter will choose the party that offers the best option today. Or the voter may ask, Am I better off now than four years ago? If not, he or she will vote against the president's party up and down the ballot. If yes, he or she will vote to keep the president and his party in power. Whichever strategy the independent voter uses, parties are essential for simplifying what is otherwise a bewildering choice.

For all voters, partisans and independents alike, the parties make it easier to hold government accountable. People can vote against the party in power in bad times and for the party in power in good times. They can vote against the party in power if that party enacts very unpopular or irresponsible legislation. Thus political parties solve one of the most important collective-action problems facing American democracy, the problem of collective responsibility. If every politician ran on his or her own, without regard to other candidates or districts or what was happening in the nation at large, each race for legislator or executive would become an isolated event. In such a setting it would be exceedingly difficult for voters to send a message to the government that they want government to go in a different direction. Parties, then, lend coherence to government and meaning to elections.[9]

The content of the labels is sustained because like-minded people sort themselves into the respective organizations. People who broadly share the principles espoused by a party and who wish to participate on a high level in politics will attend party meetings, run for leadership positions in local and state party organizations, attend state and national conventions, and even run for elected office. Surveys of those who attend national conventions as delegates and of candidates for the U.S. House find that Democratic candidates' personal views on the economy and social issues are quite liberal and that Republican candidates hold very conservative personal views on these matters.[10] Each party, then, draws on a distinct pool for activists and candidates. Each successive election reinforces the existing division between the parties.

---

[9] Morris Fiorina, "The Decline of Collective Responsibility in American Politics," *Daedalus* 109, no. 3 (Summer 1980): 25–45.

[10] Comprehensive studies of delegates were conducted by Walter J. Stone and Ronald B. Rapoport from 1980 through 1996. See Ronald B. Rapoport and Walter J. Stone, *Three's A Crowd: The Dynamic of Third Parties, Ross Perot, and Republican Resurgence* (Ann Arbor: University of Michigan Press, 1999). Surveys of candidates find similar sorting.

Influencing National Government

The ultimate test of the party system is its relationship to and influence on the institutions of government and the policy-making process. Thus it is important to examine the party system in relation to Congress and the president.

Parties and Policy.   One of the most familiar observations about American politics is that the two major parties are "big tents." They position themselves to bring in as many groups and ideas as possible. The parties make such broad coalitions as a matter of strategy, much as businesses purchase other companies to expand their market share. Positioning themselves as broad coalitions prevents effective national third parties from emerging and guarantees that the Democrats and Republicans vie for control of Congress.

The coalitions that come together in the Democratic and Republican parties shape the parties' platforms on public policy. The political coalitions that party leaders assemble determine what interests and social groups align with the parties, and also what sorts of issues can emerge. The Democratic Party today embraces a philosophy of active government intervention in the economy, based on the premise that regulation is necessary to ensure orderly economic growth, to prevent the emergence of monopolies, and to address certain costs of economic activity, such as pollution. In addition, the Democratic Party pushes for aggressive expansion and protection of civil rights, especially for women and racial minorities. The Republican Party espouses a philosophy of laissez-faire economics and a minimal government role in the economy. The coalition that Ronald Reagan built in the late 1970s paired this vision of limited government intervention in the economy with an expanded role for religion in society and strong opposition to immigration, affirmative action, and abortion.

To many European observers, the American parties appear as odd amalgams of contradictory ideas. Liberalism, as it developed as a political philosophy in Europe, naturally pairs laissez-faire economics with liberal views on civil rights. Conservatism, which maintains a respect for social and political order, would speak for a stronger role for social organizations in society, especially religions; a greater respect for existing social hierarchies, most notably social classes and higher-educated elites; and government power in the economy. The American parties, partly because of their histories, have scrambled these traditional views and developed their own political philosophies. In the Republican Party today, laissez-faire economics goes hand in hand with conservative views on civil rights and religion in society. In the Democratic Party today, liberal views on civil rights are tied to an expansive view of government in the economy. The American parties have mixed and matched different ideas as new issues have emerged and as leaders within the parties have seized opportunities. The New Deal coalition that President Franklin Delano Roosevelt assembled consisted of Progressive Republicans, who favored greater economic regulation; old-line Democrats, especially in the South; and urban political machines in northern and Midwestern cities. This peculiar coalition gave rise to the political philosophy and public policies pursued under the New Deal. It also constrained what Roosevelt could do on some issues. Most important, he could not push for expanding civil rights for blacks without losing the support of southerners. The meaning of Democratic liberalism in the United States, then, was very much a function of the history of the parties.

Even though American liberalism and conservatism do not coincide neatly with their European counterparts, they still represent distinct views about how government ought to act, and they appeal to distinctly different core constituencies. The Democratic Party at the national level seeks to unite organized labor, the poor, members of racial minorities, and liberal upper-middle-class professionals. The Republicans, by contrast, appeal to business, upper-middle- and upper-class groups in the private sector, and social conservatives. Often party leaders will seek to develop issues that they hope will add new groups to their party's constituent base. During the 1980s, for example, under the leadership of President Reagan, the Republicans devised a series of "social issues," including support for school prayer, opposition to abortion, and opposition to affirmative action, designed to cultivate the support of white southerners. This effort was extremely successful in increasing Republican strength in the once solidly Democratic South. In the 1990s, under the leadership of President Clinton, who called himself a "new Democrat," the Democratic Party sought to develop social programs designed to solidify the party's base among working-class and poor voters and somewhat conservative economic programs aimed at attracting the votes of middle- and upper-middle-class voters.

As these examples suggest, parties do not always support policies because they are favored by their constituents. Instead, party leaders can play the role of policy entrepreneurs, seeking ideas and programs that will expand their party's base of support while eroding that of the opposition. In recent years, for example, leaders of both major political parties have sought to develop ideas and programs they hoped would appeal to America's most rapidly growing electoral bloc: Latino voters. Thus President George W. Bush recommended a number of proposals designed to help Latinos secure U.S. residence and employment. Democrats, for their part, have proposed education and social service programs designed to appeal to the needs of Latino immigrants. Both parties promoted their ideas extensively within the Latino community in the 2004 presidential campaign, and although the Democrats won more Latino votes in 2004, each party claimed to be satisfied with its long-term strategy for building Latino support. The 2006 election campaign, however, produced much more one-sided results. A hard-line view on immigration, especially from Latin America, put Republicans at a competitive disadvantage. Democratic support among Latinos rose dramatically in the midterm elections, and several prominent Republican incumbents in the Southwest lost their seats as a result. The 2008 election saw a continuation of the pattern from 2006. Exit polls revealed that Democrats won 66 percent of Hispanics, a huge swing from 2004, and Hispanics continued their steady rise as a percentage of all voters. In 2000, one out of five voters was Hispanic or black; in 2008, one out of four voters was Hispanic or black.

It is one of the essential characteristics of party politics in America that a party's programs and policies often lead, rather than follow, public opinion. Like their counterparts in the business world, party leaders seek to identify and develop "products" (programs and policies) that will appeal to the public. The public, of course, has the ultimate voice. With its votes, it decides whether or not to "buy" the new policy offerings.

Through members elected to office, both parties have made efforts to translate their general goals into concrete policies. Republicans, for example, implemented tax cuts, increased defense spending, cut social spending, and enacted restrictions on abortion during the 1980s and 1990s. Democrats were able to defend consumer and environmental programs against GOP attacks and sought to expand domestic social programs in the late 1990s. During his two terms in office, President George W. Bush sought substantial cuts in federal taxes, "privatization" of the Social Security system, and a larger role for Republican-allied faith-based organizations in the administration of federal social programs. In the context of the nation's campaign against terrorism, Bush sought to shift America's defense posture from an emphasis on deterrence to a doctrine of preemptive strikes against perceived threats.

The Parties and Congress.   Congress, in particular, depends more on the party system than is generally recognized. First, the speakership of the House is essentially a party office. All the members of the House take part in the election of the Speaker, but the actual selection is made by the **majority party**. When the majority party caucus presents a nominee to the entire House, its choice is invariably ratified in a straight party-line vote.

The committee system of both houses of Congress is also a product of the two-party system. Although the rules organizing committees and the rules defining the jurisdiction of each committee are adopted like ordinary legislation by the whole membership, all other features of the committees are shaped by the parties. For example, each party is assigned a quota of members for each committee, depending on the percentage of total seats held by the party. On the rare occasions when an independent or third-party candidate is elected, the leaders of the two parties must agree against whose quota this member's committee assignments will count. Presumably, the member will not be able to serve on any committee until the question of quota is settled.[11]

As we saw in Chapter 5, the assignment of individual members to congressional committees is a party decision. Each party has a "committee on committees" to make such decisions. Whether to grant permission to transfer to another committee is also a party decision. Moreover, who will advance up the committee ladder toward the chair is a party decision. Since the late nineteenth century, most advancements have been automatic, based on the length of continuous service on the committee. This seniority system has survived only because of the support of the two parties, and each party can depart from it by a simple vote. During the 1970s, both parties reinstituted the practice of reviewing each chairmanship, voting anew every two years on whether each chair would be continued. In 2001, Republicans lived up to their 1995 pledge to limit House committee chairs to three terms. Existing chairs were forced to step down but were generally replaced by the next most senior Republican member of each committee. (Even after they were reduced to minority status in the 2006 elections, Republicans stuck to this policy. Republican chairs in the 109th Congress who had served three terms were not permitted to serve as ranking minority member in the 110th Congress.)

majority party
The party that holds the majority of legislative seats in either the House or the Senate.

---

[11] Scott A. Frisch and Sean Q. Kelly, *Committee Assignment Politics in the U.S. House of Representatives* (Norman: University of Oklahoma Press, 2006).

President and Party.   As we saw earlier, the party that wins the White House is always led, in title anyway, by the president. The president normally depends on fellow party members in Congress to support legislative initiatives. At the same time, members of the president's party in Congress hope that the president's programs and personal prestige will help them raise campaign funds and secure reelection. During his two terms in office, President Clinton had a mixed record as party leader. In the realm of trade policy, Clinton sometimes found more support among Republicans than among Democrats. In addition, although Clinton proved to be an extremely successful fund-raiser, congressional Democrats often complained that he failed to share his largesse with them. At the same time, however, a number of Clinton's policy initiatives seemed calculated to strengthen the Democratic Party as a whole. Clinton's early health-care initiative would have linked millions of voters to the Democrats for years to come, much as Franklin Roosevelt's Social Security program had done in a previous era. But by the middle of Clinton's second term, the president's acknowledgement of his sexual affair with a White House intern threatened his position as party leader. Initially, Democratic candidates nationwide feared that the scandal would undermine their chances for election, and many moved to distance themselves from the president. Nonetheless, the Democrats' surprisingly good showing in the 1998 elections strengthened Clinton's position and gave him another chance to shape the Democratic agenda.

Between the 1998 and 2000 elections, however, the president's initiatives on Social Security and nuclear disarmament failed to make much headway in a Republican-controlled Congress. The GOP was not prepared to give Clinton anything for which Democrats could claim credit in the 2000 elections. Lacking strong congressional leadership, however, the GOP did agree to many of Clinton's budgetary proposals in 1999 and dropped its own plan for large-scale cuts in federal taxes.

When he assumed office in 2001, President George W. Bush called for a new era of bipartisan cooperation, and the new president did receive the support of some Democratic conservatives. Generally, however, Bush depended on near-unanimous backing from his own party in Congress to implement his plans for cutting taxes as well as other elements of his program. After the terrorist attacks of September 11, both parties united behind Bush's military response. By the end of the president's first term, however, the parties were sharply divided on the administration's policies in Iraq, economic policy, Social Security reform, abortion, other social issues, and the need for enhanced governmental law-enforcement powers to combat terrorism. Ultimately, Bush relied mainly on Republican support to achieve his goals.

PARTIES AND THE ELECTORATE

party identification An individual voter's psychological ties to one party or another.

Political parties are more than just organizations and leaders; they are made up of millions of rank-and-file members. As we saw in Chapter 10's discussion of elections, individual voters tend to develop **party identification** with one of the political parties. Party identification partly reflects a psychological attachment developed in childhood or adolescence and carried throughout life. Party identification also has a rational component, rooted in evaluations of the performance of the parties in government, the policies they will pursue, and an individual's interest and ideology.[12] Voters generally form attachments to parties that reflect their views and interests. Once those attachments are formed, however, they are likely to persist and even be handed down to children unless some very strong factors convince individuals that their party is no longer an appropriate object of their affections. In some sense, party identification is similar to brand loyalty in the marketplace: Consumers choose a brand of automobile for its appearance or mechanical characteristics and stick with it out of loyalty, habit, and unwillingness to reexamine their choices constantly, but they may eventually switch if the old brand no longer serves their interests.

Although the strength of partisan ties in the United States seems to have declined in the 1960s and 1970s, most Americans continue to identify with either the Republican Party or the Democratic Party (Figure 11.2). The "Analyzing the Evidence" unit in this chapter takes a closer look at how political scientists study trends in partisanship. Party identification gives citizens a stake in election outcomes that goes beyond the race at hand. This is why strong party identifiers (that is, people who identify strongly with one party) are more likely than other Americans to go

FIGURE 11.2 AMERICANS' PARTY IDENTIFICATION

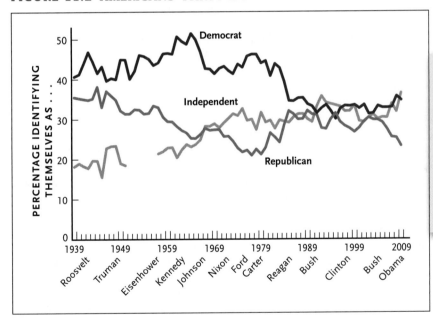

SOURCE: "Party Identification Trend," Pew Research Center for the People & the Press, http://people-press.org/party-identification-trend (accessed 7/1/09).

ANALYZING THE EVIDENCE

In 1952, Democrats outnumbered Republicans nearly two to one. Today, the two parties appear to have nearly equal numbers of loyalists. What factors might account for this partisan transformation?

---

[12] For what is perhaps still the best discussion of the bases of party identification, see Arthur S. Goldberg, "Social Determinism and Rationality as Bases of Party Identification," *American Political Science Review* 63, no. 1 (March 1969): 5–25. For a more recent article weighing in on economic versus social determinants of party attachments, see Larry M. Bartels, "What's the Matter with *What's the Matter with Kansas?*" *Quarterly Journal of Political Science* 1 (2006): 201–26.

party activist
A partisan who contributes time, energy, and effort to support a party and its candidates.

to the polls and, of course, are more likely than others to support the party with which they identify. **Party activists** are drawn from the ranks of the strong identifiers. Activists are those who not only vote but also contribute their time, energy, and effort to party affairs. Activists ring doorbells, stuff envelopes, attend meetings, and contribute money to the party cause. No party could succeed without the thousands of volunteers who undertake the mundane tasks needed to keep the organization going. It is worth noting that attachment to a party does not guarantee voting for that party's candidates, though it does reflect a tendency. Strong identifiers do so almost always, and weak identifiers do most of the time.

Group Affiliations

The Democratic and Republican parties are America's only national parties. They are the only political organizations that draw support from most regions of the country and from Americans of every racial, economic, religious, and ethnic group. The two parties do not draw equal support from members of every social stratum, however. When we refer to the Democratic or Republican coalition, we mean the groups that generally support one or the other party. In the United States today, a variety of group characteristics are associated with party identification. These include race and ethnicity, gender, religion, class, ideology, and region.

Race and Ethnicity.   Since the 1930s and Franklin Roosevelt's New Deal, African Americans have been overwhelmingly Democratic in their party identification. More than 90 percent of African Americans describe themselves as Democrats and support Democratic candidates in national, state, and local elections. Approximately 25 percent of the Democratic Party's support in presidential races comes from African American voters.

Latino and Hispanic voters consist of people whose ancestors came from many different countries, with disparate political orientations. Mexican Americans are the single largest group. They have historically aligned with the Democratic Party, as have Puerto Ricans and Central Americans. Historically, Cuban Americans have voted heavily and identified as Republican. Over the past five years, however, Cubans have exhibited a rapid shift toward the Democratic Party. This trend appears to reflect generational differences, as younger Cuban Americans look to be as Democratic as other Hispanic and Latino groups. Asian Americans tend to be divided as well. Japanese, Chinese, Filipino, and Korean communities have been long established in the United States and have influential business communities. Higher-income Asians tend to be as Republican as higher-income whites. It is not clear whether newer Asian immigrant groups, such as the Hmong, the Vietnamese, Thais, and Indians, will follow the same trajectory as the Japanese and Chinese communities.

gender gap   A distinctive pattern of voting behavior reflecting the differences in views between women and men.

Gender.   Women are somewhat more likely to support Democrats, and men are somewhat more likely to support Republicans, in surveys of party identification and voting. This difference is known as the **gender gap**. It is somewhat new in American politics. Early studies of the women's vote in the 1920s, shortly after the extension of the franchise, found little difference in voting behavior between men and women. If anything, women tended to be slightly more Republican, and they more strongly favored the prohibition of alcohol than men did. The modern gender gap emerged full fledged in the 1980 presidential election and has ranged from a difference of 4 percentage points in how men and women voted in 1992 to a high of 11 percentage points in 1996. In the 2008 election, Barack Obama won 56 percent of the vote of women and 49 percent of the vote of men, a seven-point gap.[13]

Religion. Jews are among the Democratic Party's most loyal constituent groups and have been since the New Deal. Nearly 90 percent of all Jewish Americans describe themselves as Democrats, although the percentage is declining among younger Jews. Catholics were once a strongly pro-Democratic group as well but have been shifting toward the Republican Party since the 1970s, when the GOP began to focus on abortion and other social issues deemed important to Catholics. Protestants are more likely to identify with the Republicans than with the Democrats. Protestant fundamentalists, in particular, have been drawn to the GOP's conservative stands on social issues, such as school prayer and abortion. The importance of religious conservatives to the Republican Party became quite evident in 2001. After his victory in the 2000 election, George W. Bush announced that his administration would seek to award federal grants and contracts to religious groups. By using so-called faith-based groups as federal contractors, Bush was seeking to reward religious conservatives for their loyalty to the GOP and to ensure that they would have a continuing stake in Republican success.

Class. Upper-income Americans are considerably more likely to affiliate with the Republicans, whereas lower-income Americans are far more likely to identify with the Democrats. This divide reflects the differences between the two parties on economic issues. In general, the Republicans support cutting taxes and social spending—positions that reflect the interests of the wealthy. The Democrats, however, favor increased social spending, even if this requires increasing taxes—a position consistent with the interests of less-affluent Americans. One important exception to this principle is that relatively affluent individuals who work in the public sector or such related institutions as foundations and universities also tend to affiliate with the Democrats. Such individuals are likely to appreciate the Democratic Party's support for an expanded role of government and high levels of public spending. White voters with less than a college education (a measure of class) have become less strongly affiliated with the Democrats over time, but this trend is restricted almost entirely to the South. (Outside the South, voters with less than a college education have declined in their support of Democratic presidential candidates by only one percentage point in the last fifty years.)[14]

Ideology. Ideology and party identification are very closely linked. Most individuals who describe themselves as conservatives identify with the Republican Party,

---

[13] Susan Carroll, *Women and American Politics: New Questions, New Directions* (Oxford: Oxford University Press, 2003).

[14] Andrew Gelman et al., *Red State, Blue State, Rich State, Poor State: Why Americans Vote the Way They Do* (Princeton, N.J.: Princeton University Press, 2008).

FIGURE 11.3 PARTY IDENTIFICATION BY SOCIAL GROUPS, 2008

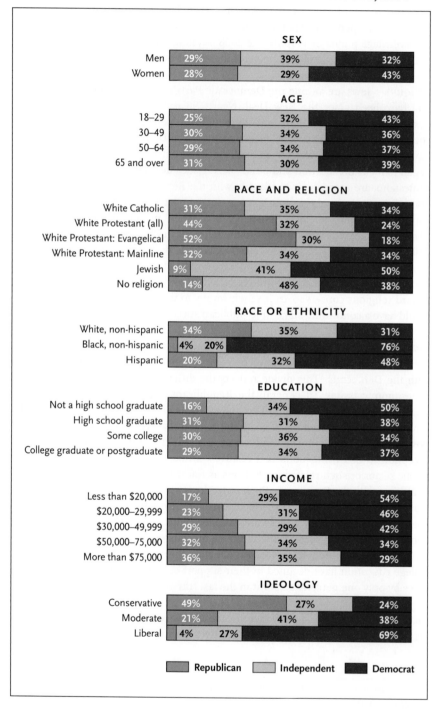

SOURCE: "November 2008 Election weekend survey," Pew Research Center for the People and the Press, October 28, 2008, http://people-press.org/.

whereas most who call themselves liberals support the Democrats. This division has increased in recent years as the two parties have taken very different positions on social and economic issues. Before the 1970s, when party differences were more blurred, it was not uncommon to find Democratic conservatives and Republican liberals. Both of these species are rare today. The Voting Rights Act of 1965 was a watershed event in American politics. Over the next two decades, African American voting in the South grew dramatically, and Republicans began offering southern whites alternatives to the Democratic Party. One consequence is that each party became clearer ideologically, leaving little room for conservative Democrats or moderate Republicans.

Region.   Between the Civil War and the 1960s, the "Solid South" was a Democratic bastion. Today much of the South has become solidly Republican, as have much of the West and Southwest. The area of greatest Democratic Party strength is the Northeast. The Midwest is a battleground, more or less evenly divided between the two parties.

The explanations for these regional variations are complex. Southern Republicanism has come about because conservative white southerners identify the Democratic Party with the civil rights movement and liberal positions on abortion, school prayer, and other social issues. Republican strength in the South and the West is related to the weakness of organized labor in these regions, as well as to the dependence of the two regions on military programs supported by the Republicans. Democratic strength in the Northeast is a function of the continuing influence of organized labor in the large cities of this region, as well as the region's large population of minority and elderly voters, who benefit from Democratic social programs. In the 2006 and 2008 elections, one of the biggest shifts toward the Democrats occurred in the Rocky Mountain West, where Democrats unexpectedly won a number of congressional races and governorships. This trend reflects in part the shift in the population to this region, including in particular people who value the environment and demand public services.

Age.   Age is another factor associated with partisanship. At the present time, individuals younger than fifty are fairly evenly divided between Democrats and Republicans, whereas those older than fifty are much more likely to be Democrats. There is nothing about a particular numerical age that leads to a particular party loyalty. Instead, individuals from the same age cohort are likely to have experienced a similar set of events during the period when they formed their party loyalties. Thus Americans between the ages of fifty and sixty-four came of political age during the Cold War, the Vietnam War, and the civil rights movement, and those older than sixty-five are the product of the Great Depression and World War II. Apparently among voters whose initial perceptions of politics were shaped during these periods, more responded favorably to the role played by the Democrats than to the actions of the Republicans. It is interesting that among the youngest group of Americans, a group that came of age during an era of political scandals that tainted both parties, the majority describe themselves as independents.

Figure 11.3 indicates the relationship between party identification and a number of social criteria. Race, religion, and income seem to have the greatest influence

How Stable Is Party Identification?

An individual's identification with a party, Democratic or Republican, is thought to be a fundamental psychological attachment and, thus, extremely stable from year to year and election to election. Yet, as we saw in Figure 11.2. Substantial changes in the percentage of people who identify with one of the two parties do occur. Particularly large changes in party identifications occurred in the mid-1960s and the early 1980s, and between 2005 and 2008. Here lies a puzzle. If individuals' party attachments are stable, why do the aggregate percentages of people who identify with one party or the other vary so much?

Two distinct arguments are often proposed to explain this puzzle and account for broad trends in partisanship. (1) *Generational replacement* may account for the change. By this account, individual party identifications don't change much throughout one's adulthood, but the composition of the electorate changes as new generations emerge and older generations fade. (2) *Conversion* of individuals from one party to the other from one election to the next may contribute to fluctuations in aggregate trends in party attachments. It may be the case that party identification is less stable than political scientists have thought, and that people do change their party allegiances in response to immediate political choices offered by the parties and their assessments of the current president.

Political scientists measure changes in individuals' opinions and attitudes using panel surveys of the same individuals at different points in time. The Cooperative Congressional Election Study conducted an annual survey of the same 2,000 people in 2006, 2007, and 2008, a period that overlaps with the most recent significant shift in party identifications (between 2005 and 2008). The table to the right shows how people changed from 2006 to 2008. Each row of the table shows the identities of respondents in 2006. The percentages in each row show the loyalty and defection rates of those people, that is, the percent of those with a given identity in 2006 who stayed with that identity in

▶

TRANSITIONS FROM 2006 to 2008

		2008 Party Identification		
		D	**I**	**R**
2006 Party Identification	**D**	89%	8%	3%
	I	20%	72%	8%
	R	4%	14%	82%

2008 or chose an alternate identification. The partisans are quite loyal, with 89 percent of Democrats and 82 percent of Republicans maintaining their loyalties. There is also very little switching between parties, and it appears to be symmetric—approximately the same percent switch from D to R as from R to D (about 3–4 percent). Most of the defection from each of the two parties is to the category of Independent, with Republicans becoming Independents at a much higher rate than Democrats (14 percent versus 8 percent). And Independents are the source of the uptick in Democratic identifications.

Can the decline in Republican identification between 2000 and 2008 be traced to the conversion of individuals, or is it attributed to newer, more Democratic generations replacing older, Republican generations? To answer such questions, political scientists conduct a *cohort analysis*. First, we define each generation in terms of when it came of age politically. Over the past several decades the main generations identified by social scientists are the pre–New Deal, New Deal, Baby Boom, Gen X, Gen Y, and Internet generations. Using survey data from each election (in this case, the American National Election Study), we then measure the party identification of the people in each generation, in this case, the percent Democratic minus the percent Republican. In the graph, a higher value on the vertical axis signifies more Democrats. ▼

COHORT PARTY ID, 1956–2008

Legend:
- Pre–New Deal (1889–1913)
- New Deal (1914–43)
- Baby Boom (1944–57)
- Gen X (1958–78)
- Gen Y (1979–88)
- Internet Age (1989–90)

*(Dem. = 1, Ind. = 0, Rep. = 1)

The generational replacement argument would predict that each generation doesn't vary in its net party attachments, because the people don't change much. We would expect each generation to be a horizontal line over time. The conversion hypothesis (in its extreme version) predicts that generations really don't differ in their baseline party attachments and that all generations show the same fluctuations in net party attachments. The graph above reveals that both arguments are in play. The generations clearly differ. The New Deal generation is consistently among the most Democratic, and Gen X is consistently among the most Republican. The net party attachments of the generations also show dramatic ups and downs, and the swings are correlated. All the generations move in the Democratic direction in Democratic years and in the Republican direction in Republican years. The Baby Boomer generation shows the most radical swings in party attachments.

Some simple calculations reveal that the changes in overall party identification in the electorate since 2000 are due to conversion. Overall, Democratic identifications minus Republican identifications rose by 18 percentage points. Consider a hypothetical change that would arise only with replacement. Suppose that the identification of each group remained as it was in 2000, but that only the composition of the electorate changed. That is, suppose that the New Deal generation shrank as a percent of the electorate and that the Gen Y and the Internet generation entered the electorate, but that the party identifications of all the generations remained as they had been in 2000. If only the composition of the electorate had changed from 2000 to 2008, then aggregate party identification would have moved 2 points in the Republican direction!

on Americans' party affiliations. None of these social characteristics is inevitably linked to partisan identification, however. There are union Republicans and business Democrats, black nonchurchgoing Republicans and white born-again Democrats, Democrats in Utah, and Republicans in Rhode Island. The general party identifications just discussed are broad tendencies that both reflect and reinforce the issue and policy positions the two parties take in the national and local political arenas.

PARTY SYSTEMS

Our understanding of political parties would be incomplete if we considered only their composition and roles. America's political parties compete with each other for offices, policies, and power and as malleable institutions have adapted to the demands of the time and age. In short, the history of each party is inextricably linked to that of its major rival. Historians often call the constellation of parties that are important at any given moment a nation's party system. The most obvious feature of a party system is the number of major parties competing for power. Usually the United States has had a two-party system, meaning that only two parties have a serious chance to win national elections. Of course, we have not always had the same two parties, and as we shall see, minor parties often put forward candidates.

The term *party system*, however, refers to more than just the number of parties competing for power. It also connotes the organization of the parties, the balance of power between and within party coalitions, the parties' social and institutional bases, and the issues and policies around which party competition is organized. Seen from this broader perspective, the character of a nation's party system can change even though the number of parties may remain the same and even when the same two parties seem to be competing for power. Today's American party system is very different from the party system of fifty years ago, even though the Democrats and the Republicans continue to be the major competing forces (Figure 11.4). The character of a nation's party system can have profound consequences for the relative influence of social forces, the importance of political institutions, and even the types of issues and policies that reach the nation's political agenda. For example, the contemporary American political parties mainly compete for the support of different groups of middle-class Americans. One reason for this is that less affluent Americans participate less often in the political process than do wealthier Americans (see Figure 10.3). As a result, issues that concern the middle and upper-middle classes—such as the environment, health care, retirement benefits, and taxation—are very much on the political agenda, whereas issues that concern working-class and poorer Americans, such as welfare and housing, receive short shrift from both parties.[15] Of course, throughout America's history the creation of new issues did not just happen. Rather, they were the fruit of political entrepreneurs looking

---

[15] See Matthew Crenson and Benjamin Ginsberg, *Downsizing Democracy: How America Sidelined Its Citizens and Privatized Its Public* (Baltimore: Johns Hopkins University Press, 2002).

FIGURE 11.4 HOW THE PARTY SYSTEM EVOLVED

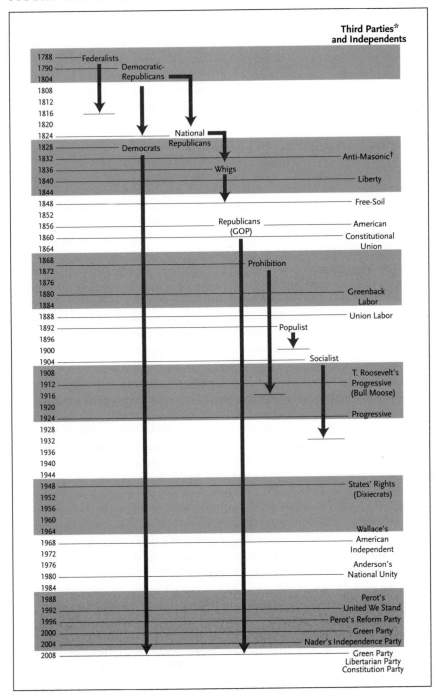

*In some cases, there was even a fourth party. Most of the parties listed here existed for only one term.

†The Anti-Masonics not only had the distinction of being the first third party but also were the first party to hold a national nominating convention and the first to announce a party platform.

for opportunities to undermine the prevailing political orthodoxy and its political beneficiaries.[16]

Over the course of American history, changes in political forces and alignments have produced six party systems, each with distinctive political institutions, issues, and patterns of political power and participation. Of course, some political phenomena have persisted across party systems. Conflicts over the distribution of wealth, for example, are an enduring feature of American political life. But even such phenomena manifest themselves in different ways during different political eras.

The First Party System: Federalists and Democratic-Republicans

Although George Washington and, in fact, many other leaders of the time deplored partisan politics, the two-party system emerged early in the history of the new Republic. Competition in Congress between northeastern mercantile and southern agrarian factions led Alexander Hamilton and the northeasterners to form a cohesive voting bloc within Congress. The southerners, led by Thomas Jefferson and James Madison, responded by attempting to organize a popular following to change the balance of power within Congress. When the northeasterners replied to this southern strategy, the result was the birth of America's first national parties—the Democratic-Republicans, whose primary base was in the South, and the Federalists, whose strength was greatest in the New England states. The Federalists spoke mainly for New England mercantile groups and supported protective tariffs to encourage manufacturers, the assumption of the states' Revolutionary War debts, the creation of a national bank, and resumption of commercial ties with England. The Democratic-Republicans opposed these policies, favoring instead free trade, the promotion of agrarian over commercial interests, and friendship with France.

The rationale behind the formation of both parties was primarily that they would be a means by which to institutionalize existing voting blocs in Congress around a cohesive policy agenda. Although the Federalists and the Democratic-Republicans competed in elections, their ties to the electorate were loose. In 1800, the American electorate was small, and deference was an important political factor, with voters generally expected to follow the lead of local political and religious leaders and community notables. Nominations were informal, without rules or regulations. Local party leaders would simply gather the party elites, and they would agree on the person, usually one of them, who would be the candidate. The meetings where candidates were nominated were generally called caucuses. In this era, before the introduction of the secret ballot, many voters were reluctant publicly to defy the views of influential members of their community. In this context, the

---

[16] Such entrepreneurial efforts are not always successful; history mainly tends to remember the successful ones. For an intriguing development of this notion, see William H. Riker, *Liberalism against Populism: A Confrontation between the Theory of Democracy and the Theory of Social Choice* (San Francisco: Freeman, 1982), esp. chaps. 8 and 9. See also Andrew J. Polsky, "When Business Speaks: Political Entrepreneurship, Discourse, and Mobilization in American Partisan Regimes," *Journal of Theoretical Politics* 12 (2002): 451–72; and Kenneth A. Shepsle, "Losers in Politics (and How They Sometimes Become Winners): William Riker's Heresthetic," *Perspectives on Politics* 1 (2003): 307–15.

Democratic-Republicans and the Federalists organized political clubs and developed newspapers and newsletters designed to mobilize elite opinion and relied on local elites to bring along their followers. In the election of 1800, Jefferson defeated the incumbent Federalist president, John Adams, and led his party to power. Over the ensuing years, the Federalists gradually weakened. The party disappeared altogether after the pro-British sympathies of some Federalist leaders during the War of 1812 led to charges that the party was guilty of treason.

The Second Party System: Democrats and Whigs

From the collapse of the Federalists until the 1830s, America had only one political party, the Democratic-Republicans. This period of one-party politics is sometimes known as the Era of Good Feeling, to indicate the absence of party competition. Throughout this period, however, there was intense factional conflict within the Democratic-Republican Party, particularly between the supporters and opponents of General Andrew Jackson, America's great military hero of the War of 1812. Jackson was one of five significant candidates for president in 1824 and won the most popular and electoral votes but a majority of neither, throwing the election into the House of Representatives. Jackson's opponents united to deny him the presidency, but Jackson won election in 1828 and again in 1832.

Jackson was greatly admired by millions of ordinary Americans living on the nation's farms and in its villages, and the Jacksonians made the most of the general's appeal to the common people by embarking on a program of suffrage expansion that would give Jackson's impecunious but numerous supporters the right to vote. To bring growing numbers of voters to the polls, the Jacksonians built political clubs and held mass rallies and parades, laying the groundwork for a new and more popular politics. Jackson's vice president and eventual successor, Martin Van Buren, was the organizational genius behind the Jacksonian movement, establishing a central party committee, state party organizations, and party newspapers. In response to widespread complaints about cliques of party leaders dominating the nominations at party caucuses and leaving no place for other party members who wanted to participate, the Jacksonians also established the state and national party conventions as the forums for nominating presidential candidates. The conventions gave control of the presidential nominating process to the new state party organizations that the Jacksonians had created and expected to control. As the political scientist John Aldrich has argued, unlike any political leader before him, Van Buren appreciated the possibilities for mass mobilization and the necessity of a well-oiled national organization to overcome free riding and other collective-action problems.[17] With a keen sense of what it took to organize a party for electoral competition, Van Buren produced institutional solutions to collective-action problems, leaving as a historical legacy the blueprint for the modern mass-based political party.

---

[17] See Aldrich, *Why Parties? The Origin and Transformation of Party Politics in America* (Chicago: University of Chicago Press, 1995), chap. 4.

The Jacksonians, whose party came to be known as the Democratic Party, were not without opponents, however, especially in the New England states. During the 1830s groups opposing Jackson for reasons of personality and politics united to form a new political force—the Whig Party—thus giving rise to the second American party system. During the 1830s and 1840s, the Democrats and the Whigs built party organizations throughout the nation, and both sought to enlarge their bases of support by expanding the suffrage through the elimination of property restrictions and other barriers to voting—at least voting by white men. This would not be the last time that party competition paved the way for expansion of the electorate. Support for the new Whig Party was stronger in the Northeast than in the South and the West and stronger among mercantile groups than among small farmers. Hence to some extent the Whigs were the successors of the Federalists. Many, though not all, Whigs favored a national bank, a protective tariff, and federally sponsored internal improvements. The Jacksonians opposed all three policies. Yet conflict between the two parties revolved around personalities as much as policies. The Whigs were a diverse group, united more by opposition to the Democrats than by agreement on programs. In 1840, the Whigs won their first presidential election under the leadership of General William Henry Harrison, a military hero known as Old Tippecanoe. The 1840 election marked the first time in American history that two parties competed for the presidency in every state in the Union. The Whig campaign carefully avoided issues—because different party factions disagreed on most matters—and emphasized the personal qualities and heroism of the candidate. The Whigs also invested heavily in campaign rallies and entertainment to win the hearts, if not exactly the minds, of the voters. The 1840 campaign came to be called the hard-cider campaign to denote the then-common practice of using food and, especially, drink to elicit electoral favor.

In the late 1840s and early 1850s, conflicts over slavery produced sharp divisions within both the Whig and the Democratic parties, despite the efforts of party leaders such as Henry Clay and Stephen A. Douglas to develop sectional compromises that would bridge the widening gulf between the North and the South. By 1856, the Whig Party had all but disintegrated under the strain. The 1854 Kansas-Nebraska Act overturned the Missouri Compromise of 1820 and the Compromise of 1850, which together had hindered the expansion of slavery in the American territories. The Kansas-Nebraska Act gave each territory the right to decide whether to permit slavery. Opposition to this policy led to the formation of a number of antislavery parties, with the Republicans emerging as the strongest of the new forces.[18] They drew their membership from existing political groups—former Whigs, Know-Nothings of the American Party, free soilers, and antislavery Democrats. In 1856, the party's first presidential candidate, John C. Frémont, won one-third of the popular vote and carried eleven states.

The early Republican platforms appealed to commercial as well as antislavery interests. The Republicans favored homesteading, internal improvements, the

---

[18] See William E. Gienapp, *The Origins of the Republican Party, 1852–1856* (New York: Oxford University Press, 1994).

construction of a transcontinental railroad, and protective tariffs, as well as the containment of slavery. In 1858, the Republican party won control of the House of Representatives; in 1860, the Republican presidential candidate, Abraham Lincoln, was victorious. Lincoln's victory strengthened southern calls for secession from the Union and led, soon thereafter, to all-out civil war.

The Third Party System: Republicans and Democrats, 1860–96

During the course of the war, President Lincoln depended heavily on Republican governors and state legislatures to raise troops, provide funding, and maintain popular support for a long and bloody military conflict. The secession of the South had stripped the Democratic Party of many of its leaders and supporters, but the Democrats nevertheless remained politically competitive throughout the war and nearly won the 1864 presidential election due to war weariness on the part of the northern public. With the defeat of the Confederacy in 1865, some congressional Republicans sought to convert the South into a Republican bastion through Reconstruction, a program that enfranchised newly freed slaves while disenfranchising many white voters and disqualifying many white politicians from seeking office. Reconstruction collapsed in the 1870s as a result of divisions within the Republican Party in Congress and violent resistance to the program by southern whites. With the end of Reconstruction, the former Confederate states regained full membership in the Union and full control of their internal affairs. Throughout the South, African Americans were deprived of political rights, including the right to vote, despite post–Civil War constitutional guarantees to the contrary. The post–Civil War South was solidly Democratic in its political affiliation, and with a firm southern base, the national Democratic Party was able to confront the Republicans on a more or less equal basis. From the end of the Civil War to the 1890s, the Republican Party remained the party of the North, with strong business and middle-class support, while the Democratic Party was the party of the South, with support from working-class and immigrant groups in the North. Republican candidates campaigned by waving the "bloody shirt" of the Civil War and urging their supporters to "vote the way you shot." Democrats emphasized the issue of the tariff, which they claimed was ruinous to agricultural interests.

Party Machines as a Strategic Innovation.   It was during the third party system that party entrepreneurs were most successful at turning party organizations into well-oiled machines. In the nineteenth and early twentieth centuries, many cities and counties, and even a few states on occasion, had such well organized parties that they were called **party machines** and their leaders were called bosses. Party machines depended heavily on the patronage of the spoils system, the party's power to control government jobs. Patronage worked as a selective benefit for anyone the party wished to attract to its side. With thousands of jobs to dispense to the party faithful, party bosses were able to recruit armies of political workers, who in turn mobilized millions of voters. During the height of the party machines, party and government were virtually interchangeable. Just as the creation of mass

party machine In the late nineteenth and early twentieth centuries, a local party organization that controlled local politics through patronage and the nomination process.

parties by Van Buren and other political entrepreneurs of the second party system solved a collective-action problem, the well-oiled machines used the selective incentives of patronage and nomination to maintain their organizations and diminish free riding. Many organizational aspects of party politics, in short, involve the ingenuity of rational politicians and leaders grappling with problems of coordination and collective action, as the rationality principle and the collective-action principle suggest.

Many critics condemned party machines as antidemocratic and corrupt. They argued that machines served the interests of powerful businesses and did not help the working people who voted for them. But one of the most notorious machine leaders in American political history, George Washington Plunkitt of New York City's Tammany Hall, considered machine politics and the spoils system to be "patriotic." Plunkitt grasped a simple, central fact about purposeful behavior and overcoming the collective-action problem. To create and retain political influence and power, "you must study human nature and act accordin'." He argued with some acumen that the country was built by political parties, that the parties needed such patronage to operate and thrive, and that if patronage was withdrawn, the parties would "go to pieces." As we shall see next, Plunkitt was somewhat prescient in making this observation.

Institutional Reforms of the Progressives. As the nineteenth century gave way to the twentieth, the excessive powers and abuses of party machines and their bosses led to one of the great reform movements in American history, the so-called Progressive Era. Many Progressive reformers were undoubtedly motivated by a sincere desire to rid politics of corruption and improve the quality and efficiency of government in the United States. But simultaneously, from the perspective of middle- and upper-class Progressives and the financial, commercial, and industrial elites with whom they were often associated, the weakening or elimination of party organization would also mean that power could more readily be acquired and retained by the "best men"—that is, those with wealth, position, and education.

The list of antiparty reforms of the Progressive Era is a familiar one. As we saw in Chapter 10, the introduction of voter registration laws required eligible voters to register in person well before an election. The Australian-ballot reform took away the parties' privilege of printing and distributing ballots and thus introduced the possibility of split-ticket voting (see also Chapter 10). The introduction of nonpartisan local elections eroded grassroots party organization. The extension of "merit systems" for administrative appointments stripped party organizations of their vitally important access to patronage and thus reduced party leaders' capacity to control the nomination of candidates.

These reforms obviously did not destroy political parties as entities, but taken together they did substantially weaken party organizations in the United States. After the beginning of the twentieth century, the strength of American political parties gradually diminished, and voter turnout declined precipitously. Between the two world wars, organization remained the major tool available to contending electoral forces, but in most areas of the country the "reformed" state and local parties that survived the Progressive Era gradually lost their organizational vitality and coherence and became less effective campaign tools. Although most areas of the nation continued to boast Democratic and Republican Party groupings, reform did mean the elimination of the permanent mass organizations that had been the parties' principal campaign weapons.

The Fourth Party System, 1896–1932

During the 1890s, profound and rapid social and economic changes led to the emergence of a variety of protest parties, including the Populist Party, which won the support of hundreds of thousands of voters in the South and the West. The Populists appealed mainly to small farmers but also attracted western mining interests and urban workers. In the 1892 presidential election, the Populist Party carried four states and elected governors in eight states. In 1896, the Democrats in effect adopted the Populist Party platform and nominated William Jennings Bryan, a Democratic senator with pronounced Populist sympathies, for the presidency. The Republicans nominated the conservative senator William McKinley. In the ensuing campaign, northern and midwestern business made an all-out effort to defeat what it saw as a radical threat from the Populist-Democratic alliance. When the dust settled, the Republicans had won a resounding victory. In the nation's metropolitan regions, especially in the Northeast and upper Midwest, workers became convinced that the Populist-Democratic alliance threatened the industries that provided their jobs, while immigrants were frightened by the nativist rhetoric employed by some Populist orators and writers. The GOP had carried the northern and midwestern states and confined the Democrats to their bastions in the South and the Far West. For the next thirty-six years, the Republicans were the nation's majority party, carrying seven of nine presidential elections and controlling both houses of Congress in fifteen of eighteen contests. The Republican Party of this era was very much the party of American business, advocating low taxes, high tariffs, and a minimum of government regulation. The Democrats were far too weak to offer much opposition. Southern Democrats, moreover, were more concerned with maintaining the region's autonomy on issues of race to challenge the Republicans on other fronts.

The Fifth Party System: The New Deal Coalition, 1932–68

Soon after the Republican candidate Herbert Hoover won the 1928 presidential election, the nation's economy collapsed. The Great Depression, which produced unprecedented economic hardship, stemmed from a variety of causes, but from the perspective of millions of Americans the Republican Party had not done enough to promote economic recovery. In 1932, Americans elected Franklin D. Roosevelt and a solidly Democratic Congress. FDR developed a program for economic recovery that he dubbed the New Deal, under the auspices of which the size and reach of America's national government was substantially increased. The federal government took responsibility for economic management and social welfare to an extent that was unprecedented in American history. FDR designed many of his programs specifically to expand the political base of the Democratic Party. He rebuilt the party around a nucleus of unionized workers, upper-middle-class intellectuals and professionals, southern farmers, Jews, Catholics, and northern African Americans (few blacks in the South could vote) that made the Democrats the nation's majority party for thirty-six years. Republicans groped for a response to the New Deal but often wound up supporting popular New Deal programs such as Social Security in what was sometimes derided as "me-too" Republicanism.

The New Deal coalition was severely strained during the 1960s by conflicts over President Lyndon Johnson's Great Society initiative, civil rights, and the Vietnam War. A number of Johnson's Great Society programs, designed to fight poverty and racial discrimination, involved the empowerment of local groups that were often at odds with established city and county governments. These programs touched off battles between local Democratic political machines and the national administration that split the Democratic coalition. For its part, the struggle over civil rights initially divided northern Democrats, who supported the civil rights cause, and white southern Democrats, who defended the system of racial segregation. Subsequently, as the civil rights movement launched a northern campaign aimed at securing access to jobs and education and an end to racial discrimination in such realms as housing, northern Democrats also experienced a split, often along class lines, with blue-collar workers tending to vote Republican. The struggle over the Vietnam War further divided the Democrats, with upper-income liberal Democrats strongly opposing the Johnson administration's decision to send U.S. forces to fight in Southeast Asia. These schisms within the Democratic Party provided an opportunity for the GOP to return to power, which it did in 1968 under the leadership of Richard Nixon.

The Sixth Party System?

In the 1960s, conservative Republicans argued that me-tooism was a recipe for continual failure and sought to reposition the GOP as a genuine alternative to the Democrats. In 1964, for example, the Republican presidential candidate, Barry Goldwater, author of a book titled *The Conscience of a Conservative,* argued in favor of substantially reduced levels of taxation and spending, less government regulation of the economy, and the elimination of many federal social programs. Although Goldwater was defeated by Lyndon Johnson, the ideas he espoused continue to be major themes of the Republican Party. The Goldwater message, however, was not enough to lead Republicans to victory. As discussed in Chapter 10, it took Richard Nixon's "southern strategy" to give the GOP the votes it needed to end Democratic dominance of the political process. Nixon appealed strongly to disaffected white southerners and, with the help of the independent candidate and former Alabama governor George Wallace, sparked the shift of voters that eventually gave the once-hated "party of Lincoln" a strong position in all the states of the former Confederacy. In the 1980s, under the leadership of Ronald Reagan, Republicans added another important group to their coalition: religious conservatives who were offended by Democratic support of abortion rights as well as alleged Democratic disdain for traditional cultural and religious values.

While Republicans built a political base with economic and social conservatives and white southerners, the Democratic Party maintained its support among unionized workers and upper-middle-class intellectuals and professionals. Democrats also appealed strongly to racial minorities. The 1965 Voting Rights Act had greatly increased the participation of black voters in the South and helped the Democratic Party retain some congressional and Senate seats in the South. And while the GOP appealed to social conservatives, the Democrats appealed strongly to Americans concerned about abortion rights, gay rights, feminism, environmentalism, and other progressive social causes. The results have been something of a draw. Democrats have won the presidency four out of the eleven elections since the passage of the Voting Rights Act, but held at least one chamber of Congress for most of that time. That apparent stalemate masked dramatic changes in the regional bases of the parties. Republicans surged in the south, making the southern states the foundation of their presidential and congressional victories. Those gains came at the expense of the old-line Republicans in the northeast. New England, once the bedrock of the GOP, had not one Republican U.S. House Member after the 2008 election.

The shift of much of the South from the Democratic to the Republican camp, along with the other developments mentioned above, meant that each political party became ideologically more homogeneous after the 1980s. Today as we've noted before, there are few liberal Republicans or conservative Democrats. One consequence of this development is that party loyalty in Congress, which had been weak between the 1950s and the 1970s, became a more potent force. The 1990s witnessed a dramatic resurgence of party-line voting in Congress. A simple measure of party developed by Professor Stuart Rice in the 1920s and tracked by *Congressional Quarterly* since the 1950s is the party unity score. This is the percentage of bills on which a majority of a party votes against a majority of the other party. Between the 1950s and the 1970s, unity hovered around 70 percent. Since the 1980s it has regularly exceeded 90 percent.[19]

To some extent, ideology has replaced organization as the glue holding together each party's coalition. But in the long run, ideology is often an unreliable basis for party unity. Although the activists within each party grouping are united by some beliefs, ideological divisions also plague both camps. Within the Republican coalition, social conservatives are often at odds with economic conservatives, whereas among Democrats proponents of regulatory reform and economic internationalism are frequently at odds with traditional liberals, who favor big government and protecting American workers from foreign competition. The party workers of yesteryear supported the leadership almost no matter what. Today's more ideologically motivated party activists give their leaders only very conditional backing and feel free to withhold support if they disagree with the leadership's goals and plans. Because of internal divisions in the Republican Party, for example, GOP congressional

---

[19] The classic statement of the connection between cohesive legislative parties and ideological homogeneity within party ranks is found in David W. Rohde, *Parties and Leaders in the Post-reform House* (Chicago: University of Chicago Press, 1991). An elaboration of this argument is presented in Gary W. Cox and Mathew D. McCubbins, *Setting the Agenda: Responsible Party Government in the U.S. House of Representatives* (New York: Cambridge University Press, 2005). See also Nolan McCarty, Keith Poole, and Howard Rosenthal, *Polarized America: The Dance of Inequality and Unequal Riches* (Cambridge, Mass.: MIT Press, 2006).

leaders have adopted a strategy of avoiding votes on the many issues that might split the party.[20] The price of unity based on ideology can be the inability to act.

The ideological gap between the two parties has been exacerbated by two other factors: each party's dependence on ideologically motivated activists and the changes in the presidential nominating system that were introduced during the 1970s. As for the first of these, Democratic political candidates depend heavily on the support of liberal activists—such as feminists, environmentalists, and civil libertarians—to organize and finance their campaigns, while Republican political candidates depend equally on the support of conservative activists, including religious fundamentalists. In the nineteenth century, political activists were motivated more by party loyalty and political patronage than by programmatic concerns. Today's issue-oriented activists, by contrast, demand that politicians demonstrate strong commitments to moral principles and political causes in exchange for their support. The demands of party activists have tended to push Democrats further to the political left and Republicans further to the political right. Often efforts by politicians to reach compromises on key issues are attacked by party activists as "sellouts," leading to stalemates on such matters as the budget and judicial appointments.

The second factor exacerbating the parties' ideological split, the changes in the presidential nominating system, took place in response to the Democratic Party's defeat in 1968. Liberal forces, guided by the so-called McGovern-Fraser Commission on party reform, succeeded in changing the rules governing Democratic presidential nominations to reduce the power of party officials and party professionals while increasing the role of issue-oriented activists. Among other changes, the new rules required national convention delegates to be chosen in primaries and caucuses rather than by each state party's central committee, as had previously been the practice in many states. Subsequently, Republican activists were able to bring about similar changes in the GOP's rules, so that today in both parties presidential nominating processes are strongly influenced by precisely the sorts of grassroots activists who are often inclined to oppose centrist or pragmatic politicians in favor of those appearing to manifest ideological purity. As a result, elections have tended to pit liberal Democrats against conservative Republicans. Observers of post–World War II American political parties often dubbed them Tweedledum and Tweedledee, but the two parties today differ sharply on a number of social, economic, and foreign-policy issues. Compare, for example, Democratic and Republican legislative priorities at the opening of the 110th Congress, in January 2007. Republicans emphasized support of Iraq war policy, immigration reform, and new laws to strengthen marriage and discourage abortion. The Democrats emphasized expanding social programs, protecting the jobs of unionized workers, bringing an end to operations in Iraq, and strengthening abortion rights. These competing agendas set the stage for a contentious legislative session. At the advent of the 111th Congress in 2009, the legislature was focused squarely on reviving the U.S. economy, but the parties' other priorities hadn't changed appreciably. The GOP was willing to slow the appointment of cabinet officials for their positions on

---

[20] Isaiah J. Poole, "Votes Echo Electoral Themes," *Congressional Quarterly Weekly Report*, December 11, 2004, pp. 2906–8.

abortion and gay rights, while Democrats pushed for aggressive action on health reform, government regulation, and global warming.

American Third Parties

Although the United States is said to possess a two-party system, we have always had more than two parties. Typically, **third parties** in the United States have represented social and economic protests that, for one or another reason, were not given voice by the two major parties.[21] Such parties have had a good deal of influence on ideas and elections in the United States. The Populists, a party centered in the rural areas of the West and the Midwest during the late nineteenth century, and the Progressives, spokesmen for the urban middle classes in the late nineteenth and early twentieth centuries, are among the most important examples. More recently, Ross Perot, who ran in 1992 and 1996 as an independent, impressed some voters with his folksy style in the presidential debates and garnered almost 19 percent of the votes cast in the 1992 presidential election. Earlier, the independent candidate George Wallace received almost 10 percent of the vote in 1968, and John Anderson received about 5 percent in 1980.

Table 11.1 lists all the parties that offered candidates in one or more states in the presidential election of 2008, as well as independent candidates. The third-party and independent candidates together polled barely 1 million votes. They gained no electoral votes for president, and most of them disappeared immediately after the presidential election. The significance of the table is that it demonstrates the large number of third parties running candidates and appealing to voters. Third-party candidacies also arise at the state and local levels. In New York, the Liberal and Conservative parties have been on the ballot for decades. In 1998, Minnesota elected a third-party governor, the former professional wrestler Jesse Ventura.

Although the Republican Party, founded as a third party in the 1850s, was only the third American political party ever to make itself permanent (by replacing the Whigs and becoming the Democrats' major competitor), other third parties have enjoyed an influence far beyond their electoral size. That is because large parts of their programs were adopted by one or both of the major parties, which sought to appeal to the voters mobilized by the new party and so expand their own electoral strength. The Democratic Party, for example, became a great deal more liberal when it adopted most of the Progressive program early in the twentieth century. Many socialists felt that President Roosevelt's New Deal had adopted most of their party's program, including old-age pensions, unemployment compensation, an agricultural marketing program, and laws guaranteeing workers the right to organize into unions.

This kind of influence explains the short lives of third parties. Their causes are usually eliminated by the ability of the major parties to absorb their programs and draw their supporters into the mainstream. There are, of course, additional reasons for the short duration of most third parties. One is the typical limitation of their electoral support to one or two regions. Populist support, for example,

third party
A party that organizes to compete against the two major American political parties.

---

[21] For a discussion of third parties in the United States, see Daniel A. Mazmanian, *Third Parties in Presidential Elections* (Washington, D.C.: Brookings Institution, 1974).

TABLE 11.1 PARTIES AND CANDIDATES, 2008

ANALYZING THE EVIDENCE

Though the Democrats and the Republicans are America's dominant political forces, many minor parties nominate candidates for the presidency. Why are there so many minor parties? Why don't these parties represent much of a threat to the major parties?

Candidate	Party	Vote Total	Percent of Vote
Barack Obama	Democrat	69,456,897	52.38%
John McCain	Republican	59,934,814	45.20%
Ralph Nader	Independent	736,804	0.56%
Robert Barr	Libertarian	524,524	0.40%
Charles Baldwin	Constitution	196,461	0.00%
Cynthia McKinney	Green	161,195	0.15%
Richard Duncan	Independent	3,902	0.12%
John Polachek	New Party	1,149	0.00%
Frank McEnulty	New American Independent	828	0.00%
Jeffrey Wamboldt	We the People	764	0.00%
Jeffrey Boss	Vote Here Party	639	0.00%
George Phillies	Libertarian (New Hampshire)	522	0.00%
Ted Weill	Reform	481	0.00%
Bradford Lyttle	U.S. Pacifist	110	0.00%

Total Turnout = 132,588,514

SOURCE: www.census.gov

was primarily midwestern. The 1948 Progressive Party, with Henry Wallace as its candidate, drew nearly half its votes from the state of New York. The American Independent Party polled nearly 10 million popular votes and 45 electoral votes for George Wallace in 1968—the most electoral votes ever polled by a third-party candidate. But all of Wallace's electoral votes and the majority of his popular vote came from the states of the Deep South.

Americans usually assume that only the candidates nominated by one of the two major parties have any chance of winning an election. Thus a vote cast for a third-party or an independent candidate is often seen as a wasted vote. Voters who would prefer a third-party candidate may feel compelled to vote for the major party candidate whom they regard as the lesser of two evils to avoid wasting their votes in a futile gesture. Third-party candidates must struggle—usually without success—to overcome the perception that they cannot win. Thus in 2004, many liberals who admired Ralph Nader nevertheless urged him not to mount an independent bid for the presidency for fear he would siphon liberal votes from the Democrats, as he had in 2000. Some former Naderites participated in efforts to keep Nader off the ballot in a number of states. Ultimately Nader did mount a presidential campaign but received 2.5 million fewer votes in 2004 than in 2000. Most of his former adherents, knowing he could not win and might prevent their second-choice candidate from winning, voted for John Kerry.

As many scholars have pointed out, third-party prospects are also hampered by America's **single-member-district** plurality election system. In many other nations, several individuals can be elected to represent each legislative district. This is called a system of **multiple-member districts.** With this type of system, the candidates of weaker parties have a better chance of winning at least some seats. For their part, voters are less concerned about wasting ballots and usually more willing to support minor-party candidates.

Reinforcing the effects of the single-member district (as noted in Chapter 10), plurality voting rules generally have the effect of setting what could be called a high threshold for victory. To win a plurality race, candidates usually must secure many more votes than they would need under most European systems of proportional representation. For example, to win an American plurality election in a single-member district with only two candidates, a politician must win more than 50 percent of the votes cast. To win a seat in a European multimember district under proportional-representation rules, a candidate may need to win only 15 or 20 percent of the votes cast. This high threshold in American elections discourages minor parties and encourages the various political factions that might otherwise form minor parties to minimize their differences and remain within the major-party coalitions.[22]

It would nevertheless be incorrect to assert (as some scholars have maintained) that America's single-member plurality election system guarantees that only two parties will compete for power in all regions of the country. All that can be said is that American election law depresses the number of parties likely to survive over long periods of time in the United States. There is nothing magical about two. Indeed, the single-member plurality election system can also discourage second parties. After all, if one party consistently receives a large plurality of the vote, people may eventually come to see their vote even for the second party as a wasted effort. This happened to the Republican Party in the Deep South before World War II.

Of the two most successful third-party efforts of the last half century, by George Wallace in 1968 and Ross Perot in 1992, it is useful to compare the candidates' relative fates. In the last Gallup public opinion poll before the 1968 election, Hubert Humphrey, the Democrat, and Richard Nixon, the Republican, were in a near dead heat, with 43 percent and 42 percent of the vote respectively. George Wallace was the preferred choice of about 14 percent of the electorate, with some voters still undecided. In the actual balloting, Nixon barely won the popular vote, and Wallace's share shrank to less than 10 percent: Wallace lost more than one-third of his support. Fast forward to 1992, when the final Gallup poll showed the Democrat, Bill Clinton, leading the Republican, George H. W. Bush, by about five percentage

single-member district An electorate that is allowed to elect only one representative from each district—the typical method of representation in the United States.

multiple-member district An electorate that selects several candidates at large from an entire district, with each voter given the number of votes equivalent to the number of seats to be filled.

---

[22] See Maurice Duverger, *Political Parties: Their Organization and Activity in the Modern State*, Barbara North and Robert North, trans. (New York: Wiley, 1954).

points (43–38). Perot was the first preference of about 19 percent. In the final balloting, Perot got approximately that share—there was virtually no loss of support such as Wallace experienced in 1968. In each case, the third-party candidate had little chance of winning. But in the Humphrey-Nixon contest, the margin was razor thin, and many Wallace supporters, not wanting to waste their vote, opted for the lesser evil. In the Clinton-Bush race, Clinton was comfortably in the lead at the end, so Perot supporters felt less pressure to desert their favorite in order to make a difference in the contest between the two leaders. In each case, voters reflected the rationality principle in their deliberations. Indeed, there is evidence in the 2000 race between Al Gore, the Democrat, and George W. Bush, the Republican, that the third-party candidate Ralph Nader did better in those states where either Bush or Gore was nearly certain of winning, whereas his support dwindled in more closely contested states.

THE ROLE OF PARTIES TODAY

As a result of Progressive reform, American party organizations entered the twentieth century with rickety substructures. As the use of civil service, primary elections, and the other Progressive innovations spread during the period between the two world wars, the strength of party organizations continued to be eroded. By the end of World War II, political scientists were already bemoaning the absence of party discipline and "party responsibility" in the United States.

Contemporary Party Organizations

In the United States, party organizations exist at virtually every level of government (Figure 11.5). These organizations are usually committees made up of a number of active party members. State law and party rules prescribe how such committees are constituted. Usually, committee members are elected at a local party meeting—called a **political caucus**—or as part of the regular primary election. The best-known examples of these committees are at the national level: the Democratic National Committee and the Republican National Committee.

political caucus
A normally closed meeting of a political or legislative group to select candidates, plan strategy, or make decisions regarding legislative matters.

The National Convention. At the national level, the party's most important institution is the national convention. The convention is attended by delegates from each of the states; as a group, they nominate the party's presidential and vice-presidential candidates, draft the party's campaign platform for the presidential race, and approve changes in the rules and regulations governing party procedures. Before World War II, presidential nominations occupied most of the time, energy, and effort expended at the national convention. The nomination process required days of negotiation and compromise among state party leaders and often required many ballots before a nominee was selected. In recent years, however, presidential candidates have essentially nominated themselves by winning enough delegate support in primary elections to win the official nomination on the first ballot. The convention itself has played little or no role in selecting the candidates.

FIGURE 11.5 HOW AMERICAN PARTIES ARE ORGANIZED

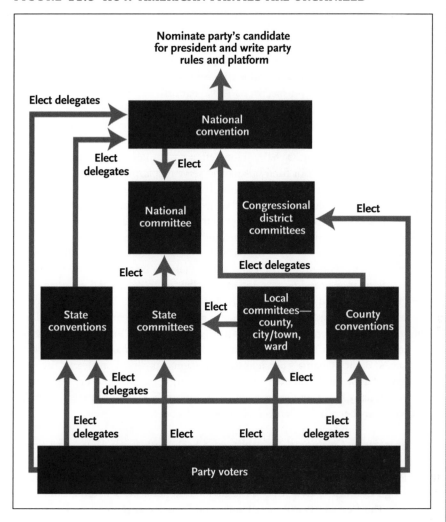

The convention's other two tasks, establishing the party's rules and establishing its platform, remain important. Party rules can determine the relative influence of competing factions within the party and can increase or decrease the party's chances for electoral success. In 1972, for example, the Democratic National Convention adopted a new set of rules favored by the party's liberal wing, according to which state delegations to the Democratic convention are required to include women and members of minority groups in rough proportion to those groups' representation among the party's membership in their state. The convention also approves the party platform. Platforms are often dismissed as platitude-laden documents that are seldom read by voters. Furthermore, the parties' presidential candidates make little use of the platforms in their campaigns; usually they prefer to develop and promote their own themes. Nonetheless, the platform should be understood as a "treaty" in which the various party factions attending the convention state their terms for supporting the ticket.

The National Committee.   Between conventions, each national political party is technically headed by its national committee. For the Democrats and Republicans, these are called the Democratic National Committee (DNC) and the Republican National Committee (RNC), respectively. These national committees raise campaign funds, head off factional disputes within the party, and endeavor to enhance the party's media image. Since 1972, the size of staff and the amount of money raised have increased substantially for both national committees. The actual work of each committee is overseen by its chairperson. Other committee members are generally major party contributors or fund-raisers and serve in a largely ceremonial capacity.

For the party that controls the White House, the national committee chair is appointed by the president. Typically, this means that that party's national committee becomes little more than an adjunct to the White House staff. For a first-term president, the committee devotes the bulk of its energy to the reelection campaign. The national committee chair of the party that is not in control of the White House is selected by the committee itself and usually takes a broader view of the party's needs, raising money and performing other activities on behalf of the party's members in Congress and in the state legislatures. In 2006, the DNC was headed by Howard Dean, whose failed but impressive presidential bid in 2004 launched him onto the national scene. Dean crafted a fifty-state strategy for the 2006 midterm elections in an effort to build party strength and recruit quality candidates in all fifty states. Barack Obama's presidential campaign capitalized on Dean's fifty-state strategy. Obama developed extensive grassroots organizations in every state, which registered many new Democratic voters in traditionally Republican areas, a change that will likely benefit the Democrats for years to come.

Congressional Campaign Committees.   Each party forms House and Senate campaign committees to raise funds for the House and Senate election campaigns. The Republicans call their House and Senate committees the National Republican Campaign Committee (NRCC) and the National Republican Senatorial Committee (NRSC). The Democrats call their House and Senate committees the Democratic Congressional Campaign Committee (DCCC) and the Democratic Senatorial Campaign Committee (DSCC). These organizations also have professional staff devoted to raising and distributing funds, developing strategies, recruiting candidates, and conducting on-the-ground campaigns. These organizations, however, are accountable to the caucuses inside the House and Senate. The chairs of these committees come from within their respective chambers and rank high in the party leadership hierarchy. The current chairs are Representative Chris Van Hollen (D-Md.) and Senator Charles Schumer (D-N.Y.) on the Democratic side and Representative Tom Cole (R-Okla.) and Senator John Ensign (D-Nev.) on the Republican side. The national committees and the congressional committees are sometimes rivals. Both groups seek donations from the same pool of people but for different candidates: the national committee seeks funds primarily for the presidential race, whereas the congressional campaign committees focus on House and Senate seats.

State and Local Party Organizations. Each of the two major parties has a central committee in each state. The parties traditionally also have county committees and, in some instances, state senate district committees, judicial district committees, and in larger cities, citywide party committees and local assembly district "ward" committees as well. Congressional districts may also have party committees. Some cities also have precinct committees.[23]

State and local party organizations are very active in recruiting candidates, conducting voter registration drives, and providing financial assistance to candidates. In many respects, federal election law has given state and local party organizations new life, permitting them to spend unlimited amounts of money on "party-building" activities such as voter registration and get-out-the-vote drives. As a result, the national party organizations, which have enormous fund-raising abilities but are limited by law in the amount of money they can spend on candidates, transfer millions of dollars each year to the state and local organizations. The state and local parties, in turn, spend these funds, sometimes called soft money, to promote the candidacies of national, state, and local candidates. In this process, as local organizations have become linked financially to the national parties, American political parties have become somewhat more integrated and nationalized than ever before. At the same time, the state and local party organizations have come to control large financial resources and play important roles in elections despite the collapse of the old patronage machines.

The Contemporary Party as Service Provider to Candidates

Party leaders have adapted parties to the modern age. Parties as organizations are more professional, better financed, and better organized than ever before.[24] Political scientists argue that parties have evolved into "service organizations," which, although they no longer hold a monopoly over campaigns, still provide services to candidates, without which it would be extremely difficult for them to win and hold office.

Many politicians, however, are able to raise funds, attract volunteers, and win office without much help from the local party organizations. Once in office, these politicians often refuse to submit to party discipline; instead, they steer an independent course. They are often supported by voters who see independence as a virtue and party discipline as "boss rule." Analysts refer to this pattern as a candidate-centered politics, to distinguish it from a political process in which parties are the dominant forces. The problem with a candidate-centered politics is that it tends to be associated with low turnout, high levels of special-interest influence, and a lack of effective decision making. In short, many of the problems that have plagued American politics in recent years can be traced directly to the independence of

---

[23] Well-organized political parties—especially the famous old machines of New York, Chicago, and Boston—provided for "precinct captains" and a fairly tight group of party members around them. Precinct captains were usually members of long standing in neighborhood party clubhouses.

[24] See Aldrich, *Why Parties?*, chap. 8.

American voters and politicians and the candidate-centered nature of American national politics.

Politicians, especially legislative politicians, have a collective-action problem. Because they possess considerable independence, they are able to chart an independent political course—hence candidate-centered politics. But so, too, can their fellow partisans. The result is that the party label, on which all rely, is undermined and comes to stand for nothing. (It is thus no accident that more and more voters call themselves independents as parties have become big tents from which a cacophony of signals is emitted.) Legislative leaders, in an effort to protect the party label, provide entrepreneurial direction to their copartisans. They seek to reduce the exercise of "too much" independence because every such instance entails negative external effects on the party's reputation. Legislative leadership, in short, enables partisans to rein in each other's independence (which each is so sorely tempted to exercise). Although each politician is thus constrained (somewhat) in the fine-tuning of his or her political behavior to meet the needs of individual constituencies, he or she nevertheless benefits from maintaining an unblemished party label. As party delegations in Congress have become more homogeneous in recent years, party leaders have been in a better position to exercise this type of control, ultimately to the benefit of copartisans. This scenario is but another aspect of the "service-organization" conception of the modern political party.[25]

Conclusion: Parties and Democracy

Political parties help make democracy work. We often do not appreciate that democratic government is a contradiction in terms. Government implies policies, programs, and decisive action. Democracy, on the other hand, implies an opportunity for all citizens to participate fully in the governmental process. Full participation by everyone is inconsistent with getting things done in an efficient and timely manner. How can we balance the ideals of democracy and efficiency in government? How can we make certain that popular participation will result in a government capable of making decisions and developing needed policies? At what point should participation stop and government begin? Strong political parties are a partial antidote to the inherent contradiction between participation and governance. Strong parties can both encourage popular involvement and convert participation into effective government.

As we've seen, parties simplify the electoral process. They set the electoral agenda by laying out party platforms, broad statements of ideas and policies that the party's candidates will pursue in office. They recruit candidates, accumulate and distribute campaign resources, and they register and mobilize people to vote. Party control of the nominating process and the pressures toward two-party politics in the United States mean that most voters must decide between just two meaningful or plausible choices in any election. Parties, thus, serve as sort of an

---

[25] This argument is developed in great detail in Rohde, *Parties and Leaders in the Post-reform House*, and in the two books by Gary W. Cox and Mathew D. McCubbins, *Legislative Leviathan: Party Government in the House* (Berkeley: University of California Press, 1993), and *Setting the Agenda: Responsible Party Government in the U.S. House of Representatives* (New York: Cambridge University Press, 2005).

informal institution in elections and government. They structure electoral choices and manage the legislative agenda, and they serve as a bridge between elections and government.

This in turn facilitates voters' decision making. Voters can reasonably expect what sorts of policies a candidate who has a party's endorsement will represent if elected. Even before a given candidate has received the nomination, most voters have already sorted themselves into one of the two competing camps, Democratic or Republican. They know for whom they will vote before the election begins. This may seem like a gross simplification of politics. It reduces the many complex interests in our society to just two competing teams, whose policy platforms must be watered down to accommodate the many subtle differences or ideological nuances among the groups inside the party. It further reduces politics into warring factions that have little hope of finding compromise or common ground. However, what the two-party system does accomplish is that it gives meaning to the vote. It empowers the voter to say, I want to stay the course with the party in power, or, I want to go in a new direction.

FOR FURTHER READING

Aldrich, John H. *Why Parties? The Origin and Transformation of Party Politics in America.* Chicago: University of Chicago Press, 1995.   ○ reader selection

Beck, Paul Allen, and Marjorie Randon Hershey. *Party Politics in America.* 10th ed. New York: Longman, 2003.

Chambers, William N., and Walter Dean Burnham, eds. *The American Party Systems: Stages of Political Development.* 2nd ed. New York: Oxford University Press, 1975.

Coleman, John J. *Party Decline in America: Policy, Politics, and the Fiscal State.* Princeton, N.J.: Princeton University Press, 1996.

Cox, Gary W., and Mathew D. McCubbins. *Legislative Leviathan: Party Government in the House.* Berkeley: University of California Press, 1993.

Cox, Gary W., and Mathew D. McCubbins. *Setting the Agenda: Responsible Party Government in the U.S. House of Representatives.* New York: Cambridge University Press, 2005.   ○ reader selection

Hofstadter, Richard. *The Idea of a Party System: The Rise of Legitimate Opposition in the United States, 1780–1840.* Berkeley: University of California Press, 1969.

Mayhew, David. *Electoral Realignments: A Critique of an American Genre.* New Haven, Conn.: Yale University Press, 2007.

Rohde, David W. *Parties and Leaders in the Post-reform House.* Chicago: University of Chicago Press, 1991.

Sundquist, James L. *Dynamics of the Party System: Alignment and Realignment of Political Parties in the United States.* Washington, D.C.: Brookings Institution, 1983.

Wattenberg, Martin P. *The Decline of American Political Parties, 1952–1996.* Cambridge, Mass.: Harvard University Press, 1998.

Ⓢ Additional study and review materials are available online at wwnorton.com/studyspace/

12

Groups and Interests

Democratic politics in the United States does not end with elections. Federal, state, and local governments provide many additional avenues through which individuals and organizations can express their preferences. People may, for example, contact elected officials, their staff, and bureaucrats directly about a particular decision or problem. They may participate in public meetings about legislation or administrative rulings; some private citizens are even selected to serve on special government commissions because of their expertise or particular concerns. They may file lawsuits to request a government agency to take a particular action or to prevent it from doing so. They may give their time and money to elect candidates to their liking. They may express their opinions in newspapers, on television and the Internet, or through other venues, and hold public protests, all without fear of persecution. Individuals, organizations and even governments make frequent use of these many points of access. Their actions are purposive—they seek something from government that is of benefit to them. Many of these encounters with government are episodic, as when an individual contacts an agency to solve a particular problem. But a substantial amount of political activity in the United States occurs through enduring, organized efforts that bring together many individuals into collective action to seek a common goal.

Both a push and a pull are behind the activity of organized political interests in the United States. The push comes from the willingness and ability of people to contact government. The pull comes from the government's need to collect information about the impact of decisions on various constituencies or sectors of society.

Individuals, firms, and other organizations engage in political activity for very definite purposes. Elections do not fully capture the intensity and range of people's preferences. Those who care a great deal about what government does or are particularly affected by government decisions are usually willing to do more than just vote in order to have their opinions heard. The 1970s, for example, witnessed a massive upsurge in business activity in Washington, D.C., in response to new labor and environmental regulations. The debate over health-care reform, which has stretched out over the better part of two decades, has resulted in a massive new prescription-drug benefit and drawn the pharmaceutical industry into Washington politics. The firms and associations in that industry are acutely aware of the economic consequences of particular regulations and benefits (such as the prescription-drug benefit); support for and opposition to particular bills reflects the economic gains the firms expect to reap.[1]

Those seeking access to the government may benefit in two distinct ways—by shaping policy and by gathering information. It is widely understood that organizations try to affect government policy decisions in the legislative, administrative, and legal arenas, but gathering information from agencies and

---

[1] Thomas B. Edsall, "Two Bills Would Benefit Top Bush Fundraisers," *Washington Post*, November 22, 2003, page 1; Jeffrey H. Birnbaum, "In the Loop on K Street," *Washington Post*, January 16, 2007, page A17.

CHAPTER OUTLINE

CORE OF THE ANALYSIS

- Individuals, firms, and other organizations engage in a wide variety of political activities, including contacting elected officials, attending government meetings, engaging in campaign activities, and contributing money in order to shape how those in office make and implement laws.

- These activities help government solve an important problem—the problem of how to learn about what problems are important to the society and how government actions might affect the society.

- There is a clear orientation of interest groups toward those segments of society with better education or more economic resources, or those most directly affected by government actions, especially corporations.

- Collective organization of interests is difficult, as there are strong incentives for any single individual to free ride. As a result, interests in the society, especially very broad interests such as "all consumers" or "the middle class," often lack effective organizations that can express their preferences.

departments may be just as important. For instance, when a commission or department issues a new regulation, firms that are potentially affected must figure out whether the regulation applies to them, how to comply if they are affected, and the exact interpretation of the regulations. That often involves many interactions between the agency and representatives of the firms and sometimes further rulings from agencies clarifying the procedures. Firms frequently hire representation in Washington or the state capital just to stay on top of such matters. One influential study discovered that half of the activities and efforts of businessmen who contacted the government consisted of gathering information and half consisted of advocacy for a particular policy or action.[2] Information gathering seems innocuous. The organizations are just trying to figure out how the regulations work. Influencing policy, on the other hand, is a matter of concern, because it may lead to government policies that protect relatively narrow or special interests at the expense of the majority. Both sorts of benefits, however, may motivate firms, unions, and other organizations to engage in political action.

The government itself encourages participation by such groups. Government agencies and representatives need information about the effects of public policies. Frequent elections provide some guidance from the public, but elected representatives may need more refined information about how a given decision will affect particular constituencies and whether those constituencies, even if not a majority, will be sufficiently affected by a decision to base their future electoral behavior—including campaign contributions and votes—on that decision. Bureaucrats typically do not have the time and resources to study all potential problems. Instead

---

[2] Raymond Bauer, Ithiel de Sola Pool, and Lewis Dexter, *American Business and Public Policy* (Chicago: Atherton Press, 1972).

they rely on information from individuals, firms, and other organizations to gauge the importance of a given problem and to learn about the consequences of particular decisions. A responsive government needs more subtle and refined information about how a decision will affect people or society or about the best way to implement a law. The solution in American government is to allow, indeed encourage, an open government with many points of access for competing views. The process for approving administrative rulings involves advisory commissions and open meetings. The process for developing legislation involves multiple committee hearings, open communication from constituents, and public debate on the floor of Congress that is widely broadcast on television. The legal process is open to all comers and allows those affected by government actions to settle disputes or even to challenge the law.

The demand for greater influence among some sectors of society and the need for information among governments creates an opportunity to organize. Even the simplest attempt to influence the government—such as writing a letter to a member of Congress or calling an agency—takes time and effort. More complex problems, such as offering an expert assessment of the costs and benefits of a proposed power plant or other facility, require investment of considerable amounts of time and money, resources beyond most individuals' means. Such problems, however, affect large numbers of people. If a group of individuals can pool their modest resources, they can mount a more effective effort to express their preferences and interests to the government. Such a group might hire an attorney or consultant to represent their interests in Washington, D.C., or a state capital, or they might decide to form their own professional nonprofit organization.

Organized advocacy of political interests, commonly known as lobbying, is a $3 billion-a-year industry in Washington, D.C., alone, involving 16,000 individuals, firms, and other organizations. Who is a lobbyist? According to the 1995 Federal Lobbying Disclosure Act any person who makes at least one lobbying contact with either the legislative or executive branch in a year, any individual who spends 20 percent of his or her time in support of such activities, or any firm that devotes 10 percent of its budget to such activities must register as a lobbyist. They must report what topics they discussed with the government, though not which particular individuals or offices they contacted. The industry that spent the most on lobbying between 1998 and 2008 was the pharmaceuticals and health products industry (nearly $1.5 billion), followed by the insurance industry ($1.1 billion), electric utilities ($1 billion), the computers/Internet industry ($840 million), business associations ($780 million), and education groups ($740 million).[3] These industries often do not speak with a common voice. Rather they encompass hundreds of firms and other organizations who advocate for and defend their own particular interests, often in conflict with other firms in the same industry.

Interest-group politics involves thousands of groups and individuals competing for the attention of elected representatives and government officials and, once they have that attention, competing with other groups and individuals to influence particular government decisions. Recognizing the importance of institutions in influencing

---

[3] These figures are compiled by the Center for Responsive Politics, www.opensecrets.org.

political outcomes, groups strategically seek out institutional venues they believe will be most hospitable to their goals and interests. A group may succeed in one domain, such as a House committee, only to find itself blocked elsewhere.

This is pluralism at work. It is messy and often disliked by the public at large, but it is an essential feature of American government. The Constitution of the United States embraces this idea fully. The more competition there is among many different interests the less likely it is that any one will triumph and the more likely it is that representatives and government officials will learn what they need to know.[4]

In this chapter we examine some of the antecedents and consequences of interest group politics in the United States. We analyze the social basis of organizations, the problems that result from collective action, and some solutions to these problems. We seek to understand the character and balance of the interests promoted through the pluralistic political system in the United States. We further examine the tremendous growth of interest groups in their number, resources, and activity in recent American political history, especially the emergence of public interest groups. Finally, we examine the strategies that groups use to influence politics and whether their influence in the political process has become excessive.

WHAT ARE THE CHARACTERISTICS OF INTEREST GROUPS?

interest group
An organized group of individuals or organizations that makes policy-related appeals to government.

An **interest group** is an organized group of individuals or organizations that makes policy-related appeals to government. Individuals form groups and engage in collective action to increase the chance that their views will be heard and their interests treated favorably by the government. Interest groups are organized to influence governmental decisions; they are sometimes referred to as lobbies.

Interest groups are sometimes confused with political action committees (see Chapter 10). The difference is that PACs focus on winning elections, and interest groups focus on influencing elected officials. Another distinction we should make is that interest groups differ from political parties: Interest groups tend to concern themselves with the *policies* of government; parties tend to concern themselves with the *personnel* of government.

Interest Groups Not Only Enhance Democracy . . .

There are an enormous number of interest groups in the United States, and millions of Americans are members of one or more groups, at least to the extent of paying dues or attending an occasional meeting. By representing the interests of such large numbers of people and encouraging political participation, organized groups can and do enhance American democracy. Organized groups educate their members about issues that affect them. Groups lobby members of Congress and the executive branch, engage in litigation, and generally represent their members'

---

[4]This sentiment is expressed most eloquently in *Federalist 10*.

interests in the political arena. Groups mobilize their members for elections and grassroots lobbying efforts, thus encouraging participation. Interest groups also monitor government programs to make certain that they do not adversely affect their members. In all these ways, organized interests can be said to promote democratic politics.

But Also Represent the Evils of Faction

The framers of the American Constitution feared the power that could be wielded by organized interests. James Madison wrote:

> The public good is disregarded in the conflict of rival [factions], . . . citizens . . . who are united and actuated by some common impulse of passion, or of interest, adverse to the rights of other citizens, or to the permanent and aggregate interests of the community.[5]

Yet the Founders believed that interest groups thrived because of freedom—the freedom, enjoyed by all Americans, to organize and express their views. To the framers, this problem presented a dilemma. If the government were given the power to regulate or in any way forbid efforts by organized interests to interfere in the political process, it would in effect have the power to suppress freedom. The solution to this dilemma was presented by Madison:

> Take in a greater variety of parties and interest [and] you make it less probable that a majority of the whole will have a common motive to invade the rights of other citizens. . . . [Hence the advantage] enjoyed by a large over a small republic.[6]

According to the Madisonian theory, a good constitution encourages multitudes of interests so that no single interest can ever tyrannize the others. The basic assumption is that competition among interests will produce balance and compromise, with all the interests regulating each other.[7] Today this Madisonian principle of regulation is called **pluralism**. According to pluralist theory, all interests are and should be free to compete for influence in the United States. Moreover, according to pluralist doctrine, the outcome of this competition is compromise and moderation, because no group is likely to be able to achieve any of its goals without accommodating itself to some of the views of its many competitors.[8]

There are tens of thousands of organized groups in the United States, but the huge number of interest groups competing for influence does not mean that all interests are fully and equally represented in the American political process. As we shall see, the political deck is heavily stacked in favor of those interests able to organize and wield substantial economic, social, and institutional resources on behalf

pluralism
The theory that all interests are and should be free to compete for influence in the government. The outcome of this competition is compromise and moderation.

---

[5] Alexander Hamilton, James Madison, and John Jay, *The Federalist Papers*, Clinton L. Rossiter, ed. (New York: New American Library, 1961), no. 10, p. 78.

[6] *Federalist 10*, p. 83.

[7] *Federalist 10*.

[8] The best statement of the pluralist view is in David B. Truman, *The Governmental Process: Political Interests and Public Opinion* (New York: Knopf, 1951), chap. 2.

of their cause. This means that within the universe of interest-group politics, it is political power—not some abstract conception of the public good—that is likely to prevail. Moreover, this means that interest-group politics, taken as a whole, is a political format that works more to the advantage of some types of interests than others. In general, a politics in which interest groups predominate is a politics with a distinctly upper-class bias.

Organized Interests Are Predominantly Economic

When most people think about interest groups, they immediately think of groups with a direct and private economic interest in governmental actions, and, indeed, economic interest is one of the main purposes for which individuals and groups engage in political action. Interest groups are generally supported by groups of producers or manufacturers in a particular economic sector. Examples of this type of group include the National Petrochemical Refiners Association, the American Farm Bureau Federation, and the National Federation of Independent Business, which represents small-business owners. At the same time that broadly representative groups such as these are active in Washington, specific companies—such as Disney, Shell, IBM, and General Motors—may be active on certain issues that are of particular concern to them.

Labor organizations are equally active lobbyists. The AFL-CIO, the United Mine Workers, and the International Brotherhood of Teamsters are all groups that lobby on behalf of organized labor. In recent years, lobbies have arisen to further the interests of public employees, the most significant among these being the American Federation of State, County, and Municipal Employees.

Professional lobbies such as the American Bar Association and the American Medical Association have been particularly successful in furthering their interests in state and federal legislatures. Financial institutions, represented by organizations such as the American Bankers Association and America's Community Bankers, although often less visible than other lobbies, also play an important role in shaping legislative policy.

Recent years have witnessed the growth of a powerful "public interest" lobby purporting to represent interests whose concerns are not addressed by traditional lobbies. These groups have been most visible in the consumer protection and environmental policy areas, although public interest groups cover a broad range of issues. The Natural Resources Defense Council, the Union of Concerned Scientists, and Common Cause are all examples of public interest groups.

The perceived need for representation on Capitol Hill has generated a public-sector lobby, including the National League of Cities and the "research" lobby. The latter group comprises universities and think tanks, such as Harvard University, the Brookings Institution, and the American Enterprise Institute, that have an interest in obtaining government funds for research and support. Indeed, universities have expanded their lobbying efforts even as they have reduced faculty positions and course offerings and increased tuition.[9]

---

[9] Betsy Wagner and David Bowermaster, "B.S. Economics," *Washington Monthly* (November 1992): 19–21.

All Groups Require Money and Leadership, and Most Need Members

Although there are many kinds of interest groups, most share certain key organizational components. First, most groups must attract and keep members. Usually, groups appeal to members not only by promoting political goals or policies that they favor but also by providing them with direct economic or social benefits. Thus, for example, AARP, which promotes the interests of senior citizens, at the same time offers members a variety of insurance benefits and commercial discounts. Similarly, many groups whose goals are chiefly economic or political also seek to attract members through social interaction and good fellowship. Thus the local chapters of many national groups provide their members with a congenial social environment while collecting dues that finance the national office's political efforts.

Second, every group must build a financial structure capable of sustaining an organization and funding the group's activities. Most interest groups rely on yearly membership dues and voluntary contributions from sympathizers. Many also sell members some ancillary services, such as insurance and vacation tours. Third, every group must have a leadership and decision-making structure. For some groups, this structure is very simple. For others, it can involve hundreds of local chapters that are melded into a national apparatus. Finally, most groups include an agency that actually carries out the group's tasks. This may be a research organization, a public relations office, or a lobbying office in Washington or a state capital.

Group Membership Has an Upper-Class Bias

Membership in interest groups is not randomly distributed in the population. People with higher incomes, higher levels of education, and management or professional occupations are much more likely to become members of groups than are those who occupy the lower rungs on the socioeconomic ladder.[10] Well-educated upper-income business and professional people are more likely to have the time and the money, and to have acquired through the educational process the concerns and skills, needed to play a role in a group or association. Moreover, for business and professional people, group membership may provide personal contacts and access to information that can help advance their careers. At the same time, corporate entities—businesses and the like—usually have ample resources to form or participate in groups that seek to advance their causes.

The result is that interest-group politics in the United States tends to have a pronounced upper-class bias. Certainly, many interest groups and political associations have a working-class or lower-class membership—labor organizations or welfare-rights organizations, for example—but the great majority of interest groups and their members are drawn from the middle and upper-middle classes. In general, the "interests" served by interest groups are the interests of society's haves. Even when interest groups take opposing positions on issues and policies, the

---

[10] Kay Lehman Schlozman and John T. Tierney, *Organized Interests and American Democracy* (New York: Harper & Row, 1986), p. 60.

conflicting positions they espouse usually reflect divisions among upper-income strata rather than conflicts between upper and lower classes.

In general, to obtain adequate political representation, forces from the bottom rungs of the socioeconomic ladder must be organized on the massive scale associated with political parties. Parties can organize and mobilize the collective energies of large numbers of people who, as individuals, may have very limited resources. Interest groups, on the other hand, generally organize smaller numbers of the better-to-do. Thus the relative importance of political parties and interest groups in American politics has far-ranging implications for the distribution of political power in the United States. As we saw in Chapter 11, after a period of relative weakness in the 1970s, political parties have witnessed a resurgence over the past twenty-five years, especially in Congress. Interest groups, as we shall see shortly, have also become more numerous, more active, and more influential in American politics.

Groups Form in Response to Changes in the Political Environment

If interest groups and our concerns about them were a new phenomenon, we would not have begun this chapter with James Madison. As long as there is government, as long as government makes policies that add value or impose costs, and as long as there is liberty to organize, interest groups will abound. And if government expands, so will interest groups. For example, a spurt of growth in the national government occurred during the 1880s and 1890s, arising largely from the first government efforts at economic intervention to fight large monopolies and regulate some aspects of interstate commerce. In the latter decade, a parallel spurt of growth occurred in national interest groups, including the imposing National Association of Manufacturers and numerous other trade associations. Many groups organized around specific agricultural commodities as well. This period also marked the beginning of the expansion of trade unions as interest groups. Later, in the 1930s, interest groups with headquarters and representation in Washington began to grow significantly, concurrent with that decade's expansion of the national government.

Over the past forty years, there has been an enormous increase both in the number of interest groups seeking to play a role in the American political process and in the extent of their opportunity to influence that process. The total number of interest groups in the United States today is not known. There are certainly tens of thousands of groups at the national, state, and local levels. One indication of the proliferation of such groups' activity is the growth over time in the number of PACs attempting to influence U.S. elections. Nearly six times as many PACs operated in 2006 as in the 1970s (Figure 12.1). A *New York Times* report, for example, noted that during the 1970s, expanded federal regulation of the automobile, oil, gas, education, and health care industries impelled each of these interests to increase substantially its efforts to influence the government's behavior. These efforts, in turn, had the effect of spurring the organization of other groups to augment or counter the activities of the first.[11] Similarly, federal social programs have occasionally

---

[11] John Herbers, "Special Interests Gaining Power as Voter Disillusionment Grows," *New York Times*, November 14, 1978.

FIGURE 12.1 PAC COUNT, 1974–2008

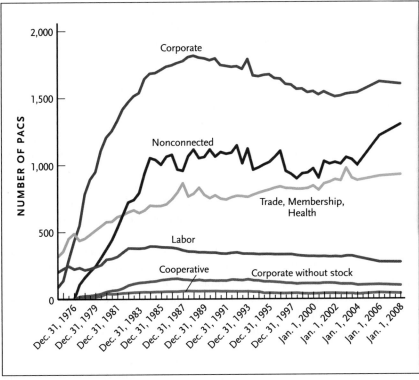

SOURCE: Federal Election Commission, "FEC Records Slight Increase in the Number of PACs," January 17, 2008, www.fec.gov/press/press2008/20080117paccount.shtml.

ANALYZING THE EVIDENCE

Since the 1970s, the number of PACs in the United States has sextupled. PACs are not the only type of interest group, but their proliferation suggests that interest-group activity has been on the rise. What factors account for the rise in interest-group activity?

sparked political organization and action on the part of clientele groups seeking to influence the distribution of benefits and, in turn, the organization of groups opposed to the programs or their cost. For example, federal programs and court decisions in such areas as abortion and school prayer were the stimuli for political action and organization by fundamentalist religious groups. These groups include the Christian Coalition of America, the Family Research Council, the Traditional Values Coalition, Focus on the Family, and Christian Voice. Struggles over such issues as abortion and gay marriage have helped these groups expand their membership roles and build a network of state and local chapters. As we have noted, religious conservatives played key roles in George W. Bush's presidential victories in both 2000 and 2004. In response, Bush launched his so-called faith-based initiative. Under the terms of this program, federal grants and contracts were given to religious organizations to provide social services to children, seniors, and others. By using so-called faith-based groups as federal contractors, Bush sought to reward religious conservatives for their loyalty to the GOP and to ensure that these groups have a continuing stake in Republican success.

Another factor accounting for the explosion of interest-group activity in recent decades was the emergence of new social and political movements. The civil rights and antiwar movements of the 1960s and the reactions against them created a generation of upper-middle-class professionals and intellectuals who have seen themselves as a political force in opposition to the public policies and politicians associated with the nation's postwar regime. Following close on the heels of these movements came the decade-long debate over the Equal Rights Amendment, the Sagebrush Rebellion (concerned with land use in the West), the nuclear disarmament movement, and the antiabortion movement. Such groups sought to make change in social behavior and public policy, usually through civil disobedience.

Members of these movements constructed or strengthened public interest groups such as Common Cause, the Sierra Club, the Environmental Defense Fund, Physicians for Social Responsibility, the National Organization for Women, and the various organizations formed by the consumer activist Ralph Nader. These groups were able to influence the media, Congress, and even the judiciary and enjoyed a remarkable degree of success during the late 1960s and early 1970s in securing the enactment of policies they favored. New politics activists also played a major role in securing the enactment of environmental, consumer, and occupational health and safety legislation.

Among the factors contributing to the rise and success of new politics forces was technology. In the 1970s and 1980s, computerized direct-mail campaigns allowed public interest groups to reach hundreds of thousands of potential sympathizers and contributors. Today the Internet and e-mail serve the same function. Electronic communication allows relatively small groups to efficiently identify and mobilize their adherents throughout the nation. Individuals with perspectives that might be in the minority everywhere can become conscious of each other and mobilize for national political action through the magic of electronic politics. For example, a relatively small number of Americans scattered across the nation might be intensely concerned with the protection of whales and other aquatic mammals. These individuals form an active and vocal community on the Internet, however. They communicate with one another, reach out to potential sympathizers, and bombard politicians with e-mail. In this way, the Internet can facilitate group formation and political action, overcoming the limitations of geography and numbers.

HOW AND WHY DO INTEREST GROUPS FORM?

Pluralist theory argues that because individuals in the United States are free to join or form groups that reflect their common interests, interest groups should easily form whenever a change in the political environment warrants their formation. If this argument is correct, groups should form roughly in proportion to people's interests. We should find a greater number of organizations around interests shared by a greater number of people. The evidence for this pluralist hypothesis is weak, however. Kay Schlozman and John Tierney examined interest groups that represent people's occupations and economic roles.[12] Using census data and lists

---

[12] Kay Schlozman and John Tierney, *Organized Interests and American Democracy* (New York: Harper-Collins, 1986).

TABLE 12.1 WHO IS REPRESENTED BY ORGANIZED INTERESTS?

Economic Role of the Individual	U.S. Adults (%)	Orgs. (%)	Type of Org. in Washington	Ratio of Orgs. to Adults
Managerial/administrative	7	71.0	Business association	10.10
Professional/technical	9	17.0	Professional association	1.90
Student/teacher	4	4.0	Educational organization	1.00
Farmworker	2	1.5	Agricultural workers' organization	0.75
Unable to work	2	0.6	Organization for the handicapped	0.30
Other nonfarm workers	41	4.0	Union	0.10
Homemaker	19	1.8	Women's organization	0.09
Retired	12	0.8	Senior citizens' organization	0.07
Looking for work	4	0.1	Unemployment organization	0.03

ANALYZING THE EVIDENCE

What types of interests are most likely to be represented by interest groups? If interest-group politics is biased in favor of the wealthy and the powerful, should we curb group politics? What was James Madison's answer? Do you agree with Madison?

of interest groups, they compared how many people in the United States have particular economic roles with how many organizations represent those roles in Washington. For example, they found that (in the mid-1980s) 4 percent of the population was looking for work, but only a handful of organizations represented the unemployed in Washington.[13]

There is a considerable disparity in Washington representation across categories of individuals in the population, as Table 12.1 suggests. Schlozman and Tierney note, for example, that there are at least a dozen groups representing senior citizens, but none for the middle-aged. Ducks Unlimited is an organization dedicated to the preservation of ducks and their habitats; turkeys, on the other hand, have no one working on their behalf. The pluralists' inability to explain why groups form around some interests and not others led some scholars to investigate the dynamics of collective action. Mancur Olson's work, mentioned in Chapter 1 and discussed later in this chapter, is the most well-known challenge to the pluralists. It is in Olson's insights that we find the basis for interest-group formation.

Interest Groups Facilitate Cooperation

Groups of individuals pursuing some common interest or shared objective—maintenance of a hunting and fishing habitat, creation of a network for sharing computer software, lobbying for favorable legislation, playing a Beethoven symphony,

---

[13] Of course, the *number* of organizations is at best only a rough measure of the extent to which various categories of citizens are represented in the interest-group world of Washington.

and so on—consist of individuals who bear some cost or make some contribution on behalf of the joint goal. Each member of the Possum Hollow Rod and Gun Club may, for example, pay annual dues and devote one weekend a year to cleaning up the rivers and forests of the club-owned game preserve.

We can think of this in an analytic fashion, somewhat removed from any of these examples, as an instance of two-person cooperation writ large. Accordingly, each one of a very large number of individuals has, in the simplest situation, two options in his or her behavioral repertoire: "contribute" or "don't contribute" to achieving the jointly shared objective. If the number of contributors to the group enterprise is sufficiently large, a group goal is achieved. However, there is a twist. If the group goal is achieved, then every member of the group enjoys its benefits, whether he or she contributed to its achievement or not.

The Prisoner's Dilemma and Free Riding.   Researchers often rely on the metaphor of the prisoner's dilemma when theorizing about social situations of collective action. This is similar to the fence-mending example in Chapter 1's discussion of bargaining failure. In the prisoner's dilemma, two prisoners (A and B) who are accused of jointly committing a crime are kept in separate interview rooms. The arresting officers do not have enough evidence to persuade a judge to give the prisoners the maximum sentence, so the officers hope that one of the prisoners will provide the additional evidence they require. The prisoners know that the officers have scant evidence against them and that they will probably receive a less severe sentence or escape punishment altogether if they remain silent. Each prisoner is offered the same plea bargain: "Testify against the other prisoner in exchange for freedom, provided that your accomplice does not also testify against you. Remain silent, and you will possibly get the maximum sentence if your accomplice testifies against you."

If you assume that prisoners A and B are self-interested, rational actors (who, given the choice between the two alternatives, will choose the one that offers the best deal) and that they prefer less jail time to more, then they will face an unpleasant choice. Notice that in Figure 12.2, prisoner A is better off choosing to snitch no matter what prisoner B does. If B chooses to snitch, then A's choice to snitch gets A a three-year jail term, but a don't-snitch choice by A results in six years for A—clearly worse. On the other hand, if B chooses not to snitch, then A gets no jail

FIGURE 12.2 THE PRISONER'S DILEMMA

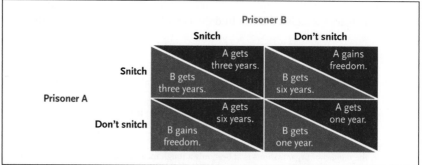

time if he snitches instead of one year if he also chooses not to snitch. In short, A is always better off snitching. But this situation is symmetrical, so it follows that B is better off snitching, too. If both prisoners snitch, the prosecutor is able to convict both of them, and each serves three years. If they had both been *irrational* and kept silent, they would have gotten only one year each! In terms of game theory (from which the prisoner's dilemma is drawn), each player has a dominant strategy—snitching is best no matter what the other player does—and this leads paradoxically to an outcome in which each player is *worse* off.

The prisoner's dilemma provides the insight that rational individual behavior does not always lead to rational collective results. The logic of this situation is very compelling—if A appreciates the dilemma and realizes that B appreciates the dilemma, then A will still be drawn to the choice of snitching. The reasons for this are the temptation to get off scot free (if he testifies and his accomplice doesn't) and the *fear* of being suckered. The dilemma is brilliant because it applies to a wide range of circumstances.

Consider the swamp-clearing example described in Chapter 1, in which each person benefits from a drained swamp even if he or she does not provide the required effort. As long as enough other people do so, any individual can ride free on the efforts of the others. This is a multiperson prisoner's dilemma because not providing effort, like snitching, is a dominant strategy, yet if everyone avails himself or herself of it, it leads to an unwanted outcome: a mosquito-infested swamp. The prospect of free riding, as we shall see next, is the bane of collective action.

The Logic of Collective Action.   The economist Mancur Olson, writing in 1965, essentially took on the political science establishment by noting that the pluralist assumption of the time—that common interests among individuals are automatically transformed into group organization and collective action—was problematic. Individuals are tempted to free ride on the efforts of others, have difficulty coordinating multiple objectives, and may even have differences of opinion about which common interest to pursue (conflicts of interest).

Olson was at his most persuasive when talking about large groups and mass collective action, such as many of the antiwar demonstrations and civil rights rallies of the 1960s. In these circumstances, the world of politics is a bit like the swamp-clearing example, where each individual has a rational strategy of not contributing. The logic of collective action makes it difficult to induce participation in and contribution to collective goals.

Olson claimed that this difficulty is most severe in large groups, for three reasons. First, large groups tend to be anonymous. Each household in a city is a taxpaying unit and may share the wish to see property taxes lowered. It is difficult, however, to forge a group identity or induce households to contribute effort or activity for the cause of lower taxes on such a basis. Second, in the anonymity of the large-group context, it is especially plausible to claim that no one individual's contribution makes much difference. Should an individual citizen kill the better part of a morning writing a letter to his city council member in support of lower property taxes? Will it make much difference? If hardly anyone else writes, then the council member is unlikely to pay much heed to this one letter; on the other hand, if the council member is inundated with letters, would one more have a significant additional effect? Finally, there is the problem of enforcement. In a large group, are other group members going to punish a slacker? By definition, they cannot prevent the slacker from receiving the benefits of collective action, should those benefits materialize. (Every property owner's taxes will be lowered if anyone's are.) But more to the point, in a large, anonymous group it is often hard to know who has and who has not contributed, and because there is only the most limited sort of group identity, it is hard for contributors to identify, much less take action against, slackers. As a consequence, many large groups that share common interests fail to mobilize at all—they remain *latent*.

This same problem plagues small groups, too, as the swamp-clearing problem in Chapter 1 reveals. But Olson argued that small groups manage to overcome the problem of collective action more frequently and to a greater extent than their larger counterparts. Small groups are more personal, and their members are therefore more vulnerable to interpersonal persuasion. In small groups, individual contributions may make a more noticeable difference, so that individuals feel that their contributions are more essential. Contributors in small groups, moreover, often know who they are and who the slackers are. Thus punishment, ranging from subtle judgmental pressure to social ostracism, is easier to effect.

Contrasting large groups that often remain latent to smaller ones, Olson called these small groups *privileged*, because of their advantage in overcoming the free-riding, coordination, and conflict-of-interest problems of collective action. It is for these perhaps counterintuitive reasons that small groups often prevail over, or enjoy greater privileges relative to, larger groups. These reasons, therefore, help explain why we so often see producers win out over consumers, owners of capital win out over owners of labor, and a party's elite win out over its mass members.

Selective Benefits: A Solution to the Collective-Action Problem

Despite the free-rider problem, interest groups offer numerous incentives to join. Most important, as Olson shrewdly noted, they make various "selective benefits" available only to group members (see Chapter 1). These benefits can be informational, material, solidary, or purposive. Table 12.2 gives some examples of the range of benefits in each of these categories.

Informational benefits are the most widespread and important category of selective benefits offered to group members. Information is provided through conferences, training programs, and newsletters and other periodicals sent automatically to those who have paid membership dues.

Material benefits include anything that can be measured monetarily, such as special services, goods, and even money. A broad range of material benefits can be offered by groups to attract members. These benefits often include discount purchasing, shared advertising, and perhaps most valuable of all, health and retirement insurance.

Another option identified in Table 12.2 is that of **solidary benefits**. The most notable of this class of benefits are the friendship and "networking" opportunities that membership provides. Another benefit that has been important to many nonprofit and citizens' groups is what has come to be called consciousness-raising.

TABLE 12.2 SELECTIVE BENEFITS OF INTEREST-GROUP MEMBERSHIP

Category	Benefits
Informational benefits	Conferences Professional contacts Training programs Publications Coordination among organizations Research Legal help Professional codes Collective bargaining
Material benefits	Travel packages Insurance Discounts on consumer goods
Solidary benefits	Friendship Networking opportunities
Purposive benefits	Advocacy Representation before government Participation in public affairs

SOURCE: Adapted from Jack L. Walker, Jr., *Mobilizing Interest Groups in America: Patrons, Professions, and Social Movements* (Ann Arbor: University of Michigan Press, 1991), p. 86.

One example of this can be seen in the claims of many women's organizations that active participation conveys to each member of the organization an enhanced sense of her own value and a stronger ability to advance individual as well as collective civil rights.

A fourth type of benefit involves the appeal of the purpose of an interest group. The benefits of religious interest groups provide us with the best examples of such **purposive benefits**. The Christian right is a powerful movement made up of a number of interest groups that offer virtually no material benefits to their members. The growth and the success of these groups depend on the religious identification and affirmation of their members. Many such religiously based interest groups have arisen, especially at state and local levels, throughout American history. For example, both the abolition and the prohibition movements were driven by religious interest groups whose main attractions were nonmaterial benefits.

Ideology itself, or the sharing of a commonly developed ideology, is another important nonmaterial benefit. Many of the most successful interest groups of the past twenty years have been citizens' groups or public interest groups whose members are brought together largely around shared ideological goals, including government reform, election and campaign reform, civil rights, economic equality, "family values," or even opposition to government itself.

purposive benefits Selective benefits of group membership that emphasize the purpose and accomplishments of the group.

Political Entrepreneurs Organize and Maintain Groups

In a review of Olson's book, the economist Richard Wagner noticed that Olson's arguments about groups and politics in general, and his theory of selective incentives in particular, had very little to say about the internal workings of groups.[14] In Wagner's experience, however, groups often came into being and then were maintained in good working order, not only because of selective incentives but also because of the extraordinary efforts of specific individuals—leaders, in ordinary language, or "political entrepreneurs" in Wagner's more colorful expression.

Wagner was motivated to raise the issue of group leaders because, in his view, Olson's theory was too pessimistic. Mass organizations in the real world—labor unions, consumer associations, senior citizens' groups, environmental organizations—all exist, some persisting and prospering over long periods. Contrary to Olson's suggestions, they seem somehow to get jump-started in the real world. Wagner suggests that a special kind of theory of selective incentives is called for. Specifically, he argues that certain selective benefits may accrue to those who organize and maintain otherwise latent groups.

Senator Robert Wagner (no relation) in the 1930s and Congressman Claude Pepper in the 1970s each had private reasons—electoral incentives—to try to organize laborers and the elderly, respectively. Wagner, a Democrat from New York, had a large constituency of working men and women who would reward him by reelecting him if he bore the cost of organizing workers (or at least bore the cost of facilitating their organization). And this he did. The law that bears his name, the Wagner Act of 1935, made it much easier for unions to organize in the industrial North.[15] Likewise, Claude Pepper, a Democratic congressman with a large number of elderly constituents in his South Miami district, saw it as serving his own electoral interests to provide the initial investment of effort to organize the elderly as a political force.

In general, a political entrepreneur is someone who sees a prospective dividend from cooperation. This is another way of saying that there is a latent group that, if it were to become manifest, would enjoy the fruits of collective action. For a price, whether in votes (as in the cases of Wagner and Pepper), a percentage of the dividend, nonmaterial glory, or other perks, the entrepreneur bears the costs of organizing, expends effort to monitor individuals for slacker behavior, and sometimes even imposes punishment on slackers (such as expelling them from the group and denying them any of its selective benefits).

An illustration of this phenomenon is a story about a British tourist who visited China in the late nineteenth century. She was appalled to see teams of men pulling barges along the Chang (Yangtze) River, overseen by whip-wielding masters. She remarked to her guide that such an uncivilized state of affairs would

---

[14] Richard Wagner, "Pressure Groups and Political Entrepreneurs," *Papers on Non-market Decision Making* 1 (1966): 161–70.

[15] The Wagner Act made it possible for unions to organize by legalizing the so-called closed shop. If a worker took a job in a closed shop or plant, he or she was *required* to join the union there. "Do not contribute" was no longer an option, so that workers in closed shops could not free ride on the efforts made by others to improve wages and working conditions.

never be tolerated in modern societies like those in the West. The guide, anxious to please but concerned that his employer had come to a wildly erroneous conclusion, hastily responded, "Madam, I think you misunderstand. The man carrying the whip is *employed* by those pulling the barge. He noticed that it is generally difficult, if you are pulling your weight along a tow path, to detect whether any of your team members are pulling theirs or, instead, whether they are free riding on your labors. He convinced the workers that his entrepreneurial services were required and that they should hire him. For an agreed-on compensation, he monitors each team member's effort level, whipping those who shirk in their responsibilities. Notice, madam, that he rarely ever uses the whip. His mere presence is sufficient to get the group to accomplish the task."

Thus political entrepreneurs, such as the whip-wielding driver, may be thought of as complements to Olsonian selective incentives in that both provide ways of motivating groups to accomplish collective objectives. Indeed, if selective incentives *resolve* the paradox of collective action, then political entrepreneurs *dissolve* the paradox. Both are helpful, and sometimes both are needed to initiate and maintain collective action. Groups that manage, perhaps on their own, to get themselves organized with a low level of activity often take the next step of creating leaders and leadership institutions to increase the activity level and the resulting cooperation dividends. Richard Wagner, in other words, took Olson's theory of selective incentives and suggested an alternative explanation, one that made room for institutional solutions to the problem of collective action.

HOW DO INTEREST GROUPS INFLUENCE POLICY?

Interest groups work to improve the probability that they and their policy interests will be heard and treated favorably by all branches and levels of the government. The quest for political influence of power takes many forms. We can roughly divide these strategies into "insider strategies" and "outsider strategies."

Insider strategies include gaining access to key decision makers and using the courts. Influencing policy through traditional political institutions, of course, requires understanding how those institutions work. A lobbyist who wishes to have Congress address a problem with legislation will try to find a sympathetic member of Congress, preferably on a committee with jurisdiction over the problem, and will work directly with the member's staff. If an organization decides to bring suit in the courts, it may want to sue in a jurisdiction where it has a good chance of getting a judge favorable to the case or where the immediate appellate courts are likely to support the case. Gaining access is not easy. Legislators and bureaucrats have little time and many requests to juggle; courts have full dockets. Interest groups themselves have limited budgets and staff. They must choose their battles well and map out the strategy most likely to succeed.

Outsider strategies include going public and using electoral tactics. Just as politicians can gain an electoral edge by informing voters, so too can groups. A well-planned public information campaign or targeted campaign activities and contributions can have as much influence as working the corridors of Congress.

Many groups employ a mix of insider and outsider strategies. For example, environmental groups such as the Sierra Club lobby members of Congress and key congressional staff members, participate in bureaucratic rule making by offering comments and suggestions to agencies on new environmental rules, and bring lawsuits under various environmental acts, such as the Endangered Species Act, which authorizes groups and citizens to come to court if they believe the act is being violated. At the same time, the Sierra Club attempts to influence public opinion through media campaigns and to influence electoral politics by supporting candidates who they believe share their environmental views and by opposing candidates who they view as foes of environmentalism.

The Center for Responsive Politics estimates that the total cost of lobbying activities at the federal level was $2.8 billion in 2007 and $3.2 billion in 2008. This figure includes grassroots organizations that spent a few thousand dollars and organizations such as the U.S. Chamber of Commerce, which spent $57.9 million.[16] The federal figure does not include campaign contributions or lobbying at the state and local levels, but the amount spent to influence state legislatures is also substantial. For example, in 2005, according to the Center for Public Integrity, lobbyists spent $240 million to influence California lawmakers, $175 million in Texas, $150 million in New York, $130 million in Pennsylvania, and more than $50 million apiece in Massachusetts and Minnesota. All told, $1.16 billion was spent in forty-two states that require lobbyists to report their expenditures. The total resources devoted to lobbying at the state and federal level, then, is approximately $4 billion a year.[17]

Whether an excessively large amount of money is devoted to lobbying is subject to some dispute. Those engaged in lobbying provide a valued service for the firms and other organizations that they represent by helping to shape legislation, influence administrative decisions, and advocate in court. Anyone who spends time in state or federal government quickly encounters lobbyists and others working on behalf of special interests. But as an economic matter, the amount of money spent on political activity by firms seems small. The value of goods purchased in a market is approximately equal to the amount of money someone is willing to pay for them, and many industries in the United States generate far more than $4 billion a year selling their goods and services. As a fraction of total government expenditures, total lobbying expenditures equal less than one-tenth of 1 percent, and lobbying is only a trace amount of the total revenue of firms' total expenses. This has led some researchers to question whether the total influence of groups can be substantial.[18] Nevertheless, the effects of lobbying on the economy as a whole may be substantial, because the gains won by individual firms could have substantial effects on other firms, consumers, society, or the environment.

---

[16] Center for Responsive Politics, Lobbying Database, www.opensecrets.org/lobby/index.php (accessed 4/7/09).

[17] Center for Public Integrity, http://projects.publicintegrity.org/lobby (accessed 5/7/09).

[18] See Stephen Ansolabehere, John de Figueiredo, and James M. Snyder, Jr., "Why Is There So Little Money in U.S. Politics?" *Journal of Economic Perspectives* 17, no. 1 (Winter 2003): 105–30.

Direct Lobbying

Lobbying is an attempt by a group to influence the policy process through persuasion of government officials. Most Americans tend to believe that interest groups exert their influence through direct contact with members of Congress, but lobbying encompasses a broad range of activities that groups engage in with all sorts of government officials and the public as a whole.

lobbying An attempt by a group to influence the policy process through persuasion of government officials.

The 1946 Federal Regulation of Lobbying Act defined a lobbyist as "any person who shall engage himself for pay or any consideration for the purpose of attempting to influence the passage or defeat of any legislation of the Congress of the United States." The 1995 Lobbying Disclosure Act requires all organizations employing lobbyists to register with Congress and disclose whom they represent, whom they lobby, what they are lobbying for, and how much they are paid. More than 7,000 organizations, collectively employing many thousands of lobbyists, are currently registered.

Lobbying involves a great deal of activity on the part of someone speaking for an interest. Lobbyists badger and buttonhole legislators, administrators, and committee staff members with facts about pertinent issues and facts or claims about public support of them.[19] Lobbyists can serve a useful purpose in the legislative and administrative process by providing this kind of information. In 1978, during debate on a bill to expand the requirement for lobbying disclosures, Democratic senators Edward Kennedy of Massachusetts and Dick Clark of Iowa joined with Republican senator Robert Stafford of Vermont to issue the following statement: "Government without lobbying could not function. The flow of information to Congress and to every federal agency is a vital part of our democratic system."[20]

Lobbying Members of Congress. Interest groups also have substantial influence in setting the legislative agenda and in helping craft the language of legislation (Figure 12.3). Today sophisticated lobbyists win influence by providing information about policies to busy members of Congress. As one lobbyist noted, "You can't get access without knowledge. . . . I can go in to see John Dingell [chairman of the House Committee on Energy and Commerce], but if I have nothing to offer or nothing to say, he's not going to want to see me."[21] In recent years, interest groups have also begun to build broader coalitions and comprehensive campaigns around particular policy issues.[22] These coalitions do not rise from the grass roots but instead are put together by Washington lobbyists who launch comprehensive

---

[19] For discussions of lobbying, see Jeffrey M. Berry, *Lobbying for the People: The Political Behavior of Public Interest Groups* (Princeton, N.J.: Princeton University Press, 1977); and John R. Wright, *Interest Groups and Congress: Lobbying, Contributions, and Influence* (Boston: Allyn & Bacon, 1996).

[20] "The Swarming Lobbyists," *Time*, August 7, 1978, p. 15.

[21] Daniel Franklin, "Tommy Boggs and the Death of Health Care Reform," *Washington Monthly* (April 1995): 36.

[22] Marie Hojnacki, "Interest Groups' Decisions to Join Alliances or Work Alone," *American Journal of Political Science* 41 (1997): 61–87; Kevin W. Hula, *Lobbying Together: Interest Group Coalitions in Legislative Politics* (Washington, D.C.: Georgetown University Press, 1999).

FIGURE 12.3 HOW INTEREST GROUPS INFLUENCE CONGRESS

**ANALYZING
THE EVIDENCE**

Interest groups can
influence members
of Congress in a
variety of ways.
They may seek to
mobilize popular
support in the form
of grassroots cam-
paigns; they may try
to generate publicity
favorable to their
cause; they may
work through con-
gressional staffers;
or they may seek to
lobby the member
of Congress directly.
How might these
various strategies
work together? What
pitfalls might an
interest group en-
counter in trying to
influence members
of Congress?

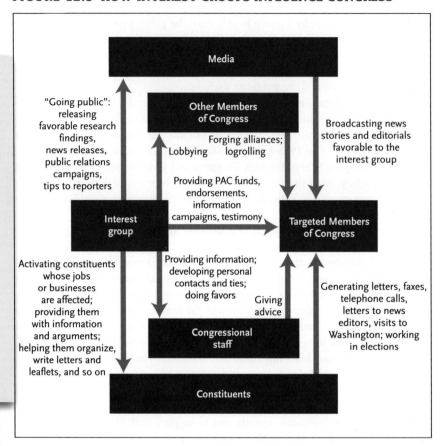

campaigns that combine simulated grassroots activity with information and campaign funding for members of Congress.

Some interest groups are able to place their lobbyists directly on congressional
staffs. In 2007, several experienced lobbyists and Washington insiders were "borrowed" by the new Democratic leadership to help organize the business of the new
Congress. For example, Dennis Fitzgibbons, a lobbyist for DaimlerChrysler, was
hired as chief of staff of the House Energy and Commerce Committee. In his capacity as an auto lobbyist, Fitzgibbons attempted to block efforts to force automakers to make vehicles more fuel efficient or to manufacture vehicles that would use
alternative fuels. In his new job, Fitzgibbons plays a powerful role on the panel that
will make the legislative decisions about these issues. At the same time, the House
Democratic whip, James Clyburn of South Carolina, appointed Matt Gelman a senior adviser. Gelman will be on leave from Microsoft Corporation, where he serves
as director of federal government affairs, a position to which he plans to return.[23]

---

[23] Birnbaum, "In the Loop on K Street."

Both Fitzgibbons and Gelman said that they would not allow their roles as lobbyists to affect their new positions. These individuals, however, could be seen as "stealth lobbyists," unlikely to forget the needs of the corporations for which they recently worked and to which they are likely to return.

Not every interest group can embed a stealth lobbyist in Congress. Many, however, do the next best thing: They hire the spouses and relatives of members of Congress or important staffers to lobby for them. One extensive study of the congressional appropriations process conducted in 2006 found thirty instances in which lobbyists related to members and senior staffers of the House and Senate appropriations committees sought money in the appropriation bills their family members helped to write. In twenty-two cases, relatives were able to get specific language inserted in bills that guaranteed money for their clients.[24] Important members of Congress married to lobbyists include Representative John Dingell (D-Mich.), Senator Joe Lieberman (ID-Conn.), and Representative Roy Blunt (R-Mo.).

Some interest groups have strong ties to the Democrats and others to the Republicans. Most interest groups, however, endeavor to maintain good relations with both political parties and are prepared to work with the party in power to achieve their legislative goals. When Republicans controlled Congress, trade associations and corporate interests hired Republican lobbyists and built close ties to the GOP leadership. In 2007, as Democrats returned to power, the same interest groups hired Democratic lobbyists and worked to build close ties to the new Democratic leadership. And when it came to campaign contributions, corporate interests cheerfully backed both sides, making sure to befriend the winners, whoever they might be.[25]

What happens to interests that do not engage in extensive lobbying? They often find themselves "Microsofted." In 1998, the software giant was facing antitrust action from the Justice Department and had few friends in Congress. One member of the House, Representative Billy Tauzin (R-La.), told Microsoft's chairman's, Bill Gates, that without an extensive investment in lobbying, the corporation would continue to be "demonized." Gates responded by quadrupling Microsoft's lobbying expenditures and hiring a group of lobbyists with strong ties to Congress. The result was congressional pressure on the Justice Department, resulting in a settlement of the Microsoft suit on terms favorable to the company. Similarly, in 1999, members of Congress advised Wal-Mart that its efforts to win approval to operate savings and loans in its stores were doomed to failure if the retailer did not greatly increase its lobbying efforts. "They don't give money. They don't have congressional representation—so nobody here cares about them," said one influential member. Like Microsoft, Wal-Mart learned its lesson, hired more lobbyists, and got what it wanted.[26]

Providing access is only one of the many services lobbyists perform. Lobbyists often testify on behalf of their clients at congressional committee and agency

---

[24] Matt Kelley and Peter Eisler, "Relatives Have Inside Track in Lobbying for Tax Dollars," *USA Today*, October 17, 2006, p. 1.

[25] "Cash Flow: Congress Changes Hands—or Does It?" *Washington Post*, January 7, 2007, p. B2.

[26] Common Cause, "The Microsoft Playbook: A Report from Common Cause," September 25, 2000.

hearings; lobbyists sometimes help their clients identify potential allies with whom to construct coalitions; lobbyists provide research and information to government officials; lobbyists often draft proposed legislation or regulations to be introduced by friendly lawmakers; lobbyists talk to reporters, place ads in newspapers, and organize letter-writing, e-mail, and telegram campaigns. Lobbyists also play an important role in fund-raising, helping to direct clients' contributions to members of Congress and presidential candidates.

Lobbying the President. All these efforts and more are needed when the target of a lobbying campaign is the president of the United States. So many individuals and groups clamor for the president's time and attention that only the most skilled and well-connected members of the lobbying community can hope to influence presidential decisions. When running for president, Barack Obama laid down a bold promist to "free the executive branch from special-interest influence." No political appointee, the Obama team promised, "will be permitted to work on regulations or contracts directly and substantially related to their prior employer for two years." That promise proved exceedingly difficult to keep as many in the Obama transition team, including the nominee for Health and Human Services Secretary and ex-Senate majority leader Thomas Daschle, had close ties to lobbyists or had worked for lobbying firms.[27]

Lobbying the Executive Branch. Even when an interest group is very successful at getting its bill passed by Congress and signed by the president, the prospect of full and faithful implementation of that law is not guaranteed. Often a group and its allies do not pack up and go home as soon as the president turns their lobbied-for law over to the appropriate agency. On average, 40 percent of interest-group representatives regularly contact both legislative and executive branch organizations, whereas 13 percent contact only the legislative branch and 16 percent contact only the executive branch.[28]

In some respects, interest-group access to the executive branch is promoted by federal law. The Administrative Procedure Act, first enacted in 1946 and frequently amended, requires most federal agencies to provide notice and an opportunity for comment before implementing proposed rules and regulations. So-called notice-and-comment rule making is designed to allow interests an opportunity to make their views known and participate in the implementation of federal legislation that affects them. In 1990, Congress enacted the Negotiated Rulemaking Act to encourage administrative agencies to engage in direct and open negotiations with affected interests when developing new regulations. These two pieces of legislation, which have been strongly enforced by the federal courts, have played an important role

---

[27] Chris Frates, "Daschle Lobby Ties Bump Obama Vow," *Politico*, November 30, 2008, www.politico.com/news/stories/1108/16015.html (accessed 4/7/09); David Kirkpatrick, "In Transition, Ties to Lobbying," *New York Times*, November 15, 2008, www.nytimes.com/2008/11/15/us/politics/15transition.html (accessed 4/7/09).

[28] John P. Heinz, Edward O. Laumann, Robert L. Nelson, and Robert H. Salisbury, *The Hollow Core: Private Interests in National Policy Making* (Cambridge, Mass.: Harvard University Press, 1993).

in opening the bureaucratic process to interest-group influence. Today few federal agencies would consider attempting to implement a new rule without consulting affected interests, which are sometimes known in Washington as "stakeholders."[29]

Cultivating Access.   Exerting influence on Congress or government agencies by providing their members with information about issues, support, and even threats of retaliation requires easy and constant access to decision makers. One interesting example of why groups need to cultivate and maintain access is provided by the dairy farmers. Through the 1960s, dairy farmers were part of the powerful coalition of agricultural interests that had full access to Congress and the Department of Agriculture. During the 1960s, a series of disputes over commodities prices broke out between the dairy farmers and the producers of corn, grain, and other agricultural commodities. Dairy farmers, whose cows consume grain, prefer low commodities prices, whereas grain producers obviously prefer high prices. The commodities producers won the battle, and Congress raised commodities prices, in part at the expense of the dairy farmers. In the 1970s, the dairy farmers left the agriculture coalition, set up their own lobby and political action groups, and became heavily involved in public relations campaigns and both congressional and presidential elections. Thus the dairy farmers lost their traditional access and had to pursue an "outsider" strategy. Indeed, the political fortunes of the dairy operations were badly hurt when they were accused of making illegal contributions to President Richard Nixon's reelection campaign in 1972.

Cultivating access usually requires considerable time and effort, and a successful long-term strategy for gaining access may entail the sacrifice of short-run influence. For example, many of the most important organized interests in agriculture devote far more time and resources to cultivating the staff and trustees of state agriculture schools and county agents back home than to buttonholing members of Congress or bureaucrats in Washington.

Regulations on Lobbying.   As a result of the constant access to important decision makers that lobbyists seek out and require, stricter guidelines regulating the actions of lobbyists have been adopted in the last decade. For example, as of 1993, businesses may no longer deduct from their taxes the cost of lobbying. Trade associations must report to members the proportion of their dues that goes to lobbying, and that proportion may not be reported as a business expense. The most important attempt to limit the influence of lobbyists was the 1995 Lobbying Disclosure Act, which significantly broadened the definition of people and organizations that must register as lobbyists. According to the filings under this act, almost 11,500 lobbyists were working the halls of Congress in 2006.

In 1996, Congress passed legislation limiting gifts from a single source to $50 and no more than $100 annually. It also banned the practice of honoraria, which had been used by special interests to supplement congressional salaries. But Congress did not limit the travel of representatives, senators, their spouses, or congressional

---

[29] For an excellent discussion of the political origins of the Administrative Procedure Act, see Martin Shapiro, "APA: Past, Present, Future," *Virginia Law Review* 72 (1986): 447–92.

staff members. Interest groups can pay for congressional travel as long as a trip is related to legislative business and is disclosed on congressional reports within thirty days. On these trips, meals and entertainment expenses are not limited to $50 per event and $100 annually. The rules of Congress allow its members to travel on corporate jets as long as they pay an amount equal to first-class airfare.

In 2007, congressional Democrats secured the enactment of a package of ethics rules designed to fulfill their 2006 campaign promise to bring an end to lobbying abuses. The new rules prohibited lobbyists from paying for most meals, trips, parties, and gifts for members of Congress. Lobbyists were also required to disclose the amounts and sources of small campaign contributions they collected from clients and "bundled" into large contributions. And interest groups were required to disclose the funds they used to rally voters to support or oppose legislative proposals. As soon as these new rules were enacted, lobbyists and politicians hurried to find ways to cirumvent them, and it remains to be seen whether these reforms will have any major impact.

Using the Courts

Interest groups sometimes turn to the courts to augment other avenues of access. They can use the courts to affect public policy in at least three ways: (1) by bringing suit directly on behalf of the group itself, (2) by financing suits brought by individuals, and (3) by filing a companion brief as *amicus curiae* (literally, "friend of the court") to an existing court case.

Among the most significant modern illustrations of the use of the courts as a strategy for political influence are those that accompanied the "sexual revolution" of the 1960s and the emergence of the movement for women's rights. Beginning in the mid-1960s, a series of cases was brought into the federal courts in an effort to force the definition of a right to privacy in sexual matters. The effort began with a challenge to state restrictions on obtaining contraceptives for nonmedical purposes, a challenge that was effectively made in *Griswold v. Connecticut*, in which the Supreme Court held that states could neither prohibit the dissemination of information about, nor prohibit the actual use of, contraceptives by married couples. That case was soon followed by *Eisenstadt v. Baird*, in which the Court held that the states could not prohibit the use of contraceptives by single persons any more than it could prohibit their use by married couples. One year later, in the 1973 case of *Roe v. Wade*, the Court held that states could not impose an absolute ban on voluntary abortions. Each of these cases, as well as others, were part of the Court's enunciation of a constitutional doctrine of privacy.[30]

The 1973 abortion case sparked a controversy that brought conservatives to the fore on a national level. Conservative groups then made extensive use of the courts to whittle away the scope of the privacy doctrine. They obtained rulings, for example, that prohibit the use of federal funds to pay for voluntary abortions. And in 1989, right-to-life groups were able to use a strategy of litigation

---

[30] *Griswold v. Connecticut*, 381 U.S. 479 (1965); *Eisenstadt v. Baird*, 405 U.S. 438 (1972); *Roe v. Wade*, 410 U.S. 113 (1973).

that significantly undermined the *Roe v. Wade* decision—namely, in the case of *Webster v. Reproductive Health Services*, which restored the right of states to place restrictions on abortion.[31]

Another extremely significant set of contemporary illustrations of the use of the courts as a strategy for political influence are those found in the history of the National Association for the Advancement of Colored People. The most important of these court cases was *Brown v. Board of Education*, in which the Supreme Court held that legal segregation of the schools was unconstitutional.[32]

Business groups are also frequent users of the courts, because of the number of government programs that apply to them. Litigation involving large businesses is most mountainous in such areas as taxation, antitrust issues, interstate transportation, patents, and product quality and standardization. Often a business is brought to litigation against its will by virtue of initiatives taken against it by other businesses or by government agencies. But many individual businesses bring suit themselves to influence government policy. Major corporations and their trade associations pay tremendous amounts of money each year in fees to the most prestigious Washington law firms. Some of this money is expended in gaining access. A great proportion of it, however, is used to keep the best and most experienced lawyers prepared to represent the corporations in court or before administrative agencies when necessary.

The forces of the new politics movement made significant use of the courts during the 1970s and 1980s, and judicial decisions were instrumental in advancing their goals. Facilitated by changes in the rules governing access to the courts (the rules of standing are discussed in Chapter 8), the new politics agenda was clearly visible in court decisions handed down in several key policy areas. In environmental policy, new politics groups were able to force federal agencies to pay attention to environmental issues even when the agencies were not directly involved in activities related to environmental quality. By the 2000s, the courts often were the battleground on which those in the new political movements waged their fights. Perhaps the most dramatic were a string of lawsuits spanning twenty years (from 1986 to 2006) in which antiabortion protest organizations, such as Pro-Life Action Network and Operation Rescue, and the National Organization of Women repeatedly took each other to court to establish the rules governing clinic protests. Ultimately, the U.S. Supreme Court sided with the antiabortion organizations, but not before deciding three separate cases on the matter, at extremely high cost to both sides.[33]

Mobilizing Public Opinion

Organizations try to bring pressure to bear on politicians through a variety of methods designed to mobilize public opinion. This strategy is known as **going public**. When groups go public, they use their various resources to try to persuade large numbers of people to pay attention to their concerns. They hope that greater

going public
The act of launching a media campaign to build popular support.

---

[31] *Webster v. Reproductive Health Services*, 492 U.S. 490 (1989).

[32] *Brown v. Board of Education*, 347 U.S. 483 (1954).

[33] *Scheidler v. National Organization of Women et al.*, 547 U.S. 9 (2006).

visibility and public support will help underline the importance of such issues to those in power. Advertising campaigns, protests, and grassroots lobbying efforts are all examples of going public. An increased use of this kind of strategy is traced to the rise of modern advertising at the beginning of the twentieth century. As early as the 1930s, political analysts distinguished between the "old lobby" of direct group representation before Congress and the "new lobby" of public-relations professionals addressing the public at large in order to reach Congress indirectly.[34] Going public, then, differs from other strategies that interest groups use to influence public policy. The "new lobby" techniques are designed to change the way people think, rather than just changing the actions of insiders.

One way of going public that groups often use is conventional advertising. For example, a casual scan of major newspapers, magazines, and Web sites will immediately reveal numerous examples of expensive, well-designed ads by major companies and industry associations, such as those from the oil and gas, automobile, and health and pharmaceutical companies. Such ads are often intended to show what the firms do for the country, not merely the products they develop. Their purpose is to create and maintain a strongly positive association between the organization and the community at large in the hope that the community's favorable feelings can be drawn on as needed in specific political controversies later.

Sometimes groups advertise expressly to shift public opinion on a question. One of the most famous such advertising campaigns was run by the Health Insurance Association of America in 1993 and 1994 in opposition to President Bill Clinton's proposed national health insurance plan. These ads featured a couple, Harry and Louise (played by the actors Harry Johnson and Louise Caire Clark), sitting at their kitchen table disparaging the excessive red tape and bureaucratic problems that they would face under Clinton's plan. The Harry and Louise ads are widely attributed with turning public opinion against Clinton's plan, which never even got off the ground in Congress. A decade later, when President George W. Bush proposed a prescription drug benefit as part of Medicare, the health insurance industry brought Harry and Louise back briefly. By then, however, the situation in the health care industry had changed, and the benefits to the industry in Bush's prescription drug benefit plan had brought the Health Insurance Association of America on board. Harry and Louise came back for one more cameo during the 2008 Democratic National Convention and the 2008 Republican National Convention. This time, ironically enough, they came to promote health care reform as the top priority for the next president.[35]

A second strategy that groups use to bring public pressure to bear on a problem is grassroots lobbying. Grassroots lobbyists use many of the same organizing methods we see in political campaigns—developing lists of supporters and urging those supporters to voice their concern with an issue and to recruit others to do so.

---

[34] Pendleton Herring, *Group Representation before Congress* (1928; repr.: New York: Russell & Russell, 1967). See also Kenneth W. Kollman, *Outside Lobbying: Public Opinion and Interests Group Strategies* (Princeton, N.J.: Princeton University Press, 1998).

[35] Jeffrey Birnbaum, "Returning to the Genre He Started," *Washington Post*, November 24, 2004; "Harry and Louise Icons Return to Promote Health Care Reform in New Ad," *Reuters*, August 15, 2008, www. reuters.com/article/pressRelease/idUS191533+15-Aug-2008+PRN20080815 (accessed 4/7/09).

It is common today to send direct mail that includes a draft letter that the recipient can adapt and then send to his or her representative in Congress, or to send e-mails urging people to contact their member of Congress regarding a particular bill or controversy. A grassroots campaign can cost anywhere from $40,000 to attempt to sway the votes of one or two crucial members of a committee or subcommittee to millions of dollars to mount a national effort aimed at Congress as a whole. Such grassroots campaigns are often organized around controversial, prominent appointments, especially to fill vacancies on the U.S. Supreme Court.

Grassroots lobbying campaigns have been so effective in recent years that a number of Washington consulting firms specialize in them. Firms such as Bonner and Associates, for example, will generate grassroots telephone campaigns on behalf of or in opposition to important legislative proposals.

Grassroots lobbying has become more prevalent in Washington over the last couple of decades because the adoption of congressional rules limiting gifts to members has made traditional lobbying more difficult. This circumstance makes all the more compelling the question of whether grassroots campaigning has reached an intolerable extreme. One case in particular illustrates the extremes of "Astroturf" lobbying (a play on the brand name of an artificial grass used on many sports fields). In 1992, ten giant companies in the financial services, manufacturing, and high-tech industries began a grassroots campaign and spent millions of dollars to influence a decision in Congress to limit the ability of investors to sue for fraud. Retaining an expensive consulting firm, these corporations paid for the use of specialized computer software to persuade Congress that there was "an outpouring of popular support for the proposal." Thousands of letters from individuals flooded Capitol Hill. Many of the letters were written and sent by people who sincerely believed that investor lawsuits are often frivolous and should be curtailed. But much of the mail was phony, generated by the Washington-based campaign consultants; the letters came from people who had no strong feelings, or even no opinion at all, about the issue. More and more people, including leading members of Congress, are questioning such methods, charging that these are not genuine *grassroots* campaigns but instead are *Astroturf* lobbying. Such "Astroturf" campaigns have increased in frequency in recent years as members of Congress grow more and more skeptical of Washington lobbyists and far more concerned about demonstrations of support for a particular issue by their constituents. But after the firms spent millions of dollars and generated thousands of letters to members of Congress in their attempt to influence legislation affecting investors' ability to sue for fraud, they came to the somber conclusion that "it's more effective to have 100 letters from your district where constituents took the time to write and understand the issue," because "Congress is sophisticated enough to know the difference."[36]

Finally, groups often organize protests as a means of bringing attention to an issue or pressure on the government. Protests, in fact, are the oldest means of going public. Those who lack other resources, such as money, contacts, and expertise, can always resort to protest as a means of making their concerns public.

---

[36] Jane Fritsch, "The Grass Roots, Just a Free Phone Call Away," *New York Times*, June 23, 1995, pp. A1 and A22.

Indeed, the right to assembly is protected in the First Amendment of the Constitution of the United States.

Protests may have many different consequences, depending on how they are managed. One basic consequence of a well-run protest is that it attracts attention. Peaceful demonstrations at city hall, the state legislature, Congress, the Supreme Court, or some other location typically involve people holding signs and chanting slogans. Passersby certainly notice, and occasionally news outlets cover the event in newspapers or on television, and the larger the protest the more likely it is to attract attention. By getting on the news, the protesters hope to attract attention to their issue and possibly raise the sympathies of others and bring them into their movement.

Organized protests also create a sense of community and common interest among those involved and raise the consciousness of people outside the protest. Civil rights protests during the 1960s brought hundreds of thousands of people to march in the nation's capitol. Newspapers and television news programs across the country carried images of Martin Luther King, Jr. and other civil rights leaders speaking to an audience that stretched from the Lincoln Memorial across the Washington Mall and surrounded the Reflecting Pool. That image wrapped the civil rights movement in the symbolism of the nation; it was not a violent confrontation between protesters and police but a peaceful plea for equal voting and civil rights. Forty years later, similar marches brought protesters for immigrants' rights to the nation's capital and to the states. In spring 2006, hundreds of thousands of people, organized mainly by Hispanic and Latino groups, as well as unions and local churches, marched in Washington, D.C. and in several state capitals to protest anti-immigration policies. That movement drew attention to immigrants' concerns in a political environment that was increasingly hostile, and it influenced the political debate over the issue. It also engaged large numbers of Hispanics and Latinos. According to the Pew Hispanic Center, one in four Hispanics participated in these protests.[37]

Finally, protests often attempt to impose costs on others by disrupting traffic or commerce, thereby forcing people to bargain with protesters. Labor strikes are a form of political action against companies, industries, or the government. Workers in a labor strike refuse to work, costing the company the revenue it would have gained from services rendered. In an industry such as automotives, the companies may have enough existing stock of cars and parts to allow for weeks or maybe months of negotiations without disrupting sales. However, in an industry such as education or the airlines, once the teachers or pilots go on strike, all service stops. On rare occasions labor organizations can instigate a general strike—all workers in the entire industry, a city, or a nation stay home from work, bringing all commerce to a stop. Such strikes have a significant effect on businesses and the larger economy and are called to remind the government and industry leaders of the political pull of labor.

Unions aren't the only groups that organize protests designed to disrupt normal activities. One impressive demonstration occurred during the winter of 1977–78.

---

[37] Pew Hispanic Center and Pew Forum on Religion & Public Life, "Changing Faiths: Latinos and the Transformation of American Religion," 2007, http://pewhispanic.org/files/reports/75.pdf (accessed 4/7/09).

American farmers were frustrated with federal agricultural policies and increasing failures of family farms. The farmers' frustration culminated in the organization of a convoy of 600 tractors and other farm vehicles to Washington, D.C. The tractor procession was peaceful but highly disruptive. It snarled traffic for weeks and tore up the grass mall running between the Lincoln Memorial and the Capitol. The protest made for compelling news photographs and was covered extensively in national newsmagazines and newspapers. The farmers did not get a revision of the 1977 Farm Bill, but they did get a promise from the Federal Housing Administration (FHA) temporarily to cease seizures of land and equipment of farmers who could not repay loans.[38] Farmers' protests, teachers' strikes, and other activities disrupt government and business activity in order to force negotiation of a better deal.

Protests may spill over and become riots or even civil conflict, or they may be confronted by counterprotests. Companies affected by protests and the government have an interest in containing or breaking up demonstrations and strikes. However, the First Amendment is generally interpreted as protecting free expression through protests and strikes so long as they do not erupt into open rioting. Courts are often asked to rule on whether a protest is lawful or unlawful. For example, during George W. Bush's second inauguration, on January 20, 2005, about 250 to 300 people conducted a protest against the war in Iraq by marching through the streets of the Adams Morgan neighborhood in Washington, D.C. Police broke up the march with mass arrests. Some of the protesters sued to overturn their convictions and complained of alleged damages from police actions. The district court agreed with the protesters, reasoning that they were engaged in a peaceful protest, but had they been involved in riotous behavior, police actions may have been justified.[39]

Using Electoral Politics

In addition to attempting to influence members of Congress and other government officials, interest groups seek to use the electoral process to elect the right legislators in the first place and ensure that those who are elected will owe them a debt of gratitude for their support. To put matters into perspective, groups invest far more resources in lobbying than in electoral politics. Nevertheless, financial support and campaign activism can be important tools for organized interests.

Political Action Committees.   By far, the most common electoral strategy employed by interest groups is that of giving financial support to the parties or to particular candidates. But such support can easily cross the threshold into outright bribery. Therefore, Congress has occasionally made an effort to regulate this strategy. For example, the Federal Election Campaign Act of 1971 (amended in 1974) limits campaign contributions and requires each candidate or campaign

---

38 "Furious Farmers," *Time*, December 19, 1977, www.time.com/time/magazine/article/0,9171,945836,00 .html (accessed 4/7/09); Marty Strange, *Family Farming: A New Economic Vision* (Lincoln: University of Nebraska Press, 1988).

39 *Carr et al. v. District of Columbia*, U.S. District Court of the District of Columbia, Civil Action, No 2006-0098, July 15, 2008, https://ecf.dcd.uscourts.gov/cgi-bin/show_public_doc?2006cv0098-69 (accessed 4/7/09).

committee to provide the full name and address, occupation, and principal business of each person who contributes more than $100. These provisions have been effective up to a point, considering the rather large number of embarrassments, indictments, resignations, and criminal convictions in the aftermath of the Watergate scandal.

The Watergate scandal itself was triggered when Republican "dirty tricksters" were caught breaking into the office of the Democratic National Committee in the Watergate apartment complex in Washington. An investigation quickly revealed numerous violations of campaign finance laws, involving millions of dollars that was passed from corporate executives to President Nixon's reelection committee. Many of these revelations were made by the famous Ervin Committee, whose official name and jurisdiction was the Senate Select Committee on Presidential Campaign Activities.

Reaction to Watergate produced further legislation on campaign finance in 1974 and 1976, but the effect has been to restrict individual rather than interest-group campaign activity. Individuals may now contribute no more than $2,300 to any candidate for federal office in any primary or general election. A political action committee, however, can contribute $5,000, provided it contributes to at least five different federal candidates each year.[40] Beyond this, the laws permit corporations, unions, and other interest groups to form **political action committees (PACs)** and pay the costs of soliciting funds from private citizens for the PACs.

Electoral spending by interest groups has increased steadily despite the campaign finance reforms that followed the Watergate scandal. Table 12.3 presents the total amounts contributed by interest groups to campaign organizations or spent on campaigns as well as the distribution of the money across House, Senate, and presidential races. Total PAC contributions continue to rise, increasing from nearly $260 million in 2000 to just under $413 million in 2008. Interest groups also pursue their electoral strategies by spending money on advertising, get out the vote efforts, and other forms of direct campaigning in support of or against candidates. Such spending is called independent expenditure because it is done independently of the candidates' campaigns totaled just $21 million in 2000, but rose to $135 million in 2008. Interest groups also give to political parties, especially through non-federal (mainly state) committees. Such "soft money" donations were restricted after 2004, and totaled almost $22 million in 2008.

Interest groups focus their direct contributions on Congress, especially the U.S. House. Given the enormous cost of running modern political campaigns (see Chapter 11), most politicians are eager to receive PAC contributions. A typical U.S. House incumbent receives half of his or her campaign funds from interest groups. There is little evidence that interest groups buy roll call votes or other favors from members of Congress with their donations. Group donations do, however, help to keep those who are sympathetic to groups' interests and views in office.[41]

political action committees (PACs) Private groups that raise and distribute funds for use in election campaigns.

---

[40] Federal Election Commission, "Contribution Limits 2009–10," www.fec.gov/pages/brochures/contriblimits.shtml (accessed 4/7/09).

[41] See Stephen Ansolabehere, John de Figueiredo, and James M. Snyder, Jr., "Why Is There So Little Money in U.S. Politics?" *Journal of Economic Perspectives* 17 (2006): 105–30.

TABLE 12.3 PRESIDENTIAL CAMPAIGN RECEIPTS FOR PAC CONTRIBUTIONS (IN MILLIONS OF DOLLARS)

	2000	2004	2008
PAC Contributions			
All Candidates	259.8	310.5	412.8
House	193.4	225.4	301.6
Senate	51.9	63.7	79.9
President + Party	14.5	21.4	31.3
Independent Expenditures			
All	20.6	55.9	134.6
House	7.7	5.4	21.6
Senate	6.8	7.1	14.3
President	6.1	43.4	98.7
Nonfederal (Soft) Party Donations	26.4	144.5	21.8

SOURCE: Federal Election Commission, www.fec.gov.

The potential influence of interest group campaign donations and expenditures over the legislature has prompted frequent calls from reformers to abolish PACs or limit their activities. The challenge is how to regulate the participation of groups without violating their members' rights to free speech and free association. In 1976, the U.S. Supreme Court weighed in on this matter in the case *Buckley v. Valeo*, which questioned the constitutionality of the 1974 Federal Elections Campaign Act. In its decision to let the act stand, the majority on the Court ruled that donors' rights of expression are at stake, but that these must be weighed against the government's interest in limiting corruption, or the perception of corruption. The Court has repeatedly upheld the key tenets of its 1976 decision: (1) That money is a form of speech but (2) that speech rights must be weighed against concerns about corruption. Most recently the Court upheld the Bipartisan Campaign Reform Act's (BCRA) restrictions on donations to nonfederal (e.g., state party) accounts as a necessary reform to limit corruption. Continued growth of PAC contributions since the passage of BCRA in 2002 has raised continued concerns about the campaign finance laws in the United States and their capacity to limit interest group influence. The challenge for future efforts at reform is to find the balance between the speech rights of interest groups and the interests in limiting corruption. It is especially hard to get the right balance because those who write the regulations, sitting members of Congress, have a profound stake in the current campaign finance system. For a fuller discussion of the rules governing campaign finance see Chapter 10.

Campaign Activism.   Financial support is not the only way in which organized groups seek influence through the electoral process. Sometimes activism can be even more important than campaign contributions.

Interest Groups and Representation

Americans have long been suspicious of organized interests and the possibly deleterious effects of campaign contributions. Political action committees (PACs) donate large amounts of money to members of Congress for their reelection campaigns. In turn, many observers worry that members may pay closer attention to the desires of the special interest groups than to their constituents.

One can get a sense of the magnitude of PAC contributions from this table. Each row shows the contribution by an industry to members of the committee that has jurisdiction over policies that most concern the industry, as well as contributions to members who are not on the committee. Notice that while the contributions to all members are quite sizable, industries tend to direct most of their money to committee members who are most involved with issues that are important to the industry. Assuming PACs are not making these contributions out of a purely charitable instinct, one can surmise that they expect something in return for their money.

INDUSTRY CONTRIBUTIONS TO HOUSE COMMITTEE MEMBERS, 2008 ELECTION CYCLE

Committee & Industry	Average Amount to Committee Members ($)	Average Amount to Non-Committee Members ($)	Ratio
Agricultural Committee, Agricultural Services and Products	$37,955	$5,877	6.5
Armed Services Committee, Defense Aerospace	$28,289	$11,216	2.5
Education and Labor Committee, Education	$19,523	$11,415	1.7
Energy and Commerce Committee, Health Professionals	$104,616	$56,578	1.8
Financial Services Committee, Commercial Banks	$49,843	$18,387	2.7
Natural Resources Committee, Oil and Gas	$31,098	$18,198	1.7

Source: Center for Responsive Politics, www.opensecrets.org (accessed 5/12/09).

The framers were attuned to the potential problems of factions and special interests. In *Federalist 10* Madison proposed the "extended sphere" of a large and diverse republic as an institutional solution. In a diverse republic, Madison argued, any single faction acting alone would have little influence as competition between the many various groups would prevent any one group from dominating. In addition, in a large republic, representation would "refine and enlarge" public opinion because these opinions pass through a select body.[1] Madison, however, did not foresee our current system of campaign finance. Is there any evidence that this institutional solution works in modern times?

Madison's prescience, perhaps, can be seen in recent research by Kevin Esterling.[2] Esterling shows that PACs tend to direct their contributions to members who have high "analytical capacity," or those members who are attentive to research and analysis in their work in committees. Esterling limited his study to committees with jurisdiction over health policies. We saw in the previous table that health interest groups tend to direct their contributions to these members, and this figure shows they contribute most heavily to members with high analytical capacity (see the red curve in the graph), or the ones who are most likely to "refine and enlarge" public opinion. In addition, these same members tend to attract more contributions from groups that are not health-related (see the blue curve), suggesting that members with high analytical capacity are pressured by groups with diverse interests, exactly as envisioned in Madison's "extended sphere."

While it may be that the groups intend to advance their special interests, the overall pattern of contributions seems to reward legislators who try to inform legislation with research and analysis.

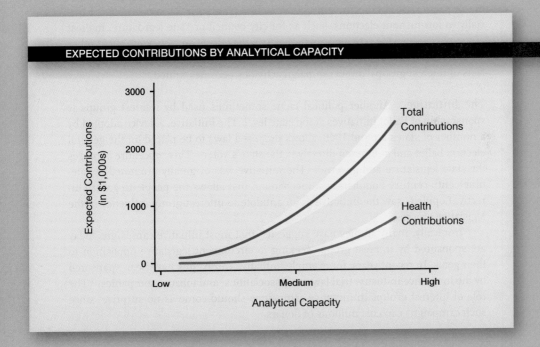

EXPECTED CONTRIBUTIONS BY ANALYTICAL CAPACITY

[1]James Madison, Federalist 10, in the *Federalist Papers*, Clinton Rossiter, ed. (New York: Peguin, 1961), pp. 82–83.
[2]Kevin M. Esterling, "Buying Expertise: Campaign Contributions and Attention to Policy Analysis in Congressional Committees," *American Political Science Review* 101 (February 2007): 93–109.

Perhaps the most notable instance of such activism occurs on behalf of the Democratic Party and candidates through unions. Labor unions regularly engage in massive get out the vote drives during political campaigns. The largest such activities come from the Service Employees International Union (SEIU), which represents works ranging from hotel and restaurant workers to clerical staff, and the United Auto Workers (UAW). SEIU, for instance, spent in excess of $30 million to support Barack Obama. Other sorts of groups routinely line up behind the Democratic and Republican campaigns. The National Right to Life Committee, for example, spent $26 million on behalf of John McCain's 2008 presidential campaign. Moveon.org reported that they spent in excess of $7 million on direct campaigning in the 2008 presidential race.

The cumulative effect of such independent campaign activism is difficult to judge. One important research initiative within political science seeks to measure systematically the marginal effectiveness of campaign contact. Professors Alan Gerber and Donald Green have developed a program of field experiments in which campaigns agree to randomly assign direct campaign activity to some neighborhoods but not others. They have been able to measure the marginal effect of an additional piece of mail, direct canvasser, or phone call. In a typical election context, it costs about $40 to get an additional voter to the polls. Professors Gerber and Green further find that campaign activism can have initially large impact, but after six or so attempted contacts the effects of campaign contact diminish dramatically. This important empirical research has given campaigns and reformers some sense of the effectiveness of campaign activism in stimulating turnout and possibly influence elections. Especially in low-turnout elections, such as for city council or state legislature, interest group get out the vote activities can have very large effects on who wins, but as other money enters the scene, especially candidates own campaign expenditures, the effects of interest groups' direct campaign activities becomes muted.[42]

The Initiative.   Another political tactic sometimes used by interest groups is sponsorship of ballot initiatives at the state level. The **initiative**, a device adopted by a number of states around 1900, allows proposed laws to be placed on the general election ballot and submitted directly to the state's voters. This procedure bypasses the state legislature and governor. The initiative was originally promoted by late-nineteenth-century Populists as a mechanism that allows the people to govern directly. Populists saw the initiative as an antidote to interest-group influence in the legislative process.

Ironically, many studies have suggested that most initiative campaigns today are sponsored by interest groups seeking to circumvent legislative opposition to their goals. In recent years, for example, initiative campaigns have been sponsored by the insurance industry, trial lawyers' associations, and tobacco companies.[43] The role of interest groups in initiative campaigns should come as no surprise, since such campaigns can cost millions of dollars.

initiative
A process by which citizens may petition to place a policy proposal on the ballot for public vote.

---

[42] Donald Green and Alan Gerber, *Get Out the Vote: How to Increase Voter Turnout.* 2nd ed. (Washington D.C.: Brookings Institution Press, 2008).

[43] Elisabeth R. Gerber, *The Populist Paradox: Interest Group Influence and the Promise of Direct Legislation* (Princeton, N.J.: Princeton University Press, 1999), p. 6.

Interest Groups: Are They Effective?

Do interest groups have an effect on government and policy? The short answer is yes. One of the best academic studies of the impact of lobbying was conducted in 2001 by John de Figueiredo of the Massachusetts Institute of Technology and Brian Silverman of the University of Toronto.[44] Figueiredo and Silverman focused on a particular form of lobbying: efforts by lobbyists to obtain "earmarks" (special, often disguised congressional appropriations) for colleges and universities on whose behalf they are working. Millions of dollars in earmarks are written into law every year.

The authors discovered that lobbying had an impact. The more money schools spent on lobbying activities, the larger the total quantity of earmarked funds they received. The extent of the effect, however, varied with institutional factors. Schools in states with a senator on the Senate Appropriations Committee received $18 to $29 in earmarks for every $1 spent on lobbying. Schools in congressional districts whose representative served on the House Appropriations Committee received between $49 and $55 for every $1 spent on lobbying. On the other hand, schools lacking such representation averaged only about $1 for every $1 spent on lobbying—hardly worth the effort.

These results suggest, as is so often the case, that institutions and politics are profoundly related. Schools without access to members of Congress in positions to help them cannot gain much from lobbying. Schools with such access still need to lobby to take advantage of the potential that representation on the Senate and House Appropriations Committees can give them. But if they do so, the potential return from lobbying is substantial.

CONCLUSION

The institutions of American government embrace an open and democratic process in order to ensure that government is responsive to the public's preferences and needs. The Bill of Rights provides for the rights of free speech, freedom of the press, and freedom of assembly. The laws of the land have only further cemented this commitment, providing for open meetings, citizen advisory commissions, lobbying, direct contact from constituents, contributions from interested individuals and groups, an open legal system, protests, and many other routes through which individuals and groups may advocate for their interests. Through these many points of access, representatives and government officials learn how their decisions affect groups and individuals. Politics, then, becomes the arena in which these many interests compete for the attention and support of the government; sometimes they succeed in coming together to find common ground.

Such a system creates an opportunity for those who have the willingness and capacity to use their resources to represent their interests before the government.

---

[44] John de Figueiredo and Brian S. Silverman, "Academic Earmarks and the Returns to Lobbying" working paper 9064, National Bureau of Economic Research, 2002; substantially rev., 2003, http://web.mit.edu/jdefig/www/papers/academic_earmarks.pdf (accessed 4/7/09).

Problems of collective action and free riding prevent many latent interests from developing permanent political organizations capable of bringing concerted pressure on the government. Businesses, unions, and professional and industry associations usually have less trouble overcoming the obstacles to organization and group maintenance that many volunteer associations may face. Interest-group politics in Washington and state legislatures, consequently, tends to reflect the interests of and conflicts among those engaged in economic activity in the country.

Although firms, unions, and other organizations can solve the collective action problem, they do not necessarily succeed in the political arena. They often find politics unfamiliar, even hostile, terrain in which to pursue organizational goals. Unlike economic activity, politics involves power derived from the ability to vote on measures, to introduce legislation or rules, or to block actions from happening. Interest groups are necessarily outsiders that can do none of these things directly. Nonetheless, these organizations seek out support in the appropriate institutions, such as a court with a sympathetic judge or a subcommittee of Congress where the chairman holds views similar to those of the group. And the way to success is usually quite subtle. Often, groups succeed not by "bringing pressure" but by providing expertise to the government and by learning from those in office about the impact of new rules and regulations.

Over the past thirty to forty years, interest groups have increasingly found that the best route to power is through public action and public opinion. It is not enough for a group to hire a lobbyist to advocate on its behalf in the halls of government. Real pressure may be brought to bear on politicians by shaping what others think. Through advertising, protests, and grassroots networks, interest groups have increasingly brought their issues to the attention of the public. Through public pressure, they have been able to influence politics. These new means of shaping public policy and government decision making are increasingly remote from traditional politics. Likewise, it becomes increasingly difficult for an organization to trace its influence in the political arena. Tens of thousands of organizations compete in the political sphere, alternately pursuing insider and outsider strategies, and each claiming credit for favorable policies and ducking blame for failures.

Interest-group politics at the beginning of the twenty-first century does not fit stereotypical notions cleanly. There are certainly as many lobbyists as ever, but the backroom dealings of the "old lobby" are an anachronism. Interest-group politics is diffuse, spread across all branches of government and involving many different interests vying for the attention of politicians in an increasingly crowded and active interest-group ecology. Those who are organized gain the advantages of pooling resources, but an interest group's political action today constitutes only one aspect of the debate over any given political issue or decision. Other interests and voices making competing claims may very well cancel out a given organization's efforts. And the activities of all groups amount to just one facet of legislators', judges', and executives' deliberations. Those who must ultimately make political decisions and be held accountable for those decisions consider other voices as well, especially the opinions and preferences of their constituents. Perhaps a better contemporary characterization is that the organized and disorganized interests participating in politics today are really contributing to a much broader sphere of political discourse and debate. That debate takes place inside the institutions of government—Congress, courts, executives, and elections. It also takes place in another arena, the media. That forum is the final leg of our discussion of democracy in America, and to that subject we now turn.

FOR FURTHER READING

Ainsworth, Scott. *Analyzing Interest Groups.* New York: Norton, 2002.

Alexander, Robert, ed. *The Classics of Interest Group Behavior.* New York: Wadsworth, 2005.

Ansolabehere, Stephen, John M. de Figueiredo, and James M. Snyder, Jr. "Why Is There So Little Money in U.S. Politics?" *Journal of Economic Perspectives* 17, no. 1 (Winter 2003): 105–30.

Baumgartner, Frank, Jeffrey M. Berry, Beth L. Leech, David C. Kimball, and Marie Hojnacki. *Lobbying and Policy Change: Who Wins, Who Loses, and Why.* Chicago: University of Chicago Press, 2009.

Esterling, Kevin. *The Political Economy of Expertise.* Ann Arbor: University of Michigan Press, 2004.

Galanter, Marc. "Why the 'Haves' Come Out Ahead: Speculations on the Limits of Legal Change." *Law and Society Review* 9, no. 1 (1974): 95–160.

Kollman, Kenneth W. *Outside Lobbying: Public Opinion and Interest Group Strategies.* Princeton, N.J.: Princeton University Press, 1998. ○ reader selection

Lowi, Theodore J. *The End of Liberalism: The Second Republic of the United States.* 2nd ed. New York: Norton, 1979.

Moe, Terry M. *The Organization of Interests: Incentives and the Internal Dynamics of Political Interest Groups.* Chicago: University of Chicago Press, 1980. ○ reader selection

Nownes, Anthony. *Total Lobbying: What Lobbyists Want and How They Try to Get It.* New York: Cambridge University Press, 2006.

Olson, Mancur, Jr. *The Logic of Collective Action: Public Goods and the Theory of Groups.* 1965. Reprinted with new preface and appendix. Cambridge, Mass.: Harvard University Press, 1965.

Rosenthal, Alan. *The Third House: Lobbyists and Lobbying in the States.* Washington, D.C.: Congressional Quarterly Press, 2001.

Rozell, Mark, Clyde Wilcox, and David Madland. *Interest Groups in American Campaigns.* Washington, D.C.: Congressional Quarterly Press, 2005.

Sheingate, Adam. *The Rise of the Agricultural Welfare State: Institutions and Interest Group Power in the United States, France, and Japan.* Princeton, N.J.: Princeton University Press, 2003.

Strolovitch, Dara. *Affirmative Advocacy: Race, Class, and Gender in Interest Group Politics.* Chicago: University of Chicago Press, 2007. ○ reader selection

Ⓢ Additional study and review materials are available online at wwnorton.com/studyspace/

13

The Media

The media make up one of the most unusual institutions of American democracy. The media are really an industry, employing thousands of writers, researchers, editors, managers, graphic designers, and others working for newspapers, book publishers, magazines, television studios and stations, radio stations, and Internet and telecommunications firms. This industry exists not for political purposes, but for communication and entertainment, and it derives the lion's share of its revenue from product advertising. The primary business model is simple enough. Using communication technologies such as the printing press and Internet, media firms develop and distribute content—news articles, TV shows, Web sites, and the like—to attract an audience. The audience—the public—is willing to pay for access to content by purchasing subscriptions, paying cover prices and access charges, and buying computers, televisions, and radios. More significant still, other businesses, organizations, and individuals want to have access to that audience, and they will pay media firms to advertise their messages. Most media revenue derives from advertising, from selling access to the audience attracted by television and radio, newspapers and magazines, and the Internet.[1] And the audience is huge. Nearly every household in the United States has at least one television; three-quarters have Internet access. The typical American adult watches four hours of television a day.

Early in their development, American media discovered the importance of politics to their business. People are willing to pay for information about politics and

---

[1] Roughly 80 percent of newspaper revenue comes from advertising, and 20 percent from subscriptions. See Ben Scott, "A Contemporary History of Digital Journalism," *New Media & Television* 6, no. 1 (February 2005): 89–126.

public affairs (or pay for access to such information), and politicians and organized interests are willing to pay to reach that audience. Individuals buy newspapers, read Web sites, watch television, and listen to radio programs about politics and current events, and politicians and organized interests purchase advertising time and, in some rare cases, purchase media outlets.[2] Most major media outlets today offer news coverage and analysis as a way to attract readers and listeners. The major television networks—ABC, CBS, NBC, CNN, and Fox—offer approximately six hours of news programming every day, and some media organizations are devoted exclusively to politics and public affairs. The cost of news programs to consumers is minimal, even free, and the content is presented in a widely accessible manner. In this way, the media offer most people an easy way to learn about the important actions of the government, the state of the nation, and the choices in an election.

The media, then, address one of the most important problems of democracy—the problem of creating

---

[2]The most prominent case of a politician owning a media outlet is the Italian prime minister Silvio Berlusconi, who owned print newspapers and publishing houses and used his wealth and political position to form the party Forza Italia.

- The primary objective of the American media is to make profits. They create and distribute content to attract an audience and earn revenues by selling access to that audience to advertisers and by charging fees for content.

- The market for news is extremely large, as most Americans rely on the media to find out about important issues, the activities of the government, and electoral choices. The centrality of the news media in informing the public makes this private industry into an important part of the public sphere.

- Reporters and journalists rely on politicians, government agencies, organizations, and average people as sources of information. This provides politicians, bureaucrats, organized interests, and private citizens the opportunity to try to shape how the media portray public issues.

- Rather than try to run the media as a public trust, the U.S. government takes a comparatively light hand in regulating media ownership and operation and instead relies on the marketplace to produce a robust flow of information about politics and government affairs.

an informed electorate. As we discussed in Chapters 9 and 10, democratic politics assumes some awareness among the electorate about who is in power, what problems the nation faces, and what actions and policies the government has taken. If you were to try to keep up with politics by attending meetings and corresponding with representatives, you would have time for little else. The news media make information about politics and public affairs readily and widely accessible, even entertaining. It takes relatively little effort to keep up with politics through newspapers, television news, and the Internet. Indeed, most of what people know about politics comes from mass media sources.

The massive audience for American media presents a tremendous political opportunity. The media provide the means through which those in government and those who want to influence the government can communicate with the public, they offer channels through which candidates for office can appeal to potential voters, and they are the main venue for public debate over important issues of the day. Given the importance of the media in American democracy, indeed in any political system, it is not surprising that those in government and those wishing to influence government have long sought to shape how journalists present information and what subjects they report. In some societies, governments control the media or limit ownership. Even in democracies, governments commonly regulate what the press may report, censoring stories unfavorable to the government and discouraging reports on sensitive subjects.

The United States takes a distinctive approach to political communication, one based on the marketplace. The American view, rooted in the First Amendment guarantee of free speech and a free press, espouses a commitment to free and robust competition in the media industry as the best way to guarantee an informed electorate, open discussion of political questions, and a government that can be held accountable for its actions. Commitment to that ideal has not always been easy, especially where questions of national security are at stake. When conflicts about the rights of journalists and editors and media firms arise, the courts have most often sided with the media rather than the government in asserting the right to a free press as essential to the practice of democracy in America. Unlike in many other countries, the legislative and executive branches of government have very little direct control over the media, and media organizations operate with very few regulations or controls. Journalists and news organizations in the United States operate as free agents and enjoy considerable protection from the courts.

In the United States, where the media operate as a private industry, communication is not immune to political manipulation. Politicians and interest groups try to shape the content and flow of communication through two routes—paid media and free media. Examples of paid media are advertisements and publications purchased by the government, politicians, party organizations, and interest groups to push a particular message. Thirty-second political commercials on television have become a staple of American political campaigns. Between campaigns, interest groups often purchase advertisements to put their views before the public. And increasingly, campaigns and interest groups use the Internet to interact with people through their own Web sites and online distribution of advertisements and videos.

Free media, which typically means news coverage, can be more important to politicians than paid media, which generally means political advertisements. News and other programming about politics attracts viewers. What the media report about individual politicians and government decisions is a sort of free advertising, though not all of it is favorable. Politicians try to shape the news, just as reporters try to cover it. Executives and legislative leaders—from the president and Congress to governors and state legislatures to mayors and city councils—hire professional staff to deal with media relations. The major press outlets assign reporters to cover the presidency, Congress, state governments, and the courts. The political staff in charge of press relations in each of these institutions try to attract press attention to their activities and initiatives and to manage what the journalists report.

Journalists, for their part, are mindful of what they are reporting and where their information comes from. Because government officials are often good sources for information about politics, there is a tendency for reporting to reflect what those in office say. To counterweight or check this tendency, professional journalists have developed standards and norms of reporting, including use of multiple sources and specifying sources. Competitive pressures on reporters and media outlets can also diminish bias in what gets covered and how. Being the first to break a story attracts an audience for the media outlet and kudos for the reporter. With newspapers, television and radio stations, and Internet outlets competing for audiences, it is exceedingly difficult for journalists to avoid reporting a particular story that is of interest to the public or for government officials to keep a story out of the press or guarantee that the story has a particular slant.[3]

---

[3] See Stephen Ansolabehere, Roy Behr, and Shanto Iyengar, *The Media Game: American Politics in the Television Age* (New York: Macmillan, 1993).

The marketplace of ideas—the principle governing media politics in America—rests on the assumption that the media serve the public best when they operate as a private industry unfettered by government control over content. Journalists, candidates, groups, and private citizens can say whatever they want in a free and open exchange of views about politics. A large number of media outlets are available to any consumer, and many of these offer reporting and coverage of politics. They do not all cover the same events in the same ways; nor do they target the same audiences. But collectively the media present a vast range of ideas, opinions, and information and make it easily accessible to everyone. It is hard for Congress, agencies, and courts to judge what information people need or want, what information is true or false, what information is good for the nation, and what is dangerous. Rather, the general philosophy governing media regulation in the United States is that it is best determined by the consumers of information, the public. Any consumer may choose to watch, read, or listen to what he or she wants. Those media that do not attract consumers fail, whereas those that offer people what they want succeed. This system does not always provide the ideal outcome, but, at least in theory, it is considered the best way to guarantee an adequately informed public.[4]

An alternate view of the media is more widely embraced in other countries but also finds expression in the United States. That view holds that owing to the necessity of maintaining an informed electorate, media firms and journalists must act responsibly. Slander and libel laws prevent people from saying and printing material that is harmful and false. The notion of a responsible press goes much farther; it implies that the media must do the utmost to create a fully informed electorate. In the United States, the Federal Communications Commission has at various times in our history required television stations to give equal time to all candidates in a campaign and to present all sides of an issue. Those norms of equal time and fair coverage exert themselves in the daily practice and professional codes of journalists and in the presentation of important political events. For example, after the president's State of the Union address, the opposition party in Congress is provided media time for a rebuttal. The media cover both the Democratic National Convention and the Republican National Convention equally. Television and radio stations provide free coverage of debates between candidates running for office. In other countries, the notion of responsible media has led to limitations on the number of televisions channels and licensing requirements that those channels provide extensive public-affairs programming.

Whether the "marketplace of ideas" works well in practice has long been a matter of debate. Observers are concerned that the market lacks local competition, that owners skew the coverage of news, and that the marketplace does not provide sufficient coverage of politics. Today, for example, very few cities are served by more than one local newspaper, raising the possibility of monopolies over the news that may give owners, editors, and journalists excessive political power in local markets. There is also concern that the Internet is driving many newspapers into bankruptcy, which could lead to a lack of any print news services. Should the

---

[4] This idea is most elegantly expressed in the majority opinion in the Supreme Court case *New York Times v. Sullivan*, 376 U.S. 254 (1964).

government subsidize newspapers to maintain more competition? What are the consequences for local communities if they have no printed newspapers in circulation? Media firms, Congress, and executive agencies (especially the Federal Communications Commission) must deal with these and other complex questions over the coming decades as new communications technologies transform the media industry in the United States and the ways that people become informed about and engage in politics.

THE MEDIA AS A POLITICAL INSTITUTION

Perhaps the most salient feature of the American media, as an industry and as a political institution, is the diversity of sources, firms, and technologies. There are approximately 1,400 daily newspapers in the United States and 1,500 television stations affiliated with seven major broadcasting networks. Hundreds of weekly magazines are devoted to national politics, along with hundreds of independent television stations and affiliates of smaller networks. Countless Web sites stream news from sources throughout the world. These media reach every community in the United States and provide information in every language.

Types of Media

There is some order to the apparent chaos. The American media are organized into three categories—print, broadcast, and Internet. Regulations of the media follow these lines. Print media, such as newspapers and magazines, have long enjoyed strong First Amendment protections and provide the ideal case for the "marketplace of ideas." The technology of printing presses and digital reproduction makes it quite easy for new papers to enter local markets, and that fact has led the courts to stay the hand of those pushing for regulation of print media. Newspapers, magazines, and other print media are distributed locally through delivery services or vendors or nationally through the mail, though most are owned by national media organizations and firms.

Broadcast and cablecast media, by contrast, have historically faced technological limits that have led to restrictions on ownership, distribution, and at times content. With the advent of radio in the 1920s, the need for regulation immediately became evident. Broadcasters would vary the strength of their signal and the part of the radio-frequency spectrum over which they broadcast to find audiences and squelch other broadcasters. That behavior was ruining the medium, because consumers could not reliably find the programming that they wanted. In 1927, then commerce secretary Herbert Hoover introduced the first regulations of broadcast media, requiring every broadcaster to secure a license from the U.S. government and to agree to send its signal only over a narrow band of the spectrum (which would be allocated to that station within a certain region). The U.S. government could revoke that license for failure to comply with spectrum regulations. In the late 1940s, concern about the use of the spectrum in emerging television technology led the federal government to freeze the development of that nascent industry for four years while the Federal Communications Commission (FCC) worked out a distribution and ownership plan. Regulation of the broadcast spectrum continues to dictate federal communications policy to this day. This view of broadcasting and cablecasting asserts the idea that in the broadcast and cable domains, media firms serve a public trust and bear responsibility for their actions.[5]

Since the mid-1990s, a third media sector has arisen, one driven by Internet technology. Internet technology blurs the line between the other two media sectors. It requires governance for the assignment of Web domains, but it otherwise operates as perhaps the most open and competitive of the three sectors. The Internet sector is still developing its distinctive identity as a mode of communication, especially political communication. For the first two decades of its existence, the traditional media have dominated the Internet provision of content, as print and broadcast firms have moved their content online. But since 2000 an increasingly unique and distinctive form of Web-based political communication has emerged, including blogs and citizen journalism, which many fear is supplanting traditional media and the norms of professional journalism.[6] The 2008 election marked the true arrival of the Internet as one of the three pillars of "the media." In 2008, for the first time, more people reported that they got news online than from newspapers.

Broadcast Media. Television news reaches more Americans than any other single news source. Tens of millions of individuals watch national and local news programs every day. Television news, however, covers relatively few topics and provides little depth of coverage. Television news is more like a series of newspaper headlines connected to pictures. It serves the extremely important function of alerting viewers to issues and events but provides little else.

The twenty-four-hour news stations such as Cable News Network (CNN) offer more detail and commentary than the networks' half-hour evening news shows. In 2003, at the start of the war in Iraq, CNN, Fox, and MSNBC provided twenty-four-hour-a-day coverage of the war, including on-the-scene reports from embedded reporters, expert commentary, and interviews with government officials. In this instance, these networks' depth of coverage rivaled that of the print media. Normally, however, CNN and the others offer more headlines than analysis, especially during their prime-time broadcasts. In recent years, cable has been growing in importance as a news source (Table 13.1).

Radio news is essentially a headline service without pictures. In the short time—usually five minutes per hour—that they devote to news, radio stations announce the day's major events without providing much detail. In major cities, all-news stations provide a bit more coverage of major stories, but for the most part

---

[5] Perhaps the best account of these developments is Erik Barnouw's excellent three-volume history *A Tower in Babel: A History of Broadcasting in the United States to 1933; The Golden Web: A History of Broadcasting in the United States, 1933 to 1953*; and *The Image Empire: A History of Broadcasting in the United States from 1953* (New York: Oxford University Press, 1966, 1968, and 1970).

[6] Cass R. Sunstein, *Republic.com 2.0* (Princeton, N.J.: Princeton University Press, 2007).

TABLE 13.1 THE TREND IN REGULAR NEWS CONSUMPTION, 1993–2008

	1993 (%)	1996 (%)	2000 (%)	2002 (%)	2004 (%)	2006 (%)	2008 (%)
Local TV news	77	65	56	57	59	54	52
Cable TV news	–	–	–	33	38	34	34
Nightly network news	60	42	30	32	34	28	29
Radio*	47†	44	43	41	40	36	35
Newspaper*	58†	50	47	41	42	40	34
Online news‡	–	2§	23	25	29	31	37

*Based on use the previous day.
†Data from 1994.
‡Viewed at least three days per week.
§Data from 1995.
SOURCE: Pew Research Center for People and the Press, "Key News Audiences Now Blend Online and Traditional Sources," August 17, 2008, http://people-press.org/report/444/news-media (accessed 4/9/09).

ANALYZING THE EVIDENCE

The percentage of Americans who say they regularly watch the broadcast news or read newspapers has declined, whereas cable TV and the Internet have grown in importance. Does this matter? How might online news content differ from print and broadcast news? Will everyone see the same news online?

these stations fill the day with repetition rather than detail. All-news stations such as WTOP (Washington, D.C.) and WCBS (New York City) assume that most listeners are in their cars and that, as a result, the people who constitute the audience change markedly throughout the day as they reach their destinations. Thus, rather than use their time to flesh out a given set of stories, these stations repeat the same stories each hour to present them to new listeners. In recent years, radio talk shows have become important sources of commentary and opinion. A number of conservative radio hosts, such as Rush Limbaugh, have huge audiences and have helped mobilize support for conservative political causes and candidates. Liberals have had less success in the world of talk radio and have complained that biased coverage helped bring about Democratic defeats in 2000 and 2002. In 2003, however, a group of wealthy liberal political activists led by Anita Drobny, a major Democratic Party donor, created Air America, a liberal talk-radio network designed to combat conservative dominance of this important medium. One executive of the new network said, "There are so many right-wing talk shows, we think it created a hole in the market you could drive a truck through." Liberals hoped their network would be entertaining as well as informative, specializing in parody and political satire.[7] In 2007, however, Air America filed for Chapter 11 bankruptcy protection and was later sold.

---

[7] CNN.com/Inside Politics, "Liberal Radio Network Planned," February 18, 2003, www.cnn.com/2003/ALLPOLITICS/02/17/radio.politics.ap.

In recent years, much of the content of the news, especially local news, has shifted away from politics and public affairs toward "soft news"—coverage focusing on celebrities, health tips, advice to consumers, and other topics more likely to provide entertainment than enlightenment. Even a good deal of political coverage is soft. For example, articles about the Obamas' choice of their dog Bo outnumbered stories about the Iraq war by 3 to 2 during April 2009.[8]

Softer even than soft news is a category of programming sometimes called infotainment. This term refers to material that purports to combine information with entertainment. For example, in 2003, Arnold Schwarzenegger appeared on the *Tonight Show*, exchanged jokes and insults with the host, Jay Leno, and announced that he would be a candidate for governor of California. A currently popular infotainment program is the *Daily Show with Jon Stewart*, which presents comedic parodies of political figures and has called itself America's "most trusted name in fake news." Although purveyors of the "true" news often sneer at the *Daily Show* and other infotainment programs, one recent survey suggested that *Daily Show* viewers do receive a surprising quantity of correct information along with their fake news. Perhaps the *Daily Show* producers are right—we understand politicians better when we see how funny they are.

Print Media. Newspapers remain an important source of news even though they are not the primary news source for most Americans. The print media are important for two reasons. First, as we shall see later in this chapter, the broadcast media rely on leading newspapers such as the *New York Times* and the *Washington Post* to set their news agenda. The broadcast media engage in very little actual reporting; they primarily cover stories that have been "broken," or initially reported, by the print media. For example, sensational charges that President Bill Clinton had an affair with a White House intern were reported first by the *Washington Post* and *Newsweek* before being trumpeted around the world by the broadcast media. It is only a slight exaggeration to observe that if an event is not covered in the *New York Times*, it is not likely to appear on the *CBS Evening News*. One important exception, obviously, is the case of "breaking" news, which can be carried by the broadcast media as it unfolds or soon after, whereas the print media are forced to catch up later in the day. Recall the dramatic real-time videos of the collapsing World Trade Center towers seen by tens of millions of Americans. Second, the print media provide more detailed and more complete information, offering a better context for analysis. Third, the print media are also important because they are the prime source of news for educated and influential individuals. The nation's economic, social, and political elites rely on the detailed coverage provided by the print media to inform and influence their views about important public matters. The print media may have a smaller audience than their cousins in broadcasting, but they have an audience that matters.

Today, however, the newspaper industry is in serious economic trouble. The rise of Web sites advertising jobs, items for sale, and personal ads has dramatically

---

[8] Project for Excellence in Journalism, "The Dog Days of Spring," http://journalism.org/TheDogDays ofSpring+ (accessed 5/7/09).

reduced newspapers' revenues from traditional advertising, such as "help wanted" and personal ads. The *Rocky Mountain News* in Denver closed in 2008, and in 2009 the *Seattle Post-Intelligencer* announced it would adopt an online format only. Major newspapers serving dozens of large U.S. cities and metropolitan areas confirmed in 2008 and 2009 that they faced serious financial difficulties, including the *Philadelphia Inquirer*, the *Minneapolis Star Tribune*, the *Miami Herald*, the *Boston Globe*, and the *San Francisco Chronicle*. Each of these papers indicated that it might close entirely or shut down its print operations and issue only online editions. Such closures would leave many cities with one or possibly no daily print newspapers. It is widely believed that the troubles experienced by these papers are the beginning of a wider transformation of the print media in the United States, which may leave the country with few or no print newspapers—the traditional "press"—in the future. The great unknown is whether other venues, such as the Internet, can adequately replace newspapers, especially in the provision of news about local area politics and public affairs.[9] The "Analyzing the Evidence" unit for this chapter explores the apparent decline of newspapers.

The possible demise of major city newspapers raises important questions. Since the beginning of the Republic, newspapers have been ingrained in the way we think about political communication. The First Amendment specifically protects a "Free Press," and legal doctrines and laws concerning political communication in the United States have evolved around the idea of a robust press serving every community. Many cities now face the prospect of no significant press, in the conventional sense. These changes will likely force a rethinking of the laws governing many aspects of political communication in this country, from campaign finance laws to obscenity standards to ownership guidelines. The U.S. Supreme Court has not extended the same set of free press protections to broadcasters.[10]

This transformation of print media may change the extent to which people are informed about politics and public affairs. The media that will replace newspapers may raise the overall level of information among the mass public or create further differences between those in the know and those who decide to tune out politics. The Internet, television, radio, and other outlets that replace newspapers may reach more people with similar content, or they may segment the audience further, reducing the number of people aware of public affairs. Social science research so far suggests that the decline of newspapers is changing newsgathering behavior. Rather than rely on a single source—the daily paper—Americans are sampling many different sources, "grazing" as a recent study by the Pew Research Center calls it. And that behavior is facilitated by the Internet.[11]

The Internet.   A relatively new source of news is the Internet. Every day several million Americans, especially younger Americans, scan one of many news sites on the

---

[9] 24/7 Wall Street, "The 10 Most Endangered Newspapers in America," *Time*, March 9, 2009, www.time .com/time/business/article/0,8599,1883785,00.html (accessed 5/7/09).

[10] *Red Lion Broadcasting Company v. Federal Communications Commission*, 395 U.S. 367 (1969).

[11] "Key News Audience Now Blend Online and Traditional Sources," Pew Research Center for the People and the Press, August 17, 2008, http://people-press.org/report/444/news-media (accesed 5/7/09).

The End of Newspapers?

Newspapers and the press enjoy a special place in American democracy. In the landmark case *New York Times v. Sullivan* (1963), Justice William Brennan defended the First Amendment's guarantee of freedom of the press as essential to an informed public, healthy deliberation, and democratic elections. A precipitous decline in newspaper readership in 2008, then, came as a shock to many observers. According to *Editor & Publisher*, a leading journal that tracks the industry, daily newspaper circulations fell by 7 percent in 2008 alone, with most of the major cities' newspapers showing decreases in readership of 10 to 20 percent and many papers threatening to close. Some observers went so far as to call for a public takeover of the newspapers in order to maintain this important source of information. Did this decline portend the end of newspapers in the United States? What was causing the decline? And what might it mean for our democracy?

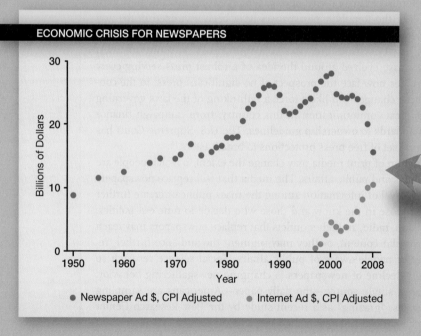

ECONOMIC CRISIS FOR NEWSPAPERS

● Newspaper Ad $, CPI Adjusted ● Internet Ad $, CPI Adjusted

The economic difficulties of newspapers are best reflected in their balance sheets. There are approximately 1,400 daily newspapers in the United States, a figure that has been roughly the same since 1970. Their main source of revenue is advertising, which accounts for about 90 percent of the revenue generated by a print newspaper. From 2000 to 2008, real revenues of newspapers decreased by over $14 billion, a 50 percent decline, and their losses appear to be accelerating. Over the same period, Internet advertising revenue increased by $7 billion. These trends lead many observers to expect Internet advertising to overtake newspapers before 2015. Advertisers, of course, are seeking the audience. The decline in revenues is widely seen as an indicator of eroding newspaper readership, and the pattern since 2000 suggests that the Internet is largely to blame.

A longer-term perspective shows that the decline in newspaper reading started long before the late 1990s, when the Internet emerged. At their peak in the 1950s, approximately 35 newspapers were sold for every 100 people in the United States. Today that figure is roughly 15 newspapers for every 100 persons, and falling.

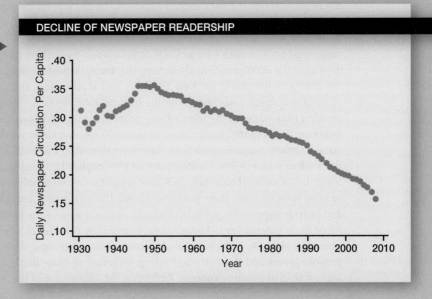

DECLINE OF NEWSPAPER READERSHIP

The Internet, however, does reflect a more general account of the problems facing newspapers—competition. Internet advertisers and Web sites have competed with newspapers for revenues and audience in recent years. Since the 1950s, television has competed with newspapers for the leisure time and attention of the American public. Television, and over the past few years the Internet, have gradually won over the newspaper audience.

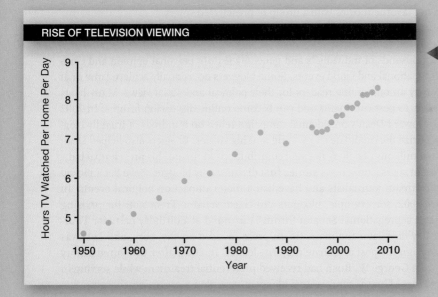

RISE OF TELEVISION VIEWING

Sources: Newspaper circulation and revenue: Editor & Publisher, *Editor & Publisher Yearbook*, various years. Internet Revenue: Internet Advertising Bureau, Internet Advertising Report, 2008 Full-Year Results, March 2009, www.iab.net/media/file/IAB_PwC_2008_full_year.pdf (accessed 7/16/09). Television Audience: Nielsen Media Research, NTI Annual Averages, reported by Television Bureau of Advertising, Trends in Television, various years. Matthew Gentzkow and Jesse M. Shapiro, "Competition and Truth in the Market for News," *Journal of Economic Perspectives* 22, no. 2 (2008): 133–54.

Internet for coverage of current events. For the most part, however, the Internet provides electronic versions of coverage offered by print sources. One great advantage of the Internet is that it allows frequent updating. It can potentially combine the depth of coverage of a newspaper with the timeliness of television and radio. Most political candidates and interest groups have sites on the World Wide Web. Many Americans relied on Web sites such as CNN.com for up-to-the-minute election news in the days after the 2000 presidential election, the dramatic postelection battle in Florida, the 2001 terrorist attacks on New York City and Washington, D.C., the war in Iraq, Hurricane Katrina, and throughout the historic 2008 election.[12] Acknowledging the growing importance of the Internet as a political communications medium, the U.S. Supreme Court posted its decisions in the 2000 election cases as soon as they were issued. Online magazines such as *Slate* have a growing audience and often feature the work of major political writers such as Christopher Hitchens and Ed Finn. Also, a number of political entrepreneurs have sought to organize online advocacy groups to raise money, make their positions known through e-mail and letter campaigns, and provide support for politicians who accept their views. One of the most successful of these enterprises is MoveOn.org, founded by two liberal Silicon Valley entrepreneurs. MoveOn seeks to build electronic advocacy groups, allowing members to propose issues and strategies and acting on behalf of those that appear to have the highest level of member support. Reflecting the importance of the Internet, in January 2007, two days after announcing her bid for the 2008 Democratic presidential nomination, Senator Hillary Rodham Clinton fielded questions from voters in an online chat. Speaking into a webcam, Clinton discussed health care, energy policy, and even her favorite movies with a group of preselected voters.

In addition, hundreds of thousands of readers turn to more informal sources of Internet news and commentary: Web logs, or blogs. Blogs are intermittently published online by thousands of individuals and generally feature personal opinion and commentary on national and world events. Some bloggers occasionally achieve fame or at least notoriety among online readers for their political and social views. Many blogs invite readers to post comments and can become online discussion forums. In 2002 and 2003, Howard Dean's presidential campaign relied on hundreds of friendly bloggers to publicize the candidate's views and tout his virtues. Bloggers also helped Dean raise tens of millions of dollars in small contributions to finance his presidential bid.

In recent years, some news stories first discussed by bloggers have been picked up by mainstream journalists and have had a major impact on political events. In December 2002, for example, bloggers criticized Senator Trent Lott for praising the one-time segregationist Senator Strom Thurmond at a birthday party for Thurmond. A few days later the mainstream press focused on the story, and Lott was forced to resign his post as Senate majority leader. In 2004, after CBS aired a story claiming that George W. Bush had received preferential treatment while serving in the Air National Guard, conservative bloggers mounted a campaign charging that

---

[12] For a discussion of the growing role of the Internet, see Leslie Wayne, "On Web, Voters Reinvent Grass-Roots Activism," *New York Times*, May 21, 2000, p. 22. See also James Fallows, "Internet Illusions," *New York Review of Books*, November 16, 2000, p. 28.

the documents presented by CBS had been forged. The network ultimately admitted that the documents had not been properly authenticated, and the CBS anchor Dan Rather was forced to resign. In 2006, liberal bloggers attacked the Democratic senator Joe Lieberman, whom they called a "cheerleader" for President Bush's policies in Iraq. Lieberman was defeated in Connecticut's Democratic primary, although he later won the general election, running as an independent. Also in 2006, bloggers and other avid Internet users, sometimes called netroot activists, helped bring about the defeat of the Virginia Republican senator and presidential hopeful George Allen. After it was shown on the YouTube Web site, a video clip of Allen directing what appeared to be a racial slur at a Democratic campaign worker was downloaded to hundreds of thousands of computers and discussed by thousands of bloggers. The story was then featured by the television networks. Allen was defeated in his bid for reelection and saw his presidential hopes destroyed.

In 2003, Republicans sought to counter what they viewed as liberal dominance of the "blogosphere" by launching Blogs for Bush, an online community of bloggers who support the president. Calling itself "the White House of the Blogosphere," Blogs for Bush was active in the 2004 presidential election and continues to provide online support for GOP initiatives. In 2005, Blogs for Bush played an active role in the battle over the president's Supreme Court nominees, seeking to mobilize grassroots support and counter Democratic bloggers who criticized the president's efforts. In 2007, Blogs for Bush praised the president's plan to send more troops to Iraq and waged online battles with Democratic bloggers who castigated the president's policies. With the Bush presidency winding down in 2008, and the McCain campaign in full swing, Blogs for Bush became Blogs for Victory.

Variations in Media Coverage

Coverage of politicians varies across media and across politicians. A study by the Pew Project for Excellence in Journalism revealed that President Barack Obama received much more favorable coverage during his first hundred days in office than did either George W. Bush or Bill Clinton. For Clinton and Bush, the bulk of coverage was neutral. Forty-nine percent of the stories about Bush and 44 percent of the stories about Clinton were neutral. Network television and newspaper coverage of these two presidents' first hundred days in office was much more neutral than cable TV News and Internet reporting.[13] Obama, on the other hand, was given more positive coverage than his two predecessors, especially by newspapers and network television. Bush and Clinton received positive stories only 23 percent of the time from newspapers and network television; Obama received positive stories from these outlets 41 percent of the time. Cable TV News and Internet outlets offered reporting on Obama's first hundred days that was on the whole neutral.[14]

---

[13] Pew Research Center's Project for Excellence in Journalism, "The First 100 Days: How Bush Versus Clinton Fared in the Press," April 30, 2001, http://journalism.org/files/100days.pdf (accessed 5/7/09).

[14] Pew Research Center's Project for Excellence in Journalism, "Obama's First 100 Days: How the President Fared in the Press vs. Clinton and Bush," April 28, 2009, http://journalism.org/files/100%20 DAYS.pdf (accessed 5/7/09).

Regulation of the Broadcast and Electronic Media

In some countries, the government controls media content. In other countries, the government owns the broadcast media but does not tell the media what to say (as is the case with the BBC in Great Britain). In the United States, the government neither owns nor controls the communications networks, but it does regulate the content and ownership of the broadcast media.

The print media in the United States are essentially free from government interference. The broadcast media, on the other hand, are subject to federal regulation. American radio and television are regulated by the Federal Communications Commission (FCC), an independent regulatory agency established in 1934. Radio and TV stations must renew their FCC licenses every five years. Licensing provides a mechanism for allocating radio and TV frequencies in such a way as to prevent broadcasts from interfering with and garbling each other. License renewals are almost always granted automatically by the FCC. Indeed, renewal requests are now filed online.

Through regulations prohibiting obscenity, indecency, and profanity, the FCC has also sought to prohibit radio and television stations from airing explicit sexual and excretory references between 6 A.M. and 10 P.M., the hours when children are most likely to be in the audience. The FCC has enforced these rules haphazardly. Since 1990, nearly half the $5 million in fines levied by the agency have involved Howard Stern, the shock jock whose programs are built around sexually explicit material. In 2004, after another set of FCC fines, Stern's program was dropped by a major outlet, Clear Channel Communications. Stern charged that the Bush administration had singled him out for censure because of his known opposition to the president.

For more than sixty years, the FCC also sought to regulate and promote competition in the broadcast industry, but in 1996 Congress passed the Telecommunications Act, a broad effort to do away with most regulations in effect since 1934. The act loosened restrictions on media ownership and allowed for telephone companies, cable television providers, and broadcasters to compete with one another for the provision of telecommunication services. Following the passage of the act, several mergers between telephone and cable companies and between different segments of the entertainment media produced an even greater concentration of media ownership.

The Telecommunications Act of 1996 also included an attempt to regulate the content of material transmitted via the Internet. This law, known as the Communications Decency Act, made it illegal to make "indecent" sexual material on the Internet accessible to anyone under eighteen years of age. The act was immediately denounced by civil libertarians and brought to court as an infringement of free speech. The case reached the Supreme Court in 1997 and the act was ruled an unconstitutional infringement of the First Amendment's guarantee of freedom of speech.

Although the government's ability to regulate the content of the electronic media on the Internet has been questioned, the federal government has used its licensing power to impose several regulations that can affect the political content of radio and TV broadcasts. The first of these is the **equal time rule**, under which broadcasters must provide candidates for the same political office equal opportunities to

equal time rule
The requirement that broadcasters provide candidates for the same political office an equal opportunity to communicate their messages to the public.

communicate their messages to the public. If, for example, a television station sells commercial time to a state's Republican gubernatorial candidate, it may not refuse to sell time to the Democratic candidate for the same position.

The second regulation affecting the content of broadcasts is the **right of rebuttal,** which requires that individuals be given the opportunity to respond to personal attacks. In the 1969 case of *Red Lion Broadcasting Company v. FCC,* for example, the U.S. Supreme Court upheld the FCC's determination that a radio station was required to provide a liberal author with an opportunity to respond to an attack by a conservative commentator that the station had aired.[15]

For many years, a third important federal regulation was the **fairness doctrine**—under which broadcasters who aired programs on controversial issues were required to provide air time for opposing views. In 1985, the FCC stopped enforcing the fairness doctrine on the grounds that there were so many radio and television stations—to say nothing of newspapers and newsmagazines—that in all likelihood many different viewpoints were being presented even without the requirement that each station present all sides of an argument. Critics of this FCC decision charge that in many media markets the number of competing viewpoints is small. Nevertheless, a congressional effort to require the FCC to enforce the fairness doctrine was blocked by the administration of President Ronald Reagan in 1987.

The emergence of the Internet since the mid-1990s has presented a set of regulatory questions as well, though they have a somewhat different flavor. One of the main controversies concerns property rights and the profitability of the media industry, most famously addressed in *A&M Records v. Napster.*[16] Napster's technology allowed users to download and play any song on any computer connected to the Internet. A&M Records sued Napster to recover royalties, claiming that the record company owned those recordings. A&M Records won, leading to a series of legal decisions that make Web distribution of content similar to other forms of distribution.

An even deeper issue concerns the regulation of domains and Web servers and the setting of standards for this technology. Here the Internet breaks sharply with broadcasting and print media. The Internet emerged out of research technology developed under the auspices of the Department of Defense, largely at universities. In the mid-1990s, Tim Berners-Lee organized researchers, firms, and government agencies involved in the development of the Internet in the international World Wide Web Consortium, to set standards and make other governmental decisions for the Web.[17] This form of self-regulation has been vital for the development of the technology. It is yielding new concepts of intellectual property, such as Creative Commons, and pushing this technology to develop in ways quite different from print media and, especially, broadcast media.[18] The philosophy behind the World

right of rebuttal
An FCC regulation giving individuals the right to have the opportunity to respond to personal attacks made on a radio or TV broadcast.

fairness doctrine
An FCC requirement that broadcasters who air programs on controversial issues provide time for opposing views.

---

[15] *Red Lion Broadcasting Company v. Federal Communications Commission,* 395 U.S. 367 (1969).

[16] *A&M Records v. Napster,* 239 F.3d 104 (9th Circuit 2001)

[17] Tim Berners-Lee with Mark Fischetti, *Weaving the Web: The Original Design and Ultimate Destiny of the World Wide Web by Its Inventor* (New York: HarperBusiness, 1999).

[18] See http://creativecommons.org (accessed 5/7/09).

Wide Web Consortium calls for much less government regulation than accompanies broadcasting but has a much more communal flavor than the philosophy of competitive markets that lies behind America's view of print media.

Freedom of the Press

Unlike the broadcast media, the print media are not subject to federal regulation. Indeed, the great principle underlying the federal government's relationship with the press is the doctrine against **prior restraint.** Beginning with the landmark 1931 case of *Near v. Minnesota,* the U.S. Supreme Court has held that, except under the most extraordinary circumstances, the First Amendment of the Constitution prohibits government agencies from seeking to prevent newspapers or magazines from publishing whatever they wish.[19] Indeed, in the case of *New York Times v. United States,* the so-called Pentagon Papers case, the Supreme Court ruled that the government could not even block publication of secret Defense Department documents furnished to the *New York Times* by an opponent of the Vietnam War who had obtained the documents illegally.[20] In a 1990 case, however, the Supreme Court upheld a lower-court order restraining CNN from broadcasting tapes of conversations between the former Panamanian leader Manuel Noriega and his lawyer, supposedly recorded by the U.S. government. By a vote of 7–2, the Court held that CNN could be restrained from broadcasting the tapes until the trial court in the Noriega case had listened to them and decided whether their broadcast would violate Noriega's right to a fair trial. This case would seem to weaken the "no-prior-restraint" doctrine. But whether the same standard will apply to the print media has yet to be tested in the courts. In 1994, the Supreme Court ruled that cable television systems were entitled to essentially the same First Amendment protections as the print media.[21]

Even though newspapers may not be restrained from publishing whatever they want, they may be subject to sanctions after the fact. Historically, newspapers have been subject to the law of libel, which provides that newspapers that print false and malicious stories can be compelled to pay damages to those they defame. In recent years, however, American courts have greatly narrowed the meaning of libel and made it extremely difficult, particularly for politicians and other public figures, to win a libel case against a newspaper. The most important case on this topic is the 1964 Supreme Court case of *New York Times v. Sullivan,* in which the Court held that to be deemed libelous, a story about a public official not only had to be untrue but also had to result from "actual malice" or "reckless disregard" for the truth.[22] In other words, the newspaper had to deliberately print false and malicious material. In practice, it is nearly impossible to prove that a paper deliberately printed false and damaging information, and as conservatives discovered in the 1980s, it is very

---

[19] *Near v. Minnesota ex rel.,* 283 U.S. 697 (1931).

[20] *New York Times v. United States,* 403 U.S. 713 (1971).

[21] *Cable News Network v. Noriega,* 498 U.S. 976 (1990); *Turner Broadcasting v. Federal Communications Commission,* 512 U.S. 622 (1994).

[22] *New York Times v. Sullivan,* 376 U.S. 254 (1964).

difficult for a politician or other public figure to win a libel case. Libel suits against CBS News by General William Westmoreland and against *Time* magazine by Ariel Sharon of Israel, both financed by conservative legal foundations that hoped to embarrass the media, were defeated in court because they failed to show "actual malice." In the 1991 case of *Masson v. New Yorker Magazine,* this tradition was again affirmed by the Court's opinion that fabricated quotations attributed to a public figure were libelous only if the fabricated account "materially changed" the meaning of what the person said.[23] To all intents and purposes, the print media can publish anything they want about a public figure.

Organization and Ownership of the Media

The United States boasts more than 2,000 television stations, approximately 1,400 daily newspapers, and more than 13,000 radio stations. Even though the number of TV and radio stations and daily newspapers reporting news in the United States is enormous, and local coverage varies greatly from place to place, the number of sources of national news is actually quite small: one wire service, five broadcast networks, public radio and television, three elite newspapers, three newsmagazines, and a scattering of other sources, such as the national correspondents of a few large local papers and the small independent radio networks. Most of the national news that is published by local newspapers is provided by one wire service, the Associated Press. More than 500 of the nation's TV stations are affiliated with one of the five networks and carry its evening news reports. Dozens of others carry Public Broadcasting Service (PBS) news. Several hundred local radio stations also carry network news or National Public Radio (NPR) news broadcasts. At the same time, although there are only three truly national newspapers, the *Wall Street Journal,* the *Christian Science Monitor,* and *USA Today,* two other papers, the *New York Times* and the *Washington Post,* are read by political leaders and other influential Americans throughout the nation. Such is the influence of these two "elite" newspapers that their news coverage, plus that of the *Wall Street Journal,* sets the standard for virtually all other news outlets. Stories carried in the *New York Times* or the *Washington Post* influence the content of many other papers as well as the network news. Note how often this textbook, like most others, relies on *New York Times* and *Washington Post* stories as sources for contemporary events.

National news is also carried to millions of Americans by the three major newsmagazines: *Time, Newsweek,* and *U.S. News & World Report.* Beginning in the late 1980s, CNN became another major news source. The importance of CNN increased dramatically after its spectacular coverage of the Persian Gulf War. At one point, CNN was able to provide live coverage of American bombing raids on Baghdad after the major networks' correspondents had been forced to flee to bomb shelters. By 2003, though, Fox had displaced CNN as the nation's primary cable news source. The rise of Fox had important political implications because its coverage and commentators are considerably more conservative than CNN's. The emergence of Fox also demonstrates the importance of the existence of more, rather

---

[23] *Masson v. New Yorker Magazine, Inc.,* 501 U.S. 496 (1991).

than fewer, news sources. When there are few sources of news, each is likely to appeal to the same broad national audience and, accordingly, to maintain a middle-of-the-road stance. When there are more sources, each is likely to position itself within a discrete ideological or partisan niche, increasing the diversity of viewpoints presented to listeners and viewers.

The trend toward homogenization of national news has been hastened by dramatic changes in media ownership, which became possible in part as a result of the relaxation of government regulations since the 1980s. The enactment of the 1996 Telecommunications Act opened the way for additional consolidation in the media industry, and a wave of mergers and consolidations has further reduced the field of independent media across the country. Since that time, among the major news networks ABC was bought by the Walt Disney Company; CBS was bought by Westinghouse and later merged with Viacom, the owner of MTV and Paramount Communications; and CNN was bought by Time Warner. NBC has been owned by General Electric since 1985. The Australian press baron Rupert Murdoch owns the Fox Network plus a host of radio, television, and newspaper properties around the world. A small number of giant corporations now control a wide swath of media holdings, including television networks, movie studios, record companies, cable channels and local cable providers, book publishers, magazines, and newspapers.

FIGURE 13.1 NUMBER OF CORPORATIONS THAT CONTROL THE MAJORITY OF U.S. MEDIA

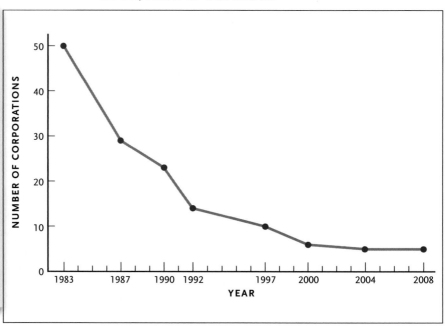

NOTE: Included are newspapers, magazines, TV and radio stations, books, music, movies, videos, wire services, and photo agencies.

SOURCE: Media Reform Information Center, www.corporations.org/media.

This development has prompted questions about whether enough competition exists among the media to produce a diverse set of views on political and corporate matters or whether the United States has become the prisoner of media monopolies (Figure 13.1).[24]

In June 2003, the FCC announced a set of new rules that seemed to pave the way for even more concentration in the media industry. It mandated that the major networks could own TV stations that collectively reached 45 percent of all viewers, up from 35 percent under the old rule. The new FCC rule also permits a single company to own the leading newspaper, as well as multiple television and radio outlets, in a single market. In the largest cities, this could include a newspaper, three television stations, and as many as eight radio stations.[25] Major media companies, which had long lobbied for the right to expand their activities, welcomed the new FCC rule. Critics, however, expressed grave concern that a decision would result in a narrowing of the range of views and issues presented to the general public. Congressional opponents of the FCC's action sought to overturn the rule but were stymied by opposition from the House Republican leadership as well as a threatened presidential veto. However, a federal appeals court placed the new regulation on hold, and in January 2005 the Bush administration decided not to appeal the case to Supreme Court. The FCC debuted new rules in 2007 to comply with the court's ruling. The cross-ownership rule, however, might outlive the newspaper itself.

WHAT AFFECTS NEWS COVERAGE?

Because of the important role the media can play in national politics, it is essential to understand the factors that affect media coverage.[26] What accounts for the media's agenda of issues and topics? What explains the character of coverage—why does a politician receive good or bad press? What factors determine the interpretation, or spin, that a particular story will receive? Although a host of minor factors plays a role, there are three major factors: (1) journalists or producers of the news, (2) politicians or other sources of the news, and (3) consumers.

Journalists

First, the character of the news is shaped by the institutions that produce it. Media content and news coverage are inevitably affected by the views, ideals, and interests of the individuals and organizations that seek out, write, and produce news and

---

[24] For a criticism of the increasing consolidation of the media, see the essays in Erik Barnouw et al., *Conglomerates and the Media* (New York: New Press, 1997).

[25] David Lieberman, "How Will FCC's Action Affect Consumers?" *USA Today*, June 4, 2003, p. 48.

[26] See the discussions in Michael Parenti, *Inventing Reality: The Politics of the Mass Media* (New York: St. Martin's Press, 1986); Herbert Gans, *Deciding What's News: A Study of CBS Evening News, NBC Nightly News, Newsweek, and Time* (New York: Vintage, 1980); and W. Lance Bennett, *News: The Politics of Illusion*, 5th ed. (New York: Longman, 2002).

other stories. At one time, newspaper publishers exercised a great deal of influence over their papers' news content. Publishers such as William Randolph Hearst and Joseph Pulitzer became political powers through their manipulation of news coverage. Hearst, for example, almost single-handedly pushed the United States into war with Spain in 1898 through his newspapers' relentless coverage of the alleged brutality employed by Spain in its efforts to suppress a rebellion in Cuba, then a Spanish colony. The sinking of the American battleship *Maine* in Havana Harbor under mysterious circumstances gave Hearst the ammunition he needed to force a reluctant president William McKinley to lead the nation into war. Today few publishers have that kind of power. Most are more concerned with the business end of the paper than its editorial content, although a few continue to impose their interests and tastes on the news.

More important than publishers, for the most part, are the reporters. The goals and incentives of journalists are varied, but they often include considerations of ratings, career success and professional prestige, and political influence. For all of these reasons, journalists seek not only to report the news but also to interpret it. Journalists' goals have a good deal of influence on what is created and reported as news.

Those journalists who cover the news for the national media generally have a lot of discretion or freedom to interpret stories and, as a result, have an opportunity to interject their own views and ideals into news stories. For example, some reporters' personal friendship with and respect for Franklin Roosevelt and John F. Kennedy helped generate more favorable news coverage for those presidents. On the other hand, many reporters' dislike of and distrust for Richard Nixon was also communicated to the public. In the case of Ronald Reagan, the disdain that many journalists felt for the president was communicated in stories suggesting that he was often asleep or inattentive when important decisions were made.

Conservatives have long charged that the liberal biases of reporters and journalists result in distorted news coverage. This charge was supported in a 2005 academic study by the economist Timothy Groseclose and the political scientist Jeffrey Milyo, who found a pronounced liberal bias in the news presented by many major papers and all but one broadcast network (Fox).[27] In a similar vein, a 1996 study of Washington newspaper bureau chiefs and correspondents conducted by the Roper Center and the Freedom Forum, a conservative foundation, found that 61 percent of the bureau chiefs and correspondents who were polled called themselves "liberal" or "liberal to moderate." Only 9 percent called themselves "conservative" or "conservative to moderate." And 89 percent said that they had voted for Bill Clinton in 1992, whereas only 7 percent indicated that they had voted for George H. W. Bush. Approximately 50 percent said they were Democrats, and only 4 percent claimed to be Republicans.[28] Another survey has indicated that even among the radio talk-show hosts lambasted by President Clinton, Democrats outnumber Republicans by a wide margin: Of 112 hosts surveyed, 39 percent had voted for

---

[27] Timothy Groseclose and Tom Milyo, "A Measure of Media Bias," *Quarterly Journal of Economics* 120 (2005): 1191–1237.

[28] Rowan Scarborough, "Leftist Press? Reporters Working in Washington Acknowledge Liberal Leanings in Poll," *Washington Times,* April 18, 1996, p. 1.

FIGURE 13.2 NEWSPAPER ENDORSEMENTS

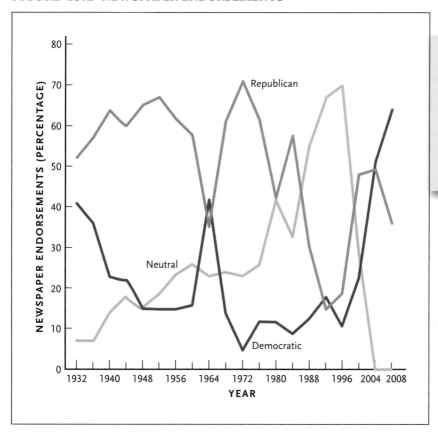

SOURCE: Harold W. Stanley and Richard G. Niemi, *Vital Statistics on American Politics, 2001–2002* (Washington, D.C.: Congressional Quarterly Press, 2001), pp. 194–95; 2004 and 2008 data from *Editor and Publisher*, www.editorandpublisher.com.

ANALYZING
THE EVIDENCE
More newspapers support the GOP, but in 2008 Obama received more editorial endorsements than McCain. Does this show a liberal or a conservative bias in the media?

Clinton in 1992, and only 23 percent had supported George H. W. Bush.[29] Generally speaking, reporters for major national news outlets tend to be more liberal than their local counterparts, who often profess moderate or even conservative views.

The link between journalists and liberal ideas is by no means absolute. The most important national newspapers, such as the *New York Times* and the *Washington Post*, have a liberal and Democratic orientation, but many other papers support the Republicans or have no particular leaning. Newspaper endorsements bear this out. Since the 1960s, newspaper endorsements for president, the U.S. Senate, the U.S. House, and statewide offices have on average balanced out between the Democrats and Republicans. To the extent that there is a bias, it is toward those already

[29] Michael Kinsley, "Bias and Baloney," *Washington Post*, November 26, 1992, p. A29; and John H. Fund, "Why Clinton Shouldn't Be Steamed at Talk Radio," *Wall Street Journal*, July 7, 1994, p. A12.

in office.[30] In 2004, for example, John Kerry received endorsements of 51 percent of papers throughout the country, compared with 49 percent for Bush. The 2008 election departed from this pattern radically. Nearly 70 percent of the newspapers in the country that endorsed a candidate for president picked Obama. These papers had a total circulation of over 40 million people, compared with 12 million people for the papers that endorsed McCain.[31]

In addition, most reporters attempt to maintain some measure of balance or objectivity, whatever their personal views. Moreover, over the past several years a conservative media complex has emerged in opposition to the liberal media. This complex includes two major newspapers, the *Wall Street Journal* and the *Washington Times;* several magazines, such as the *American Spectator* and the *Weekly Standard;* and a host of conservative radio and television talk programs. Also important is the media baron Rupert Murdoch, the creator of the Fox News Channel and the financial force behind the *Weekly Standard.* The emergence of this conservative media complex has meant that liberal policies and politicians are virtually certain to come under attack even when the "liberal media" are sympathetic to them.

selection bias (in the media) The predisposition of consumers to choose particular types of stories.

Probably more important than ideological bias is a **selection bias (in the media)** in favor of news that the media view as having a great deal of audience appeal because of its dramatic or entertainment value. In practice, this bias often results in news coverage that focuses on crimes and scandals, especially those involving prominent individuals, despite the fact that the public obviously looks to the media for information about important political debates.[32] For example, even though most journalists may be Democrats, this partisan predisposition did not prevent an enormous media frenzy in January 1998 when reports surfaced that President Clinton might have had an affair with Monica Lewinsky. Once a hint of blood appeared in the water, partisanship and ideology were swept away by the piranhalike instincts often manifested by journalists.

News Sources

News coverage is also influenced by politicians, public officials, and other news sources whose interests and activities are actual or potential news topics. Politicians want to be seen by the public as trustworthy, energetic, caring, and generally able to discharge the public duties with which they have been or hope to be entrusted. Accordingly, most politicians will seize or, if necessary, create opportunities for media coverage they deem likely to contribute to the public image they wish to fashion. Presidents, for example, know that their speeches on important topics will be televised throughout the nation. Thus they have an opportunity to use the media to demonstrate that they possess strong leadership qualities and fully understand

---

[30] Stephen Ansolabehere, Rebecca Lessem, and James M. Snyder, Jr., "The Orientation of Newspaper Endorsements 1940–2002," *Quarterly Journal of Political Science* 1, no. 4 (October 2006): 393–404, http://dx.doi.org/10.1561/100.00000009 (accessed 5/8/09).

[31] "Final Tally of Newspaper Endorsements—Obama Landslide at 287–159," Editor and Publisher, November 9, 2008, www.editorandpublisher.com.

[32] See Joseph N. Cappella and Kathleen Hall Jamieson, *Spiral of Cynicism: The Press and the Public Good* (New York: Oxford University Press, 1997).

the problems and issues facing the nation. President George W. Bush's speech in the wake of the September 11 terrorist attacks, for example, was designed to reassure Americans and demonstrate that he was firmly in command. In a similar vein, presidents and other politicians know that the media will give considerable coverage to floods, hurricanes, earthquakes, and other natural disasters. Thus, as a general rule, politicians are drawn to natural disasters like bees to honey. Indeed, the televised official inspection tour of a disaster site is a staple of American politics. This tour consists of the president and the affected state's governor, senator, or other politician, trailed by staff and reporters, all of whom first fly over the scene of the disaster and then land—at a safe location—so that the politicians can offer condolences to survivors and, finally, pledge to devote the resources of the government to make things right. Politicians hope that viewers will see them as compassionate problem solvers, certainly worthy of the public's trust. President Bush's failure to make a prompt visit to New Orleans and other disaster sites in the wake of Hurricane Katrina in 2005 was widely criticized and cited by the media as an example of the president's lack of empathy for common citizens—or at least his inability to give the appearance of having such empathy.

Politicians use many other techniques to develop favorable media images. President John F. Kennedy sought to develop strong relationships with influential journalists. Bill Clinton thought that appearances on soft news and entertainment programs allowed him to connect with ordinary Americans and show them that their president was not aloof or out of touch. Thus Clinton famously tooted his saxophone on a late-night entertainment program and discussed his choice of underwear with teenage reporters on MTV.

Politicians, interest groups, government officials, and other news sources employ a variety of techniques in their efforts to shape news coverage. These include news leaks, news releases, and in some instances cash payments to journalists. Although the news media are not oblivious to the efforts of sources to manipulate them, journalists and editors sometimes have a stake in allowing themselves to be manipulated. Journalists may publish leaked information in order to maintain good relations with important sources even when they know the source is pursuing his or her own political agenda. Editors and publishers have a financial stake in relying heavily on press releases even though they know the information they present is not objective. In such ways, the institutional stakes of the media may interfere with the unbiased and objective presentation of the news.

News Leaks.   A news leak is the disclosure of confidential information to the news media. Leaks may emanate from a variety of sources, including whistle-blowers, lower-level officials who hope to publicize what they view as their bosses' improper activities. In 1971, for example, a minor Defense Department staffer named Daniel Ellsberg sought to discredit official justifications for America's involvement in Vietnam by leaking top-secret documents to the press. The so-called Pentagon Papers were published by the *New York Times* and the *Washington Post* after the U.S. Supreme Court ruled that the government could not block release of the documents. In a similar vein, President George W. Bush was infuriated in 2005 when he learned that a still-unidentified source, presumed to be a whistler-blower, had leaked information concerning the president's secret orders authorizing the

National Security Agency to conduct clandestine surveillance of suspected terrorists without obtaining authorization from the special federal tribunal created for that purpose. Bush ordered the Justice Department to launch a probe of the leak. In 2006, a still-unidentified source leaked to the press part of a secret intelligence summary that seemed to contradict the administration's claims of progress in the war in Iraq. The president claimed the leaked portion of the report did not accurately reflect the full report. The administration proceeded to declassify other portions of the report, which seemed to support its claims about the war.

Most leaks, though, originate not with low-level whistle-blowers but, rather, with senior government officials and prominent politicians and political activists. Such persons often cultivate long-term relationships with journalists, to whom they regularly leak confidential information, knowing that it is likely to be published on a priority basis in a form acceptable to them. Their confidence is based on the fact that journalists are likely to regard high-level sources of confidential information as valuable assets whose favor must be retained. For example, I. Lewis "Scooter" Libby, former vice president Dick Cheney's former chief of staff, was apparently such a valuable source of leaks to so many prominent journalists that his name was seldom mentioned in the newspapers despite his prominence in Washington and his importance as a decision maker.[33] And the more recipients of leaked information strive to keep their sources secret, the more difficulty other journalists will have in checking the validity of the information.

Through such tacit alliances with journalists, prominent figures can manipulate news coverage and secure the publication of stories that serve their purposes. One recent case that revealed the complexities of this culture of leaks was the 2005 Valerie Plame affair. Plame was an undercover CIA analyst who happened to be married to Joseph Wilson, a prominent career diplomat. Wilson had angered the Bush White House by making a number of statements that were critical of the president's policies in Iraq. In an apparent effort to discredit Wilson, one or more administration officials informed prominent journalists that Plame had improperly used her position to help Wilson. In so doing, these officials may have violated a federal statute prohibiting the disclosure of the identities of covert intelligence operatives. The subsequent investigation revealed that the story had been leaked to several journalists, including the *Washington Post*'s Bob Woodward, who did not use it, and the *New York Times*'s Judith Miller, who did. Miller spent several months in jail for contempt of court after initially refusing to testify before a federal grand jury looking into the leak. After Miller finally testified, Libby was charged and convicted of lying and obstruction for his role in the affair, although it later emerged that the information was actually leaked by a former State Department official, Richard Armitage. The leak in the Plame case came to light only because it might have been illegal. Thousands of other leaks each year are quietly and seamlessly incorporated into the news.

The Press Release.   Also seamlessly incorporated into daily news reports each year are thousands of press releases. The press release, sometimes called a news

---

[33] Michael Massing, "The Press: The Enemy Within," *New York Review of Books*, December 15, 2005, p. 36.

release, is a story written by an advocate or publicist and distributed to the media in the hope that journalists will publish it under their own bylines with little or no revision. The inventor of the press release was a New York public relations consultant named Ivy Lee. In 1906, a train operated by one of Lee's clients, the Pennsylvania Railroad, was involved in a serious wreck. Lee quickly wrote a story about the accident that presented the railroad in a favorable light and distributed the account to reporters. Many papers published Lee's slanted story as their own objective account of events, and the railroad's reputation for quality and safety remained intact.

Consistent with Lee's example, today's press release presents facts and perspectives that serve an advocate's interests but is written in a way that mimics the factual news style of the paper, periodical, or television news program to which it has been sent. It is quite difficult for the audience to distinguish a well-designed press release from a news story. For example, a recent posting by PharmaWatch, a blog monitoring the pharmaceutical industry, identified an article published in the *New York Times* Science Times section that rehashed a news release issued by Pfizer, the giant pharmaceutical corporation. "A lawyer in New York has had to deal with what is politely referred to as 'bladder control' for as long as she can remember," the article began. "Even as a teenager she woke up at night feeling the urge to urinate but not always making it to the toilet in time." Fortunately, thanks to the press release it copied, the article was able to propose a solution. "Urge incontinence is often treated with drugs like tolterodine, sold as Detrol."[34] Not surprisingly, the drug touted in this helpful news story is sold by Pfizer.

To take another example, an April 2005 article sent to thousands of newspapers by the Associated Press (AP) was headlined "Fed Unveils Financial Education Website." Apparently written by an AP reporter, the article discussed the various ways in which a new Web site developed by the Federal Reserve could help consumers make informed decisions. The article did not mention that the information was basically a slight revision of a press release that could be found on the Fed's Web site.[35] Similarly, a *Houston Chronicle* story on teacher training claimed that students taught by teachers provided by Teach for America and other nontraditional sources performed significantly worse on standardized tests than students taught by traditionally certified instructors. The article failed to note that it was essentially a copy of a Stanford University press release touting the work of a Stanford professor who directed a traditional teacher training program.[36] And what about the June 2005 *Los Angeles Times* story "County Homeless Number 90,000"? This article claimed, without offering an explanation, that the number of homeless individuals in Los Angeles County had quintupled since the previous year. In presenting this shocking news of the increase in homelessness, though, the reporter neglected to mention that the data came from a press release issued by the Los Angeles Homeless Services Authority (LAHSA), whose budget is tied to the number of clients it serves. For the LAHSA, more homelessness equals more money and more staff. Indeed,

---

[34] Martica Heaner, "Enduring Incontinence in Silence," *New York Times,* October 25, 2005, www.nytimes.com/2005/10/25/health/25inco.html?_r=1 (accessed 5/8/09).

[35] Brian Montopoli, "Press Release Journalism," *Columbia Journalism Review Daily,* April 18, 2005.

[36] Anne Linehan, "Another Example of Press Release Journalism?" BlogHouston, April 18, 2005, www.bloghouston.net/item/1048 (accessed 4/9/09).

on its own Web site, it indicated that it had undertaken its new count of homeless individuals in part to "increase funding for homeless services in our community."[37] These should not be seen as isolated examples. According to some experts, more than 50 percent of the articles in a newspaper on any given day are based on press releases. Indeed, more than 75 percent of the journalists responding to a recent survey acknowledged using press releases for their stories.[38]

Journalists are certainly aware of the fact that the authors of press releases have their own agendas and are hardly unbiased reporters of the news. Nevertheless, the economics of publishing and broadcasting dictate that large numbers of stories will always be based on press releases. Newspapers and television stations are businesses, and for many the financial bottom line is more important than journalistic integrity.[39] The use of press releases allows a newspaper or a broadcast network to present more stories without paying more staff or incurring the other costs associated with investigating and writing the news. As one newspaper executive said, the public relations people who generally write news releases are our "unpaid reporters."[40]

In recent years, the simple printed press release has been joined by the video news release, which is designed especially for television stations. The video release is a taped report, usually about ninety seconds long, the typical length of a television news story, designed to look and sound like any other broadcast news segment. In exchange for airing material that serves the interests of some advocate, the television station airing the video release is relieved of the considerable expense and bother of identifying and filming its own news story. The audience is usually unaware that the "news" it is watching is someone's canned publicity footage.

One example of a video news release was a pair of ninety-second segments funded by the U.S. Department of Health and Human Services (HHS) in 2004. After Congress enacted legislation adding a prescription drug benefit to the Medicare program, HHS sent a video release designed to look like a news report to local TV stations around the nation. Forty television stations aired the report without indicating that it had come from the government. The segment was introduced by the local news anchor reading from a government-suggested script. Referring to the new Medicare law, the anchor read, "Reporter Karen Ryan helps sort through the details." Then, against the backdrop of film showing President Bush signing the law and the reactions of apparently grateful senior citizens, an unseen narrator, speaking like a reporter, presented the new law in a positive light: "The new law, say officials, simply offers people with Medicare ways to make their health coverage more affordable." The segment concluded with the sign off "In Washington,

---

[37] "LA Times: County Homeless Population Tops Two Kazillion, No Further Reporting Required," IndependentSources, June 16, 2005, http://independentsources.com/2005/06/16/la-times-county-homeless-population-tops-two-kazillion-no-further-reporting-required (accessed 4/9/09).

[38] Dennis L. Wilcox and Glen T. Cameron, *Public Relations: Strategy and Tactics*, 8th ed. (Boston: Allyn & Bacon, 2006), p. 357.

[39] See, for example, Davis Merritt, *Knightfall: Knight Ridder and How the Erosion of Newspaper Journalism Is Putting Democracy at Risk* (New York: Amacom Books, 2005).

[40] Quoted in Wilcox and Cameron, *Public Relations*, p. 357.

I'm Karen Ryan reporting." Viewers were not told that the entire story was distributed by the government. Nor were viewers informed that Karen Ryan was not a reporter at all. She was an employee of the ad agency hired by the government to create the video release. In response to criticism, an HHS spokesperson pointed out that the same sort of video news releases had often been used by the Clinton administration and was commonly used by a number of firms and interest groups. "The use of video news releases is a common, routine practice in government and the private sector," he said. "Anyone who has questions about this practice needs to do some research on modern public information tools."[41]

Hiring Reporters. From creating phony reporters to reading make-believe news stories, it is but a small step to hiring real reporters to present sham accounts. And this step has been taken frequently by both the government and private advocates. A number of cases have come to light in recent years in which the government or a private concern has paid journalists to write favorable accounts of its activities and efforts. Late in 2005, for example, the U.S. military acknowledged that contractors in its employ had regularly paid Iraqi newspapers to carry positive news about American efforts in that nation. The Washington-based Lincoln Group, a public relations firm working under contract to the federal government, says it placed more than 1,000 news stories in the Arab press since 2001.[42] Iraqis reading the articles would have had no way of knowing that the material presented was produced at the behest of the American authorities.

The government's practice of hiring journalists is not limited to operations abroad. In recent years, federal agencies have paid several journalists and commentators to report favorably on government initiatives and programs in the United States. The Department of Education, for example, paid the commentator Armstrong Williams $241,000 to promote President Bush's No Child Left Behind Act. Williams wrote favorably about the law in his newspaper column, commented positively about it during his cable television appearances, and urged other commentators to interview Education Secretary Roderick Paige.[43] Williams did not disclose his financial relationship with the agency whose programs he was touting. Similarly, the Department of Health and Human Services paid the syndicated columnist Maggie Gallagher $20,000 to promote the administration's views on marriage. Gallagher wrote several columns on the topic without revealing her financial relationship with the administration.

Williams and Gallagher worked for the government, but the private sector is also active in this area. Corporations, trade associations, and interest groups have been known to provide gratuities to journalists. For example, in 2005 one well-known columnist was forced to resign his position with the Cato Institute after it was revealed that he had accepted payment from a prominent Washington lobbyist in exchange for writing newspaper columns favorable to the interests of some of

---

[41] Quoted in Ben Fritz, Bryan Keefer, and Brendan Nyhan, *All the President's Spin* (New York: Touchstone Books, 2004), pp. 252–53, 357.

[42] Jeff Gerth, "Military's Information War Is Vast and Often Secretive," *New York Times*, December 11, 2005, p. 1.

[43] Howard Kurtz, "Administration Paid Commentator," *Washington Post*, January 8, 2005, p. 1.

the lobbyist's clients. The lobbyist, Jack Abramoff, who in 2006 pleaded guilty to a number of violations of federal lobbying laws, had paid the writer, Doug Bandow, to promote the causes of the Northern Marianas Islands, the Choctaw Indians, and other Abramoff clients. In one nationally syndicated Copley News Service column, Bandow defended the Choctaws' operation of gambling casinos, asserting, "There's certainly no evidence that Indian gambling operations harm the local community." Abramoff had been arguing just that point to lawmakers. In another column, Bandow opposed federal "economic meddling" in the Marianas, precisely the position the Marianas government was paying Abramoff to advocate on Capitol Hill.[44]

There have been several other recent cases in which reporters and columnists were found to have received payment from industries and interests about which they wrote. In 2005, the Indiana Wesleyan University professor Tom Lehman published a piece in *The Hill*, a magazine read by congressional staffers and members, praising so-called payday loans. It turned out that Lehman had accepted money from the industry that provides these high-risk loans to poor people.[45] In another case, the syndicated columnist Michael Fumento praised Monsanto, a huge agribusiness enterprise, in his columns and in a book. Fumento, it turned out, received $60,000 from Monsanto, although he denied that the payment influenced his writing. Fumento's weekly column was canceled by the Scripps Howard News Service after the revelation.[46]

One group especially noted for paying writers and reporters for favorable coverage is the pharmaceutical industry. As the Detrol example suggests, many of the articles that appear in popular—and even scientific—journals reporting favorably on particular drugs are written by the drug companies themselves. In some cases, the writers are actually paid by the drug companies; in other reported instances, the writer cited in the story's byline is not the actual author of the account. Often a ghostwriter employed by a drug company writes the story while the nominal author is paid for the use of his or her name.[47]

But, of course, although politicians try to use the media for their purposes, reporters often have their own agenda. Often enough, hostile or merely determined journalists will break through the smoke screens thrown up by the politicians and report annoying truths. Thus, for example, despite the Bush administration's best efforts to manage the news from Iraq, journalists filed accounts of Iraqi resistance, abuse of Iraqi prisoners, and other unpleasant facts that the administration might have preferred to keep off the table.

Consumers

The print and broadcast media are businesses that, in general, seek to show a profit. This means that like any other business they must cater to the preferences of

---

[44] Anne E. Kornblut and Philip Shenon, "Columnist Resigns His Post Admitting Lobbyist Paid Him," *New York Times*, December 17, 2005, p. A15.

[45] Eamon Javers, "This Opinion Brought to You By . . . ," *Business Week*, January 20, 2006, p. 35.

[46] Javers, "This Opinion," p. 36.

[47] Anna Wilde Matthews, "At Medical Journals, Writers Paid by Industry Play Big Role," *Wall Street Journal*, December 13, 2005, p. 1.

TABLE 13.2 EDUCATION AND ATTENTION TO THE NEWS

Level of Education	Level of Attention to Hard News*		
	High (%)	Medium (%)	Low (%)
College graduate	36	59	6
Some college	30	59	11
High school graduate	23	59	18
Not a high school graduate	12	60	28

*People with high levels of attention to hard news follow international, national, local, and business news closely; those with low levels do not follow the news.

SOURCE: Compiled by authors from Pew Research Center for the People & the Press, "Audience Segments in a Changing News Environment," Pew Research Center Biennial News Consumption Survey, August 17, 2008, http://people-press.org/reports/pdf/444.pdf (accessed 5/8/09).

ANALYZING THE EVIDENCE

Educated Americans are far more attentive to news programming than their less well-educated fellow citizens. How does this affect the type of news reported? Which issues are most likely to receive attention? Which issues are most likely to be overlooked?

consumers. Their doing so has very important consequences for the content and character of the news media.

Catering to the Upscale Audience. In general and especially in the political realm, the print and broadcast media and the publishing industry are not only responsive to the interests of consumers generally but are also particularly responsive to the interests and views of the better-educated and more affluent segments of the audience. The preferences of these segments have a profound effect on the content and orientation of the press, of radio and television programming, and books, especially in the areas of news and public affairs.[48]

Although affluent consumers do watch television programs and read periodicals whose content is designed simply to amuse or entertain, the one area that most directly appeals to the upscale audience is that of news and public affairs. The affluent—who are also typically well educated—are the core audience of newsmagazines, journals of opinion, books dealing with public affairs, serious newspapers such as the *New York Times* and the *Washington Post,* and broadcast news and evening and weekend public-affairs programming. Although other segments of the public also read newspapers and watch the television news, their level of interest in world events, national political issues, and the like is closely related to their level of education (Table 13.2). As a result, upscale Americans are overrepresented in the news and public-affairs audience. The concentration of these strata in the audience

---

[48] See Tom Burnes, "The Organization of Public Opinion," in *Mass Communication and Society,* James Curran, Michael Gurevitch, and Janet Woollacott, eds. (Beverly Hills, Calif.: Sage, 1979), pp. 44–230. See also David L. Altheide, *Creating Reality: How TV News Distorts Events* (Beverly Hills, Calif.: Sage, 1976).

makes news, politics, and public affairs potentially very attractive topics to advertisers, publishers, radio broadcasters, and television executives.

Entire categories of events, issues, and phenomena of interest to lower-, middle-, and working-class Americans receive scant attention from the national print and broadcast media. For example, trade union news and events are discussed only in the context of major strikes or revelations of corruption. No network or national periodical routinely covers labor organizations. Religious and church affairs receive little coverage (unless scandal is involved, as was the case in 2002 and 2003 in many dioceses of the Roman Catholic Church). The activities of veterans', fraternal, ethnic, and patriotic organizations are also generally ignored.

The Media and Conflict. Although the media respond most to the upscale audience, groups that cannot afford the services of media consultants and issues managers can publicize their views and interests through protest. Frequently, the media are accused of encouraging conflict and even violence in response to the fact that their audiences mostly watch news for the entertainment value that conflict can provide. Clearly, conflict can be an important vehicle for attracting the attention and interest of the media and thus may provide an opportunity for media attention to groups otherwise lacking the financial or organizational resources to broadcast their views. But although conflict and protest can succeed in drawing media attention, these methods ultimately do not allow groups from the bottom of the social ladder to compete effectively in the media.

The chief problem with protest as a media technique is that, in general, the media on which the protesters depend have considerable discretion in reporting and interpreting the events they cover. For example, should the media focus on the conflict itself, rather than on the issues or concerns created by the conflict? The answer to this question is typically determined by the media, not by the protesters. Therefore, media interpretation of protest activities is more a reflection of the views of the groups and forces to which the media are responsive—which, as we have seen, are usually segments of the upper middle class—than it is a function of the wishes of the protesters themselves. It is worth noting that civil rights protesters received their most favorable media coverage when a segment of the white upper-middle class saw blacks as potential political allies in the Democratic Party.

Typically, upper-middle-class protesters—student demonstrators and the like—have little difficulty securing favorable publicity for themselves and their causes. They are often more skilled than their lower-class counterparts in the techniques of media manipulation. That is, they typically have a better sense—often as a result of formal courses on the subject—of how to package messages for media consumption. For example, it is important to know what time of day a protest should occur if it is to be carried on the evening news. Similarly, the setting, definition of the issues, character of the rhetoric used, and so on all help determine whether a protest will receive favorable media coverage, unfavorable coverage, or no coverage at all. Moreover, upper-middle-class protesters can often produce their own media coverage through "underground" newspapers, college papers, student radio and television stations, and the Internet. The same resources and skills that generally allow upper-middle-class people to publicize their ideas are usually not left behind when segments of this class choose to engage in disruptive forms of political action. Note the media attention given antiwar protesters in 2003 even though polls indicated that such groups were a minor force in American politics.

CONCLUSION: MEDIA POWER AND RESPONSIBILITY

The content and character of news and public-affairs programming—what the media choose to present and how they present it—can have far-reaching political consequences. Media disclosures can greatly enhance or fatally damage the careers of public officials. Media coverage can rally support for or intensify opposition to national policies. The media choose what issues to cover and how and, as discussed in Chapter 9, set the national political agenda and frame political discourse.

The media have played a central role in shaping some of the most significant events in recent American political history. News media were critically important in the civil rights movement of the 1950s and 1960s. Television footage and photographs of civil rights marchers attacked by club-swinging police galvanized public support for the civil rights movement among northern whites and greatly increased pressure on Congress to bring an end to segregation.[49] The media were central actors in the Watergate affair, which ultimately forced President Richard Nixon, the landslide victor in the 1972 presidential election, to resign from office in disgrace. The relentless series of investigations launched by the *Washington Post*, the *New York Times*, and the television networks led to the disclosure of various abuses of power by those in the White House, ultimately forcing Nixon to resign.[50]

Mass media have been central to every election of the past century. They cover the emergence and activities of the candidates, political debates and conventions, and election-night returns. They are the vehicles for political advertising. They even generate their own campaign news, especially by conducting public opinion polls and reporting who is ahead and who is behind, who is gaining momentum and who is fading.

And the media go to war along with the U.S. military. Since the American Civil War, news reporting and photography have brought wars home. Graphic depictions of the atrocities in Vietnam, including the My Lai massacre, and of American war dead and wounded helped turn popular sentiment against the war, which compelled the government to negotiate an end to the conflict.[51] Video of precision bombs destroying targets in Baghdad and of the rout of Saddam Hussein's army in 1991 pushed up President George H. W. Bush's popularity and solidified his

---

[49] David J. Garrow, *Protest at Selma: Martin Luther King, Jr., and the Voting Rights Act of 1965* (New Haven, Conn: Yale University Press, 1978).

[50] Todd Gitlin, *The Whole World Is Watching: Mass Media in the Making and Unmaking of the New Left* (Berkeley: University of California Press, 2003).

[51] Willim M. Hammond, *Reporting Vietnam: Media and Military at War* (Lawrence: University of Kansas Press, 1998).

reputation as commander in chief.[52] News coverage of the Iraq war in 2003 portrayed the toppling of Saddam Hussein's statue in Baghdad, and President George W. Bush's announcement of "Mission Accomplished" at the end of combat in 2003 would later be used against the president as the military struggled for years to restore a modicum of stability in Iraq.

The tremendous power that reporters and editors sometimes wield emanates from the free hand that the press have in American politics. So long as they do not overstep the bounds of libel, journalists can (and often do) criticize the American government openly. Given the diversity of media outlets today, especially after the rise of cable television and the Internet, it is not uncommon to find defenders and critics of the government or of particular political decisions, and often those on either side of the debate argue their positions side by side. The rise of the new media has brought more voices to the fore and a broader potential debate over public policy. Wide-open debate and criticism of public officials is essential, but it sometimes exacts a social cost.

Free media are essential to democratic government. We depend on the media to investigate wrongdoing, publicize and explain governmental actions, evaluate programs and politicians, and bring to light matters that might otherwise be known only to a handful of governmental insiders. In short, without free and active media, popular government would be virtually impossible. Citizens would have few means of knowing or assessing the government's actions—other than the claims or pronouncements of the government itself. Moreover, without active—indeed, aggressive—media, citizens would be hard pressed to make informed choices among competing candidates at the polls. Often enough, the media reveal discrepancies between candidates' claims and their records and between the images that candidates seek to project and the underlying realities.

At the same time, politicians have become ever more reliant on news coverage, especially favorable coverage. National political leaders and journalists have had symbiotic relationships, at least since FDR's presidency. Initially, politicians were the senior partners. Thus, for example, reporters did not publicize potentially embarrassing information, widely known in Washington, D.C., about the personal lives of such figures as FDR and John F. Kennedy. Today, the balance has shifted. Often it seems the journalists have the upper hand. Now that individual politicians have become heavily dependent on media to reach their constituents, journalists no longer need fear that their access to information can be restricted in retaliation for negative coverage. It is not uncommon today to hear the White House press corps challenge the president's press liaison or even the president himself.

Freedom gives the media enormous power. The media can make or break reputations, help launch or destroy political careers, and build support for or rally opposition against programs and institutions.[53] Wherever there is so much power, at least the potential for its abuse or overly zealous use exists. All things considered, free media are so critically important to the maintenance of a democratic society

[52] Jon Krosnik and L. A. Brannon, "The Impact of the Gulf War on the Ingredients of Presidential Evaluations," *American Political Science Review* 87 (1993): 963–75.

[53] See Martin Linsky, *Impact: How the Press Affects Federal Policy Making* (New York: Norton, 1991).

that we may be willing to take the risk that the media will occasionally abuse their power. The forms of government control that would prevent the media from misusing their power would also certainly pose a serious risk to our freedom.

FOR FURTHER READING

Ansolabehere, Stephen, Roy Behr, and Shanto Iyengar. *The Media Game: American Politics in the Television Age*. New York: Macmillan, 1993.

Arnold, R. Douglas. *Congress, the Press, and Political Accountability*. Princeton, N.J.: Princeton University Press, 2004.

Bagdikian, Ben. *The New Media Monopoly*. Boston: Beacon Press, 2004.

Cook, Timothy. *Governing with the News: The News Media as a Political Institution*. Chicago: University of Chicago Press, 1997.

Fenton, Tom. *Bad News: The Decline of Reporting, the Business of News, and the Danger to Us All*. New York: HarperCollins, 2005.

Fritz, Ben, Bryan Keefer, and Brendan Nyhan. *All the President's Spin*. New York: Touchstone Books, 2004.

Goldberg, Bernard. *Bias: A CBS Insider Exposes How the Media Distort the News*. New York: Regnery, 2002.

Groseclose, Timothy, and Jeffrey Milyo. "A Measure of Media Bias." *The Quarterly Journal of Economics* 120, no. 4 (November 2005): 1191–1237.   ○ reader selection

Hamilton, James T. *All the News That's Fit to Sell: How the Market Transforms Information into News*. Princeton, N.J.: Princeton University Press, 2003.

Iyengar, Shanto and Jennifer McGrady. *Media Politics: A Citizen's Guide*. New York: Norton, 2007.

Kellner, Douglas. *Media Spectacle and the Crisis of Democracy: Terrorism, War, and Election Battles*. Boulder, Colo.: Paradigm, 2005.

Merritt, Davis. *Knightfall: Knight Ridder and How the Erosion of Newspaper Journalism Is Putting Democracy at Risk*. New York: Amacom Books, 2005.

Norris, Pippa, Montague Kern, and Marion R. Just, eds. *Framing Terrorism: The News Media, the Government, and the Public*. New York: Routledge, 2003.

Schudson, Michael. "The News Media as Political Institutions." *Annual Review of Political Science* 5 (June 2002): 249–69.

Shogan, Robert. *Bad News: Where the Press Goes Wrong in the Making of the President*. Chicago: Dee, 2001.

Starr, Paul. *The Creation of the Media*. New York: Basic Books, 2004.

Trippi, Joe. *The Revolution Will Not Be Televised: Democracy, the Internet, and the Overthrow of Everything*. New York: Regan Books, 2004.

Ⓢ Additional study and review materials are available online at wwnorton.com/studyspace/

Analyzing the 2010 Midterm Elections

The 2010 elections shifted the balance of power in American government. Approaching the congressional election of November 2010, the Democratic Party enjoyed solid majorities in the U.S. Senate and House of Representatives. In 2010, the Democrats held 59 of 100 Senate seats, including the seats of two independent senators who aligned with the Democratic caucus. In the House, the Democrats, with 257 of 435 seats, held 59 percent as well. But after four years of Democratic control in the House and Senate, the 2010 midterm elections gave Republicans a solid majority in the House and increased their numbers in the Senate. With the House of Representatives now controlled by Republicans, Representative John Boehner (R-OH), the Republican leader, ascended to the position of Speaker of the House, replacing two-term speaker Nancy Pelosi (D-CA). In analyzing what happened in the 2010 elections, why it happened, and what the consequences may be, we observe many of the concepts and principles from Part 3 in action.

WHAT HAPPENED?

Our analysis of the 2010 elections begins with a simple accounting of where Democrats lost races for the House and Senate. Understanding this basic data will take us a long way toward understanding the outcomes of the 2010 elections. We will look first at the races for the Senate and then at the races for the House.

The Senate

In 2010, 37 U.S. Senate races took place. Elections for full six-year terms were held for 34 seats, and 3 other seats had special elections to fill out the remainder of existing six-year terms. New York and Delaware held special elections to complete the terms vacated by Hillary Clinton and Joe Biden, who left the Senate for the positions of secretary of state and vice president, respectively. West Virginia held a special election to fill the remainder of the term of the late senator Robert Byrd, who died in office.

Electoral contests can be divided into open-seat races and non-open-seat races. A Senate seat becomes open when senators retire, leave the Senate for other offices, or lose primary battles. Republican pick-ups in 2010 came both from open-seat elections and from victories over Democratic incumbents.

There were an unusually large number of open Senate seats in 2010. Six Republicans and 6 Democrats retired. In addition, Republican senators Robert Bennett of Utah and Lisa Murkowski of Alaska and Democratic senator Arlen Specter lost their nomination contests. As a result, 12 Democratic incumbents and 10 Republican incumbents stood for reelection. Not a single incumbent Republican senator lost in the general elections. In one of the wildest races of the year, incumbent senator Lisa Murkowski of Alaska lost the Republican primary to a challenger but staged a major comeback in the general election. She mounted a write-in campaign and won more votes than Republican-nominee Joe Miller, the Tea Party favorite who had beaten her in the primary, and Democrat Scott McAdams. Two Democratic incumbents lost. In conservative Arkansas, Senator Blanche Lincoln, first

▲ *Surveys showed Senate majority leader Harry Reid lagging among voters in the days before the November 2010 election, but when the votes were tallied, he held onto his seat. Despite losing several seats in the Senate to Republicans, Democrats held onto a majority.*

elected in 1998, lost to Republican challenger Representative John Boozman, who left his seat in the House to run against Lincoln. In Wisconsin, Democrat Russ Feingold lost to businessman Ron Johnson.

Republicans' biggest gains, though, came in the open Senate seats. The GOP picked up 4 of 7 seats left open by retiring Democrats. These party changes took place in Illinois, Indiana, North Dakota, and Pennsylvania. Of these, the Pennsylvania contest was most unusual, as the seat was previously held by Arlen Specter, who was last elected as a Republican in 2004, then defected to the Democratic Party in 2009, only to lose a primary battle against Representative Joe Sestak. Though Pennsylvania trended Democratic in the last election cycles, voters opted for former congressman Pat Toomey, a Republican, over Sestak. In Illinois, Republican House member Mark Kirk edged by State Treasurer Alexi Giannoulias to take the Senate seat formerly held by President Barack Obama. Democrats won 3 remaining Democratic open seats—in Connecticut, Delaware, and West Virginia. Republican candidates won all 8 of the seats vacated by Republican senators. With two wins against incumbents and four wins in open seats, the Republicans won a total of 6 seats they had not previously held.

The new Senate, with 51 Democrats and 47 Republicans, also has 2 Independents, Bernie Sanders of Vermont and Joe Lieberman of Connecticut, who join the Democratic caucus when the Senate convenes. That brings the Democrats' edge to 53–47. This division is rather typical of the Senate. It is not the filibuster-proof majority that the Democrats won in 2008, nor is it the evenly split Senate that George Bush worked with. The composition of the new Senate is unusual in one important respect. In a body known for its folkways and traditions, nearly half of the 100 senators are in their first term of office. Past senators have often made headlines for their long tenures. For example, Robert Byrd of West Virginia, who died in 2010, served for 51 years. Other recent and current members, such as Strom Thurmond (SC), Daniel Inouye (HI), and Ted Kennedy (MA), served nearly as long. However, a host of retirements and defeats in 2006, 2008, and 2010 have led to a Senate with many more freshmen than is typical. Whether the large number of new members will have any direct political or policy consequences is an open question.

The new Senate remains overwhelmingly white and male. For instance, while just over 50 percent of the country is female, only 17 of the 100 senators in the 112th Congress are female, the same number as in the 111th Congress. Approximately one-quarter of U.S. citizens are nonwhite, but only 4 members of the U.S. Senate are nonwhite: Bob Menendez of New Jersey, Marco Rubio of Florida, and Daniel Inouye and Daniel Akaka, both of Hawaii.

The House

The 2010 elections produced a split Congress. Democrats held their Senate majority, but Republicans gained a majority of seats in the House of Representatives. Coming into the election, Democrats had to defend many more seats than Republicans, and more seats in hostile territory. Democrats held 67 seats in districts that John McCain won in 2008, while Republicans held 8 seats in districts that Barack Obama won. Making matters worse, Democrats did not field as many challengers as Republicans. Republicans failed to field a challenger for only 5 seats, but Democrats did not recruit a challenger in 24 races, and you can't beat somebody with nobody.

One important feature of the 2010 electoral landscape helped buoy the Democrats. Relatively few Democrats retired or were defeated in their primaries. Only 20 of 256 Democratic-held seats were open seats (no incumbent running in the general election), and Republicans had 21 open seats. Incumbents tend to win higher vote margins than nonincumbents. The incumbency advantage has hovered around 8 percentage points since 1990, and 2010 was no exception. Consider, for example, the Florida 12th and 13th congressional districts. In both districts, Republican presidential candidates won, on average, 55 percent of the vote from 2000 through 2008. In 2010, the Florida 12th Congressional District had an open-seat race, and Republican Dennis Ross won 54 percent of the two-party vote to beat Democrat Lori Edwards. In the neighboring 13th, incumbent Republican Vern Buchanan represented the Florida 13th and beat the Democratic challenger 69 percent to 31 percent. Comparing the two suggests a very large incumbency advantage. But even incumbency was not enough to help many House Democrats keep their seats, especially in a year in which economic woes produced high levels of dissatisfaction with the president and in those districts where a Democratic incumbent represented a traditionally Republican constituency.

Many of the Democratic losses in 2010 came from districts that Democrats had won from Republicans in 2006 and 2008. Arizona is a case in point. Prior to the 2006 midterm election, Republicans held 6 of the state's 8 congressional districts. From losses in 2006 and 2008, Republicans held only 3 of those 8 seats. Two of the 3 seats that the Republicans lost were regained in 2010. A similar story can be told about Ohio. In the previous two election cycles, Democrats gained 4 seats in Ohio and lost none. All 4 of these seats were returned to Republicans in 2010. Of the 30 seats that Democrats gained in 2006, only one, held by Joe Courtney of Connecticut, was considered a safe seat in 2010.[1]

The 2010 elections also bore out the continuing regional orientation of the two major political parties in the United States. In House elections, Republicans won the largest majorities in the South, where they took 61 percent of the vote. Democrats, meanwhile, had their strongest showing in the Northeast, where they won 54 percent of the vote. Other regions split more evenly, with the West voting slightly more Democratic and the Midwest voting slightly more Republican.

In addition to Democrats and Republicans representing different regions of the country, the parties represent different kinds of districts within states. In particular, Democrats tend to represent urban districts and Republicans tend to represent rural districts. All congressional districts are required to represent roughly the same number of people. Hence, the smaller the district in physical size, the more densely populated it is. Congressional districts vary greatly in size. The 15th district of New York, in New York City, is only 10 square miles, whereas the at-large district of Alaska is over 570,000 square miles. The median district is about 2,300 square miles in size. Democratic and Republican districts are very different. The 112th Congress continues the trend toward regional separation of Republican and Democratic representatives. Democrats are now even more highly concentrated in urban areas than they were after the 2008 election, and Republicans represent an even larger number of rural districts.

WHY?

We can identify two broad, macro-level reasons for the Democratic losses in 2010. First, we can see the 2010 midterm elections as a "correction" of the 2006 and 2008 elections. Democrats took a net 54 seats from the Republicans in 2006 and 2008, many of them in districts that traditionally leaned Republican. In 2006, the sitting president, George W. Bush, was unpopular; the U.S. war in Iraq was not going well; and several Republicans were involved in scandals. The 2006 election resulted in Democratic control of the House for the first time since 1994 and control of the Senate for the first time since 2002.

As Table 1 shows, from 2006 to 2008, the Democrats expanded the small majorities that they had gained in both chambers of Congress. Riding the coattails of a popular presidential candidate, Barack Obama, and in the midst of an economic crisis, the Democrats made sharp gains in 2008. In the House, the Democrats added 21 seats to their majority. In the Senate, following a contested election and recount for a seat in Minnesota (eventually won by Democrat Al Franken), the Democrats

---

[1] John F. Harris, "Rahm Emanuel's Class of 2006 in Jeopardy," *Politico,* October 14, 2010.

TABLE 1 CONGRESSIONAL ELECTION RESULTS, 1994–2010

HOUSE OF REPRESENTATIVES

Year	Turnout	Party Ratio	Seat Shift	Democrats Reelected	Republicans Reelected
1994	41.1%	204 D, 230 R	+54 R	89.3%	99.4%
1996	51.7	207 D, 227 R	+3 D	98.3	91.4
1998	38.1	211 D, 223 R	+4 D	99.5	97.2
2000	54.2	212 D, 222 R	+1 D	98.0	97.5
2002	39.5	205 D, 229 R	+8 R	97.4	97.5
2004	60.3	201 D, 232 R	+3 R	97.4	99.0
2006	40.2	233 D, 202 R	+30 D	100	89.6
2008	61.0	254 D, 173 R	+21 D	97.9	92.1
2010*	40.3	191 D, 244 R	+71R	78.8	98.7

SOURCE: Michael McDonald, United States Election Project, http://elections.gmu.edu/2010_vote
_forecasts.html (accessed 11/4/2010).
*Data for 2010 are preliminary estimates.

went from a 51–49 majority to a "filibuster-proof" majority of 60 seats. This advantage in the Senate, however, was short-lived. The sixtieth vote of Al Franken came not in January 2009, when the other new legislators were sworn into office, but in July 2009, after a lengthy post-election dispute. And after the death of Senator Ted Kennedy less than two months later, the Massachusetts Democrat was replaced in January 2010 by Republican Scott Brown, thus leaving the Democrats with 59 seats for the remainder of the 111th Congress.

That the Democrats controlled an unusually high number of seats going into the 2010 elections is the first reason why they lost so many seats. In the previous two elections, Democratic candidates won seats in districts that normally did not favor Democrats. This means that many incumbent Democrats in 2010 were on the defensive in conservative districts. A useful way to characterize this is by counting the number of congressional districts that were won by Republican presidential candidates but were held by Democratic members of Congress and, vice-versa, the number won by Democratic presidential candidates and held by Republican members of Congress. Districts represented by a politician of one party but won by the presidential candidate of the opposite party may be places where the legislative incumbents are particularly vulnerable. Indeed, going into the 2010 election, 47 Democratic members represented districts that George W. Bush won in 2004 and John McCain won in 2008. Conversely, only 6 Republican members held seats that John Kerry won in 2004 and Barack Obama won in 2008.[2] Thus, Democrats were

[2] James E. Campbell, "The Seats in Trouble Forecast of the 2010 Elections to the U.S. House," *PS: Political Science and Politics* (2010), 43: 627-630.

TABLE 1 (CONT.) CONGRESSIONAL ELECTION RESULTS, 1994–2010

			SENATE		
Year	Turnout	Party Ratio	Seat Shift	Democrats Reelected	Republicans Reelected
1994	41.1%	47 D, 53 R	+10 R	87.5%	80.0%
1996	51.7	45 D, 55 R	—	100	85.7
1998	38.1	45 D, 55 R	—	92.3	87.5
2000	54.2	50 D, 50 R	+5 D	93.3	64.3
2002	39.5	48 D, 51 R	+1 R	83.3	93.3
2004	60.3	44 D, 55 R	+4 R	92.9	100
2006	40.2	50 D, 49 R	+6 D	100	57.1
2008	61.0	59 D, 41 R	+8 D	100	66.7
2010*	40.3	53 D, 47 R	+16 R	76.9	100

disproportionately defending seats in areas inclined toward the opposite party. The degree of Democratic vulnerability appears even larger when considering the average presidential vote in the congressional districts from 2000 through 2008. Democrats had to defend seats in nearly 70 Republican-leaning constituencies, while Republicans had fewer than 10 seats in Democrat-leaning constituencies.

A second important, macro-level explanation for losses by the Democratic Party in 2010 is that in midterm elections, the sitting president's party almost always suffers losses in Congress. With just a few notable exceptions, such as Republican gains in 2002, candidates of the president's party tend to do worse in off-year election cycles.[3] This pattern is also visible in Table 1. This regularity in American politics is often explained by the notion that voters collectively penalize the president in power, who inevitably fails to live up to promises made on the campaign trail.

Public disaffection in 2010 can be traced to many things, including a lingering war in Afghanistan, but most important was the state of the economy. Approaching the 2010 elections, the country had not yet recovered from the longest economic recession since the Great Depression. Nearly 10 percent of the workforce was unemployed at the time of the elections, and the unemployment rate had been that high for almost two years. The Democrats' control of the presidency and both chambers of Congress made them a greater target for blame in the recession.

But it wasn't just that the Democrats happened to be in office at the wrong time. In early 2009, President Obama had shepherded through Congress a massive economic stimulus package, which his chief economic advisor, Christina Romer, predicted would help reduce unemployment to 8 percent by 2010, thereby setting up an expectation that was not met. Areas particularly hard-hit by the recession and

---

[3] The 2002 election is widely thought to be unusual in this regard, coming just a year after 9/11.

related collapse of housing and other industries included Arizona, Nevada, Ohio, Indiana, and Florida. In these states Democrats had an especially hard time.

The 2010 Electorate

While at the macro-level the Republicans' 2010 electoral gains can be explained in part by the Democrats' unusual success in Republican areas in 2006 and 2008 and the usual pattern of midterm loss of the president's party, we can also look for explanations at the level of the voters themselves. First, elections are won and lost in part because of who actually shows up on Election Day and, as importantly, who abstains. In the beginning of Chapter 10, we learned that not everyone eligible to vote actually votes. The group that chooses to vote in any particular election is not static—in each election a somewhat different conglomeration of citizens decides to vote, and the differences between the composition of the electorate in each election may influence who wins and who loses.

Turnout in midterm elections is always lower than in presidential election years. Presidential elections capture the public's attention in a way that congressional and gubernatorial elections do not. Voters tend to be more animated by the presidential race than by the congressional and gubernatorial races that top the ballot in off-years. In 2010, approximately 40 percent of adults cast a ballot. This turnout rate is on par with the last midterm election, in 2006, when 40 percent of adults also voted. These midterm turnout rates contrast sharply with the rate in the 2008 presidential election, in which 61 percent of adults voted.

In comparing the electorates across election cycles, let us focus on two important demographic variables: race and age. Racial groups in American politics have different partisan tendencies: African Americans are overwhelmingly Democratic; Latinos are moderately Democratic; whites lean Republican; and Asian voters are split fairly evenly. Because of these differences, even small compositional shifts from one election to the next can affect who wins and loses. Between 2006 and 2008, the fraction of minority voters in the electorate grew by 5 percentage points. And, by 2008, whites made up 74 percent of all voters, according to exit polls. However, in 2010, that trend reversed, with whites composing 78 percent of voters (see Table 2).

We see a similar story with respect to the ages of voters. Currently in American politics, younger people are more likely than older people to vote for Democrats. According to the 2008 national exit polls, over 60 percent of voters under age 30 voted Democratic, whereas only 48 percent of voters over 50 voted for Obama. The composition of the electorate in the 2008 general election contained a higher percentage of young voters more amenable to Democratic candidates than in the 2006 or 2010 elections. In 2006, 12 percent of the voters were under 30 years old. In 2008, the proportion of voters under 30 increased to 18 percent. And in 2010, the participation of young people dropped back down, and just 11 percent of all voters were under 30.

Thus, compared to the 2006 midterm elections and the presidential contest of 2008, the 2010 midterm elections brought fewer young people and fewer minorities to the polls. Because both of these groups tend to vote Democratic, this compositional change in the electorate might have made the difference between winners

TABLE 2 2006 AND 2010 EXIT POLLS, BY DEMOGRAPHICS

	2006			2010		
	% of Group Voting		Group Size	% of Group Voting		Group Size
	D	R	% of Voters	D	R	% of Voters
Gender						
Male	50	47	49	42	56	47
Female	55	43	51	48	49	53
Race						
White	47	51	79	37	60	78
Black	89	10	10	90	9	10
Hispanic	69	30	8	64	34	8
Age						
Under 30	60	38	12	57	40	11
30–59	53	46	58	46	52	59
60+	50	48	29	38	59	29
Religion						
Protestant	44	54	55	39	60	54
Catholic	55	44	26	44	54	25
Other	71	25	6	73	25	8
None	47	22	11	66	32	12
Income						
< $50,000	60	38	40	53	44	37
$50–100,000	51	48	38	44	54	37
>$100,000	47	52	22	40	58	26

and losers in some close races. This element of campaign politics is often referred to as mobilization. With the help of campaign appeals and news media attention, people can be mobilized to vote. As we have seen, the kinds of people that are mobilized to vote can change the composition of the electorate, and thereby change the outcomes of elections.

Another factor in the 2010 elections related to the electorate is the choices made by voters who did go to the polls. Electoral swings are explained not only by who votes, but also by how those people vote. Many voters lend unwavering support to one party, regardless of circumstances. In a typical election 85 to 90 percent of Democratic and Republican identifiers remain loyal. Though some partisans do deflect from their party on occasion, the most closely watched group are Independents. Their votes are less predictable, and candidates often fight hard to win this pivotal voting bloc, just as they campaign hard to get their own supporters to the polls. In 2006 and 2008, Democrats won convincing majorities of the Independent vote in House elections, and they lost this group in 2010 (see Table 3).

TABLE 3 2006 AND 2010 EXIT POLLS, BY POLITICAL ORIENTATION

	2006			2010		
	% of Group Voting		Group Size	% of Group Voting		Group Size
	Dem.	Rep.	% of Voters	Dem.	Rep.	% of Voters
Party ID						
Democrat	93	7	38	92	7	36
Republican	8	91	36	4	95	36
Independent	57	39	26	38	56	28
Ideology						
Liberal	87	11	20	90	8	20
Moderate	60	38	47	55	42	39
Conservative	20	78	32	14	84	41

Such losses reflect the natural correction that usually occurs in midterm elections and the poor state of the economy in 2010. They also reflect the fact that the Republican Party, or more properly a faction within the Republican Party, had energized and organized many core Republican voters.

The Role of the Tea Party

In the year leading up to the 2010 midterm elections, a movement of conservative citizens, angered by Obama and the Democrats' economic and health care policies, gained force. The Tea Party, organized by both grassroots leaders and professional political elites, held its first nationwide protest on February 27, 2009.[4] By April of the following year, nearly 500,000 people had voted online for what they believed should be the key tenets of the Tea Party platform. The platform's main tenets are demands for a balanced budget, lower taxes, and less government spending. However, the platform also demands a repeal of the healthcare reform bill passed during the 111th Congress and a rejection of cap-and-trade environmental regulation.[5]

Two weeks before the elections, the *New York Times* reported that 138 candidates for the U.S. House and Senate, all running as Republicans, were identified with the Tea Party movement. Of these, more than half were running in solidly Democratic districts where they had little chance of winning the general election.

---

[4]Judson Berger, "Modern-Day Tea Parties Give Taxpayers Chance to Scream for Better Representation," *Foxnews.com*, April 9, 2009.

[5]Bernie Becker, "A Revised Contract for America, Minus 'With' and Newt," *New York Times*, April 14, 2010.

The Tea Party movement emerged in early 2009 in ▶ *response to Obama and the Democrats' "bail out" of Wall Street. Tea Party groups helped mobilize Republican voters in the 2010 elections.*

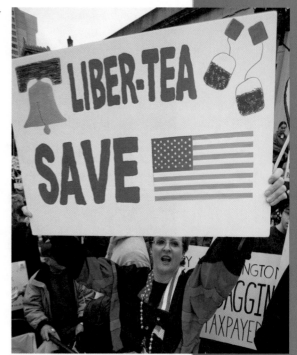

But 33 House candidates and 8 Senate candidates identified with the Tea Party movement were competitive or even dominating in their races.[6] What kinds of Americans participated in the Tea Party movement? What effect did they have on the 2010 elections?

According to a September 2010 poll by NBC News and the *Wall Street Journal*, 30 percent of Americans have a favorable view of the Tea Party, 20 percent have a neutral view, 36 percent have a negative view, and the remainder have no view or are not sure. Among self-identified Republicans, 71 percent were either Tea Party supporters, had a favorable view of the movement, and/or hoped Tea Party candidates would win.[7]

With broad support among Republican voters, outsider, Tea Party-affiliated Republican candidates were able to defeat more moderate incumbents who had the support of the Republican elites. Sitting Republican senators Lisa Murkowski of Alaska and Robert Bennett of Utah lost primary fights against Tea Party candidates. While Bennett retired from politics, Murkowski mounted a general election write-in candidacy against the candidate who had beaten her in the primary, and won the general election as an Independent. In Delaware, early polls showed that the endorsed Republican candidate, Representative Mike Castle, could easily win the general election for the seat vacated by Vice President Joe Biden. However, Castle lost the Republican primary to Tea Party candidate Christine O'Donnell, whose policy priorities were far to the right of Delaware's general election voters. O'Donnell lost decisively to her Democratic opponent, Chris Coons, who had seemed to stand no chance had Representative Castle been the Republican nominee instead.

The Tea Party is a geographically disperse movement led not by a single group but by several organizations that donate money to candidates, offer endorsements, and organize rallies. However, several key Republican figureheads are at the center of the movement and act as de facto leaders. Most prominently, Sarah Palin, former vice-presidential candidate and former governor of Alaska, stumped for Tea Party Republican candidates around the country on a "Tea Party Express" bus tour.

---

[6]Kate Zernike, "Tea Party Set to Win Enough Races for Wide Influence," *New York Times*, October 14, 2010.

[7]Peter Wallsten and Danny Yadron, "Tea-Party Movement Gains Strength," *Wall Street Journal*, September 29, 2010.

▲ *Christine O'Donnell was one of several Tea Party-backed candidates who won primary elections by appealing to dissatisfied Republican voters, but whose positions on many issues made it difficult to win the general election.*

The other prominent figure in the movement was Fox News host Glenn Beck, who promoted Tea Party activities on his show and attended Tea Party events. Beck also held his own rally in Washington D.C. in August 2010 that drew tens of thousands of activists.

The Tea Party movement played prominently in the news stories of the 2010 elections, but in the days following the elections, it was still unclear whether the movement will have a long-term impact. Will the newly elected Tea Party-backed candidates, such as Senator Marco Rubio of Florida and Senator Mike Lee of Utah, have different policy priorities and vote differently in Congress than Republicans unaffiliated with the Tea Party? Will the Tea Party movement play a prominent role in the next election cycle, or will it fade?

Money in the 2010 General Election

Campaign spending was higher in 2010 than in any other congressional election. In January 2010, in a 5–4 decision, the U.S. Supreme Court ruled on a case called *Citizens United v. Federal Election Commission*. The ruling held that part of the 2002 campaign finance law passed by Congress was unconstitutional. In particular, under the 2002 law, known informally as the McCain-Feingold Act (see Chapter 10), corporations were forbidden to electioneer in the two months before an election. A private entity could not, for example, run a television commercial encouraging viewers to vote for or against a candidate. In 2010, in *Citizens United,* the Court found that this restriction violated the free speech clause of the First Amendment of the Constitution.

The Court ruling drew the attention of critics, including President Obama, who took the unusual step of publicly opposing the case during the 2010 State of the Union address, in the presence of the justices. The case was also mentioned in political campaign ads that criticized the role of anonymous corporate donors in the elections process.

In addition to the money candidates raise in their campaign accounts or from personal wealth, most money spent on campaigns comes from political parties and interest groups. The Democratic and Republican campaign committees for House and Senate candidates collectively spent over $86 million during the 2010 cycle. Other big spenders include business groups, like the U.S. Chamber of Commerce; unions, such as the Service Employees International Union (SEIU); and independent groups, such as American Crossroads, a conservative group advised by leaders from George W. Bush's administration, Karl Rove and Ed Gillespie. With few exceptions, most of the groups taking part in political campaigns support candidates from only one party. All in all, in 2010 political spending was fairly even between Democratic candidates and parties and Republican candidates and parties. However, interest group spending in 2010 strongly favored Republican candidates.

TRENDS IN VOTING METHODS

A trend toward early voting and voting by mail continued in 2010. Until recently, almost all voters in the United States cast a paper ballot in person on Election Day. If a voter wanted to mail in a ballot ahead of the election, he or she needed to provide a valid excuse, such as a religious conflict, illness, or absence from his or her hometown. In the last several elections, alternative voting methods have gained in popularity. Thirty states plus Washington D.C. now permit "no-excuse" absentee voting. In these states, a voter can request a ballot by mail without providing a reason. In three of these states—California, Colorado, and Montana—voters can sign up to be on a permanent absentee ballot list and will then be automatically mailed a ballot for each election. In addition, thirty-two states have in-person early voting. In these states, a voter can visit the election office ahead of Election Day and cast a ballot. In some of these states, early voting takes place not only at government offices but also in churches, community centers, and other satellite locations.

According to state voting records, 10 percent of all voters in the 2008 election voted early in person, and 16 percent voted by mail. The Early Voting Information Center at Reed College estimates that in eleven states, the majority of ballots are cast before Election Day. Early estimates of nontraditional voting in the 2010 elections show that these newer forms of voting are increasing in popularity. Professor

Michael McDonald of George Mason University projects that 29 percent of all ballots cast in 2010 were absentee or early.[8]

Early and absentee voting for the 2010 elections began up to seven weeks before Election Day in some places. For campaigns, these new forms of voting reduce the amount of mobilization work that has to be done on Election Day itself. Campaign volunteers and professionals can go door-to-door, make phone calls, visit community events, and try to convince their supporters to vote before Election Day. Once people cast early votes, campaigns can ask the state and county election authorities for a list that shows which citizens have voted early, and with this list, the campaigns can focus their Election Day Get-Out-The-Vote (GOTV) efforts on those who have not yet cast a ballot. With over 50 percent of voters casting early ballots in some states, campaigns can dramatically increase their overall efficiency in the time leading up to and including Election Day.

Early and absentee voting is more popular in certain regions of the country and among certain demographic groups than others. For instance, in the Northeast fewer than 7 percent of voters cast ballots ahead of Election Day, according to a late October 2010 Gallup poll.[9] In contrast, more than half of voters in the West and nearly a third of voters in the South cast ballots ahead of time. Older voters—those over 65—are the most likely to use these new voting methods. For older citizens who are less mobile, voting by mail makes it easier to cast a ballot than does venturing to the polls in November. In contrast to age and region, there is very little relationship between use of early voting and political affiliation. According to the Gallup poll, Democrats and Republicans tend to use early voting methods at similar rates.

As nontraditional voting opportunities become more available and more popular, there will be a number of questions for scholars, policymakers, and activists. Under what circumstances does early voting increase turnout? Is early voting cost-effective? Does early voting make elections more or less susceptible to fraud? Does early voting reduce the amount of privacy in the voting process? These questions will be of growing importance as more Americans opt for nontraditional voting methods.

ISSUES AND MANDATES

Going into the 2010 elections, the biggest issue for most voters was the economy. With high unemployment and a shaky economy in the two years leading up to the elections, it is not surprising that 57 percent of registered voters told a Gallup poll in spring 2010 that the economy was extremely important to their vote. Republicans, Democrats, and Independents were all likely to focus more on the economy than on any other issue. Health care was the second-most dominant issue, with just under 50 percent of registered voters identifying it as extremely important to their vote.[10]

---

[8]See http://elections.gmu.edu/2010_vote_forecasts.html (accessed 11/4/2010).

[9]Frank Newport. "Early Voting Highest among Older Voters. Those in the West,"*Gallup.com.* October 27, 2010.

[10]Jeffrey M. Jones, "Voters Rate Economy as Top Issue for 2010," *Gallup*, April 8, 2010.

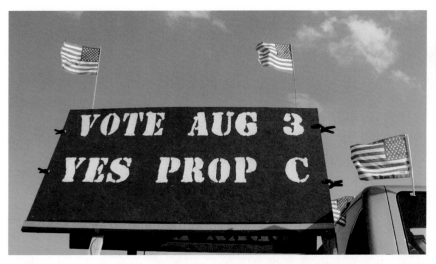

▲ *In August 2010, Missouri voters approved a referendum, Proposition C, that banned the federal government from mandating health insurance. Although the referendum had little legal impact, it was indicative of strong opposition among conservative voters to Obama's health care plan.*

During the 2010 campaign, candidates discussed both the economy and health care. On the economic front, a key issue was whether candidates supported a tax increase on wealthy Americans. At the start of his first term, George W. Bush signed into law a tax break for virtually all Americans. That tax decrease, however, would only last through 2010. When he took office, President Obama proposed that the Bush-era tax rate stay the same for most Americans but revert to its former, higher rate for the wealthiest Americans. When asked how they would vote on this issue in the 112th Congress, the candidates split along partisan lines, with most Democrats seeking increased taxation for the wealthy and most Republicans seeking an extension of the Bush-era tax rate for all.

As for health care, one of the central tenets of the Tea Party movement calls for a repeal of the health care reform bill passed in the 111th Congress, so it is likely that Republican members of the 112th Congress will advocate for scaling back or even repealing the law. However, given the Democratic control of the Senate and the presidency, a major change in the health care law is unlikely.

CONSEQUENCES FOR AMERICAN GOVERNMENT

If the electorate's choice to replace many Democrats with Republicans was fairly predictable, the elections' results seemed unlikely to produce a clear response from the government. The 2010 elections ushered in a period of divided government with the Democrats controlling the Senate and the White House and the Republicans dominating the House of Representatives. Periods of divided government have occurred frequently in American politics, and history (as well as the nature of the institutions) suggests that with control of only one house of Congress, the

▲ *As a new Republican majority took control of the House of Representatives, led by incoming Speaker John Boehner of Ohio, it was unclear how much of their agenda they would be able to implement under divided government.*

GOP will have little chance to implement an agenda of its own. The Republican Party will have to settle for either obstructing the Democrats or reaching out to the president's party in areas amenable to compromise. Given the highly confrontational tone of the 2010 campaign, the former seems to be the more likely approach. Indeed, some Republicans have stated that their major goal will be to block the Obama agenda and have suggested a need to launch legislative investigations into the administration's activities of 2009–2010.

As for the Democrats, with the GOP controlling the House of Representatives, the chance that any substantial portion of the Democratic agenda will be enacted after 2010 seems remote. President Obama has indicated that, like his predecessors, he will make increased use of such presidential tools as executive orders and regulatory review to implement programs whose congressional passage can no longer be secured.

While there remains the chance for the Republican House and the Democratic president and Senate to find common ground on key pieces of legislation like energy reform, the most likely scenario is that both sides will prevent the other from enacting any major changes to existing law as they gear up for another showdown in November 2012.

PART FOUR

Governance

14

Economic Policy

Few Americans realize how much their economic freedom owes to government action. Americans often point with pride to their "free market" economy and view governmental institutions and policies as intrusions on the freedom of the marketplace. Yet the very existence of what we regard as a free market depends heavily on public policies and institutions. Ironically, without ongoing collective action coordinated by the government, individual market freedom would be difficult to exercise and might be limited to small-scale barter and trade. America's huge free-market economy could not exist without the government. Even our increasingly global economy depends on international economic institutions and cooperation among national governments. In the economic realm, as in the realm of national security, maintaining individual freedom ultimately rests on our capacity for collective action.

Consider, for example, the case of home ownership. To many Americans, home ownership and personal freedom are inextricably linked. "A person's home is their castle" is a traditional adage that reflects long-held American beliefs. Yet the truth is that "ownership" implies a legal status enforced by the government. There can be no property ownership without collective action. In difficult times, moreover, as in the 2008–2009 financial crisis, millions of Americans demanded that the government help them restructure their mortgages to enable them to keep their homes. The Obama administration responded with billions of dollars in assistance. Once again, individual freedom was closely linked to collective action.

This dependence is brought home during times of economic crisis, but the government's role in maintaining the free market is not simply a matter of occasional crisis intervention. In point of fact, government action actually makes a market economy possible by setting the rules that allow markets to function, as well as maintaining the institutions needed to sustain a market economy. As we will see in this chapter, several prerequisites for a market economy are especially important and illustrate the ways in which collective action is needed to make individual economic freedom possible.

The job of this and the succeeding two chapters of this book is to look at the purposive actions of government—the policies. **Public policy** can be defined simply as an officially expressed intention backed by a sanction, which can be a reward or a punishment. Thus a public policy is a law, a rule, a statute, an edict, a regulation, or an order. Its purpose is to provide incentives, whether carrotlike rewards or sticklike punishments, to induce people to change what they are currently doing and do something else or to do more or less of what they are currently doing. In the first section of this chapter, we discuss the rationale for government's involvement in the economy. In the next section, we look at the goals of national economic policies. These policies have been organized into three categories: (1) policies that protect public order and private property, (2) policies that control or influence markets, and (3) policies that are designed to defend or enhance the vitality of our capitalist economy.

As we said in Chapter 1 and emphasized elsewhere, governments do what they do in part because

- Public policies create incentives for people to alter their behavior.

- In economic policy, government can play an important role in establishing the rules and institutions that allow a market economy to function

- Government has numerous tools with which to affect the economy, but there is considerable political conflict over which tools to use, how to use them, and when to use them.

- Historical events such as the Great Depression can spur government officials to make significant changes in economic policies.

public policy
A law, rule, statute, or edict that expresses the government's goals and provides for rewards and punishments to promote their attainment.

of the concerns, ambitions, and goals of politicians and other government officials and the institutional contexts in which these concerns, ambitions, and goals get played out. Since the policy-making process affords many opportunities to change the goals of government, politicians and officials constantly take advantage of their capacities as agenda setters. But policy change requires success at every step of the rather lengthy and intricate policy-making process. The institutional arrangements of a government create hurdles that a proposed change in policy must clear. This often means that change is nearly impossible. Because change is difficult, policies—once put in place—possess a degree of durability. This durability, in turn, provides a semblance of order and predictability in an otherwise uncertain world.

HOW DOES GOVERNMENT MAKE A MARKET ECONOMY POSSIBLE?

Prerequisites for a Market Economy

Establishing Law and Order.   The first feature of a market economy is inherent in the very idea of government. That is, there must be a minimal degree of predictability about the basic rules of social interaction. In other words, there must be a system of law and order. Participants in the market must be able to assume not only that they can get to the market safely—that they won't be robbed on the way—but also that, having arrived, the people with whom they are dealing will behave predictably and will be bound by some number of calculable laws.

Defining Rules of Property.   The second feature that encourages people to participate in the market has to do with defining and dealing with property. If the market involves exchanges of ownership, there must be clear laws about what constitutes property. Property may be many things—your labor or your ideas or the bed you sleep in—but the very concept of property is inconceivable without laws that define what you can call your own.

The existence of property ownership means that we can exercise dominion over something that we have declared our own, and it is defined by laws that enable us to exercise that dominion. Something is not our own unless we can be reasonably certain that someone else cannot walk away with it. Trespass laws, for example, give concrete meaning to what constitutes property: A trespass law confers on us a legal right to keep others away from certain kinds of property. It is clear, then, that laws or rules that define property are an essential part of the political economy. Before we can enter a market and participate in an exchange, we must be able to expect not only that we can lay claim to something but also that those around us will respect that claim. In this sense, private property has a public component. The probability of enjoying property would be remote without laws that were widely enforced and accepted.

Enforcing Contracts.   A third prerequisite that must be met before a market economy can operate involves rules governing the enforcement of contracts. There are, of course, societies that do not have a recognizable concept of contract, but our Western economy is highly dependent on such notions.

Contracts are closely related to property in that they are necessary only in connection with exchanges of property, broadly construed. A contract is a voluntary agreement between two or more private persons that governs future conduct. And although the agreement may be private, it has a distinctively public component: A contract must be enforceable, or it is meaningless.

Governing Rules of Exchange.   The fourth prerequisite for the emergence or creation of a market economy is closely tied to the contract requirement. A market exists only when exchanges occur, and there must be rules governing exchange itself. Laws of exchange structure how, when, and under what conditions you can sell your property. You might think that once the laws of property have defined what you own, you ought to be able to transfer it, but that transfer is surrounded by rules that govern the transfer itself.

Certain kinds of exchanges are deemed off limits altogether. For example, you own your own body, but under what conditions can you sell it? Laws about prostitution limit the selling or renting of one's body.

Setting Market Standards.   The fifth prerequisite for the emergence of the modern free market is related to the fourth. When people engage in exchanges that are not face to face—where they can't point to a good and say, "I want that tomato or that fish"—both parties must have some way of understanding what the goods are that they are bargaining over. To do that, terminology must be standardized, and one of the essential acts of any government is to establish standard weights and measures.

With modern products, the standards must go beyond weights and measures; buyers and sellers must be able to specify both the quantity and the quality of goods before they enter into their contracts. These buyers and sellers must know, for example, what is meant by long- and short-staple cotton and everything in between; they must know what they are getting when they order automobile tires of a particular quality. Many of these standards today are developed by private-sector trade associations, of course, but those standards are often incorporated into government regulations, and so they acquire governmental status—or, more important, they are protected by governmental action through the courts. If a member of the porcelain enamel association, for example, agrees to produce a certain type of enamel according to the trade association's specifications, the member can be sued if he or she cuts corners and evades those standards.

Providing Public Goods. The sixth prerequisite to the operation of a market economy involves the provision of **public goods**. As we saw in Chapter 1, *public good* refers to facilities that the government may provide because no single participant can afford or is willing to provide them himself or herself. The provision of public goods extends from supplying the physical marketplace itself—like the common in New England towns—to building and maintaining an interstate highway system to stimulate the trucking industry. The provision of public goods is essential to market operation, and the manner in which the government provides those goods affects the market's character.

> **public goods**
> Goods that, first, may be enjoyed by anyone if it is provided and, second, may not be denied to anyone once it has been provided.

In the United States, public goods related to transportation have been particularly important in promoting economic development. From the first canal systems that spread commerce into the interior of the country to the contemporary public role in supporting and regulating air transportation, government has created the conditions for reliable and efficient business activity. In some cases, government will supply a public good to stimulate the economy and then allow private companies to take over. The federal government brought electricity to rural areas in the 1930s to promote economic development, but over time the provision of electricity has been taken over by private companies. Government often supplies public goods that are too big or too risky for private actors to tackle. Major dams and hydroelectric projects are an example. By bringing water and energy to new areas, such public projects transformed the American West. More recently, government-supplied public goods have enhanced public security through such measures as the federal takeover of airport security, the creation of a pharmaceutical stockpile to protect against bioterrorism and epidemics, and the support for research to develop new vaccines.

Creating a Labor Force. The seventh prerequisite to the emergence of a market economy is the creation of a labor force. Every society has provisions that force people to work. One of the best, albeit most recent, examples of such provisions is the requirement for universal compulsory education: In this society, people are educated so that they can learn the skills necessary to function in the market. Long before education laws, however, we had poorhouses, vagrancy laws, and other more police-oriented means of forcing people to work; these rules meant that people might starve or suffer punishment if they failed to earn their own keep. Our welfare system today serves the same purpose: We adjust the welfare system in cycles to be sure that the support we give is uncomfortable enough that people will prefer working to retiring on the low income they get from welfare.

Ameliorating Externalities. Another prerequisite is not always obvious, but it is nonetheless critical to creating the conditions for a market economy. That is, to allow the market economy to operate, there must be provisions for allocating responsibility when the social cost of some behavior far exceeds the private cost. For instance, the cost of driving a gas-guzzling car may be more than the total of the monthly payments, insurance, and gasoline, because the social cost also includes the widely distributed impact of smog and the effects of carbon monoxide emissions. Negative external effects, such as pollution, that can result from market activities are called **externalities**. When individuals or firms engage in private behavior that has broad social consequences, these externalities provide government with an additional rationale for regulating the economy.

externalities The differences between the private cost and the social cost of economic behavior.

Promoting Competition.   Finally, once markets emerge, they must be maintained. This means that it should be reasonably easy for a producer to enter and freely compete in the market. If this is not the case, as when one company has established a **monopoly**, the efficiency of the market and the equitable distribution of its benefits are threatened. Decreased competition provides government with another reason for getting involved in the economy: to function as a watchdog over potential monopoly control.

monopoly The existence in a market of a single firm that provides all the goods and services of that market; the absence of competition.

Market Failures and Collective Responses

Satisfying the prerequisites for a free market does not guarantee that the market will always operate smoothly and effectively. Markets sometimes fail to deliver all they promise—the efficient allocation of society's economic resources—because of imperfections of various sorts. For example, a seller may possess information about his or her product of which a prospective buyer is unaware. This is a problem of incomplete information. This lack of information may lead more or fewer transactions than might have taken place under conditions of full and complete information. In this instance of **market failure**, the market has misallocated resources because incomplete information has misled market participants.

market failure An instance when the market fails to produce an efficient outcome.

Another and often devastating form of market failure occurs when speculative buying drives the price of major commodities such as real estate, securities, or natural resources to levels far exceeding their intrinsic value. This situation can be referred to as a *bubble*. As the bubble grows, more and more capital is misallocated and eventually wiped out in the crash that almost inevitably follows the "bursting" of the bubble. Occasional bubbles seem to be inherent features of market economies—unfortunate by-products of unfettered individual choices.[1] The collapse of a major bubble almost always leads to demands for government intervention to alleviate the economic distress left in the bubble's wake.

The most recent example of this phenomenon is the ongoing global financial crisis resulting in large part from the collapse of America's housing bubble. For several years, banks and financial institutions borrowed heavily to invest in mortgage-based securities whose value seemed to rise steadily as the value of real estate rose. In 2006–2007, the housing bubble burst and housing prices dropped sharply, setting off a chain reaction that led to a collapse in stock prices and nearly $10 trillion in losses for investors. Major banks and financial institutions failed or were

---

[1] Vernon L. Smith, Gerry Suchanek, and Arlington W. Williams, "Bubbles, Crashes, and Endogenous Expectations in Experimental Spot Asset Markets," *Econometrica* 56, no. 5 (September 1988): 1119–51.

threatened with failure; unemployment rose; major industrial corporations, such as America's automakers, unable to sell enough of their products or borrow money, faced bankruptcy. The Chrysler Corporation declared bankruptcy in May 2009 and General Motors followed.

Beginning in 2008, this crisis led to government action on a number of fronts. The Federal Reserve Board (which will be discussed in more detail later in this chapter) slashed interest rates and moved in other ways to make credit more readily available and to encourage banks to lend money to customers. Congress enacted emergency legislation that included a $700 billion plan called the Troubled Assets Relief Program (TARP) authorizing the Treasury Department to purchase some of the now worthless assets that were threatening the solvency of a number of banks and to otherwise inject capital into troubled banking corporations. The Federal Reserve and the Treasury also worked to bail out several major financial institutions; forced several weak banks to merge with stronger institutions; and took over management of Fannie Mae and Freddie Mac, the two giant lenders that serve as the linchpins of the nation's housing market. At the end of November 2008, the Treasury and the Federal Reserve announced that they were planning $800 billion in new lending programs to lower consumer interest and home mortgage rates. The Bush administration committed the nation to nearly $8 trillion dollars in spending, loans, and guarantees to bolster the economy in the last months of Bush's presidency. The new Obama administration promised further efforts to revive America's faltering economy, including a massive stimulus package designed to step up business and consumer spending. During his first few months in office, President Obama secured the enactment of a $787 billion economic stimulus package designed to pump money into the economy and to encourage banks to increase the supply of credit available to businesses and other borrowers. Several of the nation's largest banks and two of the nation's auto companies—General Motors and Chrysler—received multibillion dollar federal loans in an attempt to keep them in business. The Obama administration also assumed a major role in directing the operations of the banks and automakers that received federal dollars. In spring 2009, the administration took over General Motors and presided over Chrysler's bankruptcy as a prelude to turning over the company's operations to Italy's Fiat Corporation. The ultimate goal of these programs was the restoration of the health and vitality of the free market. Again, however, collective action was necessary to bolster individual freedom.

In the following section, we will examine the fundamental goals that the government seeks to achieve through its role in the economy.

THE GOALS OF ECONOMIC POLICY

Government has become involved in many aspects of the economy in order to promote the public well-being. Of course, there is often vigorous disagreement about the extent to which government should intervene in the economy to promote the public welfare. In addition, beliefs about which forms of government intervention in the economy are most necessary and most effective have changed over time. Although the policies have changed, government intervention in the economy has sought to achieve four fundamental goals. The first goal is to promote economic stability, the second is to stimulate economic growth, the third is to promote business development, and the fourth is to protect employees and consumers.

Promoting Stable Markets

One of the central reasons for government involvement in the economy is to protect the welfare and property of individuals and businesses. Because the threats to welfare and property change as the economy grows and new technologies emerge, government actions are constantly being updated and adapted to meet new conditions.

Maintenance of law and order is one of the most important ways that government can protect welfare and property. The federal government has also enacted laws designed to protect individuals and businesses in economic transactions. Federal antiracketeering laws, for example, aim to end criminal efforts to control businesses through such illegal means as extortion and kickbacks.

Another way in which the government promotes economic stability is by regulating competition. Beginning in the nineteenth century, as many sectors of the national economy flourished, certain companies began to exert monopolistic control over those sectors. Decreased competition threatened the efficiency of the market and the equitable distribution of its benefits. As a result, the national government stepped in to "level the playing field."

Another major reason that Congress began to adopt national business regulatory policies was that the regulated companies themselves felt burdened by the inconsistencies among the states. These companies often preferred a single, national regulatory authority, no matter how burdensome, because it would ensure consistency throughout the United States; the companies could thereby treat the nation as a single market.[2]

Political shifts and advances in technology make the regulation of competition a moving target. In 1913, when telephone service was becoming widely available, the federal government sanctioned AT&T's status as a publicly regulated monopoly. It believed that a single company—publicly regulated—could provide the best service in this industry. By the 1980s, views about the necessity and effectiveness of such monopoly control had changed, and the federal government moved to break up AT&T and open the field to new competitors. Creating competition in the telephone industry, the government hoped, would reduce prices and make the industry more responsive to consumers. And indeed, although consumers have many complaints about telephone companies, prices dropped dramatically as competitors arose. In the late 1990s, there was considerable concern about emerging monopolies in high technology. A federal lawsuit charged that Microsoft Corporation's monopoly position would stifle future innovation in software. The subsequent settlement, however, did little to alter Microsoft's market dominance.

---

[2] Compare with Gabriel Kolko, *The Triumph of Conservatism* (New York: Free Press, 1963), chap. 6.

As we've seen, the government also promotes economic stability by providing public goods. One seemingly mundane but vitally important public good provided by the federal government is weather forecasting. The National Weather Service, which is located within the U.S. Commerce Department's National Ocean and Atmospheric Administration (NOAA), seeks to provide accurate and timely forecasts of weather conditions throughout the world. NOAA makes use of orbiting satellites, radar, and computers to observe and forecast, and has developed complex computer models to predict future weather conditions. For many of us, such predictions have no importance beyond their impact on plans to go to the beach or ski slopes. NOAA's forecasts, though, have enormous economic significance. The airline, shipping, and trucking industries, for example, rely on NOAA forecasts to reduce the impact of storms on the movement of their planes, ships, and trucks. The energy industry consults NOAA models to predict future energy demands, and business firms in areas affected by hurricanes, floods, and other forms of severe weather rely upon NOAA forecasts to help them plan to minimize the damage they are likely to suffer. Predicting the weather is one way the government shelters the economy from rainy days.

Promoting Economic Prosperity

In addition to setting the basic conditions that allow markets to function, governments may actively intervene in the economy to promote economic growth. Although the idea that government should stimulate economic growth can be traced back to Alexander Hamilton's views about promoting industry, it was not until the twentieth century that the federal government assumed a central role in promoting economic growth.

Measuring Economic Growth. Since the 1930s, the federal government has carefully tracked national economic growth. Economic growth is measured in several different ways. The two most important measures are the Gross National Product (GNP), which is the market value of the goods and services produced in the economy, and the **gross domestic product (GDP)**, the same measure but excluding income from foreign investments. In the late 1990s, the American economy grew at a rate of over 4 percent a year, a rate considered high by modern standards (see Figure 14.1). Growth fell to 0.5 percent during the recession in 2001. It briefly rose but began to fall again, rising to a modest 2.2 percent in 2007.

The engine of American economic growth has shifted over the centuries. In the 1800s, our nation's rich endowment of natural resources was especially important in propelling growth. Manufacturing industries became the driving force of economic growth during the late nineteenth century as mass production made it possible to manufacture goods at a pace that was once unimaginable. In more recent times, the high-technology boom fostered unanticipated and vigorous economic growth that made the United States the envy of the world. Despite these very different economic engines, the basic prerequisites of growth are similar in each case: strong investment, technological innovation, and a productive workforce. Throughout the nation's history, the federal government has adopted policies to promote each of these conditions needed to sustain economic growth.

gross domestic product (GDP) The total value of goods and services produced within a country.

FIGURE 14.1 CHANGES IN REAL GROSS DOMESTIC PRODUCT, 1960–2008

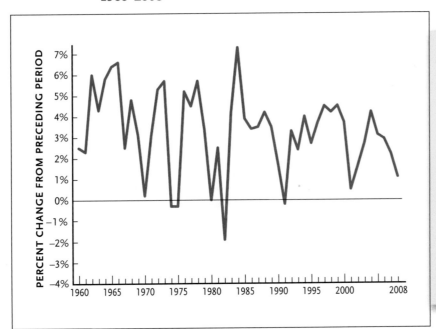

SOURCE: U.S. Department of Commerce, www.bea.gov/national/index.htm#gdp (accessed 5/19/09).

The most fundamental way that government affects investment is by promoting business, investor, and consumer confidence. When businesses fear political instability, unpredictable government action, or widespread disregard of the law, they are unlikely to invest. When consumers are insecure about the future, they are unlikely to spend. Government officials monitor surveys of business and consumer confidence as they devise economic policy. After the terrorist attacks of 2001, the federal government moved quickly to reassure the financial markets, businesses, and consumers. The Federal Reserve responded with interest-rate cuts aimed at promoting spending and investment. In 2008, the federal government enacted a $700 billion rescue plan in order to restore investor confidence after several large banks failed.

Businesses also need access to new sources of capital in order to grow. The federal government promotes reliable access to new investment through its regulation of financial markets. The most important federal agency in this regard is the Securities and Exchange Commission (SEC), created after the stock market crash of 1929. The SEC requires companies to disclose information about the stocks and bonds they are selling, inform buyers of the investment risks, and protect investors against fraud. In this way, the SEC helps to maintain investor confidence and a strong supply of capital for American business. The SEC came in for harsh criticism during the financial crisis in 2008 and 2009. Analysts pointed to weak SEC oversight and regulation as an important factor in driving the financial sector to the brink of collapse. Congressional critics called for tougher SEC regulation of Wall Street in the future.

Public investment is another important source of growth in the American economy. Such investment can be expressly designed to promote growth in accordance with the Keynesian principles outlined later in this chapter. In the 1930s and again in the late 1970s, the federal government promoted public investment as a means to spark economic growth. Some kinds of public investment promote growth as a by-product of other more central objectives. One of the most important of these is military spending. Many analysts credited the rise in military spending associated with the war in Iraq with helping to spur economic growth in 2003.

The second important condition for economic growth is innovation. The federal government has sought to support innovation in a variety of ways. One of the most important is through the National Science Foundation. Created in 1950, the National Science Foundation supports basic research across a range of scientific fields. The aim is to advance fundamental knowledge that may be useful in many different applications.[3] Federal government sponsorship of health research began in the late 1800s. Today, the National Institutes of Health (NIH) conduct basic and applied research in biomedicine. The Human Genome Project—the effort to map the basic genetic structure of human life—was initiated by government researchers and only later taken up by private corporations. Recently, the NIH has taken the lead in basic research to counter bioterrorism. Its efforts to understand the biology of various infectious agents and to develop vaccines are expected to produce important new knowledge about the human immune system. Research sponsored by the military has long been an important source of innovation for the American economy. Such key twentieth-century innovations as radar and nuclear power stemmed from military research. Military research also created the technology for the twenty-first century with ARPANET, the precursor of the Internet.

A third fundamental condition for economic growth is a sufficient and productive workforce. Federal immigration policy has played a key role in ensuring an adequate supply of labor throughout American history. Immigration laws routinely give special priority to workers who have skills that are in demand among American employers. Immigrants with nursing degrees, for example, have long received special priority.

Today, a productive workforce is a highly educated workforce. Education, as we will see in Chapter 15, is primarily the responsibility of state and local governments, though the federal government has taken an increasing role. The federal government, however, supports the development of a productive workforce with a variety of programs to support higher education, such as educational grants, tax breaks, and loans. The federal government also sponsors a limited array of job-training programs that focus primarily on low-skilled workers. Some analysts argue that the federal government must do much more to support the development of

---

[3] See David M. Hart, *Forged Consensus: Science, Technology and Economic Policy in the United States, 1921–1953* (Princeton, N.J.: Princeton University Press, 1998).

a highly skilled workforce if the United States is to sustain economic growth in the future.

Full Employment.   Before the 1930s, neither the federal nor the state governments sought to promote full employment. Unemployment was widely viewed as an unfortunate occurrence that government could do little to alter. The New Deal response to the prolonged and massive unemployment of the Great Depression changed that view. The federal government put millions of people back to work on public projects sponsored by such programs as the Works Progress Administration (WPA). The bridges, walkways, and buildings they constructed can still be seen across the United States today. The federal government viewed these programs as temporary measures, however. As the buildup for World War II boosted the economy and unemployment melted away, the employment programs were dismantled.

The New Deal and government wartime spending, however, showed that government could help ensure full employment. Public expectations changed as well: Americans looked to the federal government to reduce unemployment after the war. Moreover, economic theory now supported their expectations. The British economist John Maynard Keynes's theories that government could boost employment by stimulating demand had become very influential.

Federal policy placed the most emphasis on achieving full employment during the 1960s. Keynesian economists in the Council of Economic Advisers convinced President Kennedy to enact the first tax cut designed to stimulate the economy and promote full employment.[4] The policy was widely seen as a success, and unemployment declined to a low of 3.4 percent in 1968.

Favorable economic conditions in the 1990s reduced unemployment to record lows once again. Many analysts contended that the economy had changed so much that the old trade-offs between inflation and unemployment had ceased to exist. When the economy fell into recession in 2001, it was apparent that the boom of the 1990s—and many of the economic speculations it generated—were only temporary. The new economic worry was the "jobless recovery." Throughout 2003, as economic growth surged, job creation lagged far behind. Economists and politicians alike remained puzzled by the sluggish job market, speculating about the impact of foreign trade and growing productivity on limiting new hires. Not until the middle of 2005 did the number of private-sector jobs surpass the level in March 2001, the peak of the last economic expansion. As the economy fell into recession in 2008, unemployment began once again to climb.

Low Inflation.   During the 1970s and early 1980s, **inflation**, a consistent increase in the general level of prices, was one of America's most vexing problems. There was much disagreement over what to do about it—what public policies were most appropriate and effective. The first effort, beginning in 1971, was the adoption of

inflation A consistent increase in the general level of prices.

---

[4] See Margaret Weir, *Politics and Jobs: The Boundaries of Employment Policy in the United States* (Princeton, N.J.: Princeton University Press, 1992).

strict controls over wages, prices, dividends, and rents—that is, authorizing an agency in the executive branch to place limits on what wage people could be paid for their work, what rent their real estate could bring, and what interest they could get on their money. After two years of effort, these particular policies were fairly well discredited, and the search resumed for one or more other policies to fight inflation. Since oil prices had become so clearly a major source of inflation in the late 1970s, President Carter experimented with the licensing of imports of oil from the Middle East, with tariffs and excise taxes on unusually large oil profits made by producers, and with sales taxes on gasoline at the pump to discourage all casual consumption of gasoline. President Carter also attempted to reduce consumer spending in general by raising income taxes, especially Social Security taxes on employees.

The continuing high rate of inflation paved the way to an entirely different approach by President Reagan in the early 1980s. In place of oil import licensing and selective tax increases, President Reagan proposed and got a general tax cut. The Reagan theory was that if tax cuts were deep enough and were guaranteed to endure, they would increase the "supply" of money, would change people's psychology from pessimism to optimism, and would thereby encourage individuals and corporations to invest enough and produce enough to get the country out of inflation. At the same time, President Reagan supported the continuation of the high Social Security taxes enacted during the Carter administration, which probably went further than any other method to fight inflation by discouraging consumption. Inflation is caused by too many dollars chasing too few goods, bidding up prices. Any tax will take dollars out of consumption, but since the Social Security tax hits middle- and lower-middle-income people the hardest, and since these middle-income people are the heaviest consumers, such a tax reduces consumer dollars. Another policy supported by the Reagan administration was restraining the amount of credit in the economy by pushing up interest rates.

Inflation was finally reduced from its historic highs of nearly 20 percent down toward 2 and 3 percent each year. Noting that the 1970s were America's only "peacetime inflation," the economist Bradford DeLong contends that it wasn't until inflation had risen to dizzying heights late in the decade that the Federal Reserve truly had a mandate to reduce inflation.[5] Once it had full political support for reducing inflation in 1979, the Federal Reserve raised interest rates sharply and brought inflation rates down at the same time that it provoked a sharp recession.

Promoting Business Development

During the nineteenth century, the national government was a promoter of markets. National roads and canals were built to tie states and regions together. National tariff policies promoted domestic markets by restricting imported goods; a tax on an import raised its price and weakened its ability to compete with similar

---

[5] Bradford DeLong, "America's Only Peacetime Inflation: The 1970s," University of California at Berkeley and National Bureau of Economic Research, December 19, 1995, www.j-bradford-delong.net/pdf_files/Peacetime_Inflation.pdf (accessed 4/17/09).

domestic products. The national government also heavily subsidized the railroad system. Until the 1840s, railroads were thought to be of limited commercial value. But between 1850 and 1872, Congress granted over 100 million acres of public-domain land to railroad interests, and state and local governments pitched in an estimated $280 million in cash and credit. Before the end of the century, 35,000 miles of track had been built—almost half the world's total at the time.

Railroads were not the only clients of federal support for the private markets. Many sectors of agriculture began receiving federal subsidies during the nineteenth century. Agriculture remains highly subsidized. In 2001, an environmental group caused a stir by putting the exact amounts of subsidies received by individual farmers on a widely publicized Web site. In 2005, 40 percent of farms in the United States received subsidies; by 2006 the total subsidy was estimated at more than $20 billion. One of the many criticisms of the farm subsidy program is that it disproportionately supports large-scale farmers rather than small family farmers. The list of farm subsidy recipients includes many large corporations.

The national government also promotes business development indirectly through **categorical grants-in-aid** (see Chapter 3), whereby the national government offers grants to states on condition that the state (or local) government undertake a particular activity. Thus, in order to use motor transportation to improve national markets, a 900,000-mile national highway system was built during the 1930s, based on a formula whereby the national government would pay 50 percent of the cost if the state would provide the other 50 percent. Over twenty years, beginning in the late 1950s, the federal government constructed an additional 45,000 miles of interstate highways. In this program, the national government agreed to pay 90 percent of the construction costs on the condition that each state provide 10 percent of the costs of any portion of a highway built within its boundaries.[6] The tremendous growth of highways was a major boon to the automobile and trucking industries.

The federal government supports specific business sectors with direct subsidies, loans, and tax breaks. In 1953, the Small Business Administration (SBA) was created to offer loans, loan guarantees, and disaster assistance to small businesses. Recognizing that such businesses often find it harder to obtain financing and to recover from unexpected events such as fires, the federal government has provided assistance where the market would not. Today, the SBA provides more than $45 billion in such assistance to small businesses.

Among the many contemporary examples of policies promoting private industry, Sematech may be the most instructive. Sematech is a nonprofit, research and development (R&D) consortium of major U.S. computer microchip manufacturers, set up in 1987 to work with government and academic institutions to reestablish U.S. leadership in semiconductor manufacturing. (The United States appeared to be in danger of losing out to the Japanese in this area during the 1980s.) The results of its research were distributed among the consortium members.[7] For nine

categorical grants-in-aid Funds given by Congress to a state locality that are earmarked by law for specific categories, such as education or crime prevention.

---

[6] The act of 1955 officially designated the interstate highways as the National System of Interstate and Defense Highways. It was indirectly a major part of President Dwight Eisenhower's defense program. But it was just as obviously a "pork-barrel" policy as any rivers and harbors legislation.

[7] The members included AMD, Digital, Hewlett-Packard, Intel, IBM, Lucent, Motorola, National Semiconductor, Rockwell, and Texas Instruments.

years, industry and government together spent $1.7 billion to make the American microchip industry the leader in the world. The government contributed about half of the total expenditures. In 1997, federal funding was phased out. Industry leaders, convinced they no longer needed federal support, themselves initiated the break with government. At a critical moment, the federal government had stepped in to save the chip industry; it stepped out once that goal had been achieved.

Since September 11, 2001, the federal government has taken on a major role in promoting technological innovation related to national security. Even before the September 11 terrorist attacks, the CIA had set up its own venture-capital firm, In-Q-Tel (the "Q" stands for a character in the James Bond movies), to invest in high-tech start-ups whose work could enhance intelligence efforts. With defense and homeland security at the top of the national agenda, military spending increased by 20 percent during the first two years of the George W. Bush administration. A new emphasis on technological innovation accompanied the increase in spending. As a way to promote its access to the latest technology, the Department of Defense runs a $1.1 billion program that funds the early stages of research and development for innovative small firms.

Protecting Employees and Consumers

Stable relations between business and labor are important elements of a productive economy. During the latter half of the nineteenth century, strikes over low wages or working conditions became a standard feature of American economic life. In fact, the United States has one of the most violent histories of labor relations in the world. Yet for most of American history, the federal government did little to regulate relations between business and labor. Local governments and courts often weighed in on the side of business by prohibiting strikes and arresting strikers.

As the economic depression enveloped the United States in the 1930s, plummeting wages and massive strikes for union recognition prompted the federal government to take action. Congress passed the 1935 National Labor Relations Act, which set up a new framework for industrial relations. The new law created a permanent agency, the National Labor Relations Board (NLRB), charged with overseeing union elections and collective bargaining between labor and industry. The federal government weighed in further on the side of organized labor in 1938, when it passed the Fair Labor Standards Act, which created the minimum wage. Because it is not indexed to inflation, the value of the minimum wage declines if it is not raised periodically. Since 1938, conflicts over increasing the minimum wage have been a regular feature of American politics.

During the 1950s and 1960s, the federal government played an active role in industrial relations. The Department of Labor and occasionally even the president directly intervened in labor-management disputes to ensure peaceful industrial relations. Although Democrats were generally seen as more supportive of labor, both parties sought to achieve a balance between business and labor that would promote a strong stable economy.

President Reagan made a decisive break with this tradition of compromise in 1981 when he fired striking air traffic controllers and hired permanent replacements to take their jobs. Politicians are now much less likely to intervene in labor relations.

Economic policies also protect consumers. The idea that the federal government should protect consumers emerged in the first decade of the 1900s. Upton Sinclair's graphic exposé about the unsanitary practices of the meatpacking industry, *The Jungle*, published in 1906, galvanized public concern about unsanitary food processing. These concerns prompted the U.S. Department of Agriculture to inspect packing plants and the meat they produced, stamping approved meats with the now familiar "USDA" certification. Similar concern about food and drug safety led to the creation of the Food and Drug Administration in 1927.

The movement for consumer protection took off again in the 1960s. The consumer advocate Ralph Nader's 1965 book *Unsafe at Any Speed* helped spark new demands for federal action. Nader's book showed that design flaws in the Corvair, a popular car model, had caused deaths that could have been prevented. Nader's book not only led to the demise of the Corvair but also galvanized calls for more federal action to protect consumers. The first response was the 1966 National Traffic and Motor Vehicle Safety Act, which gave the Department of Transportation responsibility for ensuring vehicle safety. Federal responsibility for consumer safety expanded in 1972 when Congress created the Consumer Product Safety Commission. The Commission, which is an independent agency, informs consumers about hazards associated with products and works with industry to set product standards. In cases where safety concerns are severe, it will see that such products are recalled. Through the Consumer Product Safety Commission, the Department of Transportation, and the Food and Drug Administration (which regulates food, drugs, and cosmetics), the federal government continues to play an active role in protecting the public from unsafe products.

In 2007, the Consumer Product Safety Commission became the target of vigorous criticism for failing to protect consumers from hazardous products. Recalls of popular children's toys, reports of injuries to children from magnetic toys, dogs and cats dying from tainted pet food, and reported dangers from imported toothpaste all raised questions about the agency's effectiveness. Congressional hearings probed the capacity of the agency to monitor consumer safety, given that its staff had declined from more than 800 in 1980 to 420 in 2007. At the same time that the staff declined, the growth of consumer products manufactured in China made the agency's job tougher. In 2006, 20 percent of America's consumer goods had been manufactured in China, and 55 percent of all recalled products came from China, where rapid economic expansion and fewer consumer protections contributed to the problem.[8] Ensuring the safety of goods manufactured in China is a formidable challenge that will require a much greater capacity than the Consumer Product Safety Commission currently has.

Four Schools of Economic Thought

Not surprisingly, there are deep differences of opinion about whether, how much, and in what ways government should be involved in the economy, and to what extent

---

[8] Eric Lipton, "Safety Agency Faces Scrutiny Amid Changes," *New York Times*, September 2, 2007, p. A1.

government should emphasize each of the goals discussed in this section. Ideas about the appropriate role for government have shifted in response to unanticipated or tenacious economic problems such as recession or inflation. As politicians, interest groups, and the public debate which goals are most important and appropriate for economic policy to achieve, their views are informed by underlying theories. Different theories about how the economy works present quite distinct roles for government.

The idea that government should have only a minimal role in the economy is often called **laissez-faire capitalism**. Proponents of laissez-faire (literally, "let to do") argue that the economy will flourish if the government leaves it alone. The argument for laissez-faire was first elaborated in the late 1700s by the great Scottish economist Adam Smith. Smith believed that most government involvement in the economy—such as the government-authorized monopolies that dominated trade in his day—depressed economic growth. Instead, he argued that competition among free enterprises would unleash economic energy, fostering growth and innovation. In his view, the self-seeking behavior of individuals, when subject to the discipline of market competition, would create products that consumers want at the best possible price. Smith praised the "invisible hand" of the market, by which he meant that millions of individual economic transactions together create a greater good—far better than the government could create. Smith believed that the government role should be restricted to national defense, establishing law and order (including the protection of private property), and providing basic public goods (such as roads) that facilitate commerce.

In the 1930s, the ideas of the British economist John Maynard Keynes laid the foundation for a revolution in thinking about the role of the government in the economy during periodic downturns. **Keynesians** argue that by pumping money into the economy, government can stimulate demand and create a cycle of increased production and jobs that will pull the economy out of recession. Governments can do this in several ways. For one, they can increase public spending through such measures as public works or public employment. Alternatively, governments can stimulate demand through temporary tax cuts. Tax cuts will allow workers to keep more of their earnings; their increased spending power will boost consumption and increase demand.[9]

After World War II, Keynesian ideas guided economic policy making across the industrialized world. By the 1960s, Keynesians believed they could ensure ongoing prosperity by "fine-tuning" the economy: policy makers could stimulate demand with spending or tax cuts when recession loomed and then cut back on spending or increase taxes when inflation threatened. Then Republican president Richard Nixon reflected the strong consensus behind Keynesian ideas when he remarked, "I am now a Keynesian."

Yet by the time Keynesian ideas became the accepted wisdom, new economic conditions threatened their effectiveness. Many observers argued that increased international trade made Keynesian remedies less useful. Confidence that the government can fine-tune the economy had diminished, and Keynesians lost the great influence they once had in economic policy.

laissez-faire capitalism An economic system in which the means of production and distribution are privately owned and operated for profit with minimal or no government interference.

Keynesian A follower of the economic theories of John Maynard Keynes, who argued that the government can stimulate the economy by increasing public spending or by cutting taxes.

---

[9] For a good summary of Keynes's ideas see Robert Lekachman, *The Age of Keynes* (New York: McGraw-Hill, 1966).

In contrast to Keynesians, **monetarists** believe that the role of the government in managing the economy should be limited to regulating the supply of money. More active government management of the economy, monetarists argue, either has little effect or actually makes the economy worse. Monetarists do not believe that government can act quickly enough to fine-tune the economy. Instead, they maintain that government should promote economic stability by regulating the money supply. The most prominent monetarist in the United States, the late economist Milton Friedman, recommended that the federal government let the growth in the money supply match the rate of economic growth. In this way, inflation could be kept low even as economic growth continued. This strict version of monetarism envisions a hands-off approach for the government; the theory calls for little exercise of discretion on the part of government officials. Instead, they must follow a simple rule about how much to increase the supply of money.

In the late 1970s, when high levels of inflation plagued the American economy, monetarists became especially influential in economic policy making. However, today it is impractical to implement a strict version of monetarism. Instead, economic policy makers have sought to manipulate interest rates to ensure a healthy and stable economy.

Proponents of **supply-side economics** believe that reducing the role of government in the economy will promote investment and spur economic growth. Reducing tax rates is the centerpiece of the supply-side economic strategy. Supply-side arguments maintain that lower tax rates create incentives for more productive and efficient use of resources. When individuals know they can keep more of their earnings, they are more likely to be productive workers and creative investors. The ideas behind supply-side economics emerged in the 1970s, when Keynesian solutions appeared to have little impact on the high rates of inflation and a sluggish economy.

Key thinkers associated with developing the ideas behind supply-side economics include the economists Robert Mundell, who won the Nobel Prize, and Arthur B. Laffer. Laffer became know for the "Laffer curve," which posited that there was an optimal rate of taxation. If taxes went above the optimal rate, tax revenues would shrink because economic activity would decline. In this perspective, lowering taxes could yield more tax revenue by spurring economic activity. This view marked a shift for conservatives by placing more emphasis on tax cuts and less on budget deficits. Supply-side ideas were very influential in the administrations of the Republican presidents Ronald Reagan and George W. Bush, both of whom pointed to supply-side ideas as a sound reason for enacting significant tax cuts.

monetarist A follower of economic theories that contend that the role of the government in the economy should be limited to regulating the supply of money.

supply-side economics Posits that reducing the marginal rate of taxation will create a productive economy by promoting levels of work and investment that would otherwise be discouraged by higher taxes.

THE TOOLS OF ECONOMIC POLICY

The U.S. economy is no accident; it is the result of specific policies that have expanded American markets and sustained massive economic growth. The Constitution provides that Congress shall have the power

To lay and collect Taxes, . . . to pay the Debts and provide for the common Defence and general Welfare; . . . To borrow Money; . . . To coin Money [and] regulate the Value thereof. . . .

These clauses of Article I, Section 8, are the constitutional sources of the fiscal and monetary policies of the national government. The Constitution says nothing, however, about *how* these powers can be used, although the way they are used shapes the economy. As it works to meet the multiple goals of economic policy outlined above, the federal government relies on a broad set of tools that has evolved over time. Let us now turn to the actual tools designed to accomplish the goals of economic policy.

Monetary Policies

Monetary policies manipulate the growth of the entire economy by controlling the availability of money to banks. With a very few exceptions, banks in the United States are privately owned and locally operated. Until well into the twentieth century, banks were regulated, if at all, by state legislatures. Each bank was granted a charter, giving it permission to make loans, hold deposits, and make investments within that state. Although more than 25,000 banks continue to be state-chartered banks, they are less important than they used to be in the overall financial picture, as the most important banks now are members of the federal banking system.

But banks did not become the core of American capitalism without intense political controversy. The Federalist majority in Congress, led by Alexander Hamilton, did in fact establish a Bank of the United States in 1791, but it was vigorously opposed by agrarian interests led by Thomas Jefferson, who feared that the interests of urban, industrial capitalism would dominate such a bank. The Bank of the United States was terminated during the administration of Andrew Jackson, but the fear of a central, public bank lingered eight decades later, when Congress in 1913 established an institution—the **Federal Reserve System**—to integrate private banks into a single national system. The Federal Reserve System did not become a central bank in the European tradition but rather is composed of twelve Federal Reserve banks, each located in a major commercial city. The Federal Reserve banks are not ordinary banks; they are banker's banks that make loans to other banks, clear checks, and supply the economy with currency and coins. They also play a regulatory role over the member banks. Every national bank must be a member of the Federal Reserve System and must follow national banking rules. State banks and savings and loan associations may also join if they accept national rules. At the top of the system is the Federal Reserve Board—"the Fed"—comprising seven members appointed by the president (with Senate confirmation) for fourteen-year terms. The chairman of the Fed is selected by the president from among the seven members of the board for a four-year term. In all other concerns, however, the Fed is an independent agency inasmuch as its members cannot be removed during their terms except "for cause," and the president's executive power does not extend to them or their policies. Nonetheless, observers charged the longtime Federal Reserve chairman, Alan Greenspan, with being attentive to politics, for example, in his endorsement of President George W. Bush's tax cuts. In his 2005 confirmation hearings to head the Fed, economist Ben Bernanke promised Congress that he would be "strictly independent of all political influences."[10]

The major advantage that a bank gains from being in the Federal Reserve System is that it can borrow from the system. This enables banks to expand their loan operations continually, as long as there is demand for loans in the economy. On the other hand, it is this very access of member banks to the Federal Reserve System that gives the Fed its power: the ability to expand and contract the *amount of credit* available in the United States.

The Fed can affect the total amount of credit through the interest (called the discount rate) it charges on the loans it extends to member banks. If the Fed significantly decreases the discount rate, it can give a boost to a sagging economy. During 2001, the Fed cut interest rates eleven times to combat the combined effects of recession and the terrorist attacks. As the economy began to sag in late 2007, all eyes were on the Fed to reduce interest rates. By March 2008, the Fed had cut rates six times from their high in September 2007. If the Fed raises the discount rate, it can put a brake on the economy because the higher discount rate also increases the general interest rates charged by leading private banks to their customers. Although the Federal Reserve is responsible for ensuring high employment as well as price stability, it has been particularly important in fighting inflation. During the late 1970s and early 1980s, with inflation at record high levels, Federal Reserve Chairman Paul Volcker aggressively raised interest rates in order to dampen inflation. Although his actions provoked a sharp recession, they raised the stature of the Fed, demonstrating its ability to manage the economy. Because the Fed is so closely associated with inflation fighting, Senate Democrats pressed Ben Bernanke, President Bush's nominee to head the Fed, to indicate that he would view maximum employment as a goal of equal importance to that of fighting inflation.

A second power of the Fed is control over the **reserve requirement**—the amount of cash and negotiable securities every bank must hold readily available to cover withdrawals and checks written by its depositors. When the Fed decides to increase the reserve requirement, it can decrease significantly the amount of money banks have to lend; conversely, if the Fed lowers the reserve requirement, banks can be more liberal in extending more loans.[11]

A third power of the Fed is called **open-market operations,** whereby the Fed buys and sells government securities to increase or decrease the supply of money in the economy. When the Fed buys government securities in the open market, it increases the amount of money available to consumers to spend or invest; when it sells securities, it is reducing the money supply.

reserve requirement The amount of liquid assets and ready cash that banks are required to hold to meet depositors' demands for their money.

open-market operations The method by which the Open Market Committee of the Federal Reserve System buys and sells government securities, etc., to help finance government operations and to reduce or increase the total amount of money circulating in the economy.

---

[10] Kevin G. Hall, "Bernanke to Stay on Greenspan Path, But Not All the Way," *Seattle Times*, November 16, 2005, p. C1.

[11] As a rule of thumb, in a growing economy where there is demand for credit, and assuming a reserve requirement of 20 percent, a deposit of $100 will create nearly $500 of new credit. This is called the "multiplier effect," because the bank can lend out $80 of the original $100 deposit to a new borrower; that becomes another $80 deposit, 20 percent of which ($64) can be lent to another borrower, and so on until the original $100 grows to approximately $500 of new credit.

Finally, a fourth power is derived from one of the important services the Federal Reserve System renders, which is the opportunity for member banks to borrow from each other. One of the original reasons for creating a Federal Reserve System was to balance regions of the country that might be vigorously expanding with other areas that might be fairly dormant: the national system would enable the banks in a growing region, facing great demand for credit, to borrow money from banks in regions of the country where the demand for credit is much lower. This exchange is called the "federal funds market," and the interest rate charged by one bank to another, the **federal funds rate**, can be manipulated just like the discount rate, to expand or contract credit.[12]

The federal government also provides insurance to foster credit and encourage private capital investment. The Federal Deposit Insurance Corporation (FDIC) insures bank deposits up to $100,000. Another important promoter of investment is the federal insurance of home mortgages through the Department of Housing and Urban Development (HUD). By guaranteeing mortgages, the government can reduce the risks that banks run in making such loans, thus allowing banks to lower their interest rates and make such loans more affordable to middle- and lower-income families. Such programs have enabled millions of families who could not have otherwise afforded it to finance the purchase of a home.

This system began to unravel in the first decade of the 2000s with the growth of the subprime market for lending. This market made home loans available to people who could not otherwise afford to buy a home. At the same time, however, it created new instabilities in the market by offering risky loans that would become more costly due to adjustable interest rates. The slowing housing market in 2007 set off a wave of foreclosures as many homeowners discovered that they could not pay back their loans.[13]

The foreclosure crisis in turn set shock waves through the financial system, as investment banks found themselves holding worthless loans. One casualty of the home loan meltdown was the Wall Street investment bank Bear Stearns, which faced bankruptcy early in March 2008. Seeking to limit the harm to the broader economy that such a bankruptcy would cause, Fed chairman Bernanke arranged for Bear Stearns to be bought—at a bargain-basement price—by JP Morgan Chase, another investment bank. In making this move, Bernanke was exercising powers of the Federal Reserve Act that had not been used since the 1930s.[14] By the fall of 2008 several other investment banks and insurance companies were close to insolvency. In September 2008, the Treasury and the Federal Reserve announced

federal funds rate The interest rate on loans between banks that the Federal Reserve Board influences by affecting the supply of money available.

---

[12] Good treatments of the Federal Reserve System and monetary policy can be found in Donald Kettl, *Leadership at the Fed* (New Haven, Conn.: Yale University Press, 1986); and Albert T. Sommers, *The U.S. Economy Demystified* (Lexington, Mass.: Lexington Books, 1988), especially chap. 5.

[13] Majority Staff of the Joint Economic Committee, Senator Charles E. Schumer, Chairman, Rep. Carolyn B. Maloney, Vice Chair, *The Subprime Lending Crisis: The Economic Impact on Wealth, Property Values and Tax Revenues, and How We Got Here,* Report and Recommendations, October 2007, p. 1, www.jec .senate.gov/index.cfm?FuseAction=Reports.Reports&ContentRecord_id=c6627bb2-7e9c-9af9-7ac7-32b94d398d27&Region_id=&Issue_id= (accessed 4/20/09).

[14] Steven R. Wesiman, "Bernanke Faces Bear Stearns Queries," *New York Times,* April 2, 2008, p. C1.

a rescue package in which the federal government made up to $700 billion dollars in emergency credit and capital available. After taking office, President Obama pushed a $787 billion financial bailout plan through Congress. Much of this money was also aimed at helping the banks.

The president's actions are an excellent illustration of the policy principle from Chapter 1. Just as President Bush had done in September 2001, President Obama used the power of his office to respond forcefully to a crisis. Like Bush, Obama knew that he would be judged by his ability to deal with the threat facing the nation—in this case an economic threat. Accordingly, President Obama mobilized the relevant institutions, including the Congress, the Treasury Department and the Federal Reserve to craft a response to the threatened collapse of the nation's economy. The resulting programs could well be described by our principle: ambition plus institutions equals policy.

Fiscal Policies

Fiscal policy includes the government's taxing and spending powers. Personal and corporate income taxes, which raise most of the U.S. government's revenues, are the most prominent examples. Although the direct purpose of an income tax is to raise revenue, each tax has a different impact on the economy, and government can attempt to plan for that impact. After passing major tax cuts in 2001, President Bush proposed and Congress passed a sweeping new round of cuts in 2003. Bush's plan was intended to promote investment by reducing taxes on most stock dividends, to spur business activity by offering tax breaks to small businesses, and to stimulate the economy by reducing the tax rates for all taxpayers. In 2006, Congress extended the rate reductions on dividends and capital gains, a move that estimates show will cost the treasury $70 billion over five years. The Bush administration tax cuts were criticized on several grounds. Many Democrats argued that the tax cuts were simply a giveaway to the wealthy and to corporations, and that they did nothing to promote growth. There has been concern that the tax cuts are partly responsible for the large federal deficits: the federal budget moved from running surpluses in 2000 to steep deficits only four years later.

The administration of fiscal policy occurs primarily in the Treasury Department. In addition to collecting income, corporate, and other taxes, the Treasury also manages the enormous national debt—$12 trillion in 2009. (The national debt was a mere $710 billion in 1980.)[15] Debt is not simply something the country owes; it is something a country has to manage and administer. The debt is also a fiscal instrument in the hands of the federal government that can be used—through manipulation of interest rates and through the buying and selling of government bonds—to slow down or to speed up the activity of the entire national economy, as well as to defend the value of the dollar in international trade.

fiscal policy The government's use of taxing, monetary, and spending powers to manipulate the economy.

---

[15] U.S. Department of the Treasury, "The Debt to the Penny and Who Holds It," www.treasurydirect.gov/NP/BPDLogin?application=np (accessed 4/20/09). About 60 percent of the debt is held by the public, corporations, foreign governments, and other creditors. About 40 percent of the debt consists of "intragovernmental holdings." These are funds borrowed by the Treasury from other government agencies, in particular the Social Security and Medicare trust funds, which serve as a major source of funding for the federal government's major expenditures.

TABLE 14.1 FEDERAL REVENUES BY TYPE OF TAX AS PERCENTAGE OF TOTAL RECEIPTS, 1960–2008

ANALYZING THE EVIDENCE

The federal government collects revenue from a variety of different taxes. Most important is the individual income tax. Since 1960, revenues from the corporation income tax have fallen significantly. At the same time, taxes for social insurance and retirement programs have grown substantially. Does the federal government draw more of its revenue from progressive taxes or from regressive taxes?

Year	Individual Income Tax	Corporation Income Tax	Social Insurance and Retirement Receipts	Excise Taxes	Other
1960	44.0	23.2	15.9	12.6	4.2
1970	46.9	17.1	23.0	8.1	4.9
1980	47.2	12.5	30.5	4.7	5.1
1990	45.2	9.1	36.8	3.4	5.4
2000	49.6	10.2	32.2	3.4	4.5
2004	43.0	10.1	39.0	3.7	4.2
2005	43.0	12.9	36.9	3.4	3.8
2006	43.4	14.7	34.8	3.1	4.1
2007	45.3	14.4	33.9	2.5	3.9
2008 (est)	48.4	13.7	36.1	2.7	−0.9

SOURCE: Office of Management and Budget, www.whitehouse.gov/omb/budget/fy2009/pdf/hist.pdf (accessed 4/13/09).

tariff A tax on imported goods.

Taxation.   During the nineteenth century, the federal government received most of its revenue from a single tax, the **tariff**. It also relied on excise taxes, which are taxes levied on specific products, such as tobacco and alcohol. As federal activities expanded in the 1900s, the federal government added new sources of tax revenue. The most important was the income tax, proposed by Congress in 1909, ratified by the states, and added to the Constitution in 1913 as the Sixteenth Amendment. The income tax is levied on individuals as well as corporations. With the creation of the Social Security system in 1935, social insurance taxes became an additional source of federal revenue.

Before World War II, individual income taxes accounted for only 14 percent of federal revenues.[16] The need to raise revenue for World War II made the income tax much more important. Congress expanded the base of the income tax so that most Americans paid income taxes after World War II. Table 14.1 shows several notable shifts that have occurred in taxes since 1960. Social insurance taxes now make up a much greater share of federal revenues, rising from 15.9 percent of revenues in 1960 to 36.1 percent in 2008. Receipts from corporate income taxes have

---

[16] Executive Office of the President of the United States, GPO Access, "Budget of the United States Government Historical Tables Fiscal Year 2009," Table 2.2—Percentage Composition of Receipts by Source: 1934–2013, http://origin.www.gpoaccess.gov/usbudget/fy09/hist.html (accessed 4/20/09).

declined over the same time period, dropping from 23.2 percent of receipts in 1960 to 13.7 in 2008. The share of the federal individual income tax has remained fairly stable; it was 44 percent in 1960 and 48.4 percent in 2008.

One of the most important features of the American income tax is that it is a "progressive," or "graduated," tax, with the heaviest burden carried by those most able to pay. A tax is called **progressive** if the rate of taxation goes up with each higher income bracket. A tax is called **regressive** if people in lower income brackets pay a higher proportion of their income toward the tax than people in higher income brackets. For example, a sales tax is deemed regressive because everybody pays at the same rate, so that the proportion of total income paid in taxes goes down as the total income goes up (assuming, as is generally the case, that as total income goes up the amount spent on sales-taxable purchases increases at a slower rate). The Social Security tax is another example of a regressive tax. In 2008, Social Security law applied a tax of 6.2 percent on the first $102,000 of income for the retirement program and an additional 1.45 percent on all income (without limit) for Medicare benefits, for a total of 7.65 percent in Social Security taxes. This means that a person earning an income of $102,000 pays $7,803 in Social Security taxes, a rate of 7.65 percent. But someone earning twice that income, $204,000, pays a total of $10,761 in Social Security taxes, a rate of 5.3 percent. As one's income continues to rise, the amount of Social Security taxes also rises (until the cap is reached), but the rate, or the percentage of one's income that goes to taxes, declines.

Although the primary purpose of the graduated income tax is, of course, to raise revenue, an important second objective may be to collect revenue in such a way as to reduce the disparities of wealth between the lowest and the highest income brackets. We call this a policy of **redistribution**. The "Analyzing the Evidence" unit in this chapter examines the success of this policy. Another policy objective of the income tax is the encouragement of the capitalist economy by rewarding investment. The tax laws allow individuals or companies to deduct from their taxable income any money they can justify as an investment or a "business expense"; this gives an incentive to individuals and companies to spend money to expand their production, their advertising, or their staff, and reduces the income taxes businesses have to pay. These kinds of deductions are called incentives or "equity" by those who support them; others call them "loopholes." The tax laws of the 1980s actually closed a number of important loopholes in U.S. tax laws. But others still exist—on home mortgages and on business expenses, for example—and others will return, because there is a strong consensus among members of Congress, both Democrats and Republicans, that businesses often need such incentives. The differences between the two parties focus largely on which incentives are justifiable.[17]

The tax reform laws of 1981 and 1986 significantly reduced the progressiveness of the federal income tax. Drastic rate reductions were instituted in 1986.

progressive taxation Taxation that hits upper income brackets more heavily.

regressive taxation Taxation that hits lower income brackets more heavily.

redistribution A policy whose objective is to tax or spend in such a way as to reduce the disparities of wealth between the lowest and the highest income brackets.

---

[17] For a systematic account of the role of government in providing incentives and inducements to business, see C. E. Lindblom, *Politics and Markets* (New York: Basic Books, 1977), chap. 13. For a detailed account of the dramatic Reagan tax cuts and reforms, see Jeffrey Birnbaum and Alan Murray, *Showdown at Gucci Gulch: Lawmakers, Lobbyists, and the Unlikely Triumph of Tax Reform* (New York: Random House, 1987).

Before George W. Bush's 2001 reform, there were five tax brackets, ranging from a 15 percent tax on those in the lowest income bracket to 39.6 percent on those in the highest income bracket. Prior to the 1980s, the highest tax brackets sometimes were taxed at a rate of 90 percent on the last $1 million of taxable income earned in a given year. Meanwhile, Social Security taxes—the most regressive taxes of all—remain high and are likely to be increased.[18]

As we have seen, taxes were a controversial issue during the George W. Bush administration. President Bush made tax reduction the centerpiece of his administration and enacted major tax cuts. The argument for the tax cuts was largely a supply-side argument: the cuts would make for a prosperous economy. The president and his supporters pointed to the expanding economy and lower taxes for all as the fruit of the tax cuts. Opponents charged that it made no sense to cut taxes since the benefits of tax cuts primarily go to the wealthy. They argued that not only did the rich already benefit from unequal patterns of growth that sent their income skyrocketing, but tax cuts that disproportionately benefit the wealthy do not stimulate the economy, as supply-side theory predicts. Critics also charged that the tax cuts caused the federal budget, which had a surplus when Bush took office, to fall into deficit.[19]

These tax breaks were scheduled to expire in 2010. As the economy dipped into recession in early 2008, Bush urged making the cuts permanent: "The smartest thing we can do is to keep taxes low. In a time of economic uncertainty, we don't need to be taking money out of your pocket."[20] Democratic politicians, on the other hand, argued that the tax cuts benefited the rich too much. They argued that moving back to higher tax rates on the wealthy would help fund crucial public programs, such as improving the health-care system.

Spending and Budgeting.   The federal government's power to spend is one of the most important tools of economic policy. Decisions about how much to spend affect the overall health of the economy. They also affect every aspect of American life from the distribution of income to the availability of different modes of transportation to the level of education in society. Not surprisingly, the fight for control over spending is one of the most contentious in Washington, as interest groups and politicians strive to determine the priorities and appropriate levels of spending. Decisions about spending are made as part of the annual budget process. During the 1990s, when the federal **budget deficit** first became a major political issue and when parties were deeply split on spending, the budget process became the focal point of the entire policy-making process. Even though the budget deficit disappeared in the late 1990s, the budget continued to dominate the attention of policy makers (Figure 14.2). With the rapid swing from budget surpluses in 2000 to

budget deficit
The amount by which government spending exceeds government revenue in a fiscal year.

---

[18] For further background, see David E. Rosenbaum, "Cutting the Deficit Overshadows Clinton's Promise to Cut Taxes," *New York Times,* January 12, 1993, p. A1; and "Clinton Weighing Freeze or New Tax on Social Security," *New York Times,* January 31, 1993, p. A1.

[19] Center on Budget and Policy Priorities, "Tax Cuts: Myths and Realities," updated May 9, 2008, www .cbpp.org/cms/?fa=view&id=692 (accessed 4/20/09).

[20] "Bush Urges Permanent Tax Cuts Amid 'Economic Uncertainty,'" *New York Times,* January 8, 2008.

FIGURE 14.2 U.S. BUDGET DEFICITS AND SURPLUSES, 1962–2009*

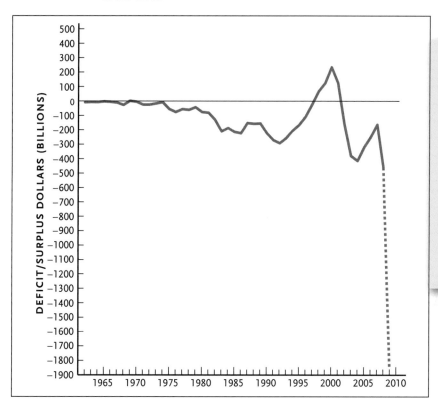

*2009 deficit is an estimate

SOURCE: Office of Management and Budget, http://origin.www.gpoaccess.gov/usbudget/fy09/hist.html (accessed 5/20/09).

record deficits by 2003, deficits once again emerged as a political issue. This time, however, Republican leaders, who had made deficits the focal point of politics in the mid-1990s, largely dismissed their importance. As then House majority leader Tom DeLay put it, "The Soviet Union had a balanced budget. Well, you can raise taxes until you balance it, but the economy will go into the toilet."[21] Nonetheless, with deficits identified as causing future reductions in Social Security and other programs, deficits are likely to remain on the political agenda.

Institutions and Policies

The budget process involves both the president and Congress. Each branch has created institutions and procedures designed to fulfill its budgetary responsibilities

---

[21] Andrew Taylor, "With Half-Trillion in Red Ink, U.S. Inc. Looks Bad on Paper," *Congressional Quarterly Weekly*, January 17, 2004, p. 132.

and to assert control over the budget process. Each branch has sought to expand the jurisdiction of its budgetary institution and to use its institution to enhance its own agenda and veto power over the budget. As we noted in Chapter 1, institutions provide political actors with authority for their policy preferences. The president and Congress use their budget institutions to promote their own budgetary preferences and priorities. The Office of Management and Budget (OMB) in the Executive Office of the President is responsible for preparing the president's budget. This budget contains the president's spending priorities and the estimated costs of the president's policy proposals. It is viewed as the starting point for the annual debate over the budget. When different parties control the presidency and Congress, the president's budget may have little influence on the budget that is ultimately adopted. Members of the president's own party also may have different priorities. In 2002, members of Congress from both parties resisted the president's efforts to cut spending for domestic programs. A key Republican staffer defended congressional prerogatives to shape the budget, declaring, "Our job is not to rubber-stamp what OMB says."[22]

Congress has its own budget institutions. Congress created the Congressional Budget Office (CBO) in 1974 so that it could have reliable information about the costs and economic impact of the policies it considers. At the same time, Congress established a budget process designed to establish spending priorities and to consider individual expenditures in light of the entire budget. A key element of the process is the annual budget resolution, which designates broad targets for spending. By estimating the costs of policy proposals, Congress hoped to control spending and to reduce deficits. When the congressional budget process proved unable to hold down deficits in the 1980s, Congress established stricter measures to control spending, including "spending caps" that limit spending on some types of programs.

A very large and growing proportion of the annual federal budget is **mandatory spending**, expenditures that are, in the words of the OMB, "relatively uncontrollable." Interest payments on the national debt, for example, are determined by the actual size of the national debt. Legislation has mandated payment rates for such programs as retirement under Social Security, retirement for federal employees, unemployment assistance, Medicare, and farm price supports (see Figures 14.3 and 14.4). These payments increase with the cost of living; they increase as the average age of the population goes up; they increase as national and world agricultural surpluses go up. In 1970, 38.5 percent of the total federal budget was made up of these **uncontrollables**; in 1975, 52.5 percent fell into that category; and by 2008, around 61.2 percent was in the uncontrollable category. This means that the national government now has very little **discretionary spending**, which would allow it to counteract fluctuations in the business cycle.

Government spending as a fiscal policy works fairly well when deliberate deficit spending is used to stop a recession and to speed up the recovery period, but it does not work very well in fighting inflation, because elected politicians are politically unable to make the drastic expenditure cuts necessary to balance the budget, much less to produce a budgetary surplus.

mandatory spending Federal spending that is made up of "uncontrollables," budget items that cannot be controlled through the regular budget process.

uncontrollable A budgetary item that is beyond the control of budgetary committees and can be controlled only by substantive legislative action in Congress. Some uncontrollables, such as interest on the debt, are beyond the power of Congress, because the terms of payments are set in contracts.

discretionary spending Federal spending on programs that are controlled through the regular budget process.

---

[22] Karen Masterson, "Bush's Budget Promise Goes Bust," *Houston Chronicle*, May 7, 2002, p. A1.

FIGURE 14.3 UNCONTROLLABLES AS A PERCENTAGE OF TOTAL FEDERAL BUDGET, 1962–2009

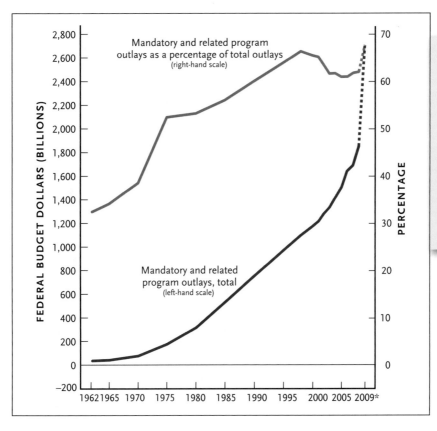

*Estimate

SOURCE: Office of Management and Budget, http://origin.www.gpoaccess.gov/usbudget/fy09/hist.html (accessed 5/20/09).

ANALYZING THE EVIDENCE

Spending on mandatory programs—such as Social Security and Medicare—has grown dramatically since 1970. These popular programs accounted for over 60 percent of the federal budget in 2008. What drives the increase in spending on these programs?

Regulation and Antitrust Policy

Americans have long been suspicious of concentrations of economic power. Federal economic regulation aims to protect the public against potential abuses by concentrated economic power in two ways. First, the federal government can establish conditions that govern the operation of big businesses to ensure fair competition. For example, it can require business to make information about its activities and account books available to the public. Second, the federal government can force a large business to break up into smaller companies if it finds that the company has established a **monopoly**. This is called **antitrust policy**. In addition to economic regulation, the federal government engages in social regulation. Social regulation establishes conditions on businesses in order to protect workers, the environment, and consumers.

Federal regulatory policy was a reaction to public demands. As the American economy prospered throughout the nineteenth century, some companies grew so

monopoly The existence of a single firm in a market that controls all the goods and services of that market; absence of competition.

antitrust policy Government regulation of large businesses that have established monopolies.

FIGURE 14.4 BUDGET OUTLAYS OF THE FEDERAL GOVERNMENT BY FUNCTION, 2009*

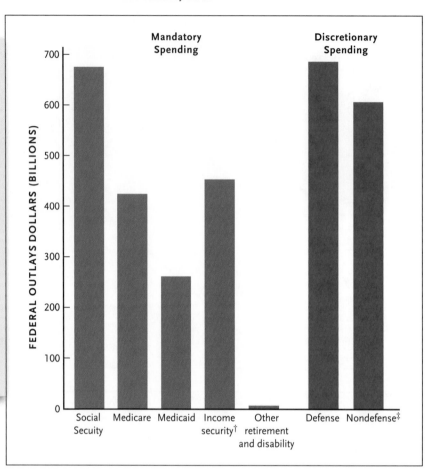

*Estimate

†Includes unemployment compensation, food and nutrition assistance, Supplemental Security Income, earned income tax credits, family and other support assistance, foster care and adoption assistance, and housing assistance.

‡Includes appropriations for all domestic programs, for example, agriculture, transportation, labor, interior, Health and Human Services, education, housing, and homeland security.

SOURCE: Office of Management and Budget, www.whitehouse.gov/omb/budget/fy2009/pdf/hist.pdf (accesssed 5/20/09).

large that they were recognized as possessing "market power." This meant that they were powerful enough to eliminate competitors and to impose conditions on consumers rather than catering to consumer demand. The growth of billion-dollar corporations led to collusion among companies to control prices, much to the dismay of smaller businesses and ordinary consumers. Small businesses, laborers, farmers, and consumers all began to clamor for protective regulation. Although the states had been regulating businesses in one way or another all along, interest groups turned to Washington as economic problems appeared to be beyond the reach of the individual state governments. If markets were national, there would have to be national regulation.[23]

The first national regulatory policy was the Interstate Commerce Act of 1887, which created the first national independent regulatory commission, the Interstate Commerce Commission (ICC), designed to control the monopolistic practices of the railroads. Two years later, the Sherman Antitrust Act extended regulatory power to cover all monopolistic practices, including "trusts" or any other agreement between companies to eliminate competition. These were strengthened in 1914 with the enactment of the Federal Trade Act (creating the Federal Trade Commission, or FTC) and the Clayton Act. The only significant addition of economic regulatory policy beyond regulation of interstate trade, however, was the establishment in 1913 of the Federal Reserve System, which was given powers to regulate the banking industry along with its general monetary powers. At the same time, public demands for consumer protection led the federal government to enact a more limited number of social regulations. As we have seen, Upton Sinclair's best-seller about the meatpacking industry, *The Jungle*, led to the federal meat inspection program in 1906. Two decades later, the Food and Drug Administration was set up to test and regulate products viewed as essential to public health.

The modern epoch of comprehensive national regulation began in the 1930s. Most of the regulatory programs of the 1930s were established to regulate the conduct of companies within specifically designated sectors of American industry. For example, the jurisdiction of one agency was the securities industry; the jurisdiction of another was the radio (and eventually television) industry. Another was banking. Another was coal mining; still another was agriculture. At this time, Congress also set the basic framework of American labor regulation, including the rules for collective bargaining and the minimum wage.

When Congress turned once again to regulatory policies in the 1970s, it became still bolder, moving beyond the effort to regulate specific sectors of industry toward regulating some aspect of the entire economy. The scope or jurisdiction of such agencies as the Occupational Safety and Health Administration (OSHA), the Consumer Product Safety Commission (CPSC), and the Environmental Protection Agency (EPA) is as broad and as wide as the entire economy, indeed the entire society.

One important example of federal economic regulation was the government's case against Microsoft. Faced with strong competition from Netscape's Navigator browser software, Microsoft used its near-monopoly of the market for personal computer operating systems to require that computers run by Microsoft's Windows 98 operating system present users with a preloaded icon for Internet Explorer. Computer manufacturing companies would have to comply or they would "lose their Windows license and thus lose their business."[24] The Justice Department's Antitrust Division charged Microsoft with "product tying," a violation of antitrust law (the oldest of federal economic regulations). Initial court rulings found Microsoft guilty of using its monopoly power to harm the consumer by reducing competition and stifling innovation. At first it appeared that Microsoft would be subject to

---

[23] For an account of the relationship between mechanization and law, see Lawrence Friedman, *A History of American Law* (New York: Simon & Schuster, 1973), 409–29.

[24] Quoted from the *Economist*, January 31, 1998, pp. 65–66.

severe penalties, including possibly splitting the company in two. Instead, the Justice Department settled the case, requiring only minor concessions on Microsoft's part. Microsoft now has to disclose parts of its Windows code and allow computer manufacturers to install competing software on their machines. Critics charged that these measures would do little to change Microsoft's anticompetitive business practices. The changes did not help Netscape Navigator, which went offline in 2008.

Despite occasional high-profile regulatory cases such as the one against Microsoft, the trend since the late 1970s has been against regulation. Businesses complained about the burden of the new regulations they confronted, and many economists began to argue that excessive regulation was hurting the economy. Congress and the president responded with a wave of **deregulation**. For example, President Reagan went about the task of changing the direction of regulation by way of "presidential oversight." Shortly after taking office, he gave the OMB authority to review all executive-branch proposals for new regulations. By this means, Reagan reduced the total number of regulations issued by federal agencies, dropping the number of pages in the *Federal Register* from 74,000 in 1980 to 49,600 in 1987.[25] By 2007 the *Federal Register* had grown again to more than 74,000 pages. Nonetheless, the movement for deregulation became steadily more controversial during the presidency of George W. Bush. In the late 1980s and 1990s, many states had opened their electrical power markets to competition, resulting in lower prices. But in 2001, severe energy shortages in California caused power outages and skyrocketing prices. California officials charged that Enron and other out-of-state suppliers had used their market power to drive up the price of energy and then used their political clout to dissuade federal regulators from intervening.

Calls for tighter regulation of the finance industry surged in 2008, when weaknesses in the subprime mortgage business triggered a worldwide crisis of confidence. Banks and other companies had devised new ways of bundling individual mortgage loans into complex securities known as derivatives. Since mortgages were thought to be solid investments, the investment banks borrowed capital to purchase and resell them in high volume. As some homeowners started finding it difficult to keep up with their payments, however, the banks suddenly appeared overextended. Other investors became reluctant to lend. Congress decided it had little choice but to approve the massive rescue plan proposed by the Treasury and the Federal Reserve. But an unmistakable movement had by then taken shape for a thorough overhaul of the country's regulatory architecture of the financial system. Such an overhaul was enacted in 2010, subjecting banks to tighter regulation and prohibiting them from engaging in a number of risky activities. The new law also established a consumer protection agency to oversee consumer lending and the practices of credit card issuers.

Subsidies and Contracting

Subsidies and contracting are the carrots of economic policy. Their purpose is to encourage people to do something they might not otherwise do or to get people to

---

[25] The *Federal Register* is the daily publication of all official acts of Congress, the president, and the administrative agencies. A law or executive order is not legally binding until it is published in the *Federal Register*.

do more of what they are already doing. Sometimes the purpose is merely to compensate people for something done in the past.

Subsidies. **Subsidies** are simply government grants of cash or other valuable commodities, such as land. Although subsidies are often denounced as "giveaways," they have played a fundamental role in the history of government in the United States. Subsidies were the dominant form of public policy of the national government and the state and local governments throughout the nineteenth century. They continue to be an important category of public policy at all levels of government. The first planning document ever written for the national government, Alexander Hamilton's *Report on Manufactures,* was based almost entirely on Hamilton's assumption that American industry could be encouraged by federal subsidies and that these were not only desirable but constitutional.

The thrust of Hamilton's plan was not lost on later policy makers. Subsidies in the form of land grants were given to farmers and to railroad companies to encourage western settlement. Substantial cash subsidies have traditionally been given to shipbuilders to help build the commercial fleet and to guarantee the use of their ships as military personnel carriers in time of war. Policies using the subsidy technique continued to be plentiful in the twentieth century, even after the 1990s, in spite of widespread public and official hostility toward subsidies. For example, in 2005, the annual value of corporate subsidies not including agriculture was estimated at more than $75 billion.[26] Crop subsidies alone, implemented by the Department of Agriculture, amounted to about $18 billion in 2007.

Politicians have always favored subsidies because subsidies can be treated as "benefits" that can be spread widely in response to many demands that might otherwise produce profound political conflict. Subsidies can, in other words, be used to buy off the opposition.

Another secret to the popularity of subsidies is that those who receive the benefits do not always perceive the controls inherent in them. In the first place, most of the resources available for subsidies come from taxation. (During the nineteenth century, there was a lot of public land to distribute, but that is no longer the case.) Second, the effect of any subsidy has to be measured somewhat indirectly in terms of what people *would be doing* if the subsidy were not available. For example, many thousands of people settled in lands west of the Mississippi only because land subsidies were available. Similarly, hundreds of research laboratories exist in universities and corporations only because certain types of research subsidies from the government are available to fund them.

Contracting. Like any corporation, a government agency must purchase goods and services by contract. The law requires open bidding for a substantial proportion of these contracts because government contracts are extremely valuable to businesses in the private sector and because the opportunities and incentives for abuse surrounding contracting are very great. But contracting is more than a method of buying goods and services. Contracting is also an important technique of policy

subsidy A government grant of cash or other valuable commodities, such as land, to an individual or an organization; used to promote activities desired by the government, to reward political support, or to buy off political opposition.

---

[26] Cato Institute, Cato Handbook for Congress 6th ed., 9. Corporate Welfare (2005), www.cato.org/pubs/handbook/hb105-9.html (accessed 4/20/09).

contracting power The power of government to set conditions on companies seeking to sell goods or services to government agencies.

because government agencies are often authorized to use their **contracting power** as a means of encouraging corporations to improve themselves, as a means of helping to build up whole sectors of the economy, and as a means of encouraging certain desirable goals or behavior, such as equal employment opportunity. For example, the infant airline industry of the 1930s was nurtured by the national government's lucrative contracts to carry airmail. A more recent example is the use of government contracting to encourage industries, universities, and other organizations to engage in research and development on a wide range of issues in basic and applied science.

Military contracting has long been a major element in government spending. So tight was the connection between defense contractors and the federal government during the Cold War that as he was leaving office, President Eisenhower warned the nation to beware of the powerful "military-industrial complex." After the Cold War, as military spending and production declined, major defense contractors began to look for alternative business activities to supplement the reduced demand for weapons. For example, Lockheed Martin, the nation's largest defense contractor, began to bid on contracts related to welfare reform. After the terrorist attacks of 2001, however, the military budget was awash in new funds and military contractors were flooded with business. President Bush increased the Pentagon budget by more than 7 percent a year, requesting so many weapons systems that one observer called the budget a "weapons smorgasbord."[27] Military contractors geared up to produce not only weapons for foreign warfare but also surveillance systems to enhance domestic security.

The government's growing use of contractors can sometimes illustrate what we called the dark side of the principal-agent relationship. Recall that when we create institutions to solve collective action problems, we are delegating decision-making power to them. We are the principals, and our governmental institutions are the agents. Inherent in all such delegations is the possibility that the agent will not act in the interest of the principal. Legislative institutions, for example, may enact laws desired by lobbyists rather than programs demanded by public opinion. Our system of government includes numerous checks—such as frequent elections—to compel agents to pay attention to the wishes of the principals.

The principal-agent problem is compounded in the case of government contracting. Here, our agent—the Congress of the United States—has delegated power to a secondary agent, a government bureaucracy, which has, in turn delegated power to a tertiary agent—a private contractor. Thus, the agent of the agent of our agent undertakes actions on behalf of the citizens of the United States. We often discover that these tertiary agents are hardly controlled by the bureaucracies that employ them, much less by Congress or the citizenry. Military contractors, for example, were responsible for a number of acts of violence against Iraqi civilians that helped to turn Arab opinion against the United States. President Obama has declared that the government will rely less on contractors and more on civil servants to carry out its responsibilities. The government's dependence on contractors is so great, however, that it seems unlikely that the role of these agents of our agents' agents will truly be diminished.

---

[27] James Dao, "The Nation; Big Bucks Trip Up the Lean New Army," *New York Times*, February 10, 2002, sec. 4, p. 5.

THE ENVIRONMENT AND THE ECONOMY

Federal interest in environmental conservation stretches back to the early 1900s, with the creation of the National Park Service and other efforts to preserve natural beauty. But it was not until the 1970s that environmental policy emerged as a major component of federal action, with the passage of new laws reaching into many aspects of the economy. Today, concern about global warming has put environmental issues front and center in debates about the economy. Not only must policy makers grapple with the costs of combating global warming, they must also assess the long-term impact of warming on the American economy and society. This is a fundamental challenge because the effects of global warming are likely to be very widely felt. At the same time, however, the specific consequences and the timing of their impact remain very uncertain.

The wave of environmental policy enacted in the 1970s stemmed in large part from American prosperity in the 1960s. An affluent America with more time for leisure grew concerned about the quality of the environment and the need to preserve natural beauty. The consequences of economic growth that paid little attention to environmental impact were evident all over America. In 1969, Cleveland's Cayuhoga River, long a dumping ground for industrial waste, caught fire. Images of the burning river became especially vivid symbols of environmental neglect. The first "Earth Day" in 1970 celebrated this new set of concerns, which would become a major feature of American politics in the coming decades.[28]

A wave of new laws wrote environmental goals into policy. The 1969 National Environmental Policy Act (NEPA), the Clean Air Act Amendments of 1970, the 1972 Clean Water Act, and the 1974 Safe Drinking Water Act together established a new set of goals and procedures for protecting the environment. They are properly considered part of economic policy because they regulate the activities of virtually every aspect of the economy. NEPA, for example, requires federal agencies to prepare an environmental impact statement for every major development project that they propose. In this way, environmental impacts routinely become factored into considerations about whether a particular project is feasible or desirable.

Environmental disasters have often drawn attention to new environmental hazards and have prompted greater federal regulation. For example, during the mid-1970s the residents of the Love Canal neighborhood in Buffalo, New York, discovered that their neighborhood had been built on a toxic waste dump. Many of the chemicals in the soil were suspected carcinogens. At federal and state cost, residents were moved to new homes. Partly as a result of this highly publicized incident, Congress passed legislation to facilitate cleanup of hazardous waste sites. Yet government action and corporate liability are often bitterly contested issues in this area. As the book and film *A Civil Action*—about toxic waste in a Massachusetts community—demonstrated, identifying the sources of toxic pollution and linking such pollution to health hazards can be very difficult.[29]

---

[28] See Samuel P. Hays, *Beauty, Health, and Permanence: Environmental Politics in the United States, 1955–1985* (Cambridge: Cambridge University Press, 1987).

[29] Jonathan Harr, *A Civil Action* (New York: Vintage, 1996).

Protecting the environment presents policy makers with difficult trade-offs. Compliance with environmental regulations can be very costly. Moreover, critics maintain that federal standards are sometimes too high. How clean should the air be? What is the difference between pure drinking water and safe drinking water? Who should bear the costs of providing environmental benefits? Not only do citizens, consumers, and businesses take different perspectives on these questions but the goals themselves often present a moving target. As new scientific evidence shows (or fails to find evidence for) new or suspected environmental hazards, conflicts over the proper government role emerge.

The Debate on Global Warming

Nowhere have these conflicts been more acute than in the debate over global warming. A large and growing body of scientific evidence suggests that greenhouse gas emissions from cars, power plants, and other human-made sources are causing temperatures on earth to rise.[30] The projected environmental consequences are dire: melting polar ice caps, extreme weather, droughts, fire, rising sea levels, and disease. All would have profound economic consequences. Yet these projections come with considerable uncertainty: how likely are most catastrophic scenarios? Should we prepare for the most damaging outcomes or only the most likely outcomes of global warming?[31] These questions are important because the costs of transforming the world's carbon-based technologies through lower energy use and newer green technologies are enormous. These questions are especially salient for the United States, which has the world's largest economy and is responsible for 25 percent of the world's greenhouse gas emissions but has only 10 percent of the world's population.[32] And because the United States relies so heavily on fossil fuels for its energy sources, the effort to reduce carbon emission requires a major shift in how we obtain and use energy.

As scientists have learned more about the effects of human activity on the climate, the issue of global warming has risen on the national agenda. The issue attracted broad attention in 2006 with the success of former vice president Al Gore's film *An Inconvenient Truth*. In 2007, the film won an Academy Award, and Gore, along with the UN's International Panel on Climate Change, received the Nobel Peace Prize for arousing public awareness about the dangers of global warming. American public opinion reflected the growing salience of global warming as a policy issue. For example, in 2007, 84 percent of Americans reported believing that human activity was at least a contributing factor in global warming.[33] In the same

---

[30] Pew Center on Global Climate Change, "Climate Change 101: The Science and Impacts," www .pewclimate.org/docUploads/101_Science_Impacts.pdf (accessed 4/20/09).

[31] See the discussion in Peter R. Orszag, "Issues in Climate Change," Congressional Budget Office, November 16, 2007, www.cbo.gov/ftpdocs/88xx/doc8819/11-16-ClimateChangeConf.pdf (accessed 4/20/09).

[32] Energy Information Administration, "Greenhouse Gases, Climate Change, and Energy," www.eia .doe.gov/bookshelf/brochures/greenhouse/Chapter1.htm (accessed 4/20/09).

[33] John M. Broder and Marjorie Connelly, "Public Says Warming Is a Problem, But Remains Split on Response," *New York Times*, April 27, 2007, p. 20.

survey, just over half of the public said that they would support protecting the environment over stimulating the economy, while 36 percent chose the economy.[34] When asked whether or not the issue would affect their votes, just under half of the public said that global warming would be "extremely" or "very important" to their vote for president.[35] Some corporate leaders have also become increasingly concerned about global warming, sponsoring events to learn more about the problem and joining coalitions to press for solutions. Moreover, many political leaders who were skeptical about the reality and causes of global warming have come to accept that it poses a threat that must be addressed. For much of his administration, former president George W. Bush resisted pressure to address global warming. Instead, concern about the availability and cost of energy drove his administration to press for securing new oil resources, such as the controversial and unsuccessful effort to open the Arctic Natural Wildlife Refuge to oil drilling. But by the end of his term, Bush had come to accept the importance of addressing global warming, warding off critics with his declaration, "I take the issue seriously."[36]

When he campaigned for office in 2008, Barack Obama emphasized the need to protect the environment, backing legislation to cut greenhouse gas emissions, and called for more rapid development of renewable energy sources such as wind, solar, and geothermal. During his first months in office, Obama directed billions of dollars to the Department of Energy for a number of renewable-energy projects.

Environmental Policies

But how can the goal of a "greener America" be reached? Agreeing on policies to reduce greenhouse gas emissions remains extremely difficult. Policy makers charged with devising approaches to global warming have identified three basic policy approaches. The first is mitigation, or reduction of greenhouse gas emissions. The second is large-scale research and development to promote alternative technologies. The third consists of measures that allow us to adapt to a warmer climate. Each of these strategies entails potentially gargantuan costs in the form of higher energy prices, subsidies to industry, infrastructure projects, and relocation decisions. When specific policy proposals are discussed and these costs become apparent, the consensus for addressing global warming breaks down.

Mitigation: Reducing Emissions. The mitigation approach, which seeks to reduce greenhouse gas emissions, has garnered the most attention from policy makers. Two policies that aim to achieve this goal are tougher standards for auto fuel mileage and higher taxes on gasoline. Both have been very controversial. Although the public strongly supports higher gas-mileage standards, auto companies resisted such standards for nearly thirty years after they were first put into place in the early 1970s. The 2007 energy bill's requirement that automobiles raise fuel

---

[34] Broder and Connelly, "Public Says Warming Is a Problem."

[35] Survey by Cable News Network, conducted by Opinion Research Corporation, November 2–4, 2007 and based on telephone interviews with a national adult sample of 1,024. [USORC.110707.R05L]

[36] Peter Baker, "In Bush's Final Year, the Agenda Gets Greener," *Washington Post*, December 29, 2007, p. A1.

efficiency rates by 40 percent—to 35 miles per gallon by 2020—was a breakthrough on this issue. Even so, when California and fifteen other states sought to require even tougher standards for fuel mileage, the Environmental Protection Agency rejected their request, citing the need for a single national standard. Proposals to increase gasoline taxes have so far been political nonstarters. Public opinion polls routinely show that a majority of Americans oppose a tax on gasoline as a way to reduce emissions, and few politicians want to sponsor such an unpopular policy.[37]

International agreements on climate change, such as the Kyoto Protocol, seek to reduce carbon emissions by establishing mandatory caps on the total amount of emissions developed countries can emit. Although the United States signed the protocol in 1997, congressional and presidential opposition prevented any effort to implement its provisions. Policy makers have since considered several ways to reduce carbon emissions. One of the most effective is a "carbon tax," which would tax the producers of energy. The higher costs would then be passed onto consumers. Yet only a handful of politicians have expressed interest in supporting carbon taxes, which could substantially raise the costs of all sorts of consumer products.

Perhaps the most politically feasible strategy for reducing carbon emissions is a cap-and-trade system. This approach sets a target for carbon emissions for each industry but allows companies to trade "carbon credits" with each other. This market-based system is attractive to political leaders because it achieves its goals by creating incentives for private actors and allows them flexibility as they seek to reduce emissions. More than twenty-three large firms, including leading auto makers, have joined environmentalists in a coalition called the U.S. Climate Action Partnership (USCAP) to press for a cap-and-trade system to reduce carbon emissions.[38] In 2007, Senators Joe Lieberman (Ind.-Conn.) and John Warner (R-Va.) introduced a cap-and-trade bill. Dubbed "America's Climate Security Act," the measure reflected the growing consensus on this market-based approach, which effectively "puts a price on pollution" to reduce greenhouse gas emissions.[39] The Lieberman-Warner bill set the stage for future debates over how to attack global warming through mitigation. For example, the 2009 Waxman-Markley comprehensive energy bill supported by many House Democrats echoed the cap-and-trade approach developed by the Lieberman-Warner bill.

Promoting Alternative Technologies.   Many analysts and politicians, however, prefer a second strategy, which centers on increasing research and development to promote alternative technologies. Former president Bush supported this approach in his 2007 State of the Union address, which called for a 22 percent increase in funding for clean energy initiatives.[40] A particularly popular type of green technology has been the hybrid car. In 2007, almost every major auto manufacturer had plans for producing a hybrid car, and over 350,000 hybrid vehicles were sold in the

---

[37] Broder and Connelly, "Public Says Warming Is a Problem."

[38] Environmental Defense Fund, "Blueprint Lays Out Clear Path for Climate Action," updated January 21, 2009, www.edf.org/article.cfm?contentID=5828 (accessed 4/20/09).

[39] "Climate Change on Capitol Hill," *Washington Post,* October 22, 2007, p. A22.

[40] White House, "President Bush Delivers State of the Union Address," January 23, 2007, http://georgew bush-whitehouse.archives.gov/news/releases/2007/01/20070123-2.html (accessed 4/20/09).

United States.[41] Other kinds of green technologies include recycling, solar power, and hydrogen fuel cells.

Green technologies may prove to be a boon for the American economy. Because highly skilled labor is required to produce most green technologies, America has a competitive advantage over many other countries. To be more precise, the production of green technologies—unlike other kinds of goods—cannot be outsourced to developing countries.

In addition to enhancing environmental quality and promoting economic growth, a move toward green technologies could significantly improve American national security. Indeed, because most oil money goes to Saudi Arabia and Iran, some argue that adopting more fuel-efficient technologies would take money away from regimes that support terrorism against the United States. As the *New York Times* columnist Thomas Friedman put it, "Green is the new red, white and blue."[42]

Part of the attraction of green technologies is that they appear to entail fewer politically difficult costs. A closer look, however, reveals that green technologies do impose unpopular costs. For example, the search for cleaner technologies has renewed interest in nuclear power. But nuclear power has long suffered from NIMBY (Not In My Backyard) problems: few people want a nuclear power plant close by. The question of how to dispose of nuclear waste poses similar problems. Current plans to deposit nuclear waste in Nevada's Yucca Mountain have been the target of considerable controversy, not only by people close by but also by those concerned with the dangers of transporting nuclear waste to Nevada. Even less dangerous technologies, such as wind farms, attract opposition, as the effort to establish a large wind farm off Cape Cod demonstrated. Other alternatives, such as the use of ethanol to replace gasoline, have different problems. In 2007, as corn farmers sought to produce corn for the ethanol market, Americans experienced rising food prices.[43]

Development of green technologies will no doubt be an important component of America's efforts to combat climate change. However, opposition to some of the new technologies and the time required to develop these alternatives mean that they are not the magic bullet that many proponents wish they were.

Adaptation Policies. A final approach to climate change is adaptation to a warmer climate. Adaptation would entail a diverse set of policies, including establishment of green corridors, pest and disease control, water conservation to deal with drought, and new infrastructure such as seawalls to cope with rising sea levels.[44] Even more controversial measures, such as moving people away from low-lying areas, would be part of an adaptation strategy.

Many aspects of a deliberate adaptation strategy would be difficult to implement in the market-oriented, decentralized context of the United States. Although some European countries, such as the low-lying Netherlands, are relocating people

---

[41] HybridCars, "December 2007 Dashboard," www.hybridcars.com/market-dashboard/dec07-overview .html (accessed 4/20/09).

[42] Thomas L. Friedman, "The Power of Green," *New York Times*, April 15, 2007.

[43] Andrew Martin, "Food and Fuel Compete for Land," *New York Times*, December 18, 2007.

[44] Orszag, "Issues in Climate Change."

as part of their adaptation strategy, American politicians have little stomach for initiating such controversial measures. Moreover, the combination of conservation and new infrastructure requires considerable public resources and broad coordination across multiple public agencies. Both are hard to achieve in the context of American politics. For example, the environmentally sensitive Sacramento Delta is extremely vulnerable to rising sea levels. The delta, a swath of land that lies below sea level, is economically important because it supplies much of northern California, including California agribusiness, with water. Yet decisions about what happens in the delta involve more than 200 government agencies.[45]

When deliberate adaptation does not occur, *de facto* adaptation may. Although no single event such as Hurricane Katrina can be attributed to climate change, the consequences of Katrina are relevant to global-warming scenarios. As in New Orleans, the most vulnerable people with the fewest resources will likely suffer the worst consequences of adaptation as they lose their homes and livelihoods. As in New Orleans and in recent urban heat waves, many may die. Many scientists believe that deliberate adaptation has to be part of our approach to climate change because even if we take major steps to mitigate carbon emissions and pour resources into developing new technologies, global warming has already arrived.[46]

Global climate change poses a difficult economic challenge for the United States. It presents the opportunity for American industry to take the lead in developing green technologies, placing the nation's economic prosperity on a fundamentally new base. Yet it also calls for government to enforce the reduction of carbon emissions and adapt current practices to a changing world. Many industries have expressed support for action to address climate change, but such a major economic transformation creates winners and losers. Firms, such as the auto companies, whose profits are jeopardized and workers whose jobs are threatened by change have successfully blocked bold action in the past. The diffuse long-term harms that global warming poses are hard to pit against the specific concentrated costs that face industries today. Nonetheless, growing recognition that climate change is real and poses potentially catastrophic consequences ensures that economic policy and environmental policy will be ever more closely intertwined in the future.

THE POLITICS OF ECONOMIC POLICY MAKING

Addressing economic challenges and maintaining a healthy economy are extremely important to political leaders. As presidents from Herbert Hoover (who presided over the beginning of the Great Depression of the 1930s) to Jimmy Carter (who faced double-digit inflation) discovered, voters will punish politicians for poor

---

[45] Joe Palca, "California Turns to Holland for Flood Expertise," National Public Radio, January 14, 2008. www.npr.org/templates/story/story.php?storyId=18080442 (accessed 4/20/09).

[46] Roger Pielke, Jr., Gwyn Prins, Steve Rayner, and Daniel Sarewitz, "Climate Change 2007: Lifting the Taboo on Adaptation," *Nature*, February 8, 2007, pp. 597–98.

economic performance. Yet even though all politicians want a healthy economy, they often differ in their views about how to attain it. Moreover, politicians disagree about what the priorities of economic policy should be. Democrats and Republicans alike want to promote economic growth, but Democrats are generally more concerned about equality and unemployment than are Republicans. Republicans stress the importance of economic freedom for maintaining a healthy economy, whereas Democrats are often more willing to support economic regulation to attain social objectives. Such differences along party lines are not hard and fast divisions, however. The politics of economic policy making are also greatly influenced by economic ideas.

Until 1929, most Americans believed that government had little to do with actively managing the economy. The world was guided by the theory that the economy, if left to its own devices, would produce full employment and maximum production. This traditional view of the relationship between government and the economy crumbled in 1929 before the stark reality of the Great Depression of 1929–33. Some misfortune befell nearly everyone. Around 20 percent of the workforce became unemployed, and few of these individuals had any monetary resources or the old family farm to fall back on. Banks failed, wiping out the savings of millions who had been prudent enough or fortunate enough to have any. Thousands of businesses failed, throwing middle-class Americans onto the bread lines alongside unemployed laborers and dispossessed farmers. The Great Depression proved to Americans that imperfections in the economic system could exist.

Demands grew for the federal government to act. In Congress, some Democrats proposed that the federal government finance public works to aid the economy and put people back to work. Other members introduced legislation to provide federal grants to the states to assist their relief efforts.

When President Franklin D. Roosevelt took office in 1933, he energetically threw the federal government into the business of fighting the Depression. He proposed a variety of temporary measures to provide federal relief and work programs. Most of the programs he proposed were to be financed by the federal government but administered by the states. In addition to these temporary measures, Roosevelt presided over the creation of several important federal programs designed to provide future economic security for Americans. Since that time, the government has been instrumental in ensuring that the economy will never again collapse as it did during the Depression.

The experience of the 1930s transformed public expectations about federal government involvement in the economy. Since that time, the public has held the government—and the president in particular—responsible for ensuring a healthy economy.

As we have seen, Keynesian ideas, which applied spending and tax policy to promote growth and low unemployment, dominated economic policy during the 1960s and during the first half of the 1970s. The Council of Economic Advisers (CEA) played a central role in economic policy during that time because the president relied on its advice about whether to stimulate or depress the economy. As Keynesian prescriptions became less effective, however, the CEA began to lose its central role. Since the late 1970s, when President Carter began to emphasize monetary policy, the chairman of the Federal Reserve has occupied the pivotal position in economic policy making. The long run of economic prosperity in the 1990s made the former Fed chairman Alan Greenspan into something of a cult figure. Universally praised by Democrats and Republicans alike for his management of the economy, Greenspan served four four-year terms as head of the Federal Reserve. As the economy fell into recession in the early 2000s, critics complained that Greenspan had lost his touch and had helped create the conditions for recession.

Presidents who preside over periods of economic downturn are generally punished by the electorate. In 1992, economic recession and relatively high levels of unemployment greatly improved the challenger Bill Clinton's presidential prospects, even though he was not widely known when he started campaigning. Clinton's campaign took as a central theme the unofficial slogan, "It's the economy, stupid." The uncertain direction of the economy made it an issue in the 2004 presidential campaign. Anxious not to repeat his father's experience in 1992, President George W. Bush claimed in 2004 that his policies were creating new jobs and touted the benefits of his tax cuts for middle-income families. Democrats countered that Bush's policies benefited the wealthy but left most Americans economically worse off.

The groups that influence decisions about economic policy are as wide ranging as the objectives of policy. Consumer groups, environmentalists, businesses, and labor all attempt to shape economic policy. Of these groups, organized labor and business are the most consistent actors that weigh in across the spectrum of policies. In the past, organized labor was much more important in influencing economic policy than it is today. At the height of their strength in the 1950s, unions represented some 35 percent of the labor force. Today, labor unions, representing 12.5 percent of the labor force, are much less powerful in influencing economic policy. Democratic presidents continue to court labor because unions control resources and votes important to Democratic politicians, but labor's overall power has waned. On particular issues, organized labor can still exercise significant influence. For example, labor played a key role in Congress's decision to increase the minimum wage in 1996. Labor has recently sought to boost its political profile and has particularly sought to influence trade policy.

Business organizations are the most consistently powerful actors in economic policy. Business groups are most united around the goal of reducing government regulation. Organizations such as the U.S. Chamber of Commerce, which represents small business, and the Business Roundtable and the National Association of Manufacturers, which represent big business, actively worked to roll back government regulation in the 1970s and 1980s.

In addition to subsidies and tax breaks, business also relies on the federal government for protection against unfair foreign competition. For example, over the past several years, the film-production industry has lobbied Washington to help it compete with other countries where films can be made more cheaply than in the United States. This country loses an estimated $10 billion in annual revenues to these foreign competitors. Television shows and films with American locales are routinely filmed in Canada, where tax incentives and lower costs make production considerably cheaper. Industry representatives, fearing that Los Angeles could turn into a "rust belt" for film production, have sought legislation to secure wage credits.[47] The Screen Actors Guild went so far as to ask the federal government to investigate Canada for unfair trade practices.

WHAT IS THE BEST DIRECTION FOR ECONOMIC POLICY?

Historically, Americans have been more concerned with ensuring economic liberty than with promoting economic equality. The widespread perception of openness and opportunity in American society has made Americans more tolerant of economic inequality than Europeans. American economic policy has rarely aimed to promote economic equality. Instead, economic policy has sought to ensure fairness in the marketplace and protect against the worst side effects of the free market. One of the central ways to ensure fair markets is to guard against the emergence of businesses so large that they can control markets. As we have seen, antitrust policy aims to break up such concentrations of power in the name of free and fair competition. The laws designed to strengthen labor in the 1930s likewise aimed to limit the power of big business by creating a countervailing power; they did not attempt directly to create equality. Consumer and environmental regulations are key economic policy protections against the worst side effects of the free market. Over time, as Americans have grown more concerned about the quality of life, policies in these areas have placed greater restrictions on the market. In a sense, economic prosperity and market success laid the foundation for such restrictions. As Americans felt more economically secure, they could afford to worry about how the economy affected the nonmaterial aspects of their lives, such as the environment. It is no accident that social regulation of the economy took off after the unprecedented prosperity of the 1960s.

The growth in economic inequality over the past three decades raises new questions about economic policy. Increased global competition, computerization, and the decline of unions and worker skills have all been identified as sources of the growth of inequality.[48] Taxes are another policy area that affects inequality. Depending on how they are designed, tax policies put relatively more money in the pockets of people with lower incomes or people with higher incomes. For example, tax cuts on investment income and reductions in the estate tax are more likely to increase the after-tax income of the wealthy because this group derives more of its income from investments and inheritances than do people with lower incomes.[49]

---

[47] Megan Garvey, "Company Town; SAG Says Canada Film Policies Illegal, Seeks Federal Inquiry," *Los Angeles Times,* August 22, 2001, part 3, p. 5.

[48] David H. Autor, Lawrence F. Katz, and Melissa S. Kearney, "The Polarization of the U.S. Labor Market," *American Economic Review* 96, no. 2 (May 2006): 189–94 (6).

[49] Thomas Piketty and Emmanuel Saez credit the progressive income tax with reducing income inequality in the United States since the 1930s. See their argument in "Income Inequality in the United States, 1913–1998," *Quarterly Journal of Economics* 118, no. 1 (February 2003): 1–39.

FIGURE 14.5 TWO PERSPECTIVES ON TAX CUTS

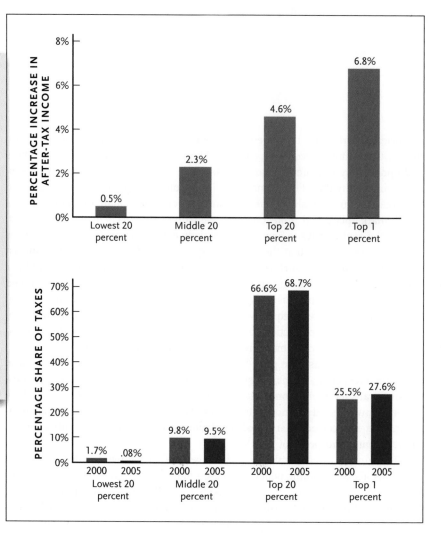

SOURCES: Center on Budget and Policy Priorities, www.cbpp.org/3-19-07tax.htm; Congressional Budget Office, www.cbo.gov/ftpdocs/61xx/doc6133/03-01-EffectiveTaxRates.pdf; and www.cbo.gov/ftpdocs/88xx/doc8885/EffectiveTaxRates.shtml (accessed 3/22/08).

Likewise, income-tax rates can be reduced for all groups, but depending on the proportion of tax cuts for each group, some income brackets may benefit more than others. One of the major criticisms of the tax cuts of 2001, 2003, and 2006 is that they increased the gap between rich and poor by allowing the rich to retain a greater proportion of their after-tax income than did middle- and lower-income taxpayers. The liberal Center for Budget and Policy Priorities analyzed the impact of these tax cuts. As Figure 14.5 shows, the tax cuts allowed households in the bottom fifth of the income range to keep an additional 0.5 percent of their pretax

FIGURE 14.6 CHANGE IN AVERAGE AFTER-TAX INCOME, 1979–2005

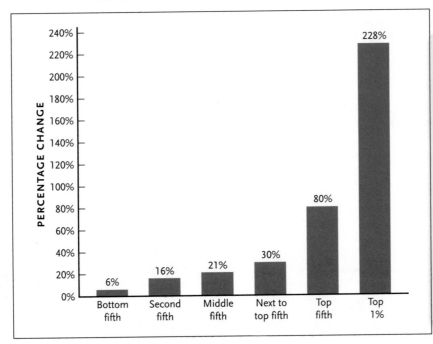

SOURCE: Center on Budget and Policy Priorities, www.cbpp.org/12-14-07inc.htm (accessed 3/19/08).

ANALYZING THE EVIDENCE

Income inequality has grown substantially as the gains from growth have gone disproportionately to the wealthy. The income of the top 1 percent of earners increased by well over 200 percent, whereas that of the bottom fifth of the income distribution has increased by only 6 percent since 1979. What has happened to the income of the middle class over this time period?

income. For the middle-income group, after-tax income grew by 2.3 percent, while the top 20 percent gained 4.6 in after-tax income. The gains for the top 1 percent of households was much larger: an increase of 6.8 percent of after-tax income each year.[50] These differences matter because long-terms trends in growth are widening the gap between rich and poor, as Figure 14.6 shows. Because after-tax incomes are *more unequal* as a consequence of the tax changes, liberals identify them as a regressive tax change. The "Analyzing the Evidence" section on the following page takes a closer look at the income gap.

Conservatives take a different view. They argue that even with these changes, the rich paid by far the greatest share of federal taxes. In fact, as the second half of Figure 14.5 shows, in 2005, the top fifth of households paid 68.7 percent of all taxes, whereas the bottom fifth paid less than 1 percent. Most crucial in judging the impact of the tax cuts, the rich paid a *larger share* of the total federal tax bill after the tax cuts than before. As Figure 14.5 shows, the share of the total tax bill fell for households in the lowest- and middle-income categories, but it increased for the top categories. Therefore, although the lowest group paid .09 percent *less* as a share of total taxes, the top 20 percent of earners paid 2.1 percent *more*.

---

[50] Tax Policy Center, Table T06-0279, Combined Effect of the 2001–2006 Tax Cuts, Distribution of Federal Tax Change by Cash Income Percentile, 2006, November 13, 2006, www.taxpolicycenter.org/numbers/displayatab.cfm?Docid=1361&DocTypeID=2 (accessed 4/20/09).

The Income Gap

Examined carefully, data often raise more questions than they answer. When viewing a table or figure, especially in the context of policy debates, it is usually prudent to make a list of the questions raised by the data presented rather than simply accepting the interpretation offered by the analyst presenting the data. Take, for example, the so-called income gap that has become a major issue in contemporary American politics. As indicated by the table below, in the last several years the difference or "gap" between the share of America's income going to the richest and poorest segments of the population has been increasing. Many Democrats blame Republican tax cuts for making the rich richer and the poor poorer and assert that major changes in tax policy are needed to restore a measure of equality to American society.

THE PROPORTION OF MONEY INCOME GOING TO EACH FIFTH OF THE POPULATION									
Family Income Bracket	1929 (%)	1934 (%)	1944 (%)	1950 (%)	1960 (%)	1970 (%)	1980 (%)	1990 (%)	2006 (%)
Lowest fifth	5.4	5.9	4.9	4.5	4.8	4.1	4.3	3.9	3.4
Second fifth	10.1	11.5	10.9	12.0	12.2	10.8	10.3	9.6	8.6
Third fifth	14.4	15.5	16.2	17.4	17.8	17.4	16.9	15.9	14.5
Fourth fifth	18.8	20.4	22.2	23.5	24.0	24.5	24.9	24.0	22.9
Highest fifth	51.3	49.7	45.8	42.6	41.3	43.3	43.7	46.6	50.5
Gap between lowest and highest fifths	45.9	43.8	40.9	38.1	36.5	39.2	39.4	42.7	47.1

Note: Figures are not strictly comparable because of difference in calculating procedures.

Source: Data for 1929–50, Allan Rosenbaum, "State Government, Political Power, and Public Policy: The Case of Illinois" (Ph.D. diss., University of Chicago, 1974), chaps. 10–11, used by permission; for 1960–2006, *Statistical Abstract of the U.S.*, 2009, Table 675.

These data may indicate an emergent social problem in the United States, but at least two questions must be answered before we can draw any meaningful conclusions from them and before we can make policy recommendations. First, the data deal with differences among income groups but they do not show the absolute income of any group. It is possible that all income groups are better off today than they were in prior years. If everyone is better off, perhaps we do not want to change our tax policies, even if they tend to increase income inequality. This possibility is at least partially borne out by census data: Between 1980 and 2004, the average incomes of every income group increased—though the incomes of the wealthiest Americans increased more sharply than those of any others.

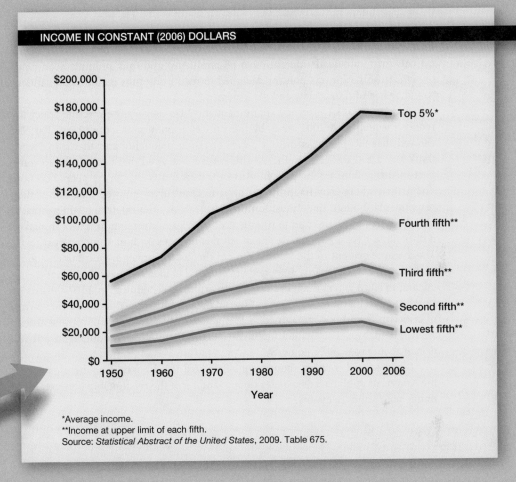

INCOME IN CONSTANT (2006) DOLLARS

Top 5%*

Fourth fifth**

Third fifth**

Second fifth**

Lowest fifth**

Year

*Average income.
**Income at upper limit of each fifth.
Source: *Statistical Abstract of the United States*, 2009. Table 675.

A second consideration is that the data showing a growing income gap deal with aggregates, not individuals. We cannot know from the data presented whether families are generally locked into a particular income quartile or are likely to move from year to year. If the latter, then the apparent increase in inequality shown in the first table is at least mitigated by social mobility. In recent years, for example, the percentage of black families in the lowest income group has decreased more sharply than the percentage of white families in that group. At the same time, the percentage of black families in the highest income group has increased more substantially than their white counterparts, suggesting that there is social mobility across the income groups.[1] Thus, in considering the income gap, we may want to consider whether policies designed to reduce inequality might interfere with social mobility.

[1]*Statistical Abstract of the United States*, 2007. Table 676.

What is fair? So long as the rich still pay a higher proportion of their income in taxes, should we worry that the tax cuts are making after-tax income distribution more unequal? After all, as the rich have gotten richer, they have paid an ever higher share of the total federal tax bill. The answer to this question depends on different views about the consequences of income inequality. Those who believe that the growth of income inequality harms the middle class by increasing prices or undermines democracy believe that tax policy should be designed to decrease these inequalities.[51] Those who think that inequality is not a major problem believe that tax cuts give individuals incentives to be productive and thus promote economic growth. In this view, tax policies designed to reduce after-tax income inequalities would be harmful to society and the economy.[52]

Are Americans concerned about inequality? Do they want economic policy to reduce inequality? A 2003 study by the Princeton political scientist Larry Bartels showed that the public is indeed aware of rising inequality and that a majority think it is a bad thing. Nonetheless, his research showed that people "fail to connect inequality and public policy." Part of the reason is that many people do not understand where they fit in the tax system. One survey showed that half of the respondents thought that "most families" have to pay the estate tax, when in fact only 2 percent of estates had to pay the tax. Americans' aversion to taxes can make it difficult to have a national debate about raising taxes on higher-income earners. This became evident in the waning days of the 2008 campaign. Questioned about his tax plan, Barack Obama defended his proposal to increase taxes for higher earners and to allow many Bush-era tax cuts to expire as scheduled, in 2010. Obama's casual remark that it made sense to "spread the wealth around" ignited a firestorm of criticism from his opponent John McCain, who had pledged not to raise taxes at all. The debate that ensued highlighted the difficulties in conducting a public debate about taxes and inequality.

If widespread concern about inequality is to drive changes in economic policy, the American public needs a better understanding of the relationship between economic policy and inequality.

CONCLUSION: HISTORY AND OPPORTUNITY IN ECONOMIC POLICY

Increased government intervention in the economy is often brought about by the economic crises engendered by market failures such as collapsing "bubbles." Such crises often are opportunities for the introduction of new programs and policies

---

[51] Robert H. Frank, *Falling Behind: How Rising Inequality Harms the Middle Class* (Berkeley: University of California Press, 2007).

[52] For a classic statement, see Milton Friedman and Rose Friedman, *Free to Choose* (New York: Harvest Books, 1990). See also Bruce Bartlett, "Is Income Inequality Really a Problem?" *New York Times*, January 24, 2007, http://bartlett.blogs.nytimes.com/2007/01/24/is-income-inequality-really-a-problem/ (accessed 4/20/09).

that had been rejected as misguided or too radical in normal times. During times of crisis, the iron hand of historical precedent is relaxed, and policy makers are offered opportunities to try new approaches. Thus, during the Great Depression of the 1930s, the Roosevelt administration experimented with new forms of economic policy, such as wage and price controls, that had previously been seen as inconsistent with American peacetime tradition.

As Obama took office in 2009, his administration indicated that it would be considering new economic policies such as "industrial policy," which entails government efforts to promote certain favored industries; energy policies that would compel firms to develop and use solar, wind, and biomass power; and financial policies that would require banks seeking government assistance to increase their lending activities and to halt foreclosures. President Obama's former chief of staff, Rahm Emanuel, called the economic crisis "an opportunity to do things you could not do before." Emanuel observed that, "You never want a serious crisis to go to waste."[53] History always matters, but at some times it matters less than at other times.

FOR FURTHER READING

Barth, James, Gerard Caprio, and Ross Levine. *Rethinking Bank Regulation*. New York: Cambridge University Press, 2005.

Farrier, Jasmine. *Passing the Buck: Congress, the Budget, and Deficits*. Lexington: University Press of Kentucky, 2004.

Ingham, Geoffrey. *The Nature of Money*. New York: Polity, 2004.

Keith, Robert, and Allen Schick. *The Federal Budget Process*. New York: Nova, 2003.

Madrick, Jeff. *The Case for Big Government*. Princeton, N.J.: Princeton University Press, 2008.

Meyers, Annette. *Evolution of United States Budgeting*. New York: Praeger, 2002.

Sachs, Jeffrey. *The End of Poverty: Economic Possibilities for Our Time*. New York: Penguin, 2006.

Stern, Gary, and Ron Feldman. *Too Big to Fail: The Hazards of Bank Bailouts*. Washington, D.C.: Brookings Institution, 2004.

Stiglitz, Joseph. *Making Globalization Work*. New York: Norton, 2006.

Wells, Donald. *The Federal Reserve System*. Jefferson, N.C.: McFarland, 2004.

Wilson, Graham. *Business and Politics*. Washington, D.C.: Congressional Quarterly Press, 2003.

reader selection

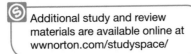

Additional study and review materials are available online at wwnorton.com/studyspace/

---

[53] Jonathan Weisman, "Wider U.S. Interventions Would Yield Winners, Losers as Industries Realign," *Wall Street Journal*, November 20, 2008, p. A6.

15

Social Policy

One policy area in which history has made America different from other Western democracies is the domain of social policy. Unlike people in many other Western democracies, Americans do not have a long history of taking public responsibility for inequalities of opportunity. The United States was, in fact, one of the last Western democracies to enter this realm of social policy, for a number of reasons. First, Americans' faith in individualism was extremely strong. Second, that faith was long fed by the existence of the frontier, which was so enticing that poverty was seen as a temporary condition that could be alleviated by moving westward. Third, Americans conceived of poverty as belonging in two separate classes: the "deserving poor" and the "undeserving poor." The deserving poor were the widows, orphans, and others rendered dependent by some misfortune beyond their control, such as national disaster, injury in the course of honest labor, or the effects of war. The undeserving poor were able-bodied persons unwilling to work, transients, or others of whom, for various reasons, the community did not approve. An extensive system of private charity developed during the nineteenth century on the basis of the distinction between the deserving poor and the undeserving poor. Most of this welfare came from churches, related religious groups, and to an extent, ethnic and fraternal societies. It was called charity, or "Christian love," and was often coupled with a high moral sense of obligation.

Until the end of the nineteenth century, government involvement in charitable activities, or what we today call *welfare*, was slight, not only because of Americans' preference for individual endeavors and private, voluntary approaches to charity, but also because Americans believed that all the deserving poor would be taken care of by private efforts. Congress did enact pensions for Civil War veterans and their dependents, and for its day this was considered a generous social policy. But those pension policies were badly undercut by a patronage-ridden administration responsible for the benefits, thus damaging the system and depriving a large segment of American citizens of federal aid.[1] Congress also attempted to reach lower-income groups with policies that would eliminate child labor, and a number of states joined in with attempts to eliminate the most dangerous and unsanitary working conditions. But these efforts were soon declared unconstitutional by the Supreme Court. Other efforts, such as the experiment with mothers' pensions and additional protective labor policies, were adopted by a few progressive states. But even as late as 1928, only 11.6 percent of all relief granted in fifteen of the largest cities came from public funds.[2]

The traditional approach, dominated by the private sector, with its severe distinction between deserving and undeserving poor, crumbled in 1929 before the stark reality of the Great Depression. During the

---

[1] See Suzanne Mettler, *Divided Citizens: Gender and Federalism in New Deal Public Policy* (Ithaca, N.Y.: Cornell University Press, 1998), p. 2. See also Theda Skocpol, *Protecting Soldiers and Mothers: The Political Origins of Social Policy in the United States* (Cambridge, Mass.: Harvard University Press, 1992).

[2] Merle Fainsod, Lincoln Gordon, and Joseph C. Palamountain, Jr., *Government and the American Economy*, 3rd ed. (New York: Norton, 1959), p. 769, based on a WPA study by Ann E. Geddes.

CORE OF THE ANALYSIS

- After the Great Depression and the New Deal, the national government assumed greater responsibility for social policies related to broadening opportunity and addressing poverty.

- However, because social policies are often redistributive, it can be difficult to get social issues on the government's agenda.

- Critics of social welfare policies have argued that these policies create a moral hazard by providing the wrong incentives to recipients.

- But reducing or changing the social welfare system is difficult, given the size and strength of the groups who benefit from contributory programs like Social Security and could oppose any attempt to eliminate such programs.

Depression, misfortune became widespread and private wealth shrank so drastically that private charity was out of the question. The Great Depression proved to Americans that poverty could be a result of imperfections in the economic system rather than a result of individual irresponsibility. Americans held to their distinction between the deserving and the undeserving poor but significantly altered their standard of who was deserving and who was not.

Once poverty and dependency were accepted as problems inherent in the economy, a large-scale public policy approach became practical. Indeed, there was no longer any real question about whether the national government would assume a major responsibility for poverty; from that time forward, it was a question of how generous or restrictive the government was going to be about the welfare of the poor. The national government's efforts to improve the welfare of the poor can be divided into two responses. First, it instituted policies that attempted to change the economic rules about the conditions of work for those who were working and could work. Second, it set in place policies seeking to change the economic rules determining the quality of life of those who could not (and, in some cases, would not) work. The first response comes under the heading of policies for labor regulation. We dealt with some of these policies in Chapter 3, showing how the Constitution itself, especially the commerce clause, had to be interpreted in a fundamentally different way to reach into local plants and firms to improve the conditions and rewards of work. Since the adoption of the 1935 National Labor Relations Act (the Wagner Act), there have been revisions (for example, the Taft-Hartley Labor-Management Relations Act of 1947 and the Landrum-Griffin Labor-Management Reporting and Disclosure Act of 1959), but there has been no real change in the economic rules established in 1935. These rules were designed to protect laborers so that they could organize and bargain collectively with their employers rather than (according to the older economic rules) being forced to negotiate as individuals under vastly unequal conditions.

That same year, 1935, Congress also adopted the historic Social Security Act. As defined and detailed later in this chapter, the program applied to a far larger segment of the population than the Wagner Act, which applied almost exclusively to wage workers in heavy industry who were represented by trade unions. At the start, and as later expanded, Social Security programs covered the vast majority of Americans: all wage earners, temporarily unemployed workers seeking work, survivors of eligible workers, the elderly, and disabled persons. Later Congress enacted the minimum wage, which had a modest beginning in the Fair Labor Standards Act of 1938. Efforts were made several times to establish a minimum annual income. Although these efforts failed, a program accomplishing part of the same objective, the earned income tax credit (EITC), was adopted in 1975. Aimed at working families near the officially recognized poverty line, EITC gives a tax credit for each dollar earned up to a certain point, and then the payments are phased out as the worker's income rises. As of 2008, the income levels set for eligibility for EITC payments ranged from $12,880 for a married couple without children to $38,646 for a couple with two or more children.

The grip of history and Americans' traditional views about individual responsibility and poverty were relaxed but never released by the Great Depression. As in the realm of economic policy, a crisis created opportunities for new policy directions. However, America never truly lost its historic discomfort with social policy, and the United States still spends a far lower percentage of its wealth on social programs than do other Western governments. In the United States, social spending amounts to less than 20 percent of the nation's gross domestic product (GDP). In most of the European Union, social spending accounts for nearly 30 percent of national GDPs.

WHAT IS SOCIAL POLICY?

The term *social policy* refers to programs promoting a range of public goals. The first is to protect against the risks and insecurities that most people face over the course of their lives. These include illness, disability, temporary unemployment, and the reduced earning capability that comes with old age. Most spending on social welfare in the United States goes to programs such as Social Security and medical insurance for the elderly that serve these purposes. These are widely regarded as successful and popular programs. They are the least controversial areas of social spending, although the debates about funding Social Security reveal that even widely agreed-on policies can generate conflict. Such conflicts over how to balance security against risks have prevented the United States from adopting universal health insurance. Despite the fact that most Americans support a public role in guaranteeing health coverage, disputes over how such coverage should be provided have blocked repeated efforts at health-care reform.

More controversial have been the other two goals of social policy: promoting **equality of opportunity** and assisting the poor. Although Americans admire the ideal of equal opportunity, there is no general agreement about what government should do to address inequalities: Groups that have suffered from past inequality generally support much more extensive governmental action to promote equality of opportunity than do others. Yet most Americans favor some governmental action, especially in the area of education.

equality of opportunity
A universally shared American ideal, according to which all have the freedom to use whatever talents and wealth they possess to reach their full potential.

The third goal of social policy—to alleviate poverty—has long generated controversy in the United States. Americans take pride in their strong work ethic and prize the value of self-sufficiency. As a result, the majority of Americans seem to suspect that the able-bodied poor will not try to support themselves if they are offered "too much" assistance or if they receive the wrong kind. Yet there is also recognition that poverty may be the product of past inequality of opportunity. Since the 1960s, a variety of educational programs and income-assistance policies have sought to end poverty and promote equal opportunity. Much progress has been made toward these goals. However, the disproportionate rates of poverty among minorities suggest that our policies have not solved the problem of unequal opportunity. Likewise, the high rates of poverty among children challenge us to find new ways to assist the poor.

There is no way to know precisely when the government ought to be called on and what the government ought to do to help individuals secure the right to pursue their own happiness. Economic and social transformations pose new challenges and often alter public views about what government should do. In the 1930s, a deep and widespread economic depression created broad public support for new federal programs such as unemployment insurance. Today the increased number of women in the labor force and the growth in single-parent households have prompted calls for more government assistance to help people combine work and family responsibilities more effectively. Yet there is no agreement on what government should do. Likewise, as the economy has changed, inequality among working people has grown. Should the government address such inequality? If so, with what measures? When patterns of risk and opportunity are shifted, citizens make new demands, thereby placing social policy issues at the center of national politics.

The first section of this chapter deals with the politics of social policy. The second section deals with policies concerned with increasing security by reducing the risk of poverty and dependence. Most of these policies come under the conventional label of "social security" or "social insurance," which concerns the *contributory* part of the welfare state. The third section focuses on welfare or the welfare system, which is also concerned with the alleviation of poverty and dependence but is the *noncontributory*, or "means-tested" dimension—eligibility to receive benefits is based on demonstrated need. The two dimensions together—contributory and noncontributory—make up the "welfare state." This section concludes with a consideration of recent efforts to reform the system. The fourth section deals with social policies that fall outside the realm of civil rights policies but are nevertheless concerned primarily with increasing opportunities for the poor and the underprivileged. The final section is a dialogue on the welfare state, including a discussion of efforts at reform by its supporters and opponents throughout its history.

THE POLITICS OF SOCIAL POLICY

There is no way to predict when political leaders will decide to put a social issue on the policy agenda. Such predictions are especially difficult to make when issues involve questions of rights. The unprecedented crisis of the Great Depression made it possible to put Social Security and the welfare state on the policy agenda. The foundations of the welfare state were in place by 1935. But ten years later, at the end of World War II, when women and African Americans had emerged as true participants in American society, not a single new social policy had been produced. The postwar economy broke all records for growth, but poverty and minority unrest also increased—without a single step being made to address the expectations and demands of these new groups. One of the most important documents in the history of social policy in the United States is *To Secure These Rights*, composed by President Harry Truman's Committee on Civil Rights and published in 1947. It set the terms of discourse for the ensuing five years and helped spur the litigation by the National Association for the Advancement of Colored People and its famous special counsel, Thurgood Marshall, who would take *Brown v. Board of Education* to the Supreme Court in 1954.[3] Marshall was later nominated to the Supreme Court and became the nation's first black justice. But that stunning and unusually well-written Truman committee document, coupled with the brilliant legal maneuverings of Marshall and his associates, did not put civil rights and equal opportunity on any public policy agenda at the time. A sense of urgency did not produce widespread agreement on what the government ought to do. Should we address inequality at all? If so, with what measures and techniques? What to do and when to do it? How to do it? To what end?

The process of forging social policy sounds like the usual noise of democratic politics: Interest groups, mass opinions, political parties, and public appeals interact at all levels with representative institutions, culminating in legislation that passes into the agencies of the executive branch for implementation. However, it is important to note that social policies are redistributive. Redistributive policies form a special category of public policy, which we identified and discussed, along with promotional and regulatory policies, in Chapter 14. For example, a tiny increase in the tax liability of the top income earners or a tiny increase in Social Security benefits for those with the lowest incomes can result in a significant transfer of income from the upper income brackets to the lower. Or a tiny boost or reduction in interest rates can redistribute economic opportunities, as well as hard cash, shifting them between the investing classes and the working classes. Because of their potential redistributive effect, it is extremely difficult to get social policies on the agenda of the president and Congress, who fear the wrath of negatively affected groups. For the same reason, once a social policy is adopted, it tends to remain on the statute books as though it were untouchable. This is why in recent years social policies have often been referred to as the "third rail" of American politics.

To repeat for the sake of clarity, redistributive policies are special because their effect cuts across class lines. *Class* is not limited to rich versus poor or employees versus employers. Other major cleavages in society are worthy of the term *class,* such as labor-intensive industries versus capital-intensive industries. Other significant class cleavages are age versus youth, female versus male, white versus black, agricultural versus commercial, and even, very generally, seaboard (blue states) versus interior (red states). Many critics of social policy raise the specter

---

[3] *Brown v. Board of Education,* 347 U.S. 483 (1954).

of "class warfare" whenever a new social policy is proposed. But class cleavage does not have to be warfare. In fact, the interest-group politics that tends to be the prevailing pattern characterizing regulatory and promotional policies can be a lot more intense than class politics. For example, on issues of the regulation and sale of guns and the registration of gun owners, the formidable National Rifle Association—one of the most influential interest groups in the country—rises up as if going into battle, arguing that even the smallest intrusion on "the right to bear arms" would destroy the Constitution and our society itself. In contrast, on Social Security reform, AARP—probably the *most* influential and largest of all interest groups—speaks with a single voice, "as a class," for all retired persons and those soon to retire. AARP was the leading foe of President Bush's Social Security reforms. In the last two weeks of March 2005, AARP reportedly spent $5 million on anti-Bush ads, nearly three times as much as all expenditures of all groups supporting President Bush on Social Security. AARP was, of course, denounced by the other side, yet key White House aides worked with AARP in an effort to find "common ground," and AARP officials let it be known that they were not averse to changing Social Security but were mainly opposing the Bush plan for private accounts.[4]

It is also fair to compare recent Social Security–type issues with the politics of President Bush's proposal for caps on the fees that tort lawyers can charge for winning product-liability, doctor-negligence, and other damage suits, especially class action suits. In response, tort lawyers mobilized around their national association and became the leading interest group opposing caps, pitting their efforts against those of other divisions of the American Bar Association, the insurance companies, doctors (especially gynecologists and obstetricians), hospital associations, and so on. Another case of the politics of regulatory economic policy, the regulation of pharmaceuticals, is one subset of the larger issue of product liability. Manufacturers of medications such as Vioxx and Celebrex are a formidable interest group battling the trial lawyers and a variety of consumer groups and alternate drug producers to keep Congress from tightening safety measures, especially expensive and time-consuming testing procedures. Competition among interest groups often comes close to warfare.

Care should be taken here not to let the politics of policy making overshadow a prior phase: the *agenda*. Policy making is the end of a long process. Chapter 5 lays out how a bill becomes a law, but before that, and just as important, is how a bill becomes a bill. Any member of Congress can propose a bill. It is read once by the presiding officer and then referred to a committee, where it can die after a long waiting period. To survive, it has to be moved up to a higher priority, the real agenda of Congress.

An agenda is simply a list of things to be done. Many people call their appointment book their agenda. But in collective decision making, an agenda remains a list of things to be done, and getting on the policy agenda of a legislature or a

---

[4] See especially Jeffrey H. Birnbaum, "Listen to the Wallet—AARP Has Become a Formidable Foe of President Bush's Social Security Plan," *Washington Post*, national weekly edition, April 4–10, 2005, pp. 11–12.

president is difficult—and probably the most creative phase of the entire policy-making process. In this institutional context, the agenda can be seen as the current list of agreements on what to discuss and debate.

Lacking the capacity to agree on what to debate, a legislative assembly is doomed. The popular picture of representative government presents a legislature made up of representatives, all equal in having been elected from a "constituency," who debate for as long as necessary, then call for a vote on the bill. But if the legislature is to be what the name implies, a giver of the laws, it must depart from that ideal of equality among representatives and organize itself in a way that allows it to control the order of the items to be considered—which comes first, second, and third; the rules of debate and amendment; and the terms of when the debate will be closed and the vote taken. Moreover, the yea-or-nay vote after formal debate is the end process; important issues are not born in a simple two-part debate format. It is a prime function of the two major parties, probably their most important function, to compose the agenda, enforce the order of priority, control the time allotted, and provide and police the procedures governing debate and passage. None of this has anything to do with which side of the issue one is on. The two major parties have to operate in virtual unanimity to make the legislative process work, largely because the agenda requires nonpartisan, bipartisan, virtual unanimous agreement.

We may oversimplify politics and make bad judgments about political power by adding up who got what in the policies produced by government. We also have to take into account what kinds of issues are kept off the agenda and never come up for any attention whatsoever.[5] For example, it took the 1954 Supreme Court decision and ten years of mass movements coupled with the assassination of John F. Kennedy to get the first serious civil rights bill on Congress's agenda. For another, more complex example, it takes a majority of members to get an issue of any sort assigned to a congressional committee agenda and then placed on Congress's formal agenda (the Calendar), but given the filibuster rule in the Senate, it takes a three-fifths vote (sixty senators) to get it on the *real* agenda for debate and an up-or-down roll-call vote. Republicans kept many of President Bill Clinton's judicial nominees off the agenda by bottling up their names in the Senate Judiciary Committee. Democrats paid them back, keeping a number of President George W. Bush's judicial nominees off the agenda by threatening to filibuster any nominee reported from the Republican-controlled Judiciary Committee to the Senate. A lot of power is at stake in that workaday word *agenda*.

Agenda is equally a presidential concern. The president's party and indeed the entire membership of Congress depend on the president to mobilize the public in support of key issues. This is part of what is sometimes called presidential initiative. As President Obama took office in 2009, he brought with him an extensive set of plans for economic and social policy changes that would shape Congress's

---

[5] A classic argument on this point is Peter Bachrach and M. S. Baratz, "Two Faces of Power," *American Political Science Review* 56, no. 4 (December 1962): 947–52. On the basis of their research, Bachrach and Baratz conclude that pluralism is not very democratic because, despite vigorous competition among interest groups and the universalization of suffrage, groups representing lower or less-respected classes do not have power because their demands rarely get on the agenda at all.

agenda. The presidential initiative is not only the mobilization of one issue and one proposal at a time; Congress also depends on the president to coordinate and set priorities for issues. Since the 1950s, this aspect of the president's role has come to be called the president's program. That concept was virtually the first insight that led to recognition of the transformation of the "new American state" from a "congressional government" to a "presidential government."[6]

Presidential initiative is most important when the policy at issue is a redistributive social policy. This is because mass support on either side of such an issue is so much more difficult to mobilize than the support that is already mobilized and well organized by the interest groups that dominate in the regulatory and promotion field of public policy. An entire class of people is too large and too diffuse to become suddenly organized when an issue arises. This is why issues such as Social Security and welfare and income tax structure get on the national agenda only once in ten or twenty years. It has been nearly twenty years since Social Security was last up for serious reconsideration. And, despite the fact that President Bush made Social Security reform a major campaign issue in 2004 and gave it high priority in his State of the Union address of 2005, coupled with an intensive nationwide campaign for Social Security reform in early 2005, it did not reach the agenda for full consideration in the House and Senate that year, and by October 2005 the president had to admit that Social Security reform was dead for the forseeable future. For another example, the "noncontributory" welfare programs (discussed below) had *never* been on Congress's agenda for fundamental reform until 1996, and they came up then only because Republicans broke all modern records by winning control of Congress in 1994 and convincing President Clinton that cooperation with conservatives was the only way to survive the 1996 election. Finally, Medicare reform was put on the agenda in 2004 for the first time since 1972–73.

In contrast, regulatory and promotional policy issues in such important economic areas as energy, the environment, communications, agriculture, and international trade get regular airings because virtually every sector of the economy is represented by highly specialized interest groups. Their proposals are not always adopted as new law, but interest groups represented by prominent Washington lobbyists can get their issues on the agenda, accompanied by thoroughly researched documents and the participation of experts in hearings by congressional committees, and then on to the floor for debate.

We turn now to the most important of those policies that seek to change the rules regarding (1) who shall be poor, (2) how poor the government will allow them to be, and (3) who, for whatever reason, will be provided for because they cannot work or otherwise find the means to provide for themselves. These policies together make up what we have come to call the welfare state.

---

[6]Two classic articles on this development of the president's program were published by Richard Neustadt: "Presidency and Legislation: The Growth of Central Clearance," *American Political Science Review* 48, no. 3 (September 1954): 641–71; and "Presidency and Legislation: Planning the President's Program," *American Political Science Review* 49, no. 4 (December 1955): 980–1021.

WHAT ARE THE FOUNDATIONS OF THE SOCIAL WELFARE SYSTEM?

The foundations of the American welfare system were established by the Social Security Act of 1935. Table 15.1 presents an outline of the key programs in the social welfare system.

Social Security

Contributory programs are financed by taxation, which justifiably can be called forced savings. These contributory programs are what most people have in mind when they refer to **Social Security**, or social insurance. Under the original retirement program, Old-Age Insurance, the employer and the employee were required to pay equal amounts, which in 1937 was set at 1 percent of the first $3,000 of wages, to be deducted from the paycheck of each employee and matched by the employer. This percentage has increased over the years; the total contribution is now 7.65 percent, subdivided as follows: 6.2 percent on the first $87,900 of income for Social Security benefits, plus 1.45 percent on all earnings for Medicare.[7]

Social Security is a rather conservative approach to welfare. In effect, the Federal Insurance Contributions Act (FICA) tax, as Social Security is formally known, sends a message that people cannot be trusted to save voluntarily to take care of their retirement needs. But in another sense, it is quite radical. Social Security is not real insurance: Workers' contributions do not accumulate in a personal account as an annuity does. Consequently, contributors do not receive benefits in proportion to their contributions, and this means that there is a redistribution of wealth. In brief, contributory Social Security mildly redistributes wealth from higher- to lower-income people, and it significantly redistributes wealth from younger workers to older retirees. Since 1972, Social Security benefits and costs have been adjusted through **indexing**, whereby benefits paid out under contributory programs are modified annually by cost-of-living adjustments (COLAs) based on changes in the consumer price index, so that benefits increase automatically as the cost of living rises. And to pay for these automatic adjustments, Social Security taxes (contributions) also increased. These changes made Social Security, in the words of one observer, "a politically ideal program. It bridged partisan conflict by providing liberal benefits under conservative financial auspices."[8] In other words, conservatives could more readily yield to the demands of the well-organized and expanding constituency of elderly voters if benefit increases were guaranteed and automatic, and liberals could cement conservative support by agreeing to finance the expanded

contributory program A social program financed in whole or in part by taxation or other mandatory contributions by its present or future recipients. The most important example is Social Security, which is financed by a payroll tax.

Social Security A contributory welfare program into which working Americans place a percentage of their wages and from which they receive cash benefits after retirement.

indexing The process of periodically adjusting social benefits or wages to account for increases in the cost of living.

---

[7] The figures cited are for 2004. Although on paper the employer is taxed, the full amount is part of forced savings because in reality the employer's contribution is nothing more than a mandatory wage supplement that the employee never sees or touches before it goes into the trust funds held exclusively for the contributory programs.

[8] Edward J. Harpham, "Fiscal Crisis and the Politics of Social Security Reform," in *The Attack on the Welfare State*, Anthony Champagne and Edward J. Harpham, eds. (Prospect Heights, Ill.: Waveland Press, 1984), p. 13.

TABLE 15.1 PUBLIC WELFARE PROGRAMS

	Year Enacted	Federal Outlays (2008 estimate in billions of dollars)	Federal Outlays (2009 estimate in billions of dollars)	Federal Outlays (2010 estimate in billions of dollars)
Contributory				
Old-Age and Survivors Insurance; Disability Insurance (Social Security)	1935	617	652	690
Medicare	1965	403	413	427
Unemployment compensation	1935	37	43	41
Noncontributory				
Medicaid	1965	204	216	230
Food Stamps	1964	39	40	41
Supplemental Security Income	1974	38	40	42
National School Lunch Program (listed as Child Nutrition and Special Milk Programs)	1946	14	15	15
Temporary Assistance for Needy Families (TANF, listed as Family Support Payments to States)	1996	21	21	21

SOURCE: Office of Management and Budget, *Budget of the U.S. Government, Fiscal Year 2008, Historical Tables* (Washington, D.C.: Government Printing Office, 2007), Table 11.3, pp. 205–229.

benefits through increases in the regressive Social Security tax rather than through general revenues from the more progressive income tax.

The Politics of Reforming Social Security. In 2007, nearly 50 million Americans received almost $525 billion in Social Security benefits, distributed to 42 million retirees and dependents or survivors and 8 million disabled people—up by more than 2 million since 2003.[9] For more than half of all American workers, Social Security is their only pension plan. And if there were no Social Security, half of all

---

[9] See www.socialsecurity.gov.

senior citizens would be living below the poverty line. No wonder Social Security is called the untouchable "third rail" of American politics.

Social Security has had its moments of potential crisis, but the only real crisis was in the late 1970s, triggered by the earlier decision to index benefits to the cost of living. The historic (for America) inflation of the 1970s caused the crisis, and it was readily "fixed" by increasing the payroll tax and the level of earnings (the cap) to which the tax applied. But a more fundamental reform would have to come as the ratio between contributing workers and retirees declined, from a comfortable sixteen contributors to one retiree downward toward three contributors to one retiree. With the record-breaking retirement of the baby boomers beginning around 2010, the ratio of contributors to workers is expected to drop toward two to one in coming years. Fear is therefore growing in all circles that contributions today will not pay for the retirements of tomorrow. Up to now, the system has run with a surplus. But the low ratio of contributors to retirees coupled with projected higher life expectancies could bankrupt the system. That is, without reform.

Bankruptcy will never be permitted, not only because it would be a national moment of shame but also because retired persons are already too large a class to permit it, and their political clout will be greater still as baby boomers retire. All contributions are to be deposited in a Social Security Trust Fund, which officially earns interest at the average level for U.S. government securities. But that is a myth. The U.S. Treasury regularly borrows money from the trust fund and leaves IOUs to hide—or soften the impression of—the true national debt in this country. Thus the Social Security system, through no fault of its own but due to the irresponsibility of successive Democratic and Republican administrations, turned out to be a pay-as-you-go program in which today's youth take care of today's aged. That is what we mean when we say that Social Security provides for the redistribution of some wealth from the youth to the elderly.

Reforms have been proposed but tossed aside. One of the best ideas—and certainly the earliest, going back to the 1940s, when the system was just beginning to take hold—was to safeguard the reserve (the trust fund) by having the Treasury invest the contributions in *private* securities, earning interest and at the same time keeping the reserve safely away from politics and government. One of the elder statesmen of that time retorted, "Why, that would be socialism!" A more recent reform, on which Al Gore staked his 2000 presidential campaign, was simply to respect the trust fund by keeping it in interest-bearing government securities but in a "locked box," unavailable to serve as a hidden part of the national debt. Gore's position was ridiculed.

Social Security got its boost to the top of the domestic policy agenda from President George W. Bush, not during his first term but after his reelection in 2004. And he pushed reform all the more intensely because of his awareness that 2005 might be his only chance to succeed—since AARP was campaigning to make 2006 an election year that would frighten a large number of Republican representatives in whose districts there were a significant number of retired persons, who are any election's most likely voters. As the *Economist* put it, "If [Social Security is] the third rail of American politics, the AARP generates much of the lethal current."[10] That threat called for equal intensity in return from Bush. The president began with a

---

[10] "The AARP—Still the Biggest Bruiser?" *Economist*, February 5, 2005, p. 26.

The Social Security Crisis: Arguing From the Evidence

Policy advocates often present evidence designed to convince readers that a particular set of programs and policies is needed to deal with a problem or to avert some future disaster. One common form of evidence is the projection. In a projection, data are arrayed to indicate what is likely to happen in the future if present trends continue. Projections should be read cautiously. First, present trends do not always continue, and second, the same evidence can support a number of alternative policy recommendations—not simply the one offered by the particular advocate. Take the case of Social Security.

Since Franklin D. Roosevelt signed the Social Security Act into law in 1935, millions of Americans have come to depend on monthly Social Security checks as their chief source of retirement income. Benefits are based on the number of years an individual worked and the amount of income he or she earned prior to retirement. Individuals can retire as early as age 62 and be eligible for Social Security benefits. However, the amount they receive each month increases if they delay retirement for several years. In 2006, the U.S. Social Security program payed out more than $500 billion in retirement, health care, and disability benefits. The Social Security program is funded through payroll taxes called FICA (after the Federal Insurance Contributions Act), which are collected through payroll withholding from nearly every wage earner in the United States and matched by their employers. At the present time, revenues collected by FICA exceed program expenditures by nearly $50 billion per year. However, government projections indicate that by 2019 Social Security expenditures will exceed revenues and the system will gradually become unable to meet its obligations to retirees. Social Security, according to some analysts, will be "bankrupt," relegating millions of retirees to a state of poverty.

These and similar projections of a Social Security crisis are often used to support plans for overhauling the nation's pension system, including a total or partial substitution of private retirement accounts for Social Security. Polls suggest that many Americans are concerned that there may be no pension for them when they retire.

The idea, however, that Social Security can go bankrupt is based on the mistaken assumption that Social Security is an insurance program whose revenues must exceed its expenditures. Social Security is actually a spending program funded by tax revenues. In that sense, it is the equivalent of the defense program, the farm program, or the space program. If tax revenues become inadequate to fund Social Security, Congress can increase taxes, cut spending, or shift money from other programs. Whatever projections may show, the Social Security Administration cannot land in bankruptcy court.

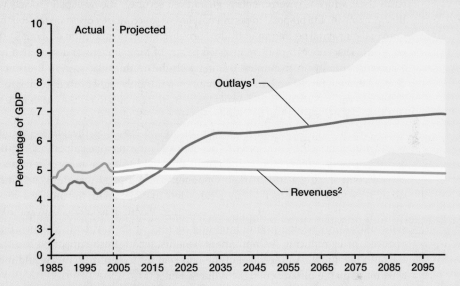

PROJECTED SOCIAL SECURITY OUTLAYS AND REVENUES UNDER CURRENT LAW, 1985–2103

Actual | Projected

Percentage of GDP

Outlays[1]

Revenues[2]

[1] Scheduled benefits and administrative costs.
[2] Payroll taxes and revenues from taxation of benefits.
Source: Congressional Budget Office, 2004

The red and blue lines indicate projections by the Congressional Budget Office (CBO) of expected outcomes. In these projections, annual Social Security outlays exceed revenues starting in 2019, and scheduled benefits cannot be paid beginning in 2053. Lighter areas indicate the 80 percent range of uncertainty around each projection. (In other words, there is a 10 percent chance that actual values will be above that range, a 10 percent chance they will be below it, and an 80 percent chance that they will fall within the range. These uncertainty ranges are based on a distribution of 500 simulations from CBO's long-term model.)

warning that unless something drastic is done now, the system will be paying out more than it takes in by 2018 and will certainly end up in bankruptcy by the 2040s. This stark warning appeared to have the same objective as his proclamation in 2003 of Iraq's imminent nuclear capacity—galvanizing the country to action through fear. That projection of Social Security doom, especially in his February 2005 State of the Union address, was followed by a cross-country campaign blitz, mainly in the "red states." He was showing his willingness to "spend the political capital" that he claimed to have earned by his reelection.

Oddly enough, Bush's campaign contained no new and startling changes in Social Security itself. The radical part of his reform was his commitment to "the ownership society," which has no bearing whatsoever on the operating parts of the Social Security system. The ownership society is, instead, an effort to alter the principle of Social Security itself, which is governmentally guaranteed security. The ownership society was Bush's name for the proposal to permit employees to voluntarily divert up to about one third of their payroll tax into an individual private account (a maximum of about $1,000 per year). That money would be invested in any of three options and converted into a personal annuity on retirement (ending with the death of the owner). Proponents claimed that the private account would return significantly higher earnings than those of the government accounts and would more than compensate for the cut in benefits that made up the second and less-publicized part of President Bush's plan.

Those who opposed the Bush reform argued first that the private account would outperform the government's account only during a sustained bull market and could yield a punishing reduction in the value of the annuity if retirement should come during a bad market. Opponents also argued that the government would have to go into stupendously greater debt to make up for the money diverted from the contributions into the private accounts. Payment would have to come the same old way, by raising payroll taxes and increasing the cap, both of which Bush opposed, or by reducing the retirement benefits, which Bush supported based on the faith that growth in the value of the personal retirement accounts would more than make up the difference in the reduced benefits.

There were merits on both sides, even though the reform proponents did not offer many details while inviting doubters to come forward and bargain with alternatives. Bush's partially hidden agenda was to get the principle of personal investment accounts adopted so that it might become a first step toward a completely privatized retirement pension system. In other words, this 30 percent diversion in contributions would jump-start the most radical social policy idea since Social Security was conceived, because it aimed to alter the entire principle of the Social Security system.

Medicare

In February 2005, as President Bush was launching his nationwide campaign for Social Security reform, the semiofficial and ordinarily restrained *Congressional Quarterly* led off its cover story with this headline: "The Real Crisis Waits Its Turn: Looming Medicare Crunch Dwarfs the . . . Social Security Shortfall."[11]

---

[11] "The Real Crisis Waits Its Turn," *Congressional Quarterly*, February 21, 2005, p. 446.

Medicare was the biggest expansion in contributory programs after 1935. Established in 1965, it was set up to provide substantial medical services to elderly persons. Like Social Security, Medicare is not means tested. (Means-tested non-contributory programs are discussed in the next section.) It was set up to provide substantial medical services to elderly persons who are already eligible to receive Old-Age, Survivors, and Disability Insurance through their contributions under the original Social Security system. Medicare provides hospital insurance but allows beneficiaries to choose whether or not to participate in the government-assisted program to cover doctors' fees. A major role is given to the private health-care industry by essentially limiting Medicare to the role of third-party payer. In other words, program recipients purchase all their health services in the free market, and then they or their doctors and hospitals are reimbursed by Medicare. As a result, there is little government control over the quality of the services and the level of fees that health-care providers charge. That is definitely a major reason that Medicare costs expanded to such a great degree.

> **Medicare**
> National health insurance for the elderly and the disabled.

Today, more than 45 million senior citizens are covered by Medicare. However, the spectacular increase in the cost of Medicare is only partly attributable to the growing number of participants; much of the increase is due to the rising cost of health care, whose rate has risen much more sharply than inflation.

Another more recent boost in the cost of health care was provided by none other than President Bush and his Republican Party control of Congress. As the *Congressional Quarterly* put it, "Far from trimming Medicare's spending, the legislation that Congress passed in 2003 may have made the program better for seniors, but it piled on billions of dollars in new spending and trillions of dollars in long-term liabilities."[12] But even if the drug benefit had not been added to the program in 2003, there would be a crisis in Medicare costs because of the revolution in health care. The drug benefit was recognition of the medical revolution, but nobody anticipated the change in the health-care industry itself. Back when Medicare was established, hospitalization was a much more common part of the health-care process. Then along came new drugs and new methods and therefore new expectations of disease prevention, and those drugs and methods became the preferred form of medical care for seniors.

As a consequence, although Social Security can anticipate a $3.7 trillion gap during the next seventy-five years between the benefits promised and the cost of those benefits, Medicare confronts a $27.8 trillion gap. The liabilities added by the Bush Medicare prescription drug benefit alone come to an estimated $8.1 trillion.[13]

The Politics of Medicare Reform. Having dealt with Medicare in late 2003 to its satisfaction, the Bush administration not only opposed further action but also hoped to discourage further Democratic efforts by moving as quickly as possible to Social Security reform. Democratic leaders complained bitterly about the arm twisting to get prescription drug benefits, accusing the Republicans of softening the sticker shock of added costs to the program by providing drug discount cards,

---

[12] "The Real Crisis Waits Its Turn."

[13] "The Real Crisis Waits Its Turn," p. 447.

which were available at a cost of $30 per year, with savings projected up to 10 percent and possibly 20 percent. Democrats also cried foul over the Republicans' rosy estimates and demanded amendments, including elimination of tax breaks for health savings accounts, expansion of drugs covered in the program, reduced payments to private plans, and permission to import prescription drugs from Canada, a tactic that promised substantial savings. In fact, many in Congress, Republicans as well as Democrats, feared that if Medicare were not fully confronted now, it would be off the agenda for years. Others, including Alan Greenspan, then chairman of the Fed, favored postponement of further treatment of Medicare in hopes that the science and technology of pharmaceuticals might produce still another revolution in treatment, as well as one in reduced costs.

Meanwhile, the states were getting into the act. Since 2001, about half the states have adopted a policy of demanding rebates from drug companies beyond those required by federal law. Some states went further, forming consortiums to allow large-lot or wholesale purchase at discounted prices. The National Conference of State Legislatures reported that in 2004 alone over 320 bills and resolutions were introduced in state legislatures for the adoption of policies aimed at generating and negotiating discounts, subsidies, and other cost-reducing and cost-containing results. And a movement emerged among state governors and mayors to find ways of sponsoring and facilitating imports of lower-cost drugs from Canada.

The Pharmaceutical Research and Manufacturers of America (PhRMA), the trade association of the drug industry, of course mobilized in response. Always a major contributor to federal congressional campaigns, PhRMA began more recently to pump unprecedented amounts of money into state legislative elections and state lobbying.[14]

Welfare: Means-Tested Public-Assistance Policy

Programs to which beneficiaries do not have to contribute—**noncontributory programs**—are also known as public-assistance programs, or "welfare." Until 1996, the most important noncontributory program was **Aid to Families with Dependent Children (AFDC**, originally called Aid to Dependent Children, or ADC), which was founded in 1935 by the original Social Security Act. In 1996, Congress abolished AFDC and replaced it with the Temporary Assistance for Needy Families (TANF) block grant. Eligibility for public assistance is determined by **means testing**, a procedure that requires applicants to show a financial need for assistance. Between 1935 and 1965, the government created programs to provide housing assistance, school lunches, and food stamps to other needy Americans.

Like contributory programs, the noncontributory public-assistance programs made their most significant advances in the 1960s and 1970s. The largest single category of expansion was the establishment in 1965 of **Medicaid**, a program that provides extended medical services to all low-income persons who have already established eligibility through means testing under TANF. Noncontributory

---

noncontributory program A social program that assists people based on demonstrated need rather than contributions they have made; also known as a public assistance program.

Aid to Families with Dependent Children (AFDC) Federal funds for children in families that fall below state standards of need. In 1996, Congress abolished AFDC, the largest federal cash-transfer program, and replaced it with the Temporary Assistance for Needy Families (TANF) block grant.

means testing A procedure that determines eligibility for government public-assistance programs. A potential beneficiary must show a need and an inability to provide for that need.

Medicaid A federally financed, state-operated program for medical services to low-income people.

---

[14] Barbara Dreyfuss, "Almost Heaven? The Pharmaceutical Lobby Is Taking Its Fight to the States," *American Prospect*, February 2005, p. 26.

FIGURE 15.1 VARIATIONS IN STATE SPENDING ON TANF BENEFITS

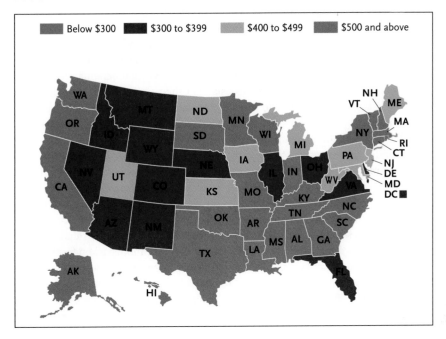

SOURCE: U.S. House of Representatives, Ways and Means Committee, *2003 Green Book*, http://waysandmeans.house.gov/media/pdf/greenbook2003/section7.pdf (accessed 4/16/09).

programs underwent another major transformation in the 1970s in the level of benefits they provided. Besides being means tested, noncontributory programs are federal rather than national; grants-in-aid are provided by the national government to the states as incentives to establish the programs (see Chapter 3). Thus from the beginning, there were considerable disparities in benefits from state to state. The national government sought to rectify the disparities in levels of old-age benefits in 1974 by creating **Supplemental Security Income (SSI)** to augment benefits for the aged, the blind, and the disabled. SSI provides uniform minimum benefits across the entire nation and includes mandatory COLAs. States are allowed to be more generous if they wish, but no state is permitted to provide benefits below the minimum level set by the national government. As a result, twenty-five states increased their SSI benefits to the mandated level.

The new TANF program is also administered by the states, and like the old-age benefits just discussed, benefit levels vary widely from state to state (Figure 15.1). For example, in 2003, the states' monthly TANF benefits varied from $170 in Mississippi to $923 in Alaska.[15] Even the most generous TANF payments are well below the federal poverty line. In 2008, the poverty level for a family of three included an income of less than $17,600, or $1,466 a month.

> Supplemental Security Income (SSI) A program providing a minimum monthly income to people who pass a means test and are sixty-five years old or older, blind, or disabled. SSI is financed from general revenues that are not Social Security contributions.

---

[15] Ways and Means Committee, *2003 Greenbook* U.S. House of Representatives, http://waysandmeans. house.gov/media/pdf/greenbook2003/section7.pdf (accessed 4/16/09).

The number of people receiving AFDC benefits expanded in the 1970s, in part because new welfare programs had been established in the mid-1960s: Medicaid (discussed earlier) and **food stamps**, which are coupons that can be exchanged for food at most grocery stores. These programs provide what are called **in-kind benefits**—noncash goods and services that would otherwise have to be paid for in cash by the beneficiary. The possibility of receiving Medicaid benefits provided an incentive for many poor Americans to establish their eligibility for AFDC, which also established their eligibility to receive Medicaid. At the same time, the government significantly expanded its publicity efforts to encourage the dependent unemployed to establish their eligibility for these programs.

Another, more complex reason for the growth of AFDC in the 1970s was that it became more difficult for the government to terminate AFDC benefits for lack of eligibility. In the 1970 case of *Goldberg v. Kelly,* the Supreme Court held that the financial benefits of AFDC could not be revoked without due process—that is, a hearing at which evidence is presented.[16] This ruling inaugurated the concept of **entitlement,** a class of government benefits with a status similar to that of property (which, according to the Fourteenth Amendment, cannot be taken from people "without due process of law"). *Goldberg v. Kelly* did not provide that the beneficiary had a "right" to government benefits; it provided that once a person's eligibility for AFDC was established, and as long as the program was in effect, that person could not be denied benefits without due process. The decision left open the possibility that Congress could terminate the program and its benefits by passing legislation. If the welfare benefit were truly a property right, Congress would have no authority to deny it by a mere majority vote.

Thus the establishment of in-kind benefit programs and the legal obstacles involved in terminating benefits contributed to the growth of the welfare state. But it is important to note that real federal spending on AFDC did not rise after the mid-1970s. Unlike Social Security, AFDC was not indexed to inflation; without COLAs, the value of AFDC benefits fell by more than one third. Moreover, the largest noncontributory welfare program, Medicaid (see Table 15.1), actually devotes less than one-third of its expenditures to poor families; the rest goes to the disabled and the elderly in nursing homes.[17] Together, these programs have significantly increased the security of the poor and the vulnerable and must be included in a genuine assessment of the redistributive influence and the cost of the welfare system today.

The Politics of Welfare Reform.   The unpopularity of welfare led to widespread calls for reform as early as the 1960s. Public opinion polls consistently showed that Americans disliked welfare more than any other government program. Although a series of modest reforms were implemented starting in the late 1960s, it took thirty years for Congress to enact a major transformation in the program. Why did welfare become so unpopular, and why was it so hard to reform? How has the 1996 law that replaced AFDC with TANF changed welfare?

---

[16] *Goldberg v. Kelly,* 397 U.S. 254 (1970).

[17] See U.S. House of Representatives, Committee on Ways and Means, *Where Your Money Goes: The 1994–95 Greenbook* (Washington, D.C.: Brassey's, 1994), pp. 325, 802.

From the 1960s to the 1990s, opinion polls consistently showed that the public viewed welfare beneficiaries as "undeserving."[18] Underlying that judgment was the belief that welfare recipients did not want to work. The Progressive Era reformers who first designed AFDC wanted single mothers to stay at home with their children. Motivated by horror stories of children killed in accidents while their mothers were off working or of children tied up at home all day to keep them safe, these reformers believed that it was better for the child if the mother did not work. By the 1960s, as more women were entering the labor force and welfare rolls were rising, welfare recipients appeared in a more unfavorable light. Common criticisms charged that welfare recipients were taking advantage of the system, that they were irresponsible people who refused to work. These negative assessments were amplified by racial stereotypes. By 1973, approximately 46 percent of welfare recipients were African American. Although the majority of recipients were white, media portrayals helped create the widespread perception that the vast majority of welfare recipients were black. A careful study by Martin Gilens has shown how racial stereotypes of blacks as uncommitted to the work ethic reinforced public opposition to welfare.[19]

Despite public opposition, it proved difficult to reform welfare. Congress added modest work requirements in 1967, but little changed in the administration of welfare. A more significant reform in 1988 imposed stricter work requirements but also provided additional support services, such as child care and transportation assistance. This compromise legislation reflected a growing consensus that effective reform entailed a combination of sticks (work requirements) and carrots (extra services to make work possible). The 1988 reform also created a new system to identify absent parents (usually fathers) and enforce child-support payments.

These reforms were barely implemented when welfare rolls rose again with the recession of the early 1990s, reaching an all-time high in 1994. Sensing continuing public frustration with welfare, presidential candidate Bill Clinton vowed "to end welfare as we know it," an unusual promise for a Democrat. Once in office, Clinton found it difficult to design a plan that would provide an adequate safety net for recipients who were unable to find work. One possibility—to provide government jobs as a last resort—was rejected as too expensive. Clinton's major achievement in the welfare field was to increase the earned income tax credit. This credit allows working parents whose annual income falls below approximately $32,000 to file through their income tax return for an income supplement of up to $4,000, depending on the size of the family. It was a first step toward realizing Clinton's campaign promise to ensure that "if you work, you shouldn't be poor."

Congressional Republicans proposed a much more dramatic reform of welfare, and Clinton, faced with reelection in 1996, signed the legislation. The Personal Responsibility and Work Opportunity Reconciliation Act repealed AFDC. In place of the individual entitlement to assistance, the new law created block grants to the states and allowed states much more discretion in designing their cash-assistance

---

[18] See Martin Gilens, *Why Americans Hate Welfare: Race, Media, and the Politics of Antipoverty Policy* (Chicago: University of Chicago Press, 1999), chaps. 3–4.

[19] Gilens, *Why Americans Hate Welfare.*

FIGURE 15.2 AVERAGE MONTHLY AFDC/TANF CASELOAD

ANALYZING THE EVIDENCE

Welfare caseloads dropped dramatically after 1994. What accounted for this? What are the positive and negative consequences of the policy change that reduced welfare rolls?

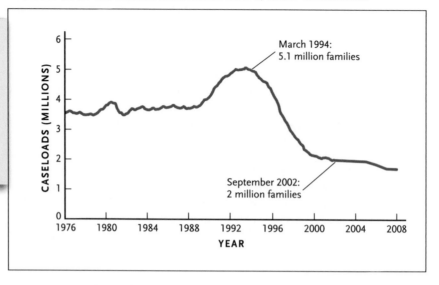

SOURCE: Congressional Research Service, based on data from U.S. Department of Health and Human Services.

programs to needy families. The new law also established time limits, restricting recipients to two years of assistance and creating a lifetime limit of five years. It imposed new work requirements on those receiving welfare, and it kept most legal immigrants from receiving benefits. The aim of the new law was to reduce welfare caseloads, promote work, and reduce out-of-wedlock births. Notably, reducing poverty was not one of its stated objectives.

After this law was enacted, the number of families receiving assistance dropped by 61 percent nationwide (Figure 15.2). The sharp decline in the number of recipients was widely hailed as a sign that welfare reform was working. Indeed, former welfare recipients have been more successful at finding and keeping jobs than many critics of the law predicted. The law has been less successful in other respects: Researchers have found no evidence that it has helped reduce out-of-wedlock births. And critics point out that most former welfare recipients are not paid enough to pull their families out of poverty. Moreover, many families eligible for food stamps and Medicaid stopped receiving these benefits when they left the welfare rolls. The law has helped reduce welfare caseloads, but it has done little to reduce poverty.[20]

As Congress prepared to reauthorize the welfare law in 2002, two perspectives emerged. Democrats proposed changes that would make the welfare law "an antipoverty weapon."[21] They sought to increase spending on child care, allow more

---

[20] See the discussion of the law and the data presented in U.S. House of Representatives, Ways and Means Committee, *2000 Greenbook*, www.gpoaccess.gov/wmprints/green/2000.html (accessed 4/16/09).

[21] Robert Pear, "House Democrats Propose Making the '96 Welfare Law an Antipoverty Weapon," *New York Times*, January 24, 2002, p. A22.

education and training, and relax time limits for those working and receiving welfare benefits. Republicans, by contrast, proposed stricter work requirements and advocated programs designed to promote marriage among welfare recipients.[22] Neither party challenged the basic features of the 1996 reform. Nonetheless, as caseloads began to rise again in 2001 as a result of the combined effects of the recession and the terrorist attacks, both sides were attentive to new problems. Because of the nation's economic downturn, welfare rolls surged in 2009, straining many state welfare budgets. To cope with the crisis, the federal government made $5 billion in stimulus funds available to the states to help meet welfare needs and extended unemployment benefits.

ANALYZING THE WELFARE SYSTEM

Arguments against It

1. The first argument is the simplest: The welfare state costs too much. The contributory programs will sooner (say the Republicans) or later (say the Democrats) come into their second or third financial crisis. But both parties agree that the crisis will come because too little account has been taken of demographic factors, with a ratio of workers to retirees approaching two to one. And that does not take into account increased life expectancy. Another factor affecting cost is the indexing of benefits to the cost-of-living index, which reflects inflation and in fact contributes to inflation.

2. A major factor contributing to cost escalation, especially in health-care benefits paid by both Medicare and Medicaid, was the adoption of a third-party structure of repayment. The systems that allowed doctors and patients to establish a relationship, with the fees being paid by the government, relieved both doctors and patients of almost any concern at all about the cost of services.

3. The welfare state is too paternalistic. The contributory programs are based on forced savings, leaving all individuals with some degree of concern for their future. The noncontributory programs are also paternalistic even though it is true that people in poverty usually have no choice to save.

4. The welfare state is an example of moral hazard—the danger that a policy will encourage the behavior or bring about the problem that it is supposed to ward off. For example, many people whose cars are insured will take less care than those whose cars are uninsured to prevent their cars from being damaged or stolen. Another example is the increase of safety factors in both automobiles and contact-sports equipment. The tendency is to push the envelope with higher speeds and faster turns in cars and the use of often ineffective headgear and protective padding in violent sports. But the safety net might be a moral hazard if it can be shown to weaken self-reliance and individual responsibility. That is why the sponsors of the 1996 welfare reform included "personal

---

[22] Robin Toner, "Welfare Chief Is Hoping to Promote Marriage," *New York Times*, February 19, 2002, p. A1.

responsibility" in the title of the legislation. A second argument is that entitlement to benefits weakens the work incentive. Even the strong supporters of noncontributory public assistance agree that care has to be taken to keep the benefits high enough for subsistence but not so high that people will prefer receiving benefits to taking a job. Finally, entitlement to child support, so the argument goes, "brings more babies into the world."[23]

5. The welfare system lays most of the blame for society's woes on "the system." Consequently, it removes the morality (or immorality) from poverty and relieves employers of a large part of their traditional responsibility to take care of their employees. Meanwhile, the employees to a large extent are relieved of personal responsibility.

These critiques are not subject to scientific proof or disproof. Like a good lawyer preparing a case for court, the critic of the welfare state is summoning up the best examples and the best logic available in the hopes that "the preponderance of evidence" will convince the jury—that is, the public and the policy makers. But the strength of those arguments is that they are based more on moral principles than on science and empirical demonstration.

Arguments for It

1. The welfare system is good fiscal policy. As discussed in the previous chapter, the welfare system is one of the "automatic stabilizers." When the economy is declining, welfare payments go up enough to help maintain consumer demand. In contrast, during inflationary periods, welfare taxes take an extra bite out of consumers' dollars, thereby dampening inflation somewhat (Figure 15.3).

2. The welfare system is paternalistic. A vice to the critics of welfare, paternalism is a virtue to its supporters because it is a notorious fact that Americans don't save enough. Welfare taxation has produced a system of universal saving, which is a safety net for employers just as much as for employees. Social Security, unemployment compensation, disability benefits, and other features of contributory and noncontributory welfare have cushioned employers, especially those operating on narrow profit margins in our globalizing economy. It is no paradox that the employers who at first opposed the welfare state quickly accepted it once it was established.

3. As a consequence of the first and second arguments, many believe that the welfare system is the savior of capitalism. Every title in the original Social Security Act creating the welfare system identified a particular imperfection of capitalism and sought to cope with it: age, unemployment, widowhood, disability for injury, illness, birth defects, inadequate education or training, and so on. The welfare system is not anticapitalist. It recognizes that capitalism is neither

---

[23] The strongest arguments for all these points are probably those of Charles Murray, *Losing Ground: American Social Policy, 1950–1980*, 2nd ed. (New York: Basic Books, 1994), and "Does Welfare Bring More Babies?" 2nd ed. *Public Interest* 114 (Spring 1994): 17–31. Another influential critic of the welfare state is George Guilder. See his *Wealth and Poverty* (New York: Basic Books, 1981), chap. 10.

FIGURE 15.3 THE INCREASING COST OF ENTITLEMENT PROGRAMS

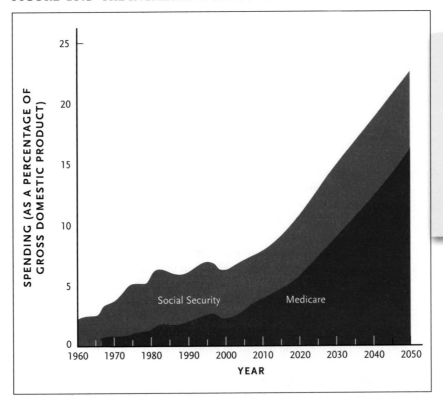

SOURCE: Congressional Budget Office.

ANALYZING
THE EVIDENCE
Under current eligi-
bility requirements,
federal spending
on entitlement
programs, particu-
larly Medicare, will
grow enormously
in the future. What
accounts for this
growth? What are
the arguments for
and against the wel-
fare state?

perfect nor self-perfecting and therefore needs various deliberate, public means of dealing with its imperfections.

4. The welfare system lays most of the blame for society's woes on the system. In other words, it removes the morality (or immorality) from poverty and relieves employers of a large part of their traditional responsibility to take care of their employees. This is the brighter side of the "personal responsibility" complaint covered by the critics' arguments 2 and 3. Welfare-system proponents have to agree that there are many chiselers and abusers in the contributory and noncontributory parts of the system, but cheating abounds in the private sector as well and need not discredit welfare any more than it discredits business. Roughly half the people on welfare at any one time are off it within one year. It should also be noted that a large proportion of recipients of the more respectable Social Security retirement system receive far more in benefits than they contribute in taxes, especially if they live ten or more years beyond their retirement. This gives rise to an interesting question: Which of us isn't taking welfare?[24]

[24] Ruth Rosen, "Which of Us Isn't Taking 'Welfare'?" *Los Angeles Times,* December 27, 1994, p. B5; source of data: Jan Tin, "Who Gets Assistance?" *Current Population Reports,* Household Economic Studies, series P70–58, U.S. Bureau of the Census, July 1996, www.census.gov/prod/2/pop/p70/p70–58.pdf (accessed 4/16/09).

5. The welfare system is politically essential. As the pro-welfare-system conservative George Will put the case:

> Two conservatives (Disraeli and Bismarck) pioneered the welfare state, and did so for impeccably conservative reasons: to reconcile the masses to the vicissitudes and hazards of a dynamic and hierarchical industrial economy. They acted on the principle of "economy of exertion," using government power judiciously to prevent less discriminating, more disruptive uses of power.[25]

In Otto von Bismarck's own words, in a speech to the Reichstag in 1899:

> I will consider it a great advantage when we have 700,000 small pensioners drawing their annuities from the state, especially if they belong to those classes who otherwise do not have much to lose by an upheaval and erroneously believe they can actually gain much by it.[26]

> If this appears to be cynical, so be it. It may be difficult to sympathize in this epoch of relative prosperity and stability, but the likelihood of great social and political disorder, if not revolution, was very much on the minds of American political leaders in 1933–35, the years leading up to the passage of the Social Security Act. In the spring of 1933, for example, Secretary of Labor Frances Perkins was urged by an influential friend to leave Washington for the summer if she possibly could because of expectations of widespread violence.[27]

There is obviously no simple solution to the welfare system. Most critics and defenders make cogent arguments for their side largely because they emphasize different aspects of the beast.[28] The welfare system was not a solution in the first place. It was a series of improvisations to some intractable problems that every nation faces when it tries, in George Will's words, "to reconcile the masses to the . . . hazards of . . . industrial economy," especially when those come to a head as quickly as they did in the early 1930s.[29] The welfare state is an institution of many parts, and no single approach to the whole will work.

---

[25] George F. Will, *Statecraft as Soulcraft: What Government Does* (New York: Simon & Schuster, 1983), p. 126.

[26] Quoted in Gaston V. Rimlinger, *Welfare Policy and Industrialization in Europe, America, and Russia* (New York: Wiley, 1971), p. 121.

[27] Episode reported in Theodore J. Lowi, *The End of Liberalism: Ideology, Policy, and the Crisis of Public Authority* (New York: Norton, 1969), p. 200. For an entirely different view of the same political phenomenon, see Frances Fox Piven and Richard A. Cloward; *The New Class War: Reagan's Attack on the Welfare State and Its Consequences* (New York: Pantheon Books, 1982).

[28] From the Right, one serious academic critique is Lawrence M. Mead, *The New Politics of Poverty: The Nonworking Poor in America* (New York: Basic Books, 1992). A defense of the welfare system is John E. Schwarz and Thomas J. Volgy, *The Forgotten Americans: Thirty Million Working Poor in the Land of Opportunity* (New York: Norton, 1993).

[29] Will, *Statecraft as Soulcraft.*

HOW CAN GOVERNMENT CREATE OPPORTUNITY?

The welfare system not only supplies a measure of economic security but also provides opportunity. The American belief in equality of opportunity makes such programs particularly important. Programs that provide opportunity keep people from falling into poverty, and they offer a hand up to those who are poor. At their best, opportunity policies allow all individuals to rise as high as their talents will take them. Two types of policy stand out as most effective in opening opportunity: education policy and health policy.

Education Policies and Their Politics

Most education of the American people is provided by the public policies of state and local governments. What may be less obvious is that these education policies—especially the policy of universal compulsory public education—are the most important single force in the distribution and redistribution of opportunity in America.

Compared with state and local efforts, *national* education policy pales. With just a few exceptions, the national government did not involve itself at all in education for the first century of its existence as an independent republic (Table 15.2).

TABLE 15.2 GROWTH OF THE WELFARE SYSTEM

Welfare	Education	Health and Housing
State Era (1789–1935)		
Private and local charity	Northwest Ordinance (1787, federal)	Local public health ordinances
State child labor laws	Local academies	
State unemployment and injury compensation	Local public schools	
State mothers' pensions	State compulsory-education laws	
	Morrill Act (1862) for land-grant colleges (federal)	
Federal Era (1935–present)		
Social Security (federal)	GI Bill of Rights	Public housing
Disability insurance	National Defense Education Act (1958)	Hospital construction
Volunteers in Service to America, Office of Economic Opportunity	Elementary and Secondary Education Act (1965)	School lunch program
Supplemental Security Income	School desegregation	Food Stamps
Cost-of-living adjustment (indexing)	Head Start	Medicare
		Medicaid

The first two of these exceptions preceded the Constitution—the Land Ordinance of 1785, followed by the Northwest Ordinance of 1787. These provided for a survey of all the public lands in the Northwest Territory and required that four of the thirty-six sections in each township be reserved for public schools and their maintenance. It was not until 1862, with the adoption of the Morrill Act, that Congress took a third step, establishing the land-grant colleges and universities. Later in the nineteenth century, more federal programs were created for the education of farmers and other rural residents. But the most important national education policies did not come until after World War II: the GI Bill of Rights of 1944, the National Defense Education Act (NDEA) of 1958, the Elementary and Secondary Education Act (ESEA) of 1965, and various youth and adult vocational training acts since 1958. Note, however, that since the GI Bill was aimed almost entirely at postsecondary schooling, the national government did not really enter the field of elementary education until after 1957.[30]

What finally brought the national government into elementary education was embarrassment over the Soviets' beating us into space with the launching of *Sputnik.* The national policy under the NDEA was aimed specifically at improving education in science and mathematics. General federal aid for education did not come until 1965, with ESEA, which allocated funds to school districts with a substantial number of children whose families were unemployed or earning less than $2,000 a year.

President Ronald Reagan's administration signaled a new focus for federal education policy: the pursuit of higher standards. In 1983, the Department of Education issued *A Nation at Risk,* an influential report that identified low educational standards as the cause of America's declining international economic competitiveness. The report did not suggest any changes in federal policy, but it urged states to make excellence in education their primary goal. This theme was picked up again by President George H. W. Bush. Calling himself the "education president," Bush convened the nation's governors for a highly publicized retreat designed to promote the development of state educational standards. Because Republicans have historically opposed a strong federal role in education, the initiatives of Reagan and Bush remained primarily advisory. But they were influential in focusing educational reform on standards and testing, now widely practiced across the states.

Bill Clinton and George W. Bush further energized the movement for educational achievement. The standards remained voluntary, however; the federal government restricted its role to providing grants to states that developed standards programs.[31] The federal role was substantially increased by President George W. Bush's signature education act, the No Child Left Behind Act of 2002, which created stronger federal requirements for testing and school accountability. It requires that every child in grades 3 through 8 be tested yearly for proficiency in math and

---

[30] There were a couple of minor precedents. First was the Smith-Hughes Act of 1917, which made federal funds available to the states for vocational education at the elementary and secondary levels. Second, the Lanham Act of 1940 made federal funds available to schools in "federally impacted areas"—that is, areas with an unusually large number of government employees and/or areas where the local tax base was reduced by a large amount of government-owned property.

[31] See Diane Ravitch, *National Standards in American Education: A Citizen's Guide* (Washington, D.C.: Brookings Institution, 1995).

reading. Individual schools are judged on the basis of how well their students perform on these tests. Parents whose child is in a failing school have the right to transfer the child to a better school. Students in failing schools can also get access to special funds for tutoring and summer programs. Because there was strong congressional opposition to creating a national test, the states are responsible for setting standards and devising appropriate tests.

Although there was strong bipartisan support for the program, the act was difficult to implement. Many states were plainly unable to move to a new system of standards and testing. But the big problem was that the federal government was demanding major improvements without providing sufficient funding to pay for them. There was some embarrassment in Republican Party circles because for years Republicans had complained about "unfunded mandates" that Democratic Congresses were imposing on the states. Now they found themselves doing the same thing in the area of education.

Despite the compromises and confusions in the new program, federal money aimed at the poorest students did increase by one-third. Local educators argue it is not enough to meet the high standard the law requires, but money is at least forthcoming. In addition, many education experts contend that yearly test results are too volatile to provide a good measure of school performance and that failing schools have been made weaker as motivated parents transferred their children out of them.[32]

The federal program got a boost after the 2004 election because Bush saw his reelection as a vindication—indeed, a mandate for—the program that had been so prominent on his agenda. In early 2005, Bush requested $1.5 billion to extend the coverage of the law to high schools up to grade 11 and to expand and improve college preparatory courses and programs aimed at keeping students from dropping out. Through 2005, there continued to be doubt that Bush would get the increase he sought, first because many thought the problems of inadequate high schools and dropout rates still resulted from weaknesses in the primary schools and second because of the embarrassment over the mushrooming budget deficits.

Hesitation and doubt in Washington despite the strong rhetoric and the promise of some financial backing put the question of primary and secondary education back in the hands of the states—in particular, in the hands of the governors. Having been a two-term governor of Texas and a Republican for states' rights, President Bush could hardly go against the initiatives that the governors were prepared to take. Moreover, the governors were not only acting independently for their own states; they were also acting with sufficient bipartisanship to be able to act through their own "interest group," the National Governors Association. In their first meeting in 2005 after Bush's request for an additional $1.5 billion, the National Governors Association released a report concluding that although graduation requirements are lax and four in ten graduates are not adequately prepared for college or the job market, billions of dollars in remedial schooling would be required to address the situation and much of that would have to come from the

---

[32] For a critique of the act's provisions, see Thomas Toch, "Bush's Big Test," *Washington Monthly*, November 2001, pp. 12–18.

national government. This was not a happy message for the conservative wing of the Republican Party. As recently as the mid-1990s, in the inspirational moment of the Gingrich revolution and the Contract with America, their message of smaller government, states' rights, and the abolition of the Department of Education was one of the most popular songs being sung. Thus despite the "political capital" that President Bush was willing to spend on No Child Left Behind, education policy in his second term was stalemated, due to cleavages within the Republican Party and a deeply partisan cleavage between the Republican and Democratic parties.[33]

Education: The Policy Principle In Action

In Chapter 1 we presented the policy principle, which suggests that policy is a result of political goals and ambitions played out in a context of institutional processes (ambition + institutions = policies). In the case of education, former president Bush was eager to make his mark by improving the performance of America's schoolchildren. Initially, Bush was an advocate of national testing for school children. However, there was strong opposition in the Republican Party to the idea of the national government's taking over what had traditionally been a state responsibility. As a result, Bush's signature No Child Left Behind act required the states to set standards and develop tests of educational performance.

Initially, the states favored the new law. But soon they objected to the expensive new obligations the law placed upon their schools. Under the law, the sates were required to improve student performance by providing such new services as supplemental tutoring, longer school days, and additional summer schools. By 2004, several states were refusing to implement No Child Left Behind, claiming that they could not afford to comply with the law's provisions. Several states, along with the National Education Association, sued the federal government on the grounds that that Congress had not provided enough money to pay for the testing and other services required by the law. As President Bush left office, the incoming Obama administration promised to revisit the increasingly controversial law.

No Child Left Behind is a case in which the institutional context worked against a policy maker's ambitions. Ambition and institutions undermined policy because the institutions chosen to implement the president's program, namely the states, were not fully convinced of the value of the effort and certainly were not willing to spend their own funds to achieve the president's goals. It remains to be seen whether the Obama administration will abandon the program or will, instead, endeavor to change the program's institutional context either by providing the states with incentives to carry out federal mandates or shifting the program's administration to a federal bureaucracy.

Another controversial topic in education policy is the issue of "school choice." Here again the political cleavages occur within and between the major parties, as well as within the well-established ideological groups. One issue of school choice is the simple one of permitting parents to move their children from a local public

---

[33] Good coverage of the politics of education policy in Bush's second term is found in Bill Swindell, "States Eager to Retake Lead in School Policy," *Congressional Quarterly*, February 28, 2005, pp. 492–93.

school that has been defined as failing to a public school in another district anywhere in the area. A far more controversial issue is the school-voucher movement, which calls for parents to be given vouchers to enroll their children in the school of their choice, whether public or private. The vouchers could be used to help defray the cost of tuition at a chosen private school. Supporters of vouchers claim that the public education system is too bureaucratic to provide quality education and does not give parents enough control over the education of their children. After several years of trial use, vouchers remain fairly popular in principle, but the data on their comparative success are not clear enough to provide a verdict.

Finally, there is the issue of the charter school. Charter schools are publicly funded schools that are free from the bureaucratic rules and regulations of the school district in which they are located. They are called charter schools because there must be an organization to form one, it must present its proposal to state authorities, and it must receive a charter as a kind of corporation that gives it the legal opportunity to operate. Charter schools are free to design specialized curricula and use resources in ways that their administrators think most effective. Since the creation of the first charter schools in Minnesota in 1990, states across the country have passed legislation to allow such schools. But here again, there are many charges against charter schools, as there are against vouchers, as being "class biased." The fear persists that the opportunity for school choice will skim off the best students in the problem schools and thus doom those schools to continued mediocrity or failure.

We can safely predict that the politics of education policy will continue to be heated as long as the technological revolutions and globalized markets in the new economy push ahead of the education and training that the schools can provide. (United States policy makers had a similar national curriculum crisis after World War I and yet another one after World War II, when policy makers finally got serious about equal education opportunities for minorities.) And the politics of education policy continues to resemble the politics of redistributive policy, which we encountered in the politics of the welfare state.

Health Policies and Their Politics

Until recently, no government in the United States—national, state, or local—concerned itself directly with individuals' health. But public responsibility was always accepted for *public* health. After New York City's newly created Board of Health was credited with holding down a cholera epidemic in 1867, most states established statewide public-health agencies. Within a decade, the results were obvious. Between 1884 and 1894, for example, the rate of infant mortality in Massachusetts dropped from 161.3 per 1,000 to 141.4 per 1,000.[34] Reductions in mortality rates produced by local public-health programs during the late nineteenth century may be the most significant contribution ever made by government to human welfare.

---

[34] Morton Keller, *Affairs of State: Public Life in Late Nineteenth Century America* (Cambridge, Mass.: Belknap, Harvard University Press, 1977), p. 500.

The U.S. Public Health Service (USPHS) has been in existence since 1798 but was a small part of public-health policy until after World War II. Created in 1930 but little noticed for twenty years was the National Institutes of Health (NIH), an agency within USPHS created to do biomedical research. Between 1950 and 2006, the national government's expenditures on behalf of the NIH increased from $160 million to more than $28 billion. NIH research on the link between smoking and disease led to one of the most visible public-health campaigns in American history. The NIH then focused on cancer and AIDS. As with smoking, its work on AIDS resulted in massive public-health education as well as new products and regulations.

More recent commitments to the improvement of public health are evident in the numerous laws, now mainly under the jurisdiction of the Environmental Protection Agency (established in 1970), addressing hazardous air and water pollutants along with degradation of the natural environment. The Occupational Safety and Health Administration (also created in 1970) was set up to make the workplace safer from air pollutants as well as threats from machinery and its operation. Laws attempting to improve the safety of consumer products were created in 1972 and housed under the aegis of the Consumer Product Safety Commission.

But by far the most important commitments to public health were made in 1965, with the creation of Medicare and Medicaid. Medicare services are available to all persons already eligible under the Social Security insurance program (and it becomes automatic for retired persons when they reach the age of sixty-five). Although there are nutritional programs for the poor, particularly food stamps and the National School Lunch Program, Medicaid is far and away the most important health program for this group.

But public health is only half the health policy area. The other half is the health-care system—that is, delivery of services by individual doctors to individual patients. Early in his administration, President Clinton announced a plan with two key objectives: to limit the rising costs of the American health-care system and to provide health insurance coverage for all Americans (almost 40 million Americans lacked health insurance at that time). Clinton's plan at first garnered enormous public support and seemed likely to win congressional approval in some form. But the plan, which entailed a major expansion of federal administration of the health-care system, gradually lost momentum as resistance to it took root among those who feared changes in a system that worked well for them. After the president's failure on health care, Congress passed a much smaller program expanding health-insurance coverage for low-income children not already receiving Medicaid. Called the State Children's Health Insurance Program (SCHIP), the law provides federal funds to states so that they can offer health insurance to more children in low-income families. The results have been uneven: Some states have greatly expanded coverage of uninsured children and have even sought to insure their parents. Other states have been far less aggressive and have not significantly increased the number of insured children. In 2010, Barack Obama and a Democratic Congress succeeded in passing legislation that gave the federal government a much larger role in the provision of health care (see the section on "Obama's First Two Years" following page 358).

WHO IS POOR? WHAT CAN GOVERNMENT DO?

When we study social policies from a group perspective, we see that minorities, women, and children are disproportionately poor. Much of this poverty is the result of disadvantages that stem from the position of these groups in the labor market. African Americans and Latinos tend to be economically less well off than the rest of the American population. Much of this economic inequality stems from the fact that minority workers tend to have low-wage jobs. Minorities are also more likely to become unemployed and remain unemployed for longer periods of time than are white Americans. African Americans, for example, typically have experienced twice as much unemployment as other Americans. The combination of low-wage jobs and unemployment often means that minorities are less likely to have jobs that give them access to the shadow welfare state. They are more likely to fall into the precarious categories of the working poor or the nonworking poor.

In the past several decades, policy analysts have begun to talk about the "feminization of poverty," or the fact that women are more likely to be poor than men are. This problem is particularly acute for single mothers, who are more than twice as likely as the average American to fall below the poverty line. When the Social Security Act was passed in 1935, the main programs for poor women were ADC and Survivors Insurance for widows. The framers of the act believed that ADC would gradually disappear as more women became eligible for Survivors Insurance. The social model behind the Social Security Act was that of a male breadwinner with a wife and children. Women were not expected to work, and if a woman's husband died, ADC or Survivors Insurance would help her stay at home and raise her children. The framers of Social Security did not envision today's large number of single women heading families. Nor did they envision that so many women with children would be working. This combination of changes helped make AFDC (the successor to ADC) more controversial. Many people ask, Why shouldn't welfare recipients work if the majority of women who are not on welfare work?

Controversies over the welfare state have led to adaptations in welfare policy in recent years. Similar controversies over affirmative action policies—those that partially determine "who shall be poor"—have led to gradual changes in civil rights policies. But although the problems of rights in America are agonizing, we can look at them optimistically. The United States has a long way to go before it constructs a truly just, "equally protected" society. But it has also come very far in a relatively short time. Groups pressing for equality have been able to use government to change a variety of discriminatory practices. The federal government has become an active partner in ensuring civil rights and political equality. All explicit *de jure* barriers to minorities have been dismantled. Many *de facto* barriers have also been dismantled, and thousands upon thousands of new opportunities have been created.

James Madison set the tone for this chapter in *Federalist 51*, in prose that has more the character of poetry:

> Justice is the end of government
> It is the end of civil society

It ever has been and ever will be pursued
　Until it be obtained,
　Or until liberty be lost in the pursuit.

Equality of opportunity has produced unequal results, and the unequal results of one generation can be visited upon later generations. Considerable inequality is accepted unless the advantages are maintained through laws and rules that favor those already in positions of power and through prejudices that tend to develop against any group that has long been on the lower rungs of society. Yet efforts to reduce the inequalities or eliminate the consequences of prejudice can produce their own injustices if government intervention is poorly planned or too heavy handed.

CONCLUSION: HISTORY VERSUS COLLECTIVE ACTION IN SOCIAL POLICY

Social policy is a realm in which history and collective action are frequently at odds with one another. Alleviation, or even amelioration, of poverty in the United States would require an enormous collective effort to expand welfare, educational, health-care, and other programs. Americans, though, have qualms about the desirability of such an effort. Although we certainly do not want our fellow citizens to be poor, hungry, and uneducated, our history and traditional views tell us that poverty is alleviated through individual rather than collective effort. The story of impoverished immigrants rising "from rags to riches" is deeply ingrained in our psyches. The notion of America as a land of opportunity where any hard-working and deserving individual can succeed implies that those who do not succeed are neither hard working nor deserving. Even as President Barack Obama avers that we should do more in the realm of social policy, his own family history signals to millions of Americans that individual self-help is still the key to success in America. Thus, history and collective action are often at war in America's social policy arena. Our history tells us that anyone can succeed in America. Our eyes and ears tell us that many do not succeed on their own and require the rest of us to help them, but what kind and how much help should government provide?

The severe economic recession that began with the collapse of the housing bubble in 2008 and continued with a financial crisis and the bankruptcy of a number of major corporations such as the venerable Chrysler, has led more and more Americans to turn to the national government for help. The Obama administration has launched new initiatives in health care and other arenas of social policy that expand the welfare state. Americans continue to be inspired by the idea of rugged individualism, but when they lose their jobs and their health insurance they turn to the government. Just as there are no atheists in fox holes, there are no rugged individualists in the unemployment line.

FOR FURTHER READING

Beland, Daniel. *Social Security: History and Politics from the New Deal to the Privatization Debate.* Lawrence: University Press of Kansas, 2007.

Ehrenreich, Barbara. *Nickel and Dimed: On (Not) Getting By in America.* New York: Holt, 2001.

Epsing-Andersen, Gosta. *Why We Need a New Welfare State.* New York: Oxford University Press, 2002.

Gilbert, Neil. *Transformation of the Welfare State.* New York: Oxford University Press, 2004.

Hacker, Jacob. *The Divided Welfare State: The Battle over Public and Private Social Benefits in the United States.* New York: Cambridge University Press, 2002.

Levi, Margaret. "Organizing Power: The Prospects for an American Labor Movement." *Perspectives on Politics* (March 2003): 45–68.   ○ reader selection

McCarty, Nolan, Keith Poole, and Howard Rosenthal. *Polarized America: The Dance of Unequal Riches.* Cambridge, Mass.: MIT Press, 2006.   ○ reader selection

Murray, Charles. *In Our Hands: A Plan to Remake the Welfare State.* Washington, D.C.: American Enterprise Institute Press, 2006.

Shipler, David. *The Working Poor.* New York: Vintage, 2005.

Skocpol, Theda. *The Missing Middle: Working Families and the Future of American Social Policy.* New York: Norton, 2000.

Trattner, Walter. *From Poor Law to Welfare State.* 6th ed. New York: Free Press, 1998.

Weir, Margaret, ed. *The Social Divide: Political Parties and the Future of Activist Government.* Washington, D.C.: Brookings Institution, 1998.

Ⓢ Additional study and review materials are available online at wwnorton.com/studyspace/

16

Foreign Policy

Accomplishing any policy goal requires collective action, but in the arena of foreign policy, in particular, we expect Americans to accept the need for collective effort on behalf of the "national interest." Certainly, Americans are expected to shoulder the enormous tax burdens associated with our nation's huge military forces. When it comes to foreign policy, questions of the collective or national interest figure more prominently than in most domestic policy debates. To be sure, advocates of competing social and economic policies argue that their preferred programs promote the interests of the nation as a whole. Yet such pronouncements are usually taken with a grain of salt, and we are usually prepared to forgive advocates whose preferred economic or social policies turn out to serve discrete constituencies rather than the entire nation.

In the realm of foreign policy, though, the collective interest looms larger. In a world where entities ranging from rival nation states to shadowy terrorist groups present genuine threats to the security of the entire nation, advocates of particular foreign policies are more likely than their domestic counterparts to be asked to demonstrate that the policies they espouse serve broad national interests. In foreign policy, unlike, say, health-care reform, advocates can and do accuse each other of threatening the nation's security and demonstrating outright disloyalty.

An old American adage asserts that "politics stops at the water's edge." The point of this saying is that if we fail to work together to protect our nation's political, economic, and security interests in the wider world, we will all suffer. However, this does not mean that collective-action problems don't arise in the foreign-policy realm. All Americans benefit from policies that effectively safeguard the nation's security. But Americans may not all agree on the most effective national-security programs—or who should pay for them. Indeed, national security is the quintessential public good. If the nation is safe, we all benefit, and each individual's contribution to the nation's security is slight. Hence, many Americans hope that someone else will shoulder the tax burdens and make the other sacrifices needed to maintain the nation's security.

Also, as in other policy areas, when it comes to foreign policy, history matters. Foreign policy is often influenced by historical events, experiences, and commitments. Debates over foreign policy tend to be strongly affected by competing historical perceptions. For example, those who argue in favor of confronting Iran, North Korea, and other potentially hostile powers often refer to the disastrous consequences of pre–World War II efforts by Britain and France to appease Nazi Germany. On the other hand, those who favor quickly withdrawing American forces from Iraq cite the parallels to America's failed efforts in Vietnam. Each group's view of the present is strongly shaped by its understanding of the past.

The foreign-policy arena is also affected by America's historic wariness of foreign commitments and the difficulties of making and justifying what are often cold, harsh, calculating foreign-policy decisions in the context of America's historic commitment to

- The goals of American foreign policy include security, economic prosperity, and—to a lesser extent—humanitarian objectives.

- Foreign policy is shaped by domestic actors—such as the president, the bureaucracy, Congress and interest groups—and through strategic interactions with foreign actors.

- The instruments that the government uses to implement foreign policy may include economic, diplomatic, institutional, or military means. These instruments are deployed strategically to serve the interests of the United States.

liberal democracy. Ever since George Washington, in his Farewell Address, warned the American people "to have . . . as little political connection as possible" to foreign nations and to "steer clear of permanent alliances," Americans have been distrustful of foreign policy. Though America is now a great world power, many Americans continue to agree with Washington that we should tend to our own affairs and leave other nations to their own devices. Doubt about ongoing foreign commitments may be one reason why many Americans question U.S. participation in the United Nations.[1]

The term *foreign policy* refers to the programs and policies that determine America's relations with other nations and foreign entities. Foreign policy includes diplomacy, military and security policy, international human rights policies, and various forms of economic policy, such as trade policy and international energy policy. Of course, foreign policy and domestic policy are not completely separate categories but are instead closely intertwined. Take security policy, for example. Defending the nation requires the design and manufacture of tens of billions of dollars worth of military hardware. The manufacture and procurement of this military equipment involves a host of economic policies, and paying for it shapes America's fiscal policies.

Many of the basic contours of the foreign-policy arena are similar to those of America's other policy domains. The nation's chief foreign-policy makers are the president, Congress, and the bureaucracy. Just as in economic and social policy, battles over foreign policy often erupt between and within these institutions as competing politicians and a variety of organized groups and rival political forces pursue their own versions of the national interest or their own narrower purposes, which they seek to present as the national interest. In many instances, the outcome of these battles among competing forces depends on the relative power of the institutions they control. Institutions affect foreign as well as domestic policy outcomes. In the foreign-policy arena, the institutional powers of the presidency give

---

[1] Alynna Lyon, "Rejecting One's Protégé? American Media, Public Opinion and the United Nations" (paper presented to the annual meeting of the International Studies Association, San Francisco, March 26, 2008).

presidents and their allies an advantage over political forces based in Congress, although Congress is not without institutional resources of its own through which to influence the conduct of foreign policy. Moreover, like domestic-policy matters, foreign-policy issues often figure prominently in public debate and national election campaigns as competing forces seek to mobilize popular support for their positions, or at least to castigate the opposition for the putative shortcomings of its policies.

In this chapter, we will first examine the main goals and purposes of American foreign policy. We will then discuss the actors and institutions that shape foreign policy. Next, we will analyze the instruments that policy makers have at their disposal to implement foreign policy.

THE GOALS OF FOREIGN POLICY

Although U.S. foreign policy has a number of purposes, three main goals stand out. These are security, prosperity, and the creation of a better world. These goals are, of course, closely intertwined and can never be pursued fully in isolation from each other.

Security

To many Americans, the chief purpose of the nation's foreign policy is protection of America's security in an often hostile world. Traditionally, the United States has been concerned about threats that might emanate from other nations, such as Nazi Germany during the 1940s and then Soviet Russia until the Soviet Union's collapse in the late 1980s. Today, American security policy is concerned not only with the actions of other nations but also with the activities of terrorist groups and other hostile **non-state actors**.[2] To protect the nation's security from foreign threats, the United States has built an enormous military apparatus and a complex array of intelligence-gathering institutions, such as the Central Intelligence Agency (CIA), charged with evaluating and anticipating challenges from abroad.[3]

Security is, of course, a broad term. Policy makers must be concerned with Americans' physical security. The 9/11 terrorist attacks killed and injured thousands of Americans and the government constantly fears that new attacks could be even more catastrophic. Policy makers must also be concerned with such matters as the security of America's food supplies, transportation infrastructure, and energy supplies. Many of our efforts in the Middle East, for example, are aimed at ensuring continuing American access to vital oil fields. In recent years, cyberspace has become a new security concern. The nation's dependence on computers means that

non-state actor
A group other than a nation-state that attempts to play a role in the international system. Terrorist groups are one type of non-state actor.

---

[2] Rupert Smith, *The Utility of Force: The Art of War in the Modern World* (New York: Vintage, 2008).

[3] D. Robert Worley, *Shaping U.S. Military Forces: Revolution or Relevance in a Post–Cold War World* (Westport, Conn.: Praeger Security International, 2006).

the government must be alert to efforts by hostile governments, groups, or even individual "hackers" to damage computer networks. Some thinkers also believe that the spread of democracy to other countries is a key component in promoting security (see "Analyzing the Evidence" on page 674).

During the nineteenth century, the United States believed that its security was based on its geographic isolation. We were separated by two oceans from European and Asian powers, and many Americans thought that our security would be best preserved by remaining aloof from international power struggles. This policy was known as **isolationism**. In the twentieth century, technology made oceans less of a barrier to foreign threats, and the world's growing economic interdependence meant that the United States could no longer ignore events abroad. At the beginning of the twentieth century, despite its isolationist sentiments, the United States entered World War I on the side of Great Britain when the Wilson administration concluded that America's economic and security interests would be adversely affected by a German victory. In 1941, America was drawn into World War II when Japan attacked the U.S. Pacific fleet anchored at Pearl Harbor, Hawaii. Even before the Japanese attack forced America to fight, the Roosevelt administration had already concluded that the United States must come to Britain's aid to prevent a victory by the German-Japanese-Italian Axis alliance. Until the Japanese attack, however, President Roosevelt had not been able to overcome proponents of American isolationism, who declared that our security was best served by leaving foreigners to their own devices. With their attack, the Japanese proved that the Pacific Ocean could not protect the United States from foreign foes and effectively discredited isolationism as a security policy.

In the aftermath of World War II, the United States developed a new security policy known as **deterrence**. Following the war, the power of the Soviet Union seemed to grow exponentially. By the end of the 1940s, the Soviets had built a huge empire and enormous military forces. Most threatening of all, the Soviet Union had built nuclear weapons and intercontinental bombers capable of attacking the United States. Some Americans argued that we should attack the Soviets before it was too late. This policy is known as **preventive war**. Others said that we should show our peaceful intentions and attempt to placate the Soviets. This policy is called **appeasement**.

The policy that the United States actually adopted, deterrence, could be seen as midway between preventive war and appeasement. A nation pursuing a policy of deterrence, on the one hand, signals its peaceful intentions, but on the other hand indicates its willingness and ability to fight if attacked. Thus, during the era of confrontation with the Soviet Union, known as the **Cold War**, the United States frequently asserted that it had no intention of attacking the Soviet Union. At the same time, however, the United States built a huge military force, including an arsenal of nuclear weapons and intercontinental missiles, and frequently asserted that in the event of a Soviet attack, it had the ability and will to respond with overwhelming force. The Soviet Union announced that its nuclear weapons were also intended for deterrent purposes. Eventually the two sides possessed such enormous arsenals of nuclear missiles that each potentially had the ability to destroy the other in the event of war. This heavily armed standoff came to be called a posture of mutually assured destruction.

isolationism
The desire to avoid involvement in the affairs of other nations.

deterrence The development and maintenance of military strength as a means of discouraging attack.

preventive war The policy of striking first when a nation fears that a foreign foe is comtemplating hostile action.

appeasement An effort to forestall war by giving in to the demands of a hostile power.

Cold War The period of struggle between the United States and the former Soviet Union between the late 1940s and about 1990.

A policy of deterrence not only requires the possession of large military forces but also requires the nation pursuing such a policy to convince potential adversaries that it is willing to fight. France had a large army in the 1930s, but Nazi Germany was not deterred from pursuing its expansionist goals in Europe because the German chancellor, Adolf Hitler, did not believe that the French were actually willing to fight. Thus, as part of its policy of deterrence, the United States engaged in wars in Korea, Vietnam, and elsewhere in response to what it believed to be Soviet aggression. Though the United States had no particular interests in Korea or Vietnam, American policy makers believed that if the United States did not fight in these areas, the Soviets would be emboldened to pursue an expansionist policy elsewhere, thinking that the Americans would not respond. Through military deterrence, the United States hoped to "contain" the Soviet Union and prevent futher increases in its power and territory.

During the 1990s, the Soviet Union collapsed, partly because its huge military expenditures undermined its creaky and inefficient centrally planned economy. The new Russia, though still a formidable and sometimes unfriendly power, seemed to pose less of a threat to the United States. Americans celebrated the end of the Cold War and believed that the enormous expense of America's own military forces might be reduced. Within a few years of the Soviet collapse, however, a new set of security threats emerged, requiring new policy responses. The September 11 terrorist attacks demonstrated a threat against which security scholars had long warned. The threat was that non-state actors and so-called rogue states might acquire significant military capabilities, including nuclear weapons, and would not be affected by America's deterrent capabilities.

A policy of deterrence assumes certainty and rationality. Certainty means that a potential adversary must know for sure that the United States will reply with force if attacked. Rationality means that, to be deterred, a potential adversary must be capable of rationally assessing the risks and costs of aggression against the United States. These two assumptions, which were valid when we faced the Soviet Union, may not be appropriate in the face of contemporary security threats. Unlike **nation-states**, countries with governments and fixed borders, terrorist groups are non-state actors having no fixed geographic location that can be attacked. Terrorists may believe that they can attack and melt away, leaving the United States with no one against whom to retaliate. Hence, the threat of massive retaliation does not deter them. "Rogue states" are nations with unstable and erratic leaders who seem to pursue policies driven by ideological or religious fervor rather than careful consideration of economic or human costs. The United States considers North Korea and Iran to be rogue states. Such states are difficult to deter because they may be willing to accept or may not fully grasp the potential costs of their actions.

To counter these new security threats, the United States shifted from a policy of deterrence to one of **preemption**. Preemption is often used as another name for preventive war or willingness to strike first in order to prevent an enemy attack. The United States has declared that it will not wait to be attacked but will, if necessary, take action to disable terrorist groups and rogue states before they can do us harm. The Bush administration's "global war on terror" was an expression of this notion of preemption, as was the U.S. invasion of Iraq. The United States has also refused to rule out the possibility that it would attack North Korea or Iran if it deemed those

nation-state
A political entity consisting of a people with some common cultural experience (nation) who also share a common political authority (state), recognized by other sovereignties (nation-states).

preemption The willingness to strike first in order to prevent an enemy attack.

The Democratic Peace and Foreign Policy

In 1795, the philosopher Immanuel Kant proposed the idea that representative governments were far less likely than other types of regimes to initiate wars. Hence, if representative governments replaced monarchies and other autocracies throughout the world, the result would be "perpetual peace." Today, Kant's idea is called democratic peace theory and has considerable support among scholars, commentators, and government officials.

Immanuel Kant

This idea has significant implications for foreign policy. For example, the Bush administration argued that transforming Iraq into a democracy would help to promote peace in the Middle East. And many policy makers believe that by helping China develop a more open and responsive government, the United States can increase the likelihood of peace with that nation.

Proponents of democratic peace theory assert that democracies seldom, if ever, fight one another. Many argue that democracies are usually reluctant to attack nondemocracies, as well. The core logic of democratic peace theory is that ordinary citizens bear the burdens of war and are usually not eager to send their children to fight unless it is absolutely necessary. Thus, to the extent that governments answer to ordinary citizens, they will be constrained from going to war. Critics of the theory point out that even in democracies, wars are often initially popular, though citizens may eventually become disenchanted with the bloodshed. Many scholars have attempted to collect data on the involvement of democracies in wars.

The table on the following page is a fairly comprehensive list of military conflicts involving democratic regimes. Whether these data support or call into question democratic peace theory depends on how the information is assessed. Relatively few conflicts have pitted one democracy against another.Yet, on many occasions, democracies have launched attacks against other nations. Does this mean that if all the world's regimes were democracies there would be no more wars, or could there be other factors at work? For example, the contemporary democracies might be members of the same trade and military alliances and these alliances, rather than their democratic constitutions, could keep them at peace with one another.

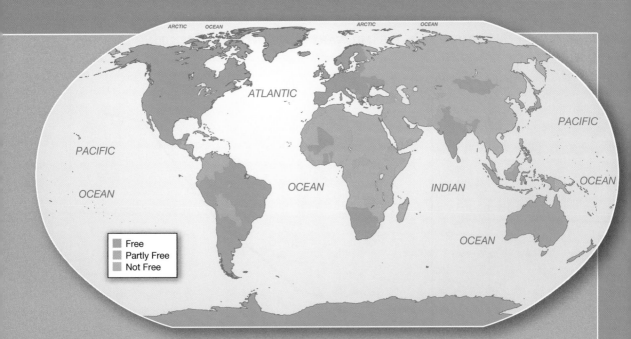

Free
Partly Free
Not Free

Freedom House ranks 89 countries in the worlds as "free" electoral democracies and 58 countries as "partly free" electoral democracies*, yet many of these countries have been involved in wars at some point since adopting democratic regimes.

MILITARY CONFLICTS INVOLVING DEMOCRATIC REGIMES

American Revolutionary War	1775–1783	World War II	1939–1945
War of 1812	1812–1815	Continuation War	1941–1944
Mexican-American War	1846–1848	Indo-Pakistani War of 1947	1947–1948
Sonderbund War	1847	1948 Arab-Israeli War	1947–1949
French Second Republic vs. Roman Republic (19th century)	1849	Cod Wars	1958–1976
		Operation Power Pack	1965
Ecuadorian-Colombian War	1863	Six-Day War	1967
War of the Pacific	1879–1884	Turkish invasion of Cyprus	1974
First Boer War	1880–1881	Paquisha War	1981
Spanish-American War	1898	Yugoslav Wars	1991–1999
Philippine-American War	1899–1913	Cenepa War	1995
Second Boer War	1899–1902	Eritrean-Ethiopian War	1998–2000
World War I	1914–1918	Kargil War	1999
Irish War of Independence	1919–1921	2006 Lebanon War	2006
Polish-Lithuanian War	1920		

*Source: Freedom House, Map of Freedom in the World, 2009 Edition, www.freedomhouse.org.
Photo: The Granger Collection, NY

FIGURE 16.1 U.S. MILITARY EXPENDITURE SINCE 2001

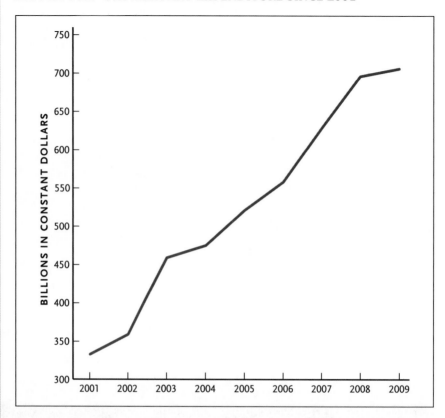

NOTE: Figure includes Department of Defense spending, Department of Energy's nuclear weapons program, the costs of the wars in Iraq and Afghanistan, and DoD-related spending by other agencies.

SOURCE: Center for Arms Control and Non-Proliferation, www.armscontrolcenter.org/policy/securityspending/articles/defense_spending_since_2001/index.html (accessed 4/21/09).

nations' nuclear programs to be an imminent threat to American security interests. Accompanying this shift in military doctrines has been an enormous increase in overall U.S. military spending (see Figure 16.1). It remains to be seen whether America's doctrine of preemption will successfully counter threats. The Obama Administration declared that it would endeavor to establish constructive dialogues with North Korea, Iran, and other hostile states. However, Obama did not necessarily renounce the Bush Doctrine for those who refused to become constructively engaged.

Economic Prosperity

A second major goal of U.S. foreign policy is promoting American prosperity. America's international economic policies are intended to expand employment opportunities in the United States, to maintain access to foreign energy supplies at a reasonable cost, to promote foreign investment in the United States, and to lower the prices Americans pay for goods and services.

Among the most visible and important elements of U.S. international economic policy is trade policy. The promotion and advertising of American goods and services abroad is a long-standing goal of U.S. trade policy, and it is one of the major obligations of the Department of Commerce. Yet modern trade policy involves a complex arrangement of treaties, tariffs, and other mechanisms of policy formation. For example, the United States has a long-standing policy of granting **most favored nation status** to certain countries—that is, the United States offers to another country the same tariff rate it already gives to its most favored trading partner, in return for trade (and sometimes other) concessions. In 1998, to avoid any suggestion that "most favored nation" implied some special relationship with an undemocratic country (China, for example), President Clinton changed the term from "most favored nation" to "normal trade relations."[4]

The most important international organization for promoting free trade is the **World Trade Organization (WTO)**, which officially came into being in 1995. The WTO grew out of the **General Agreement on Tariffs and Trade (GATT)**. Since World War II, GATT had brought together a wide range of nations for regular negotiations designed to reduce barriers to trade. Such barriers, many believed, had contributed to the breakdown of the world economy in the 1930s and had helped to cause World War II. The WTO has 151 members worldwide; decisions about trade are made by the Ministerial Conference, which meets every two years. Similar policy goals are pursued in regional arrangements, such as the **North American Free Trade Agreement (NAFTA)**, a trade treaty among the United States, Canada, and Mexico.

Working toward freer trade has been an important goal of each presidential administration since World War II. Yet as globalization has advanced, concerns about free trade and about the operation of the WTO, in particular, have grown. The WTO meetings held in Seattle in 1999 provoked unprecedented protests by groups that included environmentalists and labor unions. Tens of thousands of protesters denounced the undemocratic decision-making process of the WTO, which, they charged, was dominated by the concerns of business. These critics believe that the WTO does not pay sufficient attention to the concerns of developing nations and to such issues as environmental degradation, human rights, and labor practices, including the use of child labor in many countries. The Seattle meetings were adjourned with no agreement having been reached. Since the Seattle meetings, the major problem in WTO negotiations has been conflicts between poor, developing nations and rich, developed countries. Countries in the developing world accuse the United States and Europe of hypocrisy, preaching free trade but then using patents and subsidies to protect their own markets. There have been some successes on these issues, notably new WTO guidelines that allow poor countries to override expensive patents. Such patents make desperately needed drugs unavailable to most of the developing world. It has been more difficult to reach agreement on

most favored nation status An agreement to offer a trading partner the lowest tariff rate offered to other trading partners.

World Trade Organization (WTO) The international trade agency promoting free trade that grew out of the General Agreement on Tariffs and Trade.

General Agreement on Tariffs and Trade (GATT) The international trade organization, in existence from 1947 to 1995, that set many of the rules governing international trade.

North American Free Trade Agreement (NAFTA) A trade treaty among the United States, Canada, and Mexico to lower and eliminate tariffs among the three countries.

---

[4]This was done quietly in an amendment to the Internal Revenue Service Reform Act (PL 105-206), June 22, 1998. But it was not accomplished easily. See Bob Gravely, "Normal Trade with China Wins Approval," *Congressional Quarterly Weekly Report*, July 25, 1998; and Richard Dunham, "MFN by any other name is . . . NTR?," Business Week online news flash, June 19, 1997.

agricultural subsidies. Both the United States and Europe provide massive subsidies to their own agricultural industries. The prospects of resolving this issue are dim. The developed world has been reluctant to confront the economic dislocations and political costs of reducing the subsidies.

For over a half century, the United States has led the world in supporting free trade as the best route to growth and prosperity. Yet the American government, too, has sought to protect domestic industry when it is politically necessary. Subsidies, as we have seen, have long boosted American agriculture, artificially lowering the price of American products on world markets. In 2002 President George W. Bush, a vocal advocate of free trade, angered the rest of the world when he imposed protective tariffs on imported steel. Accused of hypocrisy and faced with retaliation from trading partners, the administration defended its actions by pointing to the damage that imports were doing to the domestic steel industry. When the WTO ruled that the steel tariffs violated WTO rules, Bush faced an unhappy choice. He could allow the European Union to retaliate by imposing tariffs, many of them on goods produced in politically important states. Or he could lift the tariffs, thus angering steel producers and workers. The president chose to lift the steel tariffs.

Trade was also an issue in the 2008 election. During their third debate, John McCain accused Barack Obama of promoting protectionist policies, whereas Obama said Republicans had exported American jobs abroad and allowed an enormous trade deficit to develop. The U.S. trade deficit was projected to reach $60 billion (see Figure 16.2), and job growth in the United States had been low for several years. Analysts predicted that many of the 2.8 million manufacturing jobs lost in the recession of the early 2000s would never return to the United States. Moreover, outsourcing—the practice of moving jobs to other countries—began to hit the white-collar workforce, as jobs for workers such as call-center operators and computer programmers moved to India and other countries with cheaper labor forces. There is much disagreement about the impact that outsourcing will have on American jobs. Some studies suggest that 20 percent of all jobs in the developed world could be affected by outsourcing including "all American librarians, statisticians, chemical engineers and air traffic controllers."[5] Other observers say that the impact will be felt more as pressure to reduce American wages. Still others suggest that concern about outsourcing has been overblown, arguing that it will be many decades before outsourcing has a major impact on American workers. All of these uncertainties have made trade a controversial policy area. As one political observer declared, "Trade is the new third rail of U.S. politics—touch it and die."[6]

International Humanitarian Policies

A third goal of American policy is to make the world a better place for all its inhabitants. The main forms of policy that address this goal are international environmental policy, international human rights policy, and international peacekeeping. The United States also contributes to international organizations such as the World

---

[5] Eduardo Porter, "True or False: Outsourcing Is a Crisis," *New York Times*, June 19, 2005, sec. 3, p. 4.

[6] Deborah McGregor, "Democrats Set Trail Alight with Attacks on Free Trade," *Financial Times*, February 4, 2004, p. 9.

FIGURE 16.2 U.S. INTERNATIONAL TRADE IN GOODS AND SERVICES

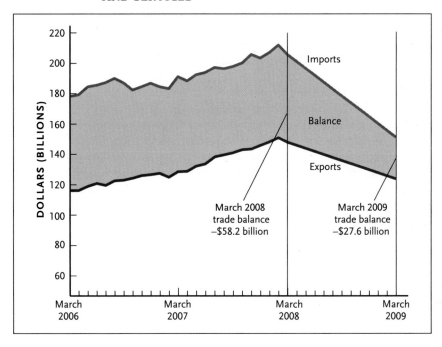

SOURCE: U.S. Census Bureau, www.census.gov/indicator/www/ustrade.html (accessed 5/20/09).

Health Organization that work for global health and against hunger. These policies are often seen as secondary to the other goals of American foreign policy, forced to give way if they interfere with security or foreign economic policy. Moreover, although the United States spends billions annually on security policy and hundreds of millions on trade policy, we spend relatively little on environmental, human rights, and peacekeeping efforts. Some critics charge that America has the wrong priorities, spending far more to make war than to protect human rights and the global environment. Nevertheless, a number of important American foreign policy efforts are, at least in part, designed to make the world a better place.

In the realm of international environmental policy, the United States supports a number of international efforts to protect the environment. These include the United Nations Framework Convention on Climate Change, an international agreement to study and ameliorate harmful changes in the global environment, and the Montreal Protocol, an agreement signed by more than 150 countries to limit the production of substances potentially harmful to the world's ozone layer. Other nations have severely criticized the United States for withdrawing from the 1997 Kyoto Protocol, an agreement setting limits on emissions of greenhouse gases from industrial countries. The United States has asserted that the Kyoto Protocol would be harmful to American economic interests. Although the United States is concerned with the global environment, national economic interests took precedence in this case. Since the Kyoto agreement is due to expire in 2012, the issue may soon be moot.

The same national priorities seem apparent in the area of human rights policy. The United States has a long-standing commitment to human rights and is a party to most major international agreements concerning human rights. These include the International Covenant on Civil and Political Rights, the International Convention Against Torture, the Convention on the Elimination of All Forms of Racial Discrimination, and various agreements to protect children. The State Department's Bureau of Democracy, Human Rights, and Labor works cooperatively with international organizations to investigate and focus attention on human rights abuses. In 1998, the United States enacted the International Religious Freedom Act, which calls on all governments to respect religious freedom. The act lists a number of sanctions that the United States and other signatories can employ to punish nations found to be in violation.

Although the United States is committed to promoting human rights, this commitment has a lower priority in American foreign policy than the nation's security concerns and economic interests. Thus, the United States is likely to overlook human rights violations by its major trading partners, such as China, and remain silent in the face of human rights violations by such allies as Saudi Arabia. Nevertheless, human rights concerns do play a role in American foreign policy. For example, beginning in 2007, the United States has made available several million dollars annually in small grants to pay medical and legal expenses incurred by individuals who have been the victims of retaliation in their own countries for working against their governments' repressive practices. In this small way, the United States is backing its often-asserted principles.

Another form of U.S. policy designed to improve the condition of the world is support for international peacekeeping efforts. At any time, a number of border wars, civil wars, and guerilla conflicts flare up somewhere in the world, usually in its poorer regions. These wars often generate humanitarian crises in the form of casualties, disease, and refugees. In cooperation with international agencies and other nations, the United States funds a number of efforts to keep the peace in volatile regions and to deal with the health-care and refugee problems associated with conflict. In 2007, the United States provided more than $1 billion in funding for United Nations peacekeeping operations in Bosnia, Kosovo, Sierra Leone, Lebanon, the Democratic Republic of Congo, and East Timor.

America's humanitarian policies are important. Without American efforts and funding, many international humanitarian programs would be far less successful than they are today. In general, though, security and economic interests take precedence in the eyes of U.S. policy makers over humanitarian concerns. The U.S. government is far more likely to decry abuses of religious freedom in Iran—an adversary—than in Saudi Arabia—an ally.

WHO MAKES AMERICAN FOREIGN POLICY?

As we have seen, domestic policies are made by governmental institutions and influenced by a variety of interest groups, political movements, and even the mass media. The same is true in the realm of foreign policy. The president and his chief advisors are the principal architects of U.S. foreign policy. However, Congress, the bureaucracy, the courts, political parties, interest groups, and trade associations also play important roles in this realm. Often, the president and Congress are at odds over foreign policy. When the Democrats took control of Congress in 2006, they vowed to force the president to end the war in Iraq. The president vowed to resist the Democrats' efforts and generally prevailed. Ethnic lobbies such as the pro-Israel lobby and the Armenian lobby also seek to affect foreign policy. In 2007, the Armenian lobby persuaded Congress to condemn Turkey's actions in 1915, which led to the deaths of more than one million Armenians. The president feared that Turkey, an important U.S. ally, would be offended and blocked the effort. Let us examine the major institutions and forces shaping American foreign policy.

Institutions are created to solve collective-action problems. In the realm of foreign policy, most Americans view the presidency as the institution best able to take action on the nation's behalf. Though they have many advisers, presidents are unitary actors and are capable of making decisions more quickly and efficiently than other governmental institutions. Thus, when collective action is needed to deal with emergencies such as the 9/11 terrorist attacks on the United States, we generally expect the president to take the lead in defending the nation's interests. Presidents have made use of this institutional advantage to expand their powers in the international and domestic realms. When we rely heavily on an institution to solve important collective-action problems, we are inclined to empower that institution above others. Thus, let us begin our discussion of who makes American foreign policy with the president.

The President

Most American presidents have been domestic politicians who set out to make their place in history through achievements in domestic policy. A standard joke during Bill Clinton's 1992 campaign, extending well into his first year, was that he had learned his foreign policy at the International House of Pancakes. Thus, it was not unusual that President George W. Bush had virtually no foreign-policy preparation prior to taking office. He had traveled very little outside the United States, and he had had virtually no foreign experience as governor of Texas.

Nonetheless, Bush was decisive in the initiatives he took to define America's national interest for his administration. Examples include revival of the controversial nuclear missile shield ("Star Wars"); his readiness to abandon the Anti-Ballistic Missile (ABM) treaty, which meant a serious and ugly confrontation with the Russians; changes in policy priorities away from humanitarian and environmental goals with a far stronger emphasis on goals more specifically within the realm of national security; and turning America's concerns (by degree or emphasis) away from Europe toward an "Asia-first" policy.

September 11 and its aftermath immensely accentuated the president's role and his place in foreign policy.[7] By 2002, foreign policy was the centerpiece of the Bush administration's agenda. In a June 1 speech at West Point, the **"Bush Doctrine"**

Bush Doctrine
Foreign policy based on the idea that the United States should take preemptive action against threats to its national security.

---

[7] Matthew Crenson and Benjamin Ginsberg, *Presidential Power: Unchecked and Unbalanced* (New York: Norton, 2007).

of preemptive war was announced. Bush argued that "our security will require all Americans . . . to be ready for preemptive action when necessary to defend our liberty and to defend our lives." Bush's statement was clearly intended to justify his administration's plans to invade Iraq, but it had much wider implications for international relations, including the central role of the American president in guiding foreign policy.

In 2008, the Republican presidential candidate John McCain was an exception to the usual rule of emphasizing domestic priorities. During his presidential race, McCain emphasized his foreign-policy expertise. Democrats countered by naming Senator Joseph Biden, chairman of the Senate Foreign Relations Committee, as their vice-presidential candidate. After his election, President Obama surrounded himself with experienced foreign policy advisers such as General James Jones, appointed to serve as national security adviser, and Robert Gates, asked to stay on as defense secretary. In October 2010, Jones announced his resignation and was replaced by Thomas E. Donilon.

The Bureaucracy

The major foreign-policy actors in the bureaucracy are the secretaries of the departments of State, Defense, and the Treasury; the Joint Chiefs of Staff (JCOS), especially the chair of the JCOS; and the director of the Central Intelligence Agency (CIA). Since 1947, a separate unit in the White House has overseen the vast foreign-policy establishment for the purpose of synthesizing all the messages arising out of the bureaucracy and helping the president make his own foreign policy. This is the National Security Council (NSC). It is a "subcabinet" made up of the major players just listed, plus two or three others each president was given the authority to add. Since the profound shake-up of September 11, two additional key players have been added. The first of these was the secretary of the new Department of Homeland Security (DHS), composed of twenty-two existing agencies relocated from all over the executive branch on the theory that their expertise could be better coordinated, more rational, and more efficient in a single organization designed to fight international terrorism and domestic natural disasters. The second was imposed at the top as the war in Iraq was becoming a quagmire: a director of national intelligence, to collate and coordinate intelligence coming in from multiple sources.

Since the creation of the CIA and the Department of Defense in 1947, the secretary of defense and the director of the CIA have often been rivals engaged in power struggles for control of the intelligence community.[8] For the most part, secretaries of defense have prevailed in these battles, and the Defense Department today controls more than 80 percent of the nation's intelligence capabilities and funds. The creation of the position of director of national intelligence in 2005 to coordinate all intelligence activities set off new Washington power struggles as the "intelligence czar" faced opposition from both the CIA and the Department of Defense. As of 2008, the Defense Department continued to resist cooperating with civilian

---

[8] Benjamin Ginsberg, *The American Lie: Government by the People and Other Political Fables* (Boulder, Colo.: Paradigm, 2007).

intelligence agencies and moved to expand its own intelligence capabilities at their expense, though in a 2008 executive order the president sought to increase the power of the director of national intelligence.

In addition to these top cabinet-level officials, key lower-level staff members have policy-making influence as strong as that of the Cabinet secretaries. Some may occasionally exceed Cabinet influence. These include the two or three specialized national security advisers in the White House, the staff of the NSC (headed by the national security adviser), and a few other career bureaucrats in the departments of State and Defense whose influence varies according to their specialty and to the foreign policy issue at hand. A few civilian intelligence agencies are also involved in foreign policy and national security, the most important of which are the Federal Bureau of Investigation (FBI), the U.S. Citizenship and Immigration Services, and the Internal Revenue Service (IRS).

In the wake of 9/11, military and law-enforcement agencies have increased their role in America's foreign policy making.[9] To a significant extent, American foreign policy is driven by military and antiterrorist concerns, and the agencies deemed capable of addressing these concerns are coming to play a larger and larger role in American foreign policy. For example, in recent years, American ambassadors have complained that they have been relegated to secondary status as the White House has looked to military commanders for information, advice, and policy implementation. For every region of the world, the U.S. military has assigned a "combatant commander," usually a senior general or admiral, to take charge of operations in that area. In many instances, these combatant commanders, who control troops, equipment, and intelligence capabilities, have become the real eyes, ears, and spokespersons for American foreign policy in their designated regions.

Congress

Although the Constitution gives Congress the power to declare war (see Table 16.1), Congress has exercised this power on only five occasions: the War of 1812, the Mexican War (1846), the Spanish-American War (1898), World War I (1917), and World War II (1941). For the first 150 years of American history, Congress's role was limited because the United States' role in world affairs was limited. During this time, the Senate was the only important congressional foreign-policy player because of its constitutional role in reviewing and approving treaties. The treaty power is still the primary entrée of the Senate into foreign-policy making. But since World War II and the continual involvement of the United States in international security and foreign aid, Congress as a whole has become a major foreign-policy maker because most modern foreign policies require financing, which requires action by both the House of Representatives and the Senate. For example, Congress's first act after September 11 was to authorize the president to use "all necessary and appropriate force," coupled with a $40 billion emergency appropriations bill for homeland defense. And although President Bush believed he possessed the constitutional authority to invade Iraq, he still sought congressional approval, which he

---

[9] Paul R. Pillar, *Terrorism and American Foreign Policy* (Washington, D.C.: Brookings Institution Press, 2003).

TABLE 16.1 PRINCIPAL FOREIGN-POLICY PROVISIONS OF THE CONSTITUTION

	Power Granted To:	
	President	Congress
War power	Commander in chief of armed forces	Provide for the common defense; declare war
Treaties	Negotiate treaties	Ratification of treaties, by two-thirds majority (Senate)
Appointments	Nominate high-level government officials	Confirm president's appointments (Senate)
Foreign commerce	No explicit powers, but treaty negotiation and appointment powers pertain	Explicit power "to regulate foreign commerce"
General powers	Executive power; veto	Legislative power; power of the purse; oversight and investigation

received in October 2002. After the Democrats took control of Congress in 2007, the Democratic leadership proposed a new resolution opposing President Bush's policies in Iraq. The president asserted that he would not be bound by such a vote. Democratic leaders also discussed ways of reducing at least some funding for the war. In principle, Congress's "power of the purse" is its ultimate weapon. However, reducing funding for troops already in battle is a difficult undertaking, one that can leave Congress vulnerable to the charge of endangering American lives. The president's 2007 budget proposal demanded increased funding for the war in Iraq. Initially, Congress sought to tie increased funding to a timetable for troop withdrawal. After a battle with the president, however, it was Congress that was forced to withdraw, and in May 2007, Congress acceded to Bush's demands.

Not only does the president need Congress to provide funding for foreign and military policy initiatives but, under the Constitution, many presidential agreements with foreign nations also have to be approved by Congress. Article II, Section 2 of the Constitution declares that proposed treaties with other nations must be submitted by the president to the Senate and approved by a two-thirds vote. Because this "supermajority" is usually difficult to achieve, presidents generally prefer a different type of agreement with other nations called an **executive agreement**. An executive agreement is similar to a treaty and has the force of law but usually requires only a plurality vote (that is, 50 percent plus one) in both houses of Congress for approval. In recent years, Congress has approved thousands of executive agreements, including such cornerstones of American trade policy as the North American Free Trade Agreement (NAFTA).

executive agreement An agreement, made between the president and another country, that has the force of a treaty but does not require the Senate's "advice and consent."

Another aspect of Congress's role in foreign policy is the Senate's power to confirm the president's nominations of Cabinet members, ambassadors, and other high-ranking officials (such as the director of the CIA, but not the director of the NSC). A final constitutional power of Congress is the regulation of "commerce with foreign nations."

Other congressional players are the foreign-policy and military-policy committees: In the Senate, these are the Foreign Relations Committee, the Armed Services Committee, and the Homeland Security and Governmental Affairs Committee; in the House, these are the Foreign Affairs and Homeland Security Committee and the Armed Services Committee. Usually, a few members of these committees who have spent years specializing in foreign affairs become trusted members of the foreign-policy establishment and are influential makers of foreign policy. In fact, several members of Congress have left the legislature to become key foreign-affairs cabinet members. After September 11, congressional committees conducted hearings on the failure of the intelligence agencies, but at the time most members of Congress were reluctant to take on these agencies or a popular president. In 2007, though, with Congress under Democratic control and the president's popularity fading, a number of congressional committees launched inquiries into the conduct of the war in Iraq and the more general operations of the intelligence and defense communities. Within weeks, congressional testimony revealed flaws in military procurement procedures, military planning, and other aspects of the administration's programs and policies. Congressional investigations and the publicity they generate are weapons Congress frequently uses to blunt presidential power.

Interest Groups

Although the president, the executive-branch "bureaucracy," and Congress are the true makers of foreign policy, the "foreign-policy establishment" is a much larger arena, including what can properly be called the shapers of foreign policy—a host of unofficial, informal players, people who possess varying degrees of influence, depending on their prestige, their reputation, their socioeconomic standing, and—most important—the party and ideology that are dominant at a given moment.

By far the most important category of nonofficial player is the interest group—that is, the interest group to which one or more foreign-policy issues are of long-standing and vital relevance. The type of interest group with the reputation for the most influence is the economic interest group. Yet the myths about its influence far outnumber and outweigh the realities. The actual influence of organized economic interest groups in foreign policy varies enormously from issue to issue and year to year. Most of these groups are "single-issue" groups and are therefore most active when their particular issue is on the agenda. On many of the broader and more sustained policy issues—such as the North American Free Trade Agreement (NAFTA) or the general question of American involvement in international trade—the larger interest groups, sometimes called peak associations, find it difficult to maintain tight enough control of their many members to speak with a single voice. The most systematic study of international trade policies and their interest groups concluded that the leaders of these large economic interest groups spend more time maintaining consensus among their members than they do lobbying Congress or pressuring major players in the executive branch.[10] The more successful economic interest groups, in terms of influencing foreign policy, are the narrower, single-issue groups such as the tobacco industry, which over the years has successfully kept American foreign policy from putting heavy restrictions on international trade in and advertising of tobacco products; and the computer hardware and software industries, which have successfully hardened the American attitude toward Chinese piracy of intellectual property rights.

Another type of interest group with a well-founded reputation for influence in foreign policy is made up of people with strong attachments to and identification with their country of national origin. The interest group with the reputation for the greatest influence is Jewish Americans, whose family and emotional ties to Israel make them one of the most alert and active interest groups in the whole field of foreign policy. But note once again how narrowly specialized that interest is—it focuses almost entirely on policies toward Israel. Similarly, Americans of Irish heritage, despite having lived in the United States for two, three, or four generations, still maintain vigilance about American policies toward Ireland and Northern Ireland; some even contribute to the Irish Republican Army. Many other ethnic and national interest groups wield similar influence over American foreign policy.

These ethnic or national-origin interest groups are more influential than their counterparts in other democratic countries. This is a kind of dual loyalty that Americans generally welcome as a worthy sentiment. But there are limits, especially when national origin is coupled with or tied to countries in which a single religion is dominant. For example, Jews with strong ties to Israel and Catholics with connections to Ireland have on occasion been blocked from group influence on foreign policy because "dual loyalty" can be taken by other groups as "doubtful loyalty."[11] Nevertheless, Irish and Jewish groups, as well as a variety of other ethnic American interest groups, are vigorously involved in salient aspects of foreign policy, and it is an irrational or nonrational elected politician who disregards their signals. It is quite possible that the "electoral connection"[12] and the politics of representation in Congress (and the White House) are at their most intense when national origin is linked to a foreign-policy issue. Many will argue that the rationality principle "need not . . . be equated with such narrowly self-serving actions."[13] However, the nationality interest is often the strongest electoral connection.

A third type of interest group, one with a reputation that has been growing in the past two decades, is devoted to human rights. Such groups are made up of people who, instead of having self-serving economic or ethnic interests in foreign

---

[10] Raymond A. Bauer, Ithiel de Sola Pool, and Lewis Anthony Dexter, *American Business and Public Policy: The Politics of Foreign Trade*, 2nd ed. (Chicago: Aldine-Atherton, 1972).

[11] For a good treatment of this in regard to Irish Catholics and Catholics in general, see Timothy Byrnes, *Catholic Bishops and American Politics* (Princeton, N.J.: Princeton University Press, 1991). For a (controversial) discussion of the role of Jewish groups, see John J. Mearsheimer and Stephen M. Walt, *The Israel Lobby and U.S. Foreign Policy* (New York: Farrar, Straus and Giroux, 2007).

[12] This felicitous term is from David R. Mayhew, *Congress: The Electoral Connection* (New Haven, Conn.: Yale University Press, 1974).

[13] John H. Aldrich, *Why Parties? The Origin and Transformation of Political Parties in America* (Chicago: University of Chicago Press, 1995), 278.

policy, are genuinely concerned about the welfare and treatment of people throughout the world—particularly those who suffer under harsh political regimes. A relatively small but often quite influential example is Amnesty International, whose exposés of human-rights abuses have altered the practices of many regimes around the world. In recent years, the Christian right has been a vocal advocate for the human rights of Christians who are persecuted in other parts of the world, most notably in China, for their religious beliefs. For example, the Christian Coalition joined groups such as Amnesty International in lobbying Congress to restrict trade with countries that permit attacks against religious believers.

A related type of group with rapidly growing influence is the ecological or environmental group, sometimes collectively called "greens". Groups of this nature often depend more on demonstrations than on the usual forms and strategies of influence in Washington—lobbying and using electoral politics, for example. Demonstrations in strategically located areas can have significant influence on American foreign policy. The most recent examples were the 1999 protests in Seattle and the 2001 protest in Genoa, Italy, against the World Trade Organization (WTO) and its authority to impose limits and restrictions on sovereign nations (even the United States).

The Media

Each part of the media has its own character and mode of operations, and as a consequence each may represent a different source of anguish and a different source of opportunity in making and implementing foreign policy. This makes the media a very special problem for every president because—as George Washington warned—once we become "entangled" with other nations, the media have to be "managed" to a certain extent, or persuaded to present a single, national voice. And managing can come close to a violation of the First Amendment's freedom of the press guarantee. Such management, then, becomes an overwhelming problem during times of war, cold war, or any other sustained threat to national security, including these years following September 11.

The balancing of security against freedom of the press has become increasingly difficult with the increased power of the media, which has resulted from significant developments in communications and information technology. Iraq is of course the most important case in point. During the first few weeks of the invasion in 2003, nearly 600 embedded journalists (plus a number of "free-floating" U.S. and non-U.S. journalists) provided the most intensive coverage in the history of war, and without any question for the first time the coverage was instantaneous, visual, annotated, and in color—not only on television but on the front pages of the major newspapers and online as well.

Take special note of the word *embedded*. No matter how delicately put, embedding involved the management of the journalists in a deal to provide access and protection in return for "responsible" reporting, a deal that led to the widespread suspicion and fear that not only the journalists but also the news itself was being managed. The suspicion grew as the war changed after the regime of Saddam Hussein was deposed, the Iraqi armed forces dispersed, and the entire civil government that had been dominated by the Hussein Baathist Party was decommissioned. Quite simply, the situation changed from a conventional, organized war to an ambiguous, insurgent war. This was the end of any practice of embedding and the beginning of fewer but freer-floating journalists, a change that also meant the expansion of dissent and open criticism accompanying the reports. "News management" to any degree was no longer possible.

As casualties mounted and the insurgency dragged on, reporting from Iraq (and the entire Middle East) began to demonstrate the true plurality of the term *media*. Considerable support remained—among Americans at home and journalists reporting from the scene—for maintaining America's commitment to Iraq and for sustaining and increasing American military and economic support of Iraq. But as reports critical of America's policy—and, even more, of the policy's implementation—expanded in number, scale, and intensity, the reaction to the unmanaged reporting also increased. Inevitably, self-designated conservative and neoconservative critics charged that ideology was driving the opposition to the war and that the media—especially certain national newspapers, periodicals, and television syndicates—were nothing more than channels for "liberal bias."

Putting It Together

What can we say about who really makes American foreign policy? First, except for the president, the influence of players and shapers varies from case to case—this is a good reason to look with some care at each example of foreign policy in this chapter. Second, because the one constant influence is the centrality of the president in foreign-policy making, it is best to evaluate other actors and factors as they interact with the president.[14] Third, the reason influence varies from case to case is that each case arises under different conditions and with vastly different time constraints: For issues that arise and are resolved quickly, the opportunity for influence is limited. Fourth, foreign-policy experts will usually disagree about the level of influence any player or type of player has on policy making.

But just to get started, let's make a few tentative generalizations and then put them to the test with the substance and experience reported in the remainder of this chapter. First, when an important foreign-policy decision has to be made under conditions of crisis—where time is of the essence—the influence of the presidency is at its strongest. Second, within those time constraints, access to the decision is limited almost exclusively to the narrowest definition of the foreign-policy establishment. The arena for participation is tiny; any discussion at all is limited to the officially and constitutionally designated players. To put this another way, in a crisis the foreign-policy establishment works as it is supposed to.[15] As time becomes less

---

[14] A very good brief outline of the centrality of the president in foreign policy is found in Paul E. Peterson, "The President's Dominance in Foreign Policy Making," *Political Science Quarterly* 109 (Summer 1994): 215–34.

[15] One confirmation of this is found in Theodore Lowi, *The End of Liberalism: The Second Republic of the United States*, 2nd ed. (New York: Norton, 1979), 127–30; another is found in Stephen Krasner, "Are Bureaucracies Important?" *Foreign Policy 7* (Summer 1972): 159–79. However, it should be noted that Krasner was writing his article in disagreement with Graham T. Allison, "Conceptual Models and the Cuban Missile Crisis," *American Political Science Review* 63, no. 3 (September 1969): 689–718.

restricted, even when the decision to be made is of great importance, the arena of participation expands to include more government players and more nonofficial, informal players—the most concerned interest groups and the most important journalists. In other words, the arena becomes more pluralistic and, therefore, less distinguishable from the politics of domestic-policy making. Third, because there are so many other countries with power and interests on any given issue, there are severe limits on the choices the United States can make. That is, in sharp contrast to domestic politics, U.S. policy makers in the foreign-policy realm are engaged not only in infighting but also in strategic interaction with policy makers in other nations; their choices are made both in reaction to and in anticipation of these strategic interactions. As one author concludes, in foreign affairs, "policy takes precedence over politics."[16] Thus, even though foreign-policy making in noncrisis situations may closely resemble the pluralistic politics of domestic-policy making, foreign-policy making is still a narrower arena with fewer participants.

THE INSTRUMENTS OF MODERN AMERICAN FOREIGN POLICY

Any government has at hand certain instruments, or tools, to use in implementing its foreign policy. An instrument is neutral, capable of serving many goals. There have been many instruments of American foreign policy, and we can deal here only with those instruments we deem to be most important in the modern epoch: diplomacy, the United Nations, the international monetary structure, economic aid, collective security, and military deterrence. Each of these instruments will be evaluated in this section for its utility in the conduct of American foreign policy, and each will be assessed in light of the history and development of American values.

Diplomacy

We begin this treatment of instruments with diplomacy because it is the instrument to which all other instruments should be subordinated, although they seldom are. **Diplomacy** is the representation of a government to other foreign governments. Its purpose is to promote national values or interests by peaceful means. According to Hans Morgenthau, "a diplomacy that ends in war has failed in its primary objective."[17]

The first effort to create a modern diplomatic service in the United States was made through the Rogers Act of 1924, which established the initial framework for a professional foreign-service staff. But it took World War II and the Foreign Service Act of 1946 to forge the foreign service into a fully professional diplomatic corps.

diplomacy The representation of a government to other foreign governments.

---

[16] Peterson, "The President's Dominance in Foreign Policy Making," p. 232.

[17] Hans Morgenthau, *Politics among Nations*, 2nd ed. (New York: Knopf, 1956), p. 505.

Diplomacy, by its very nature, is overshadowed by spectacular international events, dramatic initiatives, and meetings among heads of state or their direct personal representatives. The traditional American distrust of diplomacy continues today, albeit in weaker form. Impatience with or downright distrust of diplomacy has been built into not only all the other instruments of foreign policy but also the modern presidential system itself.[18] So much personal responsibility has been heaped on the presidency that it is difficult for presidents to entrust any of their authority or responsibility in foreign policy to professional diplomats in the State Department and other bureaucracies.

Distrust of diplomacy has also produced a tendency among all recent presidents to turn frequently to military and civilian personnel outside the State Department to take on a special diplomatic role as direct personal representatives of the president. As discouraging as it is to those who have dedicated their careers to foreign service to have personal appointees chosen over their heads, it is probably even more discouraging when they are displaced from a foreign-policy issue as soon as relations with the country they are posted to begin to heat up. When a special personal representative is sent abroad to represent the president, that envoy holds a status higher than that of the local ambassador, and the embassy becomes the envoy's temporary residence and base of operation. Despite the impressive professionalization of the American foreign service—with advanced training, competitive exams, language requirements, and career commitment—this practice of displacing career ambassadors with political appointees and with special personal presidential representatives continues. For instance, when President Clinton in 1998 sought to boost the peace process in Northern Ireland, he called on the former senator George Mitchell. Mitchell received almost unanimous praise for his skill and patience in chairing the Northern Ireland peace talks. The caliber of his work in Northern Ireland led to Senator Mitchell's becoming involved in another of the world's apparently unsolvable conflicts, that between the Israelis and the Palestinians.

Despite the United States' track record of distrust of diplomacy, immediately following the terrorist attacks of September 11, 2001, questions arose about how we could go after terrorist networks without the active cooperation of dozens of governments. Getting access to terrorists in various countries, plus putting together and keeping together the worldwide alliance of governments to fight terrorism, was a diplomatic, not a military, chore. In calls to more than eighty nations, former Secretary of State Colin Powell helped to extract dozens of pledges that would have been more difficult to get months later, when sympathy for America began to wane. In short, global unity and success in fighting terrorism required constant diplomatic efforts, not only by Powell, but also by other leading players, including President Bush himself.

In 2008, both parties' presidential candidates criticized the Bush administration for having failed to use diplomacy to secure greater international support for the Iraq war. Both promised to revitalize American diplomacy. President Obama

---

[18] See Theodore Lowi, *The Personal President: Power Invested, Promise Unfulfilled* (Ithaca, N.Y.: Cornell University Press, 1985), pp. 167–69.

appointed Hillary Clinton as his secretary of state in part to underline the importance he attached to diplomacy by appointing such a prominent figure as America's chief diplomat.

The significance of diplomacy and its vulnerability to politics may be better appreciated as we proceed to the other instruments. Diplomacy was an instrument more or less imposed on Americans as the prevailing method of dealing among nation-states in the nineteenth century. The other instruments to be identified and assessed below are instruments that Americans self-consciously crafted for themselves to take care of their own chosen place in the world affairs of the second half of the twentieth century and beyond. They therefore better reflect American culture and values than diplomacy does.

The United Nations

The utility of the **United Nations (UN)** to the United States as an instrument of foreign policy can be too easily underestimated, because the United Nations is a very large and unwieldy institution with few powers and no armed forces to implement its rules and resolutions. Its supreme body is the UN General Assembly, comprising one representative of each of the 192 member states; each member representative has one vote, regardless of the size of the country. Important issues require a two-thirds majority vote, and the annual session of the General Assembly runs only from September to December (although it can call extra sessions). It has little organization that can make it an effective decision-making body, with only six standing committees, few tight rules of procedure, and no political parties to provide priorities and discipline. Its defenders are quick to add that although it lacks armed forces, it relies on the power of world opinion; and this is not to be taken lightly. The powers of the United Nations devolve mainly to its "executive committee," the UN Security Council, which alone has the real power to make decisions and rulings that member states are obligated by the UN Charter to implement. The Security Council may be called into session at any time, and each member (or a designated alternate) must be present at UN Headquarters in New York at all times. It is composed of fifteen members: five are permanent (the victors of World War II), and ten are elected by the General Assembly for two-year, nonrepeatable terms. The five permanent members are China, France, Russia, the United Kingdom, and the United States. Each of the fifteen members has only one vote, and a nine-vote majority of the fifteen is required on all substantive matters. But each of the five permanent members also has a negative vote, a "veto," and one veto is sufficient to reject any substantive proposal.

The UN can be a useful forum for international discussions and an instrument for multilateral action. Most peacekeeping efforts to which the United States contributes, for example, are undertaken under UN auspices.

The International Monetary Structure

Fear of a repeat of the economic devastation that followed World War I brought the United States together with its allies (except the USSR) to Bretton Woods, New Hampshire, in 1944 to create a new international economic structure for

United Nations (UN) An organization of nations founded in 1945 to be a channel for negotiation and a means of settling international disputes peaceably. The UN has had frequent successes in providing a forum for negotiation and on some occasions a means of preventing international conflicts from spreading. On a number of occasions, the UN has been a convenient cover for U.S. foreign-policy goals.

the postwar world. The result was two institutions: the International Bank for Reconstruction and Development (commonly called the World Bank) and the International Monetary Fund.

The World Bank was set up to finance long-term capital. Leading nations took on the obligation of contributing funds to enable the World Bank to make loans to capital-hungry countries. (The U.S. quota has been about one-third of the total.)

The **International Monetary Fund (IMF)** was set up to provide for the short-term flow of money. After the war, the dollar, instead of gold, was the chief means by which the currencies of one country would be "changed into" currencies of another country for purposes of making international transactions. To permit debtor countries with no international balances to make purchases and investments, the IMF was set up to lend dollars or other appropriate currencies to needy member countries to help them overcome temporary trade deficits. For many years after World War II, the IMF, along with U.S. foreign aid, in effect constituted the only international medium of exchange.

During the 1990s, the IMF returned to a position of enhanced importance through its efforts to reform some of the largest debtor nations and formerly communist countries, to bring them more fully into the global capitalist economy. For example, in the early 1990s, Russia and thirteen other former Soviet republics were invited to join the IMF and the World Bank with the expectation of receiving $10.5 billion from these two agencies, primarily for a currency-stabilization fund. Each republic was to get a permanent IMF representative, and the IMF increased its staff by at least 10 percent to provide the expertise necessary to cope with the problems of these emerging capitalist economies.[19]

The IMF, with tens of billions of dollars contributed by its members, has more money to lend poor countries than do the United States, Europe, or Japan (the three leading IMF shareholders) individually. It makes its policy decisions in ways that are generally consonant with the interests of the leading shareholders.[20] Two weeks after September 11, 2001, the IMF had approved a $135 million loan to economically troubled Pakistan, a key player in the war against the Taliban government of Afghanistan because of its strategic location. Turkey, also because of its strategic location in the Middle East, was likewise put back in the IMF pipeline.[21] The future of the IMF, the World Bank, and all other private sources of international investment will depend in part on extension of more credit to the Third World and other developing countries, because credit means investment and productivity. But the future may depend even more on reducing the debt that is already there from previous extensions of credit.

International Monetary Fund (IMF)   An institution established in 1944 that provides loans and facilitates international monetary exchange.

---

[19] "IMF: Sleeve-Rolling Time," *Economist*, May 2, 1992, pp. 98–99.

[20] James Dao and Patrick E. Tyler, "U.S. Says Military Strikes Are Just a Part of Big Plan," *The Alliance*, September 27, 2001; and Joseph Kahn, "A Nation Challenged: Global Dollars," *New York Times*, September 20, 2001, p. B1.

[21] Turkey was desperate for help to extricate its economy from its worst recession since 1945. The Afghanistan crisis was going to hurt Turkey all the more; its strategic location helped its case with IMF. "Official Says Turkey Is Advancing in Drive for I.M.F. Financing," *New York Times*, October 6, 2001, p. A7.

Economic Aid and Sanctions

Every year, the United States provides nearly $30 billion in economic assistance to other nations. Some aid has a humanitarian purpose, such as helping to provide health care, shelter for refugees, or famine relief. A good deal of American aid, however, is designed to promote American security interests or economic concerns. For example, the United States provides military assistance to a number of its allies in the form of advanced weapons or loans to help them purchase advanced weapons. Such loans generally stipulate that the recipient must purchase the designated weapons from American firms. In this way, the United States hopes to bolster its security and economic interests with one grant. The two largest recipients of American military assistance are Israel and Egypt, American allies that fought two wars against one another. The United States believes that its military assistance allows both to feel sufficiently secure to remain at peace with one another.

Aid is an economic carrot. Sanctions are an economic stick. Economic sanctions that the United States employs against other nations include trade embargoes, bans on investment, and efforts to prevent the World Bank or other international institutions from extending credit to a nation against which the United States has a grievance. Sanctions are most often employed when the United States seeks to weaken what it considers a hostile regime or when it is attempting to compel some particular action by another regime. Thus, for example, in order to weaken the Castro government, the United States has long prohibited American firms from doing business with Cuba. In recent years, the United States has maintained economic sanctions against Iran and North Korea in an effort to prevent those nations from pursuing nuclear weapons programs.

Unilateral sanctions by the United States usually have little effect, since the target can usually trade elsewhere, sometimes even with foreign affiliates of U.S. firms. If, however, the United States is able to convince its allies to cooperate, sanctions have a better chance of success. International sanctions applied to Libya, for example, played a role in the regime's decision to enter into negotiations with the United States over Libyan responsibility for a number of terrorist attacks.

Collective Security

In 1947, most Americans hoped that the United States could meet its world obligations through the United Nations and economic structures alone. But most foreign-policy makers recognized that was a vain hope even as they were permitting and encouraging Americans to believe it. They had anticipated the need for military entanglements at the time of drafting the original UN Charter by insisting on language that recognized the right of all nations to provide for their mutual defense independent of the United Nations. And almost immediately after enactment of the Marshall Plan, designed to promote European economic recovery, the White House and a parade of State and Defense Department officials followed up with an urgent request to the Senate to ratify, and to both houses of Congress to finance, mutual defense alliances.

At first quite reluctant to approve treaties providing for national security alliances, the Senate ultimately agreed with the executive branch. The first collective security agreement was the Rio Treaty (ratified by the Senate in September 1947), which created the Organization of American States (OAS). This was the model treaty, anticipating all succeeding collective security treaties by providing that an armed attack against any of its members "shall be considered as an attack against all the American States," including the United States. A more significant break with U.S. tradition against peacetime entanglements came with the North Atlantic Treaty (signed in April 1949), which created the **North Atlantic Treaty Organization (NATO)**. ANZUS, a treaty tying Australia and New Zealand to the United States, was signed in September 1951. Three years later, the Southeast Asia Treaty created the Southeast Asia Treaty Organization (SEATO).

In addition to these multilateral treaties, the United States entered into a number of **bilateral treaties**—treaties between two countries. As one author has observed, the United States has been a *producer* of security, whereas most of its allies have been *consumers* of security.[22]

This pattern has continued in the post–Cold War era, and its best illustration is in the Persian Gulf War. The United States provided the initiative, the leadership, and most of the armed forces, even though its allies were obliged to reimburse over 90 percent of the cost.

It is difficult to evaluate collective security and its treaties, because the purpose of collective security as an instrument of foreign policy is prevention, and success of this kind has to be measured in terms of what did *not* happen. Critics have argued that U.S. collective-security treaties posed a threat of encirclement to the Soviet Union, forcing it to ensure its own collective security, particularly the Warsaw Pact.[23] Nevertheless, no one can deny the counterargument that more than sixty years have passed without a world war.

In 1998, the expansion of NATO took its first steps toward former Warsaw Pact members, extending membership to Poland, Hungary, and the Czech Republic. Most of Washington embraced this expansion as the true and fitting end of the Cold War, and the U.S. Senate echoed this with a resounding 80-to-19 vote to induct these three former Soviet satellites into NATO. The expansion was also welcomed among European member nations, which quickly approved the move, hailing it as the final closing of the book on Yalta, the 1945 treaty that divided Europe into Western and Soviet spheres of influence after the defeat of Germany. Expanded membership seems to have made NATO less threatening and more acceptable to Russia. Russia became a partner when the NATO-Russia Council was formed in 2002. Finally, although the expanded NATO membership (twenty-eight countries in 2009) reduces the threat to Russia, it also reduces the utility of NATO as a military alliance. The September 11 attack on the United States was the first time in its fifty-plus-year history that Article 5 of the North Atlantic Treaty had to be invoked; it provides that an attack on one country is an attack on all the member countries. In fighting the war on terror, the Bush administration recognized that no matter how preponderant American power was, some aspects of its foreign policy could not be

---

North Atlantic Treaty Organization (NATO)
A treaty organization, comprising the United States, Canada, and most of Western Europe, formed in 1948 to counter the perceived threat from the Soviet Union.

bilateral treaty
A treaty made between two nations.

---

[22] George Quester, *The Continuing Problem of International Politics* (Hinsdale, Ill: Dryden Press, 1974), 229.

[23] The Warsaw Pact was signed in 1955 by the Soviet Union, the German Democratic Republic (East Germany), Poland, Hungary, Czechoslovakia, Romania, Bulgaria, and Albania. Albania later dropped out. The Warsaw Pact was terminated in 1991.

achieved without multilateral cooperation. On the other hand, the United States did not want to be constrained by its alliances. The global coalition initially forged after September 11 numbered over 170 countries. Not all joined the war effort in Afghanistan, but most if not all provided some form of support for some aspect of the war on terrorism, such as economic sanctions and intelligence. The war in Iraq, however, put the "coalition of the willing" to a test. The Bush administration was determined not to make its decision to go to war subject to the UN or NATO or any other international organization. The breadth of the United States' coalition was deemed secondary to its being nonconstraining. As a result, other than the British government, no major power supported the United States' actions.

Military Force

The most visible instrument of foreign policy is, of course, military force. The United States has built the world's most imposing military, with army, navy, marine, and air force units stationed in virtually every corner of the globe. The United States spends nearly as much on military might as the rest of the world combined (Figure 16.3). The famous Prussian military strategist Carl von Clausewitz

FIGURE 16.3 MILITARY SPENDING, 2008

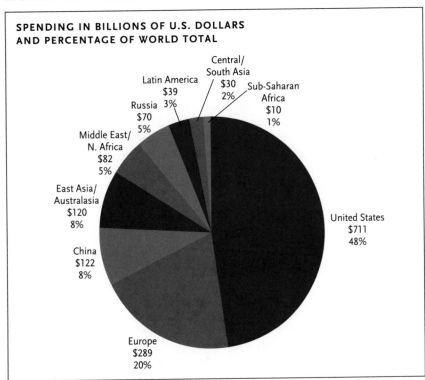

SPENDING IN BILLIONS OF U.S. DOLLARS
AND PERCENTAGE OF WORLD TOTAL

Central/South Asia $30 2%
Sub-Saharan Africa $10 1%
Latin America $39 3%
Russia $70 5%
Middle East/N. Africa $82 5%
East Asia/Australasia $120 8%
China $122 8%
Europe $289 20%
United States $711 48%

NOTE: 2008 total military spending: $1.473 trillion

SOURCE: Center for Arms Control and Non-Proliferation, www.armscontrolcenter.org/policy/securityspending/articles/fy09_dod_request_global/ (accessed 4/22/09).

called war "politics by other means." By this he meant that nations used force not simply to demonstrate their capacity for violence. Rather, force or the threat of force is a tool nations must sometimes use to achieve their foreign-policy goals. Military force may be needed to protect a nation's security interests and economic concerns. Ironically, force may also be needed to achieve humanitarian goals. For example, without international military protection, the Africans who have taken refuge in Darfur camps would be at the mercy of the violent Sudanese regime.

Though force is sometimes necessary, military force is generally seen as a last resort and avoided if possible because of a number of problems commonly associated with its use. First, the use of military force is extremely costly in both human and financial terms. In the past fifty years, tens of thousands of Americans have been killed and hundreds of billions of dollars spent in America's military operations. Before they employ military force to achieve national goals, policy makers must be certain that achieving these goals is essential and that other means are unlikely to succeed.

Second, the use of military force is inherently fraught with risk. However carefully policy makers and generals plan for military operations, results can seldom be fully anticipated. Variables ranging from the weather to unexpected weapons and tactics deployed by opponents may upset the most careful calculations and turn military operations into costly disasters. Covert maneuvers that were expected to be quick and decisive may turn into long, drawn-out, expensive struggles. For example, American policy makers expected to defeat the Iraqi army quickly and easily in 2003—and they did. Policy makers did not anticipate, however, that American forces would still be struggling years later to defeat the insurgency that arose in the war's aftermath.

Finally, in a democracy, any government that chooses to address policy problems through military means is almost certain to encounter political difficulties. Generally speaking, the American public will support relatively short and decisive military engagements. If, however, a conflict drags on, producing casualties and expenses with no clear outcome, the public loses patience, and opposition politicians point to the government's lies and ineptitude. Korea, Vietnam, and Iraq are all examples of protracted conflicts whose domestic political repercussions brought down the governments that decided military force was needed.

Thus, military force remains a major foreign policy tool, and the United States currently possesses a more powerful and effective set of military forces than any other nation. Nevertheless, even for the United States, the use of military force is fraught with risk and is not to be undertaken lightly.

Arbitration

The final foreign-policy tool we will consider is dispute arbitration. Arbitration means referring an international disagreement to a neutral third party for resolution. Arbitration is sometimes seen as a form of "soft power" as distinguished from military force, economic sanctions, and other coercive foreign-policy instruments. The United States will occasionally turn to international tribunals to resolve disputes with other countries. For example, in February 2008, the U.S. government asked the International Court of Justice to resolve a long-standing dispute with Italy over American property confiscated by the Italian government more than forty years ago. To take another example, in 1981 the United States and Iran established an arbitral tribunal to deal with claims arising from Iran's seizure of the U.S. embassy in Tehran in 1979.

More important, the United States relies heavily on the work of arbitral panels to maintain the flow of international trade on which America's economy depends. American firms would be reluctant to do business abroad if they could not be certain that their property and contractual rights would be honored by other nations. Arbitration helps produce that certainty. Almost every international contract contains an arbitration clause requiring that disputes between the parties will be resolved not by foreign governments, but by impartial arbitral panels accepted by both sides. By the terms of the New York Convention, virtually every nation in the world has agreed to accept and enforce arbitral verdicts. The United States has incorporated the terms of the New York Convention into federal law, and U.S. courts vigorously enforce arbitral judgements. The United States may not be happy with the outcome of every arbitral proceeding, but the arbitral system is essential to America's economic interests.

FOREIGN POLICY AND AMERICA'S PLACE IN THE WORLD

When policy makers choose courses of action and select the policy instruments they will employ, they do not begin with a blank slate. Presidents and other policy makers are generally guided by some overall vision of America's national interest and the nation's place in the world. Some recent presidents, Jimmy Carter for example, have seen America as a great power in decline, compelled to act cautiously on the world stage. Others, such as Ronald Reagan, have seen America as a rising power—"It's morning in America" was Reagan's slogan—capable of undertaking bold and decisive foreign policy moves.

Four Visions of America's Role in the World

In general terms, it is possible to identify four distinct visions of America's world role that, at various times, have guided recent presidents. These are:

The Napoleonic Role.   The **Napoleonic role** takes its name from the role that postrevolutionary France played under Napoleon. The French at that time felt not only that their new democratic system of government was the best on earth but also that France would not be safe until democracy was adopted universally. If this meant intervention in the internal affairs of France's neighbors, and if that meant warlike reactions, then so be it. President Woodrow Wilson expressed a

Napoleonic role   A strategy pursued by a powerful nation to prevent aggressive actions against it by improving the internal state of affairs of a particular country, even if this means encouraging revolution in that country.

similar viewpoint when he supported the U.S. declaration of war in 1917 with his argument that "the world must be made safe for democracy." Obviously any powerful nation can adopt such a position as a rationalization for intervening at its convenience in the internal affairs of another country. But it can also be sincerely espoused, and in the United States it has from time to time enjoyed broad popular consensus. We played the Napoleonic role most recently in ousting the Philippine dictator Ferdinand Marcos (February 1986), the Panamanian leader Manuel Noriega (December 1989), the Sandinista government of Nicaragua (February 1990), the military rulers of Haiti (September 1994), the Taliban government of Afghanistan (2001), and Iraq's Saddam Hussein (2003).

The Holy Alliance Role.   The concept of the **Holy Alliance role** emerged out of the defeat of Napoleon and the agreement by the leaders of Great Britain, Russia, Austria, and Prussia to preserve the social order against *all* revolution, including democratic revolution, at whatever cost. (Post-Napoleonic France also joined it.) The Holy Alliance made use of every kind of political instrument available—including political suppression, espionage, sabotage, and outright military intervention—to keep existing governments in power. The Holy Alliance role is comparable to the Napoleonic role in that each is based on the assumption that intervention into the internal affairs of other countries is justified for the maintenance of peace. But Napoleonic intervention is motivated by fear of dictatorship, and it can accept and even encourage revolution. In contrast, Holy Alliance intervention is antagonistic to any form of political change, even when this means supporting an existing dictatorship.[24]

The Balance-of-Power Role.   The **balance-of-power role** is basically an effort by the major powers to play off each other so that no great power or combination of great and lesser powers can impose conditions on others. The most relevant example of the use of this strategy is found in the nineteenth century, especially the latter half. What makes the balance-of-power role most distinct from the two previously identified roles is that this role accepts the political system of each country, asking no questions except whether the country will join an alliance and will use its resources to ensure that each country will respect the borders and interests of all the others.[25]

The Economic Expansionist Role.   The **economic expansionist role**, also called the capitalist role, shares with the balance-of-power role the attitude that the political system or ideology of a country is irrelevant; the only questions are whether a

---

[24] For a thorough and instructive exposition of the original Holy Alliance pattern, see Paul M. Kennedy, *The Rise and Fall of the Great Powers: Economic Change and Military Conflict from 1500 to 2000* (New York: Random House, 1987), pp. 159–60. And for a comparison of the Holy Alliance role with the balance-of-power role, to be discussed next, see Karl Polanyi, *The Great Transformation* (New York: Rinehart, 1944; Beacon paperback edition, 1957), pp. 5–11 and 259–62.

[25] Felix Gilbert et al., *The Norton History of Modern Europe* (New York: Norton, 1971), pp. 1222–24.

Holy Alliance role A strategy pursued by a super-power to prevent any change in the existing distribution of power among nation-states, even if this requires intervention into the internal affairs of another country in order to keep a ruler from being overthrown.

balance-of-power role The strategy whereby many countries form alliances with one or more countries in order to counterbalance the behavior of other, usually more powerful, nation-states.

economic expansionist role The strategy often pursued by capitalist countries to adopt foreign policies that will maximize the success of domestic corporations in their dealings with other countries.

country has anything to buy or sell and whether its entrepreneurs, corporations, and government agencies will honor their contracts. Governments and their armies are occasionally drawn into economic expansionist relationships in order to establish, reopen, or expand trade relationships, and to keep the lines of commerce open. But the role is political, too. For example, the United States played an economic expansionist role in Latin and Central America until the Cold War pushed us toward a Holy Alliance role with most Latin nations.

Like arms control, however, economic expansion does not happen spontaneously. In the past, economic expansion owed a great deal to military backing because contracts do not enforce themselves, trade deficits are not paid automatically, and new regimes do not always honor the commitments made by regimes they replace. The only way to expand economic relationships is through diplomacy.

AMERICA'S ROLE IN THE WORLD TODAY

Let us examine how each of these visions of America's world role has helped policy makers shape America's actions on the international stage.

The Cold War and the Holy Alliance Role

The emergence of the Soviet Union as a superpower had an overwhelming influence on American foreign policy thinking in the post–World War II era. The distribution of power in the world was "bipolar," and Americans saw the world as separated in two, with an "iron curtain" dividing the communist world from the free world. Immediately after the war, America's foreign-policy goal had been "prodemocracy," a Napoleonic role dominated by the Marshall Plan and the genuine hope for a democratic world. This quickly shifted toward a Holy Alliance role, with "containment" as the primary foreign-policy criterion.[26] Containment was fundamentally a Holy Alliance concept. According to the foreign-policy expert Richard Barnet, during the 1950s and 1960s, "the United States used its military or paramilitary power on an average of once every eighteen months either to prevent a government deemed undesirable from coming to power or to overthrow a revolutionary or reformist government considered inimical to America's interests."[27] Although Barnet did not refer to a Holy Alliance, his description fits the model perfectly.

During the 1970s, the United States played the Holy Alliance role less frequently, not so much because of the outcome of the Vietnam War as because of

---

[26] The original theory of containment was articulated by former ambassador and scholar George Kennan in a famous article published under the pseudonym X, "The Sources of Soviet Conduct," *Foreign Affairs* 25 (1947): 556.

[27] Richard Barnet, "Reflections," *New Yorker*, March 9, 1987, p. 82.

the emergence of a multipolar world. In 1972, the United States accepted (and later recognized) the communist government of the People's Republic of China and broke forever its pure bipolar, Cold War view of world-power distribution. Other powers became politically important as well, including Japan, the European Economic Community (now the European Union), India, and, depending on their own resolve, the countries making up the Organization of Petroleum Exporting Countries (OPEC). The United States experimented with all four of the previously identified roles, depending on which was appropriate to a specific region of the world. In the Middle East, America tended to play an almost classic balance-of-power role, appearing sometimes cool in its relations with Israel and playing off one Arab country against another. The United States has been able to do this despite the fact that every country in the Middle East recognizes that for cultural, domestic, and geostrategic reasons, the United States has always considered Israel its most durable and important ally in the region and has unwaveringly committed itself to Israel's survival in a very hostile environment. President Nixon introduced balance-of-power considerations in the Far East by "playing the China card." In other parts of the world, particularly in Latin America, we tended to hold to the Holy Alliance and Napoleonic roles.

This multipolar phase ended after 1989, with the collapse of the Soviet Union and the end of the Cold War. Soon thereafter the Warsaw Pact collapsed too, ending armed confrontation in Europe. With almost equal suddenness, the popular demand for "self-determination" produced several new nation-states and the demand for still more. On the one hand, it was indeed encouraging to witness the reemergence of some twenty-five major nationalities after anywhere from forty-five to seventy-five years of suppression. On the other hand, policy makers with a sense of history are aware that this new world order bears a strong resemblance to the world of 1914. Then, the trend was known as "Balkanization." Balkanization meant nationhood and self-determination, but it also meant war. The Soviet Union after World War I and Yugoslavia after World War II kept more than twenty nationalities from making war against each other for several decades. In 1989 and the years that followed, the world was caught unprepared for the dangers of a new disorder that the reemergence of these nationalities produced.

The Post–Cold War Era and Global Capitalism

The abrupt end of the Cold War unleashed another dynamic factor, the globalization of markets; one could call it the globalization of capitalism. This is good news, but it has its problematic side because the free market can disrupt nationhood. Although the globalization of markets is enormously productive, countries like to enjoy its benefits while attempting at the same time to prevent international economic influences from affecting local jobs, local families, and established class and tribal relationships.

This struggle between capitalism and nationhood produces a new kind of bipolarity in the world. The old world order was shaped by *external bipolarity*—of West versus East. This seems to have been replaced by *internal bipolarity*, wherein each country is struggling to make its own hard policy choices to preserve its cultural uniqueness while competing effectively in the global marketplace.

Approval of the North American Free Trade Agreement (NAFTA) is the best example of this struggle within the United States. NAFTA was supported by a majority of Democrats and Republicans on the grounds that a freer, global market was in America's national interest. But even as large bipartisan majorities in Congress were embracing NAFTA, three important factions were rising to fight it. The former presidential candidate Pat Buchanan led a large segment of conservative Americans to fight NAFTA because, he argued, communities and families would be threatened by job losses and by competition from legal and illegal immigrant workers. Another large faction, led by Ross Perot, opposed NAFTA largely on the theory that American companies would move their operations to Mexico, where labor costs are lower. Organized labor also joined the fight against NAFTA.

Another form of internal bipolarity became evident in 1999 over the World Trade Organization (WTO) and its authority to impose limits and restrictions on sovereign nations, even the United States. The WTO had existed since 1994, when it was set up by the major trading nations to facilitate implementation of treaties made under the General Agreement on Tariffs and Trade (GATT). But protesters in Seattle saw the WTO as a threat to local ways of life and a contributor to job loss, environmental degradation, and violation of human rights.

These battles are examples of the "internal bipolarity" that is coming to the fore around the world. As the *New York Times* foreign affairs columnist Thomas Friedman put it, "Now that the free market is triumphing on a global basis, the most interesting conflicts are between the winners and losers within countries. It is these internal battles that will increasingly shape international affairs."[28]

The global market is here to stay. American values have changed enough to incorporate it, despite the toll it may take on community and family tradition. Meanwhile, many of the elements of foreign policy created during the Cold War have persisted because they turned out to be good adjustments to the modern era. The Marshall Plan and the various forms of international economic aid that succeeded it continue to this day. Although appropriations for foreign aid have been shrinking, only a small minority of members of the Senate and the House favor the outright abolition of foreign aid programs. NATO and other collective security arrangements continue, as do some aspects of containment, even though there is no longer a Soviet Union, because collective security arrangements have, as we shall see, proven useful in dealing with new democracies and other nations seeking to join the global market. Even though the former Soviet Union is now more often an ally than an adversary, the United States still quite frequently uses unilateral and multilateral means of keeping civil wars contained within their own borders, so that conflict does not spread into neighboring states. America is practicing a new form of containment, but one that is based on the values and institutions of Cold War containment.

---

[28]Thomas L. Friedman, "14 Big Macs Later . . . ," *New York Times*, December 31, 1995, sec. 4, p. 9.

The quest for a global market is more than a search for world prosperity. Economic globalization carries with it the hope that economic competition will displace armed conflict, perhaps even reducing if not eliminating the need for traditional diplomacy. But since there are too many instances in world history when economic competition actually led to war rather than avoided it, the United States has added democratization to the recipe of globalization because of the fairly well-supported hypothesis that democracies never go to war against each other. Thus, democratization is a genuine and strongly committed goal of U.S. foreign policy, even if it is secondary to economic expansion. Meanwhile, we play the economic card in hopes that capitalism will contribute not only to world prosperity but also to the expansion of democratization.

One of the first indications of the post–Cold War American foreign policy was President George H. W. Bush's conciliatory approach to the dictatorial regime of the People's Republic of China after its brutal military suppression of the democratic student movement in Tiananmen Square in June 1989. Subsequently, President Clinton also maintained friendly relations with the dictatorial regime, and both presidents continued to grant the Chinese "normal trade relations" status. Their policy was to separate China's trade status from its human rights record, arguing that economic growth provided the only effective means to bring about political reform in a country as large and as powerful as China.

The Holy Alliance or the Napoleonic Role in the Post–Cold War Era?

During the Cold War era, the purpose of the Holy Alliance role was to keep regimes in power as long as they did not espouse Soviet foreign-policy goals. In the post–Cold War world, the purpose of the Holy Alliance role is still to keep regimes in power, but only as long as they maintain general stability, keep their nationalities contained within their own borders, and encourage their economies to attain some level of participation in the global market. If countries fail to satisfy these conditions, the United States has shown signs of reverting to its Napoleonic role. The United States has also continued to confront unfriendly dictators by adopting a Napoleonic strategy of intervention.

One case of the Holy Alliance role in the post–Cold War era is Iraq's invasion of Kuwait and our Desert Storm response to it. Iraq's invasion of Kuwait occurred in July 1990, but Desert Storm was not undertaken until January 1991. In the interim, President Bush was mobilizing Congress and the American people, not only in case the United States had to intervene militarily, but also in hopes that the possibility of such action might convince Saddam Hussein to withdraw voluntarily. President Bush was also putting together a worldwide alliance of twenty-nine nations—he had no intention of leading the United States into Desert Storm without this alliance, even though most of its members did not send troops but instead sent political approval plus what amounted to a monetary subscription. Bush had initially taken a Napoleonic position, urging the people of Iraq to "take matters into their own hands" and to force Hussein to "step aside." But after America withdrew its troops and uprisings inside Iraq began to emerge, President Bush backed away.

It was enough that the Iraqis stayed within their borders, although regular over-flights and occasional shootings by American pilots in the northern and southern "no-fly" zones of Iraq later appeared to be Napoleonic departures from the Holy Alliance role.

Regarding Bosnia, at first the United States refused to exert leadership, and it deferred to the European nations when civil war erupted after Croatia and Bosnia-Herzegovina declared independence from Yugoslavia. When Europe failed to address the problem adequately, the United States and the United Kingdom stepped in, again to no avail. Although the Americans' surprise bombing in 1995 was virtually unilateral, what emerged was a new alliance of twenty-five nations acting "in concert" to separate the warring factions from one another. And al-though one-third of the sixty thousand occupying troops and virtually all the navy and air force units were American, twenty-four other nations established and maintained a physical presence in the field, all in order to maintain the status quo, including leaving the Yugoslav president Slobodan Milosevic in power. Almost everything about the Bosnian operation was an acting out of the traditional Holy Alliance role.

Kosovo (part of Yugoslavia) in 1999 was perhaps the most spectacular case of post–Cold War Holy Alliance policy—although history may prove that the United States and virtually the entire Western world stumbled into this war.[29] Throughout 1998 and early 1999, ethnic cleansing proceeded in Kosovo, but the United States would not go it alone, and the NATO nations (except for Great Britain) were not willing to intervene in Kosovo. As late as January 1999, the CIA reported to President Clinton that "[Yugoslav President Milosevic] doesn't believe NATO is going to bomb."[30] It is clear that these delays were due less to American indecision than to America's or President Clinton's inability to forge a European, multicountry alliance. Prospects of embarrassment at the upcoming fiftieth anniversary of NATO may have forced some European leaders to reconsider an alliance—but even so, only if the United States took the lead, and then only if it promised to limit the assault to an air war, which guaranteed a minimum of casualties, especially on the allied side.

So the United States got its alliance—for NATO, a precedent-setting one—but without any ground troops.[31] But there are inherent limits to multinational coalitions. NATO is simply a more formalized version of a multicountry alliance with the same fundamental problem of any such alliance: *The power of decision tends toward the weakest member.* Opposition within the NATO alliance to intervene in Kosovo came mostly from the weaker and more internally divided Italy and Greece rather than from Britain, France, or Germany.

---

[29] See, for example, the cover story of the *Economist*, "Stumbling into War," March 27–April 2, 1999, pp. 17, 27, 49, 50.

[30] Quoted in Elaine Sciolino and Ethan Bronner, "How a President, Distracted by Scandal, Entered Balkan War," *New York Times*, April 18, 1999, p. 12.

[31] Note once again the title of the previously cited article, "How a President, Distracted by Scandal, Entered Balkan War."

The Kosovo campaign validates what we have been observing throughout this chapter: Holy Alliance politics has been the prevailing American role internationally since the Cold War, and the United States draws virtually all its allies and potential allies into that role at one point or another. In 2008, Russia reacted to American efforts to draw states along its borders into the American alliance structure by invading Georgia, a formed Soviet republic. Georgia had welcomed close relations with the United States and even discussed possibly joining NATO. The Russians saw an attack on Georgia as a warning to other former Soviet republics and satellite states, Poland in particular, against linking themselves closely to America.

The War on Terror: From Holy Alliance to Napoleonic Unilateralism

In the immediate aftermath of the 9/11 terrorist attacks, the United States had no difficulty in securing pledges of support from a number of other nations. Although the United States took the lead in launching attacks against Afghanistan's Taliban regime, which had harbored the leadership of the Al Qaeda terrorist group that planned the attacks, many other nations contributed diplomatic, military, and financial support.

However, when the Bush administration made it clear that it intended to invade Iraq to topple the dictator Saddam Hussein, only Great Britain offered unequivocal support and significant military cooperation. Most of the world's leaders expressed doubt about the wisdom of America's actions and declined to endorse or support the Bush administration's policies. President Bush averred that America was prepared to lead a "coalition of the willing" into battle. In other words, the president indicated that he did not care whether other nations joined the United States or not. Those who were willing were welcome to participate. Those not willing were welcome to stay home.

Most Europeans and many Americans were dismayed by the administration's unilateralism, but Congress supported the president, and American forces struck into Iraq. The Iraqi army was quickly defeated and, after a search, Saddam Hussein was located, placed under arrest, and eventually tried and executed for his brutal crimes against the Iraqi people. Thus, initially, the Bush administration's unilateralist foreign policy appeared to be succeeding. Not long after the Iraqi army collapsed. However, continuing to the present time, a guerilla insurgency, aided by terrorist groups and armed by Iran, began to harass American and British occupation forces, inflicting casualties on British and American troops on a daily basis. Even the steadfast British began to waver. It seemed more and more likely that the "coalition of the willing" would consist of the United States, alone.

The Bush administration's policies in Iraq illustrate the advantages and disadvantages of Napoleonic unilateralism. The major advantage is that not having to deal with allies allows the United States to do as it sees fit. The disadvantage, though, is that as problems develop, the capacity of even a great power such as the United States to go it alone becomes more and more doubtful. During the 2008 presidential campaign, candidates presented their formulae to resolve America's problems in Iraq. We shall see how a new president deals with the fallout from Napoleonic unilateralism.

CONCLUSION: THE CLASH OF HISTORY AND RATIONALITY

The nineteenth-century British statesman Lord Palmerston famously said, "Nations have no permanent friends or allies; they only have permanent interests." Palmerston's comment illustrates what is sometimes known as the "realist" view of foreign policy. The realist school holds that foreign policies should be guided by the national interest—mainly security and economic interest—and that policy makers should steel themselves to the necessity of making decisions that might be viewed from the outside as cold and ruthless if they serve the nation's interests. Although many public officials have denounced such views in public—especially if they were running for office—many have become realists once in power. Every one of America's post–World War II presidents, liberals and conservatives, Democrats and Republicans alike, have been willing to order young Americans into battle and to visit death and destruction on the citizens of foreign states if they believed the national interest required it.

The harsh rationality of foreign policy often clashes with America's history and ideals. Our democratic and liberal traditions lead us to hope for a world in which ideals rather than naked interests govern foreign policy and in which our leaders pay heed to ideals. The ideals that Americans have historically espoused (though not always lived by) assert that our foreign policies should have a higher purpose than the pursuit of interest and that America is to use force only as a last resort. Since the realities of our foreign policy often clash with these historic ideals, our policy makers often struggle to explain their actions and avoid admitting to motivations that don't embody those ideals.

"I have previously stated and I repeat now that the United States plans no military intervention in Cuba." said President John F. Kennedy in 1961 as he planned military action in Cuba. "As president, it is my duty to the American people to report that renewed hostile actions against United States ships on the high seas in the Gulf of Tonkin have today required me to order the military forces of the United States to take action in reply," said President Lyndon Johnson in 1964 referring to a fabricated incident used to justify expansion of American involvement in Vietnam. "We did not, I repeat, did not trade weapons or anything else [to Iran] for hostages, nor will we," said President Ronald Reagan in November 1986, four months before admitting that U.S. arms had been traded to Iran in exchange for Americans being held hostage there. "Simply stated, there is no doubt that Saddam Hussein now has weapons of mass destruction," said Vice President Dick Cheney in 2002. When it turned out that these weapons did not exist, Assistant Defense Secretary Paul Wolfowitz explained, "For bureaucratic reasons, we settled on one issue, weapons of mass destruction [as justification for invading Iraq] because it was the one reason everyone could agree on."[32] These false statements may hide discrepancies between our historic ideals and rationality, but they do not resolve them.

The ever-present conflicts between ideals and harsh realities manifested themselves again in 2009. As a candidate for the presidency, Barack Obama was praised for denouncing the Bush administration's treatment of enemy combatants. Obama was especially critical of the Guantánamo detention facility, where some alleged enemy combatants were incarcerated, and the creation of military tribunals, outside the regular court system, to hear their cases. Once in office, however, Obama did not rush to close the Guantánamo facility—though he continued to plan for the facility's eventual closure. As for the tribunals, the Obama administration indicated in May 2009 that it might employ them after all, not wishing to bring the enemy combatant cases to the regular courts. Ideals seemed to have given way to interests again.

FOR FURTHER READING

Bacevich, Andrew. *The New American Militarism: How Americans Are Seduced by War.* New York: Oxford University Press, 2006.

———. *The Limits of Power: The End of American Exceptionalism.* New York: Metropolitan Books, 2008.

Berman, Paul. *Terror and Liberalism.* New York: Norton, 2004.

Daalder, Ivo H., and James M. Lindsay. *America Unbound—The Bush Revolution in Foreign Policy.* Washington, D.C.: Brookings Institution Press, 2003.

Drezner, Daniel. "The Realist Tradition in American Public Opinion." *Perspectives on Politics* (March 2008): 51–70.

Fisk, Robert. *The Great War for Civilisation: The Conquest of the Middle East.* New York: Knopf, 2005.

Gaddis, John L. *The Cold War: A New History.* New York: Penguin, 2005.

Jentleson, Bruce. *American Foreign Policy—The Dynamics of Choice in the Twenty-First Century.* 2nd ed. New York: Norton, 2004.

Johnson, Chalmers. *The Sorrows of Empire.* New York: Holt, 2004.

Kagan, Robert. *Dangerous Nation.* New York: Knopf, 2006.

Kennan, George F. *Around the Cragged Hill: A Personal and Political Philosophy.* New York: Norton, 1993.

Mandelbaum, Michael. *The Case for Goliath: How America Acts as the World's Government in the Twenty-First Century.* Washington, D.C.: Public Affairs Press, 2005.

Mann, James. *Rise of the Vulcans.* New York: Penguin, 2004.

Mayer, Jane. *The Dark Side: The Inside Story of How the War on Terror Turned into a War on American Identity.* New York: Doubleday, 2008.

---

[32] Benjamin Ginsberg, *The American Lie: Government by the People and Other Political Fables* (Boulder, Colo.: Paradigm Press, 2007).

Mayhew, David. "Wars and American Politics." *Perspectives on Politics* (September 2005): 473–93.

Reid, T. R. *The United States of Europe—The New Superpower and the End of American Supremacy*. New York: Penguin, 2004.

Yoo, John. *The Powers of War and Peace*. Chicago: University of Chicago Press, 2005.

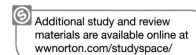

Additional study and review materials are available online at wwnorton.com/studyspace/

reader selection

Appendix

The Declaration of Independence

In Congress, July 4, 1776

When in the course of human events, it becomes necessary for one people to dissolve the political bands which have connected them with another, and to assume among the Powers of the earth, the separate and equal station to which the Laws of Nature and of Nature's God entitle them, a decent respect to the opinions of mankind requires that they should declare the causes which impel them to the separation.

We hold these truths to be self-evident, that all men are created equal, that they are endowed by their Creator with certain unalienable rights, that among these are Life, Liberty, and the pursuit of Happiness. That to secure these rights, Governments are instituted among Men, deriving their just powers from the consent of the governed. That whenever any Form of Government becomes destructive of these ends, it is the Right of the People to alter or to abolish it, and to institute new Government, laying its foundation on such principles and organizing its powers in such form, as to them shall seem most likely to effect their Safety and Happiness. Prudence, indeed, will dictate that Governments long established should not be changed for light and transient causes; and accordingly all experience hath shown, that mankind are more disposed to suffer, while evils are sufferable, than to right themselves by abolishing the forms to which they are accustomed. But when a long train of abuses and usurpations, pursuing invariably the same Object evinces a design to reduce them under absolute Despotism, it is their right, it is their duty, to throw off such Government, and to provide new Guards for their future security.— Such has been the patient sufferance of these Colonies; and such is now the necessity which constrains them to alter their former Systems of Government. The history of the present King of Great Britain is a history of repeated injuries and usurpations, all having in direct object the establishment of an absolute Tyranny over these States. To prove this, let Facts be submitted to a candid world.

He has refused his Assent to Laws, the most wholesome and necessary for the public good.

He has forbidden his Governors to pass Laws of immediate and pressing importance, unless suspended in their operation till his Assent should be obtained; and when so suspended, he has utterly neglected to attend to them.

He has refused to pass other Laws for the accommodation of large districts of people, unless those people would relinquish the right of Representation in the Legislature, a right inestimable to them and formidable to tyrants only.

He has called together legislative bodies at places unusual, uncomfortable, and distant from the depository of their public Records, for the sole purpose of fatiguing them into compliance with his measures.

He has dissolved Representative Houses repeatedly, for opposing with manly firmness his invasions on the rights of the people.

He has refused for a long time, after such dissolutions, to cause others to be elected; whereby the Legislative powers, incapable of Annihilation, have returned to the People at large for their exercise; the State remaining in the mean time exposed to all dangers of invasion from without, and convulsions within.

He has endeavored to prevent the population of these States; for that purpose obstructing the Laws of Naturalization of Foreigners; refusing to pass others to encourage their migrations hither, and raising the conditions of new Appropriations of Lands.

He has obstructed the Administration of Justice, by refusing his Assent to Laws for establishing Judiciary powers.

He has made Judges dependent on his Will alone, for the tenure of their offices, and the amount and payment of their salaries.

He has erected a multitude of New Offices, and sent hither swarms of Officers to harass our People, and eat out their substance.

He has kept among us, in times of peace, Standing Armies without the Consent of our legislature.

He has affected to render the Military independent of and superior to the Civil Power.

He has combined with others to subject us to a jurisdiction foreign to our constitution, and unacknowledged by our laws; giving his Assent to their Acts of pretended Legislation:

For quartering large bodies of armed troops among us:

For protecting them, by a mock Trial, from Punishment for any Murders which they should commit on the Inhabitants of these States:

For cutting off our Trade with all parts of the world:

For imposing taxes on us without our Consent:

For depriving us in many cases, of the benefits of Trial by jury:

For transporting us beyond Seas to be tried for pretended offences:

For abolishing the free System of English Laws in a neighboring Province, establishing therein an Arbitrary government, and enlarging its Boundaries so as to render it at once an example and fit instrument for introducing the same absolute rule into these Colonies:

For taking away our Charters, abolishing our most valuable Laws, and altering fundamentally the Forms of our Governments:

For suspending our own Legislatures, and declaring themselves invested with Power to legislate for us in all cases whatsoever.

He has abdicated Government here, by declaring us out of his Protection and waging War against us.

He has plundered our seas, ravaged our Coasts, burnt our towns, and destroyed the lives of our people.

He is at this time transporting large armies of foreign mercenaries to compleat the works of death, desolation, and tyranny, already begun with circumstances of Cruelty & perfidy scarcely paralleled in the most barbarous ages, and totally unworthy the Head of a civilized nation.

He has constrained our fellow Citizens taken Captive on the high Seas to bear Arms against their Country, to become the executioners of their friends and Brethren, or to fall themselves by their Hands.

He has excited domestic insurrections amongst us, and has endeavored to bring on the inhabitants of our frontiers, the merciless Indian Savages, whose known rule of warfare, is an undistinguished destruction of all ages, sexes, and conditions.

In every stage of these Oppressions We have Petitioned for Redress in the most humble terms: Our repeated Petitions have been answered only by repeated injury. A Prince, whose character is thus marked by every act which may define a Tyrant, is unfit to be the ruler of a free people.

Nor have We been wanting in attention to our British brethren. We have warned them from time to time of attempts by their legislature to extend an unwarrantable jurisdiction over us. We have reminded them of the circumstances of our emigration and settlement here. We have appealed to their native justice and magnanimity, and we have conjured them by the ties of our common kindred to disavow these usurpations, which, would inevitably interrupt our connections and correspondence. They too must have been deaf to the voice of justice and of consanguinity. We must, therefore, acquiesce in the necessity, which denounces our Separation, and hold them, as we hold the rest of mankind, Enemies in War, in Peace Friends.

WE, THEREFORE, the Representatives of the UNITED STATES OF AMERICA, in General Congress, Assembled, appealing to the Supreme Judge of the world for the rectitude of our intentions, do, in the Name, and by Authority of the good People of these Colonies, solemnly publish and declare, That these United Colonies are, and of Right ought to be FREE AND INDEPENDENT STATES; that they are Absolved from all Allegiance to the British Crown, and that all political connection between them and the State of Great Britain, is and ought to be totally dissolved; and that as Free and Independent States, they have full Power to levy War, conclude Peace, contract Alliances, establish Commerce, and to do all other Acts and Things which Independent States may of right do. And for the support of this Declaration, with a firm reliance on the Protection of Divine Providence, we mutually pledge to each other our Lives, our Fortunes, and our sacred Honor.

The foregoing Declaration was, by order of Congress, engrossed, and signed by the following members:

John Hancock

NEW HAMPSHIRE
Josiah Bartlett
William Whipple
Matthew Thornton

MASSACHUSETTS BAY
Samuel Adams
John Adams
Robert Treat Paine
Elbridge Gerry

RHODE ISLAND
Stephen Hopkins
William Ellery

CONNECTICUT
Roger Sherman
Samuel Huntington
William Williams
Oliver Wolcott

NEW YORK
William Floyd
Philip Livingston
Francis Lewis
Lewis Morris

NEW JERSEY
Richard Stockton
John Witherspoon
Francis Hopkinson
John Hart
Abraham Clark

PENNSYLVANIA
Robert Morris
Benjamin Rush
Benjamin Franklin
John Morton
George Clymer
James Smith
George Taylor
James Wilson
George Ross

DELAWARE
Caesar Rodney
George Read
Thomas M'Kean

MARYLAND
Samuel Chase
William Paca
Thomas Stone
Charles Carroll,
*   of Carrollton*

VIRGINIA
George Wythe
Richard Henry Lee
Thomas Jefferson
Benjamin Harrison
Thomas Nelson, Jr.
Francis Lightfoot Lee
Carter Braxton

NORTH CAROLINA
William Hooper
Joseph Hewes
John Penn

SOUTH CAROLINA
Edward Rutledge
Thomas Heyward, Jr.
Thomas Lynch, Jr.
Arthur Middleton

GEORGIA
Button Gwinnett
Lyman Hall
George Walton

Resolved, That copies of the Declaration be sent to the several assemblies, conventions, and committees, or councils of safety, and to the several commanding officers of the continental troops; that it be proclaimed in each of the United States, at the head of the army.

The Articles of Confederation

Agreed to by Congress November 15, 1777; ratified and in force
March 1, 1781

To all whom these Presents shall come, we the undersigned Delegates of the States affixed to our Names send greeting. Whereas the Delegates of the United States of America in Congress assembled did on the fifteenth day of November in the Year of our Lord One Thousand Seven Hundred and Seventy seven, and in the Second Year of the Independence of America agree to certain articles of Confederation and perpetual Union between the States of Newhampshire, Massachusetts-bay, Rhodeisland and Providence Plantations, Connecticut, New-York, New-Jersey, Pennsylvania, Delaware, Maryland, Virginia, North-Carolina, South-Carolina and Georgia in the Words following, viz. "Articles of Confederation and perpetual Union between the states of Newhampshire, Massachusetts-bay, Rhodeisland and Providence Plantations, Connecticut, New-York, New-Jersey, Pennsylvania, Delaware, Maryland, Virginia, North-Carolina, South-Carolina and Georgia.

Art. I. The Stile of this confederacy shall be "The United States of America."

Art. II. Each state retains its sovereignty, freedom and independence, and every Power, Jurisdiction and right, which is not by this confederation expressly delegated to the United States, in Congress assembled.

Art. III. The said states hereby severally enter into a firm league of friendship with each other, for their common defence, the security of their Liberties, and their mutual and general welfare, binding themselves to assist each other, against all force offered to, or attacks made upon them, or any of them, on account of religion, sovereignty, trade, or any other pretence whatever.

Art. IV. The better to secure and perpetuate mutual friendship and intercourse among the people of the different states in this union, the free inhabitants of each of these states, paupers, vagabonds and fugitives from Justice excepted, shall be entitled to all privileges and immunities of free citizens in the several states; and the people of each state shall have free ingress and regress to and from any other state, and shall enjoy therein all the privileges of trade and commerce, subject to the same duties, impositions and restrictions as the inhabitants thereof respectively, provided that such restriction shall not extend so far as to prevent the removal of property imported into any state, to any other state of which the Owner is an inhabitant; provided also that no imposition, duties or restriction shall be laid by any state, on the property of the united states, or either of them.

If any Person guilty of, or charged with treason, felony, or other high misdemeanor in any state, shall flee from Justice, and be found in any of the united states, he shall upon demand of the Governor or executive power, of the state from which he fled, be delivered up and removed to the state having jurisdiction of his offence.

Full faith and credit shall be given in each of these states to the records, acts and judicial proceedings of the courts and magistrates of every other state.

Art. V. For the more convenient management of the general interests of the united states, delegates shall be annually appointed in such manner as the legislature of each state shall direct, to meet in Congress on the first Monday in November, in every year, with a power reserved to each state, to recall its delegates, or any of them, at any time within the year, and to send others in their stead, for the remainder of the Year.

No state shall be represented in Congress by less than two, nor by more than seven Members; and no person shall be capable of being a delegate for more than three years in any term of six years; nor shall any person, being a delegate, be capable of holding any office under the united states, for which he, or another for his benefit receives any salary, fees or emolument of any kind.

Each state shall maintain its own delegates in a meeting of the states, and while they act as members of the committee of the states.

In determining questions in the united states, in Congress assembled, each state shall have one vote.

Freedom of speech and debate in Congress shall not be impeached or questioned in any Court, or place out of Congress, and the members of congress shall be protected in their persons from arrests and imprisonments, during the time of their going to and from, and attendance on congress, except for treason, felony, or breach of the peace.

Art. VI. No state without the Consent of the united states in congress assembled, shall send any embassy to, or receive any embassy from, or enter into any conference, agreement, or alliance or treaty with any King, prince or state; nor shall any person holding any office or profit or trust under the united states, or any of them, accept of any present, emolument, office or title of any kind whatever from any king, prince or foreign state; nor shall the united states in congress assembled, or any of them, grant any title of nobility.

No two or more states shall enter into any treaty, confederation or alliance whatever between them, without the consent of the united states in congress assembled, specifying accurately the purposes for which the same is to be entered into, and how long it shall continue.

No state shall lay any imposts or duties, which may interfere with any stipulations in treaties, entered into by the united states in congress assembled, with any king, prince or state, in pursuance of any treaties already proposed by congress, to the courts of France and Spain.

No vessels of war shall be kept up in time of peace by any state, except such number only, as shall be deemed necessary by the united states in congress assembled, for the defence of such state, or its trade; nor shall any body of forces be kept up by any state, in time of peace, except such number only, as in the judgment of the united states, in congress assembled, shall be deemed requisite to garrison the forts necessary for the defence of such state; but every state shall always keep up a well regulated and disciplined militia, sufficiently armed and accoutred, and shall provide and constantly have ready for use, in public stores, a due number of field pieces and tents, and a proper quantity of arms, ammunition and camp equipage.

No state shall engage in any war without the consent of the united states in congress assembled, unless such state be actually invaded by enemies, or shall have received certain advice of a resolution being formed by some nation of Indians to invade such state, and the danger is so imminent as not to admit of a delay, till the united states in congress asssembled can be consulted; nor shall any state grant commissions to any ships or vessels of war, nor letters of marque or reprisal, except it be after a declaration of war by the united states in congress assembled, and then only against the kingdom or state and the subjects thereof, against which war has been so declared, and under such regulations as shall be established by the united states in congress assembled, unless such state be infested by pirates; in which case vessels of war may be fitted out for that occasion, and kept so long as the danger shall continue, or until the united states in congress assembled shall determine otherwise.

Art. VII. When land-forces are raised by any state for the common defence, all officers of or under the rank of colonel, shall be appointed by the legislature of each state respectively by whom such forces shall be raised, or in such manner as such state shall direct, and all vacancies shall be filled up by the state which first made the appointment.

Art. VIII. All charges of war, and all other expences that shall be incurred for the common defence or general welfare, and allowed by the united states in congress assembled, shall be defrayed out of a common treasury, which shall be supplied by the several states, in proportion to the value of all land within each state, granted to or surveyed for any Person, as such land and the buildings and improvements thereon shall be estimated according to such mode as the united states in congress assembled, shall from time to time direct and appoint. The taxes for paying that proportion shall be laid and levied by the authority and direction of the legislatures of the several states within the time agreed upon by the united states in congress assembled.

Art. IX. The united states in congress assembled, shall have the sole and exclusive right and power of determining on peace and war, except in the cases mentioned in the sixth article—of sending and receiving ambassadors—entering into treaties and alliances, provided that no treaty of commerce shall be made whereby the legislative power of the respective states shall be restrained from imposing such imposts and duties on foreigners, as their own people are subjected to, or from prohibiting the exportation of any species of goods or commodities whatsoever—of establishing rules for deciding in all cases, what captures on land or water shall be legal, and in what manner prizes taken by land or naval forces in the service of the united states shall be divided or appropriated—of granting letters of marque and reprisal in times of peace—appointing courts for the trial of piracies and felonies committed on the high seas and establishing courts for receiving and determining finally appeals in all cases of captures, provided that no member of congress shall be appointed a judge of any of the said courts.

The united states in congress assembled shall also be the last resort on appeal in all disputes and differences now subsisting or that hereafter may arise between two or more states concerning boundary, jurisdiction or any other cause whatever; which authority shall always be exercised in the manner following. Whenever the legislative or executive authority or lawful agent of any state in controversy with another shall present a petition to congress stating the matter in question and praying for a hearing, notice thereof shall be given by order of congress to the legislative or executive authority of the other state in controversy, and a day assigned for the appearance of the parties by their lawful agents, who shall then be directed to appoint by joint consent, commissioners or judges to constitute a court for hearing and determining the matter in question: but if they cannot agree, congress shall name three persons out of each of the united states, and from the list of such persons each party shall alternately strike out one, the petitioners beginning, until the number shall be reduced to thirteen; and from that number not less than seven, nor more than nine names as congress shall direct, shall in the presence of congress be drawn out by lot, and the persons whose names shall be so drawn or any five of them, shall be commissioners or judges, to hear and finally determine the controversy, so always as a major part of the judges who shall hear the cause shall agree in the determination: and if either party shall neglect to attend at the day appointed, without shewing reasons, which congress shall judge sufficient, or being present shall refuse to strike, the congress shall proceed to nominate three persons out of each state, and the secretary of congress shall strike in behalf of such party absent or refusing; and the judgment and sentence of the court to be appointed, in the manner before prescribed, shall be final and conclusive; and if any of the parties shall refuse to submit to the authority of such court, or to appear to defend their claim or cause, the court shall nevertheless proceed to pronounce sentence, or judgment, which shall in like manner be final and decisive, the judgment or sentence and other proceedings being in either case transmitted to congress, and lodged among the acts of congress for the security of the parties concerned: provided that every commissioner, before he sits in judgment, shall take an oath to be administered by one of the judges of the supreme or superior court of the state, where the cause shall be tried, "well and truly to hear and determine the matter in question, according to the best of his judgment, without favour, affection or hope of reward:" provided also that no state shall be deprived of territory for the benefit of the united states.

All controversies concerning the private right of soil claimed under different grants of two or more states, whose jurisdictions as they may respect such lands, and the states which passed such grants are adjusted, the said grants or either of them being at the same time claimed to have originated antecedent to such settlement of jurisdiction, shall on the petition of either party to the congress of the united states, be finally determined as near as may be in the same manner as is before prescribed for deciding disputes respecting territorial jurisdiction between different states.

The united states in congress assembled shall also have the sole and exclusive right and power of regulating the alloy and value of coin struck by their own authority, or by that of the respective states—fixing the standard of weights and measures throughout the united states—regulating the trade and managing all affairs with the Indians, not members of any of the states, provided that the legislative right of any state within its own limits be not infringed or violated—establishing and regulating post-offices from one state to another, throughout all the united states, and exacting such postage on the papers passing thro' the same as may be requisite to defray the expences of the said office—appointing all officers of the land forces, in the service of the united states, except regimental officers—appointing all the officers of the united states—making rules for the government and regulation of the said land and naval forces, and directing their operations.

The united states in congress assembled shall have the authority to appoint a committee, to sit in the recess of congress, to be denominated "A Committee of the States," and to consist of one delegate from each state; and to appoint such other committees and civil officers as may be necessary for managing the general affairs of the united states under their direction—to appoint one of their number to preside, provided that no person be allowed to serve in the office of president more than one year in any term of three years; to ascertain the necessary sums of Money to be raised for the service of the united states, and to appropriate and apply the same for defraying the public expences—to borrow money, or emit bills on the credit of the united states, transmitting every half year to the respective states an account of the sums of money so borrowed or emitted,—to build and equip a navy—to agree upon the number of land forces, and to make requisitions from each state for its quota, in proportion to the number of white inhabitants in such state; which requisition shall be binding, and thereupon the legislature of each state shall appoint the regimental officers, raise the men and cloath, arm and equip them in a soldier like manner, at the expence of the united states, and the officers and men so cloathed, armed and equipped shall march to the place appointed, and within the time agreed on by the united states in congress assembled: But if the united states in congress assembled shall, on consideration of circumstances judge proper that any state should not raise men, or should raise a smaller number than its quota, and that any other state should raise a greater number of men than the quota thereof, such extra number shall be raised, officered, cloathed, armed and equipped in the same manner as the quota of such state, unless the legislature of such state shall judge that such extra number cannot be safely spared out of the same, in which case they shall raise, officer, cloath, arm and equip as many of such extra number as they judge can be safely spared. And the officers and men so cloathed, armed and equipped, shall march to the place appointed, and within the time agreed on by the united states in congress assembled.

The united states in congress assembled shall never engage in a war, nor grant letters of marque and reprisal in time of peace, nor enter into any treaties or alliances, nor coin money, nor regulate the value thereof, nor ascertain the sums and expences necessary for the defence and welfare of the united states, or any of them, nor emit bills, nor borrow money on the credit of the united states, nor appropriate money, nor agree upon the number of vessels of war, to be built or purchased, or the number of land or sea forces to be raised, nor appoint a commander in chief of the army or navy, unless nine states assent to the same: nor shall a question on any other point, except for adjourning from day to day be determined, unless by the votes of a majority of the united states in congress assembled.

The congress of the united states shall have power to adjourn to any time within the year, and to any place within the united states, so that no period of adjournment be for a longer duration than the space of six Months, and shall publish the Journal of their proceedings monthly, except such parts thereof relating to treaties, alliances or military operations as in their judgment require secresy; and the yeas and nays of the delegates of each state on any question shall be entered on the Journal, when it is desired by any delegate; and the delegates of a state, or any of them, at his or their request shall be furnished with a transcript of the said Journal, except such parts as are above excepted to lay before the legislatures of the several states.

Art. X. The committee of the states, or any nine of them, shall be authorised to execute, in the recess of congress, such of the powers of congress as the united states in congress assembled, by the consent of nine states, shall from time to time think expedient to vest them with; provided that no power be delegated to the said committee, for the exercise of which, by the articles of confederation, the voice of nine states in the congress of the united states assembled is requisite.

Art. XI. Canada acceding to this confederation, and joining in the measures of the united states, shall be admitted into, and entitled to all the advantages of this union: but no other colony shall be admitted into the same, unless such admission be agreed to by nine states.

Art. XII. All bills of credit emitted, monies borrowed and debts contracted by, or under the authority of congress, before the assembling of the united states, in pursuance of the present confederation, shall be deemed and considered as a charge against the united states, for payment and satisfaction whereof the said united states and the public faith are hereby solemnly pledged.

Art. XIII. Every state shall abide by the determinations of the united states in congress assembled, on all questions which by this confederation are submitted to them. And the Articles of this confederation shall be inviolably observed by every state, and the union shall be perpetual; nor shall any alteration at any time hereafter be made in any of them; unless such alteration be agreed to in a congress of the united states, and be afterwards confirmed by the legislatures of every state.

AND WHEREAS it hath pleased the Great Governor of the World to incline the hearts of the legislatures we respectively represent in congress, to approve of, and to authorize us to ratify the said articles of confederation and perpetual union. KNOW YE that we the undersigned delegates, by virtue of the power and authority to us given for that purpose, do by these presents, in the name and in behalf of our respective constituents, fully and entirely ratify and confirm each and every of the said articles of confederation and perpetual union, and all and singular the matters and things therein contained: And we do further solemnly plight and engage the faith of our respective constituents, that they shall abide by the determination of the united states in congress assembled, on all questions, which by the said confederation are submitted to them. And that the articles thereof shall be inviolably observed by the states we respectively represent, and that the union shall be perpetual. In Witness whereof we have hereunto set our hands in Congress. Done at Philadelphia in the state of Pennsylvania the ninth Day of July in the Year of our Lord one Thousand seven Hundred and Seventy-eight and in the third year of the independence of America.

The Constitution of the United States of America

Annotated with references to *The Federalist Papers*

[PREAMBLE]

We the People of the United States, in Order to form a more perfect Union, establish Justice, insure domestic Tranquility, provide for the common defence, promote the general Welfare, and secure the Blessings of Liberty to ourselves and our Posterity, do ordain and establish this Constitution for the United States of America.

84 (Hamilton)

ARTICLE I

Section 1
[LEGISLATIVE POWERS]

All legislative Powers herein granted shall be vested in a Congress of the United States, which shall consist of a Senate and House of Representatives.

10, 45 (Madison)

Section 2
[HOUSE OF REPRESENTATIVES, HOW CONSTITUTED, POWER OF IMPEACHMENT]

The House of Representatives shall be composed of Members chosen every second Year by the People of the several States, and the Electors in each State shall have the Qualifications requisite for Electors of the most numerous Branch of the State Legislature.

39, 45, 52–53, 57 (Madison)

No Person shall be a Representative who shall not have attained to the Age of twenty-five Years, and been seven Years a Citizen of the United States, and who shall not, when elected, be an inhabitant of that State in which he shall be chosen.

52 (Madison)

Representatives and *direct Taxes*[1] shall be apportioned among the several States which may be included within this Union, according to their respective Numbers, *which shall be determined by adding to the whole Number of free Persons, including those bound to Service for a Term of Years, and excluding Indians not taxed, three-fifths of all other Persons.*[2] The actual Enumeration shall be made within three Years after the first Meeting of the Congress of the United States, and within every subsequent Term of ten Years, in such Manner as they shall by Law direct. The Number of Representatives shall not exceed one for every thirty Thousand, but each State shall have at Least one Representative; *and until such enumeration shall be made, the State of New Hampshire shall be entitled to chuse three, Massachusetts eight, Rhode-Island*

60 (Hamilton)
54, 58 (Madison)

55–56 (Madison)

---

[1] Modified by Sixteenth Amendment.

[2] Modified by Fourteenth Amendment.

and Providence Plantations one, Connecticut five, New-York six, New Jersey four, Pennsylvania eight, Delaware one, Maryland six, Virginia ten, North Carolina five, South Carolina five, and Georgia three.[3]

When vacancies happen in the Representation from any State, the Executive Authority thereof shall issue Writs of Election to fill such Vacancies.

The House of Representatives shall chuse their Speaker and other Officers; and shall have the sole Power of Impeachment.

Section 3
[THE SENATE, HOW CONSTITUTED, IMPEACHMENT TRIALS]

The Senate of the United States shall be composed of two Senators from each State, *chosen by the Legislature thereof,*[4] for six Years; and each Senator shall have one Vote.

Immediately after they shall be assembled in Consequence of the first Election, they shall be divided as equally as may be into three Classes. The Seats of the Senators of the first Class shall be vacated at the Expiration of the second Year, of the second Class at the Expiration of the fourth Year, and of the third Class at the Expiration of the sixth Year, so that one third may be chosen every second Year: *and if vacancies happen by Resignation, or otherwise, during the Recess of the Legislature of any State, the Executive thereof may make temporary Appointments until the next Meeting of the Legislature, which shall then fill such Vacancies.*[5]

No person shall be a Senator who shall not have attained to the Age of thirty Years, and been nine Years a Citizen of the United States, and who shall not, when elected, be an Inhabitant of that State for which he shall be chosen.

The Vice-President of the United States shall be President of the Senate, but shall have no Vote, unless they be equally divided.

The Senate shall chuse their other Officers, and also a President pro tempore, in the Absence of the Vice-President, or when he shall exercise the Office of President of the United States.

The Senate shall have the sole Power to try all Impeachments. When sitting for that Purpose, they shall be on Oath or Affirmation. When the President of the United States is tried, the Chief Justice shall preside: And no Person shall be convicted without the Concurrence of two-thirds of the Members present.

Judgment in Cases of Impeachment shall not extend further than to removal from Office, and disqualification to hold and enjoy any Office of honor, Trust or Profit under the United States: but the Party convicted shall nevertheless be liable and subject to Indictment, Trial, Judgment and Punishment, according to Law.

Section 4
[ELECTION OF SENATORS AND REPRESENTATIVES]

The Times, Places and Manner of holding Elections for Senators and Representatives, shall be prescribed in each State by the Legislature thereof; but the

---

[3] Temporary provision.

[4] Modified by Seventeenth Amendment.

[5] Modified by Seventeenth Amendment.

79 (Hamilton)

39, 45 (Madison)
60 (Hamilton)

62–63 (Madison)
59, 68 (Hamilton)

62 (Madison)
64 (Jay)

39 (Madison)
65–67, 79
(Hamilton)

84 (Hamilton)

59–61 (Hamilton)

Congress may at any time by Law make or alter such Regulations, except as to the Places of chusing Senators.

The Congress shall assemble at least once in every Year, and such Meeting shall be on the first Monday in December, unless they shall by Law appoint a different Day.[6]

Section 5
[QUORUM, JOURNALS, MEETINGS, ADJOURNMENTS]

Each House shall be the Judge of the Elections, Returns and Qualifications of its own Members, and a Majority of each shall constitute a Quorum to do Business; but a smaller Number may adjourn from day to day, and may be authorized to compel the Attendance of absent Members, in such Manner, and under the Penalties as each House may provide.

Each House may determine the Rules of its Proceedings, punish its Members for disorderly Behavior, and, with the Concurrence of two-thirds, expel a Member.

Each House shall keep a Journal of its Proceedings, and from time to time publish the same, excepting such Parts as may in their Judgment require Secrecy; and the Yeas and Nays of the Members of either House on any questions shall, at the Desire of one-fifth of the present, be entered on the Journal.

Neither House, during the Session of Congress, shall, without the Consent of the other, adjourn for more than three days, nor to any other Place than that in which the two Houses shall be sitting.

Section 6
[COMPENSATION, PRIVILEGES, DISABILITIES]

The Senators and Representatives shall receive a Compensation for their Services, to be ascertained by Law, and paid out of the Treasury of the United States. They shall in all Cases, except Treason, Felony and Breach of the Peace, be privileged from Arrest during their Attendance at the Session of their respective Houses, and in going to and returning from the same; and for any Speech or Debate in either House, they shall not be questioned in any other Place.

No Senator or Representative shall, during the time for which he was elected, be appointed to any civil Office under the authority of the United States, which shall have been created, or the Emoluments whereof shall have been encreased during such time; and no Person holding any Office under the United States, shall be a Member of either House during his Continuance in Office.

55 (Madison)
76 (Hamilton)

Section 7
[PROCEDURE IN PASSING BILLS AND RESOLUTIONS]

All Bills for raising Revenue shall originate in the House of Representatives; but the Senate may propose or concur with Amendments as on other Bills.

66 (Hamilton)

Every Bill which shall have passed the House of Representatives and the Senate, shall, before it become a Law, be presented to the President of the United States; if he approve he shall sign it, but if not he shall return it, with his Objections to that House in which it shall have originated, who shall enter the Objections at

69, 73 (Hamilton)

---

[6] Modified by Twentieth Amendment.

large on their Journal, and proceed to reconsider it. If after such Reconsideration two-thirds of that House shall agree to pass the Bill, it shall be sent, together with the Objections, to the other House, by which it shall likewise be reconsidered, and if approved by two-thirds of that House it shall become a Law. But in all such Cases the Votes of both Houses shall be determined by Yeas and Nays, and the Names of the Persons voting for and against the Bill shall be entered on the Journal of each House respectively. If any Bill shall not be returned by the President within ten Days (Sundays excepted) after it shall have been presented to him, the Same shall be a Law, in like Manner as if he had signed it, unless the Congress by their Adjournment prevent its Return, in which Case it shall not be a Law.

69, 73 (Hamilton)

Every Order, Resolution, or Vote to which the Concurrence of the Senate and House of Representatives may be necessary (except on a question of Adjournment) shall be presented to the President of the United States; and before the Same shall take Effect, shall be approved by him, or being disapproved by him, shall be repassed by two-thirds of the Senate and House of Representatives, according to the Rules and Limitations prescribed in the Case of a Bill.

Section 8
[POWERS OF CONGRESS]

The Congress shall have Power

30–36 (Hamilton)
41 (Madison)

To lay and collect Taxes, Duties, Imposts and Excises, to pay the Debts and provide for the common Defence and general Welfare of the United States; but all Duties, Imposts and excises shall be uniform throughout the United States;

To borrow Money on the Credit of the United States;

56 (Madison)
42, 45, 56 (Madison)

To regulate Commerce with foreign Nations, and among the several States, and with the Indian Tribes;

32 (Hamilton)

To establish an uniform Rule of Naturalization, and uniform Laws on the subject of Bankruptcies throughout the United States;

42 (Madison)

To coin Money, regulate the Value thereof, and of foreign Coin, and fix the Standard of Weights and Measures;

42 (Madison)

To provide for the Punishment of counterfeiting the Securities and current Coin of the United States;

To establish Post Offices and post Roads;

42 (Madison)
42, 43 (Madison)

To promote the Progress of Science and useful Arts, by securing for limited Times to Authors and Inventors the exclusive Right to their respective Writings and Discoveries;

81 (Hamilton)
42 (Madison)

To constitute Tribunals inferior to the supreme Court;

To define and Punish Piracies and Felonies committed on the high Seas, and Offences against the Law of Nations;

41 (Madison)

To declare War, grant Letters of Marque and Reprisal, and make Rules concerning Captures on Land and Water;

23, 24, 26 (Hamilton)

To raise and support Armies, but no Appropriation of Money to that Use shall be for a longer Term than two Years;

41 (Madison)

To provide and maintain a Navy;

To make Rules for the Government and Regulation of the land and naval forces;

29 (Hamilton)

To provide for calling for the Militia to execute the Laws of the Union, suppress Insurrections and repel Invasions;

To provide for organizing, arming, and disciplining, the Militia, and for governing such Part of them as may be employed in the Service of the United States, reserving to the States respectively, the Appointment of the Officers, and the Authority of training the Militia according to the discipline prescribed by Congress;

29 (Hamilton)
56 (Madison)

To exercise exclusive Legislation in all Cases whatsoever, over such District (not exceeding ten Miles square) as may, by Cession of particular States, and the Acceptance of Congress, become the Seat of the Government of the United States, and to exercise like Authority over all Places purchased by the Consent of the Legislature of the State in which the Same shall be, for the Erection of Forts, Magazines, Arsenals, dock-Yards, and other needful Buildings;—And

32 (Hamilton)
43 (Madison)

To make all Laws which shall be necessary and proper for carrying into Execution the foregoing Powers, and all other Powers vested by this Constitution in the Government of the United States, or in any Department or Officer thereof.

29, 33 (Hamilton)
44 (Madison)

Section 9
[SOME RESTRICTIONS ON FEDERAL POWER]

The Migration or Importation of such Persons as any of the States now existing shall think proper to admit, shall not be prohibited by the Congress prior to the Year one thousand eight hundred and eight, but a Tax or Duty may be imposed on such Importation, not exceeding ten dollars for each Person.[7]

42 (Madison)

The privilege of the Writ of *Habeas Corpus* shall not be suspended, unless when in Cases of Rebellion or Invasion the public Safety may require it.

83, 84 (Hamilton)

No Bill of Attainder or ex post facto Law shall be passed.

84 (Hamilton)

No Capitation, or other direct, Tax shall be laid, unless in Proportion to the Census or Enumeration herein before directed to be taken.[8]

No Tax or Duty shall be laid on Articles exported from any State.

No Preference shall be given by any Regulation of Commerce or Revenue to the Ports of one State over those of another; nor shall vessels bound to, or from, one State, be obliged to enter, clear, or pay Duties in another.

32 (Hamilton)

No Money shall be drawn from the Treasury, but in Consequence of Appropriations made by Law; and a regular Statement and Account of the Receipts and Expenditures of all public Money shall be published from time to time.

No Title of Nobility shall be granted by the United States: And no Person holding any Office of Profit or Trust under them, shall, without the Consent of the Congress, accept of any present, Emolument, Office or Title, of any kind whatever, from any King, Prince, or foreign State.

39 (Madison)
84 (Hamilton)

Section 10
[RESTRICTIONS UPON POWERS OF STATES]

No State shall enter into any Treaty, Alliance, or Confederation; grant Letters of Marque and Reprisal; coin Money; emit Bills of Credit; make any Thing but gold and silver Coin a Tender in Payment of Debts; pass any Bill of Attainder, ex post facto Law, or Law impairing the Obligation of Contracts, or grant any Title of Nobility.

33 (Hamilton)
44 (Madison)

---

[7] Temporary provision.

[8] Modified by Sixteenth Amendment.

32 (Hamilton)
44 (Madison)

No State shall, without the Consent of the Congress, lay any Imposts or Duties on Imports or Exports, except what may be absolutely necessary for executing its inspection Laws: and the net Produce of all Duties and Imposts, laid by any State on Imports or Exports, shall be for the Use of the Treasury of the United States; and all such Laws shall be subject to the Revision and Control of the Congress.

No State shall, without the Consent of Congress, lay any Duty of Tonnage, keep Troops, or Ships of War in time of Peace, enter into any Agreement or Compact with another State, or with a foreign Power, or engage in War, unless actually invaded, or in such imminent Danger as will not admit of Delay.

ARTICLE II

Section 1
[EXECUTIVE POWER, ELECTION, QUALIFICATIONS OF THE PRESIDENT]

39 (Madison)
70, 71, 84
(Hamilton)

68, 69, 71, 77
(Hamilton)
39, 45 (Madison)

The executive Power shall be vested in a President of the United States of America. *He shall hold his Office during the Term of four years and, together with the Vice-President, chosen for the same Term, be elected, as follows:*[9]

Each State shall appoint, in such Manner as the Legislature thereof may direct, a Number of Electors, equal to the whole Number of Senators and Representatives to which the State may be entitled in the Congress: but no Senator or Representative, or Person holding an Office of Trust or Profit under the United States, shall be appointed an Elector.

66 (Hamilton)

The electors shall meet in their respective States, and vote by ballot for two Persons, of whom one at least shall not be an Inhabitant of the same State with themselves. And they shall make a List of all the Persons voted for, and of the Number of Votes for each; which List they shall sign and certify, and transmit sealed to the Seat of the Government of the United States, directed to the President of the Senate. The President of the Senate shall, in the Presence of the Senate and House of Representatives, open all the Certificates, and the Votes shall then be counted. The Person having the greatest Number of Votes shall be the President, if such Number be a Majority of the whole Number of Electors appointed; and if there be more than one who have such Majority and have an equal Number of Votes, then the House of Representatives shall immediately chuse by Ballot one of them for President; and if no person have a Majority, then from the five highest on the List the said House shall in like Manner chuse the President. But in chusing the President, the Votes shall be taken by States, the Representation from each State having one Vote; A quorum for this Purpose shall consist of a Member or Members from two-thirds of the States, and a Majority of all the States shall be necessary to a Choice. In every Case, after the Choice of the President, the person having the greatest Number of Votes of the Electors shall be the Vice-President. But if there should remain two or more who have equal vote, the Senate shall chuse from them by Ballot the Vice-President.[10]

The Congress may determine the Time of chusing the Electors, and the Day on which they shall give their Votes; which Day shall be the same throughout the United States.

---

[9] Number of terms limited to two by Twenty-second Amendment.

[10] Modified by Twelfth and Twentieth Amendments.

No Person except a natural born Citizen, or a Citizen of the United States, at the time of the Adoption of this Constitution, shall be eligible to the Office of President; neither shall any Person be eligible to that Office who shall not have attained to the Age of thirty-five Years, and been fourteen Years a Resident within the United States.

64 (Jay)

In Case of the Removal of the President from Office, or his Death, Resignation, or Inability to discharge the Powers and Duties of the said Office, the same shall devolve on the Vice-President, and the Congress may by Law provide for the Case of Removal, Death, Resignation, or Inability, both of the President and Vice-President, declaring what Officer shall then act as President, and such Officer shall act accordingly, until the Disability be removed, or a President shall be elected.

The President shall, at stated Times, receive for his Services, a Compensation, which shall neither be encreased nor diminished during the Period for which he shall have been elected, and he shall not receive within that Period any other Emolument from the United States, or any of them.

73, 79 (Hamilton)

Before he enter on the Execution of his Office, he shall take the following Oath or Affirmation:—"I do solemnly swear (or affirm) that I will faithfully execute the Office of President of the United States, and will to the best of my Ability, preserve, protect and defend the Constitution of the United States."

Section 2
[POWERS OF THE PRESIDENT]

The President shall be Commander in Chief of the Army and Navy of the United States, and of the Militia of the several States, when called into the actual Service of the United States; he may require the Opinion, in writing, of the principal Officer in each of the executive Departments, upon any Subject relating to the Duties of their respective Offices, and he shall have Power to grant Reprieves and Pardons for Offences against the United States, except in Cases of Impeachment.

69, 74 (Hamilton)

He shall have Power, by and with the Advice and Consent of the Senate, to make Treaties, provided two-thirds of the Senators present concur; and he shall nominate, and by and with the Advice and Consent of the Senate, shall appoint Ambassadors, other public Ministers and Consuls, Judges of the Supreme Court, and all other Officers of the United States, whose Appointments are not herein otherwise provided for, and which shall be established by Law: but the Congress may by Law vest the Appointment of such inferior Officers, as they think proper, in the President alone, in the Courts of Law, or in the Heads of Departments.

42 (Madison)
64 (Jay)
66, 69, 76, 77 (Hamilton)

The President shall have Power to fill up all Vacancies that may happen during the Recess of the Senate, by granting Commissions which shall expire at the End of their next Session.

67, 76 (Hamilton)

Section 3
[POWERS AND DUTIES OF THE PRESIDENT]

He shall from time to time give to the Congress Information of the State of the Union, and recommend to their Consideration such Measures as he shall judge necessary and expedient; he may, on extraordinary Occasions, convene both Houses, or either of them, and in Case of Disagreement between them, with Respect to the Time of Adjournment, he may adjourn them to such Time as he shall

69, 77, 78 (Hamilton)
42 (Madison)

think proper; he shall receive Ambassadors and other public Ministers; he shall take Care that the Laws be faithfully executed, and shall Commission all the Officers of the United States.

Section 4
[IMPEACHMENT]

39 (Madison)
69 (Hamilton)

The President, Vice-President and all civil Officers of the United States shall be removed from Office on Impeachment for, and Conviction of, Treason, Bribery, or other high Crimes and Misdemeanors.

ARTICLE III

Section 1
[JUDICIAL POWER, TENURE OF OFFICE]

65, 78, 79, 81, 82
(Hamilton)

The judicial Power of the United States, shall be vested in one supreme Court, and in such inferior Courts as the Congress may from time to time ordain and establish. The Judges, both of the supreme and inferior Courts, shall hold their Offices during good Behavior, and shall, at stated Times, receive for their Services, a Compensation, which shall not be diminished during their Continuance in Office.

Section 2
[JURISDICTION]

80 (Hamilton)

The judicial Power shall extend to all Cases, in Law and Equity, arising under this Constitution, the Laws of the United States, and Treaties made, or which shall be made, under their Authority;—to all Cases affecting Ambassadors, other public Ministers and Consuls;—to all Cases of admiralty and maritime Jurisdiction;—to Controversies to which the United States shall be a party;—to Controversies between two or more States;—*between a State and Citizens of another State;*—between Citizens of different States,—between Citizens of the same State claiming Lands under Grants of different States, *and between a State,* or the Citizens thereof, *and foreign States, Citizens or Subjects.*[11]

81 (Hamilton)

In all Cases affecting Ambassadors, other public Ministers and Consuls, and those in which a State shall be Party, the supreme Court shall have original Jurisdiction. In all the other Cases before mentioned, the supreme Court shall have appellate Jurisdiction, both as to Law and Fact, with such Exceptions, and under such Regulations as Congress shall make.

83, 84
(Hamilton)

The Trial of all Crimes, except in Cases of Impeachment, shall be by Jury; and such Trial shall be held in the State where the said Crimes shall have been committed; but when not committed within any State, the Trial shall be at such Place or Places as the Congress may by Law have directed.

---

[11] Modified by Eleventh Amendment.

Section 3
[TREASON, PROOF, AND PUNISHMENT]

Treason against the United States, shall consist only in levying War against them, or in adhering to their Enemies, giving them Aid and Comfort. No Person shall be convicted of Treason unless on the Testimony of two Witnesses to the same overt Act, or on Confession in open Court.

43 (Madison)
84 (Hamilton)

The Congress shall have Power to declare the Punishment of Treason, but no Attainder of Treason shall work Corruption of Blood, or Forfeiture except during the Life of the Person attained.

43 (Madison)
84 (Hamilton)

ARTICLE IV

Section 1
[FAITH AND CREDIT AMONG STATES]

Full Faith and Credit shall be given in each State to the public Acts, Records, and judicial Proceedings of every other State. And the Congress may by general Laws prescribe the Manner in which such Acts, Records and Proceedings shall be proved, and the Effect thereof.

42 (Madison)

Section 2
[PRIVILEGES AND IMMUNITIES, FUGITIVES]

The Citizens of each State shall be entitled to all Privileges and Immunities of Citizens in the several States.

80 (Hamilton)

A person charged in any State with Treason, Felony or other Crime, who shall flee from Justice, and be found in another State, shall on Demand of the executive Authority of the State from which he fled, be delivered up to be removed to the State having Jurisdiction of the Crime.

No person held to Service or Labour in one State, under the Laws thereof, escaping into another, shall, in Consequence of any Law or Regulation therein, be discharged from such Service or Labour, but shall be delivered up on Claim of the Party to whom such Service or Labour may be due.[12]

Section 3
[ADMISSION OF NEW STATES]

New States may be admitted by the Congress into this Union; but no new State shall be formed or erected within the Jurisdiction of any other State; nor any State be formed by the Junction of two or more States, or Parts of States, without the Consent of the Legislatures of the States concerned as well as of the Congress.

43 (Madison)

The Congress shall have Power to dispose of and make all needful Rules and Regulations respecting the Territory or other Property belonging to the United States; and nothing in this Constitution shall be so construed as to Prejudice any Claims of the United States, or of any particular State.

43 (Madison)

---

[12] Repealed by Thirteenth Amendment.

Section 4

[GUARANTEE OF REPUBLICAN GOVERNMENT]

39, 43
(Madison)

The United States shall guarantee to every State in this Union a Republican Form of Government, and shall protect each of them against Invasion; and on Application of the Legislature, or of the Executive (when the Legislature cannot be convened) against domestic Violence.

ARTICLE V

[AMENDMENT OF THE CONSTITUTION]

39, 43 (Madison)
85 (Hamilton)

The Congress, whenever two-thirds of both Houses shall deem it necessary, shall propose Amendments to this Constitution, or, on the Application of the Legislatures of two-thirds of the several States, shall call a Convention for proposing Amendments, which, in either Case, shall be valid to all Intents and Purposes, as Part of this Constitution, when ratified by the Legislatures of three-fourths of the several States, or by Conventions in three-fourths thereof, as the one or the other Mode of Ratification may be proposed by the Congress; *Provided that no Amendment which may be made prior to the Year One thousand eight hundred and eight shall in any Manner affect the first and fourth Clauses in the Ninth Section of the first Article;*[13] and that no State, without its Consent, shall be deprived of its equal Suffrage in the Senate.

ARTICLE VI

[DEBTS, SUPREMACY, OATH]

43 (Madison)

All Debts contracted and Engagements entered into, before the Adoption of this Constitution, shall be as valid against the United States under this Constitution, as under the Confederation.

27, 33 (Hamilton)
39, 44 (Madison)

This Constitution, and the Laws of the United States which shall be made in Pursuance thereof; and all Treaties made, or which shall be made, under the Authority of the United States, shall be the supreme Law of the Land; and the Judges in every State shall be bound thereby, any Thing in the Constitution or Laws of any State to the Contrary notwithstanding.

27 (Hamilton)
44 (Madison)

The Senators and Representatives before mentioned, and the Members of the several State Legislatures, and all executive and judicial Officers, both of the United States and of the several States, shall be bound by Oath or Affirmation, to support this Constitution; but no religious Test shall be required as a Qualification to any Office or public Trust under the United States.

ARTICLE VII

[RATIFICATION AND ESTABLISHMENT]

39, 40, 43
(Madison)

The Ratification of the Conventions of nine States, shall be sufficient for the Establishment of this Constitution between the States so ratifying the Same.[14]

---

[13] Temporary provision.

[14] The Constitution was submitted on September 17, 1787, by the Constitutional Convention, was ratified by the conventions of several states at various dates up to May 29, 1790, and became effective on March 4, 1789.

Done in Convention by the Unanimous Consent of the States present the Seventeenth Day of September in the Year of our Lord one thousand seven hundred and Eighty seven and of the Independence of the United States of America the Twelfth. *In Witness* whereof We have hereunto subscribed our Names,

G:^{0} WASHINGTON—
*Presidt, and Deputy
from Virginia*

New Hampshire	JOHN LANGDON	Maryland	JAMES MCHENRY
	NICHOLAS GILMAN		DAN OF ST THOS. JENIFER
			DANL CARROLL
Massachusetts	NATHANIEL GORHAM		
	RUFUS KING	Virginia	JOHN BLAIR—
			JAMES MADISON JR.
Connecticut	WM SAML JOHNSON		
	ROGER SHERMAN	North Carolina	WM BLOUNT
			RICHD DOBBS SPAIGHT
New York	ALEXANDER HAMILTON		HU WILLIAMSON
New Jersey	WIL: LIVINGSTON	South Carolina	J. RUTLEDGE
	DAVID BREARLEY		CHARLES
	WM PATERSON		COTESWORTH PINCKNEY
	JONA: DAYTON		CHARLES PINCKNEY
			PIERCE BUTLER
Pennsylvania	B FRANKLIN		
	THOMAS MIFFLIN	Georgia	WILLIAM FEW
	ROBT MORRIS		ABR BALDWIN
	GEO. CLYMER		
	THOS. FITZSIMONS		
	JARED INGERSOLL		
	JAMES WILSON		
	GOUV MORRIS		
Delaware	GEO READ		
	GUNNING BEDFOR JUN		
	JOHN DICKINSON		
	RICHARD BASSETT		
	JACO: BROOM		

Amendments to the Constitution

Proposed by Congress and Ratified by the Legislatures of the Several States, Pursuant to Article V of the Original Constitution.

Amendments I–X, known as the Bill of Rights, were proposed by Congress on September 25, 1789, and ratified on December 15, 1791. *The Federalist Papers* comments, mainly in opposition to a Bill of Rights, can be found in number 84 (Hamilton).

AMENDMENT I
[FREEDOM OF RELIGION, OF SPEECH, AND OF THE PRESS]

Congress shall make no law respecting an establishment of religion, or prohibiting the free exercise thereof; or abridging the freedom of speech, or of the press; or the right of the people peaceably to assemble, and to petition the Government for a redress of grievances.

AMENDMENT II
[RIGHT TO KEEP AND BEAR ARMS]

A well regulated Militia, being necessary to the security of a free State, the right of the people to keep and bear Arms, shall not be infringed.

AMENDMENT III
[QUARTERING OF SOLDIERS]

No Soldier shall, in time of peace be quartered in any house, without the consent of the Owner, nor in time of war, but in a manner to be prescribed by law.

AMENDMENT IV
[SECURITY FROM UNWARRANTABLE SEARCH AND SEIZURE]

The right of the people to be secure in their persons, houses, papers, and effects, against unreasonable searches and seizures, shall not be violated, and no Warrants shall issue, but upon probable cause, supported by Oath or affirmation, and particularly describing the place to be searched, and the persons or things to be seized.

AMENDMENT V
[RIGHTS OF ACCUSED PERSONS IN CRIMINAL PROCEEDINGS]

No person shall be held to answer for a capital, or otherwise infamous crime, unless on a presentment or indictment of a Grand Jury, except in cases arising in the land or naval forces, or in the Militia, when in actual service in time of War or in public danger; nor shall any person be subject for the same offence to be twice put in jeopardy of life or limb; nor shall be compelled in any Criminal Case to be a witness against himself, nor be deprived of life, liberty, or property, without due process of law; nor shall private property be taken for public use, without just compensation.

AMENDMENT VI
[RIGHT TO SPEEDY TRIAL, WITNESSES, ETC.]

In all criminal prosecutions, the accused shall enjoy the right to a speedy and public trial, by an impartial jury of the State and district wherein the crime shall have been committed, which district shall have been previously ascertained by law, and to be informed of the nature and cause of the accusation; to be confronted with the witnesses against him; to have compulsory process for obtaining Witnesses in his favor, and to have the Assistance of Counsel for his defence.

AMENDMENT VII
[TRIAL BY JURY IN CIVIL CASES]

In suits at common law, where the value in controversy shall exceed twenty dollars, the right of trial by jury shall be preserved, and no fact tried by a jury shall be otherwise re-examined in any Court of the United States, than according to the rules of the common law.

AMENDMENT VIII
[BAILS, FINES, PUNISHMENTS]

Excessive bail shall not be required, nor excessive fines imposed, nor cruel and unusual punishments inflicted.

AMENDMENT IX
[RESERVATION OF RIGHTS OF PEOPLE]

The enumeration in the Constitution, of certain rights, shall not be construed to deny or disparage others retained by the people.

AMENDMENT X
[POWERS RESERVED TO STATES OR PEOPLE]

The powers not delegated to the United States by the Constitution, nor prohibited by it to the States, are reserved to the States respectively, or to the people.

AMENDMENT XI
[Proposed by Congress on March 4, 1794; declared ratified on January 8, 1798.]
[RESTRICTION OF JUDICIAL POWER]

The Judicial power of the United States shall not be construed to extend to any suit in law or equity, commenced or prosecuted against one of the United States by Citizens of another State, or by Citizens or Subjects of any Foreign State.

AMENDMENT XII

[Proposed by Congress on December 9, 1803; declared ratified on September 25, 1804.]

[ELECTION OF PRESIDENT AND VICE-PRESIDENT]

The Electors shall meet in their respective states, and vote by ballot for President and Vice-President, one of whom, at least, shall not be an inhabitant of the same state with themselves; they shall name in their ballots the person voted for as President, and in distinct ballots the person voted for as Vice-President, and they shall make distinct lists of all persons voted for as President, and of all persons voted for as Vice-President, and of the number of votes for each, which lists they shall sign and certify, and transmit sealed to the seat of the government of the United States, directed to the President of the Senate;—The President of the Senate shall, in presence of the Senate and House of Representatives, open all the certificates and the votes shall then be counted;—The person having the greatest number of votes for President, shall be the President, if such number be a majority of the whole number of Electors appointed; and if no person have such majority, then from the persons having the highest numbers not exceeding three on the list of those voted for as President, the House of Representatives shall choose immediately, by ballot, the President. But in choosing the President, the votes shall be taken by states, the representation from each state having one vote; a quorum for this purpose shall consist of a member or members from two-thirds of the states, and a majority of all states shall be necessary to a choice. And if the House of Representatives shall not choose a President whenever the right of choice shall devolve upon them, before the fourth day of March next following, then the Vice-President, shall act as President, as in the case of the death or other constitutional disability of the President. The person having the greatest number of votes as Vice-President, shall be the Vice-President, if such a number be a majority of the whole number of Electors appointed, and if no person have a majority, then from the two highest numbers on the list, the Senate shall choose the Vice-President; a quorum for the purpose shall consist of two-thirds of the whole number of Senators, and a majority of the whole number shall be necessary to a choice. But no person constitutionally ineligible to the office of President shall be eligible to that of Vice-President of the United States.

AMENDMENT XIII

[Proposed by Congress on January 31, 1865; declared ratified on December 18, 1865.]

Section 1
[ABOLITION OF SLAVERY]

Neither slavery nor involuntary servitude, except as a punishment for crime whereof the party shall have been duly convicted, shall exist within the United States, or any place subject to their jurisdiction.

Section 2
[POWER TO ENFORCE THIS ARTICLE]

Congress shall have power to enforce this article by appropriate legislation.

AMENDMENT XIV

[Proposed by Congress on June 13, 1866; declared ratified on July 28, 1868.]

Section 1
[CITIZENSHIP RIGHTS NOT TO BE ABRIDGED BY STATES]

All persons born or naturalized in the United States, and subject to the jurisdiction thereof, are citizens of the United States and of the State wherein they reside. No state shall make or enforce any law which shall abridge the privileges or immunities of citizens of the United States; nor shall any State deprive any person of life, liberty, or property, without due process of law; nor deny to any person within its jurisdiction the equal protection of the laws.

Section 2
[APPORTIONMENT OF REPRESENTATIVES IN CONGRESS]

Representatives shall be apportioned among the several States according to their respective numbers, counting the whole number of persons in each State, excluding Indians not taxed. But when the right to vote at any election for the choice of electors for President and Vice-President of the United States, Representatives in Congress, the Executive and Judicial officers of a State, or the members of the Legislature thereof, is denied to any of the male inhabitants of such State, being twenty-one years of age, and citizens of the United States, or in any way abridged, except for participation in rebellion, or other crime, the basis of representation therein shall be reduced in the proportion which the number of such male citizens shall bear to the whole number of male citizens twenty-one years of age in such State.

Section 3
[PERSONS DISQUALIFIED FROM HOLDING OFFICE]

No person shall be a Senator or Representative in Congress, or elector of President and Vice-President, or hold any office, civil or military, under the United States, or under any State, who, having previously taken an oath, as a member of Congress, or as an officer of the United States, or as a member of any State legislature, or as an executive or judicial officer of any State, to support the Constitution of the United States, shall have engaged in insurrection or rebellion against the same, or given aid or comfort to the enemies thereof. But Congress may by a vote of two-thirds of each House, remove such disability.

Section 4
[WHAT PUBLIC DEBTS ARE VALID]

The validity of the public debt of the United States, authorized by law, including debts incurred for payment of pensions and bounties for services in suppressing insurrection or rebellion, shall not be questioned. But neither the United States nor any State shall assume or pay any debt or obligation incurred in aid of insurrection or rebellion against the United States, or any claim for the loss or emancipation of any slave; but all such debts, obligations and claims shall be held illegal and void.

Section 5
[POWER TO ENFORCE THIS ARTICLE]

The Congress shall have power to enforce, by appropriate legislation, the provisions of this article.

AMENDMENT XV
[Proposed by Congress on February 26, 1869; declared ratified on March 30, 1870.]

Section 1
[NEGRO SUFFRAGE]

The right of citizens of the United States to vote shall not be denied or abridged by the United States or by any State on account of race, color, or previous condition of servitude.

Section 2
[POWER TO ENFORCE THIS ARTICLE]

The Congress shall have power to enforce this article by appropriate legislation.

AMENDMENT XVI
[Proposed by Congress on July 12, 1909; declared ratified on February 25, 1913.]

[AUTHORIZING INCOME TAXES]

The Congress shall have power to lay and collect taxes on incomes, from whatever source derived, without apportionment among the several States, and without regard to any census or enumeration.

AMENDMENT XVII
[Proposed by Congress on May 13, 1912; declared ratified on May 31, 1913.]

[POPULAR ELECTION OF SENATORS]

The Senate of the United States shall be composed of two Senators from each State, elected by the people thereof, for six years; and each Senator shall have one vote. The electors in each State shall have the qualifications requisite for electors of the most numerous branch of the State Legislature.

When vacancies happen in the representation of any State in the Senate, the executive authority of such State shall issue writs of election to fill such vacancies: Provided, That the Legislature of any State may empower the executive thereof to make temporary appointment until the people fill the vacancies by election as the Legislature may direct.

This amendment shall not be so construed as to affect the election or term of any Senator chosen before it becomes valid as part of the Constitution.

AMENDMENT XVIII

[Proposed by Congress December 18, 1917; declared ratified on January 29, 1919.]

Section 1
[NATIONAL LIQUOR PROHIBITION]

After one year from the ratification of this article the manufacture, sale, or transportation of intoxicating liquors within, the importation thereof into, or the exportation thereof from the United States and all territory subject to the jurisdiction thereof for beverage purposes is hereby prohibited.

Section 2
[POWER TO ENFORCE THIS ARTICLE]

The Congress and the several states shall have concurrent power to enforce this article by appropriate legislation.

Section 3
[RATIFICATION WITHIN SEVEN YEARS]

This article shall be inoperative unless it shall have been ratified as an amendment to the Constitution by the legislatures of the several states, as provided in the Constitution, within seven years from the date of the submission hereof to the states by the Congress.[15]

AMENDMENT XIX

[Proposed by Congress on June 4, 1919; declared ratified on August 26, 1920.]

[WOMAN SUFFRAGE]

The right of the citizens of the United States to vote shall not be denied or abridged by the United States or by any state on account of sex.

Congress shall have power to enforce this article by appropriate legislation.

AMENDMENT XX

[Proposed by Congress on March 2, 1932; declared ratified on February 6, 1933.]

Section 1
[TERMS OF OFFICE]

The terms of the President and Vice-President shall end at noon on the 20th day of January, and the terms of the Senators and Representatives at noon on the 3rd day of January, of the years in which such terms would have ended if this article had not been ratified; and the terms of their successors shall then begin.

---

[15] Repealed by Twenty-first Amendment.

Section 2
[TIME OF CONVENING CONGRESS]

The Congress shall assemble at least once in every year, and such meeting shall begin at noon on the 3rd day of January, unless they shall by law appoint a different day.

Section 3
[DEATH OF PRESIDENT-ELECT]

If, at the time fixed for the beginning of the term of the President, the President-elect shall have died, the Vice-President-elect shall become President. If a President shall not have been chosen before the time fixed for the beginning of his term, or if the President-elect shall have failed to qualify, then the Vice-President-elect shall act as President until a President shall have qualified; and the Congress may by law provide for the case wherein neither a President-elect nor a Vice-President-elect shall have qualified, declaring who shall then act as President, or the manner in which one who is to act shall be selected, and such person shall act accordingly until a President or Vice President shall have qualified.

Section 4
[ELECTION OF THE PRESIDENT]

The Congress may by law provide for the case of the death of any of the persons from whom the House of Representatives may choose a President whenever the right of choice shall have devolved upon them, and for the case of the death of any of the persons from whom the Senate may choose a Vice-President whenever the right of choice shall have devolved upon them.

Section 5
[AMENDMENT TAKES EFFECT]

Sections 1 and 2 shall take effect on the 15th day of October following ratification of this article.

Section 6
[RATIFICATION WITHIN SEVEN YEARS]

This article shall be inoperative unless it shall have been ratified as an amendment to the Constitution by the legislatures of three-fourths of the several States within seven years from the date of its submission.

AMENDMENT XXI
[Proposed by Congress on February 20, 1933; declared ratified on December 5, 1933.]

Section 1
[NATIONAL LIQUOR PROHIBITION REPEALED]

The eighteenth article of amendment to the Constitution of the United States is hereby repealed.

Section 2
[TRANSPORTATION OF LIQUOR INTO "DRY" STATES]

The transportation or importation into any State, Territory, or Possession of the United States for delivery or use therein of intoxicating liquors, in violation of the laws thereof, is hereby prohibited.

Section 3
[RATIFICATION WITHIN SEVEN YEARS]

This article shall be inoperative unless it shall have been ratified as an amendment to the Constitution by conventions in the several States, as provided in the Constitution, within seven years from the date of the submission hereof to the States by the Congress.

AMENDMENT XXII
[Proposed by Congress on March 21, 1947; declared ratified on February 26, 1951.]

Section 1
[TENURE OF PRESIDENT LIMITED]

No person shall be elected to the office of President more than twice, and no person who has held the office of President or acted as President for more than two years of a term to which some other person was elected President shall be elected to the Office of the President more than once. But this Article shall not apply to any person holding the office of President when this Article was proposed by the Congress, and shall not prevent any person who may be holding the office of President, or acting as President, during the term within which this Article becomes operative from holding the office of President or acting as President during the remainder of such term.

Section 2
[RATIFICATION WITHIN SEVEN YEARS]

This Article shall be inoperative unless it shall have been ratified as an amendment to the Constitution by the legislatures of three-fourths of the several states within seven years from the date of its submission to the States by the Congress.

AMENDMENT XXIII
[Proposed by Congress on June 21, 1960; declared ratified on March 29, 1961.]

Section 1
[ELECTORAL COLLEGE VOTES FOR THE DISTRICT OF COLUMBIA]

The District constituting the seat of Government of the United States shall appoint in such manner as the Congress may direct:

A number of electors of President and Vice-President equal to the whole number of Senators and Representatives in Congress to which the District would be entitled if it were a State, but in no event more than the least populous State; they shall be in addition to those appointed by the States, but they shall be considered, for the purposes of the election of President and Vice-President, to be electors appointed by a State; and they shall meet in the District and perform such duties as provided by the twelfth article of amendment.

Section 2
[POWER TO ENFORCE THIS ARTICLE]

The Congress shall have power to enforce this article by appropriate legislation.

AMENDMENT XXIV
[Proposed by Congress on August 27, 1963; declared ratified on January 23, 1964.]

Section 1
[ANTI-POLL TAX]

The right of citizens of the United States to vote in any primary or other election for President or Vice-President, for electors for President or Vice-President, or for Senator or Representative of Congress, shall not be denied or abridged by the United States or any State by reasons of failure to pay any poll tax or other tax.

Section 2
[POWER TO ENFORCE THIS ARTICLE]

The Congress shall have power to enforce this article by appropriate legislation.

AMENDMENT XXV
[Proposed by Congress on July 7, 1965; declared ratified on February 10, 1967.]

Section 1
[VICE-PRESIDENT TO BECOME PRESIDENT]

In case of the removal of the President from office or his death or resignation, the Vice-President shall become President.

Section 2
[CHOICE OF A NEW VICE-PRESIDENT]

Whenever there is a vacancy in the office of the Vice-President, the President shall nominate a Vice-President who shall take the office upon confirmation by a majority vote of both houses of Congress.

Section 3
[PRESIDENT MAY DECLARE OWN DISABILITY]

Whenever the President transmits to the President pro tempore of the Senate and the Speaker of the House of Representatives his written declaration that he is unable to discharge the powers and duties of his office, and until he transmits to them a written declaration to the contrary, such powers and duties shall be discharged by the Vice-President as Acting President.

Section 4
[ALTERNATE PROCEDURES TO DECLARE AND TO END PRESIDENTIAL DISABILITY]

Whenever the Vice-President and a majority of either the principal officers of the executive departments, or of such other body as Congress may by law provide, transmit to the President pro tempore of the Senate and the Speaker of the House of Representatives their written declaration that the President is unable to discharge the powers and duties of his office, the Vice-President shall immediately assume the powers and duties of the office as Acting President.

Thereafter, when the President transmits to the President pro tempore of the Senate and the Speaker of the House of Representatives his written declaration that no inability exists, he shall resume the powers and duties of his office unless the Vice-President and a majority of either the principal officers of the executive departments, or of such other body as Congress may by law provide, transmit within four days to the President pro tempore of the Senate and the Speaker of the House of Representatives their written declaration that the President is unable to discharge the powers and duties of his office. Thereupon Congress shall decide the issue, assembling within 48 hours for that purpose if not in session. If the Congress, within 21 days after receipt of the latter written declaration, or, if Congress is not in session, within 21 days after Congress is required to assemble, determines by two-thirds vote of both houses that the President is unable to discharge the powers and duties of his office, the Vice-President shall continue to discharge the same as Acting President; otherwise, the President shall resume the powers and duties of his office.

AMENDMENT XXVI
[Proposed by Congress on March 23, 1971; declared ratified on June 30, 1971.]

Section 1
[EIGHTEEN-YEAR-OLD VOTE]

The right of citizens of the United States, who are eighteen years of age or older, to vote shall not be denied or abridged by the United States or by any State on account of age.

Section 2
[POWER TO ENFORCE THIS ARTICLE]

The Congress shall have power to enforce this article by appropriate legislation.

AMENDMENT XXVII
[Proposed by Congress on September 25, 1789; ratified on May 7, 1992.]

No law varying the compensation for the services of the Senators and Representatives shall take effect until an election of Representatives shall have intervened.

Federalist Papers

NO. 10: MADISON

Among the numerous advantages promised by a well-constructed Union, none deserves to be more accurately developed than its tendency to break and control the violence of faction. The friend of popular governments never finds himself so much alarmed for their character and fate as when he contemplates their propensity to this dangerous vice. He will not fail, therefore, to set a due value on any plan which, without violating the principles to which he is attached, provides a proper cure for it. The instability, injustice, and confusion introduced into the public councils have, in truth, been the mortal diseases under which popular governments have everywhere perished, as they continue to be the favorite and fruitful topics from which the adversaries to liberty derive their most specious declamations. The valuable improvements made by the American constitutions on the popular models, both ancient and modern, cannot certainly be too much admired; but it would be an unwarrantable partiality to contend that they have as effectually obviated the danger on this side, as was wished and expected. Complaints are everywhere heard from our most considerate and virtuous citizens, equally the friends of public and private faith and of public and personal liberty, that our governments are too unstable, that the public good is disregarded in the conflicts of rival parties, and that measures are too often decided, not according to the rules of justice and the rights of the minor party, but by the superior force of an interested and overbearing majority. However anxiously we may wish that these complaints had no foundation, the evidence of known facts will not permit us to deny that they are in some degree true. It will be found, indeed, on a candid review of our situation, that some of the distresses under which we labor have been erroneously charged on the operation of our governments; but it will be found, at the same time, that other causes will not alone account for many of our heaviest misfortunes; and, particularly, for that prevailing and increasing distrust of public engagements and alarm for private rights which are echoed from one end of the continent to the other. These must be chiefly, if not wholly, effects of the unsteadiness and injustice with which a factious spirit has tainted our public administration.

By a faction I understand a number of citizens, whether amounting to a majority or minority of the whole, who are united and actuated by some common impulse of passion, or of interest, adverse to the rights of other citizens, or to the permanent and aggregate interests of the community.

There are two methods of curing the mischiefs of faction: the one, by removing its causes; the other, by controlling its effects.

There are again two methods of removing the causes of faction: the one, by destroying the liberty which is essential to its existence; the other, by giving to every citizen the same opinions, the same passions, and the same interests.

It could never be more truly said than of the first remedy that it was worse than the disease. Liberty is to faction what air is to fire, an aliment without which it instantly expires. But it could not be a less folly to abolish liberty, which is essential to political life, because it nourishes faction than it would be to wish the annihilation of air, which is essential to animal life, because it imparts to fire its destructive agency.

The second expedient is as impracticable as the first would be unwise. As long as the reason of man continues fallible, and he is at liberty to exercise it, different opinions will be formed. As long as the connection subsists between his reason and his self-love, his opinions and his passions will have a reciprocal influence on each other; and the former will be objects to which the latter will attach themselves. The diversity in the faculties of men, from which the rights of property originate, is not less an insuperable obstacle to a uniformity of interests. The protection of these faculties is the first object of government. From the protection of different and unequal faculties of acquiring property, the possession of different degrees and kinds of property immediately results; and from the influence of these on the sentiments and views of the respective proprietors ensues a division of the society into different interests and parties.

The latent causes of faction are thus sown in the nature of man; and we see them everywhere brought into different degrees of activity, according to the different circumstances of civil society. A zeal for different opinions concerning religion, concerning government, and many other points, as well of speculation as of practice; an attachment to different leaders ambitiously contending for preeminence and power; or to persons of other descriptions whose fortunes have been interesting to the human passions, have, in turn, divided mankind into parties, inflamed them with mutual animosity, and rendered them much more disposed to vex and oppress each other than to co-operate for their common good. So strong is this propensity of mankind to fall into mutual animosities that where no substantial occasion presents itself the most frivolous and fanciful distinctions have been sufficient to kindle their unfriendly passions and excite their most violent conflicts. But the most common and durable source of factions has been the various and unequal distribution of property. Those who hold and those who are without property have ever formed distinct interests in society. Those who are creditors, and those who are debtors, fall under a like discrimination. A landed interest, a manufacturing interest, a mercantile interest, a moneyed interest, with many lesser interests, grow up of necessity in civilized nations, and divide them into different classes, actuated by different sentiments and views. The regulation of these various and interfering interests forms the principal task of modern legislation and involves the spirit of party and faction in the necessary and ordinary operations of government.

No man is allowed to be judge in his own cause, because his interest would certainly bias his judgment and, not improbably, corrupt his integrity. With equal, nay with greater reason, a body of men are unfit to be both judges and parties at the same time; yet what are many of the most important acts of legislation but so many judicial determinations, not indeed concerning the rights of single persons, but concerning the rights of large bodies of citizens? And what are the different classes of legislators but advocates and parties to the causes which they determine? Is a law proposed concerning private debts? It is a question to which the creditors are parties on one side and the debtors on the other. Justice ought to hold the balance between them. Yet the parties are, and must be, themselves the judges; and the most numerous party, or in other words, the most powerful faction must be expected to prevail. Shall domestic manufacturers be encouraged, and in what degree, by restrictions on foreign manufacturers? are questions which would be differently decided by the landed and the manufacturing classes, and probably by neither with a sole regard to justice and the public good. The apportionment of taxes on the various descriptions of property is an act which seems to require the most exact impartiality; yet there is, perhaps, no legislative act in which greater opportunity and temptation are given to a predominant party to trample on the rules of justice. Every shilling with which they overburden the inferior number is a shilling saved to their own pockets.

It is in vain to say that enlightened statesmen will be able to adjust these clashing interests and render them all subservient to the public good. Enlightened statesmen will not always be at the helm. Nor, in many cases, can such an adjustment be made at all without taking into view indirect and remote considerations, which will rarely prevail over the immediate interest which one party may find in disregarding the rights of another or the good of the whole.

The inference to which we are brought is that the *causes* of faction cannot be removed and that relief is only to be sought in the means of controlling its *effects*.

If a faction consists of less than a majority, relief is supplied by the republican principle, which enables the majority to defeat its sinister views by regular vote. It may clog the administration, it may convulse the society; but it will be unable to execute and mask its violence under the forms of the Constitution. When a majority is included in a faction, the form of popular government, on the other hand, enables it to sacrifice to its ruling passion or interest both the public good and the rights of other citizens. To secure the public good and private rights against the danger of such a faction, and at the same time to preserve the spirit and the form of popular government, is then the great object to which our inquiries are directed. Let me add that it is the great desideratum by which alone this form of government can be rescued from the opprobrium under which it has so long labored and be recommended to the esteem and adoption of mankind.

By what means is this object attainable? Evidently by one of two only. Either the existence of the same passion or interest in a majority at the same time must be prevented, or the majority, having such coexistent passion or interest, must be rendered, by their number and local situation, unable to concert and carry into effect schemes of oppression. If the impulse and the opportunity be suffered to coincide, we well know that neither moral nor religious motives can be relied on as an adequate control. They are not found to be such on the injustice and violence of individuals, and lose their efficacy in proportion to the number combined together, that is, in proportion as their efficacy becomes needful.

From this view of the subject it may be concluded that a pure democracy, by which I mean a society consisting of a small number of citizens, who assemble and administer the government in person, can admit of no cure for the mischiefs of faction. A common passion or interest will, in almost every case, be felt by a majority of the whole; a communication and concert results from the form of government itself; and there is nothing to check the inducements to sacrifice the weaker party or an obnoxious individual. Hence it is that such democracies have ever been spectacles of turbulence and contention; have ever been found incompatible with personal security or the rights of property; and have in general been as short in their lives as they have been violent in their deaths. Theoretic politicians, who have patronized this species of government, have erroneously supposed that by reducing mankind to a perfect equality in their political rights, they would at the same time be perfectly equalized and assimilated in their possessions, their opinions, and their passions.

A republic, by which I mean a government in which the scheme of representation takes place, opens a different prospect and promises the cure for which we are seeking. Let us examine the points in which it varies from pure democracy, and we shall comprehend both the nature of the cure and the efficacy which it must derive from the Union.

The two great points of difference between a democracy and a republic are: first, the delegation of the government, in the latter, to a small number of citizens elected by the rest; secondly, the greater number of citizens and greater sphere of country over which the latter may be extended.

The effect of the first difference is, on the one hand, to refine and enlarge the public views by passing them through the medium of a chosen body of citizens, whose wisdom may best discern the true interest of their country and whose patriotism and love of justice will be least likely to sacrifice it to temporary or partial considerations. Under such a regulation it may well happen that the public voice, pronounced by the representatives of the people, will be more consonant to the public good than if pronounced by the people themselves, convened for the purpose. On the other hand, the effect may be inverted. Men of factious tempers, of local prejudices, or of sinister designs, may, by intrigue, by corruption, or by other means, first obtain the suffrages, and then betray the interests of the people. The question resulting is, whether small or extensive republics are most favorable to the election of proper guardians of the public weal; and it is clearly decided in favor of the latter by two obvious considerations.

In the first place it is to be remarked that however small the republic may be the representatives must be raised to a certain number in order to guard against the cabals of a few; and that however large it may be they must be limited to a certain number in order to guard against the confusion of a multitude. Hence, the number of representatives in the two cases not being in proportion to that of the constituents, and being proportionally greatest in the small republic, it follows that if the proportion of fit characters be not less in the large than in the small republic, the former will present a greater option, and consequently a greater probability of a fit choice.

In the next place, as each representative will be chosen by a greater number of citizens in the large than in the small republic, it will be more difficult for unworthy candidates to practise with success the vicious arts by which elections are too often carried; and the suffrages of the people being more free, will be more likely to center on men who possess the most attractive merit and the most diffusive and established characters.

It must be confessed that in this, as in most other cases, there is a mean, on both sides of which inconveniencies will be found to lie. By enlarging too much the number of electors, you render the representative too little acquainted with all their local circumstances and lesser interests; as by reducing it too much, you render him unduly attached to these, and too little fit to comprehend and pursue great and national objects. The federal Constitution forms a happy combination in this respect; the great and aggregate interests being referred to the national, the local and particular to the State legislatures.

The other point of difference is the greater number of citizens and extent of territory which may be brought within the compass of republican than of democratic government; and it is this circumstance principally which renders factious combinations less to be dreaded in the former than in the latter. The smaller the society, the fewer probably will be the distinct parties and interests composing it; the fewer the distinct parties and interests, the more frequently will a majority be found of the same party; and the smaller the number of individuals composing a majority, and the smaller the compass within which they are placed, the more easily will they concert and execute their plans of oppression. Extend the sphere and you take in a greater variety of parties and interests; you make it less probable that a majority of the whole will have a common motive to invade the rights of other citizens; or if such a common motive exists, it will be more difficult for all who feel it to discover their own strength and to act in unison with each other. Besides other impediments, it may be remarked that, where there is a consciousness of unjust or dishonorable purposes, communication is always checked by distrust in proportion to the number whose concurrence is necessary.

Hence, it clearly appears that the same advantage which a republic has over a democracy in controlling the effects of faction is enjoyed by a large over a small republic—is enjoyed by the Union over the States composing it. Does this advantage consist in the substitution of representatives whose enlightened views and virtuous sentiments render them superior to local prejudices and to schemes of injustice? It will not be denied that the representation of the Union will be most likely to possess these requisite endowments. Does it consist in the greater security afforded by a greater variety of parties, against the event of any one party being able to outnumber and oppress the rest? In an equal degree does the increased variety of parties comprised within the Union increase this security? Does it, in fine, consist in the greater obstacles opposed to the concert and accomplishment of the secret wishes of an unjust and interested majority? Here again the extent of the Union gives it the most palpable advantage.

The influence of factious leaders may kindle a flame within their particular States but will be unable to spread a general conflagration through the other States. A religious sect may degenerate into a political faction in a part of the Confederacy; but the variety of sects dispersed over the entire face of it must secure the national councils against any danger from that source. A rage for paper money, for an abolition of debts, for an equal division of property, or for any other improper or wicked project, will be less apt to pervade the whole body of the Union than a particular member of it, in the same proportion as such a malady is more likely to taint a particular county or district than an entire State.

In the extent and proper structure of the Union, therefore, we behold a republican remedy for the diseases most incident to republican government. And according to the degree of pleasure and pride we feel in being republicans ought to be our zeal in cherishing the spirit and supporting the character of federalist.

PUBLIUS

NO. 51: MADISON

To what expedient, then, shall we finally resort, for maintaining in practice the necessary partition of power among the several departments as laid down in the Constitution? The only answer that can be given is that as all these exterior provisions are found to be inadequate the defect must be supplied, by so contriving the interior structure of the government as that its several constituent parts may, by their mutual relations, be the means of keeping each other in their proper places. Without presuming to undertake a full development of this important idea I will hazard a few general observations which may perhaps place it in a clearer light, and enable us to form a more correct judgment of the principles and structure of the government planned by the convention.

In order to lay a due foundation for that separate and distinct exercise of the different powers of government, which to a certain extent is admitted on all hands to be essential to the preservation of liberty, it is evident that each department should have a will of its own; and consequently should be so constituted that the members of each should have as little agency as possible in the appointment of the members of the others. Were this principle rigorously adhered to, it would require that all the appointments for the supreme executive, legislative, and judiciary magistracies should be drawn from the same fountain of authority, the people, through channels having no communication whatever with one another. Perhaps such a plan of constructing the several departments would be less difficult in practice than it may in contemplation appear. Some difficulties, however, and some additional expense would attend the execution of it. Some deviations, therefore, from the principle must be admitted. In the constitution of the judiciary department in particular, it might be inexpedient to insist rigorously on the principle: first, because peculiar qualifications being essential in the members, the primary consideration ought to be to select that mode of choice which best secures these qualifications; second, because the permanent tenure by which the appointments are held in that department must soon destroy all sense of dependence on the authority conferring them.

It is equally evident that the members of each department should be as little dependent as possible on those of the others for the emoluments annexed to their offices. Were the executive magistrate, or the judges, not independent of the legislature in this particular, their independence in every other would be merely nominal.

But the great security against a gradual concentration of the several powers in the same department consists in giving to those who administer each department the necessary constitutional means and personal motives to resist encroachments of the others. The provision for defense must in this, as in all other cases, be made commensurate to the danger of attack. Ambition must be made to counteract ambition. The interest of the man must be connected with the constitutional rights of the place. It may be a reflection on human nature that such devices should be necessary to control the abuses of government. But what is government itself but the greatest of all reflections on human nature? If men were angels, no government would be necessary. If angels were to govern men, neither external nor internal controls on government would be necessary. In framing a government which is to be administered by men over men, the great difficulty lies in this: you must first enable the government to control the governed; and in the next place oblige it to control itself. A dependence on the people is, no doubt, the primary control on the government; but experience has taught mankind the necessity of auxiliary precautions.

This policy of supplying, by opposite and rival interests, the defect of better motives, might be traced through the whole system of human affairs, private as well as public. We see it particularly displayed in all the subordinate distributions of power, where the constant aim is to divide and arrange the several offices in such a manner as that each may be a check on the other—that the private interest of every individual may be a sentinel over the public rights. These inventions of prudence cannot be less requisite in the distribution of the supreme powers of the State.

But it is not possible to give to each department an equal power of self-defense. In republican government, the legislative authority necessarily predominates. The remedy for this inconveniency is to divide the legislature into different branches; and to render them, by different modes of election and different principles of action, as little connected with each other as the nature of their common functions and their common dependence on the society will admit. It may even be necessary to guard against dangerous encroachments by still further precautions. As the weight of the legislative authority requires that it should be thus divided, the weakness of the executive may require, on the other hand, that it should be fortified. An absolute negative on the legislature appears, at first view, to be the natural defense with which the executive magistrate should be armed. But perhaps it would be neither altogether safe nor alone sufficient. On ordinary occasions it might not be exerted with the requisite firmness, and on extraordinary occasions it might be perfidiously abused. May not this defect of an absolute negative be supplied by some qualified connection between this weaker branch of the stronger department, by which the latter may be led to support the constitutional rights of the former, without being too much detached from the rights of its own department?

If the principles on which these observations are founded be just, as I persuade myself they are, and they be applied as a criterion to the several State constitutions, and to the federal Constitution, it will be found that if the latter does not perfectly correspond with them, the former are infinitely less able to bear such a test.

There are, moreover, two considerations particularly applicable to the federal system of America, which place that system in a very interesting point of view.

First. In a single republic, all the power surrendered by the people is submitted to the administration of a single government; and the usurpations are guarded against by a division of the government into distinct and separate departments. In the compound republic of America, the power surrendered by the people is first divided between two distinct governments, and then the portion allotted to each subdivided among distinct and separate departments. Hence a double security arises to the rights of the people. The different governments will control each other, at the same time that each will be controlled by itself.

Second. It is of great importance in a republic not only to guard the society against the oppression of its rulers, but to guard one part of the society against the injustice of the other part. Different interests necessarily exist in different classes of citizens. If a majority be united by a common interest, the rights of the minority will be insecure. There are but two methods of providing against this evil: the one by creating a will in the community independent of the majority—that is, of the society itself; the other, by comprehending in the society so many separate descriptions of citizens as will render an unjust combination of a majority of the whole very improbable, if not impracticable. The first method prevails in all governments possessing an hereditary or self-appointed authority. This, at best, is but a precarious security; because a power independent of the society may as well espouse the unjust views of the major as the rightful interests of the minor party, and may possibly be turned against both parties. The second method will be exemplified in the federal republic of the United States. Whilst all authority in it will be derived from and dependent on the society, the society itself will be broken into so many parts, interests and classes of citizens, that the rights of individuals, or of the minority, will be in little danger from interested combinations of the majority. In a free government the security for civil rights must be the same as that for religious rights. It consists in the one case in the multiplicity of interests, and in the other in the multiplicity of sects. The degree of security in both cases will depend on the number of interests and sects; and this may be presumed to depend on the extent of country and number of people comprehended under the same government. This view of the subject must particularly recommend a proper federal system to all the sincere and considerate friends of republican government, since it shows that in exact proportion as the territory of the Union may be formed into more circumscribed Confederacies, or States, oppressive combinations of a majority will be facilitated; the best security, under the republican forms, for the rights of every class of citizen, will be diminished; and consequently the stability and independence of some member of the government, the only other security, must be proportionally increased. Justice is the end of government. It is the end of civil society. It ever has been and ever will be pursued until it be obtained, or until liberty be lost in the pursuit. In a society under the forms of which the stronger faction can readily unite and oppress the weaker, anarchy may as truly be said to reign as in a state of nature, where the weaker individual is not secured against the violence of the stronger; and as, in the latter state, even the stronger individuals are prompted, by the uncertainty of their condition, to submit to a government which may protect the weak as well as themselves; so, in the former state, will the more powerful factions or parties be gradually induced, by a like motive, to wish for a government which will protect all parties, the weaker as well as the more powerful. It can be little doubted that if the State of Rhode Island was separated from the Confederacy and left to itself, the insecurity of rights under the popular form of government within such narrow limits would be displayed by such reiterated oppressions of factious majorities that some power altogether independent of the people would soon be called for by the voice of the very factions whose misrule had proved the necessity of it. In the extended republic of the United States, and among the great variety of interests, parties, and sects which it embraces, a coalition of a majority of the whole society could seldom take place on any other principles than those of justice and the general good; whilst there being thus less danger to a minor from the will of a major party, there must be less pretext, also, to provide for the security of the former, by introducing into the government a will not dependent on the latter, or, in other words, a will independent of the society itself. It is no less certain than it is important, notwithstanding the contrary opinions which have been entertained, that the larger the society, provided it lie within a practicable sphere, the more duly capable it will be of self-government. And happily for the *republican cause,* the practicable sphere may be carried to a very great extent by a judicious modification and mixture of the *federal principle.*

PUBLIUS

Glossary

administrative adjudication The application of rules and precedents to specific cases to settle disputes with regulated parties.

administrative legislation Rules made by **regulatory agencies** and commissions.

adverse selection The problem of incomplete information—of choosing alternatives without fully knowing the details of available options.

affirmative action A policy or program designed to redress historic injustices committed against specific groups by making special efforts to provide members of these groups with access to educational and employment opportunities.

after-the-fact authority The authority to follow up on the fate of a proposal once it has been approved by the full chamber.

agents of socialization The social institutions, including families and schools, that help shape individuals' basic political **beliefs** and **values.**

agency loss The difference between what a principal would like an agent to do and the agent's performance.

agency representation The type of representation according to which representatives are held accountable to their constituents if they fail to represent them properly. That is, constituents have the power to hire and fire their representatives. This is the incentive for good representation even when the personal backgrounds, views, and interests of the representatives differ from their constituents'.

agenda power The control over what a group will consider for discussion.

Aid to Families with Dependent Children (AFDC) Federal funds for children in families that fall below state standards of need. In 1996, Congress abolished AFDC, the largest federal cash-transfer program, and replaced it with the **Temporary Assistance to Needy Families (TANF) block grant.**

amicus curiae "Friend of the court," an individual or group who is not party to a lawsuit but seeks to assist the court in reaching a decision by presenting an additional brief.

antitrust policy Government regulation of large businesses that have established **monopolies.**

appeasement An effort to forestall war by giving into the demands of a hostile power.

Articles of Confederation and Perpetual Union America's first written constitution. Adopted by the Continental Congress in 1777, the Articles of Confederation and Perpetual Union were the formal basis for America's national **government** until 1789, when they were superseded by the Constitution.

Australian ballot An electoral format that presents the names of all the candidates for any given office on the same ballot. Introduced at the end of the eighteenth century, the Australian ballot replaced the partisan ballot and facilitated split-ticket voting.

authoritarian government A system of rule in which the **government** recognizes no formal limits but may nevertheless be restrained by the power of other social institutions.

autocracy A form of **government** in which a single individual rules.

balance-of-power role The strategy whereby countries form alliances with one or more countries in order to counterbalance the behavior of other, usually more powerful, nation-states.

bandwagon effect A shift in electoral support to the candidate whom public opinion polls report as the front-runner.

bicameralism The division of a legislative assembly into two chambers, or houses.

bicameral legislature A legislative assembly composed of two chambers, or houses.

bilateral treaty A treaty made between two nations.

Bill of Rights The first ten amendments to the U.S. Constitution, adopted in 1791. The Bill of Rights ensures certain rights and liberties to the people.

block grants Federal funds given to state **governments** to pay for goods, services, or programs, with relatively few restrictions on how the funds may be spent.

brief A written document in which an attorney explains—using case precedents—why the Court should rule in favor of his or her client.

budget deficit The amount by which **government** spending exceeds government revenue in a fiscal year.

bureaucracy The complex structure of offices, tasks, rules, and principles of organization that are employed by all large-scale institutions to coordinate the work of their personnel.

bureaucratic drift The oft-observed phenomenon of bureaucratic implementation that produces policy more to the liking of the **bureaucracy** than faithful to the original intention of the legislation that created it, but without triggering a political reaction from elected officials.

Bush doctrine Foreign policy based on the idea that the United States should take preemptive action against threats to its national security.

by-product theory The idea that groups provide members with private benefits to attract membership. The possibility of group **collective action** emerges as a consequence.

Cabinet The secretaries, or chief administrators, of the major departments of the federal **government.** Cabinet secretaries are appointed by the president with the consent of the Senate.

casework An effort by members of Congress to gain the trust and support of constituents by providing personal service. One important type of casework consists of helping constituents obtain favorable treatment from the federal **bureaucracy.**

categorical grants-in-aid Funds given by Congress to states and localities that are earmarked by law for specific categories, such as education or crime prevention.

caucus system A normally closed meeting of a political or legislative group to select candidates, plan strategy, or make decisions regarding legislative matters.

checks and balances The mechanisms through which each branch of **government** is able to participate in and influence the activities of the other branches.

chief justice The justice on the **Supreme Court** who presides over the Court's public sessions.

civil law A system of jurisprudence, including private law and governmental actions, for settling disputes that do not involve criminal penalties.

civil liberties The protection of citizens from improper governmental action.

civil rights The legal or moral claims that citizens are entitled to make on the **government.**

class-action suit A lawsuit in which a large number of persons with common interests join together under a representative party to bring or defend a lawsuit, as when hundreds of workers join together to sue a company.

clear and present danger The criterion used to determine whether speech is protected or unprotected, based on its capacity to present a "clear and present danger" to society.

clientele agency A department or bureau of **government** whose mission is to promote, serve, or represent a particular interest.

closed primary A primary election in which voters can participate in the nomination of only those candidates of the party in which they have been enrolled for a period of time before primary day. Contrast with **open primary.**

closed rule The provision by the House Rules Committee that prohibits the introduction of amendments during debate.

cloture A rule allowing a supermajority of the members of a legislative body to set a time limit on debate over a given bill.

coalitional drift The prospect that enacted policy will change because the composition of the enacting coalition is temporary and provisional.

Cold War The period of struggle between the United States and the former Soviet Union between the late 1940s and about 1990.

collective action The pooling of resources and the coordination of effort and activity by a group of people (often a large one) to achieve common goals.

commander in chief The power of the president as commander of the national military and the state national guard units (when called into service).

commerce clause Article I, Section 8, of the Constitution, which delegates to Congress the power "to regulate Commerce with foreign Nations, and among the several States, and with the Indian Tribes." This clause was interpreted by the **Supreme Court** to favor national power over the economy.

concurrent powers The authority possessed by *both* state and national **governments,** such as the power to levy taxes.

conference committee A joint committee created to work out a compromise for House and Senate versions of a piece of legislation.

congressional caucus An association of members of Congress based on party, interest, or social characteristics such as gender or race.

conservative Today this term refers to those who generally support the social and economic status quo and are suspicious of efforts to introduce new political formulas and economic arrangements. Many conservatives also believe that a large and powerful **government** poses a threat to citizens' freedoms.

constituency The district making up the area from which an official is elected.

constitutional government A system of rule in which formal and effective limits are placed on the power of the **government.**

contracting power The power of **government** to set conditions on companies seeking to sell goods or services to government agencies.

contributory program A social program financed in whole or in part by taxation or other mandatory contributions by its present or future recipients. The most important example is **Social Security,** which is financed by a payroll tax.

cooperative federalism A type of **federalism** existing since the New Deal era, in which **grants-in-aid** have been used strategically to encourage states and localities (without commanding them) to pursue nationally defined goals. Also known as intergovernmental cooperation.

court of appeals (appellate court) A court that hears the appeals of trial-court decisions.

criminal law The branch of law that deals with disputes or actions involving criminal penalties (as opposed to **civil law**). It regulates the conduct of individuals, defines crimes, and provides punishment for criminal acts.

de facto segregation Racial segregation that is not a direct result of law or **government** policy but is, instead, a reflection of residential patterns, income distributions, or other social factors.

de jure segregation Racial segregation that is a direct result of law or official policy.

delegate A representative who votes according to the preferences of his or her **constituency.**

delegated powers Constitutional powers assigned to one governmental agency but exercised by another agency with the express permission of the first.

delegation The transmission of authority to some other official or body for the latter's use (though often with the right of review and revision).

democracy A system of rule that permits citizens to play a significant part in the governmental process, usually through the selection of key public officials.

deregulation The policy of reducing or eliminating regulatory restraints on the conduct of individuals or private institutions.

deterrence The development and maintenance of military strength as a means of discouraging attack.

devolution The policy of removing a program from one level of **government** by deregulating it or passing it down to a lower level, such as from the national government to the state and local governments.

diplomacy The representation of a government to other foreign governments.

discretionary spending Federal spending on programs that are controlled through the regular budget process.

dissenting opinion A decision written by a justice who voted with the minority opinion in a particular case, in which the justice fully explains the reasoning behind his or her opinion.

distributive tendency The tendency of Congress to spread the benefits of a policy over a wide range of members' districts.

divided government The condition in American **government** in which the presidency is controlled by one party while the opposing party controls one or both houses of Congress.

double jeopardy The Fifth Amendment right providing that a person cannot be tried twice for the same crime.

dual federalism The system of **government** that prevailed in the United States from 1789 to 1937, in which most fundamental governmental powers were shared between the federal and state governments, with the states exercising the most important powers. Compare with **cooperative federalism.**

due process The guarantee that no citizen may be subjected to arbitrary action by national or state **governments.**

Duverger's Law Law of politics, formalized by Maurice Duverger, stating that plurality-rule electoral systems will tend to have two political parties.

economic-expansionist role The strategy often pursued by capitalist countries to adopt foreign policies that will maximize the success of domestic corporations in their dealings with other countries.

electoral college The presidential electors from each state who meet in their respective state capitals after the popular election to cast ballots for president and vice president.

eminent domain The right of the **government** to take private property for public use, with reasonable compensation awarded for the property.

entitlement The eligibility for benefits by virtue of a category defined by law. Categories can be changed only by legislation; deprivation of individual benefits can be determined only through **due process** in court.

equality of opportunity A universally shared American ideal, according to which all have the freedom to use whatever talents and wealth they possess to reach their full potential.

equal protection clause The provision of the Fourteenth Amendment guaranteeing citizens "the equal protection of the laws." This clause has served as the basis for the **civil rights** of African Americans, women, and other groups.

equal time rule The requirement that broadcasters provide candidates for the same political office an equal opportunity to communicate their messages to the public.

establishment clause The First Amendment clause that says, "Congress shall make no law respecting an establishment of religion." This law means that a wall of separation exists between church and state.

exclusionary rule The ability of courts to exclude evidence obtained in violation of the Fourth Amendment.

executive agreement An agreement between the president and another country that has the force of a treaty but does not require the Senate's "advice and consent."

Executive Office of the President (EOP) The permanent agencies that perform defined management tasks for the president. Created in 1939, the EOP includes the Office of Management and Budget, the Council of Economic Advisers, the National Security Council, and other agencies.

executive order The rule or regulation issued by the president that have the effect and formal status of legislation.

executive privilege The claim that confidential communications between the president and the president's close advisers should not be revealed without the consent of the president.

expressed powers The notion that the Constitution grants to the federal government only those powers specifically named in its text.

externality The differences between the private cost and the social cost of economic behavior.

fairness doctrine An FCC requirement that broadcasters who air programs on controversial issues provide time for opposing views.

federal funds rate The interest rate on loans between banks that the Federal Reserve Board influences by affecting the supply of money available.

federalism The system of **government** in which a constitution divides power between a central government and regional governments.

Federal Reserve System (the Fed) Consisting of twelve Federal Reserve districts, the Fed facilitates exchanges of cash, checks, and credit; it regulates member banks; and it deploys monetary policies to fight inflation and deflation.

fighting words Speech that directly incites damaging conduct.

filibuster A tactic used by members of the Senate to prevent action on legislation they oppose by continuously holding the floor and speaking until the majority backs down. Once given the floor,

senators have unlimited time to speak, and it requires a **cloture** vote of three-fifths of the Senate to end a filibuster.

fiscal policies Policies that use spending and taxing to accomplish policy purposes.

food stamps The largest **in-kind benefits** program, administered by the Department of Agriculture, providing coupons to individuals and families who satisfy a **means test.** Food Stamps can be exchanged for food at most grocery stores.

formula grants **Grants-in-aid** in which a formula is used to determine the amount of federal funds a state or local **government** will receive.

framing The power of the media to influence how events and issues are interpreted.

free exercise clause The First Amendment clause that protects a citizen's right to believe and practice whatever religion he or she chooses.

free riding Enjoying the benefits of some good or action while letting others bear the costs. See also **public good.**

full faith and credit clause The provision in Article IV, Section I, of the Constitution requiring that each state normally honors the public acts and judicial decisions that take place in another state.

gatekeeping authority The right and power to decide if a change in policy will be considered.

gender gap A distinctive pattern of voting behavior reflecting the differences in views between women and men.

General Agreement on Tariffs and Trade (GATT) The international trade organization in existence from 1947 to 1995, that set many of the rules governing international trade.

gerrymandering The apportionment of voters in districts in such a way as to give unfair advantage to one political party.

going public The act of launching a media campaign to build popular support.

government The institutions and procedures through which a land and its people are ruled.

grand jury A jury that determines whether sufficient evidence is available to justify a trial. Grand juries do not rule on the accused's guilt or innocence.

grants-in-aid A general term for funds given by Congress to state and local **governments**. See also **categorical grants-in-aid.**

Great Compromise An agreement reached at the Constitutional Convention of 1787 that gave each state an equal number of senators regardless of its population but linked representation in the House of Representatives to population.

gross domestic product (GDP) The total value of goods and services produced within a country.

Holy Alliance role A strategy pursued by a super-power to prevent any change in the existing distribution of power among nation-states, even if this requires intervention in the internal affairs of the country in order to keep a ruler from being overthrown.

home rule The power delegated by the state to a local unit of **government** to manage its own affairs.

illusion of salience The impression conveyed by polls that something is important to the public when it actually is not.

impeachment The charging of a governmental official (president or otherwise) with "Treason, Bribery, or other high Crimes and Misdemeanors" and bringing him or her before Congress to determine guilt.

implementation The efforts of departments and agencies to translate laws into specific bureaucratic routines.

implied powers Powers derived from the **necessary and proper clause** (Article I, Section 8) of the Constitution. Such powers are not specifically **expressed** but are **implied** through the expansive interpretation of **delegated powers.**

incumbency Holding a political office for which one is running.

indexing The process of periodically adjusting social benefits or wages to account for increases in the cost of living.

inflation A consistent increase in the general level of prices.

informational benefits Special newsletters, periodicals, training programs, conferences, and other information provided to members of groups to entice others to join.

inherent powers Powers claimed by a president that are not expressed in the Constitution but are inferred from it.

initiative A process by which citizens may petition to place a policy proposal on the ballot for public vote.

in-kind benefits Goods and services provided to needy individuals and families by the federal **government,** as contrasted with cash benefits. The largest in-kind federal welfare program is **food stamps.**

institutions The rules and procedures that provide incentives for political behavior, thereby shaping politics.

instrumental Done with purpose, sometimes with forethought, and even with calculation.

interest group An organized group of individuals or organizations that makes policy-related appeals to **government.**

intermediate scrutiny The test used by the Supreme Court in gender discrimination cases. Intermediate scrutiny places the burden of proof partially on the government and partially on the challengers to show that the law in question is constitutional.

International Monetary Fund (IMF) An institution established in 1944 that provides loans and facilitates international monetary exchange.

isolationism The desire to avoid involvement in the affairs of other nations.

issue voting An individual's propensity to select candidates or parties based on the extent to which the individual agrees with one candidate more than others on specific issues.

judicial activism The judicial philosophy that posits that the Court should see beyond the text of the Constitution or a statute to consider broader societal implications for its decisions.

judicial restraint The judicial philosophy whose adherents refuse to go beyond the text of the Constitution in interpreting its meaning.

judicial review The power of the courts to declare actions of the legislative and executive branches invalid or unconstitutional. The **Supreme Court** asserted this power in *Marbury v. Madison* (1803).

Keynsian A follower of the economic theories of John Maynard Keynes, who argued that the government can stimulate the economy by increasing public spending or by cutting taxes.

kitchen cabinet An informal group of advisers to whom the president turns for counsel and guidance. Members of the official **cabinet** may or may not also be members of the Kitchen Cabinet.

laissez-faire capitalism An economic system in which the means of production and distribution are privately owned and operated for profit with minimal or no government interference.

legislative initiative The president's inherent power to bring a legislative agenda before Congress.

legislative supremacy The preeminent position assigned to Congress by the Constitution.

Lemon test Rule articulated in *Lemon v. Kurtzman* according to which governmental action in respect to religion is permissible if it is secular in purpose, does not lead to "excessive entanglement" with religion, and neither promotes nor inhibits the practice of religion.

libel A written statement made in "reckless disregard of the truth" and considered damaging to a victim because it is "malicious, scandalous, and defamatory."

liberal A liberal today generally supports political and social reform; extensive government intervention in the economy; the expansion of federal social services; more vigorous efforts on behalf of the poor, minorities, and women; and greater concern for consumers and the environment.

line-item veto The power of the executive to veto specific provisions (lines) of a bill passed by the legislature.

lobbying An attempt by a group to influence the policy process through persuasion of **government** officials.

logrolling A legislative practice wherein reciprocal agreements are made between legislators, usually in voting for or against a bill. In contrast to bargaining, logrolling unites parties that have nothing in common but their desire to exchange support.

majority leader The elected leader of the party holding a majority of the seats in the House of Representatives or the

Senate. In the House, the majority leader is subordinate in the party hierarchy to the Speaker.

majority party The party that holds the majority of legislative seats in either the House or the Senate.

majority rule A type of electoral system in which, to win a seat in a representative body, a candidate must receive a majority (50 percent plus 1) of all the votes cast in the relevant district.

mandate A claim by a victorious candidate that the electorate has given him or her special authority to carry out promises made during the campaign.

mandatory spending Federal spending that is made up of **"uncontrollables,"** budget items that cannot be controlled through the regular budget process.

market failure An instance when the market fails to produce an efficient outcome.

material benefits Special goods, services, or money provided to members of groups to entice others to join.

means testing A procedure that determines eligibility for **government** public-assistance programs. A potential beneficiary must show a need and an inability to provide for that need.

measurement error The failure to identify the true distribution of opinion within a population because of errors such as ambiguous or poorly worded questions.

median-voter theorem A proposition predicting that when policy options can be arrayed along a single dimension, majority rule will pick the policy most preferred by the voter whose ideal policy is to the left of half of the voters and to the right of exactly half of the voters.

Medicaid A federally financed, state-operated program for medical services to low-income people.

Medicare National health insurance for the elderly and the disabled.

minority leader The elected leader of the party holding less than a majority of the seats in the House or Senate.

Miranda rule The convention derived from the **Supreme Court**'s 1966 ruling in the case of *Miranda v. Arizona* whereby persons under arrest must be informed of their legal rights, including their right to counsel, before undergoing police interrogation.

monetarist A follower of economic theories that contend that the role of the government in the economy should be limited to regulating the supply of money.

monetary policies Policies that control the supply of money, the price of money (interest rate), and the availability of credit.

monopoly The existence in a market of a single firm that provides all the goods and services of that market; the absence of competition.

mootness A criterion used by courts to avoid hearing cases that no longer require resolution.

moral hazard Not knowing all aspects of the actions taken by an agent (nominally on behalf of the principal but potentially at the principal's expense).

most favored nation status An agreement to offer a trading partner the lowest tariff rate offered to other trading partners.

multiple-member district An electorate that selects several candidates at large from an entire district, with each voter given the number of votes equivalent to the number of seats to be filled.

Napoleonic role A strategy pursued by a powerful nation to prevent aggressive actions against itself by improving the internal state of affairs of a particular country, even if this means encouraging revolution in that country. This strategy is based on the assumption that countries with comparable political systems will never go to war against each other.

National Security Council (NSC) A presidential foreign policy advisory council composed of the president, the vice president, the secretaries of state, defense, and the treasury, the attorney general, and other officials invited by the president.

nation-state A political entity consisting of a people with some common cultural experience (nation) who also share a common political authority (state), recognized by other sovereignties (nation-states).

necessary and proper clause Article I, Section 8, of the Constitution, which enumerates the powers of Congress and provides Congress with the authority to make all laws "necessary and proper" to carry them out; also referred to as the elastic clause.

nomination The process by which political parties select their candidates for election to public office.

noncontributory program A social program that assists people based on demonstrated need rather than contributions they have made. Also known as a public assistance program.

non-state actor A group other than a nation-state that attempts to play a role in the international system. Terrorist groups are one type of non-state actor.

North American Free Trade Agreement (NAFTA) A trade treaty among the United States, Canada, and Mexico to lower and eliminate tariffs among the three countries.

North Atlantic Treaty Organization (NATO) A treaty organization, comprising the United States, Canada, and most of Western Europe, formed in 1948 to counter the perceived threat from the Soviet Union.

oligarchy A form of **government** in which a small group of landowners, military officers, or wealthy merchants controls most of the governing decisions.

open-market operations The process whereby the Federal Open Market Committee of the **Federal Reserve** buys and sells **government** securities and the like to help finance government operations and loosen or tighten the total amount of credit circulating in the economy.

open primary A primary election in which voters can choose on the day of the primary which party to enroll in to select candidates for the general election. Contrast with **closed primary**.

open rule The provision by the House Rules Committee that permits floor debate and the addition of amendments to a bill.

opinion The written explanation of the **Supreme Court**'s decision in a particular case.

oral argument The stage in **Supreme Court** proceedings in which attorneys for both sides appear before the Court to present their positions and answer questions posed by the justices.

oversight The effort by Congress, through hearings, investigations, and other techniques, to exercise control over the activities of executive agencies.

party activist A partisan who contributes time, energy, and effort to support a party and its candidates.

party caucus (party conference) A normally closed meeting of a political or legislative group to select candidates or leaders, plan strategy, or make decisions regarding legislative matters.

party identification An individual's attachment to a particular political party, which might be based on issues or ideology, past experience, or upbringing.

party machine In the late nineteenth and early twentieth centuries, the local party organization that controlled local politics through patronage and the nominations process.

party vote A **roll-call vote** in the House or Senate in which at least 50 percent of the members of one party take a particular position and are opposed by at least 50 percent of the members of the other party. Party votes are less common today than they were in the nineteenth century.

path dependency The idea that certain possibilities are made more or less likely because of the historical path taken.

patronage The resources available to higher officials, usually opportunities to make partisan appointments to offices and confer grants, licenses, or special favors to supporters.

pluralism The theory that all interests are and should be free to compete for influence in the **government.** The outcome of this competition is compromise and moderation.

plurality rule A type of electoral system in which victory goes to the individual who gets the most votes in an election, but not necessarily a majority of the votes cast.

pocket veto A veto that is effected when Congress adjourns during the time a president has to approve a bill and the president takes no action on it. See also **veto.**

police power The power reserved to the **government** to regulate the health, safety, and morals of its citizens.

political action committee (PAC) A private group that raises and distributes funds for use in election campaigns.

political caucus A normally closed meeting of a political or legislative group to select candidates, plan strategy, or make decisions regarding legislative matters.

political party An organized group that attempts to influence government by electing its members to office.

political socialization The induction of individuals into the political culture; the process of learning the underlying **beliefs** and **values** on which the political system is based.

politics The conflicts and struggles over the leadership, structure, and policies of government.

pork-barrel legislation The appropriations made by legislative bodies for local projects that often are not needed but are created so that local representatives can carry their home district in the next election.

precedents Prior cases whose principles are used by judges as the bases for their decisions in present cases.

preemption The willingness to strike first in order to prevent an enemy attack.

preventive war The policy of striking first when a nation fears that a foreign foe is contemplating hostile action.

priming A process of preparing the public to take a particular view of an event or a political actor.

principal-agent relationship The relationship between a principal and his or her agent. This relationship may be affected by the fact that each is motivated by self-interest, yet their interests may not be well aligned.

prior restraint An effort by a government agency to block the publication of material it deems libelous or harmful in some other way; censorship. In the United States, the courts forbid prior restraint except under the most extraordinary circumstances.

privatization The act of moving all or part of a program from the public sector to the private sector.

privileges and immunities The provision from Article IV, Section 2, of the Constitution stating that a state cannot discriminate against someone from another state or give its own residents special privileges.

probability sampling A method used by pollsters to select a representative sample in which every individual in the population has an equal probability of being selected as a respondent.

progressive taxation Taxation that hits the upper income brackets more heavily.

project grants Grant programs in which state and local **governments** submit proposals to federal agencies and for which funding is provided on a competitive basis.

proportional representation (PR) A multiple-member district system that allows each political party representation in proportion to its percentage of the vote.

proposal power The capacity to bring a proposal before the full legislature.

prospective voting Voting based on the imagined future performance of a candidate.

public good A good that, first, may be enjoyed by anyone if it is provided and, second, may not be denied to anyone once it has been provided. See also **free riding**.

public law Cases involving the action of public agencies or officials.

public opinion Citizens' attitudes about political issues, leaders, institutions, and events.

public-opinion poll The scientific instrument for measuring public opinion.

public policy A law, rule, statute, or edict that expresses the **government**'s goals and provides for rewards and punishments to promote their attainment.

purposive benefits Selective benefits of group membership that emphasize the purpose and accomplishments of the group.

push polling A polling technique in which the questions are designed to shape the respondent's opinion.

random digit dialing A poll in which respondents are selected at random from a list of ten-digit telephone numbers, with every effort made to avoid bias in the construction of the sample.

recall The removal of a public official by popular vote.

redistribution A policy whose objective is to tax or spend in such a way as to reduce the disparities of wealth between the lowest and highest income brackets.

referendum A measure proposed or passed by a legislature to the vote of the electorate for approval or rejection.

regressive taxation Taxation that hits the lower income brackets more heavily.

regulatory agency A department, bureau, or independent agency whose primary mission is to eliminate or restrict certain behaviors defined as negative in themselves or negative in their consequences.

reserved powers Powers, derived from the Tenth Amendment to the Constitution, that are not specifically **delegated** to the national government or denied to the states.

reserve requirement The amount of liquid assets and ready cash that the **Federal Reserve** requires banks to hold to meet depositors' demands for their money. The ratio fluctuates from above to below 20 percent of all deposits, with the rest being available for new loans.

retrospective voting Voting based on the past performance of a candidate.

right to privacy The right to be let alone, which has been interpreted by the Supreme Court to entail free access to birth control and abortions.

right of rebuttal An FCC regulation giving individuals the right to have the opportunity to respond to personal attacks made on a radio or TV broadcast.

roll-call votes Votes in which each legislator's yes or no vote is recorded.

rule making A quasi-legislative administrative process that produces regulations by **government** agencies.

rule of four The rule that *certiorari* will be granted only if four justices vote in favor of the petition.

salient interest An attitude or view that is especially important to the individual holding it.

sample A small group selected by researchers to represent the most important characteristics of an entire population.

sampling error A polling error that arises on account of the small size of the sample.

selection bias A polling error in which the sample is not representative of the population being studied, so that some opinions are over- or underrepresented.

selection bias (in the media) The predisposition of consumers to choose particular types of stories.

selective benefits Benefits that do not go to everyone but, rather, are distributed selectively—only to those who contribute to the group enterprise.

senatorial courtesy The practice whereby the president, before formally nominating a person for a federal judgeship, finds out whether the senators from the candidate's state support the nomination.

seniority The priority or status ranking given to an individual on the basis of length of continuous service on a congressional committee.

"separate but equal" rule The doctrine that public accommodations could be segregated by race but still be equal.

separation of powers The division of governmental power among several institutions that must cooperate in decision making.

signing statement Announcement made by the president when a bill is signed into law.

single-member district An electorate that is allowed to elect only one representative from each district—the typical method of representation in the United States.

slander An oral statement made in "reckless disregard of the truth" and considered damaging to a victim because it is "malicious, scandalous, and defamatory."

Social Security A **contributory** welfare **program** into which working Americans place a percentage of their wages and from which they receive cash benefits after retirement.

solidary benefits Selective benefits of group membership that emphasize friendship, networking, and consciousness-raising.

sovereignty Supreme and independent political authority.

spatial issue An issue for which a range of possible options or policies can be ordered, say, from liberal to conservative or from most expensive to least expensive.

Speaker of the House The chief presiding officer of the House of Representatives. The Speaker is elected at the beginning of every Congress on a straight **party vote.** He or she is the most important party and House leader and can influence the legislative agenda, the fate of individual pieces of legislation, and members' positions within the House.

speech plus Speech accompanied by activities such as sit-ins, picketing, and demonstrations. Protection of this form of speech under the First Amendment is conditional, and restrictions imposed by state or local authorities are acceptable if properly balanced by considerations of public order.

staff agencies The agencies responsible for providing Congress with independent expertise, administration, and **oversight** capability.

standing The right of an individual or an organization to initiate a court case.

standing committee A permanent legislative committee that considers legislation within its designated subject area; the basic unit of deliberation in the House and Senate.

stare decisis Literally "let the decision stand." The doctrine whereby a previous decision by a court applies as a precedent in similar cases until that decision is overruled.

state sovereign immunity A legal doctrine holding that states cannot be sued for violating an act of Congress.

states' rights The principle that states should oppose increases in the authority of the national **government**. This view was most popular before the Civil War.

subsidy A government grant of cash or other valuable commodities, such as land, to an individual or organization; used to promote activities desired by the **government**, to reward political support, or to buy off political opposition.

Supplemental Security Income (SSI) A program providing a minimum monthly income to people who pass a

means **test** and are sixty-five years old or older, blind, or disabled. Financed from general revenues that are not **Social Security** contributions.

supply-side economics Posits that reducing the marginal rate of taxation will create a productive economy by promoting levels of work and investment that would otherwise be discouraged by higher taxes.

supremacy clause A clause of Article VI of the Constitution, that states that all laws passed by the national **government** and all treaties are the supreme laws of the land and superior to all laws adopted by any state or any subdivision.

supreme court The highest court in a particular state or in the United States. This court primarily serves an appellate function.

tariff A tax on imported goods.

Temporary Assistance to Needy Families (TANF) *See* **Aid to Families with Dependent Children (AFDC).**

third party A party that organizes to compete against the two major American political parties.

Three-fifths Compromise An agreement reached at the Constitutional Convention of 1787 stipulating that for purposes of the apportionment of congressional seats, every slave would be counted as three fifths of a person.

totalitarian government A system of rule in which the **government** recognizes no formal limits on its power and seeks to absorb or eliminate other social institutions that might challenge it.

transaction costs The cost of clarifying each aspect of a principal-agent relationship and monitoring it to make sure arrangements are complied with.

trial court The first court to hear a criminal or civil case.

trustee A representative who votes based on what he or she thinks is best for his or her **constituency.**

tyranny Oppressive **government** that employs the cruel and unjust use of power and authority.

uncontrollable A budgetary item that is beyond the control of budgetary committees and can be controlled only by substantive legislative action in Congress. Some uncontrollables, such as interest on the debt, are beyond the power of Congress because the terms of payments are set in contracts.

unfunded mandates National standards or programs imposed on state and local **governments** by the federal government without accompanying funding or reimbursement.

United Nations (UN) An organization of nations founded in 1945 to be a channel for negotiation and a means of settling international disputes peaceably.

valence issue An issue or aspect of a choice for which all voters prefer a higher value, in contrast to a spatial issue. For example, voters prefer their politicans to be honest, and honesty is a valence issue.

veto The president's constitutional power to turn down acts of Congress within ten days of their passage while Congress is in session. A presidential veto may be overridden by a two-thirds vote of each house of Congress.

veto power The ability to defeat something even if it has made it on to the agenda of an institution.

War Powers Resolution A resolution of Congress declaring that the president can send troops into action abroad only by authorization of Congress or if U.S. troops are already under attack or seriously threatened.

whip system A communications network in each house of Congress. Whips poll the membership to learn their intentions on specific legislative issues and assist the **majority** and **minority leaders** in various tasks.

White House staff The analysts and advisers to the president, often given the title "special assistant."

World Trade Organization (WTO) The international trade agency promoting free trade that grew out of the General Agreement on Tariffs and Trade.

writ of *certiorari* A formal request by an appellant to have the Supreme Court review a decision of a lower court. *Certiorari* is from a Latin word meaning "to make more certain."

writ of *habeas corpus* A court order demanding that an individual in custody be brought into court and shown the cause for detention. *Habeas corpus* is guaranteed by the Constitution and can be suspended only in cases of rebellion or invasion.

Index

executive orders issued
by, 262–63
executive privilege
claimed by, 232, 332
faith based initiatives
policy of, 521
federalism of, 84
filibuster threat and, 254
foreign policy
inexperience of, 681
global warming and, 621
Homeland Security
Department created
by, 258
hurricanes and, 230, 573
Iraq war and, 229, 249,
394, 408, 541, 563, 582,
673, 683–84, 695, 704
judicial appointments
of, 215–16, 324–26,
349, 641
judicial nominations
of, 206
Latino Americans
and, 482
management strategy
of, 295
Medicare and, 252, 253,
254, 649
Miers nomination
and, 325
military tribunals set up
by, 135–36, 317
national protection
and, 227
No Child Left Behind Act
and, 82
partisanship and, 210
Pentagon spending
and, 618
policies of, 482
preemptive attacks
and, 676
prescription drug plan
and, 403, 538
public opinion and,
366–67, 388
Reagan's popularity
and, 360, 460
senate partisanship
and, 172

September 11 terrorist
attacks and, 272,
484, 573
Social Security reform
and, 200, 385, 483,
640, 642, 645–46, 649
stem-cell research and,
203, 268, 269
tax policies of, 385, 604,
607, 610
in 2000 election, 4, 506
veto and, 235
war on terrorism of,
135–36, 237, 240, 252,
332–33, 381
Bush doctrine, 681–82
Bush v. Gore, 4, 344
business development,
598–600
Business Roundtable, 626
Butler, Pierce, 43
by-product theory, 17
Byrd, Robert, 213*n*

cabinet, 247–49, 282,
683, 685
Cable News Network
(CNN), 118, 391, 551,
556, 566, 567–68
Calendar, Congressional,
641
California, 425, 465,
530, 616
environment and,
622, 623
gerrymandering in, 181
illegal alien referendum
in, 436
immigration in, 151–53
Proposition 187 in, 151
Proposition 209 in, 404
recall election in, 437
same-sex marriage and,
71–72, 157
welfare in, 84
California, University of,
157
California Civil Rights
Initiative, 161
Cambodia, 6
Cameron, Charles M., 251

campaign finance, 452–53,
455–56, 464
Supreme Court and, 456
campaigns, political,
411–12, 413, 418, 420,
443, 451–57, 461–65
canvassing, 451, 465
financing of, 452–53,
455–56, 464
independent, 456,
459, 480
length of, 452
media in, 451–52
organization of, 451
public funding of,
455–56, 464
registration lists and, 420
Campbell, John, 424
Canada, 38, 677
prescription drugs
from, 650
canals, 594, 598
cancer, 664
candidates, political
campaigns and, 411,
413, 418, 420, 476–78
Cantor, Eric, 186
canvassing, 451, 465
cap-and-trade system, 622
Cape Cod, 623
capitalism, 602, 656, 702
globalization of, 700–702
tax laws and, 609
see also market economy
capitalization, nationhood
and, 700
capital punishment, 130–32
Capuano, Mike, 178
"carbon tax," 622
Cardozo, Benjamin,
108, 126
Carter, Jimmy, 222, 249,
624, 625, 697
draft evaders pardoned
by, 231
foreign policy and, 697
Case Act (1972), 217
casework, 175
Castro, Fidel, 474, 693
categorical grants-in-aid,
77–79, 78, 81, 599

class:
and class warfare, 639
in party identity, 487, 489
social policy and, 639
class action suits, 355–56,
640
Clausewitz, Carl von, 695
Clay, Henry, 496
Clayton Act (1914), 615
Clean Air Act Amendments
(1970), 619
Clean Water Act (1972),
619
"clear and present danger"
test, 115
Clear Channel
Communications, 564
clientele agency, 285
Clinton, Bill, 90, 222, 223,
229, 231, 249, 256, 268,
271, 280, 390, 394, *397*,
403, 463, 505, 506, 538
affirmative action and,
158, 159
budget victories of, 263
cabinet of, 247
campaigns of, 444
China and, 702
Democratic support
for, 474
"Don't ask, don't tell"
policy of, 156
economy and, 626
education policies of, 660
elections of, 210
European Community
and, 703
executive agencies
and, 260
executive orders issued
by, 262
executive privilege
claimed by, 332
foreign policy
inexperience of, 681
Gore as vice president
of, 251
health care initiative of,
208, 214, 484, 664
impeachment of,
172, 217

judicial appointments of,
323, 324, 326, 349, 641
line-item veto used
by, 234
management strategy
of, 295
media and, 558, 563
military base closings
proposed by, 287
Motor Voter bill signed
by, 418
on MTV, 573
as "new Democrat," 482
new federalism and, 83
"normal trade relations"
and, 677
Northern Ireland and,
690
as party leader, 484
reporters and, 570–71,
572, 573
scandals of, 94, 558, 572
scrutiny of private life of,
447, 449
September 11 terrorist
attacks and, 272
signing of statements
and, 265
veto and, 235
welfare reform of,
642, 653
Clinton, George, 53, 69
Clinton, Hillary Rodham,
422, 435, 456, 458
in 2008 primary, 422,
435, 462–63, 562
as secretary of state, 691
Clinton administration,
public relations efforts
of, 386
closed primary, 478
closed rule, 201
cloture, 202, 206
Clyburn, James, 186, 532
CNN (Cable News
Network), 118, 391,
551, 556, 566, 567–68
CNN.com, 562
coalitional drift, 293
Cochran, Thad, 207
coercion, 70, 71

COLAs (cost-of-living
adjustments), 643,
651, 652
Cold War, 112, 304, 441,
618, 672, 694, 699–704
foreign policy and, 701
Holy Alliance and,
699–700, 702–4
post–Cold War era and,
700–702
Cole, Tom, 508
Coleman, Norm, 396
collective action, 13–19, *15*,
16–19
benefits of, 526–27, *527*
logic of, 525–26
see also interest groups
collective-action principle,
13–19, 22
American Revolution
and, 35
benefits as solutions in,
526–27
*Brown v. Board of
Education* and, 141
bureaucracy and, 292
candidate-centered
politics and, 510
civil liberties and,
161–62
civil rights movement
and, 141, 162
coalitional drift and,
293–94
Congress and, 186, 203,
213, 253
Constitution and, 63
at Constitutional
Convention, 43
dilemmas, 15–16, *15*
foreign policy and, 681
grants-in-aid and, 78
interest groups and, 209,
389, 548
logrolling and, 213–14
parties and, 186, 469,
472–74, 480
political speech and,
115–16
president and,
251–52, 253

legislative priorities
of, 502
lobbying of, 199, 208,
531–34
logrolling in, 213–14
loss of power by, 246–47
Medicare spending
of, 650
military tribunals
authorized by, 136
NAFTA and, 701
in nineteenth century,
218
Nixon and, 232
No Child Left Behind Act
and, 82–83
103rd, 210
104th, 120, 199, 302
107th, 199
110th, 176, 203
organization of, 171–73,
171, 185–200, *193*
oversight and, 295–99
party system and,
468–72, 483–84
Pledge of Allegiance
changed by, 112–13
political struggles in, 4
"presidential
government" and,
246–47
presidential nomination
by, 225–26
presidential power and,
11, 48, 51, 90, 167,
168, *254*
procedural rules of,
200–207
ratification and, 693
religious freedom and,
113–14
representation in,
169–84, *169*
seniority rule in, 195
September 11 terrorist
attacks and, 224
social policies and, 639
Social Security reform
of, 642
staff system in, 186,
199–200

standing committees
in, 10
Supreme Court size
decided by, 323
Supreme Court's
relationship with, 345,
348–49, 355
terrorism resolution
passed by, 94
uncontrollable spending
and, 612
veto and, 233–37
Vietnam War and, 216
war powers of, 97,
228–29
welfare reform and, 653,
654–55
whip system in, 213
see also House of
Representatives, U.S.;
Senate, U.S.
Congressional Black
Caucus, 200
Congressional Budget
Office, 82, 200,
296, 612
Congressional Caucus for
Women's Issues, 200
Congressional Government
(Wilson), 243, 246
Congressional Quarterly,
501, 648, 649
Congressional Research
Service, 200, 296
Congressional Review Act
(CRA; 1996), 266
congressional staff, 186,
199–200
Connecticut:
Palko case in, 107–8
privacy rights in,
132, 331
Ricci case in, 161
Virginia Plan opposition
of, 41
Connecticut Compromise,
42, 425
*Conscience of a Conservative,
The* (Goldwater), 500
consent of Congress, 72
Conservative Party, 503

conservatives,
conservatism, 369,
380–82, 384, 405, 442,
471, 479, 481–82, 629,
705
college professors
and, 380
defining of, 381
Iraq war and, 688
in media, 557
as Republican base, 481,
487, 489, 500
Social Security and, 643
Tenth Amendment
and, 85
constituency, 169, 360,
366, 368
Constitution, U.S., 2–3,
30–32, 314, 403, 517
Article I, 46, 59, 64, 72,
75, 94, 109, 166, 233,
319, 604
Article II, 47, 100, 225,
226–28, 231, 233,
424, 684
Article III, 48–49, 59,
100, 317–19, 335
Article IV, 49, 71, 72, 229
Article V, 49, 58,
100, 425
Article VI, 49, 70, 330
Article VII, 50
commerce clause in,
75–77, 636
Congress in, 75, 171–73
equality and, 378
executive branch in,
47–48, 225–42, 244
expressed powers in, 70
foreign policy and, 684
impeachment power
of, 217
implied powers in, 70
institutions in, 10, 13
interest and principle
in, 40
judicial branch in,
48–50, 310, 322–23,
328–30, 335
legislative branch in,
46–47, 166, 228–29

issues:
  spatial, 444–46
  valence, 447
  voting and, 443–47
Italy, 703
  totalitarian government
  in, 6

Jackson, Andrew, 351
  Bank of the United
    States and, 604
  Democratic party
    founded by, 495
  as strong president, 243,
    270
Jackson, Jesse, 434
Jackson, Robert, 342
Jacksonian period,
  495–96
Japan, 672
  elections in, 453
  in IMF, 692
  totalitarian government
    in, 6
Japanese Americans,
  internment of, 261
Jay, John, 54
JCOS (Joint Chiefs of
  Staff), 250, 682
Jefferson, Thomas, 36, 64,
  75, 101, 102, 111, 494,
  495, 604
  executive branch
    under, 243
Jehovah's Witnesses, 132
Jewish Americans, 21–22
  Israel and, 686
"Jim Crow" laws, 414
"jobless recovery," 597
jobs, see employment
"Joe Sixpack," 463
Johnson, Andrew, 255
  Confederate amnesty
    given by, 230
  impeachment of, 217,
    218, 255
Johnson, Lyndon B., 84,
  222, 268, 298, 368,
  459–60, 500
  affirmative action
    implemented by, 157

Civil Rights Act order
  of, 262
Great Society of, 218,
  252, 500
polls and, 395
vice presidency of, 250
Vietnam War and, 705
Johnson, Tim, 174
Johnston, J. Bennett, 214
Joint Chiefs of Staff
  (JCOS), 250, 682
Jones, James, 682
Jones & Laughlin Steel
  Corporation, 245
journalists:
  embedded, 687–88
  free-floating, 687–88
JP Morgan Chase, 606
judges, 314
  appointment of, 310,
    323–26
  diversity of, 349, 350
judicial activism, 312, 345
judicial branch, 310–57
  in Constitution, 48–49,
    310, 322–23, 328–30,
    335
  executive branch vs., 51,
    89, 311
  legislative branch vs.,
    51, 89
  and separation of
    powers, 310
  see also Supreme
    Court, U.S.
judicial discretion, 136
judicial restraint, 345
judicial review, 49, 94–95,
  114, 310–13, 328–34,
  329
  of Congress, 310–13,
    328–30
  of federal agency action,
    331–32
  lawmaking and, 333–34
  presidential power and,
    135, 332–33
  of state actions, 302–31
Judiciary Act (1789), 330
Jungle, The (Sinclair),
  601, 615

jurisdiction, 10–11, 12, 68,
  100, 284, 317–21
  of congressional
    committees, 192–93
  of federal courts, 49
  of federal government,
    69–77, 101
Jury Theorem, 363
Justice Department, U.S.,
  159, 284, 285, 286, 296,
  324, 338
  Microsoft antitrust suits
    and, 533

Kansas, school segregation
  in, 139, 330
Kansas-Nebraska Act
  (1854), 496
Katrina, Hurricane, 84,
  230, 295, 573, 623
Kennedy, Anthony, 136,
  324, 344, 345
Kennedy, Edward, 82, 531
Kennedy, John F., 178,
  459–60
  assassination of, 641
  Cuba and, 705
  election of, 250
  New Frontier of, 218
  personal life of, 582
  reporters and, 570,
    573, 582
Kennedy, John Patrick, 178
Kerry, John, 325, 372
  "flip-flopper" accusations
    and, 449
  on Iraq war, 445
  media endorsements
    of, 572
  Nader and, 505
  as war hero, 572
Keynes, John Maynard,
  597, 602
Keynesian economics, 596,
  597, 602, 625
  definition of, 602
Khmer Rouge, 6
King, Martin Luther, Jr.,
  141, 540
King Caucus, 226
Kissinger, Henry, 250

Lobbying Disclosure Act (1995), 515, 531, 535
Lockheed Martin, 618
logrolling, 213–14
London, 30
loopholes, 609
Los Angeles, 626
Los Angeles Homeless Service Authority (LAHSA), 575
Los Angeles Times, 575
Lott, Trent, 562
Louisiana, 433
  affirmative action in, 159
  same-sex marriage banned in, 157
Louisiana Purchase, 261
Love Canal pollution, 619
Loving v. Virginia, 330–31

McCain, John, 250–51, 265, 368–69, 435, 440, 452, 455, 456, 457–65, 474, 546, 563, 572, 632, 678, 682
McCain-Feingold Act, *see* Bipartisan Campaign Reform Act
McConnell, Mitch, 187
McConnell v. Federal Election Commission, 116, 344
McCubbins, Mathew D., 297, 473*n*
McCulloch v. Maryland, 75
McGovern-Fraser Commission, 502
McKinley, William, 499, 570
Madison, James, 32, 41, 54, 56, 64, 101, 268, 289, 329–30, 370, 494, 665
  on class conflict, 378
  on pluralism, 517
  on Senate, 47
  on separation of powers, 57, 87
  see also Marbury v. Madison
Maine, 439
Maine, 570

majority leader, 186
majority-minority districts, 426
majority party, 483
majority system, 433
MALDEF (Mexican American Legal Defense and Education Fund), 152, 153
managerial presidency, 294–95
Mandate Monitor, 82
mandates, 252, 276
  unfunded, 81–83
mandatory spending, 612
manufacturing, 594
Mapp, Dollree (Dolly), 125
Mapp v. Ohio, 109, 125
Marbury, William, 329
Marbury v. Madison, 91, 329
March on Washington, 141
Marcos, Ferdinand, 698
market economy, 586–87, 588–92, 613–16
  failure of, 591–92
  global, 701
  "marketplace of ideas," 554
market power, 615
  see also monopolies; trusts
marriage, same-sex, 71–72, 156–57, *376,* 376
  see also civil unions
Marshall, John, 91, 330
  Bill of Rights and, 104
  on Commerce clause, 75–76
  on implied powers, 75–76
  Jackson and, 351
  nationalizing court of, 86
Marshall, Thurgood, 340, 639
Marshall Plan, 693, 699, 701
Maryland:
  bank tax and, 75
  slavery in, 42
Mason, George, 101
Massachusetts, 427, 530
  cholera in, 663
  Federalists in, 101

same-sex marriage in, 71–72, 156–57
toxic waste in, 619
Virginia Plan and, 41
Masson v. New Yorker Magazine, Inc., 567
mass popularity, *258*
Matalin, Mary, 388
material benefits, 526
"means-tested" part of welfare state, 638, 649, 650–55
media, 388–89, 391–94, 512, 550–83, *564*
  bias in, 553, 570, 572
  Bill Clinton and, 558, 563
  "blogosphere" and, 563
  broadcast, 555, 556–58
  censorship of, 552, 564
  conflict and, 580–81
  consumers of, 578–81
  definition of, 550
  education level and, 579, *579*
  elections and, 581
  First Amendment and, 552
  foreign policy and, 687–88
  functions of, 550–55
  government's disputes with, 386
  G. W. Bush and, 562–63
  informed electorate and, 552
  journalists and, 569–71
  leaks of information to, 574–77
  licensing of, 555, 564
  as "marketplace of ideas," 554
  media/press relations and, 553
  netroot activism and, 563
  Obama and, 563, 572
  ownership of, 567–69, *568*
  political campaigns and, 451–52
  political struggles and, 4, 5

Republican Party,
Republicans *(cont.)*
budget and, 612
candidate image and, 449
conservative base of, 500
on contributory
programs, 655
Democrats' differences
with, 408, 479, 480
education policies of, 660
environmental policy
and, 625–26
funding of, 508
Gingrich's support
by, 187
G. W. Bush and, 325
as hawkish, 377
history of, 495–503
House committee pledge
of, 483
House committee system
reformed by, 199
and Israel, 21
Johnson's impeachment
and, 217
Latino support for, 375
legislative priorities
of, 502
media and, 570–71
Medicare and, 649
members of, 209, 211
NAFTA and, 701
1994 election victories of,
180, 215, 218
in 104th Congress, 199
PACs and, *543*
partisanship and,
210–11, *212*
primary elections, 435
Progressive, 470,
473, 481
religious conservatives
in, 500
reporters in, 570–71
social issues of, 481, 482
Social Security
irresponsibility of, 645
tax cuts engineered by,
607, 610
Texas redistricting by,
181–84, 432

two-party system and,
469–72
war and, 705
welfare reform and,
654–55
white southerners in,
380, 489, 500
Republican Party
(Jeffersonian), 494–95
research and development
(R&D), 599, 600
reserved powers
amendment, 70
reserve requirement, 605
restrictive covenants,
138–39
"retail" politics, 8–9
retrospective voting, 444
RFRA (Religious Freedom
Restoration Act; 1993),
113–14
Rhode Island, 50
Constitutional
Convention and, 39
radical control of, 38, 43
Ricci v. DeStefano, 161
Rice, Condoleezza, 461
Rice, Stuart, 501
Rich, Marc, 269
Richardson, Bill, 462
right of rebuttal, 565
"rights of Englishmen," 63
right to bear arms, 124
right to counsel, 129–30
right to die, 134–35
right to privacy, 110,
132–37, 331
war on terrorism
and, 135
Rio Treaty (1947), 694
Rita, Hurricane, 230
RNC (Republican National
Committee), 451,
506, 508
roads, 602
Roberts, John G., 87, 122,
216, 325, 345
Rocky Mountain News, 559
Roe v. Wade, 537
Blackmun's opinion
in, 345

G. W. Bush's opposition
to, 326, 354
mootness and, 336
right to privacy and,
133, 345
Rogers Act (1924), 689
rogue states, 673
Rohde, David, 188
roll-call vote, 210
Roman Catholic
Church, 580
Romer v. Evans, 156
Romney, Mitt, 435, 462
Roosevelt, Franklin D., 22
Committee on
Administrative
Management of, 294
court packing plan of,
323, 331, 349
election of, 499
Great Depression
and, 625
loyalty towards, 379
national protection
and, 227
New Deal of, 87, 218,
226, 244–46, 252, 481,
486, 499–500, 503,
625, 633
1936 poll and, 396
personal life of, 582
proposals for legislative
action by, 233
public appeals used by,
255–56
reporters and, 570
Social Security and, 484
as strong president, 270
United Kingdom
and, 672
White House staff of, 249
Roosevelt, Theodore,
popular mobilization
and, 255
Roper Center, 570
Roper polls, 395
royalists, 32–34
rule interpretation, courts
and, 327–28
rulemaking, 280
rule of four, 352